China's Civil War

China's Civil War is the first book of its kind to offer a social history in English of the Civil War in 1945–1949 that brought the Chinese Communist Party to power. Integrating history and memory, it surveys a period of intense upheaval and chaos to show how the Communist Party and its armies succeeded in overthrowing the Nationalist government to bring political and social revolution to China. Drawing from a collection of biographies, memoirs, illustrations and oral histories, Diana Lary gives a voice to those who experienced the war first-hand, exemplifying the direct effects of warfare – the separations and divisions, the exiles and losses, and the social upheaval that resulted from the conflict. Lary explores the long-term impact on Chinese societies on the Mainland, Taiwan and Hong Kong, which have all diverged far from pre-war Chinese society.

DIANA LARY is Emeritus Professor of History at the University of British Columbia, Vancouver.

New Approaches to Asian History

This dynamic new series publishes books on the milestones in Asian history, those that have come to define particular periods or to mark turning points in the political, cultural and social evolution of the region. The books in this series are intended as introductions for students to be used in the classroom. They are written by scholars whose credentials are well-established in their particular fields and who have, in many cases, taught the subject across a number of years.

Books in the series

China's Civil War

A Social History, 1945–1949

Diana Lary

University of British Columbia, Vancouver

CAMBRIDGE
UNIVERSITY PRESS

CAMBRIDGE
UNIVERSITY PRESS

University Printing House, Cambridge CB2 8BS, United Kingdom

One Liberty Plaza, 20th Floor, New York, NY 10006, USA

477 Williamstown Road, Port Melbourne, VIC 3207, Australia

4843/24, 2nd Floor, Ansari Road, Daryaganj, Delhi - 110002, India

79 Anson Road, #06-04/06, Singapore 079906

Cambridge University Press is part of the University of Cambridge.

It furthers the University's mission by disseminating knowledge in the pursuit of education, learning and research at the highest international levels of excellence.

www.cambridge.org
Information on this title: www.cambridge.org/9781107678262

© Diana Lary 2015

First published 2015

A catalogue record for this publication is available from the British Library

Library of Congress Cataloging in Publication data
Lary, Diana.
China's civil war : a social history, 1945–1949 / Diana Lary,
University of British Columbia, Vancouver.
  pages   cm. – (New approaches to Asian history)
Includes bibliographical references and index.
ISBN 978-1-107-05467-7 (hbk) – ISBN 978-1-107-67826-2 (pbk)
1. China–History–Civil War, 1945–1949.   2. China–History–Civil War, 1945–1949–Social aspects.   3. China–Social conditions–1912–1949.   I. Title.
DS777.54.L36 2015
951.04′2–dc23
2014043077

ISBN 978-1-107-05467-7 Hardback
ISBN 978-1-107-67826-2 Paperback

This book is dedicated to the many Chinese who believed in progress and change for the country they loved, but, after the Civil War, were denied the chance to contribute their talents. They were persecuted in China, or forced to leave or to stay away from the country.

Contents

Figures

Tables

Maps

Acknowledgements

I have had the idea of this book in my mind for a long time, ever since I first realised what an enormous impact the Civil War had had on Chinese society. But the war was so complicated, and so full of contradictions, that it has taken me until the last stage of my career to feel able to write it. Over that long time many people have helped me with the writing, by telling me of their own experiences, and by helping me with the research for it.

I have learnt most of all from my beloved teacher Jerome Ch'en (Chen Zhirang), whose own life was so influenced by the war. I will never be able to thank him enough for all the help he has given me. As a scholar and as someone who lived through the war his knowledge and insights have been invaluable to me.

In Beijing in 1964–1965, several people whose lives were changed by the Civil War gave me my earliest understanding of the effects of the war: Cao Richang, Selma Vos Tsao, Peng Ping, Pi Ge, Tang Kai, Yang Xianyi, Gladys Yang. These people were devoted to the creation of the new China, and paid very high prices for their devotion. All of them were cruelly victimised in the Cultural Revolution.

Over many years in Beijing and in Haadchao Samaran, Endymion Wilkinson has been a wonderful source of knowledge and the most perceptive and challenging person with whom to discuss ideas.

In Beijing over the past three decades many people have helped me. Wang Bingsheng introduced me to *chengyu*, a field in which he is a master. Li Zongyi, who died much too young, and Qi Wenxin have given me deep insights. Yang Tianshi has been a constant help and advisor.

In Hong Kong, Hai Chi-yuet, David Jones, C.C. Kwong, Kenzie Kwong, Willy Lam, Gianni Mok and Elizabeth Sinn have all given me help and helped me to an understanding of Hong Kong's experience during and after the Civil War.

In Fujian, Li Minghuan and Wang Lianmao have helped me to understand the impact of the Civil War on Overseas Chinese.

In Vancouver, Alison Bailey, Phoebe Chow, Chu Shao-kang, Peter Eng, Colin Green, Jing Zhichun, Judy Lam Maxwell, Jing Liu, Joanne Poon, Shaun Wang, Alexander Woodside, Wu Yang, Dominic Yang, Helen Yu, Henry Yu, John Yu and Eleanor Yuen have all helped me in different, invaluable ways.

In Cambridge, Marigold Acland and Lucy Rhymer, at Cambridge University Press, have been the most astute and helpful of editors.

I give all these people my deepest thanks. My thanks go too to the Social Sciences and Humanities Research Council of Canada, whose financial support made this project possible.

Introduction

戰亂

Zhanluan

The chaos of war

The chaos of war is a visitation that China has endured many times, chaos created either by the invasion of outsiders or, even worse, by civil war. Between 1945 and 1949 one of the most bitter civil wars in China's long history was fought across the country. The outcome, the victory of the Chinese Communist Party (CCP), changed China forever. The incoming state was determined on revolution, on a complete transformation of the state and society. The arrival of the CCP also created a huge upheaval in global politics; communism was established in the world's most populous country.

The Civil War is still not formally over. The two sides in the war remain technically at war. The People's Republic of China (PRC) government in Beijing rules over all of Mainland China, but the Republic of China, now in its 103rd year, is still firmly in existence in Taiwan. The PRC government calls Taiwan a 'renegade province', but that rather threatening term does not alter the reality of two separate Chinese polities, two polities still firmly tied together by their common history and culture, and by the legacy of the tragedies of modern history. The most difficult and painful part of the common history is the history of the Civil War.

Civil war is the most horrible form of war. It has a hideous intimacy to it that inter-state wars do not. Those who are killed, ruined or exiled during a civil war are the victims of their own compatriots. People connected to each other by history and nationality turn against each other, driven by divisions that transcend their attachment to the nation. The basis for these divisions varies. In the Russian Civil War (1917–1922) the divides were class and ideology, between those who opposed the tsarist autocracy and those who were loyal to it. In the Rwandan Civil War (1990–1994) the division was ethnicity, between the Hutu and Tutsi, two distinct groups who were manipulated into murderous hostility. The divide may be religion, as it was in the long-running conflict between Catholics and Protestants in Northern Ireland. Civil war may be the outcome of recurrent struggles between political factions, breaking out when one or other of equally matched factions take their turn in a 'regular massacre of compatriots', as has happened with dismal regularity in the history of Colombia.[1]

Civil war often follows on the heels of an inter-state war that has weakened the existing regime. In Russia, the Civil War started in the chaos of the last year of the First World War, when soldiers of the tsarist armies were no longer willing to risk their lives for the regime, and 'voted with their feet' – i.e., left the battle fronts and precipitated a civil war that had been brewing for some time. In Vietnam, the communist Vietcong's fight against first France and then the USA was a civil war embedded in an international war, in which parts of Vietnamese society fought with the foreign powers.

China has her own particular pattern of civil war, a very long one. The war between Xiang Yu and Liu Bang in the third century BCE (206–202) came only 15 years after the Chinese state was unified by Qin Shihuang. The war is one of the most celebrated conflicts in all of Chinese history, a war in which the brutal, crude Liu Bang, from north China, defeated a man of culture and refinement, Xiang Yu, from the south.[2] Liu's victory brought about the establishment of one of China's most glorious dynasties, the Han; Liu Bang made himself the first emperor, Han Gaozu.

Over China's history there has been a sickening sense of inevitability to civil war, as an unavoidable stage in the dynastic cycle, the path followed by many of the imperial dynasties. Civil wars were triggered as a dynasty went into decline, nearing the end of the cycle. The start of civil war, often a peasant rising, was a sign that the ruling dynasty had lost the mandate of heaven, and was no longer able to hold the state together, or to keep control of the divisive elements within the vast state. A recent civil war between the Confucian order and new political forces was the Taiping Rising (1850–1864), in which a huge movement under the banner of a Chinese form of Christianity took over much of southern and central China. The Qing Dynasty managed to quell the rising, with great savagery, but the dynasty was critically weakened and its days were numbered. It fell less than 50 years later, in 1911.

---

[1] Juan Gabriel Gasquest, *The Secret History of Costaguana* (London: Bloomsbury, 2010), p. 64.

[2] Xiang Yu is an enormously popular cultural icon. One of the best-known Peking operas *Bawang bieji* (*The Autocrat Bids Farewell to his Concubine*) tells his story. A film based on the opera, *Farewell My Concubine* (director Chen Kaige), came out in 1993.

During the two decades after the establishment of the Republic in 1912, China was divided into a patchwork of military satraps, under an assortment of military figures known collectively as the warlords. This was a form of disseminated militarism rather than a full-scale civil war. Some parts of China were fought over frequently, others were untouched. There was no question of ideology, only of control. In 1928 a powerful nationalist movement, the Guomindang (GMD), unified the country. It set up its capital in Nanjing, the southern capital, to distinguish the new government from the old imperial regime whose capital was in Beijing, the northern capital. The unification was only partial; there were still large areas under the control of militarists – and there was a small but tenacious communist movement, named by the GMD as an insurgency led by the CCP, which *did* see itself as involved in a civil war, a fight for a socialist China.

Chinese civil wars have had two critical elements. The first element is the regional divide, between the north and the south. The conquests that accompanied dynastic change in China usually showed a marked distinction between north and south. In civil war the two sides often distilled out along the regional divide. In the Taiping Rising the movement moved rapidly from south to north. In the communist conquest in 1949 the north triumphed over the south, as Liu Bang had triumphed over Xiang Yu. The second common element to civil wars in China is the urban/rural divide. Many of the dynastic changes in China's history were sparked by peasant rebellions. The CCP conquered China by, in its own words, 'surrounding the cities with countryside'; the party was brought to power by peasants and peasant armies.

农村包围城市
Nongcun baowei chengshi
The countryside surrounds the cities

By contrast Chinese civil wars have lacked two of the most common elements of civil wars elsewhere – religious conflict and ethnic hostility. Ethnic hostility has shown itself in the incursions of the Han state into the borderlands, but seldom within China itself. What is shared by civil wars in China with civil wars in other countries is the tremendous human cost. These costs are measured in terms of death, disruption, exile and bitter, lasting divisions that continue over generations. During the Russian Civil War close to a million soldiers on both sides died; a much larger number of civilians, possibly eight million, died as direct and indirect results of the war. More than two million people, later known as White Russians, fled from the new Soviet state in the immediate aftermath of the war; a large number of them went across Siberia into China.[3] The deaths and the exiles from the Chinese Civil War between 1945 and 1949 surpassed the number in Russia. The losses were less catastrophic, however, in proportion to population, than the deaths in the Vietnam War, in which more than a million soldiers died, and perhaps half a million civilians, out of a population of less than 50 million.

The deaths and exiles are the most easily measureable part of the cost of civil war. Other costs are real but less amenable to cold statistical measurement. Civil war leaves behind profoundly damaged societies, and a legacy of grief and injury that the passage of time cannot heal completely.

The long Civil War

The 1945–1949 Civil War was the last stage of a conflict that had been going on for almost two decades, between the GMD and the CCP. The start of the long Civil War can be dated precisely to April 1927. In the early 1920s the GMD and the CCP were closely linked by a formal alliance, the First United Front, and through the personal ties between the youthful leaders, who had trained together in Guangdong. Both parties considered themselves revolutionary, both shared the goal of uniting and then transforming China. The major difference between them was ideology. The GMD's ideology was the rather general *Sanmin zhuyi* (*Three Principles of the People*), the thinking of the revolutionary leader Sun Yat-sen, which was designed to encompass as many people as possible, and would now be called 'big-tent' thinking. The CCP ascribed to a tougher, universalist and highly evolved political theory, Marxism-Leninism, which was based on the conviction that the victory of socialism was inevitable, and that 'all revolutionary wars are just'.[4]

The two parties fought the first half of the Northern Expedition together (1926–1928), with a shared aim to put an end to warlordism and re-establish China's international status. Then in April 1927 came what the GMD called the 'great cleansing' (*qingdang*), what the CCP called the 'counter-revolution'. The much more powerful partner in the United Front, the GMD, launched a sudden and deadly attack on the CCP, intent on eradicating the party and its members. The White Terror in the late spring and early summer of 1927 took the lives of thousands

---

[3] Orlando Figes, *A People's Tragedy: A History of the Russian Revolution* (New York: Viking, 1996), p. 774.

[4] Mao Zedong, 'Problems of Strategy in China's Revolutionary War' (December 1936) *Marxists Internet Archive*, I.

of communists; only a handful managed to escape. The extermination campaign was run by a man whom foreigners in China had labelled until then as a 'Red', Chiang Kai-shek.

The 1927 purge virtually destroyed the CCP, a literal decimation. It left lasting personal bitterness and a total distrust of the GMD that could never be altered. The tiny rump of communists who survived withdrew into a few bases across the country, all in remote fastnesses in the border regions between provinces. These survivors were condemned to isolation, completely cut off from their previous lives and from their families. There was no going back to their previous lives; only death awaited them. They had to live with the knowledge that their family members were in danger because of them, hunted down and often killed. Mao Zedong's second wife, Yang Kaihui, was killed in 1930. Years later he commemorated her in one of his most famous poems.

Mao Zedong's poem

This poem was written in 1957, as an epitaph for Liu Zhixun, sent to his widow. The surname Liu means willow. The poplar (Yang means poplar) is Mao's much-loved second wife, Yang Kaihui, who was killed by Guomindang forces early in the revolution.

我失骄杨君失柳，
杨柳轻扬直上重霄九。
问讯吴刚何所有，
吴刚捧出桂花酒。
寂寞嫦娥舒广袖，
万里长空且为忠魂舞。
忽报人间曾伏虎，
泪飞顿作倾盆雨。

I lost my proud poplar, you lost your willow.
The poplar and willow have ascended to the Ninth Heaven.
Wu Gang is asked what he can offer,
And serves them laurel wine.
The solitary moon goddess spreads her broad sleeves
To dance in boundless space for these loyal souls.
On earth there is a sudden report that tigers have been subdued,
Tears fly and fall as mighty rain.

The purge seemed to be the end of communism in China. It was not. The CCP survived, although always under threat of destruction. In the early 1930s its bases were battered and almost destroyed in a series of encirclement campaigns that the GMD government launched against them. In 1934 the Central Soviet base in Jiangxi was abandoned and the CCP was forced on to the Long March, an epic withdrawal that took the CCP to safety in the remote northwest – and also created a potent myth of survival.

A far greater threat to China than the CCP was on the horizon. Japan took advantage of China's internal struggles to encroach on Chinese territory. The Japanese threat became so severe that one of Chiang Kai-shek's own military allies, Zhang Xueliang, kidnapped him in late 1936, in the ancient capital of Xi'an, to force him to make a stand against Japan. To get his release Chiang had to agree to the Second United Front with the CCP, to resist Japan. Chiang could not forgive the humiliation of being kidnapped (in his nightshirt). He kept his kidnapper Zhang Xueliang under house arrest for the rest of his own life. Zhang was released only after Chiang's death (1975).

Names of a war

The warfare that engulfed China from 1937 to 1945 has been given a variety of names. In Chinese, on the Mainland and in Taiwan, the 1937–1945 war is known as the *KangRi zhanzheng*, the War of Resistance to Japan, shortened to *Kangzhan*, Resistance War. In Japan and in the West the war is now often called by the less emotive name, the Second Sino-Japanese War. The First Sino-Japanese War was that of 1894–1895, known in Chinese as the *Jiawu zhanzheng*, for the year name in the traditional Chinese dating cycle. In a wider context the 1937–1945 war is often conflated with the global conflict, the Second World War (1939–1945). The Second World War itself is problematic. It started in Europe, and for countries closely allied to Britain, in 1939. The USA did not enter the war until the end of 1941.

The full-scale Japanese invasion of China in July 1937 triggered the Resistance War, which lasted for eight long years. At the beginning of that war there seemed to be some rapprochement between the GMD and CCP, but it was not a happy alliance. The CCP hated and distrusted the GMD, while the GMD, much more powerful than the CCP, was deeply hostile to a party it had been fighting so long. By the middle of the war it was clear that the rapprochement had been only a hiatus in the unchanged hostility. By 1945, after the Japanese surrender, the hostility flared back up in its full virulence. There was a major rider: the balance between the two parties had shifted dramatically.

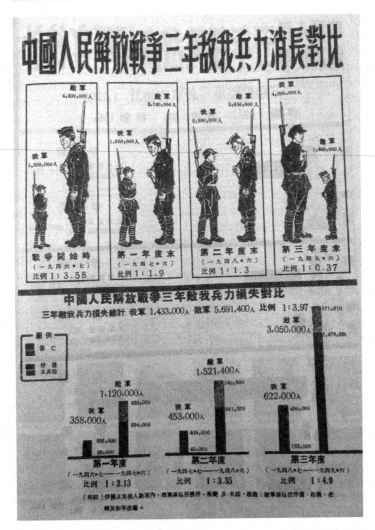

Fig. 1 Comparative military strengths

The course of the eight-year Resistance War, which damaged the GMD far more than it did the CCP, meant that at its end the CCP was strong enough to take on the GMD. In 1972 Mao Zedong thanked the then Japanese prime minister Tanaka Kakui for helping the CCP to power. Japan had fought the war under the pretext of containing communism. Instead, the brutal treatment of much of the population of the occupied areas pushed people, especially peasants, into the arms of a party committed to resistance to Japan – the CCP and its guerrilla fighters. Chalmers Johnson argues persuasively that the alliance between Party and peasantry in the resistance to Japan brought nationalism to the villages, taught peasants to understand how oppressed they were under the old order and gave them a sense of belonging to a nation.[5] The wartime mobilisation of the peasants was the beginning of the process of 'surrounding the cities (the GMD) with the countryside (the CCP)'.

The four-year Civil War, 1945–1949

The acute, four-year Civil War started at the end of a long global war, World War Two (1939–1945). Asia was in chaos. Colonialism was dying. Countries were suddenly liberated from Japanese colonialism (Korea, Taiwan) or occupation (China, Southeast Asia). Some countries were still technically colonies but the colonial masters, the British, French and Dutch, were incapable of resuming their old colonial rule given the ravages of the war in Europe as well as Asia and the nationalist movements in the colonies. The USA was the new superpower, in charge of the occupation administration of Japan, and involved in other places, including China, in preventing nascent conflicts from flaring up. The USSR had suffered greater damage from the Second World War than any other state, and was in recovery, but flexing its muscle in a mood of revenge and of promoting the spread of communism.

The Civil War that started even before the Resistance War was over was, in a formal sense, an ideological war, fought between two radically different worldviews. Both the GMD and the CCP saw themselves as representing the true China. Each side called the other 'bandit': the CCP called the GMD *guofei*, the GMD called the CCP *gongfei*. Neither called the war a civil war. For the CCP the war was fought for socialism and revolution, and so was called the War of Liberation (*Jiefang zhanzheng*). For the GMD the war was fought against communism and the spread of Soviet influence; it was a war of counter-insurgency. For the CCP the war brought the glorious Liberation of China. For GMD the war brought either the 'strategic withdrawal (*chetui*)', or the 'occupation by the enemy (*lunxian*)' of Mainland China. The war was a foreign-directed catastrophe; *Soviet Russia in China* was the title of Chiang Kai-shek's later apologia.[6]

---

[5] Chalmers Johnson, *Peasant Nationalism and Communist Power: The Emergence of Revolutionary China, 1937–1945* (Stanford: Stanford University Press, 1963), pp. i, 19, 31.

[6] Chiang Kai-shek, *Soviet Russia in China* (New York: Farrar, 1957).

The GMD fought the Civil War in a state of ideological confusion and decline, no longer certain about its own beliefs after the terrible losses of the Resistance War. Its leaders were fearful for the future, anguished and bitter about what might have been – the society they believed they were on the way to creating before 1937. The CCP fought the war detesting the past and longing for a new world, their ideological hatred of the old society coupled with bitterness over their own failures and humiliation between 1927 and 1937. In the Civil War the CCP conveyed a strong sense of renewal and redemption that was profoundly moving especially to young people who had grown up during China's darkest days and saw around them older people who were defeated, cynical or corrupt.

There is an irony to the ideological conflict. The outcome of the war was decided not in an ideological struggle, but by soldiers on the battlefields, where the CCP's army, the People's Liberation Army, won. Neither side has ever formally recognised that ideological issues were actually less important in the course of the war than were military ones. Ideology still had a key role, but it was less the victory of a formal ideology, Marxism-Leninism, than it was the winning over of popular support. Beyond the fighting on the battlefields was a propaganda struggle for the hearts and minds of key elements of the Chinese population, a battle that the CCP won.

Both the GMD and CCP had their own internecine quarrels to deal with while they fought each other. Chiang Kai-shek distrusted most of the GMD's senior military figures and spurned many political figures. The only people he trusted belonged to a small coterie with tight personal connections to himself, men who had studied under him at the Whampoa Military Academy. In the CCP Mao's harshness in dealing with his political opponents during the Yan'an period had succeeded in entrenching his tight control over the party. His harshness was slightly less in evidence in dealing with his generals, in whom he seems to have had enough confidence to allow them to argue with him with relative impunity.

Between those Chinese loyal to the GMD and those supporting the CCP was a vast space. At the start of the Civil War the two sides together commanded the loyalty of only a small proportion of Chinese; the mass of people were caught in the space between the two sides. Those who were aware of what was happening in the war looked on in anxiety, tinged by hope or fear, of what was to come. Older people thought with nostalgia for the past that seemed to be lost forever. Most people simply longed for stability, even a harsh one.

The polarisation between the GMD and the CCP can be seen as a wilful failure to find a peaceful solution to their mutual animosity. This was General George Marshall's view, as he presided over negotiations to prevent civil war. The insanity of starting a civil war after eight years of invasion was hard for outsiders to grasp but, even though both sides took part in negotiations to stop the war, both sides actually wanted war. The two leaders were implacably determined to fight.

Marshall mission

President Harry Truman sent General George Marshall, the only five-star general in the US Army, to China to prevent the outbreak of civil war. The mission lasted just over a year, from December 1945 to January 1947. It ended in failure, even though Marshall was able to impose a ceasefire early in the civil war (June 1946). The reasons for the failure have been discussed at enormous length. Marshall's insistence on a ceasefire, when the GMD seemed close to defeating the CCP in Manchuria, prompted Joseph McCarthy to label him pro-communist during the anti-communist witch hunts in America in the early 1950s. The probable reason for the failure is more prosaic: China was not America's to lose. Marshall laboured hard and sincerely to prevent a war that was inevitable because the two parties wanted it so badly. Marshall returned to Washington, became secretary of state and presided over a much more rewarding project, the Marshall Plan to restore Europe's economy.

Some of the savagery and extremism of the Civil War can be attributed to the huge egos of the leaders on either side. Both Chiang Kai-shek and Mao Zedong showed megalomaniac tendencies, in the long Chinese tradition of powerful, ruthless leaders, *bawang*, dictators or autocrats. The most famous of the *bawang* was Qin Shihuang, the first emperor of China, the ruthless man who burned books and killed scholars – but still united the state. The megalomaniac tendencies manifested themselves in an inability to trust others, or to share control, and a reliance on harsh tactics to ensure their rule. With two such individuals at the top of the opposing parties, the room for mediation or for compromise was next to nothing. Part of the tragedy of the Civil War is that it was fought under the leadership of two men whose personal ambitions drove them to seek victory at all costs – regardless of the havoc and death that would come in the process.

Until now, the Civil War has been difficult to discuss or write about. For most Chinese the war still seems too painful and too confusing to

Fig. 2 Chiang Kai-shek and Mao Zedong

analyse, except in broad terms. No objective Chinese-language history
exists as yet. There are two fine studies of the Civil War in English. The
first, by Suzanne Pepper, covers the political and economic aspects of
the war. The second, by Odd Arne Westad, covers the military and political course of the war, and discusses in detail the positions of Chiang

Kai-shek and Mao Zedong.[7] But the war tends to get limited coverage in more general histories and biographies. The most recent study on Mao Zedong, for example, by Alexander Pantsov and Steven Levine, devotes only 16 pages out of almost 600 to the Civil War. The book's major interest is in ideology and political theory, not the complexity and messiness of civil war.[8]

My study focuses on the painful and divisive social impacts of the war, impacts that deepened the process of fundamental, jarring change that had started in the Resistance War.

The social effects of the Civil War

Warfare is one of the most powerful stimuli to social change. The violence and upheaval that accompanies war, especially civil war, means almost inevitably that the old order is weakened, undermined or destroyed. This was as true of the Civil War in China as it was of the Civil War in Russia, where the First World War created such disruption and misery within Russia that even before the world war ended, the incompetent Russian autocracy was overthrown, and with it the whole old social order.

In the Resistance War, Chinese society had been subjected to eight years of continuous stress and to forces that led to disintegration of parts of the old social order. The Resistance War stretched the old order to breaking point, creating a fragmented society full of confusion and uncertainty, no longer sure what its social values were, or how they connected to the past, to values such as conformity, obedience, respect for elders and subordination of women. The process of moderate change, often associated with the term 'modernisation', had started in the 1920s and 1930s; it was derailed in the turbulence of war. There was no relief after the Japanese defeat. The Civil War intensified the process of social disintegration. The war was everywhere, unavoidable. There was no place to escape for the vast mass of people who hated war, or had simply had enough of war after eight years. War stalked the whole nation.

The process of social disintegration was seen at its most acute in siege warfare. The CCP used the strategy of siege in many of north China's cities and towns – most of which, including Beiping, were still surrounded by high walls. Changchun, Shenyang, Beiping and Taiyuan

---

[7] Suzanne Pepper, *Civil War in China: The Political Struggle, 1945–1949* (Berkeley: University of California Press, 1978); Odd Arne Westad, *Decisive Encounters: The Chinese Civil War, 1946–1950* (Stanford: Stanford University Press, 2003).
[8] Alexander Pantsov and Steven Levine, *Mao: The Real Story* (New York: Simon & Schuster, 2012), pp. 343–359.

were all besieged during the war. Siege is a highly effective way of defeating an enemy and at the same time winning over a civilian population that has been driven to despair. During a siege civilians come to hate the defending military, in this case the GMD, that has brought the siege upon them – and which gets first call on dwindling supplies of food and fuel. Civilians have to watch the weaker members of their families – the elderly, children – dying. When a siege is lifted, the physical damage to the city seems very limited. The besieged city appears intact; the citizens are not bitter towards the incomers, as they might be in a city that had been bombed, but grateful to the people who bring them food and other supplies. The besiegers are even given praise for having spared the city, for not destroying it. At the most cynical, one might see the siege strategy as a harsh but brilliant way of winning the hearts of civilians.

A different, less visible form of social disintegration was the crumbling of the old family. One of the most profound social effects of the Civil War was family separation. Innumerable families were divided in the chaos of war. For some, division meant losing touch with family members; the painful term *shizong* (literally 'lost footprint') carried the meaning that families had no idea if members were alive or dead. Other separations occurred when members of a family fled into exile while others stayed behind; these separations seemed at the outset to be short term but often turned out to last for decades. The emotional costs of family separation were enormous, and so painful that they were hard to talk about, and were often kept secret. In this book we have examples of families separated for up to four decades. The concept of family separation as inevitably painful is deeply imbedded in Chinese culture. As the ethnographer Charles Stafford puts it, in his vivid descriptions of the rituals of parting, separation and reunion, the 'many practices and cultural objects – festivals, greetings, leave-takings, religious rituals, funerals, weddings, poems, banquets, novels, doors, political speeches and newspaper articles – which suggest, when taken together, that separation is a common theme, even an obsession in Chinese culture'. And to underline the sadness of separation he adds 'the emotions of separation are actually *intensified* in China, by the many explicit and sometimes very moving, practices and idioms related to parting and return'.[9]

Family division was political as well as physical. The ascendancy of a revolutionary ideology, communism, was a huge shock to the social system.

---

[9] Charles Stafford, *Living with Separation in China* (London: Routledge, 2003), pp. 174, 178.

It went against the widespread belief that an egalitarian, class-based ideology could not transcend the Chinese attachment to family and locality. This turned out to be wrong. The young were far less committed to the old order than were their seniors. The appeal of communism had a strong generational bias. Young people turned towards the CCP during the war, either openly or covertly. They put their ideological beliefs first, their family ties – the bedrock of the traditional society – second.

The divides within small communities, specifically villages, were different than those within families. They were less spontaneous, and relied on direct CCP involvement. In much of north China, even while the Civil War was still raging, attacks on the old rural elite were a critical part of rural reform and class warfare. The old elites had been critically weakened during the Resistance War, and did not recover their status at the start of the Civil War, which saw first of all the settling of accounts from the Resistance War in the once-occupied areas, and then the start of rural revolution.

The Civil War undermined the economic life of innumerable families. Economic chaos and hyperinflation brought huge changes in family economies, especially in the cities and towns. Inflation was, for most Chinese urban populations, how the war was experienced from day to day. It caused generalised, acute anxiety. Incomes never kept pace with prices. The tension created by the inability of a husband earning a salary or a wage to support his dependants was enormous. Families were forced to be hard-hearted, in terms of how many members a single unit could support; in times of chronic insecurity, the number of mouths eligible for support had to be reduced. The key question was who was going to be given priority. The answer was often cutting out members of the extended family, including siblings and the elderly, in favour of the immediate, nuclear family, parents and children.

The status of women, which had shifted during the Resistance War as women had had to take on greater family responsibilities, continued to change during the Civil War. The deaths of soldiers and the loss of men taken away as forced labour or as military conscripts deprived families of their income, and forced more and more women to work outside the family. This might be industrial work in the big cities or entrepreneurship. For many women the wars brought a form of emancipation, which, although not always voluntary, was real. They had to make decisions for themselves, to look for their own opportunities, even to abandon a husband in favour of a man better able to support them. There were few role models for women on either side of the political divide. The GMD had the most celebrated woman in China at its head, the elegant, accomplished Song Meiling, Madame Chiang Kai-shek, the CCP had her older sister, Song Qingling. Neither could offer much by way of a model to ordinary women. The CCP did, however, make efforts to involve women in its revolutionary struggle; the GMD ignored them. This book will have examples of how women's lives changed during the war.

Neither side in the war had a strong handle on the chaotic process of social change under way in the Civil War. There was nothing in the GMD's policies that spoke to social issues. And though social revolution was very much part of the CCP's long-term vision of revolution, many of the wartime changes were beyond its plans.

In the long historical view it is not clear whether the wartime social changes destroyed the 'bedrock' of Chinese social values, the Confucian values that were already under attack in limited, privileged circles of Chinese society before the start of 12 years of war. The wartime changes predated the dramatic, ideological transformation of most of Chinese society that came with the post-1949 CCP policies for a new socialist order. Put together, the wartime changes and the CCP's policies might seem to have destroyed the old order completely. Now that the social-ist order itself is dead, that turns out not to be the case. Confucian and/ or traditional values are again being promoted by the government of China.[10] It is hard to say which changes were permanent, which were transitory – and how much social change comes from quite different sources, such as economic and technological change.

What can be said about the Civil War is that it brought out, to its utmost, the capacity for endurance of the Chinese people. It forced them to demonstrate their courage and their resilience. Battered by the waves of upheaval and destruction that the Civil War brought, the Chinese people showed an extraordinary ability to transcend the trauma of the war. Nevertheless the war left deep anguish, often unspoken. Resilience is often achieved not by facing the past but by burying it and ignoring the agonies of the past. In China's modern history there are two peri-ods in the lives of individuals and families that are often passed over in silence: the Civil War and the Cultural Revolution.

Voices

The aim of this book is to give voices to some of those who lived through the cataclysm of the Civil War. This seems to be the right time to do it. Whatever the memories, of triumph at victory on the CCP side, or of pride in survival, or of the sadness of loss, the people who remember

---

[10] The promotion is quite overt. The centres set up by the PRC government to promote a friendly vision of China abroad are called Confucius Institutes.

the events of the Civil War directly are now old. Over the past two or three decades, they have begun to express themselves, to write down their memories. There has been a recent spate of memoirs, published in China, Taiwan and Hong Kong, written by elderly people who do not want the past to die with them. Their voices have little in common – except that they all agree that the Civil War was a key turning point in their lives. Some have even been written as blogs. Cheng Tang, a retired teacher in Taiwan, decided, in his eighties and in ill-health, that there were things he did not want to be forgotten. He telephoned his daughter, the writer Cheng Yingshu, every day and dictated his memories, which she then put online as a blog. They were later published as a book.[11]

The personal memoirs are coming out after decades of suppression of memory in both the Mainland and Taiwan, when the Civil War was a black hole that could not be remembered publicly. The voices of those who experienced the war are finally being heard.

The personal stories recounted in this book are informed by powerful emotions. There are the voices of those people, young in the late 1940s, who were full of enthusiasm for the revolution, and saw themselves at the time as participating in a glorious adventure. Then there are apprehensive voices, of those who had no intention of leaving China but did not know how the revolution would affect them. There are voices of deep sadness, those of people who left China but left behind them too much to be simply relieved that they had escaped from a new world in which there would be no place for them. And there are voices of foreigners, some of them fairly objective journalists and diplomats, others pro-communist, both Marxists and people inspired more by their disgust at the GMD than by a deep commitment to socialism.

Oral history has become an important source for the history of the war, especially in Taiwan. *Chinese Women in the Fires of War* consists of interviews with women in Taiwan who were in their twenties during the Civil War.[12] *One Inch of River and Mountain, One Inch of Blood* is made up of interviews with elderly GMD veterans.[13] Joshua Fan's *China's Homeless Generation: Voices from the Veterans of the Chinese Civil War* deals with the experiences of GMD soldiers.[14] The collection of memories of

[11] Cheng Tang, *Wo ceng shi liuwang xuesheng (I Was a Refugee Student)* (Taibei: Lianhe wenxue, 2009), p. 5.

[12] Lo Jiu-jung, Yu Chien-ming and Chiu Hei-yuan (eds.), *Fenghuo suiyue xia de Zhongguo funu (Chinese Women in the Fires of War)* (Taibei: Zhongyang yanjiuyuan Jindaishi yanjiu-suo, 2004).

[13] Guoshiguan, *Yicun shanhe yicun xue (One Inch of River and Mountain, One Inch of Blood)* (Taibei: Guoshiguan, 2001).

[14] Joshua Fan, *China's Homeless Generation: Voices from the Veterans of China's Civil War* (New York: Routledge, 2011).

Taiwanese soldiers in GMD armies who were stuck in China after 1949, *Scars and Tears*, deals with a small but especially unfortunate group of men.[15] Lung Ying-t'ai's wonderful account of the year 1949, *Da Jiang Da Hai 1949*, gives a compelling account of how sudden and arbitrary the family separations of the time were.[16] Marlon Meyer's moving oral histories of now-elderly Mainlanders, *Remembering China from Taiwan*, deals with the terrible sense of loss and hidden grief these people have carried with them.[17]

Oral history is also appearing on the Mainland. Zhang Zhenglong's two remarkable histories of the war in Manchuria are based not only on the author's own knowledge, as a retired People's Liberation Army (PLA) officer, but on extensive interviews with survivors. Zhang's work is particularly impressive in that his work contains implicit but very deep criticism of the PLA.[18] There are other oral history collections that tend to glorify the CCP conquest, such as a recent volume on the return to China of Overseas Chinese after 1949.[19]

These recent memoirs join those memoirs written much earlier, by people who played significant roles in the war and wanted to give their own version of what happened. These include the memoirs of political figures, men such as Li Zongren, Chang Kia-ngau and Carsun Chang. To complement them are contemporary accounts by Westerners, journalists, diplomats, missionaries, businessmen, pilots and doctors, describing the extraordinary events they witnessed.

Biographies and autobiographies are another rich source of memory of the Civil War. One of the finest is Joseph Esherick's biography of the Ye family, which covers multiple generations of a distinguished family.[20]

One major source is missing – accounts of the war in fiction and poetry, the traditional vehicles for carrying the sad and tragic parts of Chinese history. The cost of the building of the Great Wall has been known to

---

[15] Guoshi guan, *Shanghen xuelei* (*Scars and Tears*) (Taibei: Guoshiguan, 2006).

[16] Lung Ying-t'ai, *Da Jiang Da Hai 1949* (*Great River Great Sea, 1949*) (Taibei: Tianxia zazhi, 2010).

[17] Marlon Meyer, *Remembering China from Taiwan* (Hong Kong: Hong Kong University Press, 2012).

[18] Zhang Zhenglong, *Xuebai xuehong* (*Snow White, Blood Red*) (Beijing: Jiefangjun chubanshe, 1989). This impassioned account of a great tragedy was written by a courageous retired PLA officer, from the point of view of Yunnanese soldiers. The book is a less-than-flattering picture of the PLA, and was banned in China shortly after its publication. Zhang Zhenglong, *Yingxiong shi* (*Heroic City*) (Shenyang: Baishan, 2011).

[19] Wang Yixin, *Women guojia: Xin Zhongguo chuqi huaqiao huiguo* (*Our Nation: Overseas Chinese Return to China in the Early Years of New China*) (Jinan: Shandong renmin chubanshe, 2013).

[20] Joseph Esherick, *Ancestral Leaves: A Family Journey Through Chinese History* (Berkeley: University of California Press, 2011).

countless generations not through formal history but through the folk story of Meng Jiang Nu. She wept so hard and so long in her search for her husband, captured as a slave labourer and forced to work on the wall, that her tears caused it to collapse. China's poets have commemorated loss and separation for millennia. The Civil War has provided very little in the way of literature or myth. It was so awful that it seems to have silenced China's writers; there are almost no literary works that cover the pain of the war. The only literary expression of those caught up in the war was the quotation of Tang poems.

Theories

It is hard to find an appropriate theoretical approach to the study of a period of great confusion. The winning contemporary Chinese approach, the Marxist belief in the inevitability of the triumph of socialism, has never appealed to me – and is now rejected by the CCP itself – although it did influence the work of some historians. Other Western theories are not much more helpful. Post-modernism tends to stay away from chaotic situations, especially war. The chaos of war seems to interfere with and even defy theoretical rationality. Trauma theory has more to say about the effects of war. It recognises that trauma goes beyond the experiences of individuals and families and applies to communities or to a whole society. Collective trauma is carried in collective memory. The concept of trauma in trauma theory includes physical and psychological damage, and the destruction of social and moral fabric. It resonates with Chinese thinking; there are two Chinese terms for trauma, *chuangshang* and *shangtong*, both of which speak of acute and chronic pain and injury, a recognised part of China's historical experience.

I have been deeply influenced by the brilliant writing of Tony Judt, especially in *Postwar*.[21] His aim was to record what happened in Europe in the years after World War Two, and to describe the depth of the trauma that Europe experienced. His work exists less in a theory world than in a sphere of passionate compilation, putting together, from an encyclopaedic knowledge, an account of the traumatic history of Europe during and just after the Nazi period.

There are parallels for the devastation and loss that characterised post-war Europe in the damage suffered in China. Long-term trauma emerges in accounts of the Civil War and its aftermath. Here is one poignant example. Ang Lee, the great filmmaker, whose family was divided at

---

[21] Tony Judt, *Postwar: A History of Europe Since 1945* (New York: Penguin, 2005).

the end of the Civil War, speaks of the long-lasting effects of the trauma visited on his family by it being on the losing side in the Civil War:

My father's family were liquidated during the Cultural Revolution in China because they were landowners. He was the only one to escape. I was born and brought up in Taiwan. But you absorb the trauma. My parents had no sense of security. It was as if the world could turn against them at any moment.[22]

This is a story replicated again and again in Chinese families, grief and trauma sometimes so deep that the only way to deal with them is to close down memory of the past. It is a silence that demands respect. I have on occasion felt intrusive when talking to people who have been willing to talk to me about their experiences. But almost always I found that people *did* want to talk about the past, however painful it had been. Their stories needed to be told.

Regions

It is impossible to cover all of China in a brief study. Examples used in the book focus on the following regions and places, each chosen for its representative value:

Table 0.1 *Selected regions of China*

Beiping/ Beijing	The old capital, centre of culture and universities. Occupied by the Japanese between 1937 and 1945.
Shanghai	International, cosmopolitan city. Parts occupied for the whole of the Resistance War, others only for a few years.
Manchuria	Northeastern heartland of Japanese rule until August 1945. Rich natural and industrial resources. Occupied by the USSR in August 1945.
Yan'an	The CCP capital in northwest China. Crucible of revolutionary change.
Shandong	Eastern province, the cities occupied by the Japanese in 1937. Major communist bases in the rural areas by the end of the Resistance War.
Guangxi	Southwestern province. Major supplier of troops for the Resistance War. Devastated at the end of the war.
Fujian	Homeland of many Overseas Chinese. Economically hard hit by the wartime separation from the Overseas communities.
Taiwan	Japanese colony from 1895 to 1945. Economically developed, socially quite distinct from Mainland China.

---

[22] *Ang Lee Biography*, IMDb.

Case studies of individuals, communities or regions may seem to be idiosyncratic, rather than microcosms of China during the Civil War. It is impossible to overcome this risk completely, but I have taken care to try and make sure that, between them, the regions cover the universal trauma of the Civil War.

The Civil War still haunts China. One thing that all regions, communities and people share in common is that the Civil War was one of the most tumultuous periods in all of China's long history. It changed China in fundamental ways. It changed East Asia. It changed the face of communism. The political division between China and Taiwan remains in place, despite the close economic connections between the two.

More than six decades after the CCP came to power, China is still ruled by the party, which now has more than 80 million members; they occupy every position of significance in the country. Although the party has abandoned radical socialism in favour of a form of capitalism known as 'socialism with Chinese characteristics', it is true to its Leninist origins. It is secretive and hierarchical, autocratic and harsh. It operates almost entirely outside the public realm. Its leaders, in their sixties, are bland and faceless, unknown in China or beyond. They govern as true Leninists and, ironically, at the same time in the tradition of remoteness of imperial mandarins – although without, at the moment, an emperor. They and their children have benefited to the tune of billions of dollars, some of the money now salted away in offshore accounts.[23] Taiwan, meanwhile, is democratic, a vigorous, raucous democracy that puts the lie to the Beijing's contention that Chinese people are not suited to democracy.

The division between the People's Republic and the Republic may persist, but neither of the two wartime leaders has fared well in historical memory. Mao Zedong still presides over Tiananmen, although his reputation is low, and those who remember the days when they saw him as a godhead are embarrassed at their own youthful adulation of the Great Helmsman. The flood of medallions and pictures of him made during his life are now souvenirs rather than talismans. Chiang Kai-shek has not fared better. His grandiose memorial hall in the middle of Taibei is usually closed to the public nowadays. The airport once named for him has been renamed Taoyuan International Airport, for the place where it is located. But although their reputations are low, neither man has been held to account for the tragedy of the Civil War.

---

[23] Documents published recently by the International Consortium of Investigative Journalists, January 2014, give details on wealth held by relatives of current CCP leaders in offshore accounts.

The damage of the Civil War

The Civil War did lasting damage to Chinese society. The disruption of society, the innumerable separations within families and communities, the loss of property, all left a society impoverished by the war. The war brought to power a government that promised a new heaven on earth. That dream failed. After three decades of increasingly frantic experiments with socialism, the CCP has reverted to 'socialism with Chinese characteristics', a nebulous term that includes a renewed reverence for Confucianism.

The damage to one specific sector of society stands out: the sad fates of many of the liberal and intellectual people who came to support the CCP in the Civil War. Throughout this book there are references to the idealistic and patriotic people who believed that they could help to make China a better place. They were denied the chance. Instead, in the late 1950s (Anti-Rightist Movement) and in the 1960s (Cultural Revolution), these people became the victims of the revolution. Many of them died. Others lived to see their talents and their abilities wasted, sacrificed on the altar of Maoist extremism. The losses to the Chinese intellectual and creative world can only be compared to the terrible damage wrought by the man Mao admired so much, the first emperor Qin Shihuang.

This book is dedicated to those Chinese who believed in progress and change for their country, but after the Civil War were denied the chance to contribute their talents. It is also dedicated to those Chinese who had to leave, or to stay away from, a country that they loved.

兵久而国利者未之有也

Bing jiu er guo li zhe mo zhi you ye
There is no instance of a state benefitting from prolonged warfare

This concise statement from the strategist and philosopher Sunzi was written in the sixth century BCE, during the Warring States period. It refers just as well to twentieth-century China. China was engulfed in war. The conflict that became the Second World War began in China. The Japanese invasion of China in 1937 started the Resistance War. The world war ended in Asia, with Japan's unconditional surrender in 1945. For China eight years of war were over. There was great relief but little celebration after the brief demonstrations that followed the actual Japanese surrender in August. There were too many post-war problems to resolve, for the state, for communities and for families and individuals. Beyond the immediate problems and almost dwarfing them was the recognition, now that the war was over, of the terrible costs it had brought.

The Chinese state, GMD or CCP, has found it difficult to deal openly with the scale of the losses, in human lives or in material loss. The formal recognition of those who died in the Resistance War did not come for a long time. On the Mainland the CCP waited several decades to commemorate the war. The major national memorials to the war dead were not built for four decades (the Nanjing Massacre Memorial Hall in 1985, the Lugouqiao Memorial Museum in 1987). In Taiwan the Martyrs' Memorial, which commemorates the dead of many wars, was not built until the late 1960s. Work on the Heroes' Memorial in Tiananmen (Beijing) did start earlier, in 1952, but, like the Taiwan memorial, it commemorated all those who had died over the previous century in the struggle for the revolution; the heroes of the Resistance War accounted for only a small proportion of all the heroes.

The reason for the long delay in commemorating what had been the most costly war in Chinese history was political. It was clear well before the end of the Resistance War that the war going to be followed by a civil war, which would divide the nation again after the brief period of national unity during the Resistance War. Neither the GMD nor the CCP had the time or the inclination to commemorate those who had just died. And the CCP did not want to commemorate the millions of soldiers who had fought and died for China under the GMD banner. This pattern of thinking hardened into permanency after 1949.

Casualties and damage of the Resistance War

In October 1945 General He Yingqin reported on the military casualties of the war. 1,800,000 officers and men had been killed, another 1,770,000 wounded.[1] The civilian casualties were far larger; figures as high 20,000,000 were widely cited at the time, deaths caused by fighting and bombing, and by war-induced famine and disease.[2]

China's physical infrastructure was shattered by the war. In addition to the damage to the cities in unoccupied China that had been bombed throughout the war, there was recent damage from bombing in occupied China; during the last year of the war, occupied cities were bombed not by Japanese but by US bombers. Many of the railway bridges in eastern China were taken out in the last months of the war. The Japanese forces were in the position that China had been in at the beginning of the war, facing an enemy with overwhelming air power – the USA; their own air force was virtually gone.[3] As the Japanese started to recognise the coming defeat, their troops were pulled back from southern China and their civilians started to flee towards the ports. Almost any vessel that could float, most of them Chinese-owned, was used to ship people back to Japan. The lack of shipping was a body-blow to China in terms of economic recovery.

In late 1945 China's cities were in a terrible state. Chongqing and Wuhan had been bombed almost to ruins. Hong Kong had been ransacked and its population reduced to about 20 per cent of its pre-war size; most of the inhabitants had fled after the Japanese occupation in late 1941 into the unoccupied areas of Guangdong. The once-occupied cities – Nanjing, Shanghai, Beiping and Tianjin – seemed to have survived the war unscathed but were run-down and shabby after the long years

[1] *China Newsweek*, 159 (18 October 1945), p. 4.
[2] Diana Lary, *The Chinese People at War* (New York: Cambridge University Press, 2010), pp. 171–173; Odd Arne Westad, *Decisive Encounters: The Chinese Civil War, 1949–1950* (Stanford: Stanford University Press, 2003), p. 20.
[3] Victor Odlum to MacKenzie King, April 1945, *Monthly Reports, National Archives of Canada*, p. 349076.

of Japanese occupation that saw little maintenance or restoration and almost no new building.

土崩瓦解
Tu beng wa jie
Things gone to rack and ruin

Port cities (Xiamen, Fuzhou, Qingdao, Yantai) had sunk into inactivity during the war, as the international trade on which they depended had dried up. The Manchurian cities were the only ones in China unscathed at the time of the Japanese surrender, although the grandiose new capital of Manzhouguo, Xinjing (Changchun) was less than half finished. The relatively good situation of the Manchurian cities continued only for a few days, until Soviet armies arrived in the first week after the Japanese surrender. The incoming Soviet armies quickly began to loot the cities of anything movable.

China's fledgling modern economy was in ruins, destroyed by bombing, the decline in trade and inflation. The one industrial region of China not damaged by bombing or the cessation of international trade, Manchuria, was in Soviet hands and no longer functioning. The areas in Guangdong and Fujian dependent on remittance income from Overseas Chinese were destitute, after years in which almost no remittances had got through from relatives abroad. The Overseas Chinese communities in Southeast Asia had themselves suffered severely under the Japanese occupation of the region. As ethnic Chinese they were treated as the enemy, their businesses expropriated and their livelihoods destroyed. Individuals were subjected to brutal treatment. At the end of the Second World War they were unable to help their families at home.[4]

Inflation

The Chinese economy's critical weakness made recovery a distant dream. The dream receded even further as the national currency went into free fall, now moving the economy from inflation into hyperinflation.[5] The government had funded the Resistance War by printing paper money, the quickest route to inflation. Even as the inflation worsened, there was little sign that the government grasped its significance, in economic or political terms. Inflation undermined its own popularity and its legitimacy,

---

[4] For a vivid fictional account of the Japanese occupation of one of the major Chinese communities in Southeast Asia, Penang, see Tan Twan Eng, *The Gift of Rain* (Newcastle: Myrmidion, 2007).
[5] Hyperinflation occurs when the monthly rate of inflation exceeds 50 per cent.

which withered as the inflation got worse. The government did not plan inflation but made little effort to stop it; instead it was 'the crude resort of a government faced with an intricate problem of cause and effect that was not fully understood'.[6]

Property

There was one economic peace bonus, a considerable one. The Chinese government was enriched by the confiscation of the enormous Japanese assets in China, built up over 50 years and now forfeit as enemy property – mines, factories, housing, shipping, railways. All of these assets could be used to generate income, or to reward followers, so long as the government could get hold of them. In much of once-occupied China this was the case, since the assets were concentrated in cities, but in Manchuria most fell into Soviet hands. In Taiwan, the treasure island (*baodao*), the rich trove of Japanese assets was deemed to include the property of Taiwanese who had worked for the Japanese over the 50 years of Japanese rule. This interpretation was a source of rancour and fury. Taiwanese had had no choice but to work for the Japanese, since the island was a Japanese colony. There were equally bitter feelings about the confiscation of 'enemy' property in Chinese cities. Much of this property had originally belonged to Chinese who had been expropriated by the Japanese. In the once-occupied areas, the concept of private property virtually disappeared. Whatever the returning government and its agents wanted, they took.

The social effects of war

The society that emerged from the Resistance War was in chaos. It bore little resemblance to the pre-war world. All across China there were omnipresent signs of a loss of social cohesion and of social disintegration. The war had destroyed much of the fabric of society. As Tony Judt described the post-war situation in Eastern Europe, the war had 'corroded the very fabric' of the state and of the society.[7] The American missionary and sinologist Frank Price gave this description of Chinese society in 1945:

Some may think that this war only aggravated the disturbed conditions that the Chinese people have long had to endure. Actually China had never before

---

[6] Chang Kia-gnau, *The Inflationary Spiral: The Experience of China, 1939–1950* (Cambridge, MA: MIT Press, 1958), p. 342.

[7] Tony Judt, *Postwar: A history of Europe Since 1945* (New York: Penguin, 2005), p. 34. This brilliant study captures the complete destruction of war in Europe. Much of what Judt says refers equally to China.

experienced such a severe disruption of her family and social life and of her inherited culture.[8]

Price was talking about the tens of millions of people who had been uprooted during the war, including the five to ten million who had fled into the west of the country at the start of the war and were still there at the end of the war. Some of them wanted to go home; others were permanently detached from their homes.

The disruption and disintegration were profoundly distressing for much of society, but especially for the elderly and the traditionally minded. For others the precipitous decline of the old social order was welcome. Many of the young people who had fled to the west in 1937 and 1938 did go east again at the end of the war, but they did not return to the world they had known before the war. The long separation had gradually detached them from the authority of their families. Many had married while they were away, to people they had chosen themselves. This was a complete break with the traditional pattern of marriage arranged by parents. For the young couples it was a great advance, for the parents it was less easy to cope with. And the free marriage of a son might leave the parents at home caring for his bride (or fiancée) from a marriage arranged in the son's childhood.

Those young people who believed in socialism and revolution were even more enthusiastic about the decline of the old order. They were ideologically opposed to the old order, to the point often of hatred. One of reasons that men like Mao Zedong had turned towards socialism in their youth was hatred for the old Confucian order, which they had experienced as an agent of repression in their own families. Their idea of the family was the new, revolutionary family, a small unit whose first aim was not the preservation of the traditional family but the promotion of socialism.

One of the key issues in the extreme disruption to the social order that the war had brought was the question of whether the old system could recover or not, whether it was resilient enough to restore itself. The CCP obviously believed it could not; it wanted revolution. The GMD meanwhile seemed to have no stated policy or strategy on social regeneration; the social issues were so complex and so multifaceted that they could only be passed over in silence, even while the symptoms of the disruption became clearer and clearer.

---

[8] Frank Price, *China: Twilight or Dawn?* (New York: Friendship Press, 1948), p. 30.

Social levelling/elite upheaval

The Resistance War had achieved a degree of social upheaval that is usually associated with political revolution. The term used by the CCP to describe the upheaval caused by their class warfare was *fanshen*, literally 'turning over the body', in English probably 'turning upside down'. The CCP took credit for the process, but in fact it was underway, without the party's intervention, during the Resistance War, as the old social order dissolved.[9] The structures at the grassroots of rural society that glued people together had withered – the extended family, the lineage (often called the clan), the village. Many of the functions once performed within these structures were critical to social cohesion: education; employment; care for the needy or destitute (orphans, widows, the elderly); maintaining public order; arranging ceremonies and rituals. These structures had been run in the past by the rural elite, men with deep, blood ties to the communities they led. This elite was already in decline, and had been for several decades. The abolition of the imperial examination system (1905) had deprived it of the formal designation of gentry (*shenshi*), a status based on the examination successes of family members. Soon 'elite' no longer carried connotations of cultural superiority; it often simply meant 'rich' (*caizhu*), and described a merchant or landowning family. Martin Yang's affectionate description of his home village, Taitou (near Qingdao, Shandong) in the 1930s showed how much the traditional institutions were eroding before the Japanese invasion; he cannot have imagined the degree to which the Resistance War would accelerate the process.[10]

Nowhere in China was the breakdown of the old order more apparent than in Shandong, where the main cities were occupied in 1937 and 1938 by Japanese armies, and chaos and violence descended on the rest of the province. This crippling collapse of public order was a major factor in the spread of communism in rural Shandong. From the beginning of the Resistance War, the CCP leadership, hundreds of miles away in remote Yan'an (Shaanxi), had recognised the strategic

---

[9] *Fanshen* is the title of a book by William Hinton, about the CCP takeover of a village in northwest China. William Hinton, *Fanshen: A Documentary of Revolution in a Chinese Village* (New York: Monthly Press, 1966). This influential book was based on Hinton's long stay in the village. Hinton was a committed Yankee radical, the nephew of the romantic revolutionary writer Ethel Voynich. Her novel *The Gadfly* (published in 1897) was one of the most popular Western books in China in the Mao era.

[10] Martin Yang, *A Chinese Village: Taitou, Shantung Province* (New York: Columbia, 1945), p. 135.

importance of Shandong. Over the course of the war the CCP was able, often through harsh measures, to transform an ill-disciplined scattering of communist activists into a disciplined, tough organisation, securely located in a number of strategic hill bases and augmented towards the end of the war by forces of the Eighth Route Army. The CCP effectively filled the vacuum created by the collapse of provincial and local government.[11]

Across the once-occupied parts of the country, the authority of the old rural elite had been compromised by its inability to deal with the stresses and emergencies of war. The decline of parts of the rural elite had been accelerated by absence. The members of the rural elite who had fled early in the Resistance War, either westwards or into the cities, were deeply compromised by their abandonment of their communities. Those who had stayed were fatally compromised; they had often been drawn into working for the Japanese, willingly or by force. When this meant providing girls for the military brothels, or young men to work as slave labour, the behaviour of village leaders was seen as betrayal of their own people. It earned them the fury and bitter resentment of peasants who had once respected them.[12] The rural elites emerged from the war critically weakened and discredited. They had failed to protect their members from the violence and predation of war. They had lost their leadership roles. The old elites did not recoup their pre-war positions. They were done for.[13]

The urban elites did not come through the war much better than the rural ones. The war had impoverished much of the urban elite. Merchants and manufacturers saw their businesses ruined by the direct damage of warfare and by the decline of trade. In a society without insurance, material losses were total. Salaried workers, including most of those who worked in the public service, could not keep up with inflation and lived in states of constant anxiety. Those who had savings saw the value of their holdings dwindle. Those who had held money in one of the occupation currencies saw theirs disappear completely. Once-wealthy or middle-class families were now poor. China's intellectuals suffered worst of all the middle classes. Those on monthly salaries (in universities

---

[11] Wu Yang, *A Revolution's Human Face: The Changing Social Make-up of Chinese Communist Party Members and their Relationship to the Larger National Organization in Two Jiaodong Counties* (PhD, University of British Columbia, 2013).

[12] Two recent studies deal with these painful issues: Peipei Qiu, Shu Zhiliang and Chen Lifei, *Chinese Comfort Women: Testimonies from Imperial Japan's Sex Slaves* (Vancouver: UBC Press, 2013) and Ju Zhifen, 'Labour Conscription in North China', in Stephen MacKinnon, Diana Lary and Ezra Vogel (eds.), *China at War: Regions of China, 1937–1945* (Stanford: Stanford University Press, 2007), pp. 207–226.

[13] Wu, *A Revolution's Human Face*, pp. 202–205.

or schools) were often destitute, since their salaries never kept up with inflation.

A critical and terrifying accompaniment of the destruction of the old order was violence. The wartime collapse of the old order had led to dramatic increases in violence, or to the reports of increased violence spread through the rumour mill, since reliable statistics on violence were not published. The situation in Shandong was worse than in many places, but not exceptional. Some of the violence was political, much of it was random. In the political arena, guerrilla actions against the Japanese, Japanese punitive raids and clashes between GMD and CCP supporters all produced horrific violence. Politically motivated violence was somehow justified (although not in the minds of its victims) as part of a larger, formal goal. Random violence, on the other hand, was a product of the anarchic situations that prevailed in many rural areas, where there had been little government administration for years. Banditry flourished, travel was dangerous. In the rural areas, women and girls were not safe, and often had to be kept at home. The few girls who might have gone to school were no longer able to do so.

The perpetrators of violence were predictable, a category dreaded at the end of any war: young men used to violence. China emerged from the war with a huge and amorphous body of disaffected young men. Most had little education, few were married and all were detached from their home societies. Some of the disaffected young men had missed out on the opportunity for an education because of the war. Others had been in one of the armed units that roamed throughout the occupied areas, militias, bandit gangs. Some men had served in the 'puppet' armies of the Japanese. Some had lost their families in the war. Some had been forced to work as slave labourers for the Japanese. Others had migrated to Manchuria but had been forced to come home when the factories and mines there closed down. All tended to be angry, most were inured to violence, both as perpetrators and as victims. They tended to be dismissed by the rest of society as *liumang* (wastrels, louts), but dismissing them did not make them go away. They were to be a key element in CCP recruitment, provided they could be organised and their anger channelled into disciplined service of the revolution.

Red Sorghum

No one has captured the violence and insecurity of rural China during the Resistance War better than the Shandong writer Mo

Yan. His first and best-known novel is *Red Sorghum*.* The story is set in his home county, Gaomi, a poor county mid-way between Jinan and Qingdao, a place famous for its folk culture and its tough, hard-drinking men. The red sorghum, a cereal crop, is used to produce a fierce liquor. Given the great height to which it grows, it has always been used to hide the movements of bandits and guerrilla fighters.

The novel describes the ferocity and the utter confusion of the struggles between Japanese forces and their 'puppet' troops (*weijun*) and the shifting, disorganised groups of local guerrillas, disbanded soldiers, bandits and tough young men. The outcomes are tragic for all of them; the only certainty is death, and it is often brutal. The novel and the film based on it are saved from complete blackness by a considerable amount of humour, a great deal of drinking and a passionate love story. The 1987 film starred two of China's best-known film stars, Gong Li and Jiang Wen, as the lovers. It was directed by the leading director Zhang Yimou.

Mo Yan's later novels deal with rough, earthy, lusty and often violent parts of Chinese life. He has been able to write much more frankly than other writers because he is not only a peasant by birth, but he served for a long time in the People's Liberation Army. Mo Yan won the Nobel Prize for Literature in 2012.

* Mo Yan, *Red Sorghum* (New York: Viking, 1993). The Chinese original, *Hong Gaoliang*, appeared in 1986.

The disruption and violence at the end of the Resistance War were not unique to China. The degree of social upheaval was similar to the situation in parts of post-war Europe, which had experienced 'the liquidation of old social and economic elites':

Some countries – Poland, the Baltic States, Greece, Yugoslavia – were occupied three times, in five years. With each succeeding invasion the previous regime was destroyed, its authority dismantled, its elites reduced. The result in some cases was a clean slate, with all the old hierarchies discredited and their representatives compromised.[14]

In China at the end of the war it was clear that there could be no return to the pre-war social order. In the once-occupied areas of China the mass social confusion and the loss of possible leadership by the old elite paved the way for the new, disciplined order of the CCP.

[14] Judt, *Postwar*, p. 34

Social polarisation

The CCP, with its promise of a new social order based on Marxist ideology, could fill the vacuum in social control only in the rural areas of north China it controlled militarily. In other areas different new social strata emerged and found their own opportunities in the post-war chaos. In the cities and in the commercial world, war and inflation gave birth to a noxious stratum of opportunists, black marketeers, hoarders and profiteers, quick, slippery people who saw their chance to get rich very quickly and seized it. Black marketeers traded in any goods in short supply. The most lucrative were goods brought in from the US, as aid to the Chinese people, which somehow were 'detached' from their rightful recipients. Hoarders, slightly less venial, bought up goods, stored them away and then sold them on when inflation had taken the prices up. Profiteers played all markets, but especially the currency markets.

Inflation and shortages of commodities created the ideal conditions for the enrichment of the unscrupulous. The press was still free, and news reports, plus rampant gossip, made the situation clear to all those in the money economy, many of whom existed in states of chronic rage about how they were being cheated at every turn. The government was aware of the situation, but none of its promised actions to rein in the black marketeers, hoarders and profiteers had any effect. The lack of restriction on the racketeers and profiteers convinced much of the urban population that the government was enabling their activities, or at least condoning them. Even worse, it was widely believed that many of these hated men were actually within the governing GMD elite, that the GMD had become corrupt during the war.

The taint of government corruption separated the GMD from what should have been its natural constituencies, the urban middle class, intellectuals, business people, students; these were the people who bore the brunt of corruption.

Separations

妻離子散
Qi li zi san
The wife has left, the sons are scattered

The long years of the Resistance War had created family separations that dragged on and on; until the last months of the war there seemed no prospect of them ever ending. In the immediate aftermath of the war, the possibility of reuniting suddenly seemed real. People longed to get back to their homes, to see their families again, and to pay their respects at the graves of their relatives who had died during the war. Many people did make it home, but such a long and turbulent time had elapsed that some separations could not be repaired. Writing just after the war the sociologist Fei Xiaotong wrote with deep sadness of his permanent separation from his home Wujiang, in the beautiful 'land of fish and rice' south of the Yangzi. Neither he nor his three brothers, nor any of the seven people from his home county who had studied abroad, went home after the war. All of them had fled into the west at the beginning of the war, leaving their elderly parents at home:

In the occupied areas the old people longed for the return of their children from whom they had been separated for so long. To do what? To reclaim the derelict land, to rebuild the destroyed buildings. The whole of the shattered countryside had to be restored. But what did they get? Was it their own sons who came back, the ones in whose veins their own blood flowed? No. Things had changed. It was ruthless outsiders who came and brought even greater hardships.[15]

The now-adult children had, because of the war, been permanently detached from home. The ruthless outsiders were the carpet-baggers and the profiteers who came in after the Japanese had left to 'clean up' the areas that had been occupied. The children had not only been separated from their parents, but had left them unprotected, first from the Japanese and then from the new menace. There was a permanent divide between the generations.

The divide was brought on by separation. Beyond it there was disgust that many young people felt for the state of Chinese society and politics, for which they blamed the old order and the crippling conservatism of the old family system. The fact that many of their elders were now hard-up and no longer had financial control over the younger generations contributed to the generational divide. There was a mood switch. Older people were tired and often cynical at the end of eight years of war. Many of the young were full of passion and ready to embrace the kind of idealism that had spurred an earlier generation towards revolution in the years before the Xinhai Revolution in 1911.

Foreigners in China had also gone through long wartime separations. Most of those in China in 1937 spent the next eight years there, unable to leave once ocean transport ceased. Those from Allied countries (USA, UK, Australia, Canada, New Zealand) were interned after Pearl Harbor in Japanese concentration camps. Immediately after the war the Allied

---

[15] Fei Xiaotong, *Fei Xiaotong wenji* (*Collection of Fei Xiaotong's Writings*) (Beijing: Qunyan chubanshe, 1999), p. 465.

internees came out of the camps, most to be repatriated to their home countries. The end of the war was also the end of their lives in China. Many missionaries resumed their work, but the old business communities in the former treaty ports were a shadow of their former selves. The largest group of foreigners who remained in China were the White Russians.

Jiang Fangliang

The great majority of Russians in China during the Resistance War were White Russians, refugees from the revolution in Russia and their children. Most were in Manchuria, some in Shanghai and Tianjin. Many claimed to be aristocrats by birth, but in China they were poor and dispossessed. There was one notable exception, a very different Russian woman. Raina Ipatevna Vakhreva is generally known by her Chinese name, Jiang Fangliang. She was from an ordinary family in Belarus. In China, however, her status was very high. She was the wife of Jiang Jingguo and the daughter-in-law of Chiang Kai-shek.

She married Jiang Jingguo in 1935, while she was still a teenager. He had been sent to study in the Soviet Union in 1927, and then 'retained' there by Stalin as a hostage for his father. In 1936 the young couple were allowed to travel to China with their son. Jiang Jingguo was quickly given major appointments by his father, while his wife retired into domestic obscurity, raising their four children. She was given no other role in her husband's family. Jiang Jingguo later had two more sons with another woman, who was not, however, given the status of a concubine. The Christian values of his father and stepmother, Song Meiling, prevented open polygamy. Jiang Fangliang's presence was sensed rather than visible. Her rather sad and mysterious life underlined the dysfunctional nature of Chiang Kai-shek's family.

The psychosocial effects of war

The Resistance War had a permanent effect on people's sense of security and psychological well-being. The overwhelming long-term psychosocial effects of the war were insecurity, and intense self-involvement derived from the self-protection that had been essential for wartime survival. Living in insecurity meant breaking many of the unwritten norms of society; to look after oneself and those closest to one, one had to abandon old niceties of social behaviour, to go on the black market, to hoard goods and to loot or steal as the opportunity arose. This was acute social fragmentation.

The fragmentation was intensified by the omnipresence of violence. During the war most Chinese had lived under the threat of violence, many had actually experienced it. Violence and the threat of violence had changed fundamental mindsets. As Tony Judt wrote: 'Violence precipitated cynicism. As occupying forces the Nazis and Soviets precipitated a war of all against all. They discouraged not just allegiance to the authority of the previous regime or state, but any sense of civility or bond between individuals, and on the whole they were successful.'[16]

One of the most insidious psychosocial effects of this breakdown was a general lack of trust, except of those very close to an individual, the immediate family. The extended family had lost much of its force and could no longer be relied on for financial help. The old circles of trust, based on hallowed ties (fellow-student, fellow-local (*laoxiang*), fellow-provincial) had lost their viability. And the old courtesies and customs that had oiled the traditional society were gone. Now the dominant need was to survive. The attitudes and behaviours created by the war continued into the Civil War period, but with a bitter intensification; the foreign enemy had disappeared and the only enemies now were other Chinese.

There seemed to be few places to which people in distress could turn to for help. Even the gods seemed to have let people down. The deities of Buddhism, Daoism and of folk religion had not protected people from the ravages of the war. Many people had lost faith in them, even to the point of anger.

Punishing the gods

William Hinton observed the punishment of a Buddhist deity in a village in Shanxi, part of the CCP campaign against superstition, and equally a statement of popular fury that the god had not helped the peasants, despite all the reverence and the donations he had been given. A group of young men and women from the Peasants' Association led the action:

They went to the temple, pulled the god out of his shrine, and carried him to the village office. Before a mass meeting they 'settled accounts' with him by proving that he had squandered their wealth without giving them

---

[16] Judt, *Postwar*, p. 34.

protection in return. Then they smashed his mud image with sticks and stones.*

The damage and losses of the Resistance War seemed, here and in other places, to be at least a partial indictment against the gods who seemed to be indifferent to the suffering of the people who worshipped them.

*Hinton, *Fanshen*, p. 190.

There was no help for people in distress and confusion from the established political order. The GMD was unable to offer any real hope of revival or, as Madame Chiang Kai-shek, true to her Christian beliefs, called it, 'resurrection'. The only ideology that offered a way forward was communism, a fierce task-master, but one that promised a new, proud, clean world for China. The new faith promised a better life for China.

Biographies

Liang Sicheng and Lin Huiyin

In the 1930s Liang Sicheng and Lin Huiyin made a poster couple for the new, Republican China. Both were from wealthy and influential families (Liang's father was the great reformer Liang Qichao), both were highly intelligent, foreign-educated and multilingual. They met, fell in love and married while they were studying in North America. They were both architectural historians, passionately involved in preserving the Chinese built past and adapting it to the modern world. At the start of the war their affluent, cultivated life disappeared. With the members of their institute of the Academia Sinica they fled to the west, and lived for most of the war in Li Jiang, a remote riverside village in Sichuan, where conditions were primitive. The once-privileged young couple did their own housework, cooked, sewed their own clothes, cared for their children and for each other. Lin and several other members of the community were chronically ill with tuberculosis, exacerbated by the foetid climate; there was no medical help for the sick. Although Liang and Lin coped with their diminished circumstances with good humour, many of their fellow exiles did not; there was constant bickering and frequent quarrelling in their 'lonely island' community. Lin recounted some of this in her letters to her close friend Wilma Fairbank. Just after the end of the war she wrote to Wilma about the long-term effects of the war on themselves and on mutual friends:

We have all aged greatly, gone through a peculiar form of poverty and sickness, endured long wars and poor communications and are now apprehending a great national strife and a difficult future... We are torn and shattered. We have emerged through various trials with new integrity, good bad or indifferent. We have not only tasted life but been tested by its grimness and hardship. We have lost much of our health though none of our faith. We now know for certain that enjoyment of life and suffering are one.[17]

The Gong sisters

One of the successes of the CCP lay in the charm and persuasiveness of the people who were its public face to the foreign world. Two of the most famous of these were sisters from Shanghai, Gong Pusheng and Gong Peng. They were early converts to communism. In the student movement at Yenching (Yanjing) University just before the start of the Resistance War they became radicals, but although they turned against their affluent background, they did not lose their sophistication; both were beautiful, elegant and spoke fluent English. During the war the older sister, Gong Pusheng, went to study in the USA, and made contacts with a range of important women, including Eleanor Roosevelt. Gong Peng was in Chongqing, as Zhou Enlai's mouthpiece for foreign journalists and diplomats.[18] She and her husband Qiao Guanhua were key parts of Zhou's brilliant propaganda campaign in Chongqing; the young, attractive and passionate couple made a huge impression on susceptible Westerners in Chongqing, many of whom had lost faith in the GMD. The two sisters went on to become diplomats in the PRC. Gong Pusheng was the PRC's first woman ambassador; her husband was another senior diplomat, Zhang Hanfu.

Lao She

The great writer Lao She seemed exhausted and pessimistic about the future of China at the end of the Resistance War. He had been an active and patriotic voice throughout the war, but now he could see little positive or optimistic about the future, above all for his beloved Beijing. His pessimism appeared in the words of a character in his great novel, *Four Generations Under One Roof*, which started to appear in instalments in 1946:

[17] Wilma Fairbank, *Liang and Lin: Partners in Exploring China's Architectural Past* (Philadelphia: University of Pennsylvania Press, 1992), pp. 144–145.
[18] Zhou's role in Chongqing was to represent the CCP in the United Front and to maintain international contacts for the CCP.

Our traditional maxim of 'climbing up the official ladder and making a fortune', our feudalistic thinking, which encourages one to become a high official but at the same time a contented slave, our family system, our educational methods and our habit of seeking shameful security at whatever cost – all these are hereditary national diseases.[19]

These national diseases had become worse, not better, during the war. There seemed to be no possibility of them being cured in the even greater post-war insecurity. Even though Lao She had suffered greatly during the war from his separation from his family in Beijing, he now left them again. He resolved his gloom about the future of China by leaving China. He accepted an official invitation from Washington to visit the USA. The visit gradually became permanent and he settled in New York City. As a young man he had spent many years in England. This was his second stay abroad.[20]

The Ballard family

J.G. Ballard's novel *The Empire of the Sun* was turned into a spectacular film by Stephen Spielberg (1987). It showed the Japanese attack on Shanghai, and then recounted the life of a young boy on the run in occupied Shanghai, before he was interned in a prison camp. The young Ballard, child of an affluent English family settled in Shanghai, spent three years in the Longhua Internment Camp near Shanghai. He came out of the camp in late August 1945, with his parents and sister. The family's house in Shanghai had survived undamaged, occupied by a puppet general, although his friend's house had been reduced to a shell: 'I reached for the doorbell and looked through the open door at the sky.' Shanghai revived rapidly. The Ballard's German neighbour disappeared, and was replaced by 'two very likeable American intelligence officers'. At the end of the year he, his mother and sister were evacuated to England, the first time he had been there. It was a horrible contrast to the vivid life of Shanghai: 'everything seemed to be crumbling and shabby, unpainted for years... A steady drizzle fell for most of the time, and the sky was slate grey with soot lifting over the streets from tens of thousands of chimneys.'[21]

---

[19] Quoted in C.T. Hsia, *A History of Modern Chinese Fiction* (New Haven: Yale University Press, 1961), p. 373.

[20] *Lao She Yingwen shuxin ji (Collection of Lao She's Letters in English)* (Beijing: Jinshilu, 1993), p. 100.

[21] J.G. Ballard, *Miracles of Life: Shanghai to Shepperton* (London: Fourth Estate, 2008), pp. 108, 113, 122–123.

2 Ending one war, beginning another: August 1945–June 1946

Ending one war

In sombre tones Chiang Kai-shek broadcast to the nation on 15 August 1945, the date of the Japanese surrender. His message started with a disturbing warning: 'We may feel that the problems of peace that descend on us are more trying even than those we met during the war.' He was conciliatory; he called on Chinese not to turn against 'our fellow countrymen in the enemy-occupied areas', who have endured 'a long night of devastation and disgrace'.[1]

Victory could not disguise the terrible state that the war had left China in, her society in chaos, her economy in tatters. Millions of people were away from their homes. As much as a quarter of the population had been displaced at some stage during the war, some for long periods, others only briefly.[2]

哀鴻遍野
Ai hong pian ye
A land swarming with refugees

The transport system was almost completely disrupted, roads and railways destroyed. Agricultural yields were right down in many parts of the country; famine was already acute in Hunan, where millions were starving. Famine was looming in Sichuan, Guangxi and Guangdong. The country seemed to be almost destroyed.

There was no real peace. The re-establishment of political order in China was fragile. The central government now technically regained control of all the areas occupied by Japan, but in fact did not. The bulk of the GMD armed forces were far away, in the west. The GMD government

---

[1] Victor Odlum to Mackenzie King, 8 August 1945, *National Archives of Canada*, C-9878, p. 349148. The broadcast may not have been heard by many people, given the rudimentary nature of the radio network, and Chiang's impenetrable Zhejiang accent.

[2] Diana Lary, *The Chinese People at War* (New York: Cambridge University Press, 2010), pp. 175–176, gives estimates of the total number of refugees during the Resistance War.

stayed in Chongqing, where all major government activities took place until its final return to its pre-war capital Nanjing in April 1946. These included the negotiations between the GMD and the CCP to avoid civil war. When the government did arrive in Nanjing it had to disassociate itself from the Wang Jingwei puppet regime that had been in place there until August 1945, using the same name of the GMD. Chiang Kai-shek moved into the Central Military Academy, rather than live in the new palace built by Wang, which became the American Club.

Wang Jingwei

Wang Jingwei was a close supporter of Sun Yat-sen during the early years of the GMD's rise to power. A handsome, charismatic figure, he seemed destined for leadership of the party, but he was a civilian and was side-lined by Chiang Kai-shek and the military side of the party. Even so, he held a series of important positions in the national government in Nanjing, and was widely admired. He went west with the rest of the government to Chongqing. Then, in a shocking departure, he left Chongqing in late 1938 and went back into Japanese-occupied China. He seems to have believed that Japanese victory was inevitable and permanent. He was head of the Japanese-sponsored government in Nanjing, generally referred to as a puppet government. He died shortly before the end of the war, in Japan. Wang has never been forgiven for his collaboration with the Japanese occupiers, and is still seen by virtually all Chinese as a traitor.

All over eastern, northern and southern China local groups took power. In Qingdao, the key port of Shandong, Liu Xianlong, a GMD guerrilla leader, came down from the Laoshan Hills east of the city; he had been there with 10,000 armed men for the duration of the war.[3] He became mayor of Qingdao; GMD forces did not arrive for another two months. In many of the small towns and villages of northern China it was the CCP that took control, or was already in control. There was no certainty, however, that CCP control was permanent.

Manchuria was under the control of the Soviet armies. The GMD's opportunity to re-establish its leadership of the nation was compromised by the delays and uncertainties that accompanied the end of the war, and by the need to deal with a host of other compelling issues connected to the sudden end of the war.

[3] *China Newsweek*, 24 January 1946, pp. 6–7.

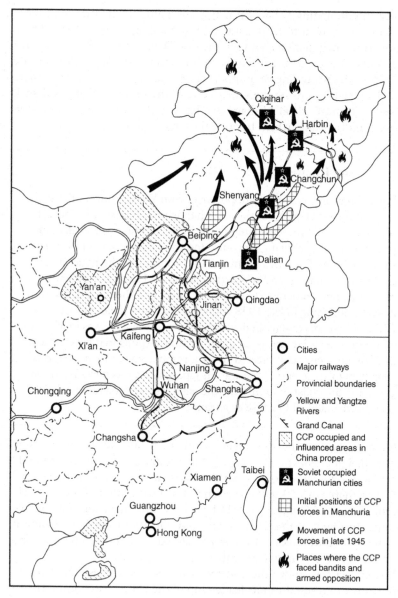

Map 1 CCP-controlled and influenced areas, late 1945

The defeated Japanese

One of the first issues was arranging the departure of the millions of soldiers of the defeated Japanese armies. The units in China proper surrendered to the GMD over a period of several months, during which many units continued in service 'keeping order' until the GMD could take over. More than half a million Japanese soldiers were captured in Manchuria by the Red Army and taken as slave labour into the USSR. The rest of the Japanese armies led the southward rush out of Manchuria in August 1945. The Japanese military had been severely shaken by its defeat by the Soviets at Nomonhan (1939) and feared a return engagement. The Red Army performed a symbolic act in Harbin: the newly built Yamato Shrine, the symbol of the expansionist Japanese state, was destroyed. For good measure the Soviet Army blew up the anti-communist monument erected by the White Russian community.

The Japanese authorities had made no arrangements for Japanese civilians in Manchuria to leave at the end of the war. They were repatriated to Japan over the next year and a half, largely by the US. Civilians were brought down to the island of Huludao, a port that the Japanese had just built on the Liaoning coast, and then shipped to Japan, with only what they could carry. In the end, more than two million Japanese civilians were repatriated; almost none were left in China.[4]

The Japanese had brought large numbers of Korean and Taiwanese into China. The future of the two million or so Koreans who had been brought into Manchuria as peasants by their colonial masters was up in the air, but many of the Taiwanese (Japanese citizens until the end of the war) left China precipitately at the end of the war. These included soldiers, merchants and intellectuals – men such as Zhang Wojun, the father of the celebrated archaeologist Zhang Guangzhi (K.C. Chang), who had been a professor of Japanese literature at Peking University.[5]

The Zhang family

The celebrated archaeologist Zhang Guangzhi (K.C. Chang) was born in 1932 in Beijing (then Beiping), the second of four sons of a Taiwanese professor, Zhang Wojun, and his wife, who was from Hubei. The father was a major figure in the Taiwanese literary

---

[4] Lary, *The Chinese People at War*, p. 189.
[5] Robert Murowchick, *Kwang-chih Chang: A Biographical Memoir* (Washington: National Academy of Sciences, 2012).

world, in Taiwan and later in Beiping; the family house there was a centre for Taiwanese intellectuals living in the Japanese-occupied city. As Taiwanese, they were Japanese citizens. The four boys lived idyllic childhood years in the ancient city. In his autobiography, Zhang remembered climbing about on the great walls and gates of the city. He described in mouth-watering detail the delicious street food of the city, especially the buns and pastries that can never be found except in Beijing. The sesame buns (*xiaobing*) that anyone who has lived in the city longs for are the equivalent of Marcel Proust's *madeleines*. The young boy was an excellent student, but his happy childhood had an unreality to it; the Zhang boys lived in a world untouched by the war. It was a time out of time. As soon as the Japanese were defeated, his father left for Taiwan; the rest of the family followed a year later – but without the oldest son, who had already left the city to join the CCP in the JinChaJi border region. The idyllic childhood vanished.

His family's enmeshment in the turmoil of Chinese politics made Zhang Guangzhi reflect, years later, on his own identity. He decided that he was Taiwanese first, then from Minnan (the part of southern China from which the native Taiwanese came), then Chinese. For this reason he called his biography *The Story of a Sweet Potato*, the sobriquet that Taiwanese use for themselves to distinguish them from the Mainlanders who started arriving on the island in 1945 and are known as 'taro (*yuzi*)'.★

★ Zhang Guangzhi, *Fanshu de gushi* (*The Story of a Sweet Potato*) (Taibei: Lianjing, 1998), pp. 3, 12–14, 27.

There was a relative lack of vengeance towards Japanese in China, certainly as compared to the Soviet vengeance on Germany earlier in 1945. Retreating Japanese forces destroyed much of the evidence of war crimes; large parts of the Unit 731 chemical and biological weapons station outside Harbin were blown up just before the retreat. In Shenyang and other places in Manchuria Japanese archives were burnt.

There was a parallel process in Asia to the Nuremberg Trials for the prosecution of Japanese war criminals. The International Military Tribunal for the Far East (the Tokyo Trials) started work in January 1946, with an international panel of judges. Twenty-eight men were indicted as Class A war criminals, including Generals Matsui Iwane and Doihara Kenji, indicted for crimes in China. Both were executed. The tribunal was wound up in 1948.

The tribunal satisfied few people. In China it seemed that too few men had been held responsible for eight years of suffering. In Japan the accusation was levelled that the tribunal represented 'victor's justice'. The dissatisfaction has continued. Many Chinese believe that Japan has not recognised the effect of her army's actions in China. And some right-wing Japanese continue to believe that Japan's real crime was to be defeated. The commemoration of Matsui and Doihara in the Yasukuni Shrine in Tokyo, and official visits to the shrine, has led to recurrent friction between Japan and China, most recently in January 2014, after prime minister Abe Shinzo's visit.

In Hong Kong, which passed back under British control almost casually at the end of the war, several dozen men accused of working actively with the Japanese occupiers were tried in military and civilian courts. Five were eventually executed, including a Japanese Canadian, Inouye Kanao, who had worked in Hong Kong as an interpreter for the Japanese secret police, the Kempeitai.[6]

Chinese who had worked with the Japanese

An immediate problem for the Chinese government was what to do with Chinese who had worked with the Japanese. The most egregious were those labelled traitors (hanjian).[7] Wang Jingwei made things easy for the GMD. He died in Japan in 1944 and could not be prosecuted. His remains were not spared; in 1945 his grave near Nanjing was vandalised.

Vengeance on Wang Jingwei's body

In Chinese tradition the bodies of those who have committed crimes for which they were not punished in life were exhumed and the bones crushed. Vengeance was taken against Wang Jingwei's body. Chan Cheong-Choo, nephew of Wang's wife Chen Bijun, described what happened to Wang's remains, which had been buried the year before, after the GMD came back into Nanjing:

One night, soon after the return of Chiang Kai-shek to Nanking [Nanjing], a loud explosion was heard coming from the 'Plum Flower Hill'. Vandals had

---

[6] G.B. Endacott, *Hong Kong Eclipse* (Hong Kong: Oxford University Press, 1978), pp. 242–247. Inouye was not convicted of war crimes, but of treason under British law, since he was a Canadian citizen.

[7] This is a loaded term; in terms of prosecution it was reserved for people who had worked actively for the Japanese at fairly senior levels.

laid explosives to the grave, the concrete compartment was blasted, the lid forced open, and Fourth Brother's [Wang Jingwei] remains had disappeared. Rumours had it that the body was hacked to pieces and taken away in a sack to be dumped in a secret place known only to the perpetrators or thrown in to the Yangtse [Yangzi]. Who did it, and why the desecration? It could only have been done on explicit orders from the highest authority.*

* Chan Cheong-Choo, *Memoirs of a Citizen of Early XX Century China* (Willowdale, Ontario: Self-published, 1967), p. 177.

Several of the most prominent *hanjian* were put on trial soon after the war.

Table 2.1 *Prominent Chinese prosecuted for treachery*

	Wartime position	Fate
Chen Pijun	Wang Jingwei's wife	Sentenced to life imprisonment. Died in jail 1959.
Zhou Fohai	Wang's second-in-command	Sentenced to death 1946; commuted. Died in jail 1948.
Wang Kemin	Head of Beiping puppet government	Tried for treason; committed suicide in jail December 1945
Chu Minyi	Foreign minister under Wang	Tried for treason, executed 1946.
Chen Gongbo	Wang's successor	Tried for treason, executed 1946.
Zhou Zuoren	Writer; brother of Lu Xun	Arrested 1945. Served four years in jail.

The number of *hanjian* executed was quite small. Their trials were given enormous media coverage, with full and often grisly details of the manner of their deaths, so that – although the executions were not public – there was little doubt about what had happened.

One of the most flamboyant *hanjian* was Aisin Gioro Xianyu, known as the Asian Mata Hari. She was a Manchu princess who had worked closely with the puppet Manzhouguo government. She was arrested in late 1945, tried and executed in 1948.[8] The most notorious Manchu,

[8] Shao Dan, *Remote Homeland, Recovered Borderland: Manchus, Manchoukuo and Manchuria, 1907–1935* (Honolulu: University of Hawaii Press, 2011), pp. 221–224. This account of Xianyu is based on the extensive evidence given at her trial.

Aisin Gioro Pu Yi, the emperor of Manzhouguo, was arrested by the Soviets in August 1945 and taken to the USSR. He was returned to China after the CCP won the Civil War, and served a lengthy prison sentence, at the end of which he lived quietly in Beijing and worked as a gardener.

Dealing with those people not formally labelled as *hanjian*, but who had worked for or lived quietly under the Japanese, and with the puppet forces (*weijun*), was problematic. These two categories amounted to a huge number of people. Many officials were dismissed from their positions, although others were allowed to stay because they were needed. According to General Li Zongren, in command in Beiping, sacking people who had worked under the Japanese was sanctioned by the government, and amounted to a form of 'terrorism purposely created by the secret service'. Those doctors at the famous Peking Union Medical College who had stayed on in Beiping after the Japanese arrived in 1937 were all fired by the incoming GMD. Li arranged for them to go and work in his native province, Guangxi.[9]

Others whose records vis-à-vis the Japanese were unclear suffered only embarrassment. The reputation of the writer Zhang Ailing (Eileen Chang) was tarnished by her husband's; Hu Lancheng was a major collaborator. For her admirers her political contamination was diminished by the elegance of her writing and by the message, as seen in her story *Lust and Precepts*, that passion overcomes 'moral and national obligations'. 'Justice, righteousness, comradeship, nation, duty and morality – all become irrelevant.'[10]

Confiscation and looting

In late 1945 and into 1946 there was a tidal wave of confiscation throughout the once-occupied regions. Confiscation technically referred only to enemy and *hanjian* property, but it quickly degenerated into general looting. Many people with no dubious record under the Japanese had their property expropriated. The stigma of having lived under occupation was used to squeeze people, in Shanghai, Nanjing and other once-occupied cities.

---

[9] T'ong Te-kang and Li Tsung-jen, *The Memoirs of Li Tsung-jen* (Boulder, CO: Westview, 1979), pp. 440–441. This is the transcript of lengthy oral interviews with Li.

[10] Nicole Huang, *Women, War and Domesticity: Shanghai Literature and Popular Culture in the 1940s* (Boston: Brill, 2005), pp. 212–213, 218. Ang Lee's film *Lust Caution* (2007) is based on Zhang's story. Hu Lancheng went into hiding in 1945, and eventually managed to get to Japan.

To many in Shanghai, the GMD takeover felt more like the onslaught of a plague of locusts than a liberation. The takeover of Japanese property – factories, businesses, houses, vehicles – was one thing, but the expropriation of Chinese property was quite another. And yet within a short time, so many houses, businesses, cars and private possessions had been lost by the locals to the incomers from Chongqing that there was widespread disillusion and anger, expressed in a classic play on words. For the word *jieshou* (takeover) were substituted two words, almost homophones: *jieshou* (hand-over) and *jieshou* (plunder).[11] The GMD made no concessions to the big industrialists and capitalists, who might seem their natural allies; they were squeezed just as hard as less wealthy people.

In Taiwan the takeover was particularly harsh. All Japanese property was confiscated, giving the incoming government enormous assets, including as much as a third of the arable land, railways, government buildings, factories, schools, hospitals and a huge supply of housing. This was not enough for the incomers. The government and its soldiers treated the entire local population as active collaborators with the Japanese, which meant that they could be – and often were – fired from their jobs, stripped of their property, their businesses and their farms.

The people of Manchuria suffered just as harsh treatment as the Taiwanese did. It was as if they were being punished for the fact that they had suffered less than other parts of China during the Resistance War. Expropriation was exacted not by Chinese but by the Soviets. Starting in the 'August Storm', Soviet troops took over all Japanese property as war booty, and started a mass shipment of industrial machinery back to the USSR, in confiscated rolling-stock drawn by confiscated locomotives. Thousands of plants, the largest being the steel mills at Anshan, were completely dismantled and their machinery sent off to the USSR. Indirectly the GMD helped in the process. The Soviet presence in Manchuria, supposedly temporary, was extended at the request of the GMD, to allow the GMD to get more troops into Manchuria, 'a concession which permitted them [the Soviets] to carry away with them, as prizes of war, all the heavy machinery, machine tools, railroad ties and even office furniture'.[12] The outcome of the looting was observed by the American journalist George Moorad, in early 1946: 'Mukden [Shenyang] was mile after mile of skeletons and emptiness, shells of

---

[11] Suzanne Pepper, *Civil War in China* (Berkeley: University of California Press, 1978), p. 8.

[12] Lionel Chassin, *La conquete de la Chine par Mao Tse-tung* (*The Conquest of China by Mao Zedong*) (Paris: Payot, 1952. English translation: Cambridge, MA: Harvard University Press, 1965), p. 66.

buildings, frameworks of factories, in which great holes had been gouged to permit the exit of the machinery.' The only factories working were those producing beer, cigarettes and vodka for the Soviet troops.[13]

The Soviets focused on machinery and railway equipment. The incoming Chinese soldiers and civilians who started to arrive in the late autumn, after the Soviets had had their pick, confiscated and looted anything else – houses, furniture, cars, chattels. In January 1946, Chiang Kia-ngau (Jiang Jia'ao) went to the Kangde Palace in Changchun, once the Manzhougo emperor Pu Yi's residence. It had been looted, even down to the light bulbs.[14]

Looted palace in Changchun

When he went to Changchun in late 1945 to negotiate with the Soviet commanders in control there, the distinguished economist Chang Kia-ngua (Jiang Jia'ao) visited the little Kangde Palace built for Pu Yi, the last emperor of China (until 1917), and the puppet emperor of Manzhouguo under the Japanese (1932 to 1945). Pu Yi had in his possession a large collection of treasures from the Forbidden City in Beijing. This is what Chang found:

[In the library] the floor was littered with crates for books and paintings, as well as split strips of wood. When I lifted one or two wooden strips I saw that underneath were several books. Browsing through them I found that they were all Ming Dynasty editions. I took these books with me.

The looters had taken away scrolls of paintings and calligraphy after tearing off the cylindrical pieces of wood.*

It was not clear whether the looters were the departing Japanese, the incoming Soviets or local people. Whoever they were, some very great imperial treasures were lost at the time.

* Chang, *Last Chance in Manchuria*, p. 15. Dai Sijie's spell-binding novel *Once on a Moonless Night* (2007) is, in part, about the search for one of the treasures lost from Pu Yi's collection.

---

[13] George Moorad, *Lost Peace in China* (New York: Dutton, 1949), p. 161. Moorad, a gifted and adventurous journalist, died in a plane crash in the same week that his book was published.

[14] Chang Kia-ngau, *Last Chance in Manchuria* (Stanford: Hoover Institution Press, 1989), p. 15. Chang was the chief of the Northeast Economic Commission in Manchuria at the time. He was a banker, former head of the Bank of China.

Very little of the post-war looting was formally sanctioned. The GMD government looked the other way, not least because many of its own people were involved. One of the few official actions on looting went in the opposite direction, to recover art treasures taken during the war that had ended up in the hands of *hanjian* or in Japan. In early 1946, the Commission for the Protection and Salvage of Cultural Objects in the War Areas was set up. The collections of art held by major *hanjian* Chen Gongbo and Chen Bijun were recovered.[15] Other cultural objects that had been taken to Japan have yet to be recovered, including many rare books from the Nanjing City Library. Meanwhile, cultural losses were still going on. The Soviet Army removed one of the four surviving copies of the great Qing encyclopaedia, the *Siku quanshu*, from the old Manchu palace in Shenyang. The Soviets seem to have recognised the cultural importance of this work; transporting it cannot have been easy: it consists of more than 30,000 volumes.[16]

Occupation currencies

One of the most damaging decisions that the GMD made in the immediate post-war period was one that impoverished all those who held occupation currency, principally the middle classes of the occupied areas. At the end of the war the occupation currency and the *Fabi*, China's official currency, were almost at parity. Then the official exchange rate was suddenly changed to 200:1. 'With a single executive order, thousands of innocent people under the puppet government became bankrupt overnight.'[17] The occupation money was almost worthless, bank balances melted away. Holders of *Fabi*, that is those people who were returning from the west or were connected to the government, were suddenly at a huge advantage over those who had stayed in the occupied areas. Those who lost their money saw the new exchange rate as a vengeful act by their liberators for the time they had lived under the Japanese; they were being punished by the incoming GMD.

Economic collapse

Immediately after the end of the war, the wartime inflationary spiral reversed itself briefly. Prices of consumer goods fell suddenly as hoarders

---

[15] *China Newsweek*, 27 July 1946, pp. 4–5.

[16] Endymion Wilkinson, *Chinese History: A New Manual* (Cambridge, MA: Harvard University Asia Centre, 2013), p. 947. The volumes were later returned to China and are now in Lanzhou (Gansu).

[17] T'ong and Li, *Memoirs*, p. 438.

unloaded their stashes, in panic. But within two months prices were on the rise again.[18] The hope that the end of war would bring a resumption of manufacturing and trade was illusory. The peace brought a brief upsurge in late 1945 and early 1946, but by the end of 1946 it was over, the result of currency confusion and of inflation.[19] Throughout China inflation roared out of hand, the sometimes heavy-handed tactics used by the government to control it all ineffective.

Inflation and currency confusion were enough on their own to damage manufacturing and trade. To make matters worse, China's transport system remained in shambles. Water travel was tremendously limited by the fact that the Japanese had taken every vessel they could lay their hands on as they fled in the summer of 1945. Vessels still available were needed to bring back refugees from the west, to repatriate Japanese civilians and to move troops into Manchuria. The railway system was heavily damaged. Bridges and tracks had been destroyed at the end of the war, and locomotives and rolling stock had disappeared, many of them to the USSR. Between 1945 and 1946 the number of working locomotives in the vast rail network of Manchuria declined by two-thirds, from 2,403 to 808. Rail track in Manchuria in workable order declined from 6,890 miles to 1,677.[20]

Inflation, coupled with the breakdown of the communications system, brought with it insecurity, uncertainty and above all corruption. The beneficiaries of the economic chaos were primary producers (i.e., peasants), who could either demand higher prices or barter what they produced, and profiteers, who could do very well through hoarding, corruption and currency manipulation. The rural economy might be slightly better-off; other parts of the traditional economy were disabled. The coastal fishing industry had died in many places, because the boats were gone. In Xiamen in September 1945 all but two of the large fishing vessels were gone, either destroyed in the war or taken to repatriate people to Taiwan.[21]

One of the few bright spots on the economic front was Hong Kong. In the autumn of 1945 the population grew by about 3,000 people a day. In November it was already up to 700,000, although still only half of its

[18] Chang, *Last Chance in Manchuria*, p. 69.
[19] Marie-Claire Bergère, *Shanghai: China's Gateway to Modernity* (Stanford: Stanford University Press, 2009), pp. 327–329.
[20] Chang Kia-ngau, *The Inflationary Spiral: The Experience of China, 1939–1950* (Cambridge, MA: MIT Press, 1958), p. 226.
[21] Hong Puren, *Kangzhan shiqi de Xiamen* (*Xiamen during the Resistance War*) (Xiamen: Xiamenshi zhengxie weiyuanhui, 1995), p. 182.

pre-war population. Hong Kong people, back in their homes, were full of energy and determination to get going again.[22]

Stranded foreigners

China had to deal with a large number of stranded foreigners. There were 16,000 stateless refugees in Shanghai, 67 per cent German, 23 per cent Austrian, almost all Jewish. They were being supported temporarily by Jewish charitable organisations in New York. They wanted to leave, for the USA, Australia or Canada; gradually most were able to do so.[23] Thousands of liberated Western internees from the Japanese camps had been repatriated immediately after the end of the war.

Citizens of Japan's allies – Germans, Austrians, Italians and Vichy French – also had to be repatriated. A group of German priests and nuns had a strange meeting near Qingdao with an Austrian Jewish doctor working with the CCP. He was delighted, after five years with the communist armies, to eat fresh bread, baked by the nuns. They were distraught that their 40-year mission in China was finished.[24] In Manchuria there was the question of what to do with the White Russians. The USSR encouraged them to go home to Russia, the last thing many wanted to do. They too started to leave China, making not for the hated USSR but for the USA and Australia.

One thing was clear to all. The days of foreign dominance and privilege in China were gone for good.

Beginning another war

Political polarisation

In late 1945, political polarisation was acute. The GMD and the CCP were both gripped by an equally steely determination to use the end of one war to start an even more vital one, for control of China. The stakes were enormous. From early in Chinese history it was understood that the way to power was through success in war. Zhuangzi, the Daoist philosopher (fourth century BCE) put it one way:

---

[22] *China Critic*, XXXII, 13 (24 November 1945), p. 191.
[23] *China Newsweek*, 7 March 1946, pp. 5–6.
[24] Gerd Kaminski (ed.), *Ich Kannte Sie Alle: das Tagebuch des Chinesischen General Jakob Rosenfeld* (*I Knew Them All: The Diary of the Chinese General Jakob Rosenfeld*) (Vienna: Locker, 2002), p. 57.

竊鈎者誅 竊國者候

Qiegouzhe zhu, qieguozhe hou
Steal a hook and be executed, steal a country and become a marquis

Over two millennia later Mao Zedong put it more bluntly (1938):

抢杆子里出政权

Qiang ganzili chu zhengquan
Political power comes from the barrel of a gun

The determinations of the two sides to fight ignored the desires of the vast majority of the population. The GMD made no effort to be popular. The lack of popularity started at the top. Chiang Kai-shek was stiff and remote. He embraced the military and the traditional elite culture, neither of which spoke to the mood of a nation recovering from war. He promised nothing to the nation – no democracy, no peace bonus, no stability. His lack of popularity as a national leader meant that the GMD could not rebuild itself as a popular party, nor could it count on its one-time constituencies in the middle and upper strata of society. Its social capital was diminishing. In the toxic atmosphere of internal GMD politics, dominated by virulent gossip and back-stabbing, the almost suicidal loss of morale could not have been more acute. The American diplomat John Melby's comments in late 1945 summed up the situation in Chongqing.

The GMD's loss of morale

The US diplomat John Melby, attached to the US mission in Chongqing, described the GMD's loss of morale towards the end of the Resistance War, and the CCP's contrasting rise in self-confidence:

One of the great mysteries to me is why one group of people retains faith, whereas another from much the same origins and experience loses it. Over the years the Communists have absorbed an incredible amount of punishment, have been guilty of their own share of atrocities, and yet still have retained a kind of integrity, faith in their destiny and will to prevail. By contrast the Kuomintang [GMD] has also gone through astonishing tribulations, has committed its excesses, has survived a major war with unbelievable prestige and is now throwing everything away at a frightening rate because the revolutionary faith is gone and has been replaced by the smell of corruption and decay.*

* John Melby, *The Mandate of Heaven: Record of a Civil War* (Toronto: University of Toronto Press, 1968), p. 44.

As the GMD's morale declined, the CCP's was on the upswing. Yan'an, under Mao Zedong, now controlled the whole CCP throughout the country; all internal opposition had been suppressed. Its strength was now considerable. The well-informed French military attaché Jacques Guillermaz estimated that it controlled at least 100,000,000 people, had an army of 910,000 men and another two million militiamen.[25] Its power was concentrated in poor, rural areas, not in towns, but this was an advantage in times of inflation. The rural economy could function at a low level, through self-sufficiency and using bartering to replace monetised trade. The CCP's spartan, self-confident ideology made it attractive to people already living through very hard times; it almost glorified poverty. Yan'an was taken seriously now by foreign observers, its leaders regarded by some as moderate agrarian reformers rather than real revolutionaries.

One of the CCP's greatest strengths was on the propaganda front. To the urban populations, through covert means, it presented a carefully constructed image that combined equity, decency and patriotism. This image won discreet support from left-leaning intellectuals and artists. For the peasants the focus was on traditional folk culture. The CCP's cultural arm adapted traditional folk arts (songs, wood block prints, theatre) to enhance the political message. The CCP's cultural arm used the tales of earthy heroism contained in the *Romance of the Three Kingdoms* (*Sanguo yanyi*) and the *Water Margin* (*Shuihu zhuan*) to draw to the party the vast population who knew and loved these works. The CCP also continued to benefit from the back-handed advantage it had acquired during the war; communism had been virulently and continuously attacked by the Japanese for almost a decade. The enemy's enemy appeared in a favourable light. Above all the CCP also had the huge advantage of Mao Zedong's boundless confidence in ultimate success.

'The Foolish Old Man who Removed the Mountains'

Mao Zedong, in his speech at the 7th Congress of the CCP in June 1945, showed how skilled he was at interweaving stories from the popular tradition with a new revolutionary message.

There is an ancient Chinese fable called 'The Foolish Old Man Who Removed the Mountains'. It tells of an old man who lived in northern China long, long ago and was known as the Foolish Old Man of North Mountain. His house faced south and beyond his doorway stood the two great peaks,

---

[25] Jacques Guillermaz, *Une vie pour la Chine* (*A Life for China*) (Paris: Robert Laffont, 1968), p. 140.

Taihang and Wangwu, obstructing the way. He called his sons, and hoe in hand they began to dig up these mountains with great determination. Another graybeard, known as the Wise Old Man, saw them and said derisively, 'How silly of you to do this! It is quite impossible for you few to dig up those two huge mountains.' The Foolish Old Man replied, 'When I die, my sons will carry on; when they die, there will be my grandsons, and then their sons and grandsons, and so on to infinity. High as they are, the mountains cannot grow any higher and with every bit we dig, they will be that much lower. Why can't we clear them away?' Having refuted the Wise Old Man's wrong view, he went on digging every day, unshaken in his conviction. God was moved by this, and he sent down two angels, who carried the mountains away on their backs. Today, two big mountains lie like a dead weight on the Chinese people. One is imperialism, the other is feudalism. The Chinese Communist Party has long made up its mind to dig them up. We must persevere and work unceasingly, and we, too, will touch God's heart. Our God is none other than the masses of the Chinese people. If they stand up and dig together with us, why can't these two mountains be cleared away?*

The role of the supernatural (the angels) in removing the mountain is mysterious, since Mao, as a communist and a materialist, had to be opposed to manifestations of supernatural forces.

* http://afe.easia.columbia.edu/special/china_1900_mao_speeches.htm

Mao was equally confident in himself. In 1945, when he was in Chongqing, he arranged for the publication of a poem he had written ten years before, *Snow*. In it he tacitly compared himself to a long list of great rulers of the past, Qin Shihuang, Han Wudi, Tang Taizu and others: 'They are all gone into history. The real great hero is rising now.'[26] His audacity was breathtaking, showing someone on the verge of megalomania.

In its relations with foreign countries, the CCP benefitted greatly from the charm of one man – Zhou Enlai, the CCP's chief post-war negotiator in Chongqing. He was suave, sophisticated and handsome. He had been in France and spoke French. He was charming and gracious. Although cynical voices would later doubt his sincerity – 'he had a talent for telling blatant lies with an angelic suavity'[27] – at the time he seemed to be a voice of moderation, a man who made communism seem unthreatening. He captivated everyone, from grizzled veterans such as General George Marshall to young and idealistic Chinese. Zhou and his talented,

[26] Mao Zedong, *Turning Point in China* (New York: New Century, 1948).
[27] The comment is from Simon Leys, *The Hall of Uselessness* (New York: New York Review of Books, 2014), pp. 179–182. Leys has the distinction of being one of the few sinologists to have been (sadly) right about Mao Zedong's China.

attractive team, including his beautiful interpreter Gong Peng, were the public face of the revolution outside the immediate confines of the CCP.

Equally important in its success was the secret war, an often vicious war conducted outside any civilised norms. The CCP's highly efficient intelligence arm was under control of the sinister and dreaded Kang Sheng, known as Mao Zedong's Beria. He collected detailed information on the GMD and on his colleagues in the CCP, information that allowed Mao to continue to exercise his iron grip on the party. The GMD lost its own fearsome intelligence head, Dai Li, in a mysterious plane crash in March 1946. His intelligence network did not recover. GMD agents were thugs rather than ideologues, capable of brutality but without vision. The GMD lost the secret war with the CCP.

Kang Sheng and Dai Li

The two dreaded intelligence chiefs were equally feared and hated, although their origins and their methods were rather different. Kang, the CCP's black hand, was born in Shandong, was educated and became a teacher. He spent a long period as an underground communist in Shanghai before going to Moscow in the 1930s for special training. He became an expert in the sinister arts of ferreting out 'internal enemies', i.e., people within the CCP who opposed his master, Mao Zedong. He is hated more for his destruction of people *within* the CCP than outside it. He was a connoisseur of the arts, and lived in the Mao Era in a beautiful Beijing complex, the Bamboo Garden (now an up-market hotel), surrounded by plundered works of art.

Dai Li started out as a street fighter and gang member in Shanghai. His street smarts were a great assistance to his master Chiang Kai-shek, whom he served as head of the Bureau of Military Statistics, an intelligence-collecting agency, and, equally importantly, as the organiser of a brutal band of agents who carried out assassinations of suspected communists. He died in 1946 in a mysterious plane crash, assumed to be an act of revenge sabotage carried out by CCP agents.

In the polarised political world in China there was no place for intermediate positions. Both the GMD and the CCP were taking increasingly hard positions. In between their two poles those who believed in liberal, democratic and open politics were seen as soft and naïve. Some organisations such as the Democratic League existed, but they were not influential in politics or the military. The CCP ignored them, the GMD regarded them as proto-communists. Chiang Mon-lin (Jiang Menglin), former president of Peking University and the leading proponent of a middle way, was the face of a loose group that saw itself as representing the exhausted Chinese people, who wanted only peace. The poet Wen Yiduo remarked on the GMD government's insistence on seeing supporters of liberalism as traitors:

Well, if they [GMD] believe we are the tail of the Communist Party, that's their affair. They make up their beliefs as they go along. Myself, I believe we are the tail of the Chinese people and we'll keep on wagging.[28]

Sadly there was no room for a tail. Both sides were determined on fighting each other. Hard-line protagonists had no interest in a middle ground except to occupy it. The sudden end of the world war had come as a surprise to both, but both were determined on civil war. The two sides knew each other only too well, and were bound together by long-running, deep animosity that had to do with their past together over two decades.

The peace negotiations

Peace negotiations between the GMD and the CCP started in September 1945. In spite of the great difference in strength between the two parties, with the GMD overwhelmingly stronger, the CCP negotiated as if from strength. Mao Zedong demanded what was effectively a Two-China policy, a parallel to previous divisions of China, in the Nanbei Chao (fifth–sixth centuries) and the Southern Song Dynasty (twelfth–thirteenth centuries). Mao proposed that the CCP be given the governorships of the northern provinces of Hebei, Henan, Shandong, Shanxi and Chahar, i.e., control over a swathe of north China.[29]

The negotiations dragged on until the middle of 1946 and then broke down, not before they had shown the over-weaning confidence of the CCP and of Mao.[30] The November 1945 appointment of General George Marshall to head a mission to drive the negotiations and to prevent civil war in China was a blow to the GMD. Marshall was known to be close to his West Point classmate, the now-disgraced General Joseph Stillwell, the American general who found Chiang Kai-shek insufferable,

---

[28] Robert Payne, *China Awake* (London: Heinemann, 1947), p. 290. The book was dedicated to Payne's friend, Wen Yiduo, who was assassinated in Kunming in 1946.
[29] Victor Odlum to MacKenzie King, 12 September 1945, *National Archives of Canada*, C-9878, pp. 349169–349170.
[30] Mao was present for only part of the Chongqing negotiations. Not long after his return to Yan'an he came down with neurasthenia (nervous exhaustion), and was out of action for a while.

a sentiment strongly reciprocated by Chiang. Marshall knew China, but he may have been out of his depth in trying to reconcile bitter enemies. He was described succinctly by Jacques Guillermaz as a 'great soldier but a mediocre diplomat'.[31]

Marshall's mission lasted for just over a year. He went back to Washington to become the US secretary of state. He admitted the failure of his mission, which he blamed on the intransigence of both sides: 'the greatest obstacle has been the complete, almost overwhelming suspicion with which the CCP and the Kuomintang [GMD] regard each other.' He believed that there were liberals on both sides, who were being blocked by 'reactionaries' (GMD) and 'dyed in the wool' ideologues (CCP).[32]

Foreign involvement in the lead-up to the Civil War has been exaggerated, particularly in the discourse on America's 'loss' of China. China was less subject to external pressure than she had been for a long while. At this point she stood high in the world, a founder member of the United Nations, one of the victorious allies. She was not at the forefront of concern to other countries, but was under less foreign pressure than for a long while. The Soviet Union was close to despair, a despair brought on by the terrible casualties and destruction of the war. Europe was in ruins, facing massive economic and refugee crises. Imperialism was over in Asia. The unequal treaties with China were abrogated during the war. India was on the brink of independence, and the British were obsessed with the impending loss of the 'jewel in the crown'. The Japanese empire had vanished as if it had never been, the French were in deep trouble in Indo-China, the Dutch were on their way out of Indonesia. The only great power in Asia was the USA. It had become the state to which every other one turned for help. The USA was the main funder of the UNRRA (United Nations Relief and Rehabilitation Agency), of which China was the largest recipient. The Chinese government received massive direct US support but, in spite of this largesse, Washington seemed increasingly impatient with the GMD.

The start of fighting

In late 1945 the GMD armies were far stronger than the CCP's, although the geographic location of troops was the key issue.

The GMD's main forces were far away in the west, while the CCP's previous isolation in the northwest had suddenly become advantageous, with Manchuria and north China within reach of CCP armies. The CCP forces in Shandong were even closer to Manchuria.

---

[31] Guillermaz, *Une vie pour la Chine*, p. 156.

[32] General George Marshall, report to President Truman, published in Washington and cited in *China Newsweek*, 16 January 1947, pp. 4–5.

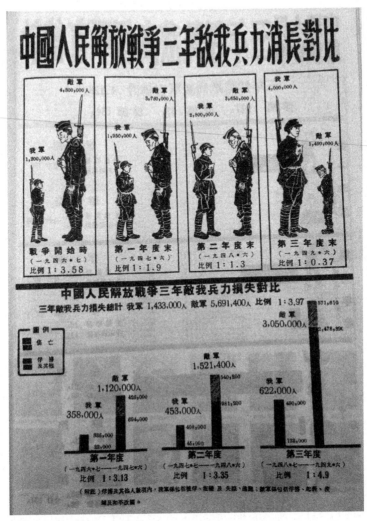

Fig. 3 Comparative military strengths 1946, Column 1

The CCP's armies were now combined as the People's Liberation Army (PLA). Soviet forces were in control of Manchuria and, although technically allied with the GMD under the Sino-Soviet Friendship Treaty, it was widely believed that they were discreetly helping the CCP.[33] This help, and the location of its forces, gave the CCP some initial advantage.

[33] The treaty was signed on 14 August, in the last days of the Second World War. Its name is almost identical to a treaty signed six years later with the new CCP government.

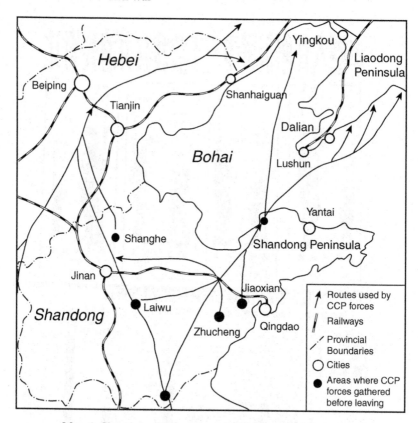

Map 2 Shandong Peninsula and Liaodong Peninsula

There was no big bang to start the Civil War, no declaration of war. Before and after the Japanese surrender, there was a flurry of skirmishes between the two sides. One of the earliest clashes was north of Xi'an (Shaanxi), between CCP forces coming south from Yan'an and a skeleton GMD garrison, left behind when better GMD units were pulled out to move to Manchuria.[34] In that clash the GMD came out on top, but in others, across north China, they lost. These battles occurred on the edge of the hills, with the CCP troops coming down from their bases. In a large battle at Shangdang (Shanxi), Liu Bocheng and Deng Xiaoping commanded a major force against regular GMD forces; more than 100,000 men were involved on the two sides. The GMD forces were routed. Then came the Handan Campaign, which was even larger.

[34] Victor Odlum to MacKenzie King, 28 July 1945, *National Archives of Canada*, C-9878, p. 349132.

Liu Bocheng's reputation as a strategist and tactician grew exponentially, along with his sobriquet, the One-eyed Dragon.[35]

Manchuria

There was a shared conviction in the GMD and in the CCP that the real civil war should start in Manchuria. Mao Zedong demanded an exclusive concentration (duba) on Manchuria. This was where the war with Japan had begun in 1931, making it the first of the lost territories. The richness of the natural resources (coal, iron, timber, agriculture) and the industrial plant left by the Japanese made the region seem the key to China's post-war recovery.

In retrospect, the focus on Manchuria was a critical mistake for the GMD. It meant the neglect of north China, particularly of Shandong. Manchuria was remote and had been cut off from China for 15 years. Shandong was much closer to the GMD centre, and the key strategic province between central China and Manchuria.

In 1945 neither the GMD nor the CCP had any troops in Manchuria, nor any deep connections there. Both had to deal with the contrary Soviet occupiers. Delegates from both sides went to meet the Soviets and were soon immersed in immensely complex diplomatic and military dances, in which they were manipulated with great skill by the Soviets:

前門拒虎 後門進狼

Qianmen ju hu houmen jin lang
As the tiger is driven from the front door the wolf comes in at the back

The GMD had no popular support in Manchuria. This failure has to be put down in part to Chiang Kai-shek's personal vendetta against the former leader of Manchuria, Zhang Xueliang. He kept the man who could have been key to regaining GMD control of Manchuria under house arrest in Chongqing. Zhang was not to be forgiven for arresting Chiang in 1936. Without the natural leader of Manchuria, the likelihood of the GMD being welcome in Manchuria was remote. The GMD reinforced its unpopularity by showing contempt for Manchurians in the cities it took over. They were treated as lackeys of the Japanese. 'Their property and personal possessions are therefore considered legitimate war booty.'[36]

---

[35] Liu Bocheng was blind in his right eye, the result of a battle injury early in his career.
[36] Chester Ronning, *A Memoir of China in Revolution* (New York: Pantheon, 1974), p. 108. Ronning, born in China, was a diplomat in the Canadian Embassy in Chongqing and Nanjing.

In late 1945 the GMD and the CCP both poured troops into Manchuria – just at the time of year that the region was preparing for its bitter winter. The GMD was given help by the USA in moving troops, although the efforts were often blocked by the USSR. Both the GMD and CCP were intent on rearming, by picking up abandoned Japanese weapons. Table 2.2 lists the military *materiel* seized from the Japanese armies (mostly in Manchuria) by the GMD.[37]

Table 2.2 *Military* materiel *seized from the Japanese armies by the GMD*

Rifles/carbines	685,877
Ammunition	180,000,000 rounds
Tanks	383
Trucks	15,785
Horses	74,159
Aircraft	1,068
Bombs	6,000 tons
Ships (small)	1,400
Armoured cars	150

The CCP also stood to benefit enormously from Japanese war booty. In Manchuria vast quantities of weapons and trucks, taken from the defeated Japanese by the USSR, were likely to be available to the PLA.[38]

The CCP moved soldiers in on foot, from Shanxi, and by boat across the Gulf of Bohai. It took over vessels in Shandong, including the 481-ton *Xiandai* (*Modern*), from the Japanese to move troops between Shandong and Manchuria. The vessel, the oldest on the Lloyd's Registry, was built in 1840 in St Petersburg, as a yacht.[39] By the end of 1945 almost 100,000 CCP soldiers had been ferried across from Shandong. The CCP rapidly picked up additional troops in Manchuria. Some were local anti-Japanese guerrillas, others were former puppet troops. These men would have been willing to go over to the GMD, but had been rejected and disbanded. They went instead to the CCP.[40] 100,000 men were recruited by two of Zhang Xueliang's brothers, Zhang Xueming and Zhang Xuesi, on the CCP's promise of an autonomous state of Manchuria run by the Zhang family.[41]

---

[37] *China Newsweek*, 14 March 1946, p. 10.

[38] Lai Xiaogang, *A Springboard to Victory: Shandong Province and Chinese Communist Military and Financial Strengths, 1937–1945* (Leiden: Brill, 2011), p. 237; Carsun Chang, *Third Force in China* (New York: Bookman, 1952), p. 171. Carsun Chang (Zhang Junmai) was a leading moderate. He was the brother of Chang Kia-ngau (Zhang Jiaao).

[39] *China Review*, II, 1 (December 1948), p. 9.

[40] Chang, *Third Force in China*, p. 169; T'ong and Li, *Memoirs*, pp. 436–437, p.470.

[41] Victor Odlum to Mackenzie King, 25 November 1945, *National Archives of Canada*, C-9879, pp. 249215–249216. There were eight Zhang brothers, from four mothers. Xueliang and Xueming were born to their father's first wife, Xuesi to his third wife.

Table 2.3 *Military* materiel *seized from the Japanese armies by the USSR*

Aircraft	925
Tanks	369
Artillery	1,226
Machine guns	4,836
Rifles	300,000
Motor cars	2,300
Horses/mules	17,497
Supply vehicles	21,084

Zhang Xuesi, already a communist, was appointed to the fictive post of governor of Liaoning and head of the Democratic Army of the Northeast.[42]

The military outlook was still poor for the CCP. Late in November 1945, Huang Kecheng, just arrived in Manchuria from Shandong with 35,000 men, complained to Mao Zedong that the situation in Manchuria amounted to 'seven nos – no Party organisation, no mass support, no political power, no grain, no money, no medicine, no shoes, no clothing'.[43] The soldiers fought in terrible conditions. Unlike the campaigns of Napoleon and the Nazis into Russia, when the bitter winter came to Russia's aid, the Manchurian winter helped neither side in the fighting in Manchuria. In the brutal winter almost none of the soldiers coming in from the south had adequate clothing. Dr Jakob Rosenfeld had to carry out hundreds upon hundreds of amputations for frostbite, 'a horrible task even for a hardened surgeon'.[44]

Serious fighting

As the Soviets withdrew in the early spring of 1946, after several delays, the fight was on for the control of the Manchurian cities. The PLA took over many of the cities from the Soviets in March. As the Red Army withdrew its commanders 'reduced the guards' on armouries, allowing for the 'theft' of weapons.[45] The PLA's position was tenuous, however. The GMD went on to the offensive, claiming its right to take over territory held less than a year before by Japan. The PLA was soon driven back under intense pressure from the better-trained GMD forces. The PLA

---

[42] Chassin, *La conquete de la Chine*, p. 67.
[43] Cited in Harold Tanner, 'Guerrilla, Mobile and Base Warfare in Communist military operations in Manchuria, 1945–1947', *Journal of Military History*, LXVII, 4 (October 2003), p. 1196.
[44] Kaminski, *Ich Kannte Sie Alle*, p. 161.
[45] T'ong and Li, *Memoirs*, p. 469.

took huge losses. The PLA abandoned the key railway junction of Siping in mid-May, after 40,000 men, half their strength, were killed; many others deserted.[46] Shortly afterwards the much larger city of Changchun fell to the GMD. GMD troops rushed north, almost to the last great city in Manchuria, Harbin. Lin Biao was so devastated by the losses that he considered leaving the army.[47] The GMD's success was credited by many observers to the strategic brilliance of the legendary 'Xiao Zhuge' Bai Chongxi, who stepped into direct the latter stages of the campaign.[48]

The GMD victory quickly turned sour. The PLA was already withdrawing from Harbin when the unthinkable happened – Chiang Kai-shek declared a ceasefire on 6 June. The ceasefire, originally for two weeks, lasted for four months and allowed the PLA to recoup its strength. The GMD had snatched defeat from the jaws of victory. The effect on GMD morale was so great, and the relief felt by the CCP so enormous, that Siping must be regarded as the turning point in the war. Many of Chiang's senior commanders lost confidence in Chiang's ability to direct the war, while Lin Biao's reputation, which had been almost mortally damaged, recovered.

The ceasefire decision

The decision for a sudden ceasefire in the summer of 1946 prevented GMD troops from pursuing Lin Biao's forces to Harbin. It was a turning point in the war, the point at which, in retrospect, the GMD started to falter and ultimately to lose the war. The decision has been ascribed to pressure from the USA, notably from General George Marshall, on Chiang Kai-shek; Marshall has been blamed for 'betraying' the GMD cause.*

There are other possibilities. One is that Chiang believed that the CCP armies were already finished and could not recover – so that taking Changchun alone would be sufficient to control Manchuria; there was no need to go further north to Harbin. Another explanation, at a baser level, is that Chiang could not bear to see Bai Chongxi score another victory and win control over Manchuria. The strategic brilliance of Xiao Zhuge had several times before put

---

[46] Zhang Zhenglong, *Yingxiong shi* (*Heroic City*) (Shenyang: Baishan, 2011) gives gripping descriptions of the capture of Siping (also known as Sipingjie) in this battle. The wretched Siping was fought over another three times during the Civil War, and completely destroyed. It became 'a coffin without a lid' (*Ibid*, p. 225).

[47] Chang, *Last Chance in Manchuria*, pp. 50–51.

[48] A reference to Zhuge Liang, China's greatest strategist, in the Three Kingdoms period. For detailed description of the battle, see Harold Tanner, *The Battle for Manchuria and the Fate of China: Siping, 1946* (Bloomington: Indiana University Press, 2013).

Chiang in the shadow. It was less than 20 years since Bai had taken Beijing, at the end of the Northern Expedition (1928). Soon after that Chiang had turned on Bai, starting a period of almost a decade when Bai was excluded from the central GMD military. He returned to the GMD fold in 1937. He was famous for two of the few Chinese victories during the war with Japan – Taierzhuang and Kunlunguan. Chiang's intense dislike of Bai is revealed very clearly in his references to Bai in his diary. The tragedy is that this animus deprived the GMD of its greatest military commander.**

    * Tanner, *The Battle for Manchuria*, pp. 6–7.
  ** Bai Xianyong, *Fuqin yu Minguo* (*Father and the Republic*) (Tiabei: Shibao, 2012), pp. 236–239.

The focus on Manchuria turned out to be a disaster for the GMD. Even the apparent victories of 1946 meant little. Fighting there was terribly demanding, especially in winter. Conditions for soldiers were appalling; many were from the south, and had never seen snow before, let alone dealt with bitter cold. No success was permanent. Much of the fighting was for railway lines and junctions. The GMD, which captured the junctions and held them with ease, was vulnerable if the lines between them were cut and the cities at the junctions isolated and besieged. Manchuria was a taste of what was to come: for the GMD the loss of a war that they seemed destined to win; for the CCP the victory that seemed impossible, except to the most dedicated of ideologues.

War and society

At the start of the Civil War, Chinese society was completely disrupted after the Resistance War. This situation did not change in 1945–1946. There was little possibility of a return to the pre-war world. There was a general post-war malaise. Prolonged war had reduced many communities to misery. A missionary reporting from a village in Beiying (Hebei), mid-way between Beijing and Tianjin, noted that the community was in deep gloom. The entire population was impoverished. Much of the arable land was no longer cultivated. All the draught animals and carts had been taken, by one army or another. The peasants were listless, as if in the grips of a deep depression, no longer even bothering to plant vegetables, but subsisting on a diet of coarse grains.[49]

[49] Frank Price, *The Rural Church in China* (New York: Agricultural Missions, 1948), pp. 238–239.

Fig. 4 Zhou Zuoren

The leadership of the traditional social order was gone in much of China, its members either absent during the war or compromised by connections to the Japanese. The gradual movement towards reform and social progress underway before the war, especially in the eastern cities, was a forgotten dream. In the CCP-controlled areas radical social revolution was looming, not gradual change.

The collapse at the top of the social scale was visible. Traditional clothing for elite men, the long gown and jacket (*changpao magua*), almost disappeared after the Resistance War; it had been contaminated by the members of the pro-Japanese elites in Nanjing and Beiping, who wore it regularly. The writer Zhou Zuoren went to his trial for treason in a simple long gown. The traditional outfits for men were replaced by business suits and military uniforms, in the GMD and in the cities, and by baggy cotton jackets and loose pants in the CCP world. Men who continued to wear traditional clothes were making a statement about their distaste for the contemporary world, not just wearing the standard clothing of the day. The great painter Zhang Daqian was a rare example of someone who continued to wear gowns. They had become a symbol of a lost world.

In late 1945 and 1946 the fundamental changes in society were dwarfed by immediate social questions.

Getting home

The most obvious social issue in late 1945 was family reunion. Millions of people were away from home, many in the western areas. Getting home was a problem of gigantic proportions. Almost no one wanted to stay in the west, and very few people in the west wanted the unwelcome guests to stay any longer.

胜利东流
Shengli dongliu
Flowing east in victory

The return journey was described in terms of 'flowing east [along the Yangzi] in victory' (*shengli dongliu*). Millions of people struggled to get home, pouring eastwards in a chaotic flood by boat, road or even on foot. Most people went home by boat, a perilous trip down through the Yangzi Gorges. The young couple Yang Xianyi and Gladys Yang, like thousands of others, made their way from Chongqing to Nanjing in the summer of 1946, crowded with their colleagues on to a ramshackle junk. A second vessel, carrying all their possessions, sank in the Yangzi Gorges.[50]

Very few people could fly, effectively only those with government connections. There were no rail connections into West China at the time, but it was possible to go north by road from Sichuan, and make it to the east–west Long/Hai railway, which connected to both north–south routes. The railways were difficult for civilians to use; their main task at the time was to transport troops. The government set up 500 transit stations for refugees along the east-bound routes, but only for those in dire need. The stations provided food, delousing and help with onward transport. The government requested $35,000,000 from UNRRA to cover their costs.[51] Everyone who could afford it was expected to make their own arrangements for the trip home.

Many journeys were odysseys, taking weeks or months. The Beiping universities moved back to their home campuses over the course of many months. Jerome Ch'en (Chen Zhirang) travelled for weeks from Kunming (Yunnan) first by truck, then by train to get from the south to the north of the country, to Beiping and his university job. He did not have time to go to his family home in Chengdu, although he passed quite close by. For him, as for many young people, the definition of home was changing. Their home was now their university, the close community they had lived with during the war. They had been away from their

---

[50] Yang Xianyi, *White Tiger* (Hong Kong: Chinese University Press, 2002), p. 149.
[51] *China Newsweek*, 10 January 1946, pp. 5–7.

families for so long that their original home was remote from them, as Fei Xiaotong noted in the previous chapter.

Many of the peasant refugees who had been resettled during the Resistance War wanted to get back to their home villages. One huge group was made up of the hundreds of thousands who had been displaced by the Yellow River flood (1938). Their return would be helped by the UNRRA work on closing the breach on the river's dike at Huayuankou. Henan peasants who had been resettled in the Huanglongshan reclamation area tried to get home from an area that even by the standards of poverty-stricken Henan was poor and disease ridden. Keshan Disease, a heart and lung disease caused by malnutrition, had taken a heavy toll among refugee settlers.[52]

For many Hebei and Shanxi peasants there was no village to return to. The Japanese army had razed thousands of villages in Hebei and Shanxi along the Great Wall and created a 'no-man's land (*wurenqu*)' as a defensive band. The hundred thousand or so peasants who were evicted from their homes could only return if they were willing and able to rebuild their shattered communities.[53]

Reunions/separations

One of the greatest social stresses during the war had been separation from family and friends. This had meant not only physical separation, but also lack of news. In an era before the telephone, the only reliable means of communication was by post, which had its own difficulties; many people were illiterate, others had no settled address. At the end of the war, many of those who had been separated were longing to be reunited with their families, or at least to discover whether they were still alive. Finding missing relatives was not easy, as the columns of names of missing people listed in newspapers showed.[54] The fear was always that they might be dead.

For many people there was no reunion. This was especially true of the millions of GMD soldiers. Most of them were still on active service, but others had disappeared without a trace (*shi zong*). Almost 50 years after the end of the war, in 1999, an old soldier, Peng Guiqun, lamented: 'My elder brother (Peng Guiqin) joined the army in 1939, but to this day, nobody knows whether he is dead or alive.'[55] The families of the hundreds

---

[52] Micah Muscolino, 'Refugees, land reclamation and militarized landscapes in wartime China: Huanglongshan Shaanxi, 1937–45', *Journal of Asian Studies* LXIX, 2 (May 2010), p. 471. Muscolino's brilliant study of the ecological impact of the use of the Yellow River as a weapon of war, *The Ecology of War in China*, will be published shortly by Cambridge University Press.

[53] Chen Jianhui, *Wurenqu* (*No Man's Land*) (Beijing: Zhongyang biance chubanshe, 2005).

[54] These lists appeared again after the opening up of the Mainland in the 1980s, when people in Taiwan were once again allowed to look for lost relatives.

[55] *Taipei Times*, 26 October 1999, p. 1.

of thousands of soldiers who had been taken prisoner by Japanese forces had to accept that they were almost certainly lost forever. After the war it became apparent that there were virtually no surviving prisoners of war, no camps to be liberated. Captured Chinese soldiers were either killed on capture, taken into the puppet armies or used as slave labour. The Japanese justification for not treating Chinese prisoners as POWs was that first, there was no formal declaration of war in China until 1941 and, second, although Japan had signed the Geneva Convention on the Treatment of Prisoners of War, she had never ratified it.

Many of the forced labourers taken to Japan, Korea and Taiwan did not survive, but in late 1945 some of those who did started to arrive back in China. Huang Guoming arrived in Tianjin from Japan. He was given a train ticket for Shijiazhuang (Hebei), and then walked the rest of the way to his home village from there. Cui Jincai, with a group of other released slave labourers, walked alongside the railway from Tianjin to his village in Shandong; the journey home took them almost a month. Their families had heard nothing of them since they were seized, and had suffered terrible anxiety and economic hardship at the loss of their main income earner.[56]

Efforts to resume the old life

Forced labourers returning from Japan to north China had few expectations about returning to their old lives, but people returning from exile in the west to the Yangzi Valley cities did. They saw themselves as the victims of the war. They now deserved compensation from those who had 'chosen' to stay under the Japanese. There was little sympathy or understanding for those who had lived under occupation. Many of the family reunions were unhappy, the joy at meeting again soon tarnished by the quite different experiences over the years.

Marital reunions had their particular problems. Trust had often been broken. Eight years of separation had been the death knell for many once-loving marriages. Wives whose husbands could no longer support them had moved on to other partners; this was considered a fundamental breach of morality When separated husbands had taken second wives while they were away from home, this was considered a less serious breach of social norms, since polygamy for men was still acceptable. But to a devoted wife the discovery that a husband had taken another wife was heart-breaking. The iconic film The Spring River Flows East (Yijiang

---

[56] Liu Baochen, *Riben luyi Zhongguo zhanfu laogong diaocha yanjiu* (*Survey of Prisoners of War used as Forced Labour*) (Baoding: Hebei daxue chubanshe, 2002), pp. 231–232.

chunshui xiang dong liu), sometimes called China's *Gone with the Wind*, dealt with that theme. A loyal wife who stayed in Shanghai during the war to look after her son and her mother-in-law kills herself when her much-loved husband returns from Chongqing, now a rich profiteer with a flashy new wife. The first wife, played by the beautiful Bai Yang, throws herself into the Huangpu River. The refrain of the long film, constantly repeated through the film, is a phrase first used in the turbulent Yuan Dynasty:

千幸万苦

Qian xing wan ku
A thousand misfortunes ten thousand bitternesses

The film was one of many made in Shanghai in the two years after the Resistance War, most dealing not with the joy of coming home but with disappointment, pain and betrayal.[57]

In Fujian and Guangdong, the left-behind wives (*fankeshen*) of Overseas Chinese had struggled to survive for several years without remittances from their husbands in the Nanyang – the Pacific War had effectively broken off all connections between migrants and their home communities (*qiaoxiang*). The end of the war did not improve matters very much. Some of the husbands came home penniless, others sent news that they had married another wife in the Nanyang.[58] Very few Overseas Chinese in North America returned to China immediately after the end of the war; trans-Pacific ship traffic had not fully resumed, and flights were prohibitively expensive.

Friendships were as much compromised by long separations as were family relationships. Old friendships between people who had stayed and those who had fled could often not be revived; the clouds of suspicion about what those who had stayed had done during the war were too thick to blow away. The universal breakdown of trust showed up in acute form in recovering lost property.

Recovering property

Property abandoned at the time of flight now had to be reclaimed by people returning from the west, taken back from the people who now held it – squatters, relatives, friends or colleagues. There was little hope

---

[57] These films included *Heaven Spring Dream, The Dress Returns in Glory, Diary of Returning Home, Eight Thousand Li of Cloud and Moon, Quick Son-in-law.* Jay Leyda, *Dianying* (Cambridge, MA: MIT Press, 1972), pp. 266–268. *Yi jiang chunshui* is sometimes known in English as *Tears of the Yangzi*.

[58] Shen Huifen, *China's Left-behind Wives* (Honolulu: University of Hawaii Press, 2012) deals with left-behind wives in Quanzhou, Fujian.

of retrieving movable property – it was gone for good. The most people could hope for was to recover immovable property such as houses or land. Many properties whose owners had fled had not been maintained for the duration of the war. When Rose Xiong (Hsiung) returned to the Xiong mansion in Beiping in the late spring of 1946, she found it almost ruined, parts of it burnt out, others simply derelict. There were strangers squatting in many of the innumerable courtyards. In other courts were mysterious caches of UNRRA flour. Every stick of furniture that could be moved had gone, looted either by the Japanese or the servants and elderly relatives who had stayed there during the war.[59]

In rural north China, in places not already under CCP control, landlords who had fled at the start of the war caused outrage when they came back after the end of the war. They demanded back rents from their tenants, just as returning local officials were demanding back taxes.[60] No actions were more likely to push peasants into the arms of the CCP.

Loss of property seems less serious than loss of life, but it has long-term effects. Those who have lost possessions react either by becoming indifferent to material property, or by developing deep, even obsessive attachment to their possessions. They often exaggerate the amount and value of what they have lost. They nurse feelings of deep grievance. In post-war China, as in much of Europe, the ownership of property was not a strictly legal matter. Formal documents showing ownership were quite inadequate, especially for inherited property. Getting property back was contingent on political influence: whether the government in charge decided to let one have it back or not.[61]

The reclaiming of property often went beyond personal property; it involved enterprises that provided employment. The Japanese confiscation of factories, banks, stores, mines, ships was sometimes reversed after the war and returned to its previous owners. Sometimes it was not. The inability to reclaim property perpetuated unemployment; enterprises could not reopen. It also, in a convoluted way, prepared China for the state ownership of property after 1949. The actual ownership of so much property was still in doubt that the new CCP government had no difficulty in putting enterprises under state control.

Demands for a new life

In the immediate aftermath of the Resistance War the gulf between the generations that had developed during the war opened up even further.

---

[59] Payne, *China Awake*, pp. 411–412. Rose Hsiung was married to Payne.
[60] Chan, *Memoirs of a Citizen*, p. 171.
[61] Tony Judt, *Postwar: A History of Europe Since 1945* (New York: Penguin, 2005), p. 38.

The GMD leaders, like the CCP leaders, were still, in comparison to other national leaders, quite young, on either side of 50, but they were now of the parental generation. The GMD leaders seemed to have made little effort to appeal to the young; the CCP took the opposite tack.

Many young people had no memory of the old world for which their elders were so nostalgic. They had lived only in the turmoil of war and were eager for a new life. Some young people saw the end of the war as the chance for escape into hedonism and self-indulgence. Many others were taken by an idealistic vision of a new world, a vision that led them towards the CCP.

The most vocal of young people, impoverished students, spent a great deal of their time now on protests and demonstrations; those who were back in the academic capital of China, Beiping, were particularly vocal. Their demonstrations were not at first directed against the Chinese government, but against the British (for not giving back Hong Kong), the USA (especially after the reported rape of a Beiping student by US soldiers) and the USSR (for the occupation of Manchuria). Later the student protests were targeted against inflation and government corruption. Essentially the students were protesting about their own misery and the lack of any sense of a future. They saw themselves, as Chinese students often have, as voicing the misery of the nation.

The CCP used student discontent very skilfully. It brought young people over to the CCP not by overt propaganda, impossible at the time, but through discreet or covert approaches. CCP organisers had a hidden hand in many of the demonstrations. Their success in recruiting young people was a quiet triumph, especially when the young people were well-connected and well-educated. A few became spies against their own parents, providing invaluable intelligence to the CCP.

The CCP had equally great success in recruiting soldiers and local officials who had been close to the Japanese. These men were critical to the PLA's military success, to fill the army ranks and to provide the logistical support for the army. The method relied on stressing redemption, promising men that if they turned to the 'right way' they could 'make themselves new (zixin)'. The idea that people could rescue themselves from their past and be born again had a strong quasi-religious aspect to it, which made it very potent; it was a great inducement for what amounted to conversion to the CCP cause.[62] The GMD took an almost opposite approach, refusing to recruit many people whom it saw

---

[62] Two decades later it turned out to have been a dangerous conversion. Wartime association with the Japanese or the GMD had not been forgotten, but was a major pretext for persecution in the Cultural Revolution.

as having been contaminated by working for the Japanese, as soldiers or civilians.

Class struggle

The CCP had learnt from its failures in the late 1920s and 1930s that it would have to base its victory in China on rural revolution, not on the industrial proletariat that Marxism saw as the leading revolutionary class. The CCP's costly failures to mobilise China's tiny (proportionately) working class had taught the party a bitter lesson.

Rural revolution involved introducing peasants to the concepts of class warfare. It turned out to be a difficult concept to introduce to villages that were organised along lineage and family lines. The concept of class was alien; even with outside activists brought in to show peasants the way, the process was fraught with complications.

At the Japanese surrender, the CCP already controlled large parts of rural Shandong, referred to as the Liberated Areas (*jiefang qu*). Work on instigating class struggle had already started in some villages, but it was a painstaking and often contradictory process, not helped by the fact that the province was in an acute economic crisis. The incomes of the millions of men working in Manchuria stopped after the closure of Japanese factories and mines there. Remittances on which many villages lived stopped. The CCP found a strategy to introduce class struggle and at the same time to assuage some of the economic needs.

The Anti-traitor Speak Bitterness (*Fanjian suku*) Campaign started in the coastal areas of the province as soon as the Japanese had left. It followed on CCP-led 'traitor elimination' groups that had operated during the Japanese occupation, attacking people who could be accused of being pro-Japanese. Since many local elites had collaborated with the Japanese, either actively or involuntarily, and had been involved in the last years of the war in such dreadful actions as helping the Japanese to round up forced labour and sex slaves, they had already attracted a great deal of anger in their communities. In Longkou, on the southern shore of the Bo Hai, the CCP organised nearly 2,000 mass meetings against traitors, mainly members of the old elite, starting in the early autumn of 1945. By the beginning of the following year they had all been expropriated; some were executed, not on the grounds that they were class enemies, but on the grounds that they had collaborated with the Japanese.[63] In Penglai

---

[63] Zhonggong Longkou shiwei Dangshiwei, *Zhonggong Longkoushi Dangshi dashiji, 1930–1949* (*Chronology of Major Events in the History of the Longkou Communist Party*) (Longkou: Longkou dangshihui, 1990), p. 95.

Fig. 5 A traitor

on the northeastern coast of the province, the movement aimed at confiscating and distributing 'traitor' property. By the end of 1945 rents had been reduced, and 174,064 kilograms of grain confiscated. In the spring of 1946 the movement picked up steam. By June 2,854,414 kilograms of grain had been confiscated.[64]

In the campaigns 'traitors' were publicly attacked. They stood before their communities tied up, with placards round their necks. The purpose was total humiliation. Similar actions took place in other recently liberated villages. In Long Bow (Zhang Zhuang) in Shanxi, the anti-traitor movement began in late 1945. The two leading collaborators were summarily executed. Many others, including people whose collaboration had been minimal or even forced, had their property confiscated. The property was then to be distributed to the poorest people in the village. The process did not go smoothly. There were injustices in the confiscations and, even worse from the point of view of the activists who oversaw the process, a general unwillingness to accept confiscated property. The potential beneficiaries were not certain how long the communists would last. 'If the

[64] Zhongong Laiyang shiwei Dangshi yanjiushi, *Laiyang geming douzheng shi (History of the Revolutionary Struggle in Laiyang)* (Laiyang, 2002), p. 79.

counter-revolution should gather enough strength to strike back, those who had property that originally belonged to the collaborators would be the first to suffer.'[65]

The anti-traitor movement and the actions that followed aimed to create class divisions that had not been visible before. The targets of the campaign were senior members of tight, common-descent, lineage groups. The word 'jia' (family) is often incorporated into a village name (Lijia Zhuang, Wangjia Gou, Fengjia Cun); Long Bow Village has the family name Zhang. Many small villages had only one surname, larger ones only two or three. The surnames were shared by people at every economic level, a proof of common descent, i.e., blood ties. The concepts of family and place were intertwined so closely that they seemed indivisible.

The role of the lineage was strengthened by a number of ingrained traditions: the ban on same-surname marriage; the importance of cultural artefacts such as genealogies, graveyards and lineage temples; the assumption, at least in theory, that the richer members of a lineage would look after poorer members, see to the education of bright boys, take some care of the elderly and preside over key rituals, such as the rites for the common ancestors.

The Resistance War had diluted the power of the blood connection. Leaders of lineages had not been able to defend the people of their common descent group or to continue their traditional roles. They had lost much of their personal prestige. Providing young men and girls to the Japanese army for forced labour and for sex slavery was treachery. The punishment of traitors was so popular among those who had suffered through the Japanese occupation that it enabled the introduction of what before the war would have been almost unthinkable and unnatural: socialist class divisions in communities based on common descent.

The situation of women

The exigencies of war had created great changes in the situation of women, and in their relative status in their families and communities. Many had acquired greater independence from their menfolk, whether they wanted it or not. Many had been forced into self-sufficiency by the death or absence of their fathers or husbands, and they had survived, becoming stronger in the process. For women in the Japanese-controlled areas, the war had been terribly dangerous; the fear of rape encouraged

[65] William Hinton, *Fanshen: A Documentary of Revolution in a Chinese Village* (New York: Monthly Review, 1966; reissued 2008), pp. 123–124.

them to stay out of sight. But for other young women, the war had brought an unexpected freedom – to choose their own husbands. In the turmoil of the war it was often impossible for parents to arrange their children's marriages, or to go through with marriages already arranged. Young people had a freedom not dreamt of before.

Comradely marriage

The CCP was opposed to arranged marriage, and urged young people to marry for love. In a society with no tradition of dating, it was difficult to find love on one's own. Wu Yun-to (Yunduo), a young miner who joined the CCP during the Resistance War, worked in a small rural armoury, along with Lu Ping, a girl whose family had been killed by the Japanese. Their relationship developed slowly:

As I saw it, she was a good comrade, a good worker and a real pal. While we were together there was nothing special between us, but when she was away I felt as if something had gone out of my life. I didn't put it any stronger than that at first. Only later did it dawn on me it might be love.*

The head of their section *did* realise that it was love, and arranged a marriage for them. This was a cautious move away from traditional arranged marriage, in which the couple did not meet until their wedding, to a modified form of arranged marriage, in which the couple already knew each other and were compatible.

* Wu Yun-to, *Son of the Working Class* (Beijing: Foreign Languages Press, 1956), p. 176.

The demands of survival, plus the new freedom of marriage, marked a key stage in the emancipation of Chinese women at all levels of society. Previously the new freedom for women in the early Republic was limited to the wealthy, living in Westernised parts of China. The war brought it to far more women.

Peasant women were a particular target of communist activism. Married women were the most crushed, maltreated by their husbands and their mothers-in-law, suspected of immorality if they got involved in any activity outside the home. The CCP tried to set up women's associations in the places they had come to control. One of the most dramatic activities of the associations was a campaign against wife-beating, a sad routine in many families. In Long Bow, the association led a direct action against a notorious wife-beater. 'They [the women] rushed at him from all sides, knocked him down, kicked him, tore his clothes, scratched his face, pulled his hair and pummeled him until he could no longer breathe.'[66] He became a reformed character.

Lack of change

The picture of social change and turbulence did not refer to all regions of China. In some of the provinces in the south and southwest the presence of the Japanese had been brief or non-existent. The direct impact of the war had been limited in time, occurring in Guangxi, for example, only in the last year of the war, during Operation Ichigo. The province had still suffered a great impoverishment during the Resistance War, not least because so many men were away fighting.

In Fujian much of the province had never been occupied, but the major parts of the province had been ruined by the collapse of connections to the Overseas Chinese world. The effect of the war was profound. Although the government realised the importance of the remittances of Overseas Chinese to China's economic revival, there was no way to ensure that this would happen. In Fujian the remittances came principally from the Nanyang, countries that themselves were recovering from the war.

Both Guangxi and Fujian, already poor, had been further impoverished by the war. And both were scarred by loss. The family separations had been long, and did not end at the end of the war. They seemed to be lasting an eternity, and many actually were forever. Hundreds of thousands of soldiers went north from Guangxi from 1937 on. The provincial government reported in 1946 that almost a million people, soldiers and civilians, had died in the war.[67] In Fujian the loss of the Overseas world took much of the vitality out of the society, at the same time that it brought poverty. The two provinces were left only with a profound sense of waste at the end of the war.

Enforced change

In some of the areas once controlled by Japan, social change was profound and enforced, nowhere more so than in Taiwan. Local Taiwanese lived through a period of nightmare after they were 'liberated' from the Japanese in 1945.[68] From having been abandoned by China in 1895, when Taiwan was surrendered to Japan in exchange for the territories the Japanese had won in Manchuria, they were now forced to be

---

[66] Hinton, *Fanshen*, p. 158.
[67] Lary, *The Chinese People at War*, p. 173.
[68] The word used by the government for the recovery of Taiwan was *guangfu*, 'light restored'.

Chinese again, and to give up anything Japanese, including the Japanese language, their surnames, their educational qualifications, the currency. From October 1945, when the GMD formally took over, the Taiwanese went through a series of horrible, jolting shocks.

Japanese soldiers and civilians (about 400,000) were rapidly repatriated from the island. The incoming Chinese found an island that seemed very Japanese. Many people wore Japanese clothing, and spoke only Taiwanese and Japanese – two languages that very few of the incomers spoke. The incomers started to strip away all evidence of the Japanese. Street names were changed to the names of Chinese provinces. The old occupational structure for Taiwanese disappeared; incoming Mainlanders took many of the best jobs. With the loss of livelihood the Taiwanese, who were used to a fairly prosperous life under the Japanese, were reduced to dire poverty, and to every conceivable form of lawlessness. Taiwan seemed to have passed from one alien rule to another – but the new one provided no security.[69]

Formosa betrayed

George Kerr, a young American diplomat who had been on General MacArthur's staff and had served in Taiwan throughout the transfer of power from the Japanese to the GMD, voiced the outraged feelings of many native Taiwanese at what he saw. The takeover process seemed a form of colonisation, in which the Taiwanese were forced to abase themselves before a new ruler.

In the Japanese era a portrait of the reigning emperor had to be placed in every school. It had to be treated with the utmost show of reverence. And there were weekly services at which all government employees and school children had to bow reverentially before the imperial portrait or toward the imperial palace in Tokyo, 'worshipping from afar'. Now, under the new Nationalist regime, portraits of Sun Yat-sen, the 'national father', or of Chiang Kai-shek, the 'national leader', had simply replaced the Japanese Emperor's portrait everywhere. On Monday morning in every week, all government offices, all military posts and all Party organisations were required to hold an hour-long Memorial Service. Participants were required to bow three times before Sun's portrait and before the flags of the nation and the Party.*

* George Kerr, *Formosa Betrayed* (Taipei: Taiwan Publishing, 1992), p. 118.

---

[69] The 1989 movie *City of Sadness* (*Beijing chengshi*) (director Hou Hsiao-hsien) is a brilliant portrayal of the period in Taiwan.

In February 1947 these feelings of bitterness would erupted into open protest, which was met with ferocious state violence.

Biographies

Wen Yiduo

Robert Payne, who lived through the Resistance War in China, wrote a powerful eulogy for Wen Yiduo five days after 'the cold and abstract violence of the Kuomintang [GMD]' brought about his death in 1946. Here are some excerpts from the eulogy:

> He was the greatest man I met in China, the most scrupulous, the most happy in his work, the most popular of all the professors at Lianta [Xinan Lianda, Southwest United University], the man with the sweetest smile and the most mature brain. His name was Wen Yi-tuo [Wen Yiduo], which means 'the one and the many of learning', and hence, by implication, all that can be understood by learning.
>
> His classrooms were always filled to overflowing, and there would be perhaps forty students hanging listening through the windows. He had a quiet contempt for the professors who thought it unnecessary to speak with the students about political problems. He believed the present government of China to be corrupt, and said so openly, with no shadow of fear on the fine high-boned face.
>
> He had led the long march of the students from Peking [Beijing] to the southwest, and we had thought of him always as the man who would lead them back again. It was no more than we had expected of him. But we did not expect him to die in the way he did, shot down in cold blood by four gangsters with American silent revolvers.[70]

Dong Zhujun[71]

The CCP's ability to attract undercover supporters was invaluable in its conquest of China. These included people whose sympathies were so deeply hidden that they could never be suspected by GMD agents. These people could help the CCP in providing intelligence. One of the more unlikely was Dong Zhujun, a feisty woman entrepreneur from Sichuan who owned an up-market restaurant in Shanghai, the Jinjiang, named for the river that flows through her home town, Chengdu. She used the restaurant as a secret hiding place for CCP operatives, and arranged for the publication and distribution of CCP propaganda. Dong's daring and her talent for deception were the stuff of a romantic vision of the communist

---

[70] Payne, *China Awake*, pp. 417–419.
[71] Dong Zhujun, *Wode yige shiji* (*My Times*) (Beijing: Shenghuo dushu, 1992).

success – a success won by cleverness, by the kind of guile and strata-
gem so much loved in traditional storytelling, rather than by violence. To
recognise her contributions, the Jinjiang Restaurant was expanded after
1949 into the Jinjiang Hotel.

The flight of Japanese civilians

For Japanese civilians who had spent their entire lives in China, the end of
the war brought terror and loss. They knew that Japan's defeat meant that
they would have to go 'home', but the suddenness of their forced departures still came as a shock. A Japanese girl who had spent all her short life
in a small town north of Dalian gave her vivid memory of the day she left:

The town was deathly silent, deserted. Since our house was at the foot of the
mountain, it was the first thing we encountered. Our house, or what had been
our house ten or twelve hours ago, was now a skeleton. From the roof tiles to
the *tatami* floor mats, the looters had stripped the house to its bare frame. Not
a piece of furniture, not a shred of rag was left. The knocked out doorways, hollow windows, crushed roof, trampled yard made it a ghost of a house, cursed by
hatred. No one uttered a sound. This was shock, a terror far more direct and real
than the emperor's announcement had been. This was the physical manifestation
of the unconditional surrender.[72]

Chan Cheong-Choo

The younger brother of Chen Pijun, Wang Jingwei's wife, was born in
Malaya, but spent much of his youth and adult life with his sister and
Wang Jingwei. During the war the rather effete young man achieved start-
lingly high office; he was made first head of the tiny air force of the puppet Nanjing government, and then president of the Central University.
At the end of the war he was arrested and jailed. Then suddenly, in late
1948, he was released. He fled first to Hong Kong and then to Canada.
He continued to believe that Wang Jingwei was a true patriot. 'His only
aim was to save China from the Japanese imperialists and bring peace to
his country, and to this end he staked his honour and prestige. But how
distressed he was to be, at the realisation that he could accomplish nothing worthwhile. His helplessness was pathetic to see.'[73] Chan's position
has not been shared by many other Chinese. Wang Jingwei is still excori-
ated by almost all of his contemporaries and by later historians.

---

[72] Kazuko Kuramoto, *Manchurian Legacy: Memoirs of a Japanese Colonist* (East
Lansing: Michigan State University, 1999), pp. 50–51.
[73] Chan, *Memoirs of a Citizen*, p. 200.

Soldier families

Chinese armies did not grant their soldiers regular leaves, and there were virtually none during the eight years of the war. Nor were there good systems for paying soldiers' families. Sending home money to the families of soldiers had not worked well during the chaos of the Resistance War. Now that the war was over, many soldiers wanted to go home, at least for a short while. Many had been away from home since 1937, at the start of the war. Those who had gone into the army as young men (probably a majority) were eager to marry the girls to whom they were already engaged. They also needed to care for their parents or, if they were dead, to perform the proper rituals, all of which has been suspended for the duration of the war. Those who were married and had children needed to rejoin families that had survived through the help of the extended family or through the women working themselves; in some of the CCP-controlled areas the party required neighbours to work soldiers' land. The families at home now wanted desperately to see their men, at least to confirm that they were still alive and uninjured. The reunions did not take place. The movement towards Civil War meant that neither the GMD nor the CCP allowed any disbandment of their own men.

3   Turning points: July 1946–June 1947

Politics and the war

In the summer of 1946 there was a brief respite from war, a sense across China of breath being held. The Civil War was apparently on hold, after the declaration of a ceasefire in June. The CCP was in retreat in Manchuria, and the GMD did not pursue its advantage.

按兵不動

An bing bu dong
Armies at a standstill

The CCP, although at first deeply chagrined by its military defeats, used the setback to boost its morale. Mao Zedong's stress on the triumph of the will was making itself felt. He came up with one of his most famous statements on the power of will in August 1946: 'All reactionaries are paper tigers. In appearance, the reactionaries are terrifying, but in reality, they are not so powerful. From a long-term point of view, it is not the reactionaries but the people who are powerful.'[1] This was one of the slogans that made his followers believe that the CCP could win the war, whatever the odds.

By contrast there seemed to be a hiatus in decision-making at the top of the GMD. Chiang Kai-shek was absent from the political scene. He spent 69 days of the summer in the hill-top resort of Guling, almost in seclusion. He did not attend his sixtieth birthday celebrations in Nanjing, a lavish affair that included a fly-past of 60 planes.[2]

The GMD was still unquestionably in charge of the country, but it was not united within itself. Chiang Kai-shek did not trust most of the GMD generals, and continued to rely on the members of the Whampao clique. The internal divisions were festering, the subject of insatiable gossip in political circles.

---

[1] Interview with Anna Louise Strong, Yan'an, August 1946. Strong, a radical American journalist, was a semi-official spokesperson for the CCP.
[2] *China Newsweek*, 7 November 1946, p. 3.

On the international front the GMD was still very much a partner of the victorious Allies. This meant in practice the USA. The US had a strong presence in Nanjing (including the military mission, which went under the unfortunate acronym MAGIC). Much of Washington's attention, however, was focused elsewhere. The US had embarked on a post-war mission to reconstruct and democratise Europe and Japan. The massive US help to Japan was hard to understand in China. The GMD thought that help should go to the victors in World War Two, not to the defeated. The CCP was disquieted by the overtly anti-communist aims of US policy, and the disquiet was increased by the November 1946 Treaty of Friendship between China (i.e., the GMD government) and the USA. The CCP, in reaction, refused to participate in the national assembly that was to bring in a new constitution, to be the foundation document of a new China.

Elsewhere in Asia the process of ending European colonialism was gaining speed. India was on the verge of independence. The Dutch had already left Indonesia, and France was barely hanging on in Indo-China. The status of Hong Kong as a British colony was anomalous, as was Macao's as a Portuguese one.

Irredentism

The GMD was in the grips of a powerful irredentism, a desire to recoup and reintegrate the territories lost through weakness of previous Chinese governments. The GMD and CCP shared the view that the 'lost' regions were 'inalienable parts of China'. One of the great slogans of the Resistance War had been 'return our rivers and mountains (*huan wo he shan*)'. A key 'lost territory' was Taiwan. The island was back under Chinese control, but unhappily; after a little over a year of GMD control, the situation there was very poor. In February 1947 the GMD made one of its greatest political mistakes.

The protests that started on Taiwan on 28 February began a terrible period in which the GMD clamped down on its 'enemies'. The 'enemies' were not the communists, but the outraged people of Taiwan who had become increasingly convinced that since 1945 they had been occupied by a colonial regime harsher than the Japanese one. There was fury about the way they had been treated by the incoming Mainlanders, not as victims, to be liberated, but as collaborators of the Japanese, to be punished. Treating the Taiwanese as collaborators was the justification for the incomers to go on a rampant campaign of carpet-bagging, expropriation, looting and dismissal from work.

On 28 February a minor incident, an attack by GMD police on a Taiwanese woman selling cigarettes against the rules of the state monopoly, mushroomed into full-scale repression and the killing of many members of the Taiwanese elite. Between 20,000 and 30,000 people lost their lives (see 'Biographies' below). In the process the Taiwanese independence movement, still strongly alive today, was created.

In Manchuria the GMD irredentist desire to get back what had been lost was equally strong. The GMD's grand strategy was to reintegrate the region into China – even though Manchuria was a remote, harsh world, one that few Chinese knew or had cared about until it was seized by Japan in 1931. Manchuria became a vision of renewed prosperity for all of China. One of the major cinematic successes of 1947 was *Along the Sungari River (Songhuajiang shang)*, an epic that started with a lyrical portrayal of Manchurian life before the Japanese occupation. This vivid film, which showed the beauty but not the cold of winter, was made in the modern film studios abandoned by the Japanese in Changchun.

The GMD was determined, eventually, to restore full control over Tibet and Xinjiang, but the remote western regions were still essentially autonomous, and the GMD had insufficient strength to get them back, for the time being.

Fighting

The winter of 1946/1947 was a period of strategic and forced retreats for the CCP armies. The CCP lost control of 174,000 square kilometres in north China and Manchuria, 165 towns and thousands of villages that they had held before the Japanese defeat or had taken control of in late 1945. The losses were especially great in Shandong. As many PLA units were transferred from Shandong to Manchuria, so the CCP lost control of parts of the province, to the GMD or to local power-holders.[3]

Nanjing was preparing for war and continued to pour troops into Manchuria, many of them southerners who were completely unsuited to fighting in the bitter winter. They were also unable to understand why they still had to go on fighting *after* the Japanese had been defeated. Morale was very low, command was weak. The GMD armies were well-equipped but highly vulnerable. They occupied only the Manchurian cities.

Transport was the big issue in Manchuria. There were few passable roads, and even those there were difficult to use for parts of the year, the freeze-up and the thaw. The great river systems flowed northeast. They

---

[3] Odd Arne Westad, *Decisive Encounters* (Stanford: Stanford University Press, 2003), pp. 61–62.

Fig. 6 Winter campaign

had limited use in the short period of each year when they were not frozen. Railway lines were what counted, built by Chinese and Japanese concerns to open up the vast territory. No one on the GMD side seemed to have realised the vulnerability of the railway lines, strung out across the vast plains. The distances between cities were huge; Changchun was almost 300 kilometres from Shenyang, for example, and Harbin about the same distance further north. Connections by air were vital, but limited.

Civil Air Transport

Civil Air Transport* (CAT) was founded in 1946 by the American aviator General Claire Chennault, the flamboyant commander of the wartime Flying Tigers. Many of Flying Tiger pilots moved on to CAT after the war. They were bold, daring-do, cowboy types, hard-living and hard-drinking, including while at the controls of their planes. The airline flew millions of miles between 1946 and 1949, taking GMD soldiers and supplies to the battlefields, and bringing out refugees and commodities. In Henan, CAT planes flew in supplies for the UNRRA relief effort and brought cotton out. CAT flew sturdy Curtiss-Wright C-46 cargo planes, which had a long-range and a large cargo capacity. There were few seats; passengers had to cling to the ledge round the edges of the planes or hold on to the cargo. CAT flew right up to the last stages of the Civil War; its planes evacuated people from one city after another. The pilots had a bird's-eye view of the war; they flew low and saw the war from above. One of the most flamboyant pilots was James 'Earthquake' Magoon, named for the Al Kapp's Lil Abner cartoon character. He was killed flying supplies into the besieged French outpost in Vietnam, Dien Bien Phu, in 1954.

* Felix Smith, *China Pilot: Flying for Chiang and Chennault* (Washington: Brassey's, 1995).

Manchuria was *terra incognita* to GMD generals. The PLA on the other hand had learned a harsh lesson from the defeat at Siping in the late spring of 1946. The PLA commanders now started to train their forces in more modern military techniques, made possible by their improved war *materiel* situation after the Soviet armies had withdrawn. Over the 1946–1947 winter, forces still under Lin Biao made a series of flanking advances east towards the border with Korea, fighting in brutal conditions to gain a stronghold over eastern Manchuria.

Meanwhile the CCP's strength was growing in rural north China. In early 1947 some of the parts of Shandong lost in late 1946 were brought back under CCP control. The GMD successes there had been temporary, as was their occupation of the CCP capital. GMD forces did oust the CCP from Yan'an in March, but this apparent victory changed little. The CCP was mobile enough to simply relocate its capital. Much of rural Henan and Hebei were now under CCP control, and the critical north–south railway line from Beiping to Wuhan was often cut. Beiping and Tianjin were still in GMD hands, as was the railway between them, but the hills and rural areas surrounding the cities were more and more under the control of the CCP. Bit by bit, the north of the country was being cut off from the south, accessible only by plane or the precarious railway lines.

Hearts and minds

Off the battlefields another war was heating up, for the hearts and minds of the Chinese people.

This was a war that the GMD largely ignored, except for virulent propaganda campaigns against the CCP and attacks on its critics. The GMD

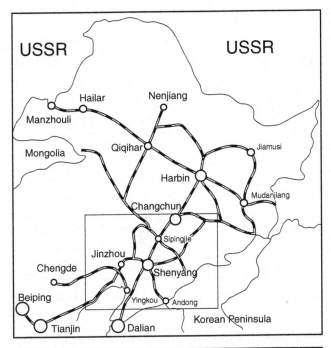

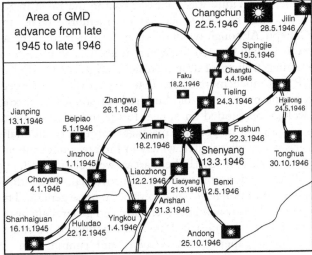

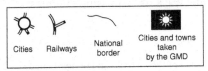

Map 3 Manchuria 1946

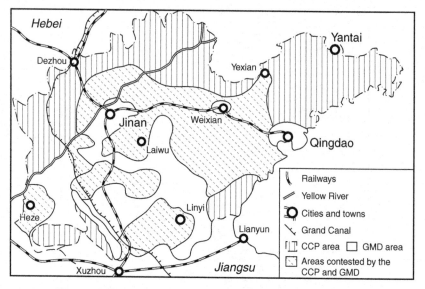

Map 4 CCP-controlled areas in Shandong, mid-1947

took harsh steps against anyone thought to be communist or a sympathiser. In July the poet Wen Yiduo was gunned down in the street in Kunming, execution-style, after he had spoken at the memorial to his murdered friend Li Gongpu. Although two individuals were named as the assassins, the GMD was widely blamed for Wen's death. The murders aroused in many intellectuals feelings of deep revulsion against the GMD.

The CCP was much more aware than the GMD of the need to win over the common people, the 'old hundred surnames (*lao baixing*)'. The Marxist ideology demanded an appeal to the masses. The party found the means to transmit its political messages through traditional cultural forms. Their slogans, distributed widely in the areas under their control and pasted up at night in GMD-held areas, were about food, peace and freedom – all deeply desirable and non-controversial.[4] The pithy slogans, modelled on the traditional *chengyu*, were often quite general. The slogan 'serve the people (*wei renmin fuwu*)' encouraged general altruism, caring for others rather than for oneself. Mao Zedong mocked his enemies with the earthy epithets 'paper tiger (*zhi laohu*)' and 'running dog (*zougou*)', direct, contemptuous ways of dismissing enemies.

---

[4] Liao Kai-lung, *From Yenan to Peking* (Peking: Foreign Languages Press, 1954), p. 59.

Fig. 7 CCP propaganda

Serve the People

Mao Zedong had a knack for combining the Chinese proverbs (*chengyu*) with his Marxist beliefs. He connected China's past to a foreign ideology, Marxism. *Chengyu* are pithy, often drawn from classical works of literature and philosophy. Mao used the traditional ones frequently, and he also came up with what in effect were new ones – political slogans, early sound-bites. A famous example is a rather bland slogan, one that could be used in almost any setting. In his 1944 essay *Wei renmin fuwu* (*Serve the People*), a eulogy for a dead soldier, Mao quoted a famous saying by China's first historian, Sima Qian: 'A person only has one death. It may be as heavy as Mount Tai, or as light as a feather.' The gloss on this traditional *chengyu* was that to die for a cause was glorious, that death should be embraced. (Mount Tai, one of China's sacred mountains, lies near the native place of Confucius.) This was what the heroic soldier had done – and at the same time he had served the people. By taking the tradition and embellishing it, Mao showed how close he was to the Chinese past, and how it could be used for the current cause.

The slogans were accompanied by vivid posters and cartoons, many of them wood block prints, an ingenious reinvention of the traditional folk prints. Just as striking were the revolutionary *nianhua*. *Nianhua* were wood block prints, produced in massive quantities in traditional China for the lunar New Year (*nian*). Even the poorest family would try to buy new ones to paste on the doors and walls of their houses. The traditional *nianhua* featured gods and fertility symbols, and were very colourful. Political *nianhua* had appeared before the CCP came along, often with anti-foreign messages. The centre of *nianhua* production was in the villages around Wei xian, in eastern Shandong.

Now the same colours and bold designs were used to promote the values of the new society. These are some of the titles of *nianhua* produced in 1947: 'Husband and Wife Learn to Read', 'Land Reform', 'Sending Husband to Join the Army'. Again, they were produced in huge quantities.[5] And, like their traditional predecessors, they were pasted on the wall of even the humblest home.

The more complex socialist vision, which included class struggle and the overthrow of the old social order, was less widely disseminated. Reading Marxist texts required a degree of literacy, and skilled teachers, to comprehend. The complex message was focused on educated young people, who had never known peace and who despised the corruption they saw all around them. The CCP had a discreet band of undercover recruiters in the GMD-controlled areas. Their role was to identify people, many of them young, who might be important or useful to the CCP, and to work on them quietly to bring them on-side. The political message was that by turning towards socialism – and often against their parents – they would be doing something courageous and altruistic, breaking the bonds of feudalism. The recruiters were looking for young, educated people who would help staff the revolution. These future cadres (*ganbu*) would provide a balance to the overwhelming number of illiterate or semi-literate converts to communism in the rural areas.[6] The recruitment campaign is one indication of how far ahead of the GMD the CCP was in its strategic planning. The GMD seemed more intent on alienating young people than on winning them over.

The CCP's propaganda campaigns, overt and covert, were significant factors in its success. In the later stages of the Civil War, more and more people emerged as communist converts and supporters, including many

---

[5] James Flath, *The Cult of Happiness: Nianhua Art and History in Rural North China* (Vancouver: University of British Columbia Press, 2004), pp. 141–143.

[6] *Ganbu* was a neologism, the term for all those who worked in administrative capacities for the CCP, essentially a replacement of the term *guanyuan* (official).

who had given no previous sign of their new allegiance. The CCP's appeal was to idealism, mixed with nationalism, the idea of cleansing society of all the dirt and dross that had attached to it during the Resistance War. Without great difficulty it was possible to portray the GMD as irremediably corrupt and polluted. At this early stage there was already a small number of opportunistic converts, who sensed which way the wind might be blowing, and decided to express at least some secret sympathy for the CCP, just in case it won in the end.

The economy

In late 1946 and 1947 there was no economic recovery in sight for China. World trade had not rebounded after the Second World War and so large-scale exports, seen as the driver of the future Chinese manufacturing economy, could not resume. Internal trade was miniscule, a result of the dire combination of broken transport systems, inflation and continuing instability. The Yangzi, China's key trade artery, was dead. The American diplomat John Melby noted in June that

despite some reconstruction, Hankow [Hankou], the second port of China, a thousand miles up the Yangtse [Yangzi], is still in the grips of an advanced stage of dry rot, which is all too familiar in China. The waterfront, once a showplace of wharves and commercial and office buildings, remains largely the rubble which our B52 strikes made it at the end of the war.[7]

There were few jobs left in manufacturing, trade or commerce; great numbers of workers were unemployed. Peasants fared better so long as they were not directly affected by fighting, because many of them were at least partially self-sufficient. In Manchuria the economic situation was particularly acute. The industrial and mining sectors were dead; these forms of economic activity had been closely associated with Japanese businesses and had collapsed when they left. The industrial plant they left behind, the white hope for future growth, was unusable; the industrial machinery was gone to the USSR. At the other end of the country the remittances from Overseas Chinese, which had fuelled the economies of Guangdong and Fujian before the war, had not resumed to any significant degree.

Inflation was gaining speed at a fantastic pace, a terrifying phenomenon for anyone involved in the money economy. Table 3.1 details the market rates for the Chinese currency (*Fabi*) and for the wholesale price

---

[7] John Melby, *The Mandate of Heaven: Record of a Civil War* (Toronto: University of Toronto Press, 1968), p. 218.

index in Shanghai for June 1946 to June 1947, stark figures that belie the misery that inflation brought with it:[8]

Table 3.1 *Fabi to US dollar and wholesale price index at Shanghai, 1946–1947*

	Rate to US dollar	WPI
June 1946	2,655	378,217
December 1946	6,063	681,563
March 1947	14,000	1,386,593
June 1947	36,826	2,905,790

Inflation is deeply preoccupying for people caught in its grip. Fear about the declining value of money drives people into frantic searches for any goods that can be bought before they go up in price and then hoarded. It makes people delay paying bills or settling debts; the longer they wait, the less they pay. It kills trust in government. Early in 1947 the Nanjing government did try to curb inflation by a series of wage and price controls, but it lacked either the will or the capacity to implement them, with the consequence that hoarding, black-marketeering and currency manipulation all increased, and Nanjing's economic credibility declined even further. The emergency measures had been effective for only a month.[9]

The desperate state of the economy was not uppermost in the minds of the GMD leaders. Their focus was on waging war. And the costs of that war were such a huge drag on the economy that they guaranteed continuing economic misery. In 1946 the military budget accounted for 60 per cent of all government spending; even that huge amount was used up in the first five months of the year.[10] In January 1947 the US ambassador John Leighton Stuart noted that the war was costing 'approximately eighty per cent of a budget in which expenditures were three or four times the current revenue'.[11] Inflation was much less of a problem for the CCP; the fact that many of the areas it controlled were rural, subsistence economies made the economic crisis less severe.

China did get international help, particularly from the UNRRA's post-war relief programme, but only for specific projects. The largest project worldwide was the return of the Yellow River to its original channel; it had flowed south since the opening of the southern dike in the

[8] Chang Kia-ngau, *The Inflationary Spiral: The Experience of China, 1939–1950* (Cambridge, MA: MIT Press, 1958), p. 79.
[9] *Ibid*, p. 73.
[10] *Ibid*, p. 156.
[11] John Leighton Stuart, *Fifty Years in China* (New York: Random House, 1954), p. 187.

river at Huayuankou in 1938.[12] The work on the project was done, by 200,000 workers, over the winter of 1946–1947, when the river was flowing low. The mile-wide breach was closed through a combination of dike reinforcement and the building of a long trestle into which new dike materials were fitted. Twenty-two million cubic metres of soil were moved for the breach closure and for dike reinforcement.[13]

The scale and brilliance of the engineering was almost lost in the conflict going on across the river. The northern bank was under CCP control, while the southern bank, where the breach was, was under the GMD. The GMD held a solemn ceremony to mark the closure of the gap, on 4 May 1947; a sumptuous volume was published to mark the ceremony.[14] The celebration was illusory. The GMD controlled only the area immediately around the breach. CCP influence had already spread into the rural areas south of the breach. The millions of peasants who had been displaced by the 1938 flood came back to their homes in the areas that had been inundated, to find them already under *de facto* CCP-control. Meanwhile the hundreds of thousands of peasants who had settled in the fertile soil of the old river bed after 1938 were refugees once the river returned to its old course.

War and society

In the second half of 1946 and the first of 1947 Chinese society continued in a state of acute disruption. Most parts of the country were affected, not only those that were directly engulfed in warfare.

Return migrations

All across the nation the people who had been uprooted from their home communities during the Resistance War were still trying to re-establish themselves in their homes. A year after the end of the Resistance War there were still tens of millions who wanted to get home. Almost a decade had gone by since the Japanese invasion, a long time in the lives of communities and families. The people who came home were strangers to their relatives. They had not shared the sufferings of the occupation. In places that had been under Japanese control, the occupation had acted

---

[12] Diana Lary, 'Drowned Earth: The Breaching of the Yellow River Dikes, 1938', *War in History*, VIII, 2 (2001), pp. 191–207.
[13] George Woodbridge, *UNRRA: The History of the United Nations Relief and Rehabilitation Administration* (New York: Columbia University Press, 1950), II, pp. 430–436.
[14] *Huang He Huayuankou helong jinian ce* (*Volume to Commemorate the Closing of the Dike on the Yellow River at Huayuankou*) (Shanghai: Huayuankou dukou futi gongchengju, 1947).

as a brutal form of social engineering: the ties that bound the old world together had been broken.

In early 1947 Feng Zikai went home to Shimenwan (Zhejiang), after almost ten years away in the west. It was a terrible homecoming. Feng saw himself as Rip van Winkle, coming back to a world that he barely recognised. As he walked along the embankment of the Grand Canal he met no one he knew. He hardly recognised the town. The embankment, once prosperous and busy, and the canal itself, once full of boats, were now desolate, the buildings in ruins, the ruins choked with weeds. His house was gone. He searched in vain for anything left of his studio, but all he found were some small, blackened pieces of wood that might have been part of a door or window. After one day he left 'this overwhelmingly sad place (*xiaohun de difang*)', knowing that he would never go back.[15] Feng, like millions of other Chinese, had been separated by the war from his old home, his *guxiang*, forever. The separation implied an almost unbearable loss, in a society where the idea of home had been so highly prized.

The separation of China's millions of soldiers from their families was equally profound. Most soldiers had not come back from the Resistance War. Many had been killed in the fighting. Others were with units still fighting, ten years after the start of the Resistance War, now in the Civil War. Their morale was low and sinking, intensified by their anxieties about their families at home. The CCP was more careful about morale, making generous promises for help to soldiers' dependants, giving the impression that a man could leave home for the army without worry.

The sad state of GMD soldier families, and the lack of knowledge of what had happened to some of their men, dragged on into the present. More than half a century after the end of the war families were still trying to find out about their men, not expecting to find them still alive, but at least to discover what had happened to them. Since the opening-up of China in the early 1980s relatives have been putting tiny, heart-breaking announcements in regional journals published in Taiwan, asking for news of relatives. In 2011 the relatives in Guangxi of two brothers, Huang Zhenguo and Huang Zhenfang, sent a plaintive message, one of several in a single issue of *Guangxi wenxian*, the journal published by the Association of Guangxi Natives in Taiwan.

They left home at an early age to be soldiers, and have not yet returned. The family thinks of them, and hopes to be in touch. If they themselves, or their relatives and friends have good news about them, please be in touch.[16]

---

[15] Feng Zikai, 'Shengli huanxiang ji (Record of Going Home After the Victory)', in *Feng Zikai youji (Feng Zikai's Travels)* (Guilin: Guangxi shifan daxue chubanshe, 2004), pp. 49–52.

[16] *Guangxi wenxian (Guangxi Documents)*, 134 (October 2011), p. 94.

The brothers had been gone from home and family for seven decades; if they were still alive they would be at least in their late eighties – but just possibly still alive in Taiwan.

Politics kept other families apart. One small but highly influential group of people could not go home at the end of the war – those leaders of the CCP who came from parts of China held by the GMD. It would have been suicidal for Mao Zedong to go back to his home in Hunan, or for Deng Xiaoping to go back to Sichuan. Another leading figure who was separated from his family was Zhang Xueliang, still held under house arrest by Chiang Kai-shek, and not permitted to go home to his native Manchuria, to his ardent supporters and to his enormous number of siblings, the progeny of his father Zhang Zuolin and his six wives.

Destitution and social upheaval

The long-term upheaval in Chinese society was almost masked by the dire economic situation. The economic collapse exacerbated the social upheaval. Tens of millions were destitute. The country was full of people, mainly men, who had lost their livelihoods, floating aimlessly around. In Manchuria hundreds of thousands were without work. They were desperate for any form of work, simply to survive, to get something to eat and protection from the bitter winter. Their lives were completely haphazard; there were sudden opportunities to do well, equally the chance to be captured, press-ganged or killed. Their fates were quite beyond their control.

Men who had supported their families from remittances while they worked away from home could no longer do so. Most of the Shandong labourers working in Manchuria had gone home when the work dried up in Manchuria, and were no longer providing for their families. Their families were destitute.

There was little hope of improvement anywhere in China. Inflation killed all hope in the GMD areas. In the CCP-controlled areas the promised gains of rural revolution could not rapidly increase the supply of food, or bring in income to the poverty-stricken. In the south families of Overseas Chinese in Guangdong and Fujian were destitute, with the flow of remittances from family members in Southeast Asia and North America still only a trickle.

The wounded from the war made up another army of the destitute. They received almost no medical care and no pensions. If they could survive, it was only by begging or by finding some support from their families. Their situation was captured in the pictures of Feng Zikai, one of the few people to express sympathy for their lot.

War wounded

During the Resistance War hundreds of thousands of soldiers had been wounded. There was no help for them, no proper hospitals, no convalescent homes, no pensions for those who could no longer serve in the military. The general consensus was that those who died of their injuries were more fortunate than those who survived. Their families were hard put to support them or to get them medical care. Very few people in official positions in the military or government cared about them. One of the few was the artist Feng Zikai, who drew some deeply moving pictures of wounded soldiers. In some of his pictures they were beggars – the only occupation still open to them.

There was no sympathy either for soldiers whose minds were injured during their wartime service. In Western armies the idea of battle fatigue – the successor to shell shock and predecessor of post-traumatic stress disorder – was already known. In China there was no such recognition.

For all those who had lost jobs in Manchuria there were others who found themselves serving in the armies there, and almost equally unhappy. The situation of transplanted outsiders, brought in from the south by the GMD, was dire. The autobiography of Huang Yaowu, a junior GMD officer from Shaoguan, on the border between Hunan and Guangdong, gives a sense of the psychological confusion that men such as him found themselves in. He was sent north in late 1945, from Burma, and experienced complete climate shock, overwhelmed by a cold he had never imagined before. For the following months he tried every means he could to get out of the army and of Manchuria, without success.[17]

Another category of people whose livelihoods were threatened was made up of anyone in north China, Manchuria or Taiwan who had had connections to the Japanese or to 'puppet' governments. The traitors (*hanjian*) had already been dealt with by early 1947, but lesser people who had worked for the Japanese lived in fear of being arrested or expropriated. Many professionals – lawyers, doctors, managers – who had worked under the Japanese lost their livelihood; they were debarred en masse. There were few people to help those accused, but sometimes connections (*guanxi*) could help. Huang Yaowu was able to get the father of the girl he

---

[17] Huang Yaowu, *1944–1948: wode zhanzheng* (*1944–1948: My War*) (Shenyang: Beifang lianhe chubanshe, 2010).

Fig. 8 Wounded soldier, Feng Zikai

wanted to marry, Hong Nailiang, released from jail; the father had been a plant manager in a Japanese-owned factory. The intervention brought the end of her parents' opposition to the marriage.[18]

The casual, capricious nature of the fate of individuals at this most unstable time is captured in Yu Hua's brilliant novel and the film adaptation, *To Live* (*Huozhe*). In the part of the story that spans the Civil War, a dissolute young man, Xu Fugui, the son of a landlord, loses his family fortune at the gambling tables. Soon afterwards he is press-ganged into the GMD forces, and nearly killed in battle. He returns home just after the CCP takeover of his town to find that the man who bested him at the gambling table and took all his property has just been executed as a landlord. His gambling losses had actually saved his life.[19]

---

[18] *Ibid*, pp. 141–142.

[19] Yu Hua, *To Live* (*Huozhe*) (New York: Anchor, 2003). The wonderful film appeared in 1994, directed by China's leading director Zhang Yimou and starring the famous actors Ge You and Gong Li.

Disappearing elites

The Resistance War had left a vacuum at the top of many sectors of Chinese society. The war had ruined most of the old elites. The intellectual and business elites were impoverished by inflation; they saw little hope of recouping their previous positions. The rural elites in the once-occupied areas were either absent, having fled at the beginning of the war, or hopelessly compromised by having worked with the occupiers. The new elites in Chinese society were the military – and the people who profited from war, the clever, ruthless people who always do well in times of upheaval in any society.

The upheaval in the social order generated anxiety for the future. Ruined or not, former elite members feared that they would have a hard time with the communists and their already well-known promise of class warfare. The GMD did not make the old elites feel any more secure. During the Civil War the GMD's only intention seemed to be to squeeze the commercial and industrial elite. Protests met with harsh responses. In 1948 a member of the prominent Rong Family in Shanghai who criticised the GMD was seized and jailed for two months.[20]

The members of the Shanghai elite started thinking about their futures, positioning themselves and their families for an uncertain future. This meant beginning to move some of their assets out of China. Now that the unequal treaties with Western countries had been abrogated, the treaty ports that had once offered safe havens had disappeared. Hong Kong, still a British colony, was still safe. The pre-war financial and commercial connections between Shanghai and Hong Kong were reactivated and strengthened. Some of the major textile businesses diverted new machinery ordered from the United Kingdom to replace machinery lost in the Resistance War to Hong Kong, rather than face insecurity in Shanghai.[21] With the machinery, manufacturing plants were set up in Hong Kong, whose economy benefited increasingly from the turmoil in China.

Embryonic class warfare

Feng Zikai's separation from home was a consequence of the Japanese invasion. In the rural north the nature of separation was shifting, based not on physical distance but on social class. The CCP's anti-traitor

---

[20] Wong Siu-lun, *Emigrant Entrepreneurs: Shanghai Industrialists in Hong Kong* (Hong Kong: Oxford University Press, 1988), p. 19.
[21] *Ibid*, pp. 28–31.

movement immediately after the Resistance War had been partially successful in transforming rural society. The full transformation of rural society through rural revolution was much more difficult. It demanded large numbers of activists to go into villages to stimulate and organise class struggle. In many areas the political and military situation was still fluid; people were not certain that the GMD would not come back. The activists in areas of north China nominally controlled by the CCP had to be armed; 'land division with one hand, a gun in the other (*yishou naqiang, yishou fentian*)'.

Rural reform was carried out village by village. The first stage involved setting up peasant associations The next stage was the expropriation of landlords, wealthy villagers and temples. Then came the most exciting stage, the sharing of the 'fruits' – the confiscated property. The purpose of these early stages was to initiate the process of full transformation, *fanshen*. There were constant village meetings, which often dragged on for days. Peasants were encouraged to speak out, to demand justice, to right past wrongs.

The most famous account of class struggle and rural reform was given by William Hinton in his classic work *Fanshen*. The book describes in great detail the process of class struggle and land division in Long Bow Village, parts of which he witnessed himself. The village had special characteristics. It lay at the edge of the area occupied by the Japanese during the Resistance War; there had been significant collaboration there. There were no strong lineages, but there was a large Catholic community. In every other respect it was like the tens of thousands of poor villages in north China.

Outside activists were sent into Long Bow by the CCP to oversee the lengthy process, which started soon after the Japanese were defeated and the village came under CCP control. The expropriation of the rich and the 'division of fruits', at first tentative, gained momentum. Activists spread out through the village houses and confiscated items from more affluent households. The courtyard of the village temple filled up with livestock, furniture, tools, clothing, 'the whole domestic and agricultural wealth of several prosperous gentry families'.[22] When the 'fruits' were put up for division, villagers competed with each other to get their hands on items from the treasure trove.

The 'settling of accounts' (righting past wrongs) was noisy and highly emotional. The local peasants were still not sure what they were supposed to do. For guidance they relied on the young activists sent in by

---

[22] William Hinton, *Fanshen: A Documentary of Revolution in a Chinese Village* (New York: Monthly Press, 1966; reissued 2008), pp. 148–151.

the CCP. Many of these outsiders, courageous, idealistic young people, had never been in a poor village before, but they were willing to endure hardship for the greater glory of socialism:

What made village life a challenge was the dirt and the squalor which surrounded the poorest peasants and the unbearable suffering that was the lot of so many victims of disease. While the itch of lice and the welts left by bedbugs were passed off jokingly as the 'revolutionary heat,' the suppurating head sores, malarial fevers, slow deaths from tuberculosis and venereal disease were not joking matters. Land reform[23] workers slept on the same *kangs*, ate from the same bowls, and shared lice and fleas with people diseased beyond hope of recovery. Yet I never saw anyone complain.[24]

CCP organiser

William Hinton described one of the outside organisers sent into help with the class classification and land distribution in Longbow Village. She was an educated woman from a big city, the mother of two children whom she had left in a crèche in the CCP capital Yan'an:

Ch'i Yun's round, friendly face was not beautiful in any particular detail, but taken together, her features were attractive and feminine. But dress and coiffure she did nothing to enhance them, however. Her fine long hair was rolled up each morning and tucked up under a visor cap in such a way that only a few wisps ever strayed to lend a touch of charm to an otherwise austere appearance. Her bulky padded suit completely disguised her figure. Only from the small size of her feet, encased in dainty, self-made cotton slippers, could one guess that her limbs might be graceful and well-proportioned.

I often thought what a hardship it must be for such a woman to live the life of a Spartan revolutionary in the bleak North China countryside after a childhood of relative luxury and comfort in the city. Yet she seemed to pay no attention whatsoever to cold, fatigue, fleas, coarse food, or the hard wooden planks that served as her bed. For her this was all a part of 'going to the people', who alone, once they were mobilized, could build the New China of which she dreamed.*

* Hinton, *Fanshen*, p. 266.

The task of the activists was to inspire the peasants to take action against those chosen as targets, however violent the action might be. And

---

[23] The CCP often used the term land reform (*tudi gaige*) to apply to the whole process of rural revolution. It actually refers to only one part, the division of land.
[24] Hinton, *Fanshen*, p. 267.

the process of revolutionary change was extremely violent. There was no prescription against summary execution. Hinton's account is stark and chilling. It describes large numbers of executions, first of collaborators, immediately after the Japanese surrender, then of landlords, leading Catholics and GMD members once the rural revolution started in 1947. Many of these people were beaten to death at public meetings.[25] The frequent beatings and summary executions were recorded in a matter-of-fact manner; the subtext was that killing was legitimate in the revolutionary process. This was clearly the CCP policy at the time; Hinton recorded the violence dispassionately, without voicing his own feelings, without either revulsion or enthusiasm.

Land division, the ultimate goal of rural revolution, was to be based on class classification. Class was assessed largely on the basis of land ownership, i.e., a material classification. But other critical elements were in play that complicated and intensified the process of class determination: collaboration with the Japanese; membership in the GMD; membership in religious groups; clan/lineage membership; personal grievances. Another critical element was the presence, in most villages, of completely dispossessed people, gamblers, drug addicts and the angry young men, the *liumang*. In Marxist terms these were members of the lumpenproletariat, not the true beneficiaries of class warfare – but often very interested in getting something out of the process.

The class classification process in Houhua, a very different village in Neihuang (Henan), was quite similar to Long Bow, though the class divisions were even more confusing. In Houhua almost the entire population was surnamed Wang, indicating strong ties of common descent. In 1947 the village was in chaos; GMD officials and soldiers had come back briefly at the end of the Resistance War, then left again. The rural revolution started as soon as the GMD left and the CCP was in control. Two organisers were sent in from the CCP district headquarters. Four Wang families owned two-thirds of the crop land. They were stripped of their land and one of the family heads, Wang Zengduo, was shot, as much because people hated him as a person as for his landownership. His widow was strung up from a tree and beaten, to try and find where she had hidden the family's valuables.[26]

These violent scenes were replicated in tens of thousands of villages across north China. In the initial stages the drama of class struggle and rural reform created a surge of excitement in villages, and often brought

---

[25] *Ibid*, pp. 116–117; 142–145.
[26] Peter Seybolt, *Throwing the Emperor from his Horse: Portrait of a Village Leader in China* (Boulder, CO: Westview, 1996), pp. 35–37.

new support for the CCP. But the outcomes of the struggle, and even more so of the division of 'fruits', were not stable. In the immediate aftermath, many people who received shares were delighted, but others felt hard done by. Having been encouraged to speak their minds in the denunciation meetings, they kept on doing so, complaining now that they had not got what they felt they deserved. And there was the unspoken fear: would the CCP win the Civil War, or might the GMD and its allies come back? If they did, what kind of retribution would be taken against those who had benefited from the changes?

There were other huge problems that the CCP, which promised so much, could not solve. Ideology meant little in times of hardship or illness. When the CCP activists were unable to cure illness, peasants were likely to fall back on what the CCP called 'superstition', to seek help and comfort in the intertwined world of folk religion and healing. The CCP launched attacks on folk religious groups, claiming not only that they were superstitious, but that they had coexisted with the Japanese. One of the most prominent was the Yiguandao, a religious group from within the White Lotus tradition of folk religion. It was founded in 1934, in Jinan. Its membership was concentrated among small merchants and local officials. It had flourished in Shandong and other parts of north China during the Japanese occupation, providing some solace in the chaos of the war.[27] The fact that Yiguandao adherents were also likely to be class enemies made another useful conjunction for the CCP – attacks on them would combine class war with anti-superstition. Association with Christian denominations was equally dangerous for adherents; it suggested direct connection with foreign imperialism.

The process of rural reform was largely destructive. It did little to create new community, to bring specialised knowledge into the villages or to solve the overwhelming problem of poverty. Millions of people may have been killed.[28] The violence of the process was terrifying not just for the victims, but for rural society itself. An unspoken question was whether this violence was an intrinsic part of rural culture, channelled by the CCP, or something created or at least exacerbated by the CCP.

Women

The years of warfare had affected Chinese women in many different ways. For younger, educated women the turbulence of the Resistance

[27] C.K. Yang, *Religion in Chinese Society* (Berkeley: University of California Press, 1967), p. 276.
[28] For grim details of the land reform process see Frank Dikotter, *The Tragedy of Liberation* (London: Bloomsbury, 2013), pp. 63–83. It focuses on the period just after 1949.

War had brought greater independence than their mothers had ever had. Some young women had the possibility of choosing their own careers and their own husbands. For them the new freedom was exhilarating. For a majority of women, however, freedom was a chimera. With these exceptions Chinese women were worse off after the Resistance War than they had been before the war. Young women might be freer than their mothers had been, but older women were not.

The saddest category of women was made up of those whose soldier husbands or husbands-to-be had died or disappeared in the war. They were in pitiful states of poverty and anxiety. Many had no idea whether their men were still alive or not. In traditional society a virtuous woman was expected to stay faithful to her husband, even, by extension, to her betrothed, whether he was still alive or not.[29] Now with their men out of touch, many women were left in a state of limbo.

Middle-class and elite women also had to adjust to a new world in which financial security had gone, while the demands for the care of their families and households had not changed. They had not only to carry out the traditional domestic tasks of women, but they had to do it in a context that had changed greatly, with less money and less security. Many managed by sheer determination. Women had to be tough to keep their families together, housed and fed during the flights at the beginning and end of the Resistance War. The side-effects of the war, if they can be called that, turned many women into indomitable figures in the care of their families.

Women from the higher strata of society were used to the help of servants, who lived as part of the household. Even a modest household had servants. As the financial situation deteriorated, this pattern started to break down, to be replaced by a world in which once-privileged women became housewives. With the erosion of domestic service went a large number of jobs; servants were sent home to their villages, joining the ranks of the unemployed.

Mao Zedong had recognised early in his career that women carried even greater burdens of oppression in the old society than men. In his *Report on the Hunan Peasant Movement* (1927) he said that, while all were burdened down by political, family and religious forces, women were also oppressed by men. This recognition did not mean automatic improvement in the status of women living in communist areas. The CCP sent mixed messages to women. They were encouraged to abandon old roles

---

[29] Betrothals often took place very early in life, when children were quite small. The families of girls were under obligation to send their daughter to her fiancé's home for marriage, even in cases where the young man was either dead or missing.

Fig. 9 Jiang Qing, 1946

of subservience to men and forgo the outward signs of femininity. The young women who joined the CCP and went to live in Yan'an or in other base areas gave up dresses and gowns, cut their hair short and dressed very much as their male comrades, in baggy pants and jackets. The revolutionary style of dressing could still appear attractive on some women, such as Mao Zedong's (fourth) wife, Jiang Qing, but on others it looked grim.

Young women activists were also expected to put the revolution before the care of their children. Xu Jing, a young activist from a genteel background, became a zealous communist during the Resistance War. In 1947, already married, she was assigned to lead land reform in a village in Suiyuan, in the remote and poverty-stricken northwest. She gave birth to her first child virtually without help (the local custom forbade a woman from outside the family to give birth in the home) and immediately put her baby son to a wet nurse, so she could go on working for the revolution. When the wet nurse turned out to have 'impoverished landlord connections', was attacked and could not feed the baby, he was simply transferred to another wet nurse. Xu Jing cared deeply for the child, but could not bring herself to abandon her revolutionary work to look after him.[30] Xu's behaviour may seem extreme, but it was not unusual among those young women who fought for socialism.

Abandoning femininity and maternity did not add up to equality. Virtually no women rose to leading positions within the CCP, even at local levels. The role for most women in the communist world was still

[30] Mu Aiping, *Vermillion Gate* (London: Abacus, 2010), pp. 19–22.

to support men, to take over tasks done by men so that men could get on with the business of revolution, especially when this involved going into the forces and leaving home. This was the wartime role of women around the world.

Children

The wartime insecurity of children continued or was intensified in the Civil War. Warfare separated children from their parents and their extended family, sometimes temporarily, sometimes forever. Lone children were not considered orphans, in the Western sense, of having no family at all, dependent on the state or on charity, but as 'children in difficulties (*nantong*)'. The tradition in China was that children without parents would be looked after by the extended family, or placed in monasteries or nunneries. From the late nineteenth century on, a few children had been cared for in foreign-run orphanages, as in the orphanage run by Roman Catholic nuns described in Somerset Maugham's *The Painted Veil*.[31]

During the Resistance War, hundreds of thousands of *nantong* were cared for in government-run homes for children. This was one of Song Meiling's (Madame Chiang Kai-shek) favourite projects.[32] This institutional response scarcely scratched the surface of the need. Lone children often had to fend for themselves. One of the few institutions interested in them was the CCP, which took older boys into its armies as 'little devils', working as orderlies and messengers until they were old enough to go into the ranks. The young soldier Lei Feng, who was the subject of a massive propaganda campaign in the Mao era as a model for other young people, lost his parents at a young age and was raised in the army.

One group of abandoned children has received particular attention recently. These are the Japanese children abandoned in Manchuria in the chaos of the Japanese withdrawal. Several thousand were left behind and were taken in by Chinese families. Four decades later, when relations between China and Japan had improved, the Japanese government made major efforts to reunite the children with their parents, tracking them down and then taking them to Japan. The family reunions were painful; the parents and children no longer had a language in common. The

---

[31] There are two films of *The Painted Veil*. The first, made in 1934, starred Greta Garbo. The second, made in 2004, was set in Guangxi. It starred Naomi Watts, with Diana Rigg as the mother superior of the orphanage.

[32] Colette Plum, 'Orphans in the Family: Family Reform and Children's Citizenship in the Anti-Japanese War', in James Flath and Norman Smith (eds.), *Beyond Suffering* (Vancouver: University of British Columbia, 2011), pp. 186–207.

adult children had great difficulty even functioning in Japan, and some returned to China.

The education of children was another casualty of the years of war. Schools opened and closed in a spasmodic way, depending on the course of the fighting. The schools that had evacuated to the west before the Japanese advance had provided some education for their pupils. At the end of the Resistance War the relocation process for these schools was as full of difficulties as the original evacuation had been. Immediately after the war inflation took a side swipe at education. School fees either kept pace with inflation – putting education beyond many family incomes – or the schools had to close.

A lost world

One of the least visible, but saddest, consequences of war to Chinese society was the inability of millions of families to resume the family celebrations that were such an integral part of traditional family life. Fighting, financial difficulties and incipient class warfare all but prevented the return of family members to spend the New Year together, and the resumption of the elaborate and lengthy celebrations that accompanied the New Year. Weddings and funerals became much less lavish than they had been before the Resistance War. The annual ritual of 'sweeping the graves (*saomu*)' at the Qingming Festival, the key ritual of the ancestral cult, was downplayed or even discontinued, when there were no family members living close to the graves.

Biographies

Qi Baishi

The venerable painter faced a problem shared by many polygamous men – he had too large a family. In 1945 he was over 80, but he still had many mouths to feed: several wives, 12 children, the youngest quite small, and more than 40 grandchildren, with more appearing at brief intervals. Almost all his family members were totally dependent on his income from painting. He had stayed in Beiping during the war, but his income had dropped dramatically because he refused to sell his pictures to Japanese buyers. In 1946 the old man came to ask the new GMD commander in Beiping, General Li Zongren, for relief. His needs were basic – rice (Qi was Hunanese and could not manage without rice) and coal. Li gave him some staples that were assigned to his own office. In return Qi gave Li a scroll of two large red peaches, an exchange that even at the time Li recognised as valuable.[33]

Ding Ling[34]

Ding Ling was a revolutionary writer, and a true believer in a new China. She was one of the most liberated women in modern China. For her beliefs and her boldness she was persecuted by both the GMD and the CCP. She still lived to a triumphant old age.

Ding Ling was born in 1904 to a ruined gentry family in Hunan. With great effort on the part of her mother she was educated, and went to the same school in Changsha as Mao Zedong's future wife Yang Kaihui. Ding went on to university in Beijing. There she fell in love with and married the young poet Hu Yepin. This was a bold act, at a time when marriage for love was still virtually unheard of. The young couple embraced socialism – and literature. They were punished. Hu was arrested in 1931 and executed. Ding Ling herself spent years in GMD prisons, until she managed to get to Yan'an in 1936. A few years later she was in trouble there too, in the Rectification Movement that saw Mao's will imposed on intellectuals. She then took part in the land reform movement, and wrote a famous novel about it, *The Sun Shines on the Sangan River* (1948). For a while after 1949 she was in official favour with the CCP, but trouble came in the Anti-Rightist Movement (1958), when she was sent to the Great North Waste for 12 years of reform through labour.

Ding Ling's story combines, in the extreme, revolutionary idealism and political persecution. Her boldness and talent allowed her to do things that many of her generation wanted to do but did not dare to. She married three times, always by her own choice. She pursued her career as a writer fearlessly. She paid a very heavy price for what she did, but in her suffering she showed an incredible ability to survive and to keep a sense of herself.

Chen Lian, rehearsing a tragedy[35]

The brilliant daughter of Chen Bulei, Chiang Kai-shek's amanuensis, was one of the privileged young people who went over to the CCP during

---

[33] Tong Te-kang and Li Zongren, *The Memoirs of Li Tsung-jen* (Boulder, CO: Westview, 1949), p. 442. Qi Baishi's works are now almost as valuable as Pablo Picasso's. In 2011 a large painting by Qi sold for US$65,000,000.

[34] Yi-tsi Mei Feuerewerker, *Ding Ling's Fiction* (Cambridge, MA: Harvard University Press, 1982) gives a detailed account of Ding Ling's life and work.

[35] Yang Zhesheng, *Chen Bulei* (Shanghai: Shiji, 2010), pp. 273–275; and Ho Dahpon, 'Night Thoughts of a Hungry Ghost Writer: Chen Bulei and the Life of Service in Republican China', *Modern Chinese Literature and Culture*, XIX, 1 (Spring 2007).

the Resistance War. While she was a student at Xinan Lianda she married Yuan Yongxi, the son of a wealthy family with warlord connections, and an underground CCP organiser in Kunming. In early 1941 they were ordered by the CCP to leave Kunming to take part in more direct political actions; this involved blowing their cover as students. Chen Lian wrote what she called her last letter (*zuihou yifeng xin*) to her sister, to tell her about the 'rehearsal of a tragedy (*paiyan beiju*)': she was going to have to break off relations with her family. She knew what trouble and sorrow this would cause the family, and begged her sister to especially comfort their father (their mother was already dead). 'Let all the people I love forget me, or hate me, but don't let them suffer because of me. Sister, I am going to a very distant place; we may never meet again [...] The road [I am taking] will be very hard, but for the freedom of the motherland there is nothing else I can say.'[36]

Chen Bulei, in Chongqing, immediately ordered the authorities in Kunming to stop her from leaving the city, but she was already gone. He was devastated, and never got over the departure of his child, and the gulf that her choice revealed between father and daughter. He still protected her, however. She was arrested in Beiping by the GMD in early 1948, as a communist, but then mysteriously released. But there was no reunion between her and her family. In November Chen Bulei killed himself, perhaps because the GMD that he had served so loyally was losing, perhaps because he could not get over his betrayal by a beloved child. During the Cultural Revolution the connection between father and daughter was revived, in a hideous way. Chen Lian was persecuted because of who her father had been, and was done to death.

Ererba victims

The native Taiwanese who protested against the GMD in early 1947 ranged from well-educated professionals to peasants and workers. They were all descended from migrants from Fujian, just across the Taiwan Straits. There was a yawning gulf between them and the Mainlanders who came in in 1945. The Taiwanese spoke the Minnan dialect of Chinese (Taiwanese or *Taiyu*) and Japanese, the language of business and education on the island from 1895 to 1945. Few Taiwanese could speak the Chinese national language (*Guoyu*, later *Putonghua*). Even fewer of the people sent in by the GMD could speak Minnan.

During the persecution that started on 28 February, between 20,000 and 30,000 people were killed, an enormous number in a small

---

[36] Yang, *Chen Bulei*, p. 273.

population. The attacks were targeted on influential Taiwanese; many of those rounded up and murdered were doctors, lawyers and newspapermen. They were taken into custody and disappeared. Most were killed, without any legal process. Some of their bodies were never recovered. Others were dumped unceremoniously, a brutal statement of the GMD's determination to root out 'dissidence'. The body of the distinguished lawyer Wu Hongwei was found beside a road in Nangang.[37]

Ererba was a deliberate, and in the short run successful, attempt to destroy or silence the Taiwanese intelligentsia. The tragedy is captured in Hou Hsiao-xian's 1989 movie, *City of Sorrows (Beijing chengshi)*. The Ererba killings have been compared to the killings in Beijing in June 1989, commonly called *Liusi* (4 June) in China, the Tiananmen Massacre in the West. The victims of Ererba were denied any commemoration until 1995, when an official apology was issued by President Lee Teng-hui (Li Denghui), the first native-born Taiwanese to be president of the Republic of China. He himself had been arrested in 1947 as a young student, one of many picked up in 1947 and the years afterwards, under a continuing crackdown that amounted at times to a reign of terror. The archaeologist Zhang Guangzhi (K.C. Chang) was held in prison for almost a year. He, like many other talented young Taiwanese, subsequently left Taiwan for the USA.

The Ererba massacre was not, in the long run, a victory for the GMD, but a disaster. It created a permanent division between the GMD and the native Taiwanese. The victims have come to be seen as the founding fathers of the movement for Taiwanese independence and its political party, the Minjindang.

Liu Hulan

Liu Hulan was one of the early proletarian heroines of the CCP, a girl from the bottom of the old society, who became, after her early death, the ultimate symbol of political youth, an inspiration to many others, especially girls. She was born into a peasant family in Wenshi (Shanxi). She lost her parents as a young child, and this bereavement seems to have made her into a very young revolutionary. In 1946, she secretly joined the local communists, and engaged in underground activities, some of them more in the line of supporting communist troops (mending their clothes) than of active fighting. When the local GMD leader was killed,

---

[37] Li Xiaofeng, *Ererba xiaoshi de Taiwan jingying* (*The Loss of the Cream of Taiwan's Heroes at Ererba*) (Taibei: 1990). This volume is made up of biographies of some of the lawyers, journalists, businessmen and professors who were killed in 1947, some months or even years after the original demonstrations.

she and other CCP activists were arrested and beheaded in the village square. She was still not 15. Mao Zedong later summed up her life in eight characters: 'In life she was great, in death glorious (*sheng de weida, side guangrong*)'. Her death later became the subject of a major propaganda campaign, and acquired huge symbolism, an example of how a devoted communist would think nothing of laying down his or her life for the cause.

Liu Hulan was in many ways a more persuasive figure than the later youth martyr, the soldier Lei Feng. He died not at the hands of reactionaries or counter-revolutionaries, but was the victim of a telephone pole. He was directing a truck that was backing up; the truck hit the pole, which fell on him and killed him outright.

4   All-out war: July 1947–June 1948

In the summer of 1947, the fighting between GMD and CCP forces in Manchuria escalated. The PLA went from the defensive to the offensive, the GMD armies in the opposite direction. It was still not clear, however, that the GMD would lose the Civil War. The government was still strong, still clearly in control of most of China. Its armies still outnumbered the CCP's.

The GMD government still had major plans for the revival of China. The modernisation project, interrupted for eight years by the Resistance War, was revived. This included plans to modernise the economy, and to revamp the political system. The National Assembly, held at the end of 1947, was a huge exercise, in part a publicity effort to show a modernising China. It adopted a new constitution, on 25 December. There was some symbolism to the date. On the same day Chiang Kai-shek made a radio broadcast in Shanghai (perhaps on the model of the King's Christmas Day broadcast in Britain). His tone was plaintive:

In China during the last few years, we have known to the dregs of the bitter cup the meaning of national sorrow. We have suffered inestimable losses due to war and internal rebellion. We have known misrepresentation and cruel slander in its blackest form. Our motives have been misrepresented. Our faults have been distorted beyond all semblance of reality.[1]

He looked for some help to Christianity, to its ability to provide faith for the future, its trust in human character, and in its improvability. But another pronouncement, also made on 25 December, presented a quite different state of mind, totally certain, reliant on a very different belief system. In a report to the Central Committee of the CCP, Mao Zedong saw that a critical change had happened:

This is a turning point in history. It is the turning point from growth to extermination in 20 years for the counter-revolutionary rule of Chiang Kai-shek. It is the turning point from growth to extermination in more than 100 years of the role of imperialism in China.[2]

[1] *China Newsweek*, 1 January 1948, p. 9.
[2] Mao Zedong, *Turning Point in China* (New York: New Century, 1948), p. 2.

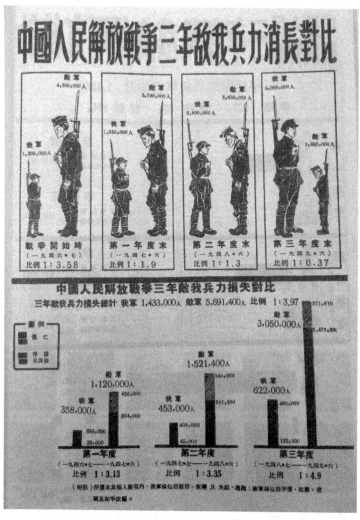

Fig. 10 Comparative military strengths 1947–1948, Column 2

It was true that Nanjing was isolated internationally. The USA was supporting the GMD government, but with less and less enthusiasm after the failure of the Marshall mission. US diplomatic opinion was more and more critical of Chiang Kai-shek, and of the cronyism and corruption within the GMD. The European powers were in recovery from their own sufferings during the war in Europe, as was the USSR. China slipped out of international headlines. The Powers were preoccupied with the march of communism in Europe, as the Iron Curtain came down, and most of Eastern Europe passed under communist control. The death knell of Western imperialism in Asia came with the independence of India in August 1947 and the violent process of partition into the states of India and Pakistan. Other Western colonies in Asia had already become independent, and more were on the verge of it. White prestige in Asia had evaporated, as the Japanese imperial enterprise had proposed – although Japan herself had not replaced the Western Powers, but had gone down to total defeat. The only 'great power' in Asia was the USA.

The course of the war

In the second half of 1947 the CCP armies went on to the offensive in Manchuria, and consolidated their positions in north China, especially in Shandong. In Manchuria, a terrible Gotterdammerung was unfolding for the GMD.

The GMD forces were isolated in the region's cities, each garrison cut off from all others, except by air. The British Embassy reported in late November that the GMD had fallen into a military quagmire, 'a government force very widely dispersed and without adequate resources, which is compelled to conform to the enemy's movements'.[3] The CCP forces had found a simple way to isolate GMD units, by cutting the railway lines. This they did by setting the wooden, tar-soaked sleepers (ties) that supported the rails on fire.

This dramatic, cheap tactic impressed the local people and others further away with its simplicity. It had something of the devastatingly simple strategies used by the great Zhuge Liang.[4] It closed the lines until timber to replace the sleepers could be brought in from northern Manchuria. In October the American diplomat John Melby was in a plane that flew along the line between Shenyang and Changchun. From the air he saw that 'the entire railroad from horizon to horizon was on fire'.[5] This was a scorched earth strategy being used aggressively, rather than, as had often been the case in the Resistance War, as the ultimate defensive strategy.

[3] R. Jarman (ed.), *China: Political Reports* (Slough: Archives Editions, 2001), VIII (1947), p. 347.
[4] Zhuge Liang was China's most brilliant strategist. During the decades of fighting in the Three Kingdoms period, he came up with simple, elegant strategies. His exploits were known to all Chinese through the *Sanguo yanyi* (*Romance of the Three Kingdoms*) and through stories, operas and comics.
[5] John Melby, *The Mandate of Heaven: Record of a Civil War* (Toronto: University of Toronto Press, 1968), p. 242.

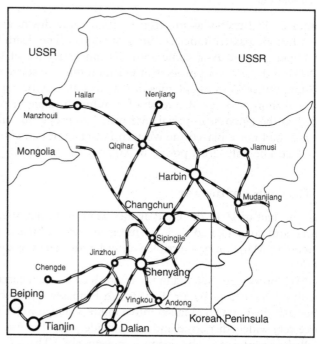

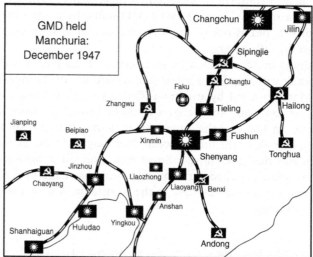

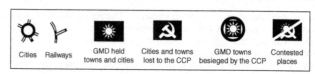

Map 5 Manchuria 1947

Fig. 11a & b Destroyed tracks

兵不血刃

Bing bu xue dao
Soldiers do not bloody their swords

By garrisoning key cities, the GMD high command had deprived its forces of any ability to take the military initiative. PLA was set on winning the war in Manchuria without too many bloody battles. Its strategists used the siege tactic several times. It was the literal version of Mao Zedong's strategy of 'surrounding the cities with the country-side', a strategy normally interpreted as a way of basing the communist revolution on China's peasants, as opposed to the Marxist belief that the urban proletariat should lead the revolution. In the case of sieges, peasant armies surrounded the cities, and put them to siege. Among civilians in the cities, sieges caused first panic, as supplies of food, water and fuel dried up, and then despair, as cold, hunger and starvation took their toll. Sieges engendered hatred of the army within the city, blamed for having brought the siege on the civilians. The armies got first call on diminishing supplies. The hostility was directed especially against senior officers who could get in and out by plane – a *de facto* form of class enmity.

The siege of Changchun lasted from the early autumn of 1947 for over a year. A huge GMD army was bottled up inside the city, while an even larger PLA army surrounded it. The tenacious refusal of either side to give up cost the lives of hundreds of thousands of people, mainly civilians. This was a silent, long drawn-out disaster for the inhabitants. The loss of life was as great, in numbers, as in the terrible attack on Nanjing by the Japanese a decade earlier (see 'The death of a city' below).

After the city fell, it was clear that the GMD could not hold Manchuria. Its hold on the cities of north China was equally threatened; the GMD's focus on Manchuria had distracted it from what was going on much closer to Nanjing. CCP forces now controlled virtually all of north China except the major cities. Tentative and very cautious talk about Two Chinas started – the idea of dividing the state at the Yangzi, the south controlled by the GMD, the north by the CCP.[6] This had been the outcome of war a millennium before for China's most cultivated dynasty, the Song; the Southern Song survived for a century and a half after the northern parts of China were lost to the alien Jin. Bu the idea of parti-tion was one that neither the GMD nor the CCP supported; both were

---

[6] Later, after 1949, 'Two-China' came to mean the Mainland and Taiwan.

determined to dominate all of China. Those who supported partition were people interested in peace, and in the security of their own regions.

Morale

By the middle of 1948 the GMD and the parts of Chinese society it ruled were suffering from growing degrees of demoralisation. There had been no real recovery from the Resistance War, nor was there any sense that there was a better (or even a possible) future. The government and its supporters seemed to have contracted a progressive, possibly fatal illness. A Canadian diplomat reported in early 1948:

The past decade of war has sapped China's admittedly under-developed central government strength, as well as the good elements of its regional administrations, to a point that might well be described as 'pernicious anaemia'.[7]

Chinese who returned from abroad were shocked at how bad the state of affairs was. The rocket scientist Qian Xuesen (Tsien Hsueh-shen) had been caught by the world war in the US, where he worked on the rocket programme. He came back to China in the late summer, on the promise that he would be made president of Jiaotong University, his alma mater. The offer turned out to be illusory, and he went back to the US disappointed – and also deeply depressed at what he saw in China, how run-down and dispirited the country that he had not seen for a decade was.[8]

The CCP's upswing in confidence, meanwhile, grew steeper. There were now two and a half million party members. There was such an influx into the party that there were concerns at the top that some of these new members were not genuine converts to socialism: 'Many landlords, rich peasants and scoundrels took this opportunity [land reform] to slip into the Party.'[9] To distinguish the true believers from the opportunists there was increasing emphasis on party discipline. This in turn gave the impression of unity and commitment to those beyond the party. The message of socialism, linked to competence and self-confidence, seemed, in the context of rampant inflation and of GMD corruption, more and more attractive. The CCP was having great success with its most valuable weapon, propaganda, particularly directed towards young people.

---

[7] D. Kilpatrick to the American Chamber of Commerce, Shanghai, 1 April 1948, *National Archives of Canada*, RG 20, TC 339, T-11968.

[8] Iris Chang, *Thread of the Silkworm* (New York: Basic, 1995), pp. 134–136.

[9] Mao, *Turning Point*, p. 14.

The CCP organised extensive underground networks of activists who lived in constant danger of arrest or execution, doing work that acquired a sinister glamour. The CCP had learnt how to touch idealistic strains in the young and the patriotic, giving them what seemed to be a chance to save China. It was dangerous to go over to the communist side, so those who did had to be brave as well as committed (see 'Generation divides' below).

There were other discreet efforts – the credit usually goes to Zhou Enlai – to identify older people who might be useful to a communist state, and to put out clandestine feelers to recruit them, not to change sides at once but to be ready to come out openly later on. The CCP recognised that some people were susceptible to appeals to their patriotism, to their vanity and to 'future considerations' – the prospect that they would benefit if and when the CCP took over the state. These were often people in positions of responsibility. In the growing political crisis a widespread phenomenon of self-protection was emerging. People who sensed the way the wind was blowing decided to move towards the CCP earlier rather than later. These people were known, often with some contempt, as members of the *fengpai* (wind faction), who would go with the wind whichever direction it blew from. This mixture of opportunism and objective calculation was a traditional way to survive in difficult times, rather like the practice in warlord times of having a store of flags in the house so that the right one could be hung out when a new occupying army arrived.

The GMD had no similar networks of persuasion in the CCP-held areas. The GMD made little effort to convert people to its cause; their only mechanisms to make people loyal were threats and punishments. To make these work, the GMD relied on an extensive network of spies and informants, many of them thuggish mercenaries, with no real commitment to the GMD. Their tactics were brutal. When secret communists were discovered, they were often executed summarily. The GMD was equally harsh in their treatment of non-communists who disagreed with GMD currency policies.

Inflation

The worst problem for the GMD was inflation. It was now completely out of hand. The value of money was declining by the day. Those who lived in the money economy and needed to buy goods (everyone except peasants) were obsessed and terrified by the inexorable rise in prices, which accelerated dramatically in the spring of 1948.

Table 4.1 lists the figures for Shanghai at three dates over little more than a year:[10]

Table 4.1 *Rise in the wholesale price index and the cost of living at Shanghai, 1947–1948*

	Wholesale price index	Cost of living
May 1947	100	100
February 1948	780	642
July 1948	11,100	5,863

The government showed little real concern about inflation. It did not reduce the amount it was spending on the military, the root cause of the inflation. The government was running a deficit so enormous that it could scarcely be grasped. The figures in Table 4.2, expressed in millions of inflating *Fabi* show the ballooning deficit:[11]

Table 4.2 *The rapidly increasing government deficit*

	Expenditures	Revenues	Deficit
1945	2,348,085	1,241,389	1,106,696
1946	7,574,790	2,876,988	4,697,802
1947	43,393,895	14,064,383	29,329,512
1948 (Jan–Jun)	655,471,087	220,905,475	434,565,612

People on salaries, paid by the month, were in desperate straits. At this stage the translator Yang Xianyi earned only enough a month as a professor to buy two sacks of flour. He and others in similar situations had to moonlight; even six or seven extra jobs were hardly enough to support a family.[12] The effect on morale was devastating.

Almost any commodity was impossibly expensive. In February 1948 Liang Sicheng asked John and Wilma Fairbank in the USA to send him a 500-sheet box of typing paper: 'It costs 10,000 *yuan* [*Fabi*] a sheet here; one box is half a month's pay.'[13]

Inflation brought out the worst in many people. Anxious consumers were obsessed with the constant rise in prices, and turned into hoarders,

[10] Chang Kai-ngau, *The Inflationary Spiral: The Experience of China, 1939–1950* (Cambridge: MIT Press, 1958), p. 356.

[11] *Ibid*, p. 71.

[12] Yang Xianyi, *White Tiger* (Hong Kong: Chinese University Press, 2002), p. 153.

[13] Wilma Fairbank, *Liang and Lin: Partners in Exploring China's Architectural Past* (Philadelphia: University of Pennsylvania, 1994), p. 158.

crafty and mean-spirited, unwilling to share their hoard with anyone except their immediate family members. People would do almost anything to acquire US dollars, the only safe haven. To get the dollars people used government contacts, or attached themselves to the many Americans working in China. An American friend was a prize beyond gold. The Americans, especially the younger ones, were besieged by Chinese women, hoping for money and security – and love.

Many people used a range of means from dubious to dishonest to take advantage of inflation. Speculating in commodities was common. Hoarding was standard. Failing to pay bills or wages on time meant paying less, at the cost of the recipient. Passing a bad cheque gave extra time and therefore money to the person signing the cheque, and cost the recipient the same amount. These were actions that seemed profitable as inflation raged ahead and the value of money declined, but were all destructive in terms of trust and of society as a whole.

Worst of all, for the GMD, inflation was destroying the people who made up the GMD's natural constituency – the urban population, especially the middle classes. There were clear signs that the GMD was abandoning its fundamental commitments.

The flight of cultural artefacts

One sign of how low morale was, and how much confidence had been sapped within the GMD leadership was the decision, in February 1948, not to install the treasures of the Beijing Palace Museum, the great collections of treasures once belonging the Qing emperors, in a new museum in Nanjing, but to send them to Taiwan.

Equally important, although less dramatic, was the shipping of the collections of the Institute of History and Philology to Taiwan, notably the artefacts saved at the beginning of the Resistance War from the great Shang site, the Waste of Yin, at Anyang. Private institutions and families also started to move treasures out of China. Books were shipped abroad. Some of the major university library collections of Chinese books in the West were put together in the late 1940s, purchased in China from people anxious to acquire US dollars, or to get their treasured books out of China.

War and society

Missing people

Two years after the end of the Resistance War Chinese society was still terribly disrupted. Huge numbers of people had not come home from the war. Many people still had little idea of what had happened to their family members, whether they were dead or alive, or were missing (*shizong*). The melancholy phrase often used at the time was *sheng si bu ming* ('unclear whether alive or dead').

生死不明
Sheng si bu ming
Unclear whether alive or dead

The worst case scenario was that relatives were dead, killed in battle or in bombing raids. Most would have no known grave. The Japanese armies disposed of some of those killed in mass graves. There were known to be such graves in many of the once-occupied areas. In the immediate aftermath of the Resistance War, no one wanted to open them and identify the victims, a gruesome task that would be unnecessary if some of the missing turned up. The mass grave on Pipashan, just outside Jinan (Shandong), was not excavated until 1954. When it was opened it was found to contain the remains of thousands of people.

Rural revolution

In the rural areas the CCP now held, including much of north China, more and more peasants had come under CCP control. The CCP had decided in 1946 to move from moderate rural reform to full-scale rural revolution, and land reform. After the early stages of expropriation of the wealthy and division of spoils (see Chapter 3) had been finished, a key preparatory stage for revolution and reform was to activate associations: poor peasant associations, women's associations, children's associations. This new form of social organisation transcended the old family and clan lines. Setting up associations was a key means of reshaping society – and of identifying potential leaders from among the members. When the activists leading the process were outsiders, there was unlikely to be any feeling of common cause between them and the locals. The associations provided this connection. Some of the associations were given specific tasks. Women, for example, were often given the task of sewing shoes and knitting socks for the soldiers of the PLA. The fundamental goal of each association was to enhance CCP control by giving people a sense of belonging – to a new world that would replace the one just destroyed.

As CCP control was consolidated, the full force of class warfare and land reform began to be unleashed in areas under secure CCP control. This was a dramatic and often traumatic process, one whose aim was to throw off 'thousands of years of feudalism', and to give the common people a voice. In some ways it followed the pattern of peasant revolts, which had marked all of Chinese history, but instead of being wild and chaotic, it was supposed to be orderly, directed by the CCP and initiated in individual communities by trained activists, usually outsiders.[14]

The newly 'liberated' areas had to go through the same initial processes that others had gone through earlier. Before land reform could start, the class status of each family had to be established. This was done in a variety ways, each of which relied heavily on endless mass meetings. During the winter in north China there is very little field work, so peasants could easily be got to go to meetings. In the meetings people were asked to declare their own class background – and also to denounce anyone else who seemed to be dissembling.

Establishing class status was a huge task, and often an arbitrary and unfair one. Society had already been gravely disrupted by the Resistance War. Now it was to be turned upside down. Now to be poor was good, to be rich bad. The question of the point in time at which status was assigned was critical: many people were much poorer at the end of the war than they had been before it. For them a recent classification was good. For all involved in the meetings it was time to show ingenuity and, if necessary, chicanery.

People found ingenious means to get a low classification. Those who had been rich or comfortably off tried to present themselves in a new light, difficult to do in a village where everyone knew everyone else, and many were related. Some families used their daughters as bait for the activists or the local cadres, others claimed to have been ruined by opium or gambling. Hinton's descriptions of the long-running meetings are humorous and earthy, and often entirely frustrating. In Long Bow class classification had to be done three times before the whole village was considered to have achieved the goal of *fanshen* – turning themselves over, 'had transformed themselves from passive victims of natural and social forces into active builders of a new world'.[15]

Behind the issue of class classification was one that went to the roots of the Chinese family system: heredity. All members of a family were assumed to belong to the same class. It was impossible for an individual to escape the class classification of parents and grandparents. In other words, there was a blood element to class; class status was hereditary.

The rural reform process often turned violent, a violence that meant killing. In a small village on the eastern end of the Jiaodong Peninsula

---

[14] The most famous novel about land reform was written by Ding Ling, who herself took part in land reform in a village in Chahar in 1947. *Taiyang shao zai Sanganhe shang* (*The Sun Shines on the Sangan River*) (Beijing: Foreign Languages Press, 1954).

[15] William Hinton, *Fanshen: A Documentary of Revolution in a Chinese Village* (New York: Monthly Review, 1966; reissued 2008), p. 609.

was Sam Ginsbourg, a young Russian Jew who had grown up in China and joined the CCP in a flight of youthful excitement in Shanghai. He soon found himself, to his surprise, on a trek with communist guerrillas near Qingdao. He saw a woman landlord being dragged off to her death by a group of local peasant activists: 'It was against the policy of the Party in the countryside, but such excesses did occur and were understandable.' Ginsbourg, despite his shock, loyally tried to justify the execution on the grounds of how awful the behaviour of landlords must have been in the past.[16] This was the formulaic justification of violence, that the people were so angry with their former oppressors that they killed them spontaneously. There is at least as strong a possibility that killing was a deliberate policy.

In many parts of the area where Ginsbourg was, close to the Qingdao-Jinan railway line, conversions to the CCP were still tentative. There was no guarantee, at this stage, against back-sliding among the peasants. The fear that the GMD would return was real. This would make the potential beneficiaries of land reform cautious about joining the communists. The use of terror was employed to make it more difficult for people to stay away from the communists; it helped to polarise village communities. When an individual or group was attacked, under the leadership of the party activists, the rest of the community either joined in the attacks or stood back and did nothing to stop them. Either way the whole community became complicit in the attacks. If the attacks ended with the target being killed, the community was even more deeply complicit.

The complicity had a long-term, although unstated goal: to pin down popular loyalty, which the external situation made difficult, and guarantee that loyalty even when the party promised what it could not deliver, or was unable to convert its promises of a better life into reality. Rural revolution was carried out village by village. It was a form of enclosed civil war within small communities. This was a bitter enough process, but it did not solve a major form of rural inequality: the location of a village. Although the revolution was intended to bring equality and eradicate privilege, it could do this only within the limited village context. It did not resolve large inequalities. A rich village on good land would still be much richer than a neighbouring village up on a hillside.

The increasing pace of rural revolution did not provide the CCP with any new means to solve fundamental problems. It was still unable to do anything about some of the most fundamental problems facing

---

[16] Sam Ginsbourg, *My First Sixty Years in China* (Beijing: New World Press, 1982), pp. 157–158. Ginsbourg was the brother of *Toronto Star* columnist Mark Gayn.

peasants: illness and natural disasters. In traditional China peasants visited by these horrors turned to the spirit world for help, to Buddhism, Daoism and folk religion. In Tunliu (Shanxi) there was considerable support for the CCP when activists first arrived, but the young revolutionaries could not fulfil all the needs of the people; their ideology could only deal with economic issues, not with sickness. When plague struck in early 1948, the party could do nothing; the peasants turned to the traditional healers and to folk religion, sects such as the Kongshengdao, people whom the atheistic communists regarded as charlatans.[17]

The winter of late 1947 and early 1948 was a critical time for the consolidation of the CCP's hold over rural society. Even though the actual war with the GMD was being fought on the battlefields, the CCP was deeply committed to a revolution based in rural China. Peasants were needed to man and to support the armies. In the virtual absence of an urban working class, China's peasantry had to be the revolutionary class. If the peasants could not be brought into the revolution by persuasion, they had to be coerced – and terror was a powerful weapon. A different kind of terror was reserved for urban residents: the siege, a military tactic that was aimed as much at civilians as at soldiers, and threatened the lives of civilians.

The death of a city

In the terrible siege of Changchun as many people died as perished in the Nanjing massacre (1937–1938), although they died over a much longer period, not at the hands of an invading force, but of starvation and cold. Until recently almost nothing has been known about one of the worst civilian disasters in modern warfare, comparable to the siege of Stalingrad (1942–1943).

Changchun, in the middle of Manchuria, was a new city, known until 1945 as Xinjing (New Capital), the capital of the Japanese puppet state of Manzhouguo. Unlike the majority of Chinese cities, it was not walled. It was laid out in imperial splendour on a European plan, with a grand collection of avenues, squares and circles, only partially completed in 1945. It was a key railway junction, connecting in every direction with the other main centres of Manchuria. Immediately before and just after the Soviet Red Army took Changchun at the end of World War Two, in August 1945, at least a third of the inhabitants, including all the Japanese, fled.

[17] Thi Minh and Huang Ngo, *Tunlai dans la tourmente* (*Tunliu in Torment*) (Paris: Riveneuve, 2007), pp. 45–46.

Changchun population

Changchun went through extreme fluctuations in population. From a high of three quarters of a million as the capital of Manzhouguo in 1945, it sunk to less than 200,000 at the end of the siege of the city in 1948:*

Table 4.3 *Changchun: population shifts*

Pre-August 1945	740,000	Before Japanese surrender
Post-August 1945	560,000	After Japanese surrender
April 1946	470,000	PLA captures city
May 1946	520,000	After GMD recaptures city
May 1947	390,000	Start of the siege
October 1947	179,241	End of the siege
October 1949	475,000	Establishment of the PRC

The bland statistics speak of enormous upheaval. They represent people fleeing and returning, people dying, only to be replaced by newcomers. The two figures for 1947, when no movement in or out of the city was possible, because it was besieged, show the horror to which civilian populations can be subjected. The number of casualties was lower than that of the Russian city of Stalingrad, where three quarters of million civilians were killed or injured during the German siege, but still well over half the population.

* Yan Wanshou, *Changchun shi zhi* (*A History of Changchun*) (Jilin: Jilin renmin chubanshe, 1999), p. 28.

Some of those who had actively collaborated with the Japanese, including the puppet emperor of Manzhouguo, Pu Yi, were arrested by the Soviet Red Army and taken to the USSR. The Chinese population, under Japanese control since 1931, had no political connections or loyalty either to the GMD or to the CCP – which may help to explain the extreme callousness with which both armies treated them during the siege.

Communist forces cut the railway lines north and south in the early autumn of 1947, after which the only long-range connection the 100,000 GMD defenders and the 400,000 civilians had with the outside world was by air. Some local products could still enter the city, but the city soon felt like an isolated island in a vast sea of hostility. The electricity was cut on 17 October 1947, and was not restored for a year. Winter fuel

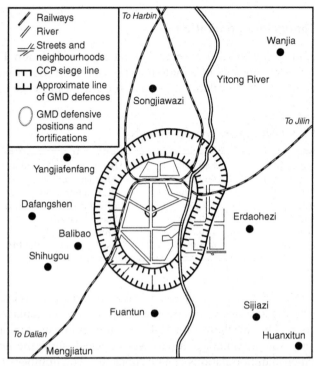

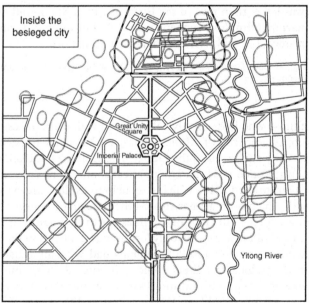

Map 6 Besieged Changchun

was in very short supply and the soldiers and civilians shivered and froze through the intense cold of a Manchurian winter (Changchun winter temperatures go as low as −30 degrees Celsius) with no electric light or heating. Anything that could be burnt for heat – furniture, floor boards – was; after that people huddled together for survival.[18] Food supplies dwindled and, by the spring, were almost exhausted.

In the spring of 1948 the siege was intensified; now even local supplies were cut. The PLA created a stranglehold on the city. The army stationed itself about two miles out from the city, along what would have been the ring road if the construction of Xinjing had been finished. PLA soldiers were often within earshot of the defenders. Irregular GMD air drops could just about feed the army, but not the civilian population. This differential between the supplies available to the soldiers and to the civilians created bitterness and despair amongst the civilians. The lines of Du Fu, written more than 1,000 years before, about the gulf between rich and poor, seemed to apply in Changchun. The people behind the crimson gates were high officials in the Tang Dynasty; in Changchun it was the GMD command that had food and warmth.

朱門酒肉臭 路有凍死骨
Zhumen jiurou chou, lu you dongsi gu
Inside the crimson gates wine and meat go to waste,
outside in the street are the bones of those who have frozen to death

Peasants in the rural areas immediately outside the city were less vulnerable during the siege than the urban residents, but they were in constant danger of having food and animals requisitioned. The order from the besieging army was: 'Do not let any grain fall into the enemy's hands, do not let enemies who are about to die be revived.'[19] This may have been an implicit recognition that the supplies of food would be taken by the PLA to feed its own men.

In spite of the slowly unfolding disaster, there was no question of the defenders surrendering. Nanjing kept sending orders to the defenders to stand fast, to defend to the death (*sishou*), apparently oblivious to the agony of the city. A cynical view from a British diplomat was that the GMD prolonged the siege so as to keep as many PLA troops as possible tied up in maintaining the siege.[20] Chiang Kai-shek had letters written

---

[18] Zhang Zhenglong, *Xue bai xue hong* (*Snow White, Blood Red*) (Beijing: Jiefangjun chubanshe, 1989), p. 465. See also Frank Dikotter, *The Tragedy of Liberation: A History of the Chinese Revolution, 1945–1957* (London: Bloomsbury, 2013), pp. 1–8.

[19] Zhang, *Xue bai xue hong*, p. 468.

[20] Jarman, *China*, VIII (September 1948), p. 620.

in his own hand dropped in to the defending commanders, to boost the resolve of the officers and men, all outsiders, who were assumed to feel no connection for the local people. Some of the soldiers did care for the city's people – they had married local girls. When the southern armies arrived in 1946, many of the unmarried men had found local girls more than willing to marry them.[21]

The CCP, despite its populist political stance, took no responsibility for the dying inhabitants. They relied instead on a constant barrage of propaganda delivered by loud-hailers and leaflets, encouraging soldiers and civilians to surrender. The GMD responded by executing men who were caught in the act of deserting.[22]

The siege did eventually end; General Zheng Dongguo surrendered in October 1948. Thirteen thousand defenders had preceded him, slipping across the lines at night. These men could not understand themselves why they were being condemned to starve to death. Their incomprehension was a gift for communist propaganda. 'We are all the sons of poor people, starving to defend the city, who for? (*women dou shi qiongku renjia zidi, e duzi shoucheng wei le shei?*)'[23] The number of soldiers who starved is not clear, but they died at a rate far below that of the civilians. By the end of the siege only 170,000 civilians were left alive; that meant that as many as 200,000 had died.[24] In 2006, while an excavation was being made for new buildings, skeletons stacked like firewood were turned up.[25]

Zheng Dongguo

In his old age General Zheng Dongguo, garrison commander of the city of death, remembered the conditions in 1948:

Changchun was once a beautiful city, but at that time the city, inside and outside, was a scene of total devastation. There were corpses everywhere, and it had become a living tomb. The people suffered an unprecedented catastrophe. For all these years, whenever I think of the tragedy of the Changchun siege, my heart beats fast and my body shakes, and above all I feel terrible pain and regret for the horrors and losses suffered by the people of Changchun.

What I regret is that I already knew quite clearly that the defeat of the army defending Changchun was not far away. In my heart I regretted even

---

[21] Zhang, *Xue bai xue hong*, p. 476.
[22] *Ibid*, p. 472.
[23] *Ibid*, p. 480.
[24] *Ibid*, pp. 494, 497.
[25] Dikotter, *The Tragedy of Liberation*, pp. 1–8.

more that I had ever come to Manchuria to fight in this civil war, but I was still dominated in my thinking by feudal ideas of loyalty and filial piety. I wrongly believed that, however corrupt the Guomindang was, however bad the situation was, I had been with Mr. Jiang [Chiang Kai-shek] for several decades, and could only use all the strength I had to fight to the end. Only then could I show the 'integrity' of a soldier, and have a clear conscience towards Mr. Jiang. So although I felt extremely anguished, and hopeless, I still maintained a calm composure, and put all my efforts in to supporting the siege, and did not in the slightest way alter my determination to defend the city. Because of my obstinate behaviour the sufferings of the people of Changchun were prolonged for a time. Later on I bitterly regretted it.*

Zheng's soldiers did not come out winners either. After their surrender their units were retrained and then sent to fight in the Korean War. Those who survived were settled, in the late 1950s, in the Great North Waste (*Beidahuang*), in northern Heilongjiang. This incredibly cold region was a bitter last home for men from the balmy province of Yunnan.

* Zheng Dongguo, *Du Yuming jiangjun* (*General Du Yuming*) (Beijing: Zhongguo wenshi chubanshe, 1986), pp. 246, 248–249.

Refugees

By this stage of the Civil War considerable flows of refugees had begun to develop. Some were made up of people fleeing from rural areas already in CCP hands or about to fall into cities and towns. Others were people fleeing south, away from the fighting. These flows consisted of people who were afraid of what the future might bring, and were moving to places where they would be safer. No one moved with ease. Much of the road and railway systems were still in ruins and when they were passable, priority was always given to the military.

The greatest pressure to leave was felt in the Manchurian cities. Very few people could manage to leave the region. The only ones who had a hope of leaving Manchuria were those with good enough connections to get on one of the flights that brought supplies into the cities. These were effectively reserved for those with GMD connections, mostly officers and their families. Other people, including the common soldiers of the bloated GMD armies, were at the mercy of fate. Some might have a chance to get away, with retreating armies, others could desert and take themselves out of the battle zones, but most were doomed to stay and hope the CCP would be merciful.

The wealthy in the cities further south were now acutely conscious of what their fate might be under communism. They started to leave China, or at least to get parts of their wealth and some of their family members out of the country. The sudden disappearances of family or friends were unnerving for those who had not yet decided what to do. An insidious draining of confidence was in progress.

Soldier families

More and more men were being drawn into the armies on both sides. This represented a new form of family division, at a time when many of the divisions from the previous war had still not been resolved. On the GMD side, very few of the soldiers had family members with them. Those who were already married when they enlisted only saw their families when they got leave to go home. There had been no leave at the end of the Resistance War. Instead many soldiers moved much further away from home than they had been before. Southern soldiers in the GMD armies were now fighting in the north. A new form of separation of soldiers from their families came in as the GMD armies press-ganged large number of men to fill the ranks of their depleted armies, and to act as porters (*lafu*).

On the CCP side, the recruitment practices stressed, on paper, the desire to sacrifice for socialism. William Hinton gave an impassioned account of the PLA soldiers he had seen marching through Long Bow. 'The soldiers were carefree yet dignified, fun-loving but not raucous, friendly but not condescending. These attitudes reflected something inside them, an inner integrity, a sense of collective pride, a confident and purposeful spirit.'[26]

This was an idealised vision, one that distinguished PLA soldiers from those who fought for the GMD. It seemed that what the PLA had achieved was what the GMD armies had not done, to instil a tight discipline on its soldiers, a discipline imbued with socialist ideology. The product was 'ideological soldiers (*zhuyi bing*)', what the GMD armies had once aspired to, under the influence of Sun Yat-sen's Three Principles of the People (*Sanmin zhuyi*). In the early parts of the Resistance War, anti-Japanese nationalism had provided an ideological stimulus to fight. Now the CCP seemed to have achieved this goal. The reality was often different. Many of the soldiers who fought for the PLA had moved into the communist armies directly from puppet armies or from GMD units. Some had gone over voluntarily, others only after they had been captured on the battlefield. Many more had simply been grabbed, by one army or another, by the accident of being in the wrong place at the wrong time.

[26] Hinton, *Fanshen*, p. 480.

Press-ganging

The GMD and CCP armies kept up their strength through normal recruiting – and through press-ganging, grabbing young men from the streets. Xu Fugui, a young man of dubious repute, was picked up on the street of his hometown. He had been in a brawl with another young man, who managed to escape:

The company commander turned round, and seeing me standing behind him, approached me with his gun held out. He pressed the barrel against my chest and said: 'You can leave too.'
My legs began to tremble uncontrollably. I figured... he'd send me to heaven with a single bullet. I pleaded 'I'll pull the canon, I'll pull the canon.'
  With my right hand I grabbed the ropes; with my left I firmly grasped the two silver coins in my pocket that Jianzhen [his wife] had given me. As we left the town I saw some thatched huts in the fields that looked like mine. I lowered my head and began to cry.*

* Yu Hua, *To Live*, trans. Michael Berry (New York: Anchor, 2003), pp. 62–63.

These soldiers, willing recruits or otherwise, were cut off from their families for the duration. As the confusion across the country intensified, it was more and more difficult to receive news of home. Reunification with families seemed far away.

Overseas Chinese

For the Overseas Chinese there were very few reunions during the Civil War. Immediately after the end of the Resistance War the problem was transport; there was very little shipping available and flights were out of the question. Over the next two years the insecurity in China persuaded many Overseas Chinese to postpone their visits home. Some were able to send money, but the very weak economy in Southeast Asia meant that may Overseas Chinese still had no money to send. For those in North America, the eight years of the war had opened up a gulf, which coincided with the improvement of their situation in the USA and Canada. The postponing of family visits gradually came to mean putting them off permanently. After 1949 going home was almost impossible. Not until the 1980s was it possible to go 'home' – a place from which all but the elderly were estranged by then.[27]

[27] Wing Chung Ng, *The Chinese in Vancouver: The Pursuit of Identity and Power* (Vancouver: University of British Columbia Press, 1999) discusses the various forms of identity in the Chinese Canadian community.

Fig. 12 New PLA recruits

Generation divides

As the fighting in the Civil War intensified, the CCP became increasingly aware of how many people would be needed to run the country if and when the CCP took over. Many of these would have to be educated, literate people – in short supply in the ranks of the CCP armies, made up largely of illiterate peasants. The CCP was already active in finding potential recruits through underground *wenxiangdui* (Smell the Fragrance Bands), which by late 1947 operated in many of the schools and universities in GMD-controlled areas.[28] The tempo of youth recruitment accelerated in 1948. Young people in the cities saw little or no future with the GMD, and no point in pursuing careers associated with it. Students spent more and more time demonstrating and protesting, less and less studying. The most radical went off to join the CCP in the areas the party already held. They knew that they would be saying goodbye to their families. The family separations based on ideology were an acute form of generational split; a process already apparent in the Resistance War was becoming even more acute.

[28] Lo Jiu-jung, Yu Chien-ming and Chiu Hei-yuan (eds.), *Fenghuo suiyuexia de Zhongguo funu* (*Chinese Women in the Fires of War*) (Taibei: Zhongyang yanjiuyuan Jindaishi yanjiu-suo, 2004), p. 54.

The role models in CCP propaganda, spread to young people, usually by word-of-mouth, were affluent, educated young people who had turned against their families' luxurious and empty lifestyles and towards the ascetic, self-denying life of socialism. Their actions were presented as the true, pure way to live, one that would bring China out of the cesspit of feudalism and decadence. The appeal to young people of a simple, shared lifestyle has often drawn them into revolutionary movements of change, in China and in many other societies, whether for religious or political causes. It is a powerful force in its initial stages. One of the young men who turned against his family and towards communism was Zhang Guangzheng, the older brother of the archaeologist Zhang Guangzhi (K.C. Chang). Just after the end of the Resistance War, the teenager had gone over to the CCP; he left his home in Beiping for one of the CCP-controlled areas in Hebei. The brothers did not meet again until 1980.[29]

In rural areas too young people were coming into their own, throwing off the control of their elders. Quite a few young women, the most celebrated Liu Hulan (see Chapter 2), went over to the CCP, even at the risk of death. In Laixi (eastern Shandong) several young women activists for the CCP were done to death in September 1947, during a brief period when GMD supporters regained control of the area. The *dizhu huanxiang dui* (returning landlord troops) seized and tortured several very young women activists. One woman village head, Sun Ruilan, was 22; another organiser of a women's group, Jie Wenliang, was only 17. All died for their new cause.[30]

The radical behaviour of the young was deeply distressing for older people. They had endured the constraints of the old society when they were young with the promise of better times as they aged; now they were threatened by the decline in the traditional respect of the young for their elders. Fathers could no longer control their children or grandchildren. Women who had been mercilessly bullied as new brides by their own mothers-in-law were less likely to dare, or even to be able, to do the same to their own daughters-in-law. It was becoming increasingly difficult for parents even to arrange their children's marriages, one of the key controls over their children. In the modernised parts of society, the idea of marriage arranged by parents, already on the way out before the Resistance War, now virtually disappeared. Some young people turned to teachers

---

[29] Robert Murowchick, *Kwang-chih Chang: A Biographical Memoir* (Washington: National Academy of Sciences, 2012).

[30] Zhonggong Laixi xianwei, *Laixi dangshi ziliao* (*Laixi Materials on Party History*) (Laixi: Laixi dangshihui, 1988).

or employers to find them a match (*duixiang*). The more adventurous looked for their own true love.

Marriage was traditionally in the purview of the family. A marriage took place when a new bride was brought into her husband's home. The character *jia*, for marriage, made up of the woman radical besides that character for family, embodies this concept of marriage.

Given that there was still no form of marriage ceremony beyond the family, one sanctioned by some civil authority, young people who choose their own partners were in a strange legal limbo, perhaps married, perhaps not. It was still a situation that for most of them was infinitely preferable to the old system.

Family separations: strategies and accidents

By this stage of the war families with the time and money to consider the future of the family were making plans, which often involved the strategic splitting of the family, for the time being at least. One strategy involved moving money and some of the family members out of the country, most often to Hong Kong. Some of China's wealthiest families planned for the future by taking several different tacks at the same time, in the hope that at least one would work and would preserve the family. One branch of the Rong Family moved most of its members to Hong Kong or the USA; a few stayed in Shanghai. This was the strategy that had served the family well towards the end of the Qing Dynasty, when some members continued in traditional scholarly roles, while others went into business (see 'Biographies' below).

Another strategy, although seldom a deliberate one, was to have some family members go over to the CCP while others waited to see what would happen. In the context of the Civil War it could not be done in a straightforwardly self-serving way, given the hatred between the two camps. Urban families whose members had gone over to the CCP had to keep their departure very quiet.

A strategy adopted by some more affluent families as they saw their world changing was to send their children abroad. The older generation knew that they could not leave China, but their children at least could get away. This strategy was very like the one used a decade before at the beginning of the Resistance War, when the young went inland and the elders stayed at home. Five of the six children of the great opera performer Zhou Xinfang and his wife Qiu Lilin went away from Shanghai one by one, to Europe and the USA, at the insistence of their determined mother. The family was last together in Shanghai in 1947. Qiu died in 1967, in the early stages of the Cultural Revolution. Zhou Xinfang and his eldest son were imprisoned. Two of the children abroad became famous, Tsai Chin as an actress and Michael Chow as a restauranteur. The family was destroyed. None of the children who went abroad saw their parents again.[31]

This was a story repeated again and again among those who left China. A strategy that seemed to call only for a short-term separation, to weather the coming storm, turned out to be a permanent one, a parting forever. It affected not only families whose young members went abroad, but also families who moved to Taiwan. There was no intent to separate the family; the separations were forced by the vicissitudes of war. The ten children of General Bai Chongxi have only one photograph of all of them all together with their parents. On 7 July 1946, the ninth anniversary of the start of the Resistance War, the family was together. Earlier the family had been separated by warfare. Later the separation was perpetuated by the Civil War and the departure of most of the children for the USA.[32]

Property and how to deal with it

In 1948 the CCP was still a long way away from taking over China, and many people still believed that it would never happen. But those with property – houses, land, chattels – had to start thinking about how to deal with it, however small the amount was. The awareness of the CCP's belief in economic equality, their contempt for displays of wealth, the simplicity of the lives of good communists, was now universal, and a threat to those who did have some property. Families had to work out how to cope with their property.

There were almost universal attempts to get hold of small, high-value items, which could be taken along should people need to flee. The most valuable of such items were US dollars, which kept on increasing in value as inflation got worse and worse. Many people were tempted to send money and valuables out of the country, notably to Hong Kong. Others converted money into jewellery and precious metals.

Those who saw no prospect except a future under communism wanted to have less rather than more property. They found ways of divesting themselves of parts of their property, by donating property to relatives or

---

[31] Tsai Chin, *Daughter of Shanghai* (New York: St. Martin's Press, 1994).
[32] Bai Xianyong, *Fuqin yu Minguo* (*Father and the Republic*) (Taibei: Shibao, 2012) xia, p. 253.

to their community. A large house could be shared with numbers of relatives and friends. Land could be handed over to relatives and neighbours. Movable valuables, jewellery, precious metals, could be hidden under floors or in the hollow walls of houses.

All of these efforts at preserving wealth, or at concealing it, showed how great the loss of confidence in the GMD was. A sense of profound gloom was enveloping much of GMD China.

Biographies

Chen Yonggui

Chen Yonggui was the outstanding peasant leader of the Mao era, the public face of the model commune Dazhai (Shanxi). In the 1950s and 1960s millions of pilgrims visited Dazhai, which became the model for agriculture (*nongye xue Dazhai*). Chen rose to be vice-premier of China. His rise was not predictable. During the Resistance War he had acted briefly as the village peace preservation representative for the local puppet (*wei*) government. His job was to deal with the Japanese if and when they came to the village. This move was later claimed to have been made on CCP instructions, which ordered him to be a 'bogus' representative, or double agent.

Chen's case was identical to that of many underground operatives of the CCP during the Japanese occupation. Their actions were courageous, but had a terrible internal flaw: who would believe them at the end of the war? Chen was haunted by his stint as 'bogus' representative. Immediately after the end of the Resistance War, he was publicly denounced as a traitor. He survived that, and the difficulties he encountered in 1947 when he applied to join the CCP. But the issue never went away. It came alive again in the 1980s, when he was on the wrong side of 'the sudden historical reversal' (i.e., the Deng Xiaoping policies of opening up); the issue was still his role working undercover with the Japanese.[33]

Fan Qishi

Fan Qishi, from the Jiaodong Peninsula, fitted in to an age-old pattern in Shandong, the leader of a band of brothers who lived and fought in the wide spaces between a legal and an illegal world. He belonged to the

---

[33] Qiu Huailu, *Ninth Heaven to Ninth Hell: The History of a Noble Chinese Experiment*, ed. William Hinton (New York: Barricade, 1995), pp. 39–44, 57–59.

model of tough, brawling men found in *The Heroes of the Marsh*. Fan and his men operated in the rural areas of Wei xian, on the railway line between Jinan and Qingdao, starting in the 1920s. They were embedded in their local community. During the Japanese occupation he was at first pro-GMD but later went over to the Japanese. He was in secret contact with local communists for much of the war, and turned a blind eye to their activities, but at the end of the war he went back to the GMD. His aim at every twist and turn had been to keep his own small unit (about 1,500 men) intact. In the spring of 1948, when the GMD seemed to be losing out to the CCP, he took his troops over to the CCP. This proved to be his last shift. The CCP accepted him, but at a cost. He and his men, now a formal regiment, were forced to undergo ideological remoulding and accept party authority. This broke the personal connections between Fan and his men. Fan's authority was undermined, he could see no future. He fled with his family in late 1948. In 1951 he was caught in Yunnan in the far southwest and executed.[34] Fan's ability to survive, with his men, came unstuck when the CCP's efforts to impose a discipline that went beyond the personal won out.

China's archaeologists

By this stage of the Civil War, it was clear to many of China's leading intellectuals that they would soon have to choose between staying in China and going abroad. The archaeologists were the stars of China's intellectuals. In the 1930s their discoveries had revealed an ancient world previously known only from myths and legends, and had brought out of the earth breathtakingly beautiful bronzes and jades. At a time when China's sense of herself was low, the archaeologists gave her a glorious past.

By 1948 many of the artefacts from the Waste of Yin (Yinxu) near Anyang that had been stored in west China since just before the Japanese overran the Anyang region in 1938 had been moved to Taiwan. The senior men, including Li Ji and Dong Zuobin, had lost confidence in being able to resume their research in China. Fieldwork was out of the question in the turbulence of the Civil War, and work on the Waste of Yin artefacts needed good working conditions and a lack of political interference; the Marxist stage theory of history would make objective analysis very difficult. These men made up their minds to leave China, for Taiwan.

---

[34] Shandongsheng Changle xian zhengxie, *Changle wenshi ziliao* (*Changle Materials on History and Literature*) (Changle: Changle zhengxie, 1989), pp. 91–109.

Some of the less senior archaeologists were discreetly contacted by agents of the CCP and offered inducements to stay in China. The professional standing of Pei Wenzhong, the young researcher who had discovered the first skull of Peking Man (*Beijing yuanren*), was already compromised. He had stayed in Beiping during the war while the others had left. He had stayed to guard the fossils of Peking Man, but they were lost in late 1941, a mysterious disappearance that has never been resolved. Pei was briefly arrested by the Japanese. When he was released he came into touch with the CCP underground; they provided medicine for his children who were sick with whooping cough. In gratitude for this help, or because he was in bad odour with his colleagues, Pei later decided to stay in Beijing. He went on to enjoy a distinguished career.[35]

Another archaeologist who stayed on the Mainland was Xia Nai. His training was in Egyptology, in London, and he had spent most of the Resistance War in Egypt. He was not part of the Yinxu group. By staying he became by default one of the leading figures in the field of archaeology in China. In 1950 he was named deputy director of the newly established Archaeology Research Institute (*Kaogu yanjiusuo*); 12 years later he became director.[36] Much of his work was devoted not to the ancient past but to the opening of the Dingling Tomb (Ming Dynasty), north of Beijing.

The split of archaeology into two camps left a sense of betrayal in archaeologists on both sides. Those who stayed in China paid terrible prices. Most were persecuted in the Cultural Revolution. The tragic story of the oracle bones specialist Chen Mingjia is beautifully told in Peter Hessler's *Oracle Bones*.[37] Those who went to Taiwan could work on the artefacts they took with them, but could never again do excavations.

The Yangs

Gladys Yang and Yang Xianyi met in the late 1930s at Oxford University. She had been born in China, the daughter of a British professor, J.B. Tayler. He was the son of a wealthy banking family in Tianjin. At Oxford the two fell in love and, in 1940, after their graduation, they made the perilous journey back to China. They worked in Chongqing, where they were married, as teachers and translators. They were a celebrity couple,

[35] Liu Houyi and Liu Qiusheng. *Faxian Zhongguo yuanren de ren: Pei Wenzhong (The Man who Discovered Peking Man: Pei Wenzhong)* (Kunming: Yunnan renmin chubanshe, 1980), pp. 64–70.

[36] *Zhongguo kaoguxue yanjiu (Chinese Research in Archaeology)* (Beijing: Wenwu chubanshe, 1986), p. 4.

[37] Peter Hessler, *Oracle Bones* (New York: HarperCollins, 2006), pp. 431–434.

handsome and accomplished. Xianyi made a reputation as a writer and translator of poetry.

They grew more and more disillusioned with the GMD and its interference with education. At the end of the Resistance War, after a wait of almost a year to get transport, they arrived in Nanjing. There they managed to survive the increasingly difficult living conditions thanks to Gladys' job with a foreign relief agency. Although they had opportunities to go abroad in 1948 and 1949, as many of their colleagues actually did, they were already in covert contact with the CCP, convinced that the party presented hope for a better future for China. Their commitment to a new China led them to stay in China.

Over the next decades they brought many of China's classics into English. Their warmth and hospitality created a wide circle of friends around them in Beijing. Their commitment to China did not spare them from terrible maltreatment, and the tragic death of their son, during the Cultural Revolution. They were examples for those of us who were lucky enough to know them of courage and of dedication to China.

The Rong Family[38]

The Rong Family was one of Shanghai's most prominent business families, and played a key role in Shanghai's economic growth. As industry developed in the late Qing Dynasty, the family elders, two brothers Rong Zongjing and Rong Desheng, realising that change was coming, diversified from government service into running cotton and flour mills. The process of diversification was a successful strategy for keeping the family alive and growing in the early Republic.

The family businesses managed to keep going during the Resistance War. As the Civil War progressed, the family embarked on another stage of diversification. Some of its members moved to Hong Kong and set up businesses there. One brother stayed in Shanghai, with one of his sons Rong Yiren, who came to be known as the 'red capitalist'.[39] After turbulent and often painful years he came into his own during the 1980s, and was vice-president of the PRC for five years. The Rongs have shown a capacity for compromise and flexibility that has made them a model for how to get through troubled times.

---

[38] Marie-Claire Bergere, *The Golden Age of the Chinese Bourgeoisie* (Cambridge: Cambridge University Press, 1989).

[39] Wong Siu-lun, *Emigrant Entrepreneurs: Shanghai Industrialists in Hong Kong* (Hong Kong: Oxford University Press, 1988), pp. 28–31.

5   Nearing the end: July 1948–January 1949

By the last half of 1948 it was clear that the GMD was going to lose the Civil War. Apart from those who believed in Marxism and were convinced that the CCP was destined for victory, the supporters of the GMD were losing hope. The GMD armies had lost the initiative. The GMD was still strong, in military terms, and it controlled an enormous government and political apparatus. It was recognised by all major foreign states and was a major international player. As one of the victorious allies in the Second World War, China was a key member of the body that was to guarantee future world peace, the United Nations. China sent a team to the 1948 Olympic Games in London. There were no medals, but the few athletes were described as 'beaten but not disgraced'.[1]

And yet deep within the GMD people felt the end was near. The American diplomat John Melby noted the feeling, almost of panic, that gripped the GMD world: 'Nanking and Shanghai are tense to the point of panic and there is still no food. Never have I seen anything like the emptiness of the stores and the lines of people hoping that something, anything will come in. In China now, where events usually move slowly, everything is moving at a fearful rate.'[2]

In the GMD military there was something close to despair about the worsening military situation. Chiang Kai-shek was intent on pursuing his own, costly strategies, concentrating huge forces in the north. He refused to let the best GMD commanders, notably Bai Chongxi, play any significant role in the grand strategy. Chiang's stubbornness was his (temporary) downfall. He lost so much support within the GMD that in January 1949 he was forced into 'retirement'; vice-president Li Zongren took over as acting president. Before he 'retired', Chiang took a hugely

---

[1] *China Review*, I, 10 (September 1948), pp. 16–17. The PRC did not participate in the Olympics until 1984.
[2] John Melby, *The Mandate of Heaven: Record of a Civil War* (Toronto: University of Toronto Press, 1968), p. 289.

significant step: he had the gold reserves of the Bank of China transferred to Taiwan.

Moving the gold*

On 1 December 1945, a young seaman, Fan Yuanjian, serving on a government customs vessel, the *Haixing*, was caught up in a secret mission. His vessel was ordered in the dark of night to move to the dock of the Bank of China, on the Bund in Shanghai. He watched in astonishment as a stream of small wooden boxes, each carried on a bamboo pole between two labourers, was brought on to the vessel. Fan and the other sailors tried to work out what the heavy boxes might contain; some guessed that it must be gold, given that the boxes were coming from the Bank of China. By 2am the loading was complete and the vessel set sail. Only after the boat had sailed was the crew informed that they were going to Taiwan. When the vessel docked in Jilong two days later, it was met by soldiers who offloaded the boxes. The vessel had carried two million ounces of gold from China, the bulk of the Bank of China reserves.

* Feng Huang, *Da baitui 1949* (*The Great Retreat 1949*) (Guangzhou: Guangdong renmin chubanshe, 2005), pp. 82–86.

This poorly kept secret underlined the widespread conviction that the GMD was drowning in corruption, which started at the very top of the party, and worked its way down to the lowest officials. The corruption was closely linked to the chronic crisis of inflation. The GMD had access to huge quantities of US dollars, by now the most highly valued currency; those with GMD connections had US dollars and rose above the misery of the great mass of people living with inflation.

Political protection for GMD members and their relatives was another key form of corruption. In the summer of 1948 Chiang Ching-kuo (Jiang Jingguo), Chiang Kai-shek's son, attempted to crack down on large-scale smugglers and black-marketeers. One of these was David Kung, son of H.H. Kung (Kong Xiangxi) and nephew of Jiang's stepmother, Song Meiling. When Jiang tried to arrest David Kung, Song Meiling intervened forcefully. Kung was not arrested, although he did have to leave the country.[3] The story was widely covered in the press, and aroused furious complaints: corruption could not have gone higher in the GMD.

[3] K.M. Pannikaar, *In Two Chinas* (London: George Allen and Unwin, 1955), pp. 32–33.

Behind the outrage was what amounted to a pro-CCP message: while altruistic young people were already communists, or were thinking of moving towards socialism, abandoning their own families, within the GMD family connections permitted malfeasance; they protected the bad young people in their own families.

The coverage was a sign of the extent to which Song Meiling's saintly image in the Resistance War had been tarnished since then. She started to spend more and more time away from China, in the USA, where, as Chiang Kai-shek's 'last weapon', she made increasingly extravagant (and unsuccessful) demands on the US government for financial and even military aid in fighting the Civil War.

No one on the GMD side dared come out in favour of the CCP, because to do so would be to invite imprisonment or assassination, but more and more people within and close to the GMD were talking about peace, about negotiations and about accommodations. Meanwhile many people who would normally be supporters of the GMD, especially the wealthy who had the means to do so, were voting with their feet, leaving China or preparing to do so.

For ordinary civilians there was little hope left in the GMD. Corrosive inflation was turning the lives of all who depended on a money economy into a daily, even hourly nightmare. Any way out of the misery, including defeat, was becoming almost acceptable.

> *The desire for peace waxes stronger as hope declines*
> Joseph Conrad, *Lord Jim*

Conrad was talking about the emotional course of a sailor as his ship seemed on the point of sinking, when there was no longer anything to be done to save it. Jim was so exhausted by the turmoil and frantic anxiety he had just gone through that all he wanted was peace. This was the feeling of much of the natural constituency of the GMD, the urban bourgeoisie and the remains of the rural elite in late 1948: all they wanted was peace.

The CCP was more confident by the day. Mao Zedong was a distant, mysterious figure, but no less formidable for the sense of mystery around him. The PLA's top generals were acquiring reputations as brilliant battlefield commanders. 'One-eyed' Liu Bocheng, the enigmatic Lin Biao and the tough Chen Yi[4] inspired admiration in many and fear in others. In the areas of China already controlled by the CCP the civilian

---

[4] There were two Chen Yis active in the late 1940s. One was the GMD general who had initiated the 228 Massacre in Taiwan. The other was the PLA general. Their names are written with different characters.

Fig. 13 Jovial PLA soldier

populations seemed to be actively supporting the CCP. The PLA's soldiers were presented as friendly, gentle giants.

As the Iron Curtain descended over Europe and the Cold War
intensified, the war in China became almost a sideshow for Western
countries. In Asia the dominant concerns were the outcome of the
independence and partition of India, and the insecurity of the remaining European colonial holdings. The USA was heavily involved in
Japan, Korea and the Philippines. President Truman was out of sympathy with Nanjing.

The course of the war

The fighting over the winter of 1948–1949 brought a series of smashing victories for the PLA, and a complete rout for the GMD armies. January 1949 was the most disastrous month of the war, with three weeks of staggering losses:[5]

Table 5.1 *PLA victories, January 1949*

10 January	Xuzhou	Key railway junction, Jiangsu
15 January	Tianjin	Key northern city
17 January	Tanggu	Port for Tianjin/Beiping
22 January	Beiping	Former capital
by 25 January	Grand Canal	All key places on the major north–south artery captured by PLA
by 31 January	North of Yangzi	Most places in CCP hands

The scale and swiftness of the victories/defeats seemed almost unbelievable. From the air American pilots flying in supplies to GMD units for Civil Air Transport saw the hopeless situation of the GMD armies, whose troops, although enormous in number, were spread out haphazardly over vast distances, suffering from shortages of supplies and from the cold.[6] The conditions – cold, distance, lack of ground transport – worked against the GMD but for the PLA.

The January gains/losses were the last of a string of victories/defeats over the autumn and winter. From September to November the PLA in Manchuria went on a series of fierce, almost surgical attacks in the LiaoShen Campaign. GMD units fell back in disarray. In October came the end of the Changchun siege, with the surrender of the defenders. It was followed not long after by the loss of Shenyang, and then all of Manchuria, essentially without major fighting. *Life Magazine* published grim pictures of defeated, demoralised soldiers walking away from the front.[7] The GMD lost 400,000 troops in Manchuria, dead, captured or defected.[8]

---

[5] R. Jarman, *China: Political Reports* (Slough: Archives Editions, 2001), IX, p. 10.

[6] The CAT pilots flew in all conditions, often fortified by alcohol against the danger and the cold.

[7] The photographs were taken by Jack Birns, one of several gifted photographers working in China at the time. Another photographer whose pictures captured the suffering of the war was Henri Cartier-Bresson.

[8] See Odd Arne Westad, *Decisive Encounters* (Stanford: Stanford University Press, 2003), pp. 192–197, for a detailed description of the campaign.

The fall of Shenyang

Just before the fall of Shenyang, Roy Rowan, *Life Magazine's* correspondent in China, reported from the city, already abandoned by the GMD forces:

This is a ghost city. Most of the government troops are encamped near rail sidings awaiting evacuation. In the heart of the metropolis freezing blasts whistle down the broad empty thoroughfares. Shop fronts, and even army pillboxes, at the main intersections, are boarded up. Jagged walls in factory areas, built by the Japanese invaders, blasted by American bombers during World War II, and later pillaged by Russian occupation forces, stand silhouetted against steel-gray sky. Mukden [Shenyang], the capital of China's richest industrial area, looks as ragged as the half-frozen refugees picking their way through the debris on few streets where people can still be found.*

* Roy Rowan, *Chasing the Dragon* (Guilford: Lyons Press, 2004), p. 107.

This was the fourth time in just over three years that the cities of Manchuria had changed hands; not since 1931 had Manchuria been ruled by its own people. The newcomers followed the Japanese, the Soviets and the GMD. The local people were beyond optimism or pessimism; they hoped only that the new regime might be more stable than the previous ones, and that there would be more food and fuel to get through the coming winter.

The HuaiHai Campaign

From November to January one of the most vicious and brutal campaigns in modern warfare took place on the cold, bleak North China Plain. The HuaiHai Campaign, known by the GMD as the XuBeng Campaign, was an even greater victory for the CCP, an even greater disaster for the GMD than the battles that had just ended.

The prelude to the campaign was the GMD defeat at Jinan (Shandong) in September 1948. The city fell soon after the defection of one of the key defenders, Wu Huawen. Vast quantities of food, weapons, ammunition and fuel were lost, as was the rail connection between north China and Nanjing. Twenty-five GMD generals were captured, a profound humiliation to the proud GMD military. These were men who had been fighting the Japanese only three years before – unlike Wu Huawen, who had commanded a puppet unit.[9]

---

[9] Xia Jicheng, *Zhongju: Guomindang gaoji zhanfu zhen xiang* (*The End: The Real Story of Elite GMD Prisoners of War*) (Beijing: Zhongguo wenshi chubanshe, 2009), p. 329.

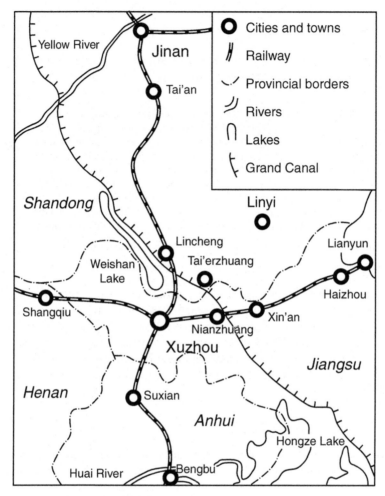

Map 7 HuaiHai Campaign

The HuaiHai battles took place over a great swathe of land whose Schwerpunkt was the railway junction at Xuzhou (Jiangsu). There was a horrible irony to the location. The battles came only a decade after the most critical battle of the Xuzhou Campaign against the invading Japanese armies, at Taierzhuang. This was one of the few victories of Chinese armies against the Japanese. In this second campaign a million troops fought on both sides. The GMD still had the better equipment, but the CCP troops fought with the determination of winners, convinced that victory was close.

Ru ru wuren zhi jing
As if entering a place where there is no one – sweeping all before one

This description of the victorious battles in *The Romance of the Three Kingdoms* could have been written to describe the HuaiHai battles. Despite the huge GMD force confronting them, the PLA turned out to be invincible. The PLA commanders showed strategic skill in fighting highly mobile positional warfare, while the GMD forces found themselves defending key positions and being virtually stuck there. To give meaning to its claims to represent the poor, the PLA was heavily supported by civilians from Shandong, now firmly under CCP control. Deng Xiaoping was in charge of the organisation of civilian coolies, who used their wheelbarrows (the universal means of carrying goods and people in north China) to bring supplies to the front, and to remove the dead and wounded. Chen Yi, the PLA commander in the campaign, said: 'It is the peasants of Shandong, with their wheelbarrows, who made our victory possible.'[10]

The GMD troop losses were horrific:[11]

Table 5.2 *GMD troop losses, January 1949*

Dead/injured	171,151
Captured	320,355
Surrendered	35,093
Mutinied	28,500

Four GMD divisions surrendered to the PLA, but many men went on fighting to the end, to be killed or taken prisoner. These included senior officers who might have had the means to get away – by plane. The Civil War losses of senior GMD commanders were astonishing. By the end of the war, almost 500 generals had been captured, the majority of them in the last stages of the war:[12]

[10] Cited in James Gao, *The Communist Conquest of Hangzhou* (Honolulu: University of Hawaii Press, 2004), pp. 43–44.
[11] Hong Ronghua, *HuaiHai zhanyi tuce* (*Illustrated Volume on the HuaiHai Campaign*) (Shanghai: Jiaoyu chubanshe, 1988), p. 109.
[12] Xia, *Zhongju*, pp. 234–263. The 50 generals for whom Xia gives full biographies served long periods in prison. They were eventually pardoned and released, in four tranches – in 1959, 1960, 1961 and 1975.

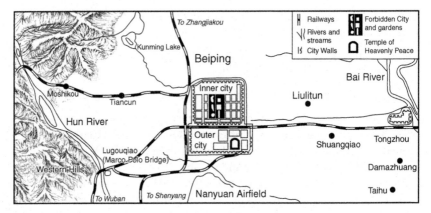

Map 8 Beiping and the Western Hills

Table 5.3 *Captured GMD generals*

1945	1946	1947	1948	1949
2	34	71	139	248

The liberation/fall of Beiping

While the HuaiHai battles were raging, the fate of the great northern cities of Beiping and Tianjin was being settled without fighting.

By the middle of 1948 PLA troops controlled the hills to the north and west of the two key northern cities, Beiping and Tianjin. They also controlled much of the local peasantry. The cities were filled with refugees from Manchuria, soldiers, government officials, middle-class people. Students had been evacuated from the Manchurian cities and from areas to the northwest threatened by the CCP. The students, including middle school students, were flown or marched out of their home places. Once they got to Beiping they were virtually abandoned. They camped in the grounds of the old imperial buildings (Temple of Heaven, Confucian Temple, Lama Temple) living in squalor, dispirited and listless. The American scholar Derk Bodde was horrified by what he saw:

all the buildings, including the Temple of Heaven itself, and the approaching gateways, are filled with hundreds of young men (also, in certain quarters, girls). They are wartime student refugees from Shansi [Shanxi], some of whom seem hardly older than twelve or thirteen. Most of the stone terraces outside, as well as the floors of the temple, are covered with their thin sleeping pads and meagre possessions.[13]

In evacuating the students, the GMD managed to upset everyone. The students were destitute, filled with anxiety, as were their parents left at home. The people of Beiping were furious at having young people whom they regarded as layabouts dumped on them (a forerunner of what people felt about the Red Guards 20 years later).

Meanwhile the local students at China's major universities were heavily involved in pro-communist propaganda work. They saw themselves fulfilling the same progressive role as the students of May 4th, 30 years before. Maria Yen, a student at Peking University (then in the centre of the city) noted that the communists 'were organised. They had discipline. They offered us leadership and the certainty of action.'[14] In the deepening confusion certainty was an invaluable gift.

On 12 December 1948 all the prisoners were released from the city jails, to make room for soldiers fleeing from the north. Eighty per cent of the prisoners had been collaborators of the Japanese.[15] This was a sign of how desperate the GMD's situation was. The city was now surrounded and besieged by CCP forces, cut off by land from the south and east as well as the north and west; the only communication with the outside world was by air. By mid-December there was no electricity or running water; people had to rely on well water. Nanyuan Airfield was used for the last time on 16 December, when nine planes flew in from Nanjing to take out important people. Shelling by PLA artillery started while the passengers were embarking. The planes took off at once, taking some of their intended passengers – but not their baggage, which was immediately looted by soldiers.[16]

There were 200,000 GMD troops in the city, many billeted on the unwilling population. Flights now landed at a tiny makeshift airfield right in the middle of the city, at Dongdan. The loyalty of the garrison troops was in doubt. The commander Fu Zuoyi was concerned more for his own men than for the leaders in Nanjing. The inhabitants of Beiping hoped only that their beautiful, ancient city be preserved. The city was running out of food and fuel. As the ancient saying, written more than

[13] Derk Bodde, *Peking Diary* (London: Jonathan Cape, 1951), pp. 32–33.
[14] Maria Yen, *The Umbrella Garden* (New York: Macmillan, 1954), p. 6. Yen's detailed description of student activities in the days before and after the CCP takeover was written after she had fled to Hong Kong.
[15] Bodde, *Peking Diary*, pp. 82–83.
[16] *Ibid*, p. 90.

Fig. 14 The PLA enters Beiping

2,000 years before in the *Zuozhuan*, prescribed, with the enemy at the walls of the city, it was time to sue for peace.[17]

城下之盟
Cheng xia zhi meng
Alliance made under the city wall

The people of Beiping cared only for the preservation of the fabric of the city; it had survived all the wars of the Republic but was now in danger. No one doubted the capacity of the GMD for ruthlessness in defence. It had used scorched earth tactics at Huayuankou and at Changsha (1938), putting defence over the interests of lives and civilians. Nanjing was not interested in suing for peace – i.e., handing the city over to the CCP – but the local authorities were, including Fu Zuoyi's own daughter, Fu Dongju, and several of his subordinates, who were secret communists. The former mayor, He Siyuan, was already conducting discreet negotiations with the CCP in the Western Hills outside the

---

[17] The *Zuozhuan* is one of the earliest works of Chinese history. It was written in the Spring and Autumn Period, probably in the fifth and fourth centuries BCE.

city. GMD agents tried to stop the process. On 18 January 1949, a bomb exploded in He's bedroom just before he went off to a negotiation session. Alert to danger, he was sleeping elsewhere, but his wife and two children were injured, and one of his daughters was killed.[18]

This murderous attempt to stop negotiations was one of the last straws. Another was the surrender of Tianjin on 15 January. Tianjin and its ports were essential for Beiping's survival. Resistance was now pointless. Fu Zuoyi surrendered to the PLA. On 31 January GMD troops left Beiping through the southern and eastern gates of the ancient city wall, while PLA troops came in through the northern and western gates. Well-disciplined soldiers marched into the city, and the anxious inhabitants breathed deep sighs of relief.[19]

The liberation of Beiping

Dr Jakob Rosenfeld entered Beiping with the PLA 4th Army. His convoy drove right across the city, from north to south. His description follows very much the CCP convention at the time:

The joy of the masses was boundless, the youthful workers and students broke through the barriers, swung themselves on to the vehicles and sat singing and waving red scarves near the canon, near the soldiers. Cigarettes and refreshments were provided to the troops, and the young people joined with delight in singing the *March of the 8th Route Army*. Over all the houses, and over the ancient walls and the countless gables of the Forbidden City of the imperial palace fluttered red flags with five golden stars, the banner of the Liberation Army. Red the colour of joy and of happiness in China, red the colour of revolution ruled the cityscape. Peking had gone red.*

* Gerd Kaminski (ed.), *Ich Kannte Sie Alle: das Tagebuch des Chinesischen General Jakob Rosenfeld* (*I Knew Them All: The Diary of the Chinese General Jakob Rosenfeld*) (Wien: Locker, 2002), p. 181.

Very little changed in the immediate aftermath of the PLA arrival. The future of the city was still unknown, whether it would become the capital of China again, and change its name back to Beijing, or whether it would go back to slumbering in its antique beauty. The stoical people of Beiping congratulated themselves on their survival. What they did not know was that, unlike Paris and Rome, cities that also survived the war

---

[18] Bodde, *Peking Diary*, p. 111.
[19] Jeremy Brown, *Dilemmas of Victory* (Cambridge: Cambridge University Press, 2011), p. 15.

intact, their beautiful city was eventually to be lost, first to socialist progress and later to 'socialism with Chinese characteristics', which together have destroyed almost everything old in the city except for a few historical sites.[20]

The economy

China's economy at this stage of the war was in a state of almost complete confusion. In the GMD-controlled areas the economy was in free fall. Government income was running at only 15 per cent of expenditures.[21] The confidence in Chinese currencies had completely evaporated. The gold *Yuan*, introduced in August 1948 to save the currency situation, started collapsing almost as soon as it was put into circulation. In late 1948 there were multiple currencies in circulation in Beiping:[22]

Table 5.4 *Beiping currencies, late 1948*

Gold *Yuan*	Little confidence left in it
US dollar	Only valued currency
Yuan Shikai silver dollar	Many coins filed down or adulterated with base metal
Mexican silver dollar	As above
Qing silver dollar	As above
Tibetan silver dollar	As above

This was hyperinflation at its worst. People in the money economy came to loathe paper money. As soon as they were paid they rushed out and bought anything there was in the shops, regardless of whether they needed it or not, just to get rid of the mountains of increasingly worthless paper. People who had anything to sell (products, services, influence) removed themselves from the money economy and went over to a barter economy, trading anything – goods and services – that could be traded. Financial transactions were nightmarish for people who depended on a wage or salary and did not have anything to sell. Inflation continued to provide golden opportunities for rogues and profiteers.

In the CCP-controlled areas the economy seemed to be settling down, but at a very low level, something close to local self-sufficiency. For the longer term it seemed that inflation might soon be over. The

---

[20] I belong to the legion of people who knew the old Beijing and deeply regret the loss of one of the world's loveliest cities.

[21] John Leighton Stuart, *Fifty Years in China* (New York: Random House, 1954), p.195.

[22] Ralph and Nancy Lapwood, *Through the Chinese Revolution* (London: Spalding and Levy, 1954), pp. 39–40.

process that the CCP used to curb inflation is still poorly understood, but it seems to have worked, especially surprising that it was managed by a party with few economists or bankers on its side. The new banking system issued a series of currencies that were quite stable. These included the currencies of the regional Beihai Yinhang, the Dongbei Yinhang, the Huazhong Yinhang and, from 1948, of a new central bank, the Zhongguo renmin yinhang. Its banknotes were printed with the date Republic 37 – which turned out to be, on the Mainland, the last year of the Republic.[23]

Culture

In terms of cultural production, the last phase of the Civil War was an empty period. China's writers were almost paralysed. They were uncertain which direction they should go in; although many favoured the left, they did not like the thought of political control. Many stopped writing. If they did write, they had little chance of publishing. Publishing, like filmmaking, had virtually collapsed; inflation made any long-term (i.e., over weeks rather than days) production impossible. Artists were withdrawing from the major cities. Fu Baoshi went off to seclusion in his remote hometown, Xinyu (Jiangxi); Zhang Daqian went back to his hometown, Neijiang (Sichuan). The flights of the two great artists were an echo of the flight of China's greatest painter, Bada Shanren, who retired to the mountains of Jiangxi at the end of the Ming Dynasty, as the Manchus invaded China.

The production of artists, particularly scrolls, on the other hand, was acquiring new value, along with antiques and curios. Small, precious items could be taken away easily – jade, jewellery, gold, scrolls – if the need for flight came. Jewellery and gold could be sewn into the seams of clothing. Many of those who left China took only such items with them, plus a few scrolls, some pieces of jade and some photographs.

Senior figures got away with much more than a few treasures. Yan Xishan, who had dominated the coal-rich province of Shanxi for almost 40 years, left China in December 1949 with a reported two tons of gold bars. So heavy was his load of treasure that he had to leave behind many of his supporters and bodyguards in order for his special plane to get off the ground.[24]

---

[23] Mao King-on, *History of the Paper Currency as Issued by the People's Republic of China* (Hong Kong: Chap Yau Print, 1972) has reproductions of all CCP banknotes from 1921 to 1965.

[24] Chen Lifu, cited in Diana Lary, *China's Republic* (Cambridge: Cambridge University Press, 2007), p. 174.

By far the largest departure of cultural artefacts was that of the Palace Museum treasures, which were shipped to Taiwan, and now form the basis of the great collection of Chinese cultural artefacts in the Taibei Palace Museum.

The Palace Museum

The Qing imperial palace was one of the great treasure houses of the world. After the fall of the dynasty in 1911, the treasures stayed in the palace in Beijing and eventually came under the control of the GMD government in Nanjing. The best of the treasures were taken to Nanjing. In 1935 the cream of that collection was sent to London for an exhibition that astonished a world that knew little of Chinese culture.

During the Resistance War many of the treasures were stored in remote locations in western China, still in the crates they had been packed in for the journey to London. In 1946 the 10,799 cases were brought back to Nanjing, but not unpacked. In 1948 2,972 of the cases, holding the very best artefacts, were sent to Taiwan for 'safe-keeping', until the GMD recovered the Mainland. They were not unpacked.* In the 1960s, when the GMD finally accepted that there would be no quick return to the Mainland, a sumptuous museum was built in Taipei. Throughout their journeys the treasures were guarded by a deeply loyal group of curators, who must be regarded as heroes of Chinese culture. The CCP inherited a lesser collection in the Imperial Palace in Beijing.

* *Zhongguo bowuguan zhi* (*China's Museums*) (Beijing: Huaxia, 1995), p. 1039.

Momentous choices

Long before the end of the war, it was clear to many people that they would have to leave China before the CCP came to power. For the core of the GMD armies and supporters, it was inevitable that they would leave for Taiwan on government orders. A great number of vessels were commandeered for the short crossings to the island from ports on the Mainland. To stay would mean being in grave danger of imprisonment or a death sentence. People who had once been associated with the CCP but had broken with the current leadership also had to flee. Zhang Guotao, the prime defector from the CCP during the Long March, went into exile in Hong Kong. Even there he did not feel safe, and later left to join his sons in Canada, where he died in complete oblivion in 1979.

Beyond the political world there were people whose class backgrounds put them at risk in a socialist world. Many of them had the means to move; now they had to decide whether to leave China or to stay. They recognised that a socialist government would probably not be kind towards the affluent – and the rumours about what was happening in the rural areas under CCP control made them fear for their safety. Intellectuals and liberals were threatened too, fearing that they would be silenced under CCP rule.

Even for those who knew they had to leave the decision was not easy. People agonised, hesitated, changed their minds repeatedly, quarrelled with each other. They asked themselves what leaving meant: would it be permanent exile, or a temporary escape from danger? Or would leaving a world they no longer understood, where they seemed not to fit, be a relief? What did staying mean? Being part of a glorious new world? Compromising or accommodating to a new order? Being punished by a new regime that denounced them?

Beyond the indecision was the role of chance or of fate. As the months passed, the ability to choose was inexorably replaced by the stark role of chance – where a person was at a certain time, what chance they had of getting away. Chance was interpreted by many as fate (*yuanfen*), the working of an unseen hand that determined what would happen in a person's life.

Leaving

In late 1948 and early 1949 people who had the ability to do so started to leave China, or to make active preparations for departure. Government officials and soldiers had no choice but to go: they were moved by the government. Increasing numbers of people in the GMD apparatus left for Taiwan, the more senior taking their dependants with them.

Business people were leaving too, but not for Taiwan. There was a widespread perception in Shanghai that the business world had been mistreated and cheated by the GMD, which seemed just as hostile to independent enterprise as was the CCP. The business people were moving to Hong Kong, now an island of calm in the seething civil war. They often took with them their best employees and, in some cases, their factory equipment. Others had already arranged for machinery ordered for their Shanghai plants in 1945 and 1946 to be diverted to Hong Kong. The North Point section of Hong Kong Island became a Shanghai quarter. It was a place where people could function in Shanghai dialect, find temporary housing and a job. And it was the start of major manufacturing in the territory.

Hong Kong was a refuge, but for the incomers it was a sad place, for one stark reason: it was not Shanghai. Adeline Yeh Ma described her grandfather's feelings as he left Shanghai in December 1948. 'Yeye's departure was heartrending. He loved his hometown and doubted if he would ever see it again. The sights, smells, sounds and memories of Shanghai were irreplaceable.'[25]

Leaving Shanghai

In 1948, just before she left the city, the young student Katherine Wei wrote about the mood in Shanghai:

In the winter months of early 1948, I noticed more signs daily of an insidious fear that was spreading through the city. Some months it appeared to be a rich man's panic. The families of my wealthier classmates were having American bills sewn in to the lining of their jackets, or moving to Bangkok, Manila or Hong Kong 'to wait,' as they put it, until the advancing Communist armies had been repulsed from the major eastern cities. The lines at the banks in the International Settlement often spilled over the Bund's avenues as people vainly tried to convert their Chinese money in to gold. And the same sense of dread had seeped into the middle- and lower-class neighbourhoods as well.*

* Katherine Wei and Terry Quinn, Second Daughter: Growing Up in China, 1930–1949 (New York: Holt Reinhart, 1984), pp. 213–214.

Southern military and political figures, from Guangdong, Guangxi and Yunnan, also moved to Hong Kong, waiting to see what would happen on the Mainland. Hong Kong was now the only one left of the traditional places of safety on the China coast available to those likely to be out of favour with an incoming regime. The old retreats of the warlord period (Shanghai, Dalian, Tianjin) were no longer available, since the unequal treaties that had made them havens for temporary exiles had been abrogated during the Resistance War. Macao, the Portuguese colony attached to the coast of Guangdong, provided a refuge for those with money but little respectability. It was the destination for the seriously seedy – gamblers, smugglers, drug and currency dealers – who were well aware of how short their lives would be under the stern moralists of the CCP.[26]

---

[25] Adeline Yeh Ma, Falling Leaves (New York: Penguin, 1997), p. 87.
[26] Six decades later Macao is a boom town like no other. Its land area has been doubled, through landfill, and every inch of it seems to be dedicated to massive, multi-storey casino palaces – the majority of whose clients come from the PRC.

China's intellectuals and artists were divided over leaving. Many, especially the younger ones, were enthusiastic about what a new regime might do. They had never known a time when China was stable, and they longed for peace, prosperity and a return of China's self-respect. Many of them were drawn to the ideology of socialism – even if not entirely to the CCP. They did not consider leaving China. Others who lived in the artistic world were too old, too grounded in Chinese culture to even consider leaving. Qi Baishi, the great painter, was over 80, and had an enormous number of dependants. He gave no thought to leaving. The opera star Mei Lanfang stopped working during the Resistance War, but did not leave China. Now he made the same decision. He knew he had no possibility of living and working outside China.

Between the two groups, the young and the traditional, were many intellectuals who had great difficulty in deciding what to do. The mental struggle of the academic dynamo, Fu Sinian, typifies the anguish that many of them went through. Fu was founder of the Institute of History and Philology and a major figure in the great archaeological discoveries of the 1930s. He was also an outspoken critic of the GMD's corruption and incompetence; he was a leader of the 'incorruptible element (*qingliu*)' in public life. In spite of this, he doubted whether, with his fiery energy and tendency to speak his own mind, he could submit to communist discipline. He knew that trouble was bound to come his way after he heard that he had been denounced by the CCP. It was time to leave. He wanted to take as many of his senior colleagues with him as possible. In December 1948 he arranged for a special plane to bring out other leading intellectuals from Beiping. When he went to the airport in Nanjing to meet the plane, almost no one came off.

During his last days in Nanjing, Fu came close to suicide, overcome by a sense of failure. He quoted over and over again Tao Yuanming's poem of regret for not having planted his trees well:

种桑长江边
三年望当采
枝条始欲茂
忽值山河改
柯叶自摧折
根株浮沧海
春蚕既无食
寒衣欲谁待
本不植高原
今日复何悔

I planted mulberry trees beside the Yangzi
For three years I watched for them to mature
Just as the branches and leaves were filling out

The hills and rivers shifted.
The branches snapped off
The roots and trunks floated away towards the sea.
If the spring silkworms have nothing to eat
Where will our winter clothes come from?
I did not plant on high ground.
What regret must I feel today.

Tao had written this poem over a millennium before. The poem alludes to the collapse of a dynasty. The shifting of the hills and rivers (i.e., the whole country) had been caused by an earthquake, a political one. The same kind of destructive force that had brought down the dynasty was now destroying the GMD. Fu was talking about his generation's failure to provide a fertile environment in which to root and nurture the young; the mulberry trees that would make for their future. Fu's regret was that the young people who had not been nurtured well enough by his generation were now turning to the communists. Fu went off sadly to Taiwan. His dynamism returned when he became head of Taiwan University, where he served only briefly; he died a little over a year later.[27]

There have been claims that not all those who moved to Taiwan went voluntarily. Some leading intellectuals left under dubious circumstances. The actor Ying Ruocheng was convinced that his father, Ying Qianli, a distinguished academic, did not leave voluntarily, but was spirited away to Taiwan on the government flight in late 1948. His conviction stemmed from the fact that his father did not say goodbye to his family, or make any effort to take members of the family with him.[28]

Staying

Many people stayed in China for ideological reasons, because they were enthusiastic about the coming change in power. Others saw their patriotic duty to stay in China. They chose to stay because they loved their country. But the great majority of people had no choice about leaving or staying; they were going to stay in China come what may. They had no means to leave. They did not have enough money to pay for tickets out of China, or to settle elsewhere. Even if they had the money, there were few ways to get out, few places where they could go. Those with heavy family responsibilities and those who were too young or too old could not even consider leaving.

---

[27] Wang Fan-sen, *Fu Ssu-nien: A Life in Chinese History and Politics* (Cambridge: Cambridge University Press, 2000), pp. 182–185.

[28] Ying Ruocheng and Claire Conceison, *Voices Carry* (Lanham: Rowman and Littlefield, 2009), pp. 63–64. Ying's father died 20 years later in Taiwan, without ever seeing a member of his family again.

In the cities the mood was less one of optimism than of resignation, mitigated with the patriotic hope that the CCP would restore China. At the very beginning of 1949, just before the PLA arrived, this was the mood at Yenching University, as reported by an English professor:

Among our staff the general attitude was of passive apprehension and resignation. They had been taught by sustained propaganda to fear the Communists; most of them came from the classes whose privileges the revolutionary movement was determined to destroy. Yet as patriotic Chinese they rejected the way of flight overseas. They intended to stay and face the music, but did not expect to enjoy it.[29]

Lin Huiyin

These are excerpts from the final letter in a long correspondence between Wilma Fairbank and Lin Huiyin. The letter was written in Beiping over several weeks in November/December 1948, shortly before communist forces occupied the city.

Now that I feel we have perhaps only a month or two to write freely to all in the USA without postal service difficulties or whatever hitch there might be, I feel a bit choked or tongue-tied. Even this letter – I hope it will get to you before Christmas or for Christmas.

Maybe we won't see each other for a long time now... Things will be very different for us, though we don't know how different, next year or next month. But as long as the younger generation have something interesting to do and can keep friends and have work, that is all that matters.*

* Wilma Fairbank, *Liang and Lin: Partners in Exploring China's Architectural Past* (Philadelphia: Pennsylvania University Press, 1994), pp. 173–175.

Further south in China there was a widespread, if subdued, recognition that things had to change, that the old world was gone. This is the courageous and sophisticated Wu Yifang, the first Chinese woman to head Ginling College in Nanjing, writing to the college's sponsors in New York City in early 1949:

Here at Ginling, we faced the question [of leaving] thoroughly last November and came to the conclusion that we should carry on no matter what changes should come to the political set-up. First of all, there is no place secure enough to justify the moving. And secondly, the rapid spread of Communism in China is due not so much to the appeal of Marxism itself as to the decay of traditional culture and complications in the international situation. On top of the revolutionary

---

[29] Lapwood and Lapwood, *Through the Chinese Revolution*, p. 41.

and evolutionary changes of the last fifty years, the government has disappointed the people since VJ Day by its inefficiency and corruption. The long years of refugeeing and struggle for mere existence have made selfishness a common practice. It is no longer possible or desirable to hope for a return to the prewar state of things. For the future of the country there has to evolve a new code of living.[30]

Turncoats, switchers and fengpai

Many of the people who stayed were quite sanguine about their decisions: they were going to move to the winning side. A significant number of people in important positions had already been approached by the CCP and offered attractive positions if they stayed. With such an incentive, the archaeologist Xia Nai decided at the last moment not to join the evacuation of his professional colleagues – and by staying went from a lowly to a leading position in the field of archaeology, impossible if his senior colleagues had not left.

In the GMD military some commanders (Wu Huawen, Fu Zuoyi) followed the established pattern from the warlord period and the Japanese invasion of going over to the enemy just in advance of certain defeat, to save themselves and their men from death or imprisonment. Their defections handed the PLA easy victories.

In 1948 and early 1949 many of the people who did not welcome the CCP were continually sniffing at the wind, to know which direction it was blowing in. Would the east, communist wind triumph? The wind faction (*fengpai*) was made up of people who would go the way the wind was blowing. After eight years of Japanese occupation they were well used to going with the wind. The Chinese metaphor is from sailing ships.

Kan feng shi duo
Steer a boat according to the wind

There were long historical precedents. At the start of the Mongol (Yuan) and Manchu (Qing) dynasties some patriots resisted the foreign conquerors, but far more people made their accommodations to the new masters. There was a sneaking admiration for the ones who resisted, but very little shame attached to the ones who did not. The neutral way of describing the behaviour of the *fengpai* is pragmatism.

Another time-honoured tactic of staying out of trouble was more difficult towards the end of the war. Waiting to see what would happen,

---

[30] Wu Yifang to New York, 5 March 1949. Cited in Jin Feng, *Ginling College: The Making of a Family Saga* (Rochester: SUNY Press, 2009), pp. 228–229.

dithering, was a less and less successful tactic as the CCP victory came closer. Those who 'sat on the wall (*qi qiang pai*)' were as likely to fall off on the wrong side as the right side.

Those who changed sides had to be clever and lucky. Whether their actions were treachery, survival or political epiphanies, they took big risks; if their timing was off they might die. As it turned out, the long-term outcomes for those who switched were poor. Many were attacked later in the Anti-Rightist Movement and the Cultural Revolution, for having bad class backgrounds or for having foreign connections (*haiwai guanxi*).

Refugee flows

Well before the end of 1948 serious refugee flows started. In September the Ministry of Social Affairs in Nanjing estimated the number of refugees within China at 55,000,000. The British Embassy reported the figure, with the comment that it was 'possibly an over-statement, but one that gives a picture of disruption and suffering on an appalling scale'.[31] The refugee flows came in the autumn from Manchuria, then from north and west China. The only way out of Manchuria was to the south, by plane; no one wanted to flee to the west into the Soviet Union. Leaving from north China in the winter meant either flying, for the very few, or walking, often alongside the train tracks on which trains no longer ran. From Shandong it was possible to get out by ship through one of the ports, particularly Qingdao, but getting there was almost impossible. The railway had been cut and the roads through the rural areas were controlled by the CCP.

Hearing by rumours of the dire situation in the north, people in central and southern China, who could still get out of China by train or boat, now realised that if they were going to leave, the time had come. Dependant family members left first, followed not long after by senior members. Most went initially to Hong Kong. Foreign residents in China did the same. Embassies, missions, businesses sent their non-essential staff away. Missions in the north and northwest had already closed.

Social issues

The chaos of the last months of the Civil War plunged Chinese society into complete confusion. The chaos hit different categories of people in

---

[31] British Embassy to London, September 1948. Cited in Jarman, *China: Political Reports*, VIII p. 622.

different ways. The implacable constraints of demography turned out to have a huge effect on how people got through the chaos.

Women

The situation of women at the later stages of the Civil War varied enormously. For a few young women it was an intoxicating period, especially for those who left home and joined the revolution. For others the war meant staying at home and taking greater and greater responsibility for themselves and their families; as the fighting intensified more and more men were away from home, and it was becoming clear that many would not be coming back. For other women the fighting itself brought fear and anxiety.

The CCP promised a new world of equality for women with men, although the message was not – or even could be – implemented at this stage. There was a small number of women revolutionaries and activists, but women did not fight in the PLA. The role of women in the areas that had passed under CCP control was providing material support, making clothing, socks and shoes for the soldiers.

Shoes

Footwear is critical for soldiers. Their ability to march and to fight is dependent on their feet being in good condition. Modern armies equip their soldiers with leather boots and woollen socks. In the GMD armies, officers had leather boots or shoes, as did some of the ordinary soldiers, especially those equipped by the USA. The PLA soldiers, however, fought in cotton or straw footwear. The cotton shoes were more like slippers than shoes. They were sewn at home by women. Many layers of cotton cloth were sewn together for the sole, and then a single piece sewn over the top to cover the upper part of the foot. For winter they were padded with cotton floss. They are comfortable, but offer no protection against rain. Throughout the CCP-controlled areas women were organised to sew shoes as a sign of their commitment to the cause. Straw shoes were more like sandals than shoes. They were made of plaited and woven grain stalks. They had many disadvantages. They were stiff and slippery, offered no protection against wet or cold and broke easily. Their only advantage was that they were not in short supply.

In the rural revolution the CCP appeared to consider women's issues seriously, promising them land on equal terms with men in the land reform, already underway in many parts of rural north China, but it was not clear what this would mean in practice, when land was being assigned to a household and its head – usually a man. Women's organisations were set up in villages; they fought less for new rights for women than for an end to bad behaviour towards women, such as the grim routine of wife-beating.

On neither the GMD nor the CCP side were there heroines in the struggle. Song Meiling, the wife of Chiang Kai-shek, played a lesser role in the Civil War than she did during the Resistance War in promoting her husband's cause. And her sister, Song Qingling, the widow of Sun Yat-sen, was still on the side-lines, although she was widely believed to be leaning towards the CCP. None of the wives of the CCP leaders had any prominence at this stage.

A generation gap started to emerge, as women looked to a new future. Young women were interested in greater freedom of choice in marriage; older women were likely to be opposed.[32] Having spent part of their lives in the misery of being a daughter-in-law, they now saw the danger of losing control over their own daughters-in-law, the most powerful role offered to ordinary women in traditional society. On the other hand the systems being introduced by the CCP required more work and political participation from younger women, all of which made older women more important in bringing up their grandchildren. Over time the CCP came to see grandmothers as primary child-carers, a role that many of them loved. One of the tightest emotional bonds as the new society developed was between grandmothers and grandchildren, often at the cost of maternal involvement. The implicit irony that the children of the new society were being brought up by women from the old society seems to have escaped the CCP's notice.

Love played a greater role in young women's lives. Among educated young women, the power of love was what drew some of them to the CCP. Fu Dongju was led to what might have been a betrayal of her father, Fu Zuoyi, by her love for her husband, as Chen Lian had turned against her father, Chen Bulei, for love of her own husband. Other young women found love within the revolution. Xue Dehong, the mother of celebrated author Jung Chang, was a young student activist in Jinzhou (southern Manchuria). Just after the town was taken over by the PLA she met a man ten years her senior who was already a seasoned revolutionary. They

---

[32] 'Older' would start about the age of 30. In a society in which women married in their mid- to late teens, they might be grandmothers by their early thirties.

were drawn to each other. She liked the fact that he brushed his teeth regularly – when she first saw him he was doing just that. He liked the fact that she was 'admirable and emancipated', but also 'pretty and feminine, even rather coquettish'. They asked the Jinzhou CCP Committee for permission to 'talk about love (*tan lianai*)'. After some delays the permission came through and the young bride moved into her new husband's living quarters, without any wedding ceremony. Living together meant that they were married.[33]

Children

The upheaval of the Civil War was a continuation of what any Chinese child under 15 had always known. No child under 15 had known peace. They had grown up in some degree of chaos, their lives far away from the well-ordered Confucian households of the past. They were engulfed in a process of very rapid change, with or without the added problem of warfare. The Chinese ambassador to the USA, Wellington Koo (Gu Weijun), described the tidal wave of change: 'Changes in Chinese social life and ideas in the past thirty years have been more rapid than those of the preceding thirty centuries.'[34] Koo may be accused of some hyperbole, but he was on the side that was opposing revolution.

Children's schooling was disrupted or cancelled. Rural schools had depended on gentry support, and the gentry were in retreat. Urban schools were in chaos. Some closed as students left, some when students could no longer afford the fees. Missionary schools were closing. This generation of children suffered educational delays, as did a later generation of children whose schooling was interrupted by the Cultural Revolution. These two periods of delay underline the critical importance of generation in modern Chinese history – some much more fortunate than others.

The children who suffered most were those who lost touch with their families in the chaos of war. Many of the inhabitants of the orphanages run by the state were evacuated to Taiwan – which meant safety, but also the death of the last hope that they might find their parents. The CCP set up its own orphanages, especially for the children whose parents had died in combat. To be an orphan was a terrible fate in China, where so much of social life and identity centred on the family. Government care could not compensate for the loss.

[33] Jung Chang, *Wild Swans: Three Daughters of China* (New York: Anchor, 1991), pp. 115–132. The marriage was very happy and produced five children.
[34] *China Newsweek*, 1 April 1948, p. 5.

The elderly

For the elderly, at that stage in China anyone over 50, the Civil War was yet another phase of upheaval in long lives of upheaval. Few of them had known any real peace, but they had held on for a long while to the traditional vision that old age would bring respect (for their accumulated wisdom), comfort (provided by their grateful children) and an honoured status in their communities. The Civil War shattered these comfortable visions. Little of the respect for age survived in the turmoil. It seemed to have evaporated in the pressure to survive.

The lives of the elderly were determined by what their children, especially their sons, decided to do. There was virtually no system of pensions or insurance in China; the elderly expected their children to care for them. If their children left China, their future was bleak in the extreme. If they went abroad with their children, they were faced with a life in a new place, with a new language.

The CCP had no specific policies for the elderly. The policies that most directly affected the elderly were those that encouraged the young to break the ties of the feudal society – i.e., to leave their families to serve the revolution, to make their own decisions about marriage. These decisions inevitably undermined the authority of older people.

Social levelling

In one respect the people of all China were being rapidly prepared for the socialist goal of equality. The chaos of late 1948 brought about social levelling on a scale not seen before. The wealthy and the middle classes were being wiped out by inflation, and (for those who were going to stay in China) by voluntary divesting of wealth. The poor meanwhile were getting relatively less poor, especially if they produced goods that went up in value with inflation. The levelling occurred without any formal policies behind it, certainly not from the GMD. It was a great help to the CCP in the formal processes that started after an area was under its full control.

Those who left China went through a major decline in their social status, unless they were at the very top of the GMD hierarchy. Most of those who moved to Hong Kong found themselves in deep poverty, living in tiny apartments or in squatter settlements on the steep hills of the colony. Wong Kar Wei's wistful film *In the Mood for Love* (2000) shows the lives of Shanghai exiles living in crowded, dark apartments, trying to maintain some semblance of the glamour of their former lives. They had not been brought quite as low as the White Russian taxi drivers and 'dance girls', who had added to the *louche* reputation of Shanghai in the 1930s, but they had fallen far from their old lives.

Soldier family separations

One of the social categories most affected by the chaos of the Civil War was the families of soldiers, many millions of them. For GMD soldier families the catastrophic defeats of late 1948 meant almost inevitable separation. For some senior military figures the separation came about after their capture by CCP forces. Because this was a civil war, there were no conventions governing the treatment of those captured. They were imprisoned for as long as the authorities thought fit. General Du Yuming was captured in the HuaiHai Campaign. He was released from prison in 1959, but was not reunited with his daughter until after relations with the USA began to improve in the early 1970s (see Chapter 6).

Other GMD soldiers were separated only from their natal families. The enterprising junior officer Huang Yaowu defected from his unit at Shenyang, in November 1948. He and his wife made it to her family in Anshan, where he found work in the steel mills. He did not see his family, in Guangdong, or his old comrades from the army for more than three decades.[35]

Huang Yaowu's flight

In 1948, Huang Yaowu was just 20 years old, a Cantonese soldier who had joined the GMD armies more by accident than by design, and had been sent to Manchuria after the Japanese defeat. In late 1948 he found himself fighting in the hopeless defence of Shenyang. In the complete chaos as PLA forces attacked the city Huang slipped away from his unit with his new wife and started to walk towards Anshan, where her family lived. Anshan was 90 kilometres away, a long walk in bitterly cold weather. He had abandoned his uniform in favour of a long padded gown, and might have passed as an ordinary person, but for the fact that his wife was wearing a *qipao*, a costume that put her in category of a *taitai* (middle class or above). They were apprehended by a PLA patrol, and he was sent to undergo 'education in socialism', in effect he

---

[35] Huang Yaowu, *1944–1948: wode zhanzheng (1944–1948: My War)* (Shenyang: Beifang lianhe chubanshe, 2010), pp. 216–217.

was taken prisoner. After a month he was told he would be joining a PLA unit. But, in another twist of fate, the unit he was sent to did not want him, and he was given a pass to proceed to Anshan. He found his wife, by another chance, back in Shenyang, and the two set off for Anshan. They stayed there for the rest of their lives. In his memoir, Huang talked about the futility and the cruelty of the Civil War. 'I didn't want to fight in that war. I felt that being a soldier was like being a tool in the war, being cannon fodder. In the end I can hardly say clearly how I got through it.'* He and his wife survived, but many of the people he knew did not.

* Huang, *1944–1948*, pp. 216–217, 226.

CCP soldiers were also separated from their families for long periods, as they campaigned further and further into the south. Their separations were somewhat easier to bear, because they were not only praised for their noble sacrifice, but also assured that their families would be given some help so long as they were away.

Social upheaval

It is hard to describe a period of such chaos and confusion as the second half of 1948 as a period of social change. What was happening was so rapid, so random and so localised that the only universal metaphors are from the natural world: hurricanes, storms, tidal surges, earthquakes. What the chaotic months did was to soften up the battered people of China for the systemic changes that were to come under the CCP's formal socialist policies.

Biographies

Lin Dai

Cheng Yueru, whose stage name was Lin Dai (often given as Linda), was the daughter of a senior member of the Guangxi Clique, Cheng Siyuan. She was born in 1934. As a teenager she was sent away from Nanjing to Hong Kong, where she was quickly discovered by the nascent Hong Kong film industry. The industry was made up largely of people who had moved down to Hong Kong from Shanghai during the Civil War. Films were made in Mandarin, not in Cantonese. Film was only one part of the cultural birth of Hong Kong; it became for the next three or four decades the freest part of the Chinese cultural world.

Lin Dai became a huge star, in films such as *Singing under the Moon* (1953) and *Scarlet Doll* (1958), but her personal life was miserable. When she killed herself in 1964, apparently in despair at her unhappy marriage, there were outpourings of grief in Hong Kong and in many Overseas Chinese communities. She has remained an iconic figure of tragedy, a little like Marilyn Monroe.

Wang Guangmei

Wang Guangmei was the sixth and last wife of Liu Shaoqi. She was born to a wealthy family in Tianjin, and was highly educated, fluent in several foreign languages. As a student she was drawn to socialism and left home to work for the CCP. She met Liu when she acted as his interpreter. She was half his age. They married in 1948. She was his trophy wife – his previous wives had all been of modest origins. As one of the most senior CCP members at the time – and the future president – Liu needed someone by his side who could present a good impression of the coming regime. In his later defence of his multiple marriages, Liu claimed that he was breaking with the feudal tradition of polygamy by practising sequential monogamy.[36]

Wu Huawen

Wu Huawen's career is one of the great demonstrations in Chinese history of the success of treachery. The most infamous is another General Wu, Wu Sangui, who, in 1644, betrayed the Ming Dynasty by opening the gates of the Great Wall to let Manchu troops in.

Wu Huawen turned his coat three times in just over a decade – and came out unscathed. In 1938, after his commander Han Fuju was executed by Chiang Kai-shek, he and his troops abandoned their connection to the GMD and operated in Shandong on their own. He later went over to the puppet government of Wang Jingwei. After the Japanese were defeated he went back to the GMD. In September 1948 he went over to the CCP at the Battle of Jinan. Twenty-five other GMD generals were captured during the battle, and many were imprisoned for decades. Wu meanwhile went on to serve as a general in the PLA, in command of the men who had followed him through each twist and turn of his career. He died a natural death.

---

[36] Hua Changming, *Condition feminine et les communistes chinois* (*Female Condition and the Chinese Communists*) (Paris: Ecole des hautes etudes, 1981), pp. 111–112.

He Siyuan

He Siyuan was the mayor of Beiping, from November 1946 to June 1948. He was a bold, creative figure. He was educated in France, worked in the Shandong provincial government in the 1930s, and then, during the Resistance War, ran a guerrilla organisation in eastern Shandong. He was a dashing figure in Beijing, with his French wife and his panache. As mayor he presided over group weddings in the Huairentang Hall in Zhongnanhai, the government complex built by Yuan Shikai in the early Republic. The brides wore white wedding dresses, the grooms traditional Chinese gowns. Sixty years later some of the surviving couples got together to pay homage to him.[37] Chiang Kai-shek detested him. In April 1948 he was shot at in the centre of Beiping near Jingshan by Nanjing agents. Even though he was fired as mayor, he devoted himself to negotiating the peaceful surrender of Beiping. Through the bitter winter of 1948–1949 he shuttled back and forth between the GMD and the CCP. One of his daughters was killed in a GMD attack on his house. For his efforts, and his courage in continuing despite the attacks on himself and his family, he earned the gratitude of the Beijing people.[38]

Chen Yi

General Chen Yi's story is one of a rapid rise followed by complete disgrace. He failed to make his way through the intrigues of GMD politics. Chen was the man widely blamed for the Ererba Repression in Taiwan. His actions were so extreme that he was relieved of his job as governor of the island and sent back to the Mainland. He was not in disgrace, however, since he was made governor of his native province, Zhejiang. Suddenly in January 1949 he was arrested, taken back to Taiwan and executed – not because of his brutality towards the Taiwanese, but because he seemed to be on the point of going over to the CCP. He was shot for one crime while being guilty of another.

---

[37] *China Daily*, 20 February 2008.
[38] He Zichuan, *Yi wei chengshi aiguo de Shandong xuezhe* (*An Honest and Loyal Shandong Scholar*) (Beijing: Beijing chubanshe, 1996), pp. 344, 350–351.

6   The end game: February–December 1949

By February 1949 the CCP was in control of almost all of north China. The end of the Civil War was in sight. Nothing seemed to stand between the PLA and victory, control over all of China.

事如破竹
Shi ru po zhu
[The fighting is] like crushing bamboo

GMD morale was at the lowest possible ebb. Total collapse was now a real possibility. Chiang Kai-shek could not avoid responsibility for the terrible battlefield failures in late 1948 and early 1949. The view of the French military attaché, Jacques Guillermaz, was harsh but widely shared: 'I do not think that the history of war offers many examples of so many strategic mistakes committed by the same man in such a short time.'[1] Added to the military losses was Chiang's complete loss of credibility within the GMD armies, underlined by the shame over the number of his senior military commanders taken prisoner.

Despite the failures, Chiang was indignant, and blamed everyone but himself, a level of hubris that was astonishing.

自取滅亡
Zi chu mie wang
Bring disaster on oneself

In Taiwan, Chiang established what amounted to a temporary presidential headquarters on Grass Mountain above Taibei. He was supposedly in retirement, but he managed to keep control over the government's military and civil affairs from his aerie.[2] The acting president, Li Zngren, was virtually powerless. Even as the GMD was collapsing, the in-fighting within the

[1] Jacques Guillermaz, *Une vie pour la Chine* (*A Life for China*) (Paris: Robert Laffont, 1989), p. 190.
[2] In 1950 Grass Mountain was renamed Yangmingshan, after Chiang's favourite philosopher, the Neo-Confucian Wang Yangming.

168

top echelons continued at fever pitch. Li Zongren was unable to stop the self-destructive and vicious in-fighting. Chiang Kai-shek's ability to stay in power even after so many disastrous losses has never been fully explained.

Respect for the GMD in the population was at rock bottom. In this desperate situation Li tried to open peace negotiations with the CCP, hoping to at least save China south of the Yangzi for the GMD. He sent informal messengers and a formal telegram to Mao Zedong.

Li Zongren's telegram to Mao Zedong, 27 January 1949 (excerpts)

The acting president sent this rather disingenuous telegram to Mao Zedong immediately after he took office. Most of the claims he made about GMD concessions were exaggerated or false.

Since the failure of the earlier political consultations, the civil war has continued for more than three years in addition to the original eight years of the resistance war. The resources of the nation have been greatly depleted and the people have suffered badly. People throughout the country now voice demands for peace.

The country has now undergone extensive damage; the people have suffered to the utmost. Countless cities, farms and homes have been destroyed; numberless people have been killed or wounded. Broken families, suffering from starvation and cold, are seen everywhere. Such are the results of the civil war.

You, sir, have repeatedly expressed your willingness to solve the problems by peaceful means. The government has now expressed its sincerity in words and deeds. Those demands that the public has voiced in the past, such as the release of political prisoners, freedom of speech, assurance of free life for the people etc., now have undeniably been put in to practice, I sincerely hope that you, sir, will also call upon the comrades of your honourable party to work for peace and that you will appoint a delegation so that peace negotiations may be resumed at an early date and at a place agreed on by both parties.

The sooner the war can be brought to an end, the more human lives will be saved and the fewer will be the future numbers of orphans and widows. If we both deal sincerely with each other, all our problems can be solved.*

* Tong Te-kong and Li Tsung-jen, *The Memoirs of Li Tsung-jen* (Boulder, CO: Westview, 1979), pp. 492–493.

His efforts were futile. The political situation was hopeless, as Li later said, 'in irreparable chaos'. Nor could anything save the economic situation in the areas still under GMD control. Inflation was now completely out of control, rampaging through the money economy like a wild beast. The value of paper money was declining hour by hour. On 8 April in Shanghai the rate of the gold *Yuan* to the US dollar was 40,000:1; a day later it was 80,000:1. The Chinese currency was in free-fall. Wherever possible, it had been abandoned. In Guangdong most transactions were now in Hong Kong dollars. In Guangxi, a much poorer province without easy access to a foreign currency, the only real currency in circulation was rice. Elsewhere the US dollar reigned supreme.

The GMD capital Nanjing was emptying out. A huge evacuation was underway: much of the air force and navy joined the government reserves of bullion and US dollars already transferred to Taiwan. The evacuation was done under the orders of the 'retired' Chiang Kai-shek, against the explicit counter-orders of Li Zongren. It was the clearest possible sign of the impending collapse on the GMD on the Mainland, and a sign that whatever happened Chiang was going to stay at the top of the party.[3]

Fighting

After the HuaiHai Campaign the end of major fighting for China was near. The GMD armies had now lost well over half their troops, dead, injured, deserted or defected. The defections involved individual units, led over to the PLA by their officers. There were various reasons for defection. In some cases officers had been secretly contacted by the CCP and offered inducements, such as positions within the CCP forces. In other cases officers had quarrelled with their superiors in the GMD armies. In most cases defeat was so close that defection seemed the only way for a commander and his unit to survive.

Whatever the reason, defections came thick and fast through the early months of 1949. Parts of the navy went over to the CCP. Defection rather than fighting was now the main cause of GMD losses and, in parallel, the main source of PLA growth. A stab in the back is known, in the old *chengyu*, as the 'hidden arrow'.

An jian shang ren
Wound a man with a hidden arrow

The GMD's losses in *materiel* were staggering. According to the US military attaché in Nanjing, quoted by Lionel Chassin, the GMD in 1948–1949 lost 400,000 rifles to the CCP (140,000 of them supplied

---

[3] R. Jarman (ed.), *China: Political Reports* (Slough: Archive Editions, 2001), 28 March 1949, IX, p. 9; and 11 April, IX, p. 54.

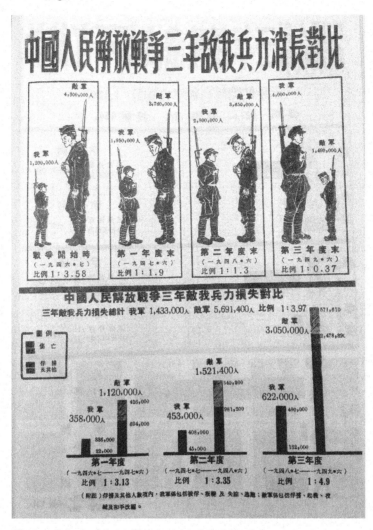

Fig. 15 Comparative military strengths 1949, Column 4

to the GMD by the US). Six hundred thousand GMD troops were integrated into the PLA, and another 400,000 used as service troops. Twenty arsenals were captured.[4] The PLA strength went in the opposite direction.

---

[4] Lionel Chassin, *La conquete de la Chine par Mao Tse-tung* (*The Conquest of China by Mao Zedong*) (Paris: Payot, 1952; English translation, Harvard University Press, 1965), p. 208.

GMD soldiers who stayed with their units were deeply demoralised, as Chassin, a French officer, noted:

The soldier of Chiang Kai-shek knew not why he fought. Against the Japanese he could fight for his country and his people, but in this civil war a peasant soldier from Kwangtung [Guangdong] had no idea why he should be fighting in Shansi [Shanxi] and Manchuria. Poorly fed, poorly paid, poorly clothed, poorly cared for, poorly armed, often short of ammunition – even at critical moments – un-sustained by any faith in a cause, the Nationalist soldier was easy prey for the clever and impassioned propaganda of the Communist.[5]

The PLA armies north of the Yangzi spent some time to gather their strength before moving on further south. By April they were ready for an operation that many had believed impossible only a short time before, crossing the Yangzi and moving into south China. Once the crossing started, along a very wide front, the GMD government and its armies abandoned their capital, only a little over a decade since they had abandoned it to the invading Japanese armies.

Into the chaos of the Lower Yangzi Valley wandered a young man from Quebec, Pierre Elliott Trudeau, the future prime minister of Canada, collecting material for his MA thesis at Harvard (never completed). He was struck by 'the extraordinary and tragic phenomenon' of Shanghai in the last days before it fell. 'The whole city was a bizarre flea market where everyone, from the poorest to the richest, was trying to peddle his or her possessions for money to flee to the south or abroad.'[6] Trudeau discovered one of his classmates at Montreal's École Jean de Brebeuf, Paul Deslierres, now a priest in the calm sanctuary of the Jesuit establishment in Shanghai. Trudeau withdrew briefly into the known world of the Jesuit house at Zijiawei before moving on to Japan.

The rout

On 22 April the last remaining government leaders and senior civil servants left Nanjing by plane for Guangzhou. They later moved on to Hankou and finally Chongqing and Chengdu. Li Zongren's government was still trying to hang on to its rapidly dwindling power. The GMD armies left by boat or on foot, going either south or east towards Shanghai, before the PLA reached the city. Some units remained intact, others dissolved, their men fending for themselves. In a sad reprise of the flight from Nanjing in

[5] *Ibid*, p. 234.
[6] Pierre Elliott Trudeau, *Memoirs* (Toronto: McClelland and Stewart, 1993), p. 59.

1937 a GMD colonel, Peng Jinchuan, abandoned his uniform and escaped westwards dressed in civilian clothes. He walked all the way to Yuezhou (Hunan), several hundred miles, then went south by train to Guangzhou.[7]

Most of the foreign diplomats stayed on in Nanjing, now an open city; they did not follow the GMD government, to which they were still accredited. Only the embassy of the Soviet Union followed Li Zongren to Guangzhou. Other foreigners, like most of the civilian population who stayed on, seemed to have accepted the inevitable and to have little fear of the CCP.

An international sideshow accompanied the crossing of the Yangzi: the Amethyst Incident started on 20 April. The quixotic attempt by a sloop of the Royal Navy to sail up the Yangzi to Nanjing to rescue British citizens ran into disaster when the vessel sailed across the front line between the GMD and the CCP armies. She was hit, disabled and ran aground. She languished on a sandbank through the hot summer until she was patched up and refloated by the crew and made her way down river to the sea.[8] The dramatic escape was not enough to prevent the incident from being a humiliation for the vaunted Royal Navy. The CCP had achieved what had been impossible for China for a century – to attack and cripple one of the foreign gunboats, the most hated symbol of imperialism in China.

In Nanjing there was no repetition of the fear and panic that had gripped the city in December 1937. The US ambassador, the gentle missionary educator turned diplomat John Leighton Stuart, was still in bed when PLA forces poured into the embassy residence at 6.30a.m. on the morning of 25 April. Several armed soldiers entered his bedroom, 'the spokesman quite politely explained that they were only looking around for fun and meant no harm'.[9]

Before that morning, while the PLA was still on its way, the population had taken things into their own hands and started to loot the offices and houses of the GMD. The American journalist Seymour Topping went out on the streets to witness the spectacle.

---

[7] Guofangbu, *Yicun shanhe yicun xue* (*One Inch of Territory, One Inch of Blood*) (Taibei: Guofangbu, 2001), p. 31.

[8] The 1957 film *Yangtse Incident* starred Richard Todd as Commander Kerans. Rather than being court-martialled for endangering his ship and his crew, Kerans was elected a Conservative MP. The film was shot in the Orwell Estuary in Essex, a pale imitation of the Yangzi.

[9] John Leighton Stuart, *Fifty Years in China* (New York: Random House, 1954), p. 239.

Looters in Nanjing

As the GMD abandoned Nanjing, the residents took over and helped themselves to what the government had left behind. The Canadian *chargé d'affaires* Chester Ronning reported:

For three days prior to the liberation, wild yet systematic looting by the people was widespread. Amidst shouting and laughing, the people stripped the residences of top Nationalist officials and army generals, carrying out the contents, ripping out plumbing, electric fixtures, doors and windows, floors and all wood for kindling. Like vultures, the looters waited patiently until the Nationalists evacuated their homes in panicky flight.*

Ronning's future son-in-law, the American journalist Seymour Topping, gave a similar report on the looting:

The looters, mostly shabbily dressed men, women and children from the slums of Fu Tze Miao [Fuzimiao], the old Chinese quarter in the southern district, were going about their thievery good-humouredly, laughing and shouting to each other. From the upper floors of the two-storey villas they were hurling sofas, carpets and bedding to the lawns below. The household goods were being hauled away on peasant carts and on the backs of excited men, women and children. A grinning soldier who had thrown away his rifle gingerly carried off a lamp in each hand. An old woman, her gray hair pulled back in a bun, happily carried off four elaborately embroidered cushions.**

* Chester Ronning, *A Memoir of China in Revolution* (New York: Pantheon, 1974), p. 136.
** Semour Topping, *Journey Between Two Chinas* (New York: Harper and Row, 2007), pp. 64–65.

The Indian ambassador, K.M. Panikkar, did not have to go outside to see what was happening. He watched from the window of his chancery as the official residence of the Nanjing mayor was systematically looted, 'in a civilised and orderly manner', with the young helping the elderly, and everyone taking no more than they could easily make off with.[10]

Shanghai soon fell to the PLA without resistance, but not without violence. Brief video clips show the execution of unnamed people on the street, as the PLA armies came in.[11] The PLA forces now spread out in simultaneous drives towards the south and west, the GMD fleeing before them.

[10] K.M. Panikkar, *In Two Chinas* (London: Allen and Unwin, 1955), p. 49.
[11] *Murder in Shanghai 1949*, YouTube.

兵败如山倒

Bing bai ru shan dao
Military defeats like mountains falling

In May and June came the retreat from the last GMD toehold in north China, the port of Qingdao. Over a few weeks 100,000 soldiers were evacuated in every kind of ship, from large steamers to fishing boats. With them went a small number, fewer than 10,000, of civilians. The crossing to Taiwan took from three days to a week. This evacuation paralleled the desperate evacuation of Allied troops from Dunkirk in 1940, although more than three times the number of men had been taken off the beaches in Dunkirk. The GMD high command held the same desperate hope that they might one day return to the Mainland. After all, Allied armies had returned to Europe in 1944.[12]

By the late summer of 1949 much of south China was in CCP hands. The remaining GMD-controlled provinces were in the far south and the west. There was still determined resistance, but no hope of victory. In a string of terrible defeats through the summer the GMD armies disintegrated as a fighting force. Soldiers deserted, others were captured. Some of those captured were taken into the PLA, but by this time the PLA had no great need for more soldiers. Some surplus soldiers were given money to go home, others were kept as prisoners.

On 1 October, Mao Zedong made the formal proclamation of the liberation of China and the establishment of the People's Republic of China. He spoke from the most symbolic of places, the Tianan Gate (Tiananmen) at the entrance to the Imperial Palace in Beijing. His thick Hunan accent was almost incomprehensible, but the symbolism of his appearance was not.[13] The city was renamed Beijing (Northern Capital), after 21 years under the demeaning name Beiping (Northern Peace). The ceremony was held nine days ahead of 10 October, the Double Ten, the national day of the Republic of China. The national day of the new China became 1 October. The Republic of China came to an end on the Mainland, in its thirty-seventh year.

It was a staggering victory. In less than a year the PLA had advanced across almost all of China. The military historian F.F. Liu gave great credit to the PLA as a 'fine fighting force', but he also saw the fighting as having been at least as much lost by the GMD as won by the PLA:

---

[12] Wang Junchang, *Jincun tuiwang (Advance and Retreat)* (Taibei: Dangan guanliju, 2010), pp. 70–72.
[13] His brief speech can be seen on YouTube.

解放區現有
面積人口城市鉄路

面積

2,962,800(方公里)

人口

279,274,000(人)

Fig. 16 CCP control, mid-1949

In the communist conquest of the vast mainland of China much of their [CCP] success must be attributed to the default of the Chinese Nationalist [GMD] military power – a great military force taxed by eight years of supreme effort against Imperial Japan and betrayed from within by corruption, maladministration and dissension in high places.[14]

[14] F.F. Liu, *A Military History of Modern China* (Princeton: Princeton University Press, 1956), p. 270. Liu served in the GMD military and was close to the Guangxi leaders Bai Chongxi and Li Zongren.

The conquest was not in doubt, but the GMD did not give up. Parts of the south and west had not been taken. The last months of 1949 were dangerous for the CCP's covert supporters there. As the PLA swept southwards, undercover communists became the targets of ferocious GMD attacks. On 27 November several hundred suspected communists were killed in Chongqing. These desperate acts could not save the GMD. The remnants of its armies were in full retreat. The last stop in the chaotic rout was the island of Hainan.[15]

残兵敗將
Can bing bai jiang
Scattered soldiers and defeated generals

Hainan

These are notes written by the American scholar Doak Barnett on what he saw in Haikou, the main city of Hainan in November 1949:

Haikow is a chaotic refugee center whose streets and sidewalks are teeming with tens of thousands of disbanded Nationalist soldiers who have fled from the Chinese mainland.

The refugee troops in Haikow [Haikou] are completely demoralised. The faces of the soldiers wading ashore through the surf or climbing on to the dilapidated concrete pier at the landing point outside of Haikow have a bleak look of hopelessness.

The 7-mile road from the pier outside the city is lined with straggling soldiers and civilian camp followers streaming in to town.

Within Haikow itself, there is almost no place that is not jammed with soldiers and their families. They have set up house-keeping in churches, public buildings, school, private homes and on the sidewalks.[*]

[*] Doak Barnett, *China on the Eve of Communist Takeover* (New York: Praeger, 1963), pp. 296–297.

CCP control over all of China seemed complete at the end of 1949 but it was not. Many of the border regions were far from being conquered. In Xinjiang, the East Turkestan administration was pressured by the USSR to accept incorporation into the Chinese state in early 1950; this was the origin of the opposition of many of the indigenous people of Xinjiang, the Uighurs, to Beijing. Tibet was not brought under Beijing's control until

---

[15] Hainan became a tropical Siberia under the CCP. The rubber plantations were worked by political prisoners. Its beaches are now lined with resorts; the island is a holiday destination, often called China's Hawaii.

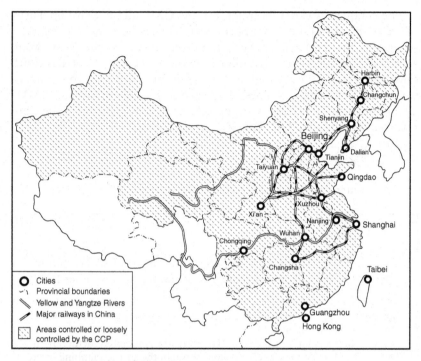

Map 9 China, December 1949

late 1950, and then only by force. In both places Beijing's control scarcely extended beyond the major cities. In the border regions in the far south hundreds of thousands of GMD troops, now labelled as 'bandits *(fei)*' held out in the hills and mountains of Guangxi and Yunnan well into the 1950s. Some had escaped south across the international borders.

Social upheaval

The last stages of the Civil War created almost total confusion within Chinese society. Nothing was certain, from day to day or even from hour to hour.

Luan qi ba zao
Chaos

This is a favourite *chengyu*, used to describe an impossibly confusing or difficult situation, when people throw up their hands as a sign of their inability to cope. Its literal meaning is 'chaos seven eight mess'. The phrase summed up what people were going through in 1949. Even where the fighting was over, the immediate relief was replaced by anxiety and uncertainty about what was to come. People waited nervously to see what would come out of the chaos.

Beyond relief and uncertainty, feelings ranged widely in the first half of 1949. Some people were delirious with excitement, that China had been liberated, that 'China had stood up'. Others were devastated. For the majority of people, whose feelings lay in between the poles of excitement and despair, relief was tinged with exhaustion and a sense of incomprehension at how much they had had to suffer through 12 years of war. There was little sympathy left for the GMD. In Nanjing, the translator Yang Xianyi, already in secret touch with the CCP, wrote that 'I was so disgusted with what I had seen and experienced under the Kuomintang [GMD] regime that I thought that living under any government would be better'.[16] In Shenyang the junior officer Huang Yaowu summed up the widespread feeling of futility and incomprehension: 'I had no particular feeling for the GMD, but I didn't understand the Communist Party either. I just felt that this war should not have been fought, and that both sides were to blame for fighting it.'[17]

Very few people had a much clearer idea about what the CCP was like. All that they heard in the GMD-controlled regions was lurid propaganda and terrifying rumours. Rumours were the only form of news.

Rumours

In a world where there was no reliable source of news ordinary people relied on rumours – 'the news of the small streets (*xiaodao xiaoxi*)' – for their information. There was no other source they could credit. Some information could be gleaned from the GMD press, not direct information, but inferences drawn from what was not said, or who was missing from the news. (This is still how people consume official media in China.)

Rumours were a valuable currency in wartime China; the more rumours a person could pass on, the higher their reputation – and the more they could, if they wanted to, profit from the frequent changes. Rumours always tend to be lurid and to get increasingly

---

[16] Yang Xianyi, *White Tiger* (Hong Kong: Chinese University Press, 2002), p. 167.
[17] Huang Yaowu, *1944–1948 Wode zhanzheng (1944–1948: My War)* (Shenyang: Chunfeng, 2010), p. 218.

so in repeated telling. Most of the rumours in the late 1940s had to do with a stock roster of topics: currency fluctuations, GMD corruption, CCP atrocities, PLA locations.

There were terrifying rumours, many of them about the incoming communists, but also, for those who knew they would have to leave with the GMD, deeply depressing rumours about Taiwan: the island was a wilderness covered in grasses taller than a man; houses had walls but no roofs; there was so little to eat that people had to eat banana skins.*

The war also saw the emergence of urban legends – 'true' stories, passed on at second hand. One I have come across several times has to do with the behaviour of peasant soldiers in a modern house with a flush toilet. The soldiers tried to wash their rice in the toilet bowl before cooking it. But when they flushed the toilet the rice disappeared. This seemingly harmless story, told about both GMD and CCP soldiers, was an implicit statement of the sophisticated urbanite's contempt for peasants, mixed with anxiety about the soldiers who had suddenly become part of their lives.**

* Lo Jiu-jung, Yu Chien-ming and Chiu Hei-yuan (eds.), *Fenghuo suiyue xia de Zhongguo funu (Chinese Women in the Fires of War)* (Taibei: Zhongyang yanjiuyuan Jindaishi yanjiusuo, 2004), p. 284.
** Maria Yen, *Umbrella Garden: A Picture of Student Life in Red China* (New York: Macmillan, 1954), p. 29; Michael David Kwan, *Things That Must Not Be Forgotten: A Childhood in Wartime China* (Toronto: MacFarlane, 2000), p. 147. The story is also cited in Frank Dikotter, *The Tragedy of the Liberation: A History of the Chinese Revolution 1945–1957* (London: Bloomsbury, 2013), p. 31.

In the areas still under GMD control there was no Chinese-language newspaper (the only mass media at the time) that gave coverage of the PLA advance. Foreign journalists were reporting on the war, both for English-language papers in Shanghai and Hong Kong, and for newspapers in their home countries, but they were not allowed to cover the PLA. The enterprising Seymour Topping made his way north along the railway line from Nanjing at the end of 1948, through the chaos of retreating GMD armies, and even got into the CCP-held area south of Xuzhou, but he was forbidden to make any observations and was immediately escorted back south of the Yangzi.[18] Jack Birns took photographs of the desolate GMD troops in retreat, but for foreign, not Chinese

[18] Topping, *Journey Between Two Chinas*, pp.29–45.

consumption.[19] There were no reliable radio broadcasts in China at the time, from either side.

Women

Neither the GMD nor the CCP paid much specific attention to women's issues in the last year of the war. For many women this period was particularly stressful. They were the mainstay of their families, a more and more difficult role in chaotic times. This was above all the case with the wives of soldiers. Those whose husbands were with the CCP armies received some help from their fellow-villagers, as part of the *daigong* (replacement labour) formula instituted in communities under CCP control.

Wives of GMD soldiers were in the opposite situation. They were now pariahs in their home communities. The GMD armies did little to evacuate families to Taiwan; dependants were not a priority. Some officers' dependants got away, often more by chance than through a formal evacuation. Polygamy created problems; there was little likelihood that more than one wife would get away. A series of oral histories of military wives who left China for Taiwan, mostly in 1949, showed that most relied on their own wits and courage to leave the Mainland.[20]

The formal CCP policy about the equality of men and women, and the concept that the revolution was being waged in the name of the poor, may have created some enthusiasm. This was less a feminist approach, a conviction that the situation of women was bound to improve than a sense that women would be able to contribute to the new world.

Another issue for a particular group of women was the CCP's promise to put an end to polygamy. Multiple marriages were still quite common. The abolition of polygamy had attractions for the future – girls would no longer be forced (often by their own families) to be the concubines of often much older men – but it was a tricky problem for existing wives and concubines: what would become of them if their husbands were obliged to have only one wife? Would the surplus wives and concubines have to find jobs? Could they find a man who was not married and would be willing to take on a woman who had been a concubine? These were issues on which there was little guidance from the CCP, only rumours and anxiety about an uncharted future.

[19] Caroline Wakeman and Ken Light (eds.), *Assignment Shanghai: Photographs on the Eve of Revolution* (Berkeley: University of California Press, 1997).

[20] Lo Jiu-jung, Yu Chien-ming and Chiu Hei-yuan (eds.), *Fenghuo suiyue xia de Zhongguo funu fangwen ji* (*Chinese Women in the Fires of War*) (Taibei: Zhongyang yanjiuyuan, 2004).

The young

One of the great successes of the CCP propaganda as it took over China
was to portray the process as a movement of youth against age. The CCP
leaders had become communists in their youth. Now the party was anxious to recruit young people and to get their enthusiastic support in overthrowing the remnants of the old order.

There were many categories of young people. One enormous group
was made up of young peasants, people who had seen no future for themselves in the old order, or had even thought about a future. They were
a key to the success of the revolution at the grassroots level. The CCP
offered them a life of excitement and gave them, for the first time in their
lives, some self-respect. By joining the revolution – which in many cases
meant joining the armed forces, PLA or militia – they had a purpose in
life. They had to be subjected to discipline, quite difficult for some of
those close to the *liumang* life of casual work and casual violence.

For China's legions of young students, at school and university, the
last few months of 1949 were an exciting time. There were communist victory parades, political rallies, propaganda campaigns, all suffused
with the feeling of a new world in birth. Education remained in a state
of virtual collapse; schools and universities functioned, but not in a serious way; teachers were waiting to see what changes were coming, and
were reluctant to resume the old teaching. The young, whatever their
age, were free to do much as they pleased. Some went to school, others
bunked off. Their teachers had other worries on their minds than taking
attendance.[21] They had to live, however, with their parents' preoccupation and anxiety, and with the continuing scrabble for food and, in the
north, for fuel for the coming winter.

Some young people left their universities or schools and went off to
join the communists as the armies moved south. When they left they
were full of enthusiasm for the revolution, driven by excitement and passionate idealism. Their idealism was brought down to earth by the tough-
ness of the communist way of life, and by the demands for discipline and
obedience.

Other young people waited to see what would happen, what the new
world would be like. All those who were still unmarried – which in much
of China would have meant quite young people, still in their mid- to late
teens – wondered about whether they would be able to choose their own
life partner, their *duixiang*. This might mean abandoning the person to

---

[21] One of the better memories of people who were school age in 1949 was that school
became optional; the dreaded discipline of a Chinese primary school was in abeyance.

whom they were already betrothed by their families. The prospect of a marriage based on choice, if not romance, and the prospect too of avoiding a fierce mother-in-law aroused tremulous excitement in many girls. The youth of China seemed to have a great deal to gain from the new government.

Departures and returns

In the last stages of the Civil War, the question of leaving or staying was critical. In most cases people made no choice about whether to leave or stay, but were simply swept along by the tidal waves of the war. Those who could choose made a range of different decisions.

Flight

Mid-1949 was the last chance for people to decide whether to stay where they were or to leave, to embrace communism or reject it. For those who decided to leave, there was nowhere close to find sanctuary, no place to which they could easily flee to escape the chaos, except Hong Kong. The foreign enclaves to which Chinese had fled in times of trouble since the Taiping Rising (1860s) no longer existed. The sanctuary offered a decade before by Christian missions throughout China for protection against the incoming Japanese was equally unavailable – the foreign missionaries themselves were leaving as the PLA advanced.

The late spring and summer of 1949 saw panicky efforts by millions of people to get out of China, by any means. The word used for their flight was *taonan*, escaping from disaster; the word used so often in China's turbulent past was now used again. Some people were able to leave for Taiwan by sea, from ports that remained in GMD hands; the vessels for these passages were organised by the GMD, so access to them required official connections. Some wealthier people managed to get tickets for foreign passenger vessels still sailing to Hong Kong. Others fled south by rail or road, going to Hong Kong as their final destination or as a stopover on their way to Taiwan. Some people fled across the southernmost border into Indo-China, others even made their way out of China through the far west and across the mountains into India.

All these departures were accompanied by acute fear and insecurity. None of the current aids to travel was available – travel agencies, bank machines, mobile phones. Bribery and the black market were often the only ways to get tickets for a train or a ship. Plane tickets could only be got through official connections – and then bribes had to be paid too. T.C. Li, an *aide-de-camp* to Li Zongren, managed to get tickets for his wife and children to leave Sichuan with him in late 1949, but only after days of efforts, which included his wife's vigorous attempts to bribe a pilot. When the family finally did get tickets, they arrived at the airport to find their plane overbooked; getting on to the plane turned out to be almost as difficult as getting the tickets.[22]

With train and plane tickets so scarce, even those who could get tickets had to make terrible decisions about who was going to go with them – a whole extended family, or only one wife and her children? What about elderly parents or young children who might not be able to withstand an arduous journey? Many had to be left behind. Chen Dunzheng, a junior official in the Ministry of National Defence, was caught in his native Changsha when the PLA took the city in August. He knew he had to leave when it became clear that his presence there was known, and that people were looking for him. He realised that he could not take his wife and five children with him. He stayed hidden for a while, and when the trains started running again in the early autumn, he disguised himself as a merchant and went south to Guangzhou and then on to Hong Kong. The parting with his family was almost unbearably painful. He promised his wife that he would get them out when he could. The time never came. He married again in Taiwan in 1956. The guilt of the abandonment of his family haunted him. He knew what his wife and children must be going through for having the worst kind of 'foreign connection', a father in Taiwan. He blamed himself for not being filial to his parents, for not giving sufficient comfort to his wife, and for not having provided sufficient education and guidance to his children.[23]

Chen at least had been able to say goodbye to his family, and had promised to try and get them out later. Others did not say goodbye. Their departures often had to be made in secret, a secret kept from those being left behind, in order not to compromise the flight.

In the end few people made sober decisions in 1949 about whether to leave or stay. Most of the associates of the GMD, soldiers and civilians, left in panic. As the year wore on it became more and more difficult to leave; the number of open borders decreased. By the end of the year the only way out was across the little river that divided Guangdong from Hong Kong.

The number of people who left was tiny in terms of the Chinese population – not more than three million out of several hundred million – but

---

[22] T.G. Li, *A China Past: Military and Diplomatic Memoirs* (Lanham: ARP, 1989), pp. 292–295.

[23] Chen Dunzheng, *Dongluan de huiyi* (*Memoirs of Chaos*) (Taibei: Wuxia shuju, 1978), pp. 118–120.

to the nation it was a highly significant number, because it included many of the best-educated and most capable members of the population. These were people who had much to offer China, as they had done in the war with Japan. The victory of the CCP made sure that they could no longer do anything for their country, but only for the island of Taiwan.

Returns

Some people came back to China in 1949. One was the writer Lao She, the man who more than any other writer is identified with Beijing. Zhou Enlai's discreet messages asking him to return to China reached him in New York on the very day that the People's Republic was established. Lao She left for China at once, and arrived there in mid-December, to be received immediately by Zhou.[24] His decision to return was driven by a desire to be back with his family again. He had been separated from his brothers for 15 years and from his wife and children for a shorter period.[25] He seemed to settle well in Beijing. He wrote the very successful drama *Dragon Beard's Ditch* and was actively engaged in supervising the translation and publication of several books.[26]

Several academics and intellectuals returned to China in 1949 and the early 1950s. The reasons varied. Sometimes it was a career move. The mathematician Hua Luogeng returned after he was offered the position as head of Qinghua University's Mathematics Department. Sometimes the reason for return was ideological. China's leading psychologist, Cao Richang, returned to China after he had finished his PhD at Cambridge University. Cao's background was unusual. He came from a peasant family in Hebei; simply by his intellectual brilliance he had acquired a university education in China. He spent the Resistance War in Kunming, then in 1945 won a Boxer Indemnity scholarship to study at Cambridge. He was already close to the CCP, and actually joined the party while he was in England. In 1951 he and his Dutch wife, Selma Vos, and two young children went back to China after a short stay in Hong Kong.[27]

---

[24] Zhang Guixing (ed.), *Lao She nianpu* (*Lao She's Chronology*) (Shanghai: Wenyi chubanshe, 1997), pp. 509–510.

[25] *Lao She Yingwen shuxin ji* (*Collection of Lao She's English Letters*) (Beijing: Jinshilu, 1993), p. 100.

[26] Lao She's return was a tragedy for him and for Chinese literature. In the 1950s he made a career as a literary bureaucrat, but he never wrote another major work. In the Cultural Revolution he was horribly persecuted. In 1967 he drowned himself in the Taiping Lake in Beijing.

[27] *Jinian Cao Richang xiansheng* (*In Memory of Mr. Cao Richang*) (Beijing: Zhongyang kexueyuan xinlisuo, 2011), pp. 11–12. The Boxer Indemnity scholarships were a legacy of the Boxer Rising in 1900. Some of the money paid by the Chinese government to

Ji Chaozhu, later Mao Zedong's interpreter, left his studies at Harvard to go back to China, to join his much older brother Ji Chaoding, a key economic advisor to the CCP who himself had returned to China a few years before. The younger Ji's motive was patriotism – encouraged by an underground network of CCP sympathisers in New York.[28]

Some young Chinese in Hong Kong and in the Overseas Chinese communities were caught up in the excitement of what was happening. Some of them went back to China (or to China for the first time) to serve the revolution. They knew that what they were doing was putting the revolution ahead of their family. The Kwan family was long-established in the Hong Kong banking world. The family had strong ties to Guangdong, and many of its members went inland during the Resistance War, to return to Hong Kong in 1945. Stanley Kwan described how the mother reacted in late 1949 when she heard that her two youngest sons were going back to the Mainland to serve socialism, 'she wept for days and was inconsolable'.[29]

Flight and return

Some of the people who fled from the Mainland just before the end of GMD rule soon returned. The Shanghai capitalist Liu Hongsheng had been unable to decide since 1948 where he and his family should be. He had fled to Chongqing during the Resistance War, and was acutely unhappy at the thought of fleeing again only a few years after his return to Shanghai. He had heavy family responsibilities as husband of two wives and father of 14 children. He wanted to keep his family together. A move to Taiwan was ruled out after the GMD's experiment with the gold *Yuan* cost him a fortune. In the spring of 1949 he decided to move most of his family to Hong Kong, except for one of his sons, who had already joined the CCP. But by the end of the year the father was back in Shanghai. He felt too old to leave home, and he did not want to be a 'white Chinese' in Hong Kong. On his return he too was welcomed by Zhou Enlai, as an example of a model capitalist.[30]

Another returnee was a senior GMD general. The GMD military authorities had made General Wei Lihuang the scapegoat for the

---

Western countries as an indemnity was put to scholarships for Chinese students. They were the best and brightest of their generation. Another Boxer scholar who went to England was the economist and historian Jerome Ch'en.

[28] Ji Chaozhu, *The Man on Mao's Right* (New York: Random House, 2008), p. 61.

[29] Stanley Kwan with Nicole Kwan, *The Dragon and the Crown: Hong Kong Memoirs* (Hong Kong: Hong Kong University Press, 2009), p. 78.

[30] Sherman Cochran and Andrew Hsieh, *The Lius of Shanghai* (Cambridge, MA: Harvard University Press, 2013), pp. 280–290.

disastrous defeats in Manchuria in 1948. He was put in cold storage in Beiping, under 'investigation'. As the CCP armies closed in on the city in December 1948, Wei decided it was time to go. He put his hands on considerable funds and managed to hire a private plane in which he, his family and 20 or 30 subordinates flew to Guangzhou. There they took over a floor of the Aiqun (Love the Masses) Hotel. He was soon discovered by GMD agents, and forced to go to Nanjing. He managed to slip away again, this time to Hong Kong. He stayed there for five years, under constant attention from GMD and PRC agents. Eventually, he went back to the Mainland and was received with great pomp as one of the most important returnees to date.[31]

Those who did not return

There is a long list of those Chinese who were working or studying abroad in 1949, and decided not to return to China, at least for the time being. The list is headed by two Nobel laureates, Franklin Yang and T.S. Lee, and by the distinguished architect I.M. Pei. The decision to stay away was often a temporary one, they were waiting to see how things turned out in China; it became permanent when it became almost impossible to have any contact with their family and friends left on the Mainland. Many Chinese students enrolled in foreign universities decided to wait until they graduated – by which time the situation would be clearer. When the time came, many decided not to go back to China.

The Overseas Chinese also waited, hoping that they would be able to go back to their home communities in the *qiaoxiang* again, but deeply worried about the CCP, knowing how hostile the party was to landowners – the very commodity that they had bought with the money they had earned abroad. The close connections built up over the past century were gradually eroded. There were exceptions. The most celebrated Overseas Chinese, Chen Jiageng (Tan Kha-khee), the Rubber King, had left Malaya ahead of the Japanese invasion in 1941 and had spent much of the Resistance War in China. Over time he had grown away from the GMD and come close to the CCP. He stayed in China in 1949 – possibly because he was unwelcome in British-held Malaya or Singapore – and lived in a modest house in the beautiful cluster of schools he had built in the 1930s at Jimei, near Xiamen. It was a lonely life; his family stayed in Singapore.

---

[31] Zhao Rongsheng, *Huiyi Wei Lihuang xiansheng* (*Remembering Mr Wei Lihuang*) (Beijing: Wenshi ziliao chubanshe, 1985), pp. 348–352, 372–373.

Reunions in China

For those who had joined the revolution early, and had been separated from their families for a long time, the end of the war brought reunion. During the eight years of the Resistance War and the four years of the Civil War, many of those who had joined the CCP were completely cut off from their families at home. From the later stages of the Resistance War on, the intensity of the GMD hatred of the CCP made it danger-ous, for their families as much as for themselves, to be in touch with their families. Now they could be reunited. For many the reunions were joyous.

The immediate months and weeks after the liberation was the ideal time to have a bona fide communist relative, an assurance of the family's correct political credentials. A bad class background could suddenly be reversed by discovering red relatives and friends, whose existence alone could mitigate against a relative's dubious background. Sometimes these reunions with red relatives were post-mortem reunions. The Qin family of Shanghai discovered, in 1952, that one of their brothers, Qin Jiajun, deeply estranged from the family, had died in battle in 1942, fighting with the New Fourth Army. His sister received a certificate that labelled him as a 'martyr in the Communist cause'. Given that the family had a strongly bourgeois background, this certificate was very useful to his siblings who had stayed on the Mainland, at least until the Cultural Revolution.[32]

Some reunions were complicated. A returning son or daughter might have married by their own choice, without the parents' permission and in breach of an existing engagement made by the family. In a society in which polygamy was not illegal, a returning husband, by marrying for love, had acquired in effect a second wife. The first wife, chosen by his parents and already living with them, was not considered divorced but still a member of the parental family.

Fourth brother's wives*

Yu Wenxiu was born in 1922. Her father was a soldier, away from home, and the family lived a modest life off their land in Yexian (northern Anhui). Her fourth brother, Yu Wenzhi (later Zhu Ningyuan), joined the CCP New Fourth Army, and served through

---

[32] Frank Ching, *Ancestors: 900 Years of a Chinese Family* (New York: Fawcett, 1989), p. 449. The author is the youngest brother of Qin Jiajun, whom he never met.

the Resistance War. In Henan, he fell ill and was left behind by his unit. He was taken in by an ordinary family. He and their daughter developed affection for each other (*ganqing*) and, despite the fact that he already had a wife at home in Anhui, they married.

He was not in touch with his family for the whole eight years of the war. He wrote to his family only in 1949, when he was part of the force taking over Nanjing for the CCP. He told his family what had happened to him, and broke the news that he had another wife and a son. His mother was furious and stormed off to Nanjing with his (childless) first wife in tow. The two had waited ten years in vain for him to return. His mother was incensed that she had supported his wife for all that time. This apparently sad story had a happy ending. The first wife was still under 30. Keeping the past secret, she changed her name and married again, quite well. She had two daughters. She never told them of her past, which remained her secret; only her sister-in-law in Taiwan seems to have known, but when she visited her almost 40 years later, she respected her secret.

* Lo *et al.*, *Fenghuo suiyue xia de Zhongguo funu*, pp. 126–128.

Some of the victorious communists did not want to be reunited with their families. The initial breach with their families in their youth seemed to have had personal as well as political causes, and they had no desire to be reunited with people to whom they felt no connection. Deng Xiaoping, for example, never went back to the childhood home (Guangan, Sichuan) that he left in his early twenties; his youthful breach with his family was permanent.

The departure of foreigners

The foreign world that had dominated the modern cities of China for almost a century did not survive the Resistance War and the Civil War. During the 12 years of war, the number of foreigners in China had dwindled. In 1949 the majority of remaining foreign residents left China. Many of the Western business concerns (Hong Kong and Shanghai Bank and Jardine's, for example) transferred their operations to Hong Kong, contributing to the start of Hong Kong's phenomenal economic growth. The European Jews who had fled to China from the Nazis were helped to leave China by Jewish charities, going either to North America or to Israel. Many Christian missionaries were withdrawn by their home churches in advance of the communist takeover. Some continued their work in Hong Kong.

In the early 1950s most of those foreigners who did not leave voluntarily were pressured into leaving by the new government. The most problematic group of foreigners was the White Russians who had fled from the Soviet Union after 1917 (see Chapter 7).

The year 1949 ended with the CCP achieving one of the most powerful goals of the Chinese nationalist movement, getting rid of foreign influence in China. The irony was that as the Western presence disappeared, so the Soviet presence grew.

Biographies

Zhang Daqian

The great painter Zhang Daqian was a deeply traditional man, always dressed in a long gown. He had few illusions that he would enjoy living under communism, but he could hardly imagine living outside China. He left China for Hong Kong in December 1948, but was soon back in Shanghai. There he came under powerful pressure from the artist Xu Beihong – who was emerging as one of the key pro-CCP figures in the art world – to go to the newly liberated Beiping. Zhang hesitated, changed his mind, then changed it again. In 1949 he was frequently in the air – a sign of his immense prestige, since getting plane tickets in China at the time was incredibly difficult. He flew to India, then to Taiwan. In November, with most of China already in CCP hands, he flew to Chengdu, capital of his home province Sichuan, picked up his wife and daughter and flew on a military plane to Taiwan. He took with him only one scroll.[33] The rest of his pictures in Sichuan, including the series based on Dunhuang cave paintings, which he had spent years painting during the Resistance War, are now in the Sichuan Provincial Museum. Family members who did not leave China donated them to the museum. For the next years Zhang roamed the world, living in Brazil, with periods in India, Argentina and the USA. When he was nearly 80, he settled in Taiwan. His wanderings gave him international prestige; he was admired in international art circles as the greatest Chinese painter.

Ji Chaoding

Ji Chaoding was one of the most brilliant economists of modern China. The son of a wealthy and highly cultivated family from Shanxi (his father

---

[33] Li Yongqiao, *Zhang Daqian nianpu* (*Zhang Daqian Chronology*) (Chengdu: Sichuansheng shehui kexueyuan, 1987), pp. 246–256. The English title on the cover of this book is *The Greatest Artist of the World*.

was a legal scholar), he went as a young man to the USA, where he became an expert in international finance and studied and wrote on Chinese history. During his time there he became, in secret, a Marxist and married an American communist. His seminal work *Key Economic Areas in Chinese History* was published in 1936. During the Resistance War he worked for the Chinese government in the USA, and seemed to be in full sympathy with the GMD. At the same time, in deep cover, he was one of the key activists for the CCP in the USA. His ability to stay undercover is incredible; he trumped the best efforts of both the GMD and US secret services. Once the Civil War was near its end he went over to the CCP. After 1949 he played a leading role in Beijing's economic thinking and in policy-making. Ji's turn to the CCP was a shock for the GMD; he was regarded as completely trustworthy, a most unlikely candidate to support socialism, but turned out to be a long-term, devout communist.[34]

Jakob Rosenfeld[35]

Rosenfeld was an Austrian Jew, a highly competent physician. His leftist views got him into trouble after the Anschluss with Germany (1938), and he spent a year in the Dachau concentration camp. He was forced to flee from Austria in 1939, and settled in Shanghai, where he practised gynaecology. He was close to other left-leaning Germans and Austrians. Through them he got in touch with CCP representatives, and in 1941 left Shanghai to work with the New 4th Army. He spent the next eight years with communist armies, in senior positions in military medical administration. As the title of his biography – *I Knew Them All* – indicates, he knew all the leaders of the CCP involved in the military. After 1950 his future was unclear. He returned (briefly) to Vienna, and then emigrated to Israel, where he died. He was refused a visa to return to China.

Rosenfeld has recently become a hero of Sino-Austrian relations. His contributions to medical care in China were far greater than those of the Canadian doctor Norman Bethune's, but Mao Zedong never mentioned him in his writings, so his fame is much less.

Du Yuming

General Du Yuming was a graduate of the first class of the Whampao Military Academy. Throughout his military career he was considered

---

[34] For details of Ji Chaoding's life, see his younger brother's autobiography: Ji, *The Man on Mao's Right*. Ji Chaochu was for a long time Mao Zedong's interpreter.

[35] Gerd Kaminski (ed.), *Ich Kannte Sie Alle: das Tagebuch des Chinesischen General Jakob Rosenfeld* (*I Knew Them All: The Diary of the Chinese General Jakob Rosenfeld*) (Wien: Locker, 2002).

to be particularly close to Chiang Kai-shek, once the commandant of the academy. After a series of major commands in the southwest during the Resistance War, in the Civil War he held important commands in Manchuria and then in Shandong. He was captured by the PLA in the HuaiHai Campaign in early 1949, the most senior GMD commander to be taken prisoner. He was released in 1959, shortly after his son-in-law Yang Zhenming (Franklin Yang), husband of his daughter Du Zhili, had won the Nobel Prize for Physics. His release was apparently a lure (unsuccessful) to bring his son-in-law back to China. The family reunion did not take place until 1973, when relations with the USA began to improve after President Nixon's visit to China. After a separation of more than a quarter of a century, Du's daughter and son-in-law were obliged to thank the party and the motherland for its welcome. Yang was received by Mao Zedong.[36]

Nanxia ganbu

The *nanxia ganbu* (southern descending cadres) were young communists, almost always men, who came south with the victorious PLA armies. Their job was to administer the newly conquered, often turbulent areas in the southern tier of provinces: Fujian, Guangdong, Guangxi, Guizhou, Sichuan and Yunnan. Most of them were serving soldiers, some were peasant activists. They were drawn from areas already under CCP control, such as Shanxi and Shandong. Sam Ginsbourg saw recruitment in Shandong. He described it in the communist vocabulary of the time:

Each of the newly-liberated towns needed thousands of seasoned revolutionary cadres, who knew well the policies of the Party, were ready to implement them, able to do work amongst the masses, capable of distinguishing the enemies from the people's masses and willing to subordinate personal interests to public interests. Shandong, with its population of fifty million, was a treasure-house of such cadres.[37]

From Shanxi 20,000 men were sent into turbulent Sichuan. Some of these men have recounted their difficult lives there in a recent collection of oral histories.[38] An equally large number left from Shandong.

---

[36] Zheng Dongguo, *Du Yuming Jiangjun* (*General Du Yuming*) (Beijing: Zhongguo wenshi chubanshe, 1986), p. 186.

[37] Sam Ginsbourg, *My First Sixty Years in China* (Beijing: New World Press, 1982), p. 185.

[38] Liu Yutai, *1949: Shanxi ganbu nanxia shilu* (*1949: The True Records of Shanxi Naxia Ganbu*) (Taiyuan: Shanxi renmin chubanshe, 2012).

The young men were sent off with little more than revolutionary zeal as a qualification to direct people who did not speak the same dialect, eat the same food, let alone believe in the same ideology. Some of these regions had a history of hostility to the CCP, such as Guangdong and Guangxi; some were areas that had never been given to obeying the word from the capital, such as Fujian; and some places were hostile to incomers, especially towards the borders where indigenous people (known as 'national minorities' in China) had very little liking for any Han people. Because their task was to serve socialism and put their own personal needs aside, the young men were not allowed to take their families (if they had them) with them. And it was very difficult for them to marry local women, given the prevailing hostility.[39] For many their lonely postings lasted until retirement or death, whichever came first. Those who retired often went back to their old homes, after three or four decades away. I met some in the hills of central Shandong in the early 1980s. Their relief to be home in the dry, cool hills, speaking their own dialect, was undisguised.

Not all the *nanxia ganbu* stayed true to their socialist beliefs. Many of the Shandong men who were sent to the southern city of Hangzhou were at first horrified by the humid climate and the softness of the people, but they soon surrendered to the limpid beauty of the place, especially after it became the winter home of state leaders. Ninety per cent of them divorced their wives at home in Shandong to marry Hangzhou women. Their families at home were left destitute.[40]

Exile

The CCP's triumph meant, for some Chinese, the sad acceptance that they were now exiles, that their world in China had come to an end. Their sadness was encapsulated in the elegiac poetry of the Tang Dynasty, in which exile was a common theme – poems dedicated to officials being sent then into exile in the borderlands of China. This is Du Fu's famous poem about exile and the loss of home, written after the fall of the Tang capital Chang'an (now Xian) to rebels at the end of the eighth century:

[39] Diana Lary, *Chinese Migrations* (Lanham: Rowman and Littlefield, 2012), p. 132.
[40] James Gao, *The Communist Takeover of Hangzhou* (Honolulu: University of Hawaii Press, 2004), pp. 75, 198–199.

春望
Chun wang
Spring View

國破山河在	The country is broken but the hills and rivers remain
城春草木深	Spring grass and trees choke the city
感時花濺淚	Feeling the sadness of the times the flowers drip tears
恨別鳥驚心	A bird's cry shocks the heart, at the pain of parting

Liu Yuxi's poem *Wuyi xiang* (*Raven Gown Alley*) also deals with the collapse of a regime, in the fourth century CE, and the loss of the capital Loyang. The poem itself was written in the Tang Dynasty, when the Tang itself was in decline. Bai Xianyong's story of the same title appeared a millennium and a half later, when his book *Taibei People* was published. The recurrence of the same theme of loss and desolation carries both deep sadness, but also a glimmer of hope that sadness may pass with time.[41]

These poems came to the minds of many people as they left China, knowing that their own capital, Nanjing, was lost and they might never return. Professor Guo Licheng gave another description of the pain of parting, as he and his fellow passengers left Shanghai on a boat sailing for Taiwan:

Once the ship left the shore, the rain started. Many people remained on the deck and did not try to hide from the rain; they cared only for the last chance to look at the land they were leaving behind. On our faces there were raindrops and teardrops.[42]

---

[41] Bai Xianyong, lecture, University of British Columbia, 3 October 2013.

[42] Joshua Fan, *China's Homeless Generation: Voices from the Veterans of the Chinese Civil War* (New York: Routledge, 2011), p. 34.

7   Immediate outcomes: the early 1950s

東方紅
Dong fang hong
The East is red

By the end of 1949, China seemed to have turned red. Most of the guns were finally silent. Twelve years of war were over. The Communist Party established a new government. For the first time since the Manchu Conquest of China in the 1640s, a new power had come into China from the north, a power that represented, as the Manchus had, a sweep 'from culturally less developed to highly developed areas'.[1]

The losses of the Civil War had cut deeply into the Chinese population. In one way only was the pain less acute than it had been at the end of the Resistance War – there were fewer civilian deaths; across the country the majority of casualties of the Civil War were military. The civilian deaths were concentrated in a few places, particularly in Manchuria.

In late 1949 the CCP launched itself on the heady process of creating a new world, remaking China in its own socialist image. It set about doing what it did best, organising the people. Across China, committees, work groups and neighbourhood groups mushroomed. Political study gradually became mandatory. Slogans covered walls and any other flat surface, carrying the messages of the new regime to the people.

Many of the messages had a strong element of nationalism; the credo was that China had regained her self-respect. The CCP drew on and intensified the mass nationalism that had come into being at the start of the Resistance War. On 1 October 1949 Mao Zedong proclaimed from the Tiananmen the portentous words that moved the hearts of all those Chinese who believed that China had been subjected to more than a century of humiliation at foreign hands:

---

[1] James Gao, *The Communist Takeover of Hangzhou* (Honolulu: University of Hawaii Press, 2004), p. 4.

中国人民站起來了

Zhongguo renmin zhanqilai le
The Chinese people have stood up

The international impact

The Western world was thrown into confusion by the CCP victory. Formally speaking, in terms of diplomatic recognition, the Civil War was not over. Very few countries recognised the new government; most Western countries continued to recognise the GMD as the legitimate government of China, as did the United Nations. The PRC was established on the Mainland, but the Republic of China (ROC) still existed on Taiwan. There was a continuing state of war in which both sides had a foreign sponsor, the USSR for the PRC and the USA for the ROC. The US government poured money and advice into Taiwan, suddenly convinced that the GMD, which the US had almost given up on a short time before, was a bulwark against the march of communism in Asia. The PRC 'leant to one side (*yi bian dao*)', and moved towards the Soviet Bloc. Tens of thousands of Soviet experts arrived in the country in the early 1950s to give advice to the Chinese 'younger brother', in the fraternal relationship of socialism, about the creation of a new society – on a Soviet model.[2]

The Taiwan Straits was the front line between the two polities. With US help, Chiang Kai-shek was able to keep alive his dream of a return to the Mainland. The ROC still controlled two islands just off the Fujian coast, Quemoy (Jinmen) and Matsu (Mazu). Repeated bombing raids were launched from Taiwan, aimed especially at Nanjing. GMD military units were still active in the southwest of China and across the borders in Laos and Thailand. Its spies were in place throughout China. In 1950, on the first anniversary of the PRC, the CCP announced that 13,797 secret agents had been arrested over the past year, and 179 radio stations 'unearthed'.[3] CCP agents were active in Taiwan, with some sad results. A monument has recently been erected in the Fragrant Hills (Xiangshan) to the northwest of Beijing to more than 1,000 CCP spies, the 'unsung heroes', executed in Taiwan in the early 1950s. The relatives of the heroes are campaigning to have their remains brought home.[4]

---

[2] In Chinese there are two words for brother: 'older brother (*gege*)' and 'younger brother (*didi*)'.
[3] *The First Year of Victory* (Peking: Foreign Languages Press, 1950), p. 13.
[4] *South China Morning Post*, 11 February 2014, p. 4.

The Korean War, the first major armed conflict of the Cold War, started in June 1950, when North Korean troops crossed the 38th Parallel, the artificial line dividing North and South drawn at the end of the Second World War. US forces arrived in South Korea in July, under a sketchy UN mandate, to prevent the total collapse of South Korea. In October PRC forces, renamed the People's Volunteer Army, crossed the Yalu River between China and North Korea, after the UN/US forces had driven North Korean troops almost to the river. The PVA and North Korea drove the UN/US forces back again. After that there were two years of stalemate, before the war ended in an armistice (still in effect).

The casualties in the Korean War were enormous, well over a million dead on both sides. Both Koreas were brought to their knees economically. The war put China firmly in the Soviet Bloc from the Western point of view, known now as 'Red China', behind the 'Bamboo Curtain'.

Almost all contact with Western countries and with Overseas Chinese was lost. The victory in the Civil War, was a sign of the degree to which China had shaken off her subjugation to the West. The old comprador capitalism, Chinese merchants cooperating with Westerners, that had dominated the treaty ports, was gone for good. The old hatred of the British was now transferred to the USA, the state that China held responsible for the Korean War, and whose 7th Fleet was preventing the PLA's crossing of the Taiwan Straits and 'restoring' Taiwan to Beijing's control.

The early revolution

The CCP had come to power on the promise of revolution and of the creation of clean government and a socialist economy. One of the immediate tasks of the new government was repairing the damage of war. Within a year much of the road and railway infrastructure had been repaired, and the transport system was working again. An early and spectacular success in restoring stability, one that even today seems almost miraculous, was halting inflation. A new currency, the People's Currency (*Renminbi*) came into being, along with tough and rigorously enforced wage and price controls. The British mission in China reported a rapid improvement in the economic situation. The new government controlled the urban food supply, levied new taxes in the towns and cities, and instituted grain levies in the rural areas. The measures were tough, but they were fair, and there was no corruption.[5] Within a short time inflation was

---

[5] R. Jarman, *China: Political Reports* (Slough: Archive Editions, 2001), 20 September 1949, IX, p. 66.

a thing of the past. The relief for consumers and producers was enormous. One of the greatest sources of insecurity was gone.

The end of inflation could not settle any of the chronic economic problems. China was still desperately poor, and now, in the absence of foreign trade, had to rely on her own resources to generate revenues. There was still a great number of unemployed. The CCP dealt with unemployment in a number of ways. One was renewal of infrastructure. Legions of people were put to work repairing the transport system. There was rapid progress in rebuilding railways and roads, and training new staff.

Motivational appeals

One of the CCP's most effective techniques for winning support was to appeal to individual motivations, not only to serve the country but also to promote careers. This was particularly important in recruiting people essential to the running of key infrastructures. This is an account of the CCP's appeal to such people, one that combined idealism and self-interest – and a first chance at self-improvement. Du Xianyang was a train driver in Manchuria. He drove the Iron Bull, one of the finest locomotives in the Manchurian railway system:

Since I was a lad I have been working on the railway for more than ten years. When the Japanese were here I had to court their favour by giving them bribes from time to time in order to hold my job. They never promoted me. The Communists came and they immediately promoted me. They sent me to a school and wanted to train me to be a better driver.*

* *China's Railways: A Story of Heroic Reconstruction* (Beijing: Foreign Languages Press, 1950), p. 26.

Another method of giving the unemployed work was using mass manpower to get rid of the detritus of war and to reverse the dilapidation into which China's public buildings and spaces had sunk during the 12 years of war. Eyesores were cleaned up. The Nanjing canals, once the haunt of prostitutes and other seedy elements, were cleaned out – both the waterways and the people who had lived in the area. Lao She's 1952 drama *Dragon Beard Ditch* showed a before-and-after street in Beijing, changed from a stinking slum into a clean, healthy community, inhabited by happy, wholesome people whose once-miserable lives had been transformed by socialism.

Dragon Beard Ditch was an example of how the state used the arts to convey its message. The CCP organised a large body of writers, poets, artists and filmmakers to create works of art for its political purposes.

These people, many of them very gifted, accepted that 'politics was in command', and that their patriotic duty was to help the CCP. One example is the work of the poet Ai Qing. He had turned against the GMD and joined the communists in 1941. He became almost an official poet, writing poems for important occasions. He shared the austere life of Yan'an, and later of Zhangjiakou (Hebei) where he worked as a professor in a new university. He took part in the land reform in several parts of Hebei. In February1949 he moved to Beijing, and became a key member of the new literary elite.[6]

The revolutionary message was spread with speed and deliberation. Within a short time the CCP despatched its agents to every school, business and organisation to start the process of transforming them to socialism. The highest positions went to people known as 'commissars', from the Soviet practice. Below them where the people called *ganbu*, a key new category in Chinese society: those whose responsibilities derived from official functions conferred by the party – and thus figures of influence, and (later) of privilege.

The CCP took the promise of dividing the spoils of victory to heart. Beyond the land divided in the rural land reform, other, urban properties were confiscated and redistributed. Large houses, temples, land, private colleges and universities became the property of the people. There was some caution in taking over factories and businesses. Unless their owners had abandoned them, by departing, or had been convicted of a formal crime, they remained for the time being partially in private control, a control that was gradually whittled away.

The old, corrupt world, deliberately associated by the CCP with the GMD and now labelled 'feudal', disappeared or went underground. Bureaucratic corruption was outlawed and, at least officially, was stopped. Nepotism, special treatment for relatives, was banned. Gambling, associated with card games and *mah-jong*, was declared to be a decadent habit. Opium smoking was made illegal, and smokers were put into compulsory rehabilitation – i.e., forced to go cold turkey. Prostitution was outlawed, brothels were closed and their occupants retrained for 'decent' occupations, a process of rebirth shown in the movie *Our Fallen Sisters Have Stood Up*.[7] Beggars were swept off the streets and sent to special

---

[6] Qi Hou, *Guanyu Ai Qing (On Ai Qing)* (Singapore: Xiling, 1984), pp. 134–138. Ai Qing's devotion to the cause was not rewarded. In 1958 he was denounced as a rightist, and he and his family were sent first to the dreaded Great North Waste (Heilongjiang) and then to Xinjiang. His son Ai Weiwei has followed his father's path of honesty even in the face of persecution.

[7] I have not seen the movie. Jay Leyda mentions what must be the same film, *Stand Up Sisters* or *Peking Prostitutes Liberated*, which he himself did not see. Jay Leyda, *Dianying* (Cambridge, MA: MIT Press, 1972), p. 186.

schools to learn trades. Religious practices were labelled 'superstition'; temples and churches were restricted in their activities, an omen of the frontal attacks on the 'opium of the people' that were to come.

The excitement that many people felt about the new world, and their hope for the future, was expressed in the choice of names for babies born in the early 1950s. The old practices of using generation names or of getting the senior male on the father's side to give names to infants gave way to anti-feudal, political naming. These are the given names of two sets of three siblings born in Beijing just after 1949: Yousu (Friend of the USSR), Youhua (Friend of China), Youkang (Friend of health); Jianguo (Establish the nation), Jianping (Establish peace), Jianmin (Establish the people). Some of these names caused their bearers embarrassment later on; for example, when China broke off relations with the USSR in the early 1960s, although not quite as much embarrassment as names later given to babies during the Cultural Revolution.

China had become a red world; red was the colour of revolution. The CCP was fortunate in that revolutionary red, transmitted with Marxism, was also a propitious colour in China. Red (*hong*) was the traditional colour of happiness, the colour of wedding costumes, of the shawls in which baby boys were wrapped, and of the paper on which messages of congratulation were written. Red is the colour of envelopes filled with money distributed at the New Year, *hongbao*.[8] Red had huge symbolic meaning in China, where it was a sign of glorious renewal, and in complete contrast to foreign views, where 'red' was the colour of the new threat to the world.

Table 7.1 *The colour red: symbolic uses*

Red Dawn	The beginning of the PRC
Red flag	National flag; automobile; major newspaper
Red Flag	Communist anthem
Red star	Star on soldiers' caps
Red Scare	US fear of communism; McCarthyism

Social currents

In the early years of the PRC Chinese society was still in turmoil. The effects of the war years were enormous and long-lasting. They were accentuated by the CCP's determination to build a new society, an

[8] Diana Lary, 'Chinese Reds', in Ian Germani and Robin Swayles (eds.), *Symbols, Myths and Images of the French Revolution: Essays in honour of James Leith* (Regina: Canadian Plains Research Centre, 1998), pp. 307–320.

enormous task that would have daunted any but the most committed ideologues. The process of establishing the new world was so complex and involved so much upheaval that it created turmoil that added to that created by war.

Refugees

As if to counter and deny the enthusiasm for the new world, the huge refugee movements that had convulsed the country in 1948 and 1949 continued. There were no restrictions as yet on internal movements. From rural China members of the old elite continued to flee to the anonymity of the cities to escape the terrors of the rural revolution. They mixed in with the millions of peasants who were moving to the cities in the hopes of a better life. And a few individuals took the traditional route of escape from trouble – only ever available to the courageous and self-sufficient – and found remote places – mountains, deserts, marshes – where they could live as hermits, cut off from most human contact.

Several million people had left China by the end of 1949, fleeing on their own or with the GMD. The flight of refugees continued in the early 1950s. The bulk of these people made their way to Hong Kong often on their way to Taiwan. The number cited for those going to Taiwan is commonly two million, although a recent, very careful analysis by Dominic Yang puts the number considerably lower, possibly only a million.[9]

Well over a million others made their own way out of China, almost always to Hong Kong. This was the only viable exit point from China; very few people wanted to cross into the Soviet Union; the French strongly discouraged refugees from moving into Indo-China. The Hong Kong population almost quadrupled between the end of the Resistance War and the early 1950s, from just over half a million to over two million. An early part of the influx was made up of refugees from Hong Kong itself returning after the end of the Resistance War. Another larger part was made up of Cantonese and people from further north who knew they could not live under communism. They flooded into the colony in the last half of 1949, as many as a million people in that period alone. Arrivals continued for many years. In 1950 as many as 100,000 refugees were coming into Hong Kong in a month. The Hong Kong authorities allowed the refugees to stay, seeing, with more far-sightedness than the

---

[9] Dominic Yang, 'Wuling niandai waisheng zhongxia jieceng junmin zai Taiwan de shehuishi chutan' ('A preliminary social history of the ordinary mainlander migrants in Taiwan during the 1950s'), in Taiwan jiaoshou xiehui (ed.), *Zhonghua minguo liuwang Taiwan liushinian ji zhanhou Taiwan guoji chujing* (*Sixty Years since the Republic's Flight to Taiwan and Leaving for Abroad in Post-war Taiwan*) (Taipei: Qianwei chubanshe, 2010), pp. 523–599.

CCP, that these people would help to build the future prosperity of the colony.

Some of the refugees brought money with them, but many were impoverished. A UN report in 1953 estimated that of the refugee 'specialists' (educated people, former police and soldiers, members of what the report called 'sedentary professions' such as lawyers and bankers), 85 per cent were unemployed and destitute.[10] On Hong Kong's steep hillsides squatter settlements mushroomed. The incomers contributed to the beginning of Hong Kong's economic boom. Cantonese refugees settled easily into a familiar world. Those from further north tended to settle in linguistic enclaves, for example the large Shanghai settlement that developed at North Point.

Some refugees were only passing through Hong Kong. Mang Yuqin, a Mongol woman married to a GMD police officer, had missed the special evacuation flight from Shenyang, for which she had a ticket, in November 1948. Her husband got away, but she was stranded. Two years later she got a clandestine message from her husband, via a friend in Beijing. She decided to leave, and with great difficulty managed to do so. She knew the journey to Hong Kong from north China would be very difficult. She took her older children with her, but left her youngest daughter with her mother, promising to return soon to pick up the child. She moved on to Taiwan from Hong Kong. She did not see her daughter again for 35 years.[11]

The precise number of departures from China just before and after the communist conquest is impossible to tell; no one was keeping exit statistics. The departures were spread out over quite a long period. But the number was certainly in the low millions, probably fewer than the number of people who fled from Russia after the Russian Revolution in 1917.

Soldiers

Millions of men and a few women who had served in the armies of both sides had to remake their lives at the end of the Civil War. There was no mass demobilisation of the PLA in 1950, because of the Korean War, but some soldiers did leave the armies. Few of them went home. Some of the best young soldiers were transferred to local administration in the south and southwest, the *nanxia ganbu*. Other PLA veterans looked for their own opportunities, some following the old tradition in Shandong

---

[10] United Nations, *Report by the High Commissioner Concerning the Question of Chinese Refugees in Hong Kong* (New York: United Nations, 1953), p. 3.

[11] Lo Jiu-jung, Yu Chien-ming and Chiu Hei-yuan (eds.), *Fenghuo suiyue xia de Zhongguo funu* (*Chinese Women in the Fires of War*) (Taibei: Zhongyang yanjiuyuan Jindaishi suo, 2004), pp. 362, 272–274.

and Hebei provinces of migrating to Manchuria. They found jobs in the factories and mines there, which were just getting going again after prolonged closure during the Civil War. 'Patriotic fighters (*aiguo zhanshi*)' were given precedence over other applicants for jobs.

The PLA divested itself of many of its weaker soldiers, especially those who had been in the puppet armies. These men were simply given train tickets to their home place. Other units remained intact, but hardly benefited from their switch to the CCP. They were drafted into the fighting in Korea from 1950 on, essentially as cannon fodder.

War Trash

Soldiers seldom write detailed accounts of their lives. Their diaries, if they keep them, are terse and unemotional. PLA soldiers were even less likely to write about their experiences, since very many of them were illiterate. This dearth of stories of war makes Ha Jin's novel *War Trash* exceptionally valuable.* Ha Jin (Jin Xuefei) is from a military family in Heilongjiang. He grew up listening to the stories of soldiers, and heard accounts that were never written down. The novel is the story of a young GMD officer who surrendered to the PLA in 1949 and was then sent to Korea, where he was soon captured on the battlefield. The next years, before he was released and returned to China, were spent in prison camps in southern Korea, in a nightmarish world in which GMD operatives appeared to try and persuade prisoners to go to Taiwan, while communist activists put pressure in the opposite direction. It is a bleak, deeply moving portrait that must be based on a close family connection. One clue is that the young officer eventually sees his beloved son move to the USA – as Ha Jin himself did.

* Ha Jin, *War Trash* (New York: Pantheon, 2004).

The GMD soldiers left behind on the Mainland were in deep trouble. Many had deserted from their units towards the end of the war, and had gone home or to the cities. They had to disguise their pasts. Those who had not surrendered and still considered themselves soldiers fled into the wilds of the border regions and into the hills and marshes, the traditional haunts of outlaws. Former GMD soldiers were active in resistance to the CCP until well into the early 1950s. Their lives were harsh, but not harsher than those of their fellow soldiers who had surrendered or been captured. Large numbers of former GMD soldiers were exiled to the military farms, organised as the Production and Construction Corps (*Shengchan jianshe bingtuan*, shortened to *Bingtuan*) in Xinjiang and other northern border regions. In northern Heilongjiang a vast, marshy region with the dismal name of the Great North Waste (Beidahuang) was designated to become China's new bread basket. There the soldier-exiles lived in the harshest conditions, enduring brutal winters and plagued by gigantic mosquitoes in summer, their lives shared after 1958 with political exiles, the victims of the Anti-Rightist purges.[12]

The soldiers who got away to Taiwan fared better. The GMD command kept its main military units around Taibei, and on the now heavily fortified west coast of the island, facing Fujian. The best troops were rotated in and out of the island of Jinmen (Quemoy), only a few miles off the Fujian coast. The island was celebrated internationally as one of the bastions in the Cold War, an Asian counterpart to West Berlin, the stand-out against communism in Europe.[13] The GMD military billeted many of its soldiers in Japanese barracks in Taiwan. Others, including veterans, were settled in new military villages (*juncun*) in remote parts of Taiwan, such as Hualian, on the rugged east coast, previously almost uninhabited. The film director Ang Lee (Li An) grew up in a *juncun* there in the 1950s. His father was school principal and also in charge of education for the veterans. Lee describes his childhood, in a world made up entirely of people from the Mainland, with warmth and affection. It brought him a good education and a strong grounding in traditional popular Chinese culture, an influence that has showed up in many of his films.[14]

Neither the CCP nor the GMD military paid much attention to wounded soldiers, either those who had suffered physical injuries or those who had been wounded psychologically – suffering from the then-unrecognised but very real syndrome of post-traumatic stress disorder. The brutalising effects of war were even stronger in the Civil War than they had been in the Resistance War. Veterans suffered the trauma of having killed or injured their own people. They had to suppress these memories. They had committed acts that could not be openly remembered, acts that reflected far worse on them than the killing of a 'devil (*guizi*)' would have done.[15]

---

[12] Wang Ning's PhD thesis, *Great Northern Wilderness: political exiles in the People's Republic of China* (Vancouver: University of British Columbia, 2005) gives detailed descriptions of the lives of those sent to Beidahuang.

[13] Michael Szonyi, *Cold War Island: Quemoy on the Front Line* (Cambridge: Cambridge University Press, 2008).

[14] Li An (Ang Lee), *Shinian yijiao: Dianying meng (A Ten-Year Dream Come True: Film)* (Taibei: Shibao wenhua, 2002), pp. 18–26.

[15] *Guizi* (ghost) was the name commonly used by Chinese people for the Japanese.

Foreigners

The number of foreigners living in China declined dramatically after 1949. The great foreign companies (*hongs*) that had dominated China's trade for a century and more had wound up their affairs in China, under persistent pressure from the new authorities to make doing business virtually impossible. Smaller businessmen left China under the same pressure, usually forced to renounce their holdings in the country. Christian missionaries left China, either under CCP pressure or because their home churches closed the missions. By 1953 almost all had left. The century of foreign efforts to convert Chinese to Christianity seemed to have failed.[16]

Some foreigners stayed on. One part of the now-tiny foreign community was made up of White Russians, the remnants of a once large community. During its occupation of Manchuria the Soviet Red Army forced some White Russians back into Siberia. Others managed to get to the USA and Australia. Those who were left behind continued to exist in the same hand-to-mouth way they had lived since they first came to China. The Russian world slowly faded away; churches, schools and restaurants that once served the community closed. In Harbin, a city whose skyline had been dominated by the elaborate spires of Russian Orthodox churches, the beautiful Church of St Nicholas was closed; it was later demolished by Red Guards in the Cultural Revolution. Other churches survived, but were closed for decades.

A number of foreign spouses of Chinese citizens stayed with their families after 1949. Most of them were wives, devoted to their husbands and children, who could not leave China. Some foreign wives had lost their citizenship on their marriage to a Chinese husband (for instance American and Dutch women). Other foreigners stayed in China out of ideological conviction, their belief in communism. Rewi Alley (New Zealand) and Anna Louise Strong (USA), the officially anointed leaders of the tiny foreign community, were active propagandists for the new government.[17] Others found careers in the propaganda world. Gerry Tannenbaum (USA) acted the imperialist villain in many movies.

---

[16] This turned out not to be the case. Over the past two decades the number of Christians in China has shot up, into the tens, possibly hundreds, of millions.

[17] Rewi Alley and Anna Louise Strong lived on different floors of the former residence of the Italian ambassador, a choice address in the centre of Beijing. They detested each other and never spoke.

The Western communists were soon heavily outnumbered by the Soviet and Eastern European communists who came to act as technical advisors to China in the 1950s. All over China large compounds of luxury apartments were built to house the experts, the Friendship Hotels (*Youyi binguan*). There they lived hermetically sealed off from the Chinese population. Soviets were the dominant foreigners in the new China – and to some people they seemed to be new imperialists, a characterisation made public in vicious propaganda after the Sino-Soviet split in 1960, after which all the advisors left China.

Continuing reunions and returns

For many Chinese the years after the end of the Civil War meant reunions with family and friends, after years of wartime separations. In the early 1950s six of the eight Ye brothers, who had been scattered all across China during the Resistance War, were back in north China, four in Beijing and two in Tianjin. One brother, Ye Duzheng, returned from America, drawn home by love of his country. The brothers' wartime experiences as young men had 'carried them far from their sheltered lives in a wealthy Tientsin [Tianjin] family'.[18] They were ready to work with and for the new regime; they welcomed the Red Dawn.

A number of Chinese students and scholars abroad in 1949 returned to China in the early 1950s, motivated by patriotism. The young academic Wu Ningkun abandoned his doctoral studies in the USA to go back to China:

I felt an inseparable bond to the ancient homeland, which had filled my early life with poverty, grief, loneliness, humiliation, insecurity and the ravages of war. The lure of a meaningful life in a brave new world outweighed the attraction of a doctorate and a comfortable life in an alien land.[19]

His reference to an 'alien land' was one that would have resonated with many Chinese intellectuals living in the West; very few of them were treated at the time in a way that their academic accomplishments merited, and many did feel 'alien' in the West to the end of their days.

---

[18] Joseph Esherick, *Ancestral Leaves: A Family Journey Through Chinese History* (Berkeley: University of California Press, 2011), pp. 218–219. For several of the brothers the choice turned out to be a bad one; they suffered horribly in the Cultural Revolution because of their class background.

[19] Wu Ningkun, *A Single Tear* (New York: Atlantic Monthly, 1993), p. 5. Wu was wrong in his optimism; the next three decades brought him and his family nothing but grief.

Some of those who returned from abroad did so because they were overtly rejected in the USA. The most famous of these was the stiff-necked missile scientist Qian Xuesen. He played a major role in the US missile programme in the 1940s, but he was stripped of his security clearance in the early 1950s, at the depth of the 'Red Scare', and spent several years in California under virtual house arrest. This insulting treatment turned him against the US for ever – and was a strategic error of major proportions for the US. Eventually in 1955 he and his wife, Jiang Ying – daughter of the famous military thinker Jiang Baili – and their two children were deported to China, taking nothing with them but Qian's intellectual brilliance and his high-level knowledge of rocketry. He put this to use in building China's space industry, and subsequently became known as the 'father of the Chinese space programme'.[20] At least two dozen other Chinese scientists left the US on the same boat as Qian. His expulsion has since been seen as one of the greatest strategic mistakes the US made during the Cold War.

Migrations

The course of the Civil War covered 3,000 kilometres from Manchuria in the far north to the far south. It brought with it massive southward movements of people. The exact figures are impossible to know, since no one was keeping statistics at the time, but they must have been in the tens of millions.

Some of the southward movers were people on their way out of China, as refugees. Others were people moved by the CCP itself, initially only soldiers, but then some of their dependants. Northern soldiers moved into the south, with or following the armies. Besides the *nanxia ganbu* ordinary soldiers were sent to the south and west, to work on major building projects, and then settled there. A third category of migrants moved of their own accord (*zifa*), looking for new opportunities, taking over positions vacated by GMD supporters in local government and education who had fled or been dismissed.

A large number of peasants saw the revolutionary upheaval as the chance they had often yearned for, to move off the land and into the cities. By 1953, 27 million people had moved off the land and into

---

[20] Iris Chang, *Thread of the Silkworm* (New York: Basic, 1995). When Qian's US security clearance was taken away, and with it his ability to work on sensitive issues, he at first tried to go back to China, but was refused permission to leave the US because of his knowledge of classified material.

the cities, amounting to about a third of the total urban population.[21] There was nothing to prevent them from moving. Their numbers put great burdens on the cities, and was one of the reasons why restrictions on freedom of movement were introduced in the late 1950s, the population registration (*hukou*) system that prevented any unsanctioned migration.

Separations

The end of the Civil War brought immediate separations to millions of Chinese families: the families of soldiers taken to Taiwan; the families of people who went to Hong Kong or abroad; the families of people close to the GMD who had been captured by the incoming communists; and the families of PLA soldiers sent to the south.

Separations were not just physical, but also emotional and economic. Family members left behind on the Mainland by refugees not only lost people they cared for, but often, especially if they were women or children, all forms of economic support. The families that GMD soldiers taken to Taiwan left behind on the Mainland had to fend for themselves. They received no army pensions, nor could the soldiers in Taiwan send money home. There was no news from them. They had turned into ghosts. One of the cruellest aspects of the separations was that no connection of any kind was permitted – no letters, phone calls, not even news of deaths. This situation continued into the late 1970s. Neither side, not the CCP nor the GMD, permitted any open connections. Some people managed to pass news via underground channels from Hong Kong, but for many there was only silence.

The political impact on the relatives at home of those abroad was severe. The existence of a relative outside China had ominous repercussions. It was potential proof of political unreliability. The words *haiwai guanxi* (foreign connections) were full of menace, and, at times of political foment, especially in the Cultural Revolution, acutely dangerous. There was little understanding of how and why people had left China. The assumption was that those who had left were deserters, unpatriotic, selfish and, worst of all, un-Chinese. In fact little of this was true. Many of those who had left were taken away by the GMD. Others happened to be caught away by the vicissitudes of the Civil War. Wang Xiangtan had a job that took him to Taiwan at the end of the Resistance War. He and his three sons were marooned in Taiwan at the end of the Civil War, while

---

[21] Cao Shuji, *Zhongguo yimin shi* (*History of Chinese Migration*) (Fuzhou: Fujian renmin chubanshe, 1997), VI, pp. 606–607.

his wife and daughter Xiaorong were left in Beijing. Like others whose relatives were known to have gone to Taiwan, the two were regarded with the greatest suspicion by the new authorities.[22]

In Taiwan and Hong Kong, the dawning realisation after 1949 that some family members and friends had stayed in the Mainland by choice was a bitter one. Those separations seemed like betrayals of those who had left China. One of the three orphaned sons of Bai Chongxi's close colleague, Yu Xingcha, whom Bai had brought up in his own household, went over to the CCP and stayed in China; he became the head of the Changchun Aeronautical College.[23]

On Taiwan, the pain of separation was intense and long-lasting. Many of the Mainlanders who settled in Taiwan were consumed with loss and guilt; although they had few details about what was happening in China, they suspected the worst, and GMD propaganda about the horrors of communism encouraged them to do so:

Many of those who came to Taiwan did so at the expense of those left behind, those who had made a sacrifice for them so that they could survive. Now these survivors couldn't face up to the guilt they carried with them, like dead corpses, like the corpses of those they now imagined rotting in Communist gaols or starving in work camps.[24]

They were right to worry, not only about how their families were coping but about what had happened to their former colleagues.

The Taiwan/Mainland separation was only one form of family separation. Many families were scattered in all directions. The Yu family were Christians, the father a professor in a Christian seminary in Nanjing and, during the Resistance War, in Chengdu. The father never thought of leaving China when the CCP came to power; he believed that there were similarities between the CCP's ideology and the Christian beliefs of equality, brotherly love and honesty. After 1949 he moved to Shanghai and worked as an editor. His four sons went in four quite different directions; the family was almost completely divided for the next four decades. The oldest brother, Yu Chengzhong, became a radical during the Civil War, stayed in

---

[22] Ji Chaozhu, *The Man on Mao's Right* (New York: Random House, 2008), pp. 162–163. Wang Xiaorong is Ji's wife.

[23] Bai Xianyong, *Fuqin yu Minguo (Father and the Republic)* (Taibei: Shibao, 2012), II, p. 80. Yu was 'struggled' so ferociously in the Cultural Revolution because of his connections in Taiwan that he committed suicide.

[24] Mahlon Meyer, *Revolutionary China from Taiwan: Divided Families and Bittersweet Reunions After the Chinese Civil War* (Hong Kong: Hong Kong University Press, 2012), p. 68. This deeply felt book is based on interviews with a series of elderly Mainlanders in Taiwan and their descendants.

Nanjing and worked as a teacher. The second brother, Yu Chengxia, had no choice but to leave China. He was in the GMD Air Force and was evacuated to Taiwan well before the end of the war. The third brother, Yu Chengjie, who was 16 at the end of the Civil War, went into the medical branch of the PLA. He left China a decade and a half later, in 1963, with his wife Helen, whose father was Canadian. The youngest brother, Yu Chengyi, went into machine tool manufacture and was sent to work in Qiqihaer (Heilongjiang). The large family had disappeared, but the brothers' existence was not forgotten, either by the brothers themselves or by others. During the Cultural Revolution both the oldest and the youngest brothers suffered severely for having brothers abroad – the dreaded *haiwai guanxi*.[25] During the years of separation the brothers did not dare to write letters to each other, and so had very little idea about each other's lives. They were reunited only in the 1980s. This kind of separation, caused by many different factors, was so common in the Mao era that it almost became the norm – a sad one, which denied the closeness of family ties.

Some family separations came about because a family member went into China from outside the country. The departure of the two brothers of Stanley Kwan for China turned out to be the end of the extended Kwan family. In the early 1950s the Mainland brothers could visit occasionally, but they gradually grew apart from the family in Hong Kong. Another brother moved to Singapore, and Stanley himself eventually moved to Canada. Kwan recognised that the old family had gone for good. 'The large family in which I grew up had started to decline in the late 1930s, and the war and the Communist revolution precipitated its dissolution. Many large traditional families in Hong Kong suffered a similar fate.'[26]

Other large families were destroyed in the wake of a member's arrest. Shen Zui, a henchman of Dai Li – head of the GMD secret service, the Juntong – was captured by the CCP in Yunnan at the very end of 1949. His wife had already gone to Hong Kong with their six children. The couple was separated permanently. She was penniless and had to marry again to survive, at which point his brother took four of the six children off to Taiwan. Of the other two, one died and another was sent back to relatives in Changsha. Shen was in jail for ten years. He was reunited

[25] Interview with John and Helen Yu, Vancouver, 8 July 2013.
[26] Stanley Kwan, *The Dragon and the Crown* (Hong Kong: Hong Kong University Press, 2009), p. 91. Stanley Kwan was one of those behind the creation of the Hang Seng Index.

with the daughter from Changsha, but never with any of the other four children.[27]

The most celebrated separated family was the Song family. Song Qingling, the widow of Sun Yat-sen, stayed on the Mainland and became, in effect, the First Lady of China; Mao Zedong's own wife, Jiang Qing, was invisible. Her sister Song Meiling, the wife of Chiang Kai-shek, went to Taiwan with her husband, the glamorous First Lady of the Republic. There was a sad irony in that the two sisters occupied almost identical positions in two regimes at bitter enmity with each other. Song Ailing, the oldest sister, and their brother Song Ziwen went to the USA almost immediately after 1949. The siblings never met together again. Song Ziwen died in 1971, Song Ailing in 1973. Song Qingling died in 1981; she was revered in China as the 'mother of the nation', but she had no family of her own to comfort her in her old age. Song Meiling lived on until 2003; she died in New York at the age of (at least) 105.[28]

Families of CCP supporters, especially those in the army, also experienced long-term separations. They were expected to go and serve the revolution wherever the party directed them to go. They might or might not be able to take their families with them. Demobilised soldiers were sent out to the south and to the borderlands. Industrial workers were sent to Manchuria to get the plants going again. Intellectuals were sent wherever they seemed to be needed. Age and marital status were often secondary considerations when someone was sent off to serve socialism. Young mothers were encouraged to leave their babies with their mothers. If they were lucky they would see them once a year at the Lunar New Year.

Along the way all these family separations helped to break down traditional parent–child and sibling relations. These had traditionally been some of the key social relationships. Now, with family members going in so many different directions, they were eroded. Love and affection might survive, but the everyday pleasure of family life was gone for many people. So too were the quarrels and disagreements, the dramas that were another common feature of family life. In the new socialist community quarrelling was frowned on, since it took away from serving socialism. Community leaders felt it their right to

[27] Shen Zui, *KMT War Criminal in New China* (Beijing: Foreign Languages Press, 1986).
[28] There was some doubt about her actual age, in the absence of birth certificates, which were not issued in China at the time of her birth.

intervene and sort people out, a task that appealed enormously to natural busybodies.

The big family has never been reborn. With the coming of birth control and the policies on strict limitation of family size, the old big family passed into history. One of the cornerstones of traditional society disappeared.

Biographies

Paul Lin

Paul Lin (Lin Daguang) was born and brought up in Vernon, British Columbia, the youngest son of an Anglican clergyman, Reverend George Lim, and his wife. He was a brilliant student, and an activist for the Chinese cause during the Resistance War; he was the head of the Chinese Christian Association of North America. While he was working on his PhD at Harvard he became increasingly enthusiastic about the brewing revolution in China. This enthusiasm got him into trouble in the USA as a 'subversive'. He abandoned his thesis and he and his family left for China. He identified not with his native country, Canada, but with the country he had never seen: 'I knew in my heart that it was time to "go home" and offer my skills for my people's future.'[29] He happened to arrive in China on the same boat as the writer Lao She, coming home from his long stay in New York. Lin was soon using his mellifluous English as a radio announcer for the English service of Radio Peking.

Lin's decision to move to China was based in great part on a profound, almost religious idealism about the future of China under socialism. The idealism diminished with time, and became 'idealistic pragmatism'. The family left China and returned to Canada just before the start of the Cultural Revolution. He remained deeply committed to China and, as China's reputation changed over time, became one of the most prominent Chinese Canadians and advocates for better relations with China. The one exception was his passionate denunciation of the government's repression of the Democracy Movement and the massacre in Beijing (*Liusi*) in 1989.

---

[29] Paul and Eileen Lin, *In the Eyes of the China Storm* (Montreal: McGill Queens, 2011), p. 59.

Fig. 17 PuYi as emperor of Manzhouguo

PuYi

Aisin-Golo Pu Yi was the last emperor of the Qing Dynasty. He abdicated in 1912, at the age of six. Two decades later the diffident and ineffectual young man was installed by the Japanese as the first (and last) emperor of the puppet state of Manzhouguo. He lived an aimless life in a mini-palace built for him in Xinjing (Changchun), accompanied by a number of wives and some elderly courtiers. In 1945 he was captured by the Soviet Army and taken into the USSR. There he stayed until the CCP came to power, when he was returned to China from the USSR. He spent another decade in detention, and was then released, to spend a quiet retirement in Beijing. With the help of historians he wrote an account of his life before 1949.[30] A lush, romantic version of

[30] Aisin-Golo PuYi, *From Emperor to Citizen* (New York: Oxford University Press, 1987).

Pu Yi's sad life was recorded in Bernardo Bertolucci's lavish film *The Last Emperor* (1987).

Sir John Keswick

Sir John Keswick, the *taipan* (chief executive) of Jardine's, one of the greatest of the China coast trading companies, stayed on in the company's headquarters in Shanghai after the communist takeover. His aim was to keep his company's trade going under the new anti-capitalist regime. He was the third generation of his family to head the company, one of the original British companies that had developed the China trade, part of which, in the nineteenth century, had involved opium. His Scottish forbears had gone through more than a century of wars and upheavals in China, always managing to keep the company's trade going. He assumed that he would be able to deal with the CCP too, but the demands made by the new regime made trading impossible. He left China in September 1951, and the company's affairs in China were wound up: 'After 120 years Jardine's were out of China, but not without hope of a new trading relationship in the future.'[31] His optimism was well-founded. Jardine's continued trading, with its headquarters now in Hong Kong, and was eventually able to get back into China, although its headquarters stayed in Hong Kong.

Esther Winnington

Esther Cheo Ying, the child of a Chinese father and an English mother, was brought up as a virtual orphan in the Midlands. Her father had returned to China, and her mother was often absent. In February 1949, aged 17, she managed with great ingenuity and bravado to get to China to look for her father. She married a young Chinese airman, who arranged for her to travel to China with him and a group of Chinese returning from England to serve the New China. Her search for her father ended disastrously. Shortly after she arrived in China she learned that he had been sentenced to eight years reform through labour in the northwest. The father and daughter never met.

Esther stayed in China, although not with her first husband. She served in the PLA and worked at the Xinhua News Agency. She went on to marry the British journalist Alan Winnington. She has written a vivid memoir

---

[31] Maggie Keswick, *The Thistle and the Jade* (London: Octopus, 1980), p. 222.

of the early days of the PRC.[32] Much later she returned to England and became the principal of a primary school.

Wu Jianxiong

Wu Jianxiong was an outstanding experimental physicist, the leading Chinese woman scientist of her generation.[33] She was born in 1912 in Shanghai. She was a brilliant child, adored and nurtured by her teacher father. She went to university in Beijing, and in 1936 went to the USA to do her PhD. Her career was stellar, particularly given that she had to overcome the dual disadvantages of being foreign and a woman. During the war she worked on the Manhattan Project. Later she moved to Columbia University. She worked closely with two other China-born physicists, Li Zongdao (T. D. Lee) and Yang Zhenning (Franklin Yang).

In 1957 Li and Yang shared the Nobel Prize for Physics; Wu's contribution was not mentioned. This oversight has been compared to the lack of recognition of the role of Rosalind Franklin in DNA research in the United Kingdom, the work for which James Watson, Francis Crick and Maurice Wilkins won a Nobel Prize. (Franklin died before that prize was awarded to Watson, Crick and Wilkins, and would not have been eligible for it, but the lack of recognition for her contributions later sparked indignation.) Yang, Li and Wu all stayed away from China for many decades, during which they achieved outstanding success in the USA. Their absence from China deprived the country of a leading role in the world of physics.

Lung Ying-t'ai (Long Yingtai)

The celebrated writer was born in Taiwan in 1952, the first child of a Mainland family to be born on the island; her given name includes the character *tai*, for Taiwan. She grew up in the south of the island, where there were few Mainlanders (known in Taiwan as *waisheng* – people from another province). She started writing as a young woman, and made a reputation as a brilliant and provocative writer. She spent part of her adult life in Germany, with her German husband and their sons. On her return to Asia she enjoyed a major career as a writer and later, in 2012, as minister of culture in Taiwan. Her recent book *Da Jiang Da Hai 1949* is

---

[32] Esther Cheo Ying, *Black Country Girl in Red China* (London: Hutchinson, 1980).
[33] Gloria Lubkin, 'Chien-hsiung Wu [Wu Jianxiong], the First Lady of Physics Research', *Smithsonian*, 1 (January 1971), pp. 52–56; and Jiang Caijian, *Wu Jianxiong: Wuli kexue de diyi furen* (*Wu Jianxiong: The First Lady of Physics*) (Taibei: Shiji wenhua, 1996).

one of the first books to deal with the tragic and often almost accidental experiences of the 1949 exiles from the Mainland. Much of the book is based on interviews with people on both sides of the Taiwan Straits. The book was a bestseller in Taiwan and Hong Kong, but has been banned on the Mainland.[34]

---

[34] Lung Ying-t'ai, *Da Jiang Da Hai 1949* (*Great River Great Ocean 1949*) (Taibei: Tianxia, 2010).

8   Social outcomes of the Civil War

In 1949 it was not entirely clear that the communist hold on China was permanent. The new government had formidable enemies, across the Taiwan Strait and across the Pacific. By the end of the Korean War (1953), however, what might have seemed to those enemies a temporary upheaval had solidified, bringing with it a series of permanent and radical changes. The changes at the top of the political system were locked in. Major parts of the economy were rapidly brought under state control. The social order was up-ended, the old bottom became the top, the old top the bottom. In Marxist terminology, 'a new world was in birth'. Whether it would be a utopia or a nightmare remained to be seen.[1]

Politics took command of all aspects of life. Mao Zedong became a godhead. Political movements roared through China in the 1950s and 1960s. Everything was black or white; no greys were allowed. China was launched on a period of intense activism, with struggle the watchword.

与天斗 与地斗 与人斗
Yu tian dou, yu di dou, yu ren dou
Struggle against heaven, against earth, against man

Struggle meant constant activity: meetings, study sessions, small and large campaigns. The state and its ideology took precedence over personal or family interests. *Geren de shi, wulun duo da, ye shi xiao shi* (personal matters, no matter how large, are small matters) – this was the watchword of the new order.

The new state was puritan. It outlawed social evils – prostitution, gambling, drug taking, sexual licence – and launched campaigns against communicable diseases, among them venereal disease. Ostentatious wealth was banned. People looked different; everyone began to wear simple,

---

[1] Frank Dikotter's recent book (which came out after this one was written) gives, in awful and relentless detail, the view of the post-1949 period as a monumental tragedy: *The Tragedy of the Chinese Revolution* (London: Bloomsbury, 2013). His view is now widely accepted in the West, although not in China. The book does not explain, however, why so many Chinese welcomed the CCP.

often dark cotton clothing, the costume of the common people. Long gowns and *qipao*, made in velvet, silk or satin, were no longer on public display. The new order was promoted as clean, virtuous and equitable. Mao Zedong's vision was that a simple life, even one of poverty, should be welcomed as the starting point for real human progress. His slogan in the early 1950s was 'poor and blank'.

一窮二白

Yi qiong er bai
One poor two blank

Yiqiong erbai meant material poverty and backwardness in culture, science and technology. Like other great thinkers, from Jesus Christ to Mahatma Ghandi, Mao grasped the enormous, often compelling, attraction of an ascetic, spare life devoted to a great cause, a life that seemed clean and pure.

Daily life changed fundamentally. Old ways of speaking to others disappeared. People now addressed each other as 'comrade' (*tongzhi*), a term literally meaning 'common will'. Life was dominated by slogans, one for almost any occasion; they were pasted on walls, blared over loudspeakers, chanted by activists and children. They were both traditional and contemporary. They were traditional in that they were derived from the *chengyu*, so much loved in popular culture, and in that they looked elegant and even artistic, especially those, such as Mao Zedong's own slogans, which were written in calligraphy. They departed from the traditional in that their meanings were socialist and often harsh. They were pithy and direct. In a few characters they called on people to overturn the old order. Slogans had a dual function, political and educational. The written form, in simple, large characters, were a way to get the vast number of illiterates (perhaps 70 per cent of the population) to understand the political message and at the same time to edge towards literacy.

This brave new world was not designed to be a happy one for the many people who were on the wrong side of the CCP. The positive vision of the future came with a need for a counterpoint; it called for enemies. The attacks on those held to be enemies (former elites, anyone with foreign connections, religious groups) were frightening. Some of them were launched under the legal rubric of the suppression of counter-revolutionaries, under a law promulgated in early 1951, but many were conducted outside any legal framework. The viciousness and venom, the intensely personal nature of the attacks on individuals and groups in the early 1950s were in theory designed to instil revolutionary discipline and fervour. They drew on the anger, envy and bitterness created by the miseries of the 12 years of war that had just ended. The vitriol spoke to a society that was deeply divided and full of unhappiness.

A class society

The Resistance War had united Chinese under the banner of nationalism and resistance to foreign invasion. After 1949 China was re-divided, not by region or by religion, but by class. The degree of division was emphasised by the new regime as it launched itself on campaigns of class struggle and the promotion of the dictatorship of the proletariat. The regime seemed obsessed with putting people into categories, and with establishing quotas of how many, or what proportion of a large population, should be in each category.

As a socialist party the CCP was committed to class struggle, a commitment it embraced with enthusiasm; the end was the reversal of the old order. Society was redesigned as an upside-down pyramid, made up of distinct strata, with the proletariat (working class) and the peasantry at the top, and the old elites at the bottom.

This process was wildly exciting for those who had been at the bottom of the old pyramid, equally fearful for those formerly at or near the top of it. Class struggle used different tactics in different parts of China. In the rural areas the Communist Party already had many years of experience in various forms of class struggle, especially in the bitter struggles of rural revolution. Class struggle implied violence. Millions of people designated as landlords, counter-revolutionaries or bad elements were executed. In the urban areas the process was less violent.

The process of class struggle was public. Public meetings, attended by whole populations, were held in villages and urban communities throughout China, a continuation of the practice in the CCP-held areas during the Civil War. The aim was to establish where people belonged in the pyramid. The meetings often involved direct attacks on those designated as 'class enemies', who were 'struggled' – i.e., ferociously attacked. Sometimes the meetings involved self-reporting, in which people had to state their class, which was then approved or refuted by others in their community. In the self-reporting many of those once prosperous or at least self-sufficient tried to get their class status reduced, closer to the former bottom.

In the rural areas, land reform, a key part of class struggle, had started in the late 1940s and continued into the early 1950s in the areas that came late under CCP control. It was a crude process. 'The land reform process involved transforming exceedingly complex property, employment and personal relationships into simple class formulas.'[2] In the many villages of China dominated by a single lineage or extended family, class classification and class struggle meant that people of the same descent and the same surname turned against each other. This was such a fraught process that it could often only be achieved by bringing in outside activists to organise class struggle meetings.

In the cities the process of class classification was less traumatic. It was often impossible to classify people into the limited number of categories available. Some members of 'bad' categories were acceptable if the designation was modified by the adjective 'patriotic', for instance 'patriotic capitalist', as opposed to 'comprador capitalist', one with foreign connections. It was difficult to make class assessments by the amount of property owned. People with a high degree of survival skills made smart adjustments in their class status. Rose Xiong, the daughter of the former prime minister Xiong Xiling, donated the massive Xiong mansion in Beijing (which had been trashed during the Resistance War) to the city and moved into a modest complex of three courtyards. She lived in one and brought in a number of 'relatives' – people with the same rather rare surname Xiong – to live in the other courtyards. Their numbers balanced out her single occupancy of a whole courtyard.[3]

The CCP showed an extraordinary bitterness and harshness towards many of its opponents who fell into its hands. This was especially true of men from the GMD armies. Captured GMD officers were referred to as 'war criminals (*zhanfan*)', even though most of their careers had been spent fighting *for* China.

The process of class classification involved artificial streamlining and simplification, since the class strata were few, but individual and family circumstances much more complicated. The general theme was clear, the implementation anything but. Class struggle turned out to be an artificial and often clumsy way of realigning society and rectifying past inequities. Every family had to be classified. The best classifications were the 'five red categories (*hong wu lei*)': worker, poor peasant, revolutionary official, revolutionary soldier, revolutionary martyr. The worst classifications were the 'four black categories (*hei si lei*)': landlord, rich peasant, counter-revolutionary, bad element. Later on two 'black' categories were added: 'rightist (*youpai*)' after 1957, and 'capitalist roader (*zouzipai*)' after 1965. In the Cultural Revolution the number of categories

[2] Joseph Esherick, 'War and Revolution', *Twentieth Century China*, XXVII (November 2001), p. 25.
[3] Interview with Rose Hsiung (Xiong), Beijing, January 1965.

rose. The additions were intellectuals, moral degenerates, renegades and enemy agents: intellectuals were known as 'stinking ninth (*chou lai jiu*)'. Under this arbitrary categorisation millions of lives were damaged or destroyed, when people were deemed 'enemies'.

No Chinese was allowed to be without a classification and a class status (*jieji chengfen*), which was almost impossible to change. Class was one of the items listed on identity cards, along with name, date of birth and province and county of origin. Class was inherited, through the 'chain of blood (*xuetong*)'. The designation was extended to their families, a practice applied across the board in class designations. Children of landlords who had already been stripped of their property became 'children of former landlords'. In the late 1950s a new political designation was applied to children whose parents were attacked in the Anti-Rightist Movement; they were *youpai ernu* (sons and daughters of rightists). These designations had severe consequences: denial of education; denial of good jobs; transfer to remote regions; refusal of permission to marry someone of a better background. Young people had to marry within their class. The state gave preference to those in the now desirable classes, and put up barriers for those descended from wealthy or landlord backgrounds.

Mainland social change

Separations

Class struggle divided Chinese society; the new socialist policies of the CCP separated people from their families. Those who had turned away from their families in political disagreement before the revolution might or might not restore relations with their families after 1949. As we have seen, Deng Xiaoping never went back to his home in Guang'an (Sichuan). The writer Mu Xiang, who had rejected his bourgeois family in Penglai (Shandong) in the 1940s, returned to his native place for the first time only in 1986, even though as a cadre he would have had no problem in going to the beautiful coastal city. Nor did he ever invite his family to visit Beijing.

The CCP made some recognition of the need for loyal cadres to see their families. Family members of senior CCP cadres were given travel money to visit them in Beijing, but this was not necessarily what the devout communist wanted. Mu Xiang's father-in-law, a polygamous landlord from Henan, came to visit his daughter, whom he had not seen for 14 years, in 1952. The old man wanted to stay for good, in the luxury of the residential compounds of the Northern Bureau of the CCP, but was persuaded to go home, where his elderly wife and concubine awaited him, after a few months.[4]

Family separations within China were a routine matter for many people in the new socialist world. The lofty banner of serving socialism specified cutting ties with the feudal past; this included attachment to the family and the locality. In practice it meant that individuals could be sent wherever they were needed. Peasants and disbanded PLA soldiers continued to be sent to live in the military settlements (*bingtuan*) in the border regions, to supervise the former GMD soldiers who were 'making themselves new (*zixin*)' there.[5] People with education or skills were assigned (*fenpei*) to jobs in places where the authorities thought they would be useful; individual preferences were not considered. These postings were permanent, as were those of the *nanxia ganbu* discussed in Chapter 6. And the CCP continued the process, promoted often in the past by central governments (and still a key issue today), of redistributing population from over-populated regions to less populated ones. From densely populated Shandong as many as five million people were moved out to emptier places in the first three decades of the PRC.[6]

In the first decade and a half of socialism, tens of millions of people were moved within China.[7] Most of the migrants were sent away from home as single people; if they already had spouses and children, these were left behind. These moves were almost always intended to be permanent. The separations might last for decades. Some of the internal migrants were allowed to go home for the New Year, but many were not. The great floods of migrants going home at the New Year, known as the 'blind flood (*mangliu*)' is a phenomenon only of the past three decades.

The fall-out of the 12 years of war from 1937 to 1949 produced its own physical divisions. Millions of people were stuck far from home, where they were at the end of the Civil War. Many of the southern soldiers sent north by the GMD in 1946 and 1947 lived their entire lives in Manchuria. Others were stranded in southern China. A group of young Taiwanese men recruited into the GMD armies in the late 1940s were captured by the PLA in early 1949. Of those who were still alive, the first soldiers to be allowed home were only able to do so in 1989. Some of

---

[4] Mu Anping, *Vermillion Gate* (London: Abacus, 2010), p. 194 ff.

[5] *Zixin* is code for a reduced punishment dependent on a convict confessing the error of his ways and promising to become a new person.

[6] Diana Lary, 'Hidden Migrations: Movement of Shandong People, 1947–1978', in Kam Wing-chan (ed.), *Internal Migration in China*, special issue of *Chinese Environment and Development* (Summer 1996), p. 59.

[7] Diana Lary, *Chinese Migrations: The Movement of People, Goods and Ideas Over Four Millennia* (Boulder: Rowman and Littlefield, 2012), pp. 129–144.

the elderly men who returned spoke with bitterness, some with something close to astonishment, at the lives that they had led. They had been powerless, buffeted by the winds of political change.[8]

While so much state-organised movement was going on inside China, almost no emigration from the country was permitted. After 1949 it became almost impossible to go abroad legally. Restrictions on foreign travel were absolute. The necessary documents were impossible to obtain; the PRC issued passports only to a tiny number of people in senior positions; the passports were only valid for travel within the Soviet Bloc. Many Western governments, led by the USA, forbade their citizens from travelling to China.

Some Overseas Chinese still travelled from Hong Kong and the Overseas communities into China, but no one moved in the other direction – legally. Hundreds of thousands did leave China illegally, getting into Hong Kong by land or on boats. The bravest swam (or, for non-swimmers, paddled in an inner tube) through the shark-infested waters between Guangdong and Hong Kong.

Many of the family separations lasted for decades, until the 1980s, dictated by the cold, harsh policies of the Mao era. Two new generations were born, the older generations died off. The longest separations were those where family members had gone abroad. Katherine Wei, daughter of the sociologist Cato Yang (Yang Kaidao), was separated from her parents for 32 years, from 1949 to 1981. She received only 14 letters from her parents in all that time, although she had regularly sent them money. She arrived for her first return visit from America to find her father on his deathbed.[9]

For some the pain of having left China and their families was so great that they forced the memories of those who had been left behind into a dark, secret place. As she grew up in Athens, Ohio, the architect Maya Lin never heard her parents mention their own parents or their wider families, 'it might have been too painful for them because they had to leave all their family, all their friends'.[10] There was an extraordinary coincidence hidden in this silence: Maya knew nothing of her aunt, Lin Huiyin (see Chapters 1 and 5). She and her husband, Liang Sicheng, stayed in China in 1949. One of their major projects was to design the Martyrs' Memorial in Tiananmen Square, a memorial as famous as Maya Lin's own Vietnam Memorial in Washington.

---

[8] Guoshiguan, *Shanghen xuelei* (*Tears and Scars*) (Taibei: Guoshiguan, 2006).
[9] Katherine Wei and Terry Quinn, *Second Daughter: Growing Up in China, 1930–1949* (New York: Holt Reinhart, 1984), pp. 3–6.
[10] Donald Langmead, *Maya Lin* (Santa Barbara: Greenwood, 2011), p. 24.

For many people the separations were permanent. Even into the 1990s men who had served as officers in the GMD forces were forbidden to travel to the Mainland, while others were forbidden to go to Taiwan. As we saw in Chapter 3, right up until the present time people in China and in Taiwan continue to seek information about missing relatives, through local authorities, newspapers and journals and now online.

Separations were not a new phenomenon in Chinese history, nor was the melancholy and pain associated with them. The enduring love for Tang poetry is due in part to one of its major themes – exile and separation.

Du Fu

月夜忆舍弟 **Thinking of My Brothers on a Moonlit Night**

戍鼓断人行 The garrison drum halts travellers
边秋一雁声 A goose calls at the autumnal border
露从今夜白 From today on the dew at night will turn to frost.
月是故乡明 The moon is brighter at home
有弟皆分散 My brothers are scattered
无家问死生 There is no home to ask whether we are dead or alive
寄书长不达 Letters are sent but do not arrive
况乃未休兵 The fighting does not stop.

The melancholy and the deep sadness of this poem convey with great poignancy the anguish of separation over a millennium after they were written.

Separation from the dead

A different form of separation after 1949 derived from the attack on the 'feudal' practice of honouring the dead. The CCP established a separation between the living and the dead; the dead were gone, not to be revered or honoured. This hard line attacked one of the most fundamental tenets of Confucianism, the ancestral cult, which required the living to make sure that the dead were properly buried, that their graves were maintained at least once a year, in the sweeping of the graves (*saomu*) at the Qing Ming Festival. After death the spirits of the deceased had to be supplied with the necessities of life, some in paper form, to be burned over their graves, some in the form of fruit and cakes.[11]

---

[11] Annual paper offerings to the departed, all made of paper, include money, houses and furniture – and more recently mobile phones, flat-screen TVs, refrigerators and air-conditioners.

Campaigns against feudal thinking gradually eroded the funeral and burial rituals central to ancestor worship; it led to the banning of burial in favour of cremation, 'transformation by fire (*huohua*)'. The ritual observance of sweeping the graves was discontinued. Existing graves were moved from agricultural land to waste land. The degree of offence that these breaches of deep-seated codes of ritual behaviour caused was shown by how strongly burial customs were revived as soon as the Mao era was over.[12]

One of the deepest regrets of those who left China in 1949 was that they were unable to perform the rituals for the dead, but in the matter of separation from the dead and the ancestors those who stayed in China suffered the same degree of pain as did those who had left.

Generation splits

The younger generation was more likely to welcome the incoming CCP than were their elders. The revolution seemed positive and exciting to many young people, it promised them a glowing future under the leadership of the party and Mao Zedong. The party displaced parents as authority figures, and encouraged children to rebel against their parents if necessary. Their hearts were to be dedicated not to the family but to the party.

Ba xin jiao gei dang
Give your heart to the party

Parents were relegated to the side-lines of young lives. In a society in which the elderly depended on their children and grandchildren for support in old age, in the absence of health insurance and pensions, the decline in respect for age threatened not only the emotional security of the elderly, but also their material security.

The progress of the decline in respect for the elderly reached its most extreme during the Cultural Revolution, when the 'old', except for Mao Zedong, became the enemy. Ironically, many of the Red Guard generation, whose rebellion was against their parents, had been born to parents who themselves had turned against their own parents.

There was a fundamental contradiction, however, in the generation divide. Children inherited their parents' class status. They were still classified by their bloodline, not by their political attitudes and behaviour.

---

[12] Two of China's communist leaders found ways of avoiding burial. Mao Zedong's body was embalmed, and still lies in a sarcophagus in a mausoleum in the centre of Beijing. Zhou Enlai's body was cremated, and his ashes scattered over the whole nation.

In the Cultural Revolution the concept of inherited bloodlines (*xuetong lun*) had tragic consequences for those from bourgeois or landlord backgrounds who had joined the revolution. Chen Lian, the daughter who had betrayed her father Chen Bulei to join the revolution, was persecuted because of her inherited class status.

One sign of the acceptance of the movement of children away from the authority of their parents was that the change in naming patterns mentioned in the last chapter was solidified in the new era. There were no more generation names, when one of two characters appeared in all the males, brothers and cousins, of one generation. Now children's names often included positive, revolutionary elements. *Hong* (red) appeared in many names, as did *xin* (new) and *jian* (establish). In Taiwan and Hong Kong, by contrast, names reflected the birth places of those born outside China. Ma Ying-cheou (Ma Yingjiu), the president of the Republic of China, was born outside China, just after 1949. The two parts of his given name represent England (*ying*) and Kowloon (*jiu*), the part of Hong Kong where he was born. The martial arts hero Jackie Chan, the child of refugees from the Mainland, was born in Hong Kong – and that is the meaning of his given name in Chinese, Gangsheng.

Property

Owning property, whether as an individual or a family, was discouraged in the new world. One basic concept was that people should only have what they needed – the Marxist principle of 'to each according to his need'. In the land division in rural China land was assigned in part according to the number of mouths (*kou*) in a household.

Throughout China people were expected to live in limited spaces. Large residential properties were divided. The traditional custom of family-owned compounds virtually disappeared. Local authorities expropriated large properties and divided them for multiple occupancy; many of the new tenants were not family members. Grand courtyard complexes were no longer the homes of single families – and if they still lived there, the former owners, as members of the former elite, were vulnerable to attack by their new neighbours. Many of the courtyard houses did not survive the decades in which they were scarcely maintained; no one was responsible for maintenance. Even fewer have survived the rapid modernisation of the past four decades. In Beijing a few have survived as restaurants, or as the homes of leading CCP figures. The cultural czar of the early CCP period, Guo Moruo, lived in a luxurious princely mansion (*wangfu*); it is now a museum dedicated to his life.[13] The Daguanyuan in Beijing is a more recent reconstruction of the complex of buildings in which the characters in China's most famous traditional novel, *The Dream of the Red Chamber*, lived their delicate and difficult lives. It was built for a lengthy television series (1987); this has been followed by a second and longer series (2010).

In the 1950s the new ideal for housing was based on a model from the Soviet Union. For increasingly large numbers of workers in the cities 'home' became synonymous with the place where they worked, the *danwei*, or work unit. The actual place of work – factory, school or offices – was surrounded by housing blocks, usually several stories high. Each family had an apartment, complete with electricity, running water and sewage – all things unknown in traditional housing. The compound included crèches for infants, kindergartens for toddlers, clubs for the elderly and a hall for meetings.

Rise in the status of women

One of the promised aims of the CCP was to raise the status of women. Mao Zedong is often credited with saying that 'women hold up half the sky', a way of recognising their value. What he actually said was more cautious, 'women *may* hold up half the sky'.[14] It was not at all clear that women would ever be the equals of men. Still crucial steps were taken to get rid of some of the most egregious abuses from which women suffered in the old society. An early act was the 1950 Marriage Law, which enshrined choice for women in marriage. Women were free to marry the man they wanted, although they did have to marry; the idea of not marrying was inconceivable. The marriage should ideally be for love or, as the phrase at the time went, for *ganqing* (good feelings).

Initially making marriages for love was difficult. There was no tradition of dating, the Western method of finding one's own true love. In the 1950s most marriages were still arranged, no longer by the couple's families through go-betweens, but by work bosses, unit leaders or teachers. Great care was taken to match class backgrounds. Lavish weddings were scaled further and further back, until a wedding became simply a registration of the new wife's change of address at the local Office of Public Security. There were no wedding costumes, besides red rosettes worn on

---

[13] Guo's five children by his first (Japanese) wife were cut off from Guo and his new family for many decades, living first in destitution in Japan and later in Dalian.

[14] Perry Link, *An Anatomy of Chinese* (Cambridge, MA: Harvard University Press, 2013), p. 304, makes this important corrective to the standard reading of Mao's statement.

the newly-weds' left lapels. The wedding banquet consisted of an offering of fruit and candy to immediate family and friends, after which the bride moved her few possessions over to her new husband's house.

The marriage law had another important effect: it outlawed polygamy. The tradition of concubinage came to an end. This was a great advantage for young women, who were no longer candidates for the invidious position of concubine. The change was less advantageous for older women who were already concubines; they had no other home but the polygamous one in which they lived. The fate of existing concubines was mixed. Some left their husbands, and went on to make their own way in life. Some were given jobs in state enterprises. Others stayed in the families into which they married. As a young boy growing up in Shanghai during the Cultural Revolution, Kevin Rao was cared for not by two but by three grandmothers – his mother's mother and his grandfather's two wives. His childhood overflowed with love and attention from all three grandmothers, which mitigated against the absence of his parents, who had been sent away to cadre schools.[15]

The end of polygamy improved the chance of poor men to find a wife; the CCP regarded it as a duty to find wives for men who had served the revolution, but because they were poor, had never been able to marry. For peasants, the acquisition of land in the land reform made them a reasonable marriage prospect (*duixiang*).

The abolition of polygamy had a particular effect on Overseas Chinese. Men who made money abroad often had more than one wife. The senior wife usually lived in China, in the case of Xiamen (Fujian) on the idyllic island of Gulangyu, which consists largely of the mansions of successful men from the Nanyang (Southeast Asia). The concubine lived with the husband abroad. After 1949 the concubine living abroad with the husband effectively became the only wife, and her children, instead of being disadvantaged as they would have been traditionally, had greater chances for education than did the children at home, who had to bear the label of being the children of a 'bad element'. Denise Chong and her four siblings in British Columbia, the grandchildren of a man from Taishan and his concubine, all went to university. None of their cousins in Guangdong, the grandchildren of the grandfather's first wife, got any serious education.[16]

Polygamy was outlawed, but serial monogamy was not. Mao Zedong married his fourth wife, Jiang Qing, in Yan'an, in the process casting off He Zizhen, the wife who had been with him on the Long March. His

[15] Personal information from Kevin Rao, Hong Kong.
[16] Denise Chong, *The Concubine's Children: The Story of a Family Living on Two Sides of the Globe* (Toronto: Penguin, 1995).

大力发展养猪事业

Fig. 18 Happy young woman

beloved second wife, Yang Kaihui, had been killed much earlier. Jiang Qing was resented by other leaders and their wives and was consigned for a long time to life in the shadows. Liu Shaoqi's beautiful sixth wife, Wang Guangmei, was a strong presence. The most devoted revolutionary couple were Zhou Enlai, the most handsome of men, and his homely wife Deng Yingchao. Wang and Deng were the closest revolutionary China came to female leaders. There were even fewer women media stars. The greatest film star of the slightly earlier period had left China. Hu Die (Butterfly Wu) was in Hong Kong, as was the new movie queen Lin Dai. The Shaw brothers, who had dominated the Chinese film industry in Shanghai and later in Singapore, did not go back to Shanghai after the Resistance War, but set up an enormous industry in Hong Kong.[17]

A longer-term change in the status of women was the expectation that women would have equal opportunities to men, in education and in work. Work became not an option but a duty. Peasant women had always worked; now urban women were expected to work as well. Their child-care tasks were taken over by grandmothers, often their own mothers.

[17] The last of the Shaw brothers, Runrun Shaw, died in Hong Kong in January 2014, aged 106.

The old division between the husband's family and the wife's family, which made the wife part of her husband's family, eroded.

Another change in women's lives, that for a long time seemed permanent, was the stern conviction that women should not enhance their looks by jewellery, make-up, beautiful clothes, coiffure or perfume. The ideal woman of the early 1950s looked robust and cheerful. She wore her hair cut short in a pudding-basin style; she dressed in indigo blue pants and jacket, her face was devoid of make-up, she wore flat black cotton shoes. Silk dresses and jackets, high-heeled shoes, long hair, lipstick, rouge – all were outlawed as 'bourgeois'.

This proletarian 'fashion' lasted into the 1980s – since when it has been swept on to the scrapheap of history, as Chinese women started to wear glamorous clothing again, to use make-up and to have their hair done. Shanghai is now one of the fashion capitals of the world. The new fashion is interchangeable with Western fashion. What has not returned is traditional women's costume. Long gowns with long slits at the sides are reserved for hostesses in hotels and restaurants. The style of dress worn by Song Meiling, long, demure gowns in beautiful fabrics, with discreet jade and coral jewellery, is no more.

The long-term rise in the status of women has been slow and halting. Women still tend to work at lower levels and for less money than men. The only famous political women, now all dead, were wives of leaders: Song Qingling, widow of Sun Yat-sen; Song Meiling, wife of Chiang Kai-shek; Deng Yingchao and Jiang Qing, who re-emerged with a vengeance in the Cultural Revolution. The only leading woman in government has been Anson Chan, chief secretary of the Hong Kong government from 1993 to 1997. Today there are virtually no senior women in the political world, although the glamorous Peng Liyuan, the wife of Xi Jinping, is herself a famous singer. Traditional ways of exploiting women have remerged. Prostitution is back in full force, as is concubinage, although it has no formal status; concubines are now known as 'little wives'.

Widows and abandoned wives

Every war leaves large numbers of widows. In some societies they are cared for by the state, through pension systems. In other societies they depend on their families or on their own wits. In 1949 there were large numbers of abandoned wives or widows in China. Many of them had no idea of whether their husbands were still alive or not – they had simply disappeared in the fog of war. Those in the most precarious situation were the wives and widows of GMD soldiers. Very few dependants got away with the GMD armies as they withdrew to Taiwan. They had few means of support; their income had gone. They were often unpopular in their home communities. Their extended families often tried to distance themselves from the miasma that emanated from the wives of 'traitors'. Their only chance of survival was to make a second marriage to an older man.

Their misery dragged on into the 1970s and 1980s. For some, whose husbands unbeknown to them had made it to the USA, the silence ended in 1971, when Henry Kissinger's visit to China was seen as a sign that it was now possible to write letters to China. Connections by mail from Taiwan took longer to restore; there was opposition from the governments on both sides. The letters from outside, and the ones written in reply, brought news of deaths, births and even remarriages. Those outside, especially in Taiwan, had to report the same kind of news, including the existence of a second wife and a second family. The family separation was over, connections were restored, money was sent into China. The process of resuming connections was joyous, but so fraught with complications that the restoration of contact with an early spouse was seldom happy for everyone involved.

Children

Most of the children of China benefitted from the communists revolution. For the first time there was a commitment to universal education, unheard of before. The state's goal was free education, for girls as well as boys. With it came the possibility of lifting the majority of Chinese out of illiteracy. To achieve this bold vision, the language was simplified, a process begun in 1952. As they learned to read and write, children were taught to be socialist citizens.

Children were enrolled into a new national organisation, started in 1949 and given its current name, the Young Pioneers (*Xiaonian xianfengdui*), in 1952. The aims of the Young Pioneers were quite similar to that of the Boy Scouts and Girl Guides, except that the two sexes were enrolled together, all wearing their red scarves with pride. The CCP was making sure that the coming generation would be loyal to the party and to socialism. One painful aspect was that the children of 'bad elements' were excluded.

Children also benefitted from changes in the family system. The outlawing of polygamy meant that one traditional source of family disharmony – constant quarrelling between wives – disappeared. It had applied only in families at the top of the old society, but its abolition was a sign that the status of wives – and mothers – was rising.

Military ascendancy

In both China and Taiwan the military ascendancy created by the Resistance War and the Civil War continued into the post-war period.

There was very little post-war demobilisation. The Civil War was not in fact over; it continued across the Taiwan Straits. The Korean War brought even more militarisation. The military lived in its own separate, dominant world. On both sides of the Straits the military took precedence in the economy, with its own version of the 'military-industrial complex'.[18]

On the Mainland the huge military bases, many of them in the middle of cities, complete with barracks, family housing and every facility, from hospitals to schools, came to be a dominant but remote part of the society – present but also invisible, as the political leaders were in their own compounds. The military bases and the party compounds were completely off-limits to civilians.

In official propaganda soldiers were kindly, brave, dedicated men (and very occasionally women), who were always ready to sacrifice themselves for the people. This broke the traditional stereotype that 'good men do not become soldiers'.

好人不当兵
Haoren bu dang bing
Good men do not become soldiers

Soldiers were presented as altruistic, self-denying men who would not, according to Mao Zedong, take so much as an apple from the people's trees. They practised the Three Eight Working Style (*samba zuofeng*), which required them to respect the common people at all times, and if necessary to lay down their lives for them.

The East is Red

In the mid-1950s, this song, sung to a rousing tune, became virtually the national anthem of China. The vainglorious words show Mao Zedong's extreme self-importance.

东方红, 太阳升	The east is red, the sun rises
中国出了个毛泽东	China has produced a Mao Zedong
他为人民谋幸福	He strives for the people
呼尔嗨哟, 他是人民大救星!	Huerhaiao, he is our saviour.
毛主席爱人民	Chairman Mao loves the people
他是我们的带路人	He is our guide
为了建设新中国	To build a new China
呼尔嗨哟,领导我们向前进!	Huerhaiao, lead us forward!

---

[18] The term was coined in 1961, by President Dwight Eisenhower in his farewell address to the USA.

Fig. 19 Officer sewing

The new image of soldiers was of simple, clear-eyed, husky men, who lived simple, decent lives. Even officers looked after their own uniforms. Much of the new image of the soldier could not have been more than propaganda. Given the levels of transport, armies, especially when on the move, had to supply themselves locally, although if the army paid for the food and animals it took, this was an advance on previous practice.

In Taiwan the GMD government went even further in stressing the dominance of the military and introduced compulsory military training for all young men. This growing number of trained soldiers was added to the hundreds of thousands of Mainland soldiers who had been brought over to Taiwan in 1949. Although most young men stayed in the armed forces only for the required period, many other young men made the military their career, especially as the veterans from the Mainland came to the end of their service. These old soldiers lived sad and difficult old ages, without families to care for them.[19]

Other military influences went beyond the actual military. On the Mainland clothing for all ages and both genders was standardised in a militaristic way, not quite a military uniform, but close. Children and adults were given quasi-military physical training, in the form of physical exercises and marching. The old cultural stereotypes of soldiers were gone. The military was, and has remained to this day, a dominant force in the Chinese world.

[19] Joshua Fan, *China's Homeless Generation: Voices from the Veterans of the Chinese Civil War* (New York: Routledge, 2011).

Religion and ritual

In the 1950s the CCP waged a bitter battle against all the traditional religions. Religion was denounced as superstitious. Priests, monks and nuns were laicised, religious buildings taken over by the state. A huge number of religious practitioners were sent to jail or to reform through labour. Family rituals, such as making offerings to the ancestors or tending their graves, were banned. Fortune tellers and geomancers were denounced.

This frontal attack on religion and ritual could not take away from the fact that there was a new godhead in China, Mao Zedong, the Great Helmsman, the Saviour of the Nation. Mao dominated much of life in China. His picture was in every home, his sayings on every wall and billboard. The new religion was the Cult of Mao.

Movements

Social change accelerated through the 1950s and 1960s, stimulated by years of political movements that brought intense and often hysterical activity, usually focussed on attacking 'enemies'. These were the largest of the movements:

Table 8.1 *Political campaigns in the early PRC*

Date	Name	Targets
1951	Three Antis (*Sanfan*)	Corruption, waste, bureaucracy
1952	Five Antis (*Wufan*)	Bribery, theft of state property, tax evasion, chiselling, theft of state information
1958–1959	Anti-Rightist Movement	Critics of the party
1958–1961	Great Leap Forward	Economic backwardness
1963	Socialist Education	Reactionary bureaucrats
1966–1976	Cultural Revolution	Opponents of Mao Zedong in the party, intellectuals

The culmination of these movements was the Cultural Revolution, in which many of those who had espoused the revolution were attacked, driven to suicide or killed. This was probably the most tragic period of all of China's modern history, one that is still almost incomprehensible.

Taiwan social change

The social fall-out of the Civil War on Taiwan was almost as complicated as that on the Mainland, although much less violent. The local Taiwanese people (*bentu*) were repressed for decades by the incomers from the Mainland. They lived under a coercive system that tried to strip them of their identity and their language. The repression had a counter-effect to its intentions. Taiwanese identity became stronger and stronger.

The Mainlanders (*waisheng*) lived in a distorted society. Only the senior members of the military and government had their families with them, and then only their immediate families. The common soldiers who had come with the armies lived half-lives, separated from their families at home, most unable to find wives in Taiwan – the implicit ban on inter-marriage with native Taiwanese was upheld by both sides. The bright spots for both sides were economic growth, good education and a strong infrastructure left by the Japanese. Over the decades Taiwan became prosperous, and almost all its citizens benefitted.

Those who had saved themselves by getting to Taiwan had an unspoken burden to bear – the anguish of the loss of relatives and friends, and with it the tacit admission that everything that they had stood for had disappeared, that their own country people had turned on them. In his brilliant set of short stories of Mainlanders living in Taibei, *Taibei People*, Bai Xianyong counterposed moments of glory and hope (the 1911 Revolution, the May 4th Movement, the Japanese surrender) with times of sadness, regret and even numbness in Taiwan, years after the great moments. The loss of the Mainland had drained the joy and excitement out of their lives. The loss was not only personal, but cultural. Bai's stories were written during the Cultural Revolution, when the PRC seemed intent on destroying traditional Chinese culture completely. They were an elegy for a lost world.[20]

The Overseas Chinese social change

The separations of the Resistance War and the Civil War between Overseas Chinese and their home communities continued in the first decades of CCP rule, so much so that they became permanent. As many as one million Overseas Chinese returned to China after 1949. This was a permanent move; they would not be allowed to leave China again, or to re-enter the countries in which they lived.[21]

The vast majority of Overseas Chinese did not go back to China. They feared that if they did they would not be able to leave again. There was

[20] Bai Xianyong, *Taibei People* (Hong Kong: Chinese University Press, 2000).

[21] Wang Yixin, *Women guojia: Xin Zhongguo chuqi huaqiao guiguo* (*Our Country: Overseas Chinese Returning to China in the First Decades of the New China*) (Jinan: Renmin chubanshe, 2013), pp. 2, 41.

a profound separation from their native places. There were no more visits, no more education for young people in China. Generations of Overseas Chinese grew up with no connection to China, which became a strange, alien place – especially during the Cultural Revolution. The many millions of Overseas Chinese were deeply affected by the political change in China. The new world order was the Cold War. Overseas Chinese in Southeast Asia were in states that were deeply hostile to communist China. The Overseas Chinese could easily be portrayed as fifth-columnists, loyal first to their now-communist ancestral country. Even before the formal CCP takeover it had been clear to many Overseas Chinese that their close relations with home, with the *qiaoxiang*, so badly damaged by 12 years of war, would not be fully restored. After 1949 the estrangement deepened.

Their relatives at home in the *qiaoxiang* were over a barrel. Many still depended on remittances from relatives abroad to live, while the proceeds of past remittances – land holdings, houses, businesses – put them in double jeopardy: they had family abroad, a cause of suspicion, and they had the land acquired through remittances, which made them landlords in the land reform and susceptible to expropriation. Some were able to keep in touch through 'informal' communications – i.e., underground and illegal – via Hong Kong; shadowy versions of the old Overseas Chinese networks kept working.

The experiences were quite different for Overseas Chinese in Southeast Asia – mainly from Fujian – than for those in other parts of the world, particularly North America. In North America the established communities, almost all originating from Guangdong, moved away from China. The effective closure of China coincided with the gradual weakening of anti-Chinese sentiment and legislation in the US and Canada. The generations born from the 1950s on felt only a minimal connection to China. The separation involved a loss of Chinese language and culture, and a change in identity, towards the countries in which they lived. China faded into the past.[22]

Hong Kong social change

With very little fanfare Hong Kong became the most successful Chinese society in the world in the 1950s and 1960s. The economy forged ahead, driven by the energy and ambition of the people. Hong Kong went from being an entrepôt for the China trade to being a major manufacturing

---

[22] Denise Chong, *Lives of the Family: Stories of Fate and Circumstance* (New York: Random House, 2013).

city, helped by the arrival of Shanghai capitalists.[23] The energy was fuelled by something close to desperation in many of the refugees, people who had lost so much and had to pull themselves up from the bottom. The story of Hong Kong from the 1950s on is made up of innumerable lives of rags to riches.

The Hong Kong government provided resources for the population that elsewhere would have been considered dangerously socialist: free education, health care, public housing, pensions. Everyone was expected to work hard, and did. From the start of the 1950s Hong Kong experienced decades of continuous growth, which eventually made it one of the most prosperous places in the world. It prospered under a combination of efficient public administration and a strict regard for the rule of law. Its society preserved many of the aspects of traditional Chinese society, although polygamy was gradually outlawed. Religion flourished, as did public morality. Gamblers had to make the short trip to Macao to indulge their habit.

Biographies

Danwei *people*

One of the groups that benefitted most from the revolutionary social changes of the early 1950s were those who moved into the idealist/socialist form of living, the *danwei* (unit). Workers lived together, worked together and played together, in enclosed worlds; *danwei* were always surrounded by walls, a continuation of the traditional fetish of building walls wherever walls could be built. The *danwei* provided for all needs. The work gave income, the income paid for modest rents and for the needs of life – food in canteens, daily necessities in small stores. Babies could be put in crèches, small children into kindergartens. In the evenings and at weekends people could hang out together, smoking and chatting – and gossiping. It seemed an ideal, comfortable world – but also one in which there was zero privacy, no escape from irritating or hostile neighbours. The social control exerted in the *danwei* was absolute. In times of political campaigns the *danwei* was claustrophobic and even terrifying. Those under attack had to live and work with their attackers; there was no relief.[24]

---

[23] Wong Siu-lun, *Emigrant Entrepreneurs: Shanghai Industrialists in Hong Kong* (Hong Kong: Oxford University Press, 1988).

[24] Lu Duanfang, *Remaking the Chinese Urban Form: Modernity, Scarcity and Space 1949–2005* (London: Routledge, 2006).

I.M. Pei (Bei Yuming)

I.M. Pei is one of the great architects of his generation. He grew up in Guangzhou and Shanghai, in a banking family, and studied at St John's School, an English-medium school attached to St John's University. The two educational establishments were run by the Episcopalian (Anglican) Church and nurtured many of Shanghai's elite boys. Some of the best-known St John's old boys were: Wellington Koo (Gu Weijun), foreign minister; T.V Soong (Song Ziwen), younger brother of Song Meiling and finance minister to Chiang Kai-shek; Lin Yutang, writer and diplomat; Rong Yiren, financier; and Lu Ping, the man responsible for the 1997 handover of Hong Kong to China.

Given his early education in English, Pei transferred with ease to the American educational system. He studied architecture. In the late 1940s and early 1950s he embarked on what became an immensely success- ful career. Among his most famous buildings are the Diamond, at the Louvre in Paris, and the Bank of China Building in Hong Kong. He did not return to China for over 40 years after he left in 1935. When he did return, it was to build the beautiful Fragrant Hills Hotel outside Beijing, a masterpiece that combines Chinese, Tibetan and Western elements.

Ang Lee (Li An)

The filmmaker Ang Lee was born in 1954 in Pingdong, southern Taiwan. His parents were both refugees from the Mainland. His father was a teacher in a settlement for soldiers; he instilled in his son a great respect for traditional culture. Ang Lee did not get into the prestigious university his father had envisaged for him, but instead studied fine arts in Taiwan and later in the USA. In the USA he married Jane Li, a molecular biolo- gist, and spent several years as a house-husband, raising their two sons. In the early 1990s his filmmaking career started in Taiwan. *The Wedding Banquet* (1993) was his first major success, enough to send him on the way to Hollywood, where his first big success was *Crouching Tiger, Hidden Dragon* (1999), a fantastic story derived from the Chinese tradition of knights-errant (*wuxia*). The film was discreetly a sign of reconciliation between Chinese from different places. Its stars were from Hong Kong (Chow Yun-fat), Singapore (Michelle Yeoh) and the Mainland (Zhang Ziyi). Lee came from Taiwan, as did much of the financing for the film. Lee has made many films with non-Chinese themes. He has won two Oscars for Best Achievement in Directing, for *Brokeback Mountain* (2005) and *Life of Pi* (2012).

Conclusion

There was no doubt at the time, nor has there been since, about who won China's Civil War. It was the CCP, under its dominant and charismatic leader Mao Zedong. The new regime immediately put its stamp on China. As at the start of imperial dynasties, the state was renamed, and the dating of history restarted. The new state was the People's Republic of China, the *Zhonghua Renmin Gonghe Guo*. The Republic of China, the *Zhonghua Minguo*, ceased to exist, except on Taiwan. The new dating system marked the break with the old system, in two ways. There was a fundamental break. The end of the Civil War was named the Liberation, *Jiefang*. China was liberated from her past. Previous or subsequent events were described as Before Liberation or After Liberation. And there was a modernist twist to the new dating. In the dynastic period, the counting of years was restarted with the accession of each new emperor, for example the First Year of the Qianlong Reign. Now the CCP switched China's dating to the Western system – or, more accurately, to the system used in the USSR. The year of liberation started as the 38th Year of the Republic and ended as 1949 of the Common Era.[1]

There was no doubt either about who lost the Civil War. It was the GMD, and its blundering, indecisive leader Chiang Kai-shek. He was blamed for the loss of the Mainland by many of his own supporters, by much of the natural consistency of the GMD, the middle classes and those with Western connections, and by much international opinion. The GMD defeat was seen, in the West as a huge victory for communism, a terrible loss to the democratic West. It was one of the worst imaginable outcomes, a sudden and terrifying intensification of the Cold War, with the state with the world's largest population gone over to the Reds.

[1] For a discussion of dating systems, see Endymion Wilkinson, *Chinese History: A New Manual* (Cambridge, MA: Harvard University Asia Centre, 2013), p. 510. The GMD did not change the dating system. So 1949 was the 38th Year of the Republic, 2014 is the 103rd Year.

The speed of victory was shocking for both sides in the war. For the CCP the victory came far faster than its leaders had hoped or imagined. The party was nowhere near ready to take over, especially in terms of the number of people available to govern its new domain. The party needed huge numbers of people to take over national, regional and local governments. This was a daunting task, since there was little continuity in government. Most of those who had worked for the GMD were either out of the country or in detention.

For the GMD the sudden collapse was a hideous humiliation. The GMD fell faster than any major dynasty had done before; the Song, Ming, Qing dynasties all took much longer to fall apart than did the Republic on the Mainland. For the GMD there has been a lasting inability to comprehend why the collapse came so fast. There were no official post-mortems. Chiang Kai-shek never took responsibility for the GMD's debacle; instead his private diary is full of bitter recriminations against others in the GMD hierarchy, particularly the last two GMD leaders left standing on the Mainland, acting president Li Zongren and General Bai Chongxi. He launched an equally bitter but more public assault on the Soviet Union, as the worldwide sponsors of communism, in his book *Soviet Russia in China*.[2] He had no direct criticism for the USA. He dared not turn against his major benefactor; his rump republic was now a client state.

For several years Chiang and his followers kept up the dream that the Mainland would be restored (*guangfu*). The Taiwan Straits became one of the most heavily militarised bodies of water in the world; the beautiful beaches on both sides of the straits were covered in fortifications, tank traps and barbed wire. On several occasions open warfare almost broke out. This continuing state of war became part of the Cold War and meant that the PRC entered into a state of deep isolation except from the Soviet Bloc.

Isolation

After 1949, China withdrew from much of the world, behind what came to be known as the Bamboo Curtain. Most foreign residents had to leave China. There were almost no family visits, no tourism. There was very little foreign trade except with the Soviet Bloc; trade within Asia almost ceased. China was politically isolated from her neighbours; the only foreign connections were now with the fraternal countries in the Soviet Bloc. With Western countries there was an almost complete lack of

---

[2] Chiang Kai-shek, *Soviet Russia in China* (New York: Farrar, 1957).

communication, although a few Western countries managed to maintain diplomatic relations, at a skeleton level.

For Chinese on the Mainland, foreign connections (*haiwai guanxi*) – which included having relatives abroad or having studied abroad – became dangerous, a likely cause of suspicion and discrimination. Relatives and friends who were outside China could only keep in touch with people at home through the post. As time went on even occasional letters became dangerous. Money could still be sent to relatives in China, but there was no confirmation that it ever arrived. These remittances were, in fact, one of China's few sources of foreign currency.

As a general rule, Chinese were not permitted to leave their country, unless on official business or as students. This meant travel to one of the Soviet Bloc countries. Many of the students went on to become major figures in the Chinese political system, including former premier Li Peng and former president Jiang Zemin, who worked at the Stalin Automobile Works in Moscow. One student did not return to China: the pianist Fu Tsong (Fu Zong) defected to the West while he was studying the piano in Warsaw.[3]

One of the most dangerous forms of foreign contact was belonging to a Christian church. By the early 1950s all missionaries had been expelled. Public religious manifestations were frowned on or attacked. Priests were arrested and sent for long periods of reform through labour. Churches were closed and turned to other uses, quite often as factories. Hospitals with religious or other foreign connections changed their names. Universities with foreign connections were taken over by the state. Yenching University, to the west of Beijing, had been founded by American missionaries. Peking University, which was set in the middle of the city, was moved out to the beautiful Yenching campus and the two combined as Peking University.[4] Yenching ceased to exists except in the memories of its legion of distinguished alumni.

The attacks on Christianity were part of a general attack on religion, Karl Marx's 'opium of the people'. All over the country Buddhist and Daoist temples and Islamic mosques were closed, and many of the monks and nuns laicised. Only the old and the bold dared perform religious rituals. In the Cultural Revolution the attacks were

---

[3] Fu Tsong's father, the distinguished translator Fu Lei, and his wife both committed suicide at the beginning of the Cultural Revolution. Fu Lei's letters to his son have had a major success in China: *Fu Lei shuxin ji* (*Letters of Fu Lei*) (Shanghai: Jiaoyu xueyuan, 1992).

[4] Peking University is permitted to use the English word 'Peking' in its title; all other institutions now use 'Beijing'.

intensified, and many religious buildings were actually destroyed. For a long time it seemed that the goal of eliminating religion had been achieved. But as soon as the new policies of opening up were introduced in the 1980s, religious adherents emerged. Faith in Christianity, as in Buddhism, Daoism and Islam, had not been destroyed, but had gone underground. According to official statistics, there are now at least 100 million religious adherents in China; unofficial estimates put the figure much higher.[5]

Winners and losers

The question of winners and losers in Chinese society in the aftermath of the Civil War and the socialist revolution is so complex that it seems almost impenetrable, but it demands to be addressed, given how great the changes were and how huge the costs to the losers. In bald socialist theory the winner was History, with a capital H. The CCP's victory was inevitable, prescribed by Marxist ideology. This view has persisted despite present-day China's retreat from socialism. A lavish volume published for the sixtieth anniversary of 1949 has as its title *History Elected the Communist Party*.[6] In practical terms this 'election' should mean victory for the poor and downtrodden, the proletariat. The new China was a workers' and peasants' state.[7] The winners in the early 1950s were presented as the peasants, the workers and the PLA soldiers, liberated from the shackles of the old, feudal society.

The losers were the old social elites, the merchant, landlord and business elites. Beyond these groups of outright losers were the people who had espoused modernity, democracy and the rule of law, and those who had converted to foreign religions. A huge group of losers was made up of those who had had connections to the GMD. Since the senior members of the GMD administration had largely got away, in practice this meant regional and local officials and their families. China's intellectuals, her writers, poets and academics, were losers; in the early 1950s they saw their creative careers end. China's modern writers – the most prominent being Mao Dun, Lao She, Shen Congwen and Ba Jin– were all effectively silenced.

---

[5] *The Independent*, 30 January 2014.

[6] Zhu Hanguo, *1949: Lishi xuancele Gongchandang* (*1949: History Elected the Communist Party*) (Taiyuan: Shanxi renmin chubanshe, 2009).

[7] It remains so today. Article 1 of the PRC Constitution states: 'The People's Republic of China is a socialist state under the people's democratic dictatorship led by the working class and based on the alliance of workers and peasants.'

On the winners' side, the joy felt by the winners did not last. The three decades that followed the Civil War were among the hardest that China has ever known. As Jacques Guillermaz, who observed much of the transition and the next two decades from Nanjing and Beijing as a French diplomat, said, 'the years that followed [1949] were less bloody but just as cruel and murderous and equally critical for the future of China'.[8] As Mao's dominance turned into megalomania, the toll that extremist politics took grew larger and larger. Tens of thousands of intellectuals and critics were punished for standing up to Mao in the Anti-Rightist Movement (1957–1959). Millions of peasants died in the famine that followed the Great Leap Forward (1958–1961). Tens of millions of lives were lost or disrupted during the Great Proletarian Cultural Revolution (1966–1976). The socialist revolution had consumed many of its early supporters.[9]

Generations

Much of how people have lived their lives in modern China has depended on what generation a person was born in to. The different experiences of the generations have been determined by political events. Those Chinese born in the early years of the Republic grew up in an unstable but largely peaceful world. Their children, born in the 1930s and 1940s, were born into war. Their grandchildren, born in the 1950s and 1960s, grew up in political turmoil. Each of these generations went through its own particular trauma. The oldest generation suffered the horrors of the Resistance War and the Civil War, and experienced the loss of the old society. The members of the second generation were in the front line of the political movements that culminated in the Cultural Revolution. Many of them had believed passionately in the new China, and worked hard for it. The members of the third generation old enough to be Red Guards behaved horribly, but paid a very high price for their excesses; they had little education and little hope to make careers.

The next generations, born at the end of the Mao era or thereafter, have been more fortunate. The reforms that started in the 1980s seemed to bring an end to almost five decades of chaos and confusion, from the Japanese invasion in 1937 on. The opening up to the outside world in the early 1980s reversed the negative connotations of foreign connections

---

[8] Jacques Guillermaz, *Une vie pour la Chine* (*A Life for China*) (Paris: Robert Laffont, 1989), p. 200.
[9] Frank Dikotter's trilogy, of which two volumes have so far appeared, provides a catalogue of all the suffering of the Chinese under the new communist state: *Mao's Great Famine* (London: Bloomsbury, 2010) and *The Tragedy of Liberation* (London: Bloomsbury, 2013).

and made them desirable again. The isolation of the 1950s and 1960s seemed to have been an aberration.

Whether the most recent generations have been affected by their parents' and grandparents' experiences is in question. I have often been told that young people 'know nothing' about the recent past. I doubt this. The sense of family has been so strongly re-established over the past three decades, in legal as well as emotional terms, that 'knowing nothing' would be quite an achievement. This is especially true now that the Resistance War, and to a lesser extent the Civil War, are so present in political statements, movies, books, blogs and online.

Accounts of the Civil War

The disasters of the Mao era still lurk in the shadows of Chinese consciousness, not confronted or analysed, but by no means forgotten. The unwillingness to confront those tragic times means that the connection between the 12 years of war, from 1937 to 1949, and the Mao era is not made explicitly, but the spate of recent accounts of the Resistance War and the Civil War all have, as a subtext, a recognition of the baleful impact of the war years on the old society, and the role of the wars in paving the way for the communist rise to power and for how the CCP government of China behaved in its first three decades.

Official versions of the Civil War

An accurate, objective history of the Civil War has yet to be written in Chinese. Both the CCP and the GMD have gone to great lengths to create official accounts of the recent past, in which historical accuracy is not a key, or even a secondary consideration. History is moulded to fit the official vision – or ignored.

The practice of reshaping the history of the Civil War started as soon as the GMD lost and the CCP came to power. The GMD insisted on the critical role of the Soviet Union, and claimed the CCP's victory in the Civil War was engineered by foreign, Marxist influences, a view shared in many minds in the USA.[10] The CCP affirmed Marxist influence, but saw it as a boon not a threat. As a communist party it believed in the inevitability of socialist victory, a linear history that omitted any inconvenient details. On the first anniversary of the victory, premier Zhou Enlai had this to say about the CCP's success in 1949:

---

[10] Some of the victims of the Red Scare in the USA were loyal American diplomats who had criticised the GMD, men such as John Service and John Melby.

Such a big victory can never be regarded as an accidental phenomenon in history, but is the inevitable outcome of the numerous revolutionary struggles of the Chinese people during the last century.[11]

The PRC's stance on recent history has changed since then; it no longer focuses on Marxist inevitability. But the desire to cover up or distort events that do not fit the official rubric has remained constant. For the Civil War and much of the Mao era amnesia is still the official rule, a political decision *not* to remember many of the events that occurred during and after the CCP's rise to power.

There is a separation between the past and history. The past is what people remember of their own lives, or what they think themselves about previous times; it may be their own past, or the past of their community and society. History is a loftier, more remote subject. To a great extent in China it is and always has been controlled by the state. The current state's desire is to downplay events of the recent past in favour of a history that deals with China's more distant, glorious past. During the Mao era the glorious past was peopled by peasant rebels; now it is peopled by great emperors. The sadness of much of modern history has no real place in official history.

This sunny view of history is not unusual. States tend to have an official history that favours a glowing past – America the *Beautiful*, *Great* Britain.[12] What is unusual are the lengths to which the Chinese state goes to sanction *only* this past, to present only a simplistic history. The Three Emperors Exhibition, opened in London in 2005–2006, showed only glory, luxury and power; the fact that the three emperors, Kangxi, Yongzheng and Qianlong, were not Han Chinese but Manchu scarcely counted, nor did the harshness with which they ruled.

How to handle the history of the Civil War is sensitive, so much so that at an official level it remains a dark hole. The war brought the CCP to power, where it remains, after 65 years, but it had little glory about it.

Official amnesia is not a guaranteed way of obliterating history. That is harder to do. The experience of other countries is that it is better to deal with a bad past than to hide it. Ian Buruma's perceptive comparison of the ways in which Germany and Japan have dealt with the evils the two countries perpetrated during the Second World War shows that West Germany's acceptance of war guilt and the efforts to make amends to at least some of the victims has been far more successful in dealing with a terrible past than has Japan's tendency to deny the recent past. Buruma's

---

[11] *The First Year of Victory* (Beijing: Foreign Languages Press, 1950), p. 3.
[12] The British prime minister David Cameron announced after Margaret Thatcher's death that she 'put the "great" back in Britain'.

book shows how much this denial has done to keep the issue of war crimes alive, at least among the countries occupied by Japan.[13]

The CCP has gone to great lengths to rectify past wrongs, on occasion. There has been a long practice of rectification (*pingfan*), reversing the unjust treatment of individuals, often after their deaths. The president of the PRC, Liu Shaoqi, done to death in 1969, was officially rehabilitated 11 years after his death. In the immediate aftermath of the Cultural Revolution major and much more widespread efforts were made to compensate victims, under the policy of restitution (*lushi zhengce*). They were compensated for lost income and for property wrongly seized; the children of victims were given jobs and education.

Taiwan has moved in the same direction of rectifying the past, but in a much more forceful and effective way. In the 1980s, as soon as the movement towards democracy was underway, the government appointed a commission to uncover what exactly happened during the Ererba massacres. Official investigations and reports were commissioned, and a major monument to the victims was erected in downtown Taibei. These actions have gone only part way to assuaging Taiwanese anger.

Although the formal, officially sanctioned history of the Civil War has yet to be written, the building blocks for a large history are being created. The period is no longer off-limits for professional historians in China. A great deal of work has been done in Taiwan, on the Civil War in general and on Ererba. These historians and ones outside China are working actively on the war and on how the CCP came to power.[14]

Memory

The state's amnesia about the tragedies of recent history is shared by many individuals. Personal memories of the Civil War are often too sad and painful to be dredged up.

悲痛歈絕

Bei tong yu jue
Agonising grief

---

[13] Ian Buruma, *The Wages of Guilt: Memories of War in Germany and Japan* (London: Phoenix, 2002). Prime minister Abe Shinzo's visit to the Yasakuni Shrine in December 2013 drew predictable condemnation from China and South Korea. The shrine contains memorials to Class A war criminals.

[14] For example Jeremy Brown, *City Versus the Countryside in Mao's China* (New York: Cambridge University Press, 2012); and Yang Wu, *A Revolution's Human Face* (PhD, University of British Columbia, 2013).

Often the only way to deal with agonising grief is to suppress the memory of what gave rise to it. Self-imposed amnesia seems preferable to the pain of memory. Personal histories of suffering and loss are hard to pass on to the younger generation, to children and grandchildren. There was for a long time a strong element of tacit consensus in the desire not to talk about the Civil War. So many people wanted to bury their memories of suffering that there was what amounted to a mass conspiracy of silence about the war. This desire to ignore the war lasted, for most people, until the end of life seemed so close to survivors that if memory was to be transmitted, it had to be done at once. Over the past two decades there has been a stream of autobiographies, out of which can be drawn the tragic, the uplifting and, above all, the arbitrary nature of the war.

Memories are difficult for victims and also for people who were revolutionary activists; they are often too embarrassing to recall. Not many people want to explain to younger generations how much they believed in socialism, or how they worshiped Mao Zedong. Personal memories of the Cultural Revolution are even more embarrassing and shame-inducing. Very few former Red Guards, as parents trying to discipline their own children, have wanted to tell their children about what they did in the Cultural Revolution.

The Red Guard generation, people in their sixties, is now in charge of the Chinese government, and sitting at the top of many institutions. Their youthful experiences are mentioned but seldom, until very recently, how they behaved as Red Guards. What members of this generation have talked about are the experiences that came afterwards, when young people were forced to spend long periods in the countryside as 'educated youth (*zhiqing*)'. The educated youth had not all been Red Guards (almost all young people were 'sent down (*xiafang*)'), but a significant proportion of them had. The amnesia about the Cultural Revolution is now lifting. The son of Marshall Chen Yi, Chen Xiaolu, has published a formal apology to the teachers at the Beijing Number Eight Middle School; as leader of the student body Chen spearheaded the persecution of the teachers during the Cultural Revolution. He also asked other Red Guards to come forward and express their shame for the horrible things that they did: 'The "Chinese Dream" cannot be realised until China accepts responsibility for the crimes and injustices committed during the Cultural Revolution.'[15]

Beyond amnesia is remembering constantly but hiding memories of the Civil War. Those who went through the war often had secrets that they kept even from their families. Three of the Chinese American writer

---

[15] *South China Morning Post*, 21 August 2013.

Amy Tan's novels hinge around the secrets brought to America by women who had fled from China at the end of the Civil War.[16] The saddest of them involved abandonment of children in China: Tan's own mother Daisy had herself left three daughters behind in China.

Amy Tan's mother*

Amy Tan's first novel, *The Joy Luck Club,* dealt with the tortuous relationships between a group of four Chinese-American girls and their China-born mothers. There are inter-generational and inter-cultural differences – and behind those there are secrets. These are about the people whom the mothers left behind in China, sometimes other children. The pain of having abandoned them, and left them to what they thought of as the horrors of communism, was so great that their existence was kept secret from the 'American' children.

One of the secrets is the existence of three daughters, born to Winnie Louie when she was married to her first husband and left behind in China when she left for America to escape communism – and to marry her second husband. Amy Tan based this story on her own mother's story. Daisy Tan, already married, fell in love with John Tan during the Resistance War. After the war her husband sued her for adultery. When she went to join Tan in the USA, she left her three daughters behind. For two decades she kept them a secret. She only revealed their existence in the turmoil following the deaths of her husband and son – Amy's father and brother. Amy was at first shocked and angry at what she saw as her mother's duplicity, but later came to understand her mother's extreme and often inexplicable behaviour in terms of the burden of loss she carried. The pain of separation from her first three daughters caused her great psychic pain. In 1978, three decades after she left them, Daisy went to China and saw her daughters. This was the earliest time that it was possible for Chinese with foreign citizenship to go back to China. Amy herself went in 1987, and felt an immediate connection with her long-lost sisters.

* May Ellen Snodgrass, *Amy Tan: A Literary Companion* (London: Macfarland, 2004) gives detailed analyses of the intersection between Tan's fictions and her family history.

---

[16] Amy Tan, *The Joy Luck Club* (New York: Putnams, 1989), *The Kitchen God's Wife* (New York: Putnams, 1991) and *The Bone Setter's Daughter* (New York: Putnams, 2001).

The memory of lost children is perhaps the one that is hardest to bring out from hiding. The abandonment of children in the last turbulent stages of the Civil War, almost always by accident, was common, both for those uprooted within China and for those who had left the country. Children of GMD personnel who fled to Taiwan were left behind, most because they were not with their parents when they left the Mainland. CCP activists had to leave their children behind at the start of the Long March, or during the Resistance War. Women cadres were expected to leave their children to be brought up by relatives, or to live in crèches. Some foreigners left children behind, usually the child of a foreign father and a Chinese mother. The German sinologist Walter Fuchs left a baby daughter behind when he left Beijing in 1947.[17] His future in Germany was uncertain, because of his Nazi activities, so he went home alone. He, like other fathers, may have hoped to return for his child and her mother once his situation was sorted out.

Both the Mainland and Taiwan have found a different way to understand what happened during the war, not through the formal writing of history but through the arts.

Art and memory

Some of the most powerful forms of public memory are carried in art, especially film and fiction. Taiwan has led the way in dealing with the Civil War period.

After the political changes in Taiwan in the 1980s, it became possible to talk openly about the Civil War period. Writers and filmmakers leapt to the task. Their focus was on Ererba, not on what happened on the Mainland. The greatest exemplar is Hou Hsiao-hsien's film *City of Sadness* (*Beijing chengshi*) in which Hou uses his consummate artistry to recount the complexity and horror of the tragedy. The film was shot in the Taiwan dialect (*Taiyu*) and not in Mandarin, an implicit statement of the gulf between the GMD and the people of Taiwan. The language barrier did not prevent the film from becoming a huge international success.

The CCP still controls film production. From its earliest days in power the party has been adept at ignoring or adjusting historical reality in film. In 1950 the first anniversary of the establishment of the PRC was celebrated with a showing of the documentary film *Liberated China*, made by Soviet cameramen; it included scenes of rural revolution,

---

[17] Wolfgang Franke, *Im Banne Chinas* (*Under the Spell of China*) (Dortmund: Project, 1977), p. 178.

'partly spontaneous, partly staged'.[18] The *Victory of the Chinese People* was another fictionalised 'documentary'.

Victory of the Chinese People

One of the areas in which the CCP sought Soviet help was in the making of movies. In 1950 the Soviet documentary filmmaker Leonid Varlamov arrived in China. His most famous films were *Moscow Strikes Back* (1942) and *The City That Stopped Hitler: Heroic Stalingrad* (1943). His first documentary in China was *The Victory of the Chinese People*. The film script, written by the Soviet war poet and writer Konstantin Simonov, proved conclusively that the Chinese revolution was a natural part of the struggle for socialism. The proof required some liberties with what had actually happened. The great campaigns in Manchuria in 1948 had been filmed as they took place, but the quality of the film was poor. After the end of the war, at Varlamov's direction, Chinese troops re-enacted the battles, all in the same location near Jinzhou (Liaoning), rather than where they had actually been fought. Even some of the generals who had directed the fighting from the GMD side took part; they were given temporary release from jail for the purpose, and went back when the filming was finished.

A 2009 film to mark the sixtieth anniversary of the communist accession to power is more sophisticated, but still a work of propaganda. *The Founding of the Republic (Jianguo daye)*[19] features both CCP and GMD figures, including almost all the senior generals who lost the Civil War. Many of China's (including Hong Kong's) leading actors and directors appeared in cameo roles: Jackie Chan, Chen Kaige, Chow Yun-fat, Ge You, Jet Li, Jiang Wen, Andy Lau. The female megastar Zhang Ziyi played Zhou Enlai's translator Gong Peng. The stars waived their fees to show their support for the project. The title of the film is notable. *Jianguo* is the term that has replaced the old term for 1949, *Jiefang* (Liberation).

Events of the Mao era are difficult to reflect in films that will satisfy the censor. Censors require a positive take on post-1949 events, something impossible for the Anti-Rightist Movement, the Great Famine or the Cultural Revolution. The filmmakers' way of dealing with tragic

---

[18] Jay Leyda, *Dianying* (Cambridge, MA: MIT Press, 1972), p. 189.
[19] *Jianguo daye*, director Huang Jianxin, 2009.

historical events is by allusion. The 2012 film *1942* deals with the terrible famine that hit Henan in that year; it is equally a tacit but clear allusion to the famine that ravaged China after the Great Leap Forward.[20]

On the Mainland to get at what has really happened in the decades since the Civil War one has to turn to fiction. One of the first implicit attacks on the excesses of the Cultural Revolution was Gu Hua's *A Small Town Called Hibiscus*. Some of the best recent novels that reveal the tragic events are the black comedies of Yan Lianke (*Serve the People, Lenin's Kisses*), Mo Yan (*The Garlic Ballads*) and Chan Koonchung (*The Fat Years*).[21] Fiction gives a freedom to writers that other creative people, let alone professional historians, do not enjoy. Writing is an occupation that requires no major financial outlays. Books may be banned in China, but they can be published in Chinese in other places – in Hong Kong, Taiwan or North America – and there is a big enough readership outside China to bring in decent earnings for successful writers. In China itself they soon appear in pirated editions. These works of fiction are one way of looking at a harsh recent past. Some official Chinese commentators attack the writers as being unpatriotic, as contributing to 'China-bashing'. But their accounts are backed up by what is written in memoirs and autobiographies.

Trauma and ghosts

There is another realm for dealing with the legacy of suffering. The clinical way now to see people who have survived horrors and been scarred by them is as victims of post-traumatic stress disorder, a condition that needs to be treated if it is not to lead to substance abuse, psychological breakdown or suicide. In the world of literature, trauma theory has evolved as a way of looking at how past tragedies are reflected in writing – and of seeing how writing about suffering can help in dealing with it.

In Chinese culture there is a traditional way of looking at past suffering: to associate grief and grievances that have not been rectified with ghosts: angry ghosts, sad ghosts or hungry ghosts. The ghosts will not let past evil disappear until the evil done to them has been propitiated. These beliefs, once outlawed as superstition, have made a comeback over the past decades.

---

[20] *1942*, director Feng Xiaogang, 2012.
[21] Gu Hua, *A Small Town Called Hibiscus* (Beijing: Chinese Literature, 1983); Yan Lianke, *Serve the People* (New York: Black Cat, 2008) and *Lenin's Kisses* (New York: Grove, 2012); Mo Yan, *The Garlic Ballads* (New York: Viking, 1995); Chan Koonchung, *The Fat Years* (New York: Doubleday, 2009).

This idea is difficult to grasp, particularly for those who think of themselves as rational and dismiss the existence of ghosts. There is a problem of language. In Chinese there are three distinct words that are translated into English as 'ghost'.

Table C.1 *Ghosts and spirits in Chinese*

ling	靈	Family ghost, good associations, there to help the living.
gui	鬼	Angry, hungry or evil spirit, determined to harass those who committed evil deeds.
shen	神	Holy figures, local spirits, well-disposed to the living.

The *ling* have to be respected; there are proper ceremonies to be performed for them, especially at the Qingming Festival when people visit the graves of their forbears to burn paper offerings to provide for them in the afterlife. These rituals, once denounced as feudalistic, have been reintroduced since the early 1980s. The *shen* live in temples and shrines. Hundreds of thousands of these places have been rebuilt over the past three decades, after the fury of destruction in the Cultural Revolution. The *gui* are more difficult to cope with. They may live on for centuries. They make their presence felt through cold currents of air, strange signs, mysterious noises. Until they are propitiated – which often requires the services of religious specialists – they will haunt those who harmed them and their descendants.

The ghosts of recent history, of the Civil War and of the Mao era, have yet to be laid.

Survival, resilience and resourcefulness

The Civil War determined much of what would happen in China over the next half century. The sombre evaluation by Odd Arne Westad, the leading Western historian of the war, sums up widely held views:

Much of what went wrong in Chinese history over the past fifty years – and in my opinion there was more wrong than right – was based on the experiences of the civil war by the generation who fought it. The militarization of society, the deification of the supreme leader and the extreme faith in the power of human will and of short, total campaigns – all came out of the lessons the Chinese Communists believed to have learned from the late 1940s. So too did their obsession with control of intellectuals, labor leaders and national minorities, their enmity with the United States and their application of Soviet models.[22]

---

[22] Odd Arne Westad, *Decisive Encounters* (Stanford: Stanford University Press, 2003), p. 328.

This was not the first time in Chinese history that brutal conquest was followed by state brutality. The glories of Chinese culture have been interspersed with grief and tragedy. Warfare has haunted Chinese history, from the Warring States period if not before. There are plenty of tyrants in Chinese history. The most terrible was also the founder of a united China, Qin Shihuang. There have been periods of mass brutality, notably the Mongol invasion, and the Ming/Qing transition. Through these cataclysms the Chinese people learned to survive and to be resilient. The ability to survive the Civil War and the political movements of the Mao era, the ability to bear hardship, was learned from this cultural inheritance and, in the immediate past, from experiences of the Resistance War.

One of the remarkable aspects of survival was physical. Many of the intellectuals who stayed on the Mainland in 1949 and endured the difficulties and persecution of the next decades still survived to great ages – Liang Shuming to 94, Ma Yinchu to 100, Fei Xiaotong to 94. Their longevity is counter-balanced by the many others who died long before they should have done, often in the despair of suicide.

Even more extraordinary was the survival of the wartime leaders into deep old age, Chiang Kai-shek, Mao Zedong and Emperor Hirohito, all of whom lived to a ripe old age and died of natural causes, in their own beds. Song Meiling lived to an even greater age, at least 105 – her exact age was never clarified.

Surviving leaders

All three of the major leaders associated with the Anti-Japanese War and the Civil War survived long after the wars, all in the same dominant positions they had risen to during their careers. All died in their beds. Chiang Kai-shek lost his country and his capital, but he continued (except for a brief period during which he was forced to resign as the Civil War was ending) as president of (a much reduced) Republic of China until his death in 1975, at the age of 87. Mao Zedong died a year later, at the age of 82, still at the top of the CCP system. He had to weather a series of major challenges to hold on to power, but he dealt with all his opponents within the CCP with great ruthlessness. Emperor Hirohito was allowed by the Allied victors in the Second World War to continue in his position as emperor, in whose name the war had been fought, although he had to announce publicly that he was a mortal and not a divine being. He died in 1989 at the age of 87. All three leaders died of illness in old age. All were accorded splendid funerals and extended official mourning. None was ever called to account for their failures or for the atrocities committed during their rules.

Resilience

Survival is often attributed to resilience. The concept of resilience may be physical – a key concept in engineering – psychological or social. In each context it speaks to the ability to bounce back, to recover from an attack or a setback, to return to the original state. Two forms of resilience, physical and social, are combined in two classic Chinese images. The first is of the bow. People can rebound (*tanxing*), just as the bow springs back after it is pulled to unleash an arrow. The second symbol of resilience is the bamboo, which bows with the wind but rights itself once the storm has passed. Trees with rigid trunks will snap in a gale, but the bamboo bends, even down to the ground, and still recovers.

The courage and endurance of the Chinese people through the agonies of the Resistance War, the Civil War and the first decades of the People's Republic is awe-inspiring. People who suffered from war, political movements, natural disasters and personal losses, as most Chinese did, have shown incredible resilience. In this resilience there is no room for self-pity. What there is instead is a will and determination to transcend misery, to move forward.

Resilience may seem a passive acceptance of maltreatment, but it may also be a practical reaction to forces beyond one's control. It has its own rewards. In traditional as well as modern China there is a pride in resilience, which makes one part of a long tradition of survival. Resilience is positive in another way. It does not mean returning to the same place, but arriving at a new equilibrium, stronger rather than weaker. Although it seems to mean going back to the *status quo ante*, which is not possible when the old system has been badly damaged or destroyed. When it has changed so radically, under stresses too great to resist, there may be no going back to the old order. Resilience then comes to mean learning from past difficulties and assaults to cope not with the old world but with a new one.

Is this resilience the same phenomenon as post-traumatic stress growth, the conception of the French psychologist Boris Cyrulnik? Cyrulnik's own childhood was deeply scarred by the horrors of war; as a Jewish child in Nazi-occupied France, he was forced to live hidden in a foster family. He survived, as many others did not, and came to believe that surviving childhood trauma had to have positive outcomes and that, although survival left deep scars, the survivor could, with help, learn to grow from past anguish and was not doomed to perpetual sadness.[23]

---

[23] Boris Cyrulnik, *La murmure des phantoms* (*The Whispering of Ghosts*) (Paris: Odile Jacob, 2003).

Resilience is heroic. The traditional Chinese treatment of suffering and trauma seems to suggest that the obliteration of past pain was not a long-term goal. In Chinese culture there has been a tradition, at times rising almost to a sacrament, of honouring people who showed the ability to transcend awful trauma and maltreatment. A woman may weep so hard for her dead husband that parts of the Great Wall come tumbling down – the legend of Meng Jiang Nu, from more than two millennia ago. A man may be wrongfully done to death, but his reputation lives on in glory. Yue Fei, the unjustly executed general of the Southern Song, a millennium ago, is one of the greatest examples of posthumous celebration; the man who conspired to bring about his death, Qin Hui, is still loathed.[24] Lovers may be separated by cruel parents and, after they elope, are caught and killed, but their spirits fly up together to the heavens – the legend immortalised in the Willow Pattern plate.[25] These stories are known to every Chinese. All are forms of resilience, of the triumph, in life or death, over adversity. They also remind people that suffering is not to be forgotten.

Resourcefulness and flexibility

Resourcefulness is an inherited cultural pattern. This example is more than two millennia old, from the Warring States. It indicates that having several ways of surviving difficulty is the only way to cope with the uncertainties of life.

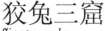

Jiao tu san ku
The clever hare has three holes to its burrow

This principle may have been more helpful than any other in surviving what modern Chinese have had to endure. Always leave yourself a way out, never get trapped down a hole, use your intelligence to foresee what bad things may happen, and be smart in choosing which hole to use to get out of trouble.[26]

Flexibility is a little different and less positive then resourcefulness. It involves determination for personal survival at all costs. It is a reaction

---

[24] Until quite recently people visiting Hangzhou could show their contempt for Qin Hui by spitting on his statue in the Yue Fei Temple. This is no longer permitted, on public health grounds.

[25] The Willow Pattern became one of the most popular designs in Western ceramics.

[26] The word *tu* can be translated as hare or rabbit but, given the negative connotations of rabbit in English, hare seems more appropriate.

to difficulties that goes back into antiquity. The survival tactics learned in the Resistance War and the Civil War came in useful. In the early decades of communist rule flexibility was as useful as it had been to earlier Chinese. Those who survived the decades of tumultuous political movements did so by going along with the prevailing line, whatever it was, often at the cost of ties of family, friendship and community. It was a barren survival; it proved, as it had done in the wars, that survival alone does little to improve or strengthen society. After the last of the movements were over, and the economic reforms started, the sense of relief was tinged with a recognition of loss. With the sense of loss came a tacit acceptance that the tumultuous events of the recent past had changed what it mean to be Chinese.

Identities

The 12 years of war that China endured between 1937 and 1949 had a permanent effect on Chinese identity. The Resistance War saw the arrival of mass nationalism and the creation of a national consciousness and a national identity that had not existed before. The Civil War, by contrast, created permanent divisions: two Chinas, on the Mainland and in Taiwan, and beyond that the separation of the Mainland from those of Chinese origin living abroad.

The permanent changes brought about the emergence of several different Chinese identities, reflected in the formal terms now used in China to distinguish between different types of people of Chinese descent: those living in China and those living in other countries:

Table C.2 *Chinese identities*

Chinese	中国人	*Zhongguoren*
person of Chinese descent	华人	*Huaren*
foreign citizen of Chinese descent	华裔	*Huayi*
Overseas Chinese	华侨	*huaqiao*
Expatriate	流落海外	*liuluo haiwai*
Hong Kong compatriot	港胞	*Gangbao*
Taiwan compatriot	台胞	*Taibao*

The actual identity of people from Hong Kong and Taiwan are not reflected in these designations. Over the long period after 1949 many people in Hong Kong began to think of themselves less as Chinese compatriots and more as belonging to Hong Kong. The change in identity in Taiwan has been different. For several decades there was a clear division. The people who had moved from the Mainland were known colloquially as *waisheng* (people from another province). The local people called themselves Taiwanese, or colloquially *bentu* (local). Over time that distinction has blurred. There is now a strong Taiwan identity, whatever the origin of earlier generations.

Further away from China the identity of people of Chinese descent has been diluted. In Southeast Asia there has been a blurring of ethnic lines, after the intense anti-Chinese hostility in some countries (notably Indonesia and Vietnam) in the 1960s and 1970s. In North America people of Chinese descent began in the 1950s to call themselves Chinese-Americans or Chinese-Canadians. Their children and grandchildren often think of themselves as Americans or Canadians.

Cultural China

A new concept has emerged that transcends the distinctions in identity. That is Cultural China, a conception that celebrates not ancestry or citizenship but a great cultural tradition. Its appeal is that it can be enjoyed by anyone willing to take the time to immerse themselves in China's cultural riches.

After 1949 traditional culture was preserved not within China, where the 'feudal order' was under attack, but in emigration, principally in Hong Kong and Taiwan. The ROC government gave massive support to traditional cultural production, and built the greatest museum of Chinese art in the world, the Palace Museum. Hong Kong became a major centre for publishing, fine arts and film production. One of the major themes of cultural production in Hong Kong has been the *wuxia*, the beloved knights-errant of traditional culture. The most famous works (all of them later filmed) are the 15 novels written by Louis Cha (Cha Liangyong) under his pen name Jin Yong.

Since the 1980s the Mainland has re-embraced many aspects of traditional culture, sometimes with the help of Chinese from outside. Bai Xianyong, from Taiwan, has done more than anyone else to revive the great opera form of *kunju*, which was almost destroyed on the Mainland in favour of revolutionary opera.

Chinese culture is now celebrated around the world. It is in a vibrant stage of creativity, flourishing in many different directions, traditional, modern and post-modern.

The Chinese language

The fundamental element of the cultural tradition, the written language, was dramatically simplified in the 1950s on the Mainland, in the interests

of promoting literacy while attacking the feudal past.[27] Traditional characters were preserved in Taiwan and Hong Kong. The changes in the
written language were great enough to make them, if not mutually unin-
telligible, still very difficult to understand for people who use one or the
other form of writing.

Traditional and simplified characters

Table C.3 *Traditional and simplified characters*

	Meaning	*Traditional*	*Simplified*
long	dragon	龍	龙
guang	broad	廣	广
du	read	讀	读
qin	close	親	亲
shu	book	書	书
zhan	war	戰	战

The spoken language has been a battleground between the governments
in both Beijing and Taibei and the people. Both governments have promoted the language known in the West as Mandarin (*Putonghua* on the
Mainland, *Guoyu* in Taiwan), but in many parts of China it remains a
second language, after the local dialect. Ideological concerns have faded.
The pragmatic outcome is bilingualism or multilingualism. An example
is the Hong Kong businesswoman Hai Chi-yuet, the just-retired managing director of the Yantian Container Terminal. In her work she used
Cantonese, Putonghua, Shanghai Dialect and English. She is slightly
unusual in being competent in four languages, but having a mastery of
three is now common.

Reunions and separations

Beijing's new policies from the 1980s on have undone many of the separations created by war and revolution, at least for those who survived.
Within China people have been able to return from the borderlands in
retirement, if they have enough money to buy a place to live; unit housing is a thing of the past. From outside China people have gone back
to visit family there. And over the past decade it has become easy for
Mainlanders to leave China as tourists or on visits to relatives abroad.

---

[27] Efforts to replace characters with the Roman alphabet through the introduction of
Hanyu pinyin have largely failed.

Bridging the gap of almost four decades has not been easy, if even possible, given how many people died while separated. In the earliest stage of reunions, many Mainlanders were glad to see long-lost relatives but also bitter over what they had endured for having relatives abroad. In the 1980s they were poor in comparison to their relatives outside China, and they wanted money from their rich relatives, and, for their children, opportunities to leave China to study.

Families had grown far apart over four or more decades. Some of the younger generation born in emigration no longer spoke any form of Chinese, nor had much idea of how life in China worked. Their own habits of life were so different that, even if they could speak to each other, they were strangers to each other. The family ties were still real, especially in Overseas Chinese communities with a tradition of separation, but the separations had been too long to re-establish emotional ties.

Ties with the dead have survived. For many people not having performed the proper rituals for a parent was a huge psychological burden. David Chang, who had fled to the USA in 1949, went to his parents' grave as soon as it was possible for him to return to China – in 1979. He gave this passionate, almost histrionic lament, which showed how deeply the failure to properly care for a parent in death was felt:

I had abandoned my mother, left her to suffer and die without my comfort, her heart broken and crying out for her lost sons, of whom I had been the youngest, dearest and most culpable for the final tragedy of her life.[28]

One of the great desires in the 1980s was to return to pray at the graves of parents and more distant forebears. In some cases this meant rebuilding a grave destroyed in the Cultural Revolution. All over China relatives have visited from abroad to see to proper graves for their forebears. The grave of General Lu Rongting in Wuming, near Nanning (Guangxi), almost destroyed by Red Guards in the late 1960s, was rebuilt and even realigned, to fit the local *fengshui* (spirits of wind and water) better. The reburial was done in close collaboration between the local authorities, who wanted to commemorate their most famous native son, and his descendants in Hong Kong.[29]

Two civil wars: the social outcomes

The two communist powers of the twentieth century, Russia and China, emerged to power from civil wars. In the aftermath of civil war both went

---

[28] David Wen-wei Chang and A.P. Carter, *The Soldier and the Tiger: A Memoir of Famine and War in Revolutionary China* (Lanham: Rowman and Littlefield, 2009), p. 162.
[29] Visit to Wuming, 1984.

through the vast and terrible process of class warfare. Both annihilated their old social elites. Both lost great numbers of their intellectual elites to persecution and to emigration. Both abandoned old social codes in favour of 'socialist morality'. Both attacked religion.

The long-term outcome of revolution was profoundly ironic: both states eventually rejected the socialist cause, the USSR explicitly, China in all but name – the Communist Party remains in power, ruling in the name of 'socialism with Chinese characteristics'. Both states have tried to revive elements of the old, pre-war order. In Russia the Orthodox Church is flourishing, and the (would-be) charismatic leader, Vladimir Putin, rules in the style of the tsars. In China Confucius is once again revered as a sage; at home he is the mentor for proper social behaviour, and abroad he is the symbol of Chinese culture (the Confucius Institutes).

The time span between the initial revolutions and the end of the socialist orders marks a critical difference between the two societies. The socialist order dominated Russia for seven decades; the old order was effectively beyond living memory. In China the gap between the CCP's victory in the Civil War and the Reform Era was four decades; memories of the old order survived. More importantly there were intact Chinese societies outside China. The millions of Russian refugees from the civil war were stateless, without a state structure to aid the maintenance of an integrated social order; within a generation or two the émigré communities died out. Chinese societies survived outside China, in Taiwan, Hong Kong and in the Overseas communities. Since the start of the Reform Era these extant Chinese communities have been used as tacit references for Mainlanders, looking to see how a Chinese society that had not been through the Mao era might look. It is embarrassing for those who share the current triumphalist vision of China to look openly at models from Hong Kong and Taiwan, but without fanfare it is happening. Terms of respect never lost abroad have crept back into the Chinese language. One example: the term *tongzhi* (comrade) has disappeared, replaced by traditional polite forms of address.[30] The concept of religious charity has reappeared, stimulated in part by the work of the Taiwan Buddhist welfare organisations Ziji (Tzu-chi) and Foguang (Fo-kuang), both of which are active on the Mainland.

The reversion to some aspects of the old social order must not be exaggerated. The changes brought about by the turbulent decades of the Mao era are profound, as are the changes brought by modernisation, such as birth control, medical improvement and electronic communication.

---

[30] *Tongzhi* is now the slang word for 'gay'.

One twist in the comparison between Russia and China: the Soviet order collapsed in the immediate aftermath of the Tiananmen Massacre in Beijing. The international revulsion and outcry against China was so strong that the Soviet regime dared not follow Beijing's tough example. All over Eastern Europe similar mass protests to those that broke out in China in the spring of 1989 were accommodated, not crushed, by the state. The outcome was that the Soviet order came to an end. The dead of Beijing helped to create a new world for the people of the former Soviet Union.

Biographies

Louis Cha

Louis Cha (Cha Liangyong) was born in 1924 in Zhejiang, the son of a distinguished literary family. His grandfather passed the highest level of the traditional examinations. Growing up in turbulent times, his devotion to his nation was profound, but his education quite limited. He became a journalist and, well before the CCP takeover, moved to Hong Kong. His journalistic career was very successful – he founded the leading Hong Kong newspaper *Ming Bao*. His great fame depended, however, on the series of 15 novels he wrote in the 1950s and 1960s under the pen name Jin Yong. These are dramatic, exciting tales of adventure, and at the same time tributes to the great popular tradition of knights-errant (*wuxia*), the bold, brave men who fought for right against evil. Many of his novels are set in the distant past, but the analogies to the present can never be missed. Although the books were banned on the Mainland for a long while, Jin Yong became the bestselling Chinese-language author worldwide.

Leaders' children

The Civil War was fought by the CCP in the name of turning against the past. In the case of the leaders' own lives their attitudes towards the traditional family were very mixed. While none was able to pass on their status to their children, a practice that would have seemed feudal, they kept to the tradition of fathering large numbers of children. Mao Zedong had four wives and ten children, many of whom died or disappeared when they were young. Liu Shaoqi had six wives and nine children. At the opposite end of the marriage spectrum, Zhou Enlai was a model of marital constancy. He was devoted to his only wife, Deng Yingchao; the couple had no children.

The leader of the GMD was less prolific. Chiang Kai-shek had at least two wives, but fathered only one child, Chiang Ching-kuo (Jiang Jingguo). Chiang Wei-kuo (Jiang Weiguo), recognised by Chiang Kai-shek as his son, was widely believed to be adopted, the child of another man. Chiang Ching-kuo did inherit his father's status. He became president of the Republic of China after his father's death – and promptly launched Taiwan on the path to democracy, something his father had steadfastly refused to do. By contrast to the Chiang family, the long-lasting marriage of GMD general Bai Chongxi and Ma Peichang was legendary for the couple's devotion to each other and for their large number of children, seven sons and three daughters.

Descendants of revolutionaries

The present generation of descendants of the early communist leaders are often referred to as 'princelings (*taizidang*)'. They are the subject of massive gossip, often accused of using their illustrious family connections to engage in money-making and influence-peddling. There is no possibility of confirming these allegations, given the absence of a free press. The importance of revolutionary connections has a special element: almost all of the members of the *taizidang* grew up seeing their fathers being persecuted in the Cultural Revolution, and themselves being persecuted because of their parentage.

Xi Jinping, the current secretary-general of the Chinese Communist Party, is the son of a veteran revolutionary. His father was purged during the political campaigns of the Mao era, and Xi spent many years working in the countryside before he was able, in the Reform Era, to go to university.

Some of the children of early revolutionaries have risen high only to crash to the ground. Bo Xilai (born 1949), the son of Bo Yibo, a prominent early member of the CCP, was until recently seen as a future leader of the entire country; he held successively more important roles in regional governments and emerged as a leading campaigner against official corruption. He is now in jail, convicted of corruption and bribery. His wife, Gu Kailai, has already received a suspended death sentence for her part in the death of an English businessman, Neil Heywood. Whatever the truth of the criminal charges, it is often suggested that political rivalries are behind the treatment of Bo and his wife.

Children of exiles

Ma Yingjiu, the current president of the Republic of China, personifies the generation of children born after their parents left the Mainland – in his case in Hong Kong. He is highly accomplished, a graduate of universities in Taiwan and the USA, fluently trilingual. He has been elected several times, as mayor of Taibei and twice as president of the ROC. Ma's success in democratic politics gives the lie to the claims made by supporters of autocracy that Chinese are unsuited to democracy.

Some of the best-known Chinese names in the cultural world in the West are the children of people who fled from China in 1949. This is a very partial list: writers Bai Xianyong, Lung Ying-tai and Amy Tan; film director Ang Lee; dress designer Vera Wang; tennis player Michael Chang. All are cosmopolitan, at home in many different places, attached to their Chinese roots but detached from the authority of the Chinese state. They belong where they choose to belong, even at the cost of never fully belonging anywhere. Ang Lee had this to say about his sense of detachment:

I was never a citizen of any particular place. My parents left China to go to Taiwan. We were outsiders there. We moved to the States. Outsiders. Back to China. Now we are outsiders there too, outsiders from America.[31]

Two last questions

Two last questions hang in the air. The first is whether China has recovered from the terrible damage of the wars of the twentieth century. On the Mainland the question is answered at the level of political power. The process of territorial recovery is still not complete, but China's political ascendency is unquestioned.

The response to the first question leads to the second question: is China unchanged? Are the changes to the structure of Chinese society that came with the Resistance War, the Civil War and the Mao era permanent and irreversible? Or is the bedrock of Chinese society untouched? Has the essence of Chinese culture and society survived? The current government, with its stress on Chinese values and on a revived Confucianism, seems to believe that the bedrock is still intact. The irony of a Confucian revival under a communist party is not lost; it seems a deeply antagonistic contradiction for a revolutionary party to emulate the old order. The cynical see a practical purpose to the stress on Confucianism; the state avoids providing social services by giving a philosophical underpinning to get people to rely on family and community for these services.

My own feeling is that, although the belief that the past was a well-ordered place may be illusory, there is still much of great value to be found in the past. If China can recover some parts of this past, then the

---

[31] Ang Lee, interview with Roger Ebert, 11 December 2005; YouTube.

terrible damages of the wars and the chaos of the first three decades of communist rule have not completely destroyed the old society.

苦盡甘來

Ku jin gan lai

When the bitterness is exhausted sweetness may come

The PLA heroes temple*

The Fujian communities on the shores of the Taiwan Straits were often shelled and strafed during the last stages of the Civil War and in the early 1950s. In one such raid on the beautiful white sand beach of Chongwen Township, a 13-year-old girl, Zeng Hen, was almost killed. She was saved by five soldiers who threw themselves on top of her as the shells rained down. All were killed. Five decades later Zeng, after a determined struggle with the local authorities to acquire the site, managed to get a temple built in memory of the 27 soldiers who died in the raid, including the five who saved her. One half is a Buddhist temple, the other a shrine to the soldiers. She raised the money herself. The temple is built in the traditional Minnan style, and stands above the beautiful beach.

To have a Buddhist temple dedicated to men serving an ideology explicitly opposed to religion has a delicious irony about it. The temple is frequently visited now by members of the PLA, retired and serving; it is the only temple dedicated to members of the PLA.

* Jiang Weixin, *Zhuangzhan ershi qi jun: Chongwu Xishawan Jiefangjun lieshimiao* (*Twenty-seven Good Fighters: The Temple to the Martyrs of the PLA in Xishawan, Chongwen*) (Chongwu: 2010).

Glossary

People

Andy Lao (see Liu Dehua)	
Ai Qing	艾青
Ai Weiwei	艾未未
Aisin Gioro Puyi	愛新覺羅溥儀
Aisin Gioro Xianyu	愛新覺羅顯玗
Ang Lee (see Li An)	
Bada shanren	八大山人
Bai Chongxi	白崇禧
Bai Xianyong (Pai Hsien-yung)	白先勇
Bai Yang	白央
Bei Yuming (I.M. Pei)	贝聿铭
Bo Xilai	薄熙来
Bo Yibo	薄一波
Cato Yang (see Yang Kaidao)	
Cao Richang	曹日昌
Cha Liangyong	查良鏞
Chan, Anson (see Fang Ansheng)	
Chan, Jackie (see Chen Gangsheng)	
Chang, Carsun (see Zhang Junmai)	
Chang Kia-ngau (see Zhang Jia'ao)	
Chen Bulei	陈布雷
Chen Gangsheng (Chan, Jackie)	陈港生
Chen Gongbo	陈公博
Chen Jiageng (Tan Kha-khee)	陈嘉庚
Chen Kaige	陈凯歌
Chen Lian	陈琏
Chen Mengjia	陈梦家
Chen Pijun	陈璧君
Chen Xiaolu	陈小鲁
Chen Yi (Communist)	陈毅

Chen Yi (Guomindang)	陈仪
Chen Yonggui	陈永贵
Chen Zhirang (Jerome Ch'en)	陈志让
Cheng Tangkou	成湯口
Cheng Yingmei	成英妹
Cheng Yueru (Lin Dai)	徥月如
Cheo Ying (see Zhou Ying)	
Chiang Kai-shek (see Jiang Jieshi)	
Chiang Monlin (see Jiang Menglin)	
Chow Yun-fat (see Zhou Runfa)	
Chu Minyi	褚民誼
Cui Jincai	崔进才
Dai Li	戴笠
Deng Xiaoping	邓小平
Deng Yingchao	邓颖超
Ding Ling	丁玲
Dong Zhujun	董竹君
Dong Zuobin	董作賓
Du Yuming	杜聿明
Du Zhili	杜致禮
Fan Qishi	范启爽
Fan Yuanjian	范元健
Fang Ansheng (Chan, Anson)	方安生
Fei Xiaotong	费孝通
Feng Zikai	丰子恺
Franklin Yang (see Yang Zhenning)	
Fu Baoshi	傅抱石
Fu Dongju	傅冬菊
Fu Lei	傅雷
Fu Sinian	傅斯年
Fu Zong	傅聰
Fu Zuoyi	傅作义
Ge You	葛优
Gong Li	巩俐
Gong Peng	龚澎
Gong Pusheng	龚普生
Gu Kailai	谷开來
Gu Weijun	顧纬鈞
Guomindang (see Chen Yi)	
Guo Moruo	郭沫若
Ha Jin	哈金
Hai Chi-yuet (see Xi Zhiyue)	

Han Gaozu	汉高祖
He Yingqin	何应钦
He Zizhen	贺子珍
Hong Nailiang	洪乃良
Hou Hsiao-hsien (see Hou Xiaoxian)	
Hou Xiaoxian (Hou Hsiao-hsien)	侯孝贤
Hu Die	胡蝶
Hua Luogeng	华罗庚
Huang Guoming	黄国明
Huang Yaowu	黄尧武
Huang Zhenfang	黄振方
Huang Zhenguo	黄振国
Jerome Ch'en (see Chen Zhirang)	
Jet Li (see Li Lianjie)	
Ji Chaoding	冀朝定
Ji Chaozhu	冀朝铸
Jiang Fangliang	蒋方良
Jiang Jieshi (Chiang Kai-shek)	蒋介石
Jiang Menglin (Chiang Monlin)	蒋梦麟
Jiang Qing	江青
Jiang Wen	姜文
Jianguo	建国
Jianmin	建民
Jianping	建平
Kang Sheng	康生
Lao She	老舍
Lee Teng-hui (see Li Denghui)	
Lee Tsung-tao (see Li Zhengdao)	
Li An (Ang Lee)	李安
Li Denghui (Lee Teng-hui)	李登辉
Li Gongpu	李公朴
Li Ji	李济
Li Lianjie (Jet Li)	李连杰
Li Peng	李鹏
Li Zhengdao (Lee Tsung-tao)	李政道
Li Zongren	李宗仁
Liang Qichao	梁启超
Liang Shuming	梁漱溟
Liang Sicheng	梁思成
Liang Siyong	梁思永
Lin Biao	林彪
Lin Daguang	林达光

Lin Dai (see Cheng Yueru)	林黛
Lin Huiyin	林徽因
Liu Bang	刘邦
Liu Bocheng	刘伯承
Liu Dehua (Andy Lao)	刘德华
Liu Hulan	刘胡兰
Liu Yuxi	刘禹锡
Long Yingtai (Lung Ying-t'ai)	龍應台
Lu Rongting	陆荣廷
Lung Ying-t'ai (see Long Yingtai)	
Lu Xun	鲁迅
Ma Peizhang	马佩璋
Ma Yingjiu (Ma Ying-cheou)	马英九
Ma Ying-cheou (see Ma Yingjiu)	
Ma Yinqu	马寅初
Mang Yuqin	莽玉琴
Mao Zedong	毛泽东
Mei Lanfang	梅兰芳
Meng Jiang Nu	孟姜女
Pai Hsien-yung (see Bai Xianyong)	
Pang Jingtang	龐鏡塘
Pei Wenzhong	裴文中
I.M. Pei (see Bei Yuming)	
Peng Jinchuan	彭金川
Peng Liyuan	彭丽媛
Qi Baishi	齐白石
Qian Xuesen (Tsien Hsueh-shen)	钱学森
Qiao Guanhua	乔冠华
Qin Shihuang	秦世皇
Rong Guiyu	荣桂玉
Rong Yiren	荣毅仁
Song Meiling	宋美龄
Song Qingling	宋庆龄
Song Ziwen	宋子文
Sun Ruilan	孙瑞兰
Sun Yat-sen	孙中山
Sunzi	孙子
Tan Kha-khee (see Chen Jiageng)	
Tao Yuanming	陶渊明
Tsai Chin (see Zhou Caiqin)	
Tsien Hsueh-shen (see Qian Xuesen)	
Wang Guangmei	王光美

Wang Kemin	王克敏
Wang Jingwei	汪精衞
Wang Zhihong	王志宏
Wei Lihuang	卫立煌
Wen Yiduo	闻一多
Wu Hongqi	吳鸿麒
Wu Huawen	吳华文
Wu Jianxiong	吳健雄
Wu Ningkun	巫宁坤
Xi Jinping	习近平
Xi Zhiyue (Hai Chi-yuet)	溪治月
Xia Nai	夏鼐
Xiang Yu	項羽
Xiong Xiling	熊希龄
Xu Beihong	徐悲鸿
Yan Lianke	阎连科
Yang Kaidao (Cato Yang)	杨开道
Yang Kaihui	杨开慧
Yang Xianyi	杨宪益
Yang Zhenning (Franklin Yang)	杨振宁
Ying Ruocheng	英若诚
Youhua	友华
Youkang	友康
Yousu	友苏
Yu Chengjie	于成節
Yu Chengxiao	于成孝
Yu Chengyi	于成義
Yu Chengzhong	于成忠
Yu Muren	于牧人
Yu Wenxiu	余文秀
Yu Xingcha	于星槎
Yuan Yongxi	袁永熙
Yue Fei	岳飞
Zeng Hen	曾恨
Zhang Ailing	张爱玲
Zhang Daqian	张大千
Zhang Guangzhi	张光直
Zhang Guotao	张国焘
Zhang Jia'ao (Chang Kia-ngau)	张嘉璈
Zhang Junmai (Chang, Carsun)	张君劢
Zhang Xueliang	张学良
Zhang Xueming	张学明

Zhang Xuesi	张学思
Zhang Yimou	张艺谋
Zhang Zhenglong	张正隆
Zhang Ziyi	章子怡
Zheng Dongguo	郑洞国
Zhou Caiqin (Tsai Chin)	周采芹
Zhou Enlai	周恩來
Zhou Fohai	周佛海
Zhou Runfa (Chow Yun-fat)	周润发
Zhou Xinfang	周信芳
Zhou Ying (Cheo Ying)	周瑛
Zhou Zuoren	周作人
Zhuangzi	莊子
Zhuge Liang	诸葛亮

Chengyu and slogans

Ai hong bian ye	哀鴻遍野
An bing bu dong	按兵不動
An jian shang ren	暗箭傷人
Ba xin jiao gei dang	把心交給党
Bei tong yu jie	悲痛歟絕
Bing bai ru shan dao	兵败如山倒
Bing bu xue dao	兵不血刃
Bing jiu er guo li zhe mo zhi you ye	兵久而国利者未之有也
Can bing bai jiang	殘兵敗將
Cheng xia zhi meng	城下之盟
Fanjian suku	反奸诉苦
Geren de shi, wulun duoda, ye shi xiaoshi	个人的事无论多大也是小事
Haoren bu dang bing	好人不当兵
Huan wo he shan	还我河山
Jiao tu san ku	狡兔三窟
Kan feng shi duo	看凤使舵
Ku jin gan lai	苦盡甘來
Luan qi ba zao	亂七八糟
Nongcun baowei chengshi	农村包維城市
Nongye xue Dazhai	农业学大寨
Qi li zi san	妻離子散
Qiang ganzi li chu zhengquan	抢杆子里出政权
Qianmen ju long houmen jin lang	前門拒虎 後門進狼
Qianxing wanku	千幸万苦
Qiegouzhe zhu, qieguozhe hou	竊鈎者誅 竊國者候

Ren ge you yi si, huo zhong yu Taishan, huo qing yu	人个有一死 或重于泰山或輕于鳥毛
Ru ru wuren zhi jing	如入无人之境
Sheng de weida, si de guangrong	生的伟大, 死的光荣
Shengsi buming	生死不明
Shi ru po zhu	事如破竹
Tu beng wa jie	土崩瓦解
Wei renmin fuwu	为人民复务
Yi jiang chunshui xiang dong liu	一江春水向东流
Yi qiong er bai	一穷二白
Yishou naqiang, yishou fentian	一手拿枪一手分田
Yu tian dou, yu di dou, yu ren dou	与天斗与地斗与人斗
Zhanluan	戰亂
Zhi laohu	紙老虎
Zhongguo renmin zhan qilai le	中国人民站起來了
Zhumen jiurou chou, lu you dongsi gu	朱門酒肉臭 路有凍死骨
Zi chu mie wang	自取滅亡

Words and terms

aiguo zhanshi	爱国战士
Baodao	宝岛
bawang	霸王
Beihai yinhang	北海银行
Beijing yuanren	北京猿人
bentu	本土
bingtuan	兵团
caizhu	财主
changpao magua	长袍马褂
chengyu	成语
chetui	撤退
chou lao jiu	臭老九
chuangshang	创傷
daigong	代工
dangji liduan	當机立断
danwei	单位
didi	弟弟
dizhu huanxiangtuan	地主还乡团
Dongbei yinhang	东北銀行
duba	独霸
duixiang	对象
Ererba	二二八
Fabi	法幣

fankeshen	番客婶
fanshen	翻身
fei	匪
fengpai	凤派
fenpei	分配
ganbu	干部
ganqing	感情
gege	哥哥
gongfei	共匪
guangfu	光复
guanyuan	官员
guxiang	古乡
guizi	鬼子
Guofei	国匪
Guomindang	国民党
Guoyu	国语
haiwai guanxi	海外关系
hanjian	汉奸
Hanyu pinyin	汉语拼音
hei si lei	黑四类
hei wu lei	黑五类
hong	紅
Huazhong yinhang	华中银行
hukou	戶口
huohua	火化
jia	家
jian	建
Jiefang	解放
Jiefang zhanzheng	解放战争
jiefangqu	解放区
jieji douzheng	阶级斗争
jieshou (take-over)	接收
jieshou (hand-over)	接受
jieshou (plunder)	劫受
juncun	军村
Juntong	军統
KangRi zhanzheng	抗日战争
Kaogu yanjiusuo	考古研究所
Kongsheng dao	孔圣道
lafu	拉夫
lao baixing	老百姓
laoxiang	老乡
liumang	流忙

Liusi	六四
lunxian	沦陷
Lushi zhengce	录事政策
mangliu	盲流
Minjindang	民近党
nantong	难童
nanxia ganbu	南下干部
nianhua	年画
paiyan beiju	排演悲剧
pingfan	平反
Putonghua	普通話
qi qiang pai	骑墙派
qiaoxiang	侨乡
qingliu	清流
Qingming jie	清明节
qipao	旗袍
Renminbi	人民币
Sanba zuofeng	三八作凤
Sanfan	三反
Sanmin zhuyi	三民主义
saomu	扫墓
shangtong	傷痛
shaobing	燒鉼
shengchan jianshe bingtuan	生产建设兵团
shengli dongliu	胜利东流
shenshi	绅士
shizong	矢碌
sishou	死守
taitai	太太
Taiyu	台语
taizidang	太子党
tan lianai	谈连愛
tanxing	弹性
taonan	逃难
tongzhi	同志
tudi gaige	土地改革
waisheng	外省
wangfu	王府
weijun	伪军
wenxiangdui	闻香队
women dou shi qiongku renjia *zidi, eduzi shoucheng weile shei?*	我们都是穷苦人家子弟, 俄肚子守城为了谁?
wufan	五反

wuren qu	无人区
wuxia	武侠
xiafang	下放
xiandai	现代
xiaodao xiaoxi	小道消息
xiaohun de difang	销魂的地方
xiaonian xianfengdui	小年先锋队
xuetong	血通
yi bian dao	一边倒
Yiguandao	一貫道
youpai	右派
Youyi binguan	友议宾馆
yuanfen	缘分
yuzi	芋子
zhanfan	战犯
zhiqing	知青
Zhonghua minguo	中华民国
Zhonghua renmin gongheguo	中华人民共和国
zhuyi bing	主义兵
zifa	自发
zixin	自新
zouzepai	走资派
zuihou yifeng xin	最后一封信

Places (not including major cities and provinces)

Beidahuang	北大荒
Chongwen	崇文
Dingling	定陵
Fuzimiao	夫子廟
Guang'an	光安
Gulangyu	鼓浪屿
Handan	邯郸
HuaiHai	淮海
Hualian	花莲
Huanglongshan	黄龙山
Huayuankou	花园口
Jinmen	金门
Kangde Palace	康得宫
Laixi	莱西
Long/Hai	龙海
Longkou	龙口
Lugouqiao	盧溝橋

Lushan	庐山
Manzhouguo	满州国
Mazu	马祖
Minnan	闽南
Nanyuan	南苑
Neijiang	内江
Penglai	蓬莱
Pingdong	屏东
Renmin yingxiong jinianbei	人民英雄纪念碑
Shangdang	上黨
Shaoguan	绍关
Siping	四平
Tunliu	屯留
Weixian	潍县
Wenshi	温室
Wujiang	吳江
Wuming	武鳴
Xiangshan	香山
Xinjing	新京
Xinyu	新余
Xubeng	徐蚌
Xuzhou	徐州
Yuezhou	岳州
Yinxu	殷墟
Zhangjiakou	张家口
Zhangzhuang	张庄

Books and films

Beijing chengshi	悲情城市
Hong gaoliang	紅高粮
Huozhe	活着
Jianguo daye	建国大业
Sanguo yanyi	三国演义
Shuihu zhuan	水湖传
Siku quanshu	四库全书
Songhuajiang shang	松花江上
Taibei ren	台北人
Wuyi xiang	鸟衣巷
Yi jiu si er	一九四二
Yijiang chunshui xiang dong liu	一江春水向东流

Index

CPSIA information can be obtained
at www.ICGtesting.com
Printed in the USA
LVOW13s1535230118
563692LV00014B/327/P

Aging, the Individual, and Society

EIGHTH EDITION

Susan M. Hillier
Sonoma State University

Georgia M. Barrow

THOMSON
™
WADSWORTH

Australia • Brazil • Canada • Mexico • Singapore • Spain
United Kingdom • United States

This labor of love is dedicated to my husband, Rod Ferreira, for his loving support; and to the memory of my father, Kenneth Lynn Hillier.

THOMSON

WADSWORTH

Aging, the Individual, and Society, Eighth Edition
Susan M. Hillier and Georgia M. Barrow

Senior Sociology Editor: Robert Jucha
Assistant Editor: Kristin Marrs
Editorial Assistant: Katia Krukowski
Technology Project Manager: Dave Lionetti
Marketing Manager: Michelle Williams
Marketing Assistant: Jaren Boland
Marketing Communications Manager: Linda Yip
Content Manager, Editorial Production: Cheri Palmer
Creative Director: Rob Hugel
Print Buyer: Becky Cross

Permissions Editor: Joohee Lee
Production Service: G & S Book Services
Text Designer: Lisa Devenish
Photo Researcher: Terri Wright
Copy Editor: Barbara Norton
Cover Designer: Yvo Riezebos Design
Cover Image: © Corbis Corporation
Compositor: G & S Book Services
Printer: West Group

Library of Congress Control Number: 2006906457

ISBN 0-534-59814-5

Thomson Higher Education
10 Davis Drive
Belmont, CA 94002-3098
USA

For more information about our products, contact us at:
Thomson Learning Academic Resource Center
1-800-423-0563

For permission to use material from this text or product, submit a request online at
http://www.thomsonrights.com.
Any additional questions about permissions can be submitted by e-mail to
thomsonrights@thomson.com.

CONTENTS

4 Theories in Social Gerontology

5 Friends, Family, and Community

6 Intimacy and Sexuality

PREFACE

The twenty-first century is an exciting time to explore the relationship of human aging, individual processes, and our American society. The study of aging has changed dramatically since the late 1960s, when a handful of scholars began seriously exploring the human and social meanings behind longevity and the demographic shift from a nation of youths to one of adults, and on to an aging nation. This text, too, has grown and stretched with grace and vision in its history.

This edition benefits from the strength of previous editions and moves on to address many of the recent shifts in the rapidly changing field of human aging. The approach of this edition is interdisciplinary—a perspective that adds a valuable dimension to the text and lends itself to a fuller description of the meaning of aging in individual and in social terms.

The tone of this edition reflects the current understanding that aging is a powerful process and that growth and development do continue in later life. Indeed, as long as an individual lives, the personality continues to develop in complexity and richness. Additionally, no previous edition of *Aging, the Individual, and Society* so directly addresses the impact on society of the increasing adult populations that are living longer.

The eighth edition presents a multidisciplinary perspective from which to view the ways biology and psychology affect social structures. It also provides strategies for understanding the ways in which social systems impact an individual's long life, now and in the future. The changes included in this edition are cutting-edge at publication and fully reflect the diverse paths of Americans who are aging into the twenty-first century. The bibliography is a broad reflection of scientific, professional, and popular literature that provides students outstanding exposure to the field.

In deference to different learning styles and various pedagogical approaches, each chapter begins with a news story providing a real-life illustration or account of a basic chapter concept. These stories are intended to help students make the connection between theory and life-as-lived. Summaries of research discoveries and snippets of information are provided in boxed sections throughout the text. These bits and pieces are designed to promote critical thinking by presenting ideas that can be explored further through library research, lecture, and/or group discussion.

Questions for discussion, for experiential learning, and for exploration on the Internet end each chapter. Each set of activities is integrated topically, theoretically, and pedagogically. They require a personal interaction of the student with material representing specific chapter concepts, thereby reinforcing the context of each chapter. The text includes an appendix of Internet addresses to assist students and faculty who seek further information on a broad range of topics.

Eighth Edition Features

- Old Is News: Designed to jump-start student interest in each chapter with a news story to help students understand the practical reality of the chapter's concepts
- Chapter key concepts: A pedagogic tool to help students and faculty keep focused on the main points of each chapter; can be used as a framework for teaching and learning key topical concepts
- Chapter summaries: An organizational tool for students to review; each summary is linked to the chapter's key concepts, thereby reinforcing the learning framework
- Key terms found in each chapter: Another student learning tool
- Discussion questions: Designed to be used either in group discussions or as assignments for written work, the questions combine the need to critically think about both theory and practice
- Suggestions for fieldwork experiences: Experiential learning opportunities to guide teaching and learning
- Online activities: Suggestions for explorations of the Internet to help students understand the complexity of available information

New to the Eighth Edition

Changes to this edition include:

- Integration of issues relevant to subgroups is woven into the conceptual framework of each chapter. For example, ethnic/cultural differences and gender differences are discussed as an integral part of each chapter rather than separated as "other"
- Subject matter has been reorganized for a more effective sequence of learning material
- Throughout, topics are tightly linked to policy, public will, and policy implementation
- Greater discussion of the role of baby boomers—certainly the most important demographic factor so far in the twenty-first century
- Greater use of learning aids such as summary tables and figures
- Extensive use of references to professional literature and Internet resources
- Expanded appendix on Internet addresses
- Text boxes and examples integrated throughout each chapter to help students understand the practicality of the subject matter

Supplements

Instructor's Manual with Test Bank

Prepare for class more quickly and effectively with such resources as chapter summaries, chapter outlines, key terms, video resources, and in-class activities. A Test Bank with 15–20 multiple-choice questions, 10–15 true/false questions, and 3–5 essay questions for each chapter saves you time creating tests.

ExamView® Computerized Testing

Quickly create customized tests that can be delivered in print or online. ExamView's simple "what you see is what you get" interface allows you to easily generate tests of up to 250 items. (It contains all the Test Bank questions electronically.)

Acknowledgments

I gratefully acknowledge the numerous people who have assisted me with the eighth edition. To begin, the text could not have been completed without the generous award of a sabbatical leave from California State University, Sonoma, in addition to that institution's very fine reference librarians. Feedback and support from my colleagues—most especially Linda Rarey, Pamela Abbott-Enz, and Jim Parks—was essential.

Special acknowledgment for their words of encouragement and their thoughtfulness during the writing process are Jennifer Bliss, Judy England, Rod Ferreira, Gabriele Huff, Carol Pollard, Jeanne Booth Ross, my octogenarian mother, Alouise, and many others who I hope truly know my appreciation for their support. It's been a ride!

Deepest gratitude is extended to Bob Jucha, my tactful, patient, ever-courteous editor, and his fine assistant editor Kristin Marrs; and to the Thomson Wadsworth Publishing Company team of Matt Ballantyne, Rob Hugel, Katia Krukowski, Cheri Palmer, and Michelle Williams.

I want to thank the following reviewers for their thoughtful comments and suggestions: Ross Andel, University of South Florida; Augustine Aryee, Fitchburg State College; Carol Bisbee, Midwestern State University; Jacquelyn Frank, Illinois State University; Diane Penner, Hostos Community College of the City University of New York; and Martha Sparks, University of Southern Indiana.

Aging in America

1

Riding the "Age Wave"

David R. Gergen

Howard Baker, who has moved beyond his distinguished career in politics but will always keep his good humor, tells the story these days of an older couple watching TV. The man stretches and says, "Honey, I think I'll go to the kitchen and get some ice cream. Would you like some?"

"Believe I would, thanks." "Would you like some chocolate sauce on it?" "Yes, I would . . . but now be sure and write that down so you won't forget." Her husband glares, shakes his head, and marches off to the kitchen.

Twenty minutes pass as the husband rustles about. Finally, he reappears, carrying a plateful of scrambled eggs. "Why," exclaims his wife, "I told you to write it down. Here you've come back and forgotten my bacon!"

It's almost as much fun to watch Baker tell his tales as to hear them. At 72, he's acting like a young pup after a year of marriage to another former senator beloved by colleagues, Nancy Kassebaum, not many years his junior. And together, they are just the opposite of the couple in search of ice cream: They head up commissions trying to improve our national life, jet hither and thither, read good books, and keep plenty of time for each other.

They are riding the top of a new wave in America—the "age wave," as author Ken Dychtwald calls it in his popular book by that title. In a country where one out of five will soon be over 65, people everywhere are finding a fresh lease on life just when it's least expected.

Billy Graham (left) and Nelson Mandela (right) are remarkable examples of elders who continue to grow in spiritual and political leadership.

Delight. Word that former publisher Katharine Graham, at age 80, had won a Pulitzer Prize for her recent autobiography brought whoops of delight across the newsroom of the *Washington Post* last week. Hard-edged veterans of the paper had watched with admiration as this woman of quiet courage had flowered over the years and has now become a role model for women everywhere.

Celebrations were also underway last week for George Mitchell, four months shy of 65, for his stunning success in negotiating a peace agreement in Northern Ireland. He and President Clinton joined in a textbook case of American leadership. It was especially poignant for Mitchell, who in 1994 had turned down the president's offer of a seat on the Supreme Court so he could attempt to win passage of health care reform. That was a debacle; this was a fitting climax to his years of public service.

Last week, too, 76-year-old John Glenn was in training in Texas for his space launch this fall, while 72-year-old Alan Greenspan was keeping the economy humming. For him, like Baker, a recent marriage has brought a wave of irrational exuberance. Meanwhile, 79-year-old Billy Graham—a man who is said to have preached to greater multitudes than anyone else alive—recently opened his own Web site. A 79-year-old Nelson Mandela is moving his nation into the sunlight. And a 77-year-old pope is nudging open the doors to freedom in Cuba. Who has greater moral authority than these men?

At 58, Jack Nicklaus hardly qualifies as an oldster, but in sports, he's darn close to Methuselah. Returning to the Masters Golf Tournament this spring for his 40th appearance (!), Nicklaus came within four strokes of the top. He even whipped Tiger Woods. Over in Baltimore, another group of "old men" is on fire, too. The Orioles have 21 players over the age of 30—Cal Ripken is a full 37—but the oldest team in baseball is off to a soaring start.

What we are seeing all about us are men and women who are practicing "successful aging." This is the title of a brand-new book that, according to health writer Jane Brody of the *New York Times*, should be featured in every newspaper and on every talk show in the country. In a project sponsored by the MacArthur Foundation, Doctors John W. Rowe and Robert L. Kahn summarize a decade of research by doctors in the United States and Sweden proving it's possible to realize the Greek ideal—as Brody puts it, "to die young, as late in life as possible."

It's the best news of the spring: Most older Americans, they find, are in reasonably good health and generally doing well; a great many are learning how to operate a computer, surf the Net, and communicate by e-mail. And they never forget the bacon.

Source: © 1998. U.S. News & World Report, L.P. Reprinted with permission.

Who is growing old? We all are! In many people's minds, however, growing old is something that happens only to others and only to individuals older than themselves. If you have not yet reached your 50s, can you imagine yourself to be 65, 75, or 90? With reasonable care and a bit of good luck, you will live to be 75 or older. With advances in medical science and technology, we all can anticipate long lives.

But what will be the quality of our lives? As we advance through life, aging may bring either despair or enhanced vitality and meaning. Indeed, at the dawn of the new millennium many social and medical issues of aging focus more on postponing **senescence** (age-related loss of function) and on ensuring a good quality of life than on ensuring old age itself. For example, research for the past 30 years on the health risks of environmental factors such as cigarette smoking or air and water quality, on genetics and genetic engineering, and on biochemical and pharmaceutical factors in health all combine to increase our longevity. Concern with living well in old age is now at least as great an issue for many people as concern with living a long life.

An Interdisciplinary Topic

The study of aging is exciting and complex, and can be examined from many perspectives: emotional, physiological, economic, social, cognitive, and philosophical, among others. **Gerontology** is the study of the human aging process from maturity to old age, as well as the study of the elderly as a special population. Each viewpoint in gerontology adds a dimension to the broader understanding of what it means, personally, socially, and globally, to age. This understanding, in turn, allows us to plan for our own well-being in later life and to consider quality-of-later-life issues on a social level.

Gerontology as a scholarly field has changed markedly since its beginnings in the early 1950s. The gerontologist John Rowe described a "new gerontology" in which the focus "goes beyond the prior preoccupation with age-related diseases . . . to include a focus on senescence . . . and physiological changes that occur with advancing age and that influence functional status as well as the development of disease" (Rowe, 1997, p. 367). To his concept of "new gerontology" we might add a focus on the social issues that are inherent in any society experiencing social and interpersonal changes as rapidly as the United States and other industrialized countries are doing now because of their changing demographics.

The term "aging" is wildly nonspecific: wine ages, babies age, galaxies age, we are all aging right now regardless of our chronological ages. Clearly that does not imply a common biological process. **Aging** in the context of this text refers to progressive changes during adult years. These changes are not necessarily negative, nor do they necessarily reduce an individual's viability. For example, gray hair is a result of aging, but does not impair a person's functioning. Because of negative stereotyping, however, gray hair might have negative social meaning in some cultures.

Mutations that may accumulate over time in certain genes in cells in the reproductive system, on the other hand, describe age-related loss of function, referred to as senescence (Rickles & Finch, 1995; Peto & Doll, 1997). Gerontologists define aging in terms of (a) *chronological aging,* or the number of years since the individual's birth; (b) *biological aging,* or changes that reduce

the efficiency of organ systems; (c) *psychological aging,* including memory, learning, adaptive capacity, personality, and mental functioning; and (d) *social aging,* or social roles, relationships, and the overall social context in which we grow old (Hooyman & Kiyak, 2002).

Perhaps the most basic discipline in the study of aging is *biology.* If it were not for the biological aging process, we could all theoretically live forever. However, the causes of biological aging are still not clearly understood.

A biological study of aging includes all kinds of animals, as well as detailed analyses of the human body. The effects of diet and exercise (lifestyle effects) on longevity are an important focus of study, and the cutting-edge field of genetics has dramatically changed our understanding of the complexity of the human organism. We can impact our biological health through attention to lifestyle. We can do nothing—at this point—about our genetic background, although recent research indicates that genes determine about one-third of our longevity (Ljungquist & Berg, 1998). That leaves two-thirds of how long we will live up to factors such as lifestyle and social environment—factors that can be addressed by individuals and by society. We are more in control of what will be our well-being in later life than we even imagine.

A second component of gerontology, the *sociological perspective,* examines the structure of society—its norms and values and their influence on how a person perceives and reacts to the aging process. Rather than focusing on individual experience, however, sociology focuses on groups of individuals and the cultural context in which they age.

The impact of context is huge: a society that gives the aging person high status can expect more positive outcomes for its aging population, whereas a society that accords the aged a low or marginal status can expect more negative outcomes. Within the sociological circle are anthropologists, who, in documenting the aging process around the world, find that cultures offer elders enormously varied roles. Also in the circle are political scientists, social policy experts, and historians. Demographic and population experts provide information on the numbers and distribution of older persons in societies and countries around the world and provide projections of population trends for consideration by politicians and generators of public policy.

A third lens through which aging may be viewed is that of *psychology*. In contrast with a sociological perspective, the locus of psychological inquiry is the individual. Psychologists are interested in the aging mind—how perception, motor skills, memory, emotions, and other mental and physical capacities change over time. The psychological constructs of motivation, adaptability, self-concept, self-efficacy, and morale all have an important impact on how we age. Psychologists bring a perspective to solving social problems that considers individuals in terms of their life span or particular places in the life span rather than in terms of one point in time. They view individuals as dynamic and interactive, existing in multiple webs of relationship, history, and culture. Psychologists focus on identifying the connections between internal (psychological) and external (social) aspects of the individual's life (American Psychological Association, 2001).

Studies of older people cannot be complete without including an understanding of *philosophy, spirituality,* and *ethics*. Virtually all theories of human development suggest that the psychological task of later life is to gain greater understanding of the life we have lived and of our own approaching death. We seem to gain greater insight into the meaning of our lives by asking the very questions that have been asked throughout the history of humankind: What was this life all about? What is the relationship of the people I am connected with to the meaning of my life? What is my understanding of death—my own as well as the deaths of others?

In a related vein, *ethical issues* are central in the care of the elderly as well as in life decisions made by elders themselves. Families are the major care providers for America's frail elders and issues of competence and decision making or autonomy, and family relationships are central to families and therefore to the larger society of which they are part (Tennstedt & Yates, 1999; Almberg & Grafstrom, 2000). Developing an understanding of ethics and values requires that psychologists and health care practitioners be culturally competent (Sue et al., 1999). *Cultural competence* refers to the ability to honor and respect styles, attitudes, behaviors, and beliefs of individuals, families, and staff that receive and provide services (Yali & Revenson, 2004). Culturally competent practitioners are thus able to support and reinforce older adults in achieving their own culturally-appropriate sense of self-efficacy, that is, to help elders develop personal mastery in a shifting internal and external environment (Fry, 2003).

Gerontologists, then, are multidisciplinary. They examine aging from a chronological perspective (age in years from birth); they study biological and psychological processes and individual meanings of aging; and they look at the social meaning of aging, including changing roles and relationships brought about by moving through the course of life. Gerontologists apply their specialty in many fields—medicine, dentistry, economics, social work, mental health, religion, education, and recreation. They are practitioners in nursing, dentistry, occupational therapy, mental health, sociology, social work, and many other fields having to do with the health and well-being of individuals and society. The field of *geriatrics*, a term sometimes confused with *gerontology,* focuses on preventing and managing illness and disease of later life. Geriatrics is less multidimensional than gerontology and looks specifically at biological and physiological health issues. Geriatrics is a medical model perspective; gerontology uses a biopsychosocial model.

Person-Environment and Social Issues Perspectives

In this text both social issues and psychological perspectives and strategies are presented as factors in understanding aging. Social situations that are problematic or undesirable for a large proportion of older adults as well as those situations and solutions that promote well-being in later life will be examined. Chapter by chapter, the text addresses social issues affecting the lives of older people—issues of status, roles, income, transportation, health, housing, physical and mental health, work, leisure, sexuality, and relationships. We discuss the strengths and contributions that elders bring to their families and communities and the perspectives from which to view widespread patterns of behavior affecting quality-of-life indicators. The causes and solutions of social problems do not remain at the individual or micro level, but must ultimately be found at a greater level—they require macro-level response. Generalized problems associated with aging and with a society that is aging lie with large numbers of people; the causes and solutions impact everyone, not just an age-identified segment of the population.

Person-environment

A person-environment approach views the environment as a continually changing context to which individuals adapt as they also adapt to the personal, psychological, and physical changes inherent in the aging process. From this perspective as the aging person adjusts to life's changes, this adaptation impacts the environment which, cycle-like, further changes the individual as well as the social context (Hooyman & Kiyak, 2002). This reciprocity of change is the person-environment model: the context changes so the individual must change; the individual changes thereby impacting his/her context, and so the environment changes.

Environmental press

Eventually the individual's ability to adapt or change will become exhausted. Let's use an example. An 84-year-old woman has become quite frail following a hip replacement and has a lingering cough and increasingly arthritic knees. She has become more cautious when she walks (internal change), and she has placed appropriate handrails and lighting throughout the house (external change). As time goes on her frailties increase, and the internal and external adaptations available to her are no longer sufficient for her to continue to live alone with safety. To maximize her quality of life the press of the environment (cooking, navigating stairs, cleaning and doing laundry, caring for her rose garden) must be alleviated by external resources.

The solution to this woman's situation requires a macro-level response. It is when the environmental press becomes too great for the individual to manage alone that family, neighbors, community, and local and state resources can be mobilized The causes of and solutions to social problems relevant to aging might be at an individual, a group, a societal, or even a global level.

No Golden Age of Aging

Nature has always been harsh with old age. Among humans, however, the ways in which the old are treated has been closely tied to the culture of their society (Cowgill, 1974, 1986; Crandall, 1980). Early in the study of aging, the sociologist Leo Simmons pointed out that in all cultures it takes both values and environmental context to provide for all age segments of a society. According to his analysis, the culture must state that aging is a positive achievement and must value the aged *as individuals* in order for the aged to have status and value (Simmons, 1949, 1960).

When old age is viewed historically and cross-culturally we get a mixed picture of the position and status of elders throughout history. In ancient times most people died before the age of 35. Our general understanding is that those who survived into their 40s were treated with respect and awe, honored ceremonially and socially as keepers of the memories.

The belief that elders were held in high status in American society has a couple of different

Racial and ethnic diversity in the population will continue to increase. The proportion of white, non-Hispanic elders is expected to decline from 87 percent in 1990 to 67 percent in 2050.

etiologies. First, honoring older people and one's ancestors is believed to have been an inherent family value. Second, because so few people lived into later life, old age came to be seen as a marker of exclusivity. Status was bestowed on a person by virtue of his or her being part of this exclusive circle.

A third theory of elder status suggests that because the aged were perceived to be closer to death, they served as mediators between this world and the next. This valued role lent prestige to age by providing a respected function to the larger community, assuming the elder's mental faculties were intact (Hooyman & Kiyak, 2002).

Not all ancient cultures equally honored old age. The difference was huge between surviving into later years with good physical and mental health and surviving with frailty. In a subsistence culture, people who outlived their usefulness were a burden, so the treatment of the frail could range anywhere from being treated cruelly or even killed to being ignored to being honored as more godlike because they were so exceptional (Glascock, 1997).

After the fifth century BC in Greek and Roman cultures old age was generally seen as a distasteful time of decline and decrepitude. This perspective emerged gradually from between the sixth and fifth centuries BC. Records from before that the sixth century BC indicate old age to have been associated with wisdom, but even this positive association seems to have been tied to material wealth and social status (deRomilly, 1968). We know next to nothing about the status of old people before the fifth century BC who were not part of the power elite—that is to say, who were peasants rather than landed gentry.

A gradual shift to a denigration of old age seems to have emerged concurrently with a belief in social equality, in that no one's status was supposed to be elevated merely because of birthright (Hooyman & Kiyak, 2002). During the classical period beauty and strength were idealized in art and in myth, and old age was considered to be a time defined by physical incompetence and mental ineptitude. Old age in the classical era was ugly.

We know very little about the treatment of elders in medieval Europe. As urbanization created population centers, **life expectancy** in medieval Europe dramatically dropped below what it had been in Greek and Roman times. Poor nutrition and sanitation and crowded living conditions, coupled with a lack of social organization appropriate to urban living, resulted in an era of tremendous social disruption. Norms and values from previous generations were no longer applicable, and new norms had not yet emerged. Art from the medieval and Renaissance eras pictured age as cruel or weak, as surely it must have been given the environmental context (Hooyman & Kiyak, 2002).

Personal and Social Definitions of Age

Social status among Americans is correlated to no small extent with education, wealth, and health—and most older people are better off in all of these categories today than they were in previous generations (National Center for Health Statistics [NCHS], 2004). With the exception of a dramatic increase in obesity among older adults, lifestyle changes, including nutrition and exercise, have helped add health and vigor to the longevity people have been experiencing since the 1990s. This trend suggests that the United States might be presently undergoing a shift in cultural values toward higher status for older people.

To understand cultural trends as quality-of-life indicators, it is important to note that several age **cohorts** exist within the elder population. The term "older people" could refer to anyone 50 years old or more, or it might refer to those 85 years and older. Specificity is important. For example, 73 percent of people in the over-65 age category—the bureaucratic definition of old age in our country—rate their health to be good to excellent (NCHS, 2004). On closer examination we find that of people 75 and older, 85 percent have chronic physical limitations, nearly 41 percent have mental (learning, remembering, or concentrating) disabilities, and over 70 percent experience difficulty going outside the home without assistance (U.S. Bureau of the Census, 2000). From the perspective of health and vigor, there are enormous differences between a cohort of 65-year-olds and a cohort of 85-year-olds, although members of both age groups are "older Americans." When gender and ethnicity are specified in the health data, we get yet another, more complete picture of the face and experience of aging.

The age of a person during a historical event of major proportion, such as the civil rights movement that began in the late 1950s, profoundly influences the social and personal meaning of the event. This is what is meant by *historical cohort*. The personal and educational and career choices available to a 35-year-old black woman in 1960 as she grew into adulthood would greatly impact her social and personal status as an 80-year-old in 2005. A woman who was 15 years old in 1960 would enter old age from a markedly different social experience. Cultural variations in the form of changing values and norms come about through historical events ranging from epidemics and wars to scientific breakthroughs and social change.

The importance of historical events to the development of a particular cohort cannot be overestimated. Consider the impact of the terrorist attacks on the United States on September 11, 2001—a date that has entered the American lexicon as 9/11. Children who were five at the time will grow into adulthood with the experience of their country under attack by amorphous "others"—terrorists. As they attempted to manage and decipher the event, they saw frightened and ill-equipped adults who themselves had few skills to cope with the magnitude of the event. Depending on such demographic factors such as proximity to the disaster, family religiosity, parental education and stability, the event took on different meanings and different importance for those children. All of them, however, experienced this historical event through the eyes of a five-year-old.

People in their adolescence at 9/11 had a very different perspective on the event than their six-year-old siblings. An adolescent's cognitive abilities to draw conclusions and make moral judgments and decisions are only one aspect of their perspective. Unlike the five-year-old, the adolescent's understanding of personal safety extends beyond the protection provided by parents and family; the worldview shifts. Terrorism, formerly a word with little personal meaning for most Americans, suddenly became a household word.

The impact of 9/11 on the lives of young adults—some of whose college education was being supported by their participation in the

National Guard—was different again from that on the younger cohorts. Apart from those whose lives were directly impacted by the bombings, the event radically modified young adults' course of life as the national economy shifted focus, job opportunities changed, and society absorbed the possibility of global warfare.

The age of individuals at the time of the historical event shapes the meaning people give to historical events of great magnitude. By the time they are 65, those who were five at the time of the disaster will essentially have lived with its outcomes for their entire lives. For those who were 65 at the time of the disaster, the event comes to be included in a lifetime of other events—its meaning is modified by other life experiences.

Historical Perspectives on Aging

Historically the status of older people was related to property ownership, which resulted in the control of political resources. Control of property by one generation created opportunity for a balanced exchange between generations: elders were cared for in their later years by their children in exchange for children's inheriting property from their parents. Clearly, this was literally the case only for property owners, but the ethic of providing care for infirm elders in exchange for some level of inheritance was the cultural norm. With the onset of industrialization, farming and the control of property became less central to a family's well-being as economic resources became more available to people independent of their age. As the economic center shifted from the family to the corporation, the status of older people also declined.

This cultural shift in the status of elders is known as *modernization theory* (Simmons, 1949; Cowgill, 1974, 1986), and it suggests that the Industrial Revolution was the linchpin to older people's decline in status. The vigor and energy of young adults, whose stamina kept the industrial sector moving, became the national icon. Youthfulness was the embodiment of the nation's progress toward increased wealth and prosperity. When their physical energy and strength began to ebb, older workers were less able to contribute to the industrial economy, and they ultimately either died on the job or were retired from work when they could no longer do their share. No substitute social role emerged for those not in the industrial workforce. The status of women was also very low; however, a substitute social role of wife and homemaker provided women access to social status depending on the incomes of their husbands and thereby the size and beauty of their homes and the quality of the lifestyles of their families.

The values of equality and individualism, coupled with crowded and costly urban living, correspondingly shifted the role of older people: no longer participants in a reciprocal system of the exchange of resources, they were now dependent on a younger generation. The growing emphasis on impersonality (equality) and efficiency (through individual effort) further contributed to the status shift of older people.

In his classic articulation of modernization theory, Cowgill (1974, 1986) identified the characteristics of modernization that contribute to lower status for elders as:

- Health technology—reduced infant mortality and prolonged adult life
- Scientific technology—creating jobs that do not depend on skills and knowledge accumulated over decades of experience
- Education—targeted toward the young

These three cultural characteristics continue to shape social values today. The aged are not perceived to be as great a "problem" today, with the advent of pension reform and the introduction of Social Security. Their special needs, however, continue to make elders an identifiable group. Elders today live longer than did the previous generation. They have lived through—and sometimes been surpassed by—major technological changes. Their education, appropriate to the twentieth century, reflects a more traditional and classical approach than one focusing on job skills and the abstractions of a society focused on information technology.

From the perspective of *social issues,* old age itself has not been seen as an issue (Brown, 1990). Until 1900 or so, only the illnesses related to old age (not actually *being* old) were defined as problems. In the seventeenth and eighteenth centuries the issues relevant to old age were understood to be the responsibility of families. At a family level, grandparents were respected—in part because there were so few older people in society. Among the Puritans in early Judeo-Christian America, long life was believed to be the result of God's favor, a blessing bestowed by the Almighty on those few who had lived truly pure lives (Achenbaum, 1996). The primary basis of the respect and power granted older people in the seventeenth century, however, was their control of property. For a nation whose economy was based on the abundance of agricultural production from family farms, the control of land provided the senior family member an especially powerful position.

With the industrialization of the late 1800s, the problems associated with growing old became reconceptualized, not just on a physical level but on social, economic, and psychological levels as well. Social change occurred at breathtaking speed, and the relative status of youth came to be elevated. Additionally in the 1800s birthrates began to drop and longevity to increase, resulting in an increase in the median age and the evolution of an identifiable category of "older" people.

By the 1930s and 1940s this new conceptualization of youth and the aged by society and by individuals themselves had created an identifiable group with physical and social problems that called for collective action. For example, the right to a decent income at retirement became an issue. In the words of the sociologist C. Wright Mills, a family's "private troubles" became "public issues" (Mills, 1959). Respon-sibility for aging individuals came to be seen as belonging to society as well as to family. Older people received more public attention, but in the process they began to be viewed as helpless and dependent. These negative images were universally applied for many years in spite of improvements in the health of those relatively "young" old, age 65 to 74, and in spite of the countless people age 75 and over who remained active and involved in society.

Ageism as a Social Problem

We have defined a social problem as a widespread negative social condition that people both create and solve. **Ageism** is such a problem. We know that the number of older persons is large and growing larger, and ageism directly affects the older population. Any social-problems approach, including the critical perspective, considers ageism in our society to be a major concern. Aversion, hatred, and prejudice toward elders, and the manifestation of these emotions in the form of discrimination on the basis of age, is *ageism,* a term coined by Robert Butler in 1975. Sister Rose Therese Bahr defined ageism as "the process of systematic stereotyping of and discrimination against people because they are old" (Bahr, 1994, p. 4). The critical perspective looks to the economic and class system and for root causes of ageism.

Ageism has been called the third "ism," following racism and sexism. Whereas racism and sexism prevent racial minorities and women—and sometimes, in what is called "reverse sexism," men—from developing their full potential as people, ageism limits the potential development of individuals on the basis of age. Ageism can oppress any age group, young or old. If you are young, you may have been told that you are too inexperienced, too immature, too untested. If you are elderly, you may have been told you are out-of-date, old-fashioned, behind the times, of no value or importance. Although ageism may affect the young as well as the old, our concern here is with the senior members of society. As Robert Butler noted, "The tragedy of old age is not that each of us must grow old and die, but that the process of doing so has been made unnecessarily and at times excruciatingly painful, humiliating, debilitating, and isolating" (Butler, 1975, pp. 2–3).

Ageism is a complex phenomenon affected by technology, industrialization, changing family patterns, increased mobility, demographic changes, increased life expectancy, and generational differences. A form of discrimination leveled by one group against another, ageism is not an inequality to be associated with biological processes alone. It is created and institutionalized by many forces—historical, social, cultural, and psychological.

Ageism Today

Our Western cultural heritage decrees that work and financial success establish individual worth. Industrialization has reinforced the high value of productivity and added further problems for the aging worker. The speed of industrial, technological, and social change tends to make skills and knowledge rapidly obsolete. Most people must struggle to keep abreast of new discoveries or skills in their fields. The media have used the term Detroit syndrome to describe older people in terms of the obsolescence that exists for cars. When younger, stronger, faster workers with newly acquired knowledge are available, employers tend to replace, rather than retrain, the older worker. Within the workforce, older persons have often been considered a surplus population. As such, they suffer the potential for being managed much like surplus commodities: devalued and discounted.

Social change can create a generation gap that contributes to ageism. Rapid social change can cause our values to be somewhat different from our parents' and significantly different from those of our grandparents. Those who grew up in a given time period may have interpretations of and orientations toward social

issues that differ from those of an earlier or later generation. For example, a person who matured in the 1940s and experienced the patriotism of World War II may be unable to understand the behavior and attitudes of those who matured in the 1960s and protested the war in Vietnam or the Persian Gulf.

People who matured in the 1990s may not understand the historical rationale for the United States' intervention in small countries such as Panama or El Salvador. These people, many of whom have postponed marriage and childbearing, may be unable to grasp the reasons for early marriage and large families held by now-elderly generations. The study of intergenerational relations, which provides insights into similarities and differences in values across generations, reveals that communicating and understanding across generations are difficult when values are different.

Ageism appears in the many euphemisms for old age and in the desire to hide one's age. The elderly themselves do not want to use the term old, as the names of their local clubs show: Fun after 50, Golden Age, 55 Plus, and Senior Citizens Club. Some forgo their "senior discounts" because they do not want to make their age public.

Fear of aging shows when men and women want to keep their age a secret. They hope that their appearance denies their age and that they project a youthful image. Many people suffer a crisis of sorts upon reaching age 30 and repeat it to some extent when entering each new decade. Some even experience an identity crisis as early as their late 20s, because they are entering an age that the youth culture considers old. Many counselors recognize "over 39" syndrome, a time when young adults come to terms with the fact that youth does not last forever but blends gradually with the responsibilities of maturity.

Greeting-card counters are filled with birthday cards that joke about adding another year. Despite their humor, they draw attention to the fear of aging that birthdays bring. Some birthday cards express the sentiment that to be older is to be better, but then add a note that says, in effect, that no one would want to be better at the price of aging. Though birthday cards often joke about physical or sexual decline, the fear in the minds of many is no joke at all. Fear of aging can damage psychological well-being and lead us to shun older people. Ageism is a destructive force for both society and the individual.

Ageism as a concept in literature has been described in a general sense, but it also has been measured in more specific ways. Alex Comfort (1976) used the term sociogenic to imply ageism in a broad sense. He described two kinds of aging: physical, which is a natural biological process; and sociogenic, which has no physical basis. Sociogenic aging is imposed on the elderly by the folklore, prejudices, and stereotypes about age that prevail in our society. Thus, age prejudice, as it exists in our minds, has become institutionalized in many sectors of our society.

We can find more specific evidence of ageism in our laws, particularly those dealing with employment, financial matters, and legal definitions relating to competency as an adult. There are differences in individuals' income, occupation, and education among the generations. One aspect of ageism is age inequality in education and occupation, caused by the fact that newer generations receive an education attuned to a highly technical and computerized society and are therefore better qualified for such jobs. Elders are easily left behind on the information highway as the high-tech knowledge of those in younger age groups rises. Income inequality based on age is caused not only by younger age groups' having more extensive formal or technical education, but also by age discrimination in employment. Gerontologists believe that ageism in employment dates back to the early 1800s. This form of age prejudice will be covered in more detail in the chapter on work and leisure.

The critical perspective in gerontology draws sharp attention to inequities in U.S. society, addressing broad and fundamental structures of U.S. society such as the class system, capitalism, racism, sex roles (sexism), and age roles (age-ism). It is the most radical sociological approach in addressing inequality and in its suggestions for completely new structures to replace failing ones. Gerontologists have made use of the critical perspective to understand the problems of aging in a broad political, social, and economic content (Minkler & Estes, 1991; Sokolovsky, 1997; Yali & Revinson, 2004).

Despite the social and personal issues arising from ageism, we must be careful not to view older people as more dependent and helpless than they are. That negative stereotype is not productive to the mission of understanding social issues and problems salient among America's elderly population. We need to understand both the strengths and the vulnerabilities of the older person in our present society, and to identify and support institutions and social structures that encourage strength and self-reliance.

Ageism Yesterday: The Early American Example

A look at older people in earlier times, when age relationships were different, provides us with a clearer view of ageism now and in the future. Generalizing about ageism in the past is not easy. Some historians believe the status of older people was higher in the colonial period—the time during which early settlers, especially the Puritans, founded America and formed the 13 colonies. In contrast, other historians point to ageism and neglect of older persons in the colonial days.

Early colonial days

According to David Fischer, author of *Growing Old in America* (1977), the power and privilege of old age were deeply rooted in colonial times, when age, not youth, was exalted. To be old was to be venerated by society and to be eligible for selection to the most important positions in the community. Meetinghouse seats were assigned primarily by age, and the elderly sat in the positions of highest status. According to Fischer, the

Today's elders are different from elders of the past. Here a 94-year-old man responds to interview questions (posted on board) from a fourth-grade classroom.

national heroes were "gray champions." Community leaders and holders of political office tended to be older men, and the elderly were honored during ceremonial occasions.

Older adults were believed to be in favor with God. Their long life was thought of as an outward sign they would be "called" or "elected" to heaven. This view was based in part on a biblical injunction: "Keep my commandments, for length of days, and long life, and peace shall they add unto thee" (Prov. 3:1, 2). The Puritans pictured Jesus as an old man with white hair, even though, according to most theologians, Jesus died in his early 30s. Respect for age was also evident in manner of dress. Increase Mather, the president of Harvard College from 1685 to

1701, wrote that old men whose attire was gay and youthful, or old women who dressed like young girls, exposed themselves to reproach and contempt. Male fashions during the 1600s, and even more in the 1700s, flattered age. The styles made men appear older than they were. Clothing was cut specifically to narrow the shoulders, to broaden the waist and hips, and to make the spine appear bent. Women covered their bodies in long dresses. Both sexes wore white, powdered wigs over their hair. Not until the 1800s did clothing styles begin to flatter the younger man or woman.

Fischer studied other historical data that indicate age status. American literature, for example, emphasized respect for old age from the

1600s until after the American Revolution. A careful examination of census data shows that in the 1700s individuals tended to report themselves as older than they actually were, in order to enhance their status. In the mid-1800s this tendency reversed itself.

The tradition of respect for the elderly was rooted not only in religious and political ideology, but also in legal and financial reality. The elders owned and controlled their own land, which did not pass to their sons until they died. The sons, therefore, had financial reason to show respect for and deference to their fathers. In these conservative times, the young had little choice other than to honor, obey, and follow the ways of the old.

A word of caution must guide our consideration of the older person's status in colonial times. "Status" is a multidimensional concept, measurable in many ways, that indicates one's social ranking in society. Deference, respect, health, economic resources, material possessions, occupation, education, and political power are all possible indicators of social status. By some measures, the colonial elders had high status. They were shown deference and respect, and they had political power and financial control of their land. But not all elderly colonial citizens had financial and political power, which was indeed held by only a very few. Colonial legal records show that widows who had no means of support wandered from one town to another trying to find food and shelter. Older lower-status immigrants and minorities, and most certainly older African Americans, had an especially difficult time because of their low economic status; many were indentured servants or slaves.

Most old people suffered from health problems that medical science was unable to cure or alleviate. Benjamin Franklin, for example, was wracked with pain in his later years because of gout and "the stone" (gallstone). Yet the old, in spite of their infirmities, were expected to be models of service and virtue to their communities. The very veneration that brought older persons respect kept them from enjoying close, intimate relationships with younger people. Relationships between youth and elders were distant and formal, and the old suffered loneliness in their elevated position.

A number of historians take exception to Fischer's rosy picture of colonial days. Haber (1983) described old age in colonial times as more dire than Fischer's work indicates. Haber believes that although select, well-to-do elderly had high status in the Puritan days, they did not live in a golden era of aging. Many not-so-well-to-do were viewed with scorn and contempt. Haber advises that a careful sociologist or historian must try not to idealize the past, but to recapture reality by examining all of its facets: political, historical, economic, and social. Quadagno (1982) and Cole (1992) make the same point as Haber, emphasizing that multiple forces, some positive and some negative, shaped life in colonial times.

Shifting status of old age

According to Fischer, change throughout the 1800s altered the system of age relationships in a negative way, leading to social problems for the aged. The most fundamental change took place in political ideology. The principles formulated in the Declaration of Independence became stronger: equality for all in legal, social, and political matters. This trend affected older persons because "lovely equality," in Jefferson's words, eradicated the hierarchy of age, and hence the respect automatically accorded the old. A study of word origins shows that most of the negative terms for old men first appeared in the late 1700s and early 1800s. *Gaffer*, originally an expression of respect, changed from a word of praise to one of contempt. Before 1780, *fogy* meant a wounded soldier; by 1830 it had become a term of disrespect for an older person. *Codger, geezer, galoot, old goat,* and *fuddy-duddy* came into general use in the early 1800s.

The preeminence of religious elders waned as doctors and other technologists began to replace preachers as the custodians of virtue and learning. The United States became more industrialized. In the 1800s the city became a means of escape from both farming and parental control. Instead of waiting for his father to provide him with land, a young man could move to the city and find work in a factory. As long as America remained a traditional agricultural society in which parents controlled property until their advanced years, older adults exercised considerable power. Urban and industrial growth led to diminished parental control over family, wealth, and possessions (Haber, 1983). By the late 1800s the young pioneer and the young cowboy had become popular heroes; Teddy Roosevelt was young, rough, and ready. The youth cult began to replace the age cult.

The older population grew rapidly during the 1800s and 1900s because of advances in medical science. Retirement gradually became more and more common. However, many older people who retired had no source of income and were often neglected. Old age became a burden to those who lived it and a social problem to those who analyzed it.

Fischer (1977) divided U.S. history into two general periods:

1. 1600–1800: an era of growing **gerontophilia.** Old age was exalted and venerated, sometimes hated and feared, but more often honored and obeyed.
2. 1800–present: an era of growing **gerontophobia.** Americans increasingly glorified youth instead of age, and the elderly often became victims (self-victims as well as social victims) of prevailing attitudes and social arrangements.

Fischer's historical analysis suggests that we may eventually enter another period of age relations, one that will create better conditions for older adults. The goal, he states, should be to make a new model—a fraternity of age and youth and a world in which "the deep eternal differences between age and youth are recognized and respected without being organized into a system of inequality" (Fischer, 1977, p. 199).

The example of colonial America illustrates that the position of elders in our society can be something other than what it is now. We can be aware of various age relationships and possibilities that are more positive than the situations we have created.

The Aging Revolution: Demographics of Aging

What was once referred to as the "graying of America" is now more accurately understood to be a revolution, whose social meaning profoundly permeates American culture. The population of Americans age 65 and older has greatly exceeded the growth of the population as a whole, and the "oldest old" (85 years and over) are the most rapidly growing age group among those over 65. The 2000 American census found that nearly one-half of Americans age 65 or older were over 74, compared with less than one-third in 1950. One in eight were 85 or older in 2000, compared with 1 in 20 in 1950 (U.S. Bureau of the Census, 2000). While people 85 or older made up only 1.5 percent of the total U.S. population in 2000, they were about 12 percent of all of those Americans over 65. These oldest old are of particular interest to gerontologists because this is the group that requires the largest number of services to remain viable in their homes and communities (Himes, 2001).

Increasing Numbers of Aged

In the past decade, the number of men and women living to age 85 years has increased dramatically; the number of those living past 85 has also substantially increased (see Figure 1.1). The total number of people in the United States under 65 has tripled in the past century; however, the number of people aged 65 or older has increased by more than a factor of 12 (U.S. Bureau of the Census, 2000). Children under five were the largest age group in 1900; in 2000 the largest five-year age groups were 35- to 39-year-olds

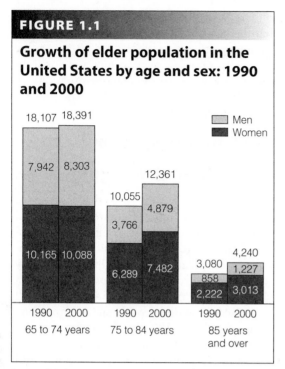

FIGURE 1.1

Growth of elder population in the United States by age and sex: 1990 and 2000

Source: U.S. Census Bureau, Census 2000 Summary File 1; 1990 Census of Population, *General Population Characteristics, United States* (1990 CP-1-1).

(8.1 percent of the total population) and 40- to 45-year-olds (8.0 percent of the total population; see Figure 1.2).

A huge jump in the over-65 population will occur from 2010 to 2030, when the leading edge of the **baby-boom generation** (those born between 1946 and 1964) reaches 65. Because of the presence of "boomers," the elderly population will grow by an average of 2.8 percent annually, compared with annual growth of 1.3 percent during the preceding 20 years (Hobbs & Damon, 1996). By mid-century, there will probably be more people over the age of 65 than there will be people 14 years or younger. This shift will profoundly affect national and regional policies on education, health, recreation, economics, and the role of government—indeed, our national self-concept will experience a shift from being a youth-oriented nation to one of mature citizenry.

The 2000 Census Bureau findings also highlight the strong growth of the older population from 1900 to 2000. Figure 1.3 reflects these changes. Notice in this **population pyramid** representing the years 1900, 1950, and 2000 the proportional change in the 85-plus age group over a century. Note both the shape of each pyramid and the length of each bar. All older age groups starting at age 65 show large increases. In general, the higher the age interval, the greater the proportional increase. In other words, the old as a group are becoming older—that is, not dying off as quickly—so the numbers of the very old will continue to mushroom. The portion of the population age 95 to 99 nearly doubled in 10 years. The centenarian group (those who reach the age of 100) grew 77 percent during the same time.

The dramatic increase in the number and proportion of elderly is increasing worldwide. In 1994, the world population of those age 65 and over was 357 million. Twenty percent of this proportion (61 million) are age 80 and older. By 2020 the numbers of the oldest old are expected to more than double to about 146 million (Hobbs & Damon, 1996).

Two major reasons for the increasing proportion of older people are increased life expectancy and a declining birthrate. We will consider each topic separately.

Increased life expectancy

Life expectancy in the United States has consistently increased throughout the nineteenth and twentieth centuries. The proportion of the population age 65 and over increased more than tenfold from 1900 to 2000 (U.S. Bureau of the Census, 2000). A dramatic increase in life expectancy occurred in the 1920s as a result of reduced infant mortality, health-care advances, and improved nutrition, although the increase is characterized by ethnic disparities. Overall, estimated life expectancy in 2000 was just over 77 years (NCHS, 2001). White males born in 1920 could expect to live to 54; white females, to

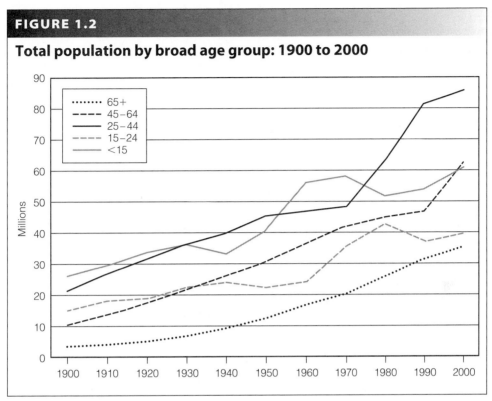

FIGURE 1.2

Total population by broad age group: 1900 to 2000

Legend:
- 65+
- 45–64
- 25–44
- 15–24
- <15

(y-axis: Millions, 0 to 90; x-axis: 1900 to 2000)

Source: U.S. Census Bureau, decennial census of population, 1900 to 2000.

56. Racial differences exist in longevity patterns: white males live more than six years longer than African American males, whose life expectancy in 1995 was just over 65. The life expectancy for African American females in 1995 was 74.

The mean life expectancy today of women at age 65 is another 20 years. Fully half of all women today in the United States who are 65 will survive to the age of 85 (Smith, 1997). Women at every age, regardless of race or ethnicity, have longer life expectancies than do men, though this discrepancy has decreased in the decades of 1990 and 2000. Table 1.1 compares changes in number of men per 100 women; note that among all people over 65 years of age, in 1990 there were 67 men per 100 women; by 2000 there were 70 men per 100 women. In the age category 75 to 84 the number of men per 100 women shifted from 60 to 65. The largest in-creases in the male-to-female ratios from 1990 to 2000 occurred in the age group 55 and over (U.S. Bureau of the Census, 2000), indicating that men are entering later life with a greater expectancy of longevity in this century than in the previous one. Still, in 2000 there were 14.4 million men and 20.6 million women age 65 and over. These numbers underscore the reality that older women are more likely to live without a life partner than are older men.

The longer a person has lived, the greater is that person's statistical life expectancy. The reasons for this have to do with **selection for survival** (Olshansky, 1995; Holliday, 1996b), meaning that members of a population are selected for survival based on their resistance to common causes of death. Those causes might be intrinsic or environmental, but studies on the genetics of long-lived people and of twins suggests

FIGURE 1.3

Total population by age and sex: 1900, 1950, and 2000

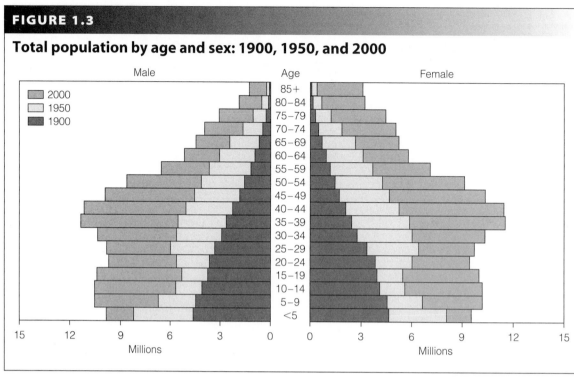

Source: U.S. Census Bureau, decennial census of population, 1900, 1950, and 2000.

that genes probably affect longevity by altering the risk of death at different ages, rather than by directly determining age at death (McGue et al., 1993; Yashin & Iachine, 1995). In other words, our genetic programming seems more aimed at the level of protection we have against mortal illness than at setting age at birth.

Over the years there have been dramatic reductions in the death rates for diseases of the heart, cerebrovascular disease, and pneumonia. Even though life expectancy for males is not as high as for females, both genders' expectancies have increased considerably over the last several decades. This increase has been driven overwhelmingly by changes in environmental factors that result in death, rather than factors intrinsic to the aging process itself. In addition to having long-lived grandparents (genetic factors), being near an ideal weight for one's stature, having low blood pressure and low cholesterol, not smok-

ing, consuming alcohol moderately, exercising vigorously four to five times a week, eating a healthy diet, and living a relaxed and unstressed life style are central predictors for a long life.

Heart disease remains the leading cause of death for older Americans; however, the proportion of deaths due to coronary heart disease has fallen in the past 10 years, and now cancer is responsible for one-third of the deaths of those between the ages of 65 and 75, especially among African Americans (NCHS, 1996; see Figure 1.4). The age-adjusted death rate for coronary heart disease declined by 16 percent from 1987 to 1993, and the death rate for stroke dropped by 12 percent. Older Americans are living longer, and they are less frail than were their parents and grandparents.

Studies comparing the longevity of men and women show that the top causes of death kill more men than women. Heart disease, lung can-

Number of men per 100 women by age, for the 65 years and over population: 1990 and 2000

Age	1990	2000
65 years and over	67	70
65 to 74 years	78	82
75 to 84 years	60	65
85 years and over	39	41

Source: U.S. Census Bureau, Census 2000 Summary File 1; 1990 Census of Population, *General Population Characteristics, United States* (1990 CP-1-1).

Note: For information on confidentiality protection, nonsampling error, and definitions, see www.census.gov/prod/cen2000/doc/sf1.pdf

Causes of death for persons in the United States aged 85 and older, 1993

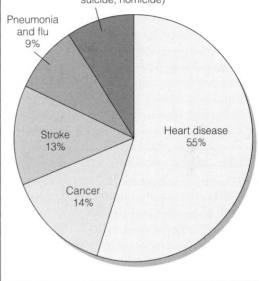

Source: U.S. Bureau of the Census. (1995). Current Population Reports, Series P-25 (U.S. Department of Commerce). Washington, DC.

cer, homicide, suicide, accidents, and cirrhosis of the liver all kill men at more than twice the rate of women (Dolnick, 1991). Each of these causes of death is linked to behaviors that our culture either encourages or finds more acceptable in males than in females: using guns, drinking alcohol, smoking, working at hazardous jobs, or appearing fearless. Such cultural expectations seem to contribute to males' elevated mortality. Men suffer three times as many homicides as women and have twice as many fatal car accidents (per mile driven) as women. Men are more likely to drive through an intersection when they should stop, are less likely to signal a turn, and are more likely to drive after drinking alcohol.

But behavior doesn't entirely explain the longevity gap. Women seem to have a genetic makeup that programs them to live longer. Some scientists think that the longevity gaps may be due to chromosomal or hormonal differences. Whatever the reasons, elderly women outnumbered their male counterparts in 1994 by a ratio of three to two—20 million to 14 million—and the difference grew with advancing age. One consequence of this gender discrepancy is that

elderly women are much more likely than men to live alone. Eight out of ten noninstitutionalized elderly living alone in 1993 were women (Hobbs & Damon, 1996).

The leading causes of death for men and women over age 65 have remained stable since the mid-1990s. Ranked in order from most to least common, they are: (1) diseases of the heart; (2) malignant neoplasms (tumors); (3) cerebrovascular disease (stroke); (4) chronic obstructive pulmonary disease; (5) pneumonia and flu; (6) chronic liver disease; (7) accidents; (8) diabetes; and (9) suicide. Men have higher death rates in all the categories except diabetes.

Decreasing birthrate

When the birthrate declines, the number of young people decreases in proportion to the number of old people. The birthrate has gradually declined since public record keeping began in the eighteenth century. A baby boom in the 1940s and 1950s increased the birthrate temporarily but did not reverse its long-term trend. In 1972, we witnessed a near zero population birthrate (2.1 children born for every couple): the number of live births nearly equaled the number of deaths, stabilizing the population. The birthrate then dipped lower until it rose slightly in the early and mid-1980s. According to the Population Reference Bureau in Washington, D.C., the 1991 birthrate evened out at 2.1 children per couple. If the United States maintains a lower birthrate, the proportion of older people will further increase. With no increase in the total population, the relative proportion of older persons will grow each year.

The post–World War II baby boomers of 1946–1964 are one of our largest age groups. Now in midlife, this age group will begin to reach age 65 in 2011, massively increasing the over-65 population. If we assume continued low birthrates and further declines in death rates, the older populations will jump tremendously by the year 2030. As we saw earlier, their numbers will double and their percentage of the population will rocket to over 20 percent.

A controversy rages over whether medical science can do anything further to extend life expectancy at birth to more than 85 years. In the past 125 years, the life expectancy of Americans has almost doubled, rising from 40 to nearly 80 years. But these gains in life expectancy, most of which have come through reducing deaths of young children (particularly infants) and of mothers in childbirth, may have been the "easy" ones. It is clear that in the twenty-first century longevity is a complex interaction of environmental, historical, and genetic factors (Francheschi et al., 2000).

The population that is presently the oldest old has had unique life experiences. This cohort survived infancy when the infant mortality rate was about 15 to 20 times the present rate, and they survived the infectious diseases of childhood when medical practice did not have much to offer. They survived at least one world war, and the females survived childbearing at a time when the maternal mortality rate was nearly 100 times its present level (Smith, 1997). The next generation of elderly will have lived their adult years with many of the advantages that were only emerging for the previous older generation, so mortality rates will continue to be lower in later life. That does not, however, appear to change the maximum human life span, which seems to have fixed limits (Finch & Pike, 1996).

Some medical experts and laboratory scientists say that the period of rapid increases in life expectancy has come to an end. They argue that advances in life-extending technologies or the alteration of aging at the molecular level, the only ways to extend life expectancy, will be either improbable or long, slow processes. And although they do agree that eliminating cancer, heart disease, and other major killers would increase life expectancy at birth by about 15 years, cures for these diseases are not in sight. Other scientists are more positive about extending life expectancy. Findings of a study by Ken Monton at Duke University, reported in 1990, predicted that Americans could very well live to age 99 if they quit smoking, drinking alcohol, and eating high-cholesterol foods. Populations with low-risk lifestyles, such as Mormons in the United States, already have achieved average life spans exceeding 80 years (Krieger, 1990).

The longest documented human life span on record is that of Jeanne Calment, a French woman who lived to be 122. There are some generally accepted records of people throughout history who have died between 110 and 120 years of age, but few that are extensively documented. The most extreme claims come from populations with the least reliable records. No evidence exists, either current or historical, that there has been much change in the rate of aging. Increases in life expectancy have been driven overwhelmingly by reductions in environmental causes of

Frenchwoman Jeanne Calment, who died in 1997 at the age of 122, was the world's oldest person with verifiable birth records.

© AP Photo Wide World/Francois Mori

TABLE 1.2

Counties exceeding the U.S. proportion 65 years and over by region: 2000

Region	Total Counties	Counties Exceeding U.S. Proportion[1]	
		Number	Percent
United States	3,141	2,263	72.0
Northeast	217	170	78.3
Midwest	1,055	869	82.4
South	1,424	980	68.8
West	445	244	54.8

Source: U.S. Census Bureau, Census 2000 Summary File 1.

Note: For information on confidentiality protection, nonsampling error, and definitions, see www.census.gov/prod/cen2000/doc/sf1.pdf

[1] U.S. proportion 65 years and over was 12.4 percent.

mortality (Austad, 1997). It appears that the maximum human life span has not increased; however, the mean life expectancy in developed countries has done so tremendously.

Our Aging Nation

Table 1.2 lists regions of the country exceeding the U.S.'s proportion of citizens over the age of 65. The Midwest has the largest number of counties with higher than national average proportions of people over 65, and the western area of the country has the lowest number of counties exceeding the national average (Table 1.2). Although California has the largest *number* of citizens over 65 (just over 3.5 million), Florida, a retirement haven, has the highest *proportion* of over-65 elders in the nation, at 17.6 percent. In several states (North and South Dakota,

Pennsylvania, Rhode Island, Iowa, Arkansas, and Maine in the 2000, census; see Figure 1.5) 14 percent or more of the total population falls into the over-65 age category. Note that elder population can increase by virtue of in-migration of elders to retirement communities (Florida, Arkansas, and Arizona, for example) or by the out-migration of younger citizens (represented by some Midwestern states). In many farm belt states, younger people are leaving farms for jobs in cities, whether those cities are in the same state or not.

The social implications of these demographics are broad. The increasing percentage of older people means that more and more families will be made up of four generations instead of two or three. Currently whites are more likely than African Americans to live in married-couple-only households, and African Americans are more likely than whites to live in multigenerational households (Coward et al., 1996), although these differences balance out somewhat as people age. It seems clear that in the next 20 years more children will grow up with the

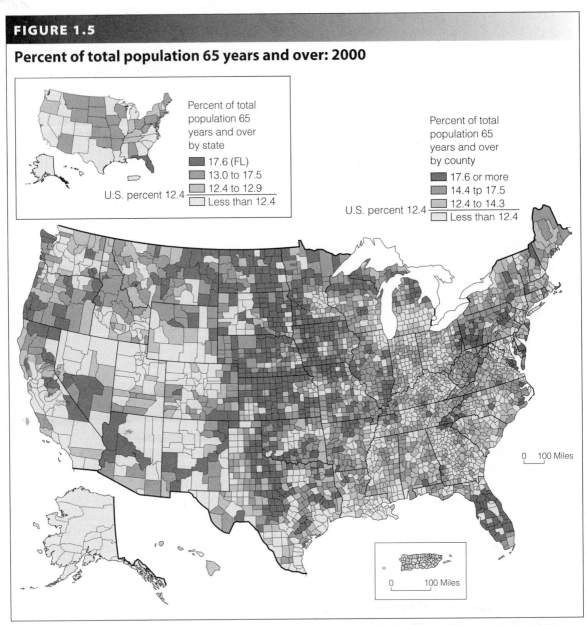

FIGURE 1.5

Percent of total population 65 years and over: 2000

Percent of total population 65 years and over by state

- 17.6 (FL)
- 13.0 to 17.5
- 12.4 to 12.9
- Less than 12.4

U.S. percent 12.4

Percent of total population 65 years and over by county

- 17.6 or more
- 14.4 tp 17.5
- 12.4 to 14.3
- Less than 12.4

U.S. percent 12.4

0   100 Miles

0   100 Miles

Source: U.S. Census Bureau, Census 2000 Summary File 1. American Factfinder at www.factfinder
.census.gov provides census data and mapping tools.

Note: For information on confidentiality protection, nonsampling error, and definitions, see
www.census.gov/prod/cen2000/doc/sf1.pdf

support of older relatives, and more people in their 60s will be called on to care for 80- and 90-year-old parents.

Population pyramids, illustrated in Figures 1.3 and 1.6, portray the effects of a population's age and gender composition on the structure of a nation's population. The horizontal bars in the pyramid represent **birth cohorts** (people born in the same year) of 10 years. The effect of the boomer cohort on the U.S. population can be clearly observed in Figure 1.6 as a bulge in the middle of the pyramid in 1997, a squaring-off of the population in 2025, and a startling increase in the over-85 population in 2050. Note the relationship between lower birthrates and lower death rates, indicating there will be fewer young people and more older people. This trend effectively reshapes the pyramid into a more boxlike image, illustrating the more balanced proportion in the population of each of the age cohorts.

Developed countries throughout the world are also experiencing an aging boom. The shape of the population pyramid for a less developed country such as Nigeria, for example, would be a large base, indicating high birthrates, and a small top, indicating a high death rate with few people surviving into old age. This pyramid was typical of the United States as a developing nation in the 1800s, and it is typical of most developing nations. Countries with this pyramid form have difficulty caring for all their young, and as a result, social policy is directed toward youth.

Countries such as Sweden and Japan, on the other hand, have an even higher proportion of elderly than the United States. They have achieved virtual zero population growth and thus would eventually have a stationary or boxlike pyramid. The social implications are that the needs of a society change with a changing age structure, as must social policy that directs national resources to various segments of the population. As the population shifts in age, housing, health care, education, and other services for elders must be balanced with services targeting younger age groups.

Ageism in the Future

For many decades our society has suffered from gerontophobia. The term comes from the Greek *geras*, "old," and *phobos*, "fear," and refers to fear of growing old or fear or hatred of the aged. To conceive of any status for elders other than that to which we are accustomed is difficult. We have accepted tension between youth and age. As a nation, the United States clearly identifies itself as youth oriented. Respect by the young for the old in our society is not a given. It is not deeply embedded in the fabric of our society.

Some people view the increasing number of older adults as a burden on society, referring to the economic burden of providing care for unemployed elders who depend on society for financial aid. The number of people age 65 and older relative to the working population (those 18 to 64) is called the old-age **dependency ratio.** If the population age 65 and older grows faster than the working population the cost to the taxpayer of providing for the elderly population rises. The ratio of elders to the working population has increased steadily, so there are proportionally fewer employed people to support older, retired people today. In 1910 there were 10 working people per older person; in 1980, 5 or 6. If the trend continues, by the year 2010 a ratio of 0.22, or about 4.5 workers per retired person, is expected (U.S. Bureau of the Census, 1994).

The larger the proportion of seniors in the population, the more Social Security and Medicare payments, and, consequently, higher taxes, are required, and indeed, Social Security taxes have slowly increased over the years. One of the many reasons is the increase of retirees in that system. This will be addressed more fully elsewhere in the text. The prospect for the future, however, rests on one simple fact: if you go to work at a young age, you will have to live a very long time to receive in benefits what you have paid into Social Security, because resources for that "enforced savings plan" will have been spent on people who are *presently* retired. If we

Population pyramid summary for the United States, 1997, 2025, 2050

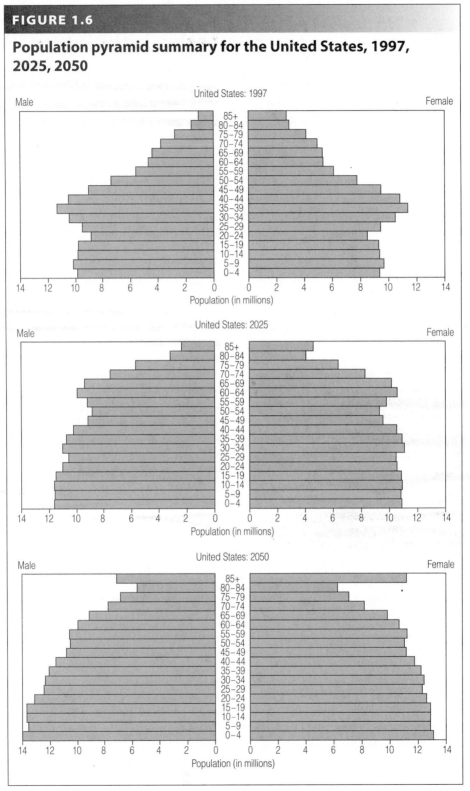

Source: U.S. Bureaus of the Census. (1994). Population pyramid summary for the U.S. *International database.* Washington, DC: U.S. Bureau of the Census. U.S. Department of Commerce.

view elders solely as an economic burden, ageism may increase as the number of retired, sick, or frail elderly increases.

Some gerontologists believe that we have become an age-segregated society, with separate schools for the young and separate retirement communities for the old. Undeniably, segregation further generates misunderstandings and conflict. Other gerontologists, alternatively, maintain that ageism is declining. They point to the improved health of seniors and to retirement communities composed of increasingly younger retirees who seem happy and content. In such contexts the image of older persons is improving. In addition, the increasing numbers of elders may be leading to a psychological shift away from a youth-oriented culture and toward a more life-course-inclusive identification.

The gerontologist and marketing consultant Ken Dychtwald (1989) believes that the increasing number of older persons is eroding the youth cult. His marketing corporation, Age Wave, took the lead in capitalizing on the demographics of an aging America. Dychtwald explains that the baby boomers of the 1940s, 1950s, and 1960s had a major impact on the economics and consumerism of the 1980s. Young adults of the 1980s, many of them "yuppies," prospered thanks to a relatively inexpensive college education and the economic expansion of the times. These same baby boomers will age in unprecedented numbers and continue to influence our lifestyle and our economy. Older people, Dychtwald contends, need not be a burden either to themselves or to the nation. The senior boom "is not a chance to be old longer but a chance to live longer" (Boynton, 1993). His prediction is that as boomers make demands on the market, our nation will modify our culture to accommodate an older population—from changing how long it takes a traffic light to turn from green to red, to modifying clothing styles, to increasing services at airports.

Dychtwald believes that businesses will stop discriminating on the basis of age when they realize that there are not enough young people to go around and that older workers are good, solid employees who, if treated well, will not choose to retire. Indeed, employers in the future may well pay to update the education of older employees rather than contend with inexperienced applicants from younger workforce. There is some support for his predictions in Japan, whose economy depends on the work and experience of its older workers, despite rapid changes in technology (Carr, 1997).

Old age can be an exciting time of contributing to others and of self-fulfillment. Dychtwald describes a framework in which less ageism, not more, can exist.

Chapter Summary

Gerontology is the multidisciplinary study of the human aging process from maturity to old age, as well as the study of the elderly as a special population. The key perspectives in gerontology are *biological, sociological,* and *psychological* processes. The text uses a *social problems approach,* examining patterns of social behavior and institutional structures that negatively affect the quality of life of the aging individual.

America has always been a youth-oriented nation; however, during the second half of the twentieth century increased longevity and lowered birthrates transformed the population to an older one. Social problems such as ageism, changing economic burdens, and the need for changes in social policy have resulted. The need to address the issues of an aging nation is upon us. Gerontologists believe that ageism can be ameliorated through education and the changing health and lifestyle of the "new" elderly, who are more healthy and vigorous than the population of elders preceding them.

Key Terms

ageism
aging
baby-boom generation
birth cohorts
cohort
critical perspective
dependency ratio
Detroit syndrome

gerontology
gerontophilia
gerontophobia
life expectancy
population pyramid
selection for survival
senescence
sociogenic aging

Questions for Discussion

1. Explore ageist attitudes within yourself, using some specific topics to focus on, such as your reaction to older drivers or your own fears of aging.
2. What are some social implications of the "aging revolution" not covered in this chapter? How will they affect advertising, fashion, or music?
3. What are some implications of increased longevity for family interactions?
4. How long do you expect to live, and how long do you want to live? Why?
5. There are different ways of looking at age. How old are you in your mental outlook on life? How old are you spiritually? Chronologically? Physically? How old are your parents in each of these categories? Your grandparents? What basis did you use for assigning the ages?

Fieldwork Suggestions

1. Browse several card shops—at least one at a local grocery store and another at a stationery store—and develop a list of the number and type of birthday cards that you find. How many do you find that joke about physical health? Memory? General negativity about age? How would you characterize the general tone of the greeting-card sections? Find one example of a birthday card directed to adults that is particularly meaningful to you and one that is particularly offensive.
2. See how many people know the meaning of the word ageism. Talk with some younger people as well as some middle-aged and older people in your investigation.
3. Survey several people about 15 to 25 years old to see how many come in contact with an elderly person daily. Survey several people 35 to 50 to see if there are differences. Determine how age segregated we are as a society.
4. Describe a chronologically young person who meets your criteria of being old.
5. Describe a chronologically old person who meets your criteria of being young.

Online Activities

Using the Internet, locate the home page for the U.S. Bureau of the Census. Go to Bureau of the Census Current Population Reports and locate data on the number of people over 65 in your home state. How does this compare with the number over 65 for your state in the 1980s? What would the population pyramid look like for your state?

Stereotypes
and Images

2

Senior Citizen Bloggers Defy Stereotypes

Carla K. Johnson

Forget shuffleboard, needlepoint, and bingo.

Web logs, usually considered the domain of alienated adolescents and home for screeds from middle-aged pundits, are gaining a foothold as a new leisure-time option for senior citizens.

There's Dad's Tomato Garden Journal, Dog-walk Musings, and, of course, the Oldest Living Blogger.

"It's too easy to sit in your own cave and let the world go by, eh?" said Vancouver's Ray Sutton, the 73-year-old Oldest Living Blogger. "It keeps the old head working a little bit so you're not just sitting there gawking at TV."

Web logs, or blogs, are online journals where people post entries on topics that interest them. They may offer links to other Web sites, photos, and opportunities for readers to comment.

Bloggers say their hobby keeps them thinking about current events, makes them friends to strangers around the globe, and gives them a voice in a society that often neglects the wisdom of the elderly.

"It brings out the best in me," said Boston-area blogger Millie Garfield, 80, who writes My Mom's Blog. "My life would be dull without it."

Three percent of online seniors have created a blog and 17 percent have read someone else's blog, according to the Pew Internet & American Life Project. Compare that to online 18- to 29-year-olds. Thirteen percent of them have created blogs

and 32 percent have read someone else's blog, according to the Pew data.

Joe Jenett, a Detroit-area Web designer who has been tracking the age of bloggers for a personal project called the Ageless Project, said he has noticed more older bloggers in the past two years.

"Isn't that phenomenal? And their writing is vibrant," Jenett said. "The Web is diverse and it breaks across generational lines."

Jenett and others noted that sites such as Blogger.com give step-by-step instructions and free hosting, making it simpler to self-publish on the Web.

"It's easy to start one if you can connect dots," said former Jesuit priest and retired newspaperman Jim Bowman, 73, of Oak Park, Ill. Bowman writes four regular blogs: one on happenings in his city, one a catchall for his opinions, one on religion, and one offering feedback on Chicago newspapers.

A recent post from his newspaper blog praised the *Chicago Tribune*'s front page stories on the White Sox World Series games:

"It's been a lovely thing, to see copy so clean and substantive enough to make E. B. White and his mentor William Strunk Jr. stand up in their graves and say Yippee," Bowman wrote.

Bowman once had eight separate blogs, but has let some lapse. The blog topics he doesn't keep up with anymore include ideas for sermons, Chicago history, and condominium life.

"Like any other hobby, you've got to make sure it doesn't take over," he said.

Mari Meehan, 64, of Coeur d'Alene, Idaho, has been blogging since July. It's given her a voice in her small resort town where, as a relative newcomer, she felt rebuffed in her efforts to get involved.

Inspired by other local bloggers she'd found on the *Spokesman-Review* (Spokane, Washington) newspaper's Web site, Meehan discovered it was easy to get started.

"If you can read, you can do it," she said. She titled her blog Dogwalk Musings and based it on the premise that she would write about her thoughts during morning walks with her St. Bernard, Bacchus. Her posts range from nature sightings of a kildeer's nest with four eggs to rants about local and national politics.

When readers started mentioning Dogwalk Musings as one of their favorites on a newspaper columnist's blog, Meehan said she felt compelled to post every day.

But now she's backing off. "Lots of times, I'll walk away from it for three or four days," Meehan said. "I'm not going to let it take over."

Response from blog readers does keep many older bloggers returning to their keyboards day after day. If they skip a day, readers will e-mail the older bloggers, asking if they're sick.

In the two years since 92-year-old Ray White started Dad's Tomato Garden Journal, the blog has been viewed more than 45,000 times. Some of those who click on the site are regular readers who know they can rely on White six days a week.

A recent post, with its original punctuation:

"How is everything going this morning with you, cheer up because today is Friday and most of you know what you can do in the morning, pull up that cover and go back to sleep for a little while. But we do have to get going for today. You know all about the coffee and tea at Dad's house, it's ready and the door is always unlocked. Let's go out there and do a good job today and then we will be able to smile when we head for home this afternoon."

White's daughter, Mary White, said the blog keeps her father interested in life. When his computer is broken, "he's just like a different person," she said. "He's sad."

The blog connects Ray White with friends he's never met in England, Portugal, Germany, Canada, and all 50 states, he said.

He's continually surprised by the response.

"You'd be surprised how many questions I get during the tomato season," he said. "There's always somebody having a problem. I try to answer all those questions. . . .

"It's just like one big family."

© 2005 Associated Press. Reprinted with permission.

Maybe you've heard or even made the following statements: "Old people are narrow-minded." "Old people are set in their ways." "Old people are terrible drivers!" These statements are negative stereotypes. Are you familiar with the phrase "a twinkle in his eye" or "old and wise"? These statements are also stereotypes. This chapter explores stereotypes based on age and provides information to explain why they exist.

Stereotypes of Aging

Stereotypes are generalized beliefs or opinions based on individual experience and often produced by irrational thinking. Stereotyping and labeling seem to fulfill our need to structure and organize situations in order to minimize ambiguity and to clarify where we stand in relation to others. Because of the complexity of our society, we need to be able to make quick assessments of situations and of people, and we usually base those judgments on our beliefs or previous experience—this is a person I can trust, this situation makes me uncomfortable, this person is probably not reliable, and so forth. These assessments are our "people skills," and they form the basis for making judgments and shaping many of our interactions in the larger society. However, when observations become rigidly categorized—I cannot trust this person because she looks like an untrustworthy person I once knew, for example—then we have fallen into making assessments based on stereotypes.

Stereotyping, whether direct or subtle, is usually inaccurate. When we generalize by putting people into categories, we tend to oversimplify reality. We ignore inconsistent information and emphasize only a few characteristics. Thus, the statement "old people sit around all day" is a generalization that does not apply to the many active older individuals who work, write, paint, are physically active, or involve themselves in community affairs.

Although stereotypes can be positive, they can also be negative. Whether positive or negative, they are emotional impressions and are not based on objective information, and they categorize people. Stereotypes can interfere with our judgment by arousing strong and sometimes negative emotions such as hatred or resentment. Hating or resenting any person or groups of people for any reason, but doing so on the basis of a trait such as age is especially ignorant and unfair.

Positive and Negative Stereotypes

Tuckman and Lorge (1953) were among the first gerontologists to study stereotypes. Using a list of statements with which subjects were asked to agree or disagree, they found that old people were perceived as being set in their ways, unproductive, a burden to their children, stubborn, grouchy, lonely, "rocking-chair types," and in their second childhood. Since the Tuckman and Lorge study, psychologists have continued to find that society stereotypes older persons (Perdue & Gurtman, 1990; Bargh, Chen, & Burrows, 1996; Hummert, 1999). Palmore (1990) summarized the negative stereotypes of aging: (1) illness, (2) impotency, (3) ugliness, (4) mental decline, (5) mental illness, (6) uselessness, (7) isolation, (8) poverty, and (9) depression (grouchiness, touchiness, crankiness). He countered all these stereotypes with factual information disproving these stereotypes for the majority of older persons. Stereotypes, however, are no longer as negative as they were in the 1950s (Palmore, 1990). Palmore and others (Luszcz & Fitzgerald, 1986; Schwald & Sedlacek, 1990) have cited studies showing increasingly positive attitudes toward elders over the last several decades. This is due in no small part to the shifting demographics discussed in chapter 1, which resulted in more exposure by the general population to older individuals as well as the improved general health of elders in the final decades of the 1900s.

Despite this positive shift in social attitude, negative stereotyping of the elderly remains a significant social issue. Two kinds of negativism are relatively common. One is an ageism that focuses only on the least capable, less healthy, and least alert aged. This focus on the sick takes attention away from the healthy aged who defy negative stereotypes. The biomedicalization of aging emerged over a century ago with the growth of scientific inquiry and subsequent breathtaking advances in medical sciences. It is the belief that problems associated with aging are biological rather than social and behavioral. The "problems of aging," therefore, can only be addressed by medical technology, if at all (Vertinsky, 1991). A biomedicalized perspective of age locks the aging process and the individual experiencing it into an irreversible decline of physical deterioration. Physical change and decline, of course, are only a piece of the process of aging; trapping society and the aging individual in this stereotype of age limits all other possibilities for physical, psychological, and spiritual growth and development in later life.

The second kind of negativism is called *compassionate stereotyping*. Binstock (1983) coined this term to describe images that portray elders as disadvantaged on some level (economic, social, or psychological), in need and deserving of help by others. This may sound harmless, but consider the reaction of disability activists to posters of the Easter Seal child—a poster designed to invoke pity for those with disabilities. No individual, including the elderly, wants pity; rather, people want the tools for being independent and self-reliant. For some, the tools for independence and self-reliance are strictly inherent qualities; for others, those inherent qualities must be supplemented with external resources such as a wheelchair, a hearing aid, or specially designed educational opportunities. Like all people, older adults want to be seen as individuals, not as a category. **Compassionate stereotypes** perpetuate dependency and low self-esteem and unnecessarily lower expectations of what older people can achieve.

A *positive stereotype* is a generalized belief that categorizes all older people in a favorable light, whereas a *negative stereotype* categorizes old people in demeaning ways. The extent to which different stereotypes elicit positive versus negative attitudes now has been studied by a number of social scientists (Linville, 1982; Crockett & Hummert, 1987; Heckhausen et al., 1989; Hummert et al., 1994; Hummert, 1999). Hummert (1995) found that the two most frequently cited **positive stereotypes** of older people were the "Golden Agers" (lively, adventurous, active, sociable, witty, independent, well informed, successful, well traveled, etc.) and "Perfect Grandparents" (kind, loving, family oriented, generous, grateful, supportive, understanding,

wise, knowledgeable, etc.). She found the most prevalent negative age stereotypes to be "Severely Impaired" (slow-thinking, incompetent, feeble, incoherent, inarticulate, senile) and "Despondent" (depressed, sad, hopeless, afraid, neglected, lonely).

The "Despondent" stereotype finding illustrates compassionate stereotyping, whereas the "Severely Impaired" stereotype reflects biomedicalization of aging. Like all stereotypes, positive and negative typecastings of elders emerge from a kernel of truth: older people *do* become more frail. Depression in later life *can* be a serious problem—in part because when it is categorized as a natural part of aging, it goes undiagnosed and untreated as a mental health issue. The tragedy of stereotyping is that the individual becomes objectified; that objectification is internalized by the person who is being victimized by it, and a vicious circle of loss of sense of self ensues. If a retired 70-year-old former CEO of a large corporation is treated by everyone in his environment as being incompetent or slow, that social reflection of who he is can profoundly impact his sense of well-being. We humans are interdependent creatures, and we derive much of our personal sense of self from our social environment. If I am treated as if I were feeble, I will identify with that kernel of feebleness that I can see in myself, rather than identifying with my continuing strengths.

The mass media are a profoundly important source of stereotypes about aging in the United States. Media influences shape the attitudes of children as well as the self-concepts of adults, and older people continue to be invisible or negatively portrayed. When they are visible, it is seldom (less than 10 percent of the time) in major roles (Robinson & Skill, 1995). Old women are even less likely to appear than are old men, and when they are present they are more likely to be characterized in negative stereotypes (Vasil & Wass, 1993; Robinson & Skill, 1995; Hilt & Lipschultz, 1996). Negative stereotyping and sexism continue to be major themes in the portrayal of elders in the electronic media.

Although the average age of Americans is increasing, most television characters are young. Elders watch more television than all other age groups, averaging 21 hours a week, or three hours a day (Levy, 2003). Many elders do not travel and are dependent on television for companionship and entertainment; for them, television is a window on the world. The more elders watch television, however, the worse they feel about themselves. Repeated exposure to negative images or to only a few images with which they can identify can be neither psychologically productive for the elderly nor in the long run economically productive for television networks, yet the trends continue. Yale researchers asked elderly television watchers to maintain evaluations of how they saw themselves portrayed on television (Levy, 2003). One outcome of that study was that elderly viewers were less likely to turn on the television than they had been previous to becoming consciously aware of how they were portrayed. Generally, elders found that older Americans either were portrayed as forgetful and ill-tempered or were simply omitted. Despite numerous findings that viewers age 50 and older were significantly more likely than younger viewers to be consumers of television news, a study of television station management described the struggle within news management regarding stories of interest to an older audience. In the Yale study, one 71-year-old viewer said of TV news: "When people were interviewed about different matters, older people were left out." Another responded, "I feel like we've been ignored. I feel like we're non-existent" (Levy, 2003). It is difficult for action-oriented television news to cover many social issues of interest to an older audience. If local television were to report more stories of interest to an older audience, viewers of all ages would have a better-developed perspective of social issues affecting a broad age range. In that way we all would be less exposed to having our stereotypes and

biases reinforced through this powerful medium. The more exposure people of all age groups have to one another, the less likely are stereotypes of any sort to develop, for it is through our exposure to others that we are reminded of the huge range of personality, values, and behaviors among human beings.

Who Is Old?

When is a person old? Do the words old, elderly, senior, mature adult, and senior citizen all mean the same thing? Or do they mean different things to different people, under different circumstances? No definition of an older person has been universally agreed upon. "Old age" means different things and is assigned on the basis of chronology (age 65, for example), biology (how well one functions), and social standards (the point at which, for example, a woman is considered "too old" to wear a bikini on the beach). Sweeping statements about a category of people ("the elderly," "the twentysomethings," "teenagers," etc.) stereotype the individuals within that category because they bypass existing vast individual differences. Some old people are frail, some are wise, some are cranky, some are jolly, and some are patient. We age just as we have lived: we do not become a different person because we have reached a chronological marker that makes us "old." Aging is a gradual process with many influences. The reality is that people age differently.

In addition to individual differences, the definition of "old" defies precision because over time new cohorts move into later life, bringing with them their unique life experiences, values, and attitudes, which have been shaped by shared sociohistorical events (natural disasters, wars, recessions, etc.) of their times. In a classic study of life-course effects of the Great Depression, Glenn Elder (1979; Elder & O'Rand, 1994) found notable differences in personality style between people who were young adolescents and those who were young adults beginning their families and careers at the time of the great stock market crash. Stereotypes of "cautious" and "conservative," for example, might be quite descriptive of one age cohort among the current "old" and completely inaccurate for another cohort, also currently "old."

In part, longevity is behind the need for more precise descriptions of just who are the "old." Those who are relatively young, about 65 to 75, are referred to as the "young old." Older people who are vigorous, fit, and healthy have been labeled the "able elderly." Those 80 and older are variously called the "old old," the "frail elderly," or the "extreme aged," depending on their health and the focus of the gerontologist's work. In the dawn of the twenty-first century the category of centenarian is commonly used by the media and the professions to address the growing numbers of people living past their hundredth year.

The Legal Definition of Old

In the 1890s, Germany's Otto von Bismarck established a social security system for German elders that benefited citizens 65 years or older. Life expectancy in the late 1800s was approximately 48 years for men and 51 years for women, so the political advantage of addressing emerging Positivist social thought by establishing social security programs far outweighed any economic disadvantages.

Nearly 60 years later, in 1935, the United States passed the Social Security Act under President Franklin D. Roosevelt. In that act, 65 was named as the onset of old age, in accordance with a tradition by then established in Europe. In line with Social Security standards, most companies as well as state and local governments developed pension programs beginning at age 65 for retiring workers.

This legal definition has become a social definition: on retirement, a person's lifestyle generally changes dramatically, creating a point of entry from one phase of life to another that has become a social event for celebration and congratulations. Retirement, in fact, is one of the few life-course transitions that is celebrated throughout the United States. "Retirement age" has become somewhat standardized legally, socially, and psychologically as initiation into "old age."

Since the 1930s, however, medical science has extended longevity and improved general health. The 65-year-old today is not the same physically or psychologically as the 65-year-old in 1935. Today's 65-year-old is likely to be healthier and better educated, for starters, and to be more intimately connected with the larger world through the media of television and radio than was his or her counterpart in 1935. Social scientists now question whether 75, 80, or 85 might more accurately mark the beginning of old age. Whatever the age, any *chronological* criterion for determining old age is too narrow and rigid, for it assumes everyone ages in the same ways and at the same time.

Biology: The Function of Age

Some authorities say aging begins at the moment of conception. Others reserve the term aging to describe the process of decline following the peak in the biological characteristics of muscle strength, skin elasticity, blood circulation, and sensory acuity. Peak functioning in most capabilities occurs at relatively early ages. After the mid-20s, for example, hearing progressively declines, and muscle strength reaches its maximum between 25 and 30 years of age.

We spend approximately one-fourth of our lives growing up and three-fourths growing old. Biological decline, a gradual process beginning in young adulthood and continuing gradually throughout the life span, varies among individuals in its speed and extent. One person may be biologically old at age 45, another may be physically fit at 80. All organs do not decline at the same rate, either. Someone may have a 30-year-old heart, a 60-year-old response rate, 80-year-old eyes—and be only 20 years old! That everyone ages in the same way and at the same pace is a myth; however, the dominance of the medical model has shaped public perception to view aging as a decremental process, one based solely on our age.

Psychology and Mental Functioning

Mental functioning includes the capacity to create, think, remember, and learn. Although we often assume that mental functioning declines with age, studies now show that this belief is too simplistic to adequately describe mental functioning in later life. Although older students enrolling in college after raising families or retiring are often concerned that they cannot keep up with younger students, most professors know that older, nontraditional-age students as a group prove to be outstanding in their classroom work. Most of us have known some men or women in their 80s or 90s whose minds are clear and alert and others who have memory lapses or confuse facts. The wide variations in the mental functioning of older people may be caused by disease, genetic makeup, or the effects of stress. We are only just beginning to realize how the aging process affects people psychologically. But like body functioning, mental functions do not automatically decline with age. Change is genetically programmed and inevitable; decline is not.

Studies of mental functioning in adulthood show tremendous heterogeneity (variability), and emphasize the need to distinguish between normal, optimal, and pathological aging. Psychologists have identified a developmental reserve capacity in later life, demonstrated for example by the ability of older people to develop in their professional lives, or to profit from practice and engage in new learning (Featherman et al.,

1990; Perlmutter, 1990; Baltes, 1991; Baltes & Lindenberger, 1997; Berry & Jobe, 2002). Newer psychological studies indicate there is generally a loss with aging in the mechanics of the mind, but that pragmatic knowledge (information-based knowledge) forms the basis of new ways of learning in later adulthood (Sternberg, 1990; Baltes et al., 1999; Berry & Jobe, 2002). Psychologists are now focusing research on the identification and meaning of wisdom as a select area of knowledge and problem solving.

The Social Construction of Aging

Self-concept is the way in which a person sees himself or herself. It is how individuals define themselves to themselves, the ongoing image we have of ourselves, and it forms the basis for the way people maintain a sense of continuity even as their bodies age and change. Even if we see ourselves changing, that change is emerging from something that is or was also part of the self-concept. Early in the study of gerontology, Bernice Neugarten (1977) cautioned her colleagues that chronological age is an "empty variable." It is the importance of the *events* that occur with the passage of time that have relevance for the study of identity development, not time itself (Vertinsky, 1991). Perhaps most important, self-concept dictates the way in which people interpret and make meaning of the events that occur in their lives. It is a complex psychological function, not just one general image, and it shapes our styles of coping and managing the world we live in.

The social construction of self addresses the idea that the way we interpret events in our lives is partially a reflection of how we are treated and partially the extent to which we have internalized the way society has defined or categorized us. So, for example, it might not be unexpected for that 70-year-old woman to believe that it is improper for her to wear a bikini on the beach. Her self-concept precludes that behavior: she sees herself as, perhaps, too dignified *at her age* to publicly expose her less-than-youthful body.

Those people who see themselves as old and accept as true the negative characteristics attributed to old age may, indeed, *be* old. As the sociologist W. I. Thomas stated, "If people define situations as real, they are real in their consequences" (1923, p. 42). Current research on self-concept emphasizes the knowledge base, or structure, that helps individuals to maintain a consistent sense of who they are throughout their life experiences (Schaie & Willis, 1996). Those who have a good sense of continuity of who they are appear to be better adjusted in later life. They are less likely to identify themselves as being "old," because they identify as being who they *always* have been. The dimensions of an individual's self-concept that deal with self-esteem and a sense of social worth are the very dimensions that our society is most likely to treat harshly.

A current focus in gerontology is to move away from scientific measurements of personality and aging processes, toward listening to the voices of aging people themselves—to their own narratives of their life processes. This methodology is referred to as **phenomenology**, in which the meaning of an event is defined by the person experiencing that event (or phenomenon), not a researcher's hypothesis. Sharon Kaufman's skillfully developed study *The Ageless Self: Sources of Meaning in Later Life* (1986) is an excellent example of using the voices of elders to develop a description of their self-concept. "I wanted to look at the meaning of aging to elderly people themselves, as it emerges in their personal reflections of growing old" (Kaufman, 1993, p. 13). Kaufman documented the finding that many older people see themselves not as old, but rather as ageless, as living *in their old age.*

The voices of older people, documented by Kaufman (1986) and in a second study by Tan-demar Research, 1988), best describe this ageless self:

> *I don't feel seventy. I feel about thirty. I wear my hair the way I did then. . . . I just saw some slides of myself and was quite taken aback. That couldn't be me. (Kaufman, 1986, p. 8)*

> *The only way I know I'm getting old is to look in the mirror . . . but I've only felt old a few times—when I'm really sick. (Kaufman, 1986, p. 12)*

> *I'm always telling my children I'm still the same inside. I just have to walk for the bus now instead of run. (Tandemar Research, 1988, p. 23)*

Kaufman summarized the process by which people maintain a solid sense of self in later life, even as their bodies, their relationships, and their social circumstances change over time:

> *[The ageless self] draws meaning from the past, interpreting and recreating it as a resource for being in the present. It also draws meaning from the structural and ideational aspects of the cultural context: social and educational background, family, work, values, ideals, and expectations. . . . [Elders] formulate and reformulate personal and cultural symbols of their past to create a meaningful coherent sense of self, and in the process they create a viable present. In this way, the ageless self emerges. Its definition is ongoing, continuous, and creative. (Kaufman, 1993, p. 14)*

Through the use of narrative methods, the personal experience of growing old is increasingly being captured by theorists as well as the media. The cognitive act of constructing a story of one's experience for another person to hear helps the narrator to organize his or her sense of that life; it also helps the listener to release preconceptions (stereotypes).

Through narrative techniques the concept of **possible selves** has emerged: we have a sense of who we were, of who we are presently, and of who we are becoming (or might become if we are not careful) (Markus & Herzog, 1991; Hooker & Kaus, 1994; McAdams et al., 1997; Bauer & McAdams, 2004). This image or projection of who we might become with time can be positive, hoped-for selves or negative, feared selves. Not surprisingly, elders who experience a threat to their health can project a negative possible self: I could become that bent, osteoporotic 80-year-old woman if I don't get my act together! Both positive and negative possible selves can be very motivating for making useful and appropriate behavioral change.

Occupation and Achievement

The age at which a person becomes old depends to some extent on the nature of his or her job. In his classic work *Age and Achievement* (1953), Harvey Lehman studied the age at which superior productivity tends to occur in different occupations. He found that in most fields, the productivity of adults peaked when they were in their 30s. Only in a few fields did it peak in those in their 40s or older. Researchers have been challenging and refining his work ever since. More recent studies show the 40s and beyond to be highly productive for a number of professions, including sales and marketing, and for fields requiring special skills and knowledge (Day, 1993; Landau & Werbel, 1995). Productivity in family farming requires physical endurance as well as historical knowledge of plants, soils, weather patterns. Farmer productivity peaks at midlife—around the time children in the family begin to take more central roles in the business. It seems that the older family farmer moves to the role of mentor as the younger generation takes over (Tauer, 1995). Novelists peak in their 50s and 60s; botanists and inventors, in their 60s; and scholars such as historians, humanists, and philosophers, in their 60s and 70s. If we can truly define old age as a time of reflection, we can understand why scholars are able to make major contributions in later life.

Prime occupational performance may occur in the 20s or at any age after that. The following list gives some trends:

Profession	Peak performance age
Football or baseball players	20s
Female models	20s and 30s
Movie actors	30s and 40s
Presidents of colleges	40s and 50s
U.S. senators	60s
Outstanding commercial and industrial leaders	60s
Philosophers	70s
Millionaires	80s

Although many people who give peak performances in early adulthood continue to produce top-notch performances throughout their lives, productivity rates do depend on the type of work an individual performs. Studies of blue-collar workers indicate that they reach their highest productivity at an earlier age than white-collar workers, because their work often requires physical skills that peak in early adulthood. In contrast, other studies show that executives see themselves as maturing slowly and believe that old age comes later for them. Clearly, the personal and cultural meaning of achievement varies with environment, age, gender, and culture (Salili, 1995; Boudreau et al., 2001; Riordan, Griffith, & Weatherly, 2003).

Coping with Stress and Illness

People who are chronologically young can be "old before their time" if they exhibit the physical and mental traits characteristic of more advanced age. An approach to studying the link between stress, illness, and physiological aging began with an attempt to estimate the amount of stress created in people by various life events (Schaie & Willis, 1996). Forty years ago Holmes and Rahe (1967) developed a rating scale to measure stress over a year's time using 43 life of anxiety, depression, migraine headaches, and peptic ulcers (Rahe & Arthur, 1978). Research has also clearly documented stress as an associated precursor of coronary heart disease and stroke (Rahe, 1995).

What stresses individuals, however, changes with the cohort. The Stressful Life Events Scale was adjusted in 1977 and again in 1995 to reflect cultural changes in perceptions of stress. Modern-day raters saw marriage, for example, as a less meaningful event than did persons 18 and 30 years earlier (Rahe, 1995). "Death of a close family member" was adjusted significantly upward in LCUs in the 1995 sample, compared with the 1965 and 1977 samples. Longevity is an important part of this adjustment: a greater proportion of adults have older parents and grandparents living—and dying—than did the 1965 sample. Similarly, economic and work-related events are more highly loaded among women in the 1990s than for women in the 1960s and 1970s. One consistent finding in the measurement of stressful life events over the past 30 years stands out, however: many of the most stressful life events occur most frequently in one's later years, including death of a spouse, death of a close family member, death of a friend, change in health or behavior of a family member, and major personal injury or illness (Rahe, 1995).

How does stress affect the individual? The individual's response to stress, including the perception of ill health itself, is the key. The mechanism connecting stress and illness is still not completely understood, but individuals who are highly stressed, who feel they have little control over their lives, and who have limited social support systems appear to be most vulnerable to disease (Krause, 1991; Brandtstadter, 1999).

To summarize, the very process of aging creates multiple life events. If the individual lacks the resources to cope with the consequent stress, illness may result or the aging process may speed up. An individual's "age," then, may depend on the number of severely stressful events he or she experiences and on the individual's ability to cope

Even after retirement, many elders work part-time or volunteer their skills in the community.

© Alan Carey / The Image Works

events, known as the Stressful Life Events Scale. Typically, it works by tabulating all the events an individual has experienced over a specific period of time (six months or one year, generally) and using that tally to predict illness in the people with higher scores. The events are weighted by stress-load: for example, in the 1967 scale death of a spouse was rated at 100 life change units, and change in financial status was 38 LCUs. We have understood for about 20 years now that psychosocial and environmental stress ages people, and stress is a well-documented cause with them. Throughout life, adjustment requires adapting to change. Some people resist change, and stress hits them particularly hard. Others, who are more flexible, compromise and adapt to whatever life brings. Psychologically, the ability to address stress by adapting to change—one's coping and adaptation resources—reflects how one will age.

Studies of Children's Attitudes

Since the mid-1960s interest has grown in studying attitudes young children and adolescents have toward the aged. The body of research developed since that time has produced varied and contradictory results, but uniformly shows that children do tend to stereotype older adults. However, those stereotypes have become incrementally less overtly negative in the past 30 years.

Children formulate attitudes about elders and the aging process at an early age. These attitudes are shaped by various outside forces: families, social interactions with peers, school influences, and media influence (Aday, Sims, & Evans, 1991). Children as young as three exhibit ageist language (Burke, 1981), and by age five they begin to have clear attitudes about aging and being old (Fullmer, 1984). In adolescence, children appear to stereotype and adopt values in a way similar to adults (Carstensen, Mason, & Caldwell, 1982; Carstensen, Gross, & Fung, 1997)

The media are a primary source of ageist messages for children. Even fairy tales instill ageist feelings in the very young. Evil, ugly, old witches and mean old stepmothers endanger children in many stories. Some books are changing this theme, emphasizing, for example, the grandparent-grandchild connection (Steinberg, 1993). In a cross-national study of children from Australia, England, North America, and Sweden, Goldman and Goldman (1981) found that children believe that the physical, psychological, socioeconomic, and sexual powers of old people decline and that old people's skills become less useful with age. These views

reflect a negative stereotype based on a biological model of decline—a decline that, of course, children can observe by watching their grandparents age and die, for example. It is particularly important that children be provided greater opportunities to develop positive interactions with older people, in part because their internalized attitudes about old age will have a significant influence on their own lives and the ways in which they see themselves as they age.

Changes in attitude

The ways in which attitudes can be changed have been extensively examined in the past 40 years (Amir, 1969; Sanders et al., 1984; Corbin, Metal-Corbin, & Barg, 1989; Bengtson & Achenbaum, 1993). Three primary ways to impact attitudes were identified in 1982 by Class and Knott: (1) through discussions with peers, (2) through direct experience with attitude objects, and (3) through increased information or knowledge. This model has been used in several projects for school-based programs to change children's attitudes toward the elderly. In one very well designed classroom experiment (Aday et al., 1996), older volunteers were paired with children to assist with a school-based task. The interactions also included structured and informal discussions designed to foster more intimate relationships between the pairs, and it tested attitude changes in one-year and five-year follow-ups. Researches found that as a result of the interactions, children and youth developed more positive attitudes about the aged and about aging, and those attitudes remained part of the children's perceptual schema five years later. Responses by the children to the question "What have you learned from the intergenerational project?" included:

> I never knew some older people were so active. . . . That not all older people are mean and stingy. . . . I learned that older people were once a young person just like me. I never thought about it before. (Aday et al., 1996, p. 150)

In response to the question "How has this project changed you?" some responses were:

I learned that everyone on this earth is equal, no matter what their age. . . . I'm not so afraid of older people. . . . It has changed my outlook on older people to a more positive one. . . . I'm not as scared of growing old as I used to be. . . . I'm more apt to smile and speak to older people. (Aday et al., 1996, p. 150)

Teachers can improve children's attitudes toward old age by telling them about old people's physical and mental capabilities. They can present accurate information about old age, and they can bring active, creative elders into the classroom. Teachers can also help children explore attitudes toward older people as they explore cultural and ethnic differences among classmates' backgrounds. Children are generally encouraged to follow the traditional values of their families' cultures, whatever that cultural heritage might be (Zandi et al., 1990). Discussing different ways parents and grandchildren interact with grandparents is a wonderful way to honor cultural differences and to identify and explore different attitudes about aging.

Studies of College Students' Attitudes

Understanding the nature of how younger adults view older adults is important because those attitudes will impact intergenerational relationships, the level of concern for social programs that benefit older adults, and the self-concept of that younger adult as he or she matures into middle age and later life.

Studies of college students' attitudes toward aging, like those of the population in general, show very mixed results. Some of this lack of consistency is methodological—different researchers ask different questions and often are not actually measuring the same thing. Attitude is a multidimensional mental schema influenced by many factors, including exposure to older people, gender, culture, and individual differences of personality. The elderly, too, do not make up a single category: vast individual differences exist among elders. A second reason for mixed findings on young adults' attitudes toward their elders is that older adults may be seen to some extent as multidimensional people, with both positive and negative attributes (Slotterback & Saarnio, 1996).

The most generalized stereotype among college students is based on a biological model of decrement and excludes personality, skill, and interactional factors. This can be a particularly problematic perspective among students training for the health and healing professions. In a study conducted by AARP and the University of Southern California in Los Angeles in 2005, 66 percent of college-aged students believed that most older people didn't have enough money to live on (compassionate stereotype), and around 61 percent believed that loneliness is a serious problem for older people, when in fact only 33 percent of people over 65 agree (Gotthardt, 2005).

The attitudes of pharmacy students (Shepherd & Erwin, 1983), medical students (Intrieri et al., 1993), nursing students (Downe-Wamboldt & Melanson, 1990; Rowland & Shoemake, 1995), and college students (Shoemake & Rowland, 1993; Barrow, 1994) have all been studied and surveyed. A conclusion drawn in one study of nursing students also summarizes the findings of other studies:

Change comes in small increments, but changes in attitudes come only after learning has occurred. Providing students opportunities to test their professional skills and meet challenges to their preconceptions of the elderly can increase the rate of change. (Rowland & Shoemake, 1995, p. 747)

Barrow (1994) conducted a study of college students in which they developed their own

Learning environments can provide a rich source of interaction between age groups.

not live their last few years of life with great happiness; it is a time of stress and unhappiness, pain, sorrow, weeping, and reversals in memory.

They have a lot to teach yet don't have a fair role in society. Some people, what I think, are just waiting to die because they're lonely. A lot of people put them aside. Cause—the amount of attention the elderly need seems to be a burden to a lot of families.

They have done and seen so much. I view old people sort of as old cars, with some parts broken, but others running as smooth as ever. I feel it is always worth it to stop and talk to an elderly person. You never know when they could teach you a valuable lesson.

descriptions of older people. In this study, stereotypes emerged directly from students' minds, **phenomenological** in method. A salient finding was that students paid the most attention to the changing physical appearance and capabilities of older people. Many students responded to the word aged with a description of physical decline. Some responded to the word aged with a social position or role description, such as "bad driver," "interesting life stories," "bingo," "grandparent," or "calm life." Still others included psychological qualities, such as "wise," "lonely," "fear of death," or "experienced." The students had a relatively balanced mix of both positive and negative stereotypes—for example, an equal number of responses of "wise" and "lonely."

In response to the question "What are your general thoughts or views about the aged?" students again displayed a range of attitudes, from negative to neutral to positive, and including positive, compassionate, and negative stereotypes defined earlier in the chapter.

Their late years may be years of dependency on physicians, drugs, institutions and ambulatory medicine. The aged sometimes do

Explaining Stereotypes

We categorize. On meeting or merely seeing a person, we determine the person's age, race, gender, and perhaps other social categories such as socioeconomic status (Whitley & Kite, 2006). We can explain the existence of stereotypes on a number of levels. On one level, the historical/cultural explanation requires the gerontologist to look at the roots and cultural context of our concepts about old age. On another level, current social explanations look at elements such as social class and the influence of the media. On yet another level, psychologists ask why some individuals, either young or old, accept the negative stereotypes of old age whereas others accept the positive ones.

Whatever new object we see, we perceive to be only a new version of our familiar experience, and we set about translating it at once into our parallel facts. We have thereby our vocabulary.

RALPH WALDO EMERSON, 1878

Historical and Cultural Explanations

Understanding the relationships between generations and exploring views about growing old in a previous era are the jobs of a historian. For example, a historian in chapter 1 described how American society's view of elders shifted from one of veneration and favor to one of scorn. The reasons for the change are extraordinarily complex and are related to larger philosophical issues, the influences of multiple cultures brought about by immigration, advancements in science and medicine, longevity, global and local economic structures, and the shift of cultural values as a result of all those factors.

Rude, insulting, or negative labels directed to anyone whom we consider "other" is not new, however, and seems to endure throughout history. The words we use to describe people provide a basis for the formation of stereotypes, and people often internalize those labels, incorporating them into their own self-concepts. Language is powerful: it shapes consciousness, and our consciousness affects our health and well-being as well as our interpersonal relationships.

Becca Levy and Ellen Langer (1994) identified a dramatic relationship between cultural beliefs and the degree of memory loss people experience in old age. They conducted memory tests with (1) old and young mainland Chinese, (2) old and young from the American Deaf culture, and (3) old and young hearing Americans. They expected that the Chinese and Deaf cultural groups would be less likely than the hearing Americans to be exposed to and accept negative stereotypes about aging. They found that younger subjects, regardless of culture, perform similarly on memory tests. Older Chinese and older Deaf participants, however, outperformed the older American hearing group. They described their findings:

> A social psychological mechanism contributes to the often-reported memory decline that accompanies aging. . . . The negative stereotypes about how old people cognitively age, to which individuals starting at a young age are exposed, become self-fulfilling prophecies. (Levy & Langer, 1994, p. 996)

An unexpected finding of the research was that the sample of old Chinese performed similarly to the sample of young Chinese. The scores for the two groups did not differ significantly even though the memory tasks that were used typically reflected those that demonstrate memory loss with age in the United States. The results were even more surprising because the older Chinese group had completed fewer years of education than the young Chinese and the samples of old and young Americans. Of the three groups studied (old and young hearing Americans, old and young Chinese, and members of the American Deaf culture), the Chinese reported the most positive and active internal image of aging. Because of this, the authors concluded that "the social psychological component of memory retention in old age may be even stronger than we believed" (p. 966). In other words, the internal self-concept, reflecting as it does society's judgments, directly impacts memory processes. If I believe on a very deep level that I am less competent now, at age 82, than I was at age 32, that prophecy becomes self-fulfilling.

> *If men describe situations as real, they are real in their consequences.*
>
> THOMAS & THOMAS, 1928

Use of ageist language is hardly unique to the twentieth century. Herbert Covey (1991) beautifully illustrated the extent to which a culture's religious and philosophical values play out in stereotypes and/or expectations in his history of the term "miser." Covey associates the miser, a social role defined as a mean or grasping person, with "avarice," one of the seven deadly sins, thought for centuries to be the chief sin of old age (Chew, 1962). He traced the image of the miser from classical literature and religious thought through to modern times, exploring both literature and art. He concludes:

> There are justifiable reasons why older people have been associated with miserly behavior, such as the need to be frugal to ensure their future survival. Other reasons accounting for this association have been proposed, such as the reluctance of older parents to surrender family wealth to their demanding offspring. In addition, social support programs for older people were not readily available and stigma was sometimes attached to those receiving benefits. The depictions of older people dying while surrounded by their worldly possessions also fueled the image of the miser. Older people were expected to surrender their worldly concerns and possessions in order to enter heaven. Those who were reluctant were viewed as misers and avaricious. (Covey, 1991, p. 677)

In a previous study of the **language of aging** used in the 1800s and earlier, Covey (1988) identified widely used terminology that augmented negative stereotypes about the elderly (see Table 2.1).

Present-day researchers observe few age-specific terms that refer positively to older people. Several examples are mature, sage, venerable, and veteran. A study conducted in the 1980s of the language of aging, however, found that even the terms aged person and elderly were considered less than positive (Barbato & Freezel, 1987). This language bias continues 30 years later—and language structures consciousness. We use the words (language) we have to describe ourselves and others. Today, just as they did 30 years ago, presidents of companies or people in a position of power typically do not want to be called aged or elderly. The core of the problem is that as long as there are negative attitudes about aging, even initially positive terms may develop into negative stereotypes.

Historians examine magazines, newspapers, poetry, sermons, and other written materials for information about aging in prior times. For

TABLE 2.1

Historical terminology used to describe older people

Terms for Old Women	Terms for Old Men	Either Sex
Old bird	Old buzzard	Old bean
Old trout	Old goat	Mouldy
Old crow	Old coot	Crone
Old hag	Old crock	Gummer
Little old lady	Old fogey	Has-been
Witch	Dirty old man	Fossil
Tabby or cat		Dodo
Old hen		Fuddy duddy
Old bag		Gink
Old biddy		
Quail		

Source: Adapted from Covey, Herbert. Historical terminology used to represent older people," *Gerontologist, 28,* 291–297.

example, sheet music of the 1800s and 1900s reflects the then-popular sentiments about age (Cohen & Kruschwitz, 1990). With few exceptions, writers of tunes popular in the late nineteenth and early twentieth centuries saw old age as a time of failing capacities; in their lyrics clearly preferred youth and dreaded growing old. In these songs, elders fear that their children will abandon them, and they worry about the death of a spouse, loneliness, disability, and their own death. The touching song "Silver Threads Among the Gold" (1873), a classic of the period, emphasizes the declines of old age. Another example is the song "Old Joe Has Had His Day" (1912).

A whole series of songs, such as "Will You Love Me When My Face Is Worn and Old?" (1914), echoes the fear of loss of attractiveness. Perhaps the most poignant of all is "Over the Hill to the Poor House" (1874), which ends:

> For I'm old and helpless and feeble
> The days of my youth have gone by

Then over the hill to the poor house
I wander alone there to die.

Only a few songs during this time period celebrated positive aging—growing old together and being young at heart, for example.

Songs of recent decades continue the themes of the past. A well-known song, the Beatles' "When I'm 64," carried ambiguities about aging: although anticipating the joys of growing old together with his wife, the singer has doubts: "Will you still need me, will you still feed me, when I'm 64?" The Alan Parsons Project saw aging as a time to simply bid life farewell in "Old and Wise" (1982): "As far as my eyes can see / There are shadows approaching me." Bette Midler's "Hello in There" evoked compassionate stereotypes with "but old people—they just grow lonely, waiting for someone to say 'Hello in there; hello.'" One of the biggest country songs of 1990, "Where've You Been?" by Kathy Mattea, finds an elderly woman lying helplessly in a hospital, waiting for death and for a last visit from her husband. We do not see the full range of the status of elders in popular music, but we do see some historical roots of both acceptance and fear. We also see various stereotypes, many of which are negative.

The fears of aging expressed in the songs at the turn of the twentieth century, such as going to the poorhouse to die, were more valid then than now. Life expectancy was lower, and so was people's overall health status. Resignation and sadness were more appropriate to them. Older people are now leading healthier, more active lives. The negative stereotypes still present in popular songs are an example of the cultural lag that makes our attitudes and cultural beliefs slower to change than the technology that has improved our longevity.

Social Forces: The Media

Sociologists study present-day situations to find explanations for negative stereotyping. The media, which can both reflect and create society's views, have a strong impact on our views of life. The boldfaced title on the cover of an issue of *Redbook* magazine read: "When It's Smart to Lie about Your Age." The article cited sexual attractiveness and career pressures as reasons to lie. The author said, "We all want to be young. Despite feminist assertions, 20 implies desirable, attractive, sexy, and 40 doesn't" (Peters, 1994). This article creates a fear of aging in its readers. The obvious message is that by the age of 40, aging has taken an insurmountable toll on women.

Television

In 1972 Lydia Bragger, the articulate former public relations director for the Rhode Island State Council of Churches, met Maggie Kuhn, founder of the Gray Panthers, a group organized to fight for the rights and interests of older persons. Following their meeting, Bragger organized the Media Watch Task Force, supported by the Gray Panthers, to identify and protest television programs that presented stereotypical and unrealistic portrayals of elderly people. In an interview in 1975, Bragger expressed her outrage at television's portrayed older people: "Look at how rarely we see older couples on TV sharing affection or, heaven forbid, making love" (Hickey, 1990). Two decades later, discussing her role with Media Watch, Bragger discussed television's negative portrayal of elders: "People would watch old people in the commercials who did nothing but take laxatives and use denture cream. . . . On TV, they were shown as helpless, toothless, sexless, and ridiculous. They were walking in a certain way, dropping things, forgetting things" (Tanenbaum, 1997). Media Watch disbanded in the late 1980s: television had moved from an industry in which younger actors portrayed older ones because it was assumed that older people would not be able to remember their lines to one in which older people were far better represented.

Industrial standards have improved the representation of older people thanks to a better

Older people are not as ill, as lonely, or as isolated as the stereotypes would lead us to believe.

© Harry Cutting

between current research in aging and the incorporation of that information into the culture.

Older women are particularly slighted by the medium of television, which consistently underrepresents them. Older female news anchors are a rare species, in contrast with their male counterparts. In a widely publicized successful lawsuit in the 1990s, Christine Craft sued a Kansas City broadcasting station for sex discrimination, claiming she was demoted for being "too old, unattractive, and not deferential enough to men." The "elderly" Craft was 38.

Television typically pairs older women romantically with men who are older, thereby avoiding role models for same-age, or older woman–younger man relationships. The singer and actress Cher, at 45, said she worried about her looks as she got older: "The roughest thing in the world is to be an older woman," she said, referring both to the entertainment world and to her personal life (DeVries, 1991). Only 8 percent of all movie roles and 9 percent of television roles go to women over 40. According to the actress Sally Field, the stigma commonly attached to aging actresses in Hollywood has been around "since the beginning of time" (Bash, 1995).

Despite the increased exposure of some older performers, including older women, television still has problems with its portrayal of older Americans. Television programming commonly and unfortunately uses a comedy gimmick—a **reversed stereotype of aging** in which older characters drive race cars, go clubbing, or make reference to their amazing sex lives. The introduction of sexual performance–enhancing drugs such as Viagra has made a huge impact on images of older men (and women) in advertising. Such images are, of course, intended to be comical or outrageous, because they are in stark contrast with the stereotype of elders with a low-energy, sedentary lifestyle.

Reversed stereotypes do more harm than good. The public tends to believe what stereotypes, reversed or not, present. Laughing at a reversed stereotype demonstrates unconscious, uncritical acceptance of the underlying negative

understanding of the shifting market potential. The Nielsen Television Index did not even regularly identify individuals over 55 years of age until 1977, but now that population is carefully examined (Greco & Swayne, 1999). There is a great distance to go, though, before ageist stereotypes are eliminated from advertising and programming. A review of the literature shows that much of the information about aging that informs advertising decisions is based on research conducted in the early 1970s and 1980s emphasizing the biological model of cognitive decline. This is another example of a cultural lag image, as does viewing sexual functioning and attraction among older people to be outrageous in a humorous way. Older respondents are even less critical than the young. Older people as a general segment of the viewing public do not complain about their television image. Older men, on seeing an advertisement for Viagra, are likely to think "Good for him!" if not become personally interested themselves. Older women whose partners are interested in performance-enhancing drugs also are likely to feel positive about choices they or others now have. And even though pelvic inflammatory disease has reached epidemic proportions among women whose partners take these drugs, the media does not inform the public of these findings. We look once again at the biomedicalization of aging: normal age-related changes, including sexual functioning, cannot merely be addressed by taking a pill. Aging in a person is not meant to be "fixed." It is to be explored and recognized for what it is, which can be and is, for many older people, an extraordinarily sensual time of life.

Aging experts believe that the television industry needs to revise its unrealistic portrayal of older Americans to reflect the current aging experience. The challenge of television is to offer a true portrait of the elderly—and that portrait is a constantly changing one, as one cohort replaces the next and the oldest cohort grows larger each decade. A sensitive, realistic portrayal is the goal. On the one hand, older adults must not be demeaned; on the other hand, television must not gloss over the real problems of aging. Portrayals should attempt to balance strengths and satisfactions with the real problems of being an older person in this society.

Television viewing time increases with age. To isolated persons, television commonly acts as a companion. The widowed and lonely often prefer programs that emphasize family solidarity and a sense of belonging. To continue to be relevant in a society that is becoming dramatically more aged, television programming will need to respond to the numbers, the values, and the perspectives of an older audience. It will be

an interesting ride to watch the ways in which images and stereotypes shift in the next decade as a new cohort of active, healthy, and well-educated people move into elderhood. Presently, television programming in the United States that features older characters generally portray them in the role of the parents of a main character (*Judging Amy* and *The Simpsons*, for example). British public television, however, better represents a broad age range, such as the outstanding *Keeping Up Appearances*, in which a ditsy mom is the main character. The parental role remains a theme, but the character development is age appropriate.

Advertising and nonverbal communication

Television advertising that urges the public to cover up the signs of aging is particularly powerful. Advertising currently tells us that aging is primarily ugly, lonely, and bothersome—unless, of course, one looks and acts young. Advertisers create markets by instilling a fear of aging or by capitalizing on existing fears. Commercials imply that the elderly are sluggish and preoccupied with irregularity, constipation, and sexual performance. As a group, they suffer from headaches, nagging backaches, and loose dentures. Men are offered alternatives to baldness; both sexes are urged to buy products that will "wash away the gray"; women are urged to soften facial wrinkles and smooth old-looking hands with creams and lotions.

Advertisers are beginning to catch on, however, and a more positive view of aging is emerging. Some active, happy older people are appearing in advertisements on television and in magazines. As the market demographics shift, manufacturers are beginning to recognize that older people are consumers; correspondingly, advertisers are devoting more advertising time and space to elders as their numbers and buying power increase.

However, advertisers must be careful not to alienate their target audience. One study showed that consumers in their 50s and 60s respond best to an actor who is around age 40. If the actors are older, advertisers may inadvertently be targeting the elderly parents of the 50-plus group (Greco & Swayne, 1999). The internalization of those negative messages has worked to cause some of the 50-year-olds—who might theoretically be opposed to ageism—to ignore ads if the actors are too old. They do not want to identify with the "old" faces they see on the screen.

Ageist messages are nonverbal as well as verbal. The use of **patronizing communication** (overaccommodation in communication based on stereotyped expectations of incompetence) can be as offensively ageist as directly derogatory language (Ryan, Hummert, & Boich, 1995). According to **communication accommodation theory,** people modify their speech and behavior based on their assessment of their communication partner. If that assessment is based on erroneous stereotypes, the communication can be patronizing and produce the opposite effect than that intended (Coupland, Coupland, & Giles, 1991).

Critics of television ads using older people are frustrated by the image of foolish, out-of-it elders. In a classic Doritos chips advertisement a gray-haired woman shuffles along munching on chips, oblivious to a steamroller behind her. Chevy Chase comes to the rescue to save the chips, and the woman is plowed into wet cement. In another classic spot for Denny's restaurants, an oldster stumbles over the name, repeatedly calling it Lenny's. In these examples, the communicated image is distinctively ageist. In another ad, a younger woman looks kindly and sympathetically at an older woman, pats her hand, and explains that the product she is being served is "good for you." The image is controlling, the younger woman's verbal communication evokes images of a young child, and the overall nonverbal behavior is patronizing and insulting (Kemper, 1994). Carol Morgan, president of the marketing group Strategic Directions, sees a "huge lack of sophistication" among people advertising to the mature market (Goldman, 1993).

Movies

The primary aim of most makers of feature-length commercial films is to reach young people, particularly males between the ages of 16 and 24. Consumer studies conclude that most moviegoers are teenagers and young adults, and studios market their products accordingly. Many commercially successfully movies seem to be rather mindless entertainment with a focus on high-speed chases and violence. Exceptions to the standard movie formula are rare. The typical movie reflects the larger society, in which youth holds much more promise than age. It is the exceptional movie that stars older persons and promotes understanding of the challenges and joys of aging. Shifts in this pattern are gradually becoming more evident, however.

The Chicago philanthropic group that gives annual Owl awards to film and television productions that treat older people with respect skipped the feature films category because it did not find a single film of merit in 1992. In 1989 and 1991 the Jessica Tandy films *Driving Miss Daisy* and *Fried Green Tomatoes* won awards (Newman, 1993). By drawing attention to outstanding training and educational films about and for older people, the organization added marketing power to films then, and films now, including:

- *Something's Gotta Give* (2003): a perennial bachelor who dates only women under 30 comes to terms with his own aging
- *About Schmidt* (2002): a man reaches several life crossroads simultaneously and begins a journey of self-discovery
- *The Straight Story* (1999): shows the power and need for reconciliation and the hero's journey in later life; is shot through the eyes of an older man and has a slow and contemplative pace
- *Tuesdays with Morrie* (1999): Morrie tells a friend, "Death ends a life, not a relationship"

- *American Beauty* (1999): a man fears growing older and not being respected by those who know him best
- *Shadrach* (1998): an elderly former slave walks over 600 miles to the place of his birth
- *Troublesome Creek: A Midwestern* (1995): a documentary in which a couple in their 70s have to sell their farm and leave the life they have led for 70-some-odd years
- *Nobody's Business* (1996): a man documents his reluctant father's life story, interspersing humorous moments with moving and revealing insights
- *Breaking Silence: The Story of the Sisters of DeSales Heights* (1994): the plot follows 12 nuns behind the walls of the 150-year-old DeSales Heights Monastery and School in West Virginia during its final year of operation
- *Complaints of a Dutiful Daughter* (1994): Oscar-nominated documentary about a daughter caring for her mother, who has Alzheimer's disease
- *The Cemetery Club* (1993): three widowed women who are best friends adjust to their new status in conflicting ways
- *Enchanted April* (1992): a snippy aristocratic widow joins three younger women in renting a vacation home on the Italian coast
- *Strangers in Good Company* (1991): seven elderly women, stranded when their bus breaks down, share their stories, fears, and dreams
- *Age-Old Friends* (1990): two buddies living in a retirement home cope with frailty; their minds remain sharp as their bodies decline

These movies describe aging, care of the ill, spousal relationships, friendships over the years, and intergenerational relationships and attempt to portray older people as complex characters, not caricatures. Some additional excellent examples can be found: for example, in the 1993 movie *Shadowlands*, the writer C. S. Lewis (played by Anthony Hopkins) was portrayed as someone willing to risk a new relationship and as having depth to his person. Paul Newman, at age 70, brought insights into the possibilities for healing family relationships in his role as Sully in the 1994 movie *Nobody's Fool*. Richard Farnsworth's portrayal of Alvin Straight in *The Straight Story* (1999) provided an outstanding example of the deepening of character over time that develops for some elders.

The Psychology of Prejudice

Those who hold negative stereotypes of aging are prejudiced against older persons. The two variables go hand in hand. To explain why an individual would subscribe to negative stereotyping is to explain why a person is prejudiced. The **psychology of prejudice** draws attention to the psychological causes of prejudice, as opposed to social causes previously discussed, such as TV and magazine advertising.

One psychological explanation is self-concept. Someone with a positive self-concept may be less prone to believe the negative stereotypes of other groups. And when that person ages, he or she may well choose to accept only positive stereotypes of age. Psychologists use the term *projection* here: if we feel negative about ourselves, we project it on to others. This might explain why prejudice against elders correlates with one's personal degree of anxiety about death (Palmore, 2001).

Three well-known theories that explain racism may also be used to explain ageism (Palmore, 1990): (1) the **authoritarian personality,** in which less-educated, rigid, untrusting, insecure persons are the ones who hold prejudices; (2) the **frustration-aggression hypothesis,** in which those who are frustrated, perhaps by poverty and low status, take it out in aggression toward others; and (3) **selective perception,** in which we see what we expect to see and selectively ignore what we do not expect to see; our perceptions then confirm our stereotypes. (For example, we "see" only old drivers driving badly. We do not "see" young drivers mishandling a vehicle. Nor do we "see" all the old drivers who do well. In fact, we may perceive as "old" only those who are stooped, feeble, or ill.)

Breaking Negative Stereotypes

The negative stereotypes of age must be disproved if we are to have a true picture of older people. One way to do this is to draw attention to people who have made significant contributions in their old age. Michelangelo, Leo Tolstoy, Sigmund Freud, Georgia O'Keeffe, Pablo Picasso, and Bertrand Russell, for example, continued to produce recognized classics until the ends of long lives. Other prominent men and women are still working productively at relatively advanced ages: the writer Norman Mailer; the nation's first female poet laureate, Mona Van Duyn; the pianist Alicia de Larrocha; the stage actress Julie Harris; the vocalist Lena Horne; the jazz musician B. B. King; the physician Jonas Salk; and the scientist and lecturer Jane Goodall. Numerous Nobel Prize winners in the sciences every year are 65 or over.

Emphasizing the Positive

Negative stereotypes must be countered with accurate information. For example, the myth that elders as a group suffer mental impairment still persists. More specifically, many people believe that the mental faculties of older people decline and that most old people are senile. However, longitudinal studies of the same persons over many years have found little overall decline in intelligence scores. Studies show that older individuals are just as capable of learning as younger people—although the learning process may take a little more time. One longitudinal study of intelligence in subjects ranging in age from 21 to 70 shows that on two out of four measures intelligence *increases* with age. The study concludes that "general intellectual decline in old age is largely a myth" (Baltes & Horgas, 1996).

The stereotype that most old people are senile simply is not true. Few ever show overt signs of senility, and those who do can often be helped by treatment. Although mental health is a problem for some, only a small percentage of the elderly have Alzheimer's disease or any other severe mental disorder. This will be addressed more fully in a later chapter.

Physical stereotypes are as common as mental ones and just as false. More positive images are replacing the "rocking chair" stereotype of old age as older Americans stay more physically active and fit. The physical fitness craze has not been lost on the over-65 generation. Aerobics classes, jogging, walking, tennis, golf, and bicycling have become very popular among this group.

Many sports now have competition in senior divisions. Tennis is one example. It's never too late for a shot at Wimbledon—"Senior Wimbledon West," that is, held annually in the western United States. Divisions of this tournament, for both men and women, exist for those in their 50s, 60s, 70s, and 80s. Golf, swimming, cycling, bowling, softball, competitive weight lifting, and basketball have senior events. Sports and physical fitness can extend throughout one's life.

The key ingredient to a long, full life, according to the psychologist Lee Hurwich, a wise elder in her 70s, is not physical health, but attitude (Opatrny, 1991). With the right attitude—one of passion about life, whether this passion is found in career, friendships, or interests—a person can enjoy some of the best and most rewarding years in later life. Hurwich interviewed active, socially committed women and discovered that her subjects live in the present, squeezing from daily life all its enjoyment. They had relationships with people of all ages. Many had suffered physical afflictions that would send most people into despair, but they had optimistic attitudes and a trust in people. One woman was studying Spanish at age 87. Why? "I want to keep the cobwebs out of my head," she told Hurwich. As they reached their 80s and 90s, Hurwich's subjects still felt life has meaning, and they were satisfied with their lives.

Consequences and Implications of Stereotyping

Negative stereotyping of old people has detrimental effects on society in general and on old people in particular. First, negative stereotyping perpetuates ageism in our society. Ageism increases when society views all old people as senile, decrepit, and rigid. These and other negative stereotypes, which do not apply to the majority of elders, reinforce prejudice and lead to discrimination. Perpetuating ageism often results in polarization (a feeling of "us" against "them") and segregation. One student in an unpublished study had this to say:

> I can't stand old people and I don't get along with them at all. To me they seem useless and without a purpose. I try to avoid the aged. (Barrow, 1994)

This opinion serves as a good example of the negative stereotyping and ageist attitudes that result in the avoidance of old people. When we avoid old people, society becomes age segregated. Real communication cannot take place in a segregated society, and the cycle of stereotyping, ageism, and polarization continues.

Ageism even affects professional objectivity. When presented with clinical vignettes in which the ages of the clients varied, clinical psychologists considered older, depressed clients to be significantly less ideal than younger clients with identical symptoms and histories, and older clients were given poorer prognoses than younger ones. However, older psychologists were more favorable toward older clients than were young psychologists (Ray, 1987). An experimental program was introduced in a medical school to improve the medical students' attitudes and skills in working with elders. In another study, an experimental group participated in four 10-minute group sessions that emphasized psychological and biological knowledge as well as communication skills. The experimental group developed more positive attitudes and more socially skilled behavior in their work with older adults than did members of a control group (Intrieri et al., 1993).

Employees could relate better to older clients if they rid themselves of negative stereotypes, especially the stereotype that older people are in their second childhood, which is a very poor way to elicit the highest potential from a person. Even if the older person has a mental disorder and is physically dependent, the second-childhood stereotype glosses over the ways in which he or she is not childlike.

Negative stereotyping fosters fear of aging in both old and young. Who wants to be "hunched over," "grouchy," "useless," "rejected," and "alone"? One study, which used agree-disagree statements to measure fear of aging, showed a clear and strong relationship between low fear of aging and subjective well-being (Klemmack & Roff, 1984). The study measured fear of aging with statements such as:

> I feel that people will ignore me when I'm old.

> I am afraid that I will be lonely when I'm old.

> I am afraid that I will be poor when I'm old.

Subjective well-being was measured by agree-disagree statements such as these:

> I have made plans for things I'll be doing a month or year from now.

> Compared to other people I get down in the dumps less often.

> The things I do now are as interesting to me as they were when I was younger.

Those who did not fear aging felt good about themselves and their lives. On the other hand, those who feared aging did not have a good personal sense of well-being.

A question asked of the aged participants in the outstanding longitudinal Berkeley Older Generation Study was: "Looking back, what period of your life brought you the most satisfaction?" This question was asked when the respondents were, on the average, 69 years old, and 14 years later, when the average age was 83. The findings remained consistent over time. Adolescence was considered the most unsatisfactory time. The decade of the respondents' 30s was named as most satisfying time period by 16 percent of the sample. The period of their 50s was second most popular, named by 15 percent of the sample. Old age was seen as more satisfying than childhood: 12 percent said their 60s brought them the most satisfaction, 13 percent named their 70s, and 5 percent described their 80s as the most satisfying period of their lives. The common stereotypes that old persons are fixated on childhood memories, that youth is best, and that old age contains few satisfactions were, thus, dispelled (Field, 1993).

Negative stereotyping stifles the potential of older people and draws attention away from happy, sociable, successful, active oldsters. A self-fulfilling prophecy is created: older people do not do anything because they assume they are not able. Their lives, therefore, are neither as satisfying nor as fulfilling as they might be.

We have hardly begun to explore the potential of elders in this society. Too often large companies try to remove older persons from the labor market to make room for the young. Too often we provide no alternative ways for them to make contributions. Too often society works against elders instead of for them. We need to put more thought and effort into conserving a valuable natural resource: older Americans.

Chapter Summary

Many stereotypes of old age exist, and a large portion are negative. Sources of negative stereotyping are the language we use to describe elders, songs, speeches, television, advertising, movies, and a complex sociohistorical heritage. The psychology of prejudice examines ageism to understand the roots of this prejudice.

Far greater public education and interaction with older people needs to take place if we are to develop a full understanding of the potential of elders in our culture. Action directed at diminishing our cultural belief in stereotypes about aging can and must take place on a personal level, as well as the level of social policy. Emphasizing the accomplishments of older scholars, scientists, and artists is helpful. Senior sports events draw attention to the physical fitness potential of elders and their ability to enjoy competition. The entire society benefits when we have a more holistic understanding of what the nation's elderly look and act like in the present, and who they will be in the future.

Key Terms

authoritarian personality
biomedicalization of aging
communication accommodation theory
compassionate stereotypes
developmental reserve capacity
frustration-aggression hypothesis
heterogeneity
language of aging
negative stereotypes

patronizing communication
phenomenology
positive stereotypes
possible selves
pragmatic knowledge
psychology of prejudice
reversed stereotype of aging
selective perception
self-concept
social construction of self
stereotypes

Questions for Discussion

1. Everyone bring one birthday card to class with an "age message." Is the message about aging positive or negative? Discuss both the explicit messages and the implicit messages of the cards. Categorize them by style and type.

2. Bring an advertisement with an "age message" to class. Write an advertisement in which you use *implicit* ageism. Write one in which you use *explicit* ageism.

3. Try to recall some children's literature that contains stories about or references to old people. What are the images portrayed? Who were your aging "models" as a child? Have these models affected you in a positive or negative way?

4. Describe yourself at age 85: what you will look like, what you will be doing, where you will live, who your friends will be.

Fieldwork Suggestions

1. List the first 10 words that come into your mind upon seeing the words *aged, middle-aged, adult,* and *adolescent.* Analyze your words. Do they reveal your personal biases and judgments about these age groups? Ask three people—preferably representing different age cohorts—to list the first 10 words that come into their minds when they see the words *aged, middle-aged, adult,* and *adolescent.* Compare your lists in a discussion group in class. What common patterns and language can you identify? What differences do you see? Can you draw any conclusions from your comparisons?

2. Design a study to identify stereotypes of aging. Identify your focus of inquiry: Popular music? Pre-school-age children? Advertisements in public places? Determine a systematic way in which you will record your observations; draw your conclusions.

3. Watch a couple of hours of prime-time television, including advertising. How is the topic of aging handled? Are old people visible? How are they characterized? To what age group is the advertising targeted? Watch the news, both local and national and including public broadcasting. In your estimation, what age group is the "target" audience? Why?

4. Study magazine ads of the 1960s, 1970s, 1980s, and 1990s in regard to aging. Do you observe any changes? Write an advertisement for an anti-aging skin cream.

Internet Activities

1. Identify the target audience for the advertisements on any search engine on the Internet. What are your criteria for determining what that audience is?

2. Use the key word "elderly" and make a list of the *range* of references—that is, the various information networks that are linked to this word.

3. Repeat this exercise, using the word "ageism," and "ageist literature." What are you finding? What are you not finding?

4. Look up the name of a recording artist with whom you are familiar and see if you can locate words to a song of his or hers that addresses ageism or that speaks to the topic of aging.

3 Theories in Adult Development

Study Challenges Image of Depressed Widows

The sad image of a grieving widow may not be entirely accurate, according to a study published on Tuesday showing that six months after the death of their partner, nearly half of older people had few symptoms of grief.

And 10 percent cheered up, according to the survey conducted by the University of Michigan and paid for by the National Institute on Aging.

The study, which followed 1,500 couples over the age of 65 for years, looked at the quality of their marriages, their attitudes toward one another, and the effects on one spouse after the other died.

Close to half—46 percent—said they had enjoyed their marriages but were able to cope with the loss of a spouse without much grieving.

"Until recently, mental health experts assumed that persons with minimal symptoms of grief were either in denial, emotionally distant, or lacked a close attachment to their spouse," Rutgers University sociologist Deborah Carr, who began analyzing the data while she was at the University of Michigan.

"But 46 percent of the widows and widowers in this study reported that they had satisfying marriages. They believed that life is fair and they accepted that death is a part of life," Carr said in a statement.

"After their partner's death, many surviving spouses said they took great comfort in their memories," she added.

"Taken together, these findings provide strong evidence that men and women who show this resilient pattern of grief are not emotionally distant or in denial, but are in fact well-adjusted individuals responding to loss in a healthy way."

In the United States, more than 900,000 adults lose spouses each year. Nearly 75 percent are over the age of 65.

The AARP, a group that represents Americans over the age of 50, says there are more than 13.7 million widowed people in the United States and more than 11 million, or 80 percent, are women.

Writing in a new book, "Spousal Bereavement in Late Life," Carr, psychiatrist Dr. Randolph Nesse, and psychologist Camille Wortman of the State University of New York at Stony Brook said they found that the death of their partner was a relief to about 10 percent of those widowed.

They were depressed before their spouse's death but were much less depressed afterward.

"These are people who felt trapped in a bad marriage or onerous caregiving duties and widowhood offered relief and escape," Carr said. "The old paradigm would have seen this absence of grief as emotional inhibition or a form of denial, but in our view, these are people for whom bereavement serves as the end of a chronic source of stress."

Another 16 percent of surviving spouses experienced chronic grief, lasting more than 18 months.

This chapter considers the human life cycle from the psychological perspective of adult development. In it, we see how developmental perspectives are useful in understanding the fear of aging and age transitions. The personality variables are studied that affect aging and are in turn affected in the aging process.

Theories help to understand and organize what we see—the empirical observations we make. Some areas of study, biology for example, have highly developed theoretical structures that allow questions, or hypotheses, to be studied with scientific precision. Gregor Mendel's theory of plant genetics integrated a series of observations and allowed for the prediction of what size or color a plant's flower would be, or how many ears a corn stalk would produce. A theory of human development would be required to have a similar capacity for outcome prediction; however, there are many competing forces affecting the growth and development of an individual. For this reason, there are many different theoretical approaches to human development.

Imagine for a moment six people watching a tennis match. The eye of a ballet dancer would probably be skilled at observing the movements of the bodies in relation to the space of the court and the ball. The artist might see color, shape, proportion, and intensity. The corporate sponsor's perspective, on the other hand, would include assessing the apparent popularity of the players by the crowd, perhaps calculating the value of corporate exposure to an audience of a given size. There are many different lenses from which to view an event, and different theoretical approaches describe that phenomenon from a slightly—or not so slightly—different lens.

Data is the information being gathered by each of the viewers above, as a means for testing or developing their perspective, whether it be economic or physical. Data might be summary scores on objective tests used to elaborate **quantitative development.** This methodology emphasizes changes in the number or amount of something. Data might also be the telling of a story, of the kinds of things that people do, or of how they do them. This approach emphasizes **qualitative development.**

The different perspectives or theories used to describe an event or process shape what is observed, and they can be described by different metaphors. A **metaphor** is a figure of speech that implies a comparison: being in "the autumn of life," for example. Metaphors can describe theories, too. The primary metaphors in personality or ego psychology are outlined in Table 3.1 and are described at length in Susan Cloninger's book *Theories of Personality* (2003).

Perhaps the metaphor most highly integrated into Western thinking is a view of the person as machine: development dictated by determining forces such as biology (the **mechanistic metaphor**). This model is based on eighteenth-century Newtonian physics, in which an object cannot move unless it is acted upon by outside forces (Cloninger, 2003).

The **organic metaphor** sees the individual as being much like an unfolding flower. All the potential of the rosebud is within itself to become a perfect rose. Our potential lies within. An associated metaphor, **information processing,** is

TABLE 3.1

Theories as metaphors

Metaphor	Description	Exemplary Theorist
Information processing	Personality relected by cognition of subjective experience, which differs among people; recognizes multiple potentials; is causal	Sperry (1980, 1990) Kelly Bandura Mischel
Mechanistic	Personality determined by external determinism; adopted from the physical sciences; biological in nature; empirically testable	Freud through behaviorists
Organic	Personality compared with growth of plants and animals; potential is within the person, not the environment	Erikson Levinson
Narrative	Personality as the story of a person's life; when personality changes, we rewrite our life stories; narrative has plot, characters, time progression, and episodes	Saarbin Kelly
Emergent self	Self-directed, willful personality from internal determinism; emphasis on choice and striving; free will, and individual behavior; future oriented, not past oriented	Adler Sappington Ziller Sperry Rychlak
Transcendent self	Individual personality is not separate and self-contained but connected with others on a plane of shared experience; experience beyond individual ego	Jung Maslow Rogers

Source: Cloninger, Susan. (2003). *Theories of personality: Understanding persons.* New York: Prentice Hall.

concerned with one person's ability to function differently than another. Theoretical models emphasizing thinking, or cognitive processes, fall into this group. Although individual competency emerges from within, this metaphor implies multiple potential that comes from both internal and external sources.

In a fairly new model using the theory of the **narrative metaphor** (Sarbin, 1986), development is thought of as the story of a person's life. Our stories are rewritten by us when we perceive ourselves as having changed; the "new" story might be only slightly modified, or it might be an entirely new story (McAdams & Bowman, 2001). Life stories have a plot, characters, time progression, and key events, all of which both describe and shape the person's development (Cloninger, 2003). The life story is somewhat parallel with

Levinson's concept of life structure, elaborated on later in this chapter.

> *Identity in adulthood is an inner story of the self that integrates the reconstructed past, perceived present, and anticipated future to provide a life with unity, purpose, and meaning.*
>
> McAdams, 1995

The **emergent self metaphor** views the individual as being highly self-directed and emphasizes choices and motivations as primary factors in shaping development. Finally, the **transcendent self metaphor** sees development as being shaped by experience beyond the individual ego, sometimes from a plane of shared experience (Cloninger, 2003). It is primarily this metaphor that allows for the concepts of spiritual development to be addressed. The transcendent self also is the "end state" or "ultimate unfolding" that occurs in organic and mechanistic perspectives. It is a particularly important metaphor in the study of aging when we attempt to deal with concepts such as wisdom, or issues concerning preparation for one's death.

Early Developmental Models

According to researchers of early human development, distinct stages or phases form the **life cycle** through which humans pass. We proceed from infancy to childhood through adolescence to adulthood and then into parenthood and grandparenthood, and the cycle begins anew for each newborn baby. The life cycle is the course of aging: individuals adapt throughout their lives to changes in their own biological, psychological, and social roles.

On the one hand, the experiences common to all people in their passage through the life cycle give life some consistency. On the other, individual variations supply a measure of uniqueness to each person. We are all different, but we are not different in all ways, nor are we necessarily different in the same ways. Yet we are like all others in that we are conceived and born in a given time period, we age, and we die.

Freud, 1856–1939

The influence of Sigmund Freud, father of the psychoanalytic perspective, on the field of psychology is profound and indisputable. Freud believed that it is not human reason, but unconscious psychological forces, that most profoundly affect our thought and behavior. These forces originate in the emotions of early childhood and continue their influence throughout our lives. According to Freud, the influences shaping all that we are or will occur in the first eight to ten years of life. From that point on, we replay the fears, the securities and insecurities, and the issues that were established through early interaction with our parent figures. Freud felt that human behavior and motivation are driven by instincts, the outcome of which can be either positive or negative, and that "these forces fuel the positive achievements of culture but also lead to war, crime, mental illness, and other human woes" (Cloninger, 2003).

Psychoanalytic theory established the impact of early life experiences on the psychology, and therefore the life choices, of the individual. The focus on the unconscious, including our understanding of sex and aggression, has transformed the way in which people in modern times understand their conscious experience.

Jung, 1875–1961

A younger contemporary of Freud's, Carl Gustav Jung initially had strong professional ties with Freud. For years they maintained an active correspondence, and they jointly presented a critically important seminar on psychoanalysis in the United States in 1909. Over time, however, Jung developed a strong intellectual disagreement with Freud based primarily on Freud's emphasis of the role of sexuality and his relative failure to address the potential of the unconscious to contribute positively to psychological growth. Freud, for his part, feared that Jung had abandoned scientific knowledge for mysticism (Cloninger, 2003). The two men, by this time both preeminent theorists in the field of psychology, developed a powerful personal conflict from which two separate schools of psychological orientation emerged. The Freudian school continued to focus on the shaping power of past events, whereas Jungians began to focus attention to the future direction of personality development.

> *We cannot live the afternoon of life according to the program of life's morning, for what was great in morning will be little at evening, and what in the morning was true will at evening have become a lie.*

JUNG, 1955

Jung was perhaps the first modern voice to focus on the possibility of adult personality development. The first three decades of development in the individual, he said, deal mainly with the **shadow**—the repressed childhood desires and attributes that Freud first discussed. Jung preferred to describe the psyche in the language of mythology rather than of science, "because this is not only more expressive but also more exact than an abstract scientific terminology, which is wont to toy with the notion that its theoretical formulations may one fine day be resolved into algebraic equations" (Jung, 1959, p. 13).

Jung believed that after 40 the individual begins to develop his or her internal self-potential. If it is able to balance competing internal opposites, the personality can reach maturity; otherwise, the personality remains in struggle, incomplete. For example, all people have both a feminine and a masculine side, produced by biological and social conditioning factors (Dolliver, 1994). As an example of the power of opposites, Jung (1916/1956) wrote that psychologically *eros* (pure love) is the opposite of the will to power. "Where love reigns, there is not will to power; and where the will to power is paramount, love is lacking. The one is the shadow of the other" (p. 63).

As individuals age, said Jung, personality **archetypes** change, and people adopt psychological traits more commonly associated with the opposite gender. Men become more nurturing, and women develop a sense of their masculine personality traits. This represents Jung's formulation of *animus* and *anima* (Markson, 2003). Likewise, a balance of **extroversion** and

The field of later life development was profoundly influenced by life partners and collaborators Joan and Erik Erikson.

© Ted Streshinsky/CORBIS

introversion is necessary for mature personality development. Over the life course, individuals move from self-in-society—a focus on social interactions and institutions—to a more internal focus, referred to by Bernice Neugarten in 1964 as **interiority.** This process of self-reflection begins taking place around midlife and is a central way in which the individual is able to prepare for life's final state, which is death. The idea initiated for us by Jung that individuals become more introverted with age has become one of the most studied issues in personality research on aging (Cavanaugh & Blanchard-Fields, 2006).

Erikson, 1902–1994

In the late 1920s Erik Erikson, then Erik Homberger, helped to develop a program to teach art to children of Freud's entourage (Cloninger, 2003). The woman who would become his wife, Joan Serson, was studying psychoanalysis; it was she who introduced him to psychoanalysis. Erikson eventually was recruited to be a "lay analyst" (because of his nonmedical training); he received his training and became part of Freud's inner circle. In 1933 he and Serson, fearful about Germany's increasing anti-Semitism, left the country first for the Netherlands, then the United States. It was at this point that Erik Homberger took the last name of his biological father, Erikson. Some scholars suggest that Erikson's career-long interest in identity emerged from his own somewhat confused identity (Cloninger, 2003).

Psychoanalytic theory was the base on which Erikson build a model of the stages of the full course of human development, incorporating the impact of the social environment on the maturing personality. He was concerned with the mechanism by which people develop an identity. Erikson emphasized interactions between genetics and the environment in personality development and developed the concept of the **epigenetic principle.** This refers to an innate structure of development in which people progress through stages as they become emotionally and intellectually more capable of interacting in a wider social radius (Erikson, 1963).

Erikson's model of the **stages of human development** extends beyond childhood and adolescence to include middle and old age, although the adult years, from roughly 20 through 60, were described by only two ego stages (Erikson, 1963). He recognized that personality continues to develop throughout the life cycle, and he believed the individual progresses through eight psychosocial stages in order to establish new orientations to self and the social world over time (see Table 3.2). Each of Erikson's stages is identified with a developmental task, or challenge, to be accomplished. There may be either a positive or a negative resolution of the challenge, and whatever ego resources we gain on completion of one stage are brought with us to the next stage of development (Richman, 1995). The first five stages are similar to Freud's stages of psychosexual development.

Erikson's last three stages deal with early, middle, and later adulthood. In early adulthood the main issue of growth and development of identity is intimacy. Relationships in friendship, sex, competition, and cooperation are emphasized. Mature, stable relationships tend to form in the late teens and twenties. The task of young adulthood is to first lose and then find oneself in another, so that affiliation and love behaviors may be learned and expressed.

In middle adulthood the ability to support others and in doing so, to create a legacy is the primary developmental task. In this stage, **generativity** involves a concern for the welfare of society rather than contentment with self-absorption. The task is to be able to create, to care for, and to share, the positive outcomes of balance in middle adulthood. Parenting and grandparenting are manifestations of generativity, but examples also include mentoring relationships and circumstances of "husbandry" in terms of tending to growing plants and concern with the environment.

Erikson's psychosocial emphasis shifts for individuals in later adulthood to considerations of being nearly finished with life and facing the reality of not being. The crisis of later adulthood is **integrity versus despair:**

> [Integrity] is acceptance of one's one and only life cycle as something that had to be and that, by necessity, permitted no substitutions. The lack or loss of this (accumulated) ego integration is signified by fear of death: the one and only life cycle is not accepted as the ultimate of life. Despair expresses the feeling that the time is now short, too short for the attempt to start another life and to try out alternate roads to integrity. Disgust hides this despair. Healthy children will not

TABLE 3.2

Erikson's stages of ego development*

Psychosocial Conflict	Age (Approx.)	Goal and Strengths
Basic trust vs. mistrust	0–1	Drive and hope
Autonomy vs. shame and doubt	1–2	Independence; self-control and will power
Initative vs. guilt	3–5	Purpose; develop language and conscience; sense of direction
Industry vs. inferiority	6–puberty	Competence; task completion
Identity vs. role confusion	Adolescence	Devotion and fidelity; integrated sense of self
Intimacy vs. isolation	Early adulthood	Affiliation and love
Generativity vs. stagnation	Middle adulthood	Mentoring and care; creativity
Ego integrity vs. despair	Old age	Reflection; creation of life narrative
Resilience vs. rigidity	Late life	Acceptance of frailty and death; spiritual development

Source:- Adapted from Erikson, E. H. (1963). *Childhood and society* (2nd ed.) New York: Norton.

*Original model modified 1997 by Joan Erikson to include a ninth stage, late life psychosocial conflict.

fear life if their elders have the integrity not to fear death. (Erikson, 1966, p. xxi)

We are fortunate if in old age our passage through the first seven stages has provided us with a balance of ego resources—tools for development of identity—appropriate to take on the final task of preparing ourselves for death. The primary and profound task of Erikson's final stage is to integrate all the experiences of our life in a way that provides meaning to that life as it has been lived. It is the time during which an individual determines, in the process of reviewing his or her life, whether that life has been "successful" to that person in a social and spiritual way. In essence, the final stage is a time when an individual asks and seeks the answer to the questions, what is the meaning of my life? and what difference has my life made? The process involves the remembering and the telling of stories—sorting through and adjusting or arranging remembered events until a cohesive life "story" can be made from all the events of life. In having a witness to that story, it becomes tangible—real—and the telling of it helps to clarify it for ourselves. The process has been

called **life review,** or **reminiscence,** and will be addressed more fully later in the text.

Positive resolution of Erikson's eighth and final stage allows the individual to interpret his or her life as having purpose. Meaning is ascribed to those many lived experiences, and the outcome of that meaning is a sense of life satisfaction. The negative resolution of this stage is one of meaninglessness and despair, the feeling that one's life has been useless. The final stage is one of reflection on major life efforts that are nearly complete. The reason for this process is to prepare the person to leave life—to die—with a sense of peace and completion. Life has had a purpose, and I have fulfilled my small part of a larger whole in a meaningful and fulfilling way. This accomplished, I can now leave.

Erikson did not consider his stage model to be **unidirectional;** he believed that in addition to moving on to the next level of development (moving in one direction only), we revisit various stages again and again throughout our life course by means of remembering. Haunting memories to which we return again and again exist, according to his model, because we are not at peace with them. We have not yet been able to make sense or have any understanding of the memory and how it fits with the rest of our life. When we are able to make meaning of those events and experiences, we are able to gain the positive outcome that experience represents and that allows us to move on to the next stage. Wisdom is the adaptive strength—the personality characteristic that allows us to face the next task, at the final stage (Feinberg, 1997). It is "a kind of informed and detached concern with life itself in the face of death itself" (Erikson, 1982, p. 61).

Erikson's model is difficult to test. In one of the few empirical studies of Erikson's model, McAdams and de St. Aubin (1992) and McAdams et al. (1994) developed an elegant measure of generativity. Their findings support the hypothesis that generativity peaks in middle life, consistent with Erikson's expectations. Another study on generativity, of Mills College and Radcliffe College graduates, looked at which personality, attitudes, and life outcome factors were related to generativity at midlife (Peterson & Klohnen, 1995). This study concluded that generative women have prosocial personality characteristics, express generative attitudes through their work, are invested in the parenting process, and exhibit an expanded radius of care.

In general, however, Jung's and Erikson's formulations give rise to more questions than conclusions concerning development of the basic personality orientations in childhood, middle age, and old age. Perhaps Erikson's most lasting gift to the field of adult development was his emphasis on the process of living, the idea of life history rather than case history, and the use of biography rather than therapy as the chief research method (Levinson, 1996).

Following Eric Erikson's death, his collaborator and wife Joan Erikson reconsidered the eight-stage model and developed a ninth stage, applicable to very late life. Based on Tornstam's (1997) theory of **gerotranscendence,** the stage emerged through Joan Erikson's experience with herself in later life as well as through her being with Eric Erikson as he was dying. She became convinced that to accomplish full identity development, the individual must go *backward* through the eight stages, focusing on the dystonic rather than the systonic outcome. One must learn to *distrust* rather than trust: my body is different than it once was; I cannot know when I walk across the street that my gait will be fast enough, that my "trick" knee will not act up. The issue of trust is challenged, and I must re-identify myself around the concept. Growth and development in personal identity comes about through a revisitation of all the developmental stages, reinterpreting each in terms of the aged person. It is the final stage of identity.

Most compelling about this modification to the Eriksons' stage model is that it views the character and sense of self of the elder as having a natural potential for transcending—going beyond—midlife reality. Traditional models simply project midlife developmental values into later life; therefore, as the elder's energies and interests shift, those shifts become interpreted as losses both by the elder and by society.

Loevinger

Jane Loevinger (1976) proposed eight stages of **ego development,** each of which provides a frame of reference to organize and give meaning to experience over the individual's life course. As the adult ego develops, she said, a sense of self-awareness emerges in which one becomes aware of discrepancies between conventions and one's own behavior. For some, development reaches a plateau and does not continue. Among others, greater ego integration and differentiation continue. Helson and Roberts (1994) describe this development as a process in which the individual gains "further internalization of rules of social intercourse, a growth of cognitive complexity, impulse control increasingly based on self-chosen, long-term motives, and an increased respect for individual autonomy and mutuality in interpersonal relations" (p. 911).

Loevinger developed a sentence completion scale to measure the nature of ego development,

(Loevinger & Wessler, 1970; Loevinger, 1976). That scale has now been used extensively to identify concepts of ego development (Helson & Roberts, 1994; Cavanaugh & Blanchard-Fields, 2006) and has helped to establish basic ego construct definitions such as conscientiouness, individualism, autonomy, and personality integration. Her model describes a continuous increase in these characteristics as higher ego development unfolds. It is worth noting that Loevinger does not necessarily associate ego level with psychological adjustment or well-being. She views ego development as emerging from previous levels of complexity but not necessarily as something that creates individual happiness or a sense of fulfillment.

Levinson, 1923–1994

Daniel Levinson's interest was development in adulthood. In 1978 he published an extraordinary longitudinal study of men's lives in which he conceived of the life cycle as a sequence of eras, each with its own biopsychosocial character. Major changes occur in our lives from one era to the next, and lesser (although equally crucial) changes occur within each era. The eras partially overlap, with one era ending as another begins. These are referred to as **cross-era transitions,** and they generally last about five years.

The eras and transitions described by Levinson form a broader **life structure:** the underlying pattern or design of a person's life at a given time. The primary components of a life structure are the person's relationships with others in the external world, identified as *central components* and *peripheral components,* depending on their significance for the self and the life.

It is through our life structure that we are able to address the question, What is my life like now? This question is crucially different from the question emerging from a theory of personality, that is, What kind of person am I? The latter question looks at the life from an egocentric perspective; the first one, from a life course perspective—seeing life *in context.*

© Glen Korenbold/Stock, Boston

People change and remain the same as they age. This woman's story is reflected in her remarkable eyes, from her youth to her old age.

Levinson's theoretical model was developed using only the life experiences of men and as such been criticized as being sexist. Levinson himself, however, addressed the need to study male and female development separately, and he chose to study men's lives first, primarily because he is male. He also described his own midlife transitional phase as a central motivator for his study of men. His writings always emphasized that this developmental model was based on men's lives only, and that it was necessary to study the lives of women to determine if it was a truly *human* developmental model, or merely a model of male gender development.

In 1996 Levinson's second major longitudinal study was published: *The Seasons of a Woman's Life.* In this study, he attempted to develop a model of the structure of women's lives, including the significance of gender. He made the "surprising discovery" (p. 6) that women and men go through the same sequence of periods at roughly the same ages, although he identified wide variations in the ways in which the genders traverse each period.

A valuable concept emerging from the second longitudinal study is what Levinson named **gender splitting**—a sharp division between feminine and masculine that permeates all aspects of life. Gender splitting, he said, takes many forms. It is

> the rigid distinction between feminine and masculine in the culture and in the psyche; the division between the domestic world and the public occupational world; the traditional marriage enterprise, with its distinction between the male husband/father/provisioner and the female wife/mother/homemaker; the linkage between masculinity and authority, which makes it "natural" that the man be head of the household, executive and leader within the occupational domain, and predominant in a patriarchal social structure. (Levinson, 1996, p. 6)

It is through this cultural and psychological process of gender splitting, Levinson postulated, that the seasons of a woman's life are primarily distinguished from seasons of the life of a man.

Transitions in Adult Life: Developmental Patterns

Psychologists have drawn attention of the need for a psychology explaining changes throughout the life span. A subdiscipline called *developmental psychology* has responded. This area of study concerns itself with continuity and discontinuity over time—in other words, stability versus change in personality and the ways stability and change play out in the context of life are concerns of the developmental perspective. Developmentalists also incorporate human biology and the impact biology has on our progression through the life course in explaining human psychological growth.

Up until about 20 years ago, "human development" in psychology actually referred to child development. The field of psychology at that time reflected the profound influence of Freud's model of development, which did not recognize growth and development in adulthood and later life. A new focus on early, middle, and later adulthood now characterizes the field of human development. Considering that we will live approximately two-thirds of our life as adults, it is reasonable that adulthood and later life are now major foci in developmental psychology.

The study of personality in middle and later life is sometimes referred to as *adult development*. The term **transitions** is used to describe points at which the person's development is moving, or transitioning, between one phase or stage and the next. The developmental perspective focuses on the unfolding developmental process of the individual. As maturity develops, attitudes and behavior change in a somewhat orderly fashion, following a path unique to each individual, yet generally similar for all people. A caution must be used regarding the term "life course," which is actually a misnomer, since there are so many. The very term implies one "correct" way for a life to pattern itself, and clearly, in the study of human lives, there are many ways to reach and live a full, productive adulthood. Additionally, a reliance on a central human tendency (such as a pattern of development) may reinforce restrictive age-based expectations and age stereotyping (Light et al., 1996).

During different periods of adulthood, we appear to have different levels of awareness of our own aging. Immediate concerns—careers, personal relationships, and leisure pursuits—tend to take up more of our time when we are younger. The most extensive preparation we may undergo for old age may come in our middle years, when we sense what is yet to happen to us, mentally and physically. As we grow older, we may experience an undercurrent of fear at the thought of aging. We might just as likely, however, experience awe, excitement, satisfaction, and anticipation. Among most people, change can foster fear and dread as well as excitement. The two emotions are part of our human experience of being and speak to the **tension of opposites** articulated by Jung and Erikson. Resolution of that tension of opposites, from the developmental perspective, is what drives ego development.

Psychologists continue to disagree over the number of stages in the adult life course and the points at which they begin—and, indeed, whether there are actual stages or not. Focusing on what happens normatively—that is, to most people—at a particular point in the life cycle can reinforce a belief that one path of development is best while another is somehow less than normal or abnormal. Despite this caveat, the movement from childhood through old age is too complex *not* to have theoretical structures that help us gain a better understanding of the process. And clearly, many "stages" are points that we observe in our own lives or in the lives of people around us. They are consistent with our empirical observations, with folk wisdom and stories, and with our cultural expectations.

Some theorists suggest that adulthood consists of four or more different life periods: young adulthood, maturity, middle age, and late adulthood (which can be divided into young old and old old). Others see only three categories: youth, middle age, and old age. Many young people think of middle age as beginning about age 35 or thereabouts, whereas older people more often think of age 40, 45, or 50 as middle age; in other words, one's own age colors one's perceptions of the stage boundaries. A current trend in psychology and sociology is to distinguish between **age identity** (a component of the self-concept) and **age group identification,** a feeling of solidarity with age peers (Sherman, 1994). In this way, the subjective sense of age is separated but included in theoretical models designed to help us understand changes in the life course. Susan Sherman provides an excellent illustration of the subjective sense of age in the voice of a 40-year-old who writes to his aunt:

I have to admit that the coming big FOUR-OH has got me thinking. None of the mir-

rors I've looked at lately has cast me back the image of a 40 year old shadow. I usually see a 35 year old cynic, sometimes I look closer and see a 30 year old idealist. . . . I can't see that self loathing 20 year old. Now and then I catch a glimpse of the unbroken teenager. (1994, p. 398)

We will now consider three broad stages of the life cycle: young adulthood, middle age, and late adulthood. First, the point must be made that the developmental tasks in each stage are generally culturally based and not clearly defined, and are becoming even less so.

The Identification of Eras, Phases, or Stages

The distinctions between life periods are blurred. Some young people postpone marriage and childbearing, and some people experience a pattern of remarriage and divorce throughout their life courses. No longer is marriage necessarily reserved for young adulthood. Parenthood may happen at age 19 or age 42 or never. Consequently, one may be a grandparent for the first time before age 40 or after age 75—or not at all.

People are also more flexible in entering and exiting jobs and careers. Some retire at age 50, whereas others start new careers at age 70 or beyond. Launching a new career is no longer the prerogative of the young, nor is education. Increasingly, people of all ages are attending school. Indeed, public education has begun to address the shifting demographics to provide relevant continued educational opportunities for older adults. The number and quality of educational programs for older adults has increased dramatically in the past 30 years (Manheimer & Moskow-McKenzie, 1997; Rogers, 2000).

Events throughout the course of life are becoming less predictable. Some teenagers face adulthood early by running away from home or by becoming emancipated minors. Others live at home for long periods, getting an education or working in their first full-time jobs, saving money to get married or for a home. Teenage pregnancy forces some girls and boys into adulthood, whereas others delay taking on heavy family responsibilities until they are nearly age 40 or perhaps older.

In some ways, even the line between childhood and adulthood is disappearing. Young girls are encouraged by advertising to rush into wearing makeup and adult clothing. Soap operas cater to young adolescents, and children are bombarded with images and messages on such once-taboo topics as sex, alcohol and drug use and abuse, suicide, and family dysfunction. Divorce, no longer taboo for the older generation, is a common occurrence among married couples of all ages. Many older persons are changing their marital status—and their lifestyle—to "single" and engaging in social activities and arrangements once reserved for young adults. Our society is more complex as many behavioral expectations lose their validity, and the developmental tasks that once seemed to be set in a clear time frame no longer are.

We develop not only a sense of personal identity as our life course progresses, but we also develop a sense of social identity, of who we are as a member of different groups or social categories. A 55-year-old African American woman, for example, might "belong" to the social categories of middle-aged American female, African American, African American woman, postmenopausal female, and woman, to name only some groupings. Our various social categories will have different meanings to us depending on our life stage, social circumstances, and so on (Williams et al., 1997). So at certain times, identifying socially and psychologically as an African American will be most salient for the woman in our example, while at other times, identifying and being identified as an American will be most salient, depending on the circumstances. The groups with which we identify impact our perspectives and our development, because each group has normative behavioral expectations.

Identification by social group is called an **intergroup perspective,** which for our purposes is concerned with people's identity as members of an age category or generation (Williams & Giles, 1997). When we categorize others in this way, it is generally in terms of salient features such as appearance, behavior, and so forth. Once the categorization occurs, we ascribe certain attributes to that category and generalize to all members of the group. This is the process of stereotyping, and it can lead to prejudicial behavior.

Nonetheless, generational or cohort categories (based on historical decade, not biology) provide an easy and intuitively valid way to generalize for the purpose of social commentary. Baby boomers, Generation X-ers, thirtysomethings, baby busters—each of these categories reflect a possible (and commonly used) sociohistorical intergroup identification. The intergroup perspective reflects the extent to which the individual shapes the historical moment and the historical moment shapes the individual. The process takes place in conjunction with biological processes, which are generally those identifiers used in human development to classify groups.

The following section provides summary descriptions of the global categories identifying the life course: young adulthood, middle age, and old age.

Young Adulthood

Young adulthood comprises the years between 18 and 35 or so. A variety of challenging tasks present themselves at this time. Late adolescence in America often involves physical separation from one's family. College or military service can be the separating factor, or the young person may leave home to share an apartment or house with friends. Young people tend to have more friends than any other age group. This is perhaps to help them with the real task, which is one of psychological separation—of becoming an independent, autonomous person. Many adolescents find the passage stormy; identities are difficult to create when many options exist. "Who am I?" can bring much inner turmoil before an answer is formed.

Family and society place many "shoulds" on young adults. After establishing an identity and an occupational goal, the young man or woman may be expected to finish his or her education, begin a job or career, get married, set up housekeeping, and have children.

The "shoulds" for getting married are not as clear as they once were. Parents are anxious for their children to become established in the economic structure; they are concerned about jobs and their children's future economic prospects. In response to this parental "should," people increasingly delay marriage, opting instead to set up shared living with their significant other while they pursue education and/or concentrate on performing in their first jobs. In effect, marriage is postponed, but the development of intimacy and affiliation, identified by Erikson as the task of young adulthood, is not.

This pattern, it must be noted, is evident among some people in the United States but does not speak for all cultural groups in the country. This caution must be kept foremost in mind as we study human development, because in the search for similarities to describe a human process, it can become easy to overlook the differences. As we look through our particular lens, we must not forget to watch also for the individuating patterns of culture that affect our lives profoundly.

The centrality of major culture values creates a particularly intense pull for minorities. Internal and family expectations, as well as the social rules in which people are embedded, are culturally mediated. Minority-culture young adults have been asked through public education in the United States to give up their cultural roots and embrace a culture that is different than their own. This is known as **acculturation,** and it serves the purpose of helping to assimilate nonmainstream cultures into the American economic reward system (Calabrese & Barton, 1995, p. 121). Acculturation, however, can place the young adult in the position of feeling the need to abandon values held by parents and grandparents and embrace the values and beliefs accepted as normative by the larger culture. This dilemma can create tremendous disruption between the generations. The task of maintaining one's sense of self over the life course is an enormous one. It is even more monumental when one's cultural identity has been systematically presented by the major culture as something to abandon.

The difficulty of maturing and finding a place in the world for young adults depends on a range of sociocultural factors, including ethnicity, family resources, place of birth, and so forth. Most people are so busy coming to terms with life they do not consciously think about growing old. But when asked, they do express attitudes and opinions about aging.

Attitudes and opinions toward aging vary, as the responses of college students show (Barrow, 1994; Hillier, 2004). Students who were asked "What is your personal reaction to growing old?" offered the following responses:

- As you get older, you become wise, less caring of time, and are not in a big rush as much as when you are younger.

- I look forward to growing old, simply to have the luxury of getting to live. I work as an AIDS hospice worker and watch young people die year after year.

- I *hate* the fact that I have to grow old. I look at old people and dread getting there. My biggest fear is looking old, being ugly and sick. . . . I'm sure that sounds shallow but that's how I feel.

- Growing old scares me because I am scared to be alone. Being alone is the scariest thing that could happen to someone.

- How wrinkled will I get? Will I still want sex? Will I become a bitter old lady? How or when will I die? I just get so scared to even think of these things.

- My life is so complex right now that I look forward to sitting back in a rocking chair and watching life go by.

Consistent with other findings on attitudes toward aging (Fleeson & Heckhausen, 1997), some responses from these young people show a degree of acceptance and anticipation of aging, while others show fear. How and why do people come to fear aging? We can assume that fear and worry about aging do not make the coming stages of the life course easier. Apprehension makes every life stage more worrisome and less enjoyable. The two persons quoted above who were worried about getting wrinkled and ugly were female. Women seem to have the most fears, because their aging is judged more harshly by society. In other words, they, indeed, have more to fear.

The Ubiquitous Midlife Crisis

Is midlife a point of transition, or is it a crisis? In 1965 the psychoanalyst Elliot Jaques coined the term "midlife crisis" in his essay "Death and the Mid-Life Crisis," He saw in men around 35 years old a struggle between basic Freudian drives: the life instinct of *eros* versus *thanatos,* or the urge toward destruction and death (Kruger, 1994). His observations were based on analyses of artists' lives and works, and he found a dramatic change of some sort around the age 35 in almost every artist he studied. This change was generally precipitated by the individual's recognition of his own mortality—often generated by the death of a parent or a long-term friend.

The phrase "midlife crisis" apparently spoke to the experiences of enough people that it took hold in the language. In addition to being intuitively compelling, it is consistent with the theoretical underpinnings of adulthood developed in the early part of the century by Jung, van Gennep, Ortega y Gasset, and Erikson (see Table 3.3). Numerous psychologists took up the popular concept and developed a more popularized literature that assumed or further developed the idea of a crisis at midlife. Three primary writers in this vein were Levinson, in his *Seasons of a Man's Life* (1978); Gould (*Transformations: Growth and Change in Adult Life* [1978]); and, just before Levinson or Gould, Gail Sheehy (1976).

When I had journeyed half of our life's way, I found myself within a shadowed forest, for I had lost the path that does not stray. Ah, it is hard to speak of what it was, that savage forest, dense and difficult, which even in recall renews my fear: So bitter—death is hardly more severe!

DANTE, 1308

Gail Sheehy's book *Passages* (1976) launched the term midlife crisis into the popular media. She named the time between ages 35 and 45 the "deadline decade." Not much thought is given to aging during the teens and 20s, wrote Sheehy; but in our 30s we realize we have reached a halfway mark; "yet even as we are reaching our prime, we begin to see there is a place where it finishes. Time starts to squeeze" (p. 244). She continues:

The loss of youth, the faltering of physical powers we have always taken for granted, the fading purpose of stereotyped roles in which we have thus far identified ourselves, the spiritual dilemma of having no answers—any or all of these shocks can give this passage the character of crisis. (Sheehy, 1976, p. 244)

Sheehy felt that the years spanning the ages of 37 and 42 are the "peak years of anxiety for almost everyone." Although she did not claim that everyone experiences a midlife crisis, she observed that many, if not most, people find it difficult to face their own aging during these years. She further stated that somewhere between the ages of 35 and 45, if we permit ourselves to do so, most of us will have a full-out authenticity crisis, during which we may, as we did in adolescence, find ourselves desperately seeking to define our identity and purpose:

I have reached some sort of meridian in my life. I had better take a survey, reexamine where I have been, and reevaluate how I am

TABLE 3.3

Models of adult development: Intellectual generation of basic concepts

Theorist	Historical/Cultural Location	Theoretical Concept
Sigmund Freud	1880s through 1930s; Austrian; father of psychoanalysis	Personality based on first 5 years of life. Divided into id, ego, and superego, representing impulsive, realistic, and moralistic tendencies. Individuals attend to conscious awareness yet are driven and motivated by the unconscious
Carl Jung	1990s through 1950s; Swiss; first modern voice in psychiatry/psychology in adult development	Inner struggles of the 20s–30s deal with the "shadow" (repressed childhood attributes); 40s deal with potentials within the self, archetypes, that are primitive until midlife
Arnold van Gennep	Early 1990s; Dutch anthropologist; *Rites of Passage,* 1908	Life cycle is a series of transitions incorporating major life events such as birth, death, marriage, divorce. People in transition are a threat to society because they are not well integrated in the group they leave or the group they enter; it is a psychologically unstable time. Ritual provides a collective vehicle for gaining personal control over anxieties generated by transitions
Jose Ortega y Gasset	Spanish historian/philosopher; *Man and Crisis,* 1933	Generational divisions (childhood, 1–15; youth, 15–30; initiation, 30–45; dominant, 45–60; old age, 60+)
Erik Erikson	German and U.S.; stages of psychosocial development; *Childhood and Society,* 1950	Human development comprised of 8 linear age-based stages from which specific ego strengths emerge. First theorist to focus on ego development in late life, e.g., *integrity vs. despair*
Daniel Levinson	1970s; U.S. psychologist; *Seasons of a Man's Life,* 1978; *Seasons of a Woman's Life,* 1996; adult development	*Life structure* is the design of a life based on what a person finds most important. *Phases,* or loose stages, are identified by approximate age; *transitions* of about 5 years' duration connect overlapping phases

Source: Adapted from Levinson, D. (1996). *The seasons of a woman's life.* New York: Knopf.

going to spend my resources from now on. Why am I doing all this? What do I really believe in? Underneath this vague feeling is the fact, as yet unacknowledged, that there is a down side to life, a back of the mountain, and that I have only so much time before the dark to find my own truth. (Sheehy, 1976, p. 242)

Sheehy clearly hit a nerve. How people felt about themselves and what they observed in other people was apparently consistent with the idea that people experience a major psychological disruption, often creating a need for change, at or around midlife. The term midlife crisis became a topic of discussion among journalists, psychologists, sociologists, television talk-show hosts, and patrons of the local cafés and coffee shops. By virtue of sheer repetition, a "midlife crisis" now existed.

Levinson's research on men's lives echoed Sheehy's sentiments:

For the great majority of men ... this period evokes tumultuous struggles within the self and with the external world. Their Midlife

Transition is a time of moderate or severe crisis. Every aspect of their lives comes into question. . . . A profound reappraisal of this kind cannot be a cool, intellectual process. It must involve emotional turmoil, despair, the sense of not knowing where to turn or of being stagnant and unable to move at all. (Levinson, 1978, p. 199)

Few corresponding scientific studies, however, could state unequivocally that age crises are to be expected within given time intervals for every individual. Soon after the publication of *Passages*, controversy ensued over whether a midlife crisis occurs or not.

I suggest that the midlife crisis is a chimera, that is . . . , "an unreal creature of the imagination, a mere wild fancy; an unfounded conception . . . a phantasm, a body"

KRUGER, 1994

Despite all the attention paid to midlife in the past 20 years, the time period is variously referred to as "the prime of life," or as a "crisis." Most studies have found that midlife is both, depending on what life sends a person's way and the coping skills and resources the person has to deal with life. Among those who clearly identify having had a crisis at midlife, it could have taken place not just between ages 35 and 45 but anytime between about 30 and 60. Even before 30 some individuals refer to an "early midlife crisis," and others after 60 to a "late midlife crisis"; therefore, midlife as a factor predictive of an age crisis is virtually meaningless.

Rosenberg et al. (1993, 1997) suggest that the midlife crisis might best be considered a narrative form providing the person with a way of shaping and understanding the events and experiences in her or his life. The midlife crisis represents a story (a plot) around which the personal narrative might be constructed. The underlying theme of the story is that there *is* a turning point—a change in the stable narrative of early

adulthood. Schaie and Willis (1996) describe the importance in this narrative of change in terms of the context—the particular historical time and culture. It is context that allows individuals to understand and describe their experiences to themselves.

The period after World War II (1950s) was one of economic expansion, a strong focus on the family, and a view of the person (particularly men) as autonomous, self-determining entities. Young adulthood for these cohorts of men was the era of "father knows best." These men entered midlife, however, at a time (late 1960s, 1970s) of marked ideological change regarding gender roles and authority relations. (pp. 73–74)

The word transition or shift, rather than crisis, more aptly describes the midlife experiences of most individuals (Levinson, 1996). Everyone agrees that we all make many transitions in life, and young adulthood to middle age is one of them. The new perspective views **midlife transitions** as normal situations likely to confront anyone. Such times, which are marked by feelings of uncertainty and instability, eventually result in some kind of adaptation. Klohnen & Vandewater (1996) conceptualize midlife as a

potential stressor that brings with it forces that impinge upon individuals. Individuals, in turn, posses mediating resources (e.g., ego-resiliency and coping styles) that aid in the creation of mediating conditions (e.g., social support systems and meaningful work involvement) that modify the impact of the potential stressor. (p. 432)

Ego resiliency (named and first measured by Block and Block [1980]) is the general capacity for flexible and resourceful adaptation to external and internal stressors. Klohnen & Vandewater, supposing it to be an important personality resource to help individuals negotiate their lives under conditions of change, assessed ego resiliency in women at age 43 and again at age 52. They found that ego resiliency at age 43 indeed predicted life adjustments at age 52. Whether a midlife age transition becomes a crisis seems to depend on several factors: the attitudes toward aging that formed early in life, the life events an individual experiences, social resources, and the coping mechanisms, including ego resiliency, that people have developed to deal with stress and ambiguity (Holahan et al., 1995; McCrae & Costa, 1995; Aldwin & Sutton, 1996).

Let us take the hypothetical story of John. The corporation John works for is downsizing, but John believes his job is secure. His younger sister recently died after a sudden myocardial infarction (heart attack). She lived in another state and was taking care of their mother, who was in frail health. The mother of John's wife, who suffers from some form of dementia, lives with them. She frequently wakes them up in the middle of the night, telling everyone to get up to get ready for work. His wife often stays awake all night with her mother. John has tried to help them at night but is afraid that sleep deprivation will keep him from being able to perform successfully at work. The death of John's sister left him very fearful of having a heart attack, and he told his doctor:

> It's all too much. My wife isn't around, and we're not making love anymore. I have no energy, and my job performance is terrible. My sister just died, and I couldn't even stay with my own mother because I had to get back to help Marti with her mother. I sometimes wish that I would just die in my sleep, but I can't even get to sleep to get away from it all.

John *is* experiencing a crisis, but is it inherent to aging? Or is it a combination of his position in the life course—a working person with aging parents (probably also with children, perhaps in college)—and the economic circumstances of this particular moment in history?

Those factors, combined with his aging biology and the symbolic indicators of age (John really hates that he is becoming bald!), can feel overwhelming.

John has sought the assistance of a psychiatrist to help him with his "sleeping disorder." His physician has determined that John is quite depressed (Samuels, 1997). Small wonder: John has multiple, significant stressors. It is stories like John's, of which there are many, that reinforce for us that a midlife crisis exists: we see these crises around us. Those in the helping professions who see the Johns and Janes of the community employ an intergroup analysis, see age-related patterns, and seek therapeutic and medical treatment patterns for patient in a midlife crisis.

There's some kind of profound something going on—a reassessment, a rethinking, a big gulp, whatever. It's not biological. It has to do with self-image and the work-place. And I find this astonishing.

A. CLURMAN, A PARTNER AT
YANKELOVICH SURVEY PARTNERS, 1995

Midlife crisis can be seen as a self-fulfilling prophecy: many people anticipate one because its existence is generally accepted (Fleeson & Heckhausen, 1997). Cultural norms create psychological and interpersonal pressures on individuals to conform to those behaviors and attitudes that express "human nature" as it should (Dannefer, 1996). A new wrinkle, not knowing any Top 40 tunes, having a doctor who looks too young to have graduated from medical school, or being the age of co-workers' parents can precipitate feelings of being out of control, of being dated. The death of a close friend or of a parent can precipitate a profound process of self-reflection: How much time do I have? What have I really accomplished? Am I clear about what happens after death?

Those are the very questions predicted by developmental theorists, including Jung and Levinson (Table 3.3), who postulate that midlife is a special time for reflection—a time when one's focus begins to become more interior as the full meaning of mortality begins to emerge and take shape in an individual's consciousness. The jury on the presence or absence of a midlife crisis is still out; however, it is clear that midlife is a uniquely identifiable period in the life course.

Middle Age

Middle age is an interesting period: the *transition* between young adulthood and old age. It is often stereotyped as either dull, boring, and routine, or consumed by a life- and lifestyle-threatening crisis. However this time of life plays out, an individual's reactions and adjustments to changes in middle age surely affect his or her reactions and adjustments to old age, just as one's response to aging at any point surely affects the points that follow.

Those in their middle years frequently accomplish or conclude certain developmental tasks. The normative expectation is that most people typically spend their 20s settling down and in their 30s, 40s, and 50s becoming further established. This frequently is when people buy a house and establish an economic base. In middle age, those who are married may feel either satisfaction or discontent, but those who have not married and settled may feel a stronger push to do so. Age norms constrain those who do not fill the appropriate social role at the appropriate time; middle age can become a time to sort through which roles one might still fill and which roles to abandon, and to deal with the feelings of loss for those roles that never will be (Foner, 1996).

Major role changes and events occur in our 40s and 50s. Our parents are likely to be in their old age, and this is our time to cope with their old age and eventual death. The older generation, in turn, must confront the reality of their children's middle age (Tillman, 1997). Many popular books are on the market to provide guidance for middle-aged children who are helping and coping with older parents.

One's grown children launch out on their own during one's middle years. This event can be sad and depressing, a relief, or a mixture of both. Though the post-parental period has often been described negatively, for many this new freedom is a cause for a celebration rather than a crisis, depending on their outlook and perhaps on their ability to redefine their goals and purpose in life.

The concept of the empty nest syndrome has been used to describe a midlife depression experienced by some women whose energies have been focused on child rearing (fathers' experience of children leaving home has unfortunately not been well studied). However, the consequences of the empty nest phenomenon, research tells us, is as varied as the individuals experiencing it. Some people perceive their lives as having little purpose once their children have left home. Others identify a new sense of life satisfaction—a time to renew the marriage relationship and to attend to personal interests that were pushed aside by the necessity of addressing the needs of children.

A relatively new social phenomenon is the return home ("empty nest refilled") by either unmarried or married adult children. This is most likely to happen in an uncertain economic environment when the adult child has lost a job or accepted a very low-paying job (Kausler & Kausler, 1996), or if the adult child has had a divorce. A survey in 1990 revealed that 16 percent of young adults age 25 to 29 were living with their parents. This proportion is probably even higher today (Kausler & Kausler, 1996). The return of adult children to the parental home is not in and of itself negative, however. For many cultural groups in the United States, adult children once again living in the home might be "traditional," as opposed to aberrant. It is, however, contrary to larger cultural expectations of the progression of the life course.

Nowadays the majority of middle-aged people have more parents than they have children.

WEISHEIT, 1994

In some families, the needs of aging parents for care are synchronous with the return of adult children—indeed, those needs become determinants in the decision to "move home." In other families, the older parent moves in with the middle-aged "child" because of the parent's frail health or for economic reasons. The impact of increased longevity substantially increases the likelihood of intergenerational responsibilities for elderly parents on the part of people in middle age (Uhlenberg, 1996). For example, in 1900, a 50-year-old had a 4 percent chance of both her parents still being alive. Today, the midlife granddaughter of that woman will have a 31 percent chance of both her parents being alive in 2010, and an 80 percent chance of having one of her parents still be living (Cutler et al., 1997).

For those in midlife who have jobs or careers, the 40s and 50s are generally also a time of experiencing peaks, or at least of evaluating a present occupation's potential for status, money, or power. Midlife is a time to come to terms with what is not possible. We may acknowledge, at this point, the impossibility of becoming president of the company or of fulfilling any of a host of goals.

Midlife is likewise a time of peak competence, professional respect, and earnings. People in midlife who have been working can look toward retirement in the first two decades of the twenty-first century with optimism. It is very possible that their needs for wealth will exceed those of their parents; however, they are better positioned for retirement than their parents were. They will have higher preretirement earnings than their parents did, and this earnings growth will increase pension benefits and allow greater savings for retirements (Manchester, 1997). Additionally, more women will be eligible for their own Social Security and pension benefits than were their mothers. This optimistic vision of a future old age might follow the pattern of the self-fulfilling prophecy and help to psychologically position midlifers for their later life.

Those who are unemployed or in low-paying jobs, however, may have more trouble squaring their dreams with reality. Aligning dreams with the facts can be a daunting task or no task at all, depending on the dreams and the degree of success we expect. Some individuals have both the inner strengths (self-confidence and motivation) and the outer resources (monetary savings and cultural support) to find new jobs or careers in their 40s and 50s. However, those seeking new lines of work sometimes must forfeit seniority and retirement benefits from the companies where their careers originated. Changing jobs may require risk taking and sacrifice and, for many, can literally be a time for starting over.

Middle age brings biological changes, as well as changes in career and family. For women, menopause—the ending of menstruation—is a major physiological change: the childbearing years have ended. The decrease in estrogen in menopausal and post-menopausal women can create numerous physical changes and symptoms, such as hot flashes, genital atrophy, urinary tract changes, and loss of bone density. Hormone replacement therapy (HRT) is chosen by some women to alleviate symptoms, but there are risks associated with it. An increase in the risk of endometrial or uterine cancer exists for women who receive estrogen over a long period of time, although this risk is reduced when estrogen is combined with progesterone. On the other hand, there is evidence of reduced stroke and hypertension, as well as strong evidence for the reduction of osteoporosis, when estrogen supplements are taken. The negative findings are frightening, however, and for all women, particularly for those with family histories of breast or uterine cancer, taking hormone supplements must be carefully thought through.

Making the decision to take or not to take hormones for the remainder of one's life is not an easy one to make. Done well, it takes a thoughtful, self-reflective approach, and therefore creates an opportunity for many women to reflect on who they see themselves as being as they come to terms with the ending of one stage of life and the beginning of another. A biologically determined experience can become a time of self-reflection and examination. Women in their 40s and 50s may mourn the loss of their fertility but at the same time be relieved. It is a profound change in the rhythm of a woman's life, and sometimes women and their partners need reassurance that menopause does not, in itself, diminish sexuality. Rather, it can free partners from concern about pregnancy; many couples report improved pleasure and joy in their sexual relationship after menopause.

A major literature review of women's personalities in middle age (Stewart & Ostrove, 1998) showed that concepts generally considered to be aspects of middle age (such as midlife crisis, generativity, empty nest, and menopause) were identified as being important in women's personalities. Additionally, however, the review identified features of midlife review, identity, and confident power that are not typically associated with middle age. These concepts were shown to be central to the personality development of middle-aged women.

Karp (1988) provides a symbolic interactionist perspective from which to view the middle-aged years from age 50 to 60. He describes these years as a decade of reminders that bring age consciousness to new heights. These reminders come from the reflections of self that come from the appraisals of other people,

a "looking-glass self" that gives rise to self-appraisals about aging. Those in their 50s whom Karp studied were surprised by their own aging. In their minds, they were young; but either their bodies or people around them were giving them different messages. A man who played on a basketball team was referred to as "sir" by a younger team member.

Each to each a looking glass
Reflects the other that doth pass.

Cooley, 1902

Self-concept is socially constructed, at least in part: "Our self-identity is the product which springs from the responses of many others and it is their collective reactions which form the underpinning of our self-concepts" (Hensley, 1996). Who we are and how we respond is mediated by the way we are treated by others, and how we believe we *ought* to be in the world. We have, according to the sociologist C. H. Cooley, a tendency to become the person others say we are.

One category of reminders is generational—fiftieth-birthday bashes focus on the fact that the birthday "boy" or "girl" has made it to the "big five-oh." Children grow up and become independent; they have children of their own. Parents die, long-term friends die, and the reality of being at or near the alpha generation is ever-present. The person in midlife is surrounded by social reminders of age: being the oldest member of a group or club; self-consciousness about going to places such as singles dances or bars where most people are young; or being old enough to be the parent or even grandparent of students, clients, or patients.

The age consciousness in Karp's study was not necessarily a negative commentary on aging. Research on the perception of self over time suggests that many people expect a peak in integrity in late life, and a peak in generativity in midlife. They anticipate high levels of well-being in midlife and later (Fleeson & Heckhausen, 1997). The way in which people anticipate their future self can profoundly affect the choices they make in the process of becoming old. A projected self-concept of well-being in later life is, perhaps, half the battle.

Late Life

In the mid-twentieth century, when psychological models of human development began to expand inquiry from child development to the adult experience, late life remained the least examined part of life. It has been characterized by decline and loss: loss of physical health, of lifelong partners and friends, of mental capacity, of creativity, of social roles—in short, it has been seen as depressing, discouraging, and barely worth spending much time on.

Late adulthood is still the least studied portion of the life course; however, the interest in social gerontology brought about by increased longevity and changing demographics since the mid-1980s has created a parallel interest in the psychological development of later life. Today, many people will spend about one-third of their entire life span in their "old age"—a fact that the French address by calling it *le troisième âge,* "the third age" (Schaie & Willis, 1996). Although the student of gerontology is still likely to be met with the incredulous question, Why are you studying *that*?, the exploration of growth and development in later life is now seen as an exciting field of inquiry attracting increased numbers of scholars.

Loss does occur in late life, but it is important to distinguish between normal, pathological, and optimal late life experience. Although physical changes do occur with advancing age, physical and mental decline are not necessarily part of normal aging. Just as wearing prescription lenses to maintain 20/20 vision is considered to be an adaptive compensation, so too are the compensations an individual develops for minor dysfunctions that accompany the normal

aging process (Schaie & Willis, 1996). Walking more slowly on a hike to compensate for a reduced energy level might be an example. Being unable to take a walk at all, however, is not a consequence of normal aging, but an indication of pathological aging—a physical state based on disease or injury rather than an outcome of the aging process. This serves as a reminder that "the aged" are a very diverse population: well-being in old age is largely a function of the physical and psychological processes that preceded it. Additionally, losses tend to be counterbalanced with gains: the death of spouse, for example, can lead to remarriage and a regeneration of a loving relationship. Retirement from a full-time career may lead to part-time work at the same place or another job elsewhere, or to the expansion of a creative hobby.

Developmentalists generally divide *le troisième âge* into categories of the young old (around 65 to 75 or 80), the old old (75 or so to about 90), and the very old (around 90 and older). This distinction is very important when we talk about "old age," because if we are talking about a 95-year-old and a 68-year-old, we are speaking of people in profoundly different developmental places. Clearly, 40 years ago this was almost a moot point, because so few people lived past what we now call the young old group. Today, the young old are more like the middle-aged than they are like the old old.

Erikson (1979, 1982) defined old age as a time when one seeks balance between the search for ego integrity and feelings of despair. Other scholars have elaborated on Erikson's theme. Havighurst (1972) developed six tasks of late life as

1. Adjusting to decreasing physical strength and health
2. Adjusting to retirement and reduced income
3. Adjusting to the death of a spouse
4. Establishing an explicit association with one's age group

5. Adopting and adapting societal roles in a flexible way

6. Establishing satisfactory physical arrangements

The function of these tasks is to promote well-being in later life—optimal aging. Note the extent of adaptation required of older people in Havighurst's model.

Extreme old age is a very special time. In his 90s, Erikson wrote from personal experience about the final stage of the life cycle model that he presented with the help of his wife, Joan, 40 years earlier. He expanded on his late life stage, "integrity versus despair," by describing the wisdom that comes with age if one completes the developmental tasks that began earlier in the life cycle. For example, the basic trust learned in infancy evolves into the knowledge in old age of how interdependent we are—of how much we need each other. In early childhood, the life cycle's second phase, learning physical autonomy and control of one's bodily functions, versus shame and doubt in not learning them, paves the way for coping with deterioration of the body in old age. Old age is basically the second phase in reverse. One must "grow" in order to avoid the shame and doubt that can accompany decline, just as one "learned" bodily development without having shame and doubt. Every stage offers lessons that can apply in old age.

In old age, we can develop humility by comparing our early hopes and dreams with the life we actually lived. **Humility** is a realistic appreciation of our limits and competencies. On the individual level, in old age, one might achieve a sense of integrity, a sense of completeness, of personal wholeness strong enough to offset the downward psychological pull of inevitable physical disintegration (Fleeson & Heckhausen, 1997).

On the social level, Erikson saw a discouraging scene: the widespread lack of regard in modern life for future generations. The only thing, he felt, that can save the species is "generativity"—the promotion of positive values in the next generation. Unfortunately, he felt, greed and the depletion of the earth's resources are accomplishing the opposite.

Transitions in late life

As a result of longer life expectancy in the late twentieth and early twenty-first centuries, most Americans can expect to pass through a number of age-linked events: long-term survival, empty nest, retirement, and, for women, an extended term of widowhood characterized by solitary living. Actually, a transition can be movement either from one age to another or from one age-linked event to another (e.g., children leave home or a spouse dies).

Every decade has its share of tasks and challenges. In later life, illness, death of a spouse, or increased frailty may take its toll; but personal growth and joy in living are still possible and probable. As Socrates awaited death in prison, at the age of 71, he was learning to play the lyre. Transitions do not end at age 65; we continue making them until the final transition. We can begin early in life to teach ourselves and our children that growing older is a natural event, one not to be feared, but rather one to be anticipated for new roles, new avenues of expressions, and new opportunities.

Continuity Theory: "You Haven't Changed One Bit"

Continuity theory is broad enough to be considered a sociological theory as well as a psychological one. Continuity theorists propose that a person's adaptations to young adulthood and middle age predict that person's general pattern of adaptation to old age. According to continuity theory, the personality formed early in life continues throughout the life span with no basic changes. This theory implies that neither activity nor disengagement theory explains adjustment to aging: adjustment depends on personality patterns of one's former years. This approach is consistent with the core of personality theory. Some therapists believe that significant personality change after about the age of 30 is unlikely. And, although some researchers continue to debate the degree to which the personality remains stable throughout the life course, continuity theory maintains that the individual achieves a core personality by adulthood. By adulthood, people have adopted coping mechanisms, established stress and frustration tolerance levels, and defined ego defenses.

Surely enduring personality traits . . . form the core of our identity. For better or worse, we are what we are, and the recognition of that fact is a crucial step in successful aging.

COSTA ET AL., 1994

Trait theorists look for consistency in the personality: **traits** are the enduring response patterns that are exhibited by a person in many different contexts. **States,** on the other hand, more accurately describes things that are transient in the personality. Not unexpectedly, trait theorists find consistency in personality development over a lifetime. They define personality in terms of the basic tendencies that are the core potential of the person.

Two of the most influential trait theorists, Paul Costa and Robert McCrae, feel that personality stability is crucial for successful aging. Personality traits are central to an individual's self-concept; they form the core of how people see themselves, and the continued sense that we are the "same" person provides the basis on which we can move on to make meaning of that life as lived. Enduring dispositions provide a dependable and necessary basis for adaptation to a changing world (Costa et al., 1994).

Trait theorists say that lives change, but personality does not. One study found, for example, that states were associated with different feelings of well-being among older people, but that traits (those more enduring personality characteristics) did not predict shifts in affect (Adkins et al., 1996). It is those more enduring traits that provide solidity for the ongoing sense of self, even in the midst of change.

Those who argue with the continuity theorists point to individuals who believe they have made dramatic personality changes later in life. Consider this quote by Elia Kazan (at age 78), a noted Hollywood film director, when interviewed about his biography:

I don't know any other biography that is so candid as mine. It was a hard journey getting to this point. For a lot of my youth, I didn't like myself. I thought, "I'm not as good as other filmmakers." But now I think I don't have to compare myself with anybody. I'm not afraid of anything and don't feel hostile to a soul in the world, which is new for me.

KAZAN IN CONVERSATION WITH
REPORTER ALVIN SANOFF, 1988

It would appear that Kazan has become more open, more self-accepting, less hostile, and less fearful. Continuity theorists might respond to this quote by saying that we can at least make minor modifications to our personalities. Studies show that personality shortcomings can be addressed and, to some extent, overcome. With effort, tempers can be controlled, fears lessened, organization learned, and social skills practiced; thus, personalities can improve with age.

Analysis of longitudinal data suggests that personality stability might be associated with generations—that is to say, stability in personality might be the result of early socialization. Schaie and Willis (1996) report that "substantial positive development toward more flexible personality styles, behaviors, and attitudes [are seen] in successive generations" (p. 213).

Most people, however, believe they remain "themselves" over time, and that belief seems to be reinforced in research studies (Gold et al.,

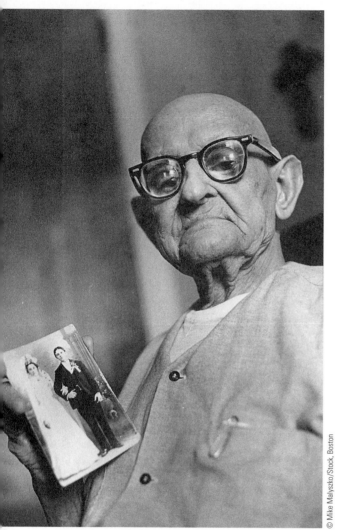

Love, courtship, marriage, and widowhood are part of the life course for many people. Each experience remains a part of a person's identity throughout his or her life.

© Mike Malyszko/Stock, Boston

1995; Parker, 1995; Onega & Tripp-Reimer, 1997; Troll & Skaff, 1997). By feeling a sense of continuity in their personalities, people are enabled to view change as connected to their past and linked to their present and future. This sense of the ongoing self is consistent with Kaufman's findings (previously reported) of the ageless self.

Two theorists in the 1980s studied adaptation skills among people who were moving from their homes into long-term care facilities (Lieberman & Tobin, 1983). They found that their respondents maintained stable self-concepts primarily by drawing on their pasts. When possible, they altered their daily activities in ways that were similar with past interests. Self-concept in very old age was described by Tobin (1991) as being "not so much a current self-picture as a view of an entire life."

These findings can help to shatter the stereotypes that older people become less flexible, more cranky, more conservative, and less satisfied with their lives. Continuity theory suggests, as do other developmental psychologists, that growing old is a process of *becoming;* who we are in late life is a culmination of who we have been throughout our lives.

Longitudinal Studies on Coping

The Maas-Kuypers Study

The Maas-Kuypers study, which observed personality change in women and men over a 40-year period, found personality to be stable throughout adulthood. Evidence in the research suggested that "qualities of life in old age are, indeed, highly associated, in complex ways, to qualities of life 40 years earlier" (Maas & Kuypers, 1977; Field, 1991). Those who had negative attributes in young adulthood had various negative personality characteristics in old age; fearful oldsters were rigid, apathetic, and melancholy as young mothers; anxious mothers were restless and dissatisfied in old age; the defensive elderly were withdrawn in early adulthood. The personality types that seemed most firmly connected to early adult-life behaviors were those with the most negative features. On the positive side, cheerfulness, lack of worries, and self-assurance in young adulthood seemed to match high self-esteem and self-satisfaction in old age.

The Elder-Liker Study

Another 40-year longitudinal study assessed the **coping** mechanisms and consequences for women who lived through the Great Depression of the 1930s (Elder & Liker, 1982). During the depression, financial losses were more severe for working-class women than for middle-class women, and many working-class women, lacking the educational, financial, or emotional resources to master their circumstances, were too hard hit to make a comeback. The researchers suggest that the hardship of the depression offered these women a trial run through the inevitable losses of old age. Economic hardships meant new challenges for women: coping with unemployed husbands, taking in boarders for pay, looking for work, borrowing money from relatives, and getting along on less by reducing purchases to a bare minimum. In short, women had to become more self-reliant.

The women under study experienced the depression as young married adults in their early childbearing years. On the whole, the depression diminished the emotional health of the lower-status women but increased that of the middle-class women. The middle-class women who struggled through hard times turned out to be more self-assured and cheerful than a "control" group of women who had not been deprived. They were also less fretful, less worrisome, and less bothered by the limitations and demands of living. Hard times left them more resourceful, with more vitality and self-confidence. In contrast, depression losses added to the psychological disadvantage of working-class women, lowering their self-esteem and increasing their feelings of insecurity and dissatisfaction with life.

The conclusion was that a life history of mastery enables women to manage traumatic experiences throughout their lives. Women like the middle-class women in the study are lucky if they have the resources for such mastery—economic resources do matter significantly. Coping skills are acquired in hard times, not in tranquil ones. One who experiences no hard times until old age may not have developed coping skills: "Neither a privileged life nor one of unrelenting deprivation assures the inner resources for successful aging" (Elder & Liker, 1982).

A review of personality research revealing dramatic support for the resiliency of personality throughout life offered two conclusions: (1) we should get help for undesirable characteristics because bad traits are unlikely to change by themselves, and (2) the well adjusted and cheerful will generally remain so for life in spite of any adverse circumstances brought about by time or aging (Costa & McCrae, 1987).

The Baltimore Study

The Baltimore Longitudinal Study of Aging, spanning 30 years, confirmed that personality remains remarkably stable with aging. A cheerful, optimistic young person usually remains so throughout life. And, conversely, a negative person maintains his or her pessimism (Shock et al., 1989). Personality, in fact, was found to be more stable than gender roles when changes in activities over the life course were examined (Verbrugge et al., 1996).

Stress appears to be a key modifier in the extent to which personality continuity takes place. One recent study developed a clear relationship between self-criticism and stress-induced changes in biochemistry, which in turn make the individual more vulnerable to ill health and depression (Gruen et al., 1997). In a 12-year study of 216 lower-middle-class people, continuity was the norm in personal functioning. Stress altered the pattern: with high exposure to stress, morale and self-concept deteriorated (Fiske & Chiriboga, 1990). Low morale, negative self-concept, and self-criticism have been found to be highly associated (Lieberman & Tobin, 1983; Troll & Skaff, 1996).

Adapting to Loss

A study monitoring the stress patterns people experienced when they were relocated to different nursing homes found the very old to be unique. Continuity theory did not apply. Their roles had changed, their bodies had declined, important people in their lives had died. Issues of finitude and death were close to their hearts. Thus, the psychology of the very old assumes new dimensions. Discontinuity with earlier periods of life is the rule as the very old adapt to stresses such as relocation. Their coping patterns have changed, and their psychological survival seems to hinge on preserving a sense of self. For those in the study, survival strategies involved adopting myths of control and turning to their past to maintain self-identity. In other words, imagining themselves to be in control of their health and surroundings and "living in the past" were successful coping strategies (Lieberman & Tobin, 1983; Parker, 1995).

Emotional problems are not physical in origin, but they may be related to physical losses. The older one is, the more likely one is to face physical disability and imminent death. Loss of hearing, loss of vision, and loss of the use of limbs have a strong psychological impact at any age. So does being told you have only five years, six months, or two weeks to live. Denial, depression, anger, even rage are common responses.

Other age-related losses are the death of a spouse, the deaths of siblings, and the deaths of friends. Retirement, the loss of one's driver's license, the sale of the home, or a move to an institution are the types of losses that scare people about aging. They do not happen to every older person, but the longer a person lives, the more likely they are to happen. There is a considerable difference between the young old (65 to 74) and the old old (75 and over) as to the losses they can expect. In fact, by comparison, the young old experience very few losses.

Numerous studies have shown that older persons, on the whole, adapt well to loss. Most elderly persons adapt to the loss of their spouse without severe psychiatric repercussions. However, the initial period of widowhood can be especially difficult. During the first year of widowhood, there are a high incidence of psychological and physical symptoms, an increase in the use of psychiatric services, and an increased risk of suicide.

Those who experience emotional problems with widowhood and with other losses should reach out for help. A therapist, for example, may counsel an older woman who has undergone a mastectomy. The woman may feel a loss of femininity as a result of her surgery; she may be depressed, angry, or anxious. If family members are supportive and her attitude is positive, her loss can be minimized. However, if her husband, for example, is negative or rejecting, then she will have greater problems recovering emotionally.

Those in counseling and related fields should not regard elders as untreatable, nor should they have expectations for recovery that are too high or too low. Older persons can—and do—rebound after grieving over loss.

Personality Theory

There are certain stereotypes of personality change in old age, none of which are supported conclusively by research findings. Old people were once thought to become more rigid or set in their ways, stubborn, grouchy, and crotchety. Studies lend little or no support to such changes as a natural consequence of the aging process.

With regard to learning, personality is an influential variable. Interest, motivation, self-esteem, rigidity, flexibility, cautiousness, fearfulness, and anxiety all affect one's ability to learn. Old people vary in personality characteristics just as young people do.

Personality theory focuses on the many traits of individual personality, such as friendliness, shyness, humor, and aggressiveness. The study of personality has been a major focus of developmentalists who analyze personality and its change over the life course. Theorists have used personality variables to explain why some older individuals withdraw from society whereas others do not, and why some individuals are satisfied with an active lifestyle whereas others prefer noninvolvement. Personality theorists generally use personality characteristics to explain why some people readily adapt to and cope with aging and why others have problems.

Personality studies show that many older individuals are mature, focused types, happy and satisfied with life. But others are striving, defensive about aging, and discontented. Some are very passive types who depend on others. They may be apathetic and bored much of the time. They may see the world as collapsing and become preoccupied with holding on to what they have. The most disorganized personalities suffer major impairments to their mental health and cannot function outside a mental hospital.

A constricted or rigid personality type has a difficult time dealing with change. In contrast, a flexible personality type adapts to change, whether it be positive or negative (such as widowhood, ailing health, or shrinking finances).

An extensive longitudinal study of personalities grouped them into five categories:

1. Neurotic—characterized by feelings of anxiety, worry, hostility, and depression.

2. Extroverted—characterized by a tendency to be outgoing, active, and assertive.

3. Open—characterized by receptiveness to new experiences, new ideas, and change.

4. Agreeable versus Antagonistic—Antagonistic types tend to set themselves against the grain and be opposed to others, whereas agreeable types are pleasers. Antagonists may be skeptical, mistrustful, stubborn, and rude.

5. Conscientious versus Undirected—The conscientious are hardworking and responsible. They have a drive to achieve. The undirected have no focus and tend to be lackadaisical and aimless (Costa & McCrae, 1987).

The personality traits in the many studies reviewed by Costa and McCrae show astonishing stability. The traits remained consistent over time, and individuals who were extroverted and open experienced less stress as they aged.

Locus of Control

The personality characteristic known as locus of control is a concept that came under heavy scrutiny in the 1980s and continues to be examined. The locus, or center, of control may be perceived as internal if the person sees that his or her own actions bring about a reward or positive change. If, however, the person sees rewards as due to fate, luck, change, or powerful others, the locus of control is external. Research has found locus of control to be a long-standing personality component developed over years of positive and negative reinforcement. A person with an internal locus of control feels more control over the environment and is more likely to attempt to improve his or her condition.

Studies show that older people experience higher life satisfaction if they possess an internal locus of control. Thus, both psychologists and sociologists have reason to study locus of control. Changes in the social environment can facilitate the development of internal control. By allowing older individuals more self-determination and administration on policies that affect them and by increasing their involvement, control, and power in all aspects of their social and political lives, we can help them to develop greater satisfaction with their lives.

An older person who has received positive support from a cohesive family tends to have a strong internal locus of control. Social support, such as tangible assistance and emotional help, also tends to increase feelings of control, but only to a point. Beyond this point, additional support can *decrease* feelings of personal control. We need a word of caution concerning beliefs about both extreme internal and external loci of control: both extremes may hinder older adults' abilities to cope with stressful life events.

Gender Development

The developmental model emphasizes the psychology of the individual. Developmental psychologists who look at how individuals change over the life course focus on the individual by studying variables such as personality, motivation, cognition, and morale. Social and cultural factors are examined for their role in personality changes. Maturation, or some inherent biological mechanism, may also be a strong force in creating change in persons as they progress through life. As theoretical models of aging are set forth, empirical studies test and refine them. The question of which attitudes, behaviors, and individual characteristics are **intrinsic** (biologically mandated) and which are **extrinsic** (formed by changes in social structure and roles) is still an issue for study and discussion.

One example of the question of intrinsic or extrinsic causality is that of gender differences. Carl Jung postulated the existence of opposites in our personalities, with young adults generally expressing only one sexual aspect as they developed into adulthood. The expression of that sexual self is usually defined by sex-role stereotypes.

As a person ages, he or she may become more self-accepting and more comfortable exploring all sides of his or her personality. Both sexes, according to Jung, move psychologically closer to the middle ground.

The psychologist David Gutmann (1987) believes that this path toward the opposite characteristic is intrinsic. Regardless of the cause of the initial gender behavior, he says, at around midlife, generally all males begin to grow more nurturing, and all women become gradually more "executive." This finding is cross-cultural, according to Gutmann's research (1977, 1987). In effect, there is a "cross-over effect" from one gender-defined set of behaviors closer to the other, which he names the **post-parental transition** (1992). Older men become freer in expressing behaviors that would be considered feminine, and women show more "masculine" behaviors.

Gutmann proposed the initial reason for gender role differentiation (and the subsequent cultural norms for male and female behaviors) is the "parental emergency," in which the arrival of children requires an extensive period of "parental service" during which clearly differentiated gender roles are necessary. Therefore, for the good of society, women become the nurturers, and fathers, the providers. When this period of time is over, men and women can expect the release of previously unused potential (James et al., 1995).

Perhaps so; perhaps not. Later studies on Guttman's hypothesis reveal that findings do not always converge. Some studies clearly do not support a crossover, some find only marginal support, and some find that it may exist for some people some of the time (James et al., 1995). Older men may have time to give the love and tenderness to their grandchildren that they were not able to with their own children. Older women may become more assertive and confident not because of the aging process, but because they have ended parenting roles and

Rather than internalizing negative messages about old age, some people defy the belief that they cannot learn or cannot be active and effective citizens; these people become community leaders in their elderhood.

entered the job market, or because they are now in a role that does not require them to simultaneously balance the different needs of many individuals. One provocative implication of Gutmann's hypothesis is that the mother role and the role of worker and provider are inherently incompatible. On the other hand, research based on interviews with older adults often identify a "shift in the politics of self," in Gutmann's words (1987, p. 203).

We have all seen the old person who is bitter, depressed, and very anxious about life and living. We have also all seen the old person who has clarity and grace, with a special understanding of the meaning of their existence and a willingness to share the story of their understandings.

Clearly, we want to be like the latter person when *we* are 70 or 80 or 90. Psychologists are only beginning to ask some of the questions that are central to a better understanding of the development of well-being in later life. They are not in agreement about which theoretical perspectives most accurately describe the growth and development taking place in later life, possibly because there is no single unifying theory to be found. The human life and the human psyche are dynamic and infinitely resilient. We return, after crushing life events, after multiple experiences and cultural ways of interpreting those experiences, to a central human core. It is the task of gerontological psychology to better understand and describe that core, as well as the process for getting there.

Chapter Summary

This chapter considers the progression to late life from the perspective of developmental psychology. In this view, individuals move through stages, or identifiable eras, in their development. A complex interaction of internal (biological) and external (social) factors combine to shape the person as we age. Expected behavior patterns exist at every level of adulthood, whether young adulthood or advanced middle age. Ageism in a society can be internalized to fear of aging within the individual. Some individuals experience a traumatic transitional crisis at midlife, but it is unclear whether this crisis affects all people, whether it affects every person in the same way, and whether it affects every person in every culture. Psychologists coming from a biological perspective say it is universal to our human condition; psychologists coming from a social perspective say it is cultural; increasingly more psychologists say it is both.

Personality theory draws attention to how personality changes as a function of age and how individual variations in personality may affect one's own aging process. Continuity theory suggests that personality remains stable throughout life. Personality and the struggle to cope with the world interact to shape the aging process. Studies of locus of control determine the degree to which older people feel in control of their lives.

Perhaps most important, psychologists believe there is a profoundly important human task to be dealt with in later life, and that is the hard work of making coherent meaning of all of life's experiences. It is the task of pulling together a meaningful life story, ending with a sense of *integrity*.

Key Terms

acculturation
age group identification
age identity
archetypes
coping
cross-era transitions
data
ego development
ego resiliency
emergent self metaphor
epigenetic principle
extrinsic
extroversion
gender splitting
generativity
gerotranscendence
humility
information processing
integrity versus despair
intergroup perspective
interiority
intrinsic
introversion
life cycle
life review
life structure
mechanistic metaphor
metaphor
midlife transitions
narrative metaphor
organic metaphor
personality theory
post-parental transition
qualitative development
quantitative development
reminiscence
shadow
stages of human development
states
tension of opposites
theories
traits
transcendent self metaphor
transitions
unidirectional

Questions for Discussion

1. Is there a midlife crisis? In small groups, take a position either in support of or against a midlife crisis and argue it. Substantiate your position with evidence, both empirical (your observations) and from the studies presented in the chapter.

2. Why do some individuals have difficulty making the transition from early adulthood to middle age? From middle age to old age?

3. Discuss Erikson's final two stages, adding Havighurst's elaboration of the stage of generativity versus stagnation. Do these stages describe your observations? Do you think they represent experiences of people from a culture different than your own? Why or why not?

4. What personality variables would you choose to examine in a longitudinal study of students throughout their lives? Why?

Fieldwork Suggestions

1. Interview someone who is age 65 or older. Ask that person if he or she believes he or she has changed, and if so to what extent, in the past 30 years. In the past 40 years?

2. Interview a young woman about her expectations about menopause. Does she have expectations about her physical appearance? Symptoms? Self-concept?

3. Ask six middle-aged or older women their ages. Did you violate a norm? Did they answer you? What was their reaction? Ask six middle-aged men their ages. Are their responses the same as the women's? What did you expect?

Internet Activities ✍

1. Beginning with the key search words "narrative therapy," search the Internet for information about this emerging therapeutic field. Repeat this, using key words "Jung" or "Jungian psychology" and see what comes up.

2. Locate the Internet site of a university that is not in your state. Find a psychology department that has a faculty member doing research in human aging. What are the research interests of this professor? What classes does the department have that would provide more specific information about some of the topics touched on in this chapter?

4 Theories in Social Gerontology

Caregiving throughout Life

Joseph Shapiro

Older people do a lot of caregiving for elderly family members and friends. Among Americans 75 and older, one in five say they do some caregiving. And sometimes it's the very old who help out—like Clarice Morant. She's 101.

In Morant's small and tidy living room, photographs of family crowd the walls, tables, and shelves. Morant coaxes her elderly brother, Ira Barber, to get up off the couch for lunch.

Barber can't speak, as the result of a stroke. He's a handsome man sharply dressed in gray pants and matching shirt. Just a few steps away is the dining room table. At the head of the table there's a plate of chicken, collard greens, and macaroni and cheese.

Morant can't get her brother to pull himself up on his walker and take those few steps to the dining room. "Your dinner will get cold if you don't eat now," she tells him. "Come on, honey. Come on, eat something."

Morant lives in her brick row house with her brother and her sister, who's in the next room in a hospital bed.

Her sister, Rozzie Laney, is 89. Her brother is 95. And Morant, who cares for them, is 101.

"I'll be 102 the 29th of August, this year," she says. "If I'm here, thank the Lord."

But can a 101-year-old woman give good care? And do it without putting her own health in danger?

Morant cooks for her brother and sister. She does their laundry, bathes them, and gets up in the night to turn and change them.

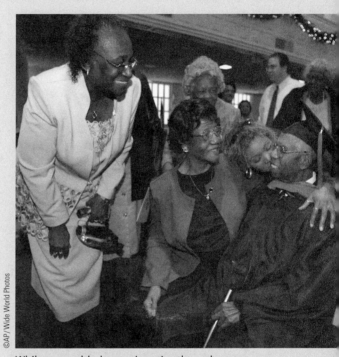

©AP / Wide World Photos

While some elderly remain active through caregiving, others seek out different pursuits. Here, Eugene Florence, 100, receives his master of divinity degree, surrounded by his family.

She's a small woman. But she stands up straight. Her friends and family don't call her by her given name, they call her Classie.

According to a recent study by the Urban Institute, people 75 and older provide more hours of caregiving than people in any other age group.

After her husband died, Morant moved into this house, which belongs to her sister. Laney, her sister, is blind and in the terminal phase of Alzheimer's disease.

"I've been taking care of my sister for 20 years, and my brother for about 6 now," says Morant.

Morant says there's a simple reason why she does the hard work of caregiving: "I made a promise to the Lord. If he gives me the health, the strength, the life to do for them. Take care of them, keep them from going in a home, I would do it. And as long as he gives it to me, I will give it to them."

The lifting, pulling, and all-through-the-night work of caregiving can take a physical toll on anyone.

Last fall, Morant got sick and was hospitalized for congestive heart failure.

Other family stepped in to take over the caregiving: a goddaughter from Baltimore, and her brother's son and his wife, who came to town from California.

When Morant got out of the hospital four days later, it wasn't clear whether she'd regain the strength to ever again care for her brother and sister.

"She still maintained that schedule where she'd get up three to four times a night," says Monica Thomas, a social worker for a medical program that cares for Morant's brother and sister. "I didn't think there was any way she could do that."

Thomas arranged for an aide to come in on the overnight shift, and after six weeks, Morant bounced back.

"She got better," says Thomas. "She did, miraculously. She improved. She really did."

Today, Thomas worries how long Morant can continue to provide good care to her brother and sister.

"It would be difficult for any person to do this," she says, "much less when you're 101 and have some medical conditions of your own. But it's also hard to tell whether or not the fact that she has this purpose is what's keeping her alive at 101 and what motivates her to get better and stay as strong as she possibly can."

Morant and her siblings all sleep just steps away from each other. Morant's fold-out couch is an arm's length from her sister's hospital bed. Their brother is steps away, on the other side of a thin glass door.

"Well, I don't get too much sleep," says Morant. "Some nights I sleep more than others. Some nights, I don't think [Laney] feels too good. She's restless. She's making noises. She'll call me. Either one of them makes a noise, I hear it."

Government programs, family, and friends help them get by.

On weekdays, Morant gets important assistance from in-home aides. One comes three hours on Monday, Wednesday, and Friday to care for her sister. Another aide cares for her brother, 12 hours a day, Monday through Friday.

There's also a neighbor who helps with meals and cleaning.

But at night and on Saturdays and Sundays, Morant is on her own, the lone caregiver for her sister and brother.

"I think they're getting superb care at home," says Dr. George Taler, Laney and Barber's doctor. Taler says his patients who go to nursing homes tend to die in about two years. Morant's brother and sister have lived much longer.

"Miss Laney is really at the end stages of Alzheimer's disease, and has been maintained at home now for many years," says Taler. "She is totally dependent and needs to be fed. She's been bedbound for more than 10 years. And Mr. Barber's had progressive strokes. The fact is, he's not deteriorating as fast as one would expect given his age and his illnesses."

Taler says the difference is Morant's close attention. The way—during the day—she pulls her sister to a sitting position. Just sitting up keeps muscles strong. The way Morant gets up at night to clean her brother and sister and help them move their bodies in bed. As a result, neither has gotten a bedsore. Bedsores, which are painful and sometimes even deadly breakdowns of the skin, can be common for such frail, elderly people.

Taler says it's not uncommon for family members—old or young—to do even most of the medical care.

"This happens with families. They couldn't conceive of themselves picking up on things like wound care or managing people on vents or feed-ing tubes. But when the need is there, they step up and find the ability to do that," says Tayler.

Morant's brother and sister can no longer speak. They can't say how they feel about their sister's continued devotion. And Morant—at 101—says she isn't sure what they'd say if they could.

"I really don't know," but probably, she adds, they'd say "thank you."

What happens to people as they grow old? What methods can we use to study old people—their bodies, their perceptions, their motivations, their relationship to society? These topics are the subject matter of gerontology. By omitting the physiology and biology of aging, we narrow the field to social aspects of aging. **Social gerontology,** the study of aging from a social-science perspective, has been recognized as a distinct area of study for less than 60 years. Aging and related subjects have received limited attention since the mid-1940s, but now the sharp rise in the number of older persons, along with their increased visibility, has increased interest in the development of theory and in research. Social gerontology will continue to grow in importance as it becomes increasingly able to explain the phenomenon of aging.

In an effort to explain aging, social gerontologists have developed numerous theories to examine how people respond to the aging process. Theoretical models most commonly used to explain social gerontology include seven theoretical perspectives most frequently referenced in academic journals: (1) social constructionist, (2) social exchange, (3) life course, (4), feminist, (5) age stratification (age and society), (6) political economy of aging, and (7) critical theory. These theories are summarized in Table 4.1 (Bengtson et al., 1997).

Scientists never entirely prove or disprove a theory. They merely develop greater confidence in the theory or move closer to rejecting it by proving that parts of it are untrue. Traditionally a theory does not rest on a single proposition but on a series of propositions, any one of which may be partially erroneous. Any single proposition contained in a theory, or hypothesis, can be subjected to testing by empirical research, which collects evidence that may or may not support the hypothesis. Through this testing, scientists formulate new questions that require further research. Also, social theories can be used to predict what would happen if society maintained its present course and to suggest ways the social world could be altered to achieve specific results. The **theoretical frameworks** we examine in this chapter attempt to identify the important factors in aging and offer guidelines for further inquiry.

Historical Foundations: Activity versus Disengagement

Controversy over two contradictory theories of aging shaped the field of social gerontology in the 1960s. Both activity theory and disengagement theory attempt to predict how one might respond to old age. Activity theory was the first social theory of aging, but only after the development of disengagement theory did it receive both its name and recognition as a distinct theory.

TABLE 4.1

Theoretical models in social gerontology

Theory	Description	Key Concepts
Social constructionist	Focuses on individual agency and social behavior within larger structures of society; interest in understanding individual processes of aging as influenced by social definitions and structures	Labeling; social breakdown theory; situational features of aging
Social exchange theories	Examines exchange behavior between people of different ages as a result of the shift in roles, skills, resources that accompanies aging	Social costs and benefits; social resources; interaction; reciprocity; social power
Life course perspective	Explains the dynamic, context, and process nature of aging; age-related transitions; social meaning of aging as a process; focus on individuals, cohorts, and groups	Developmental tasks; social time clocks; social ecology; life trajectories and transitions; age roles and norms
Feminist theories	As a primary organizing principle for social life across the life course, gender is a primary consideration in understanding aging and the aged	Gender stratification; power structures; macrolevel analysis of social institutions; social networks and caregiving; family work
Age stratification	Focuses on role of social structures in the process of aging, looking at age cohort movement across time; asychrony between structural and individual change over time; interdependence of age cohorts and social structures	Age cohorts; social structures; structural lag; cohort flow
Political economy of aging	Explains how interaction of economic and political forces determines how social resources are allocated; how variations in treatment and status of elderly are reflected in policy, economic trends	Structural constraints, control of social resources, marginalization, social class
Critical theory	Focuses on humanistic dimensions of aging; structural components of aging; interested in understanding subjective and interpretive dimensions of aging, processes creating practical change, and knowledge that helps people change	Positive models of aging; power, social action, and social meaning in aging

Source: Bengtson, Vern L., Burgess, Elisabeth O., & Parrott, Tonya M. (1997). Theory, explanation, and a third generation of theoretical development in social gerontology. *Journal of Gerontology, Social Sciences*, 52B (2), S72–S88.

These two somewhat opposing theoretical models remain central in social gerontology in part because they are intuitively compelling—that is, they appeal to our common sense about people, and they are easily understood and observed in our daily lives.

Activity Theory

Because it continues to be widely accepted by social scientists, as well as by many people working with the elderly, we can say that **activity theory** is still a dominant theoretical perspective.

HANDLING TRANSITIONS IN LIFE CAN BE TOUGH

SOMETIMES IT'S LIKE GOING THROUGH A FOG BANK

IT'S HARD TO SEE ANYTHING.

BUT PERSEVERE; EVEN THE THICKEST FOG

.... WILL BURN OFF!

Activity theory implies that social activity is the essence of life for all people of all ages. Early studies found that positive personal adjustment correlates highly with activity: the more active people are—mentally, physically, socially—the better adjusted they are. Early proponents of this theory believed that normal aging involves maintaining the activities and attitudes of middle age as long as possible. Any activities and roles that the individual has been forced to give up should be replaced with new activities. Activity theory predicts that those who are able to remain socially active will be more likely to achieve a positive self-image, social integration, and satisfaction with life, and that, therefore, they will probably age successfully.

The principles of activity theory are evident in the work of most gerontologists. The writings of Ernest Burgess from the 1940s show an orientation toward activity theory. Burgess, one of the founders of social gerontology, observed that the elderly had no real place; they were left out of social activity. He described old people as having a "**roleless role**" (Burgess, 1960). Burgess felt that it was neither necessary nor appropriate for elders to be excluded from socially meaningful activity. Instead, he felt that a new role for elders should include responsibilities and obligations that could lead to a productive existence and enhance society. This stance clearly implies support for the activity theory.

The roleless role, which indicates a lack of social functions, is similar to Durkheim's concept of anomie, a condition whereby some individuals in a society are in a normless state. These individuals lack a consensus on rules to guide their behavior and therefore receive no support or guidance from society. The result is that they are excluded from participation in social activities. If this exclusion were prevented, old age would be a satisfying period. This social critique, however, did not consider gender differences (a feminist theory model) or the meaning to the individual of active involvement (the critical gerontology model, see Table 4.1). When these considerations were included in more recent research, findings were more complex. Wright (1995), for example, found that men and women are most likely to report lowest feelings of anomie when their personal networks are composed of a relative balance of men and women—despite the inclination of people to form gender-segregated social networks. Rather than being able to trace well-being to a simpler concept of connectedness, then, research seems to indicate that analyses of the integration of an individual network into a larger community might be important to understanding how people maintain a sense of belonging and well-being as their social networks change.

Generally speaking, the last 50 years of research have found a positive correlation between being active and aging successfully. In many of these studies "successful aging" was defined in relation to life satisfaction: people with strong reports or measures of life satisfaction were considered to be aging "successfully." As the complexity of human aging has become clearer, however, questions have arisen about those life satisfaction studies: What is the relationship of other important factors to life satisfaction, such as health, gender, culture, socioeconomic status, and the desire to maintain active? Might not one person's internal experience of "activity" be different from another's, based on their histories and interests? What about different cultural expectations and gender differences? Indeed, Jacob and Guarnaccia (1997), in a study of life satisfaction and social engagement, suggested that the term life satisfaction is probably a misnomer, and that the condition might better be termed momentary contentment (p. 816). They concluded that the culture reinforces disengagement among elders; therefore, commitment to new goals and relationships is less necessary to psychological health in old age than it is in early life.

Recent studies find it unnecessary for elders to maintain the same high degree of activity they had in middle age in order to have a high degree of self-esteem and life satisfaction in old age. The concept of **planned behavior,** or the extent to which an individual *intends* to perform a behavior, has been developed recently for understanding *readiness for activity* (Courneya, 1995; Chodzko-Zajko, 1997). This deals with the internal meaning and motivation structure of the individual. Among some people, not being active will have a negative impact on self-esteem because they have a strong planned behavior related to that activity: I am committed to walking one mile a day again after I feel stronger. Another study looked at different categories of activities and found that only leisure activities exerted a positive effect on self-esteem (Reiters et al., 1995). The study further found gender differences in the types of activities in which an individual engaged: activities performed alone had a positive effect on men's self-esteem, but not women's; and among women, activities had a more positive effect on self-esteem when role commitment was high (Reiters et al., 1995). This highlights the vast individual differences

that must be kept in mind as we analyze age as a category. Activities, Reiters and colleagues concluded, *might* enable people to confirm their identities and participate in roles they highly value. In those cases, activity is likely to bolster self-esteem and life satisfaction.

Many older people seek a more relaxed lifestyle and are quite happy when they achieve it. For example, a 65-year-old woman may long for the time when she can work half-time instead of full-time, sleep in, and devote more time to her aerobics classes and to reading the newspaper at a local coffeehouse.

Disengagement Theory

Disengagement theory is an explicit theory developed through research and explained in the book *Growing Old* (1961) by Elaine Cumming and William E. Henry. This book, one of the best known in the history of social gerontology, contends that it is both normal and inevitable for people to decrease their activity and seek more passive roles as they age. Disengagement is a mutual withdrawal of the elderly from society and society from the elderly in order to ensure the optimal functioning of both the individual and society. Aging individuals, wishing to escape the stress of recognizing their own diminishing capacity, collaborate in the withdrawal.

The exact time and form of disengagement varies from individual to individual. The process involves loosening social ties through lessened social interaction. Knowing that the time preceding death is foreshortened, feeling that the life experience is narrowing, and sensing a loss of self-esteem all signal the onset of disengagement. Ultimately, society's need for persons with new energy and skills, rather than the wishes of the older individual, dictates when disengagement occurs. In other words, as people approach their 70s, they become gradually disengaged from society owing to their declining energy and their desire for role loss. After an initial period of anxiety and depression, they accept their new status as disengaged and regain a sense of tranquility and self-worth.

The disengagement theory has generated a great deal of criticism. Some say the theory is ethnocentric in that it reflects the bias of a male-dominant industrial society. Others have suggested that it discourages interventions to help old people. Still others have questioned why some elderly choose to disengage and others do not, contending that society pressures people into disengagement against their will. However, it must be remembered that the theory emerged from a particular context of social thought—one in which biology-as-destiny prevailed, and the extent to which a number of variables (such as gender, socioeconomic, and cultural factors) interacted with the process of aging was not yet clearly understood (Achenbaum & Bengtson, 1994).

> *The relation between biological and social factors is recognized in that physiological and psychological measures of capacity are . . . used [to study] the relation of declining capacity to problems of individual adjustment in old age.*
>
> Pollak, 1948

Do relationships and our need to be connected in order to maintain psychological well-being alter with time? Particularly in most recent research, support is emerging for a more complex form of disengagement. In 1994, Lars Tornstam used the term **gerotranscendence** to refer to the elderly as selectively investing in some relationships over others, rather than comprehensively withdrawing. In his model, elders do seem to disengage, but do so more at will, choosing where their priorities lie and divesting themselves of superfluous relationships to focus on a more transcendent view of experience. According to Quinnan (1997) in his study of elderly religious men:

> *Thus the elderly demonstrate a higher degree of autonomy by dispensing with forms of social intercourse which have little value for them. This exercise of autonomy, rather than breaking connectedness, selectively enhances those relationships which the gero-transcendent find filled with meaning. (p. 118)*

Gerotranscendence is rooted in stage theories such as Erikson's (see chapter 3), which postulates a movement from dependence to greater autonomy with maturity. From this perspective, growth in autonomy takes place through a shift in connections—for example, reducing connection (the process of individuating) from the family occurs among adolescents in conjunction with a growing connection with peers and people outside the family (Quinnan, 1997).

In a related line of inquiry, comfort in being alone was found to be related to lower depression, fewer physical symptoms, and greater life satisfaction in a survey of 500 U.S. adults in 1995 (Larson & Lee, 1995). This finding is also consistent with our intuitive observations: some people deal with stress by secluding themselves from social contact, spending time reflecting, and engaging in self-care activities. Clearly this does not imply that it is healthy to be involuntarily isolated from others, but consistent reports continue that people do spend less time with others as they age, and those who are able to enjoy this segment of their lives are better adjusted and have a greater sense of well-being. An anthropological study of patterns of interaction in a nursing home, where elders have little choice to pull away from social contact, showed residents to engage in what the author referred to as "sitting" time and "giving" time (Gamliel, 2001). Sitting time was characterized by silence in which "[residents] transcended the borders of past and future time to live in a 'sacred present' or a 'limbo' time" (p. 107). Giving time was characterized by "limitless concern" for the health and well-being of one another. The author concluded that "sitting time" and "giving time" combined to help residents transcend the circumstances of their own health and environment. In this way, the nursing home residents were able to maintain a higher degree of self-controlled social activity and thus a higher degree of life satisfaction than they would otherwise experience, consistent with Tornstam's theory of gerotranscendence (1997).

Spending time alone, in thoughtful reflection, can be cherished time for some elders.

> *The habit of retiring into myself eventually made me immune to the ills that beset me.*
>
> JEAN-JACQUES ROUSSEAU, 1778

Some research finds that disengagement occurs at differing rates and in different aspects of behavior. Other research indicates that it is the increased physical and social stress that can accompany aging, rather than age per se, that creates disengagement. One commentator observed that the very model of the Great American Individualist is one who can move on, cut all losses, and leave situations (including people) that are not sustaining (Harris, 1996). His advice in support of "quitters"—a nonscientific term for disengagement—included being reasonable (think about the process) and going slow (ease from one set of priorities to another set). We have cultural support for disengaging from one set of activities in order to do something else, Harris's comments suggest, and his light recommendations to "quitters" are remarkably consistent with more serious explorations of human connectedness and well-being.

Despite these more positive findings, the controversy over disengagement theory continues. Unanswered questions remain about each of the major aspects of disengagement: the role of the individual, the role of society, and satisfaction versus dissatisfaction with disengagement.

The role of the individual

Disengagement is not inevitable with old age. Some elders disengage; others do not. Yet, according to disengagement theory, the individual's inner processes lead to a loosening of social ties, which is a relatively natural process. This process is "primarily intrinsic, and secondarily responsive" (Cumming & Henry, 1961). Research should perhaps concentrate on the very old. If disengagement is a process preparing both the individual and society for the ultimate release of the elderly member, why should it begin at the relatively early age of 65? If disengagement is in fact a developmental task of old age, perhaps it actually begins in the 80s or 90s, when one is nearer death. We do not universally enter stages of life at a given age.

The role of society

According to disengagement theory, society must withdraw from its older members to ensure the smooth operation and survival of the social system. Yet one can question this assumption. That disengaging older people from employment or other active roles is in society's best interest remains to be demonstrated. One might easily argue that the disengagement of older people is wasteful or dysfunctional because it removes many experienced, knowledgeable, and capable members. One might just as well speak of society excluding its older members as disengaging them; perhaps the older people who withdraw are merely reacting to a society that would exclude them anyway.

Disengagement: Positive or negative?

Neither activity theory nor disengagement theory fully explains successful or well-adjusted aging. More variables must be examined to explain why some people are happy in an active old age whereas others are content to narrow their activities and involvement in life. Getting rid of negative or unrewarding activities and events alone does not seem to be adequate to promote well-being—it seems to also take specifically positive interactions to promote a healthy existence (Stallings et al., 1997). This implies that eliminating (disengaging from) interactions that are not satisfying in order to pursue satisfying activities is an indicator of appropriate and positive aging, as long as something satisfying is added. Those newer activities being engaged in, however, might very well include exploring solitude (Larson, 1997).

Psychological Well-Being

Well-being itself is a complex variable. It is one of the most popular, most persistently investigated issues in the social scientific study of aging. A major focus in gerontology over the last 50 years has been to define and measure well-being and to identify factors that will increase it in the older population. Generally speaking, well-being means feeling good, or having good mental health. Oftentimes, researchers use the phrase subjective well-being. The word subjective indicates a personal evaluation based on how the respondent feels, not an evaluation based on external criteria, such as visits to mental hospitals or psychologists' evaluations.

Psychological well-being is a broad term that has different meanings for different social scientists. Linda George (1981) offered a definition that differentiated among three concepts that measure well-being—morale (courage, discipline, confidence, enthusiasm, etc.), happiness (mood of gaiety or euphoria), and **life satisfaction** (an assessment of overall conditions

of existence or progress toward desired goals). One critical reason to develop a clear definition of well-being is to develop assessment tools to help elders and people working with elders to make the best decisions (George, 2005). An assessment describes the client in terms of characteristics relevant to the service being offered and gathers the information needed to tailor programs specifically to the needs of an individual. Cummins (1996) further defined life satisfaction as "subjective life quality" and identified seven domains of satisfaction: material well-being, health, productivity, intimacy, safety, community, and emotional well-being. This definition includes psychological security as well as physical and environmental security and well-being. In the helping professions, merely knowing how a person interprets his or her life situation is not adequate. Understanding the different domains of that sense of quality of life can help the individual and the helper to better focus on strengths and needs.

The Life Satisfaction Index A (LSIA), the most frequently used scale in social gerontology, offers another method of defining well-being. One of the best-known instruments for measuring well-being, the LSIA, as originally developed by Neugarten et al. (1961), consisted of 20 items representing five components: zest for life versus apathy; resolution and fortitude versus merely accepting that which life has given; congruence between desired and achieved goals; self-concept; and mood tone of optimism versus pessimism.

Researchers continue to refine the LSIA. They still debate whether the scale is **valid** (whether it measures what it is supposed to measure) and **reliable** (whether its results are consistent). They also continue to question whether the scale is unidimensional (measuring only the concept of life satisfaction) or multidimensional (measuring more than one concept). Table 4.2 shows the model developed from the LSIA measure by Liang (1984) to identify the three domains of mood tone, zest for life, congruence, and a generalized "other" category.

TABLE 4.2

A proposed use of the 20 LSIA items

Agree or Disagree with Each Item

Mood tone
  This is the dreariest time of my life.
  I am just as happy now as when I was younger.
  My life could be happier than it is now.
  These are the best years of my life.
  Compared to other people, I get down in the dumps too often.

Zest for life
  As I look back on my life, I am fairly well satisfied.
  I would not change my past life even if I could.
  I have gotten pretty much what I expected out of my life.
  I have gotten more breaks in life than most of the people I know.
  When I think back over my life, I didn't get most of the important things I wanted.

Other items (originated by Neugarten)
  In spite of what people say, the lot of the average person is getting worse.
  I feel my age but it does not bother me.
  Compared to other people my age, I've made a lot of foolish decisions in my life.

Note that this measure deals less with the context and more with the internal meaning the individual makes of his or her life.

Some studies, combining personal narrative with the psychometric measure LSIA, report that life satisfaction appears to be the construct being measured (Hawkins et al., 1995; Rosen et al., 1995; Sherrard, 1997). Other researchers believe that the measure taps a multidimensional concept that contains life satisfaction but does not measure that alone (Kahana et al., 1995).

The items in the LSIA, however, do seem to provide us with a general overview of a person's psychological well-being. Increasingly, current research in the United States seems to converge on the domains of positive interactions, negative interactions, and stress management as primary factors in life satisfaction and well-being (Kahana et al., 1995; Krause, 1995; Glass & Jolly, 1997; Lawton, 1997). This research is consistent with findings from other industrialized countries as well (Liang et al., 1992; Shmotkin & Hadari, 1996; Allain et al., 1996). This convergence of research concludes that the presence of negative interactions is separate from positive self-assessment. Eliminating negative conditions in life doesn't in and of itself promote well-being. It reduces depression, low self-esteem, and general negative mood tone. But it takes positive interactions and conditions to have high life satisfaction and to experience well-being. Clearly much work needs to be done on the concept of happiness in life: if we had the key to well-being, we could use it to create more happiness for everyone.

Morale and well-being in later life have been extensively studied. Studies by Neal Krause (1991, 1995) have tested the relationship between general evaluations of life satisfaction and evaluations of specific domains. Krause presented two hypotheses. The "top-down" hypothesis suggested that a person's ongoing sense of satisfaction with life as a whole predisposes him or her to develop similar feelings about specific domains such as health and employment. The "bottom-up" hypothesis maintained that satisfaction with the specific areas of one's life synthesize to form an overall sense of satisfaction with life as a whole. Krause, whose findings supported this latter theory, expresses concern that survey self-assessment scales are the major tools used to study subjective well-being.

Current life satisfaction research includes a broad range of predictors of high morale and life satisfaction indicators, reflecting the theoretical perspective of the investigator. These include activities, relationships, health, and income (Kahana et al., 1995); subjective health and health self-image (Sherrard, 1997); reduced barriers to participation (Hawkins et al., 1995); having a spouse, participating in community activities, and interacting with friends; and interacting

Most elders choose to remain actively engaged with friends and in the community. Shared lifetime experiences form the basis for meaningful relationships in later life.

with one's children (Hong & Duff, 1997). Ardelt (1997), summarizing research on wisdom (Pascual-Leone, 1990; Achenbaum & Bengston, 1993), made a particularly strong argument for including the construct of wisdom in studies of life satisfaction. "I [propose] that people experience satisfaction and a sense of fulfillment in old age as a consequence of achieving greater wisdom over the life course and that wisdom, rather than objective life conditions, explains most of the variation in life satisfaction during old age" (p. P16). In her argument, happiness in later life is strongly related to the life we have lived and to the way we integrate it with our present sense of self.

That body of literature also contains predictors of low morale and life satisfaction, including limited choice, limited responsibility, limited social resources, poor physical health, lack of personal meaning, and lack of optimism (Reker, 1997); as well as envy, a need to control, complaining and critical thought, a sense of entitlement, regret, perfectionism, and unrealistically high expectations (Hosen, 1996). Eliminating predictors of low morale does not create high life satisfaction, but it does seem to be strongly associated with health.

Clinical observations and qualitative data derived from narrative methodologies will add an important and perhaps clarifying perspective to the burgeoning body of knowledge about morale and life satisfaction. It is one thing to measure someone's attitudes and feelings; it is quite another to systematically record that person's self-perception. The field is poised to take on the latter charge.

Structural-Functional Frameworks

Sociologists study society—social factors such as values, norms, roles, social structures, institutions, stratification, and subcultures. Social gerontologists study these factors as they affect elders. The studies that fall under this broad category delve into every social group in an older person's life. Studies have included economic structure, the family, race, and demography. Studies on the historical context of aging, the media, work, friendship, and communication networks provide data on the social context of aging.

Sociological theories of aging use the same concepts as those used in contemporary general sociological theory. One dominant framework in sociological theory is the structural-functional framework, which views societies as systems and subsystems of social rules and roles. Members become socialized by internalizing the social system's norms and values, and the entire system functions in a reasonably orderly fashion if its structures are organized and intact. The activity theory of aging and the disengagement theory are structural-functional in that they deal with systems of rules and roles for the aged in society. Three more structural-functional concepts for understanding aging are here: considered age stratification, role theory, and age grading.

Age Stratification

The **age stratification** theory studies older persons in relation to all other age groups, or age strata, in a society, examining the differences between the age strata and studying the way in which society allocates opportunities, social roles, rights, privileges, status, power, and entitlements on the basis of age. The persons in an age stratum have similar characteristics because they are at the same stage in the life course and share a common history. Changing social environments produce different patterns of ad-

© Gary Walts / The Image Works

Being alone does not necessarily mean being lonely. Here a businessman reads while enjoying a quiet lunch.

aptation in successive age groups, and cultures vary in the extent to and manner in which they are stratified by age (Bowling, 1997; Liu et al., 1995). Age stratification theory has been used to explain power and status inequities between young and old in given societies. For example, sociologists have used the theory to analyze the power—and lack of it—in younger generations in China.

Roles, Gender, and Ethnicity

Role is one of the most basic concepts in all of sociology, one that you will find used in almost every sociological framework. Sociologists are quick to point out that the word role is a concept, not a theory. A role is a status or position, which carries known attributes, accorded to an individual in a given social system. "Doctor," "mommy," "sports fan," and "churchgoer" are all roles.

In studies of aging we find analysis of age roles, role transitions, role acquisitions, role relinquishment, and socialization to and from roles (Dannefer & Uhlenberg, 1999; Quadagno & Reid, 1999). Roles are modified, redefined, and transformed as people age. Roles in marriage, families, careers, and community change throughout the life course. The interplay of race, gender, and ethnicity serve to shape life opportunities and lifestyles. They have formal roles in institutional settings such as schools and hospitals and more informal roles in less structured settings such as friendship and neighboring. Role exit was once a major focus of aging studies, but role transition now seems a more appropriate term.

Gender roles have to do with the cultural aspects of being male or female. Being male and female in every culture is linked to specific roles, attitudes, and behaviors. Because aging men and women are looked on differently in our society and in other cultures around the world, the study of gender is very important. Clearly, the experience of being old is a different one for men than it is for women.

Ethnic diversity has become a major focus of gerontology. **Ethnicity** refers to one's identification with a subgroup in society having a unique set of values, traditions, or language, often originating in another country. The role of ethnicity as it affects aging and the aged is often overlooked in the studies of gerontology. Particularly among earlier studies, generalizations were made on the basis of white, middle-class respondents, but clearly these generalizations did not apply to all racial and ethnic groups. Numerous international studies are now adding richness to our understanding of aging (Liu et al., 1995; Allain et al., 1996; Shmotkin & Hadari, 1996; Bowling et al., 1995), and newer studies of cultural groups within the United States (Liang et al., 1992; Uehara, 1995; Guyotte, 1997) further develop a true understanding of the experience of all U.S. elders. Looking at older people in diverse groups has added to the richness and complexity of the research of aging.

Age Grading

We live in an age-graded society. **Age grading** means that age is a prime criterion in determining the opportunities people may enjoy. Our age partially establishes the roles we may play. Both children and old people are welcomed to or barred from various opportunities because of the often stereotyped images that society forms of the young and the old. Such beliefs often prevent the young and the old from expressing individual differences and thereby lead to injustices. In other words, older people may be less active not because of their biology or the aging process, but because they are expected to present an image of idleness; indeed, social roles sometimes do not permit elders to be active and involved. Role expectations at various age levels are called **age norms**. Society pressures individuals to engage in activities such as marriage, schooling, and child rearing at socially approved ages. One way to determine the presence of age norms would be to ask questions such as the following:

- Would you approve of a woman who decided to have a child at age 42? Age 60?
- Would you approve of a couple who moved across the country to live near their married children when the couple was 50? 65? What about 80?

Answers to these and similar questions would reveal age norms for child rearing and other activities. Age norms affecting the older population can be studied by asking a sample group whether situations such as the following are appropriate or inappropriate:

- A very old man buys and drives a flashy new sports car
- An older woman dresses in very modern youth fashion, including a nose ring
- A couple in their 70s sunbathe on a public beach in their bikinis

We can view age norms as a form of social control. If one follows the age norms, one receives approval; if not, disapproval and possibly negative sanctions result.

Studies show a continuing shift toward a loosening of age grading and age norms in the United States. Lives are becoming more fluid. There is no longer a definite age at which one marries, enters the labor market, goes to school, or has children. It no longer surprises us to hear of a 23-year-old computer company owner, a 34-year-old governor, a 36-year-old grandmother, or a retiree of 52. No one is shocked at a 60-year-old college student, a 50-year-old man who becomes a father for the first time, or an 80-year-old who launches a new business. Our ever-advancing technologies continue to test and stretch the limits of what people find acceptable—for example, medical developments now permit the implantation of a fertilized donated egg in a postmenopausal woman.

Age Groupings
Studying Cohorts and Generations

Studies of cohorts and generations are conducted by demographers, sociologists who study social change, and social psychologists studying the life course. A major problem in understanding age differences is determining whether change is due to "age" or "period" effects. A change due to an age effect is caused by maturation, that is, biological change from the physical aging process. Period effects are changes in different age groups resulting from historical events that have affected one age group differently than another.

Age Cohort

For our purposes, an **age cohort** is a group of individuals exposed to a similar set of life experiences and historical events. Demographers often use cohort analysis to compare groups of people born during specific time periods, usu-

ally separated by 5- or 10-year intervals. We expect that age cohorts will show similarities to one another. Cohort analysis permits the sociologist to study the effects that events or demographics may have on a broad group of individuals, all of whom have experienced the same events at a similar state of biological and physical development.

With the tendency of the media to homogenize social groups, a cultural image has evolved of baby boomers as the free-loving hippie generation that dodged the draft, protested against the Vietnam War, attended Woodstock, and enjoyed economic prosperity (Williams et al., 1997). Likewise, young adult cohorts in their 20s have been referred to by the media as **Generation X** (Keil, 1998). The "twentysomethings" who represent Generation X are stereotyped as whiners and slackers, complaining about the national debt they have inherited and totally unappreciative of "how good they have it." This cohort has watched more television and as a result has probably witnessed more violence and murder than any generation in history; its members have passed more time alone as young children, and it is the first generation to have spent considerable time in day care (Losyk, 1997). Many of them grew up with stepparents, stepsiblings, half-siblings, and with both parents in full-time employment.

Generation X is the smallest cohort since the early 1950s and is thus labeled a "baby bust" generation, as opposed to their boomer parents. They are the first generation in the United States to be smaller than the generation that precedes them (Williams et al., 1997). For this reason, their chances in the job market are increased, and if the higher productivity of American business continues into the new century, and if homes stay affordable, Generation X should do well compared with the cohorts before them (Miniter, 1997).

Another important first with the Generation X cohort: the media are profoundly powerful in their lives. All of the characterizations outlined above are media created and media reinforced. Social scientists have been woefully silent as characterizations have been reinforced into stereotypes of all the generational cohorts.

Despite the many similarities in individuals as members of cohorts, the result of their growing into maturity within a specific cultural and economic moment in history, the differences among people remain greater than their similarities, and the reminder to avoid overgeneralization must be restated. Subgroups within a cohort experience the world in different ways based on such variables as class, gender, ethnic background, or region of residence

Generations and Events

The concept of a **generation** is more complex than the concept of a cohort. The print and electronic media have used the term widely (and loosely) to indicate the differences in values between parents and children (the so-called generation gap). Others have used the term to identify the values of those who are older or younger than some arbitrary age—the "over-30 generation" or the "under-30 generation," for instance. Historians and sociologists have applied the term in additional ways. For them, the term generation may mean distinctive life patterns and values as they emerge by age, or it may connote not only distinctive life patterns but also a collective mentality that sets one age group apart from another.

Karl Mannheim (1952, 1993) formulated the latter definition and described the process by which group consciousness of generations develops. According to Mannheim, generations are not an arbitrarily defined number of years imposed by researchers; instead, they represent a reflection of historical events and social change. For example, the invention of the automobile may have led to the formation of two generations—those who grew up with access to cars and those who did not. And children's use of computers may lead non-computer-using parents to feel as if they are truly from another generation in this sense.

An age group that has lived through a major social event, such as the Great Depression, may exhibit characteristics that are not due to internal or biological aging and that are not found in other age groups. The impact of widespread social events on their survivors has not received enough systematic investigation, even though events that your parents or you have experienced may well continue to influence your lives. What, for example, are the effects of having lived through the Vietnam or Watergate era? The wars in the Persian Gulf? If you were a young adult during the Iran-contra affair or the savings and loan crisis, will you be more skeptical of politicians than your children, assuming no comparable incidents occur in their early adulthood? Would a young adult of the Vietnam War era be less patriotic than you, if you were a young adult during the post-9/11 war in Iraq? If so, one might conclude that events, rather than the aging process, made you more skeptical or more patriotic. Events of our younger years play an especially important role in shaping feelings and attitudes that persist throughout our lives.

According to Mannheim, broad social movements, including somewhat trivial changes in fads and fashions, are concrete manifestations of a generation's social reality. Consequently, if social change is rapid, then different generations could theoretically appear every few years. Conversely, if social change is slow, then the same generation might exist for several decades. **Mannheim's "generation"** is defined quite specifically: birth cohorts do not form "true generations" unless they develop not only a distinctive life pattern but also a collective identity and a political consciousness of themselves as a unique group.

Some social scientists speak of the post–World War II generation, as opposed to the World War II generation, in the sense Mannheim describes. Those who remember the patriotism that World War II generated are not the same as those who were born too late to have experienced it. The post–World War II generation is described as less patriotic, less traditional, more alienated, and more skeptical of war. Collectively, in contrast, those who experienced World War II are more optimistic about the U.S. role in world politics and political leadership and show more

What gives meaning in life depends on the individual. For many people, grandchildren are a profound source of meaning.

© James L. Shaffer

support and respect for the president. During the 1991 war in the Persian Gulf, this patriotic mentality seemed to assert itself once again: perhaps a new "generation" was born. Social commentators define as a "new" generation those who use computerized equipment—computers, digital cameras, satellite TV, digital music players—with ease. New technologies can indeed make one feel a generation removed, hopelessly dated and at odds with changing times. With motivation and training, however, one can join the new generation.

Lineage

Sociologists use the concept **lineage** to discuss generations within families. Parents transmit values to children, and continuity or discontinuity may distinguish the transmission of specific values within a particular family or families. Social, political, or technological events may intervene in this transmission and thereby alter roles and values within the family context. Consequently, the authority of older family members may be strengthened, weakened, or changed in a way that also alters parent-child relationships.

Given the increase in life expectancy in the United States today, four- and even five-generation families are quite common. Although this interaction of family members can be a source of great personal enrichment, differences in values can produce tension and conflict among the family's generations. These value differences may be a source of age prejudice, or ageism, within the family. We may reduce these age prejudices in our own families by understanding the social and historical development of other family members' generations.

Explaining the Generation Gap

When a **generation gap** exists between young adults of, say, 20 and adults age 50 and over, the cause may be biological maturation, historical or social events, or personal change such as education.

Biology

A 50-year-old mother may have acted like her 20-year-old daughter or son when she was the same age. That 20-year-old child may, in the process of aging, take on the same traits as the mother's. Thus, this generation gap between mother and child may be the result of differences in biological maturation or the biological aging process.

Historical and Social Events

Suppose a mother grew up in a conservative time period when say, early marriage was expected for women. We would probably label her values traditional. We would consider her child, who grew up in a later time period that might be called more liberal, as having modern values—for example, a couple that lives together instead of getting married. In this case, history or social events cause the generation gap.

Social change may be a major cause of age prejudice, principally because the more rapid the social change, the greater the possibility of value clashes. Social observers may sometimes overestimate the rapidity of social change. Studies have shown that basic value orientations remain fairly constant across several generations. For example, analysis of the generation gap in the late 1960s, a time of considerable social unrest, showed that politically liberal students tended to have politically liberal parents. Thus, measured in terms of differences between a specific parent and child, the generation gap of the 1960s was not as extreme as it appeared overall. The generation gap in such countries as Israel, Russia, and Korea is greater than the gap in the United States because value systems for the young and the old show greater extremes in these countries and because many of these countries are undergoing rapid social change.

Personal Change

A generation gap caused by personal change is an individual matter that does not necessarily reflect widespread cultural changes. If one child, for example, moves from a cattle ranch to the city to get an education and, upon returning to visit her parents, announces that she is now a vegetarian and that killing animals is morally wrong, the cattle-raising father may comment with exasperation about the "generation gap" between himself and his daughter. This single occurrence, however, is an example of shifting values within a family. It does not necessarily reflect a larger social pattern indicating that young people are becoming vegetarians. It is therefore not consistent with Mannheim's use of the term generation.

Although a number of studies have examined generational differences, most have focused on middle-aged parents and children. Few have focused on the very old. A generation gap can exist between middle-aged offspring and their parents, or between elders and their grandchildren or great-grandchildren. We generally think of young people when we hear the "generation gap." But differences between the beliefs and values of the middle-aged and oldsters can be as real as the differences between the beliefs and values of the old and the young.

Cross-Sectional versus Longitudinal Studies

Two helpful methods of studying different cohorts or generations have been cross-sectional and longitudinal studies. A **cross-sectional study** samples, at a given point in time, persons belonging to different cohorts or generations and observes the differences. **Longitudinal studies,** in contrast, sample individuals or cohorts and follow them over a long period of time. In general, longitudinal studies have been more fruitful than cross-sectional studies in analyzing change over the life course, because social scientists have drawn many erroneous conclusions by using cross-sectional studies of different age groups at a single point in time.

In general, longitudinal research is more accurate than cross-sectional research. Although cross-sectional research offers the social scientist the unique opportunity of simultaneously studying the young, the middle-aged, and the old, it cannot account for the *process* of change. Differences in attitude or behavior may be due to the aging process or to other factors, but cause and effect are quite difficult to determine in a cross-sectional study. For example, if old persons attend church more often than younger people, can we assume that individuals become more religious with age? Not really. The older people have possibly always been faithful in attending church, even as youngsters; and the young who do not now attend church also may

TABLE 4.3

Longitudinal study method

Three cohorts are studied in the year 2000. Those same cohorts are studied 20 years later.

Year of study: 2000	Cohort 1: 20-year-olds	Cohort 2: 40-year-olds	Cohort 3: 60-year-olds
Year of study: 2020	Cohort 1: 40-year-olds	Cohort 2: 60-year-olds	Cohort 3: 80-year-olds

not do so in old age. Longitudinal studies are superior to studies conducted at any given point in time because they can follow the change (or lack of change) in individuals.

Generalizing about cause and effect may become more reliable with longitudinal study. Several years ago, an assumption that IQ decreased with age was based on cross-sectional studies that showed older people to have lower IQs than younger adults. However, these older individuals had left school at a relatively young age during an era when many children did not have an opportunity to attend high school, such as people usually have today. Differences in education (a cohort effect) explained much of the presumed decline found in the cross-sectional studies. In fact, longitudinal studies show that IQ does not decrease with age but remains stable into one's 70s. Many of our misconceptions about aging may be blamed on cross-sectional research.

Separating the effects of age (maturation that comes with the aging process), period (history and events), and cohort (differences in social class, education, and occupation) can be difficult. To do so, one must first consider cross-sectional differences, then longitudinal differences. Let us use Table 4.3 as an example. The top row of 20-year-olds, 40-year-olds, and 60-year-olds represents one cross-sectional study, which could compare all three age groups at once in 1990. The downward arrows, in contrast, represent longitudinal studies. A study using the model in Table 4.3 would provide a basis for many interesting comparisons and would produce findings about the effects of the aging process, "the times" (external social forces), and cohort differences. If such a model were used to study

voting behavior, fear of aging, personal contentment with life, or political alienation, what do you think the results would show? In the final analysis, one would have:

One cohort of 20-year-olds

Two cohorts of 40-year-olds

Two cohorts of 60-year-olds

One cohort of 80-year-olds

Comparisons could be made within and between all these groups. If, for example, the two groups of 40-year-olds scored dramatically differently on a political alienation scale, one could assume that the time period during which they were raised, not biological aging, was a key factor. These massive studies incorporating both cross-sectional and longitudinal approaches may allow us to unravel the complicated effects of age, period, and cohort differences.

Exchange Theory

Exchange theory is based on the premises that individuals and groups act to maximize rewards and minimize costs; that such interaction will be maintained if it continues to be more rewarding than costly; and that when one person is dependent on another, the first person loses power. This model explains decreased interaction between the old and the young in terms of the older generation having fewer resources to offer in the social exchanges and thus less to bring to the encounter (Dowd, 1975; Bengtson & Dowd, 1981).

Power is thus derived from imbalances in social exchange. Social exchanges are more than

People from several generations combine forces in a Walk to End Hunger. Here participants stop for lunch during a daylong walk.

economic transactions. They involve psychological satisfaction and need gratification. Though this perspective sounds rather cold and calculating, social life according to exchange theory is a series of exchanges that add to or subtract from one's store of power and prestige. The concept has become particularly useful recently in studies of leadership (Williams et al., 1996; Gerstner & Day, 1997) and of friendship (Burger et al., 1997; Roberto, 1997).

The first gerontologist to apply exchange theory was J. David Martin (1971), who used the theory to aid in understanding visiting patterns among family members. Some older individuals have little power. Families feel an obligation to visit but may not really want to. The older person's persistent complaints that relatives do not visit may motivate some visiting behavior, but the complaints may also decrease any pleasure and satisfaction felt by those who visit. Those elders who have other sources of power, such as financial resources or having interesting stories to tell, are in a better position. In fact, they could hold "power" positions over "dependent" relatives. Similar equity considera-

tions have been applied to the study of shifts in roles, skills, and resources that accompany advancing age (Hendricks, 1995). Another way of discussing change is to use a concept popular among anthropologists: reciprocity. The **norm of reciprocity** involves maintaining balance in relationships by paying for goods or deeds with equivalent goods or deeds. It is a social rule that requires us to return favors to those who do something nice for us. It does not imply an open-ended obligation to return a favor. Rather, it requires only that acts of kindness be returned within a reasonable period of time (Burger et al., 1997). It can be applied in business or in relationships with family and friends For example, I'll trade you this radio and five cassettes for that stereo: the goods' values are equal; we're "balanced." The goods might be less tangible: I will come to stay with your frail mother while you go shopping, because you were there for me when my husband was ill; a kindness is exchanged for a kindness. One study used exchange theory to interpret differences over time in a group of older women's close friendships (Roberto, 1997). They found that the essential elements of the women's friendships (understanding, affection, trust, and acceptance) endured over time, although the balance of the exchanges of those elements shifted: I can be trusted to keep your confidence because, in the past, I have been able to trust you.

Some groups in society are unable to repay what they receive—children and mentally disabled people are two examples. In these cases, beneficence becomes the norm. The person who does the giving in this case does not expect a material reward but does expect love or gratitude. The **norm of beneficence** calls into play such nonrational sentiments as loyalty, gratitude, and faithfulness. The norm is particularly relevant for care providers of frail and vulnerable people. One study comparing the use of restraints in chronic and acute patient care found that fewer restraints and a greater range of alternatives were used by chronic care nurses (Bryant & Fernald, 1997). The authors concluded that the differences were due in part to the norm of beneficence that chronic care nurses must honor to be effective in their professions.

Dowd (1984) asserts that the very old—but not the young old—in our society benefit from the norm of beneficence. He directs his attention not to personal relationships but to social ones, noting that benefits from the government, such as Medicaid, Meals on Wheels, and other social services are being less strongly supported and becoming increasingly unavailable to the young old. In a classic analysis of interactions made more than four decades ago, Gouldner (1960) distinguished between reciprocity as a pattern of social exchange and reciprocity as a general moral belief. The reciprocity norm dictates that one not gain at the expense of another's beneficial acts (a moral belief). **Equity theory** suggests that people react equally negatively to under- and to overbenefiting. Balanced benefit is the moral standard. Studies on African American women, midwestern rural elderly, and the very old in Appalachia, however, conclude that people have far greater concern about overbenefiting, or being on the receiving end of the

balance (McCulloch & Kivet, 1995; Uehara, 1995). This finding has implications both for service providers and for those who receive senior services. Exchange theory and the norms of reciprocity and beneficence remain valuable concepts for understanding the position of elders. We can apply exchange theory at a small-group level, between one older individual and another person, or at a societal level.

Meaning in Everyday Life

Studies of the meaning in everyday life come to us from philosophy, phenomenology, symbolic interaction, and social psychology. The studies that form this body of information are diverse, but they intersect at the point of seeking to understand, from person to person, the meaning we attach to living our lives and the communications we have with others. Symbolic interaction, for example, examines the way in which people attach meaning to their own behavior. This meaning is based partly on their perceptions of others with whom they interact.

Gerontologists concerned with psychological well-being are becoming increasingly concerned with what aging means to the individual experiencing it. One scholar describes the findings of old age as a paradox: although old age is often negatively described as a marginal status, this seems to have little effect on the everyday lives and feelings of older people (Ward, 1984). Old age may be derogated, yet old people are often happy with themselves and their circumstances. Ward explains this paradox with the term **salience**—the degree to which something is central, important, or meaningful. If age is not salient to older people, they may not think about their age or feel the marginal status they supposedly hold. Older individuals may not feel that their age is a prominent trait, even though gerontologists and others think it is.

Learning what is salient to individuals requires listening to what they say. What elders have to say frequently emerges in the telling of stories—of sorting through memories, making sense of the present in terms of the past. This is the artful skill of drawing from the community and from past experience to help construct a positive self-image in the present (Encandela, 1997). The meanings represented in life stories might be work in progress, might already be a clear part of the individual's meaning structure, or might represent a dilemma on which the individual is working—aspects of the self that are not yet coherent or well integrated (Luborsky, 1993).

In life stories, the narrator shows how [an] event takes on new meaning as the self is realigned in relation to some larger collective body and ideology.

GINSBURG & HEINEMANN, 1989

In a recent study designed to test psychometric measures, an interesting finding emerged that is remarkably consistent with phenomenological research, which pulls its conclusions from people's own voices. Van Ranst and Marcoen (1997) began their research with the premise that one's need for personal meaning should increase with age. Their findings, based on statistical analysis of the Life Regard Index, concluded that there were age differences in the experienced meaning in life. The older the individual, the better able was that person to see life within some perspective, and the more that person considered him or herself as having fulfilled or as being in the process of fulfilling life goals. Young adults, on the other hand, seemed to experience less meaning in life than did the elders. Perhaps the *work* of making meaning was less salient for the young adults than it was for the older adults. Examples of the 30 items in the measure are purpose in living, clear direction, philosophy of life, accomplishment, attainment of goals, and the value of potential (Debats et al., 1993).

Older people may not feel that their age changes their circumstances or their personal "worlds." Age is, in essence, irrelevant to who they are. To better understand aging as experienced by those who are aged, gerontologists need to understand more clearly when age is relevant to individuals, what the consequences of that relevance is, and what the function of friendship networks is in aging.

Many studies of meaning in everyday life derive their basic approach from the school of sociological theory known as phenomenology. The **phenomenological theory** of aging is primarily concerned with the meaning that life and growing old have for aging people. Rather than constructing a theory about aging, phenomenologists attempt to define growing old through close association with those who are actively participating in the process. A major methodology of the phenomenological approach is to observe older people. Rather than, say, give the elders statements with which to agree or disagree, this approach would let their words or actions speak for themselves.

Sociologists have lived in the settings they studied. Early in the history of social gerontology, Gubrium (1975) constructed the meaning of living in a nursing home by documenting the lives of the participants, who included patients, residents, staff, administrators, and visitors. Jacobs (1975) followed a similar strategy in studying two other housing arrangements for elders—a middle-class retirement community and a high-rise apartment building in an urban environment. His more recent studies have focused on aspects of everyday life of which people have little conscious awareness—the small routine aspects of life. His studies direct attention to the "nontrivial nature of trivia"—the everyday, taken-for-granted knowledge, skills, and interactions of which most social life is composed (Jacobs, 1994).

Whether the study takes a phenomenological approach or not, researchers who study meaning in everyday life typically try to use techniques that do not allow the researcher's perspective or presence to influence the subjects' words and actions. The goal is to encourage respondents to articulate a life perspective free of any bias the researcher's theoretical framework might cause.

A significant study using phenomenological methods entitled *The Ageless Self: Sources of Meaning in Late Life* was published in 1986 by Sharon Kaufman. Kaufman used open-ended questions as she conducted lengthy interviews with 60 aged people in their own homes. In studying the 60 people, Kaufman looked for themes that arose from *their* voices—not her theory—to discover what gave them a sense of life meaning. What Kaufman discovered was what she called an "ageless self."

For 80-year-old Millie, life gained its meaning from close, emotional ties:

My mother cherished me. . . . I adored my father and he clung to me. . . . I adored my principal. . . . I was attached to the other children in the neighborhood. I took care of all of them. . . . I loved my piano teacher. . . . (Kaufman, 1986, p. 34)

Millie's meaning in life came from the positive feelings she got from relationships with others.

For others, meaning in life came from a variety of sources: making money, overcoming alcoholism, or achieving status. Dorfman's study (1994) of Franklin Village is, in her words,

a personal odyssey into the inner experience of aging. The journey began with my immersion into a community of elders and the honing of my observational skills. It ends with a clearer understanding of the phenomenology of aging—one that is divested of ageist myths and stereotypes and that highlights the significance of aspirations and values in late life. (p. xiii)

Franklin Village is a continuing-care retirement community in which the researcher lived, and she took part in the daily life of the community. What resulted is an ethnography (field research study) encompassing in-depth interviews, case studies, and participant observation.

Eighty-one residents shared their aspirations with her in both prearranged interviews and informal chats. When she left, she had spent 1,000 hours talking to people who ultimately became her friends, in addition to providing her with a look into the inner experience of aging. Examples of residents' aspirations were to be independent, to have new experiences, to have intimate contact, to recreate past experiences, and to have a quick, easy death when the time came (Dorfman, 1994).

Symbolic interaction, another theoretical framework, also studies meaning in everyday life. Symbolic interaction examines interactions that individuals have with each other—ways that verbal and nonverbal messages are communicated by one party to another and how these messages are understood by the other party. Such interaction modifies one's self-concept and one's view of the other interactant and, on a larger scale, of the social order. Symbolic interaction offers a dynamic rather than a static view of social life. Individuals continually change their self-concepts and their views of others based on continuing interactions.

Life is a vapor. It passes in a blink of an eye.

Sarah Delany, age 107, in Delany & Hearth, 1997

Meaning in life can also be gleaned from poems, diaries, journals, and other sources of life history narratives. Older people who are not able to write may give their life history orally. Two sisters, Sarah and Elizabeth (Bessie) Delany, when they were over 100 years old, told their life history of being born the children of former slaves, getting their education, and becoming educators themselves. On September 25, 1995, Bessie Delany died in her sleep at home. Life's meaning is beautifully and poignantly reflected by her sister, Sarah, in her subsequent book, *On My Own at 107: Reflections on Life without Bessie* (Delany & Hearth, 1997). In it, she speaks to her sister:

> *I'm very conscious of being alone. . . . The winter after you left us was the longest, coldest, snowiest one that anyone had ever seen in these parts. It seemed fitting, somehow. But once the spring came I began to feel better. How can you not feel optimistic when the days are longer and warmer? And the birds are singing? The spring reminded me,* Life goes on. *(p. 32)*

Life narratives have wide appeal because they promote the ideal of freeing people to reflect on their life and share personal meanings. Constructing a life story is thought to be therapeutic for older people, but gerontologists caution that the telling of life stories does not always enhance well-being for the aged person. It can bring distress if the memories are negative or painful. Another problem in this area of research is that very rarely is the entire text of the tale printed. Instead it is glimpsed in fragments selected by authors, despite its being upheld as a means to empower individual voices (Luborsky, 1993). Qualitative research raises new issues about context, process, and meaning (Abel & Sankar, 1995). According to another expert on qualitative research, experience and voice should be represented from those studied—whether it be caregivers, care receivers, family members, or significant others. This requires that researchers keep subjects and their worlds at center stage, never (not even late in the research process) in the background (Gubrium & Holstein, 1995).

The use of qualitative research is particularly cogent for studies on aging. Bernice Neugarten (1985) summarizes:

> *If ever there was an area of inquiry that should be approached from the perspective of interpretive social science, this is one. It is apparent even to the most casual observer that aging has multiple biological, psychological, and sociological components; that neither the behavior of older people nor the status of older people can be understood otherwise; and that the primary need is for explication of contexts and for multiplicity of methods. (p. 294)*

Qualitative research is a means for *connecting* lives—of understanding more fully how individual experience shapes a life. This understanding provides the perspective necessary to design programs and policy interventions that have the capacity to respond to particular, as well as to general, needs (Holstein, 1995).

The particulars of any story in a narrative may not have ever occurred, or may have occurred quite differently to another participant than to the person remembering it. This does not mean that the storyteller is lying. Understanding another's story is the true test of the axiom that "the truth is relative." One person's truth or interpretation of an event might be very different from another's. It is our interpretation that we remember, not necessarily the cold, hard facts. The storyteller may believe the story, but memory and circumstances may have altered the actual facts. However, if the storyteller and his or her listener believe it is true, they behave with each other as if it were. Whether exact in terms of the cold, hard facts or not, the truth as spoken has symbolic meaning to the speaker, and therefore to the receptive listener.

Things perceived as real are real in their consequences.

THOMAS, 1927

Critical Gerontology

Critical gerontology evolved from critical sociology, which uses a neo-Marxian theory to critique the social fabric. Marxian theory looks to economic structures as the root cause of social manifestations. Members of society form an individual or group consciousness of their struggle against powerful economic forces. Only then can they unite to fight against these forces. The focus in this perspective on individual and group consciousness borrows from symbolic interaction theory. The main goal of the critical gerontology perspective is to identify wider social influences on problems that individuals experience. In 1989, for example, Cohen and Sokolovsky used a critical gerontology perspective in their report describing how the living conditions of men in the Bowery became defined in individual terms, not in terms of the larger social and political context. The critical perspective says that as long as social problems are defined in individual terms, change cannot happen. The analysis moves issues from "feed a man a fish" and "teach a man to fish" to "examine the environment in which fish might thrive, so a man can both fish and eat."

Current and future generations of the elderly are part of a quiet revolution . . . of older individuals representing the broadest range of ethnic, racial . . . and [regional and class] diversity ever witnessed. . . . This diversity challenges us to evaluate the applicability of existing research, policy and programs to emerging elderly populations.

BURTON, 1992

The **political economy of aging** draws attention to the political side of economics with regard to the aged—how political power affects the amount of money given to fund social services for elders. For example, critical theory posits that capitalism and the profit motive shortchange elders. It criticizes the class structure for perpetuating poverty among older women and minorities. Programs that address individuals fail to address the larger issue of social inequity (Estes, 1991). The causes are rooted in market and class structures—in other words, American capitalist institutions.

Minkler and Estes (1991) described the American values that undermine true reform as the ethic of individual responsibility, the negative view so many citizens hold of centralized government, and the individualistic view of social problems. These perceptions "obscure an understanding of aging as a socially generated problem and status" (Estes, 1983, p. 171). Laws (1995) argues that ageism is rooted in values that devalue the aged body. She wants to use critical theory to understand the way morality and values place their stamp upon our conceptions of the aging body.

The critical approach focuses on the negative experiences of aging, with the premise that the problems of aging are social and, thus, can be corrected with political and social action. A structural explanation is, therefore, tied to activism. Other branches of critical gerontology are working to identify wide social influences that shape what gets defined as a problem, how the problem gets looked at, and the consequences of different patterns of research. The worldviews of gerontologists should come under study as well as the people they are studying (Luborsky & Sankar, 1993). These studies can overlap with philosophy. They are important in directing our attention to biases that affect our choice of what to study, how to study, and even our choice of concepts and the wording of hypotheses.

Concludes Minkler (1996): "For gerontology to reach its full potential, . . . the important work that continues to take place in the biological and psychological aspects of ageing must be complemented by critical perspectives from political economy, feminist scholarship, and the humanities, coupled with newer, culturally relevant ways of thinking about ageing in multicultural societies."

Pure versus Applied Research

Pure research is the search for knowledge in the most unbiased fashion possible. The natural, physical, and social sciences use the scientific method to test hypotheses objectively and to accept or reject hypotheses using clearly defined criteria. The pure researcher first formulates a theory; then he or she generates hypotheses and devises a plan for testing them. The researcher must find ways of empirically measuring theoretical concepts or variables.

Let us consider an example from the activity/disengagement controversy. A researcher might want to test the hypothesis that the morale of an older person increases with the number of activities in which he or she is involved. To do so, at least two variables must be measured—morale and number of activities. This task may seem easy, but it is not. Morale is a complex variable, hard to define and hard to scale in a meaningful way. The number-of-activities variable is somewhat easier to deal with, but it can present problems. The researcher must decide, for example, if watching television or reading should be regarded as activities. Once variables are defined and scaled, the pure researcher must then identify the sample group.

A study of all elderly persons is impossible, so some smaller group, or sample, must be identified and selected. The sample should be chosen on a random basis so that no particular selective factor confuses the issue. Next, methods of collecting the data from this sample must be devised. Typical methods for collecting data are the interview and the questionnaire. After the social scientist has collected all the data, he or she uses methods of analysis, which often involve statistical techniques, to tabulate the results of the study.

The objective of all this work is to produce a study that is valid (accurate) and replicable (capable of yielding the same results when repeated). The data analysis will usually determine whether the initial hypothesis should be accepted or rejected, but the study's validity and replicability are just as important in determining the authority and persuasiveness of the conclusions about the hypothesis drawn from the study.

Using scales and tabulating totals is known as **quantitative research.** Survey research is typically quantitative. Another kind of research

widely used in the study of people is called **qualitative research.** Making observations in a retirement setting or nursing home, conducting lengthy oral interviews to get oral histories, or asking open-ended questions that explore the meaning of life may not yield results that can be scaled or analyzed statistically; yet these observations and interviews are scientific studies. They represent qualitative studies rather than quantitative ones. One qualitative study consisted of taped interviews, an approach the researcher called "retrospective life span analysis" (Job, 1983). Very old persons answered open-ended questions and told of important and meaningful life events. This model incorporates ethnographic methods developed by anthropologists in which narrative data, or people's stories about their lives, are the units of analysis (Gubrium & Holstein, 1995).

Gerontologists do not agree on the best approach to study, or even that there is a best approach. In a sense, each one has a camera set up in a different position, getting a different angle on the subject.

The applied branch of any science is concerned with using the findings of pure research to improve the quality of life. **Applied research,** to state it simply, yields practical solutions to a particular problem and is not concerned with theoretical speculation as to why the problem exists. Are most elderly poorly nourished, poorly housed, victims of high crime rates, and living below the poverty line? If they are, what is the best way to solve these problems? Just as physicians apply findings from biological science to help people get well and engineers apply findings from the physical and natural sciences to build better dams, bridges, and buildings, the applied social scientist might analyze the delivery of services or devise ways to improve the social environment in which people live. Of course, individuals may have differing ideas of what constitutes an improvement. Applied gerontology should be used to evaluate housing, transportation, pensions, employment programs, and Older Americans Act services. Scholarly consideration should also be given to how government regulations affect older people (Kane, 1992; Minkler, 1996).

One might think that the pure and applied approaches are separate and distinct, yet in gerontological study the pure and applied are often used together. Some theories present obvious value judgments and imply how the research can be applied. The everyday-life approach may or may not imply intervention. It can be pure research in the sense of its goal: to study the meaning that life has for old people. Yet some of the findings from this theoretical approach also imply ways for improving the lot of older people. Thus, the distinction between pure and applied research is often arbitrary. Applied research can identify and suggest ways to solve existing problems. Pure research can question why the problems exist. If solutions are implemented, applied research can then investigate the effectiveness of the solutions. All in all, pure and applied research stimulate each other.

The Future of Social Gerontology

Social theories of aging come from two principal viewpoints—the psychological and the sociological—or from some combination of the two. Gerontology has been more interdisciplinary than many fields of study. Subjective well-being adds a psychological dimension to studies of aging, for example, whereas age stratification emphasizes the sociological dimension.

Sometimes the distinction between the psychological and sociological can be quite arbi-trary, and this can be confusing to students just beginning their study of gerontology. If one can imagine gerontologists as photographers taking pictures of aging from many different angles, one can go on to conceptualize theorists looking at the lives of older people from many different angles. The pictures have a great deal in common, but the angles offer shades of difference and meaning. Theories overlap, but each one has its unique emphasis.

Because older people face so many practical problems that demand immediate solutions, research in the field of gerontology has often been applied rather than purely theoretical. Researchers have invested much of their time in seeking effective social solutions, often ignoring the broader theoretical questions.

The 1960s brought forth a flurry of research instigated by the activity/disengagement controversy, whereas the 1970s and 1980s saw a greater diversity of theoretical frameworks. The 1990s fostered an even wider and richer array of theories and concepts to the study of gerontology, with special emphasis on issues relevant to our extraordinary diversity of culture. At the beginning of the twenty-first century, the voices of scholars now call for acknowledgment that societies and cultures are woven together in complex strands, thus highlighting the need to study and understand that interdependence.

Likewise, as the percentage of older persons continues to climb, society needs more workers in fields such as education, outreach, and long-term care. We have many more research questions to answer before our society can fulfill the physical, psychological, and social needs of our older population.

Chapter Summary

Social gerontology studies social aspects of aging. Various theoretical frameworks have been used to study aging from a social science perspective. Controversy over the activity theory versus the disengagement theory of aging shaped the field of social gerontology in the 1960s. The controversy has never been resolved, though the activity theory seems to be favored. The most often studied variable in all of gerontology is psychological well-being. The implications of this concept are deep and numerous. Sociologists study how societies are stratified by age and how roles are differentiated by age. Society imposes age norms or age constraints, which also shape the way we behave at any given age. Every level of adulthood, whether young adulthood or advanced middle age, has expected behavior patterns. Exchange theory has been developed by sociologists and social psychologists and has been used to show that elders in society suffer from an imbalance of power. Balancing operations could bring more power and, thus, equality to the aged in the United States. A phenomenological perspective studies the meaning that elders find in life—in everyday events and in their relationships with others. Finally, from critical anthropology and sociology comes critical gerontology: the perspective that basic capitalist institutions interfere with the status and power of elders.

Key Terms

activity theory	Mannheim's
age cohort	"generation"
age grading	norm of beneficence
age norms	norm of reciprocity
age stratification	phenomenological
applied research	theory
critical gerontology	planned behavior
cross-sectional study	political economy
disengagement theory	of aging
equity theory	pure research
ethnicity	qualitative research
exchange theory	quantitative research
gender roles	reliable
generation	role
generation gap	roleless role
Generation X	salience
gerotranscendence	social gerontology
life satisfaction	symbolic interaction
lineage	theoretical frameworks
longitudinal studies	valid

Questions for Discussion

1. If you were to study aging from a sociological perspective, which theoretical framework would you choose and why?

2. How do our value systems affect the theoretical frameworks we design?

3. Do you personally expect to remain active or to disengage at age 65? At age 95? Explain.

4. Would you prefer to work in pure or applied social gerontology? Why?

Fieldwork Suggestions

1. Develop a measure of life satisfaction, beginning with your definition of the term. Interview three older adults to determine their degree of life satisfaction. What are some of their sources of satisfaction or dissatisfaction? Ask them what they thought about your measure and how they might have changed the way you went about getting your information.

2. Following a "meaning in everyday life" framework, make a visit to a nursing home. How would you describe the feelings and reactions of the elderly people there? Are they finding meaning in life? If so, how? In what way is your own perspective—your lens—shaping what you see?

Internet Activities

1. Look up the American Anthropological Association home page and see what you might find about critical anthropology. Does this give you any information about the use of life story and narrative to study aging?

2. Look up the home page for the Gerontological Society of America. How much information can you glean about methodology from this site and its links?

3. Using one of the Key Terms, conduct an information search. See if you can categorize the sources you find by "scholarly," "popular," and other appropriate groupings. Do some levels of information seem more solid or believable than others? How do you distinguish between off-the-cuff opinion and thoughtful, informed discourse?

5

Friends, Family, and Community

Family Development in Later Life

Elders in the Kin Structure

Social Networks

Religion and Spirituality

Strengthening Social Bonds

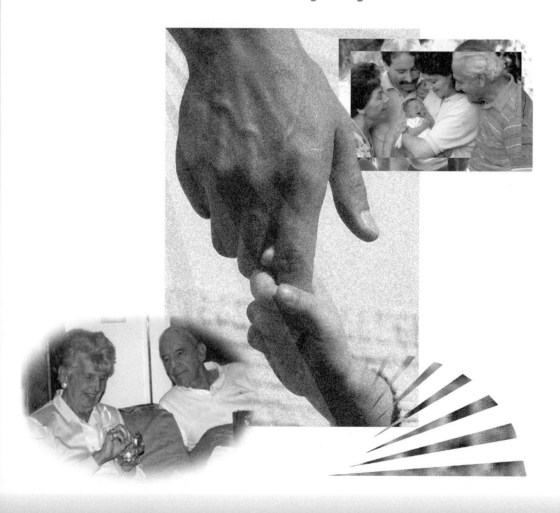

Lonely Deaths of Elderly Shock Australia

Michael Perry

They were five lonely deaths and only discovered because of the stench of decomposing bodies, but the realization that someone can die in their Sydney home unnoticed for months has shocked Australia's biggest city.

In the past 10 days, the bodies of five elderly Australians have been found in their loungeroom or bedroom—one a mere skeleton after dying an estimated eight months ago.

The latest two, an elderly couple in their 80s, were found in their apartment on Tuesday on Sydney's affluent north shore, police said Wednesday.

"What sort of a heartless society can it be in which elderly are so irrelevant and unimportant that they can die alone and unnoticed, unmissed for months on end?," asked Sydney's *Daily Telegraph* newspaper in its editorial on Wednesday.

"A society like ours, obviously."

Sydney won an international reputation as a warm and friendly city during the 2000 Olympics, but the elderly deaths have left many wondering what happened to their community.

"We have to come back to being a community, not only those that surround the older person living by themselves to make sure they are not isolated," Lillian Jeter, spokeswoman for the Elder Abuse Prevention Association, told reporters on Tuesday.

Sydney's radio bristled on Tuesday with discussion on whether the city of 4 million people had become mean spirited.

A newspaper survey this week found half of Australians feel their country has become a meaner place in the past 10 years since Prime Minister John Howard first came to power in 1996.

The *Sydney Morning Herald* survey also found that one in 10 people felt Australia was a "less fair society."

The survey found the overwhelming majority supported Howard's economic stewardship, with Australia enjoying 15 years of growth, and his stand against terrorism, but 55 percent of people regarded the prime minister as divisive.

News of the elderly deaths in Sydney coincided with media reports that four elderly women suffering dementia, one aged 98, were allegedly raped while being cared for in nursing homes in the southern state of Victoria.

Police have charged one man with alleged sexual assault.

The Australian government has ordered an urgent summit on the country's care system for the aged following the rape reports.

The Australian Minister for Aging, Santo Santoro, said on Tuesday he will consider mandatory reporting of elderly abuse, with some pro-elderly groups claiming thousands of abuse cases a year.

"There can be no guarantees because bad people do bad things when you least expect them," Santoro told Australian television.

Family and friendship connections take on a special significance when it becomes clear that they might not be in our life throughout *all* our life. Those significant connections include romantic and sexual relationships. Maintaining relationships can be a challenge when people become ill or frail, when friends die or move, or when family pressures for traditional grandparenthood take precedence over developing an independent lifestyle in later life.

Family Development in Later Life

Later life is not a static, stagnant time for the older family member. Transition events such as widowhood, retirement, remarriage, or a child's departure punctuate the life course. Transitions lead to changed perceptions, ways of behaving, and interdependence shifts with kin and community. The older person's life is also influenced by family development events in the past, such as whether he or she was childless or a parent, the person's culture, and certainly, the gender of the older person.

All these events add to the ever-changing character of the older person's role as a family member. Older persons may face adjustments equal to or more difficult than those younger family members face. For the newly married couple, the birth of a first child may require a difficult adjustment; but for the middle-aged or elderly couple, learning to relate to an independent adult offspring who was once "my baby" might be equally traumatic. Adjusting to the death of a spouse can be the most challenging of all changes in the life cycle. Each event in the life cycle calls for relating to others in new ways and facing the problems inherent in every transition.

Because of increased survival through childhood, adulthood, and into old age, Americans experience predictably longer lives. Marriages are more likely to last 50 or 60 years, and

parents are more likely to survive to see their children become adults and to see their grandchildren grow up. Whole stages of life that were brief and rare in the past, such as the postparental stage, are now long lasting. Many kin relationships last much longer now than they did in past generations.

Elders in the Kin Structure

The family is a vital part of the older person's life. Elders give a great deal to their families, and they receive a great deal in return. Family members tend to exchange emotional and financial support throughout their lives. A person's confidant in life is typically a close family member—a spouse or a child. Only when a closely related family member is unavailable does a friend rather than a relative act as confidant (Kendig & Wells, 1988). In this section, we will discuss siblings and grandparenthood. Parent-child ties are discussed in the next chapter.

Blood is thicker than water.

Shakespeare, 1581

The Elder Sibling

Brothers and sisters are brothers and sisters for life, no matter how intimate or how estranged they might be. The relationship with siblings, solid or shaky, is likely to be the longest relationship in an individual's life. If we have a brother or sister, it is likely that we will be a **sibling** and have a sibling from the time we are very young through to the time either we or they die. In later life, because of the duration and the shared experiences of childhood, the sibling relationship can be emotionally very intense, and that intensity can be either positive and life-confirming or bitter. There are as many different types of sibling relationships as there are types of families, but the fact remains that a sibling is a close kin connection over which we have no choice, and from which we can gain pleasure, irritation, or rage.

Although siblings may cause problems for one another at any time in the life course, they can also extend support to one another in a social environment that does not always foster the development of social bonds (Connidis, 1994). Bonds between siblings typically extend throughout life and are reported to be second only to mother-child ties in intensity and complexity.

Family systems in particular, because of their culturally ascribed and socially recognized status, implicate or entangle their members in a form of involuntary membership.

SPREY, 1991

Most elders have a living sibling. The parents of today's elderly produced more children than did the elders themselves; any given married adult probably has more siblings than offspring. If the birthrate is now at the replacement level of two children per couple, we can expect there will be fewer children, and thus fewer siblings, in the future. In fact, the baby boomers will be the first cohort in history that has more siblings than children (Selzer, 1989). The family support system will be smaller in the years ahead, and for this reason alone, the responsibility one family member feels for another is likely to increase with time. If there are no other resources for you, and you are my sister (or brother), can I *not* be there? Because adult siblings fall outside the nuclear family structure, their impact in the life course has been woefully overlooked by family researchers.

Exploring the sibling tie can highlight the importance of continuing family ties over time. Many family scholars have pointed out that there remains a conceptual distinction between feelings that siblings may harbor for one another and the obligations that are shared by virtue of family ties (Connidis & Campbell, 1995). When sibling ties are ranked by level of obligation within the family, the sibling tie is typically

less binding than that of marriage or of parent to child, but it is present nonetheless (Rossi & Rossi, 1990). The tie is important, and it is unique: siblings share biological and/or familial characteristics, values, and experiences under comparatively egalitarian status (Robinson & Mahon, 1997). Given their shared experiences, siblings can be a major resource for life review among older adults (Hays et al., 1997).

Studies on sibling relationships have had somewhat inconsistent conclusions regarding sister-sister, sister-brother, and brother-brother interactions. The variety of combinations of sibling units is nearly overwhelming, if we consider variables such as marital status, birth order, proximity, number of siblings in the family, living (or non-living) siblings and their birth order, blended families, and so forth. Theory helps to identify some key defining characteristics of being a sibling, however, to guide investigations.

Connidis and Campbell (1995) established the hypotheses for a study on sibling relationships after conducting a major review of the literature on sibling relationships in middle and later life. Using interviews with 678 people over 55 years of age, the researchers wanted to understand more about the relationship of sibling gender, marital status, emotional closeness, and geographic proximity. Their conclusions, generally consistent with most of the less recent studies in the literature, are itemized in Table 5.1. Their findings imply that to understand the support and emotional closeness of family in later life we must also understand sibling relationships. Because siblings are not considered to be extended family, their impact can be underestimated—both as providers of instrumental assistance and as assistants in maintaining a continuing sense of self when a sibling is in physical or emotional trauma, such as bereavement in widowhood.

Elders do in fact have brothers and sisters. In an earlier review of the literature by Cicirelli (1981), between 78 and 94 percent of older people reported having a sibling. A review of the literature on siblings (Bank & Kahn, 1994; Bank, 1995; Cicirelli, 1997) indicates that siblings

TABLE 5.1

Closeness, confiding, and contact among middle-aged and older siblings

Variable	Finding
Gender differences	1. Women's ties with siblings are more involved than those of men.
	2. The greater emotional attachment of women to their siblings was confirmed.
	3. Respondents with sisters only are closer on average to their siblings than those whose networks include brothers and sisters.
	4. Women are closer to their brother(s) and their sister(s) than are men.
	5. Telephone contact is more frequent if the highest contact sibling is a sister.
	6. Women seem to have greater emotional investment in their ties to siblings and are more engaged in sibling ties—possibly due to an assumed level of obligation.
Marital status	1. Contact is more frequent between single siblings.
	2. Emotionally closer ties among those whose closest sib is widowed than among those whose closest sibling is single.
	3. Being single affects overall level of involvement with both the sibling network and the sibling seen most often, but does not alter feelings about siblings.
Parent status	1. Childless respondents confide more in their primary sibling confidant and in siblings overall than do parents.
	2. Respondents with networks including parents and childless siblings confide in their siblings more than those whose siblings are all childless.
	3. No greater emotional closeness to siblings among the childless.
	4. Childless seem to have greater emotional investment in their siblings (higher levels of confiding).
Emotional closeness	A powerful relationship to confiding, telephone contact, and personal contact; emotional closeness appears to be a primary love/friendship binding tie.
Relationship over time; education; proximity; sibling number	1. Growing attachment to sibling network as a whole, over time.
	2. Higher education is associated with greater closeness to closest siblings, but not sibling network overall.
	3. Educational level inversely related to contact with sibling network overall.
	4. Proximity enhances emotional closeness, but not to emotionally closest sibling.
	5. Greater opportunity for selectivity within larger families.
	6. Network size not related to overall closeness and confiding.

Source: Connidis, Ingrid Arnet, & Campbell, Lori D. (1995). Closeness, confiding, and contact among siblings in middle and late adulthood. *Journal of Family Issues, 16*(6), 722–745.

generally maintain contact with one another, and that contact increases in old age. In all of the studies it was quite rare for siblings to lose contact, and in no study did more than 10 percent of the respondents report they had completely lost contact with their siblings. Gold and colleagues (1990) reported that the majority of elder siblings view their relations with their brothers and sisters positively. Indeed, Gold reported

that one of the greatest life regrets reported by elder siblings is a failed sibling relationship.

Older people are more likely to confront the death of a sibling than that of any other kin, and that loss can be profound (Cicirelli, 1997). The two highest times of interest and involvement in the life course in a sibling relationship are youth and late life. When an elderly person experiences the death of a sibling, the loss can be far more

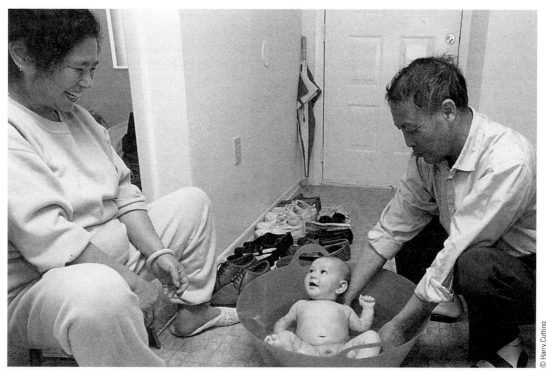

How to be a grandparent depends on one's family relationships, ethnic customs, health and age, and whether grandchildren live nearby. Many grandparents have close, indulgent relationships with their grandchildren.

consequential than it might have been earlier in life (Hays et al., 1997). Parents die, children grow and leave home, friends die or move, and health becomes more frail, yet the sibling bond endures. Research literature reports the bond of siblings to be more forgiving, mutually warmer, and more interested in one another in the last years of life (Bank, 1995).

Variations in Kin Relations

The demography of the kin system varies widely. Some older people have large and extensive kinship systems, with many relatives nearby, whereas others have managed to outlive siblings, children, spouse, and other kin. The relationships among kin members vary by sex, social class, and locale (urban or rural).

Gender differences are very apparent in family relationships. Females maintain closer rela-

tionships with other family members than do males. There appear to be stronger norms of obligation and feelings of attachment to extended family members among women than among men, as well as what might be called an ethos of support among women in a family (Connidis & Rosenthal, 1996). Families with more sisters have an increased likelihood that parents—both fathers and mothers—will have assistance from their children. While having more brothers in a family decreases the likelihood that one of them will be the primary care provider for a frail parent or parents, having more sisters in a family does not decrease the likelihood of their being primary care providers, but increases the level of care to the parents (Connidis & Rosenthal, 1996). This finding supports the conclusion that family contact remains consistent and intact through the parents for many years after children reach adulthood.

Blue-collar families tend to have close extended family ties, which members maintain by living near each other. Visits from kin often constitute the major, if not the only, form of social activity for such families. White-collar family ties are also fairly strong; however, such families are more likely to be geographically scattered by career opportunities. Contact is often maintained in spite of distance, however, through the use of e-mail and holiday vacations and visits.

Literature in gerontology is inconsistent in reported differences between rural and urban families. On the one hand, rural areas are shown to be bastions of traditional values including family responsibility and respect for elders. We can picture rural family reunions at which the elders are celebrities looking with pride at the family line of children, grandchildren, and great-grandchildren. In this picture, kinship ties are strong and meaningful. Small-town newspapers often reflect the apparent importance of family and neighborly ties by featuring articles on who has visited whom, who is in the hospital, or who went out of town to visit relatives.

Another picture of rural areas is one of poverty, isolation, and despair. In spite of the assumed traditional values, rural elders interact less with their children than do their urban counterparts. Studies have shown that, compared with urban older people, rural elders have substantially smaller incomes, are more restricted in terms of mobility, experience poorer physical health, and have a more negative outlook on life. Kin ties should be promoted and supported in a society where they are so threatened by social and demographic change.

Grandparenthood

The three-generation family is becoming common, and four- and five-generation families are on the increase. Rossi and Rossi (1990) found, though, that two- and three-generational lineages are most common. About 80 percent of those over 65 have living children, and 80 percent of those, or 60 percent of all older people, have at least one grandchild. If one becomes a parent at age 25, one may well be a grandparent at age 50. If parenthood at age 25 continues for the next generation, the individual would be a great-grandparent at age 75, thus creating a four-generation family.

Note that middle age, not old age, is the typical time for becoming a grandparent—indeed, half of Americans become grandparents by age 50 (Szinovacz, 1998). Most grandparents do not fit the stereotypic image of jolly, white-haired, bespectacled old people with shawls and canes: many are in their 40s and 50s.

My grandmother was the radiant angel of my childhood, and, you know, now my grandchildren are just the same. They are the part of my life that is most joyous, that gives me most pleasure.

GRANDFATHER, QUOTED IN KIVNICK, 1982

The rapid cultural changes characteristic of the second half of the twentieth century profoundly affected the American family. Some analysts say these changes are negative for the family, some say the changes are for the better, and some say they are simply *change*—not necessarily positive or negative, but clearly something to which people and society must adapt. In the tapestry of life, the color and design are variations brought about by change, but it is the continuity across generations that forms the fundamental shape and form. It is through that continuity that people learn how to be a grandchild, how to be a parent, and how to be a grandparent. The degree to which grandparents are involved in playing their role and just what that role will be with respect to their grandchildren is significantly influenced by their having known their own grandparents (King & Elder, 1997).

Living with intergenerational relationships is critical to the passing on of that cultural and family continuity, for these intergenerational exchanges serve as socializing influences as well as emotional influences (Wiscott & Kopera-Fryer, 2000). Grandparents can be playmates, storytellers, friends, advocates, providers of unconditional support, and mentors (Lussier et al., 2002).

There are as many different ways of being a grandparent as there are family types and styles. Grandparents can be a point of reference and identity for the grandchild; they expand the age range and number of adult role models available to children. They can be that connection that provides a sense of historical and cultural rootedness for the child; and they can provide a secure and loving adult-child relationship for their grandchild (Kennedy, 1996).

For some, grandparenting is a time to have childish fun or to indulge grandchildren, or perhaps even a chance to re-experience one's youth—the **fun-seeker** grandparent. At the opposite end of the spectrum would be the more formal, distant grandparent—perhaps one who tries to be a role model or the repository of family wisdom—the grandparent children go to for the best cookie recipe or for stories about their parents, aunts, and uncles. For some, grandparenthood is personally meaningful because it represents the continuation of the family line—it provides a sense of purpose and identity and a source of self-esteem when the grandparent has the role of the keeper of family history. The grandparent role can be central to helping children maintain identity in stepfamilies. But as in any role, there are vast individual differences. One grandparent might find great joy and meaning in the role of grandparent, whereas for another grandparenting has little relevant meaning.

The role of some grandparents is essentially that of substitute parent. Because their adult child is unable or unavailable to parent—because of drug abuse, death, divorce, AIDS, a mental health problem, career choice, or a host of other modern-day complications—grandparents sometimes end up with full-time care of their grandchildren. The pattern of young children being raised by grandparents has slowly but distinctly increased in the past 30 years, from about 3.2 percent of children in 1975 to 5.5 percent in 1997 (Szinovacz et al., 1999).

The emotional responsibility of raising grandchildren can be complicated by the complex relationships with the adult child of that grandparent. Fully two-thirds of children living with grandparents live in homes in which at least one of the child's parents also live (Fuller-Thomson et al., 1997). This means that grandparents who have taken responsibility for raising grandchildren also have responsibilities for (or the residential impact of) that child's parent. The stress of this complex set of relationships can be enormous. One-third of grandparent caregivers report their health to have deteriorated since becoming primary caregivers, and a vast majority (over 72 percent) reported "feeling depressed" in the week prior to data collection in one major study (Minkler & Roe, 1993).

Research has variously described grandparents who parent their grandchildren to be extraordinarily committed to child rearing; angry; in despair about their own child; guilt ridden about their role as parent to their "failed" child; and frustrated regarding the imposition of unexpected child-rearing responsibilities in later life (Kelly, 1997; Burnette, 1999). The full range of these feelings is likely to be experienced.

Women are much more likely than men to look forward to the role of grandparent. Women often visualize themselves as grandparents well ahead of the birth of the first grandchild, and the grandmother role is positive and desirable to most women, even though it can make young grandmothers feel old. Men typically become grandfathers when their primary identity is still with the work role. Consequently, they may postpone involvement with their grandchildren until retirement.

The anthropologist Dorothy Dorian Apple (1956) explored grandparent-grandchildren relationships in 75 twentieth-century societies and found that in societies where grandparents retain considerable household authority, the relationship between grandparents and grandchildren tended to be stiff and formal. In societies such as the United States, where grandparents retain little control or authority over grandchildren, the relationship is friendly and informal. Others have likewise observed that American grandparents, more than grandparents in other societies, engage in companionable and indulgent relationships with their grandchildren and usually do not assume any direct responsibility for their behavior.

One of the most representative samples of grandparents of teenagers affirmed many of these results. Grandparents often played a background, supportive role, helping most during times of crisis (Cherlin & Furstenberg, 1994). A recent study of psychological adjustment among youth from divorced families found that attachment to maternal grandmothers provided a protective factor to the children during and just following the divorce of their parents (Henderson, 2003). Among many families, the role of grandparent is somewhat distant and does not including disciplining the grandchildren, for example, but in a family crisis the grandparent is there with financial and/or instrumental support for the grandchildren. Additionally, even if they do not live with their grandparents, millions of American children receive child care from their grandparents each day (U.S. Bureau of the Census, 2002), and many grandparents express gratitude for the companionship of their grandchildren (Hayslip et al., 1998).

Grandparents are the child's roots, a sense of belonging to a larger family and a larger community. Grandparents are there when things go wrong for the child—sometimes the child needs that protection.

GRANDMOTHER, QUOTED IN KRUK, 1994

One can conclude that grandparenthood carries meaning for some elders but not for others. This meaning may be biological, social, or personal. The degree of involvement with grandchildren varies. Current evidence seems to indicate that in the United States grandparenthood for many is not a primary role, although it is enjoyed by most. It may be a primary role, however, for grandparents who provide the majority of care for their families' children. Becoming a grandparent is not going to fill voids left by shortcomings in marriage, work, or friendships.

The Impact of Divorce on Grandparenthood

The consequences experienced by grandparents when their children divorce is currently a topic under study by sociologists and under legal scrutiny in the courtroom. If a couple divorces and the in-law has custody of the offspring, grandparents often cannot enjoy the relationship they desire with their grandchildren. Existing patterns of contact with grandchildren as well as gender of the custodial parent and composition of the family influence the role grandparents will take upon the divorce of their child (Dench et al., 1999; Drew & Smith, 1999).

In some families, grandparents are emotionally distant enough from their adult children's lives to maintain cordial relations with former sons- and daughters-in-law. One study found half of the grandparents interviewed to be "friendly" with their child's former spouse. These grandparents tended to be friendly if the ex-spouse was a female, but they tended to lose contact if the ex-spouse was male, even if he had custody of the grandchildren. A recent study of grandparents and grandchildren of divorce indicated that grandchildren and grandparents saw their relationships in highly similar ways. They desired increases in time together as well as time together spent in specific activities. The two groups associated emotional bonding with the grandparents' listening and keeping them safe and with gift giving. Grandparents felt a good relationship with the custodial parent was essential (Schutter et al., 1997). The study further identified "healthy" and "less healthy" subgroups. The healthiest group was related to geographic proximity, being female for both parties, and being married and employed full-time for grandparents. Grandparents who were related by blood to the custodial parent and had a good relationship with them were also more likely to have a healthy relationship.

Matilda White Riley writes about the "matrix of voluntary kin relationships." Given the emphasis on individualism and social ties based on mutual interest, kinship can be complex in U.S. society. These social norms make the negotiation of kin relationships a necessary task. Good relationships with former daughters-in-law, for example, may determine whether grandparents can remain close to grandchildren. If informal negotiation fails, more and more people may be arguing in court for the right to spend time with a given child.

Grandparents who have been denied access to their grandchildren have traditionally had no standing in cases involving visitation and adoption of grandchildren, and the courts have upheld the supremacy of the parent-child relationship. Traditionally, a legal relationship between grandparent and grandchild existed only when both parents were incapable or dead, meaning that the courts had to judge the child's parents unfit before the grandparents had any rights.

Today, at least one legal precedent has been set: if provisions for visiting grandparents had been made prior to divorce, visitation is generally permitted after divorce. Thus, grandparents can, under limited circumstances, get visitation rights. (They have no rights, however, if parents choose to give their children up for adoption.) Grandparents are increasingly pressing for rights with regard to their grandchildren. The recent growth of the "grandparent rights" movement in North America suggests that a significant proportion of grandparents have concern about difficulties having access to and loss of contact with their grandchildren following divorce or in other situations. Current social policy is inadequate to address the phenomenon of grandparent-grandchild contact loss, although it has become an issue in the legal system for family mediators. At this time, legal mediation

is seen as the best possibility for resolution of grandparent-grandchild access problems.

We should also note that elders add new relatives to their kinship system when their adult children remarry. Remarriage, which may take place more than once, brings not only new sons- and daughters-in-law but may bring stepgrandchildren. When older parents can maintain ties with their children's former spouse(s), grandchildren lead more stable lives. Grandparents who can remain flexible and friendly have the benefit of enjoying an expanded kinship system. This "new extended family" (Cherlin & Furstenberg, 1994) created by stepgrandparenthood may lead to close kin ties. Some grandparents report that there is no difference between stepgrandchildren and biological grandchildren. Often, younger grandchildren and those who live close will develop more involved relationships.

Social Networks

One stereotypical picture of old age is that of a solitary person, in a tiny hotel room, staring silently into space. Another is of oldsters in a rest home, propped up in adjacent armchairs but worlds apart. Either way, the picture is one of isolation and loneliness. Do the elderly have friends—really good friends—they can count on? Simply stated, like other age groups, most do but some do not. Numerous factors affect the likelihood of close friendships in old age.

Elders as Friends and Neighbors

Friendship is extremely important in the lives of older people. Let us contradict one stereotype about friendships among elders by saying that most older people maintain active social lives. In one of the first major studies of friendship formation in widowhood, respondents were asked how many times in the past year friends had helped them with transportation, household repairs, housekeeping, shopping, yard work, illness, car care, important decisions, legal assistance, and financial aid. They also were asked how many times they had given help. Only 8 percent of the respondents indicated that they did not have a close friend. For the first close friend, 84 percent of the respondents named a woman. The average length of acquaintance with the friend was over 20 years; 81 percent keep in touch at least weekly (Roberto & Scott,1984–1985).

Although nationally in the past two decades there has been an increase in geographic mobility, older people are still most likely to live in the communities in which they raised their children (Lussier et al., 2002). Note that the date of the Roberto and Scott study was the mid-1980s. It has only been in the past 20 years that the role of friendship in later life has been seen as an important enough factor in well-being in later life to be a topic of research. This is not necessarily because social science research is insensitive to later-life development. It is because, once again, we can see a consequence of longevity in the patterning of our lives. Friends have clearly always been important; however (as we were reminded earlier), the adage that "blood is thicker than water" is culturally ingrained, and it becomes easy to overlook the true impact that friends—particularly friendships of very long duration—have on our psychological and social well-being.

Roberto and Scott (1984–1985) used **equity theory** to formulate hypotheses and analyze results. According to equity theory, which says that an equitable relationship exists if all participants are receiving gains, participants will be distressed if they contribute too much to, or receive too little from, a friendship. Equity is related to high morale, and, as expected, the equitably benefited women had the highest morale. An unexpected finding was that the overbenefited (those who received more help than they gave) had the lowest morale: receiving goods and services that one cannot repay may leave one feeling uncomfortable or inferior, resulting in lower morale. Also unexpected was the high morale that existed among the underbenefited, the ones giving more than they received. Perhaps

Interactions with neighbors can provide companionship and be a source of connection for older people. These men meet regularly in a local park to "talk shop."

the underbenefited woman feels good that she does not need help and enjoys giving without receiving. Single women who lived alone compensated for lack of a marriage companion through extensive and meaningful friendship networks with other women.

A differentiation can be made between a confidant and a companion. A **confidant** is someone to confide in and share personal problems with, whereas a **companion** is one who regularly shares in activities and pastimes. A companion may be a confidant, but this is not necessarily the case. The objective of one study that examined older women's friendships was to identify changes and stabilities in the qualities older women attributed to their close friendships (Roberto, 1997). They found that, over time, women's interactions with friends did change, and the change was based on the woman's work, marital, and health status. Although those interactions changed, they also found that the essential elements of friendship—understanding, affection, trust, and acceptance—endured over time. It appears that the expressive domain of friendships in later life predominates (Roberto, 1997).

Social Organizations

Are elders "joiners"? At what rates do they participate socially in voluntary organizations? Many, in fact the majority, join and are actively involved in voluntary organizations (nonprofit groups that elders join only if they choose to do so).

Lodges and fraternal organizations such as the Moose Lodge, the Elks, Eastern Star, and the like are the most commonly joined volunteer associations. Membership in them tends to increase with age, and leadership positions are concentrated among older persons, perhaps because these organizations have a respect for elders that other organizations lack. The second most frequently reported form of participation is in the church. Church-related activities involve more than attending services; they include participation in church-sponsored groups such as missionary societies and Bible study classes. Except for lodges and church, people's participation in other voluntary associations generally declines with age. When studies are controlled for social class, however, no decline is evident. This means that being a "joiner" is related to a middle- or upper-class lifestyle, and aging by itself does not necessarily change this lifestyle.

Senior centers, as opposed to clubs, offer services and activities in addition to recreation—libraries, music rooms, health services, counseling, physical exercise, and education. Many senior centers operate under the auspices of churches, unions, or fraternal organizations. Often individuals who began senior centers in

their own communities find them successful and popular years later.

The demand for senior clubs and centers continues to rise. Someday every community may have a senior center, and it will be as natural for older people to use their senior center as it is for children to go to school.

Network Analysis

We can conceive of the combination of social ties—organization memberships, friends, neighbors, and family—as a social network. Each person has some kind of social network. The process of analyzing the strengths and weaknesses and the sources of various functions of an older person's social network, called **network analysis,** enables caretakers to tell whether social or health intervention might be necessary. A distinction might be made between social support and social network. **Social network** describes the structural characteristics of support relationships (e.g., size, composition). **Social support,** on the other hand, is assessed as a more qualitative aspect of the relationship, including how satisfied individuals are with the support they receive and whether supportive others understand them (Antonucci et al., 1997).

In recent years, a great deal of research has focused on social networks. A study using the **convoy model** provides us with detailed information showing that older individuals are in frequent contact with both family and friends. The term convoy (Antonucci & Akiyama, 1987) is used to evoke the image of a protective layer of family and friends who surround a person and offer support. Convoys are made up of those family and friends who travel through time with the individual; some members of the convoy travel the entire way, some drop out along the way, and some enter the convoy after it has begun. In the late 1980s the average older convoy was reported in one major study of older persons to consist of about nine members who offer themselves as confidants, give reassurance and respect, provide care when ill, talk when upset, and discuss health (Antonucci & Akiyama, 1987).

The role of women as keepers of the network emerges in many ways when the networks of older people are examined. This finding is to some extent an effect of the difference in longevity between men and women: more older people are women, so women are more available as friends and family members. It is also due to social expectations and learning. Women tend to be more engaged in network support activities across the life span than are men. The caregiving role of daughters to aging parents has been well documented, as has the finding that married older people tend to maintain closest relationships with their same-sex children and siblings—a finding consistent with the **sex commonality principle**. Women play more central roles in the network of unmarried people (including widowed parents), a pattern referred to as the **femaleness principle** in network analysis (Akiyama et al., 1996).

A recent study of older people's networks (Akiyama et al., 1996) concluded that although older people tend to have more women in their network and receive more support from those women, elders are not necessarily closer—either psychologically or geographically—to the women than to the men in their networks. Their data also showed a noticeable shift from same-sex relationships to female-dominated networks when older people became widowed and required more support. When normative expectations for family member interaction were considered, the study concluded that relationship norms seem to be more powerful than sex norms—that is, the filial responsibility of a son to his parents is demonstrated by the son's interactions with aging parents.

Religion and Spirituality

The religious dimension of aging encompasses the spiritual, social, and developmental aspects of a person's life and is an important dimension of well-being for the elderly. Efforts to study the relationship of the spiritual dimension to aging are hindered by the research community's inability to use consistent terms and definitions. Inconsistent conclusions abound in the literature. As more scholars become engaged in the study of spiritual development, however, a concerted effort has been made to share definitions and methodology.

I represent a Father in heaven who owns everything. That's one of the reasons I've gotten along so well. I haven't been worried about where the next dollar was coming from.

CHARLES, 101 YEARS OLD, 1992

Thomas (1994) conceptualized an intrinsic-extrinsic pole of religiosity for the individual in which the intrinsically religious find within themselves their ultimate meaning in life. For these types, religion is the fundamental motive for living. The extrinsically religious use religion for sources of socialization, or in some instances to justify their politics and prejudices. Their religion is extrinsic to their fundamental reason for being. Other theorists have developed the concept of intrinsic-extrinsic religiosity by considering higher or lower levels of intrinsic religiosity, such as the importance of structured religion to the individual.

Fehring and colleagues (1997) conceptualized the religious dimension by differentiating between **spirituality** and **religiosity**:

Spirituality . . . connotes harmonious relationships or connections with self, neighbor, nature, God, or a higher being that draws one beyond oneself. It provides a sense of meaning and purpose, enables transcendence, and empowers individuals to be whole and to live life fully. Religion, on the other hand, is a term used for an organized system of beliefs, practices, and forms of worship. (p. 663)

By differentiating these two concepts, the study was able to show that religiosity (interaction with organized religion) and spiritual well-being (psychological sense of purpose and meaning) are independently associated with hope and positive mood states in elderly people coping with cancer. Subjects with high intrinsic religiosity and spiritual well-being had significantly higher levels of hope and lower levels of negative mood states than subjects with low spiritual well-being and low intrinsic religiosity. The researchers believed that subjects with high religiosity could use their religious patterns for coping (prayer, religious objects), and that subjects with high spirituality were able to maintain a greater sense of wholeness than those with low spirituality (Fehring et al., 1997).

Church and synagogue attendance (a traditional measure of religiosity) for older people exceeds that of other age groups. People age 65 and over are the most likely of any age group to belong to clubs, fraternal associations, and other church-affiliated organizations, such as widows' and widowers' groups, Bible study groups, and volunteer groups that serve the sick and needy. It is uncertain whether this is a cohort effect (i.e., people over 65 have been more religious throughout their lives than other cohorts) or an effect of aging. Evidence for shifts in religiosity with aging is inconsistent: some studies find that religiosity changes significantly as one ages; others find that it does not (Courtenay et al., 1992). Studies including centenarians, however, indicate that among the oldest old, the "non-organizational" aspects of religion (less active aspects of religion such as beliefs, faith, and influences of religion on daily living) are more common than the organizational aspects (Courtenay et al., 1992). This is likely due to more limited ability of the oldest old to attend organized religious functions. These findings highlight the importance of the multidimensionality of the religious dimension.

The findings from Courtenay and colleagues (1992) might differ significantly for ethnic groups. More than 75 percent of all elderly Af-rican Americans are church members, for example, and at least half attend religious services at least once a week. (Stolley & Koenig, 1997). Traditionally, religion and church have been powerful sources of social support for elderly African Americans—in fact, church attendance is *the* most significant predictor of both frequency and quantity of support received (Stolley & Koenig, 1997).

It is important to view elders in a multicultural sense. In a study of health-related decisions and the role of religion, Laurence O'Connell (1994) noted that "a healthy baby, a healthy marriage, a healthy sex life, a healthy set of social skills, a healthy appreciation of our mortality and so forth, are [all] humanly meaningful and religiously significant" (p. 30). To this we would add that they are also *culturally* significant, and it might be difficult to disentangle culture, human meaning, and religion in this context. Individuals are multicultural, and cultural and ethnic groups are heterogeneous. Knowledge of the importance of religion for ethnic groups can be critical to, say, designing intervention programs that are culture specific. However, categorizing by ethnicity comes dangerously close to stereotyping by race. It is always necessary for the practitioner working with older people to remain sensitive to variations in cultural values, including religious and spiritual states and needs, as well as to individual differences within cultural groups.

Elders benefit from the services of religious groups that minister to the needs of the sick, frail, disabled, and homebound. Carl Jung said:

Among all my patients in the second half of life—that is to say, over 35—there has not been one whose problem in the last resort was not that of finding a religious outlook on life. (Jung, 1955)

This quote brings to mind questions about who enters a "spiritual journey" in the second half of life, and why and how they do so. The awesome challenges of facing loss, suffering, pain, and death; of finding ultimate meaning and purpose; and of setting priorities and integrating the threads of one's life are possible reasons for such a quest. These are developmental tasks of aging, and religion may be useful in handling them. Jung's quote also brings to mind Erik Erikson's developmental concept of integrity versus despair, discussed in chapter 3: if a person can come to terms with life, integrity is achieved. If not, despair is the outcome.

In contrast to increased religiosity with age are the observations of a minister to elders in Cambridge, Massachusetts. He reports being distressed that so many people in old age lack "self-knowledge and spiritual discernment." He states that they are missing "the peace of soul which would make old age much more satisfying," and he believes one of the most neglected aspects of old age in America is the need for spiritual development. With spiritual development one can experience a growing benevolence and a deeper empathy with fellow human beings (Griffin, 1994). It is not a given, then, that individuals become more religious with age. More studies are needed to document the circumstances under which this occurs.

Strengthening Social Bonds

Although elders are not as lonely and isolated as stereotypes would have us believe, many live out their last years without the close emotional or social bonds that they need and desire. For some, such isolation may result from their inability to establish and maintain intimate relationships with others. For many, however, isolation results from the new social situation that old age brings. Changing family patterns means less need for the services of older members within the family. The trend toward smaller families means fewer siblings and children with whom to interact. Very old age may bring the loss of a driver's license and car, physically curtailing social opportunities. Physical disability and illness also can hinder one's social life, and if these events do not happen to one aged individual, they may happen

to his or her friends. For others, social organizations may not be available to provide the aged person with friends and companionship.

We need a greater commitment to strengthening the social bonds of elders and providing them with the resources to develop the intimate ties and friendships they need to enjoy a meaningful life. The formation of supportive associations among people with common experiences could produce age-integrated as well as age-segregated groups. Fostering connections across age groups is vital, along with encouraging alliances among older people.

We need to explore other solutions—from nightclubs and centers to communes that cater to seniors. The suggestion of nightclubs is valid not because older people need to drink, but because they have few places to interact socially. Perhaps expanding senior clubs and centers would be more to the point. The motivating factor is the same: to increase the older person's opportunities to find sociable companions, and this is the responsibility of the larger community in many ways. The availability of transportation in a community, for example, is critical to those who are homebound.

The communal concept is being emphasized in some retirement housing, designed with rooms clustered around a communal kitchen and dining facility. The elders share meals but find privacy in their own rooms. With some imagination, communal concepts could find further approval in the aged community and, in turn, enhance the social relationships of the elders who want to participate.

Social, legal, and financial pressures on older people discourage remarriage. Many retirement programs pay the surviving spouse a monthly income that remarriage voids or reduces. A second factor is pressure from children, who may discourage an aging mother or father from remarrying for fear that, upon the parent's death, his or her assets will be in the hands of the second marital partner. Reluctance to marry out of respect for the deceased spouse poses another barrier to remarriage. Finally, some people may

⁴fear ridicule or condemnation if they choose to marry in old age. The barriers to marriage or remarriage are also barriers to the formation of intimate relationships. But as living together without legal marriage becomes a more acceptable lifestyle for young people, it also becomes more acceptable for the old.

Widow-to-widow programs exist in many communities. These programs, which locate widows and help them to get together to share experiences, also provide legal assistance, social activities, and employment counseling. Churches are another source of counseling and other services for widows. We can strengthen social bonds and friendships through a genuine effort to provide these and other services and interaction that elders need.

Chapter Summary

Old or young, we all need intimacy and social bonds with others. Our social structure and values are such that old age can reduce opportunities for social interaction. Elders are at the later stages of the family life cycle and may have experienced children leaving home, retirement, job changes, the death or divorce of a spouse, the death of dear friends, remarriage, the birth and marriage of grandchildren. Despite these changes—or perhaps because of them—older people have the coping skills for getting through life's transitions. Connections with others—maintaining the ability to express intimacy, sexuality, and emotionality—are central to these coping skills.

In the area of social bonds, vast gender differences emerge. Women seem to be keepers of the support network—they are more involved with friends and family members when help is needed, and they have more friends than do men. The bonds that men do have, however, are as emotionally strong as the bonds that women make. More women than men must cope with death of their spouse and widowhood.

The importance of sibling relationships reemerges in later adulthood; aged siblings often provide support and companionship. Grandparenthood is a role that most elders experience; however, there are many different types of grandparenting, and the role of grandparent for most people is not a central one. The aged report themselves to be happier if they form intimate friendships with others. Neighbors and social organizations such as lodges, church, and senior centers are important sources of social interaction. Structured religion is a source of companionship, social stimulation, and spiritual support.

Key Terms

companion	religiosity
confidant	senior centers
convoy model	sex commonality principle
equity theory	sibling
femaleness principle	social network
fun-seeker	social support
network analysis	spirituality

Questions for Discussion

1. What are the advantages and disadvantages of being married in later life? Of being single?
2. Who offers the elderly the best chance of an intimate relationship, a family member or a friend?
3. What are the ages of those with whom you are most intimate? How much time do you share with your parents or grandparents, and they with you? How close to your parents do you expect to be in 10 or 20 years?
4. Imagine for a moment that you have just learned that your mother, living in a nursing home because of some cognitive impairment,

is "being allowed" to have a sexual relationship with another facility resident. What is your emotional response? Should you do something about it? If so, what will that be? If not, how can you be certain that her best interests are being guarded?

5. As an older person yourself, how close will you want to be to your children or relatives? Who would you like to live with in old age if you were married? If you were single?

Fieldwork Suggestions

1. Attend a social function for older people, such as a club, senior center, ballroom, or folk dancing. Or attend a National Association of Retired Persons (NARP) or American Association of Retired Persons (AARP) meeting. What were the informal topics of conversation? What kind of interaction took place? What norms and values did you observe?

2. Interview two grandmothers and two grandfathers about the closeness of their relationships with their children and grandchildren. Include questions that explore how the relationships developed. How much interaction is there across the generations for these individuals? Why is the amount of involvement higher for some and lower for others?

Internet Activities 🌐

1. Search for resources for grandparents on the Internet. Look for AARP Grandparent Information Center; Grandparents as Parents; Grandparents Who Care; National Coalition of Grandparents; and any other sources you can find. If you had a friend with sudden responsibilities for parenting their grandchildren, would you be able to provide information to them regarding these organizations?

2. See what kinds of Internet resources you can find that are designed to promote social contact specifically for older people. Keep a log of your search path. How difficult was it to find information? How accessible do you think this information is?

3. Develop the idea for an Internet home page designed to promote social interaction among seniors. Remembering that older people as a group are very heterogeneous, incorporate in your home page links to various sources that might be interesting or useful to people with different interests.

Intimacy and Sexuality

6

Older Women Talk about Sex

Beverly Johnson, Ph.D., RN

These are the words of an 83-year-old widow: "Physical satisfaction is not the only aim of sex . . . it is the nearness of someone throughout the lonely nights of people in their 70s and 80s. We need someone to hold, hug, and confide in."

A married woman age 57 said: "I believe sex is a wonderful outlet for love and physical health. It's worth trying to keep alive in advancing age . . . it makes one feel youthful and close to one's mate and pleased to still work."

A different story is told by a married 64-year-old woman: "Now that I approach retiring age, seems I am constantly compared by my spouse to other younger and attractive women. . . . I have always been affectionate and supportive. . . . I feel undesired."

These are a few of the words of more than 600 women age 50 and older who participated in a survey of women on sexuality and aging. The results are still being analyzed.

When I was an assistant professor of nursing at the University of Vermont, I invited readers of AARP's *Modern Maturity* who were age 50 and older to participate in my study of older adults' sexuality. I asked the readers to complete surveys on such topics as health, sense of self-worth, intimate relationships, and attitudes. To encourage the participants to be as open and honest as possible, I asked them not to sign their names to the questionnaires.

I also invited the participants to describe their degree of interest, participation, and satisfaction for a variety of sexual activities such as sitting and holding hands to reading or looking at erotic materials to saying, "I love (or like) you" to more physically intimate activities such as kissing, hugging, intercourse, masturbation, and oral sex. I wanted to explore sexuality in older adults from a broad perspective and not just equate sexuality with sex or sexual behaviors.

Studies looking at sexuality in this age group are especially significant as society has often seen older adults as sexually, uninterested, uninteresting, and incapable. The recent study of contemporary adult sexual behavior by University of Chicago researchers included adults between the ages of 18 and 59; the researchers used this upper age limit since they found previous research had shown both the amount and variety of sexual behaviors declined with age and financial constraints also led them to reduce the upper age limit from age 65 to age 59.

My study intentionally included items to provide a view of older female sexuality beyond frequency and type of sexual behaviors and to include other aspects of oneself such as self-esteem and intimacy.

How did these older women describe themselves? Nearly one-half of the women were married, while one-third were widowed. Three quarters of the women were satisfied with their lives in general. Their health status reports indicated that 40 percent had had a hysterectomy, while their most common health problems were arthritis and high blood pressure. Eighty-five percent of the women described their health as good.

I also found that women saw themselves from a positive self-view and as participants in intimate relationships (41 percent described their spouse as the person to whom they were most close while 33 percent said such a person was a friend). For example, 90 percent of the women reported, "I feel I have a number of good qualities," and "I take a positive attitude toward myself." Half of the women said their closest relationship provided sexual satisfaction while over 80 percent described their intimate partner as physically attractive, and both partners had a strong emotional attraction for each other.

Women also described themselves as knowledgeable about sexuality and aging and liberal in their sexual attitudes. They knew physical changes in sexual function were associated with aging and 85 percent said older adults continue their sexual interest and activity well into old age if they are healthy. Furthermore, 90 percent believed sex was not just for the young, that late life romances are good, and that sexuality continues throughout life.

In this study women described their sexual interest, participation, and satisfaction in various sexual activities. At least 50 percent reported being very interested, active in, and satisfied with activities such as sitting next to someone and talking, making oneself more attractive, hearing or saying "I love (or like) you," kissing, hugging, and caressing. Two-thirds of the women said they were "very interested" in sexual intercourse while 50 percent or less said they participated "very often" in this sexual activity. Sexual activities for which one-third of the women or less expressed being, "very interested, active in, and satisfied with" included talking about sexuality, reading or watching erotic materials, daydreaming about sex, masturbation, and oral sex.

Compared to their younger years, only 35 percent of the women said their present sexual interest had decreased, while 56 percent said their sexual participation had decreased, and 38 percent said overall sexual satisfaction had decreased. These facets of sexual behaviors do continue for this group of older women!

For this group of older women, I concluded that greater levels of sexual interest, participation, and greater levels of satisfaction characterized those women who saw themselves in a positive light, had intimate relationships, and had liberal sexual attitudes. Although the results of this study can't be generalized to the population of older U.S. women because the women had volunteered to participate and had not been randomly selected, the results do describe a view of positive and continuing sexuality of community-based older women.

Reprinted with permission from Beverly Johnson, Ph.D., RN.

The Need for Intimacy

Intimacy is the need to be close to, to be part of, and to feel familiar with another person. Old or young, we all need intimacy and social bonds with others. We may believe our ability to maintain close **relationships** is strictly a personal problem. However, from a sociological viewpoint, the social environment affects the maintenance of close or primary relationships as well as the larger network of friends and of kin. The norms, values, and social structure of a society may either foster or retard the development of social bonds.

Social scientists have long discussed the positive relationship between connection with others and psychological well-being. Those with whom we are emotionally connected might be either friends—**achieved relationships,** or people whom we have chosen to be in our networks; or kin—**ascribed relationships,** or people who are in our networks but whom we may not have chosen (Adams, 1983; Adams & Blieszner, 1994; Antonucci & Akiyama, 1995; Blieszner & Bedford, 1995). The number of friends and active family relationships a person has traditionally has been viewed as an indication of how well an individual is aging. It must be remembered, however, that the sheer number of interactions or connections is not necessarily an accurate reflection of the quality of those interactions (Adams & Blieszner, 1994). Psychological well-being is enhanced when the connections being maintained are positive and support the elder's ability to maximize potentialities, and by interactions in which the elder's self-concept is positively reflected and maintained.

Adams and Blieszner (1994) identify **friendship relationships** in terms, first, of their—process: the important attributes of the relationship, the level of enjoyment gained through the connection, and the activities conducted. Second, friendships are identified by structure: the size of the network, how similar the network members are, and the network density or the proportion of friends that know one another. Family or **kin relationships** are identified in terms of their process, which is similar to that of friendship networks; and of their structure, which refers to family size and generational composition, marital and parenthood status, household size and living arrangements, and the functions members serve for one another.

Although most older people have strong social bonds of some sort, certain events are more likely to put constraints on their relationships. Disability and illness limit visiting, as does lack of transportation. Death takes friends and neighbors and eventually a spouse. At the very point in life when retirement brings free time for social interaction, the opportunities for it may be reduced. Malcka R. Stern experienced various losses, including her husband. She moved to a nursing home and is hearing impaired, but she continues to reach out to others and respond to a warm social environment. Stern (1987) de-

scribed her intimate group of friends in an article she wrote for the *Washington Post:*

When I count the many blessings accrued to me in my long life of 93 years, high up on the list is the fact that I am a resident in the Attic Angle Tower, a senior citizens' apartment complex in Madison, Wisconsin. There are about 70 of us, average age 85, mostly widows.

We have a beautiful dining area, and when we all sit together at dinner—the one meal we take together—four of us to a table, we really present a picture of a group of elegantly coiffed and attired older women.

True, at the tables lucky enough to have among them one of our few men, there always seems to be much more animated conversation and much more gaiety. We do indeed miss our men.

Our group is impressive. We have among us professional women, all retired, of course, from all walks of life. Teachers, social workers, scientists. Many are widows of renowned professors, doctors, judges, lawyers and businessmen. In our midst we have talented artists, knitting and weaving experts, even a poet in residence.

But lest we become too smug and too satisfied with our way of life, we all remember that attached to our apartment complex is the nursing home to which sooner or later we will all have to enter at the last stop. We don't talk about it very much. . . .

Our friendships are warm and close. We have all experienced the same troubles, lived through losses of loved ones. Our own health fails. You complain to your neighbor about your arthritis and she doesn't say a word, but holds out her own gnarled and twisted hands. And we both smile and pat each other on the shoulder and go on about our business.

I am very hard of hearing and often fear that I must seem pixilated when I respond inappropriately to someone's question. One does get tired of saying "What? What?" all the time. . . .

Some of us go to a discussion group every week, and last week it was about grieving. We read James Agee's A Death in the Family, and then our group leader asked each of us to recall our first experience with grief.

When it came my turn I talked about the death of my first child, my Barbara, a baby of 2 who died of diphtheria. I began to tell them and I couldn't finish the story. To my embarrassment, I burst into tears. It was 60 years ago. It was yesterday.

Marital Status

The marital status of older people shapes a great deal of their roles, their patterns of interaction, and the social bonds they form. This section considers older couples and three categories of older singles: the widowed, the divorced, and the never married. An unknown percentage of older people live together without being married. Remarriage as a result of divorce or death of a spouse is becoming more common and is also discussed in this chapter.

Later-Life Couples

Being married is a reality for many older Americans: just under half of the population over 65 is married and lives with a spouse (U.S. Bureau of the Census, 2002). Being married is far more common among older men than among older women (Figure 6.1). Life expectancy is longer for women, who therefore are more likely to be widowed than are men, and men are more likely to be married to women younger than themselves. The total proportion of married people over 65 does not provide an accurate social picture, because 73 percent of men aged 65 and older are married, whereas about 41 percent of women in the same age group are married. In other words, older women are almost half as likely to be married as are older men. (U.S. Bureau of the Census, 2003). In many respects, the older couple can be considered lucky. Most

couples hope they can grow old together, but one or the other may die before old age.

Marriage is health maintaining: married persons tend to have higher levels of well-being and better health than unmarried persons. Among men, marriage is associated with a lower risk of coronary heart disease, and socially isolated men and widowed women seem at particular risk of a fatal cardiovascular event. The longevity advantage of marriage is nearly always greater among men than among women, indicating that men gain greater health benefits from being married than do women (Gliksman et al., 1995; Goldman et al., 1995; Preston, 1995). Regardless of gender differences, however, the elderly couple seems to be happier, less lonely, and financially more stable than older single persons (Goldman et al., 1995). Together, they can usually live out their lives in a satisfying way and be a source of comfort and support to one another. If one's social ties have decreased because of retirement or disability, the role of spouse takes on even greater importance. The relationship can become the focal point of the couple's everyday life and continue to develop in commitment, affection, cognitive intimacy (thinking about and awareness of another), and mutuality (interdependence) (Blieszner & deVries, 2001; Huyck, 2001).

The probability that an elderly spouse will need to provide caregiving for the other, more frail spouse is very high for late-life married couples. This can be deeply satisfying for both parties, for the caregiving can demonstrate a gift of love. It can also be extremely exhausting and stress producing if the caregiving partner is herself or himself afflicted with any chronic illnesses. One particularly interesting study analyzed the quality of the marital relationship and the effectiveness of caregiving for a spouse with cognitive impairment (Townsend & Franks, 1997). The study found that people providing care to a spouse with cognitive impairment had a greater sense of effectiveness if the relationship was characterized by emotional closeness. On the other hand, emotional closeness did not mediate the sense of effectiveness when the frail

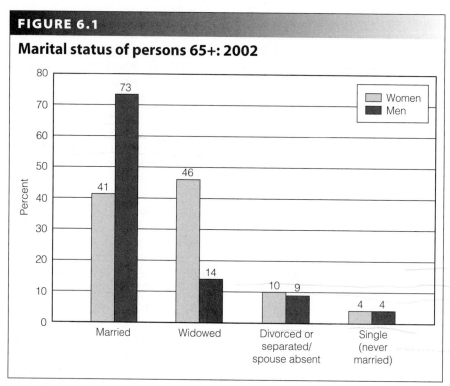

FIGURE 6.1

Marital status of persons 65+: 2002

Source: Based on Internet releases of data from the 2002 Current Population Survey of the U.S. Bureau of the Census.

spouse had a functional impairment—say, was incontinent or unable to walk without assistance. In case of either functional or cognitive impairment, conflict had a direct, negative influence on a spouse's perceived caregiving effectiveness. In other words, marital emotional closeness is a critical component to understanding spousal caregiving effectiveness. This highlights once again the necessity to examine the relationship of interpersonal ties, as well as their presence or absence, in order to gain a full understanding of the meaning of issues we examine.

It is essential to recognize that the personal and social meanings attached to erotic intimacy in earlier years have ripple effects in later life.

Huyck, 2001

Either retirement or disability might suddenly precipitate a shift in the amount of time couples spend together. Disability is clearly not a planned-for event, and it might be expected that shifts in personal and couple identity and in other patterns would be complicate a marital relationship. Research evidence consistently indicates, however, that retirement can be a major transition requiring adaptation to the loss of work and reduced income, change in social status, and changes in identity (Sharpley, 1997). In fact, early literature in gerontology emphasized retirement as a life crisis; however, more recent studies seem to indicate that it is, for most people, less a crisis than an adjustment (Hooyman & Kiyak, 1996/2003). More recent literature describes retirement not as a single transition so much as a process, including having friends who are retired, thinking about retirement, and

Physical and emotional intimacy and romance continue to the end of our lives.

© Joel Gordon

making specific plans for being retired. Planning often includes investigating possibilities for part-time work following retirement from a long-held or full-time job.

From a relationship perspective, both retirement and disability alter the couple's patterns of interaction. Prior to retirement or disability, one or both partners may have been very active outside the home; consequently, the number of hours each week they actually spent together may have been limited. It is particularly important, given the current pattern of early retirement and increased numbers of years of healthy life following retirement, to understand about spousal relationships following this life transition. People who retire involuntarily, not surprisingly, have been found to adjust more poorly to retirement than people who have planned for their retirement and have chosen the timing. This is in large part because the bulk of involuntary retirements occur when an individual

has health-related disabilities and can no longer reasonably work full time. More Type A personalities (people who attempt to control their environment and appear to be aggressive and ambitious on the job) are among those involuntary retirees than Type B personalities (people who take events more calmly and are not very assertive or ambitious in job-related situations) (Kausler & Kausler, 1996). Type A personalities are particularly susceptible to coronary diseases; the link between personality, work patterns, and adjustment at home in later life is evident in this regard. A survey in California indicated that voluntary retirees were more likely to exercise regularly, have lower stress levels, be in better physical condition, and report a higher quality of life than were involuntary retirees (Kausler & Kausler, 1996). The circumstance of the retirement, then, will have a direct effect on family relationships.

Most current research indicates no trend of increased marital strife when a husband retires and his wife is not employed. In many such cases, marital satisfaction increases following the husband's retirement—probably owing to increased recreational shared time. A slight trend toward dissatisfaction and/or conflict was evident in a recent study on marital satisfaction among wives who were still working after their husband's retirement (Kausler & Kausler, 1996). Women report that their housework increases following a husband's retirement: changing the roles of who has responsibility for management of the home appears to be as large a transition as changing from the role of worker to retiree.

In a national study of families, married people age 50 to 95 were selected for an analysis of work, housework, and marital satisfaction (Ward, 1993). High levels of marital satisfaction were reported by husbands and wives, and retirement neither enhanced or reduced marital satisfaction in this study. Although women were found to do more household work, it was the perception of unfairness rather than the division of labor that led some wives to express dissatisfaction. It would seem that traditional sex roles die hard. If these roles become more equal for young couples, we may see a more equitable division of household labor between couples in their retirement years.

One common stereotype of marriage is that, after the early stages of romantic love, the relationship begins to deteriorate. Recent studies have found the opposite—namely, an increasing enchantment with each other in the later years. Marital satisfaction appears to follow a trend that can be plotted in the shape of an inverted bell: satisfaction declines after the initial years, levels off in the middle years, and increases again during the postretirement years. Satisfaction may, in fact, return to its initial high level of the early marriage years once couples have adjusted to their new relationship.

An inverted bell-shaped pattern also charts a husband and wife's opportunity to share time and common interests and to develop greater mutual respect and understanding. The time before the birth of their first child offers husband and wife maximum opportunity for mutual involvement and marital cohesion. The increasing time demands of careers combined with the new demands of parenting substantially reduce the amount of time husband and wife can spend together in their middle years. The last child's leaving home and the retirement of the husband and wife once again allow time for greater involvement, shared activity, and marital cohesion.

Not all studies show that marital relationships become rosier with advanced old age. The deteriorating health of both husband and wife can bring problems to a relationship. Outside intervention can help troubled couples in advanced old age. Too much stress, whether financial or health related, is hard on a marriage no matter what the couple's ages.

Elderly Singles: The Widowed

Older singles may be divorced, never married, or widowed. Three-quarters of older men are married, and more than half of older women are widowed. Of women over age 75, two-thirds are widows, whereas 70 percent of men over 75 are living with their spouses (U.S. Bureau of the Census, 2000).

As shown in Table 6.1, widowhood is the predominant lifestyle for women who make up the "old old" (age 75 and above) and the "oldest old" (age 85 and over). We can expect that, in the future, three out of four women will ultimately become widows. Only if a man lives to be 85 is there an even chance of his being widowed. Women essentially can plan to be widowed in their later life, and, given the numbers, perhaps women *must* include that possibility in their planning.

The transition from married to widowed status can bring with it both personal and familial problems. The transition is not always successful. Having an intimate relationship over many years impacts an individual's sense of self: simply knowing that one matters in someone else's life can have a huge impact on well-being and personal happiness (Pearlin & LeBlanc, 1997). Childless widows especially lack support. The feelings of loss after the death of a spouse are enormous, especially if the couple had been married 30, 50, or even 60 or more years. The empty chair and the empty place in bed reinforce memories of sharing family rituals. What does one do with the memories? How does one manage the grief? Many turn to other family members for emotional support; others simply suffer alone.

Loss of a spouse may cause the most difficult role change that a person must cope with in a lifetime. The widow has lost the support and services of an intimate person in her life. If she doesn't find substitute supports, she is on her own. Her social life will be altered. She, as a single person, may be either uninvited to or feel uncomfortable in social settings where she had once been welcome. She may lose contact with her husband's friends and relatives. She then must form new relationships and make new friends. With this process in mind, Lopata

TABLE 6.1

Marital status of older people living in the community by age, race or ethnicity, and gender (percentages)

	65–74		75–84		85+	
	Men	Women	Men	Women	Men	Women
White						
(N = 26,000,000)						
Never married	5	5	4	6	3	6
Married	83	55	74	30	53	9
Widowed	8	36	19	61	42	83
Divorced	4	5	2	3	2	2
Black						
(N = 2,436,000)						
Never married	4	4	6	5	—*	6
Married	67	39	60	27	—	16
Widowed	18	47	25	67	—	76
Divorced	11	9	9	2	—	2
Hispanic Origin (any race)						
(N = 1,005,000)						
Never married	6	7	6	11	—	—
Married	78	60	69	26	—	—
Widowed	9	34	21	58	—	—
Divorced	6	10	3	5	—	—

Source: U.S. Bureau of the Census. (1990). Marital status and living arrangements: March 1989, *Current Population Reports,* Series P-20, No. 445. Washington, DC: U.S. Government Printing Office.
*Based less than 75,000.

(1988) described the **stages of widowhood** as follows:

1. Official recognition of the event
2. Temporary disengagement or withdrawal from established lines of communication
3. Limbo
4. Reengagement

Official recognition of the event of widowhood typically begins with the funeral and the initial mourning period. The term **grief work** describes healthy confrontation and acknowledgment of the emotions brought about by death. The widow must accept the finality of her loss in order to get on with living. Grief work for the widow takes time and may bring a temporary withdrawal from past social activities and responsibilities as she reassesses her life. Once she answers the question "Where do I go from here?" she can re-engage in society.

Studies of widowhood typically characterize the period beginning about six months after the spouse's death as a reorganization stage, different from the phase of intense grief that comprises the first few months after the event. Research on the later phases of coping with widowhood has zeroed in on the importance of friends and family as sources of social support. This research has emphasized the early stresses associated with grieving and the support required to help the recent widow maintain a sense of identity during profound loss. The tightly knit structure of a family network seems indicated for this kind of support. The less highly structured network of friends has been associated with help on decisions for building a new life as a single woman. A good deal of research, in fact, has taken place to describe the beneficial aspects of both of these support system types for widows. Recently, however, studies have begun to explore the finding that not all support network interactions are satisfactory.

Family dynamics, tightly knit or not, have both negative and positive aspects to them, as do friendship dynamics (Morgan et al., 1997; Schuchter & Zisook, 1993; Kanacki et al., 1996). One major study (Morgan et al., 1997) found that there seemed to be no shift from family toward friends as a time-related pattern of reliance on support networks in widowhood. Widows were given a diagram of concentric circles and asked to place people who "have either a positive or negative effect on your life" into one of three circles: an inner circle for those who had the most effect; a middle circle for those who had considerable effect but not quite so much as did those in the inner circle, and an outer circle for anyone else who still had an effect. Although this methodology did not specify what the negatives and positives were, it allowed people to identify the existence of network members who did not have a positive impact at this time in the widow's life. Family members, it was discovered, were the primary source of both positives and negatives. Differences in the number of negatives were notable because they increased over time in both family and nonfamily segments of the network. A shift was evident between those in the first year of widowhood, where only family negatives had a significant effect on depression, and those in the third year, where only nonfamily negatives had a significant effect on depression.

Clearly, the relationships of family and nonfamily have different impacts on the process of grief work among widows. As Morgan and colleagues point out, there is no theory to adequately address the finding of time and the interaction of positive and negative support. Their research serves as an important reminder that the assumption that personal networks are positively supportive is not accurate and can be myth generating, as is the belief that stressful events mobilize "positive support." Even so, research continues to support the finding that higher levels of perceived social support are related to lower depression scores for both widows and widowers (Kanacki et al., 1996).

The perception of having a supportive network, regardless of the contact and the number of exchanges made, seems to serve a critically important function for widows. "Positive illusions" (Taylor & Brown, 1988) assist in adapting to difficult situations, and we might suggest that the *belief* that one is fully supported is by far more than half the battle. Changes, be they positive or negative, will naturally occur for the widow following the death of her spouse—reduced contact with friends of the husband or with in-laws, for example, or changes in the relationship of couple-companionate friendships and new and different relationships with children (Lamme et al., 1996).

Some older widow–adult children relationships seem to have a negative side. Older widows sometimes feel unappreciated; they feel that they're making too many sacrifices for their children when their children should be offering comfort (Talbot, 1990). On the other hand, a classic finding emerging in the early 1980s is that older women are more likely to be distressed and dissatisfied if they were over-benefited by their children, that is, if their children provided them with considerably more support than they reciprocated (Beckman, 1981). Even in bereavement—or, it might be suggested, *especially* in bereavement—consistency in the parental role seems to be important to the maintenance of self-identity.

Widowhood creates changes in the widow's support system beyond that of the absence of a spouse. In one longitudinal analysis of children's responses to their mother's widowhood, Roan & Raley (1996) found that contact increased between mothers and their adult children. This is a finding we would expect, because adult children and their mothers have the intimacy of shared grief over the death of a father and death of a husband. Another study of parent-child communication shortly following the death of a parent-spouse found that both parents and children seemed concerned with protecting each other from the pain and sadness associated with the loss (Silberman et al., 1995). The study identified two types of families. In the open family, consoling and informing language was used. Less open families used language to influence and to avoid feelings and confrontation with death. In these families the surviving parent often saw the deceased partner as the competent family caregiver. Two key points are relevant to all these studies, however: that network contact is not necessarily always positive, and that study findings are generalized and can mask the vast individual differences that exist.

The role of friends can be very important to the bereaved widow. Again, however, support can be positive or negative. One woman reported:

> This business of people saying "You're doing so well:" I hated that. Or "You're so strong." Because I was really feeling terrible, and I needed someone to say, "Gee, it's really rough for you right now." (Morgan, 1989)

Friends can offer more useful support by not trying to speed recovery, emphasizing strength, and not forcing a new identity. They can just listen, not argue, and provide unconditional love.

Interviews with 300 widowed women in an urban community showed them to be self-sufficient in managing their daily lives. They did not lean heavily on anyone for help with the basic tasks of daily living unless they were in advanced age and/or experiencing poor health (O'Bryant, 1991). The research suggested that too much independence and self-sufficiency might lead to social isolation. Asking for help and giving help to others results in *interdependence,* which is the most valued lifestyle (Roan & Raley, 1996).

Different women react differently to the loss of a spouse. Women in traditional marriages, who saw their role of wife as central and who invested their identity, time, and energy primarily in this role, suffer immensely. If the marriage was close, the loss cuts most deeply into all aspects of the survivor's life. Reactions of widows may also vary by social class. The generally lower income levels of widows can promote isolation and loneliness. Indeed, many widows have lower morale and fewer social ties because they are poorer than their married counterparts and are unable to interact in as many social events as financially better off women can. Generally speaking, the higher the widow's personal resources, such as income and education, and the higher her participation in her social life and the community, the better she can cope with her status.

The process of adjustment to widowhood is a very complex path of redefinition of roles and self-concept. People may move back and forth between feeling secure and comfortable with their self-concept and feeling quite the opposite; or they may experience several feelings simultaneously. Those with previously happy marriages are more likely to consider remarriage or to make a successful life for themselves alone; in contrast, women whose marriages were not fulfilling are less likely to consider remarriage.

Darling, I am living half without you; half of me is dead.

BECK, 1965

The loss of identity experienced by a woman when she becomes a widow can be tremendous, most particularly among women who have maintained traditional marriages throughout their lives. To determine the cost of widowhood, one study used the autobiographical accounts of 10 widows (van den Hoonaard, 1997). The women described their experience as one of transformation, not one of recovery. Van den Hoonaard named the process described by the widows "identity foreclosure" to refer to the sense of shift in personal identity reflected in their writing. Some examples of this foreclosure, in the voices of the women:

> After Martin died, I had learned that my identity had been derived from him. I did not know who I was. (Caine, quoted in van den Hoonaard, 1997)

> Who am I without Judd? Who will define my existence for me? (Seskin, quoted in van den Hoonaard, 1997)

> My sense of self, to a great extent, became linked to being Leonard's wife. . . . We reassured, validated, reinforced, and encouraged. We mirrored the best part of each other. I lost that mirror when Leonard died. It was a double death. When he had said, "You're wonderful," I believed him. . . . But with Leonard gone, I felt paralysed. It was as if he had taken a major part of me with him. (Rose, quoted in van den Hoonaard, 1997)

> "Sign here," the girl in the office of vital statistics said when I went to pick up a copy of your death certificate. . . . "Right here. In the block that says widow of the deceased." The word pierced me like a lance and my sharp intake of breath was audible. . . . Later as I walked home, I tried to give voice to my new label. Widow! Widow! I mouthed the word over and over and although I could hear it thundering in my head, no sound would leave my lips. . . . Until two weeks ago, widow was only a word in the English language. Now it is me. (Dohaney, quoted in van den Hoonaard, 1997)

A number of organizations offer outreach services to widows and widowers. They may be religious, social service, or mental health groups. The American Association of Retired Persons (AARP) has a program, Widowed Persons Service (WPS), in which volunteers who have been widowed 18 months or more are trained to reach out and offer support to the newly widowed. This program is offered in 220 communities nationwide. WPS conducts special outreach to minorities and other groups who are typically less active in such programs (*Widowed Services Fact Sheet*, 1990). Participation in outreach programs can be a lifesaver for elders willing to seek help.

Gender differences in widowhood

Family sociologists disagree whether husbands or wives experience greater difficulty in coping with the death of a spouse. A husband who is the surviving partner of a traditional relationship may have the greater difficulty. He may have to learn the new role of housekeeper—learn to cook, to assume cleaning chores, and to host if he wants to entertain friends. Further, the widower is less likely than the widow to move in with his children, less likely to have a high degree of interaction with relatives, and less likely to have close friends. He is more likely to have somewhat increased interaction with sons, however, than is a widow. If the wife was the initiator of family contacts, her death typically lessens the widow's interaction with extended family members. Statistics paint a grim picture for the husband who survives his wife: widowers are four times more likely to die from suicide, three times more likely to die from accidents, ten times more likely to die from stroke, and six times more likely to die from heart disease as are married men of the same age (*Widowed Services Fact Sheet*, 1990).

On the other hand, the widow's situation may be equally difficult, both socially and psychologically (Stevens, 1995). Many widows (about half by some estimates) spend a significant period of time providing care to ill husbands before becoming widowed. They often have depleted social and emotional resources. Some social scientists believe that it would make good policy sense to shift a portion of Social Security benefits from the time both the husband and wife are alive to the time when there is only one survivor (Sandell & Iams, 1997). This might reduce some of the poverty that emerges with widowhood for many women.

The emotional costs of widowhood are high for all people. A longitudinal study of widowhood found that the long-widowed men and women (five or more years) reported more loneliness than married individuals, and for women there was less perceived life satisfaction (Lichtenstein et al., 1996). In this study, there were no effects of bereavement on how healthy the individual believed himself or herself to be; however, there was evidence for an anticipation effect for women, indicated by elevated depressive symptoms just prior to the spouse's death. Although the longitudinal analysis shows that it is more stressful to be bereaved when young old than when old old, there were no age differences in how long it took to feel well adjusted again following a spouse's death. Adjustment to bereavement appears to be multidimensional and includes personality, social, economic, and family history factors.

It seems that men and women change in different directions at the loss of a spouse. The men are more "in search of others." With time, they become more aware and appreciative of friends and relationships. Women, as the quotes above indicate, are more "in search of themselves." With time, they develop confidence, assertiveness, and independence. In general, widows were previously more wrapped up in the role of wife than were widowers in the role of husband. New relationships developed by each seemed to allow more flexible roles and less dependency. Both sexes found new excitement about the changes in their lives.

Elderly Singles: The Divorced

Divorce is now a dominant social reality in the United States. By 2010 the proportion of people 65 or older who have been divorced is projected to be 50 percent (Quadagno, 2005). In over one-third of all married-couple households, at least one spouse had a previous marriage that ended in divorce or widowhood. Couples in a first marriage constitute one-quarter of black households and just under half of all white and Hispanic households (Holden & Kuo, 1996). Implicit in these trends is the shifting role of members of the extended family in the care of a single elder parent—most especially the role of adult children and their mother.

Strains in marriage are complex and will not be dealt with completely in this review; however, it is important to keep in mind that marital strains are probably heightened by longevity. At the end of the nineteenth century, the average length of marriage when one spouse died was 28 years; now it is over 43 years. There have never before in history been so many couples attempting to live a lifetime with one another for such a long period of that lifetime. Rare and widely celebrated at one time, the golden wedding anniversary (50 years) is now reached by many couples, and although its occurrence is still celebrated and honored, it is no longer a rarity. The extent to which it is a rarity is increasingly due to the smaller proportion of marriages that last that long, but not because of the death of a spouse. One couple was overheard to be talking about celebrating 60 years of marriage between them: 22 years with his first wife, 20 years with her first husband, and 18 years together. This couple joked that the years were additive because they represented experience being brought to the present marriage. A new perspective on an old tradition is apparent in the twenty-first century.

Each year at least 50,000 people over 60 years of age dissolve marriages of 30 to 40 years' duration. Not only that, but divorce will continue to increase. The rate has climbed in the last 30 years from 5 percent to 50 percent, and a high proportion of those divorces are taking place among the baby boomers—the cohort for whom divorce has become commonplace, and the next cohort to enter the aged population (Mulroy, 1996). For the elderly person who is remarried, the risk of that marriage ending in divorce is 10 times that of an elderly person who is in his or her first

We can no longer assume a group of older women are all widows. Increasing numbers of divorced women reach later life following many years of independent living.

marriage (Lanza, 1996). The consequences of these numbers are enormous: when one considers both widowhood and divorce, only half of all women entering old age in 2025 will be in a marriage. This figure could be less than half if divorce rates continue to increase in middle and old age and if remarriage rates continue to decline (Uhlenberg, 1996).

Though divorce has gained acceptance as a solution to an unpleasant or difficult marriage, at this point in history the impact of the increasing divorce rate in old age on the financial status of elders and the conformation of kinship networks is profound. Many of the changes in social interactions and patterns of relationship that are only now being worked out—relationships with ex-in-laws, for example—will become "traditional" in the next couple of decades, and new norms will emerge. For now, though, divorce is traumatic, both economically and emotionally.

Along with new social norms, social policy will need to catch up with the social reality of multiple marriages and single status through divorce in later life. Property reform and survivorship rules regarding public and private benefits

have improved conditions of widowhood, but there is less protection against the long-term economic consequences of past and future dissolution of marriage (Holden & Kuo, 1996).

Divorce is a particularly difficult event for older people. It is rarely a sudden development and might result from many years of deepening emotional disruption. Preexisting attitudes toward marriage and divorce, probably as much as the circumstance of the dissolution, shape the adjustment to divorce. Among people for whom marriage and the family have been both vocation and avocation, divorce is not only a failed promise but also a broken covenant (Lanza, 1996). The social shame felt by some men and women at being divorced can be very powerful—particularly so among older women, for whom remarriage rates are very low. In her extensive study of divorced older women in 1988, Cain found that the length of marriage significantly contributed to postdivorce despair and slow recovery. Some women described feeling envious of widowed women they knew: society knows how to respond to the needs of a widow, but is uncertain about those of the divorcee. Widows are more likely to have the acceptance of her peers, the support of her family, economic stability, and the anticipation of living alone than are divorced women (Lanza, 1996).

Not as much support exists for the divorced single person, male or female, as for widowed elders. Men have a higher probability of remarriage, but their friends are usually in longer-term marriages, and most of those friends were friends as couples. Adult children can have a difficult time dealing with the divorce of their parents after many years. Uncomfortable and complicated family interactions commonly erupt, and the isolation of one or both of the elder parents by children and grandchildren can result. Thanksgiving might seem less uncomfortable if *neither* grandparent attends; birthday celebrations for the grandchildren are more comfortably celebrated within the nuclear family only. There are few norms for dealing with the divorce of an older couple, for the divorcing couple or their friends, or for the kin network. These norms will, fortunately or unfortunately, become better developed in the next few years, given the projected numbers of marriage dissolution.

Elderly Singles: The Never Married

Never-married persons 65 and over constituted a little more than 4 percent of the population in 2002 (see Figure 6.1). Few people who have never married do so in old age; first marriages make up less than 10 percent of all marriages of elders. One might expect elderly singles who have never married to be unhappy and lonely, but the never married have typically adjusted to being single in their younger years and are well practiced in those skills of self-reliance and independence that make living alone a desirable and workable lifestyle. They report parallel levels of life satisfaction with married persons (Bennett, 2005), and because the never married will never experience the death of a spouse, they are spared the grief and loneliness that follows such an event.

However, those who have never married do suffer from losses. To measure the connections of people who are married and those who were never married, one psychologist asked older people to write "the one person or persons who are the very closest" in the innermost of three circles on a piece of paper. People not quite as close but who are still important were to be listed in the middle circle, and those who are less close but still important were listed in the outer circle. The results were that married people had more connections in the inner and middle circles (their spouse being the most intimate), whereas singles had more outer-circle relationships (Rubenstein, 1987).

Older people who have never married often have highly valued friends and relatives, including nephews and nieces. When these important people in their lives die or drop contact, the elders suffer greatly. Like all other subgroups of older people, however, the never married are a diverse group—some *are* isolated (sometimes by choice), while others have many friends. Some wish they were married and feel they have lost out on something; others are happy and fulfilled with their lives and have no regrets.

Remarriage

Today we hear a great deal more about the occurrence of late-life marriages. Remarriage in old age is becoming more common for two reasons: more older people are divorcing, which places them in the remarriage market, and remarriage has become more acceptable for the widowed. Although remarriage of widowed and divorced women over age 65 currently constitutes only 4 percent of all marriages (U.S. Bureau of the Census, 1993), remarriage seems to work well for most older people.

Many older people have had long, reasonably happy second (or third) marriages and are glad to have found another compatible partner. They do not take relationships or marriage for granted. Older singles in search of relationships try to meet partners at church functions, local clubs and organizations, parties, and dances. The extroverted might try video dating, computerized dating, or advertise in the personal columns of newspapers. Here is a sampling:

All I want is a kind, spiritual NS/ND/ND gentleman who has a house with a garden to grow vegetables. I am 5'7", 67 and into holistic health and metaphysics. I love nature and people, too.

Single woman 60ish enjoys everything from opera to country, dining out, picnics, playing pool, horseback riding, swimming, reading and more! Would love to meet male with similar interests.

Cuddly, down to earth, emotionally and financially stable WM, 55, to share dance, movies, ocean walks, tennis, his heart and more w/very loving N/S slim SWF w/good values.

An early 70's N/S DWM seeks the companionship of a woman who manifests spirituality and intelligence. A few of my interests are theatre, Dixieland jazz, and strenuous hiking. In 1994 I traveled to Europe and China. Please respond to . . .

Tired of road kill? Desire an energized rabbit? Tall, fit, SWM, 69. Keeps going . . . and going . . . and going. (Santa Rosa Press Democrat, *The Meeting Place*, February 28, 1995, F3)

Such ads indicate that the desire for romance, courtship, and meaningful relationships lasts a lifetime. Beginning in the 1980s, researchers called for a greater effort to understand dating and mate selection in later life. However, we know little about the process of courtship in later life. Although we know that intimate relationships are important and that older people seek intimacy and meaningful relationships, we have not yet examined the process leading to remarriage.

A positive aspect of remarriage in old age is that children are grown and out of the house, so the couple does not typically experience great daily strain being stepparents. An increase in the use of prenuptial agreements, developed by family lawyers, has helped to reduce the potential for family conflict over inheritance. More attorneys are now familiar with issues of particular relevance to an older client: pension rights; whether both parties do or should have nursing home care insurance; and clarity on issues around durable medical powers of attorney, tax issues, Social Security benefits, and insurance. Some older people have bypassed remarriage because of concern for children's inheritance rights and competing filial obligations among adult stepchildren. Mediation before remarriage to establish clear understandings among all family members can help eliminate misunderstanding before it surfaces. Families are reassured, and the elders feel more secure in being able to develop their own late-life plans as a couple. Remarriage can enhance older partners' abilities to adjust

to changes in physical competence by providing steady and caring companionship (Choi & Wodarski, 1996). Feeling cared for and being touched are important factors that enhance quality of life at any age, and perhaps they are most precious in later life when the likelihood of being without them is so great.

Sexual Relationships and Sexuality

Sexuality is not simply a product of biology. Sexual identity is a complex product of emotional, developmental, and cultural aspects of life—it is part of an individual's identity and an important characteristic that is carried with us throughout our lives over the life course. Being aware of the marriage of these aspects of life at all ages can help develop an appreciation for sex as an essential part of the relationship with oneself and with others (Kaye, 1993; Drench & Losee, 1996).

Developmentally, in childhood we learn in what ways our own boundaries are separate from those of other people. Understanding those boundaries is an important part of developing a solid sense of the self. In adolescence, the developing self learns to enter into relationships of love, in which the experience of being a separate individual is simultaneous with the experience of being emotionally merged. Sexuality is an integral part of loving and bonding. The continuing aspect of sexual identity remains a dynamic part of our self-concept throughout the life course. Over time the identity shifts and changes, but it remains a central aspect of our human condition. It remains central even if we develop a chronic illness, if a spouse dies, if we are surrounded by friends and family, or if we live alone and maintain a solitary life. Fundamentally, we are sexual beings.

Our sexual identity, as part of our self-concept, is dynamic—it changes over time in terms of behavior and of interest. Numerous psychosocial factors are involved: customs; personal characteristics; religious and social considerations; educational, financial, and vocational levels; partner availability; the nature and severity of organic conditions; mobility; and effects of medications (Drench & Losee, 1996). The role models available to us as we grow into maturity are also critical. A survey of college students bears out this idea. Both young and middle-aged college undergraduates completed the Aging Sexuality Knowledge and Attitude Scale (Hillman & Stricker, 1996). Findings showed that greater knowledge about sexuality and later life was associated with more permissive attitudes. Most interesting, however, was the finding that the simple presence of a relationship with at least one grandparent was significantly and positively related to adult attitudes toward elderly sexuality. Those adults will bring their attitudes with them as they age and eventually become new cohorts of elders.

Cohort and culture clearly shape sexual relationships in later life. Modern historical analyses of marriage and marriage expectations provide an example (Dion & Dion, 1996; Botkin et al., 2000). People who were between the ages of 16 and 19 from 1937 to 1944 (the World War II cohort) grew into adolescence and adulthood with strictly defined gender roles, and a solid marriage was considered the ultimate objective of life. The "silent generation" (Sheehy, 1995), born between 1936 and 1940, is the last modern generation to respect the authority of American institutions and corporate paternalism (Huyck, 2001). Ninety-three percent of women from this generation became mothers. Following this cohort, the women's movement challenged traditional gender roles, including the value to women of marriage and childbearing. Sheehy (1995) refers to the next cohort (1946–1955) as the "Vietnam generation." They represent the leading edge of the baby boomers, and according to Margaret Huyck's analysis,

[partly] because there are so many of them . . . competition for everything has been fierce and they have responded by emphasizing individuality (to stand out from the crowd) and hard work (to get ahead of the competitors). (2001, p. 13)

In this cohort gender roles were challenged, and cohabiting—living together without marriage—became an acceptable norm (Huyck, 2001). The rules for marriage and sexuality were forever shifted.

Sheehy (1995) has named the next two cohorts the "me generation," born 1956 to 1965, who married later or not at all; and the "endangered generation," born 1966 to 1980, for whom committed relationships of marriage seem particularly difficult.

A significant change in the two decades straddling the year 2000 has been a cultural shift in recognition of same-sex romantic relationships. Driven in part as it is by the "Vietnam generation," with its strong identities of individualism and personal rights, challenges to the legal inequalities between heterosexual and homosexual partnerships shape the sociopolitical discourse in the early 2000s.

The cultural context of sexual identity, shaped in no small part on historical trends, is huge, and its ripple effects impact family composition, the workforce, and social policy, to name only a few of the institutions and organizations that respond to shifting cultural values.

Sexual Invisibility

The sexuality of older people is largely invisible. This is partly because for many older people, sex and sexuality are intensely private matters. It is also from our cultural focus on youth: that which is not youthful (or new) is not functional and of no use. The myth that older people automatically lose interest in sex distorts perceptions of older people. It also influences older people's perceptions of themselves, because we generally incorporate our culture's attitudes, norms, and values into our self-concepts unless there is some other powerful validation for being "different."

As a result, elders in our society are "sexually invisible." They are not viewed as being sexual, and therefore any suggestion of sexuality is received with derision (what does he think *he's* going to do?), condescension (did you see how *cute* he was around that young woman?), humor (did you hear the one about the old guy who . . .), shock (how could a woman her age *act* like that?), or some deadly combination of the four. Simply stated, people generally do not put themselves in positions to be treated with scorn, and therefore their sexuality becomes hidden. Invisible.

It is important to note that these assumptions need not be true, but simply believed.

FRIEND, 1987

Physical Attraction and Youth

The idea is commonplace that sexual tension is based mainly on physical attraction between the sexes and that very young men and women are the most physically or sexually attractive. Advertising, film, television, and stage promote the theme that good looks, youth, and sex go together. Models are generally young, and beauty contests usually involve those not yet out of their mid-20s.

Many people consider only the young, perfectly proportioned body to be sexually attractive. The signs of age, especially when combined with obesity or socially unacceptable features, are assumed automatically to be unattractive. When people consider older bodies to be neither sexually stimulating nor desirable, the next step is to assume that no interest in sex or sexual activity occurs in old age. Assumptions can produce self-fulfilling prophecies in which old people internalize those cultural messages about themselves.

One study, however, suggests that the self-fulfilling prophecy might not always apply. Wilcox (1997) surveyed 144 men and women age 20 to 80 in order to determine their personal body attitudes. She found that self-esteem, health, and masculinity (an instrumental orientation) were positively related to body attitudes, but these relationships did not differ by age or by gender. In other words, men and women with good self-esteem also had good body attitudes—that is, they liked their bodies, and 80-year-olds with good self-esteem liked their bodies as much as 20-year-olds with good self-esteem. Wilcox suggested that **social comparisons** (Heidrich & Ryff, 1993) are an aspect of this body attitude. They describe a process by which people compare themselves with people who are having more difficulty along a particular dimension. This is a "downward" comparison and might be a particularly functional adaptation for older adults in maintaining a good sense of body image.

Romantic Love

Although romantic love has been variously defined, it has a number of generally accepted characteristics: idealization of one's mate, a consuming interest and passion, fantasy, and desire for a blissful state of togetherness. Clichéd ideals—love at first sight and the idea that love conquers all—are often elements of romantic love. There is no inherent reason why only young people should have exclusive access to romantic love. Yet in all forms of media, romantic love is predominantly an emotion for young people. From Shakespeare's *Romeo and Juliet* to the present, passion and romance have been primarily for young lovers. Perhaps the concept came to be associated with young people because they are the ones most often involved in mate selection. However, with the increasing divorce rate and an increasing life expectancy, mate selection often continues throughout life. The belief that only young people are capable of strong passionate feeling invalidates the passions of older people.

The concept of **sexual function for procreation,** which disassociates elders and sex, was embodied in Christian Catholicism by the teach-

Older people are often treated as asexual beings. This woman looks lovely, feels lovely, and is helping to change the image of later-life sexuality.

ings of St. Augustine (Feldstein, 1970). Accordingly, a woman's femininity was measured by her ability to bear children and be a mother. Likewise, a man's masculinity was measured by the number of children he fathered. Because of the association between sexuality and procreation, men and women beyond the usual childbearing years were believed to be asexual—most clearly so for women, whose ability to procreate ends

abruptly with menopause. In current times, the sex act is considered an expression of love and happiness, with the reward being pleasure rather than children. Deeply rooted ideas take a long time to die, however. Some men still fear that a vasectomy will rob them of virility, and some women fear that menopause or a hysterectomy will rob them of femininity.

Homosexual Relationships

Stereotypes of older gay men and lesbians portray them as lonely, predatory, pitiful outcasts. Indeed, aging can be a particularly difficult course for gay men and lesbians. The psychotherapist Joel Frost (1997) states:

> *Negative myths and stereotypes about older gay men and lesbians, the dearth of positive older role models, continued discrimination in a heterosexist society, and developmental pressures without a clear model for gay aging make is especially difficult and complex for gay men and lesbian women. Indeed, many older gay men have to now struggle with being the age of the internalized homophobic stereotype of the "dirty old man" they learned to avoid when they were younger. (p. 268)*

Relatively recent political and social discussion of the civil rights of gay males and lesbians has helped to highlight some of the discrimination faced by these groups (Boxer, 1997). Particularly among younger people, there is a good deal of social activism on behalf of issues relevant to gays and lesbians, and this activism will undoubtedly shape social policy in the future. *Outing Age: Public Policy Issues Affecting Gay, Lesbian, Bisexual and Transgender Elders* (Cahill et al., 2001) identifies the following key social policy inequalities favoring "institutionalized heterosexism":

- Social Security pays survivor benefits to widows and widowers but not to surviving same-sex life partners of someone who dies

- Married spouses are eligible for Social Security spousal benefits, which can allow them to additionally receive half their spouse's Social Security benefit if it is larger than their own Social Security benefit. Unmarried partners in lifelong relationships are not eligible for spousal benefits

- Medicaid regulations protect the assets and homes of married spouses when one member of the couple enters long-term care; no such protections are offered same-sex partners

- Tax laws and other regulations of 401(k)s and pensions discriminate against same-sex partners, costing the surviving partner in a same-sex relationships tens of thousands of dollars a year

- Basic rights such as hospital visitation or the right to die in the same nursing home as one's partner are regularly denied same-sex partners

The social and psychological circumstances of most older gays and lesbians is vastly different, however, from those of younger men and women. A study in the early 1980s (Dawson, 1982) estimated the U.S. population of gay men and lesbians over the age of 60 to be 3.5 million people. These men and women developed their sexual identity and "came out" in times of social persecution and fear. They had few positive role models and were surrounded by highly negative stereotypic messages about themselves (Frost, 1997). Developmentally and socially, most older gays and lesbians are charting new waters in the twenty-first century, developing role models for younger adults in the process. It is a difficult course to chart: in addition to the impediments of social attitude and self-perception, many older people must address the ageism that still occurs in gay, lesbian, and bisexual communities (D'Augelli & Garnets, 1995).

Given the diversity and difficulty of generating representative samples for study, little is known about the older gay and lesbian population from a social-science perspective (Michaels, 1996). Most information is anecdotal, based on partisan observations of individual regions or communities. For example, contrary to popular wisdom, recent research on families and relationships caution not to assume that being partnered is more developmentally appropriate or necessarily psychologically satisfying than being single for older lesbians and gays (Hostetler & Cohler, 1997). Clearly, research on aging in lesbian and gay male communities lags behind that on heterosexual aging, and it is equally clear that the assumptions and theoretical frameworks used for one cultural group must be carefully challenged when applied to another.

Older lesbians and gay men typically live within a self-created network of friends, significant others, and selected biological family members. The Senior Action in a Gay Environment in the city of New York found that 65 percent of 253 gay and lesbian elders reported living alone—nearly two times the rate of all people 65 or older in New York City (Cahill et al., 2001). Like the general population, older women were two times as likely to live alone—42 percent compared to 21 percent of men (Brown, 2000). Another study with a more culturally diverse population found that 75 percent of gay and lesbian elders in Los Angeles lived alone (Cahill et al., 2001).

Herdt and colleagues (1997) reported finding that many people have fears about being alone in their old age. The possibility remains that as the baby-boomer generation ages, new models of living in community may become more common (Boxer, 1997).

In reality, the lifestyles and life choices of gay males and lesbians are similar to those of heterosexuals. In reports from older lesbians, although the respondents were suffering from ageism, sexism, and homophobia, they did not regret their sexual orientation. They were able, as are other groups of elders, to make a healthy adjustment and live their lives with high self-esteem (Schoonmaker, 1993).

Research on Sexuality

The **Kinsey studies** of the sexual practices of men and women were landmark, classic studies. *Sexual Behavior in the Human Male* appeared in 1948, followed by *Sexual Behavior in the Human Female* in 1953. No one had previously studied the sexual histories of so many individuals in such depth. Although very few of Kinsey's sample subjects were older men and women, Kinsey concluded that the rate of sexual activity gradually declines with age. The men in Kinsey's study were sexually most active in late adolescence (ages 16 to 20), the women in their 20s, and the rate for both genders gradually declined thereafter.

A great deal of research has followed Kinsey's stepping-stone into aging and sexual behavior. A few of the most recent studies are explored here.

Erection is chiefly caused by scuraum, eringoes, cresses, crymon, parsnips, artichokes, turnips, asparagus, candied ginger, acorns bruised to powder and drank [sic] in muscadel, scallion, sea shell fish, etc.

ARISTOTLE, 4TH CENTURY BC

Masters and Johnson

The **Masters and Johnson studies** of human sexual behavior were considered revolutionary for their time period, just as Kinsey's were for his; they studied not just sexual histories but also observed and recorded the physiological responses of couples having sexual intercourse. This research resulted in their first book, *Human Sexual Response* (1966). Their second book, *Human Sexual Inadequacy* (1970), is based on their treatment program for those suffering from sexual dysfunctions. Although their technical language is rather difficult for the layperson to understand, the discussion that follows is taken largely from a very readable book that interprets their work and was endorsed by them (Belliveau & Richter, 1970). One methodological problem relative to aging with Masters and Johnson's study is that most of their "old" subjects were between 50 and 60. They studied few individuals over 60.

Body processes slow down with age but do not stop. Masters and Johnson found that if a middle-aged husband and wife are aware of these changes and take them into account in their lovemaking, there is no reason why pleasurable sex cannot continue. For men, the body processes affected by the aging process include the length of time needed to get an erection and the firmness of the erection. The ejaculatory expulsion of semen is less forceful, and the erection may be lost faster after ejaculation. In addition, it may take longer to have another erection. If the older man is aware that these changes do not signal the end of his ability to have an erection, he can relax and enjoy sexual activity.

According to Masters and Johnson, men over 50 have many advantages over younger men. Their ejaculatory control becomes better, and they can maintain an erection for a longer period of time without the strong drive to ejaculate. As partners, many women say that longer lovemaking is more satisfying—time allows for greater opportunity to bond emotionally during sex. Sex becomes, for these women, more an act of sexuality and emotional connection than an act of physical performance.

If [a woman] . . . is normally developed mentally, and well-bred, her sexual desire is small. If this were not so, the whole world would become a brothel, and marriage and a family impossible.

J. G. RICHARDSON, M.D., 1909

The aging female is subject to all the negative attitudes of our society regarding women and sexual matters: the beliefs that a woman's sex drive is not as strong as a man's, that women are more passive, and that women are not supposed to enjoy sex as much as men. These myths become even stronger in terms of the older woman—for instance, the myth that it is unnatural for women to continue sexual relations after menopause. Far less attention has been paid to sexuality in aging women than in aging men, owing in no small part to the sexism of the male-dominated medical profession of the nineteenth and twentieth centuries (Morley & Kaiser, 1989).

Masters and Johnson reported that it is natural and beneficial for older women to continue sexual activity, without long periods of abstinence. Older women do, however, experience a slowing process, just as men do. Vaginal lubrication occurs more slowly with aging, and less lubrication is produced. While younger women take 15 to 30 seconds for lubrication, older women may take as long as four or five minutes. The clitoris may get smaller with age, but it still receives and transmits sexual excitement. There is less increase in the size of the vaginal canal. And, with age, the lining of the vaginal walls becomes thinner. Older women, like older men, generally experience a shorter orgasmic phase. Menopause alters the hormone balance, and some women benefit from hormone replacement therapy.

Masters and Johnson reported an increase in the rate of masturbation in older women. Many women are widowed or divorced and isolated from male sex partners. Particularly among older couples, husbands may be ill and unwilling to participate in sex. According to Masters and Johnson, there is no reason why women who still need release from sexual tension should not provide it for themselves.

For women, as for men, aging has advantages. Postmenopausal women are no longer concerned about the risk of pregnancy or the side effects of contraceptives. They also may be free of the anxieties and pressures of motherhood. Masters and Johnson state that there is no reason why menopause should blunt the human female's sexual capacity, performance, or drive. They found no endpoint to female or male sexuality set by advancing years.

The Duke Longitudinal Study

In spite of the small numbers of older people Masters and Johnson studied, their findings are of tremendous importance regarding the sexual potential of older people. But Masters and Johnson made no attempt to study just how many older people take advantage of their sexual potential and remain sexually active. The **Duke longitudinal study** tried to answer this question and to also assess the changes in sexual interest and activity that come with age (Verwoerdt et al., 1969). The study, which began in 1954 at Duke University, still continues. Many different researchers involved in the study are still publishing their findings. One fascinating finding is that one in six of us will be even more interested in sex as we age (Witkin, 1994).

In the Duke study, sexual activity was one of many aspects studied in the lives of 254 older people. The sample was composed of nearly equal numbers of men and women whose ages ranged between 60 and 94. Four patterns of change in sexual activity were observed throughout the 10-year longitudinal study of 1954 to 1965: inactivity, sustained activity, decreasing activity, and rising sexual activity.

The researchers found a great deal of variability in sexual behavior among the aging individuals. Approximately 15 percent of the sample fitted into the rising category, whereas unmarried women were almost totally inactive sexually. Ten years did not greatly decrease the number of elders who were sexually active. About half of the men and women who survived into their 80s and 90s reported having sexual interest. Among men surviving into their 80s and 90s, continued sexual activity was not rare, and about one-fifth of these men reported that they were still sexually active.

In summary, the Duke study shows enough sexual activity on the part of the old and the very old to illustrate the sexual potential Masters and Johnson found in older adults. On the other hand, the sexual interest of many Duke study participants exceeded their actual sexual activity. Although not clearly explained, this discrepancy was perhaps caused by ailing physical health, psychological reasons, or lack of an acceptable partner.

Other Studies

The Kinsey study has been criticized for conclusions made from its cross-sectional methodology. To make age comparisons in a cross-sectional study, researchers must compare old people who were raised in conservative times with young people raised in more permissive times. In other words, the criticism holds that Kinsey's report might accurately show patterns of interaction for different age groups at one point in time; however, it says nothing reliable about change over time.

Starr and Weiner (1981) studied responses of older individuals to a lengthy questionnaire on sex and sexuality. Elders, even those in their 70s and 80s, reported being sexually active and stated that sex was as good as or better than ever, though somewhat less frequent than previously in their lives. Three-fourths of the elders studied said their lovemaking had improved with time. Counter to popular myth, it is apparent that the need for intimacy and the desire for a sexually meaningful relationship continues throughout the lifespan.

Another opportunity for questionnaire response was provided by the Consumers' Union (Brecher, 1984); over 4,000 aged men and women responded. The responses indicated that age did not adversely affect enjoyment of sex and that most husbands and wives were currently having marital intercourse. Unhappy marriage reduced sexual activity for older couples, just as it did for younger couples. Rates of extramarital intercourse, though lower than those for younger couples, still occurred for the same reasons. Inattentive or uninterested spouses were major factors. Some couples had open marriages. Homosexual experiences were reported, some of which took place for the first time in old age. Such findings dash stereotypes of sexually inactive and uninterested elders, many of whom had struggled for sexual frankness and openness throughout their lives, fighting taboos that seem to have been stricter than those young people face today. Some elders had improved their sex lives over the years by breaking down psychological barriers; some had not. Some regretted being so sexually uninformed when they were young.

Overall, both men and women experienced only slight declines by decade in sexual activity. The percentage of sexually active married women in their 50s, 60s, and 70s is, correspondingly, 95, 89, and 81 percent. For married men, 98 percent are sexually active in their 50s, 93 percent are still active in their 60s, and 81 percent continue to be active at age 70 and over.

Respondents found a variety of ways to compensate for sexual changes brought about by aging or poor health. They slowed down the lovemaking process, emphasized oral sex and manual stimulation of the genitals, and participated in lots of fondling and cuddling. Many reported that the sensation of touch was more important, meaningful, and appreciated than in their younger years. Some women used a lubricant to compensate for lack of vaginal moisture. The biggest problem for older unmarried women was finding a partner: men their age are in small supply. Respondents generally showed a strong interest in sex and a large capacity for enjoying life.

For the very old, biological studies of changes in the male reproductive system reveal a need for greater direct penile stimulation to achieve erection, slower erection (but only a few minutes slower), briefer stage of ejaculatory inevitability, reduced amount of seminal ejaculation, and reduced need for ejaculation at each and every sexual contact (Zeiss & Kasl-Godley, 2001). If a man becomes impotent, the cause is illness or disease, not aging. New knowledge and techniques are continually being made available in dealing with either impotence or premature ejaculation. In addition, sensations become less genital, more sensual, and more diffused. In the aging female, changes include slower lubrication, greater need for direct stimulation of the clitoris, shorter orgasmic phase, and irritability of vaginal tissue and outerlying tissue with low levels of estrogen. But these issues do not mean the end of one's sex life. According to Helen Singer Kaplan, sexuality is among the last of our faculties to decline with age (Witkin, 1994).

A study in the *Johns Hopkins Medical Letter* reports that 70 percent of 68-year-old men and the majority (over 50 percent) of women in their 70s regularly engage in sexual intercourse. One of the most debilitating factors related to diminished sexual activity is the self-fulfilling prophecy mentioned earlier: the belief that sexual prowess diminishes with age. The article suggests that knowing what changes to expect with aging as well as how to deal with those changes is a key to remaining sexually active. At any age, health problems such as diabetes, alcoholism, depression, or anxiety can interfere with sexual function.

Bretschneider and McCoy (1988) studied the sexuality of a healthy population of individuals between the ages of 80 and 102. The most common activities in order of frequency were (1) touching and caressing, (2) masturbation, and (3) intercourse. Although 63 percent of the men had intercourse at least sometimes, only 30 percent of the women did. The researchers concluded that, for men, the frequency of sexual intercourse does not change greatly after age 80 compared to the previous decade. This would suggest that physiological shifts have occurred already for the 80-year-old man and assume he has an available sexual partner—probably a wife. For either men or women in general there is no decade this side of 100 in which sexual activity is totally absent.

In general, findings on sexuality show that, given good health, a positive attitude, and an acceptable partner, even those in their 80s and 90s can and do remain sexually active. Changes inherent in the aging process need not interfere with sexual activity because compensatory strategies are easily employed, and indeed most older adults have been shown to adapt easily to such changes (Zeiss & Kasl-Godley, 2001). Physically disabled or terminally ill individuals continue to be sexual beings, too, and sexual counseling is now commonly available through hospitals and clinics to assist couples with physical disabilities or impairments. Sometimes people simply need reassurance that they are sexually attractive and capable, regardless of their physical limitations. It is relatively common for heart attack and stroke victims to report fearing that sexual activity may trigger a life-threatening episode. Information, knowledge, and caring for oneself and one's partner are primary aspects of a continuing and satisfying sexual life.

We must be aware that most of what we know about aging and sexuality is from a predominantly healthy, well-off Caucasian population (Zeiss & Kasl-Godley, 2001). Although the information available on elders and sexuality is generally valid, professionals in health care and human services must honor the gap in knowledge about sexuality and subgroups.

Improving Attitudes about Aging and Sexuality

In spite of society's general taboo on romantic love for older adults, many people look for romance. Many elders enjoy dating. They can and do talk about "steadies" and become possessive about their "friends" and partners. Indeed, retired older people may have more leisure time to dance, bicycle, eat out, and date than younger individuals, whose time is taken up with jobs and careers. Most dance clubs have a majority of members who are over 60 years old. Folk and country dancing, for example, can be vigorous exercise and fun, as well as an opportunity for romance.

The old double standard of aging is still so strong that a wife five years younger than her husband is considered to be an "older woman," but a man five years older than his wife is not

© James L. Shaffer

Older men are more likely to be married than older women, but it is no longer uncommon to see a marriage between two older people. Sexuality and love persist throughout the life course.

To heighten awareness that elders do indeed have and enjoy sex, a company that makes sex education films produced a film entitled *Ripple in Time* that shows an older couple making love. The couple in the film find each other's bodies attractive and stimulating. When this film was shown to a human sexuality class, the evaluations were overwhelmingly positive. Students of all ages said that they had never seen more tenderness and love expressed or thought sex could be more beautiful than the way it was portrayed by the couple in this film. Many remarked that the movie had changed not only their conceptions about sex but also their conception of elders.

In Ruth Jacobs's book *Be an Outrageous Older Woman,* a chapter on sexuality relates her surprise and dismay at the shock evoked by her writings and seminars. Her writings, although not graphic, are open and candid about the sexual desires of older women. She believes that our definition of what is sexual has undermined older adults and needs to be changed. If being sexy is measured by frequencies of orgasms and other quantitative counts, sexuality may show some decrease with age. But if sexuality refers to one's ability to be sensual, then one can become more sexual with age.

In one of Jacobs's workshops an older woman who assumed her decreased interest in sex was due to aging discovered that the tranquilizers she had been taking for four years were responsible. Other drugs, such as the relatively new ones for depression such as Prozac and Zoloft, can severely affect the ability of a woman to have an orgasm. Individuals must check on the side effect of drugs. For example, sexual dysfunction is not an uncommon side effect for men who take certain medications for hypertension.

considered to be an "older man" (Lovenheim, 1990). In the past 20 years, however, a 50 percent increase in the number of American women marrying younger men has taken place. Bureau of the Census data for 1990 shows that in 1970 only one-sixth of women married younger men, but in 1990 nearly 25 percent did (U.S. Bureau of the Census, 1994). Although this is most common among men and women in their 30s to early 50s, the pattern itself represents a shift in normative attitudes about age. And those couples and the couples to follow will continue to age. Change is in the air for the twenty-first century.

Once I asked Grandma when did you stop liking it?, and she was 80. She said, "Child, you'll have to ask someone older than me."

Granddaughter, 1998

Remaining Sexual in Special Circumstances

We come face-to-face with cultural taboos and social prohibitions with the topic of sex in nursing home settings. The topic has been generally avoided by research, and most information is anecdotal in nature, coming from nursing assistants and floor nurses in nursing homes. Much of the information is in the form of poking fun and expressing exasperation at the "problem" old man, or the "acting-out" old woman.

Indeed, many old people continue to engage in sexual behaviors despite the lack of marital partners and living circumstances that range from incarceration-like to the more affluent life-care communities. An anonymous study of sexual practices in 10 California life-care communities disclosed that sexual thoughts and activity were frequent (Richardson & Lazur, 1995). Seventy percent of men and 50 percent of women thought often about sex and physical closeness with the opposite sex. Fifty-three percent of the men and 25 percent of the women who responded had regular sex partners, though at the time of the survey only 29 percent of the men and 14 percent of the women were married. The survey and interview methodology disclosed that the frequency and enjoyment of sexual activity in the past correlated with the sexual patterns of elderly participants. The study, then, highlights that sexual patterns and attitudes do not change much over the life course. Those who enjoyed and sought out sexual opportunities earlier in life continued to enjoy and seek out sex in their later years.

What, then, of sexual interests and activity among people living in nursing homes, rather than the more affluent life-care communities? Most studies identify the barriers to sexuality among nursing home residents. Generally, sexual activity and interest in sex in nursing homes is seen as being problematic to both staff and residents, and in any one facility the "issue" is focused on one individual as the "problem."

It is very probable that cognitively competent older people handle their sexuality in a nursing home setting by private use of masturbation and by psychological repression. One study compared the sexual attitudes of nursing home staff with those of the residents (Lauman et al., 1994). It found that residents were more likely than staff to agree that sex is not needed for women after menopause or for men after age 65; that most people over 55 years of age masturbate some of the time, and that sexually active elderly people are "dirty." It is not coincidental to these findings that approximately 98 percent of the respondents were elders. In addition to attitudes about behaviors, 61 percent of the residents did not feel sexually attractive and did not think they would enjoy sexual activity if they had a partner (Richardson & Lazur, 1995). This form of repression is probably functional in most nursing home settings—it helps people to get past any felt need for sexual expression. It also illustrates, however, the loss for nursing home residents of part of the human condition. The lack of sexual contact hurts, as well as the lost sexuality. Most tragically, it is probably unnecessary if alternative opportunities for the expression of sexuality are provided.

Living in the communal circumstances of a nursing home is difficult. Behavioral and psychological problems may result when residents are ridiculed or prevented from enjoying physical contact. When residents hold hands or say they want to marry, this may evoke laughter and sarcastic remarks, leading to humiliation. Treating an aged man and woman like children because they want to hold hands or embrace is insulting and robs them of an important aspect of their identity.

Nursing home administrators generally answer not to the elderly people in their facilities, but to the children of those elders. Adult children may have trouble accepting that their parent living in the nursing home wants intimacy with another resident. According to one study of nursing home life (Richardson & Lazur, 1995), nursing homes can address this issue of sexuality directly in several ways, including:

- Improving privacy ("do not disturb" signs, respected by staff)
- Educating staff about human sexuality in later life
- Helping to arrange for conjugal visits or home visits
- Encouraging other forms of sexual expression, such as hugging and kissing
- Evaluating complaints about sexual functioning
- Discontinuing medicines that may affect sexual function

- Providing information and counseling about sexuality to interested patients

We all need to know that the possibilities for intimacy and enchantment with another continue to the end of our lives. Sex is for life. The frequency and vigor of sex may change with age, but sex in later life remains a critically important aspect of our self-identity, in whatever way it has formed for us over the course of our lives. Regardless of age, the loving expression of it says, "I value you. I appreciate you. I like having you in my life. I trust, and want to touch you and be touched by you."

Chapter Summary

This chapter considers older couples and three categories of older singles: the widowed, the divorced, and the never married. An unknown percentage of older people live together without being married, but we do not directly address this important and growing phenomenon in this chapter. As the baby-boomer cohort begins to move into elderhood, more information on the social significance of unmarried partners will become available.

The myth that older people automatically lose interest in sex distorts perceptions of older people. Unhappy marriages reduced sexual activity for older couples who experienced them just as it did for younger couples. One large study indicated that 70 percent of men and 50 percent of women thought often about sex and physical closeness with the opposite sex, regardless of age.

Sex, feeling sexual, having intimate relationships, and being touched with care—caressed—are profoundly important human experiences, regardless of one's age. Old age separates people from marriage partners and sometimes from other relationships of intimacy, but old age does not mean asexuality.

Key Terms

achieved relationships
ascribed relationships
Duke longitudinal study
friendship relationships
grief work
intimacy
kin relationships

Kinsey studies
Masters and Johnson studies
relationships
sexual function for procreation
social comparisons
stages of widowhood

Questions for Discussion

1. What are some differences between being a widow and being a widower? What are some similarities? Do you think that gender differences somehow shape the experience of losing a partner?
2. What are the advantages and disadvantages of being married in later life? Of being single?
3. Imagine for a moment that you have just learned that your mother, who is living in a nursing home because of some cognitive impairment, is engaging in a sexual relation-

ship with another facility resident. What is your emotional response? Should you do something about it? If so, what will that be? If not, how can you be certain that her best interests are being protected?

Fieldwork Suggestions

1. Interview a person who works in a hospice program. What insights might this person give you regarding widowhood? Is what you hear consistent with your understanding of widowhood?
2. Talk with two people who have been widowed for several years. Ask each person what his or her partner was like. *Listen* to the response.

Internet Activities

1. Search for an Internet site with information on widowhood. Develop categories of the material you find: Who do you guess would use this site? What does the site market, if anything? What is the intent or purpose of the site?
2. Locate an Internet chat group specifically for older people who want to connect with other older people. What observations can you make about this site?

Physical Health and Well-Being

The Aging Body: A Description

Major Health Problems

Biological Theories of Aging

Longevity: The Role of Diet, Exercise, and Mental Health

EXPIRES CALIFORNIA
JUNE

J 875021

DISABLED PERSON

Drop in Exercise Efficiency with Age Can Be Eased

Amy Norton

Older adults may have to work harder than young people to perform the same physical activity, but regular exercise may close that age gap, research findings suggests.

In a study comparing sedentary adults in their 60s and 70s with those in their 20s and 30s, researchers found that older men and women had to use much more oxygen to walk at the same speed as their younger counterparts.

But that was before they went through a six-month exercise program. After taking up walking or jogging, biking, and stretching, the senior study participants reversed their loss of exercise "efficiency."

Exercise efficiency refers to how much energy the body expends to perform a given activity. At the start of this study, older men and women used 20 percent more oxygen to walk at the same speed as a younger person, said Dr. Wayne C. Levy of the University of Washington in Seattle, the study's senior author.

But six months of regular exercise—90 minutes, three days per week—improved older participants' exercise efficiency by 30 percent, versus only 2 percent among their younger counterparts.

The findings are published in the current issue of the *Journal of the American College of Cardiology*.

It's well known that as people age, there is a decline in exercise capacity—how much work a person can do before becoming exhausted. But the new findings suggest this is not just a product of the aging cardiovascular system being less able to send oxygen to working muscles. The older body also needs more oxygen to perform the same work as a younger one—that is, exercise efficiency declines.

But this decline appears to arise largely from inactivity, and may well be reversible.

The idea that exercise efficiency dips with age is a "relatively new concept," Levy told Reuters Health. And though younger people in his study were still better at pumping blood and oxygen to their muscles after exercise training, it was only the older exercisers who showed significant gains in exercise efficiency.

Their "disproportionately" greater improvement in this area, Levy and his colleagues write, is "new and unexpected."

It's not clear yet how intensely people need to exercise to hang on to their efficiency as they age, according to Levy. But he said he suspects that any activity done regularly, including walking, would have benefits.

© Reuters Limited.

Underscoring a fundamental truth about biological functioning, the phrase "use it or lose it" is often used to refer to physical abilities. What causes the decrease in physical activity that we see in people as they age? Is it inevitable?

Statistically, good health declines with age. However, we do not yet fully understand the role of the aging process in contrast to other factors that affect this decline. Poor diet, overeating, smoking, excessive drinking, misuse of drugs, accidents, and stress all affect our health. Some of the health problems that the elderly have may be an inevitable consequence of the aging process. Others clearly are not. Physical fitness and good nutrition are two factors that can slow the aging process.

To best fulfill their individual potentials, people of all ages, especially elders, need factual information about physical health and their body's changing dietary and exercise needs.

Did You Know . . .
Restricting food intake seems to retard aging in rats. Whether caloric intake restriction for humans would produce the same results is speculative, but some scientists believe that in the future the human life span can be increased.

Aging is a gradual process beginning at birth. As guaranteed as biological aging is to all life, we do not know for certain what causes aging. For starters, we know that our life span is finite: we will not survive indefinitely. That period between birth and death, then, is our "life," no matter how long or short it might be. The **absolute human life span** is the maximum possible chronological age that the human can live. Although currently under debate, it is considered to be about 120 years for humans (Walford, 1983; Ross, 1996). Biologists believe that we are not programmed by our genes to live indefinitely, because aging is species specific: the human maximum is around 120 years; the tortoise, about 150. The absolute life span of the domestic cat is about 30 years, and of the mouse, a little over 3 years. There may be a biological limit to the number of times human cells can divide and replace themselves, but if so, we do not know what that limit may be or whether it is possible to extend it (Barinaga, 1991).

A more useful measure of how long humans live than absolute possibility is the **mean human life span,** which is the chronological age by which 50 percent of humans will have died, according to statistical projection. That was discussed briefly when we talked about changing demographics, because it is the number that has most radically increased over the past century. Mean human life span in the United States is currently about 76 years, with gender differences of longer lives for women (approximately 81 years) than men (approximately 75); and ethnic differences, probably based on the unequal distribution of wealth and access to health care in the United States.

As a person ages, his or her body parts reach peak levels of operation or performance; their functioning then remains constant or begins a slow decline. Some peaks are reached in youth, others in young adulthood or middle age, and some in old age if the potential of the younger years was never developed. Physical declines may result not from the aging process but from various pathologies (diseases), lack of proper diet and exercise, cigarette smoking, stress, or other factors. Some declines that have generally been attributed to the aging process may take place at very different ages or not at all once disease is controlled for.

This chapter will examine only that physical debilitation that is *correlated* with age. These physical problems generally are considered to be pathological or disease related and may or may not be caused by the aging process itself.

The Aging Body: A Description

Many changes that take place in the body are observable: the skin loses its elasticity and becomes more wrinkled, the hair grays and thins out, and the body becomes less erect. Individuals get tired more easily and quickly. As early as the 30s and 40s, the eyes may develop **presbyopia,** a condition in which near vision is impaired and the fine print of a book or newspaper becomes difficult to see at close range. Hearing loss may occur. As the aging process continues, teeth may be lost or gums may develop disease. In addition, an older person tends to gain body fat and lose muscle strength, especially if he or she does not reduce caloric intake and maintain physical exercise. In most cases, the older people become, the fewer calories their bodies need. Further, the ability of the body cells to absorb calcium declines. This loss of calcium results in bones that are more brittle and more easily broken. Aging brings more wear and tear to one's bones and joints; thus, the likelihood of rheumatism and arthritis increases with age.

Some health declines are not as apparent. The capacity of the body to achieve homeostasis (physiological equilibrium) declines with age. This means that older people have greater difficulty "getting back to normal," biologically speaking, after a stressful event. Blood pressure and heart rates, for example, take longer to return to their prestress levels. Various organs operate at reduced efficiency: the lungs decrease their maximum breathing capacity; the kidneys decrease the speed at which they can filter waste out of the blood; bladder capacity declines; and the level of sex hormones decreases. The nervous system also changes: Reflex action remains constant with age, but reaction time declines. As a result, tasks take longer to perform. The digestive juices decrease in volume; consequently, the body takes longer to digest its food. The body's **immune system** decreases in its ability to protect a person from disease; hence, the older individual is less immune to contagious diseases, such as the flu, and is likely to be harder hit by them.

Although we know that these changes take place, we do not yet fully understand why. In other words, we do not know what causes aging. Some gerontologists believe that aging is not an inherent process at all, but merely describes a "medley of unhappy outcomes" (Posner, 1995, p. 17). From this perspective, age is strictly the result of illness, and if we were able to keep ourselves completely disease free, we would not age. A more useful understanding of aging, however, is to view it as a process in which bodily changes occur and there is a general physiological decline in body functioning. This model of physical decline is somewhat offset, according to some gerontologists, by an increase in intellectual and psychological competence. So, for example, at the very biological time one's metabolism is becoming less efficient, the person is intellectually (and perhaps psychologically) able to take more seriously the idea of self-care—more attuned to messages from the body.

Biological changes such as slower reaction time or shifts in visual acuity can call into question the functional ability of older adults. One question often raised, for example, is whether older adults should be permitted to drive. Of the changes the aging body undergoes, visual changes are among the most pronounced. We know, however, that chronology (age by year) is a poor indicator of functionality (ability to function). Policy declaring that people at age 70, for example, could no longer drive would be grossly unfair to those 70-year-olds whose functioning is unimpaired. This would be somewhat like declaring that 17-year-olds do not have the maturity or judgment to make quick, critical driving decisions, and therefore the driving age should be increased to 20. Although drivers age 55 to 65 are the safest drivers on the road by almost every measure, after age 75, collision rates increase dramatically. What are the social implications of age changes that might endanger the safety of others?

Although physical changes may significantly affect the ability of some older adults to drive competently, improved structural changes in driving conditions would create a safer driving environment for older adults: larger road signs with more legible lettering, raised pavement reflectors, and so on. As more and more of our citizens reach late life, we will need to adjust traditional transportation practices to accommodate this group's mobility needs.

All these physiological changes that take place with age occur so gradually that they go unnoticed much of the time. The deterioration of body organs and systems owing to age may be fairly insignificant as it relates to an individual's ability to function independently, to get around, and to carry out normal activities. Nevertheless, the process of decline proceeds.

Chronic and Acute Conditions

The key health problems facing middle-aged and older adults today are those that are chronic. Young people tend to have **acute conditions,** that is, short-term illnesses in which the cause is known and the condition is curable. Chicken pox, colds, and influenza are examples of acute diseases. **Chronic conditions,** in contrast, are long term. Acute diseases decline with age, whereas the number and severity of chronic conditions increase with age. Their causes are typically unknown, and even if the cause is known, cures are not available. The goal of chronic health care is control, maintenance, or rehabilitation. The most prevalent chronic conditions affecting elders, in order of highest frequency, are:

1. Arthritis
2. Hypertension
3. Heart conditions
4. Hearing and visual impairments
5. Cancer
6. Diabetes

A chronic condition may or may not be disabling, depending on the type and severity of the condition. Loss of teeth can be considered a chronic condition but is rarely disabling. A chronic condition may be progressively debilitating; Parkinson's disease is one example. An older person may have a number of chronic conditions but not be severely limited by any of them. Imagine the 65-year-old with mild arthritis, mild diabetes, minor visual impairment, loss of teeth, and a mild heart condition. Although this person has five chronic conditions, he or she may remain active, vigorous, and unaffected in a major way by any of them. Conversely, another older person might become completely bedridden from just one severe chronic condition.

Sometimes, the discovery of a medical cure for a disease can transform it from a chronic to an acute one. For example, some forms of cancer, now considered acute, were once thought to be chronic. Some chronic conditions do not seem to be the result of pathology (disease). Instead, they seem to be the result of the normal aging process. Several forms of arthritis fit into this category.

Health Status

The majority of persons over the age of 65 are in fairly good health. The **health status of the aged** has improved markedly in the past 50 years. Although the health status of the average 45-year-old differs from that of the average 65-year-old, this difference is not great. People do not reach age 65 and suddenly become decrepit. However, physical decline does become more apparent with advancing age. Those age 75 and over usually have noticeable physical declines compared with the middle-aged, and those over 85 have even more noticeable declines. With advanced age come more numerous and longer hospital stays, more doctor visits, and more days of disability. But declines are typically very gradual.

Ninety-five percent of Americans 65 and over live successfully or nearly successfully in the community; a small percentage are confined to institutions. Among noninstitutionalized elders, 86 percent have chronic conditions, but in the

TABLE 7.1

Characteristics of noninstitutionalized persons over 65 by disability status: 2000

Characteristic	Total	Male	Female
Population 65 and over	33,346,626	13,940,918	19,405,708
With any disability	41.9%	40.0%	43.0%
Sensory	14.2%	15.6%	13.2%
Physical	28.6%	25.8%	30.7%
Mental	10.8%	9.9%	11.4%
Self-care	9.5%	7.5%	11.0%
Difficulty going outside the home	20.4%	16.8%	23.0%

Source: U.S. Census Bureau. (2003). Economics and Statistics Administration, Washington, DC.

vast majority of older people with chronic conditions, the condition is relatively minor, and they suffer no interference with their mobility. Of the noninstitutionalized elders with chronic conditions, which range from mild arthritis conditions to totally disabling ailments, 58 percent report no activity limitation whatsoever, almost 29 percent report physical disabilities of some sort, just under 11 percent report some form of mental disability, and 20.4 percent report difficulty going outside the home (see Table 7.1). Heart conditions and arthritis impose the most limitations on older people. Statistics that indicate a high number of elders suffer from chronic conditions hide the fact that most older people manage quite well. The very old, 80 years old or more, are those who suffer most from disabilities.

The prevalence of disabilities among people over 65 has social consequences. For people under 65, the prevalence of disability among boys and men was higher than among girls and women (7.2 percent for boys under 15 and 4.3 percent for girls the same age). Among men age 16 to 64, 19.6 percent have disabilities, compared with 17.6 percent of women in that age category. Among people over 65, women with disabilities outnumber men, with 40.4 percent of men and 43.0 percent of women reporting disabilities (Waldrop & Stern, 2003). As the population

ages, the number of older people requiring medical and social assistance with disability management will increase proportionally. This will impact health care and social programs, thereby straining the existing resources established for well-being care for elders.

Table 7.1 examines the functional limitations by limiting category of persons 65 years and older. Note that differences in male and female disabilities reflect a greater disability rate among the female population than among men. This figure is related to the greater proportion of older (85-plus) women in the 65-plus population.

Major Health Problems

Although people tend to assume that old age brings sickness, this is not necessarily true. Most of the major health problems of old age result from pathology, the presence of disease, the causes of which, in many cases, lie outside the aging process. Poor living habits established early in life, inadequate diet, and too little exercise cause some of the "diseases of old age." With preventive measures, these diseases can be avoided. About 75 percent of all deaths are caused by heart disease, cancer, and stroke.

Death rates from heart disease have declined significantly over the last 20 years, owing to medical advances, modifications of the diet, reduced smoking rates, and better exercise habits. However, cancer deaths have increased, and cancer has its highest incidence in the elder population (American Cancer Society, 1996).

Differences in mortality are evident between black and white populations. Heart disease, cancer, and cerebrovascular diseases are the leading causes of death among those 65 and older for both races. The rates of mortality for African Americans are significantly higher: 5 percent, 17 percent, and 24 percent higher, respectively, for each of these conditions in 1990 (U.S. Bureau of the Census, 2000). These ethnic differences are due in no small part to the socioeconomic disadvantages experienced by African Americans, including income, education, and access to health care.

Heart Disease

Heart disease is a very general term covering many conditions. Some aspects of heart disease are pathological; that is, disease is present in the body. Other kinds of heart problems, although associated with aging, cannot be attributed to the aging process alone. Of all persons aged 65 and over, one-fourth (25 percent) are limited in their activities by heart conditions (U.S. Bureau of the Census, 1993).

The most widespread form of heart disease, **coronary artery disease** or **ischemic** (deprived of blood) **heart disease,** is now the major killing disease in the United States and in other industrialized nations as well. Its incidence increases with age, and it is *the* most common cause of death in middle-aged and older individuals. With coronary artery disease, an insufficient amount of blood reaches the heart. This deficiency, which results from the narrowing of the blood vessels, damages the heart tissue.

Two major disorders of the circulatory system are **atherosclerosis** and **hypertension.** Atherosclerosis is one form of a group of cardiovascular disorders called **arteriosclerosis,** which refers to hardening or loss of elasticity of the arteries (Kausler & Kausler, 1996). Atherosclerosis occurs when fat and cholesterol crystals, along with other substances, accumulate on the interior walls of the arteries, thereby reducing the size of these passageways. The accumulation of some deposits of fat in the arteries seems to be part of normal aging; however, the increased incidence in Western countries of heart attack suggests that excessive deposits are linked to factors such as smoking and serum cholesterol levels that might be controlled by lifestyle changes.

Hypertension refers to excessive arterial blood pressure. It is present in about 40 percent of people age 65 and older and 25 percent of those in the 45- to 64-year age range (Kausler & Kausler, 1996). Hypertension can be treated with medications that rid the body of excess fluid and sodium. Factors associated with risk of hypertension include obesity, smoking, and excessive alcohol consumption. Additionally, some pain medications (nonsteroidal anti-inflammatory drugs) may increase blood pressure when taken over a long period of time. Hypertension is responsive to diet and exercise, so once again the issue of lifestyle choices emerges in relation to healthy aging.

Excess body fat has long been considered to be a risk factor in coronary heart disease, but the exact relationship is still unclear. A recent study from the Honolulu Heart program of over 3,700 Japanese-American men age 71 to 93 suggests that the relationship of body weight to heart disease might be more complex than previously believed. The body mass index (BMI), or weight divided by height in square meters, is commonly used in research as an estimate of overall weight. The Honolulu Heart study found that among men, a high waist-to-hip ratio (WHR) accompanied by elevated cholesterol (HDL-C) was more strongly related to coronary heart disease than was "predominantly peripheral fat accumulation," or excess weight accumulated more uniformly on the body (Huang et al., 1997). Research indicates that risk factors among women are different than those among men; however, biomedical research on coronary heart disease experienced by women is still new and incomplete (Sonnichsen et al., 1993).

The solutions to difficult problems are oftentimes simple, logical, and wrong.

H. L. MENCKEN, 1939

A major health problem associated with atherosclerosis is *thrombosis,* or blood clotting. Blood clots occur when undissolved fatty deposits in the arteries cut off the blood supply to the heart. Some of the factors that lead to atherosclerosis are thought to be a high cholesterol count, a diet high in refined sugars and saturated fats, high blood pressure, obesity, stress, hereditary factors, lack of exercise, and cigarette smoking.

Forrester and Shah (1997) argued for use of serum cholesterol as a screening test for preventing coronary artery disease (CAD) for a broader range of people than that recommended by the American College of Physicians. The guidelines state that screening is not recommended for men younger than 35 or older than 75 or for women younger than 45 or older than 75, and that it is "appropriate but not mandatory" for men between 35 and 65 and for women between 45 and 65 (Garber et al., 1996). Forrester and Shah developed five arguments, based on reviews of the literature, in opposition to the ACP findings:

1. It is more cost-effective to prevent CAD than to treat it after it is clinically apparent.
2. Elevated cholesterol in young adult men establishes increased CAD over the next 40 years.
3. Lowering blood cholesterol in young hypercholesterolemic persons would decrease rates of CAD over their life span.
4. Cholesterol lowering can be accomplished at low cost.
5. Cholesterol lowering is equally effective in women and the elderly.

Research that establishes treatment guidelines must be critically reviewed because those guidelines help establish recommendations that health insurance companies use to determine whether or not particular tests and treatments will be covered by a health policy. On an individual level, medical decisions are always probabilistic, their uncertainty born of the vast individual differences inherent among people as a group (Forrester & Shah, 1997).

Coronary artery disease can vary in its severity and in the area in the body of greatest damage. Older people are known to have increased risk of vascular disease in their legs (Vogt et al., 1992). This condition is strongly associated with increased disability, and particularly complicates symptoms of diabetes (Orchard & Strandness, 1993). If coronary artery disease results in deficient blood supply to the heart, heart tissue will die, producing a dead area called an **infarct.** The disease can lead to myocardial infarction, or heart attack.

Heart attacks can be acute, sudden, painful, and clearly identifiable; or they can be more subtle, creating a more generalized dizziness, weakness, confusion, or numbness. The symptoms have a broad range, and they are different in men than in women. Men and women have similar rates of heart attack after 65, but women are less likely to suffer this event before that age than are men. Even at younger ages, women are more likely to die from a myocardial infarction than are men—a fact that is still not clearly understood because of the limited research that has been conducted on women's health issues (Hooyman & Kiyak, 2002).

Cutting-edge research using stem cells for cell infusions has had remarkable results in animal models; however, in 2005 limits were placed on studies on human models. Stem cell therapy is an experimental approach involving taking cells, sometimes from the patient's own body, sometimes from fetal embryonic stem (ES) cells, and delivering them to the ailing heart (Couzin & Vogel, 2004). Embryonic stem cell therapy transplants ES cells into a patient. The cells then search out, detect, and attempt to repair damage; they additionally release growth factors that stimulate the body's repair mechanisms (Medra, 2004). Research in Europe among (primarily) French, German, and English cardiologists has shown promising possibilities for regenerating cells in the human heart, but the research remains experimental. In animal models immature muscle cells taken from the thigh seem to aid injured hearts, but the cells do not synchronize with heart cells, indicating a dangerous possibility of arrhythmias. Research cardiologists remain excited about future possibilities for stem cell transplantation, but in the United States the ethics of using embryonic stem cells has engendered a public debate over ethical, legal, and religious questions (American Association for the Advancement of Science, 2005 [hereafter AAAS]).

Stem cell research continues in Europe and Asia; however, it is yet to be determined whether it will proceed with full federal support in the United States. From mapping the human genome to preventing, treating, and curing devastating illnesses such as Parkinson's disease, heart disease, cancer, diseases of the nervous system, and Alzheimer's disease, stem cell research is currently the most promising research for the future.

Cancer

In reality a group of several hundred diseases, cancer may affect the breast, skin, stomach, bones, blood, or other parts of the body. Its common characteristic is an uncontrolled, invasive cell growth at the expense of normal body systems. There may be numerous causes of cancer, among them perhaps the inhalation or ingestion of chemicals, smoking, diet, and radiation. Although the basic cause of cancer is not fully understood, it begins when a living cell somehow becomes a cancer cell. This cancer cell then transmits its abnormality to succeeding cell generations. When the wild growth of cancer cells is not eliminated from the body, tumors develop.

Statistics have traditionally shown that the risk of cancer increases with age. The latest research, however, now shows that cancer mortality rates at very old ages decline precipitously (Smith, 1996). This finding is available only because of the number of people living into very old age: In 1960, there were 66 cancer deaths of people age 100 and over in the United States. In 1990, 12,340 people over the age of 100 died, and of these, 524 died of cancer—just under 4 percent of the total deaths (National Center for Health Statistics, 1994). The increasing numbers reflect the larger number of people living to 100 and beyond; the proportion of cancer deaths has remained the same over time. Different kinds of cancers peak at different ages: mortality for cancer of the liver peaks between the ages of 85 and 95; lung cancer seems to plateau between 80 and 84 years of age (Smith, 1996); and the incidence of ovarian cancer has been described to decrease beginning about at 75 years of age (Yancik, 1993).

Most people do not live to be over 85 years of age, however, and cancer remains a major killer of older people in the United States. Over one-half of all deaths from cancer occur in later life (age 65 and older). Thus, cancer is the second leading cause of death among the elderly, and also a leading chronic condition among elderly. Many cancers are treated for some time before the reserve capacity of the elder is gone or the elder has passed the five-year point of "cure." This has implications for treatment: a 70-year-old woman, for example, has a remaining life expectancy of 15 years. If she has physiologic declines in addition to cancer, the impact on her ability to function in daily life is a major consideration (Cohen, 1997).

A recent study surveyed 1,647 elders with cancer to determine the impact of cancer on how well they could function, and what their utilization of health care was (Stafford & Cyr, 1997). They measured limitations in the activities of daily living (ADLs)—such as getting out of a chair—and in the instrumental activities of daily living (IADLs)—going shopping, for example. Findings revealed that cancer increased the use of health care resources and modestly reduced physical function. Elders with cancer might require the care not only of an oncologist, but also of a geriatrician, to help determine appropriate services.

Three forms of cancer treatment are surgery, radiation, and chemotherapy (treatment with drugs). Some forms of cancer can be successfully treated and effectively cured, especially following early detection—for example, breast cancer, if detected early. Other forms of cancer, such as lung cancer, are more difficult to diagnose at early stages and are therefore more difficult to treat.

Cerebrovascular Disease

A stroke occurs when there is a disruption of blood flow to the brain. **Cerebrovascular disease,** more commonly called **stroke,** is predominantly a problem of old age and is one of several chronic diseases that account for the greatest burden of physical disability and health care utilization in later life (Barker & Mullooly, 1997). It is estimated that more than half a million Americans have strokes each year; most are elders (Kausler & Kausler, 1996).

The most common causes of stroke are the same as those of coronary artery disease—atherosclerosis and arteriosclerosis. These conditions may result either in a malfunction or narrowing of the blood vessels serving the brain, or in a blood clot blocking an artery that serves the brain. Two other causes of stroke are hemorrhage (bleeding inside the brain) and blockage of an artery serving the brain as a result of a clot that has broken off from a major clot elsewhere in the body. When brain cells do not receive blood from the heart, they die. The death of brain cells indicates the occurrence of a stroke.

The severity of a stroke depends on the area of the brain affected and the total amount of brain tissue involved. Strokes may affect various parts of the brain. When the left side of the brain is affected, the symptoms will differ from those

© James L. Shaffer

Exercise is critical for health in later life. Here an elderly woman who is unable to walk unassisted still achieves cardiovascular exercise as she bowls in a modified bowling alley.

that occur when the right side of the brain is affected. Depending on the particular area of the brain and the size of the area affected, paralysis in varying degrees, speech disorders, mental confusion, or memory impairment can result. Stroke is a leading cause of first admissions to mental hospitals because of the symptoms resulting from damage to the brain.

Rehabilitation for stroke victims is successful in varying degrees. Much of the variance depends on the severity of the stroke. The victim of a stroke has a better chance of recovery if treated promptly during the initial phases. Rehabilitation and exercise training are now commonly prescribed for survivors of coronary artery and cerebrovascular diseases. Rehabilitation is remarkably successful: one study found marked improvements in exercise capacity and obesity indices and modest improvement in plasma lipids in older women, in addition to improved quality-of-life parameters (Lavie & Milani, 1997).

Rehabilitation from stroke and other life-altering diseases is also related to the personality of the individual with the disease. Morris and colleagues (1993) determined in an Australian sample of old people who experienced stroke that personality introversion and depression are associated with increased mortality following that stroke.

Stroke has become less lethal and disabling in the past 20 years, though no less common a disease. Debate rages in the medical world over whether the reduction in mortality is due to hypertension control efforts or to treatment following the event (prevention or treatment). Both appear to be factors: a sharp decrease in rates of coma among stroke cases in the 1980s (treatment) and the reduced prevalence of hypertensive heart disease among new stroke cases (prevention) probably combine to reduce fatality (Barker & Mullooly, 1997). The question, however, is an important one. The perspectives have implications for health care policy, which is increasingly determined by insurance companies. Should health care policy focus on individual treatment or on larger, more social-level programs for prevention of disease?

Accidents

A health problem of major proportions is disability or death due to accidents. Although persons over 65 make up 13 percent of the population, they represent 29 percent of all accidental deaths. Falls are the most common cause of accidental death among those 65 and over, followed closely by motor vehicle accidents. Suffocation from an object that has been ingested, surgical and medical mishaps, fires, and burns are also major causes of accidental death among elders. The 90-and-over group has an alarmingly disproportionate share of deaths due to accidents in two of these categories: falls and suffocation by ingestion of food (National Safety Council, 1993, p. 23).

Such needless tragedy among people of advanced age illustrates a need for more preventive measures. A few concerned organizations, for example, have run "falls clinics" as a preventive measure. The annual incidence of falls is approximately 30 percent in people over 65 years of age, increasing to 50 percent in those over age 80 (Steinweg, 1997). About half of those falls can be attributed to accidents (toppling from a shaky ladder) and extrinsic causes (slippery floors). The other half are from causes such as weakness of the lower extremities, gait disorders, the effects of medications, or illness (Steinweg, 1997). A great deal of attention is now being focused on ways in which stability can be enhanced in older people as a means for reducing the incidents and severity of falls. Some programs help people train for balance. Much as we learned balance as young children from walking, running, and/or skipping on a railroad track or ledge, learning and relearning skills of balance can be accomplished at any age and have shown to be quite effective with elders.

There is a real danger with falls that a hip will crack. Because we instinctively use the hip to absorb most falls and because bones are often weakened by osteoporosis, a hip fracture is a common ailment to be feared. One-third of women (those most likely to have osteoporosis) and one-sixth of men who live to age 90 will suffer a hip fracture.

About 90 percent of hip fractures are due to osteoporosis. Older women with smaller body size are at increased risk of hip fracture because of lower hipbone mineral density (Ensrud et al., 1997). Only 25 percent recover fully, and one in four dies within six months of the injury (Schideler, 1994). Compared with women, older men hospitalized with hip fracture in one study were shown to have higher mortality and more risk factors for osteoporosis. Like women, the men are usually fragile, with preexisting illnesses that contribute to an overall poor outcome (Diamond et al., 1997). Recovery can be slow and quite painful; some people never walk again, others gain mobility only with the use of a walker, and those that can heal well enough to resume a normal, active life often take years to do so.

Some other factors of age that contribute to accidental death or injury are failing eyesight and hearing; reduced muscular strength, balance, and coordination; and increased reaction time. If these limitations are combined with impaired judgment, the very old are especially vulnerable to accidents. They may try to lift loads that are too heavy or poorly balanced, or they may climb or reach overhead without sufficient strength to manage the task. Changes in automobile traffic conditions can happen too swiftly for them to react. The swallowing reflex diminishes with age, making choking on food or objects in the mouth, such as a safety pin, more likely. Danger signals of fire or leaking gas are not perceived readily, and the few minutes or seconds of delayed reaction often prove to be fatal. Accidental drownings of older persons result more often from activities around water rather than from actual swimming.

Arthritis

Arthritis, which results from the inflammation of a joint or a degenerative change in a joint, is one of the oldest diseases known. It is widespread today and affects all age groups, but mostly older persons. There are numerous types of arthritis, with different causes, different symptoms, and differing degrees of severity. Rheumatoid arthritis and gout, though rare, are painful and troubling forms. The type of arthritis that most often poses problems for those 65 and over is osteoarthritis.

Osteoarthritis, the most common form of arthritis, is fairly widespread in middle age and almost universal in old age. It is estimated that 63 percent of women and 50 percent of men over 70 have some physical evidence of arthritis (National Center for Health Statistics, 1994). Most older people have some degree of osteoarthritis. The joints most commonly affected are the weight-bearing ones: the hips, knees, and spine. The fingers and big toe are also commonly affected. With osteoarthritis, elastic tissue (cartilage) becomes soft and wears away and the underlying bones are exposed, which causes pain, stiffness, and tenderness. For some, osteoarthritis starts early in life and affects mostly the small joints. For others, osteoarthritis results from injury or vigorous wear and tear (the athletic knee is an example). It occurs later in life in the large or overused joints. Therapies for osteoarthritis include anti-inflammatory drugs, steroids, exercise, reduction of strain on critical joints, and surgical procedures such as hip and knee replacement (Hooyman & Kiyak, 2002).

Osteoporosis

Osteoporosis, another potentially severe and crippling skeletal problem, is characterized by a gradual loss of bone mass (density) that generally begins between the ages of 35 and 40. The number of victims and the severity of the disease increase with advancing age. Millions of Americans suffer from this disease, and 75 to 80 percent of them are women.

Loss of bone mass can result in diminishing height, slumped posture, the "dowager's hump," and a reduction in the strength of the bones, which makes them more susceptible to fractures. The bones may become so weak that a sudden strain will break them.

The causes of osteoporosis include inadequate diet over a long period of time (lack of calcium is a major dietary factor), reduced absorptive efficiency due to an aging digestive system, cigarette smoking, lack of vigorous physical activity, and estrogen deficiency in women. The loss of estrogen at menopause contributes to about 80 percent of osteoporosis, but men can also get this disease, and fractures related to osteoporosis in men have higher mortality rates than in women (Diamond et al., 1997). The prevention of osteoporosis must be lifelong, with attention to nutrition and activity as well as the modification of risk factors such as smoking and excessive alcohol consumption (Johansson et al., 1993).

An initial cause of osteoporosis is a decrease or upset in hormonal balance. In menopause and old age, the body may not have enough hormones to maintain its calcium balance. Some medications, such as steroids, actually cause osteoporosis to develop, and are a particular problem for older people, who are likely to be on several medications for different medical conditions.

Osteoporosis can sometimes be slowed by a high-calcium diet. Some doctors recommend calcium supplements. The vitamin D metabolite calcitrol has been shown to help correct problems with calcium absorption and has been particularly useful with steroid-induced bone loss. There is growing evidence of the effectiveness of estrogen treatment for women following menopause (Mykyta, 1997). The pharmaceutical treatment alendronate is available by prescription and has been shown to be effective in actually increasing bone mineral density in postmenopausal women (Adami et al., 1995; Chestnut et al., 1995).

Scientists continue to search for biomedical treatments of osteoporosis and arthritis. In 2004 markers were identified that are early indicators of progressive disease in rheumatoid arthritis (RA), a form of arthritis. From that information, early, aggressive baseline treatment was developed to stop or slow the development of the arthritis (Goronzy, 2004). As our biomedical understanding of the process of arthritis and musculoskeletal disease continues to develop, health and well-being in later life will be dramatically altered in a positive way.

National campaigns are mounted each year to teach about prevention of this disease. Weight-bearing exercise should start in younger years, along with a good diet, and both should be continued in old age to slow this disease. Exercise has been proven to help maintain bone strength.

Other Concerns

Other health concerns more frequently found in older populations than in younger ones are emphysema and chronic bronchitis (which often occur together), diabetes mellitus, and obesity. Emphysema is characterized by lung rigidity; thickening of the mucus of the bronchioles; and scarring of the lung walls. Smoking and inhalation of contaminants such as gases, industrial fumes, or traffic exhaust may increase the risk of emphysema. Bronchitis, on the other hand, is a condition in which the bronchial tube becomes inflamed and scarred, often resulting in chronic coughing and an excessive production of mucus. Acute infectious bronchitis is treated with antibiotics, but long-term management—appropriate for most elders—includes improving the airway passages through medications, providing supportive nutritional care, and maximizing the function of the muscles that support the respiratory process (Heath, 1993).

Diabetes mellitus is a health-related problem that requires intervention and constant monitoring. Diabetes develops when sugars and starches are not translated into energy, generally due to inadequate amounts of insulin (produced by the pancreas). The most common type of diabetes is developed late in life and is milder, pathologically, than diabetes contracted in youth or late middle age. Often in late-onset diabetes, a change of diet may be sufficient to stabilize the condition. Symptoms of diabetes include increased appetite and urination, fatigue, decreased wound healing, and excessive thirst—but these symptoms might not be present in older people. Blood sugar might be temporarily elevated under conditions of illness or stress, so it is important to conduct glucose tests under conditions of reduced stress.

Did You Know . . .
Increased serum insulin may be more strongly associated with decreased cognitive function and dementia in women than is cerebrovascular disease.

STOLK ET AL., 1997

One study with rhesus monkeys suggests an approach with humans: monkeys were provided a diet with 30 percent fewer calories than the control group but the same level of nutrition. It resulted in lowered blood sugar and insulin levels compared with age-related increases in those markers in the control group of monkeys (Kemnitz et al., 1994).

Although not considered a disease, obesity, which results from excessive food intake, strains the heart and exacerbates systemic disease factors such as emphysema, osteoporosis, and arthritis. About one out of three older adults is significantly overweight.

Biological Theories of Aging

Must we grow old? Is there any way to stop aging? Human beings have asked these questions for centuries. The longest-lived persons on record are Shirechiyo Izumi of Japan and Jeanne Calmet of France, both of whom reached 120 years. This figure, then, represents the **maximum life span** of the human species, the greatest age reached by a member of a species. Biologists refer to biological aging as *senescence,* often described as the onset of the degenerative process—a process that usually becomes apparent between the ages of 40 and 45. Graying at the temples, crow's feet around the eyes, and the need for reading glasses to correct farsightedness (presbyopia) are among the early indicators that the process is underway.

Medical technology is slowing the aging process by increasing our fitness and vigor along with our **average life span,** the average age reached by the members of a species. No physician, or anyone else, has ever saved another's life—he or she has only prolonged it. A child born today has a life expectancy of approximately 80 years. Someday, life expectancy may be 120 or more years—a span the accommodation of which will require profound social and cultural changes. The extension of life, although desirable, also challenges society to ensure that the quality of that life will justify the efforts to extend it. Why do we grow old? Although there are a number of biological theories of aging, there is, at this time, no one clear scientific reason why we age. Aging today is viewed as many processes, and the theories described here are not necessarily mutually exclusive.

Did You Know . . .
Alexander Graham Bell conducted a genealogical study of one family with thousands of descendants, and discovered that children of parents who lived to be 80 or older, lived about 20 years longer than children whose parents died before they were 60 years old.

KAUSLER & KAUSLER, 1996

Aging as Disease

Aging may be entirely due to the disease processes in the body. If so, future medical science may be able to inhibit or eradicate **aging as disease.** One major study on the causes of deaths of centenarians found that 100 percent of those over 100 years of age succumbed not to "old age" but to organic failure cause by cerebrovascular disease, respiratory illnesses, cardiovascular diseases, and gastrointestinal disorders

(Berzlanovich et al., 2005). By eliminating disease in the body as it occurs, medical intervention theoretically should be able to keep the body in good health indefinitely. Still, most scientists try to separate the aging process from disease, because people seem to age even when no disease is afflicting the body. Several ideas about the nature of aging have been put forth.

Genetics

First, let us consider the genetics of aging. Scientific studies have demonstrated that human longevity runs in families. Investigations of twins confirm that human life span is inherited. Identical twins die within a relatively short time span of one another, whereas siblings have a greater variation in life spans. Evidence indicates that 10 to 15 percent of variation in age at death is genetically determined. Thus, the longevity of our parents and grandparents is an important indicator of our own longevity. A number of genetic theories have arisen to explain differential rates of aging. One group of theories, called programmed theories, emphasizes internal programs. Some genetic theorists presuppose a **biological clock** within us that begins ticking at conception. This clock may be in the nucleus of each cell of our body, an idea that advances the proposition that the body is "programmed" by specific genes to live a certain length of time.

Scientists once speculated that the biological clock was governed by a single gene. They now believe that thousands of genes are involved. The study of genetics became dramatically more sophisticated with the advent of genetic cloning and gene splicing; science is on the cusp of identifying for the first time the genetic factors in aging.

Do we really know that the human life span cannot be extended well beyond 100 years? What is the nature of the biological clock? How does it affect growth, development, and decline? Scientists in the fields of molecular biology and genetics continue to search for answers to these questions.

Related to the search for "longevity" genes is the search for genes that are responsible for hereditary diseases. More than 150 mutant genes have been identified. An example is the one responsible for a rare hereditary disease, a thyroid cancer. Soon DNA tests are almost certain to be a part of standard medical exams. From a sample of the patient's blood, doctors will be able to spot genetic mutations that signal the approach of hereditary diseases and also breast cancer, heart disease, and diabetes. Today at least 50 genetic tests for 50 specific hereditary diseases are available. In the near future a genetic test for the breast cancer gene (BRCA1), which is responsible for 1 in 10 of all breast cancers, will be available.

Genes are being identified at a rapid rate, including mutations responsible for Alzheimer's and colon cancer. Genes of neurodegeneration have been identified in the mouse in the form of a defect in a copper ion transporter (Mori, 1997). Most likely multiple genes are involved in Alzheimer's, and all these have yet to be found. Once a gene is found, laboratories work to develop a test to determine its presence or absence in the body. Discovering the genes of longevity in mammals cannot be far behind.

It is clear that there are multiple mechanisms to aging: it is a complex biological process characterized by disorder and decline and requires the approach of integrative biology, rather than the single-focus approach of a distinct biological discipline (Jazwinski, 1996). With support for research on the human genome, however, biogerontology is rapidly becoming an exciting new field in medicine.

Genetic **error theory** holds that errors in DNA molecules are looped back to become duplicated; thus any error introduced becomes replicated in the DNA, generating further errors, and finally leading to a lethal "error catastrophe" (Holliday, 1996b). The errors can be introduced by radiation and heat, by chemicals such as alcohol, or by mutation. Although not yet ruled strictly out, recent research has concluded that "these studies culminated in a definitive demonstration that errors in protein synthesis do not increase during cellular aging" (Riabowal et al., 1995, p. 6). Holliday (1996b) calls for the science community to keep an open mind to the idea of error catastrophe, because there are still many unanswered questions.

Immune System

A most promising "programmed" theory about aging is the immune system theory. Many aspects of immune function decline with age, and this decline is related to many kinds of disease, such as cancer. If the body's immune system becomes decreasingly effective with advancing age, harmful cells are more likely to survive and do damage. The theory is that cancer and other diseases attack the body with advancing age because the body progressively loses its ability to fight off disease. Some scientists are trying to revitalize the ailing immune systems of elders with hormone therapy, specifically the hormone DHEA. Studies of mice have shown that this hormone restored their immune systems to youthful levels in warding off certain diseases such as hepatitis B. Experiments with testosterone show it to increase muscle strength and counter anemia. In addition, AIDS research is bringing us more information about strengthening the immune system that hopefully will help prolong lives.

A related immunological theory of aging suggests that as the body ages, it develops more and more autoimmune antibodies that destroy cells, even normal ones. As age increases, the immune system seems to increase its capacity for autoimmune reactions. Several diseases, such as midlife diabetes, are related to autoimmune reactions, leading to the theory that such reactions cause aging. The theory is criticized because most autoimmune diseases, in fact, begin to develop at younger ages, but the impact of their consequences affects the quality of life of elders.

The consequences of impaired immune function in old people include increased susceptibility to infectious disease, emergence of tumors, and increased autoimmune reactions (Wick &

Grubeck-Loebenstein, 1997). For this reason, a distinction between **primary immunological change** (intrinsic decline of immune responsiveness) and **secondary immunological change** (due to disease and environmental factors such as diet, drug use, physical activity, etc.) can help to develop treatment models.

Cellular Theories

A major group of theories, called error theories, directs attention to forces that damage cells (National Institutes of Health, 1993). If the forces can be controlled, the belief is that aging can be prolonged.

One of the oldest and most enduring error theories is the cellular theory of **wear and tear,** the idea that irreplaceable body parts simply wear out. The cell is viewed as a highly complex piece of machinery, like an automobile. Some organisms live longer because they maintain themselves more carefully. Those who live more recklessly will wear out sooner. This idea is difficult to test and ignores the fact that cells can repair damage caused by wear and tear. The repair aspect returns the focus to the attempt to understand DNA, how it works, and why some cells get repaired and others do not. One theory would be that the person who lives longer has a more effective DNA repair system. This area of study is complicated by the intricate multiple phases of the repair systems.

Free Radicals

People seem to vary in their ability to fend off assaults to the body such as smoking, too much fat, and alcohol abuse. Some smokers, for example, manage to live long lives with no impact on their longevity. Winston Churchill is one example. Yet others who are very health conscious, such as Adelle Davis, succumb to cancer or other diseases before reaching old age.

One explanation for variability in longevity is that some people are more susceptible to free radicals than others. Free radicals is a name given to molecules in the body that are highly reactive. They are the by-product of normal metabolism, produced as cells turn food into energy. One way to combat aging is to trap the damaging molecules before they can do harm. Free radicals invade cells throughout the body, mangling vital protein enzymes and membranes and in general damaging the body.

Recent research has been investigating the relationship of free radical theory to Alzheimer's disease. Harman (1995) hypothesized that Alzheimer's disease is caused by increased free-radical reaction levels in brain neurons that over time advance patterns of cell loss. His conclusions suggest that the incidence of Alzheimer's may be decreased by efforts to minimize free-radical reactions. Harman further recommends that antioxidant supplements taken by the general population may decrease the incidence of Alzheimer's among people who are genetically programmed to develop the disorder.

Researchers have discovered chemical agents that absorb free radicals and thus prevent cell and tissue degeneration. For example, a compound called PBN administered daily to aged gerbils restored the function of oxidized proteins in their brains. Their ability to run through mazes improved, and they had fewer strokes from brain damage. The next step is to develop compounds for humans. In the meantime scientists are looking to vitamin supplements such as A, E, and C as natural absorbers of free radicals.

Longevity: The Role of Diet, Exercise, and Mental Health

There is a saying that everyone wants to live forever, but no one wants to grow old. And there is another: "If I'd known I was going to live this long, I'd have taken better care of myself!" Research on longevity holds a fascination for all of us—wondering whether science can find the key

to knowledge that would keep each of us on the planet awhile longer. The previous section covered some biological theories that hold promise for understanding the mysteries of aging. Scientists are also looking at some other factors: diet and exercise, along with social, emotional, and environmental factors. There is no one answer to living a good long life.

Did You Know . . .
If the degree of mortality rate slowing achieved in rats by diet restriction is applied to humans, then the **median** *human life expectancy would approach the present* **absolute maximum** *of 120 years.*

Finch & Pike, 1996

Diet

Research has come up with some astonishing findings regarding diet and longevity. Scientists at the University of Wisconsin–Madison found that reducing an animal's usual diet by 50 to 70 percent could extend its life span by 30 percent or more. The animals not only live longer, but they also are healthier, exhibit less cancer and heart disease, have better immune systems, and have a much lower incidence of diabetes and cataracts (Devitt, 1991).

Calorie restriction clearly increases longevity in a number of species, though it is still unclear how this works. (Beckman, 2004). Reducing a human's food intake by 50 to 70 percent might surely cause some serious interpersonal problems, if not physiological and psychological ones. Caloric restriction to the extent used in the rat studies is not recommended for humans at this point, but some intriguing findings continue to emerge. It appears that disease and other pathology are delayed to the end of the absolute maximum life span of the animal: the animals remain remarkably healthy up to the point where they become ill and die. Morbidity has been delayed, and mortality has become compressed in these research animals.

"The outcome of caloric restriction is spectacular," stated Richard Weindruch, a gerontologist at the University of Wisconsin and a pioneer in this field. He has tested caloric restriction in animals from protozoa to rats to dogs to monkeys. The studies may be telling us we are tampering with fundamental aging processes. The animals act friskier and suffer fewer diseases. Tumor growth is reduced by at least 30 percent, and some cancers are virtually eliminated. Thus, many usual causes of death are stripped away. A 22-year study of 19,297 men revealed that those at their ideal weight (determined by height) live longer than those who are only slightly above (2 to 6 percent) their ideal weight. Those men 20 or more pounds above their ideal weight suffered a major loss in years lived (Manson & Gutfeld, 1994). And from another culture: The caloric intake of those who live on the island of Okinawa is just 60 percent of that of Japanese who eat the normal Japanese diet. People live longer on Okinawa and have half the rates of heart disease, diabetes, and cancer of those on the main island of Japan. It would seem that by restricting food intake, scientists can cause age-sensitive biological parameters—such as DNA repair, glucose regulation, and immune functions—to work better and longer. The decline in the immune function is at the root of many of the health problems faced by elders. Flu, for instance, tends to be more severe with age because immune responses are less vigorous. Low caloric intake helps protect the immune response system.

Nutrition

Only in recent years have we begun to understand the inadequacies of the food eaten by the average American. Studies have shown that nutritional adequacy in early life is related to health and well-being in later life.

Dietary patterns in the mid-twentieth century turned away from raw fruits, vegetables, dairy products, and whole grains. For too many, today's diet still is high in cholesterol, fat, sugar, refined grains, and processed food, and low in bulk, fiber, and nutrients. Many recent studies give strong evidence of the relationship of diets high in vegetables and fruits with low incidence of various types of cancer and the relationship between type of dietary fat and coronary heart disease (Willett, 1994; Walter, 1997). Data pertaining to this matter shows that older persons often have a low intake of important nutrients, such as calcium, iron, magnesium, vitamins B and C, beta-carotene, thiamine, and especially folic acid.

Our awareness of the importance of fresh fruits, vegetables, and whole grains in our diet is now increasing. Americans are decreasing their intake of salt, red meat, and saturated fat. The statistics presented in chapter 1, showing reduced rates of heart disease, bear this out. Nutritional supplements, though controversial, are often recommended to older people whose diets might not provide adequate food-source nutrition. Additionally, specific nutrients have been associated with the enhancement of physical capability. For example, a recent study of older sportsmen found that vitamin C intake was associated with maximal oxygen uptake as a measure of physical fitness (Chatard et al., 1998).

Research on diet continues to be productive, particularly that using nonhuman mammals, in which the complexity of social and environmental variables, along with the diet, can be controlled. The trace nutrient chromium, when given to rats, increased their life span by one-third. The chromium was thought to reduce the blood sugar level, which in turn reduces atherosclerosis and kidney disease (Schmidt, 1993). Results from studies such as these provide suggestions for human dietary factors. Like many health-conscious Americans, Kathy Keeton, the author of the bestseller *Longevity,* eats large portions of complex carbohydrates, especially pasta, because they are fat free and have a calming effect on the brain (Keeton, 1992).

Physiological change happens with age, but health and vigor are maintained through exercise. Many geriatricians now believe that physical flexibility is one of the most important keys to a healthy body in later life.

Good nutrition, it must be remembered, is not necessarily only an issue of preference. Between 8 percent and 16 percent of old people in the United States have experienced food insecurity in a six-month period. This means that somewhere between roughly 3 million and 5 million older people experience being hungry and/or not having access to a "nutritionally adequate, culturally compatible diet that is not obtained through emergency food programs" in a given six-month period (Wellman et al., 1997, p. S121). Though overall the economic situation of elders has improved in the past 25 years, not all Americans have made the same gains. Nearly 6 million older people were poor or nearly poor in 1994, and these numbers do not include those who are homeless or undocumented residents (Burl, 1993; Fowles, 1995).

As a group, elders fare far better than they did 40 years ago, and therefore hunger and malnutrition among the elderly has gone largely unnoticed by hunger advocacy groups. National hunger screening programs at the local level have reported rates at which elders are at risk from malnutrition ranging from 25 percent to 50 percent (Wellman et al., 1997; Whitehead & Finucane, 1997). If we include those independent elders with confusion or memory loss; the one in eight elders experiencing appetite loss due to depression; elders with poor teeth and gums or ill-fitting dentures; and the one in five elders with trouble walking, grocery shopping, and preparing food, we can better understand the large proportion of at-risk elders. Malnutrition, and especially undernutrition, are common and often unrecognized health risks among elders.

Functional and behavioral change

Physiological and sociopsychological factors can compound nutritional difficulties for the very old. Digestive processes slow down as part of the aging process. Dental problems can limit one to foods that are easily chewed. Reduced keenness of taste, sight, and smell can diminish enjoyment of food and dampen the appetite. Physical handicaps, such as arthritis, can complicate the preparation and consumption of meals. Lack of transportation to markets poses further problems.

Less obvious, but also of great importance, are social and psychological factors. For example, a widow who has spent many years cooking for and eating with her family may find little incentive to shop and cook for herself when she is living alone. Older men living alone are even less inclined to cook for themselves than are women. Older adults on limited budgets who seldom leave their homes because of fear or disdain for shopping may settle for a diet of crackers, bread, or milk. Many have lost olfactory (taste and smell) acuity as well. Even those who live with families or in institutions may not find an atmosphere conducive to good eating habits. In some institutions, the hurried, impersonal atmosphere of meals served cold at 5:00 p.m. can discourage residents from eating as they should. And as for those who do not live in institutions, we all know that American culture fosters the fast-food diet, which tends to be high in fat and lacking many needed nutrients.

Pathology and diet

Research on nutrition is now uncovering the way in which poor diet contributes to pathology (disease). Establishing the relationship between diet and disease is difficult, partly because the time that elapses before an inadequate diet results in disease can be substantial. Individuals may not be able to accurately remember their eating habits over a period of years. Nutritional cause and physical effect are difficult to determine.

Nevertheless, diet is increasingly being implicated as a factor in numerous conditions and diseases (Garber et al., 1996; Goldbourt, 1997). Saturated fat contributes to atherosclerosis. A lack of fiber in the diet is thought to be one cause of cancer of the intestine or colon. With a low-fiber diet, the cancer-causing agent remains in the intestine for a longer period of time. High fiber protects against constipation, intestinal disease, gallstones, and cancer. Diverticulitis, an infection or inflammation of the colon, may be caused by a deficiency of vegetable fiber in the diet. Research has shown that various nutritional anemias are almost certainly the result of poor diet. Similarly, studies have shown that proper dietary programs can control 80 percent of the cases of diabetes mellitus. As we grow older, our metabolic rate slows down. We require less energy intake, or fewer calories. Because of reduced kidney function, elders should eat somewhat less protein to help avoid kidney strain.

It is the function of medicine to have people die young as late as possible.

E. L. WYNDER, AMERICAN HEALTH FOUNDATION, 1995

Physical Fitness

A classic study of physical activity and health more than 40 years ago compared the incidence of coronary heart disease between London bus drivers and music conductors (Morris et al., 1953). Coronary heart disease was less by half among the conductors, compared with the bus drivers. The question arising from the study was: do specific occupations produce a differential effect on heart disease morbidity, or are healthier and sturdier men selected for one job over another? From this study and others like it in the 1950s grew research to assess the relationship of on-the-job and leisure-time physical activities and heart disease. The Framingham

Heart Study in Massachusetts is one of the better known studies of this type. More recent studies, armed with more sophisticated capabilities to measure biological functioning, replicate the findings that physical activity is positively associated with lower heart disease. Additional research establishes that physical activity is a component in rehabilitation following cardiac illness and reduces the risk of total mortality by 20 percent, of cardiovascular mortality by 22 percent, and of fatal reinfarction (second heart attack) by 25 percent (O'Connor et al., 1989). Paffenbarger and Lee (1996) summarized the current state of research:

> Since time immemorial, a physically active and fit way of life has been conceptualized as promoting health and longevity. But not until the 19th century did investigators use numerical quantification to show health benefits of physical activity by occupational categories demanding different degrees of energy output, and to demonstrate longevity differentials. (p. S12)

Research shows that patterns of exercise throughout a person's life and even exercise at any point *during* life produce positive physical and mental outcomes: some exercise is better than none. Exercising for the first time in later life is better than believing it to be "too late" and not exercising at all. For most older people, including those who are frail or ill, a program of strength-training and flexibility exercises helps maintain mobility, improve quality of life, and prolong independence (Buckwalter et al., 1993; Buckwalter, 1997). Loss of mobility is a significant cause of loss of independence among the elderly.

It is a myth that older individuals are unable to exercise or to profit from it. Actually, exercise helps maintain good health, improves circulation and respiration, diminishes stress, preserves a sense of balance, promotes body flexibility, and induces better sleeping patterns at any age. It is now clear that most old people benefit substantially from exercise. The person who exercises reduces the risk of heart attack and, should one occur, increases his or her chances of survival. Swimming, walking, running, bicycling, and tennis are all valuable and inexpensive forms of exercise. However, despite current publicity about physical fitness, some older people are not getting the exercise they need.

Much of the deterioration and many of the health problems and physical disabilities associated with age have been thought to be inevitable. However, many of the problems found in older people result directly from disuse of body systems, which results in decline. Disuse affects muscle mass, for example. Between the ages of 30 and 80, the mean strength of back, arm, and leg muscles drops as much as 60 percent. Age-related changes in joints can lead to stiffness, which leads to limited range of motion (Buckwalter et al., 1993). These trends can be slowed and in some instances actually reversed with proper exercise (Hein et al., 1994).

We commonly associate youth with supple, strong, erect bodies and old age with weak muscles, drooped posture, and low energy. One study showed that aerobic exercise increased oxygen efficiency by 30 percent among 60- to 70-year-olds within six months of participation in a program (Seals et al., 1984). Older people can have dramatic exercise benefits from strength-training exercises. One study concluded that resistance exercise may forestall declines in strength and muscle mass for decades (Klitgaard et al., 1990). Their study found that even among frail elders, strength training leads to "life enhancing improvements such as increased stair climbing and walking speed" (Buckwalter, 1997, p. 131). Older individuals who participate in physical activity that constantly works the muscles will have a larger muscle mass than younger individuals who follow no physical fitness program. All unused tissues and functions atrophy. This can happen very quickly, even in a matter of days while one is bedridden. With disuse, muscle tissue is replaced by fat tissue. Exercise prevents this from happening, but the exercise should be appropriate for the body's condition. For those who feel that high-impact aerobics are harsh, jarring, and harmful, low-impact aerobics may be ideal. Geriatric medicine should address these issues; unfortunately, there are not enough geriatric physicians in the United States at this time.

An older person does not have to run marathons or enter competitions to get exercise, feel better, and stay fit. Many programs offer more moderate degrees of exercise. Light forms of yoga, stretching, and relaxing exercises and all kinds of dance and aerobics have been standard fare for elder fitness enthusiasts. People who exercise experience increased oxygen transport capacity, lung capacity, vital capacity, and physical work capacity (Huang et al., 1997). Body fat and blood pressure may decrease with regular exercise. Nervous tension also can be reduced with vigorous physical exercise. People who become sedentary and who overeat lay the groundwork for the development of disease. Complaints of aches and pains in joints and muscles, low-back strain, high blood pressure, and other symptoms could be eased or eliminated with a physical fitness program.

A recent research report demonstrates scientifically what for health enthusiasts has long been an article of faith: regular exercise can indeed prolong life. People who are active and fit can expect to live a year or so longer than their sedentary counterparts. For each hour of physical activity, one can expect to live that hour over—and live one or two more hours to boot. The study, the most comprehensive ever to relate exercise and longevity, tracked the health and lifestyles of 16,936 men who entered Harvard from 1916 to 1950. The subjects were followed until 1978, by which time 1,413 of them had died. Correlating death rates with exercise habits, the researchers were able to quantify, for the first time, the relationship between various amounts of physical activity and length of life. Regular exercise, the researchers found, is a critical factor in determining longevity. Men who walked nine or more miles a week (burning off at least 900 calories), for example, had

a risk of death 21 percent lower than that of those who walked less than three miles a week. The optimum expenditure of energy seems to be about 3,500 calories a week, the equivalent of six to eight hours of strenuous bicycling or singles tennis. The Harvard men who worked out that much had half the risk of death of those who did little or no exercise. Moreover, the study showed that a lifetime habit of engaging in energetic activity three to four times a week could reduce the negative health effects of cigarette smoking or high blood pressure. It even partly offset an inherited tendency toward early death (Paffenbarger, 1985; Lee et al., 1995).

Changing exercise habits

What are the constraints for elders to participating in exercise programs? The mantra "diet and exercise" has been repeated sufficiently that people of all ages surely understand the primacy of these two factors in good health and healthy aging. What, then, holds people back from participating in health-enhancing activities?

Constraints to exercise appear to be both universal and individual. One particularly useful study took a phenomenological approach by asking older people what they liked or did not like about their participation in an exercise program and the option offered them to participate (Whaley & Ebbeck, 1997). Some of the constraints that were voiced by elders were not those assumed by the researchers: "I don't like this activity—it's a women's class" and "I want exercise with a *purpose*." Clear gender differences emerged. Men felt that the classes offered were "for women" and were not appropriate for them. Women were more likely to cite health-related reasons for inactivity. Women are also more likely to live in poverty and to have more chronic illnesses than men; this affects women's ability to participate. In addition, more universal themes developed that related to the **lived experience** of the participants, which includes their history and the social context of their life course. Participating in an activity that has some product, such as gardening, painting a house, or doing volunteer activity, seemed important to some study participants, whose life experience includes the Depression and a subsequent hard-work ethic.

There are many physical activities, and there is something appropriate for every age group. Speed walking is an excellent routine for the middle aged and elderly. William Evans, M.D., at Tufts University in Boston, reports that it is never too late to start a strength-training program. A study of participants 87 to 96 years old showed dramatic improvements after eight weeks; several no longer needed canes to walk, and all experienced "three-to-fourfold increases in strength" (Evans & Rosenberg, 1991). Similarly, other experimental studies of nursing home residents who began lifting weights show them to greatly improve their muscle strength, walking speed, and mobility (National Institutes of Health, 1993).

The American College of Sports Medicine now recommends a minimum exercise routine of some type of aerobic exercise for 20 minutes or more three times a week and some form of resistance training at least twice a week that exercises all the major muscle groups in sets of 8 to 12 repetitions each (Segell, 1993, part 1).

A study begun in 1987 of almost 200 master athletes age 40 and over who competed in one sanctioned event each year (e.g., runners, swimmers, field athletes) asks the question, "Just how old and how fit can one become?" The study is expected to continue 20 years but already has predicted the following: (1) speed and muscle strength will endure longer than assumed, (2) athletic performance will not decline significantly until age 60, (3) death rate will be reduced, (4) falls and injuries will be reduced, (5) the heart and lungs will not have to lose function as quickly as previously thought, and (6) the incidence of osteoporosis will be reduced. In general, we have underestimated the ability and potential of older people. The study also concludes to date that nothing can retard the aging process as much as exercise (Roan, 1993).

© Jim Harrison/Stock, Boston

Much as we have been told since childhood, to remain healthy in later life requires good genetic stock, exercise, excellent nutrition throughout one's life, and a healthy lifestyle.

Mental Health

The connection between physical well-being and mental health is strong. Most mental health professionals and geropsychologists recognize, in Niederehe's words (1997), "that biological factors become more saliently intertwined with psychosocial ones in the mental disorders of late life, relative to typical problems of younger adults" (p. 102). Biology and psychology have the paradoxical relationship of being the same and being different, simultaneously. Older people who are involved in aerobic sports—sports that increase the heartbeat and respiration—for several hours a week felt healthier and happier than people who were not involved in such exercise (van Boxtel et al., 1997). The subjective sense of being physically fit—feeling good about one's health and body—predicts better mental health (Niederehe, 1997). Being a happy, optimistic person in turn contributes to longevity. The 50-year study of Harvard graduates cited earlier (Paffenbarger & Lee, 1996) found that:

- Men who cope well with emotional trauma live longer, while men who denied their feeling or intellectualized personal problems suffered more rapid declines in health after age 50

- Optimists have better health in middle and old age than pessimists

- Good mental health (one measurement was the lack of need to take tranquilizers) predicts successful aging

A study by Costa at the National Institute on Aging found that one personality trait—"antagonistic hostility"—is a predictor of premature death. A person who exhibits this trait is easily provoked to anger and vindictive (reported in Segell, 1993). Other related personality characteristics have been determined by social scientists to be life shortening include repressed anger, depression, egocentricity, shyness, and various other negative attitudes (Morris et al., 1993; Shephard et al., 1995). One review of the study begun by Lewis Terman in the 1920s reported that the degree of psychological maladjustment was related to higher risk of all causes of mortality over a 40-year follow-up period. The review indicated that mental health problems were significantly more strongly related to deaths from injury and cardiovascular disease among men

(but not among women). The finding was not mediated by alcohol consumption, obesity, or cigarette smoking (Martin et al., 1995).

In addition to longevity-limiting psychological characteristics, within any given age population will be those who are chronically mentally ill. Mental illness of any proportion is alarming and requires appropriate intervention, and it is anticipated that with the baby boom generation moving into late adulthood in the twenty-first century, the sheer numbers of people with chronic mental illness (as opposed to late-onset mental illness) will be large. To add to the possible load for mental health professionals, increased depression and suicidal ideation in older people with serious medical diseases has been documented (Niederehe, 1997). In some instances, the difficulty of letting go—of recognizing that death is nearby—can explain the sadness and depression. In other cases, however, it cannot be understood simply as the older person's psychological reactions to the experience of illness and must be looked at from a medical, as opposed to a mental health, perspective (Zeiss & Breckenridge, 1997). Medications often are a major issue to deal with in older adults, particularly in anxious older patients: shifts in medication tolerance and negative cognitive effects are part of a psychological symptoms complex associated with older adults (Beck & Stanley, 1997). If we expect larger numbers of people requiring mental health services in the future, we must train and prepare for that in the present.

A whole set of findings revolves around stress. In a nutshell, some stress may be a positive factor in life, but too much of the wrong kind is bad. And those who are good at coping with stress will live longer. In the same vein, a good sense of humor helps, as well as a strong sense of self and purpose and a zest for life. The feeling that one is in control of one's life also adds years. Even in a nursing home, those who have choices and assert their will live longer.

In the presence of disease, "guided imagery" has been shown to lengthen life for some. They imagine their body parts getting healed—perhaps their immune cells are warriors fighting off the evil enemy. Or they picture in their minds a totally healed lung. Here, a positive mental attitude is used to get the immune system activated and fighting. Hypnotism, meditation, and other relaxation techniques are being used, with some success, to prolong life.

Social and Environmental Factors

The environment we live in plays a role in how long we live. Noise and air pollution, pesticides, radiation, secondary smoke from cigarettes, and other adverse chemicals in our air, water, and food bring disease and shorten life. The ultraviolet rays of the sun age the skin and can cause skin cancer. Living in an area of high crime can be life threatening. For rats, overcrowding in cages alters behavior and shortens life. Likewise, living in overcrowded cities may be harmful for humans.

A positive, hopeful, stimulating social environment adds years to life. Rats in cages with lots of wheels and mazes live longer than rats with no outlet for activity. Likewise, an active physical and mental environment is important for humans. Social class is correlated with longevity. Those with more money for health care live longer.

A shortened life is statistically correlated with the following: divorce (for men only); accidents (especially car accidents); a lifestyle that includes smoking, heavy use or abuse of alcohol or drugs, and too little or too much sleep; an imbalance of work and leisure; continual risk-taking or self-destructive behavior; and being a loner instead of having lots of friends.

Centenarians

Rather than study animals in a laboratory, some scientists have focused their attention on centenarians as a way of learning about longevity. Twenty-five or so centenarians, the "oldest

old," were included in the Georgia Centenarians Study (Poon, 1992). The sample population had approximately equal numbers of African American and white subjects. With regard to personality and coping, the oldest old scored high on dominance, suspiciousness, and imagination, and low on conformity, personality traits that served as protective functions. The centenarians were described as assertive and forceful. There were a number of extraordinary persons who wrote, published, performed music, gave guided tours, invested in the stock market, earned a living, and coped well regardless of the adequacy of support systems. In terms of cognitive skills, they rated high on practical problem-solving tests, but lower on intelligence and memory tests. Religion was important and a common coping device: "I don't worry about the future; it's in God's hands," said Charles C., 101 years old. Regarding nutrition, most were moderate, healthy eaters who did not go on diets. None were vegetarian; they did not smoke and drank very little; most ate big breakfasts. Surprisingly, they had a high intake of saturated fat, especially the African American men, who continued lifetime patterns of consuming pastries, soda, sugar, and whole milk. This speaks to the power of genetic predisposition: the frail and sick have died off, leaving behind a cohort with remarkable survival power.

The American demographer James Vaupel claims that genetic factors account for no more than 30 percent of variance in life spans, with the remaining 70 percent related to lifestyle and environmental factors (quoted in Kirkland, 1994). Beard (1991) found, in studying individual differences among centenarians, that long life was correlated with good health habits, stimulating physical and mental activity, spirituality, moderation, tolerance, integrity, and interacting with others. International studies of centenarians support the suggestion that heredity is important but explains far less about that which constitutes the "sturdy disposition" of these survivors into a second century of life (Italian Multicenter Study on Centenarians, 1997).

Further research on centenarians will provide us with more answers, and in the decades to come, we will have centenarians from a wider range of cultures and lifestyles from which to gather information.

As science continues to document habits that increase stress and decrease nutritional and physical health, the wellness movement will gain strength, encouraging prevention and the adoption of good health-related habits. The long-term effects may well result in larger populations of older adults who will experience fewer debilitating illnesses and, as a result, higher levels of life satisfaction.

Chapter Summary

The health status of the population aged 65 and over is far better than most people would predict. Most elders are able-bodied and not limited in a major way by physical impairments—indeed, only 5 percent of people over 65 live in nursing homes or other long-term care institutions. Poor health in old age is not caused by the aging process, but lack of exercise, inadequate diet, stress, and disease are contributors. Heart disease, hypertension, cancer, strokes, and accidents are the leading causes of death. With the elimination of these and other factors, longevity would increase. Exercise and nutrition are vital in maintaining health and longevity; however, caution is given to avoid the pitfalls of blaming the victim for lifestyles not conducive to well-being in later life. Culture, life experience, historical time, and poverty levels each have an impact on choices made and choices available to each age cohort.

Wellness is the key emerging concept in the study of aging and in planning for one's own aging. At the baby boomers enter late life in the twenty-first century, they will be the first generation to come into old age with a lifetime of information about the relationship of nutrition, exercise, and lifestyle choice on the aging process.

The wellness movement is based on anticipating and taking measures to prevent health-related problems as we age. Although modifying a person's lifelong behavior patterns is not always easy, it can be done. More and more of our young, middle-aged, and older citizens are losing weight, exercising, and monitoring their diet than ever before. Learning to avoid foods with higher levels of calories or fat, reducing hypertension, and discontinuing the use of tobacco, while simultaneously including a diet of nutritional foods and maintaining higher levels of physical activity, reduces health risks in later life. Extending the number of healthy years of life, what has been called the **health span**, has become a viable goal for all Americans.

Key Terms

absolute human life span	heart disease
absolute maximum	hypertension
acute condition	immune system
aging as disease	infarct
arteriosclerosis	ischemic heart disease
arthritis	lived experience
atherosclerosis	maximum life span
average life span	mean human life span
biological clock	median
cancer	osteoporosis
cerebrovascular disease	presbyopia
chronic condition	primary immunological change
coronary artery disease	secondary immunological change
error theory	stroke
health span	wear and tear
health status of the aged	wellness

Questions for Discussion

1. How long do you expect to live? How long did your grandparents or great-grandparents live? What are the causes of death among

those in your family who have died? What are you doing specifically to enhance the level of well-being you expect to have in later life?

2. Examine your own lifestyle in terms of your everyday habits, exercise, diet, auto safety, smoking, drinking, and stress. How healthy will you be at age 80 if you are now 50? How healthy will you be at 80 if you are now between 20 and 30?

3. Which biological model of aging makes most sense to you? Do you believe that the absolute maximum human life span can be extended to 150 years, or 200 years? Why or why not? What might be some social consequences of such longevity?

Fieldwork Suggestions

1. Survey a group of people who are older and a group that is younger to determine the kind and the quality of physical exercise they engage in. Which age groups are in better shape? Why?

2. Contact two people over the age of 65 at the close of day. Have them list everything they ate that day. Evaluate the nutritional quality of their food intake.

3. Interview three people who work in health clubs to determine (1) how many people over 65 come into the club; (2) what the activities of older club participants are; and (3) what the interviewee thinks about having older people working out. What level of training to work

with older adults do these people have? Is the club you visited a place that you would recommend to your mother, father, grandmother, or grandfather (or your great-grandmother or great-grandfather) to attend? Why or why not?

Internet Activities

One intent of the exercises is that you become able to locate sources easily on the Internet. Another intent is that you develop a sense of discrimination about the information you find: To whom is it written or addressed? How difficult or easy was it to locate the information? Who do you think the primary users of the site are?

1. Locate the home page for American Association of Retired Persons (http://www.aarp.org/index/html). What sort of practical health-related information does the site contain?

2. Log on to Senior Com: The Source for Seniors (http://www.senior.com). This is a site designed to be used by seniors to promote their health and well-being. Compare what you find and the way it is presented with the AARP site, and with other sites for and about seniors.

3. Locate the best source of information you can find on the Internet related to nutrition for older people. How persistent did you need to be to find this source? Is it a site that older people might use? Is it one that someone who plans menus for a board and care facility might use?

8

Work and Leisure

Happy 150th Birthday? New Era Looms for Aging

Modern medicine is redefining old age and may soon allow people to live regularly beyond the current upper limit of 120 years, experts said Wednesday.

It used to be thought there was some built-in limit on life span, but a group of scientists meeting at Oxford University for a conference on life extension and enhancement consigned that idea to the trash can.

Paul Hodge, director of the Harvard Generations Policy Program, said governments around the world—struggling with pension crises, graying work forces, and rising health-care costs—had to face up to the challenge now.

"Life expectancy is going to grow significantly, and current policies are going to be proven totally inadequate," he predicted.

Just how far and fast life expectancy will increase is open to debate, but the direction and the accelerating trend is clear.

Richard Miller of the Michigan University Medical School said tests on mice and rats—genetically very similar to humans—showed life span could be extended by 40 percent, simply by limiting calorie consumption.

Translated into humans, that would mean average life expectancy in rich countries rising from near 80 to 112 years, with many individuals living a lot longer.

Aubrey de Grey, a biomedical gerontologist from Cambridge University, goes much further. He believes the first person to live to 1,000 has already been born and told the meeting that periodic repairs to the body using stem cells, gene therapy, and other techniques could eventually stop the aging process entirely.

De Grey argues that if each repair lasts 30 or 40 years, science will advance enough by the next "service" date that death can be put off indefinitely—a process he calls strategies for engineered negligible senescence.

His maverick ideas are dismissed by others in the field, such as Tom Kirkwood, director of Newcastle University's Center of Aging and Nutrition, as little more than a thought experiment.

Kirkwood said the human aging process was malleable—meaning life expectancy was not set in stone—but researchers had only scratched the surface in understanding how it worked.

More Healthy Years

The real goal is not simply longer life but longer healthy life, something that is starting to happen as today's over-70s lead far more active lives than previous generations.

Jay Olshansky of the University of Illinois in Chicago is confident that longevity and health will go hand in hand and that delaying aging will translate into later onset for diseases like cancer, Alzheimer's, and heart disease.

But to get to the bottom of understanding the biology of aging will require a major step-up in investment.

Olshansky and his colleagues have called on the U.S. government to inject $3 billion a year into the field, arguing the benefits of achieving an average seven-year delay in the process of biological aging would far exceed the gains from eliminating cancer.

Ethically, the extension of life is controversial, with some philosophers arguing it goes against fundamental human nature.

But John Harris, professor of bioethics at the University of Manchester, said any society that applauded the saving of life had a duty to embrace regenerative medicine.

"Life saving is just death postponing with a positive spin," he said. "If it is right and good to postpone death for a short time, it is hard to see now it would be less right and less good to postpone it for a long while."

To work or not to work in old age: that is the question. The answer to this question has implications for both society and the older person. It also implies a choice that for many people is limited or nonexistent. Some people are forced to retire because of age discrimination or because of illness. Others must continue to work, often at menial jobs, because they cannot afford to retire. Further, the economics of supply and demand governs one's presence in or out of the job market. If there is a demand for your work, you stay; if not, you are encouraged to retire.

The issue of work and retirement is a thorny one. Retirees may either feel elated and free or devalued and depressed. Because of changes in routine, personal habits, and opportunities for social interaction, retirement can bring stress even when it is voluntary. Though studies show that most older people generally make a satisfactory adjustment to retirement, given good health and sufficient income, some do not have these benefits; and a minority are not satisfied with retirement, regardless of their health and financial status. Retirement is a dirty word to some; to others it represents freedom from a daily grind of work. But the very concept of retirement is taking on new meaning as the impact of the baby-boomer culture begins to shape another decade and shake up traditional attitudes.

In this chapter, we will explore the options of retirement, analyze discrimination against the older worker, examine the difficulties old people have in adjusting to retirement, and look to the newest cohort of retirees to examine changes in attitudes toward both work and leisure. We will look at the meaning of leisure in our culture. When we are young, our time away from work is called leisure; when we are old, it is called retirement. What is the difference?

As a social institution, retirement has been the major means of redividing the life span so that old age can be identified by a common dimension[:] as a period of inactivity on a pension.

GUILLEMARD, 1980

The Concept of Retirement

The social definition of **retirement** has changed in the past half-century. By earlier definitions (Atchley, 1976), retirement is an event that occurs when a person definitively stops working and withdraws from the formal labor market. Numerous sociologists have since pointed out that some people withdraw from the formal labor market because they lack the health to continue working, or because of age-related disabilities, or because they have become unemployed and are unable to find a new job. Retirement is quite different from struggling with the inability to work and consequently being dependent on family, charity, or public welfare for survival (Guillemard & Rein, 1993). In this chapter, retirement will be seen from the perspective of a social institution: it is a person's definitive economic inactivity, with income replaced by pensions, assets, Social Security, earnings, and other sources. It is additionally a stage in the life course, with a set of social rules and with special social meaning.

For individuals, the meaning of retirement can be broadly differential. Researchers analyzing data from a study on the problems and suggestions of retirees (Marcellini et al., 1997), summarize:

> For some, it is a way of being free from daily routine, making it possible for the person to dedicate him- or herself to more satisfying activities linked to personal interest. For others, instead, it is a difficult period of line in which [they] feel deprived of a social role, and problems regarding finances, health and loneliness can arise. For everyone, though, it is a period of great change in which lifestyle has to be restructured in many ways. (p. 377)

The outcome of retirement depends on individual characteristics—people's lifestyles and the sociocultural context in which they live. The meaning of retirement therefore is not only individually distinctive, it reflects the values of cohorts—groups of retired people who have shared unique historical events. A major survey of baby boomers by Princeton Survey Research (MetLife Foundation, 2005) indicates critical trends in attitudes toward work among this large demographic group, the leading edge of which is just now approaching retirement. Fully 65 percent of these boomers plan for work to continue to be part of their life throughout what

was formerly considered to be retirement years. This cohort is distinguished by a desire to have a second career following retirement from their first, and their attention is focused on a desire to contribute to the greater good.

> The drive toward good work comes largely from the people themselves—not the organizations that might use their time, talents, and experience. This drive contains many of the features of a social movement—and in many ways it resembles the women's movement during the 1960s. There were few supportive polities, nor much impetus from employers at that juncture. All the dynamism came from the individuals themselves. It should be little surprise then that this survey reveals that groups most ready to be pioneers in this new generation are none other than the boomer women and African Americans who broke down so many barriers earlier in their lives. (MetLife Foundation, 2005, p. 5)

The impact of the boomer generation and the values and attitudes it reinforces in society through their sheer numbers cannot be underestimated. U.S. Bureau of Labor Statistics (2004) projects the number of available 55- to 64-year-olds to increase in the labor force by 8.3 million from 2002 and 2012. At the same time, the number of 35- to 44-year-olds in the labor force will decline by 3.8 million. The systems designed to connect with older workers with socially relevant job positions are nonexistent at this time—but this will change. And it will need to change quickly as this cohort redefines a new stage of work. Increasing numbers of people who have retired from one job are moving to other jobs—paid jobs, not just volunteer positions—and the meaning of retirement is being forever changed.

In 1900 nearly 70 percent of American men over age 65 were employed. By 1963 the figure had dropped to 20.8 percent, by 1976 it had dropped to 14.2 percent, and by the year 2001 the proportion of men 70 or older participating in the labor force was 12.2 percent (U.S. Bureau of the Census, 2001). The corresponding proportion of women age 70 in the workforce was 5.9 in 1963, 4.6 in 1976, and 5.9 in 2001. Note that the proportion of older women in the workforce, though significantly lower than that of men, remained roughly the same for these three example years, whereas men's participation in the labor force precipitously declined. This observation is probably related to poverty levels among a small but significant proportion of older women. For example, in 2001 the percentage of people age 65 or older living in poverty was 10 percent. Of the total population, 7 percent of men and over 12 percent of women lived in poverty (U.S. Government, 2003).

Economists and social scientists have collected a huge array of labor market statistics in the past 50 years. Trends in labor force transitions show a precipitous drop in labor force participation among older people, especially among men. The drop in participation rates for the 25-year period of 1970 to 1995 for men aged 65 and over was nearly 18 percent. The labor market participation rates for that 25-year time period for males 65 and over dropped from 27 percent participation to 17 percent (U.S. Department of Labor, 1996). Women 55 to 64 years old in 1970 had a greater labor force participation rate than did the age group in 1950, but the labor force participation rates for women age 65 plus have remained roughly the same since 1950 through 1995. Unlike men's patterns, women's labor force participation is associated with changes in marital status, childbirth, spouse's income, and family background, so a complete picture of retirement decisions for women over this same 25-year period is less clear. Projections for future retirement statistics are made on past retirement patterns; however, cohort differences are likely to create changes in the actual patterns that emerge. These cohort differences have to do with economic and social status at the time individuals prepare for retirement and then actually do so. Current workers in middle age were educated after the end of World War II,

and retirement decisions are being made in a time of economic and labor market turbulence. For those who have retired since the mid-1970s, pension plans were less frequently provided, and Social Security benefits were lower than they currently are for middle-aged workers. Fewer retiring men had wives who were also in the workforce, and retirements did not have to be coordinated within a family. Because longevity was not as great, fewer of the retiring workers in the past had elderly parents needing care. All these factors impact retirement decisions and an individual's adaptation to retirement.

For most people in the United States, retirement is an expected life event. Even though mandatory retirement was abolished by law in 1986 for most workers, other factors are leading older workers to favor retirement. In fact, today people take retirement for granted, assuming it to be a natural part of the adult's life course. However, not all workers retire completely; in fact, more than one of every five older Americans who retire return to work at least part time (Moody, 2000).

In the agricultural era of the United States, few workers retired. Most workers were self-employed farmers or craftspeople who generally worked as hard as they could until illness or death slowed or stopped them. Stopping work, however, did not have to be abrupt. A gradual decline in the workload could occur simultaneously with a gradual decline in physical strength.

Older people who held property could usually support themselves in old age. For example, a homesteader who began to grow old and to experience difficulty doing heavy work could usually pass the work on to family, retaining his or her authority as the children assumed more and more responsibility. Because he or she remained in charge, the older farmer did not have to quit producing entirely. No one could technically force "retirement."

Before 1900, few people lived past age 65. Those who owned property lived longer than those who did not own property or did not have

Self-concept for Americans is often tied closely to life's work. For some people retirement is a welcome respite after many years of work. For others it is a loss of daily companionship, income, and meaningful activity.

helping family members. Older persons without economic resources had to do heavy work because of their need to support themselves. When they could no longer physically continue to work, they often ended up in almshouses or died of malnutrition and neglect. The "good old days" were not good for many old people.

The Industrial Revolution brought many complex changes. Increased productivity created great surpluses of food and other goods. More people ceased being self-employed and went to work in large factories and businesses. Government and bureaucracies grew. When civil service pensions for government workers were introduced in 1921, the retirement system began.

In 1935, with the passage of the Social Security Act, all conditions for institutionalizing retirement were met. The law dictated that persons over 65 who had worked certain lengths of time were eligible for benefits, and 65 became the age for retirement. Since then, employees in both the public and the private sectors of the economy have retired in increasing numbers, and retirement has come to be associated with leisure.

We need a word about women's work pattern cohorts. Women born in the early 1900s were not encouraged to enter the workforce. A Gallup poll in 1936 found 82 percent agreement for the statement that wives of employed husbands should not work (Keating & Jeffrey, 1983; Burkhauser, 1996). Not until the 1960s did the concept of work outside the home as other than a temporary role for women develop. Even then, wives' employment was often seen as a supplemental source of money for "extras."

Before the 1960s, the majority of permanently employed women were single. Married women tend to have interrupted work histories—entering the labor force and then leaving it upon the birth of a child (the "mommy track"). Thus many women who are old today (the married ones, at any rate) do not have the extensive work histories that older women in the future will have, even though many of them worked temporarily outside the home during the Depression and World War II.

Now more than 95 percent of all adults expect to retire someday. Although retirement has become an accepted feature of modern life, one must question whether retirement is wise for everyone.

Early Retirement?

A different trend is usurping retirement at age 65. In the 1990s increasing numbers of companies encouraged employees in skilled, semi-skilled, or unskilled jobs to retire before age 65 without a substantial loss of pension benefits. American industry, which seems to presume that the young have greater vitality, has steadfastly worked for **early retirement** and restrictions on work opportunities for older workers. In industry, retirement at age 55 is not uncommon, and 62 is typical. And contrary to popular belief, the trend for early retirement is not among people in poor health. In 1993–1994 the typical early Social Security beneficiary was as healthy and as wealthy as the typical worker of the same age who did not retire (Burkhauser et al., 1996).

This trend in industry has now become common in the white-collar world of work. Whether blue- or white-collar, most baby boomers say they would like to retire by age 55. Some (about 40 percent) want to retire between the ages of 56 and 65, and some, after 65 or never. The desire for and expectation of early retirement has increased over the last several decades. From 1950 to 1990 the median retirement age dropped from 67 to 63.

In 1961, early Social Security benefits were introduced. In 1960, over 79 percent of men age 61 and nearly 76 percent of men age 63 were in the labor force. In 1993 those percentages were 64 percent and 46 percent, respectively—despite improvements in mortality and morbidity (Burkhauser, 1996). In the 1970s the trend toward making pensions and other benefits available before age 65 greatly accelerated, from the government's pension system to other public and private institutions. One study indicated that those who were offered full pension benefits before age 65 were twice as likely to retire early (Burkhauser, 1996). In 1992, 38 percent of early retirements from large companies were the result of incentive offers. For the most part, companies were seeking to cut their payrolls and at the same time avoid layoffs.

Studies of companies and educational institutions show that most corporations do have early retirement inducements in their pension plans. Only a handful of organizations offer incentives to continue working beyond age 65.

The following excerpt illustrates the way in which Hewlett-Packard used early retirement to scale down its number of employees when business was off.

> *Plagued by manufacturing problems that have hurt its earnings for the last two quarters, the company announced a corporate-wide plan to offer early retirement to 2,400 workers in plants across the country. The program is available to workers who are at least 55 years of age or older and have 15 or more years with the company. Those who opt for the program, get a half-month's salary for each year of service up to a maximum of 12 months' salary. (Silver, 1990)*

Likewise, when IBM's Japan unit needed to reduce the size of its workforce, it offered an early retirement plan in hopes of removing a significant number of employees age 50 and over ("IBM's Japan Unit Offers Early Retirement Plan," 1993). These early retirement packages became typical of large corporations wishing to cut costs by downsizing their operations. Such downsizing is especially common in the cyclical high-technology industry, with its recurring booms and busts. Some workers like these packages, grabbing a retirement package at one company and then getting an equivalent or even better job elsewhere. Others wanted to retire anyway. The unhappy ones are those who feel forced to retire.

Some industry sectors have begun to question the policy of encouraging workers to retire at or before age 62. The labor pool of young workers is declining, and they sometimes cost as much to train as to retain the older workers (Cyr, 1996). Some companies are studying **late retirement incentive programs (LRIPs).** These studies show, however, that although most businesses are afraid too many workers will take advantage of LRIPs, most workers still opt for early retirement. Incentives for early rather than late retirement are still the order of the day for business and industry. The only change is that many early retirees find the "good deals" not so good after all: buyout plans are growing skimpier, and new jobs are scarce. The trend toward early retirement brings with it a number of complex issues, not the least of which are the large hidden costs of funding pension systems and the loss of older workers' skills and talents (Moody, 2000).

The Role of the Older Worker

The population of older workers roughly parallels the aging of baby boomers—that large cohort born between 1946 and 1964. At the dawn of the twenty-first century, these workers are entering their 60s and beginning to take issues of work and retirement seriously and personally. Industrial and governmental planning and policies regarding pensions, Social Security, early retirement incentives, and the like are impacted by this large population of workers and by the smaller-than-expected succeeding generation, referred to as the "baby bust" generation (Moody, 2000).

Some early retirement incentives are offers that older American workers cannot refuse, and many older workers are wondering whether they are being subjected to disguised **early retirement discrimination.** For example, at the age of 56, a man who had worked for 31 years for a large manufacturing company was hoping to work 6 more years and retire at age 62. But his corporation, like many others across the United States, decided to trim its payroll and abolish numerous jobs, including his. The company offered him half-pay retirement for the next four years, provided that he did not work elsewhere. He accepted these terms out of fear that other jobs would not be available to him.

A one-time incentive is not the same as an early retirement option. An early retirement option offers the employee the choice to stay or to go. In contrast, with the one-time incentive, the employee either accepts or gets laid off. For every employee who gladly accepts an early retirement incentive, another feels that he or she is being forced out the door. Under the **Age Discrimination in Employment Act (ADEA),** all early retirements must be voluntary (Blouin & Brent, 1996). The question remains, what is voluntary? Do you leave of your own free will if your boss drops strong hints that you are not wanted and hints at a big bonus offer if you leave early? Or if you are told that in a year your job will be phased out?

Employers are slowly starting to realize that jettisoning older workers can result in an irreparable loss of skills and expertise.

Reday-Mulvey, 1996

Along with the multinational web of new global marketplaces, new forms of industrial competition are emerging "precisely at the time the population is aging" (Minda, 1997, p. 564). Downsizing, restructuring, reengineering, outsourcing, reduction-in-force (RIF)—all are terms common to the postindustrial work environment of the last decade of the twentieth

Skills developed after many years of work can compensate for reduced physical agility or stamina of the older worker. In many jobs older workers are more productive than younger workers because they "work smarter."

century. These management shifts were all part of an economic recovery between 1990 and 1998; however, while productivity and stock market indices have growth vigorously, median family incomes have remained stagnant, and the average weekly earnings of most rank-and-file workers have fallen (Minda, 1997). Some economists and social analysts believe the definition of work that has emerged from these circumstances has created social changes as profound as those of the Industrial Revolution 200 years previously (Minda, 1997; Weaver, 1997).

In the United States, outsourcing and downsizing have shifted much labor from permanent workers to contingent workers, who are generally nonunion and less well paid than those they have replaced. Contingent, part-time workers often do not receive benefits such as health

care and corporate pensions (Minda, 1997). In the early 1980s the profile of the typical unemployed worker was of someone younger, unskilled, and blue-collar. By the 1990s, the profile of the unemployed worker included many more older, skilled, white-collar workers (Congressional Budget Office, 1993). The risk of job loss is rising for workers age 45 to 55—the age category that has suffered most as a result of corporate downsizing (U.S. Bureau of Labor Statistics, 2000).

The risk extends out internationally. When Congress amended the ADEA to apply to U.S. companies abroad, it neglected to include the entire class of American workers working for foreign employers stationed in the United States (Madden, 1997). With increased globalization of the economy the protection of all workers, including older workers, becomes more complex and yet more essential.

The pattern of easing older workers out of the labor market is seen in all industrialized nations. In the Netherlands and France, less than 60 percent of the active male population between 55 and 59 and less than 20 percent of those between 60 and 64 years of age are now part of the labor market (Reday-Mulvey, 1996). The rates are only slightly higher for Great Britain and Germany. The problem is not unique to the United States—it is an issue related to the global economy. Downsizing, the 1990s version of permanent unemployment, has become a concern for older workers throughout the globe who have devoted an entire lifetime of employment to a single employer (Minda, 1997).

The Taxpayer versus Early Retirement

People are asking, "Can we afford old age?" Business and industry are pushing for early retirement programs, and these programs are sometimes a boon for the older worker. But there is an irony involved. Life expectancy is greater than ever, and the supply of younger workers is shrinking, creating a larger percentage of older workers. Social Security would be more likely to stabilize if older workers stayed on the job longer, and the government, contrary to many companies' wishes, is attempting to see that they do. The Social Security retirement age will gradually be raised to 67 (in other words, the normal retirement age will be 67 for those who will reach age 62 after 2022), and those taking benefits early will receive 30 percent less (they currently receive 20 percent less) than those receiving benefits at the normal retirement age. In this way, federal policy is encouraging workers to extend their work lives. But the incentives from business and industry are powerful in encouraging the older worker out of the market. Economists make it very clear that most people respond to economic incentives in choosing to retire; however, more and

more large companies can no longer guarantee employment based on the patterns of the past. This introduces a dilemma for workers, who may opt for early retirement as an alternative to possible future unemployment.

Early retirement has generally been interpreted positively. It is an indication that society is able to provide economic security for a large number of older people who no longer need be in the labor market. This in itself is an historic development. Additionally, retirement has been a positive force in avoiding generational conflicts between older, employed workers and younger workers seeking employment (Morris & Caro, 1995). Despite its widespread acceptability, however, retirement poses problems for many older workers, who find themselves unemployed.

Marty Denis (1996), in an analysis of early retirement from a corporate perspective, listed six advantages of early retirement plans:

1. They can reduce the need for massive layoffs
2. Payroll costs can be reduced
3. The number of senior, more highly paid employees can be reduced
4. When done across-the-board (not targeted), employee morale may be preserved or at least not unduly disrupted
5. Because of the release component, employment discrimination claims can be minimized, if not avoided
6. Promotion channels can be opened so that other qualified employees can advance within the company

The downside of early retirement, according to Denis, is that employers "may be deluding themselves about the overall effectiveness of these programs in cutting staff and, in particular, ridding employers of their less-productive employees" (p. 66).

When employees seek redress under the law for what they believe to be discrimination, they often do not win. In a retirement case heard by the U.S. Supreme Court in 1995 (*Lockheed Corporation v. Spink*), the Court supported the corporation. Lockheed had amended its retirement plan to provide financial incentives for certain employees to retire early. The plan required that participants receiving the early retirement benefits must release any employment-related claims they may have against Lockheed. Employee Spink was eligible for the early retirement package but refused to sign the release. He retired without earning the extra benefits and subsequently sued Lockheed. The Court held that the Lockheed retirement plan was permissible but introduced the concept of "retirement sham." If the payment of early retirement benefits is purely a sham, a court might find that the plan assets were misused. Just how egregious the transaction must be to be considered a "sham" was not defined by the Court (Denis, 1996).

The economic incentives to business for introducing early retirement packages are strong. To keep older workers on the job and thereby save Social Security funds, the government will need to strengthen its measures—to increase the amount of money older workers can earn without reducing their Social Security benefits, for example. And business and industry should try harder to find a place for the older worker, who may well offer a gold mine of experience, wisdom, and loyalty. Unfortunately, workers near retirement seem expendable to most large-scale employers. But as the number and percentage of younger workers shrink, private business may finally be motivated to retain and retrain older workers. It will take collaboration between the private and public sectors to reach the proper integration of policies that accomplish (a) an extension of the working life in order to manage human resources and to finance pensions and (b) the development of well-protected and regular part-time work to sustain policies of gradual retirement (Reday-Mulvey, 1996). In the beginning of the twenty-first century, a new definition of "work" is being forged, and we must hope it will represent a balance of the public interest with that of the private.

Age Discrimination in Employment

Age discrimination in employment starts long before the traditional time for retirement. Even those still in their 30s have trouble getting into some training programs and schools, such as flight school and medical school. The problem of job discrimination is severe for older workers in spite of federal laws that prohibit it. The 1967 Age Discrimination in Employment Act (amended in 1974 and 1978) prohibits the following:

1. Failing to hire a worker between age 40 and 70 because of age

2. Discharging a person because of age

3. Discrimination in pay or other benefits because of age

4. Limiting or classifying an employee according to his or her age

5. Instructing an employment agency not to refer a person to a job because of age or to refer that person only to certain kinds of jobs

6. Placing any ad that shows preference based on age or specifies an age bracket *Exceptions:* the federal government, employers of fewer than 20 persons, or jobs where youth is a "bona fide occupational qualification," such as modeling clothes for teenagers.

Prior to 1978, the Age Discrimination in Employment Act protected employees from age 40 through age 64. The amendments adopted in 1978 extended that protection to age 70. Though all upper limits were removed for federal employees, the law does include exceptions that allow the federal government to retire air traffic controllers, law enforcement officers, and firefighters at younger ages. Nevertheless, the U.S. Supreme Court in 1985 ruled that the city of Baltimore could not force its firefighters to retire at age 55, despite federal regulations requiring retirement at 55 for most government firefighters. Other cities are easing their rules to allow firefighters, police officers, and other public safety employees to stay on the job until the age of 65 or older.

Between 1989 and 1997 the number of workers older than 50 years of age who became unemployed increased by 68 percent. This compares with about 41 percent of people under 50 years of age who became unemployed. Clearly, some of the unemployment among the 50-plus people was voluntary and planned for; however, in the same time period age discrimination claims filed with the Equal Employment Opportunity Commission jumped 34 percent (Matley, 1994). A survey of 515 verdicts of wrongful termination cases found the average award to total $302,914—surpassing awards in cases of discrimination based on race, gender, or disability (Blouin & Brent, 1996).

Interpretations in the law can be subtle. In 1996 the U.S. Supreme Court upheld the suit of a 56-year-old worker who had been replaced by a 40-year-old worker, both ages, 56 and 40, fall under ADEA protection. In *O'Connor v. Consolidated Coin Caterers Corporation,* the Court ruled that the case was discriminatory because an older person was replaced with a substantially younger worker (Blouin & Brent, 1996).

Additional protection for the older worker was legislated in 1990 with the Older Workers Benefit Protection Act. Some companies required older workers to sign a waiver agreeing not to sue before they could qualify for an early retirement bonus. Now any waiver and release signed by an older worker going through a job transition must meet certain requirements. The agreement must be clear and concisely written, and the employee must have 21 days to decide whether to accept. Additionally, the agreement must clearly specify that the worker is waiving all rights under the ADEA (Blouin & Brent, 1996).

The protection of older workers has become necessary in light of downsizing and demand for high corporate profit margins even in a time of economic growth. When layoffs are not for legitimate business reasons but rather are to eliminate one or more undesirable employees, or to eliminate employees who are highly compensated, those layoffs are not legal. When actions are not legal, the onus is on the older worker to take his or her case to court—at enormous economic and emotional cost to the "retired" or otherwise laid-off worker. It is estimated that for every case that even gets to court (much less every case in which the worker wins the suit), there are 50 cases in which the unhappy worker did not sue (Abel, 1998).

Age Discrimination in the Job Search

Age should not be a determining criterion in finding work. One's ability to do the job is what counts; however, older workers find that age discrimination in the labor market makes finding work more difficult. Because older workers have difficulty finding jobs, changing fields is even more difficult. The skills and energy of older people come to be greatly underutilized. More older people want to work than is commonly believed. One study found that

- As many as 5.4 million older Americans (55 and over)—one in seven of those not currently working—report that they are willing and able to work but do not have a job

- More than one million workers age 50 to 64 believe that they will be forced to retire before they want to

- More than half of all workers age 50 to 64 would continue working if their employer were willing to retrain them for a new job, continue making pension contributions after age 65, or to transfer them to a job with less responsibility, fewer hours, and less pay as a transition to full retirement (Commonwealth Fund, 1993)

A 1992 Harris survey revealed three reasons for older people wanting to work: (1) financial,

37 percent; (2) boredom with retirement, 21 percent; and (3) wanting to do something useful, 14 percent (Taylor et al., 1992).

Older persons who feel that they have been denied employment or have been let go because of their age can take steps to get their job back or to receive compensation by making a formal written charge of discrimination against the employer to the Wage and Hour Division of the Department of Labor. Individual cases of age discrimination are difficult to prove, however. In the investigation of the employer's hiring, firing, and retiring practices, the government tries to reveal a pattern of discrimination. For example, if an employer has hired a good many people over the past several years—but nobody over age 30—a pattern of discriminating against older workers in favor of younger ones may be documented. The older worker will have a better chance of winning if he or she hires a lawyer. A class-action suit may be filed if a number of job applicants feel they have been denied employment because of discrimination.

Resources that work diligently to help the older worker find employment are increasing. For example, in the past, employment agencies commonly violated the Age Discrimination Act by stipulating upper age limits or using words such as "junior executive," "young salesperson," or "girl" in advertising. Employment agencies also have been found guilty of failing to refer older workers to potential employers. Such violations, unfortunately, are still common practice. Now, however, employment agencies such as Kelly Services: Encore cater to people over 50 years of age. They advise older applicants that they do not have to give their date of birth on a résumé, and they remind them that potential employers may not legally ask a person's age in an interview. Other employment resources are aimed specifically at elders. One example is Operation ABLE in Chicago, which has helped thousands of people between the ages of 50 and 70 to find work. It not only matches people with jobs but also teaches them skills such as word

processing. Nevertheless, age discrimination in employment is prevalent according to one AARP study (Job Applicants, 1994), and older people are still laboring for acceptance.

In the mid-1970s, Jobs for Older Women, a branch of the National Organization for Women (NOW), began analyzing refusals to hire older women. Employers often base refusal on an older woman's appearance: a department or clothing store may be worried about projecting a youthful image, or a certain restaurant may hire only young women who will wear uniforms believed to be unattractive on older women. Older women are also rejected in favor of younger women for the more visible positions of bank tellers, receptionists, and other such jobs. The sad refrain is "I'd love to hire you, but you just won't fit in." But employers may soon lack the personnel to meet their youthful standards. As the U.S. population collectively ages, older women will begin to outnumber younger women in the job market (Crispell, 1993). The percentage of women age 55 to 59 in the job market was 55 percent in 1993, compared to 27 percent in 1950 and 46 percent in 1983 (Perkins, 1994). Middle-aged women, many of whom are heads of households, have had to settle for low-paying jobs with little chance for promotion. Studies show that age discrimination is well established by age 40 for women. (One indicator is the large number of age-discrimination lawsuits for women this age compared with men.)

More women are in the labor force more continuously than ever before, yet 60 percent of these women are segregated into three occupations: sales, service, and clerical. Of the 27 percent in administration, management, and professions, many are teachers or nursing administrators. Further, women's earnings peak at age 35 to 44, whereas men's peak later in life at age 45 to 54. One major reason is that women have the kinds of jobs that do not get rewarded with big raises. In the very near future, many employers will need to change their attitudes toward these women or risk not only legal action on the basis of age and gender discrimination, but possibly understaffing as well if the predicted labor shortage occurs.

On-the-Job Discrimination and Ageism in Layoffs

Ageism in the labor market is deeply ingrained institutionally and culturally. Ageism in employment occurs in job categories of every kind. Studies of professionals, engineers, and scientists who are unemployed show age to be a significant variable in explaining their layoffs. Ageism is a factor in both blue-collar and white-collar occupations and for both sexes. Occupations in sales and marketing may suffer the most age discrimination, because they place more emphasis on youth and a youthful image than other occupations, as do occupations requiring physical stamina, such as construction. Once out of work, older workers are likely to remain unemployed much longer than their younger co-workers and to find job hunting a nightmare. If they do find work, it is usually at a much lower salary and with fewer fringe benefits.

The number of age-discrimination charges filed with the U.S. Equal Employment Opportunity Commission (EEOC) has increased every year since the Age Discrimination in Employment Act went into effect. In 1992, 30,604 cases of age discrimination charges were filed with the EEOC, 18 percent more than in 1982. Today, workers are more likely to press charges if they feel they have been victims of discrimination. Complaints of age discrimination have been growing faster than those concerning gender or race. In these recession years, the large numbers of layoffs and reassignments have angered all workers, especially older ones. These layoffs have also been a factor in the large number of age-bias suits. And although few affirmative action programs address the concerns of middle-aged workers, a quirk in the age-discrimination law allows for jury trials, which seems to work in favor of those filing suits. In age-discrimination suits, jury members, who tend to be older, appear to see corporations as the "bad guys."

Age discrimination is still a tough charge to prove. In the last several years, thousands upon thousands of cases filed with the EEOC have led to only several hundred lawsuits, and not a high proportion have been won. However, in spite of mishandling many cases, the EEOC has obtained some very large settlements involving millions of dollars in back wages and pension benefits:

- Blue-collar workers at the Kraft General Foods plant in Evansville, Illinois, sued for bias when the plant closing led to the firing of workers (Geyelin, 1994)

- Ceridian Corporation and Control Data Corporation will pay as much as $29 million to more than 300 former employees who claimed they were fired because of their age. The 1997 court ruling favored the employees, who accused the corporation of a pattern of discrimination by laying off older workers and replacing them with younger workers. The suit was begun in 1989; the proportion of the settlement required to cover legal costs will probably be one-third of the total amount ("Ceridian, Control Data," 1997)

- Westinghouse Electric and Northrop Grumman Corporation settled two age-discrimination lawsuits in 1997 ("Westinghouse Electric," 1997)

- American Airlines and Delta have also been accused of age bias in hiring practices that discourage older pilots (O'Brian, 1993)

- A 78-year-old physician for the medical unit of the Los Angeles County Sheriff's Office was returned to his job after the county settled his claim that he was forced to retire ("Jail Doctor Wins Age-Bias Settlement," 1998)

- A news correspondent got a settlement from CBS on age discrimination (Lambert & Woo, 1994)

- Apple Computer has been sued for age discrimination in a "wrongful termination" suit ("Fired Executive Sues Apple," 1993)
- An ex-AT&T manager won just under $2 million in an age-discrimination verdict (Sandecki, 1993)

The cost in time, dollars, and personal stress required to pursue legal action is enormous. In addition, the line between discrimination and decision making for corporate well-being has become less clear. Some factors behind this lack of clarity include conservative court decisions, stockholder pressure for high corporate profit margins, and changing technology. In the past, courts have supported age-bias claims in which the layoffs had "disparate impact" on employees over the age of 40. Four federal appeals courts, however, have recently questioned the idea that people can claim age bias merely because an employer's actions had a harsher effect on older people. Instead, the courts have said, "older workers must now show that their employer intentionally discriminated against them" (McMorris, 1997). In a job market in which technological skills are important, more recently trained people probably will have the most current skills unless the company provides appropriate employee training. If a company lays off workers based on whether their skills are up to date or otherwise makes decisions that they feel further the economic stability of the corporation, is it age discrimination?

One particularly ominous struggle is taking place in the United Kingdom between Intel, the microchip manufacturer established both in Britain and in the United States, and 200 of its employees. The workers have taken the unusual step of forming a pressure group (Former and Current Employees of Intel, or FaceIntel) and publicizing their argument on the Internet. The concerns have to do with the firm's use of "ranking and rating" to assess employees. This ranks employees "equal to" or "slower than" other employees according to a movable line determined by the company. Anyone receiving either two out of three or two consecutive "slower thans" is automatically put on a disciplinary corrective action program. Those who do not reach a target set by their manager face discharge.

The employees claim that a disproportionate number of people receiving "slower thans" are older workers and workers with disabilities—two groups protected by antidiscrimination laws in the United States. Intel denies the group's allegations, saying that it remains as flexible as possible in the face of the astounding competition in the microelectronics business. This competitive environment requires the company to have employees who can work under demanding circumstances. A random sample telephone survey by FaceIntel of the 1,400 laid-off workers reportedly found that 90 percent were over 40 years old, and 40 percent had some form of disability (Welch, 1997).

The following age-discrimination complaints are typical of those reported by older workers on the job:

- Position terminated: older people are told their jobs are terminated; when they leave, younger workers are hired in their places
- Sales force downsized: the sales force is trimmed, and older workers are the ones eliminated
- Retirement credits refused: older workers reach a certain salary level, and there is no more potential for salary (or pension) increases
- Dropped for medical reasons: older people are told they are being dropped for medical reasons

In some cases older workers are passed over for promotion or are the first fired—sometimes to protect a company's pension funds, sometimes to save salary costs. The reasons for and means of discrimination against older workers vary. Employers frequently prefer younger workers—sometimes because of age prejudice, sometimes because younger workers will accept a lower wage, and sometimes because the company feels it will receive more years of work before it must pay retirement benefits. Employers in a tight job market can get by without giving substantial salary increases because the older worker, afraid of unemployment, will settle for a low salary. The older worker is highly vulnerable in a tight labor market.

Health and life insurance fees, which tend to increase with worker age, constitute a supposedly inordinate cost of retaining older workers. The older, tenured worker also tends to receive a higher salary and more vacation time. Surely companies could deal more creatively and tactfully with older employees. For example, many older people would gladly contribute toward their health and life insurance costs if it meant keeping a job; in turn, companies could be more realistic—and less paranoid—about the older workers' health concerns.

Myths about the Older Worker

Negative stereotypes of the older worker still persist. The older worker is thought to be prone to accidents or illness, to have a high absenteeism rate, to have a slow reaction time, and to possess faulty judgment. Stereotypes contribute greatly to on-the-job discrimination. Common **myths about the older worker** include the following:

- Older workers cannot produce as much as younger workers
- Older workers lack physical strength and endurance
- Older workers are set in their ways
- Older workers do not mix well with younger workers—they tend to be grouchy
- Older workers are difficult to train—they learn slowly
- Older workers lack drive and imagination—they cannot project an enthusiastic, aggressive image

Retention of older employees in the labor force will require some changes in employer attitudes. One study that looked at beliefs about older workers came to three interesting conclusions: (1) direct, frequent experience with older workers reduced negative beliefs for younger workers; (2) older workers had more positive beliefs about older workers than did younger workers, but even younger workers tended to have generally positive beliefs; and (3) older supervisors held more negative beliefs about older workers than did younger supervisors (Hassell & Perrewe, 1995). The third conclusion is rather surprising. The researchers suggested that age discrimination is so institutionalized and so unconscious that younger supervisors might have lower expectations with older workers and actually exaggerate or overreward their good performance. Older supervisors, on the other hand, choose to perceive themselves as valued members of the organization and do not identify personally as an "older" employee.

Management needs to be concerned with dispelling myths about older workers. According to the U.S. Bureau of Labor Statistics, by the turn of the century there will be more than 17 million labor force workers age 55 or older (Siegel, 1993). The impact of this process will be felt both by workers and by employees. Employers need to be aware of the following points:

- Healthy older workers may not cost more in medical benefits than younger employees who have children at home
- Use of sick leave is more highly correlated with lifetime patterns developed at a young age than with age itself. A natural selection process operates to leave healthy older workers on the job. The less fit have quit
- Older persons retain their mental faculties, can learn new skills, and are not necessarily more rigid

Age is not necessarily a determinant of the capacity to do well on the job. The fact that the age of the workforce is increasing means that opportunities for a wide variety of interactions with older workers will increase. The more frequently younger people are around older people, the less negatively they see the elderly as a group, and older people are seen more positively—as individuals, some of whom are winners and some of whom are not.

Older Worker Performance

On-the-job studies reveal individual variations in the ability of older workers. Most important, however, such studies generally show that older workers are as good as—if not better than—their younger counterparts. One study indicated that older workers have superior attendance records (less absenteeism); that they are likely to be stable, loyal, and motivated; and that their output is equal to that of younger workers (Commonwealth Fund, 1993). The work ethic of older people tends to be very high, which leads to high job satisfaction.

Experience can often offset any decrements that come with aging. The ability to do heavy labor does decline with age, but this decline is gradual, and jobs vary greatly in the physical strength they require. Furthermore, an older person in good physical condition is quite likely to outwork a younger person in poor physical condition. Studies of work loss due to illness show that workers age 65 and over have attendance records equal to or better than that of most other age groups. The U.S. Bureau of Labor reports that workers age 45 and over have better safety records than younger workers: the highest overall accident rates occur in the 18-to-44 age group (U.S. Bureau of the Census, 1991, p. 115).

Older workers may take somewhat longer to train, but considering their careful work, the investment in time should be worthwhile. Some firms who recognize this say the problem is not "How can I get rid of the older worker?" but "Where can I find more?"

Adjustment to Retirement

Just how difficult is adjustment to retirement? Though one myth claims that people get sick and die shortly after retirement, studies do not confirm this. Retirement in and of itself does not lead to poor physical health. Research shows, however, that adjustment to retirement can be difficult.

Studies of retirement adjustment show varying results in terms of adjustment, satisfaction, and happiness. A general finding is that a minority of people have serious problems with retirement, whereas the majority adjust reasonably well. The message here seems to be that of continuity. The kind of person one has been does not change significantly just because of retirement. This man is typical of those who have no problem adjusting to retirement:

> I turn 80 next February. It's always a milepost, I suppose, but no big deal. I retired about 75 percent at age 65 and then fully retired at age 70. It was easy, very easy, for me to retire. I like the freedom to do what I want, go where I want. I never understood these people who are restless and unhappy in retirement. It seems to me they haven't got much imagination. (Colburn, 1987)

Financial problems top the list of reasons for unfulfilled retirement expectations. Those at a marginal or lower income level are affected most adversely by retirement. In fact, about one-third of retired men end up going back to work, and many retirees worry that they will outlive their retirement funds (Szinovacz, 1996).

Clearly, if one's retirement income is adequate, retirement has a much greater chance of success. Good health is also a factor. If the retiree has the money and physical mobility to pursue the lifestyle of his or her choosing, adjustment comes more easily. The importance of these two factors suggests that adjusting to the role of retiree depends more on physical and monetary resources than on mindset. Lifestyle is another factor: if a person is involved with family, friends, and activities, then adjustment is usually more successful. Conversely, if a person has nothing to do and no associates, then adjustment may be poor.

Willingness to retire and attitude toward retirement are also important factors. Naturally, reluctant retirees show negative attitudes toward retirement. Those who retire voluntarily are healthier mentally and physically than those who did not feel they had had control over whether to retire (Gall et al., 1997). A positive attitude toward retirement also depends on an individual's expectations. In general, those who expect to have friends and social activities, and who expect that their retirement will be enjoyable, usually look forward to retirement.

Guillemard and Rein (1993) identified five types of retirement patterns:

1. Withdrawal—Extreme reduction of social activity; long "dead" periods exist between actions performed to ensure biological survival

2. Third-age retirement—Professional activities give way to creative activities (artistic creation, hobbies) and cultural improvement. (This term is commonly used in France. Life has three stages: childhood, adulthood, and **third age.** With each stage a new positive phase of living may begin)

3. Leisure retirement—The focus is on leisure activities (vacations, trips to museums and other exhibitions, theater shows), with an emphasis on consumption

4. Protest retirement—Characterized by political activism; much time is devoted to associations of the elderly to protect the interests of the retired

5. Acceptance retirement—Acceptance of traditional retirement values; lengthy time periods spent in daily exposure to television and other forms of mass communication

According to Guillemard, those with professional backgrounds tend to cluster in groups 2 and 3. Those with working-class backgrounds are overrepresented in the other categories.

Studies of differences in adjustment to retirement between white-collar and blue-collar employees reveal various findings. Former top managers and executives can have difficulty adjusting because they feel a loss of power and status, but on the whole, white-collar workers generally adjust fairly well because they have more resources at their command. Professional types, such as educators, often show a good adjustment to retirement. Because they are well educated, they tend to have interests and hobbies, such as community affairs, reading, travel, and art, that lend themselves well to retirement. Some professional people write or act as consultants. They seem to have many ways to spend their time fruitfully.

Blue-collar workers indicate a greater readiness to retire because their work may bring them less satisfaction. For example, a man or woman with a dull, routine factory job may look forward to leaving. However, studies show that those with the least education and the lowest incomes have the most trouble adjusting to retirement. Socioeconomic status has been found to have a major influence on retirement rates. The lower one's socioeconomic status, the earlier one retires. Individuals with less education who are employed in occupations characterized by low skills and labor oversupply tend to retire early.

Retiring persons face several adjustments that relate directly to retirement: loss of the job itself, loss of the work role in society, loss of the personal or social associations that work provides, and loss of income. In addition, events such as declining health or the loss of a spouse may coincide with retirement. When all these events occur at the same general time, adjustment is stressful and difficult.

Retirement Preparation Programs

Retirement preparation programs can aid adjustment to retirement, that "roleless social role" (Rosow, 1974). Anyone who is employed would be wise to prepare for retirement; yet few people do much beyond paying into Social Security, benefits of which average around $8,000 per year for individuals and $14,000 annually for a couple.

Retirement preparation programs have become important sources for education and planning among middle-aged workers. In addition to traditional programs, "outplacement companies" have been created to assist with layoffs and to offer assistance to laid-off employees (Marcellini et al., 1997). Most are offered by government agencies and by companies whose workers are covered by a private pension. These retirement programs fall into two categories: (1) limited programs that explain only the pension plan, the retirement timing options, and the benefit level associated with each option; and (2) comprehensive programs that go beyond financial planning to deal with topics such as physical and mental health, housing, leisure, and the legal aspects of retirement. Individuals exposed to comprehensive programs have a more satisfying retirement.

Successful adjustment to retirement from a psychological perspective depends on the ability to maintain stable and meaningful life goals and a sense of purpose (Weaver, 2000). Favorable attitudes toward retirement are therefore associated with planning, company counseling, personal discussion, and exposure to news media presentations about retirement. People need to be socialized into post-work roles just as they are socialized into other roles. Anticipatory socialization, which prepares a child for adult roles, is also necessary to prepare an adult for successful retirement in old age. We can prepare for retirement in several ways: by saving money, by deciding what our goals are, by beginning to care for and improve our health, by forming meaningful relationships with a sense of permanence, and by expanding our interests so that work is not our primary focus.

Work and Leisure Values

Even though Americans are expected to retire, our traditional value system gives higher social esteem to those who work. In the past, leisure was an accepted lifestyle only for the extremely wealthy. Adherence to the traditional work ethic, however, is not as complete as it once was.

What value older people assign to leisure is a research question with some interesting answers.

Work

The sociologist Max Weber (1958) proposed that before the Protestant Reformation in the sixteenth century, work had been regarded as a burden and something to be avoided. With the Reformation, religious reformers such as Martin Luther and John Calvin suggested that all work had an inherent dignity and value. In fact, diligence in the performance of work was part of the highest form of Christian behavior. This ethic has remained through the centuries, and although work is no longer considered to be the direct glorification of God, the Judeo-Christian culture still respects work for work's sake. New evidence suggests that a 1990s shift in the meaning of the work ethic includes both high values in hard work *and* negative and disparaging views of others who may lack a strong work ethic (Mudrack, 1997).

The **work ethic** stems from a long-standing American tradition of a relationship between religious belief and work that has helped to form the firm conviction that it is immoral not to work. The saying "Idle hands are the devil's workshop," a basic precept in the structure of the early American character, still influences our attitudes today. Work has high value not only because of its moral quality, but also because of its practical and personal value. Many people truly enjoy their work and derive pleasure from it. Work can foster interest and creativity as well as a feeling of pride and accomplishment.

To some, work is not a value in and of itself, but is rather a means to identify one's social standing. It is not work that matters, but having a job. Indeed, everyone knows that the general question "What do you do?" requires a very specific answer: to have any status, one must name some type of occupation. Work provides a means of achieving self-identification and placement in the social structure. This very fact has made many American women second-class citizens, because work at home has not traditionally been considered an occupation.

A common theme in the literature—both popular and academic—is that the work ethic has declined. A nationwide study in 1955 and again in 1980 reported a significant decline from 52 percent to over 33 percent of full-time workers in the United States who said they enjoy their work so much they have a hard time putting it aside. Additionally, workers who said they enjoyed hours on the job more than hours off the job declined from 40 percent to 24 percent. (Glen & Weaver, 1983–1984). This finding, however, might reflect an increase in the cultural value of leisure rather than a decrease in the work ethic. A follow-up to the study found that there were few fundamental changes in the work ethic in the United States from 1972–1978 to 1988–1993. The study found, in fact, that among white workers of both sexes in white-collar jobs, there is evidence for *increased* work ethic values (Weaver, 1997). Gender and ethnicity changes that did emerge included the fact that more white females in blue-collar jobs and more white men in white-collar jobs said they would continue to work if they were to get enough money to live as comfortably as they would like for the rest of their lives. More women in white-collar jobs felt that people get ahead by their own hard work than by lucky breaks or help from others; fewer men and fewer women from all ethnic groups reported being "very satisfied" with their jobs (Weaver, 1997).

Work matters to Americans. One problem with having a strong work ethic is that it may be difficult to reconcile it with retirement. Work attitudes can be so ingrained in retirees that they carry over to nonwork activities. A strong work ethic tends to be related to low retirement satisfaction. The least satisfied retirees tend to be those with high work values who do not perceive their retirement activities as being useful. Retirees with strong work values participate less in social activities because they have a hard time enjoying them. Although most eventually make a satisfactory adjustment, a 1993 survey found

retirement to be one of the most difficult transitions in life: 41 percent of retirees said the adjustment was difficult. The younger the retiree, the more likely that retirement was a difficult adjustment (Mergenbagen, 1994).

Perhaps the disparity is due to the fact that the line between one's job and "work" has grown less distinct than it once was. Extreme devotion to the work ethic does seem to be waning, and acceptance of retirement as a legitimate stage in the life course is increasing. As technology advances, the United States will need fewer workers to produce necessary goods and services, thus lowering the value of long work hours and increasing the value of other activities. With shifts in longevity, retired people will have more company, and role models for a healthy, active life following retirement are now increasingly prevalent.

Leisure

The work ethic is alive and well. The traditional conceptualization of the life course is organized around realms of preparation for work, work, and retirement from work; this is overlaid on realms of marriage, childbirth, childrearing, grandparenthood, death. Traditionally, the male "specialty" has been in the work realm, and the female "specialty" has been that of home and children, with the understanding that movement between the two realms takes place in the process of living. This model is changing. Shifts in gender role expectations, work demands, longevity, and the need for continuing education and training to update skills in a changing technology-driven marketplace have combined to shape this change. The model for the twenty-first century is very likely one in which work comes and goes throughout the adult life course, as do recreation and education. The new model brings profound changes in attitudes toward the concepts of work and leisure activity.

A Gallup poll revealed that 8 out of 10 adults of all ages think time is moving too fast for them. One benefit of retirement is having more time. The older the person, the more content they seem to be with the amount of time they have. Only 44 percent of those younger than 50 said they have enough time, whereas 68 percent of those 50 and older believed they had time enough for their tasks. According to the poll, all Americans wish they had more time for personal exercise and recreation, such as aerobics, hunting, fishing, tennis, and golf (47 percent); hobbies (47 percent); reading (45 percent); family (41 percent); and thinking or meditation (30 percent). Given more time, most Americans would relax, travel, work around the house or garden, or go back to school. **Leisure values**, that is, the acceptance of leisure pursuits as worthwhile, are becoming stronger.

Sociologists have observed that for the past several decades we have treated leisure as another commodity that is produced and consumed. The leisure industry is one of the largest segments of the American economy, and it keeps hundreds of thousands of persons employed. Ironically, Americans who become overly engrossed in working to attain the symbols and commodities of leisure must work harder to obtain them and often end up with less time to enjoy them.

In some segments of American society, older people are becoming a visible and contented leisure class as they accept the new lifestyles of the retired. The retirement community concept has, no doubt, made the role of retiree more legitimate. Elders who choose the traditional symbols of leisure—the boat, recreation vehicle, or home in a warm climate with access to a golf course and swimming pool—seem to go beyond merely owning the symbols to enjoying the lifestyles that the symbols represent.

In the past, elderly Americans have been considered "invisible consumers," a segment of the population to be ignored by marketers (Oates et al., 1996). Their presence is now being acknowledged by virtually all institutions in the economy. On the positive side, recognizing elders as consumers gives them greater visibility and legitimizes their role as people enjoying life. On the negative side, consumerism directed at older people as a group often does not recognize

© Joel Gordon

Retirement can be a time to develop skills or specialties that were previously too time-consuming to pursue. Volunteer or part-time jobs provide tremendous life satisfaction for retirees.

that they are a diverse group whose needs and wants vary dramatically (Lee et al., 1997).

The sheer size of the over-65 age group market, however, is gaining the attention of the commercial world. News that the mature market is growing and that adults will likely have excellent incomes in the future from improved pension and retirement planning, is showing up in bold print on marketing magazine covers.

Expanding Work and Leisure Opportunities

In spite of age discrimination and retirement eligibility, a substantial number of elderly are employed. Many middle-aged women are entering into the job force for the first time in their lives. And, although men have been retiring in larger and larger numbers since the turn of the century, women have not. Indeed, although the labor-force participation of women 65 and over has remained at about 8 to 9 percent since 1950, middle-aged women have entered the labor market in increasing numbers.

More older people want to be employed full time than are. Still, a more popular choice for older people is part-time work. But part-time jobs are relatively uncommon in many sectors; for example, professional, technical, administrative, and other high-paying jobs tend to be full time. According to Social Security laws, those age 65 to 69 are allowed to make only up to a prescribed amount (about $11,000 in 1994) without a cut in their payments. (The cut is $1 off their Social Security for every $2 earned.) And those younger than 65 suffer cuts at even a lower wage. These amounts are guidelines for many elders. Those who lack private pension coverage are more likely to continue working full or part time in their later years.

A nationwide study of 11,000 workers examined the work choices of those who retired. More than one-fourth of those workers who leave full-time employment will take up new employment within four years. (Typically, retirees return to work swiftly or not at all.) Most of the remainder will remain retired. The most likely work change is to take a new full-time job (11 percent of the sample); second, to take a part-time job (10 percent); and third, to work part-time at the job from which one retired (just under 5 percent). Factors that led a retirees back to full-time employment included low pensions and personal savings and, in contrast, the offer of high wages. Those who were eligible for good pensions tended to retire completely (Myers, 1991).

In another large study, workers of all economic status decreased their work hours gradually as their retirement approached (Choi, 1994a). Not unexpectedly, the extent of work reduction was based on preretirement income, since reduced work reduces earnings. The study revealed the fluid relationship between work and leisure, especially during the early years of retirement. "For many workers," the authors concluded, "the transition from work to leisure is not a very finite process, at least in the early years of retirement" (p. 6).

Among those whose income is 50 percent above poverty level and higher, interest in work following formal retirement from a job seems to be related more to people's individual characteristics and their life goals than to postretirement income (Toughill et al., 1993). Attitudes toward future employment among some retirees are very positive, and among others, quite negative: people age as they have lived. Those who look forward to retirement and have planned their leisure activities for retirement do not want work and resent it if they feel compelled for financial reasons to work again. Others plan for continued work, either part-time or full-time, and are frustrated when their job searches lead to rejection.

Where and how do older people find jobs they want? Although jobs are hard to find for any age group, they are especially so for elders. If an elder's original goal is to have leisure and a good-paying part-time job as well, opportunities are limited. Older part-timers are on track for jobs that might seem quite disappointing for some people. For example, some retail outlets recruit elders, but the pay is minimal. Fast-food chains might offer a better wage, but the working conditions can be difficult—socially, physically, and psychologically—for some older people who are more accustomed to work in which they have a valued skill or knowledge base The common occurrence of being paid less per hour as a part-timer for the same work as a full-timer can lead to low morale for part-time workers of any age.

Full-Time Work Opportunities

An obvious and far-reaching way of expanding work opportunities for seniors has already been mentioned: for private business and industry to keep their older workers and discourage, not encourage, early retirement. More older workers should be retrained and motivated to stay in the labor force.

Older workers who want to change jobs or branch out on their own need support in achieving these goals. Rather than retire, able elders sometimes shift their focus or their employers. A nuclear engineer may become an expert witness on nuclear power. A lawyer may leave a large law firm and set up practice on his or her own. A retired professor may become a lecturer, conduct workshops, or become a consultant. Consulting is a common job for retired managers, employers, and engineers.

Business leaders who look at demographics (shrinking young population, growing elders) have taken steps to hire older people. The U.S.-based hotel chain Days Inn currently employs many older persons; in fact, they are more than 30 percent of its labor force. Days Inn analyzed its Atlanta Center by comparing costs and benefits of hiring older versus younger workers. It found the following:

- After a half-day of computer familiarization training, older workers can be trained to operate sophisticated computer software in the same time as younger workers— two weeks

- Older workers stay on the job much longer than younger workers—an average of three years compared with one year. This resulted in average annual training and recruiting costs per position of $618 for older workers, compared with $1,742 for younger workers

- Older workers are better salespeople: they generate additional revenue by booking more reservations than younger workers, although they take longer to handle each call for the reservations center

- Older workers are flexible about assignments and willing to work all three shifts (Commonwealth Fund, 1993, p. 17)

All in all, the president of Days Inn reports a very positive experience hiring seniors as reservations agents. Other companies that recruit elders for full-time positions are Bay Bank Mid-dlesex of Boston and Aerospace Corporation of Los Angeles.

Many elders turn to self-employment as a way to earn money. Creativity, initiative, capital, and sometimes past business experience are needed to start a business in old age. Still, self-employment is often easier than getting hired to work for someone else. Slightly over 40 percent of all employed elders are self-employed. One retired man at age 62 started a travel agency that eventually expanded into three more. At age 60, another started an equipment leasing business. A 60-year-old woman started producing how-to videos on more than 150 subjects ranging from watercolor painting to foreign language instruction to being a magician; the videos are now distributed nationwide (Duff, 1994). Some retirees have businesses in arts and crafts, such as real grandfathers who make grandfather clocks.

A way of assisting older people in finding work is to encourage self-employment, either by helping them to start new businesses or by providing the means for advertising and selling the goods they make. One urban senior citizens' center established a shop to provide local artisans with a sales outlet for quality handmade goods. Rural towns, too, offer stores selling quilts, stitchery, wooden carvings, and other crafts made by local elders.

Part-Time Work Opportunities

Some older people welcome the opportunity to work part time, and companies such as McDonalds, Wal-Mart, and Walt Disney World all actively recruit older workers. Some "young-at-heart" retirees have found part-time work in the summer at amusement parks. Some companies, such as Travelers Insurance in Hartford, Connecticut, offer an early retirement program to the long-term workers who command the highest salaries. But Travelers hires back pensioned workers part time when they are needed. Retirees are recruited regularly at "unretirement parties" hosted by the company. Open to all retirees is a job bank offering flexible part-time temporary work. The company profits by not having either to train new workers or to create new pension funds for them. Thus, one place to look for work is in the company that retired you (Commonwealth Fund, 1993).

One company that hires older workers for new assignments is F. W. Dodge, a data-gathering firm headquartered in Kansas. Until recently, the company hired temporary part-time workers to assist in filling out forms. Because these temporary workers were not always dependable, the company redesigned the jobs as part-time permanent positions and recruited retirees. The response by oldsters was extraordinary: 90 percent of the positions were filled. Employees work several days every month. The older employees have proven to be more reliable, and the accuracy of the data has increased (American Association of Retired Persons [AARP], 1990). These patterns continue to be consistent 20 years after the program's inception.

The federal government has several small-scale work programs designed to aid retired persons by providing work to supplement their Social Security benefits. For example, the Green Thumb Program pays minimum wage to older people living near or under the poverty level to plant trees, build parks, and beautify highways. The Foster Grandparent Program also employs old people near the poverty line to work with deprived children, some mentally retarded and physically handicapped, others emotionally disturbed. The older workers try to establish meaningful relationships with the children. For their efforts as foster grandparents, the elderly receive an hourly wage, transportation costs, and one meal a day.

Work opportunities could expand if employers were more flexible in scheduling the hours and days older employees worked per week. Management consultants have suggested that workers age 55 and over be allowed gradually shrinking work weeks, with final retirement not occurring until age 75 or later. Another suggestion is that companies allow employees the op-

tion of reducing their work load to two-thirds time at age 60, one-half at 65, and one-third at 68. Still another alternative would allow the older person near retirement to work six months and retire for six months, alternating work and retirement periods until permanent retirement. **Flexible work/retirement plans** enable older persons to gradually retire and at the same time remain productive on the job even into their 70s and beyond, if they desire.

Part-time work is sometimes possible through **job sharing.** Job sharing has generally been found not only to please workers by giving them more options, but also to benefit employers. One employer stated that it increases productivity: "When people know they're working only two or three days a week or only up to four hours a day, they come in all charged up. You can bet they're much more productive." Job sharing increases job interest, lowers absenteeism, gives the company decreased turnover, and increases morale, all of which results in greater productivity. Employers' arguments against job sharing are that people may have less commitment to part-time work than to full-time work and that training and administrative costs might increase because of the greater number of people involved (Kane, 1996). Neither of these points is borne out in the literature (Turner, 1996).

Polaroid has a program offering part-time work to employees age 55 and over. Permanent part-time opportunities are available through job sharing. Varian Associates, a high-tech firm in California's Silicon Valley, offers reduced work schedules before retirement. As a rule, the reduction entails a four-day work week the first year of transition and a three-day schedule in the second year. A third year of half-time work is possible. At Corning, the "40 Percent Work Option" enables persons to retire, collect their pension, and work two days per week at 40 percent of their preretirement salary. To qualify, they must be age 58 or older and have been with the company 20 years or more.

Polaroid also has a "rehearsal for retirement program" allowing individuals to take unpaid leaves of absence. Leaves can run as long as six months. At Kollmorgen in Massachusetts, employees may reduce their time on the job to do volunteer community service while receiving full pay and benefits 12 months before retiring (AARP, 1990).

Retraining

If new technology makes older workers obsolete, they should have options for **retraining**, or updating their knowledge and skills. In the past, people assumed that professionals and their skills naturally and unavoidably became obsolete. Now, however, retraining and mid-career development programs have proven effective; and national training programs have trained older workers as successfully as younger workers, despite the fact that these training programs could work harder to consider the unique problems of adult retraining.

Career development programs for middle-aged and older workers are far too few. In our society, which generally punishes those who make job changes, the older worker who changes jobs loses most of the retirement benefits from his or her previous job. People would have much more career flexibility if retirement benefits were transferable. They would feel freer to change jobs, and companies would be more inclined to hire the middle-aged. For those whose careers require working so intensively that they become hardened and emotionally drained, spending a few years in a related field would actually increase their effectiveness in the original career if they chose to return to that field of work.

Under Title V of the Older Americans Act and with the help of the Job Training Partnership Act (JTPA), older workers are receiving some job training. The JTPA offers special training programs for economically disadvantaged older workers age 55 and older; 3 percent of the funds allotted to the act must be spent on such training. Some businesses are offering more than severance pay to laid-off workers: a change to start a new teaching career. Pacific Telesis, Chevron, AT&T, Rockwell, IBM, and Kodak, as a part of their severance program, pay tuition and expenses for retirees to go back to school to become teachers in kindergarten through twelfth grade. At PacTel, managers with undergraduate degrees in math or science who are bilingual are given priority ("Severance Offers Chance to Teach," 1991).

Other businesses offer continuing education and retraining. General Electric and AT&T have classes to teach employees the latest changes in technology. Pitney Bowes has a retirement educational assistance program in which employees and their spouses over age 50 are eligible for tuition reimbursement up to $300 per year per person, continuing for two years after retirement for a maximum of $3,000 per person. These same retirees often become teachers for classes at Pitney Bowes (AARP, 1990). The examples given here may be a drop in the bucket, but they serve as examples of how older people can be retrained, reeducated, and encouraged to stay in the workplace.

Leisure Opportunities

As we discussed previously, Americans generally use leisure for keeping busy with something, so that we rarely relax or refresh ourselves. Time away from work at any age should be a time for being, not doing. We all need conditioning to learn simply to be, to express our individual talents and interests, and to find fulfillment in the pleasure of self-realization.

Boredom does come with nothing to do, but real leisure is satisfying. Meditation, reflection, and contemplation are fun when divorced from the necessity to do them. Playing with ideas, trying to solve puzzles, or brainstorming new inventions can be relaxing and pleasurable. A group of older citizens could meet daily for lunch to share their ideas and experience: "We solve the problems of the world, but no one listens." All of us have undeveloped personal resources, talents, and abilities that could be realized. We need not limit our self-development only to what is necessary to hold a job. For example, a particular college professor likes to sit quietly and speculate. Students coming to her office say, "I see you are not doing anything." Much that can be enjoyed cannot be seen!

We should try to see the role of retiree as a valid and legitimate one, well deserving of leisure in its real sense. Our work values need to be examined and put into perspective. Pas-sively watching television, a common activity of both young and old, is hardly a form of self-realization. Our educational system, both formal and extended, should prepare us not only to work, but also to find fulfillment as human beings.

Chapter Summary

Retirement has not always been characteristic of American life. Ceasing work at a given age and receiving a pension has become more and more common for Americans after the Great Depression when Social Security was enacted. Most now expect to retire and many take an early retirement. Orientation to work and leisure are important factors influencing a person's decision to retire. The older person with a strong work ethic who enjoys status and friends on the job may continue working. Age discrimination operates against older people in employment. There are negative stereotypes of older workers. Employers may want more years of work than the older person has to give. "Youth cult" values encourage hiring the young instead of the old. Finding work in old age can be difficult.

Many factors affect one's adjustment to retirement, and the capacity to enjoy leisure is not a given. Sufficient retirement income appears to be of great significance in retirement. Work and leisure opportunities for elders in our society could be greatly expanded. More part-time options and gradual retirement programs would give older persons more choice, and hence, satisfaction with postcareer plans.

Key Terms

age discrimination
  in employment
Age Discrimination in
  Employment Act
  (ADEA)
career development
  program
early retirement
early retirement
  discrimination
flexible work/
  retirement plans
job sharing
late-retirement
  incentive
  programs (LRIPs)
leisure values
myths about the older
  worker
retirement
retirement preparation
  programs
retraining
third age
work ethic

Questions for Discussion

1. Are we becoming a more leisure-oriented society?
2. Do you see positive or negative values (or both) in retirement communities that place great emphasis on leisure activities?
3. Why would someone want to continue working beyond age 65?
4. Will discrimination in jobs on the basis of age ever be eliminated? Why or why not?
5. What do you envision for yourself in old age in terms of work and leisure?
6. Imagine yourself isolated in a cabin in the mountains for two weeks with only pencil and paper—no visitors, television, or radio. Would you enjoy it?

Fieldwork Suggestions

1. Study adjustment to retirement by talking to four retired people about their adjustment.
2. Go to a senior center in your community and talk with older retired people about what

would induce them to return to work. Are you able to draw any conclusions from your discussions?

3. Interview two older people who have remained in their professions—entrepreneurs, lawyers, writers, teachers, executives, managers, or doctors, for example. Why do they continue working? Do they have any "retirement" plans?

Internet Activities 🌐

1. Look up FaceIntel on the Internet to assess their position in terms of older workers. See if you can find an Internet response to this pressure group by Intel.

2. Locate a website with current age discrimination cases in the state in which you live. Who sponsors the site? How accurate do you believe the information is? How easy or hard was it for you to find it?

3. You are a career counselor providing assistance to a 57-year-old male who was recently laid off from his job at a nationwide hardware chain. His former job was inventory control for six stores in a certain region of the country. What websites on government programs and services will you access for information on his behalf? (Hint: begin with websites for Pension Benefit Guaranty Corporation and the Social Security Administration.)

Finances and Lifestyles

9

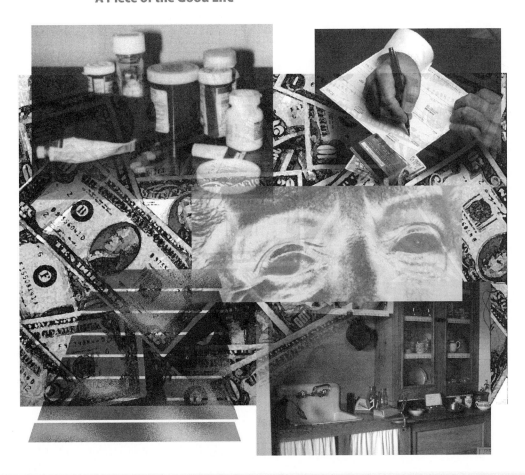

How to Ride That Aging Baby-Boomer Wave

Linda Stern

The baby boomers are starting to turn 60, and who wouldn't want to be selling whatever they're going to buy?

People approaching retirement buy second homes, cruises, investment products, health-care services, the occasional RV or (post) midlife-crisis motorcycle, and lots and lots of restaurant meals.

It seems like investors willing to place a few strategic bets might look at some of those industries. With the members of the boom numbering around 76 million, and entering—or entrenched in—their biggest earnings years, there's a lot of money to be spread around.

That is not to say that investors should throw all of their money after this demographic. The key to a successful investment plan is, after all, diversification, low fees, and a steady, long-term view.

But boomers will be aging and spending for a long time, and investors who want to spend a bit of time researching the companies and funds that might profit most from that will find a lot to like.

Here are some ideas for getting your piece of it.

Leisure

Boomers love their fun, and fun-selling companies such as lodging and travel businesses, craft stores, publishers, fishing-rod manufacturers, and casinos have profits to show for it.

Four leading mutual funds that focus on leisure company stocks have returned 32.4 percent to investors in the six years since the stock market peaked in 2000, says Lipper analyst Don Cassidy. That gain is in comparison to a 0.7 percent loss for the Standard and Poor's 500 over the same period.

The four are Icon Leisure & Consumer Staples (whose symbol is ICLEX), Fidelity Select Leisure (FDLSX), Rydex Leisure (RYLIX), and a load fund: AIM Leisure (FLISX).

He thinks leisure companies will do well for a while. "I like to be in them, in effect, to overweight those areas that the megatrends favor," he said.

Financials

This is another Cassidy favorite. From time to time analysts have looked at the shares of mutual fund companies and determined that they often do better than the mutual funds the companies sell.

Of course, simply buying shares of fund companies will not get you the kind of diversified portfolio you should get from holding a mutual fund.

But with the biggest generation ever entering its investment-obsessed years, and money managers aiming at skimming a minimum of 1 percent off the top of those portfolios, it's worth a look.

Here are some of the companies whose own share prices are beating the heck out of the SP500: Merrill Lynch & Co. (MER), T. Rowe Price (TROW), Raymond James Financial (RJF), Cohen and Steers

(CNS), Calamos Asset Management (CLMS), Janus Capital Group (JNS), Legg Mason (LM) and, of course, Ameriprise Financial (AMP), the financial services company behind those embarrassingly annoying (or is it annoyingly embarrassing?) 1960s nostalgia ads.

Health Care

More than $3 billion in knees and hips are sold every year in America. Increasing numbers of boomers are moving to the aspirin-a-day plan. Diabetes, sleep apnea, hypertension are all at epidemic levels, or at least more carefully monitored, analyzed and treated than they ever were before.

Investing in health care in the face of an aging population seems a no-brainer. And companies that sell health-care supplies, run hospitals, and make medical equipment have all been doing very well.

Mutual fund research firm Morningstar picks T. Rowe Price Health Sciences Fund (PRHSX) as the best of the bunch. Another inexpensive fund that has done well in this category is the Schwab Health Care Fund (SWHFX).

Health-care companies, says Cassidy, will benefit from the aging trend and all of the new bio-tech discoveries likely to be brought to market in the next several years.

Over the next 40 years, the number of people over 65 years of age and over will more than double, and the number of people 85 and older will increase almost five times over—from around 3 million to over 16 million (U.S. Bureau of the Census, 2002). New models of intergenerational exchange are being forged even as this is written. Family financial relationships in the twenty-first century do not look like those in the twentieth century.

In the early 1900s, older Americans were almost all poor or near-poor. They faced a variety of economic hardships that were not justified, given the generally high standard of living among the rest of the population. With the advent of Social Security and other pension programs, the financial status of the elderly improved throughout the twentieth century. Changes in Social Security in the 1960s and 1970s provided more comprehensive coverage. Still, the bulk of elders live relatively modest lifestyles. To cope with inflation, a big problem in the 1970s and early 1980s, the U.S. government raised interest rates. In the early 1990s when a recession hit, interest rates were dramatically lowered. Interest-sensitive monies are savings accounts, bonds, and utilities stocks—those very institutions in which elders have invested their savings and pension.

Financial Status

The financial status of the average older American is rather ordinary. The household income of those over age 65 is not much different from the average for all adult households. Approximately one in every six households headed by an elderly person in 2000 had an income of less than $15,000; 40 percent had incomes of $37,000 or more (American Association of Retired Persons [AARP], 2001). On average, the poverty level of elders has improved over the last several decades. The poverty rate for persons age 65 and older declined from 24.6 percent to 9.8 percent between 1970 and 2000, slightly less than the rate for people 18 to 64 (AARP, 1997; U.S. Bureau of the Census, 2002; Health Care Financing Administration [HCFA], 1996). The poverty rate is somewhat higher for older adults than for younger adults but is still below the poverty rate for children (Moody, 2000). The "greatest generation" cohort, which reached adulthood in the 1940s and 1950s, had high marriage rates, high birthrates, and low divorce rates. More women remained married throughout their lifetimes, and more children were raised by two parents. The post–World War II era is exemplified by improving opportunity, stable family life, and upward mobility.

Numbers derived from population trends, however, can be misleading. Social class, race, ethnicity, and gender all combine to unequally distribute power and wealth in the country. The circumstances over an individual's lifetime have financial consequences in later life. The poverty rate for women living alone, for example, is more than two times the average rate for all people; and poverty rates among African American women living alone is nearly 50 percent—more than four times the national average (U.S. Bureau of the Census, 2000). Eighty-five percent of people over 65 today belong to the non-Hispanic white majority; however, the minority population is growing and aging. It is projected that by the middle of this century non-Hispanic whites will constitute about 67 percent of the older population (Moody, 2000).

As a group, in 1998 2.5 million elders were classified by the U.S. government as "near-poor" (income between the poverty level and 125 percent of this level; see Table 9.1). These elders have been variously described as near-poor, deprived, or **economically vulnerable.** Such an income is inadequate to allow most people to lead a full life. Altogether, one-fifth of the older population was poor or near-poor in 1996 (AARP, 1997), and those trends remain constant in the first decade of the new century.

A major reason for the increased income (reduction in poverty) of elders over the past two decades is that Social Security payments are higher because of automatic cost of living adjustments. Additionally, more women are now

TABLE 9.1

Income of persons 65 years and over living in the community as a percentage of the poverty level: 1990, 2005, 2020

Income	1990	2005	2020
Total percent	100	100	100
Less than 100 percent	17	13	7
100–140 percent	18	14	9
150–199 percent	13	12	9
200 percent or more	52	61	75

Source: Siegel, J. (1996). *Aging into the 21st century.* National Aging Information Center, U.S. Administration on Aging: Washington, DC.

covered under pension plans and Social Security. The number of young and middle-aged women in the workforce who pay into the system has steadily increased since the 1960s, and as these women retire they receive greater benefits than did women from previous generations. Nine out of 10 households of older people rely on Social Security for some portion of income; 3 of 10 older households depend on it for four-fifths or more of their income; and 13 percent of older households have no income other than Social Security (Moody, 2000).

Aging is not a unidimensional phenomenon. The income of the head of the household tells only a small portion of the story. Generally elders live in families, families consist of generations, and family patterns include both personal and financial interactions across the generations. The financial and personal caregiving exchanges that take place over time powerfully impact the financial status of the all generations in a family. Another point to emphasize in studying finances in later life is that the upcoming cohort of baby boomers will age much differently than did their grandparents. The grandparents of boomers are their model for aging because, generally speaking, our parents and grandparents become our role models for aging. Cutler and Devlin (1996)

Retirement has many faces, depending on health, income, living environment, and other factors. For some, the opportunity to simply sit and relax or visit casually with friends is a warmly welcomed change from the working years.

discuss a "wealth span" that corresponds with the life span. Middle age is a time in one's wealth span when a variety of emotional, biological, social, and financial changes begin to emerge and are likely to form the basis of new sets of expectations and concerns and therefore of plans and financial decisions within the family unit (p. 25).

The moral economy of a society is its set of beliefs about what constitutes just exchange: not only about how economic exchange is to be conducted . . . but also . . . when poor individuals are entitled to social aid, when better off people are obligated to provide care, and what kinds of claims anyone—landowners, employers, government—can legitimately make on the surplus product of anyone else.

STONE, 1988

Wide Diversity in Financial Status

Census data suggests that the spread of wealth is great among older people. That means those 65 and over have a great diversity of rich and poor. Income, as we have pointed out, is not equally distributed among ethnic groups. One of every 11 elderly whites was poor in 1996, compared to one-fourth of elderly blacks and almost one-fourth of elderly Hispanics (AARP, 1997). Nonmetropolitan women of any ethnicity are particularly likely to be or to become poor in old age, and they have higher poverty rates and lower incomes than do women living in metropolitan areas (McLaughlin & Holden, 1993).

Disadvantaged people—the poorly educated, women, and minorities—have not shared equally in the increase in retirement income (Moody, 2000). The equalizing effects of Social Security are more than outweighed by private pensions and asset income (interest on savings), which are received mainly by those in the upper income brackets. Inequality throughout life is cumulative and becomes magnified in old age as accumulated disadvantage. In other words, the advantages of a good education and/or a good job lead to better pension coverage and savings as well as other assets in the later years.

Women, ethnic minorities, those who live alone, and the oldest old make up 90 percent of the elderly poor. Their financial distress is a function not only of aging, but also of education, race, and past employment. Single, widowed, and divorced women have a particularly difficult time because living alone is the most expensive way to manage. Because women live longer, and because many have not paid as much into Social Security, older women are many times more likely than older men to live alone in poverty.

Poverty has declined over the past several decades, but not extraordinarily given the state of the economy. Gerontologists are concerned that older Americans are being unfairly blamed for the country's huge economic deficits. The myth that all elders are down-and-out has transformed into the myth that elders are well-to-do and depriving the young of their fair share. In reality, most older people are struggling in the lower- to middle-income ranges. If the benefits of Social Security were removed from that income, many more of America's elderly would move into poverty and beyond, into destitution. The new trend toward decreased government support for social welfare places the well-being of this population in a precarious and insecure position.

Home Ownership

The net worth of a family unit or individual is the total value of all assets, minus debts. The overwhelming majority of the American population saves little for old age, does not maintain significant savings accounts, and does not hold other financial assets. However, around 78 percent of the elders owned their own homes in 1996, a figure that is 12 percent higher than a decade before. Although more older people own their homes than do younger adults, the problem for older home owners is to remain in their homes and stay financially solvent. High energy costs and the generally high cost of living can lead to difficulties. The percentage of income spent on housing, including maintenance and repair, in 2000 was higher for older persons (34 percent) than for the younger consumer population (27 percent); however, about 80 percent of older home owners in 1995 owned their homes free and clear (AARP, 1997). Many older people are "house rich and cash poor"—that is, they have minimal monthly income, but many thousands of dollars in equity in their home. The greatest asset for most elders is the value of their home. In 1988 the federal government introduced a plan of **reverse mortgages,** whereby a loan is made against home equity owned by the borrower. A borrower (the home owner) increases indebtedness while drawing down the equity in the home. The loan does not require monthly repayment and becomes repayable when the borrower ceases to use the home as a principal residence, which may be when he or she moves (to long-term care, for example) or dies. At that time the home is sold, and the lender (government and/or its agent) receives the value of the loan plus interest. In another approach to home equity conversion, a bank guarantees a monthly income to the home owner for the remainder of his or her life and claims ownership of the home upon the death of the home owner (Vitt, 1998). Money can be received in a number of reverse mortgage approaches:

- a lump-sum payment
- monthly payments for a fixed period of time—the term plan
- monthly payments over the remaining lifetime of the borrower for as long as the home is used as principal residence—the tenure plan
- a credit line up to a maximum amount that can be drawn upon at various times
- some combination of lump-sum payments, monthly payments, and a credit line.

It is estimated that more than 600,000 elderly home owners living in poverty could be raised above the poverty line if they obtained a reverse mortgage (Kutty, 1998). One study sponsored by the U.S. Department of Housing and Urban Development estimated that the poverty rate of elderly households could be reduced by three percentage points by means of reverse mortgages (Sawyer, 1996; Kutty, 1998).

Reverse mortgages are only of value for those elders who strongly desire to age in place—that is, who wish to live in their present home until their death (or a move). If an older person were willing to move, selling the home and investing the proceeds in an income-generating asset would make more sense from a strictly economic perspective (Kutty, 1998). Most older people, however, are strongly motivated to remain in their own homes for as long as possible. Houses are memory holders: one's lifescape is contained in a home. Familiar surroundings, including of the familiarity of a neighborhood—even one that has changed over time—are comforting. For many elders, a reverse mortgage option can provide exactly the right pay-off: the investment in a home over all those years is paying off for them in their old age, assisting them to remain solvent in the space of their choosing. For others, it is an option they choose not to take; still others have fewer options than this.

A number of elders own mobile homes, which are typically cheaper than houses. Many people have found the mobile-home-park lifestyle to be an affordable one. A summary of mobile-home facts and figures reveals that:

- Six percent of older Americans live in mobile homes
- Almost half the residents of manufactured housing are age 50 or older
- More than one-third of manufactured home residents are retirees or part-time workers
- More than 90 percent of older residents own their manufactured homes; 23 percent own their lots
- More than half the older residents of manufactured homes live in mobile-home parks

- California and Florida have the most manufactured homes
- "Double-wides"—composed of two sections—and even larger mobile homes are growing in popularity, accounting for half of all units produced in 1996
- Average price for a single-section home in 1992: $20,600; for a multisection home: $37,200 (Glasheen, 1994)

These figures speak for themselves as to the popularity of mobile homes and their affordability. Also is implied the owner's modest lifestyle. Residents, however, must pay rent for the space on which the mobile home sits, and these rents have risen in recent years. In many areas of California, elders are called "prisoners of paradise," because their rents have escalated at a frightening pace. Mobile-home owners and even condominium owners who pay maintenance fees are subject to cost increases over which they have no control. Older people would benefit from legislation controlling these costs.

Home Rental

A renter is more subject to inflation, enforced living conditions, involuntary moves, and other forms of control by others than is a home owner. In 1997, of the 20.8 million households headed by older people, 22 percent were renters. The median household income of older home owners was $21,629; the median household income of older renters was $10,151 (AARP, 1997). Some cities have adopted rent-control ordinances to help people like elders living on fixed incomes, but such policies are rare.

Social Security or Social Insecurity?

The United States has had a strong work ethic since its inception. In 1929 the U.S. stock market began a steep decline into a crash; subsequently, in 1931, many large financial institutions failed, and the United States entered the Great Depression. This was perhaps the first time as a nation that Americans were faced with the reality that hard work, diligent savings, and good citizenship were not enough to keep one from economic disaster. Good people—admired political and community leaders, as well as ordinary, hard-working blue-collar folk—were economically ruined overnight. The collapse was like a house of cards: businesses failed; factories shut down; people lost jobs; banks repossessed properties for which loan payments were not being made; then many of the banks failed, taking the savings of ordinary and extraordinary people alike down with them. The poverty rate in the United States was tremendous, and older people were among the very least competitive applicants for whatever jobs were available. The extent of economic interdependency was clearly driven home to the average U.S. voter: it indeed might take more than hard work, good values, and trust in the institution of banking to protect oneself economically, and society as a whole had an obligation to help out those who were most desperate.

Social Security began in 1935 to counteract the effects of the Great Depression. It was designed to provide, in the words of President Roosevelt, "some measure of protection . . . against poverty-ridden old age." The intent of the first Social Security Act was to provide a safety net for those most vulnerable to desperate poverty. It was assumed that pensions and personal savings would support people in their later years; however, in 1994—about 60 years after the act was first passed—40 percent of all income received by older people was from Social Security (Hooyman & Kiyak, 2002; also see Figure 9.1).

Social Security was designed to supplement pensions or retirement savings, rather than to provide the total income of aged people. Although everyone seems to agree that Social Security should not be and was never designed to be the sole source of retirement income, for many elders it continues to be just that. If it were

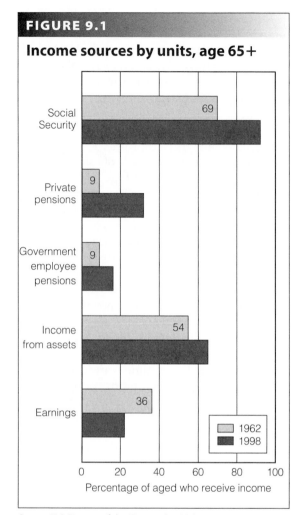

FIGURE 9.1

Income sources by units, age 65+

Source: U.S. Bureau of the Census. (1998c).

not for Social Security benefits, nearly half of our aged, rather than the current 12.4 percent, would live in poverty. In general, the lower one's income level, the more important Social Security becomes as a component of the household budget. It is the most common source of income for all races. For either blacks or Hispanics, Social Security is much less likely to be accompanied by other forms of income. Obviously, for the individual with no income from earnings, savings, stocks and bonds (asset income), or pensions, Social Security is a much higher percentage of the total income. Under these circumstances, there is no universal agreement on the adequacy of the benefits or the appropriate level of benefits. Social Security benefits currently begin at age 65, but they may begin at age 62 if the recipient chooses to accept 20 percent less per month.

The United States was one of the last industrial nations to introduce a major public system of social insurance against old-age dependency. By 1935, 27 other countries already had well-developed national retirement systems. The Social Security Act of 1935 required that employer and employee each pay into the Social Security fund 1 percent on the first $3,000 of the worker's wages. (Workers in 1991 paid 7.65 percent of their paychecks into Social Security.) Congress eventually amended the act to extend benefits on the basis of social need in addition to earned right. Amendments adopted in 1939 made certain dependents of retired workers and survivors of deceased workers eligible, too. In 1960 amendments extended benefits to all disabled persons. Over the years, the amount of money that a retired person may earn before forfeiting part of the benefit has increased.

Today the most important income sources for elders are Social Security, interest income (income from assets), and pension income—amounts directly dependent on earlier earnings.

Fewer Workers to Support More Retirees

Social Security operates on a principle of sharing: some individuals die before they are able to collect benefits, whereas others live long enough to get back much more than they contributed. The ledger supposedly balances. However, the increasing percentage of elders and their increasing life expectancy has greatly strained the Social Security system.

In 1945, for instance, 42 workers paying into Social Security supported one retiree. Today each retiree is supported by just three active taxpay-

ers. In about 30 years the huge baby-boom generation will begin to retire, creating even bigger strains. In the year 2030, there will be only two workers for every retiree. Most citizens believe that their payroll taxes go into a kind of insurance pool, which is held and invested until the day they retire. In fact, Social Security taxes are transferred almost immediately to retirees: The system takes money from workers and hands it to retirees. Americans have been receiving far more than they and their employers ever paid into the system. Most young people now will collect less after retirement than they contribute over their working lives.

Modifications to Social Security over time have tried to incorporate principles of both equity (people get back an amount proportional to their contribution) and adequacy (lower-income people receive a larger replacement proportion to compensate for lower life earnings), but debates rage because of this "compromise between two opposing values" (Moody, 2000, p. 166).

Social Security Adjustments

Social Security benefits do rise with the cost of living. This change was brought about by Social Security amendments instituted in 1972. Under the current law, this cost-of-living adjustment (COLA) occurs automatically whenever there is an increase in the Consumer Price Index in the first quarter of the year (in comparison with the same period in the previous year). Effective January 1995, for example, Social Security benefits increased 3 percent based on the 1994 increase in the Consumer Price Index from the previous year. However, even with the COLA provision, many who now receive Social Security are still living below the poverty line.

How to keep Social Security solvent is a major social issue. Some changes in Social Security have been made to restore the system's fiscal health. In 1983 compromise amendments were painfully worked out by a bipartisan committee and were subsequently adopted by Congress. For example, starting in 1988 college students between the ages of 18 and 22 can no longer draw benefits on a deceased parent who paid into Social Security. The practices designed to protect the Social Security system include:

- Accelerating Social Security tax rate increases

- Gradually raising the eligibility age for full benefits (in the year 2000, the retirement age began its increase from 65 to 67). This change affects people born in 1938 or later. For example, those born between 1943 and 1954 will not receive full benefits until age 66

- Substantially increasing tax rates for the self-employed

- Levying an income tax on higher-income Social Security beneficiaries

- Expanding coverage to newly hired federal employees

- Creating sharper decreases in starting benefits for early retirees—to a 30 percent reduction at age 62 by the year 2000

Changes in the system were seen as necessary to keep it from defaulting. The question of how close to bankruptcy the Social Security system is, is more complex than it appears to be. Social Security is said to be heading for bankruptcy because it uses earmarked taxes and has a trust fund. Presently there is more credit in the Social Security trust fund than is required for payouts; however, projections suggest that by 2025 revenue coming into the fund will fall below the benefits being paid out (Quadagno, 2002). Much of the baby-boomer generation will be receiving payments by that date; people are living longer, and therefore payments are made for more years than previously; and after the 1960s, women began having fewer children—a smaller generation of workers to pay Social Security benefits (Quadagno, 2002). Other federal programs (such as education and defense) have no earmarked taxes and no trust fund and would therefore never be perceived to be bankrupt. Those other federal programs are represented in the congressional budgetary process—a process by which program needs are presented and the budget is lobbied for by legislators, along with budget requests from other programs.

In order to protect it from prevailing political winds, Social Security was designed as a "pay-as-you-go" system. Essentially, Social Security will only become bankrupt and unable to pay benefits if taxpayers are unwilling to raise taxes to pay for those benefits—the benefits that spread the cost. An alternative to raising taxes would be to reduce benefits by increasing the number of years people must work before receiving payments, for example. Yet another alternative would be to introduce means testing. An affluence test would reduce benefits to higher-income individuals to allow for more adequate benefits to lower-income people. This model appeals to many Americans, but economists fear that it would discourage savings—for "income" includes all an individual's assets. Suppose, for example, persons 1 and 2 both earned the same salaries over their lifetimes but their standards of living were very different. Person 1 was the last of the big-time spenders, and person 2 saved and scrimped and had a substantial savings account. Through means testing, person 1 would qualify for Social Security, whereas person 2 would not.

A more radical suggestion is to eliminate Social Security all together and instead require mandatory savings: to privatize Social Security. This plan would replace today's pay-as-you-go program with a funded system of individual accounts invested in the stock market (Moody, 2000). Proposals to privatize only a portion of Social Security have also been designed. The fundamental argument for privatizing is the belief that investment in the private sector will exceed the value of future Social Security benefits.

The unknowns are enormous: to completely privatize is to tell citizens, "You're on your own," rather than to spread the risk through an insurance program model (Social Security) and help each other. On the other hand, banking regulations since the Depression have been enacted to radically minimize the possibility of a similar collapse in the future—so presumably, the individual's mandatory investments would be protected from such disaster. Regulations controlling sales commissions on investments by workers might also reassure the public.

The United States is not alone in its dilemma to provide old-age security for its citizens. While the ratio of persons 65 and over to those between 20 and 64 will rise from 21 percent in 1990 to 36 percent in 2030 in the United States, it will rise in Germany from 24 percent to 54 percent, and France is close behind that proportion (Feldstein, 1997):

> The Organization for Economic Cooperation and Development projects that government retirement benefits (excluding health costs) will exceed 16 percent of the GDP of Germany, France, and Italy by 2030, compared with about 7 percent of GDP in the United States. (Feldstein, 1997, p. 25)

The bottom line in the emerging debate is what sort of social contract the nation wants. To what extent does a nation consider itself responsible for the well-being of its citizens?

Inequities in Social Security

Under Social Security, people under age 65 and between the ages of 65 and 69 are penalized for working, although after age 70 there is no penalty on wages earned. Earned income is subject to both income and Social Security taxes, although Social Security payments are subject to neither. Nor is there a penalty for income earned through capital gains or interest on savings. In the end, the system is more beneficial to those who have money than to those who do not; however, it is far more critical to the economic quality of life for those with fewer resources.

Salaried workers are penalized the most by the present system. Older workers who need money often settle for hourly part-time jobs at minimum wage or even less so their wages will not be docked. In fact, most federal government employment programs for elders provide income only as a supplement to Social Security and pay minimum wage or less. Military, federal, and state government and other pensioned retirees, however, generally face no penalty against their pension earnings after retirement because salaries and wages are the only income subject to the penalty.

Before complete retirement, some employees receive retirement benefits (other than Social Security) from one job while receiving full salary from another—a practice called "double dipping." The end result of one of the changes in Social Security—an income tax levied on higher-income Social Security beneficiaries—is that about 20 percent of people who get Social Security have to pay taxes on their benefits. This provision affects the more well-to-do, who typically have income from a variety of sources such as salaries, interest from savings, and dividends from stocks and bonds.

Congress has considered reforming the Social Security law to eliminate the ceiling on earnings. However, this change has never been enacted. The reluctance of Congress to remove all limits on extra benefit income is due in part to uncertainty as to the effects of such a move. Congress has reasoned that an older person who could earn more than the yearly amount of unpenalized income probably does not need full Social Security benefits, thus reducing the strain on the system for the benefit of others. But this ruling works a hardship on those making a very modest living. Further, if there were no ceiling, it might reduce the number opting for early retirement by keeping them employed full time. All that would ease the strain on the system.

Still another criticism of Social Security involves the two-career family. The law favors one-earner households. Working couples pay up to twice as much in Social Security taxes as single-earner families, yet they seldom collect twice as much in benefits. A woman who has contributed throughout her working years may find that, because of her lower earning capacity, she may fare better with 50 percent of her

© K. Preuss/The Image Works

Adequate income for later life is critical, but savings and assets are unequally divided in society, reflecting income inequality during the working years. For those with adequate resources old age can be a profoundly rewarding time.

husband's benefits than with 100 percent of her own. (She is not entitled to both.) In essence, many working women receive none of the money they paid into Social Security. Another problem: Divorced men and women, particularly those who have not worked outside the home, may be left totally unprotected. To draw on an ex-spouse's benefits, a man or woman must have been married to that spouse for 10 years. For example, a woman married to one or more husbands, each for 9 years, who has not paid into Social Security is not eligible for benefits. A man or woman married 10 years to one person and 10 years to another would not qualify for benefits from both. Divorced women suffer more than divorced men because they are more likely to have worked at home and to have not paid into Social Security.

Assistance from Poverty

The definition of poverty, for purposes of social policy, is framed in terms of inadequacy, yet what is adequate might be absolute (having less than an objective minimum), relative (having less than others in society), or subjective (feeling one does not have enough to get along) (Hagenaars & de Vos, 1988). Poverty, then, must be understood in its political context, which is dynamic and changing over time. At one point in time, keeping citizens from starving to death might be the bottom-line social objective (absolute adequacy) for a society. At another time nutritious food, adequate safe shelter, and access to information for decision making is the bottom-line objective (relative adequacy). The difference in the values of those two times is primarily economic—economic strength and stability drive social policy and, to some extent, social values. It is an important concept to bear in mind while making the difficult trade-offs in cutting the budget pie.

The poverty threshold in the United States was set in the 1960s by estimating a minimally adequate food budget and multiplying by a factor of three, because research from the 1950s indicated that families spent about one-third of their income on food. Since the 1960s the threshold has been modified in prices, but not for standard of living (Meyer & Bartolomei-Hill, 1994).

In 1974 the federal program known as Old Age Assistance, which was intended to aid those not covered adequately by Social Security, was renamed **Supplemental Security Income (SSI)**. Instead of being managed by local offices, it is run by the Social Security Administration.

Funds, however, come not from Social Security, but from general U.S. Treasury funds. The program provides a minimum income for elders, the blind, and the disabled by supplementing Social Security benefits if they are below the amount stipulated by SSI. In essence, it is a guaranteed annual income, and that is very important for those who get little or no Social Security. The monthly amounts vary from state to state.

The federal SSI program makes no allowances for special circumstances. The amount is clearly defined, calculated by subtracting an individual's or a couple's income from a guaranteed level. In addition to income, individuals must pass an asset test: couples have countable assets (those that "count" in the defined allowances) of less than $2,500, and singles must have less than $1,500 to be considered eligible. Excluded in this are the value of an owner-occupied home, a car needed for transportation to medical treatment or to work, life insurance valued at less than $1,500, and personal property or household furnishings valued at less than $2,000 (McGarry, 1996).

The SSI program is designed to be a safety net for the poorest segment of the population. Although called "supplemental," benefits decrease substantially if the person or couple has other sources of income. The program has been strongly criticized because it does not consider differences in the cost of living between states and because it has no flexibility to allow for special circumstances. It has been estimated that only 56 percent of the elderly who are eligible for SSI presently receive benefits (McGarry, 1996).

Retirement Winners and Losers

Social Security payments are determined according to detailed guidelines and legislated formulas and are not based solely on need, unlike SSI payments. Depending on a person's personal circumstances or work history, the amount of a monthly Social Security check can be adequate or inadequate. Here are some hypothetical examples of people who fared differently in retirement:

Once relatively well off, Ed earned $75,000 per year as a chemical engineer. But he never stayed long enough at one job to qualify for a private pension. He spent his full salary every year on his wife and four children, hobbies, travel, and their home. He retired at age 65 with a Social Security benefit of $1,733 per month, making his annual income $18,396. How will he handle the giant financial step downward?

Jim, a former construction worker, earned an average yearly salary of $30,000; so did his wife, Jane, a teacher. Both retired in 1998. Their combined monthly Social Security check is $2,028; their union pension checks provide another $1,500; they also have a joint savings account that yields $600 in monthly interest. Now they earn almost as much as they did while working. (Their combined working salary after taxes was $50,000.) They are now making $49,536 annually and are moving to a condo in Hawaii.

Former Senator Calvin Bigg was in the air force for 20 years before joining a law firm and then entering politics. He has an annual $25,000 military pension; his years as a lawyer qualify him for Social Security; and he qualifies for a civil service pension for his years of public service as senator. His three combined pensions total more than $80,000 a year, not including interest on his savings and dividends from real estate holdings, which bring his yearly total to $130,000.

Wilona still misses her husband, who died in 1980. She was age 61 at the time and eligible for Social Security benefits as his widow. In 2000 she was 81 years old; she is healthy, and she wants to go on some cruises. But her yearly income, in spite of cost-of-living adjustments (COLA), is less than $6,000 a year—income hardly sufficient for living, let alone traveling.

At its inception, Social Security was meant to provide a stable future and a safety net for all citizens. It was never meant to be the sole source of income, which unfortunately it is for many older Americans.

Medical Expenses in Old Age

Medical expenses rise with age. Although elders represent only 13 percent of the population, they spend 25 to 30 percent of the money used for health care. Contrary to popular belief, Medicare and Medicaid do not cover all medical expenses when one is over age 65. Actually, these programs do not cover many chronic conditions, leaving the individual to pay for treatment. The "Medicare Handbook" lists the following expenses as not covered:

- Dental care and dentures
- Over-the-counter drugs and most prescribed medicine
- Eyeglasses and eye examinations
- Hearing aids and hearing examinations
- Routine foot care
- Most immunization shots
- Custodial care in the home
- Custodial long-term care (nursing homes)

Examine the list carefully. The program's coverage excludes most parts of the body that tend to change with age and require care. As medical costs rise, one's standard of living declines.

Did You Know . . .
Medicare and Medicaid are expected to grow by over 10 percent annually over the next 5 years; they will have the fastest growth of any other part of the federal budget. Together they are [projected] to constitute one-third of the federal budget in 2002.

Lynch & Minkler, 1997

Medicare and Medicaid

Medicare is a part of the Social Security system; those who are eligible for Social Security benefits are also eligible for Medicare. The vast majority of those eligible are elderly. Medicare is the main insurer of persons over 65 years of age: 95 percent of the elderly are covered by Medicare hospital insurance (Part A), and 98 percent of those have supplementary medical insurance (Part B) as well (Health Care Financing Administration [HCFA], 2000). Medicare requires deductibles and 20 percent coinsurance for most services, which must be paid for either by **Medicaid,** if the individual meets the financial criteria; supplemental private insurance (Medigap) purchased by the individual; or the individuals themselves. Medicaid has traditionally provided medical coverage for poor and disabled people.

Two interacting factors cause concern for the solvency of Medicare: the growth of the over-65 population and medical costs. People enrolled in Medicare increased from 19.5 million in 1967 to nearly 39 million in 1996—a 95 percent increase. Medicaid recipients increased by 275 percent (this proportion includes an increase of 86 percent in dependent children). The number of **dually entitled** persons (people covered by both Medicare and Medicaid) amounted to nearly 6 million in 1995 (HFCA, 1997).

Steadily rising medical costs threaten both the Social Security system and to the elderly individual. Some examples: Medicare skilled nursing facility payments increased from $7.1 billion in 1994 to $9.1 billion in 1995—an increase of 28.2 percent, and due in no small part to longevity. Home health agency benefit payments for Medicare grew from $12 billion in 1994 to $15.1 billion in 1995—a 25.8 percent increase. Medicare hospice expenditures have significantly increased, from $1.4 billion in 1994 to $1.9 billion in 1995—an increase of 35.7 percent (HFCA, 1996)!

In 1967 national health costs, including Medicaid, were $51 billion, or 6.3 percent of the gross national product. By 1995 total Health

Care Financing Administration (HCFA) outlays were $248.9 billion—16.4 percent of the federal budget. Although the elderly are increasingly scapegoated as causing the national budget deficit, nearly 20 million dependent children under 21 received Medicaid benefits in 2000. Dependent children represented 51.5 percent of the Medicaid budget in 1995. The 5 million people over 65 receiving Medicaid represent only a little over 12 percent of all recipients.

Medicare has two parts. Part A, called Hospital Insurance, covers a portion, averaging about 50 percent, of short-term hospital bills. Most people on Social Security pay no premiums for Part A. It covers hospitalization for up to 90 days plus 60 "lifetime reserve days" that can be used to extend the 90-day covered period. When the days have expired, individuals pay $194 per day. In 2000 hospital insurance paid for all covered services for the first 60 days in a hospital, except for a deductible of about $780. For days 61 to 90 in a hospital, Medicare pays a portion and the older patient pays a daily coinsurance amount. If inpatient skilled nursing or rehabilitation services are necessary after a hospital stay, Medicare pays for up to 100 days. Medicare does not pay for "custodial" care given in a facility that lacks appropriate medical staff—it is designed for a "spell of illness," or to assist with acute illness, not chronic conditions. Some hospice care is also covered. If a recipient is confined at home, Medicare can also pay for limited visits from home health workers.

Medicare Part B, called Medical Insurance, consists of optional major medical insurance for which the individual pays a monthly fee. Over 98 percent of Medicare beneficiaries also select Part B. Medical insurance helps pay for necessary doctor's office visits, outpatient services for physical and speech problems, and many medical services and supplies that are not covered by Part A. After the patient pays a deductible, medical insurance pays 80 percent of covered services.

To qualify for Medicare payments under Part A, hospital care must be "reasonable and necessary for an illness or injury." Congress established Medicare to pay a restricted portion of a citizen's medical expenses that resulted from only the most serious illnesses. That is why the most common health needs of seniors, such as routine checkups, drugs, and dentures, are not covered. In addition, the program places both a dollar limit and a time limit on what is covered. Recall, for instance, that Part A has a deductible that the patient must pay. Other restrictions and limitations get rather elaborate. Suffice it to say that many frail, sick oldsters pay thousands of their own dollars for medical care. Medicare does not usually cover all expenses, especially for long-term, chronic conditions, and private insurance plans such as Blue Cross, Kaiser, and EmCare cover only portions of either office visits or a hospital stay. Therefore medical expenses can get costly, and a person may be just a major illness away from financial disaster. Over the past several years, Medicare has tightened its system, covering less, not more, of hospital and medical costs. The patient or some other source pays the difference between what the doctor charges and what Medicare pays the doctor.

Of the 38 million Medicare beneficiaries, nearly 90 percent are using a traditional **fee-for-service** model. They pick their doctors, and Medicare pays a set fee for each service. Most beneficiaries also purchase private supplemental insurance to pay for uncovered costs. It can become an expensive proposition, even with Medicare assistance. The Public Policy Institute of the American Association of Retired Persons recently found that over 2 million elderly people at or below poverty line are using 50 percent of their yearly income or more for medical expenses that are not covered by Medicare (Stamper, 1998). These expenditures are for such things as prescription drugs, outpatient care, and premiums for private supplemental insurance.

One alternative to a fee-for-service plan is the **health maintenance organization** (HMO), also called managed care, in which approximately 11 percent of elders are currently enrolled (Nelson et al., 1997). In this model the HMO agrees to cover all an individual's medical needs for a **capitated** (all-inclusive) payment covering all Medicare-covered services (Lui et al., 1997).

In the managed-care model, the elder can use only the doctors and facilities on a limited list, but there are often additional benefits such as a broader range of coverage for pharmaceuticals and the convenience of avoiding a confusing bureaucratic billing system ("This is not a bill, but you owe X dollars"). Concerns with the HMO model have been that in an effort to control costs, access to needed care will be restricted. Some people fear that more costly services will be rationed, resulting in unequal access. Recent studies on service access have borne out some of those concerns: vulnerable subgroups such as the nonelderly disabled, the oldest old, people with functional impairments, and people in poor health or worsening health seem significantly more likely to report access problems than the general population (Brown, 1993; Ware, 1996; Nelson et al., 1997). The authors of one major study on health provision models concluded that access to home health services is particularly problematic in the managed-care model and that HMOs need to address the needs of frail and more vulnerable Medicare beneficiaries more effectively (Nelson et al., 1997).

A third option for Medicare services is called **point of service,** in which beneficiaries can visit doctors outside the network but must pay an additional cost. Another option that is growing in popularity is the **preferred provider organization (PPO)**, in which the beneficiary can visit any doctor in the health care network without a referral or see doctors outside the network at an additional cost. Medicare pays the PPO a set fee for all services for a set period of time.

The **provider-sponsored organization (PSO)** is quite new. Owned and operated by doctors and hospitals (as opposed to health insurance companies in the HMO model), PSOs are organizations similar to managed care plans in which Medicare pays the health plan a monthly fee for each recipient. In the **Medicare medical savings account,** which was not put into effect until around 1999, a high-deductible insurance policy provided by Medicare is combined with a tax-free medical savings account to help pay the deductible. At the end of the year, the beneficiary keeps any unused Medicare money.

The final option for Medicare services is the **privately contracted fee for service,** in which the beneficiary may visit any doctor or purchase any health plan but pays extra for uncovered or expensive services (Serafini, 1997).

Beyond question, those with greater financial resource have a broader range of options for health care services in later life. Because Medicare is an **entitlement** (provided categorically, not need based), people with higher income pay the same as people with limited income in terms of dollars, but the percentage of their income that they must pay is much smaller.

Extremely low-income individuals who qualify for SSI are also eligible for Medicaid in most states in the nation. Two groups of people qualify: the categorically eligible and the medically needy. The categorically eligible are people with certain characteristics (aged, blind, disabled, or a member of a family with dependent children that is headed by a female or in certain cases by an unemployed male) (Ettner, 1997). The medically eligible must have a limited income and have less than $3,000 in savings, excluding one's home and automobile, household goods, and $1,500 in burial funds. For those who qualify, Medicaid helps pay for a wide variety of hospital and other services. Medicaid often pays for services Medicare does not cover, such as eyeglasses, dental care, prescription drugs, and long-term nursing home care.

With the cost of long-term and nursing care beyond the ability of most elderly and their families to pay, Medicaid fills in the gap. In fact, over one-third of Medicaid's dollars to go long-term care received by fewer than 10 percent of all recipients. The aged account for nearly 60 percent of that total (Kaiser Commission on the Future of Medicaid, 1996). Currently, federal law requires states to cover nursing-home care for very poor elderly people judged to need that care, and it gives states the option (which all states take) to cover people above the poverty level but without resources for long-term care (Feder et al., 1997). Federal law allows but does not require states to cover long-term care at home or in the community. States have the option to cover personal care; however, New York is the only state that budgets much funding for this type of care (HFCA, 1996).

Medigap Policies

Medigap insurance policies are popular among elders who can afford them. In spite of continually rising policy costs, a majority of those on Medicare are estimated to also have a **Medigap policy.** Such policies are sold by private companies to help cover the "gaps" in health-care protection for which Medicare does not provide. Prior to 1992, insurance carriers could sell any benefits they chose as Medigap so long as minimum benefit requirements were met. The range and costs were enormous. In 1992, federal legislation was implemented to standardize policy benefits. Any company that sells Medigap coverage must offer policy A (a specified package of core benefits). Policy A is the starting point for policies B through J, with policy J having the most comprehensive coverage. Prior to standardization a typical policy paid out a maximum of $500 per year, compared to $1,250 or $3,000 after (Rice et al., 1997; Roha, 1998).

The required core benefits include:

- Daily Medicare co-payment of $191 for hospital days 61 through 90, and $382 for days 91 through 150
- Full cost of up to 365 additional hospital days during your lifetime
- 20 percent co-payment of Medicare's allowed amount for doctor charges

Table 9.2 provides a summary of the differences in each policy level. The policy level, as well as the company providing the policy, needs to be carefully chosen by the consumer. For example, policy C appeals to many seniors, but the cost from most carriers is often greater than the benefit. Policy H might be best if significant prescription drug expenses can be anticipated, but the cost of the policy must be balanced with its benefit. For the first six months after signing up for Part B of Medicare, a person can buy *any* Medigap policy sold in their area. After that time, the insurance provider has the option to turn down an applicant.

Did You Know . . .
Federally legislated Medigap insurance provisions were initiated in 1999. People who lose their coverage through no fault of their own or who move away from the area covered by the plan will have 63 days to buy any plan labeled A, B, C, or F, regardless of their health. Also introduced in 2001 were high-deductible versions of policies F and J. They will provide the same coverage as present ones but will be much less expensive because each will have a $1,500 deductible.

Consumers will find wild price differences, even within the same region: for example, the cost of policy A ranged from $436 to $1,032 for a 65-year-old man in California in 1998 (Roha, 1998). Advice to people shopping for a Medigap policy includes:

1. Comparison shop—review policies from at least three insurance carriers before purchasing
2. Ask for current premiums for 70-, 75-, 80-, and 85-year-olds—some policies increase faster with age of beneficiary than others
3. Inquire about a Medicare Select plan—a hybrid managed-care/fee-for-service system offering premiums reduced from 10 percent to 20 percent in exchange for giving up some choice of health care providers, especially hospitals (Roha, 1998)

TABLE 9.2

Medigap policy benefits summary

	Summary of Coverage
Policy A: Core benefits	• Daily copayment of $191/day hospital days 61–90; $382/day hospital days 91–150 • Full cost of hospital days up to 365 additional hospital days during one's lifetime • 20% copayment for doctor charges
Policy B	• Core benefits *plus* • Annual $100 Part B deductible for doctors' fees
Policy C	• Core benefits *plus* • Annual $100 Part B deductible for doctors' fees
Policy D	• Core benefits *plus* • Copayment for skilled nursing-home care, days 21–100 ($95.50/day) • Foreign travel emergency care • Up to $1,600/year short-term custodial care
Policy G	• All of D *plus* • 80% difference between doctor charges and Medicare approved payment
Policy H	• Core benefits *plus* • 50% cost of prescription drugs up to maximum of $1,250/year; $250/deductible
Policy J	• Core benefits *plus* • Annual $100 Part B deductible for doctors' fees • Daily copayment for skilled nursing-home care, days 21–100 ($95.50/day) • 50% outpatient prescription drugs costs up to $3,000/year, after $250 deductible • $1,600/year for short-term custodial care at home following surgery, illness, injury • 100% difference between doctor charges and amount approved by Medicare • $120/year for preventive health screenings • 80% cost of emergency care during foreign travel, $250 deductible

Source: Adapted from Roha, Ronaleen R. (1997). *Kiplinger's Personal Finance Magazine,* pp. 107–108.

No Place to Go

The aging population is the major determinant of increasing nursing home admissions: the number of elderly requiring long-term care is expected to double by 2025. Currently, 46 people per 1,000 over 65 are nursing home residents; the proportion increases to 220 per 1,000 among those 85 and over (Hicks et al., 1997). Double those proportions by 2025, and a substantial, if not alarming, increase in costs and need for facilities will result. The out-of-pocket costs for nursing home care have also dramatically increased. In 1980, the nursing home industry consumed 8.1 percent of all spending for personal health care services, a total of $17.6 billion. In 1994,

those costs came to $72.3 billion and accounted for 8.7 percent of all personal health care expenditures (Levitt et al., 1996).

For many older Americans, the cost of long-term health care is insurmountable. In a few months a couple can use up all their assets. If their income is sufficiently low, they can apply for Medicaid to cover nursing home care. This is a devastating experience, and one that more commonly occurs to the oldest old (those age 80 and over), to women, and to those living alone.

In terms of medical coverage, the forgotten minority are those elders whose income is just above the Medicaid cutoff, yet too low to cover the cost of nursing home care. Medicaid is administered by states; eligibility and dollar cov-

Although not created to be so, Social Security has become the most common source of income for all ethnic groups in the United States. If not for Social Security, nearly half of the aged would live in poverty.

erage per month vary widely. In Delaware, one of the best states for coverage, nursing homes are well reimbursed: therefore, good homes are available and willing to take even "heavy-care" patients. In contrast, a study of working- or middle-class Florida residents just above the level of Medicaid eligibility found that these elders were experiencing severe emotional, physical, and financial hardships trying to cope at home. Nursing home care, unavailable or unaffordable, was urgently needed for many (Quadagno, 1991).

With no adequate government programs to pay for nursing home care, older patients suffer, as do hospitals and frustrated care providers. Many low-income elderly patients who cannot get into nursing homes remain in hospitals even if they no longer need expensive hospital care. Hospitals that keep older patients for longer periods than Medicare or Medicaid fund rack up huge losses. The "boarder elderly" problem affects about 25 percent of the nation's hospitals, with urban hospitals hurt the most. Seventy-five percent of hospitals say that finding nursing homes for their "boarder" patients is difficult. Although "buyers" regularly visit some hospitals shopping for "profitable" elders on Medicare or Medicaid to fill their nursing homes, they have trouble finding them. A patient like 70-year-old Lucille, who suffers from seizures and is on a ventilator, does not interest them. The reimbursement for heavy-care patients does not meet the true cost of care, so nursing homes limit the heavy-care patients they take. Lucille is left to fend for herself; there is no real safety net for her.

The message here for older people is this: do not stay too long in a hospital or nursing home unless you can pay for it yourself. If you are poor and there is no government subsidy, nobody wants you and there is nowhere to go.

Private Pensions

A pension is money received upon retirement from funds into which an individual usually has paid while working. Some employers have plans to which the employee contributes; others have plans to which the employee does not have to contribute. An employee may have both a pension plan and Social Security or only one of these programs. On the average, **private pensions** provide a much lower percentage of the income of elders than does Social Security (which is, overall, 38 percent of the income of elders).

Trends in Private Pensions

Private retirement plans created in the 1980s, such as Individual Retirement Accounts (IRAs) and 401(k) pension plans, have become popular. In both plans, the benefit amounts are proportionate to the amount of money the employee contributes (and the employer matches, in the case of a 401(k) plan), as well as by how long the money is invested in the plan at the bank or with the employer. These plans transfer more of the retirement costs directly to the individual employee. For cost-cutting reasons, U.S. employers have in droves eliminated traditional pension plans for which they footed the bill, plans that guaranteed retirees a specific income based on salary and length of employment. Many employers offer no substitute; others offer 401(k) plans or similar types of individual plans (IRAs), which may or may not have a limited contribution by the employer. And they do not guarantee a monthly income for one's retirement life. Such studies show that the current generation

of workers is not going to have large retirement benefits unless they save their own money. There is also a definite shift away from fully paid health care for retirees by private employers.

Tax incentives further encouraged this avenue of retirement planning. However, the Tax Reform Act of 1986 eliminated some tax advantages, and uncertain interest rates (on which IRAs are based) have made these alternatives less reliable over the long term. When interest rates were high in the 1980s, the IRA and 401(k) (along with other savings plans, such as certificates of deposit) were seen as good sources of supplementary income to Social Security or employer pension plans. When interest rates came down in the early 1990s, these saving plans did not seem as good or as reliable as they were in the 1980s. Also, the earnings can be tied to the stock market, which carries risk for the individual who is participating. In any case, whatever is in the account when the worker retires is what he or she gets. And if it runs out before the retiree dies, too bad. One good thing is that a worker who changes jobs can take the IRA or 401(k) along—they are portable, unlike the company-sponsored pension.

Problems with Pensions

Numerous gaps exist in private pension plan coverage. Temporary or part-time employees do not typically have a pension plan offered by their employers. Some companies simply have no pension plans. And to be eligible for pension benefits in many companies, the individual must have worked for a considerable number of years. Thus, the person who changes jobs every 7 years might work for 40 or more years but accrue very small or no pension benefits from any job. The worker who changes jobs several times will typically get less in total pension income than a long-term worker, even if both earned the same pay, worked the same number of years, and were in similar pension plans.

In spite of a pension reform bill passed in 1974, many loopholes in pension plans continue. Before the Pension Reform Act of 1974, a person who lost a job before retirement might lose all the money he or she had paid into the company's pension fund. The Employee Retirement Security Act of 1974 established minimum funding for private pension plans and offered termination insurance to protect employees if their company ended the plan for any reason.

Congressional investigation of private pension plans has revealed that too many workers, after a lifetime of labor rendered on the promise of a future pension, found that their expectations were not realized. In some instances, people were laid off in their late 50s or early 60s, just previous to their retirement, and lost their pensions in the process. In other instances, corporations changed ownership—a small chain of independently owned grocery stores, for example, rotated ownership among key family members every eight years or so. Each "sale" provided a legal loophole for the company to eliminate or otherwise alter the pension fund. As more giant companies fall on hard times, retirees face a wave of broken promises. When Pan Am Airlines declared Chapter 11 bankruptcy, its pension plan was terminated. The federal government stepped in to cover employees according to the Pension Reform Act of 1974 but determined that they were obligated to pay workers only $596 per month of the $1,000 per month the workers were expecting. Pan Am and many other financially strapped companies have taken the option to "underfund" their pension programs, intending to make up for it later. General Motors is one example (Karr, 1993). For companies that go bankrupt, later never comes.

Typically, if a person leaves a job before 30 years of service or before reaching the retirement age the company specifies, benefits are drastically cut. There are other reasons for getting small pension benefits. Sometimes a company will stipulate that an employee's years of service must be uninterrupted. For example, a truck driver who belonged to the Teamsters Union for 22 years and retired anticipated that he would receive pension benefits of $400 per month.

Upon retirement, however, he was told that he was ineligible for a pension because he had been involuntarily laid off for three and a half months during one of his work years. Denied a pension he thought was rightfully his, this Teamster sued the union, claiming that he was never told of the pension plan risks. He won his case.

When not completely denied, benefits from a pension fund may be small because the recipients are either widows or widowers. Most private pension plans require the wage earner to sign a form, if he or she wishes, to allocate survivor benefits—usually considerably less than those the employee would receive—to his or her spouse. An employee who refuses to do this need not inform his or her spouse, and the spouse may have no way of learning the details of the pension. The federal government and private companies, because of privacy laws, may not divulge pension information to anyone but the employee. Consequently, a widowed homemaker cannot always count on getting something from her husband's pension.

Some retirement plans base pensions heavily on wages earned during the final three years of the worker's employment. Thus, in spite of pension plan reforms, loopholes prevent many elders from receiving equitable benefits. For example, a teacher who worked full time for 30 years but who worked on a half-time basis for the final three years might draw a pension largely based on the salary received during those last three years. Thus, the teacher's pension benefit would be considerably less per month because he or she had worked part time rather than full time—a severe penalty for trying to ease into retirement. Teacher retirement differs from state to state, and teachers must investigate provisions and restrictions on their plans. Anyone employed by an organization that offers a pension plan should become fully acquainted with the provisions of the plan.

Despite the reforms that have been enacted, current pension laws and provisions do not encourage job change. Yet, data from the field of occupational psychology indicates that with advancing technology, college graduates today will have to change careers, on an average, three times in their lives. What can be done? Young people, eager to get a job, rarely question or quibble about retirement policies, and too many young people still cannot imagine themselves getting old. However, young people *will* become old; and they must concern themselves with the retirement benefits of the jobs they accept. Perhaps in time all private plans will merge into one federal plan of Social Security, with each individual's account showing total earnings regardless of occupational mobility.

A potential problem with private pensions is that they do little to contend with inflation. How can companies offering pensions take inflation into account? That is a grave challenge for financial planners. An opposite problem in the 1990s is the recession and the dramatic lowering of interest rates. Many elders use the fixed interest on savings accounts to pay for living expenses. When interest rates are cut from, say, 10 percent to 5 percent, the income from the accounts is cut in half. Today's times bring fear and anxiety to retirees that can be alleviated only by a certainty of financial security.

Gender differences become sharply evident when postretirement income is analyzed, underscoring the finding that old women are more likely to be poor than are old men. Whether a pension is received and in what amount play a major role in differentiating the life chances of old people. Opportunities and decisions made earlier in life ripple into late life. The choices women make to marry, to withdraw from the labor market, to raise children—each of those choice points increases her likelihood of having limited pension resources in her old age (DeViney, 1995).

Did You Know . . .
A study on the status of elderly single women in 6 industrialized countries (France, Germany, the Netherlands, Sweden, Switzerland, the United States) concluded that the Netherlands and Sweden seem to have the best record in preventing poverty among older single women. France's position is next, with elevated poverty in the 75 or older age group. Germany is a greater distance behind, with Switzerland in close proximity to Germany. The United States ranks last for its protection of older single women.

Siegenthaler, 1996

Lifestyles of the Poor

What does poverty mean to you? You might say it is a small spendable income, and that would certainly be true; but how does income translate to lifestyle? It is the housing in which you cannot live, the food you cannot afford, the stores in which you cannot shop, the medical care you cannot get, the entertainment you cannot enjoy, the items (color TV, VCR, car) you cannot possess, the clothing you cannot buy, the places you cannot go, the gifts you cannot give, the holidays you cannot celebrate. These and other deprivations are the essence of poverty.

Inner cities and rural areas both contain disproportionately high shares of the older poor, yet the elders' lifestyles are different. About 4 million people in the United States are poor and old. Each day, about 1,600 people age 65 years old enter this group.

Did You Know . . .
A study of 225 homeless people in London in 1997 revealed: Two men became homeless before they were 10 years old; 5 men and 4 women first became homeless in their seventies; more than 75% of women and 50% of men had been in one town since becoming homeless; heavy drinking was not a problem for many respondents; more than 2/3 demonstrated or reported mental health problems.

Payne & Coombes, 1997

A Profile of Poverty

Rather than a sudden displacement from an upper- or middle-class economic situation to a lower class, the overall picture of the aged poor is typically a descent from a lifelong lower economic class to the lowest, culminating in total dependency on a government paycheck that is far too small.

The study of poverty among elders is more a woman's story—70 percent of the aged poor are female. Though averages show that the older poor woman is typically over 75 years old and white, the poverty rate among African American women is three times as high as it is for white women.

Below is a discussion of the poorest poor—the homeless.

The Homeless: An Urban Dilemma

Close to three-fourths of all older U.S. residents live in urban areas. Of these urban seniors, nearly half live in central cities. Although younger people are more likely to abandon a deteriorating city area, older people are attached to their area; for both emotional and financial reasons, they are not as likely to move to the suburbs. Urban issues such as crime, pollution, transportation, housing, and living costs in a large city are the issues of older people. The bulk of the older population in a central city lives in neighborhood communities, often racially and ethnically homogeneous—ethnic enclaves made up of people of European, Hispanic, or Asian ancestry.

An estimated 250,000 to 3 million Americans are homeless at any given time, and a significant proportion of those people live on the streets because they lack stable shelter (Somlai et al., 1998). An American tragedy hit large cities in the United States with a jolt in the early 1980s: homelessness. The problem grew even faster in the 1990s. High inflation in the 1970s, economic policies favoring the rich, corruption in the savings and loan industry, budget crunches at all levels of government, and lack of low-cost housing have all worked to swell the number of homeless people. The noose tightened around the desperately poor in the "greed decade" of the 1980s, during which time the dominant social paradigm became the corporate profit model. A strictly capitalistic profit model has no room for those who neither participate in production nor have an economic or familial safety net.

A new feature of poverty in the 1980s and 1990s has been the large number of homeless women and children. Though homelessness received considerable media attention, formal studies of the homeless focus more on the young than on the old. Crane, in her review of three studies on homeless elderly people, found agreement that catastrophic causes for homelessness were rare. Risk factors were more commonly discharge from an institution, release from prison, and/or exploitation and abandonment by family members. The studies each profiled older people who had "lifelong difficulties with other people, lack of a supporting family, poor education and lack of job skills, and personal problems such as alcohol abuse and criminal behavior" (Crane, 1994, p. 633). Additionally, among homeless elderly people in New York City, psychological trauma following the breakdown of a relationship or bereavement was listed as a cause of homelessness.

> *Whether portrayed as derelicts, as victims of misfortune, or as people burdened by structural forces beyond their control, the image of homeless people as reflected in most court opinions is one of weakness, helplessness, and despair.*
>
> DANIELS, 1997

In Boston, a study of homeless elders revealed an average age of 77. Many of the homeless people in this study had lived on the streets an average of 12 years—they were chronically homeless before old age. This population had an average of four chronic diseases and suffered from chronic alcoholism, severe mental illness, or both. Most resisted all efforts to place them in nursing homes (Knox, 1989).

More than one-third of Philadelphia's 252,000 elders lived below the federal poverty line in 1990. This was especially true for women, African Americans, and Hispanic Americans (Kaufman, 1991). A study in Detroit in the 1980s, "Aged, Adrift, and Alone," found an estimated 2,000 to 3,000 elders walking the streets and living in vermin-ridden abandoned homes, hungry and unable to find help. Most had incomes of $200 to $300 a month, which they got by retrieving discarded bottles and cans; most had fallen prey to crime, including rape. The study named three causes of homelessness: poverty, substance abuse, and improper release from mental hospitals and prisons (Tschirhart, 1988). To this list might be added domestic violence, which plays a major role in the increasingly visible population of homeless women (Homeless Women, 1997).

Older men and women suffer homelessness in essentially the same way. Often labeled "bag ladies," homeless women cannot afford even the most inexpensive shelter, often shun the confinement of an institution, and carry their few possessions with them, eating from garbage cans or wherever they can get a free meal. Their very existence says something profoundly tragic about the role of elders in our society. For older, homeless-men "skid rows" are common living environments. Estimates are that one-fifth of the homeless live in such areas. A skid-row resident is essentially homeless, even though he or she may not live exclusively on the streets. When they can afford it, they get cheap accommodations in run-down hotels or boarding houses. Typically, the men live on the street, periodically abuse alcohol or other drugs, may be physically or emotionally impaired, lack traditional social ties, and are poor.

A study of 281 homeless men aged 50 and over in the Bowery area of New York City provides us with a look at survival strategies (Co-hen, 1988; Cohen & Sokolovsky, 1989). The men were paid $10 upon the completion of a two-to-three-hour interview. Fifty may not be very old, but in the Bowery men look and act 10 to 20 years older than they are. Of the final group interviewed, 177 lived in flophouses, 18 in apartments, and 86 on the street. The oldest man living on the street was 78.

Perceptions of "home" are important. . . . Some individuals living in marginal accommodation develop a sense of attachment and rootedness to their housing and perceive it as "home."

CRANE, 1994

The men had developed skills that enabled them to survive in a treacherous environment. One-half of the non-street men had spent two or more years at their current address, suggesting considerable stability. The median number of years a study participant had resided in New York City was 13. Approximately half of the street men had been living on the streets for 3 years. One had been on the streets for more than 25 years. Most had very little income. One man bragged, "Sometimes I live on two bucks a month." Their lives revolved around getting food, cigarette butts, some wine, a bench to sleep on, a bit of hygiene, and a degree of safety. One man said, "I'm really tired; I'm worn out. You walk back and forth from 23rd to 42nd Street. I must walk 30 miles a day." Income sources were welfare or SSI, friends or relatives, panhandling, hustling, and odd jobs. Quite a few had long work histories. Some sought food from garbage cans or obtained scraps from restaurants. The men had their friendships with each other, counting on each other for help in times of trouble. Crimes such as muggings were their biggest fear. Though many of these men were eligible for government aid of some type, they did not apply for it, relying first on themselves, second on each other, and last on local charities such as missions. The researchers suggest that flophouses offer a better chance of survival than streets and that supporting and strengthening local service groups would help these men (Cohen, 1988). Project Bowery in Lower Manhattan has been partially successful in providing assistance—food, clothing, and job and housing referrals—to older residents (Cohen, 1992, p. 467).

Marginal and poor elders also live in single room occupancy or **SRO hotels.** The Tenderloin area of San Francisco fits the stereotyped image of the decaying central city. Although unique in some respects, it characterizes sections of all large cities. The Tenderloin is primarily a residential neighborhood where most inhabitants occupy cheap single rooms in apartment buildings, rooming houses, and hotels. The area seems to house society's discards; it is a dumping ground for prisons, hospitals, drug programs, and mental institutions.

Many residents are transients who drift in, stay a while, and drift on. The most numerous and yet least visible of those who live in this 28-block area are the elderly; most of them live alone in small rooms. During the day, they go out on short walks and for meals. A few never make it past the hotel lobby, where they sit. Others barricade themselves in their rooms and are not seen for long periods of time. Very few leave their building at night.

Higher-priced rooms usually include a private bathroom. The cheaper rooms may include a sink and toilet, but more often the bathroom is down a dimly lit hallway. Many hotel managers take no responsibility for meeting the special needs of older people; their job is simply to operate the hotel at a profit. Many of the buildings lack cooking facilities. Some residential hotels maintained specifically for elders provide food on the "continental plan," which includes three meals per day, six days per week. On Sundays, only brunch is served.

Some of the residents are alcoholics; others are lifelong loners, detached from larger social networks. Both men and women, reluctant to trust, tend to present a "tough" image and protect their privacy. The death rate is high in the Tenderloin; common causes include malnutrition, infection, and alcoholism, all of which hint at neglect, isolation, and loneliness. In spite of the negatives, some elders seem to like the independence and privacy that a hotel room in the Tenderloin can offer, much preferring their SRO quarters to an antiseptically clean room in a nursing home.

A survey of 485 aged SRO residents in New York City had similar findings. Many of the elderly residents had weak family ties, strong preferences for independence, and long-standing attachments to central city neighborhoods. The SRO hotel, although run down, was an acceptable solution for housing because more "standard" accommodations were not affordable (Crystal & Beck, 1992). Some are able to find meaning and purpose in life despite rough circumstances; others are not.

Many downtown urban areas have undergone urban renewal. The older hotels in these marginal areas have been torn down, and the residents, with their low incomes and limited housing options, face a crisis. For example, by the late 1980s Chicago's skid row no longer existed. SRO hotels were eliminated. Although an alcohol treatment center was built, no affordable housing remained, and the residents left to seek cheap shelter in other areas. Eliminating the skid row destroyed a community and a way of life. The area had been a settled community in that 30 percent of its residents had lived there four years or more. And, counter to the skid-row aging-alcoholic image, 37 percent drank no alcohol. About 60 percent had the meager economic means to make independent life in an SRO hotel a viable living arrangement, and the inhabitants needed the proximity to employment that the urban downtown environment provided. They might have liked a more pleasant room and perhaps better food, but if the hotel had a TV, lobby, working elevator, and housekeeping services and was reasonably clean, they were satisfied with the convenient location, the autonomous lifestyle, and the affordability.

But they had no power to resist redevelopment (Hoch & Slayton, 1989).

Jason DeParle (1994) provided an excellent summary of the history of SROs in the United States:

> They sprung [sic] up in downtowns during the early part of the century to house railroad workers and other transient laborers. Over time, many of them deteriorated into slum housing for drifters, drinkers, and the mentally ill. Then came developers, who, enticed by cheap land, razed the skid rows and replaced them with galleries and office towers. Over the past several decades, as many as a million cheap hotel rooms have been destroyed. (p. 53)

Some cities have begun to view their SROs as a community resource for the prevention of homelessness, rather than as a community liability that should be demolished (Shepard, 1997). Residents of SROs are, after all, only a short step away from living on the street. Perhaps the specter of people sleeping in doorways and camped out in alleyways will become too great an ethical burden for the public at large, and society will see fit to fund social programs to address homelessness.

Rural Elders

Rural is defined by the U.S. Census Bureau as territory outside places of 2,500 or more inhabitants. It includes ranches, farms, other land, and towns that are smaller than 2,500 persons. The term nonmetropolitan is much more general and refers to counties that are not metropolitan. A metropolitan county is one with an urban area of 50,000 or more and whose surrounding counties total at least 100,000 people. Elders in rural areas represent all social classes. Some are owners of large farms or ranches; others own oil fields, factories, or businesses, or have been professionals such as doctors, lawyers, and teachers. Their only commonality may be a love of the rural lifestyle, which in itself varies from the South to the Midwest to the North and East Coasts and varies by population density. Some rural areas contain small towns; others, acres and acres of farms and ranches with no towns for miles.

In 1996 the 10 states in the United States with the highest poverty rates for people over 65 were Mississippi (20 percent), Tennessee (20 percent), the District of Columbia (19 percent), Arkansas (19 percent), South Carolina (19 percent), Louisiana (18 percent), Alabama (17 percent), North Carolina (16 percent), Georgia (16 percent), and South Dakota (15 percent). Note that all except South Dakota are in the South. All except the District of Columbia are agricultural states and have large rural populations. Individuals who lived a marginal lifestyle as farm workers rather than owners tend to rely on Social Security as their only source of income when they retire, if they even have that.

The lifestyle of the rural poor is potentially more isolated than that of the urban poor. We imagine rural elders living in comfortable homes close to neighbors and family in small towns, shopping at nearby stores, and busily involving themselves in the social activities of the community; but this picture is not necessarily accurate. The older person may live miles from town or from neighbors. Housing in rural areas is often more run down than in urban areas and more likely to be substandard. The lack of a formal transportation system combined with lower income impacts the older rural person's access to services, as well as to specialty health care services, friends and family members, and participation in social activities in more distant regions (Johnson, 1996; Alexy & Belcher, 1997).

Incomes for rural elders are often lower than those of their urban counterparts. Compared with urban elders, a greater percentage of rural elders are poor and an even higher percentage are **near-poor.** This is especially true in the South. Yet income in and of itself may not be the most appropriate indicator of this group's well-being. The rural elderly have a somewhat lower cost of living and tend to be more satisfied and better able to make do with what they have. Rural elders are likely to have lived 20 or more years in their communities; they have commonly developed low expectations with regard to services, both social and medical.

Rural and urban elders construe health differently: rural persons are more tolerant of health problems (DePoy & Butler, 1996). Age, education, and marital status are apparently less related to a sense of life satisfaction among elderly rural women than are social factors over which they have no control, such as their standard of living or community changes (Butler & DePoy, 1996). One study concluded that rural women seem to feel less entitled to be satisfied with their lives ("my lot in life") than do urban women of the same age. Expectations and comparisons, in other words, shape people's perception of quality of life, and female rural elders in this study expected less (Butler & DePoy, 1996).

Rural African Americans generally tend to be particularly disadvantaged economically. They have substantially lower incomes than their rural white counterparts: for example, in 1987 the poverty rate for nonmetropolitan older African Americans was 46.5 percent, compared with 12.6 percent for whites (Spence, 1997). The disparity becomes even greater among those in the oldest-old category. Sixty-eight percent of rural African American women lived in poverty, compared to 21 percent of their white counterparts in the early 1990s (Bould et al., 1989).

The rural crisis of the last decade continues. Small farmers are being forced to abandon farming because they cannot make a living. The cost of supplies and equipment has far outpaced price increases for beef, pork, and grain. Young people have been leaving the farm life for years. Many towns and counties in the Midwest have been slowly losing population for the last 50 years. These rural changes have threatened the survival of towns, and many have become ghost towns (Johnson, 1996). Those who own businesses and homes in these now-defunct towns have lost the sense that their community is strong and thriving. As buildings have increasingly been abandoned, home and business owners have also lost a lot of money.

Government-sponsored low-income housing is less widely available in rural areas. Rural residents are likely to migrate to cities simply to improve their housing circumstances. Yet retirement complexes in large cities often do not offer a viable way of life to longtime rural dwellers. They do not really want to sacrifice the advantages of rural living, such as peace and quiet and longtime friendships, for better medical care and a more modern home. Studies of rural life tend to document a marked resilience and strength. Interviews reveal rural elders to be self-sufficient, proud, and able to survive on small Social Security checks.

The devil wipes his tail with the poor man's pride.

JOHN RAY, *ENGLISH PROVERBS*

It is life near the bone, where it is sweetest.

HENRY DAVID THOREAU, *WALDEN*

The Culture of Poverty

Location is only one way in which the lifestyles of the poor can vary. Poor people's degree of independence, pride, dignity, and happiness, and their ability to meet their physical needs and provide meaning in their lives, can also differ. Most people in the United States find it difficult to think of poverty as a stable, persistent, ongoing condition (Lewis, 1998). The **culture of poverty** refers to the abject hopelessness, despair, apathy, and alienation in poverty subcultures. The concept, which has been used to describe minority subcultures, has application to poor elders who are hopeless and despairing about their situation. Some have trouble living life with dignity, hope, happiness, and meaning. This tends to be more the case in inner cities, where elders are fearful and alienated. Elders in

Income is essential for security in later life, but it is only part of the story. This couple's choices and opportunities are reflected by the depth of appreciation they share with one another as they pose in front of their motor home.

rural areas seem to be more content with their lifestyle.

Relative Deprivation

According to the theory of **relative deprivation,** a person is deprived if his or her resources come up short in comparison with another's. This theory, which has been applied to financial adequacy, holds that the older person who compares his or her income with the income of another and feels relatively deprived is not satisfied with that income regardless of its actual amount. Applied in another way, the older person who looks back on past income and considers the former a better income than the present one may also feel relatively deprived and therefore dissatisfied.

One study hypothesized that not only real income, but also the older person's subjective interpretation of that income, affects financial satisfaction. The theory ties in with the symbolic interactionist definition of a situation: If people perceive a situation as real, its consequences become real. An older person can experience relative deprivation both in terms of comparison of oneself with others and in terms of comparison between one's present and past financial circumstances. Objective income influences financial satisfaction only indirectly: feelings of relative deprivation directly affect subjective financial well-being. Subjective feelings allow some to be satisfied with low incomes and others to be dissatisfied with high incomes. At least one study has substantiated this theory of relative deprivation as applied to the financial well-being of elders (Liang et al., 1980).

A Piece of the Good Life

In reflecting on what old people deserve in later life, we must conclude that they deserve a fair share of the "good life"—respect, dignity, comfort, and resources for experiencing new or continuing pleasures. Actually, a select number of aged in our society's upper echelons are doing quite well, having amassed great assets over their lifetimes. But they account for only 5 to 6 percent of the population age 65 and over. Many elders, especially those at the very bottom of the economic ladder, struggle to enjoy—or to simply get—their piece of the American pie.

One obstacle to attaining this good life is that older people typically have less income in retirement than when they were working. A rationale for this is that the older person is not doing anything; therefore, little money is necessary. However, this rationale is based on a negative image of nonactivity, which often becomes self-fulfilling. Actually, the retired person with plenty of leisure time needs an adequate sum of money to enjoy it. During our working years, we spend eight hours per day on the job; we spend more time traveling to and from work; and we spend still more time resting up from work. After the working years, one may justifiably need more money for pursuing leisure activities, such as travel, school, and hobbies. Elders without money most commonly fit the negative stereotypes of aging.

Businesses in cities and towns recognize the modest means of many older persons and offer discounts of all kinds. Local programs provide seniors with token assistance such as free banking services and discounts in theaters, restaurants, and transportation. In the Richmond, Virginia, area, for example, local merchants initiated a **senior discount program** in which elders who wanted to participate were issued photo identification cards. After nine months, more than 600 merchants and 19,000 older persons were participating. The AARP has a national discount directory, and some cities have a "Silver Pages" section of the Yellow Pages that lists special services and shops that cater to the "senior citizen."

Under senior discount programs, elderly individuals receive discounts from 10 to 15 percent on drugs, groceries, baked goods, taxi fares, haircuts and hairstyling, TV and radio repairs, auto tires, shoe repairs, restaurant meals, banking services, movie and theater tickets, miniature golf, cassettes and compact discs, jewelry, hearing aids, dry cleaning, electrical work, furniture and appliances, hardware, flowers, books, clothing, auto repairs and supplies, art supplies, services at health spas, and pest extermination. Merchants offer a variety of explanations for their voluntary participation in such programs; often they join because they believe such programs will promote their goods and services. In short, programs such as these indicate an awareness of the need to ease the financial burden on older persons. Although Maggie Kuhn, founder of the Gray Panthers, described contemporary programs for the elderly as "novocaine treatment" that dulls the pain without really changing anything, some are more optimistic. They feel that discount programs are a step in the right direction and are greatly appreciated by older people.

We might easily wonder why our society seems so unwilling to allow its members a comfortable passage through middle and old age. In *Critical Perspectives on Aging* (1991), Vicente Navarro, professor of health policy at Johns Hopkins University, asks, "Why is there no debate about the morality of an economic system that does not provide security, joy, and relaxation for those citizens who have built the country through their sweat and toil?" Navarro believes that most Western populations would like to see their countries' resources distributed according to need and that the unrestrained capitalism of the United States is failing in this area. He asks, "How can the United States proclaim that it is the society of human rights when basic rights such as access to health care are still denied?"

Those with a critical perspective (see chapter 1) call for a restructuring of our society to meet the needs of the whole population, not just a select few.

Chapter Summary

The poverty rate for persons age 65 and older declined precipitously from 1970 to 1996, in no small part due to the benefits of Social Security. Women, ethnic minorities, those who live alone, and the oldest old make up 90 percent of the elderly poor. Most old people are not desperately poor, but they are struggling in the lower to middle income ranges. If the benefits of Social Security were removed from their income, many more of America's elderly would move into poverty.

Under Social Security, people under age 65 and between the ages of 65 and 69 are penalized for working, although after age 70 there is no penalty on wages earned. An income tax levied on higher-income Social Security beneficiaries resulted in about 20 percent of people on Social Security paying taxes on their benefits. Supplemental Security Income provides a minimum income for elders, the blind, and the disabled by supplementing Social Security benefits if they are below the amount stipulated by SSI. It is designed to assist the very poor.

Food, shelter, personal safety, health, and the opportunity to be socially interactive are minimum requirements for a good quality of life. It is the responsibility of society as a whole to provide for all of its citizens, including poor elders whose fortunes have changed and desperately poor elders who have never experienced comfort and security.

Key Terms

capitated
cost-of-living
   adjustment (COLA)
culture of poverty
dually entitled
economically
   vulnerable
entitlement

fee-for-service
health maintenance
   organization
SRO hotels
Medicaid
Medicare
Medicare medical
   savings account

Medigap policy
near-poor
point of service
preferred provider
   organization
   (PPO)
private pension
privately contracted
   fee for service

provider-sponsored
   organization (PSO)
relative deprivation
reverse mortgages
senior discount
   program
Social Security
Supplemental Security
   Income (SSI)

Questions for Discussion

1. What is the general purpose of Social Security for older persons?
2. What are some loopholes in pension plans?
3. Why do older women have more financial problems than older men do?
4. Within the population of elders, compare the urban poor with rural poor.

Internet Activities

1. Locate Quotesmith (www.quotesmith.com) on the Internet to determine the range of Medigap policies in your state, and specifically in your region. If you were seeking Medigap insurance for your parent or grandparent, in what way would you use this resource? Find three other sources of information on Medigap insurance (hint: check out AARP, HCFA, and the insurance commissioner's office in your state).
2. You represent a 75-year-old man whose wife is in long-term care. They own their own home and have a savings account of approximately $120,000. Locate a site or sites with information on Medicare, Medical, Social Security, and/or other programs that would help you give your client some basic pointers for making economic plans.

Living Environments

10

New Jersey May Level Elderly Grandma's House

Associated Press

The city wants Anna DeFaria's home, and if she doesn't sell willingly, officials are going to take it from the 80-year-old retired pre-school teacher.

In place of her "tiny slip of a bungalow"—and two dozen other weathered, working-class beachfront homes—city officials want private developers to build upscale townhouses.

Is this the work of a cruel government? Or the best hope for resurrecting an ocean resort town that is finally showing signs of reviving after decades of hard times?

Echoes of the debate are happening across the country, after a U.S. Supreme Court decision brought new attention to governments' ability to seize property through the tool of eminent domain. Some 40 states are re-examining their laws—with action in Congress, too—after the court's unpopular ruling.

"We thought this was going to be our home forever," said DeFaria, sitting in a kitchen cozy with photos of children and grandchildren, quotes from the Bible and a game of Scrabble that she plays against herself. "Now they want to take it away. It's unfair, it's criminal, it's unconstitutional."

Not according to the Supreme Court. In a 5–4 ruling last June that was greeted with widespread criticism, the court found that New London, Connecticut, had the authority to take homes for a private development project.

The Constitution says governments cannot take private property for public use without "just compensation." Governments have traditionally used eminent domain to build public projects such as roads, reservoirs and parks. But for decades, the court has been expanding the definition of public use, allowing cities to employ eminent domain to eliminate blight.

The high court, in its ruling, also noted that states are free to ban that practice—and legislators around the country are thinking about whether they should do just that.

New Jersey state Senator Diane Allen, with bipartisan support, is pushing for a two-year ban on all eminent domain actions and for a bipartisan study group to re-examine its use in New Jersey.

"Right now government, I think, is using eminent domain to take people's private properties and hand it over to another owner," said Allen, a Republican. "It's really putting a hole in the American dream. Ownership of private property plays such a large role in that dream."

After the court ruling, four states passed laws reining in eminent domain. Roughly another 40 are considering legislation. In Congress, the House voted to deny federal funds to any project that used eminent domain to benefit a private development, and a federal study aims to examine how widely it is used.

The Washington-based Institute for Justice, a libertarian advocacy group that worked for homeowners in the New London case and in Long Branch, argues that state laws should be changed so property can only be seized for public uses like a park or a school—not urban redevelopment that benefits private developers.

Redevelopment usually depends on defining an area as "blighted" or a "slum," though definitions are vague, said Bert Gall, an attorney with the institute. Criteria can include a building's age, lack of compliance with building codes, even the size of a yard.

Abuses are widespread, Gall said, claiming that over a five-year period ending in 2002, more than 10,000 properties were threatened by eminent domain.

Municipal leaders across the country are pushing back, arguing that it's false to claim eminent domain is widely abused and warning that an emotional backlash to the court ruling is putting at risk an important tool that has helped turn around neighborhoods including Baltimore's Inner Harbor and New York's Times Square.

Elected officials have difficult decisions to make, and often must balance a community's needs with a few individuals, said Don Borut, executive director of the National League of Cities.

The plight of homeowners is hard to ignore, he said. "But at the same time . . . there are hundreds if not a couple of thousand faces of people you don't see, of people of all levels of income who as a result of the economic development will get jobs," he added. In Long Branch, there's no doubt the city needed to do something—a comeback wasn't happening on its own, Mayor Adam Schneider said.

"Most people wouldn't walk down those streets anymore. The worst neighborhood in our city was along our oceanfront. And that's been reversed," he said. Since the redevelopment effort began in earnest in 2002 after a decade of planning, new shops and homeowners have moved in, and new sidewalks have been installed—along with a new boardwalk, parks, and an ice-skating rink, he said.

"What you do is you've improved your city, you've gotten rid of decrepit housing, you've created jobs," Schneider said. "It's easy to play it out as the city is cruel and government is stealing your property. I'm used to it. . . . But this has reversed the decline that's been going on in Long Branch for more than 50 years."

Already, people are coming to new shops along the central waterfront, where the old pier burned down back in 1987. Rows and rows of new, sand-colored condominiums shadow DeFaria's one-story home when the afternoon sun sinks low.

DeFaria said she was offered $325,000 for the home she and her late husband bought in 1960 for $6,400. Where could anyone buy a waterfront view on the Jersey coast for that amount of money now?

But it's not the money, she said: $1 million wouldn't convince her. "They're taking my home away—not my house. My home. My life."

Think of the one place where you can be yourself, keep the things that mean the most to you, live in the way you prefer, and shut the world out when you feel like it. There are lots of names for it, but they all mean the same thing—home. In this chapter, we will discuss the issue of housing, which to some may mean a home and to others may mean only a shelter. Psychologically, there is a big difference between *housing* and *home.*

One of the most important challenges facing the nation in this century is that of providing safe, adaptable, quality, affordable housing for the growing elderly population. Quality-of-life concerns are never simple, and the issue of "adequate" housing options for America's elders is an example. The expanding population of elders is quite diverse: the housing needs of a 65-year-old newly retired person is likely to be quite different than the housing needs of an 85-year-old person. Between now and the year 2050, the population of people over 85 is expected to quadruple, from 5 million to 20 million. Shifts this dramatic in the age distribution of a population require that a responsible society work to understand the social implications of that shift and prepare for the well-being of its citizens. Housing is one area that profoundly affects the quality of life of an individual, and among special-needs populations, it requires study and policy-level response. This chapter will consider issues of income and affordability; competence and opportunity; the need for adaptability (of houses, of people, and of social policy); the emotional power of the meaning of home; and options, both current and future, for housing for older people.

Living Environments

Housing—where a person lives—is a primary key to that person's quality of life. Housing is comfort, safety, community, memory, and connection to family and the larger community. This is especially so for older people living on fixed incomes and those who are becoming frail. The diversity of the aged population underscores the need for many housing options.

The environment plays a very important role in the well-being and adjustment of the older person, because with age the ability to control certain environmental factors becomes more difficult. For example, 80-year-old Marge McDonald has lived in her home for 41 years. She and her husband, now deceased, bought the home and raised their three children in it—its walls hold many memories. It is a lovely, two-story home on a tree-lined street in a tidy neighborhood in middle America. Mrs. McDonald now confines herself to the downstairs portion of the house because she can no longer manage the stairs to the second floor. To make a bedroom, her sons helped her wall off the dining room. They also added a shower.

Compared with other industrialized nations, the United States has been slow to acknowledge the housing needs of its older citizens and to offer the needed options. The housing market for older people is continually changing as the older population ages and grows. Elders need appropriate housing that offers safety and comfort in a convenient, desirable location and at a cost within their budgets. Gerontologists are becoming increasingly concerned with the effect of the **living environment** on older people—not only in terms of the house structure, but in terms of the environmental context as well. The features of a residential area and its surrounding community help to determine whether an older person is going to be happy. Because older people are typically in their homes many more hours per day than younger people are, their living environments must make a positive, meaningful contribution to their lives.

Diversity in Living Arrangements

The kinds of problems elders face in housing depend to an extent on the location and type of housing they have and on their personal circumstances, such as their health and marital status. The majority (67 percent) of older non-institutionalized people lived in a family setting, according to the Department of Health and Human Services data (U.S. Dept. of Health and Human Services, 1997). About 81 percent of older men and 57 percent of older women live in families—usually with a spouse (Figure 10.1). The number of people living in a family setting, of course, decreases as widowhood increases. Single people tend to choose to live independently until there is a specific reason not to do so, which generally occurs when they become more physically frail with age. In fact, the elderly, whether single or married, are the least

Living arrangements of persons 65 and over

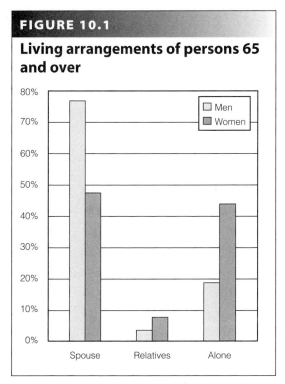

likely to change residence than other age groups: in 1994, only 6 percent of people 65 years old and older had moved since 1993, compared to 18 percent of people under 65 (Administration on Aging, 1997). Living alone or in a large home is difficult and can be unsafe if, for example, an individual is visually impaired or unable to reliably negotiate steps.

In the home are objectified both self-identity and social identity. Patterns of living, social norms and values, together with personality and biographical experiences, are hardly more clearly expressed anywhere else than in the home.

EKSTROM, 1994

About 7 percent of older people (6 percent of men and 8 percent of women) in 1995 were living not with a spouse but with children, siblings, or other relatives. An additional 2 percent of men and 2 percent of women, or 567,000 older people, lived with non-relatives in 1995. About 30 percent (9.9 million people) of non-institutionalized older people lived alone in 1995—that represents 7.6 million women and 2.3 million men, or 42 percent of older women and 17 percent of older men. Reversing a previous trend, from 1990 to 1995 the number of older persons living alone increased less rapidly (7 percent) than did the older population (9 percent) for that time period (Administration on Aging, 1997).

The trend in the 1980s showed a modest increase in the rate of home ownership for elders, whereas it showed a decrease in home ownership rates for young adults, minorities, and other first-time buyers. Rates of home ownership for elders in the 1990s stabilized or, according to some reports, declined slightly. In 1995, 78 percent of elders owned their own homes. For elders, these statistics reflect both their better health (enabling them to live in their own homes longer) and their better financial situation (enabling them to afford homes of their own). The percentage of income spent on housing by those older home owners, including maintenance and repair, was higher for older people (34 percent) than for the younger consumer population (27 percent) in 1995 (Administration on Aging, 1997).

The older population is scattered throughout the United States, although some areas and states have disproportionately high numbers. In 1996, just over half (52 percent) of people over 65 years of age lived in nine states: California (over 3 million); Florida and New York (over 2 million each); and Texas, Pennsylvania, Ohio, Illinois, Michigan, and New Jersey (over 1 million each) (Administration on Aging, 1997). The 65-plus population increased by 14 percent or more in 11 states between 1990 and 1996: Nevada (45 percent); Alaska (42 percent); Hawaii and Arizona (23 percent each); Utah, Colorado, and New Mexico (17 percent each);

Wyoming, Delaware, and North Carolina (15 percent each); and Texas (14 percent) (Administration on Aging, 1997). Inner-city areas with high percentages of elders typically house those who have "aged in place." In such areas the people have aged along with their houses.

Older people tend to reside in ordinary houses in ordinary neighborhoods, rather than in institutions or in age-segregated housing. Thus, the housing needs of elders are obscured because many are dispersed and invisible as a distinct group. Those who live alone tend to have fewer financial resources than married couples, and their housing tends to be of poorer quality. Single men have the poorest housing, in spite of having higher incomes than single women, who, after fulfilling roles as homemakers, often seem to have more of an emotional investment in their housing.

America's Older Homeless

Some elders have no home at all. Homelessness was addressed in chapter 7 in more detail, but this chapter on housing addresses the problem once again.

Although the *proportion* of men who are homeless is declining because of the increased number of women and children in this situation, the *number* of homeless men is increasing. It is estimated that over 3 percent (5.7 million) people in the United States were homeless between 1985 and 1990.

The population of homeless Americans has an "unacceptably high risk for preventable disease, progressive morbidity, and premature death" (Plumb, 1997). A study of 55 chronically homeless older men in Seattle found them to have serious health-care needs, to be subject to violence and crime, and to be facing loneliness and frail health brought about by a history of poor nutrition or overconsumption of street drugs and alcohol and/or by the general fragility of inefficient networks of social and emotional support (Goering et al., 1997).

Public homeless shelters provide the homeless a temporary sanctuary, but the rigid routines and the loss of self-esteem they suffer in such places are not conducive to their staying. Many homeless people have a lifelong pattern of being asocial "loners," with limited social skills and frail mental health. Older homeless women, increasing in number and proportion, like the men, often suffer from histories of asocial behavior and/or mental health problems (Daniels, 1997). Outreach agencies such as Project Rescue in New York and the Hostel Outreach Program in Ontario have been successful in providing respite and health care to the homeless. But little funding is available for such programs, and special-project funding is more often targeted at the severely mentally ill or to homeless families—groups that can be systematically categorized—than to the larger issue of homelessness and poverty (Buhrich & Teesson, 1996; Daniels, 1997).

We on the street have long recognized that Social Services operates under the policy of "don't make it too easy for them." . . . A county caseworker told me that before she could process my application I must bring in receipts from all the people I'd panhandled from so she could total my monthly income. But my personal all-time favorite is "provide proof of no income."

"KIM," HOMELESS VOICES PAGE, 1997

Across the United States, cities are now preparing for the consequences of the 1996 welfare "reform" bill called the Personal Responsibility and Work Opportunity Reconciliation Act. This act was designed to force people to work, its underlying assumption being that poverty and homelessness is an individual responsibility that can be addressed by the homeless person's getting a job. Some policy analysts fear that this legislation will radically increase the number of homeless persons in the next 10 years, placing even greater strain on existing health, food, and shelter programs (Golberg et al., 1997; Hwang et al., 1997). Additionally, the welfare reform bill of 1996 was accompanied by cuts in social programs that have left holes in the safety nets available for people living on the streets—both the chronically homeless and the "temporary" homeless (Plumb, 1997). The number of homeless elders is projected to double in the next 30 years, along with an overall increase in homelessness in the United States (Cohen, 1999). Just what the status of the elderly homeless and near-homeless will become, given their greater reduced opportunities for employment, is largely dependent on the attention given the issue by the American people and the government.

In old age, a home of one's own fosters the maintenance of personhood and integrity. A home not only provides shelter, but also is a symbol of permanence and identity. The loss of home is devastating to one's being. Along with the loss of self is often the loss of friends and neighbors, of support, and of a platform from which to reach out and restructure one's life. When bodies age, the desire to remain settled and safe is strong. Homeless elders symbolize the tragic nature of a competitive society where the less fit are ignored and neglected. Lack of a place to call home in one's old age is tragically incomprehensible.

Dissatisfaction with Housing

Compared to the homeless, those who have a place to live are doing well and counting their blessings. Yet older people can be dissatisfied with their housing situations for a number of reasons.

Personal Changes

It is generally not until people are in the oldest-old age grouping (85+) that the more profound effects of aging begin to affect the ways in which they can live comfortably in their homes. However, for a significant minority of elders, acute or chronic health conditions will necessitate a change in their housing (Frolik, 1996). Among those people, a decline in strength and vigor makes it inappropriate to remain in their current living situation.

Changes in one's life may lead to a housing situation that does not match one's needs. First, as the older persons' needs change, a house may become too large. A large proportion of older individuals are widows or widowers living alone. When a house that once was the appropriate size for a family is unnecessarily large and empty, a smaller house or an apartment may be more suitable.

Those with physical disabilities may not want to put their energies into keeping up a big house. Limited mobility and agility make it hard for older people to climb stairs, stand on stepladders, use bathtubs, and reach high cupboards. The person who loses a driver's license due to failing health or as a result of forgoing car ownership may be unhappy if the home is also isolated from friends and stores.

Financial Changes and Increasing Maintenance

Shrinking personal finances can lead to difficulties in paying required housing costs. The older person who retires may receive only half the income he or she received when working. For home owners, property taxes and insurance premiums take ever-increasing chunks out of fixed income; sizable rent increases may force them to move to less adequate dwellings. There is a tremendous disparity among renters and home owners, however; almost 70 percent of elderly renters pay 25 percent or more of their income for shelter, whereas only 30 percent of older home owners spend that same proportion of income (Gilderbloom & Mullins, 1995). The housing costs of taxes, insurance, and repair will increase, but property resale, over which the elder has no control, will not result in higher monthly payments for the home owner.

The home ages with the person. Older people may have lived in their homes 20, 30, 40, or more years. The older house requires more maintenance, and hiring others to perform the work is often costly. Leaking roofs must be repaired, appliances made usable, lawns mowed, and windows washed.

The amount of money spent annually on the upkeep of a home is less for home owners age

One person's castle is another's prison. Housing is appropriate for an elder if the person wants to be there, and if it is physically and psychologically safe.

65 and older than it is for younger home owners. The average home maintenance cost for people 60 and younger is about $466 annually; that cost drops to about $145 for home owners 75 and older (Kausler & Kausler, 1996). Housing that requires little upkeep is ideal, but the risk becomes that older people not do necessary home maintenance. An estimated 10 to 15 percent of elders live in dwellings that are substandard, with rural areas having the highest rates of substandard housing.

Urban Blight

The calm, quiet residential neighborhood in which inner-city residents choose to grow old often becomes a run-down area of high crime. Elders may be afraid to go out at night or afraid in their own homes. What was once an attractive residential area can deteriorate or become a "concrete jungle" of commercial buildings or factories, with extensive air and noise pollution. Drug trafficking, burglary, theft, muggings, and assault as well as rape occur with greater frequency in these areas. Victimization and fear of crime are reported as fears of older people, and it is a common stereotype that elders are more frequent victims of crime than are younger adults. The Bureau of Justice Statistics (2000), however, consistently shows that people over 65 have the lowest rates of victimization of any age group over 12. Compared to people 16 to 19 years of age, those over the age of 65 are 30 times less likely to be victims of an assault, 23 times less likely to experience a robbery, and 3 times less likely to be attacked by a purse snatcher or pickpocket (Hooyman & Kiyak, 2002).

Desire to Pursue Leisure

Old people who have no financial or health problems may wish to relocate closer to recreational amenities. Some want milder climates; others want to live among those in their own age group. Those who choose to migrate, who must go through the difficult decision of whether or not to uproot, often select a retirement community or center. Many such places exist, especially in Florida, Arizona, and southern California, where the climate is mild; but there are others scattered across the United States.

Problems in Relocating

According to an AARP study quoted by Braus (1994), the most common reasons older people gave for relocating are:

- Wanting to be closer to family, 15 percent
- Wanting a change, 10 percent
- Inability to afford current housing, 9 percent
- Buying better housing, 8 percent
- Retirement, 7 percent

Not included in this list, but a very important factor in the decision to relocate, is the physical inability to continue to live in the present environment. Whatever the reasons for deciding to relocate, there are a number of issues associated with making the move. Four of those issues are discussed here.

Shortage of Appropriate Housing

The availability of suitable housing for elders is, in some communities, woefully inadequate. A shortage exists in both low-cost housing and in housing that meets the special needs of the oldest old.

One of the biggest shortages is in low-cost housing. Demand far exceeds supply in all areas of the United States. Those with low incomes—for example, those who must live entirely on Social Security or Supplemental Security Income—often live in substandard housing. Government housing programs for elders lost their funding in the 1980s due to budget cuts. The National Affordable Housing Act of 1990 has some provisions to help older home owners. A home equity provision allows use of home equity to make home repairs (Redfoot & Gaberlavage, 1991). The equity provision is available to all home owners, regardless of income. Budget constraints at the federal, state, and local levels, however, offer little hope that other funds for housing will be forthcoming. In 1997, the status of Section 8 housing was considered fair game in the battle for budget balancing, as lawmakers struggled with the ideological issues of the degree to which government was responsible for providing its citizens with safe housing. Section 8 housing is rental assistance to specific properties, many of which are "project based," and provides assistance to more than 20,000 properties containing an estimated 3 million units across the United States (Wells, 1997). One suggested model is that project-based subsidies be replaced with tenant-based assistance—that is, the federal assistance is provided to the individual, who then locates his or her own housing, rather than subsidizing builders and housing project management. The weakness in this argument is that the private sector will have no incentive to build inexpensive housing. Sister Lillian Murphy is president of the nonprofit Mercy Housing, which operates about 3,000 units for low-income elders and families in eight states. She fears that housing for the poor will virtually disappear if there are no incentives for the for-profit industry. "The market has never served the poor, [and] it never will," she said. "If [for-profit companies] are not getting the subsidies, they will walk away" (Wells, 1997). To allow elders to remain in their original homes, some states provide property tax relief by not taxing property after the owner is a given age. When the older person dies, the tax bill is deducted from the estate. A second option, discussed at greater length in a previous chapter, is the Home Equity Conversion Mortgage Insurance program, or reverse mortgage plan ("New FHA Program," 1988). Both tax savings and reverse mortgages, however, they require that the individual own his or her own home.

Ideally, the physical structure of a house for the older person would include:

- Wide hallways and doors to allow wheelchairs to move freely
- Protective railings and dull-surfaced floors to reduce the probability of falls
- Low-hung cabinets for easy access
- Increased brightness in lighting fixtures to accommodate reduced visual acuity
- Acoustical devices to increase the volume of doorbells and telephones

The very old have little physical tolerance for extreme temperatures, so the thermal environment must be carefully regulated. The house should have no change of levels, not even a step down into a living room. Walk-in, sit-down showers rather than bathtubs are a must. Nearly as important as the services available to and the facilities of the living environment is the **surveillance zone**—the visual field outside the home that one can view from the windows or glass doors inside. A surveillance zone provides an important source of identity and participation in one's environment. The concept has implications for location, design, and landscaping.

Housing designed without consideration for the special needs of the elderly is just as inadequate as housing that has been built on an unstable foundation or that lacks adequate plumbing.

Uprooting

Relocation is difficult whether it is voluntary or not, because it involves leaving close friends and associates as well as a familiar environment. It also poses the uncertainties of change. Older people, both home owners and renters, are far more likely to have lived in their current homes for over 30 years. Only 5 percent of elders move in a given year, compared with 32 percent of adults age 20 to 29 (U.S. Department of Housing and Urban Development [HUD], 1999). Like everyone else, older people have quite varied emotional experiences to forced moves, however making a move that one has not fully chosen—moving with regrets—can have a particularly powerful emotional impact on the elder.

Most studies on the emotional impact of voluntary and involuntary moves made by elderly people have focused on stress. Stress has to do with loss of control. It is the emotional experience of being unable to manage a situation or changes that occur, and of the struggle to reshape those changes to gain a sense of competence. A complex blend of emotions, or feelings, is present in the stress of changing one's home, most especially if that change is not fully voluntary. Issues having to do with security, attachment, belonging, estrangement, anxiety—all are connected to the emotional meaning of *home*.

Mats Ekstrom (1994) developed categories of emotional states that people in his study experienced when they were forced to move from the place they called home (see Table 10.1). Coping with stress requires a reinterpretation of the meaning of the stressful situation and the development of a plan of action designed to remedy the situation. The person must reinterpret feelings of mistrust, self-estrangement, guilt and sorrow, and—most centrally—of violation, or adjustment to the stress of the move will not happen. Ekstrom provides the poignant illustration of a man who was required to make an involuntary move:

For Mr. Peterson his home was intimately associated with who he was. In spite of the fact that his wife had been dead for several years, little had been touched. Her bed was in the same place as before, the furniture

TABLE 10.1

Emotions described by an elderly population being forcibly relocated

Emotional Experience of . . .	Definition
Stress	Feeling the lack of resources to cope with, and possibilities of escaping from, considerable problems, demands and/or threatening situations. Exposure to potentially stressful situations, and also the capacity to handle them, is dependent on social context, and dispositions and patterns of actions developed over time
Trust & security	Related to the degree of dependability, continuity, stability and anonymity of the social environment in which one lives
Belonging, self-estrangement, meaninglessness	Related to the capacity to set our imprint on the environment through creative, self-expressive action; realize our thoughts in various objects; realize our possibilities of living in a place, and in the presence of objects, to which, over time, we have established a deeper relation
Guilt, shame, pride, dignity	Indirectly, also joy and sorrow; created when we regard ourselves through other people's eyes and reflect on our actions in light of other people's values and expectations
Violation	Direct exercise of power, insult and infringement of social identity; vulnerability to such actions is socially determined

Source: Adapted from Ekstrom, Mats. (1994). Elderly people's experiences of housing renewal and forced relocation: Social theories and contextual analysis in explanations of emotional experiences. *Housing Studies,* 9 (3), 369–391.

arrangement had not been changed, the ornaments had not been moved, and in the kitchen and linen-cupboard things were ordered in the way that she had ordered them. In conjunction with the move he had to dismantle all this, and he never felt able to put it together again. Several months after the move what had been his home was still largely packed in boxes that stood all over the new flat. The furniture was scattered here and there, and only in the bedroom were there curtains and pictures on the wall. His relationship to his new flat was an alienated one, at the same time as he felt that his life had been encroached upon by the landlord, for which reason he felt deeply violated. Mr. Peterson finds it hard to hold back the tears as he speaks: "They took my home away from me. . . . I was forced to take apart the home we had, and I'll never be able to put it back the way it was. . . . I
live in a furniture depository and I'm never really happy." (Ekstrom, 1994, p. 388)

Mr. Peterson's story demonstrates the importance of the home environment—the relationship of things, of placement, and of space to memories. Home has deep emotional meanings for us all, and the management of those emotions might take more resources than any one individual—especially one who is experiencing the losses of the physical self—has to give it.

Migration

More than 60 percent of older people living in their own homes have lived there 20 years or longer (Redfoot & Gaberlavage, 1991). Living in an area for a long time fosters a feeling of neighborhood integration and security, and closeness to friends and family. Yet many older persons can and do move, some very happily.

Retirement communities have sprung up throughout the country, advertising their amenities for the "golden age lifestyle." It must be kept in mind that most older people do not move at all until it becomes absolutely necessary for them to do so because they are unable to thrive in their present housing. This is projected to be particularly true for the newest cohort of older people, born between 1925 and 1942 (Brecht, 1996). By the end of the 1990s, almost all the marketing efforts and retirement services had been directed to those born before 1924. The "new generation" of elders are those born between 1925 and 1942, and their needs and interests will be different from those of their predecessors (Clark et al., 1996).

Amenity relocation (moving to an age-homogeneous community for one's retirement pleasure) is a concept realized by an industry specializing in building living. Most housing built in the 1960s and 1970s offered no nursing care or assistance with daily living. The communities focused on hospitality services such as meals, housekeeping, transportation, and activities. They targeted the newly retired (Brecht, 1996). In the 1980s and 1990s the age of those moving into independent living units was typically the late 70s and early 80s, rather than the late 60s and early 70s (Newbold, 1996). That population requires a different approach to facility amenities than did the first wave of retiree-relocators.

Among those who do move, a first move typically occurs around retirement for the young old. In any five-year period, about 5 percent of the population over age 60 make a long-distance move. Long-distance moves are more popular among "60-something" couples who have both the financial resources and the desire to relocate during their early elder years. Some retirees have planned their move for years and have vacationed in the spot many times. Though the reasons for relocation vary, they typically involve the attractive leisure amenities retirement communities offer—whether it is arts and crafts, music, golfing, boating, fishing, tennis, or social activities. Elders from the Northeast and Midwest still migrate toward the Sunbelt of the West and South.

Migration may be either permanent or seasonal (Newbold, 1996). For several decades now, Sun City, Leisure World, and other large retirement communities of the Sunbelt states have offered housing and amenities at reasonable prices. Over half the popular retirement communities are in southern states, or in the southern parts of states: Florida, Texas, Arkansas, Arizona, and California. The northern and western states of Michigan, Wisconsin, Minnesota, Oregon, and Nevada also have clusters of retirement communities. Florida still has the largest percentage of elder residents of all states.

Some older persons are **snowbirds,** living in the North for several months during the summer and going south for the winter. The opposite, those who live in the South and move north in the summer, have been labeled **sunbirds.** Sunbirds have been understudied, yet the tendency for older Arizona residents to leave in the summer is comparable to the tendency of older Minnesotans to go south during the winter. Researchers find a trend toward snowbirds' eventually making a permanent migration to the South, then becoming sunbirds. Seasonally migrant elders are more likely than non-migrants to be married and retired; they also have slightly higher levels of education and backgrounds than non-migrant workers. Studies of Sun City and similar retirement communities show that the stereotype of the older person moving away from family and friends to a foreign and unfamiliar world is largely false. Retirees generally hear about such places from relatives and friends and visit the community before moving to it.

Some people do move, but not that many. The popular belief that Snowbelt seniors will flee to warmer climates if they can afford to obscures the reality that only 5 percent actually move away from their community. Most projects attract residents from within a six- to seven-mile radius (Olson, 1998).

The pressure for a second move occurs when older people develop chronic disabilities that make it difficult to carry out everyday tasks. The presence of a spouse is helpful and may act to postpone the move, which, when made, may place the disabled elder nearer to adult children who can offer assistance or to medical facilities. With urbanization and industrialization, many grown children have moved to cities for jobs. Older parents from rural areas, if they are to be near their children, must move to the city. An example is that of a middle-aged Iowa farmer who gave up farming after years of drought and moved to the city to secure a more financially stable livelihood for his family. In the process, he left his parents, both in their 70s, behind on the farm. With increasing age and/or declining health, these older parents will need to move closer to their displaced son and his family or make arrangements for local services (if any are available). Sometimes the second move is to some type of congregate or assisted housing where the older person can maintain a degree of independence.

The 1990 census repeated the 1980 census finding that a larger number of older persons live in the suburbs than in central cities. Declining health and the need for health care are often associated with migration to suburban areas. Given the closing of rural hospitals and the inadequacy or nonexistence of rural health-care systems, worry about well-being often acts as a strong stimulus for an unwanted move to the city. The young old who do not have to worry as much about health care tend to migrate to rural areas. The old old tend to come to the suburbs or city from rural areas for necessary social and medical services.

Integration versus Segregation

The issue of **age-integrated housing** versus **age-segregated housing** concerns whether one would rather live in age-segregated communities, and thereby threaten an elder's ties with the larger society, or be integrated into the larger society,

with greater opportunity for interaction among all age groups.

Age-concentrated retirement housing has strong support from middle- to high-income elders. Interviews with elders in three apartment buildings with low, medium, and high densities of older adults revealed that residents associated high-density senior citizen housing with larger numbers of friends, more active friendships, and slightly better morale (Hinrichsen, 1985). However, the hypothesis that age-concentrated housing is the best and most desirable situation has not been proved conclusively. A study, in contrast, revealed that living environments with high densities of elders had little effect on morale, either positive or negative.

Many elders live in age-concentrated housing because they like the accommodations and amenities. Others are simply in "old" neighborhoods: age concentration is high because everyone has lived there for many years. They do not, by choice, limit their interactions to other old persons. Researchers conclude that, in general, though age-concentrated housing is a desirable alternative for some, it should not serve as a guide for housing policy at large. Some sociologists are predicting more age integration in the years to come (Riley & Riley, 1994). If the young old stay in the job market longer and continue their activities of middle age, they will not gravitate toward age-segregated housing. Some social critics view age-segregated housing as a means of insulating older people from ageism in the larger society. Here again, if ageism decreases, one would predict a decline in age-segregated housing.

Housing Options

We can view types of housing as ranging on a continuous scale from independent to dependent. Living in one's own home is the most independent lifestyle, living in a hotel-type residence is semi-independent, and living in an institution is the most dependent lifestyle.

Generally speaking, the more dependent the new lifestyle, the more difficult the adjustment. Sometimes the problem in institutionalized group housing is not the quality of care provided, but the fact that the older person really does not want to be there. Many elders are dedicated to a lifestyle of self-reliance and self-direction and have little tolerance for the regulations of a nursing home. They would like better food and shelter, but not in exchange for the freedom to decide their life's course. A truly independent person might choose to live on a menu of eggs, beer, and ice cream in a cockroach-infested hotel rather than in a nursing home.

On the other hand, an isolated, frail, disabled elder might welcome the safe haven of institutionalized care. Acknowledging the diversity in age, personality, and health of those age 65 and older opens up more and more housing alternatives for older people. The needs and requirements of the young old in good health are vastly different from the frail elders in poor health. In this section, housing options for both the young old and the oldest old are considered.

Nearly every study affirms the conventional wisdom that older people strongly prefer to age in place, to grow old within familiar territory that has provided a context for their lives, whether they live in single family dwelling, elderly housing complexes, or naturally occurring retirement communities.

SYKES, 1990

Aging in Place

Most people do not move from their own homes until they must do so for reasons of safety. The image of retiring and moving to Golden Age Village is just that: an image. Some people do retire and move; indeed, in some states elderly migration is a growth industry. Retirees are viewed as the ultimate "clean industry" (Clark et al., 1996). Moving does not reflect the first choice of most new retirees these days, however. Most people go to great lengths to remain in their own homes—a home not associated with being old or frail, or with having special needs. That home is the home of memories and is often associated with the self-concept of mature and responsible adulthood. **Aging in place** has become a popular phrase reflecting the pattern of staying in one's home as long as possible despite increasing frailty and its associated problems (Hart & Reed, 1990).

American elders have moved less frequently each year since World War II (Golant, 1994). About 84 percent of people age 55 and older say they want to stay in their longtime homes rather than move to senior housing. When they are forced to move, 63 percent prefer to remain in the same city or county, and only 11 percent prefer to move to a different state. "Their dominant preference is to stay in their homes, and not move, never move—stay there forever," said Lea Dobkin, a housing specialist with AARP. "[For developers], it means use caution. It's a more competitive environment."

Many older people already live in a type of informal retirement community known in the senior housing industry as a **naturally occurring retirement community (NORC)**. These are buildings or neighborhoods where the residents have aged over the years. There are many cases in point, in the suburbs, in the rural Midwest, and in inner cities (Newbold, 1996). The neighborhood, like the individual, goes through a life cycle of young to middle-aged to old.

Aging in place is not always easy. As people age into their 80s and 90s and beyond, more and more tasks may pose difficulties, even for those in good health—writing checks, driving a car, shopping, or bathing. Public or private agencies must be available to provide services that elders themselves and their families and friends cannot provide. Home-nursing services and homemaker services, including cooking, housecleaning, bathing, and grooming assistance, laundry, and transportation, might be required. Also, social services may be needed

Aging in place has profound psychological meaning for some elders. It is sometimes difficult for families to balance their needs for the elder to be safe and cared for with the elder's needs to age in place/die in place.

© Alan Oddie/PhotoEdit

for emotional health and support. In more and more areas, volunteers are calling older people once a day to check on their health and safety. These calls are especially important for those living alone.

Downsizing

Downsizing, or the move to a smaller home, say a condominium or a mobile home, if it is in the same town or general area, is a form of aging in place. The reasons for such a move were discussed earlier in this chapter: The upkeep is easier, taxes are lower than for a large house, and the location may be more convenient.

Mobile homes, typically smaller than conventional homes, can provide a comfortable liv-

ing environment. Perhaps the most significant factor in opting for a mobile home is related to its affordability. Mobile homes provide older adults with a sense of home ownership, privacy, and security.

Life in a mobile home may not be without problems, however. Historically, the quality of mobile homes has been suspect. In the past, owners have had little success influencing manufacturers to correct deficiencies. There has been general agreement that, overall, the quality of mobile homes has improved in recent years. In a move to protect mobile-home buyers in some states, buyers are provided with a five-year warranty, building (manufacturing) standards have been raised, and "mandatory" funds have been designed to pay for repair costs not reimbursed by unscrupulous or bankrupt businesses. Funding for these standards is borne by the state.

An additional potential problem for the majority of older mobile-home residents is related to the fact that they must purchase space in a **mobile-home park,** where they have little control over actions made by park owners. For example, in Washington State, an owner of a lush mobile-home park is planning to close his park and redevelop it for more lucrative commercial use (Glasheen, 1994), in the process dislodging all the current tenants. Other problems include space rental increases, restrictive rules, and the lack of parity between the mobile-home owners and park owners (Glasheen, 1994).

Enough people live in their RVs (recreation vehicles) the year around for the term **full-timing** to have evolved. This is one more choice that older people have. Some fulfill a lifetime retirement dream when they hit the road in their RVs and see all the places in Canada, the United States, or Mexico that draw them. It is a lifestyle that has not gone unnoticed by sociologists and gerontologists.

Adult Day Care

Adult day care offers medical and social services at a center to elders who commute from home. Many service providers call their programs "frail-elder programs," to avoid evoking an image of a child-care center with a program for adults. Centers may be nonprofit organizations, government-run centers, or profit organizations run by insurance companies such as Elderplan, Kaiser, SCAN, and Seniors Plus. Multipurpose senior centers provide health-care facilities where older persons are brought in the morning and taken home in the afternoon. These might be day hospitals that offer medical or psychiatric treatment or day-care centers that provide social and recreational services. Studies show that persons who can avail themselves of adult day care reduce their risks of hospitalization.

Some nonprofit organizations provide multiple services to elders. Through the Older Americans Act, the federal government now funds a number of multipurpose senior centers. One such organization, the Minneapolis Age and Opportunity Center, largely government funded, provides services such as daily meal deliveries, laundry, and transportation. A Touch of Home in Rochester, New York, provides respite and socialization opportunities for the frail elderly and their caregivers. The program is an example of other small nonprofit agencies that provide "therapeutic recreation that emphasize opportunities for success in a structured, safe and fun environment" as well as transportation, sometimes a meal, personal care, and transportation (Tracy, 1996).

Frail-elder programs are especially critical for people who choose to continue living in their own homes, or who are living with a spouse or adult-child caregiver. The socialization and care provision offered by these programs can make the difference in whether or not an individual can continue to live independently. Rochester's Touch of Home grew from a small program in the basement of a church in 1990 to services at three locations in the region, providing services to more than 60 people by 1996. The need is undeniably there, however the funding to support programs and subsidize program costs for individuals and families is stretched very thinly between competing social services programs. Program managers for a Touch of Care concluded that the greatest hurdles facing adult day services are

funding streams and private market acceptance. As government funds diminish and decision-making is decentralized to local governments, identification of local community-based funding streams is critical. Partnerships with employers, other service providers and public elder service agencies, as well as education and awareness-raising of local government officials, will be critical to the survival of non-profit, community-based adult day care programs. (Touch of Home, Rochester, NY, 1998, p. 41)

Insurance programs are now being offered to assist the older person in staying at home. Such plans are becoming affordable and workable. A variation of the health maintenance organization (HMO) is the SHMO—social health maintenance organization. Elderplan in New York, Kaiser in Oregon, and Seniors Plus in Minnesota offer health insurance programs that provide personal care and household assistance services at home or in day-care settings.

A new variation of health insurance policies offers LCH (Life Care at Home). Insurance agencies are tailoring LCH insurance policies that cover medical and personal costs for the older person who wishes to stay at home. One must proceed with caution in purchasing a LCH plan because the LCH involves a large initial entry fee, a monthly fee, and at least a one-year contract. Such private long-term-care insurance policies are expensive and may have restrictions that limit coverage.

The On Lok Health Center in San Francisco, patterned after the day-care system in England, provides day-care services to elders in Chinatown. A van with a hydraulic lift transports the elderly to the center, where each day begins with exercise and reality orientation. People are introduced to each other in both English and Chinese. On Lok assumes responsibility for providing all services needed by the functionally dependent. If not for On Lok, the participants would need institutional care. Though the cost per person for this service is about the same as that for institutional care, the psychological benefits and the social facilitation make the service well worth the price.

Granny Units and Shared Housing

A housing concept currently being proposed and enacted on a limited basis in the United States is actually an old concept to the Japanese and Australians: the **granny unit,** also called the granny flat or elder cottage. A granny unit, by U.S. definition, is a small living unit, built on the lot of a single-family home, where adult children can care for aging parents. Older people can also install granny units in their backyards. They can rent their home or their granny unit for income or trade for services such as nursing or homemaking.

Advocates of the granny-unit concept, such as the American Association of Retired Persons (AARP), must fight zoning laws in some towns and cities. Areas zoned for single-family homes may not welcome added granny units. The desirable features of granny units are that they allow the older person a choice of living independently. If the older person can live in a granny unit rather than in the adult child's house, there is more privacy and freedom for everyone. The "granny flats" experience in Great Britain suggests that "they have an important but limited role" in enabling people to live close to their families (Tinker, 1991). But despite cost and regulations, this housing alternative is gaining support in more countries worldwide. Canada has already endorsed the granny-unit concept (Lazarovich, 1991).

Shared housing that involves some type of group living is another concept being developed by and for elders. In Great Britain, there are over 700 Abbyfield homes—homes in the community that house several elders and are run by specialists in aging. This kind of program is being developed in the United States. Another alternative is renting a room of one's house to another person and sharing such rooms as the kitchen and living room. Such an arrangement is usually predicated by the need for financial relief, services, and companionship. Many variations are possible. An older person could rent a room of the house in return for income or services.

The difficult part is to find a good tenant—home owner match. More and more community agencies, such as Share-a-Home in Memphis, Tennessee, and Independent Living in Madison, Wisconsin, are helping to coordinate shared housing. One study, unfortunately, showed that matching is problematic. A majority of the matches dissolved in the first three months.

Adult Communities

Many towns and cities have adult communities for those over age 50. Typically, children under 18 are prohibited from living in these places; court cases have upheld the legality of the age limit. Adult mobile-home parks with age limits on younger persons are also quite popular. An **adult community** may have a grocery store, bank, medical clinic, and convenience stores within its boundaries. The sizes of adult communities within cities vary. A recent trend is for older folk with interests in common (for example, artists or gay retirees), to form their own communities.

Retirement Cities

Some older people like age-segregated **retirement cities,** because such communities offer so much. Sun City, Arizona, after which many other retirement towns have been patterned, has a population of over 46,000 and a minimum age of 50 (others, such as Youngstown, Arizona, have set the lower limit at age 60). Located 20 miles northwest of Phoenix, Sun City is a large complex on 8,900 acres with a number of social and leisure activities, such as tennis, bridge, quilting, wood carving, and language classes. The lure is the affordability and the weather. Prices for homes in 1991 started at $65,000 in Sun City West, a development started in 1978 when all of the original Sun City units had been built and sold. Residents tend to be upbeat about cities made up of all senior citizens. They get involved more easily because of the many activities shared by persons in their own age group.

Several million older people have bought or leased property in the retirement cities that have mushroomed around the country since 1950. One of the most successful retirement community developments has been Leisure World, with locations in several sections of the country. Most retirement villages have swimming pools, clubhouses for dancing or crafts, symphony orchestras, golf courses, and free bus rides to shopping centers and entertainment. One community excludes dogs and puts a three-week limit on visits by children. Such features make age-segregated housing more desirable to some older persons.

Assisted Living

Assisted living (or assisted housing), an alternative to skilled nursing facility (nursing home) residence, typically refers to community-based residential housing of some type (apartment, condominium, or semicommunal living), including supportive services to assist in the activities of daily living. It is designed to serve the needs of the frailer person who wants to live in a homelike setting but requires some assistance to do so. This level of care is a fairly new concept. Elders requiring assistance with their daily living tasks formerly had only the options of hiring home assistants or moving to skilled nursing facilities, in which, by law, "all needs" are to be provided for. The assisted living philosophy is one of individualizing and maximizing the elder's independence, privacy, and options. It is a clearly hands-off approach: people will be provided whatever assistance they need to maximize their independence. This is in stark contrast with the philosophy of skilled nursing care, which is to be hands on, providing people assistance with all their needs. Assisted living services generally include meals and the option of eating either in a dining room or in one's room, housekeeping, transportation, and help with everyday tasks such as bathing and grooming.

Growth in assisted living has come about because investors can see the emerging market and the potential for profit. It is, in fact, currently the hottest senior housing market. In 1996 construction for assisted living accounted for 54 percent of all senior housing built in the United States (Murer, 1997). Assisted living development is estimated to reach $33 billion in revenues by the turn of the century, with nearly 4.1 million beds (Olson, 1998).

In the mid-1980s hospitality corporations such as Marriott and Hyatt made substantial investments in long-term care, which had previously been seen as a health care or hospital arena. This somewhat legitimized the industry for other investors. In a recent analysis of assisted living facility development, Olson (1998) reported that "in the past 24 months there has been a tremendous increase in the money available to develop senior housing. . . . A large part of this capital comes from Real Estate Investment Trusts (REITs) seeking to diversify their portfolios" (xi). Wall Street and bonds also provide development funds, but the majority of financing comes from conventional sources such as banks (Olson, 1998). Financing provides the structures; the cost of the services is paid, separately from rent, by the resident. Not surprisingly, most of the facilities generating the greatest amount of excitement are designed for upper- and upper-middle-income elders.

Funding is also available for housing for the truly low-income elderly—those with annual incomes of about $15,000 or less. Section 42 of the Internal Revenue Tax Code provides for a low-income housing tax credit to corporations investing in low-income elder housing. Some communities use Community Development Block Grants to build low-income housing; still others look to other federal programs such as the HOME Program, established under the National Affordable Housing Act of 1990 (Nolan, 1997).

Problems arise in the options for building low-income assisted living housing for elders because of the need for assistance. Services must be funded separately, because for low-income elders those costs cannot be passed on to the resident. Some developers have used a new Medicaid home- and community-based waiver that allows for the financing of health care services in an assisted living setting (Nolan, 1997). Other areas simply compete with local service providers for the limited funding available to provide living assistance to the poor.

In its current state of development, assisted living is a Cadillac: nice to have but affordable to a relative few. Unlike a Cadillac, though, assisted living is more than "nice to have"; it is becoming a necessity for many elderly Americans who are, nevertheless, unable to afford it. Aging but still living independently, in need of support services but a long way from needing skilled care, they are natural customers for assisted living. Is gaining access to it beyond hope for them?

NOLAN, 1997

A **board and care home** is similar to an old "mom and pop" operation in a large family home, where unoccupied bedrooms become available to boarders. Relatively little attention has been paid to board and care facilities, which are variously referred to as residential care facilities, adult congregate living, rest homes, adult foster care, personal care, care facilities, and group homes (Garrard et al., 1997). Usually, the board and care facility offers a bedroom in a private home, whereas an assisted living facility offers self-contained housing units. Operators of board and care homes are typically middle-aged women who live in the homes with their spouses, many of the operators have worked previously as nurses or aides in health care settings (Kalymun, 1992).

Sunrise Retirement Homes and Communities is the country's largest operator of assisted living centers, operating more than 30 such communities (Estrada, 1994). When a husband-and-wife team started their first Sunrise Center by renovating a nursing home, the term assisted living did not exist. Now more than 2,000 elders live in their centers. One example of their efforts is the Sunrise Retirement Home near Washington, D.C., a three-story "Victorian mansion" with 42 one- and two-room units. The building has the feeling of a country inn, with a fireplace, large bay windows, and a sun room filled with wicker furniture. Residents' rooms are grouped around common living rooms and lounges. Units rent for $2,000 to $3,000 a month, which includes housekeeping, meal services, and minor medical care.

Marie Morgan, 73 years old, was withdrawing and deteriorating in a nursing home when she opted for assisted living and moved to Rackleff House in Canby, Oregon (McCarthy, 1992). Despite incontinence and a heart condition, she is thriving in her assisted living quarters. She gets out and about using her walker to circle the grounds, does her own laundry, and is able to keep her dog, a Lhasa Apso, in her private apartment. For about $2,200 a month she also gets housekeeping, meals, laundry facilities, transportation, social activities, and regular visits from nurses.

Some residents in Rackleff House have mild to moderate Alzheimer's disease, like the person who loiters by the copy machine in the office. She was a bookkeeper most of her life and finds the office bustle comforting. The staff understands and works around her. In Oregon assisted living centers have become so widespread that nursing home population has been reduced by 4 percent even though the over-65 population rose by 18 percent. There are more than 20 assisted living units in Oregon.

Rackleff House, which opened in 1990, was created by a Portland State University professor motivated by her mother's needs, not by profit. Renting a room in Rackleff House is affordable to lower-middle-income elders. The average age is 89, and half are on Medicaid. They can furnish their rooms with their own things. Rackleff looks like a big yellow farmhouse. It is not lavish, yet it has a cathedral ceiling in the dining room and a secure enclosed courtyard. A fireplace flickers in the front parlor. Traditional nursing homes have a staff-to-patient ratio of about 10 to 1: Rackleff's is one worker per three residents.

Continuing Care Retirement Communities (CCRCs)

The **continuing care retirement community** (CCRC) represents an upscale form of congregate housing that requires a strong commitment on the part of the resident. A CCRC, also known as a **life-care community (LCC)**, requires a large entry fee ($50,000 to $500,000), monthly fees of $500 to $2,000 (depending on the area of the country, quality of housing, and number of services available), and commitment to at least a yearlong contract. In return, the entrant is provided with housing, health care, social activities, and meals. Few CCRCs are currently being built because they are large (typically with a budget of $50 to $70 million per project) and the financing is complex (Olson, 1998).

Housing options will be developed if a market is perceived to be there. For example, some universities are now investigating CCRCs for alumni and faculty. According to a plan developed for Davidson College in South Carolina, residents will be able to audit classes, use campus libraries and sports facilities, and become involved in other ways with the university campus life (Olson, 1998). Part of the exchange, aside from providing a profitable and valuable service, will be that the increased investment in the university's well-being by the CCRC residents' involvement will result in an increase of bequests to the university.

The entire life-care industry has grown dramatically in the last few years. Dozens of big-name developers and corporations have built or plan to build CCRCs and other assisted living senior residences. The options are marketed in very sophisticated ways, and there is a growing concern for the need to protect older consumers.

Legislation has been passed in many states to protect the older consumer. Contracts and rental agreements are regulated, and most states have certification and registry requirements. California and Florida, for example, require extensive disclosure statements prior to certifying facilities; Indiana and Colorado require that the potential resident receive copies of such disclosure statements. Those considering life-care communities must protect themselves as much as possible by examining the facility and contract very carefully before signing.

Nursing Homes

Meeting the needs of the infirm is the responsibility of society, not just the responsibility of service providers, the government, or their families. Here we will consider what nursing homes can offer. How well they meet needs ultimately depends on how well the public informs itself concerning the problems of nursing homes and the rights and services to which residents are entitled.

Who Needs a Nursing Home?

Nursing homes are becoming large-scale operations. Since 1985, the number of nursing homes decreased by 13 percent while the number of beds increased by 9 percent (U.S. Department of Health and Human Services [DHHS], 1997). The number of nursing home residents was up only 4 percent between 1985 and 1995, however, despite an 18 percent increase in the population aged 65 and over. Before this 1995 finding by the Department of Health and Human Services,

the utilization rates had kept pace with the increase in the elderly population (DHHS, 1997). People are *not* aging in the same way they did 25 years ago.

The typical nursing home patient is female, white, widowed, and over age 80. Most of the residents come to the facility from another institution, usually a general medical hospital, rather than from their own homes. Most nursing home residents have multiple problems such as arthritis, heart trouble, diabetes, or vision or hearing impairment. In addition to physical impairments, there are often mental health problems, such as disorientation (confusion), impulse control (anger), and emotional affective disorder (depression). People living in nursing homes generally require assistance in dressing, eating, toileting, and bathing.

Making the Decision to Move

Whether an older parent, relative, or friend will need nursing home care can often be anticipated some months before the individual actually enters the facility. The limitations in behavior brought on by chronic illness or age may be progressive as well as irreversible, usually allowing the individual and the family time enough to make a thoughtful and careful selection of homes and to ease the transition from one living arrangement to another.

Unfortunately, too few people are willing to entertain the possibility of a nursing home and simply wait for circumstances to force a quick, hurried decision, usually one filled with emotional trauma for all concerned. The fact that the typical nursing home patient enters the facility from a hospital rather than from a private home indicates that nursing home care has become a necessity rather than a choice. Families often burden themselves for long periods of time trying to care for an elderly parent who could receive care as good or even better in a nursing home. They often associate guilt and even shame with any attempt to consider nursing home care until the need becomes absolutely critical.

Families can anticipate eventual need and involve all members in the decision-making process. All concerned can discuss the advantages and disadvantages of nursing home care and together can inquire about and visit potential facilities. A grandparent living with adult children may not be happy to be in the midst of bustling young people or to be the cause of unusual alterations or deviations in a family routine. Families can and should discuss these problems in an atmosphere of mutual love and concern. The older person "dumped," without discussion or plan, in a nursing home after a sudden medical crisis may well feel deserted and hurt. The American Health Care Association has published three brochures for those considering nursing home care: "The Nursing Home Dilemma," "Thinking About a Nursing Home?," and "Welcome to Our Nursing Home: A Family Guide." These brochures are available on request; they detail the many aspects of the decision-making process and can be the basis for beginning conversations about future needs (American Health Care Association, 1994). American Health Care Association websites are excellent resources for information on nursing homes and decision-making.

Finding a Nursing Home

Over 30 percent of the population in one national-level random-sample study would rather die than move to a nursing home (Olson, 1998). Some professionals and family caregivers might add that the other 70 percent simply do not know about daily life in a nursing home, cost notwithstanding.

Many nursing homes provide fine patient care and make special efforts to meet the psychosocial needs of their residents. Others are skilled in the delivery of medically related services but lack the foresight, knowledge, and skill to address the psychological and emotional needs of their residents. The better facilities generally have long waiting lists, so early planning is essential to eventual placement.

Unfortunately, most families spend little time visiting a variety of nursing homes in order to secure a satisfactory placement. There are, however, resources that can assist in the search for the right nursing home. The local Council on Aging and the local chapter of the state Health Care Association can provide the locations of licensed facilities in the area and factors to consider in choosing a home. Local ombudsman programs maintain a list of all formally reported complaints made by or on behalf of people who are residents of long-term-care facilities. The Office of Nursing Home Affairs can provide information on characteristics of good homes. Finally, the local chapter of the Gray Panthers typically has a nursing home committee, and various other watchdog groups publish information on how to choose a nursing home. The following was compiled by social workers and nursing home professionals as preliminary ideas about how to select a nursing home.

- Make at least two visits to a particular nursing home, once at a mealtime and again in mid-morning or mid-afternoon. Visit several other facilities, so you can make comparisons.

- Make sure you know what the basic rate covers. Investigate extra charges for professional services and medications.

- Take time to observe interactions among staff. Does there seem to be an easy relationship, or do you pick up any tension? The more staff seem to like one another, the greater the probability that the environment is a happy one for residents, too.

- Extend your observations to interactions between staff and residents. Are you comfortable? Does the staff extend to each resident an attitude that goes beyond mere courtesy and seem to have a genuine regard for each person? (You, after all, are "company," and "company manners" might be on display.)

- Ask to see a copy of the month's menu. Is it varied and interesting? Does the food on the menu actually get served? How is it served? Have breakfast, lunch, or dinner in the facility. How was it? How did it make you feel?

- How many hours a month does a registered dietician spend in the facility? Experts believe four hours a week should be an absolute minimum.

- Is there a registered nurse on duty on the afternoon and evening shifts? This is required by law for facilities of 100 beds or more. All facilities with more than six beds should have an RN on the daytime shift.

- Is there an activities director (required by Medicare-certified facilities)? Talk to him or her. What are the reasons for specific activities? What is the range of activities, and how often do they occur? Are there activities for bedridden residents? What are they? Do they seem interesting to you?

Death is a dramatic, one-time crisis while old age is a day-by-day and year-by-year confrontation with powerful external and internal forces, a bittersweet coming to terms with one's own personality and one's own life.

BUTLER, 1994

What Are Nursing Homes Really Like?

Virtually all of us are either directly or indirectly affected by nursing home care. Although at any given time only 5 percent of the nation's elders are in long-term-care institutions, this figure is deceptive. About 1.5 million residents were receiving care in 16,700 nursing homes in 1995. Almost 90 percent of those residents were aged 65 or older, and more than 35 percent were aged 85 and older (DHHS, 1997).

Families are also affected. Nine out of ten children can expect that one of their parents (or their spouse's parents) will spend time in a nursing home. Nursing home populations are projected to increase from the 1990 level of 1.8 million to 4 million within the next 24 years—an increase of well over 50 percent (DHHS, 1997). That means that a lot of people are going to be directly and indirectly affected by the quality standards of nursing homes.

The question remains: are all homes as bad as we imagine them to be, or is a bad nursing home relatively rare? It turns out that this question is not an easy one to answer. For starters, we can easily identify truly negligent care, but can we identify good care—"quality" care? The very concept is laden with personal judgments—good quality in Mr. Jones's estimation might not be good quality from the perspective of his wife. Bad care, on the other hand, can be obvious to the observer, or more subtle and not immediately apparent. Nursing home violations cover a broad range of conditions, just a few of which include residents being tied in chairs for hours at a time; lack of an activities program; bedridden elders lying in urine-soaked bedding; unappetizing and possibly undernourishing meals; and the use of foam drinking cups and plastic utensils, which impose a hardship on those with tremors and arthritis. Where is the line between bad and good enough, all things considered? What about quality?

Measuring Nursing Home Quality

Identifying the specific dimensions of nursing home quality in a way that makes sense to professionals, consumers, and policy makers, is a relatively new research endeavor. In a major qualitative study, Rantz and colleagues interviewed people with a variety of experiences in providing nursing home care to determine the

TABLE 10.2

Factors in nursing home quality

Nursing Home Care Components	Good Care Quality	Bad Care Quality
Environment	• Clean • No odor • Maintained • Bright/good lighting	• Odor of urine/feces • Shadowed, lighting poor
Care and treatment	• Attentive, caring, residents listened to • Treated as individuals • Restorative care, ambulating • People up, dressed, clean, and well cared for • Food is good	• Residents unkempt, exposed, not clean, unshaven, disheveled, clothes dirty, poor nail care • Complaints from residents about care, lying in urine, not being taken to toilet
Staff	• Knowledgable, professional • Busy interacting and working with residents • Open and listens to family • RNs involved in care • Education encouraged • Low turnover	• Interact inappropriately or ignore residents • Vistors can't find staff
Milieu	• Calm but active and friendly • Presence of community, volunteers, animals, and children • Residents engaged in age- and functionally-appropriate activities	• Chaos? • Residents screaming and no one paying attention • Unfriendly atmosphere • An institution, not a home
Central Focus	• Residents and family	• Surivival of agency • Leadership void • Financial gain without regard or understanding of services needed by residents

Source: Adapted from Rantz, M., et al. (1998). Nursing home care quality: A multidimensional theoretical model. *Journal of Nursing Care Quality,* 12 (3), 30–49.

variables they used to assess nursing home quality (1998). The people interviewed represented a range of responsibilities in long-term care, including administrators, nurses and activity directors, social workers, ombudsmen, state regulators, professional home care staff, and hospice and mental health personnel.

The two key indicators of quality that these experienced nursing home professionals identified were interaction and odor: caring interactions between staff and residents, and the absence of the odor of urine—an indication that residents are adequately toileted and kept clean. Table 10.2 summarizes the Rantz study findings on specific components of good and bad nursing homes. Note in the table that many of the identifiers of poor quality are subtle and might not be immediately obvious to overwhelmed family members or to the frail elder himself or herself.

The decision of when to move, where to move, and whether to move, is a loaded one for all family members. Add to that burden the uncertainty of what kind of care a facility truly will provide for this person whom you love (or yourself), and the load on that decision is enormous.

It seems apparent that quality nursing home care is something that cannot be legislated: the difference between "good enough" and "high quality" takes an organizational philosophy—a dedication to providing *care* in the nursing home. Caring incurs meeting individual needs, and meeting individual needs incurs a good deal of knowledge and understanding about the individual being cared for. This, in turn, requires a low ratio of residents per staff person and an organization dedicated to the mental as well as physical well-being of its guests. At the turn of this century, money holds quality of life hostage for the care of many of America's elders. As a nation, the United States has not made elder care a priority.

Did you know . . .
Medicare will provide only skilled nursing and rehabilitative services, and only in Medicare-approved nursing homes—fewer than 10 percent of existing facilities. Medicare Nursing Home Benefits provide:

- *First 20 days paid 100 percent by Medicare*

- *Additional 80 days, patient pays $92/ day; Medicare pays remainder*

- *Beyond 100 days, patient pays all nursing home costs*

The economics of nursing home management has another whole range of problems. The government reimburses nursing homes through two systems, both of which can be corrupted by dishonest owners. On the flat-rate system, the nursing home is paid so much per patient. The operator who wants to make a large profit on this system keeps costs as low as possible by providing cheap food, having as few registered nurses on the staff as possible, and providing no physical therapists or psychiatric counseling. Healthy residents are the most desirable under this system.

The second system is called the cost-plus system. Here, the nursing home is reimbursed for its costs, plus a "reasonable" profit. The way to make money under this system is to pad the bills—in other words, the government is billed for more goods and services than the facility received, or is billed for goods and services never delivered. Doctors and nursing homes gain if doctors perform "gang visits," stopping just long enough for a quick look at residents' charts and perhaps to visit briefly with people. The government is then billed as though each resident had a separate appointment—a task would take days rather than hours.

Who speaks for the frail, sometimes confused residents who are not objects of a television news exposé? Ombudsman Programs is an independent nonprofit agency, federally and state mandated to be an advocate for long-term-care residents. Employing a staff of well-trained volunteers, the agency investigates and resolves complaints from and on behalf of residents of nursing homes. The agencies, though seriously underfunded by federal and state sources, provide a critical watchdog role. In one northern California county in 1997, the 3-staff-person, 20-volunteer program handled 1,052 cases, including over 200 abuse cases. Volunteers made 1,429 visits to long-term-care facilities in the region, and contributed 5,155 volunteer hours (OPSC, 1998).

The debate over whether proprietary (for-profit) homes offer a lower quality of patient care than nonproprietary (nonprofit) homes goes unanswered. One study, using strict quality control measures, found no difference in the quality of care between for-profit and nonprofit facilities (Duffy, 1987). Other analyses disagree, observing that nonprofit facilities generally have greater concern for the psychological and spiritual development and well-being of their residents (Rosenkoetter, 1996). Close to three-quarters of all nursing homes, however, are operated on a for-profit basis.

Those in the business who are really concerned about elders and provide quality care deserve credit. Credit also must be given to all the honest doctors, pharmacists, nursing home inspectors, social workers, and therapists. A number of nursing homes are excellent by any standards. The Jewish Home for the Aged in San Francisco is considered to be among the best. The living quarters resemble rooms in a nicely furnished college dormitory. Virtually all residents are out of bed and dressed. The home has a beauty shop, and there are many activities and opportunities for therapeutic exercising on stationary bicycles and other equipment. "They take care of me from head to toe," said one resident.

New Trends in Nursing Homes

The majority of nursing home residents have disabling mental health conditions, such as depression, Alzheimer's disease, or a history of mental illness. As a result, many nursing home residents present behavior problems ranging from agitation and abusiveness to wandering. Nursing home care presents an increasing challenge for staff, family, and residents alike. In the past, the health care system provided scant rehabilitation for frail elders and held low expectations for older people in nursing homes. Now, however, there are positive new trends for both the physically and the mentally disabled.

Those over 65 are more likely than any other group to suffer strokes, lower-limb amputation, hip fractures, and heart disease. With rehabilitation, many can achieve a level of independence that allows frail elders to live in their own homes. Rehabilitation units represent a departure from the traditional nursing home. One nursing home with a rehabilitation unit revealed that 57 percent of its residents were discharged after an average stay of three months in the unit. The unit had a team composed of a geriatrician,

a psychiatrist, a physical therapist, a social worker, a nurse, an occupational therapist, and a nutritionist. The conclusion was that patients discharged "quicker and sicker," without rehabilitation, are likely candidates for relapse and readmission. The rehabilitation unit brought a sense of triumph to all who participated (Adelman et al., 1987).

It is estimated that 65 percent of all nursing home residents have at least one mental disorder (Lantz et al., 1997). The mentally ill, who present far more behavioral problems than other nursing home residents, need rehabilitative services. Such services have been found to be generally effective. But, according to Shea et al. (1994), fewer than 25 percent of nursing home residents with a mental disorder actually received such services in the year of the study. Furthermore, only about 5 percent of those residents with a mental disorder received *any* mental health treatment in the last one-month period. One-half of the services they received were provided for by general practitioners with very little training in geriatric psychiatry. Obviously, although services for those who receive them tend to be somewhat effective, much more must be done to provide the quality and quantity of services for those who need them. It has been argued that nursing homes, in fact, should be mental health facilities. A more in-depth preparation of staff is necessary, and a wider range of mental health professionals must be utilized to meet these needs.

Family and community involvement can improve life for elders in a nursing home. Both resident-only counseling groups and resident-and-family counseling groups reduce anxiety and increase feelings of internal control for those in institutions. Family members who strive to keep family connections, offer optimism for recovery, and help the resident to maintain dignity can do much to uplift spirits. Family members tend to judge a nursing home not so much by its technical care as by its psychological care. The views of involved family members provide the staff with good feedback that hopefully can lead to improvements. Families of nursing home residents are often unfamiliar with ways to assist their relatives. Nursing homes that establish a "partnership" with families in sharing responsibilities for the nontechnical aspects of care enhance the psychological and emotional welfare of the resident as well as that of family.

The Omnibus Budget Reconciliation Act of 1987

With the enactment of the **Omnibus Budget Reconciliation Act of 1987 (OBRA)**, the nursing home industry became one of the most highly regulated environments for health care delivery in the United States. In addition to tightening survey and certification procedures, the act strengthened patients' rights in the planning of their care and in making treatment decisions. Other requirements, such as written care plans, mandated nursing assistant training, and the employment of certified social workers, were designed to upgrade the quality of patient services and to ensure their participation in planning their care.

OBRA also intensified requirements for survey teams making routine and unscheduled audits. As a result, many past procedures, such as placing patients in restraints without medical authorization, denying patients full disclosure of their medical records and diagnoses, or failing to assure patients of their rights may become grounds for censure or, ultimately, the closing of a facility by regulatory agencies. Although OBRA does not purport to correct all problems related to the quality of care, it represents a concerted effort to upgrade and enrich services to institutionalized elders.

Enforcement of the provisions of OBRA is generally left in the hands of in general woefully understaffed state health departments, which results in only occasional audits of nursing homes to ensure that OBRA mandates are being carried out. Although it is hoped that the enactment of OBRA has led to a higher quality of care for residents, empirical evidence does not confirm that those outcomes have been achieved.

Chapter Summary

Theoretically, there are many acceptable kinds of housing currently available to those who must relocate:

- Home of a relative
- Public housing
- Deluxe high-rise apartment
- Retirement village
- Mobile home
- Apartment complex or duplex
- Hotel-type residence with meals or a board and care home
- Intermediate day care or own home at night
- Assisted living (a residential complex with many services and facilities)
- Small group residential home
- Institution

Reality, however, does not keep pace with theory. Old people are often forced into housing that is inadequate or that needlessly increases their dependence. Most prefer to live in their own homes where possible, but others enjoy the stimulation of living in retirement communities, shared housing arrangements, community care retirement centers, or similar living environments. For older adults with limited incomes, **public housing** or mobile homes may provide a practical alternative. Although the percentages are declining, many continue to live with relatives—usually a daughter or son and their families. Regardless of the type of living situation, most prefer to remain as independent as possible.

For those who decide to relocate (either voluntarily or involuntarily), problems may arise with respect to housing shortages, downsizing, decisions over whether to live in an integrated or segregated environment, or finding a community in which to live that is compatible with their lifestyles. Relocation is never a simple matter, although under optimal conditions it can enhance both the lifestyle and the life satisfaction of those who elect to do so.

For a small percentage of older adults—those who are debilitated—the nursing home is often the only viable housing option. The lack of personalization often creates dependency and the loss of personal freedoms for the resident. OBRA legislation was enacted to increase the quality of life in nursing homes by providing for resident input and by offering a broader range of higher quality services.

Everyone needs a home. The older we get, the more important a safe harbor becomes. Home is not just a place to exist, but a place to be. More needs to be done to meet this most important psychological requirement. We all deserve to live out our lives in dignity, pride, and comfort.

Key Terms

adult community
adult day care
age-integrated housing
age-segregated housing
aging in place
amenity relocation
assisted living
board and care home
continuing care
     retirement
     community (CCRC)
downsizing
full-timing
granny unit
life-care community
     (LCC)

living environment
mobile-home park
naturally occurring
     retirement commu-
     nity (NORC)
Omnibus Budget
     Reconciliation Act
     of 1987 (OBRA)
public housing
retirement city
snowbird
sunbird
surveillance zone

Questions for Discussion

1. Identify at least three reasons that adequate housing is important for older adults.
2. Think of your parents as older adults. In what type of housing environment would you like to see them live? Why? Imagine that you are 70 years of age. Where would you like to live? Why?
3. What are some of the issues associated with living in public housing? What steps would you take to increase the quality of public housing?
4. What are the disadvantages of living in a segregated community? Advantages?
5. What would you look for in selecting a nursing home for your father or mother? What alternatives, other than the nursing home, would you consider? Why?

Fieldwork Suggestions

1. Visit a senior center and interview at least three older adults. Ask each of them where they live, who lives with them, and how satisfied they feel about their housing. Do you find any themes in their responses? How consistent are the responses to material presented in this chapter?
2. Visit a public housing complex in your community. What are your first impressions? Talk to residents to find out how they feel about living there. Interview the director of housing with a focus of identifying the positives and negatives associated with that particular complex.
3. Visit a local nursing home. Using the guidelines from this chapter, outline the major strengths and weaknesses with respect to how the environment promotes quality of life for residents.
4. Visit an assisted care living complex. What is the living environment like? What is the apparent functional level of the people you observed? In what way does this environment differ from your observations of the nursing home environment?

Internet Activities

1. Locate the home page for the American Association of Homes and Services for the Aging. What resources do they have that would give you information if your private nonprofit

agency were interested in building an assisted living complex for poor elders in your community?

2. Your parents live 500 miles away from you, their closest adult child. Your mother requires extensive caregiving, and your father is very weakened from a recent heart attack. You fear that his exhaustion in trying to care for your mother will kill him. You feel that the family needs to consider placing your mother in a nursing home. Use the Internet to search out the information you need to bring to a family gathering that is being held to discuss, "What will we do with Mom?"

11 Mental Health

Mental Exercise Nearly Halves Dementia Risk

LiveScience Staff

Staying mentally and physically active throughout life is the best way to keep the mind sharp and reduce the risks of developing dementia, two recent studies show.

One large group study found that staying mentally active reduces the risk of Alzheimer's disease and other forms of dementia by nearly half by building and maintaining a reserve of stimulation.

"It is a case of 'use it or lose it,'" said study leader Michael Valenzuela from the School of Psychiatry at the University of New South Wales in Australia. "If you increase your brain reserve over your lifetime, you seem to lessen the risk of Alzheimer's and other neurodegenerative diseases."

46 Percent Risk Reduction

The study combined data from 29,000 individuals and 22 studies worldwide. It was detailed in a recent issue of the journal Psychological Medicine.

It found that individuals with high mental stimulation had a 46 percent decreased risk of dementia. The protective effect was present even in later life, so long as the individuals engaged in mentally stimulating activities.

The findings support the idea that a person's education, occupation, IQ and mental stimulation play a big role in preventing cognitive decline.

In a previous study, Valenzuela showed that after five weeks of memory-based exercise, participants increased brain chemistry markers in a direction that was opposite to that seen in Alzheimer's. The change was concentrated in the hippocampus, one of the first brain regions to be affected in dementia.

Exercise Helps Too

Another study found that older people who exercise three or more times a week had a 30 to 40 percent lower risk of developing Alzheimer's and other types of dementia. Even light activity, such as walking, seemed to help.

This study, led by Eric Larson of GroupHealth Cooperative in Seattle, was published in a recent issue of the journal Annals of Internal Medicine.

The researchers tracked 1,740 people who were 65 and older over the course of nine years. The participants were all dementia-free at the beginning of the study.

At the end of the study, 77 percent of the individuals who were still free of dementia had reported exercising three or more times a week. The study could not determine whether certain types of exercise worked better than others.

In addition to preventing dementia, mental and physical exercise has also been found to boost the mood of depressed patients and improve memory in the elderly.

Social scientists continue to unravel the effects of aging on the mind. The ultimate fate of an elderly person was once considered to be senility—whatever that meant. No one was surprised if Grandpa forgot where he put his glasses, that cousin Herman was coming to visit, or even that he was married. No one became too alarmed if old Mrs. Jones down the street saw angels in the sky or was hiding in a cave because she thought the world was going to end in six months. The reasoning went: "This is what happens when people get old—their minds go. At the very least, they become set in their ways, stubborn, and cranky." Nonconformist, bizarre behavior was tolerated and rationalized: "What can you expect at her age? Old age must take its course. What can you do but accept?" These ideas about old age still persist. Today, scientific evidence suggests that declining mental health is not a natural consequence of the aging process. The vast majority of people aged 65 and over are in good mental health. If they are not, specific causes other than the aging process itself usually can be pinpointed. This chapter will examine the psychology of aging and the most common mental health problems of older adults.

The Psychology of Aging

In this chapter, we will discuss areas traditionally covered in the behavioral aspect of the psychology of aging. These are changes with age in perception, motor performance, intelligence, learning, memory, and personality. Gerontological psychologists also study changes in the brain and central nervous system. Many psychologists have backgrounds in physiology, biology, physics, math, or some combination thereof. Others are more interested in personality characteristics and social behavior and, thus, may have social psychology backgrounds.

In the psychology of aging, one must distinguish between **age-related changes** and **biologically caused changes**. For example, a scientist

may find a positive correlation between age and depression—the older the age group, the higher the incidence of depression. In this case, depression is an age-related phenomenon. Once this statistic is staring the scientist in the face, the scientist must interpret it. Can the scientist say that the biological aging process causes depression? Certainly not without further investigation. What would be some possible causes of the correlation? Are society's values the cause? Are there cumulative stresses that some persons resist in their younger years but to which they finally succumb in old age? How do events such as retirement, poor health, or the death of a spouse affect aging? There may be other possible causes for the correlation.

The important thing to remember is that some psychological states that initially appear to be caused by the biological aging process are, upon closer examination, really related to age, in which case the scientist must look further for the cause of the correlation. For example, studies of the incidence of depression in the United States show some surprising and contradictory results. Several studies found the highest rates of depression in young adults and elders, but not in middle-aged groups. In contrast, in three other studies the oldest group showed a lower rate of depression than all younger groups when variables such as income, socioeconomic status, and gender were held constant (Lewinsohn et al., 1997). These studies suggest that the initial findings of increased depression are a consequence of the social changes that accompany aging, rather than the biological aging process itself (Bliwise, 1987). A social scientist must go beyond assumptions; preconceived notions should undergo objective testing.

Did you know . . .
Lower limb strength is a predictor of performance on cognitive texts. Strength loss results from muscle atrophy, which is caused by a loss of fibers and, to a less extent, reduction in fiber size. Anstey et al. (1997) report that

muscle fiber reduction is caused by denerva-
tion and reinnervation of individual fibers
caused by continuous loss of motor neurons
in the spinal cord, which is part of the central
nervous system. Age-related changes in the
central nervous system are also associated
with memory, reaction time, and cognition.

Cognitive Processes

Cognition is what we think about a situation. It is our awareness of the world around us—how we absorb stimuli and information and how we make sense of it. Our perception of a cause is related to our behavior in various situations. Did you see the traffic accident? Did you hear the crash? Do you know who was at fault based on what you saw? What was your response? How quickly did you react? Cognitive processes involve the use of our senses, our arousal, attention, information processing, reaction time, and motor performance. Gerontologists want to know whether people see and hear situations differently based on their age: Does attention span or speed change? Is information processed in an altered or different way due to aging?

Psychologists have compared our brains to computers. Information enters our brain, is coded, and then is stored at various levels. If our brains are working efficiently, we can retrieve information when we need it. This section deals with cognitive functioning. First, the basic senses, sensory memory, and steps of information processing are described; second, studies of intelligence are reported; and, third, learning and longer-term memory are analyzed.

Basic Cognitive Functions

Information processing in the brain is a complicated matter. The loss of memory that many people assume will occur in later life seems to be more highly related to individual differences as well as the context in which human development occurs than with age itself (Lewinsohn

et al., 1997; Luszcz et al., 1997). But memory loss does seem to occur. Some of the complex processes having to do with thinking, remembering, and making judgments (perceiving) are discussed in the next sections.

The Senses

Sensation is the process of taking information in through the senses. **The five senses** (vision, touch, hearing, smell, and taste), which relay environmental information to the brain, generally lose acuity with age; therefore, one set of pathways in which information is gathered for processing by the brain is modified as we age. Vast individual differences exist, however. Some very old people experience no sensory declines. The social and psychological consequences of sensory declines can be enormous, and it is the old old—those over age 75—who are more likely to experience noticeable declines than are the young old, or those between 65 and 75 years of age.

Older persons vary in how they deal with sensory loss. Some persons can compensate for losses in one area by stressing enjoyment from another. For example, a person losing vision might choose to focus on an existing appreciation of orchestral music. Compensation by habit and routine is probably even more frequent. Though adaptability may vary, most older people can compensate very well for minor sensory losses. For example, loss of visual acuity can be compensated for with corrective lenses, more light, less glare, and clearly printed reading material.

Those who care for the elderly could easily respond inappropriately to such sensory decline: Why fix a nice meal for one who cannot taste it, or why take a vision-impaired elder outside? Rather than encouraging withdrawal, sensory decline might challenge caretakers to find ways of enhancing life for those who have suffered losses. Perhaps the person might like spicy Mexican food, or stronger hugs, or a windy day, or a warm fire in the fireplace. Sensory decline may

Sensory Memory

Each memory starts as a sensory stimulus. You can remember certain aspects of things you see and hear for only a fraction of a second. This initial short-term sensory experience is called a **sensory memory.** Sensory memory takes in large amounts of information so rapidly that most of it gets lost. Do you recall what is on a one-dollar bill or a dime? Could you draw the details? Much information that passes through sensory memory is never processed to a storage place in the brain because we cannot pay attention to everything hitting our senses. Although not as well studied as other memory phases, research indicates that the amount of visual information one can handle at a time seems to decline with age.

Attention

Paying attention is an important part of information processing. **Selective attention** is focusing attention on the relevant information while inhibiting irrelevant information. If we pay attention to a stimulus, the experience moves from our sensory memory to be stored in our working memory. If we are distracted—unable to focus on a specific stimulus among many—our ability to code the stimulus into memory is impaired. Compared to sensory memory, working memory can handle a very small amount of input. We vary in our capacity for information to get to our working memory at any one point in time. Very old people have a smaller capacity to absorb stimuli into the working memory and thus to maintain concentration over a long period of time.

Studies of **divided attention** (doing two things at once such as watching television and reading) show that when divided-attention tasks are easy, age differences are typically absent. But when the tasks become more complicated, age differences emerge. Attention studies show that older people are more distractible and less able to disregard the clutter of irrelevant information than are younger people. Age-related differences in vigilance also exist (Wolters & Prinsen, 1997). Older adults tend to have lower physiological arousal (Mutter & Goedert, 1997), which lowers their alertness. Vigilance does not appear to be age related unless the task is sustained over an extended period of time, when, beyond age 60, fatigue can result in notable performance loss.

Perception

The process of evaluating the sensory information carried to the brain is called **perception.** Individuals may perceive the same stimuli differently; further, the same person may react differently at different times. **Sensory threshold** is the minimum intensity of a stimulus that is required for a person to perceive it. Mood, activities, and personality may all influence perception.

Sensory decline affects perception significantly. If a person is unable to hear parts of a conversation, for example, the content of the conversation is more likely to be misunderstood. Perceptual differences among age groups are frequently reported, but research does not explain the reason. The differences may be caused by biological changes, or they may be age related. Social isolation also tends to affect perception; therefore, isolation, not aging per se, may cause perceptual changes.

Psychomotor Speed

People first experience the environment through the five senses; second, they perceive what is happening; and third, they may react. A physical reaction to a stimulus is called motor performance. Motor performance may be simple, that is, a reaction requiring very little decision making or skill. Pressing a button to turn on the television and turning off a light switch are simple motor skills. Some types of motor performance, such as dancing, riding a bike, playing tennis, or driving a car, are more complex.

Very old drivers, for example, may be affected by changes in vision and hearing. Their

Some skills become enhanced with age. Age can ripen and enhance the interpretation of music, compensating for reduced physical agility.

vision does not adapt as rapidly to darkness, and they are more affected by glare. Additionally, older people take longer to read road signs. The processing of information is slower from the point of sensation (seeing the sign) to the perception (its meaning registers, and action is taken). Researchers suggest designing cars with older adults in mind: headlights with less glare, well-lit instrument panels, easy entry, and so on. They recommend large letters on signs with pictures if possible. Training programs for those with sensory decline are also advised.

Though it is commonly believed that older drivers are hazardous on the road, older drivers have far fewer accidents than do younger drivers. This is in part because older people seem to exercise greater caution (driving at reduced speeds and giving greater conscious awareness to the task), drive fewer miles, and drive at less hazardous times of the day than do younger people.

One aspect of motor performance is reaction time—the length of time between the stimulus and the response, directly related to psychomotor speed. Studies show that reaction time increases with age, at about age 26 for some tasks and not until the 70s for other tasks. The general slowing of behavior with age is one of the most reliable and well-documented age-related changes. This includes slowed **psychomotor speed** and the resultant lengthened reaction time. The more complex the task, the greater the difference in reaction time by age, generally speaking. However, individuals can differ substantially; for example, an individual 70-year-old might respond more quickly than a 30-year-old.

A noted researcher in the field of cognition has introduced two terms to categorize the variables affecting cognition:

1. **Cognitive mechanics**—the hardware of the mind—reflects the neurophysiological architecture of the brain. It involves the speed and accuracy of elementary processing of sensory information.

TABLE 11.1

Variables hypothesized to be related to slowing of information processing in old age

Genetic-biological factors
- Changes in sensation acuity
- Changes in physiological arousal to stimuli
- Changes in attention
- Changes in motor capacity (stiffness; reduced strength)
- Lower levels of physical activity
- Changes in blood flow to the brain leading to neural malnutrition
- Changes in the central nervous system
- Changes in cortical levels of the brain
- Gradual loss in brain mass
- Neural/metabolic changes
- Decline in physical health

Cultural-social factors
- Changes in self-esteem and self-confidence
- Lower levels of mental activity
- Lessened familiarity and experience with the task
- Lifestyle characteristics, such as divorce, lack of travel, lack of stimulating environment

2. **Cognitive pragmatics**—the software of the mind—reflects the knowledge and information of one's culture. It involves reading, writing, education, professional skills, and life experiences that help us master or cope with life (Baltes, 1993).

The first term represents the genetic-biological influence and the second represents the cultural-social influence. Table 11.1 itemizes the biological factors, biological mechanics, separately from the cultural-social pragmatics, factors associated with the slowing of information processing in old age. The cultural-social factors tend to be more reversible than the genetic-biological ones.

Many of these variables in Table 11.1 do not accompany universal aging. Physical pathologies (e.g., high blood pressure) do not go hand in hand with aging. Neither does reduced activity. Aerobic exercise and other forms of physical activity have been shown to increase blood flow and increase speed of reaction. Activities such as tennis and dancing are helpful. Physically fit older people have shorter reaction times than less fit young adults (Foley & Mitchell, 1997). Practice at a task can compensate for slowness. Many a grandchild has been amazed, for example, at the speed with which a grandparent can peel a potato or whittle a wooden object.

Psychologists know that the slower reactions of older people have more to do with changes in the mental processes of interpretation and decision rather than with the initial level of sensory input (Thomas, 1992). In other words, the course of slowing has a lot to do with the brain and central nervous system (CNS). It is important to remember, however, that not every older individual experiences a slowdown in reaction. It is a pattern of aging that has many exceptions.

The implications of CNS slowing for the everyday life of the older person are various. Experience and familiarity are great levelers—giving the older person an edge on the job or at various tasks at home. Very old people may need more time to get a job done, and they may need to be more cautious to avoid accidents. A speedy reaction is needed to avoid falling objects, to drive a car safely, to escape a fire, to get across a busy street, or to play a good game of ball. Many older adults would benefit from education or retraining to minimize the consequences of reduced cognitive efficiency. Environmental modifications may be in order—for example, stronger lighting, brighter colors, grab bars, hand railings, door handles as opposed to knobs, a louder telephone ring, larger and sturdier step stools. And people should not be so ready to assume that if an individual cannot think quickly, he or she cannot think well. That is a form of ageism.

Intelligence

As we compare the learning abilities of babies, elementary students, college students, or people in general, we find that within each group, some people are better able to learn than others. **Intelligence** was conceptualized by Guilford (1966) in three dimensions: *content* (figures, symbols, words), *operations* (memorizing, evaluating, coming up with solutions), and *products from the operations* (relationships, systems, implications). The dimensions are measured by various tests to determine an individual's "intelligence." Although tests have been devised to measure one's intelligence quotient (IQ), the validity of such tests has been debated for years. They have been variously criticized for being ethnocentric (biased toward the majority culture), sexist (biased toward boys and men), and ageist (inadequate to measure applied knowledge) (Cunningham et al., 1998). The jury is still out, even as tests become more clearly defined for diverse populations. Two major questions about IQ tests arise: (1) is there any such thing as intelligence; and (2) do IQ tests really measure intelligence?

The tests actually measure a number of specific intellectual abilities. Twenty-five **primary mental abilities** have been established, composed of five primary and independent abilities: number, word fluency, verbal meaning,

reasoning, and space. Tests of six or so secondary mental abilities—skills composed of several primary abilities—have also been identified. Most research focuses on two secondary mutual abilities: fluid and crystallized intelligence (Schaie & Willis, 1996).

Intelligence is most often measured by a standardized test with many multiple-choice items on vocabulary, reasoning, and the ordering of numbers and spaces. Using such a test represents the **psychometric approach,** in contrast to other tests that examine thought processes—the quality and depth of thinking and the ability to solve complex problems (the **cognitive process approach**). The most widely used psychometric test of intelligence for older adults is the Wechsler Adult Intelligence Scale (WAIS), developed in the 1950s. This test compensates for increasing age. The test norms assume declining speed with age; an older adult can perform worse than a younger adult and still have the same IQ! Critics point to the fact that this test emphasizes skills learned in school and not skills of everyday life. For this reason, all things being equal, the test favors the younger adult. This test has been revised (WAIS-R) and is used widely in clinical settings. Another IQ test, the Primary Mental Abilities Test (PMA), has often been used to examine adult intellectual development. The WAIS test measures a "verbal intelligence" aspect that involves comprehension, arithmetic, similarities, vocabulary, and the ability to recall digits; and a "performance intelligence" aspect that involves completion, block design, and assembly of objects. On the performance scale, speed is important. Bonus points are awarded for rapid solutions.

Both the WAIS-R and the PMA include tasks that evaluate fluid and crystallized intelligence. **Crystallized intelligence** is a measure of knowledge you have acquired through experience and education. Vocabulary tests are a clear example. **Fluid intelligence** refers to innate ability—the information-processing skills described in the previous section. Each of these types of intelligence taps a cluster of primary abilities. No standardization test measures one alone, although a given test can emphasize either crystallized or fluid intelligence (Kaufman & Horn, 1996).

We once assumed that a decline in intelligence with age was to be expected. Scientists are now questioning this assumption. Longitudinal studies have found that some IQ components such as verbal skills remain stable over time, and some can even increase with age. Schaie (1996) reported that virtually no individuals show deterioration on all mental abilities, even in their 80s. At age 60, 75 percent of subjects maintained their level of functioning on at least 80 percent of the mental abilities tested (as compared to seven years prior). More than 50 percent of those aged 80 had maintained 80 percent of their mental abilities over the seven-year period.

Fluid intelligence does appear to decline some with age, whereas crystallized intelligence does not. Similarly, the verbal scores of the WAIS show no declines with age, whereas the performance scores do decline with age. The high verbal score and declining performance score of older adults is so consistently found that it is called the **classic aging pattern** (Thomas, 1992). The drop in fluid intelligence indicates a decline in the ability to process information and complete tasks in an efficient manner and might reflect either the complexity of age-related changes in functions such as sensory and perceptual skills, or something as simple as lack of practice or fear of tests. More than likely, changes reflect a combination of both: neuropsychological shifts with age and the context of the individual's life.

To understand fully what happens to intelligence with age, we need to know exactly what primary mental abilities decline with age and why. We need to know at what age the onset of decline happens and what the rate of decline is. We need to know whether such changes are inevitable and whether they can be reversed. And we need to account for individual differences. Schaie (1996) found that it is not until people reach their 70s that declines in intelligence take on significance. Speed of response is the major decline. There is mounting evidence that perceptual speed may be the most age-sensitive mental ability (Stokes, 1992). Older people are as proficient as ever when it comes to situations that demand past experience or knowledge—if they are given enough time.

Though cross-sectional, "one-shot" studies of different age groups often find that older people have lower IQs than younger people, such studies may not acknowledge that young adults may have benefited from upper-level schooling. Many of the elderly studied in the 1950s and 1960s had not attended either high school or college. Some had had no formal schooling at all. Thus, cross-sectional studies that infer a decline in IQ with age are suspect. Test designers should distinguish between actual IQ (the quotient the test actually measures) and potential IQ for the young as well as for the old.

We emphasize that intelligence tests must be used with caution. IQ tests measure specific skills to generalize about an all-inclusive concept of intelligence. Their results may be biased, and scientists must continue to investigate why, how, and in what direction such instruments are biased. The evidence today supports the finding of little decline with age in skills that one acquires through education, enculturation, and personal experience. We do not really know what happens to IQ as one approaches extreme old age—say, after age 85. Although researchers believe that IQ begins to decline at some point in very old age, they have yet to determine the typical course it follows.

A problem with cross-sectional studies for the future is that young students today are not doing as well on standardized tests in their general education. If this translates into lower scores on IQ tests, then it appears that IQ increases with age because older generations today do better at test taking, and it is not necessarily true that IQ increases with age. To avoid the problems presented by cross-sectional research, longitudinal studies appear desirable.

A few words of caution about longitudinal studies: Sample size tends to be small; furthermore, repeated presentation of material, which brings about improved performance, can produce a learning effect. Additionally, the people from whom the final measures are obtained are survivors: they are more robust and healthy than were those who died over the duration of the study. In one major study on intelligence and aging, only one-sixth of the sample was left after seven years (Savage et al., 1973). One must be aware of the research methodology employed and recognize that any one study is bound to have some inadequacies in addressing issues of age-related changes.

A new area of intelligence study is practical problem solving. Researchers have done studies using tests such as the Everyday Problem Solving Inventory (Denney & Palmer, 1987) to measure ability to solve problems such as a grease fire breaking out on top of the stove. When the problems are familiar to older people, they do extremely well on these tests, but not necessarily better than middle-aged adults. Once again, let it be said that intelligence comes in various forms. Also, retraining is becoming a major focus of study. The decline in primary abilities in old age can be slowed or even reversed in many cases. Future studies will clarify which abilities can be maintained or improved and the circumstances under which it is possible (Stokes, 1992).

Further research is needed to clarify the relationship between age and intelligence. A theory of terminal decline or **terminal drop** has been proposed by a number of gerontologists (Kleemeier, 1962; White & Cunningham, 1988). According to this phenomenon, a precipitous decrease in cognitive functioning is related to the individual's distance from death rather than to chronological age. "Critical loss" in cognitive functioning is supposedly experienced up to two years before death. The theory is controversial and has not been fully substantiated by research.

Learning and Memory

Learning and memory, important components of mental functioning, are separate yet interrelated processes. When an individual can retrieve information from his or her memory storage, learning is assumed to have occurred; alternatively, if someone cannot remember, it is assumed that learning has not adequately taken place.

Learning

Learning is the process of acquiring knowledge or understanding. For purposes of psychological research, scientists speak of learning in terms of cognitive processes, which are intellectual or mental. As in studies of intelligence quotients, learning is measured by tests of performance, particularly verbal and psychomotor performance. Again, the same sort of question surfaces: do such tests really reflect learning?

Let us consider two general questions related to age: do learning skills change with age, and how do older people's skills compare with younger people's? The answers to these questions depend on the skills being learned and the conditions under which they are being learned. Up until 1960 and even later, members of the scientific community generally assumed that learning declined with age.

Many factors affect learning abilities. Pacing (the rate and speed required for learning) is an important factor. Older adults learn better with a slower pace, and they perform best with self-pacing. They also do better with a lengthened time to respond. Another factor is anxiety. Some studies suggest that older adults are more uncomfortable with the testing situation and therefore experience increased anxiety. The meaningfulness of the material makes a difference, too. Older people do better when nonsensical or abstract syllables and words are replaced with actual, concrete words. They tend to be more interested if the material makes sense to them. Further, they are more susceptible to distraction. Motivation and physical health are contributing factors as well. Here again the factors in Table 11.1 may inhibit learning. The finding that younger adults are better learners than older adults should be viewed cautiously. Under certain conditions, older people can learn as well as or better than younger people.

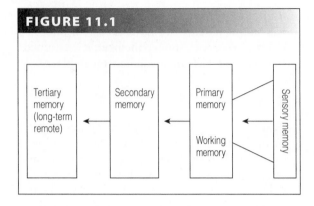

FIGURE 11.1

Tertiary
memory
(long-term
remote)

Secondary
memory

Primary
memory

Working
memory

Sensory memory

Memory

Memory varies enormously among individuals of all ages (inter-individual differences), and types of memory vary greatly in the same person (intra-individual differences). There appears to be a very slight and progressive deterioration in memory efficiency as people grow older; however, the extent of this deterioration remains controversial.

The four types of memory that have been identified by researchers are diagrammed in Figure 11.1:

1. *Sensory memory.* Sensory memory is the initial level at which all sensory information is registered but not stored. It is fleeting, lasting less than a second, unless deliberate attention is paid to the information and it is transferred to primary memory (see previous section on Basic Cognitive Functions). Countless numbers of stimuli bombard us every fraction of a second in our waking hours.

2. *Primary memory* and *working memory.* Primary memory is our current consciousness. We have only a small capacity to deal with what is being paid attention to at the moment. It may be forgotten rather quickly—for example, a phone number or joke—or it may be transformed for longer storage. The processing of our current sensate information is our working memory.

3. *Secondary memory.* Secondary memory, once called recent memory, refers to remembering the details of everyday life—friends' telephone messages, directions to the new shopping mall, the movie you saw last week, what you studied for the exam, what you need to do at work, and so on. It is the major basis for the research on memory. Hundreds and hundreds of studies are reported in this area.

4. *Tertiary memory.* **Tertiary memory** is long-term memory, sometimes called remote memory. It is the stored facts and words, learned years ago—past life experiences such as weddings, births, deaths, and episodes from childhood. Tertiary memory is studied much less often than secondary memory.

The findings on sensory memory have been described earlier in this chapter. The findings on the other levels of memory follow.

Primary Memory and Working Memory

Primary memory

The type of memory known as **primary memory** shows little change with age. Once information is stored in primary memory, people of all ages seem equal in being able to recall it. But age differences are found in **working memory,** or the processing of sensory stimuli to give it meaning and get it transferred to longer-term storage. If information does not get to storage, it cannot be recalled. Two examples of using working memory are remembering a phone number given to you orally long enough to dial the number a few seconds later and unscrambling letters of a word in your head. Some researchers believe that working memory is vital to understanding declines in the cognitive functioning of older adults (Bechara et al., 1998). Neuropsychologists generally believe that a major portion of age-related decline is due to the decreased speed of working memory in processing information. Research on working memory is relatively new but holds great promise in solving some of the mysteries of the mind.

Secondary memory

Research indicates that **secondary memory** is another major source of age-related decline. Younger adults are superior on tests of secondary memory, which is the major memory function in everyday life. The processing involved is deeper than primary memory, enabling recall to take place over a longer period of time. If the processing is too shallow, a person will not be able to recall the information a year, a month, or even a day later.

Numerous kinds of memory tasks have been developed to study secondary memory. For example, in "free recall," people are given 20 words and asked to recall as many as they can in any order they wish. The results from hundreds of studies are that younger people do better on this task. There is great variation with the type of task and pace involved. In tests of recognition, people are given a list of 20 words to look at and then given a list with those 20 words plus 40 new words. They are then asked which are old and which are new. Older people do as well as but not better than young people on this test. On some memory tests, such as those that require the subject to recall facts out of context, older persons do worse than middle-aged persons.

Starting somewhere in middle age, many persons suffer from "tip-of-the-tongue" (TOT) syndrome, which places them on the verge of recalling a name, date, or event and unable to do it. Later, when they are not trying to remember, they will recall the information. Older adults experience more TOTs and come up with more blockers (related words) during the TOT than do younger adults (Brown & Nix, 1996). In old age, interference hinders secondary memory. For example, if a neighbor rings the doorbell while an older person is reading the paper, he or she may forget what was just read. Studies suggest that eliminating distractions could optimize short-term memory for the older person. Still, some older people have excellent memories.

Older people do not usually have to engage in free recall because they have external cues, such as date books or notes or reminders on the refrigerator. A psychometric test situation may not have "ecological validity" in a real-life setting. A good deal of recent research focuses on natural memory, which includes studies of autobiographical memory. Most people believe they can remember where they were on the day of a particular historic event, such as the start of either of the Gulf Wars or the destruction of the *Challenger*. These searing historical moments, called "flashbulb memories," seem to be no more accurate three months later than any other memories (Small, 1995). Instead, flashbulb memories serve as "benchmarks in our lives that connect personal histories to cultural history" (*Science News,* quoted in Small, 1995).

Did you know . . .
It is possible, according to sleep scientists, that we sleep in order to organize efficient cortical representations of experience. Information acquired during the day is compared with older memories, and both new and old memory become somewhat modified in the process.

SEJNOWSKY, 1995

Tertiary memory

Information is stored for years in tertiary, or long-term, memory. The study of this memory has some problems: if the person constantly recalls the old days, say, going to college, is it still tertiary memory compared with someone who has not thought about his or her college days for years? Some people may retrieve certain events of the past often, whereas others never do.

Another problem is knowing the accuracy of long-term memories. Researchers often have no way to validate the memories.

One method of study is to ask people of all ages about a historic event, such as a major earthquake, or a popular television show. Typically, no age differences exist in these studies. Some autobiographical information can be verified, like naming high school classmates, for example. Again, no age differences appear in tertiary memory. What does appear to change with age is perceptual speed, or the speed at which long-term memories are processed and retrieved. When perceptual speed was controlled in one major memory study, all age-related differences in working memory span were eliminated between young adults and older adults (Fisk & Warr, 1996). The speed of retrieval, not memory itself, is the difference.

Exercising the mind is important. Learning and recalling what is learned (in other words, keeping the mind active and stimulated) is a good way to preserve memory. Learning and memory are related; memory is the ability to retain what is learned. The more one learns, as a general rule, the more one can remember. Reading books, talking to friends, and seeking new activities are fun ways to exercise the mind at any age. People adapt differently to recent memory loss. Some might compensate very well by carrying a notepad to jog the memory—keeping a written record of phone numbers, plans, and appointments. Another person might give in and permit what he or she perceives as senility to become a self-fulfilling prophecy. As is so often the case, positive attitudes and self-evaluations can lead to constructive, corrective actions.

Part of the mind/spirit's effect on healthy aging is direct and conscious. The extent to which we regard ourselves, take care of ourselves, determines whether we eat right, get enough sleep, smoke, wear seat belts, exercise, and so on. Each of these choices is conscious decisions of the mind, and controls probably 90 percent of the factors that determine our health.

SCHOTANUS, 1997

Memory retrieval skills may decline with age, but only if they are not used. If used, memory will be maintained or will even improve throughout one's lifetime. The memory expert Tony Busan (1991) advocates the use of mnemonics—techniques to improve memory. One technique is to use a vivid imagination, calling forth wild, colorful, and exaggerated images, even sexual ones, and associating them with important dates or items on a shopping list. A second technique is to use a linking system with a special list of key words to which all other items are linked.

Many studies of memory view the person as a machine that senses, acquires, processes, stores, and retrieves information. Using this image, older adults generally show a pattern of decline in the speed and efficiency with which they can process, store, and recall information. Movement from one task center to the next requires a complex set of psychoneurological communications. Error at any one of the points will create disruption in the remaining processing points. So, for example, if a person misinterprets the initial sensory information, it is moved to short-term memory (acquired), processed, stored in long-term memory, and ultimately retrieved inaccurately. Likewise, error might be introduced at any point along the way in the process.

If, however, the image of a well-oiled machine is substituted with an image that excludes speed and includes philosophy of life and the ability to integrate a lifetime of experiences, the older person makes gains with age. There may be a trade-off: an older individual may lose some details but gain a broader outlook. This has been referred to as the race between the bit and the byte, with older adults giving up the bit for the byte. We have just begun to explore the potential of the aging mind. Using our increased cultural-social knowledge, we may able to out-wit the biological limitations and deficits of old age (Baltes, 1993).

Psychopathology and the Myth of Senility

Psychopathology is the study of psychological disease, or, in other words, of mental disorders. Some mental disorders have a physical cause; others seem to be entirely emotional in nature. In still others, the physical and emotional aspects seem intertwined. A specific diagnosis, though difficult, is critical in the treatment of patients at any age.

Unfortunately, the term **senility** has been used as a catchall term for any mental disorder of the elderly. Any symptoms of confusion, anxiety, memory loss, or disorientation readily receive this label, and the labeling is done by people of all ages, including elders. Senility, however, is not an inevitable consequence of growing old. The word masks both the possibility of multiple causes of certain mental disorders and the fact that treatment for them may be available. In some cases, for example, persons diagnosed as senile actually suffer from thyroid deficiency. Thyroid hormone treatment eliminates the "senility." In other cases, the "senile" patient may be suffering from anorexia or emotional problems that antidepressant medication can alleviate.

It is particularly problematic when doctors and other health-care professionals accept the myth that the elderly become senile as a result of the aging process. This erroneous belief forms the basis for ignoring an older person's complaints, rather than attempting to diagnose the problem thoroughly. This tendency is not from disregard for the older person's well-being: it is due to medical professionals' generally inadequate training in geriatrics. In reality, the symptoms of "senility" have many causes. Older patients can show confusion and disorientation as a result of infection, pneumonia,

heart failure, heart attack, electrolyte imbalance, anemia, malnutrition, or dehydration—to name only a few causes. Older people more often have cognitive contraindications to drugs than do their younger counterparts, and they are more likely to be taking a multiplicity of drugs, including such "benign" over-the-counter drugs as decongestants. Another reason for **pseudo-senility** may be depression. Most mental illnesses can be more precisely described—and thereby treated—than the label "senile" suggests.

Functional Disorders

A reference book by the American Psychiatric Association (1994) designed to improve the diagnosis of psychiatric disorders is the *Diagnostic and Statistical Manual of Mental Disorders* (4th ed.), called *DSM-IV* for short. Psychologists use the term **functional disorder** to denote emotional problems of psychological, rather than physical, origin that interfere with daily functioning. Such disorders are more serious than the emotional problems (such as those based on widowhood or other loss) previously described. To differentiate among functional disorders, psychologists use the terms *anxiety disorders, depressive disorders, personality disorders, affective disorders,* and *schizophrenia.*

Anxiety Disorders

Anxiety is a cluster of feelings of uneasiness, nervousness, tension, and dread of the future. Trait anxiety is related to the individual's personality, and state anxiety is more related to a transitory situation. Persons with anxiety disorders tend to be anxious, rigid, or insecure personality types. There seem to be no age differences in either trait or state anxiety, as measured by psychological tests. **Anxiety disorders,** which are a clinically significant form of neurotic anxiety, are quite infrequent in elderly people (Kausler & Kausler, 1996). Among those elders with this disorder, however, it can be debilitating—especially when it is undiagnosed and assumed to be the result of aging.

Generalized anxiety disorder

When a person becomes so anxious that fear and dread of things or events begin to impair his or her ability to function, a **generalized anxiety disorder** is present, in which any real danger is exaggerated. An older person may fear being robbed or mugged. Consequently, he or she may not leave home; the person may get dozens of locks and constantly check them. Psychotherapeutic intervention would help this person face the threat—if actual—rationally and realistically.

Obsessive-compulsive disorder

A person obsessed with one act, such as washing the hands, walking back and forth across a room, looking for something, or touching something, exhibits **obsessive-compulsive disorder.** Persons who continually wash their hands may think they are dirty when they are not. The "dirt" may be internal—for example, repressed feelings of guilt that need to be resolved.

Phobia

A **phobia** is a fear that displaces fears that a person cannot face. Claustrophobia, the fear of being closed in, may, for example, mask a more potent fear, such as fear of death. Numerous kinds of phobias can manifest numerous fears, and left untreated, phobias can be especially limiting for an individual whose life circumstances includes other limits, such as physical frailty or impaired vision. Social phobias, characterized by the fear and avoidance of situations where an individual is subject to the scrutiny of others, have been shown to be more than 10-fold higher among first-degree relatives, implying a biological basis (Stein et al., 1998). A clear understanding of the relationship of biology with all phobias still eludes psychologists.

Depressive Disorders

Many people of all ages are depressed at times. A person with a **depressive disorder** feels sad, has low self-esteem, is lethargic, and believes that life is confusing, hopeless, or bereft of meaning. Physical symptoms may be insomnia or difficulty in sleeping, loss of appetite, or the inability to concentrate. Depression can be triggered by the death of family members, the loss of memory, or other disappointments accumulated over time. The person may or may not have had bouts of depression throughout his or her life. Most people over 65 who suffer from depression are not receiving any formal psychiatric treatment.

It is a common belief that older adults suffer from depression more than do younger adults. This belief, much like the belief that memory loss is a function of aging, is a myth. Early studies indicated that as much as 65 percent of the older population suffered from depression. It is now recognized that the tests used to obtain those scores were not valid for an older population. For example, emotional symptoms ("I feel sad") were included with physical symptoms ("I have difficulty sleeping"). Among younger adults a strong relationship exists between feelings of sadness and inability to sleep. Among older adults, it is now recognized, this relationship does not exist *necessarily.* More recent studies reveal that roughly 15 to 20 percent of older people suffer from mild (but noticeable) depression, and only 1 to 2 percent are clinically (severely) depressed (Kausler & Kausler, 1996). The incidence of clinical depression among older people (1 to 2 percent) is actually lower than among younger adults (4 percent) (Richardson & Hammond, 1996; Kant et al., 1997).

Depression can be treated, but first it has to be recognized. More mild forms often spontaneously disappear, but more severe (clinical) depression requires treatment. Treatment for older adults variously includes psychotherapy, especially cognitive therapy; chemical antidepressants, which can be problematic if the individual is taking any other medications; the administration of electroconvulsive therapy (ECT); or a combination of these treatments (Kausler & Kausler, 1996).

"Don't say bleed," says the Hypochondriac's First Aid Book, "say hemorrhage." This tongue-in-cheek advice sums up much of the hypochondriac's problem: it isn't that he or she imagines symptoms that don't exist; it's that they greatly overestimate the seriousness of those that do.

GREENHALGH, 1997

Hypochondria

A hypochondriac is someone who is overly concerned about his or her health. The person generally has bodily complaints for which no physical cause exists. He or she may be depressed, fear physical deterioration, need attention, or be otherwise expressing emotional issues through a series of somatic (body-oriented) complaints. Although the complaints may be real, the appropriate treatment involves dealing with the underlying emotional problem.

Personality Disorders

We age into the people we have been through our life course. Personality disorders are not characteristics of older people, but are characteristic of a group of people, some of whom have aged into late adulthood. This distinction becomes important when treatments are considered: a psychotherapeutic treatment plan for a young adult is not any more appropriate for an older adult than it is for a child.

Personality disorders are believed to occur in approximately 10 percent of the adult population, yet they are seldom diagnosed in primary care settings (Hueston et al., 1996). People who have developed extremely rigid styles of coping that make adaptive behavior difficult or impossible fall into the category of having **personality disorders.** People with personality disorders typically have held long-standing, maladaptive, and inflexible ways of relating to stress and the environment throughout adulthood. We can describe a number of personality types that lend themselves to disorders.

The *paranoid* personality is extremely suspicious and mistrustful, preoccupied with being alert to danger. A person with this personality tends to be stubborn, hostile, and defensive.

The *introverted* personality tends to be a solitary person who lacks the capacity for warm, close social relationships. Situations that call for high levels of social contact are especially stressful for the introverted individual.

The *antisocial* personality is characterized by a basically unsocialized behavior pattern that may conflict with society. Such people have difficulty with social situations that require cooperation and self-sacrifice.

These personality types and others involve behavior from childhood or adolescence that has become fixed and inflexible; for each, certain situations cause stress and unhappiness.

Affective Disorders

Affective disorders are sometimes called mood disorders because depression and mood swings are typical. *DSM-IV* uses the term bipolar disorder to describe behavior that includes both a depressed phase, characterized by sadness and slowed activity, and a manic phase, characterized by high levels of excitement and activity. An individual generally first manifests this type of disorder in his or her 20s and 30s. *Depression,* without the manic phase, is more common. Depression is most severe as an affective disorder; as an anxiety disorder, it is moderate. Some event—a great disappointment, for example—sets it off. For the older person, depression might follow the loss of a spouse or the onset of a terminal illness. In nonclinical depression, feelings of melancholy are normally appropriate for the situation; normally, the feelings will eventually wane. An inappropriate duration of depression and intense, continued sadness mark clinical depression.

Schizophrenia

Schizophrenia, another category of functional disorder, is more complicated, severe, and incapacitating than any of the disorders previously described. It may affect up to 1 percent of the general population (American Psychiatric Association, 1997). Schizophrenics typically suffer serious disturbances in thinking and behavior and are often unable to communicate coherently with others. Their language seems to be a means of self-expression rather than communication, and their talk is filled with irrelevancies. Feelings have no relation to verbal expression: fearful topics may be discussed with smiles; a bland topic may incite rage. Schizophrenia is characterized by an impaired contact with reality, at least during the disorder's active phases, and it often takes the form of hallucinations or delusions.

Late-life onset of schizophrenia is fairly rare; typically, the sufferer has evidenced the disorder in earlier years. Surprisingly little is known about the treatment needs of patients who remain symptomatic and functionally compromised in late life, despite the debilitating effects of the illness (Bartels et al., 1997). Older people with schizophrenia often develop cognitive impairment that seems similar to but less severe than that resulting from Alzheimer's disease (Davidson et al., 1995). Postmortem studies of tissue from patients who were chroni-cally hospitalized with schizophrenia, however, show notably little neurodegeneration or other pathology to explain the impairment (Arnold & Trojanowski, 1996). We apparently are not yet close to understanding the path of this devastating form of mental illness in late life.

Organic Mental Disorders

Organic disorders arise from a physical origin that impairs mental functioning. About 11 percent of older adults are believed to have mild disorders of this type (Vasavada et al., 1997), and geriatricians estimate that 6 percent of Americans over 65 have severe intellectual impairment based on physical causes. This rises to 20 percent for those over age 80 (Cohen, 1990), with some estimates running as high as 50 percent.

The difficulty in assessing the prevalence of dementia is partially due to the many different paths of brain disorder, including reversible and irreversible dementias with a multiplicity of causes and symptom clusters (Bowen et al., 1997). The diagnosis of dementia overlaps with a recently described mild cognitive impairment known as CIND, or "cognitive impairment, no dementia," which previously was believed to be a mild, initial form of dementia (Graham et al., 1997). **Dementia,** defined by the geriatrician Bruce Robinson, is

> *an acquired syndrome of progressive deterioration in global intellectual ability that interferes with the individual's ability to function in social and occupational roles.* **Global deterioration** *is . . . impairment in memory and at least one other cognitive category [such as language or visual/spatial ability].* (Robinson, 1997, p. 30)

An acute organic brain disorder is short-term and reversible. An infection, heart condition, drug reaction, liver condition, or malnutrition may cause an acute disorder. Anything that interferes with the nourishment of the brain— the supply of oxygen or nutrients through the bloodstream—can produce an acute disorder. If not treated promptly, it may become chronic.

Chronic organic disorders are brain disorders with a physical cause for which no cure is known. Such disorders characterize an irreversible, chronic, and progressive deterioration of the brain. One should not assume, however, that these disorders go hand in hand with old age; they do not. Organic brain disease is so debilitating for the minority who suffer it that we should direct our efforts to finding cures, rather than merely fostering acceptance. Of those with chronic brain disorders, 50 to 60 percent are living at home rather than in institutions and are being cared for by relatives and neighbors. More geriatric services would be helpful to all concerned.

The two manifestations of organic brain disorders are delirium and dementia, which are general terms for two syndromes or symptoms of organic brain disorders. Delirium is characterized by a lack of awareness about oneself and the surroundings, hallucinations, delusions, and disorientation. Caused by the atrophy and degeneration of brain cells, dementia was once labeled senility and was thought to accompany normal aging. Dementia is now no longer recognized as normal. Its symptoms can result from many disorders, though causes for many types of the disorder still remain a mystery. More than 10 forms of dementia have been identified—for example, years of alcohol abuse can lead to dementia. However, the largest contributor by far is Alzheimer's disease.

In the early stages of dementia, emotional responses to ordinary daily affairs, previously handled without difficulty, may be extreme to inappropriate. Memory, judgment, social functioning, and emotional control are impaired. Problems become more difficult to solve, and decisions become harder to make. One may lose interest in life and become apathetic or irritable. Further declines come as one has trouble receiving, retaining, and recalling new information. A newly acquired fact may be forgotten in minutes: a person may forget, for example, what he or she saw on a television program minutes after the program ends. As time passes, progressive disorganization of personality follows, accompanied by disorientation with respect to time, situation, and place. Some patients can no longer recognize even family, friends, and neighbors.

Did you know . . .
Alzheimer's disease is a major public health concern. It was added to the list of leading causes of death in the United States beginning with mortality data for 1994.

Alzheimer's Disease

The most common form of chronic organic brain disease, accounting for 70 percent of all such disease, is **Alzheimer's disease.** It is estimated to affect 4 million middle-aged and older persons in the United States. The standardization of diagnostic criteria has helped make estimates of the prevalence of this disease; however, estimates continue to vary widely, from 3 percent to 11 percent of those 65 years and older (Hoyert & Rosenberg, 1997).

In 1995 the disease was named on 41,419 death certificates for people of all ages, and 40,836 of those were people 65 years old and older. In 1995, Alzheimer's disease was the 14th leading cause of death for all ages combined and 9th for people age 65 and older (Hoyert & Rosenberg, 1997). The risk of developing Alzheimer's disease during one's lifetime depends on disease incidence and on life expectancy. The *incidence* of Alzheimer's disease (number of people who contract the disease) does not appear to be increasing. Its *prevalence,* however (proportion of people in a population), has increased because it is more commonly developed in later life, and more elders are living into late life. It seems to be more common among women than among men.

The Framingham Study estimated the lifetime risk of developing Alzheimer's disease and dementia based on their longitudinal population studies. For a 65-year-old woman, the lifetime risk was calculated to be 12 percent; for a man the same age, the risk was 6.3 percent. The cumulative risk was much higher from age 65 to 100, at 25.5 percent in men and 28.1 percent in women (Seshadri et al., 1997).

Named after the German physician Alois Alzheimer, who, in 1902, diagnosed the condition in a 51-year-old woman, the disease was thought to be rare and was relatively unknown as late as the 1970s. In the 1980s it emerged as the fourth leading cause of death among adults. As a result of this disease, the brain gradually atrophies, shrinking in both size and weight; neurons are lost; fibers become twisted in the neuron cell bodies; and abnormal masses develop. Affected individuals gradually lose their memory; their thought processes slow; their judgment is impaired; they develop speech disturbances; and they become disoriented. In the disease's more advanced stages, the individual suffers emotional disturbances, delusions, deterioration of personal and toilet habits, failing speech, and finally total loss of memory. This disease, which heightens anyone's fear of brain disorders, is tragic for all concerned.

The major symptoms of Alzheimer's disease are gradual declines in cognitive functioning (memory, learning, reaction time, word usage), disorientation, declines in self-care, and inappropriate social behavior such as violent outbursts. In the beginning the symptoms are mild and may mimic depression or mild paranoia, but they may develop into disruptive behaviors as the individual's cognition becomes increasingly damaged by the progression of the disease.

Extremely disruptive behaviors have been termed **catastrophic reaction,** occurring when the organism is unable to cope with a serious defect in physical and cognitive functions (Goldstein, 1980). A catastrophic reaction is defined as a "short-lasting emotional outburst characterized by anxiety, tears, aggressive behavior, swearing, displacement, refusal, renouncement, and/or compensatory boasting" embedded in physical and mental shock (Tiberti et al., 1998).

The cure for Alzheimer's disease continues to elude scientists, who hope to approach a cure by understanding more about its cause. The cause of the disease in 10 to 30 percent of people with Alzheimer's has been identified as genetic, and the fields of molecular biology and genetics currently lead the way into the 21st century for hope to finding a cure. Geneticists have discovered mutations in three different genes—APP, PS1, and PS2—which are associated with increased production of a protein that accumulates in the plaques of both "sporadic" (late onset) and familial cases of Alzheimer's disease (Haas & Selkoe, 1998).

Did you know . . .
Leaves from the ginkgo tree have been used by Chinese herbalists for several thousand years as a cure for memory problems. Research at New York Institute for Medical Research has recently found that 27 percent of people with Alzheimer's disease who took a 40-milligram ginkgo tablet for one year showed improvements in memory and social behavior. The improvements were equivalent to a 6-month delay in the progression of the disease. The results are comparable to the two drugs currently on the market to treat Alzheimer's disease.

HEALTH, 1997

In 1993, the genetic risk factor for late-onset sporadic and familial Alzheimer's was found to be in the apolipoprotein E (apoE) e4 allele. An eight-fold risk of developing the disease exists among those with this allele, compared to those bearing the common e3 allele (Corder et al. 1993, reported in Lamb et al., 1998). This breakthrough has been further developed to explore possibilities for accurate diagnosis, but reports recently published indicate that apoE genotyping does not provide sensitivity or specificity sufficient to allow it to be used alone for diagnosis (Mayeux et al., 1998).

The ethical issues of the potential for a sitting president to become a victim of Alzheimer's disease engaged a nation when former president Ronald Reagan's Alzheimer's disease was made public.

© AP/Wide World Photos

Some medical experts think it unlikely that Alzheimer's disease is the result of a single underlying cause. Genetic tracing is only part of a broad range of approaches targeting Alzheimer's disease, and research on all fronts must continue until cause and cure are determined. Exploring the possibility of environmental toxins, searching for a virus, looking at causes for the penetration of the blood-brain barrier—all of these factors continue to be explored in the search for a cure or the ability to slow the progression of the disease.

More positive news regarding Alzheimer's disease, however, is emerging. Two teams of scientists from California and from Sweden have identified brain scan and spinal fluid markers of Alzheimer's risk years before any measurable cognitive change is apparent (Seppa, 2006). Early diagnosis could increase the time available to treat the disease. According to William Jagust at the University of California, Berkeley, many people believe that treatments for Alzheimer's will be available by 2011 (Seppa, 2006). The drugs currently available to treat the disease ease its symptoms, but do not slow its progression.

Among the most intensive areas of therapeutic intervention are currently the role of cholinesterase inhibitors (tacrine HCl, donepezil, metrifonate), the possibility of hormonal control (especially estrogen), and the effect of anti-inflammatory agents, along with other approaches such as antioxidants, calcium channel blockers, and nerve growth factor (D'Epiro, 1996).

Because at this writing a preventive measure or cure for Alzheimer's disease has yet to be discovered, attention must be directed toward improving the functioning of the ailing person and helping family members to cope. The disease is gradual and progressive; the length of survival ranges from 2 to 20 years. Several stages are involved—some say seven stages: (1) normal; (2) forgetfulness; (3) early confusional; (4) late confusional; (5) early dementia; (6) middle dementia; and (7) late dementia.

Did you know . . .
The University of Kentucky Nun Study has found that women who scored poorly on measures of cognitive ability as young adults were at higher risk of Alzheimer's disease and poor cognitive function in late life. Of those nuns with confirmed Alzheimer's who died, 90 percent had low linguistic ability in early life, compared with only 13 percent of those without evidence of the disease.

NATIONAL INSTITUTES OF HEALTH, 1996

In the first stages, cognitive declines are not readily apparent. A midway stage is characterized by recent memory loss and personality changes. For example, a person may become hopelessly lost while walking to a close and familiar location. Abstract thinking can also become impaired; the difference between an apple and an orange can become confusing, for example. Ailing individuals are typically aware of their intellectual decline, becoming anxious, depressed, or angry.

The next stages of Alzheimer's disease advance the deterioration of thought processes. Further memory loss and drastic mood swings are common. Speaking may become difficult, and paranoid symptoms may appear. During this stage, complications often force the patient to relocate to housing where care is provided. He or she may have trouble remembering close family members.

The final stage is terminal and usually very brief, lasting one year or less. Though many Alzheimer's patients at this stage stop eating and communicating and are unaware of their surroundings, the year, or the season, they are still sensitive to love, affection, and tenderness. This is an enormously stressful time for friends and relatives; it is at this stage that they are most in need of support groups and counseling.

Multi-Infarct Dementia (MID)

Rising from problems with blood flow to the brain, this vascular dementia is caused by a series of small strokes (infarcts) that damage brain tissue over time. The disease is typically chronic, and a person may live with it for many years. For most, impairment is intermittent, occurring when he or she has one of these small strokes, so small that the sufferer is unaware of them. A patient may have sudden attacks of confusion but then recover. Another may remember something one minute, then forget it the next. Gait difficulty, urinary incontinence, and palsy may accompany dementia symptoms. The brain area in which the stroke occurs corresponds with the impaired ability.

Alcoholism

Lifelong alcoholism or the onset of alcoholism in late life may yield changes that indicate a dementia syndrome. For example, chronic alcoholism may cause Wernicke-Korsakoff syndrome, a type of dementia resulting from the lack of vitamin B12, which results in memory loss and disorientation.

Creutzfeld-Jacob Disease

Creutzfeld-Jacob disease, though far less common and much more rapid than Alzheimer's, follows a similar course. Within a year, the cerebral cortex degenerates to a fatal point in the sufferer. Scientists suggest that an infectious agent, possibly a virus, may be involved.

Parkinson's Disease

Parkinson's disease, which can lead to dementia, affects close to 1 million individuals in the United States. Rarely diagnosed before age 40, it increases in prevalence among those between the ages of 50 and 79. Tremors and rigidity of movement characterize the disease. Parkinson's progresses through stages, and some sufferers are eventually confined to bed or a wheelchair. Between 20 and 30 percent of patients develop dementia. Parkinson's has been treated with some success using the drug L-dopa, which relieves symptoms but is not thought to slow the progression of the disease (de Rijk et al., 1995; Turjanski et al., 1997).

Huntington's Disease

A rare disease, Huntington's disease is inherited as a defective gene. Its most famous victim was Woody Guthrie (1912–1967), a popular folksinger and composer. The disease starts unnoticed in one's 30s or 40s and proceeds over a 12- to 15-year period, ending like Alzheimer's disease with total deterioration of memory and bodily functions.

Caring for the Mentally Ill

Care for mentally ill elders can be provided in clinical settings of mental health professionals, hospitals, institutions for the mentally ill, nursing homes, or the homes of relatives. Some environments are supportive of mentally ill elders, whereas others are hostile or indifferent. Those who are mentally ill, whether living in group homes or boarding homes, have been shown to benefit by

1. Activities to keep them busy, such as music, dance, cards, and handiwork
2. Activities to get them outside the setting and into the community—even if only to have a cup of coffee
3. Programs and goals of reducing dependency and getting them out of a conforming, passive rut

Comparisons of U.S. and Canadian funding and organization of psychiatric services for elders find services to be more accessible in Canada because of universal health insurance. In Canada, for acute mental health problems hospital benefits are free of charge. The many limitations posed by Medicare in the United States do not exist there. However, in both countries, the small number of professionals trained and interested in the mental health of the elderly limits such services. In both countries, long-term care is generally inadequate, especially for those with serious behavioral disturbances.

Beginning in the mid-1970s, high-cost institutions offering basic, non-therapeutic care "dumped" the mentally ill. The ousted older persons either wandered around trying to find a place in the community or were placed in nursing homes, where they often received inadequate treatment for mental illness. Elders who were once custodial residents in mental hospitals are now cared for in nursing homes, often with not even a pretense of psychiatric care.

The burden can be great on families caring for the mentally ill elderly at home. Caretakers cannot expect expanded government programs in the immediate future; if anything, programs are being curbed. Gerontologists are looking to volunteer programs and family support groups to help the elderly infirm and their families. Fortunately, support groups for caretakers of patients with Alzheimer's and other dementias are often available and highly beneficial.

Outreach programs can serve the mental health needs of elders very effectively. A program in Iowa, for example, on request sent workers to the homes of rural mentally ill aged, most of whom were single women between the ages of 65 and 85, living alone and experiencing depression, some form of dementia, and/or adjustment problems. The program, which assessed clients, then treated them or referred them to more professional help, was deemed a success in helping older persons and in keeping them out of institutions (J. Buckwalter et al., 1993). Just about any form of therapeutic assistance is more help than many older people with histories of chronic mental illness have received in the past 15 years in the United States.

Community networks—cadres of "good people"—have helped tremendously by forming volunteer programs designed to consider the unique needs of mentally ill elders, and in organizing the assistance of friends, other residents, and family members. Through network building, programs can be expanded to involve churches, schools, and senior citizen groups in caring for the mentally ill in institutions or at home.

Peer counseling is a somewhat similar concept. Older persons are trained by a professional to reach out to other elders in need of mental health services. These volunteer peer counselors are taught to deal with a variety of problems, to offer advice, and to serve as a bridge, through referrals, to more formal mental health services. In some communities, peer counselors have organized hotlines for elders in crisis.

Good Mental Health

Most older people have good mental health. One safeguard against emotional debilitation in later years is good mental health in youth and middle age. Many mental disorders in old age represent continuing problems that have gone untreated. A second safeguard against emotional debilitation in old age is to maintain an active interest in life and to keep one's mind stimulated. A third safeguard is to seek professional health-care services when they are needed.

Getting mental health care is less likely in the older years. Ageism perpetuates the myth that mental illness in old age is untreatable. The problems of younger persons have often received more priority in mental hospitals, community organizations, and other care organizations. Older people are also more reluctant to seek help. But the mental health of the elders is beginning to receive more attention. More geriatric specialists are offering encouragement and assisting those older individuals with mild emotional problems or more severe disorders. Sharp criticism has occurred of the application of psychotropic drugs to the mental health problems of older people. Older persons do not have to tolerate depression, anxiety, or other disorders any more than younger persons do, nor must they be drugged into zombielike states in lieu of appropriate therapeutic attention. Depression and anxiety are pathologies that can be treated and cured.

At every point in our lives, we can have the goal of maximizing our potential. Even a person in a very debilitated mental state can generally respond to help. For example, individuals suffering from advanced organic brain syndrome can benefit from "reality orientation": reviewing the day of the week, one's location, and one's name. Human contact, a touch or a hug, also adds meaning to life.

Caretakers in the field of mental health can work toward maximizing a patient's potential. In the On Loc Nursing Home in San Francisco, even the most impaired attend programs, form friendships, and are encouraged to attend music groups, old movies, and arts and crafts workshops. They are fully dressed in street clothes every day, even though most are incontinent. In this hospital, the worker's goal is to help patients reach and maintain maximum functioning potential. With a constantly deteriorating patient, specific goals may have to be adjusted downward; but if the goal is to see Mrs. Smith smile or to hear Mr. Juarez sing, the task remains rewarding.

Community mental health clinics (CMHCs) are mandated to serve the old as well as the young, yet a disproportionately small number of older persons use these services. Medicare pays only a minimal amount for outpatient mental care. A tragic irony exists in that although nursing homes represent a major setting for mentally ill elders, they receive, for the most part, inadequate mental health care in these homes. Geriatric mental health is an evolving field desperately in need of growth and improvement.

Chapter Summary

The psychology of aging is a broad field covering cognition and its many aspects: perception, sensory input, information processing, psychomotor speed, intelligence, learning, and memory. Older persons generally suffer a decline in reaction time, but not necessarily in intelligence, learning, memory, and other areas. Mental health problems may be functional (have no physical basis) or organic (have a physical basis). Functional disorders may be moderately debilitating, as with a temporary emotional problem, or they may be quite severe, as with a psychotic breakdown. The most common form of organic brain disease is Alzheimer's disease. The bulk of the aged are in good mental health. A substantial minority of elders need mental health care by a professional.

Key Terms

affective disorders
age-related changes
Alzheimer's disease
anxiety disorders
biologically caused
    changes
catastrophic reaction
classic aging pattern
cognition
cognitive mechanics
cognitive pragmatics
cognitive process
    approach
crystallized intelligence
dementia
depressive disorder
divided attention
five senses, the
fluid intelligence
functional disorder
generalized anxiety
    disorders
information processing
intelligence

learning
memory
obsessive-compulsive
    disorder
organic disorders
perception
personality disorders
phobia
primary memory
primary mental
    abilities
pseudo-senility
psychometric approach
psychomotor speed
schizophrenia
secondary memory
selective attention
senility
sensation
sensory memory
sensory threshold
terminal drop
tertiary memory
working memory

Questions for Discussion

1. How does age affect intelligence, learning, and memory? How would you design a training program that would permit the capable older worker to retrain under the least stressful circumstances and to demonstrate capability?

2. What personality variables would you choose to examine in a longitudinal study of adults throughout their lives? Why?

3. Based on your present personality, what emotional problems do you anticipate in your old age?

4. How would you respond to being told you had a chronic brain disease?

5. Why do high numbers of older men commit suicide?

Fieldwork Suggestions

1. Put in earplugs and a thick pair of gloves as you go through your daily routine. Note the loss of sensory perceptions and how these losses influence your ability to function and to do things for yourself. Are you treated well by other people? Are you hesitant about going out in public? How long are you able to withstand the sensory loss? Did you find any ways to compensate for it?

2. Call your county mental health agency to find out what services are available for elders.

3. Interview a mental health worker. Ask him or her what mental disorders older people seek treatment for. Is there a percentage breakdown?

Internet Exercises

1. Locate the Internet site for the Alzheimer's Disease and Associated Disorders Association (ADRDA), and research two therapeutic treatments for the disease. Are you able to tell whose perspective represents the information you have found? (For example, was it developed by academicians or by a pharmaceutical company?) How useful is the level of material to you?

2. Find all that you can about learning from as many different sources as possible. Keep a journal of your search. Which locations are the most useful? Was it easy or more difficult for you to gather a range of material? Did your search provide you with cross-cultural resources? Cross-species resources?

3. Develop a list of Internet address links that you would use if you were designing a home page on learning and memory in later life.

12

The Oldest Old and Caregiving

The Oldest Old

Informal Caregiving

Elder Caregiving to Adult Children and Grandchildren

Solving Caregiving Problems

Alone Time with Pets Helps Seniors

Dogs apparently need no help lifting the spirits of lonely people. A study has found that nursing home residents felt much less lonely after spending time alone with a dog than when other people joined in the visit. The residents shared their problems and story in "intimate conversations" with the visiting dog, researchers said.

"It was a pretty surprising finding," said Dr. William Banks of Saint Louis University, who co-authored the study with his wife, Marian Banks, a postdoctoral fellow in nursing at Washington University at the time.

"They were happier with the one-on-one . . . bonding with the animal. It suggests human interaction is not value-added, and might be slightly detrimental."

Residents at three St. Louis nursing homes who said they wanted dog visits were divided into two groups. One group received one-on-one visits with a dog; the other group shared the dog visitor with several other residents.

Researchers suspected the visiting dog would prompt socialization—and reduce loneliness—but the residents who shared dog visits with other people reported only slightly less loneliness. The big winners were the residents who had exclusive visits with dogs. Their loneliness decreased substantially.

The research will be published in the March issue of *Anthrozoos*.

"The study also found that the loneliest individuals benefited the most from visits with dogs," William Banks said.

An earlier phase of the study, conducted by Marian Banks in Mississippi in 1997, found that nursing home residents who received one to three dog visits a week had substantial decreases in loneliness, as measured in a psychological test instrument known as the UCLA loneliness scale.

Those without dog visits had no change in loneliness.

The next phase of the study, at Saint Louis University, will look at whether robotic dogs popular in Japan have a similar effect on lonely seniors. Researchers will measure both residents' loneliness and ability to attach to the robotic dog.

Marian Banks said a Japanese study showed that the robotic dog, Aibo, elicited smiles from Alzheimer's patients.

Marian Banks said she used an academic mentor's golden retriever to conduct the first phase of the study in Mississippi.

But for the second and third studies in St. Louis, she's used Sparky, a mixed-breed dog she found four years ago in the alley behind her house.

She said his sweet disposition won her over, and she adopted and trained him. She said Sparky sits next to nursing home residents on their bed, listens to their stories, and lets them groom him.

"He sits there very nonjudgmental," she said.

"When they go to a nursing home, they lose all their possessions. They need to belong, love and be accepted. The dog gives unconditional love. They say the most incredible things in the presence of a dog."

As the population of the old old has mush-roomed, caregiving to an older person within a family setting has become more common. Informal caregiving usually precedes and sometimes accompanies or replaces the formal caregiving offered by hospitals and other institutional settings. We have no clear-cut norms or customs dictating care for older family members who need help in caring for themselves. This chapter examines the oldest old population and the caregiving that is offered in a family context.

The Oldest Old

Recently, researchers have begun separating old-age groups in their studies. As early as 1974, Bernice L. Neugarten separated the older population into the young old (age 65 to 74) and the old old (age 75 and over). Before that, studies considered all the elderly together, obscuring important differences and offering little insight into the social realities of the oldest old. Other terms for the oldest old have also come into use, and they may have slightly different meanings: the very old, the extreme aged, the dependent elderly, and the frail elderly. These terms, often used interchangeably, need to be clarified when they are used. There is no clear-cut time at which gerontologists all agree that one joins the oldest old, and the discussion in this chapter reflects that fact. Here age 75 and over and age 85 and over are both used at different times to identify the oldest old, depending on the studies cited. As longevity and the proportion of very old elders increases, however, oldest old is coming more commonly to refer to people age 85 and over.

Figure 12.1 shows the percentage distribution of four age groups among those 65 and over, the two oldest groups being those 75 to 84 and those 85 and older, for the years 1998 and 2050 (projected). People age 85 and older are the fastest growing segment of the older population, currently representing nearly 12 percent of the all Americans age 65 or older. Table 12.1 shows the projected number of people 65, 75, and 85

and older for approximately the next 100 years. Note that the number of people over 85 years of age will be more than five times as great in 2100 as in 1995; the number will be nearly one and one-half times greater in 2100 than in 2050. The table shows that were 3.8 million people age 85 and older in 1995 in the United States—a huge number, relative to existing social policy (U.S. Social Security Administration, 1997).

Another 46 percent of the older population were in the 75-to-84 age range in 1997. In the year 2000, those age 75 and older comprised 48 percent, or nearly half, of the aged population. Thus, the needs of elders age 75 and older will weigh more heavily in the future as their number and percentage of the population increase. As a society we will need to provide a viable lifestyle for this burgeoning group.

People do not necessarily decrease in functional ability with age, however. **Robust aging** is sometimes called "successful aging." It refers to aging while maintaining good mental and physical status. The most robustly aging people have certain characteristics in common: they report far more social contact than those who are not aging well, they have better health and vision, and they have experienced fewer life events in the past three years than their less well compatriots (Garfein & Herzog, 1995).

Physical Health

The 75-to-84 age group is, by and large, healthier and happier than stereotypes would have us believe. In fact, the general consensus seems to be that physical losses in old age do not begin taking a heavy toll until after age 85. The 85-and-older group uses approximately 10 times as many hospital days as those age 45 to 64, whereas those 75 and over use about 4.5 times as many (U.S. Bureau of the Census, 2001). An 85-year-old is 2.5 times more likely to enter a nursing home than is a 75-year-old.

In one of the first longitudinal studies of the health and well-being of elders (median age just under 89 years) conducted in the 1980s, only

FIGURE 12.1

Percentage of older Americans by age group

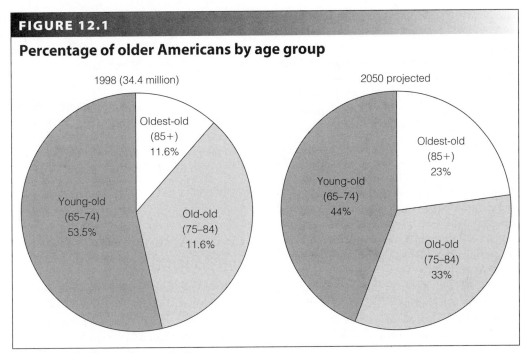

1998 (34.4 million)

Oldest-old (85+) 11.6%
Young-old (65–74) 53.5%
Old-old (75–84) 11.6%

2050 projected

Oldest-old (85+) 23%
Young-old (65–74) 44%
Old-old (75–84) 33%

Source: U.S. Administration on Aging, 2000.

TABLE 12.1

United States aged population, projected (in millions)

Age in Years	1995	2000	2025	2050	2075	2100
65 and over	34.2	35.4	60.8	74.1	83.7	89.9
75 and over	15.1	16.8	25.1	39.3	45.9	50.6
85 and over	3.8	4.4	6.3	14.7	16.9	20.1

Source: Social Security Administration, Office of Programs: Data from the Office of the Actuary, Washington, DC.

moderate declines in mental, physical, and daily living functions were found over a 10-year period (Palmore et al., 1985). The findings contradict the gloomy view held at that time that the old old experience rapid decline. In the 1990s, a mere 20 years after the first wave of the study cited above, it became clear that traditional views of aging needed rethinking. It is now recognized that people who do not suffer from illnesses or severe impairments can exhibit a broad range of healthfulness and well-being. People in their 90s and older are often very healthy and robust—and the population of centenarians grew by 160 percent in the United States during the 1980s (Perls, 1995).

Did you know . . .
Among people 65 to 79, women seem to have a slight advantage over men in cognitive abilities. A gender crossover seems to occur between the ages of 80 and 89, however, after which men are on average higher than their female counterparts. This occurs because men who are cognitively impaired generally die earlier than do women, leaving mainly mentally intact men to live into later life.

PERLS, 1995

The health of the oldest old is a basic concern. A critical measure of health is whether a person can manage daily activities alone or requires the help of others. A measure of **functional ability** is the ability to do **personal activities of daily living** (PADLs or ADLs) without help. These include bathing, eating, dressing, toileting, transferring oneself in and out of a bed or chair, and walking or getting around inside the home (see Figure 12.2). A second measure of functional disability is the ability to do **instrumental activities of daily living** (IADLs) such as shopping, housework, money management, and meal preparation (see Figure 12.3). Fewer than half of the oldest old (85 and over) need some help in performing ADLs, and about 60 percent need help with IADLs.

The oldest old have a number of chronic and disabling conditions. The most common are bone and joint problems, heart disease, osteoporosis, vision and hearing problems, mental impairment, drug intoxication (from prescribed drugs), falls, and urinary incontinence (National Center for Health Statistics [NCHS], 1999).

In spite of the chronic conditions associated with old age, many of the oldest old have no functional limitations: that is, their chronic diseases do not keep them from living alone and doing their own personal and household chores. A recent study of people over 85 years of age and living in home settings found good to excellent functioning in mental and social domains, with the largest functional impairments having to do with physical functioning (Krach et al., 1996). Common chronic diseases in this group were arthritis, hypertension, and cardiac problems. The elders in this study reported that they needed visiting nurses, home health aides, and help with shopping and transportation to maintain themselves. The implications for society of robust longevity are vastly important. As a result of better ways of life and medical advances, the "new" model of living into very old age might work to compress morbidity, mortality, and disability into a shorter period of time at the very end of the life span. This means that as

the old become very old, the massive drain on the economy to care for a growing population of frail, disabled older people that some people predict and fear will not happen.

> *As a result of . . . demographic [changes] and work-force trends, the long-term care industry has boomed over the past few decades, from just over 500,000 nursing home beds in 1963 to 1.7 million today.*
>
> COOPER, 1998

Living Arrangements and Marital Status

Only a small percentage of the oldest old are institutionalized. Of the oldest old, those age 85 and over, more than 50 percent still live at home. More than 35 percent live alone at home; in fact, about 75 percent of those 85 and over are widowed. An estimated 25 percent of the oldest old live in the household of an adult child or other person (usually a relative), and another 21 percent reside in nursing homes. For the oldest old, the most critical need in the future will be for programs and policies that reduce the risk of dependence and promote self-determination. If housing were more affordable and home help services more available, more people could live in their own homes. Most people live in their own homes. Not until elders reach age 90 are there more than 50 percent who cannot live independently. However, much of the help needed is not covered by Medicare. For example, if a medical diagnosis is osteoarthritis of the knees, the primary problem is trouble with walking. Although the problem is medical, and some help involves pain medication (to control but not cure), major help is needed with shopping and self-maintenance. Such categories of help are not "treatments" and therefore are not covered by Medicare.

The marital status of men and women at the upper age levels afford a dramatic comparison,

FIGURE 12.2

Activities of daily living (ADL) index

Physical Self-Maintenance Scale (PSMS)

Subject's Name _____ Rated by _____ Date _____

Circle one statement in each category A–F that applies to subject.

A. *Toilet*
   1. Cares for self at toilet completely, no incontinence
   2. Needs to be reminded or needs help in cleaning self, or has rare (weekly at most) accidents.
   3. Soiling or wetting while asleep more than once a week.
   4. Soiling or wetting while awake more than once a week.
   5. No control of bowels or bladder.

B. *Feeding*
   1. Eats without assistance.
   2. Eats with minor assistance at meal times and/or with special preparation of food, or help in cleaning up after meals.
   3. Feeds self with moderate assistance and is untidy.
   4. Requires extensive assistance for all meals.
   5. Does not feed self at all and resists efforts of others to feed him/her.

C. *Dressing*
   1. Dresses, undresses, and selects clothing from own wardrobe.
   2. Dresses and undresses self, with minor assistance.
   3. Needs moderate assistance in dressing or selection of clothes.
   4. Needs major assistance in dressing, but cooperates with efforts of others to help.
   5. Completely unable to dress self and resists efforts of others to help.

D. *Grooming* (neatness, hair, nails, hands, face, clothing)
   1. Always neatly dressed, well-groomed, without assistance.
   2. Grooms self adequately with occasional minor assistance, e.g., shaving.
   3. Needs moderate and regular assistance or supervision in grooming.
   4. Needs total grooming care, but can remain well-groomed after help from others.
   5. Actively negates all efforts of others to maintain grooming.

E. *Physical Ambulation*
   1. Goes about grounds or city.
   2. Ambulates within residence or about one block distant.
   3. Ambulates with assistance of (check one) a. another person _____ b. railing _____ c. cane _____ d. walker _____
      e. wheelchair _____
   4. Sits unsupported in chair or wheelchair, but cannot propel self without help.
   5. Bedridden more than half the time.

F. *Bathing*
   1. Bathes self (tub, shower, sponge bath) without help.
   2. Bathes self with help in getting in and out of tub.
   3. Washes face and hands only, but cannot bathe rest of body.
   4. Does not wash self, but is cooperative with those who bathe him/her.
   5. Does not try to wash self, and resists efforts to keep him/her clean.

Source: Adapted by M. Powell Lawton, Ph.D., Director of Research, Philadelphia Geriatric Center, Philadelphia, from *Older Americans Resource and Assessment Multidimensional Functional Assessment Questionnaire.*

Instrumental activities of daily living (IADL) scale

Name _____ Rated by _____ Date _____

1. Can you use the telephone
   without help, — 3
   with some help, or — 2
   are you completely unable to use the
   telephone? — 1

2. Can you get to places beyond walking
   distance without help, — 3
   with some help, or — 2
   are you completely unable to travel unless
   special arrangements are made? — 1

3. Can you go shopping for groceries
   without help, — 3
   with some help, or — 2
   are you completely unable to do any
   shopping? — 1

4. Can you prepare your own meals
   without help, — 3
   with some help, or — 2
   are you completely unable to prepare any
   meals? — 1

5. Can you do your own housework
   without help, — 3
   with some help, or — 2
   are you completely unable to do any
   housework? — 1

6. Can you do your own handyman work
   without help, — 3
   with some help, or — 2
   are you completely unable to do any
   handyman work? — 1

7. Can you do your own laundry
   without help, — 3
   with some help, or — 2
   are you completely unable to do
   any laundry at all? — 1

8a. Do you take medicines or use any medications?
   Yes (If yes, answer Question 8b.) — 1
   No (If no, answer Question 8c.) — 2

8b. Do you take your own medicine
   without help (in the right doses at the
   right time), — 3
   with some help (if someone prepares it for you
   and/or reminds you to take it), or — 2
   you are completely unable to take your own
   medicine? — 1

8c. If you had to take medicine, could you do it
   without
   help (in the right doses at the right time), — 1
   with some help (if someone prepared it for you
   and/or reminded you to take it), or — 2
   would you be completely unable to take your
   own medicine? — 3

9. Can you manage your own money
   without help, — 3
   with some help, or — 2
   are you completely unable to manage money? — 1

The IADL Scale evaluates more sophisticated functions than the ADL Index (see Figure 12.2). Patients or caregivers can complete the form in a few minutes. The first answer in each case—except for 8a—indicates independence; the second, capability with assistance; and the third, dependence. In this version the maximum score is 29, although scores have meaning only for a particular patient, as when declining scores over time reveal deterioration. Questions 4–7 tend to be gender-specific: modify them as you see fit.

Source: Adapted with permission from M. Powell Lawton, Ph.D. Director of Research, Philadelphia Geriatric Center, Philadelphia, from *Older Americans Resource and Assessment Multidimensional Functional Assessment Questionnaire.*

with the oldest old women much more likely to be widowed and the oldest old men more likely to be married, indicating that among women the percentage of widows is dramatically higher than is the percentage of widowers among men. Nearly 36 percent of women aged 65 to 74 are widowed. The majority of women 75 and over are widowed (65 percent), whereas the majority of men (70 percent, in fact) in the same age group are married. Widowhood is the predominant lifestyle for women 75 and over (U.S. Bureau of the Census, 2001).

Evaluation of Life

A study of the oldest old, those age 85 and over, revealed that at some point between 80 and 90 years of age, individuals became willing to describe themselves as "old" (Bould et al., 1989). There is a definite awareness that the spirit is willing, but the body is unable to cooperate. Malcolm Cowley (1980), who wrote of his personal experience with aging in *The View from Eighty*, describes this reality:

- Everything takes longer to do—bathing, shaving, getting dressed or undressed
- Travel becomes more difficult and you think twice before taking out the car
- Many of your friends have vanished . . .
- There are more and more little bottles in the medicine cabinet . . .
- (You hesitate) on the landing before walking down a flight of stairs
- (You spend) more time looking for things misplaced than using them . . .
- It becomes an achievement to do thoughtfully, step by step, what (you) once did instinctively

Evaluations of reality vary with one's age and life view. People age 85 and over who are in good health, living at home, and still driving feel lucky in life thanks to the absence of limitations. A study of 12 centenarians found a sense of comparison to be an important part of the evaluation of life: "I'm doing pretty good for my age" was a commonly heard remark (Pascucci & Loving, 1997). **Life satisfaction** is the sense of well-being experienced and identified by the individual; it cannot be recorded by measures external to the individual. To a certain extent, satisfaction in later life seems to depend on an elder's sense of self-efficacy—the extent to which a person is able to master the environment effectively and feel a sense of control in life (Jacob & Guarnaccia, 1997).

Most life satisfaction studies have focused on the young old and show that life satisfaction does not particularly change over time for an individual. This implies that life satisfaction is more a personal way of seeing the world than something affected by current circumstances. Measuring life satisfaction, however, is difficult to do—some researchers believe that self-reported measures of life satisfaction are superficial and do not actually measure an individual's subjective experience of well-being (Hogan & Nicholson, 1988; Euler, 1992). Gerontologists generally believe that phenomenological methods (interviews in which the subject's own words are used to define well-being) are more useful in studying quality of life and life satisfaction among older people.

A greater number of longitudinal studies of the old old would help us to better understand this age group. Life may or may not be different as one progresses from age 75 to 85 to 95 to 100. Among the "one hundred over 100" (Heynen, 1990) interviewed for a book about centenarians, full and meaningful lives were the norm. No single factor predicted who would live to be over 100. Some were smokers, worrywarts, or non-exercisers. Some were homebodies, others travelers. Some were religious fanatics, others skeptics. Old people are as varied a group as are younger people—there are just fewer of them, and their activities and therefore their interests are generally more limited. Studies of the very old continue to identify themes of good health, good coping patterns, and a strong sense of well-being throughout life (Poon, 1992; Wallis, 1995; Aquino et al., 1996; Krach et al., 1996; Pascucci & Loving, 1997) These qualities do *not* imply the jolly, twinkly-eyed old person of popular stereotype, however. Common qualities of the very old also include being completely willing to voice an opposing opinion if need be and being an assertive voice for self-care. The very old are a group of people who have survived because of the combination of (1) their genetic makeup, (2) the lifestyles they have both chosen and been blessed with throughout their lives, and (3) personality characteristics having to do with taking care of themselves physically, psychologically, socially, and spiritually. They are generally people who are able to experience joy in surviving and appreciation for what is available to them.

Informal Caregiving

Among those elders requiring assistance in living, a great number receive in-home care from relatives. Although the numbers vary depending on definitions, at least 17 percent of all non-institutionalized elders are in need of help. This percentage more than doubles for those age 85 and over. For every disabled person who resides in a nursing home, two or more equally impaired aged live with and are cared for by their families (Brody, 1990). An even larger number of people provide help to old people who do not share their households.

There is a myth that the extended family, especially the three-generation family, was common in the 1700s and 1800s. In fact, the three-generation family was more common in the twentieth century than it was in the two centuries before. The primary reason is due to demographics: more elders are alive today. Five percent of U.S. children today live with their grandparents or other relatives. In a third of these homes neither parent is present (Minkler & Roe, 1993). In 1993, 19 percent of all women 70 and over lived with someone other than their spouse, as did just under 7 percent of all men (U.S. Bureau of the Census, 2000). Of those, just over 12 percent of women and 4 percent of men lived with a child or children (Soldo et al., 1997). The preferred living arrangement of elders, however, is independently from adult children. The trend over the last several decades has been to encourage such independence, with more care being provided in the homes of elders, not in the homes of the adult children.

Informal caregiving is caregiving comes from relationships that exist naturally in a person's environment, such as family, friends, church,

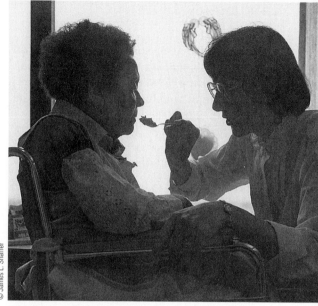

Contrary to popular belief, Americans feel a tremendous responsibility for their frail and aging parents. The tasks of caregiving can be enormous for people with careers and responsibilities for their own children.

and organizations that are not professional or financed by the government (members of a garden club, for example). The care is given by "lay" members of society, while formal care is provided by "professionals" (Pickens, 1998). **Formal caregiving** includes health care professionals, hospitals, and day care centers and nursing homes. Staff are professionals or paraprofessionals and are paid for their caregiving.

The stress of caring for a frail, disabled person is very costly in human terms among both formal and informal caregivers, but particularly for informal family caregivers, whose psychological relationship with the care recipient is generally intense and complex. It is not uncommon for an elderly caregiving spouse to die, leaving the "frail" spouse behind. Informal caregiving is most commonly carried out by a spouse, and when no spouse is available, by a daughter.

From a statistical perspective, the typical caregiver is a 46-year-old working woman who spends 18 hours a week caring for her chronically ill 77-year-old mother who lives nearby. Forty-one percent of caregivers also care for their own children under the age of 18 (Cooper, 1998). Most caregivers get help—usually from a son, daughter, or other relative—in providing services such as transportation, grocery shopping, and household chores for their relative (Adams, 1998). Despite the myth of the nonfunctional nuclear family, research has found that families generally work hard together to provide care for a frail member. That care adds a heavy toll on family caregivers, but it occurs nevertheless.

Obligations of Adult Children to Parents

The **modified nuclear family** concept describes the typical American situation. There is a great deal of family interaction—for example, visiting and exchanges of gifts and services—but no extended family household. Most elders live in separate households but are not cut off from their families. However, the standard indicators used to measure family interaction do not measure emotional closeness, nor do they measure how responsible the family feels for frail, older parents.

It's just really, really hard. It was a year and a half of unbelievable sandwich-generation problems. With the best will in the world you aren't necessarily doing the best thing because you don't know what that is. What worked yesterday won't work today, but how you're supposed to figure it out, I don't know.

ADULT CHILD CAREGIVER,
REPORTED IN COOPER, 1998

Gerontologists observe that there are no clear cultural guidelines, no specific norms for behavior, in the area of intergenerational relationships between elderly parents and adult children. Some older parents expect that (1) married children should live close to parents; (2) children should take care of sick parents; (3) if children live nearby, they should visit their parents often; and (4) children who live at a distance should write or call their parents often. Indeed, that is why the phrase "modified extended family" has been used—it describes families that keep close ties even though they do not share households. These norms or expectations of close relationships are adhered to in the typical American family.

He doesn't know us anymore. But every time I go to say goodbye it kills me. I'm so sick of saying goodbye. . . . One time when the doctors told us he wouldn't make it through the night, my mother and I actually made funeral arrangements. . . . It was so hard. I grieved. I mourned. He didn't die—and I actually got angry. I was like—when is this going to end? Of course I felt guilty.

DAUGHTER, QUOTED IN MCCARTY, 1996

Extreme financial or physical dependence of aged family members tests the limits of adult children's sense of responsibility. In seeking to determine whether there is a solid moral underpinning for filial responsibility, Canadian researchers used the vignettes in Figure 12.4 to elicit adult children's sense of responsibility for physically ill or disabled parents (Wolfson et al., 1993).

Respondents in the Canadian study were first asked what levels of assistance adult children *should* provide in each case. Second, adult children were asked to imagine that it was their own parents described in the vignettes. They were asked what levels of financial assistance, emotional support, and physical assistance that

FIGURE 12.4

Vignettes to elicit sense of responsibility of adult children for dependent parents

Vignette 1

A 64-year-old woman had a major stroke 8 months ago, causing paralysis of her right side. Because of this weakness, she is unable to get out of bed and into her wheelchair or onto the toilet without physical assistance. Her 71-year-old husband, who has some minor health problems, finds it very difficult to do this for her and is only just managing. Also, he is obviously having trouble coping emotionally with seeing his wife in such a weak condition.

Their only source of income is the government old-age pension, so they are unable to afford private help.

Vignette 2

A 76-year-old man has had Alzheimer's disease for the last 4 years. He presently lives with his wife in an apartment, where a community nurse visits him every week. Besides poor memory, his major problem is that he has no understanding of his illness. He gets quite upset, and at times aggressive, when anyone tries to get him to do something against his will. He tends to get more agitated at night and has trouble sleeping. He has reached the stage where he requires supervision for most activities and so cannot safely be left alone for any length of time.

His wife, who is 72 years old, is in reasonable physical health but is becoming exhausted with having to take care of her husband. She is unable to get a good night's sleep and cannot rest during the day because she is afraid her husband will get into trouble.

They are living on their old-age pension supplemented by a small amount of savings.

Vignette 3

An 82-year-old widower lives alone in a small second-floor apartment with no elevator. He has quite bad arthritis, causing pain in his knees and deformity in his hands. He can get about his apartment safely with specially designed canes but is unable to get outside without help. Even though he has few visitors he claims not to be lonely, but the visiting social worker thinks that he must be.

Two years ago he had an operation to remove a cancer from his bowel. Unfortunately, he required a permanent colostomy, which means that he has to wear a plastic bag on the side of the abdomen to collect his stool. Because of the arthritis in his fingers he needs help to empty and maintain the bag.

He receives the old-age pension along with a small pension from his former employer.

Source: Wolfson C. et al. (1993). Adult children's perceptions of their responsibility to provide care for dependent elderly parents, *Gerontologist,* 318.

they *could* provide if the elders in the vignettes were their own parents.

The overwhelming majority of people interviewed (almost all) felt that emotional support *should* be provided by adult children in general and *could* be provided by them for their parents. Not quite as many, but still a substantial majority, believed adult children *should* provide physical assistance; a somewhat lower percentage *could* provide physical assistance. And a majority believed adult children *should* help out financially. The lowest figure in the study was the degree to which adult children *could* help

financially, and even these scores were reasonably high. The researchers concluded that adult children feel a strong moral obligation to provide care for their disabled parents.

Another study in a similar vein asked respondents to agree or disagree with statements such as the following (Mangen & Westbrook, 1988):

> *If an old man has a medical bill of $1,000 that he cannot pay, his son or daughter is morally obligated to pay the debt.*

The purpose of the study was to reach a deeper understanding of **intergenerational**

norms, which are the standard, expected behaviors of one generation toward another. Interestingly, on the above item older generations were more likely to disagree than younger generations. Among Americans, the strong value of independence may well prevent older parents from expecting their adult children to take on any economic responsibility for them. In contrast, the majority of adult children agreed with the above statement.

Not all studies show similar expectations of aid to older parents from adult children. Intergenerational conflict was revealed in a classic study of three generations of women, using a hypothetical story about a widowed mother to ask each generation what adult children *should* do for an elderly parent (Brody et al., 1984). Respondents from each generation recommended in general that adult children not share a household with the mother. (The youngest group of women was most in favor of sharing the household, a feeling the researchers interpreted as a youthfully idealistic view of the caregiver role.)

Older parents judged female family members as acceptable to provide personal care such as meal preparation, housework, and grocery shopping, whereas male family members were judged unacceptable. Middle-aged daughters reluctant to change family schedules or give up jobs outside of the home were somewhat reluctant to become caregivers, yet the oldest mothers in the study were the most likely to expect caregiving from their middle-aged daughters.

A study recently released by Stanford University Medical Center found that the physical cost to those middle-aged daughters for caring for a frail parent can be actually greater than the physical cost to the spouse of the person requiring care. Daughters experienced a significantly greater increase in heart rates and blood pressure than did wives during social interactions with the ailing loved one, and the daughters recorded significantly more distress in interpersonal interactions (Evans, 1998). Divided energies, divided loyalties, and feelings of guilt for being unable to meet all of the demands of caregiving exact a heavy toll.

Did you know . . .
The number of extended family households in the U.S. steadily decreased from the turn of the 20th century until the 1980s, when the downward trend reversed. This shift resulted from increases in horizontally extended households among immigrants—primarily Mexican, Guatemalan, and Salvadoran. It is related to young, single adults living with relatives, and in increases in poverty rates among immigrants from these countries which precludes independent living among the newest immigrants.

GLICK ET AL., 1997

Weakened Family Support Systems

In 1977 Treas accurately predicted that the family would be more and more strained by caring for its oldest members. She cited three factors that contribute to the **weakened family support system,** which remain relevant at the turn of the century: (1) demography, (2) women's changing roles, and (3) changing intergenerational relationships.

Demography

Long-run trends in mortality and birthrates have startling consequences for the kin network. At the millennium, the aging parent, having raised fewer children, will have fewer offspring to call upon for assistance than did his or her own parents. Middle-aged children without siblings to share the care of the elderly parents will feel increased strain, and those adult children will themselves enter old age alongside their own parents, who will be then in the oldest-old category.

Kin networks offer fewer options and resources when the younger generations have fewer members. Generally speaking, an aging couple will fare better when several children can contribute to their support. And having a number of grown children increases an aging widow's odds that at least one will be able to accommodate her.

With more and more people living into their 80s and beyond, more of the old will be frail elderly, or the old old. The burden of their physical, financial, and emotional support may be considerable, especially for the young-old children of old-old parents, children whose own energy, health, and finances may be declining.

Women's Changing Roles

Traditionally, providing older parents with companionship and services has produced a sexual division of labor. The major burden of physical care and social activity has traditionally fallen on female relatives' shoulders, while the burden of instrumental care such as tax filing, medical bookkeeping, and the like has become the responsibility of male relatives. In a study of the division of caregiving responsibility among siblings, Wolf and colleagues (1997) found that the presence of siblings does reduce the workload on any one adult child; however, it is far less than a one-for-one basis. They further found that the primary predictor of parent care hours is the presence of sisters: when one's siblings include sisters, the workload on any of the siblings is less.

Changing Intergenerational Relationships

In the past, children have been expected to tend to their aging parents in return for inheriting the family farm or business. This exchange created a pattern of economic interdependence. Parents had greater certainty of care in their later life through their ownership of the family's greatest asset.

Children are now less likely to take over their parents' farm or business. They are more free to take jobs elsewhere or establish careers independent of their parents. Emotional ties, however, remain strong in the American family. Affection, gratitude, guilt, or a desire for parental approval still motivate adult children to care for their aging parents. Thus, the basis for helping is now less for economic and more for psychological reasons.

We may view these changes either as positive or negative. On one hand, the power of elders to ensure family support is reduced. On the other hand, Social Security and other governmental programs have reduced the dependence of the old on family-support systems. In the postindustrial society and the welfare state, both grown children and aged parents have been liberated from complete economic dependence on one another.

It seems that society is so enamored with the notion of "the family," that we overlook the fact that parenting can be a very painful experience. Too often, we deprive our older people of the chance to express the guilt, grief, uncertainty, fear, and uneasiness that are tied to their concern that they have not been effective parents.

BUTLER, 1977

Changes in the family, demographic shifts, and changes in the economic structure have necessitated greater levels of governmental and formal intervention in the care of older people. Programs such as day care centers, hot meals, and housekeeping services are essential to help relieve overburdened family support systems. However, these programs still suffer from high cost and limited availability.

Spousal Caregiving

Spouses provide a large percent of caregiving, with wives being more likely to be caregivers than husbands. About 40 percent of all caregiving is provided by spouses: 14 percent by

A spouse is generally the primary caregiver when one's life partner becomes frail and requires caregiving.

©Joel Gordon

to be older and in worse health than themselves. Some noninstitutionalized elders in the community are homebound, and of those, a portion are bedridden. A husband or wife, if available, is most often the primary caregiver, and if the couple is lucky, paid helpers and children provide additional assistance.

In addition to family structure, both gender and racial differences shape the caregiving experience. A recent study comparing male and female white and African American caregivers showed that men of either race are less likely to refer to caregiving in terms of emotional work, and men and African American women caregivers are less likely to acknowledge a difference in the caregiving role between males and females (Miller & Kaufman, 1996).

Sometimes the caretaking role is assumed for years and years. In the following example the husband has Alzheimer's disease:

For nearly a decade, Hildegarde Rebenack, 69, has watched her 78-year-old husband, Robert, deteriorate from Alzheimer's disease. Robert was a bank examiner, a man proud of rising above his eighth grade education. Now, he spends his days staring at a collection of stuffed animals in their Louisiana home. . . . Robert was diagnosed in 1982. By 1984, he could no longer be left alone, and, two years later, Hildegarde had to put him into a nursing home. . . . Last March, the latest price hike forced her to bring him home. "We had 37 good years together," says Hildegarde, her voice breaking. "But the last six years have been hell." (Beck et al., 1990)

husbands, 26 percent by wives (Harris, 1994). Living to very old age as a married couple represents a biological and social achievement. Nevertheless, the consequence of marriage in late life is not always blissful. If illness and chronic impairments loom large, heightened anxiety, interpersonal difficulties, and economic strains may result. Older married women often become part-time nurses for their husbands, who tend

For the spouse of an impaired person, decline challenges long-established patterns of interaction, goals, and behavior. The loss of functional capacity in one partner has reciprocal emotional effects on both partners, and those effects are highly variable, depending on the couple (Ade-Ridder & Kaplan, 1993). Spouses meet with circumstances that bring up the most intense emotional issues: life and its meaning, freedom, isolation, and death. Different styles of caregiving bring different problems and issues. Some women feel burned out by giving too much of themselves over the years, both before their husbands' health began to fail and after. Both men and women sometimes need to redefine their roles as spouse, and they may require assistance in establishing an identity as an individual as well as someone who is part of a marriage as the marital role changes with the changing health of the frail partner. In a study of husbands who were caregivers, Harris (1993) named four types:

1. *The worker:* He models his role after the work role. He plans his work schedule every day. He reads everything he can about Alzheimer's disease and has a desk where he organizes the insurance papers and other materials.

2. *Labor of love:* He provides caretaking out of deep feelings of love. He often holds his wife's hand and embraces her. He cares for her out of devotion, not duty.

3. *Sense of duty:* Caregiving stems from commitment, duty, and responsibility. He says, "She would have done the same for me. I will never abandon her."

4. *At the crossroads:* This is typical of a new caregiver who hasn't oriented to the role. He is floundering and in crisis.

Harris concluded with a variety of support recommendations: (1) educational groups led by a male caretaker and nurse clinicians; (2) support groups limited to men, because men often are not comfortable discussing personal matters in predominantly female groups; (3) computer networking programs for men who would not join groups; and (4) more quality and affordable in-home respite services. These conclusions are consistent with a second study that provided a comprehensive psychosocial intervention program available to all family members, male and female, over the entire course of an aged family member's disease (Mittelman et al., 1995).

By providing options for helping interventions, spouse caregivers were able to use services most suited to their unique situation and relationship with their spouse and their larger family. The results showed significantly lower rates of depression among the treatment group than among those in the control group. Supportive intervention can work to help ease the tremendous emotional and physical burden of caring.

Adult Children as Caregivers

Now is the first time in history that American couples have more parents than children. The number of years of caregiving a married person with children might plan for is now around 17 years for children, and 18 years for elderly parents (Stone & Keigher, 1994). These numbers are particularly dramatic for women: nearly 30 percent of aging persons who need home care receive it from adult daughters, 23 percent from wives, and 20 percent from more distant female relatives or female nonrelatives; adult sons, by contrast, provide 10 percent of home care (Older Women's League, 1989; Stoller, 1990). The greatest strain seems to be upon "women in the middle"—middle-aged women who have children and jobs and who also are responsible for the home care of parents. The demand of multiple roles on the caregiver can be profoundly stressful. That stress is mediated by the history of the relationship with the parent, by the extent of the caregiver's social support, by her coping skills, and by her self-image (Adams, 1996; McCarty, 1996). Some adult-child caregivers, for example, have long histories of conflict with the very parent for whom they now feel responsible, and these histories shape the caregiving experience for both the caregiver and the care recipient. One care-providing daughter wrote:

> When I was young my mother manipulated me until I could get away from her. To have to take responsibility for her now is quite distressing. Everyone thinks she's "cute," or "quite a character," but [they] don't under-

stand that these qualities are not endearing on a lifetime basis. In fact, they are outright distressing when they seem to take over your life. I am trapped in a circle of anger and guilt, guilt and anger, with a smattering of denial and grief. (reported in Brackley, 1994, p. 15)

Unmarried adult children who share a household with the ailing parent provide the most care. Being married and being employed decreases the amount of help given. Living apart further reduces the amount of help elders receive. Adult-child caregivers most commonly offer help with getting out of bed and going to the bathroom, shopping for food, traveling, doing laundry, preparing meals, doing housework, bathing, taking medicine, dressing, getting around the house, and providing personal and supportive communication.

Family size, socioeconomic level, and ethnicity are all determinants of family caregiving patterns. In one study of middle- and upper-socio-economic-class neighborhoods, non-Hispanic whites with no children were more likely than Mexican Americans to report other family or nonfamily as their available caregiver. Among those with five or more children, however, non-Hispanic whites were *less* likely than Mexican Americans to report nonfamily as their caregiver (Talamantes et al., 1996). These findings imply that Mexican Americans have access to a more extensive support system, especially informal support, than do non-Hispanic whites and highlight the need for services and policy to address ethnic differences.

Parent care involves a constant tension between attachment and loss, pleasing and caring, seeking to preserve an older person's dignity and exerting unaccustomed authority, overcoming resistance to care and fulfilling extravagant demands, reviving a relationship and transforming it.

ABEL, 1991

Unlike caregiving for children, who become more independent with age, caregiving for the severely impaired requires more effort as the years go by. Coping skills and management strategies become stretched to the limit. Clearly, providing care for a frail parent might promote compassion and personal growth, or it might become overwhelming, with a negative outcome for both the caregiving child and the parent.

An early study of 30 women caring for a chronically ill parent or parent-in-law along with the person receiving care observed two kinds of parent-caring roles: (1) care provision and (2) care management (Archbold, 1983). A care-provider was one who personally performed the services an older parent needed, whereas a care manager was one who identified and obtained needed services, then supervised their provision by others.

The care-providing individuals were generally more strained, had lower incomes and less knowledge of available resources, were more involved in the heavy physical work of daily care, and were less likely to provide stimulating activities and entertainment in their caregiving role. In contrast, though the care managers did not totally avoid strain and stress, they experienced less than the care-provider. The expenses care managers incurred were greater, but financial expenses were high for care-providers as well.

We might note here that the Tax Reform Act of 1986 entitles anyone who works and who pays for the care of a dependent to a federal tax credit. However, care must be for a child or other relative for whom the taxpayer provides *more than half* the needed support, and the maximum credit allowance is only 30 percent of care expenses per dependent. Therefore, the act provides very little actual relief.

Childlessness

Children were once described as one's old-age insurance. Today, however, 20 percent of the population over age 65 have no children, and this trend will accelerate with increased longevity among the baby-boom generation, which experienced decreased fertility rates and increased divorce rates (Choi, 1994b). Most studies on childlessness have addressed psychological and emotional health rather than care provision. The general profile of the childless individual, compared with the elderly parent, emerges as someone who is more financially secure and in better health; more reliant on siblings, nieces, and nephews, and on hired care providers; and experiencing no greater loneliness, isolation, or unhappiness than their counterparts with children (Cicirelli, 1981; Keith, 1983; Rempel, 1985; Ikels, 1997; Choi, 1994b). Patterns of help seem to be shaped more by marital status than by parental status (Keith, 1983).

Other researchers have found that childless elders follow the "principle of substitution" by turning to extended kin for help, but these resources are less available than are children. Childless married couples tend to rely primarily on each other and to remain otherwise independent from extended kin. Unmarried elders, having established lifetime patterns for seeking assistance, seem to be more resourceful in using a variety of people and social resources to meet their needs. The childless elderly require more easily available substitute supports (Chappell, 1991).

Elder Caregiving to Adult Children and Grandchildren

The number of older parents who care for dependent adult children and grandchildren is increasing. Census figures estimate the number of children being cared for by grandparents in the United States at just over 3 million, and project that number to steadily increase in the wake of AIDS and increased drug abuse in some population sectors (Saluter, 1992). Reduced mortality in the second half of the century among children with mental and physical disabilities has placed many older parents in the role of be-

ing care providers throughout their lives. It is no longer unusual for an 85-year-old parent in good health to be caring for a 65-year-old child with developmental disabilities or a grandchild who has been abandoned by his or her parents.

Sometimes older parents assume the caregiver role because no one else is available to care for their dependent children or grandchildren. Support groups for elderly parents have become more available in recent years to help them with their caregiving in times of stress and crisis. The impact of later-life caregiving on 105 mothers of adult children with mental illness and 208 mothers of developmentally disabled adult children was assessed to determine their experienced levels of stress (Greenberg et al., 1993). It was found that elderly mothers had the most problems with mentally ill adult children. The mentally ill children posed greater behavior problems and were less likely to have day care outside the home or be employed. The mothers' social network of friends and relatives was smaller than the that of mothers of developmentally disabled adult children.

The emotional cost of caring for a disabled child is high. Strawbridge and colleagues (1997) found differences in mental health, but not in physical health, between elderly people caring for an ailing spouse and those caring for an adult child. Grandparent caregivers in that study experienced decreases in physical health as well as mental health.

Solving Caregiving Problems

The stresses and strains of caregiving have drawn considerable attention over the last decade. The discussion that follows summarizes some of the solutions that have been offered.

Stress and Stress Management

A fierce tangle of emotions comes with parenting one's parents: anguish, frustration, inadequacy, guilt, devotion, and love. Stress comes not only

The ability to appreciate life's small graces as well as to laugh at life's absurdities is often the outcome of a long life well lived.

from these emotions, but also from work overload. **Caregiver distress** indicates the negative stresses of caretaking, including role strain, subjective burden, depression, anxiety, hostility, and other troublesome emotions. Scales such as the Zarit Burden Interview (ZBI) have been developed to measure degrees of caregiver distress (Knight et al., 1993). One specific emotion that has been widely studied is depression. Gerontologists seek to understand how much depression precedes the caregiving distress and how much is solely the result of the new added role. Those who are not depressed to begin with cope better than those who are. Personality factors have been examined, using personality inventories, for their role in one's ability to cope (Hooker et al., 1994).

Coping has been conceptualized as a response to the demands of specific stressful current situations. Coping techniques and abilities vary from person to person. These variations in ability need attention and explanation so that those with poor skills can be helped. In one study the specific stressors embedded in caring for severely impaired elders were specified. The most commonly identified characteristics of the person with Alzheimer's disease that cause stress to the caregiver are memory defects, loss of ability to communicate, and unrelenting decline (Williamson & Schulz, 1993). The process in which a caregiver travels has been identified by Opie (1992) as that of "taking on the responsibility for caregiving, its content, the relationship between various family members, and the interface between informal and formal care" (quoted in Adams, 1996, p. 705). Opie's process model does not include the well-documented grief response that accompanies caregiving. It is a heavy load.

Problems in caregiving come from (1) the strain of responsibility for direct personal care of the elder, (2) the caregivers' own current personal and health problems, (3) role strain from the demands of other work and the need for leisure, (4) intersibling problems and other strained family relationships, and (5) arranging outside help and coping with bureaucratic mix-ups. A social support network is very important to caregivers.

Although helping parents can be rewarding for many adult children, it can be accompanied by enormous burdens, both financial and emotional. The principal caregiving adult children are women pulled in many directions by competing demands on their time and energy. Brody (1990) reports that three-fourths of daughter caregivers said that they felt they were not doing enough for their mothers. Adult children often express feelings of guilt as caregivers because of a deep commitment to "repay" their parent for care given in their childhood and infancy. This is impossible, and guilt is the result.

Ellen McCarty's intensive interviews with 17 adult-child caregivers found that daughters were less likely to experience stress if they could:

1. Restructure her parents/former identities and her own prior filial relationship

2. Seek out helpful management strategies such as taking time for herself, taking it "day by day," receiving support from siblings, using humor, perceiving support from formal caregivers, and "having someone to talk to"

3. Perceive and respond to available support from family and significant others

4. Seek support from professional caregivers

5. Grieve in response to perceived losses and changes in self and others

6. Engage in positive restructuring of life beliefs in the face of reality (1996, p. 800)

Psychological Interventions and Respite Care for Caregivers

The 1980s was a time for drawing attention to the burdens of caregiving. Gerontologists have documented the problems again and again and continue to study what kind of help is most useful. A controlled study of psychosocial interventions (psychological help from paid professionals) and respite programs (programs that allow the caregiver time off) showed them generally to be moderately effective (Knight et al., 1993). The kinds of **psychosocial interventions** for the caretakers were varied: individual counseling, family counseling, support groups, educational groups, problem-solving groups for the caretaker and patient, social worker visits, and family consultants.

Support groups are typically available in larger communities at mental health clinics and also from individual counselors. They usually meet once a week for eight weeks or so, in which meetings individuals share problems and help each other with emotional support, friendship, and ideas. A paid professional leads the group. We should keep in mind that group interventions such as these work for some, but not for everyone. Counseling, either individual or family, can also be helpful if families can afford it, although, for some families suffering from poor relationships, no amount of professional help can fix the problem. In this case, emotional distancing may be the only stress-management technique that would alleviate guilt and despair. Organizations are available in most communities to offer services to caregivers or to refer them to individuals who do.

In the study cited earlier by Knight et al. (1993), respite care was somewhat more effective than psychosocial interventions. **Respite care** can mean placement of the dependent elder in a nursing home for two weeks or so, or it may involve bringing a hired home care worker into the home for one to two weeks or more while the caregiver goes on a vacation. Time off for the caregiver is very important in relieving distress. Intervention and respite care should not measure its success by the alleviation of caregiver distress only. Other important outcomes have been found: improved functioning of the dependent elder, reduced use of hospital days for the elder, and improvements in patient mortality.

Future research should direct attention to how much and what kind of intervention is necessary to achieve a desired effect (Knight et al., 1993). If interventions and respite care work, which they often do, the next step is to determine what works best at what levels of strength, with which kinds of caregivers for elders with which kinds of impairments. A broad range of ethnic differences in real and perceived family support and in coping styles exists, and social service programs must identify and address these cultural differences to adequately support the provision of family-based care (Talamantes et al., 1996; Strom et al., 1993).

The Home Care Crisis

The percentage of elders is increasing, and more family members work outside the home. Is a crisis emerging? Who will care for the very old in our society? Many gerontologists believe that a trained paraprofessional labor force for long-term care of the aged and disabled must be a national priority. Others believe the next cohort of elders will be healthier and less disabled than their parents were, and that medical and life-style advances will compress their morbidity and morality into the very end of their lives, as opposed to their living for decades with disabling diseases. Regardless of which scenario plays out in the next century, the number of Americans needing long-term care is expected to reach 9 million by 2000 and mushroom to 24 million by 2060 (Cooper, 1998). Home health care

personnel are now the fastest growing segment of the long-term care industry, and the demand for their services will continue.

Home care workers are generally poorly paid, overworked, and poorly trained. They are disproportionately middle-aged ethnic-minority women (Feldman, 1993). Wages, job conditions, and opportunities for caregiving work have typically been at the lower end of the employment scale, with no chance for advancement. Outstanding **paraprofessional caregivers** in such job categories as nurse's aid, home health aide, personal care attendant, chore worker, and homemaker should receive prospects for increased responsibility and advancement. Poorly paid **paraprofessional home care workers** are a transient work group with a high turnover rate. Paraprofessionals at present have little training. In some states they must undergo about 75 hours of training and pass a competency test. In many states, however, the requirements include fewer hours of training and no test. Given such easy entry into the field, one might expect a large labor pool, but this is not the case. Many states report having trouble delivering state-funded home care services because of worker shortages and high turnover. Increased wages and better working conditions will reduce caregiver turnover, and continuity of care will be improved.

Paraprofessional home care workers' wages lag behind those of workers with similar jobs in nursing homes and hospitals. Home care worker rates in Massachusetts are at the higher end of the pay scale, running from $11.50 to $12.50 per hour. However, large cuts in state home care funding have resulted in the loss of 500 paraprofessional home care worker jobs in that state. Another problem in the industry is the poor job image associated with the long-term care of chronically disabled elders (MacAdam, 1993b). More attention needs to be paid to upgrading the job image and recruiting, training, and retaining quality home care workers for elders (Eustis et al., 1993).

Many families do not qualify for state-funded home care workers. Nearly 46 percent of all Medicare users of home health care must purchase services in addition to those Medicare offers (Kane, 1989). Only 25 percent of the disabled elderly population getting home assistance receive skilled nursing care at home. When they have to pay out of their own pockets, many go without care. Those in need who have enough income and access to services do seek paid help (Stoller & Cutler, 1993).

Although private insurance should be available at affordable prices to cover home care, it typically is not. The gerontologist Nancy Kane states that "society should be compelled to come up with better ways to both pay for home care and provide the services" (Kane, 1989, p. 24). She proposes a managed long-term care insurance program focused on maintaining older people in their homes, a program similar to most HMOs. She estimates that 40 to 50 percent of the very old could afford such an insurance policy. The federal government could assist in a number of ways, such as subsidizing low-income elders who want to buy into the program.

The private sector has a stake in caring for elders. There were 33 million Americans age 65 or older in 1990; 70 million will reach old age in the next century, when life expectancy may increase to 90 years. Currently, about 80 percent of all in-home care received by frail elders is being provided by family members. This elder care costs business billions of dollars per year in absenteeism, lost productivity, and increased turnover (Scharlach, 1994).

Businesses are run better if caregiving adult workers receive outside help in caring for aged parents. To date, only about 3 percent of U.S. companies have policies that assist employees who care for the elderly; but many more are considering such programs. Such programs need to be developed, and quickly, for the growth in the labor force in the 1990s will come primarily from women aged 35 to 54, Brody's stressed "women in the middle."

Researches suggest that employers could provide more policies, benefits, and services for employees who are caregivers. They recommend:

1. Part-time job options such as job sharing, voluntary reduced time, or shared retirement
2. Flexible work hours, such as a spread during the day and evening, or a compressed work week with a day or two off
3. Policies encouraging working at home
4. Paid sick, vacation, and personal leave
5. Parental/family leave, paid or unpaid
6. Medical/emergency leave
7. Dependent care reimbursement plan in which the employer directly subsidizes a portion of the employee's caregiving expenses
8. Long-term care insurance that includes home care by paraprofessionals and respite for family caregivers
9. Education about caregiving
10. Resource and referral
11. Counseling
12. On-site day care
13. More tax relief for caregivers (Neal et al., 1993)

Options for care provision in later life must be developed now, before the tidal wave of the boomer generation requires care. In some families, home care with occasional paraprofessional assistance works to provide the best care for the elder; in others, broad ranges of outside assistance are necessary; in still others the needs of elders will be best met by their living in assisted living housing or long-term care facilities. Some companies such as IBM, Stride Rite, and Travelers Insurance have elder care programs.

They offer flexible work schedules to allow employees time to care for older relatives and, furthermore, pay for up to 26 weeks' leave for elder care. Adult day care costs can be lower than bringing in home health care aides, depending on how much care is needed. The elderly are a very diverse group with widely diverse needs. Services must address those needs.

Chapter Summary

This chapter extends information in the chapter on social bonds, providing an emphasis on the oldest old and on caregiving. Norms governing intergenerational relationships are not clear-cut, which leaves room for elders to feel disappointed when adult children do not live close by and act in a supportive manner. Aged women far outnumber aged men, especially at advanced ages. The existing studies show the oldest old to be healthier and more active than stereotypes would have us believe. Most manage to live outside nursing homes, either in their own homes or with adult children. Chronic conditions are common, but most people are not totally disabled by them. Caregiving by adult children is becoming more and more common as more elders live into their 80s, 90s, and 100s. The largest percentage of caregiving is provided by older wives and middle-aged daughters. A smaller but substantial percentage of caregivers consists of (older) husbands and sons. Caregiving places a great deal of stress on families because more women are employed outside the home and because families have fewer children than they once did. In spite of the burdens, the family in the United States remains strong and a major source of aid to its members. More paraprofessionals are needed in the home care field to offer quality care at a reasonable price to the oldest old.

Key Terms

caregiver distress
coping
formal caregiving
functional ability
informal caregiving
instrumental activities of
    daily living
intergenerational norms
life satisfaction
modified nuclear
    family
oldest old
paraprofessional
    caregivers
paraprofessional home
    care worker
personal activities of
    daily living
psychosocial
    interventions
respite care
robust aging
weakened family
    support system

Questions for Discussion

1. Assuming that you have or plan to have children of your own, what role do you expect them to play should you require caregiving?

2. What kind of life do you hope to live when you are one of the oldest old?

3. Based on your relationship with your parents now, what will your relationship be like if and when they become very old and need care?

4. What satisfactions could one enjoy from serving in capacities such as nurse's aide, home health aide, personal care attendant, chore worker, or homemaker?

Fieldwork Suggestions

1. Interview five people, using the vignettes listed in Figure 12.4. What were the similar responses? What were the unique responses? What conclusions can you draw from the experience of this small study?

2. Contrast the daily life of a very old person who is frail and ill with one who is active and fit. Describe the two people physically and in terms of attitude and personality.

What conclusions might you draw from your observations?

Internet Activities 🌐

1. Beginning with the home page for AHEAD (Asset and Health Dynamics Among the Oldest Old) locate current information on health factors among the oldest old in the United States. What ethnic differences are evident? (Use www.umich.edu/~hrswww/index.html for your initial address in this search.)

2. Locate three of the following resource home pages on the Internet, and prepare an outline highlighting the resources that each makes available to the consumer:
   - American Association of Homes for the Aging
   - American Association of Retired Persons
   - American Health Care Association
   - Assisted Living Facilities Association of America
   - Health Care Financing Administration
   - National Citizens' Coalition for Nursing Home Reform and
   - National Council on the Aging

Special Problems

13

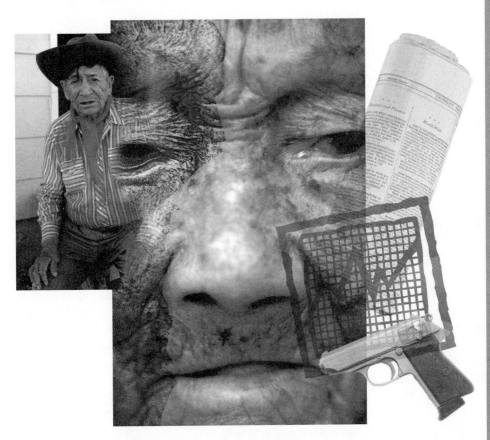

Facing Up to Elder Abuse

Charlie LeDuff

Anne DeBraw lives in fear. On a dark night not long ago, she heard the footsteps of a prowler on her roof. There was a tormented moment of silence before the intruder came crashing through the skylight.

"I felt so scared, so alone at that moment," said Mrs. DeBraw, 71, the memories tumbling out in tears. The man had been there before, but there was little she was willing to do. "He is my son and I didn't want to hurt him."

Mrs. DeBraw's is a common story, but one not often told. Many elderly parents like Mrs. DeBraw live in silent fear of their children. Quieted by shame, Mrs. DeBraw was battered and browbeaten for a decade.

People like Mrs. DeBraw, who have been abused by their children, may soon have a refuge of their own. By next spring, a Long Island City-based organization hopes to open a 20-bed emergency facility that will offer shelter, counseling and medical assistance to victims of elder abuse and their families.

"Elder abuse is New York's dirty little secret," said the Rev. Coleman Costello, founder and director of Walk the Walk, the group that plans to build the shelter. "Many of our old people are isolated and dependent on those who hurt them. Nobody wants to report that they're suffering at the hands of their children."

With $350,000 in grant money, Father Costello and his organization expect to close this week on a piece of property in Glendale, Queens, where the shelter is to be built. Father Costello, a Catholic priest, assisted Mrs. DeBraw after the court system was unable to stop her son's uninvited visits to her home.

Father Costello believes that the shelter in Glendale may be the first in the country just for victims of elder abuse. According to statistics provided by the National Center on Elder Abuse, more than 5 percent of New York City's 1.3 million people over the age of 60 are the victims of domestic mistreatment. Usually the abuse comes at the hands of an adult child and it can include physical or emotional duress, financial exploitation or abandonment. As the baby boomers age, those numbers will skyrocket, particularly in Queens and Brooklyn, where the majority of New York's elderly live.

"This is a disgrace that is not perceived of as a problem because nobody wants to talk about it," said Herbert W. Stupp, Commissioner of the New York City Department of the Aging. Although abused elderly people can take refuge in shelters for battered people, they often leave after only a few days, Mr. Stupp said.

"They have different physical and emotional needs," he said. "As difficult as it is, a young woman can start another life while a senior citizen is coming to the end of hers."

With age comes increasing frailty. With increasing frailty comes greater dependence on family and community for assistance with tasks ranging from taking the trash to the curb to home maintenance. Many frail elders, aware of their physical frailty, express feelings of vulnerability as they watch television programs and read news accounts of street crime and of gang activities. The actual commission of crime is only one aspect of the trouble; the fear of crime brings its own set of problems. Law enforcement and social agencies now recognize the crime patterns most likely to affect elders. Older people themselves are devising ways to fight back, and they are taking initiative, both as individuals and as a group, to protect and defend themselves.

As we develop our understanding of what it means to be old in our society, we must understand that it brings vulnerability due to ageism and, for some, further vulnerability due to physical and financial limitations. Here we discuss some special problems that, if not unique, occur in high frequency within the aged population. And let us not forget that older persons are not always victims; they can also be perpetrators. This topic will be covered briefly.

Suicide

Suicide is the ultimate reaction to hopelessness—the acting out of a belief that there is no promise to the future and no reason to live in it. It is inextricably linked with depression and is one of the 10 leading causes of death in the United States. The reported annual national **suicide rate** is about 12 persons per 100,000 (NCHS, 1999). Elder suicide is particularly understudied, even though the suicide rate among the elderly is the highest in the general population—perhaps double that of the general population—and white men over age 85 are the most at risk. One of every five suicides in 1997 in the United States was committed by someone over the age of 65 (Centers for Disease Control [CDC], 1999), and the highest rates are found among white males.

White men age 85 and older are at almost double the risk rate for suicide, second only to white men aged 15 to 24 (NCHS, 2000).

For four decades, the suicide rates among older Americans declined, but from 1980 to 1996 they climbed by almost 9 percent. During this time, men—predominantly white men—completed 81 percent of those suicides (Centers for Disease Control and Prevention, 1996). In 1933, the first year the National Center for Health Statistics kept suicide statistics, the suicide rate among elders was an alarming 45.3 per 100,000 compared with a national average of 15.9. Between 1950 and 1980—years in which Medicare, housing, and other social programs targeting elders were initiated—suicide among elders declined by 40 percent (Marrone, 1997). By 1981 the rates had dropped to 17.1, compared with a national average of 12 per 100,000 people. Since 1981, however, elder suicide has increased to 22 people per 100,000, compared to a national average of 12 per 100,000, and the trend continues for increased elder suicide.

Did you know . . .
Suicide notes among the elderly, more than among any other age group, often include references to loneliness, isolation, and to pain.

DARBONNE, 1969

Differences by Gender and Race

Suicide in old age is *statistically* a man's issue, and older white men are particularly vulnerable. All women 65 years and older, although reporting higher depression rates, have a disproportionately lower rate of suicide. The rates in old age for white and black women combined were about 6.5 per 100,000 people in 1986, compared with 61 suicides per 100,000 that year of white men over 85 years of age. On the other hand, the risk of suicide for men in the United States begins in the teen years and continues to increase with age, making an alarming increase in very old age. The proportion of **successful suicides** to **attempted suicides** is far greater in old age than at younger ages. Older people who express a determination to complete a suicide generally do so.

The World Health Organization reports that suicide rates throughout the world are generally higher for people over 65 years of age—often two or three times that of the national average. The highest international rates were in Hungary, Sri Lanka, Denmark, and Finland, and the lowest rates were in Colombia, Ecuador, Greece, and Venezuela. Rates for elder suicide in the United States lie somewhere in the middle (Schaie & Willis, 1996). International gender differences in suicide also exist: in Japan, for example, suicide rates for older women have risen steadily from 1980 through 2000—possibly a reflection of the progressive loss of the traditional importance of older women in that culture (World Health Organization, 2000).

Examining numbers and proportions of suicides by themselves can be misleading. For example, women outnumber men in unsuccessful attempts at suicide by about three or four to one (Schaie & Willis, 1996). Men's attempts to kill themselves are simply more successful; if suicidal intent is considered, older women outnumber older men. Men are more likely to kill themselves by violent and more certain means—guns were chosen by 74 percent of men who killed themselves in 1994, compared with 31 percent of women. Women are more likely to overdose with medications or poisons, which are clearly less effective (Marrone, 1997). Among young adults, more people attempt suicide than actually succeed. By about the age of 50 the suicide completion ratio grows larger. Even considering the ratio of suicide attempts to completion by women, when compared to younger adults older adults are more likely to kill themselves when they attempt to do so.

African American men and women have lower rates of suicide than do white men and women. The reasons for these comparatively low rates are not entirely clear, but they are thought to be related to positive views of aging, a developed tolerance for suffering, strong religious and cultural prohibitions against suicide, and the lack of a giant step downward in status that white males experience in retirement.

Did you know . . .
A study in the early 1970s subjected dogs to minor but discomforting electrical shocks that they could not escape. The animals became apathetic, seemed sad, and were unable to think or move quickly. This behavior led psychologist Martin Seligman to the concept of learned helplessness *as a source of human depression. After a series of inescapable losses, if people feel they have no mastery or control of their environment they develop a feeling of futility, even toward events they can control. The resulting emotional state is apathy, hopelessness, and depression.*

Seligman, 1975

Causes of Suicide

Some experts speculate that medical technology has introduced a quality of life that elders cannot accept. These advances give people longer lives, but not necessarily a better long life—there is greater quantity in terms of longevity, but the quality of life suffers.

Suffering and loss are factors known to be related to depression and suicide and take place on psychological, physical, and social levels. Table 13.1 outlines some risk factors related to suicide, including the psychological risk inherent in the process of interiority, physiologically mediated risks of chronic illness and pain, the social risks of isolation through repeated loss, and the behavioral risk of alcoholism—an outcome of a behavior that promotes denial (Marrone, 1997). The most significant factor, subsumed in the table under "multiple losses," is the loss of loved ones by separation or death. When children leave home, when friends and relatives

TABLE 13.1

Risk factors associated with suicide in later life

Risk Factor	Description
Interiority	A turning in toward ourselves in search of personal meaning; has both healthy and unhealthy aspects: can promote self-knowledge, spirituality, and increased satisfaction with life; or result in unhealthy self-absorption and increased social isolation.
Chronic illness	Organic and psychological decline along with chronic illness and pain contribute to depression. Seventy percent of older suicides visited a physician within 1 month of their death.
Multiple losses	Job loss, death of friends, death of a spouse, the divorce of a child, loss of health and social status—all are cumulative experiences, and can occur so rapidly that resolution of the inherent grief of loss does not happen; associated depression of recurring losses can become chronic depression.
Alcoholism	More important among males 35 to 64 than any other age group; alcohol abuse enhances depression and exacerbates negative live events. Bereaved adults report significant increase in alcohol consumption, psychological distress, and decline in physical health.

Source: Adapted from Marrone, Robert. (1997). *Death, mourning, and caring.* © 1997 West Publishing Co. by permission of Brooks/Cole Publishing Co.

die, and especially when a spouse dies, the survivor is often beset with the desperate feeling that there is no reason to continue living. Social isolation has been associated with suicide—and elders are all too often isolated both socially and psychologically by society's ageism.

Perhaps most important, physical illness, pain, or disability can prompt suicide. Aversion to the bodily changes that illness brings and worry over medical bills, coupled with the possibility of becoming a burden to one's family or to society, are typical reasons for older persons to take their own lives. Fully 70 percent of elders who commit suicide had seen a doctor the previous month. Physical illness as a cause of depression may be a common precipitating factor in completed suicides. More than 60 percent of older suicide victims have extreme medical problems (Devons, 1996).

Existential philosopher Soren Kierkegaard (1843) argues that the price we pay for not coming to terms with our own death is despair. . . . In not coming to terms with death, *the person in despair avoids the insights that life is precious, that existence is delicate, that a life filled with vibrancy, choices, and risks is the truest antidote to loneliness and despair, and that the dignity with which you live your life is the dignity with which you die.*

MARRONE, 1997

Choices

The Hemlock Society was founded by Derek Humphry in 1980 to help people make choices about how they would deal with terminal illness. The motto of the society is "Good life, good death through control and choice." Humphry gained international fame after writing *Jean's Way,* the personal account of how he helped his terminally ill wife kill herself in 1975.

Until recently, most Hemlock Society members were older people. With the advent of the AIDS epidemic, however, many younger people joined the organization. Humphry's books *Let*

After decades of inadequate funding for mental health programs, many old people have lived a lifetime of marginal existence. For some, hopelessness is a way of life.

Me Die Before I Wake (1985) and the more recent *Final Exit* (1991) describe specific methods to use to ensure a gentle, painless death. Both the 1985 book and *Final Exit* have become national best sellers, reflecting the public interest in the topic of planned suicide. The Hemlock Society believes that suicides are not necessarily the result of poor mental health but can be the result of a sound decision based on good mental health—what is called **rational suicide.** Thus, the relationship between suicide and mental health is not as clear-cut to some as it is to others.

Therapeutic intervention by skilled professionals is always recommended for a suicidal person. Depression is treatable; suicide is not. Many communities have established suicide-prevention centers that maintain 24-hour crisis lines for helping persons in distress. The National Center for Studies of Suicide Prevention has assigned a high priority to the problem of

suicide among those 65 and older. There is, however, a shortage of skilled therapists to treat self-destructive elders, and of all calls to suicide hot lines, those over 65 make only 3 percent of them—even though suicide is more common in the elderly than in other age group, it is still a relatively rare event.

Why some people can cope with stress and loss and others cannot is not fully understood, nor is the line between "rational suicide" and that emerging from hopelessness and depression very clear (Lester & Savlid, 1997). Barbara Haight (1996) found that elders being relocated to nursing homes who expressed suicidal ideation reported a strong sense of self-esteem and described suicide as a way to retain control of their lives. We do not sufficiently understand the mixed picture of the hardy survivorship qualities of old people and the isolating effect of the relentless loss of peers (Kastenbaum, 1992). All in all, the viability and allegiance to life of elders in general should not be underestimated.

Self-Destructive Behavior

The approximate 6,500 suicides per year of people 65 and over leaves a large number of survivors who grieve and mourn. The solitary act of suicide has a ripple effect, touching the lives of many. In some instances, couples who fear leaving or being left by their partner conduct **double suicides.** The most common pattern of a double suicide is the mercy killing of a frail and dying wife, followed by the husband's suicide.

Elders in nursing homes are especially vulnerable to suicidal behavior. Although the actual rate is only 16 per 100,000, the attempted rate is 63 per 100,000. The rate of death from indirect self-destructive behavior is 79 for every 100,000 people, and the rate of nonlethal, indirectly self-destructive behavior is 228 per 100,000 (Osgood, 1991). Methods included self-mutilation, ingestion of foreign substances, the refusal to eat or drink, and any repetitive act bringing physical harm or tissue damage.

Future Trends

Suicide is twice as prevalent in western states as in the East and Midwest. Older persons in the West are more likely to have moved away from friends and family, and the divorce rate is higher in western states. Although no direct relationship has been found between suicide and divorce or mobility, the trends are important (Parker et al., 1997). The trends imply that meaningful social interaction might be more difficult to come by in the West, and meaningful personal relationships are the most potent antisuicide remedies—failures and losses are burdens easier to bear in the context of close family and friends.

Health experts anticipate an even higher rate of suicide as the baby boomers reach age 65. Baby boomers have had higher rates of mental illness than their predecessors; after age 65, this group may suffer a tragically high suicide rate. The implications of this projection for mental health professionals are awesome regarding programs and services for a very diverse and large emerging portion of the population.

Crimes against Persons

Though attacks on elders have drawn increasing media attention in recent years, national surveys show that they are less likely to be victimized than younger adults. When one considers **crimes against persons,** such as robbery, rape, and assault, only one specific area shows elders victimized as frequently as younger adults—the personal larceny of purse and wallet snatchings and pocket-picking (U.S. Bureau of the Census, 1993). Despite the relatively low rates of crimes committed against them, the elderly express the greatest fear of crime of all age groups (Bureau of Justice Statistics, 1992). This fear has serious psychological, physical, and financial consequences for the elderly. Fear of crime has been found to be independent of environmental variables, such as trust of neighbors, years of residence in a location, or type of housing (Bazargan, 1994). It is a psychological state based on a sense of vulnerability, and among many elders it results in fear or avoidance of leaving home (Joseph, 1997).

Gerontologists are aware of the wide variations in victimization rates. Surveys show that a majority of violent victimizations of older people occur in or near their homes. The converse applies to younger adults, who are more likely to be attacked away from their homes. Unlike younger adults, elders tend to avoid places of danger and to restrict their use of public streets. But in spite of precautions and their tendency to stay home more, some elders still are victimized.

Their particular vulnerability may well be a reason for attacks on older individuals. Many are poor, living on fixed incomes, and dependent on public transportation. They may live in neighborhoods with relatively high crime rates or in changing neighborhoods where unemployed youths prey on them. Often they are not physically strong enough to defend themselves against their assailants. Further, they are often unable to identify attackers or may be unwilling to report crimes or press charges for fear of reprisal. Crimes against the elderly are often called **crib jobs,** because robbing an old person is supposedly like taking candy from a baby.

A 33-year-old woman decided to experience victimization by "becoming old" herself. Donning a gray wig, wearing semiopaque glasses, and putting splints and bandages on her legs, she created, at various times, three characters: a bag lady, a middle-income woman, and an affluent woman. She traveled through 116 big cities and small towns across the United States, walking the streets, eating at restaurants, and living in motels. While some people were kind to her, she was overwhelmed at the abusive and neglectful attitudes of others and by the constraints she suffered because of transportation systems inadequate for those who have difficulty walking or seeing. She was mugged twice in New York City. Today she lectures to designers and gerontologists on the needs of elders (Ryan, 1993).

Some elders defy the stereotype of being weak and easily threatened. A 73-year-old woman in New York City fought off an intruder and foiled a rape attempt in her apartment ("Woman, 73, Battles Intruder," 1991). In an elder housing project, the tenants got involved when gang members attacked 12 older women over a three-week period, choking them from behind, punching them, and stealing their money. Older tenants were instrumental in helping police set up a stakeout and came forward as witnesses to identify those arrested. Anger won out over fear as the residents who "didn't want to take this" came forward (Hevesi, 1994).

These examples are not meant to advocate fighting back in every circumstance. It is not widely recommended that *anyone* fight an armed assailant. These accounts merely remind us that not all old people are easily intimidated. If this fact were more widely known, the number of attempted attacks might decrease.

The damage an attack can do to an older person is hard to measure. Crime can destroy one's possessions, body, and emotional well-being. Attacks against persons can shatter pride and self-esteem. They can change one's view of the world from one of trust and security to one of bitterness and paranoia and can change one's concept of humanity from good to bad. The memory of an attack can disturb sleep and rest and cause continuous anxiety during waking hours. Recouping financial losses because of crime can be difficult or impossible for the older victim. And, although a bodily attack may be fatal to anyone, the danger of serious injury is even greater for frail oldsters, whose bones break more easily and for whom the shock of assault may trigger heart or respiratory failure. Sensory acuity diminished by age may be completely destroyed by a blow to the head.

Fear of Attack

The National Opinion Research Center (NORC) has conducted national surveys on the **fear of crime.** When asked, "Is there any area right around here (your home) that is within a mile where you would be afraid to walk alone at night?" more than 50 percent of those over age 65 answered yes. The image of frightened older persons barricaded behind locked doors, however, is overplayed in the media. A study in Dade County (Miami), Florida, found that the elderly did not have a statistically higher fear of crime than did younger adults (McCoy et al., 1996). This suggests that fearfulness might be less evident in relatively age-homogeneous neighborhoods, or that older people are capable of making context-based judgments of community safety. The Florida study found that dissatisfaction with neighborhood and physical vulnerability were important correlates of fear of crime, but that actual victimization experience is not the main determinant of fear.

Most literature and research find, however, that older persons are more afraid of crime than younger persons. The literature consistently reports that women are more fearful than men,

© Harry Cutting

Fear often accompanies frailty because being frail means having less personal control over life's events. Being frail, alone, and frightened is the bleak circumstance that some elders experience.

African Americans are more fearful than whites, those with less money are more fearful than those with more money, and residents of large cities are more fearful than people in smaller towns and rural areas.

The manner in which fear of crime should affect social policy is not entirely clear. On the surface, it would appear that one way to reduce fear of crime among elders would be to segregate them in walled and guarded retirement communities. But age segregation in our society could have undesirable consequences. Studies show generally that the more integrated one is in community activities, the less one fears crime. Related to this is the finding that one feels less threatened by crime if one knows and trusts one's neighbors. The social implication is that developing cohesive, close-knit communities reduces fear of crime. These two alternatives are opposites, but either may be needed depending on the possibility of elders' developing a close-knit, friendly neighborhood.

A consistent finding over the years has been that although older women fear crime more than older men, they are less likely to be victims. And though older people are more fearful than younger people, they are less likely to be victims. One explanation for this paradox may be that women and elders, considering themselves to be more vulnerable, do not as often expose themselves to risk. An additional explanation may be that they associate more minor offenses with more serious ones. For example, an older person, thinking that begging is a pretext for mugging, might be more afraid of a beggar than a younger person is. A woman might fear burglary more than a man because of the threat of rape in addition to theft. Thus, the possible consequences of the criminal act can be as frightening as the fear of victimization itself.

Fighting Back

In many cities, new programs aimed at preventing crime against the elderly, helping those older persons who have become victims, and teaching them what they can do to help themselves are receiving priority. One common approach is the use of police units trained in the problems particular to older people. Such units tip off the elderly to the latest trends in crime, help them to be on the alert for suspicious activity, and instruct them how to be effective witnesses against criminals caught in the act. Programs such as **Neighborhood Watch,** which emphasizes crime awareness in residents of all ages, have resulted in crimes being spotted while in progress.

In many cities "granny squads" of older people patrol neighborhood blocks and give lectures on how to avoid being raped, robbed, and burglarized. Granny squads, organized under titles such as Heaven's Angels and Gray Squads, recommend such precautions as:

- Report all suspicious persons and all crimes to the police

- Use automatic timers to turn on radios and lamps when you are away from home

- Do not carry a purse. Make a band to wear inside clothing to carry money

- Have Social Security and pension checks mailed directly to the bank

- Join a Neighborhood Block Watch, in which neighbors in a block meet each other and watch out for one another's person and property

Some cities provide escort services to older people when they are the most vulnerable to attack—such as on trips to stores and banks. For example, one Chicago police district, on the day that Social Security and relief checks arrive, supplies a bus and driver to pick up people from two housing projects, take them to a bank and a grocery store, and then return them safely home. New York City police, hoping to bridge the gap between young and old, use teenage volunteers to provide escort services for elderly persons. In Milwaukee, Wisconsin, neighborhood security aides patrol the streets in high-crime areas that house many older residents, walking in pairs to offer safety in numbers. Although they have no power to arrest, they carry two-way radios to call police or firefighters if they encounter suspicious persons.

Efforts to protect elders from crime exist at the state level as well. Many states offer reimbursement programs for crime victims, and some of these programs give priority to older persons. A New York state law makes a prison sentence mandatory for anyone, including a juvenile, who commits a violent crime against an elderly person. Many states have extended child-abuse laws to include elders. Other states are currently considering legislation that does

For the incarcerated elder, "aging in place" has a particularly poignant meaning. Re-entering society for the older person can be a huge mental and physical task.

not allow probation for those who commit crimes against older persons.

Aging Criminals

Although studies find that younger adults are at least 10 times more likely than elders to commit crimes, crime committed by the elderly is very much a reality. Most crimes committed by elders are misdemeanors—petty theft, sleeping on the sidewalk, alcohol violations, and traffic violations. Shoplifting is a frequent misdemeanor charge, and most shoplifters are white females. But felonies occur as well, most frequently in the form of grand theft and narcotic charges.

There is not necessarily a relationship between economic hardship and crime. Typically, older people are caught stealing lipstick, perfume, night creams, even cigars. They are not necessarily stealing to eat. Shoplifting among elders represents the combined influence of stress, age, and merchandising; fear for the future may compel some to shoplift in order to conserve money for anticipated expenses. Some steal to ease fear; others do it to get attention. Psychologically, stealing may reflect feelings of deprivation in human relationships (Dullea, 1986). Only a minority of elder shoplifters have been engaged in criminal activity throughout their lives.

In general, the older perpetrator accounts for only a minority of all crimes committed. The average percentage of elders incarcerated is 30.7 percent for men and 32.1 percent for females, with only about 6.6 percent of the U.S. prison population above the age of 50 (Camp & Camp, 1996). The proportion, however, is expected to increase, and by 2005 the population of inmates 50 and over in federal prisons is projected to be between 11.7 percent and 16 percent (Smyer et al., 1997). Their number more than doubled between 1981 and 1990 (Morton, 1992). The criminal activities most likely to be engaged in by older inmates are (1) violence against a family member, (2) white-collar crimes such as fraud, (3) drug sales, and (4) alcohol-related crimes such as vehicular manslaughter.

Older Professional Criminals

Professional criminals tend to remain active because crime represents their life's work. The longevity of some professional thieves is incredible. Joseph (Yellow Kid) Weil, a prototype for Paul Newman's role in *The Sting*, lived to be over 100 years old and was last arrested at age 72. Willie Sutton, professional bank robber, was into his 80s and still on parole when he died

(Newman, 1984). Most leaders of organized crime are in the upper registers of the age scale. Organized crime is age stratified, and the heads of "families" tend to be well over 50. Vito Genovese died in prison at age 71, still commanding his organization from his cell. Older offenders also play an important role in white-collar crime. And as the percentage of elders increases in the total population, their percentage of criminal arrests will probably increase as well.

Growing Old behind Bars

More people are being sent to prison and receiving longer sentences, increasing the number of older prisoners. In California, for example, the number of inmates over 50 increased to 6,735 (4.8 percent of the total) from 3,874 (4 percent of the total) in 1996 alone (Anderson, 1997). Older convicts are either chronic offenders who have grown old in a steady series of prison terms, offenders sentenced to long mandatory terms who have grown old in prison, or first-time offenders in their old age.

The routine of prison life starkly separates the old from the young and middle-aged. The young men tend to be muscled and heavily tattooed, have an "in-your-face" attitude, and form groups, even gangs, for friendship and safety. The old men tend to keep to themselves, trying to find quiet. The gang tensions, the chaos, the constant chatter, and the televisions going from early morning to late at night take their toll over the years. There is virtually nothing in the construction of prison life that acknowledges the needs of older prisoners.

The greater threat, beyond illness or victimization is despair. Many prisoners . . . "put their lives on hold." As they age, they begin to face the fact that they may never get out. "The dream of getting out, you equate with heaven. Dying in prison, you equate with hell."

PRISON INMATE, QUOTED IN ANDERSON, 1997

Taxpayers have reason to be alarmed by the increasing numbers, along with prison officials and humanitarians. Prison inmates are not eligible for Medicare or Medicaid. Age and illness are more strongly associated behind bars, given the prisoner's life of chronic stress, idleness, cigarettes, and heavy food. Prison costs for eyeglasses and dentures and for treatment for heart surgery, emphysema, prostate problems, strokes, and other age-related needs and conditions are rapidly growing and will continue to do so. The average annual maintenance with medical costs for inmates 55 and older in California was estimated to be $69,000 in 1997—triple that of younger prisoners (Smyer et al., 1997). An Iowa study of 119 male inmates 50 and older found increased rates of incontinence and sensory impairment, as well as 40 percent with hypertension, 97 percent with missing teeth, and 42 percent with gross physical impairment; in addition, 70 percent were smokers (Colsher, 1992).

Tish Smyer and colleagues, on reviewing the mental and physical health of elderly prison inmates, concluded that new models of incarceration are emerging, and changes must continue to be made:

> The use of medical parole/release, community placement (secure skilled nursing facilities . . .), and growing use of prison hospice programs are being implemented as an alternative to placement of the chronically ill or elderly inmate in the general prison population. Those with functional disabilities who require help with activities of daily living may require more intensive contact with skilled professionals and counselors. Their dependent status merely intensifies the meaning of violence and powerlessness to these elderly inmates within the prison environment. (Smyer et al., 1997, p. 16)

Elder Abuse

Most abuse of elders is done by the person with whom he or she lives. Often an adult child is the abuser. Though we are familiar with battered child syndrome, evidence increasingly indicates a corresponding syndrome at the other end of the age scale—**battered parent syndrome**—in which parents are attacked and abused, sometimes fatally, by their own children. Factors that increase the risk of a caregiver's becoming an abuser include alcohol and drug abuse, cognitive impairment, economic stress, caregiver inexperience, a history of family violence, a blaming personality, unrealistic expectations, and economic dependence on the elder (Allan, 1998).

Among community-dwelling elders in the United States and other Western countries, it is estimated that between 3 and 6 percent of individuals over the age of 65 report having experienced abuse, usually at the hands of family members (Ogg & Bennett, 1992; Podkieks, 1992; Lachs et al., 1997).

Abuse can be intentional (e.g., willfully withholding food or medications) or unintentional, resulting from ignorance or the genuine inability to provide the necessary care (Allan, 1998). On a national level, neglect is by far the most common form of abuse, followed by physical abuse, then financial and material exploitation (Lachs et al., 1997). Several measures of abuse have been identified:

1. *Physical abuse* is the willful infliction of pain or injury and may include beating, choking, burning, inappropriate medication, tying or locking up, and sexual assault

2. *Psychological abuse* includes threats, intimidation, and verbal abuse

3. *Financial or material abuse* means taking financial advantage of frail or ill elderly. It is the misuse of an elder's money or property: theft, deception, diversion of income, or mismanagement of funds

4. *Violation of rights.* Old people have the right to vote and the right to due process. A conservator, for example, may take away all the rights of an older person

5. *Neglect* occurs when a caregiver's failure to provide adequate food, shelter, clothing,

TABLE 13.2

Theoretical explanations of elder abuse

Theory	Description
Psychological model	Relationship of violent behavior to aggressive personality traits; at the most severe end of physical aggression, large proportions of elder abusers have histories of mental illness and/or substance abuse. Intervention is individual, focused on the caregiver.
Situational model	Abuse as a problem of caregiving; high levels of stress and burden of caregiving increase mistreatment and neglect of the frail elder. Intervention is on stress reduction of the care-provider.
Symbolic interaction model	Each person approaches in interaction with personal definitions and expectations; if behaviors match the roles expected, the interaction continues, otherwise conflict arises. The caregiver's subjective sense of stress related to the dependency tasks creates stress, not the tasks themselves. Assessment of the caring situation by caregivers is necessary for abuse prevention.
Social exchange theory	When each individual contributes equally, a fair exchange results; when one party is unable to reciprocate, the exchange is seen as being unfair. Unequal distribution of power in caregiving situations can result in abuse. In this model, intervention should focus on the abuser.
Feminist theory	Identifies violence as a tactic of entitlement and power that is deeply gendered, rather than a conflict tactic that is personal and gender neutral. This model has been more successful in explaining wife abuse than child or elder abuse.
Ecological model	Focuses on behavior within the social context and on the accommodation between the person and the environment. According to this model, mobilization of the community is the intervention strategy.
Political economy model	Elder abuse arises from the way older people are marginalized in society. These experiences are a product of the division of labor and structure of inequality in society, rather than a product of relationship and aging. Intervention focuses on change in social policy.

Source: Adapted from Wolf, Rosalie S. (1997). Elder abuse and neglect: Causes and consequences. *Journal of Geriatric Psychiatry*, 30 (1), 153–174.

and medical or dental care results in significant danger to the physical or mental health of an older person in his or her care

6. *Self-abuse and neglect.* Some old people do not adequately care for themselves. Sometimes it is intentional; other times they simply cannot adequately provide for themselves

One example of elder abuse is an active form of neglect informally called **granny dumping.** This term is used by emergency workers at hospitals to refer to the abandonment of frail elders. It has been most recorded in Florida, California, and Texas. A Tampa, Florida, emergency room staff found a woman sitting in a wheelchair with a note that said, "She's sick. Please take care of her." More commonly, the older person is brought to the hospital by family members or a nursing home. When the patient has recovered, there is no one in sight to take the patient home. Elder abandonment has increased over the last few years as medical and other costs of elder care have accelerated.

The abuse of elders, despite the cruelty of the crime, is not a well-studied topic, and therefore systematic ways to address the problem have not been developed in social policy. Table 13.2 presents a summary of existing theories of elder abuse developed by Dr. Rosalie S. Wolf, president of the National Committee for the Prevention of Elder Abuse. The table shows that resolution of the problem of elder abuse depends on the theoretical perspective taken: psychological models address caregiver personality and relationships in the family setting, while other models look to the community and to the larger society (Wolf, 1997).

The primary policy implication for the issue of elder abuse is that strained families must have more help available to them—help from social services, home care services, protective services, personal care services, and family counseling.

The profile of the typical abused elder has traditionally pointed to the frail, widowed female who is cognitively impaired and chronically ill. Subsequent studies, however, show wider variation in the at-risk older adult. In one nine-year study of more than 2,800 elders linked to abusive victimization through adult protective service records, the predictors of mistreatment were poverty, race, functional and cognitive impairment, worsening cognitive impairment, and living with someone (Lachs et al., 1997). Gender did not emerge as a profile in this study.

A common predictor of abusive behavior is economic dependence. In one case, an older woman lived with her son and supported him even though he drank all the time and abused her. In another case, an older mother cared for her epileptic daughter, who stole money from her. In some cases, wives were abused by the severely disabled husbands they were caring for. Abusers are rarely stable individuals, brought to the brink by the excessive demands of an elderly dependent; rather, these caretakers suffer emotionally and are barely able to meet their own needs, much less the needs of another person. The older person who stays in an abusive situation can see no better alternative. Under the social exchange theory, the abuser's lack of power is a factor in the abuse. The caretaker's dependency, especially his or her financial dependency, rather than the dependency of the victim, correlates most strongly with abuse.

Abuse can and does take place in nursing homes by staff. Older persons are more at risk in institutions than in their own homes because of their exceptional frailty and the danger of retaliation by caretakers (Sengstock et al., 1990). Abuse in institutions is not necessarily reported or reflected in national statistics. A survey revealed that 36 percent of the staff at several nursing homes had observed other staff psychologically abusing patients and had witnessed physical abuse that included employing excessive restraints; pushing, grabbing, kicking, or shoving patients; or throwing things at patients. Over 70 percent of the psychological abuse included yelling and swearing at patients; this abuse also included isolating patients, threatening them, and denying them food and/or privileges (Pillemer & Moore, 1989). Despite existing regulations monitoring the treatment of institutionalized elders, the need for vigilance remains. Penalties have been stiffened, county and state agencies are being given more power to investigate and prosecute, and people are being encouraged to report suspicious happenings. Signs of abuse include abrupt negative changes in physical appearance; inappropriate behavior, such as extreme fear, asking to die, or extreme anger; a bad attitude on the part of the caregiver; and deteriorated or isolated living quarters. As more people live to extreme old age and, thus, to the point of becoming physically dependent on someone else, adequate social service programming for elder care is critical.

Fraud

Any person with money is a potential victim of the huckster and the con artist. Although victims of confidence schemes and consumer frauds who file crime reports are not normally required to give their age, accounts of fraud state that the elders who constitute approximately 13 percent of the population represent approximately 30 percent of those who are swindled. Many elders have accumulated a nest egg over the years or have recently come into a large lump-sum pension or life insurance benefit. Some may be seeking investments they can make with relative ease; for some, low returns on passbook savings accounts motivate the search for new investments. And elders are more likely to be at home when a con artist calls. The following descriptions summarize some of the major kinds of fraud.

Social Referral

Some dating and marriage services seek out the lonely and the widowed to lure them into paying big fees for introductions to new friends or possible mates. A victim may pay hundreds of dollars for a video to be shown to prospective dates (and then it is never shown) or for a computerized dating service that never generates any dates. Religious cults also have targeted elders and even entire retirement communities as recruitment areas for new members (Collins & Frantz, 1994).

Land and Home Equity Fraud

In one type of **land fraud**, real-estate developers may offer lots for sale in a still-to-be-built retirement community, promising all kinds of facilities, such as swimming pools and golf courses, and describing the site in glowing phrases. None of the descriptions and promises may be accurate.

Home-equity fraud has left some elders homeless (Wallace & Williamson, 1992). Swindlers pose as financial experts who offer help in refinancing a home. The swindler ends up with the cash from the home-equity loan or actually gets the owner to unwittingly sign papers transferring title.

Fraud through Mail Order and Television

Mail-order catalogs and television advertising can be misleading and result in **mail-order fraud.** Ads, which may be hoaxes or wild exaggerations, tout nutritional miracles, breast developers, and weight-reducing and exercise devices. Mail ordering and phone ordering from television ads are particularly attractive for those who no longer have transportation. Although many firms are honest, the mail-order and television industries have yet to eliminate the racketeers in their midst.

Mail-order health insurance has, in the past, proved to be worth little. Fraudulent hospitalization policies can be filled with small-print exceptions—ifs, ands, and buts that will eliminate the policyholder when a claim is made. Coverage for the person may not exist at the very time when he or she is suffering from failing health and needs hospitalization.

In 1986, a national consumers' group filed a complaint charging 19 insurance companies with trying to sell extra health insurance to elders using deceptive mailings that bore official-sounding names and Washington, D.C., addresses. These companies sent out hundreds of letters warning people about Medicare cutbacks. Those who returned a response card, thinking they were dealing with a concerned government group, were solicited by insurance agents. The companies were given cease-and-desist orders (Reich & Morrison, 1986). In a similar case, U.S. attorneys are conducting mail fraud investigations on a direct-mail kingpin of the political Right who exploits the fears of elders by telling them their Social Security benefits are being taken away (Stone, 1993).

The "contest winner" fraud is ever present in our mail system. In some, the "winner" of a vacation, car, stereo, or other prize must either send money for postage or registration or pay to make a long-distance telephone call for more information. Twice in four months, an 88-year-old man flew, confirmation letter in hand, to

Florida to collect his $11 million "winnings." The letter read, "Final results are in, and they're official. You're our newest $11 million winner." The fine print, however, fully informed the "winner" that a specific winning number was required. In a statement to Ann Landers, the attorney general of Florida was quoted as saying, "In their zeal to sell magazines, American Family Publishers and their high-profile pitchmen have misled millions of consumers. They have clearly stepped over the line from advertising hype to unlawful deception" ("Sweepstakes' Fine Print Tells All," 1998).

Telephone Fraud

Telephone fraud is also a problem. For some elders, telephone contact is their primary source of interaction with other people. In New York, an 80-year-old woman reported that she had lost thousands of dollars to telemarketers because "I've been a widow for 19 years. It's very lonely. They were nice on the phone. They became my friends." Said a 77-year-old man, "I wasn't a victim—I was a sucker. I lost $200,000" ("Phone Swindlers Dangle Prizes," 1997). The typical story is that the elder has won a wonderful prize—a vacation in Hawaii, a new car, or substantial cash. They then are asked to send a check by overnight mail to cover taxes, postage and handling of the winnings. The same people often fall prey to more than one scheme.

Telephones are now the vehicle of choice for committing fraud. Telemarketing fraud accounts for $10 billion in investor losses annually, and southern California alone has as many as 300 **boiler rooms** (offices from which the telephone calls are made) functioning at any one time. The telephone vacation scam has lured may retirees. Callers tout fantastic-sounding Hawaiian packages for an unbelievably low price—$179 for two people for a week, for example. The "lucky traveler" need only provide his or her credit card number for reservations. But the trip is either postponed indefinitely or uses sleazy hotels with untold extra charges.

A Tennessee criminal fraud investigation team recommended to elders: (1) beware of requests for money to prepay taxes; (2) beware of requests to send a check by overnight delivery; (3) beware of requests for credit card numbers to show eligibility; (4) beware of a rush for action; and (5) to fight back, just hang up ("Phone Swindlers Dangle Prizes," 1997).

Credit Card Fraud

Credit card fraud, in which swindlers find ways to get your card number and charge items on your account, has become widespread. The increased incidence of identity-theft among all age groups through credit card use, including credit card theft through Internet purchases, has reached startling proportions. Senior centers and other community organizations, as well as credit card companies themselves, are working diligently to educate people about safe use of the credit card.

Door-to-Door Sales

Peddlers of various kinds of merchandise often target the homebound because their loneliness makes them eager for conversation. Some salespeople are honest; others sell shoddy goods or offer useless services. For example, a salesperson might scare a person into contracting for unnecessary home repairs and then flee with the down payment. Or one salesperson may make a pitch while the other robs the house (Cronk, 1998).

Life Alert, a company whose television ads used the memorable line "Help! I've fallen and I can't get up!" has been sued for deceptive advertising. The lawsuit, which contends that the company uses high-pressure sales tactics (including sales presentations that last up to six hours) and misleading ads to bully old people into buying the product, alleges that salespeople lied to senior citizens and disabled persons during sales pitches and refused to leave until a sale—the system's cost ranged from $1,700 to $5,000—was made. Misrepresentations included the claim of an emergency hotline more reliable than the public 911 system (Holding, 1991).

Investment Fraud

Many "get-rich" schemes are used to fleece older people. Older people eager to invest their savings as a hedge against inflation may become victims of numerous investment frauds involving bogus inventions or phony businesses. One California scam artist was convicted of stealing close to $700,000 from mostly older investors invited by mail to investment seminars (Brignolo, 1998).

Estate Planning Ripoffs

Some scam artists contact elders to offer services in preparing living trusts. They charge high fees, make phony pledges, and make off with money, and no living trust is provided (Crenshaw, 1992). Court-appointed guardians or conservators assigned to look after older persons are in a position to steal from them, and some do. To preserve an inheritance, children will sometimes force adult parents to live in inferior dwellings. Individual cases can become complicated when the line between generosity and friendship and fraudulent taking advantage becomes blurred. In a California case, a savings and loan manager conservator, as well as the corporation for which he works, are being sued for $10 million on behalf of family members of a woman with Alzheimer's disease, whose friendship with the thrift manager clearly preceded her mental deterioration (Mintz, 1998). Some authorities are urging the government and the courts to more closely audit estates so that abuse can be discovered. They also suggest a limit on the yearly fees that conservators can charge.

A study of guardianship revealed the following:

1. The elderly in guardianship courts are often afforded fewer rights than criminal defendants
2. The overburdened court systems puts elders' lives in the hands of others without

Because some elders experience loneliness and isolation or reduced judgment, they are a group targeted by unethical businesses. Companionship, advocacy, and legal vigilance can help protect the more vulnerable of the country's elders.

enough evidence that such placement is necessary

3. The more than 300,000 persons age 65 and over who live under guardianship are "unpersons" in that they can no longer receive money or pay bills, marry, or choose where they will live or what medical treatment they receive

Though most appointed guardians are dedicated, caring people, there are not enough safeguards against the minority who are corrupt and greedy (Associated Press, 1987).

Medicare and Medicaid Fraud

One kind of medical hoax involves outrageous abuses of the federal Medicare and state Medicaid programs. The violators are licensed physicians and registered pharmacists who file exaggerated claims for reimbursement.

Despite an elaborate system of safeguards, some experts say that the Medicare program is being bilked out of millions of dollars a year. Vague regulations, overworked investigators, swamped claims processors, and gullible consumers all play a part. Typical frauds identified by federal fraud investigation teams include (1) a 20-minute procedure being billed as a 24-hour procedure, (2) unnecessary surgery, (3) billing for multiple procedures when a single procedure was used, (4) the submission of bills for patients who are no longer living, and (5) the sale of outrageously overpriced medical equipment for which Medicare pays 80 percent.

U.S. Health and Human Services has paid out nearly $2 million to recruit and train retired professionals to fight against fraud, waste, and abuse in Medicare and Medicaid. Twelve projects have been funded to develop demonstrations to train people in uncovering federal insurance fraud. The Administration on Aging estimates that as much as 14 percent of Medicare claims ($23.2 billion) were overpaid in 1996 because of improper fee-for-service billings (Bellandi, 1997). The program trains volunteers to work with people in their communities to help them understand their benefits and look for overbilling and unnecessary care. In California, more than 500 volunteers work in 24 health insurance counseling and advocacy programs (HICAPs) to help seniors and Social Security offices navigate Medicare's explanation of benefits (Bellandi, 1997).

Confidence Games

Con artists use various tactics. In **confidence games,** the victim is tricked into giving up money voluntarily. Several games are common. Some examples are (1) the "block hustle," in which the con artist sells the victim a worthless item that he or she claims is both stolen and valuable; (2) the "pigeon drop," in which the victim is persuaded to put up money on the promise of making much more; and (3) the "lottery swindle," in which the victim pays cash for counterfeit lottery tickets. In one case a man was arrested for bilking older tenants by dunning them with fake water bills (James, 1994).

Medical Quackery

Though **medical quackery,** the misrepresentation of either health or cosmetic benefits through devices or drugs that are presumably therapeutic, can target both young and old, older people tend to be more prone to this kind of victimization. For one thing, older persons often have more ailments than younger persons; for another, the "youth culture" in the United States sometimes leads older persons on a medical quest to look younger.

Many who offer medical goods and services are honest. Some are not, however, and the elderly are often cheated. Americans spend about $27 billion a year on quack products or treatments. The top five health frauds in the United States, according to the FDA, are (1) ineffective arthritis products, (2) spurious cancer clinics (many of which are located in Mexico), (3) bogus AIDS cures (offered at underground clinics in the United States, the Caribbean, and Europe), (4) instant weight-loss schemes, and (5) fraudulent sexual aids ("The Top Ten Health Frauds," 1990). We will cover four topics here: medical devices, youth restorers and **miracle drugs,** cancer cures, and arthritis cures.

Medical Devices

According to the Federal Trade Commission, many older Americans who need such medical devices as eyeglasses, hearing aids, and dentures frequently are victims of overpricing, misrepresentation, and high-pressure sales tactics. And because Medicare does not cover the cost of these items, many persons cannot pay for the devices and must do without them. Some of the abuses include a 200 to 300 percent variation in the cost of identical eyeglasses, dentures, hearing aids; and outrageous profits for lifesaving devices such as heart pacemakers, which may sell for four times the manufacturing cost.

Youth Restorers and Miracle Drugs

Elders are likely targets for products that promise to restore the appearance of youth—cosmetics, skin treatments, hair restorers, male potency pills, wrinkle and "age spot" removers, and the like. In a society such as ours, which glamorizes youth, the desire to remain young is strong.

Like the medicine shows that once traveled from town to town offering miracle tonics and multipurpose cures, those who today provide cosmetic surgery and breast implants are enjoying a booming business. Unfortunately, the cosmetic surgery field contains many quacks. Poorly trained surgeons have mutilated patients' faces and bodies and endangered lives.

Even ads for beauty products that promise to restore wrinkled skin border on quackery. But even though the Federal Drug Administration (FDA) believes that many such claims are misleading if not absolutely false, the interpretation of the law is fuzzy, and there's not much that can be done.

The skin-care market has grown into a huge moneymaking industry. Dermatologists say that despite the claims of all the antiaging creams and lotions, there is no substance that can alter the structure or functioning of your living skin. The only thing that any product can hope to do is add some moisture to the top layer of skin. Nevertheless, advertisers are having a heyday because the FDA spends its time regulating more harmful substances.

Even products that have been FDA approved tend to be advertised with exaggerated claims. A product called Retin-A (generic name: tretinoin), originally used to treat acne, is now touted as a miraculous cure for wrinkles. Actually it is not a permanent cure. Further, use of the product, like use of any chemical product, carries some risks and side effects. The FDA-approved antibaldness medication minoxidil, under the brand name Rogaine, may not produce a perfect head of hair and does not work for everybody.

Cancer Cures

Cancer victims have been offered "cures" ranging from sea water at $3 per pint to irradiated grape juice to machines alleged to cure cancer. Scientific studies have not shown laetrile, a substance extracted from apricot seeds, to have value in treating cancer. The FDA's refusal to approve laetrile has caused many states to ban it. Yet, many cancer sufferers claim to have been helped by the drug.

Many factors account for the popularity of proven "cures" like laetrile. Because hundreds of thousands of new cancer cases are diagnosed each year and because two out of three victims will ultimately die of it, people are rightfully afraid of cancer. Conventional treatment is neither simple nor pleasant—surgery is often extensive, radiation can burn, chemotherapy can cause hair loss and vomiting. Laetrile offers a far easier treatment. It comes in tablets to be taken with large doses of vitamin C on a low-sugar diet that avoids all foods containing additives.

Fraudulent cancer cures rob the sick not only of their money. Cancer quacks also rob their victims of the most precious thing they have: time for proper treatment.

AIDS patients who can perceive no cure in the traditional medical establishment are especially willing to try unconventional treatments. In desperate efforts to prolong their lives, AIDS patients are prime targets for medical quackery. Some have spent thousands of dollars on worthless cures.

Arthritis Cures

Arthritis is the most common chronic condition of elders. An inflammation that makes joints stiff and painful to move, arthritis appears in a hundred or so forms, the most severe and crippling of which is rheumatoid arthritis. Some forms of arthritis are painless; others cause severe pain.

Because no one knows exactly what causes arthritis, doctors can do little more than prescribe pain relievers. This lack of certainty leaves the field wide open for all kinds of fake cures. Copper bracelets have been sold to cure arthritis. Wearing two kinds of metal in each shoe purportedly sets up "chemical impulses" that ward off pain. Various diets, cod-liver oil, brown vinegar with honey, "immune" milk, alfalfa tablets, megavitamins, and snake or bee venom have all been sold to "cure" arthritis.

Drug Abuse

Elders can be victims of drug abuse. Our society offers drugs—both legal and illegal—as a solution to a host of problems. The abuses discussed here are not those involving illegal drugs, such as heroin and cocaine, but those that involve legal drugs: prescription drugs, over-the-counter drugs, and alcohol.

Prescription Drugs

Though persons of all ages need prescription drugs for various health problems, elders need them in much greater proportions, because they are more likely to suffer from chronic illnesses or pain. The elderly, who comprise 13 percent of the population, consume 30 percent of all prescribed drugs (Blazer, 1990). More than 30 percent of all prescriptions for Seconal and Valium, two potent and potentially addictive sedatives, are written for persons over age 60.

With high drug usage, a more significant chance exists for adverse drug reactions and drug abuse. Health professionals are responsible for some of the drug abuse suffered by the older population. Their errors can be of two types: not prescribing a drug correctly or prescribing fewer or more drugs or a lower or higher dose than necessary. A study from Harvard University found that almost one-fourth of seniors are prescribed drugs that by themselves or in combination are dangerous or wrong (Stolberg, 1994). But such errors can sometimes seem intentional. Health professionals in nursing homes, for example, may overprescribe drugs so that patients become calm and easier to manage. When overused, drugs can stupefy, injure, and kill. Educational intervention is advised, not only for older drug consumers, but for practicing physicians and pharmacists as well.

The nation's nearly 2 million nursing home residents are perhaps its most medicated people, often suffering depression and disorientation from receiving too high a dosage of drugs such as Valium, Calpa, and Elavil or a combination of such drugs. Elderly patients both in and out of nursing homes may get prescriptions from several doctors and then have reactions from their combined ingestion. Friends may exchange prescription drugs without regard to side effects or combination (synergistic) reactions with other medications. They also may mix prescription and over-the-counter drugs without realizing that the interactions can be harmful. Or they may take the wrong amounts of their own medications. Adverse drug reactions occur more frequently in old age, and multiple drug use should be closely monitored.

Stereotypes and the negative portrayal of older people have a considerable impact on a physician's prescribing habits. In ads in physicians' magazines, such as *Geriatrics,* elders tend to be pictured as inactive and described in negative terms: aimless, apathetic, disruptive, insecure, out of control, and temperamental. Drug advertising influences the medical professional to offer drugs as a first solution to emotionally disturbed elders; viewing old people in this manner may result in a physician's giving increased prescriptions.

Over-the-Counter Drugs

Although over-the-counter (OTC) drugs may seem harmless, they are overused and consequently abused. One can either blame the drug companies, which push their products through advertising, or the poorly informed consumer. Aspirin is the most widely used OTC drug. Many old people use very high doses of aspirin for arthritis, even though aspirin is a stomach irritant and can deplete the body of essential nutrients. (Some doctors use a milder drug, suprofen, rather than aspirin, to treat arthritis, but suprofen is not available over the counter.) And, though laxatives have been advertised as "nature's way," nothing is further from the truth. Prolonged laxative use can impair normal bowel function. Nature's way is plenty of water and fiber in the diet; many people, however, become addicted to laxatives, thinking they are making the best choice. The same is true of those who take sleeping pills, which must be taken in escalating doses to be effective. Consequently, they can cause rather than cure insomnia (Kolata, 1992). Because people need less sleep as they get older, many are better off accepting this fact rather than trying to force themselves to sleep eight or more hours a night. Antacids such as Alka-Seltzer contain sodium bicarbonate, which may harm kidney function. Hemorrhoid medication ads exaggerate the effectiveness of their products, and mouthwash does little more than add to the complaints of dry mouth. These OTC drugs can be a waste of money, cause bodily harm, and delay proper treatment of potentially serious ailments.

Alcoholism

Alcoholism as a problem for elders has been largely ignored until recent years. If, after retirement, older persons lead much less visible lives, alcoholism can remain well concealed, becoming a self-generating cycle of abuse: diminished contacts and a sense of loss may trigger drinking that goes unrecognized.

Alcoholism: " . . . a primary, chronic disease with genetic, psychosocial and environmental factors influencing its development and manifestations. The disease is often progressive and fatal. It is characterized by impaired control over drinking, preoccupation with the drug alcohol, use of alcohol despite adverse consequences, and distortions in thinking, most notably denial."

NATIONAL COUNCIL ON ALCOHOLISM AND DRUG DEPENDENCE AND THE AMERICAN SOCIETY OF ADDICTION MEDICINE (REPORTED IN MORSE & FLAVIN, 1992)

Elders do *not* have higher rates of alcoholism than younger adults, however, and one review of the literature concluded that alcohol consumption goes down with age. In addition, there are fewer alcohol-related problems among heavy drinkers who were elderly than among those who were not (Liberto et al., 1992). Among those with problems, however, the strain on the body of alcoholism is profound.

Some older alcoholics began their drinking early in life; others do not drink heavily until old age. Between half and two-thirds of older alcoholics are estimated to have begun early in life (Council on Scientific Affairs, 1996). "Early-onset" alcoholics have had alcohol-related problems for years and are more identifiable because of earlier dysfunctional behavior that brought them to the attention of the medical or helping establishment. In contrast, "late-life-onset" alcoholics, who begin abusive drinking in their 50s or 60s, are often viewed as reactive drinkers, whose problem began after traumatic events such as the death of a spouse, retirement, or moving from an original home. The late-life-onset alcoholic will have fewer chronic health problems and is likely to drink alone at home. In cases where alcoholism first occurs in old age, the alcoholic will often respond readily to intervention—help for depression or loneliness, for example, may reduce the need for alcohol.

Treatment focuses on rebuilding a social support network and overcoming negative emotional states. Long-term alcoholics are more difficult, but not impossible, to help.

Psychiatric hospital and outpatient clinic records show that admission for alcoholism peaks in the 35-to-40 age group. Some researchers believe that alcoholism may be a self-limiting disease; that is, the decrease in alcoholism in the older age groups results not from treatment but from a spontaneous recovery with age due to factors such as a lowered social pressure to achieve. Others think that alcoholism kills many of its victims before they reach old age. Still, about 10 percent of elders manifest symptoms related to excessive use of alcohol. Older men are more at risk than older women. And two-thirds of older alcoholics are severe chronic alcoholics whose symptoms tend to be obvious and profound (Council on Scientific Affairs, 1996).

Risk factors for alcoholism in later life include: (1) family history of alcoholism; (2) personal history of excessive alcohol consumption; (3) discretionary time and money and/or opportunities to drink; (4) age-related volume of alcohol distribution in the body; (5) increased central nervous system sensitivity to alcohol; (6) pain or insomnia secondary to chronic medical disorders; and (7) other psychiatric disorders, such as schizophrenia and depression (Goldstein et al., 1996).

Alcoholics Anonymous (AA) and other groups can be instrumental in stopping heavy drinking. Countless people have benefited from AA. Addiction can touch even the powerful and the famous. The former first lady Betty Ford described her cross-addiction to alcohol and painkillers as "insidious." She went public about her multiple drug abuse and eventually founded the Betty Ford Rehabilitation Center. Many people, including the actors Mary Tyler Moore, Elizabeth Taylor, and Tony Curtis, have attended the clinic and gotten help for their drug abuse.

Promoting Consumer Education

Consumer education is vital in helping individuals to avoid fraud, medical quackery, and drug abuse. Adult education programs are one way of reaching the public. Videotapes and DVDs now provide advice on a variety of topics, such as how to buy a used car without being swindled, how to handle the estate of a deceased relative, or how to recognize and avoid con artists. Books and magazines offer consumer information aimed at the older population, covering topics such as prescription drugs and their side effects, as well as the use and abuse of over-the-counter drugs and alcohol. Consumer action groups are available for persons of all ages who want to support the creation of stricter consumer-protection laws and the enforcement of existing laws.

Chapter Summary

Suicide continues to be a significant problem among those 65 and over. The suicide *attempt* rate for older women is much higher than for older men, yet older men (white males, that is), have the highest rate of *actual* suicides of any age group. Many factors may be involved, especially dependency, depression, physical illness, and social isolation.

The dimensions of the problem of crime against elders are being studied by law enforcement and social agencies. National surveys show that elders are less likely to be victimized than younger adults, except in the area of personal larceny (e.g., purse and wallet snatchings), where attacks on elders are considerable. Over half of the violent victimizations occur in or near one's home. Fear of crime is widespread among elders and exists to a greater degree than the actual crime rate against them would suggest. It is the metropolitan elderly on whom fear of crime takes its greatest toll. Elders themselves can be the victimizers. Older criminals come from two groups: those who started at a young age engaging in illegal activities, and those who committed offenses for the first time in their later years. The older prison population is growing, but adequate medical care is lacking in jails and prisons.

Elders are the potential victims of hucksters and con artists. Land fraud, mail-order fraud, mail-order health insurance, and confidence games are used to deceive and cheat people out of money. Medical quackery often entices the sick and ailing. Medical devices, youth restorers, and cancer and arthritis cures have robbed many of their money. Elders are sometimes victims of drug abuse—both prescription and nonprescription drugs.

Education, self-help groups, and professional help should be available to assist elders with their special problems. Consumer education is useful in learning to detect frauds and gaining knowledge about over-the-counter and prescription drugs.

Key Terms

attempted suicides
battered parent
  syndrome
boiler rooms
confidence games
credit card fraud
crib job
crimes against persons
double suicides
fear of crime

granny dumping
home-equity fraud
land fraud
mail-order fraud
medical quackery
miracle drugs
Neighborhood Watch
rational suicide
successful suicides
suicide rate

Questions for Discussion

1. How does fear of crime affect one's behavior?
2. Imagine that you are an old person and your adult offspring is taking advantage of you in some way. How would you handle the situation?
3. Why might some elders be susceptible to con artists?
4. Imagine that you have just been cheated of $1,000 by a con artist who has promised that your money will be quadrupled in four days. What would you do?

Fieldwork Suggestions

Clip articles from magazines and newspapers that advertise goods and health insurance that are probably fraudulent. Find other evidence of fraud, such as letters from funeral homes, that border on the unethical.

Internet Activities

1. Locate a grief forum on the Internet. What themes do you find? What ages do you guess are represented among the correspondents? Can you find a source of Internet discussion about depression, death, and suicide that reflects the perspectives of older adults?
2. Write a content analysis of the Hemlock Society's Internet home page. What resources are linked? Why? How would you characterize the tone of the information presented?
3. Search a website that would provide useful and appropriate information for a family member concerned about alcohol consumption of an elderly person in the family. (Hint: try the American Medical Association and Alcoholics Anonymous home pages.)

14 Ethnicity, Gender, and Culture

Women

African Americans

Hispanic Americans

Asian Americans

Native Americans

Improving the Status of Ethnic Elders

Maya Angelou Offers the Grace of Good Advice

Paul Craig

The scope of Maya Angelou's life is breathtaking.

She has been during her 65 years an actress, dancer, journalist, educator, author, screenwriter and TV and movie director-producer. She also has served on federal commissions and, at the inauguration of President Clinton, delivered her poem, "On the Pulse of Morning."

Angelou's book, *Wouldn't Take Nothing for My Journey Now,* offers some of her thoughts on what the years have taught. From her comparatively tranquil vantage point as a professor at Wake Forest University in Winston-Salem, N.C., Angelou (pronounced AngeLOW) comments on everything from the status of women to tired phrases she hates.

Above all, Angelou issues a plea for honoring diversity as the country grows into a more varied mixture of peoples and creeds: "It is a time for the preachers, the rabbis, the priests and pundits and the professors to believe in the awesome wonder of diversity so that they can teach those who follow them. It is a time for parents to teach young people early on that in diversity there is beauty and there is strength."

Angelou admits she ponders death "with alarming frequency" but fears the loss of others more than her eventual demise, recommends forgiveness but no patience with fools and heartily recommends taking a day off now and then just for fun. She even suggests that paranoia can have its valid uses.

Maya Angelou, author, actress, political activist, teacher, philosopher, and spokesperson for honoring diversity in America.

On the less serious side, Angelou, always a woman who dresses in cheerful colors she says make her happy, writes of fashion's intimidation of those who "are imprisoned by powerful dictates on what is right and proper to wear. Those decisions made by others and sometimes at their convenience are not truly meant to make life better or finer or more graceful or more gracious. Many times they stem from greed, insensitivity and the need for control."

She also warns the whiners of the world, "Whining is not only graceless, but can be dangerous. It can alert a brute that a victim is in the neighborhood."

Some of her accomplishments?

She toured Europe with the cast of *Porgy and Bess* in 1952; has been an editor and writer in Cairo and in Ghana's capital, Accra; was northern coordinator of Martin Luther King Jr.'s Southern Christian Leadership Conference at the start of the 1960s; worked on commissions under Presidents Ford and Carter; acted in TV's *Roots;* and has seen her autobiographical works, such as *I Know Why the Caged Bird Sings,* adapted for television.

Additionally, she appeared in such plays as *Mother Courage* and *The Blacks,* was nominated for a Tony Award for her stage role in *Look Away,* and received a Pulitzer nomination for her book *Just Give Me a Cool Drink of Water 'Fore I Diiie.* (Yes, "i" three times is how she wanted to spell it.

Her career in education has included teaching in Italy, Ghana and Israel, as well as in American universities, including an appearance as distinguished visiting professor at California State University, Sacramento. And she has clear-cut evidence of her welcome at Wake Forest—the professorship is for life.

Her thoughtful work soars far above most "what I have learned" books. Angelou has things to say and says them gracefully. Her book is an excellent learning investment for any reader.

Author's Note: Born in 1928 as Marguerite Johnson, Maya Angelou was raised in rural Arkansas. She married a South African freedom fighter and lived for 5 years in Cairo, Egypt. During that time she became the editor of *The Arab Observer,* the only English-language news weekly in the Middle East; she taught in Ghana; and she was the feature editor of *The African Review.* In the 1960s she remarked that being black, female, non-Muslim, non-Arab, six feet tall, and American made for some interesting experiences in Africa! In addition to her profile talents in the English language, Dr. Angelou speaks French, Spanish, Italian, and West African Fanti.

Source: © 1993 *The Sacramento Bee.* Reprinted by permission.

Culture is "the shared values, traditions, norms, customs, arts, history, folklore, and institutions of a group of people" (Administration on Aging, 2001). This focus corrects a past tendency to ignore the diversity and richness that **ethnic groups** have added to American life and to assume that Americans' experiences are relatively similar, despite their roots, origins, and cultural traditions. Until recently the study of aging America was a study of the older white Americans who made up nearly 90 percent of America's elderly population, while the many ethnic and cultural groups were ignored. Generalizing from the larger population to all subcultures of elders is misleading, incorrect, and insensitive. Understanding culture helps people to understand how others see their world, and therefore to better understand one another's behaviors and attitudes. Being old and a member of a minority group, or being an old white woman, is to experience the political economy—the context of aging—in ways strikingly different than that experienced by older whites, particularly white males.

Cultural competence is defined as "a set of cultural behaviors and attitudes integrated into the practice methods of a system, agency, or its professionals" (Administration on Aging, 2001).

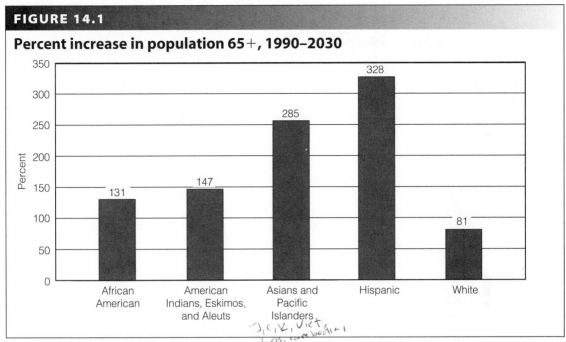

FIGURE 14.1

Percent increase in population 65+, 1990–2030

Source: U.S. Census Bureau, population projections of the United States by age, sex, race, Hispanic origin, and nativity: 1999 to 2100; published January 2000.

When human service providers and other professionals have an integrated knowledge about groups of people, a far greater understanding of their values, motivations, and behaviors emerges. Traditional Chinese culture, for example, values keeping from a patient the severity of his or her condition. This is in direct conflict with Western medicine (Administration on Aging, 2001), and lack of cultural competence in this situation might cause serious miscommunication between doctor, patient, and the patient's family.

By 2030 there will be about 70 million people over 65 in this country—more than two times their number in 1996 (Administration on Aging, 2001). This population represents a rich cultural and ethnic mix; Figure 14.1 shows the percentage increase in elders from 1990 to 2030 by ethnicity. From 1990 to 2030 the non-Hispanic white population will increase 81 percent. As illustrated in the figure, the Hispanic elder population will increase by 328 percent, the Asian

and Pacific Islander population by 285 percent, Native Americans by 147 percent, and African Americans by 131 percent. With every passing year the ethnic aged become a larger proportion of aging America. Figure 14.2 illustrates the projected distribution of the over-65 age category by race from the year 2000 to 2050. Note that although there are huge relative projected increases in minority growth, non-Hispanic whites remain by far the largest group of elders for the next 40 to 50 years. It is perhaps for these reasons that professionals and service providers must develop and target services appropriate to the nonwhite population. Until recently, most programs—developed and supported for funding by the majority culture—have not adequately developed services appropriate to non-majority populations.

The categorization of minorities, however useful it might be for bureaucratic purposes, often flies in the face of group identification. Ko-

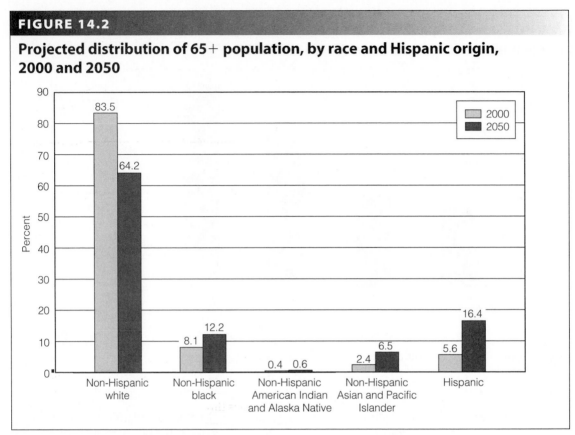

FIGURE 14.2

Projected distribution of 65+ population, by race and Hispanic origin, 2000 and 2050

Source: U.S. Census Bureau, population projections of the United States by age, sex, race, Hispanic origin, and nativity; published January 2000.

reans, for example, identify strongly as Koreans and most certainly do not identify with, say, Japanese. Both groups, however, are considered Asian by the U.S. government. For this reason, understanding culture helps service providers and professionals avoid stereotypes and biases.

Ethnicity involves (1) a culture and an internalized heritage not shared by outsiders, (2) social status, and (3) the composition and function of support systems (Hooyman & Kiyak, 2002). Discrimination is not necessarily associated with ethnicity: some German, Scandinavian, Eastern bloc, and southern European immigrants have retained close cultural ties with their ethnic backgrounds but do not necessarily hold minority status.

Minorities in this context are ethnic elders identified by language, physical, or cultural characteristics who, based on those characteristics, have experienced unequal treatment in certain segments of society. It is critical to remember two important issues regarding ethnic minority elders: (1) each cohort has a unique historic calendar of life events that impacts the group members' lifestyles, many of which events are positive, not negative; and (2) there is a cumulative negative effect of racism, ageism, discrimination, and prolonged poverty on each cohort and on each individual (Hooyman & Kiyak, 2002).

A particular challenge to American society in the twenty-first century will be that its aged population is relatively homogeneous, but its younger population is quite heterogeneous, and this diverse population of younger adults will be responsible for developing national policy that affects a homogeneous older age group. It will not be until around 2010 that the older population will begin to reflect the diversity of the larger population. By 2050, elder diversity will be established: more than 60 percent of the elder population will be non-Hispanic white; less than 1 percent will be American Indians, or Native Americans; 12 percent will be black; about 16 percent will be Hispanic; and nearly 7 percent will be Asian (Hobbs & Stoops, 2002).

Acknowledging the limitations of the "ethnic" concept and the vagaries of group identification, we consider here five groups: women of any ethnicity, African Americans, Hispanics, Asian, and Native Americans. Women, although not an ethnic minority group, hold a lower status in our culture than men. Therefore, women have been judged a minority group not in terms of numbers, but in terms of status. Older women are considered first in this chapter, after which comes the section on ethnic minority elders.

Women

The minority status of women is based on sexism. For older women, sexism is compounded by ageism. Older women have trouble finding acceptance and equality in the work world, in politics, and in romance. Women are making progress in these areas; however, hundreds of years of established patterns cannot be changed overnight.

One advantage for women is their willingness to reach out and get help: from each other, from books and seminars, from re-entry programs at colleges, and from various counseling services. Models of positive aging such as Meryl Streep and Susan Sarandon, in their 50s; Jane Fonda and Erica Jong, in their 60s; and Gloria Steinem, a leader of the feminist movement, 70 in 2004, all are looked to for advice and inspiration.

The present generation of older women is receiving more attention and validation than previous generations. Roles for older women, which historically were narrowly constructed in the United States, are broadening. Even the topic of menopause, previously considered a process that was experienced individually and silently, is out of the closet as women begin to view menopause not as a marker to the end, but as a bridge to a new stage of adulthood. Increasingly, older women have more options for experiencing a rewarding and fulfilling later life. Two areas of struggle for older women are discussed in this section of the text: finances and the double standard of aging.

Financial Status

A huge economic discrepancy exists among elders. Poverty is unevenly distributed, with women being among the poorest in the United States and women of color being the most poverty-stricken of all. Poverty among married women is fairly low; poverty among unmarried women is three to four times higher than in their married counterparts, reflecting their work and marital histories. The high percentage of women and their children among the poor has been referred to as the feminization of poverty. Of all individuals poor enough to receive Supplemental Security Income (SSI), two-thirds are women. Over 40 percent of men are covered by pensions, but fewer than 20 percent of women have pensions, and of that 20 percent, benefits are approximately half those of men because of salary differentials over the working years (Hooyman & Kiyak, 2002).

A special report on women's issues by the American Association of Retired Persons (AARP, 1995) listed some of the major ways in which women's lives become compromised in later life, including:

- *Limited training and educational opportunities.* Women have historically lacked the training and educational opportunities available to men. Most colleges and training programs are now available to women, but disparities still remain—"male" fields pay 20 to 30 percent more and offer better benefits than fields in which women predominate

- *Inequities in the workplace.* Women still make only 80 percent of what men do, and the wage gap widens with age

- *Low retirement income.* Women are more likely than men to leave jobs before becoming vested in retirement plans; low wages mean many women cannot save for retirement

- *Lack of financial planning skills.* Managing money was traditionally left to husbands; without money management skills, women are jeopardizing their long-range security and independence, yet older women in particular lack these skills

- *Need for public benefits:.* Women are almost twice as likely to be poor than men. This means they are far more likely to need public services to survive in later life

- *Caregiving responsibilities.* Women provide three-quarters of family caregiving; for 12 percent of working caregivers, the demands are so intense they leave paid employment

- *Inadequate housing.* Because of longer life spans, women are more likely to live alone in old age than are men. Added to the lower incomes of women, affordable housing is a challenge to living independently for many older women

Middle-Aged Displaced Homemakers

Financial problems for women frequently originate in middle age or even earlier. A typical displaced homemaker is middle-aged and has been a homemaker for most of her adult life, dependent on her husband for her income and

© Deborah Kahn Kalas/Stock, Boston

Spotty and low-paying work histories among unmarried women who are currently old have resulted in negligible pensions. Many unmarried female elders have no source of income other than welfare.

security. She finds herself suddenly alone with little or no income and with limited marketable skills. In 1993, 30 percent of all women in the 45 to 64 age category were single, widowed, or divorced.

The middle-aged woman who can save some money (or, at a minimum, pay into Social Security) improves her chances for a fulfilling old age. Though middle-aged women are now in the workforce in large numbers, a pay gap persists for these women and for older women. They tend to be in low-paying "women's jobs," working as secretaries, sales clerks, waitresses, nurses, or teachers.

Single, Widowed, and Divorced Older Women

Single women

More than 25 percent of women 65 and older who live alone or with nonrelatives live below the poverty level (U.S. Bureau of the Census, 1993). This percentage would almost double if the Federal Poverty Index were updated as experts recommend. In contrast, 8 percent of those living with their husbands are poor. Those married and living with their husbands have the benefits of another income. Those single women receiving Social Security receive lower pensions than men because the earnings on which they contributed to the program tend to be lower than the earnings of men of their generation. Women who are 65 years old today are still paying for the wage and social discrimination they suffered in their earlier working years.

Widows

Widows constitute nearly one-half of all women 65 and over. Of women 65 and over who live alone, 85 percent are widows. Some widowed women depended on their husbands' incomes, and, when retired, on their husbands' private pension plans or Social Security. More often than not, private pension plans fall sharply when a retired spouse dies. The death of a spouse also lowers the amount of Social Security benefits. In this case, widows' low incomes expose them to greater social and economic risks than other segments of the elder population. Data from a national sample of widows of all ages found that widowhood decreased living standards by 18 percent and pushed into poverty 10 percent of women whose prewidowhood incomes were above the poverty line. The problem is so great that some laws have been passed to protect women during times of marital transition, including the Consolidated Omnibus Budget Reconciliation Act (COBRA), which allows women to keep their health insurance coverage under their husbands' plans, at their own expense, for up to three years after divorce, separation, or widowhood.

The opportunity for older widows to remarry is quite limited, owing to the relatively small number of eligible males in their age group. Older females who are eligible for marriage outnumber eligible males by a ratio of three to one. In addition, males who marry after age 65 tend to marry women from younger age groups.

Divorced women

The socioeconomic well-being of divorced women is significantly below that of married or even widowed women. Given current statistics and expected trends in marriage, divorce, and widowhood, the numbers of married and widowed older women will decline, but the proportion of divorced older women will dramatically increase. Included in the increasing divorce rate are divorces involving women over age 40. And, although 7 percent of women over age 60 are divorced (and not remarried), this statistic is increasing: in 1993, 1.5 percent of all married women over 65 divorced their spouse (Lanza, 1996). Each year, at least 50,000 persons older than 60 dissolve marriages of 30 to 40 years' duration.

For women, the probability of remarriage after divorce declines steeply with age and is quite low after age 45. In 1990, for example, fewer than 5 out of every 100 divorced women between the ages of 45 and 64 remarried within the year. If current rates persist, few women who enter midlife divorced, or who divorce after midlife, will ever remarry. Remarriage rates have fallen dramatically since 1965; they have fallen by half for women between the ages of 45 and 64.

According to rough projections, by 2025 no more than 37 percent of women between the ages of 65 and 69 will be in their first marriage. Half will not be in any marriage; this figure could be considerably higher if the divorce rate after age 40 continues to increase and the remarriage rate continues to decline (Uhlenberg, 1996). There is good reason for public concern over these statistics. Older women living outside marriage, especially those who are divorced, have much lower standards of living than married women. The high divorce rates of adult children can compound the strain on family resources, as well, as their needs and the needs of grandchildren are often addressed from a family, not an individual, perspective.

Upgrading the Financial Status of Older Women

In our society, in spite of positive steps toward equality, women in the workforce and in politics remain in inferior positions. Their lower incomes reflect this fact. Inequalities in income for older women will not totally disappear until women achieve equality in the workplace from the beginning of their careers.

If women are homemakers or caretakers of children or elder parents during their working years, they suffer financially in old age. Being removed from the paid labor market reduces their Social Security benefits (Devlin & Arye, 1997). They could be compensated in a number of ways. One way would be for women to receive full credit for their nonmarket labor in pension plans, including Social Security (Quadagno, 1996). Another plan suggests combining the wage earner's 100 percent benefits with the dependent homemaker's 50 percent benefits. The wage earner and the homemaker could then divide the resulting 150 percent into equal shares of 75 percent that they would receive regardless of gender or family earning roles, and they could place the equal shares in separate accounts under their own names and Social Security numbers. The funds would thus remain unaffected by possible divorce or separation.

A feminist perspective on retirement— taking into account sociocultural variables— would include a mandate to "examine the connections between family and work roles (public and private); investigate the personal and politi-

cal spheres in order to free women from a substantial investment in unpaid work (caregiving, home labor); and promote parity among men and women during retirement" (Richardson, 1999, quoted in Hooyman & Kiyak, 2002).

Some centers provide job counseling, training, placement services, legal counseling, and outreach and information services to middle-aged and older women. Policies that encourage work and ensure adequate survivor benefits improve the financial status of older retired women.

Double Standard of Aging

Susan Sontag coined the term **double standard of aging** in 1972. By implication, the standard of aging for a woman progressively destroys her sense of beauty and self-worth, whereas the standard of aging for a man is much less wounding. More recent literature questions the belief that changes in body self-concept are more difficult for women than for men, but opinion is unified around the issue of intense social standards for women's appearance (Cohn & Adler, 1992; Harris, 1994; Wilcox, 1997).

"Like wolves, women are sometimes discussed as though only a certain temperament, only a certain restrained appetite, is acceptable. And too often added to that is an attribution of moral goodness or badness according to whether a woman's size, height, gait, and shape conform to a singular or exclusionary ideal. When women are relegated to moods, mannerisms, and contours that conform to a single ideal of beauty and behavior, they are captured in both body and soul, and are no longer free."

ESTES, 1992

Society trains women from an early age to care about their physical beauty. As a result, women spend a tremendous amount of time and money on their appearance. Women are very concerned about being "fat" or "ugly"—

indeed, dieting and eating disorders are far more a woman's issue than a man's (Abbott et al., 1998). Cosmetic and plastic surgery and face-lifts are performed more often on women than on men. Many women's exercise programs emphasize appearance rather than strength or endurance: in the self-help section at any local video store, note the number of cassettes and DVDs that promise shapelier breasts, thighs, or buttocks. Or attend an aerobics class at a local health club and note the female clients' concerns about their exercise clothing.

The youth culture in our society exerts intense social pressure for women to remain young. In a personal account of her own aging, Ruth Thone, an activist from Lincoln, Nebraska, gave her reason for writing her book: the "subtle, deep, pervasive, unspoken distaste and derision" for old Americans in general and old women in particular (Thone, 1993). She wrote of her own "internalized aging," in which she is filled with self-loathing and anxiety about aging. She is also furious at being sexually invisible to men and being patronized by younger people. She is sensitive about any jokes putting down older women. She gave this account.

> My husband found a joke in a magazine, that he added to his repertoire, about two women in a nursing home who decided to streak their fellow residents. Two startled old men looked up and one asked, "What was that?" "I don't know," the other replied, "but whatever they were wearing sure needs ironing." My husband did not understand how hurt I was by that joke, by that ridicule of women's aging skin and by the double standard that does not make a mockery of men's aging skin. He insisted it was my feminism, not any ageism in him that kept me from knowing the joke was harmless. (Thone, 1993, p. 54)

She wondered, "Am I an object of scorn as my body ages?" She dealt with self-criticism, self-rejection, and self-hate, coming to terms with aging by writing in her journal, meditating,

and becoming more spiritual. In a chapter titled "The Grief of Aging" she described working through her sadness at the loss of her youth.

Not all women can confront their aging so directly and honestly. They buy into the idea that they must stay young and beautiful in appearance forever, and when physiological and health changes occur to alter that image, healthy adjustment to aging becomes difficult. Self-neglect in old age is thought to come about because of the negative self-concept that results in part from comparing one's physical condition and personal competence to a standard that is unattainable (Rathbone-McCuan, 1996; Karpinski, 1997).

The successful exploitation of women's fears of growing older has been called **age terrorism.** Pearlman (1993) speaks of **late midlife astonishment**—a developmental crisis in which women aged 50 to 60 work through society's devaluation of their physical appearance. Women suffer a loss of self-esteem, depression, and feelings of shame and self-consciousness. Feminist therapists believe that body image disturbances are not limited to eating-disordered clients and that they occur among women of all ages. One example is Helen Gurley Brown, former editor of *Cosmopolitan,* the "Cosmo Girl" who at age 71 referred to age as the great destroyer. She admits to silicone injections, cosmetic surgery, shrink sessions, endless dieting, and a 90-minute daily "killer" exercise regime. She says:

> I'm afraid of losing my sexuality. I'm desperately afraid of retirement. I fear that with age, I'll cease being a woman, that I'll be neuter. I fear losing my looks and ending up looking like . . . like an old crumb. (quoted in an interview with Marian Christy, 1993)

One dangerous outcome of negative shifts in self-image can be self-neglect. Women's fear of age-related physical changes can take on a pathological flavor, since personal changes can cause a woman to doubt her social capability, which leads to low self-assessment, leading to low self-esteem, leading to self-neglect (Rathbone-

McCuan, 1996; Watson, 1997). Self-concept itself, however, does not seem to undergo age-related change. The key to successful aging appears to be that women develop adequate strategies to maintain their self-identities even as key aspects of their bodies, their minds, and their health change (Matthews, 1979; Kaufman, 1986; Barusch, 1997).

African Americans

African Americans constitute the largest population of color in the United States; however, only about 8 percent of that population is 65 years or older, compared to 14 percent of the white population (U.S. Bureau of the Census, 2001). It is a diverse group, yet some overall pictures do emerge. A majority of elder African Americans (53 percent) live in the South. There are fewer males than females. Older men tend to be married; women tend to be divorced or widowed. African American elders are less likely to be married than any other ethnic group, but all ethnic elderly, including African Americans, are more likely to live with other family members (not counting the spouse) than whites. The oldest-old women are the most rapidly growing segment of the population, and they have the longest average remaining life span (National Institutes of Health [NIH], 2000).

African Americans as a group differ widely in socioeconomic factors. As a result of the civil rights movement, African Americans have gained a large middle class, a class that has now grown so large that it outnumbers the African American poor. As comparatively well-off African Americans move to better neighborhoods, they leave behind an African American "underclass"—chronic welfare recipients, the unemployed, high school dropouts, and single-parent families. Although many African Americans moved into the upper middle class in the 1980s, one-third remained locked in deprivation. As a result, a deep class division now exists among African Americans. Elders in inner cities are

African Americans have gained a large middle class that now outnumbers the African American poor.

often left to cope with deteriorating neighborhoods, high crime rates, and the threat of violence; or they are left in rural areas to struggle with poverty and a lack of medical and social services.

Income and Housing

Compared with Caucasian and other **minority elders, African American elders** have less adequate income, and poorer quality housing. Over 26 percent of non-Hispanic blacks lived in poverty in 1998, compared with 21 percent of Hispanics, 16 percent of Asians, and about 8 percent of non-Hispanic whites (Administration on Aging, 2002). This constitutes a serious social problem, because elderly cannot easily move elsewhere due to those limited incomes and because they face a stronger likelihood of housing discrimination (Golant & LaGreca, 1994). Although the income level for older African Americans has improved over the past 30 years, the improvement rate has not been as rapid as that for older whites. Unemployment rates for African Americans of all ages are far higher than those for whites and have been for many years. Again, in elderhood, it is the *cumu-*

lative function of poverty over a lifetime that seriously disadvantages poor elders.

A small percentage of retired African Americans are from the upper class, having owned large businesses or real estate, headed large corporations, or worked in the highest levels of industry. Other retired African Americans are middle class, having been schoolteachers, owners of small businesses, or government employees. Still others are retired from manual labor or domestic service jobs. Overall, however, older black Americans suffer appalling levels of poverty, having not paid as much into Social Security as whites and having worked predominantly in jobs that offer no pensions. In general, retirement benefits for older African Americans will be less in old age than those of older white Americans due to patterns of limited employment opportunities and periods of unemployment throughout their lives.

African American elders are slightly more likely to be looking for work after age 65, because of inadequate retirement income. Older African American men have higher unemployment rates than older white men. Elders in the lower socioeconomic groups, regardless of race, have a different understanding of retirement. Health permitting, they often must work at lower-paying jobs well beyond retirement age in order to meet basic expenses for food, medical care, and housing. Studies of work patterns among African Americans revealed a large group of "unretired retirees" age 55 and over who need jobs but cannot find them. They do find occasional work well into old age—but it is usually part-time and temporary. Those under age 62 are not eligible for Social Security or other pension programs and, therefore, without work, are more financially needy than those eligible for pensions.

Studies of African American retirees age 65 and over show that those who receive Social Security have relatively high morale—higher, in fact, than that of their counterparts who are still working. This finding is reversed for whites. One explanation for the high morale of retired African Americans is the undesirable work they often face should they remain employed (Gibson, 1993).

Older African Americans are more likely than older whites to reside within decaying central cities and to live in substandard housing. They are also more likely than whites to live in public housing. Those who work with minority elders must be able to advise them accurately on low-cost public housing, low-interest housing loans, and other forms of available property relief.

Older African Americans are admitted to nursing homes at between one-half and three-quarters of the rate of whites. Although black elders have at least the same proportion of chronic physical illnesses as white elders, low use of long-term care cannot be explained only with the statement that African Americans prefer to care for elders within their families. The economic option of choosing long-term care is not available to many black American families.

Health Care and Life Expectancy

Low-income African American elders have health care problems. Many poor elders have lacked the resources for adequate health care throughout their lives, which has resulted in a life expectancy rate that is much lower than that of whites. Older African Americans experience some disease processes more frequently than do their white peers, though the differences are greatest at age 45 and decline with age (Hooyman & Kiyak, 2002). These diseases include heart disease, stroke, and diabetes. Diabetes rates are alarmingly high among black women—nearly twice that of white women (NIH, 2000)—and kidney failure, which is associated with hypertension and diabetes, is more common (Freeman & Payne, 2000). In general, heart disease is over two times more common among older African Americans than among white elders. Being either black or poor is a powerful predictor of mortality.

Life expectancy for white Americans at birth in 1997 was a bit over 77 years; for black

Americans, it was just over 71 years. Life expectancy for these two groups reverses by age 85, however: it is 6.2 years for whites and 6.4 years for blacks. This finding is largely because people at 85 years of age are survivors. Those African Americans who survive into their eighth decade and beyond generally have survived far less advantageous life circumstances than their white counterparts. They are individuals of exceptionally strong physical and mental character.

Between 1986 and 1991, life expectancy for African Americans actually *dropped.* Though African Americans had been sharing in life expectancy increases over the decades, the trend reversed in the late 1980s. One major reason is the high number of African American babies who die in their first year. But this is only one factor. Thousands of African Americans die in the prime of life from illnesses that could be cured or treated by routine medical care: appendicitis, pneumonia, hypertension, cervical cancer, tuberculosis, and influenza are examples. Given early detection and good treatment, all these illnesses are curable; few should be dying of curable diseases and those headed off by early detection.

The experience of profound, personally directed racial discrimination is a lifelong experience for almost every older African American. Assuming that low social status generates repressed negative emotions and inner tensions, some gerontologists believe the high incidence of hypertension among black Americans reflects the pressures of low social status. Both physical and mental illnesses can result from the chronic stress of prejudicial attitudes and behavior of others. Combined with the possibility of genetic predisposition toward hypertension, the health of older African Americans is precarious for tragically unjust reasons.

Whatever the cause, the incidence of high blood pressure among African Americans is nearly two and a half times that of whites, and the mortality rate from high blood pressure is higher for African Americans than for whites (U.S. Bureau of the Census, 1993). Though yoga, aerobics, and biofeedback programs to reduce blood pressure have typically been attended by white, middle-class persons, African Americans are now joining them.

Family and Social Relationships

More than 40 percent of African American women 65 and over live in poverty. Some groups urge African American women to become politically active, to lobby for equality on behalf of themselves and their mothers, aunts, and sisters. Organizations such as the National Association for the Advancement of Colored People (NAACP) and the National Black Women's Political Caucus can speak and work on behalf of issues most salient to black Americans.

Despite racism and economic woes, African Americans possess a resolve to persevere. The solid family ties, which are one source of this strength, are indicated in the concept of **familism**—a notion of family extending beyond the immediate household. Family network roles are flexible and interchangeable. A young mother, an aunt, a grandfather, or an older couple may head a family. Grandmothers often help raise children while their parents work. The high divorce rate has encouraged reliance on older relatives. Additionally, families tend to value their elder members because they have survived in the face of hardship and because they play important roles within the family (Choi, 1996; Mullen, 1996). A study of 154 African American and white grandparents rearing their children's children as a consequence of the biological parents' neglect and drug addiction showed that grandparents bore a far larger burden for this support than did their white counterparts (Kelley et al., 1997). It was emotionally rewarding but exacted many costs, both psychological and financial. Similar findings appear in studies of grandmothers raising grandchildren during the crack cocaine epidemic (Burton, 1992; Minkler & Roe, 1993).

Religion has also been a resource of support in the African American family (Walls, 1992; Nye, 1993). The black American church has been a source of strength for coping with racial oppression and has played a vital role in the survival and advancement of African Americans. The church has provided a place of importance and belonging. Within the church, elders receive recognition as members, choir singers, deacons, and treasurers. A study of a Pennsylvania church, which revealed that church membership contributed to feelings of well-being among older African Americans, recommended that these churches act as a link between families and agencies that deal with issues of aging. The church is a likely information and referral institution because so many older individuals are active participants (Walls & Zarit, 1991).

A spirit of survival has seen older African Americans through hard times. Thankful to have survived, they are more likely to appreciate aging; thus, they accept it more easily than those who have not experienced such hardship.

Future Outlook

Though data on the lives of African American elders are becoming more available, our knowledge is still far from adequate. We are gaining knowledge about their lifestyles, roles, and adaptations to living environments, but the information on whites that pertains to these topics still far exceeds that about minorities.

Studies of fear of crime and victimization show much higher rates of fear for African Americans than for whites, and, in fact, their rates of victimization are significantly higher than those for white Americans. The major reason is thought to be geographic location—more of them, compared with white American elders, live in high-crime areas such as the inner city and in or near public housing. And because feelings of alienation and mistrust of police may have existed from their youth, these elders are less likely than their white counterparts to reach out

TABLE 14.1

Social and economic characteristics of white and African American population, 1992

Characteristic	Percent	
	White	Black
Age 65 and over	13.0	8.3
Homeowner	67.5	42.3
College, 4 years or more	22.1	11.9
Income of $50,000 and over	34.1	14.9
Unemployed	4.3	8.9
Living below poverty level	10.3	33.8

Source: U.S. Bureau of the Census (1993). *Statistical Abstract of the United States, 1993.* Washington, DC: Bureau of the Census.

for help. Social policy experts suggest Neighborhood Watch programs to unite residents and also recommend age-segregated housing with more safety features (Barazan, 1994).

Despite the impact of affirmative action in the United States, the economic outlook for large numbers of older African Americans is bleak. Table 14.1 reflects some characteristics that are related to economic inequality and shared by other elder populations of color. Persons of color are still disproportionately clustered in peripheral industries that pay lower wages: agriculture, retail trade, nonunionized small businesses, and low-profit companies that pay minimum wage. In contrast, white Americans are still clustered in better-paying "core" industries, such as the automobile industry, construction, and other high-profit, unionized industries. Although some improvement can be expected by the twenty-first century, it will be small: between 1982 and 1992, the ratio of African American family income to white family income actually declined. In 1996, the average income of whites was $29,470 a year; of African Americans, $21,068 (Administration on Aging,

1997). If young and middle-aged working African Americans cannot fare as well as whites, they will not compare much more favorably in old age. Only through major economic changes that promote the hiring of minorities in major businesses and industries will they begin to achieve economic parity in middle and old age.

Hispanic Americans

Older Hispanics, the *ancianos,* are the largest ethnic minority population in the country following African Americans; they are also the fastest-growing group in the United States. They are not, however, homogeneous. This highly diverse group includes many subgroups of people, each with its own national and cultural heritage: Mexicans, Puerto Ricans, Cubans, Central or South Americans, and native Mexican Americans—many of whom have lived in the United States for several generations. Professionals and service providers often are unprepared for the cultural and socioeconomic diversity of the Hispanic community. One of the obstacles preventing **Hispanic elders** from being understood and served is the lack of a clear-cut definition of who they are. Census counting often uses two inclusive terms that exacerbate the problem: Spanish heritage (having Spanish blood or antecedents) and Spanish origin (having been born in a Spanish-speaking country or having antecedents who were). Theoretically, then, a person could be of Spanish origin but not of Spanish heritage, or vice versa. The term Hispanic will be used here to mean Spanish people in a broad sense including both terms.

Demographics

From 1980 to 2000, the Hispanic population more than doubled in the United States. In 1990, more than 22 million persons in the United States were of Hispanic origin. Of these, 5.5 percent were aged 65 or older, and this figure will rise to 7.2 percent by 2010 and 10.9 percent by 2025

(U.S. Bureau of the Census, 2000). Mexican Americans are the largest Hispanic group in the United States—more than half of all Hispanics combined.

The Hispanic population is expected to be the largest U.S. minority group soon after the year 2000. Under Census Bureau projections, the elderly Hispanic population will more than double from 1990 to 2010 and will be 11 times greater by 2050. In 1990 the Hispanic elderly numbered less than half the black elderly population; however, in 2030 the number of Hispanic elderly (7.6 million) will be larger than the elderly African American population of 6.8 million (Hobbs & Damon, 1996).

Minority Status

Several social factors indicate the minority status of Hispanic elders: (1) high percentage living below the poverty level, (2) inadequate health care, (3) high illiteracy rates (second only to rates among Native American elders), and (4) low occupational levels such as skilled and unskilled laborers, and farm workers. These job categories have few benefits, including retirement and pension benefits. Some Mexican-American elders are unlikely to seek social services support because they entered the country illegally or are uncertain about their legal status and fear detection and expulsion.

Migration Patterns

The majority of Mexican American elders were born in this country; other Hispanic elders are more likely to be foreign born. Accordingly, foreign-born Hispanics are not as acculturated as native-born citizens. Immigrants require greater assistance in order to understand and utilize services and to develop a comfort level appropriate to their well-being with the delivery of services in the United States. As previously described, it is essential that services and programs acknowledge the traditions and values the population has retained.

Differing patterns of migration have brought Hispanics to various locations in the United States. Hispanic-American immigrants tend to live in urban areas. Immigrants from 6 of the 12 Hispanic nations identified in the 1990 census have more than 80 percent of their populations in the nation's 20 largest cities (New York, Los Angeles, Chicago, Miami, Washington, D.C., Boston, Philadelphia, and San Diego, for example), and three others have between 70 percent and 79 percent in the 20 largest cities. Because so many Mexican Americans were born in the United States, they are not as extensively urbanized as immigrant Hispanics (including Mexican immigrants), who tend to locate in urban areas. In Texas, for example, the older urban immigrants outnumber their rural counterparts by a ratio of five to one. San Antonio, Houston, and Dallas have large numbers of Mexican Americans who are foreign born.

Puerto Rican and Cuban elders are almost exclusively city dwellers. The Hispanic populations of Florida and the Northeast are more urbanized than those in the Southwest.

The American Experience

Hispanic elders today are an ethnic composite that has suffered major linguistic and cultural barriers to assimilation and has occupied a low socioeconomic status. Forty-five percent of Hispanic elders are not proficient in English (Seelye, 1997). In 1998, 21 percent of persons of Hispanic origin age 65 and over lived below the poverty level (Administration on Aging, 2002). A major reason for the financial disadvantages of older Hispanics is the lack of pension plan coverage during their working lives: their coverage rates are lower than those for whites or African Americans. Health problems such as diabetes and obesity are more common among Hispanic elders than in the aged population as a whole, and those health problems generally are not addressed from a prevention perspective because of the costs of medical assistance and cultural issues such as language barriers.

Utilization of Services

Hispanic elders are generally somewhat suspicious of governmental institutions and of service workers and researchers not of their culture. Their suspicion, along with a lack of education and money, results in isolation and nonutilization of available services. This underutilization tends to conceal their very real need. Further, because the census undercounts minorities, underutilization is even greater than is generally recognized. One example is in nursing home care, where Hispanic elders are greatly underrepresented (Mui & Burnette, 1994). Social program providers need to develop greater sensitivity to and communication skills with Hispanic seniors. Popular beliefs characterize Mexican Americans as living in extended families, and, in fact, Hispanic families do tend to be larger than Anglo families in the United States. But that does not mean that the extended family system runs smoothly. Generally speaking, the more acculturated the family members, the less extensive the family interaction, and the more complete the breakdown of extended family. Traditionally, adult children provide a great deal of support to Hispanic parents in terms of chores such as laundry, housework, transportation, and shopping. Both cultural values (the needs of the larger family go above one's individual needs) and economic need dictate these close family ties. The patterns of intergenerational assistance are strong compared to white Americans, for example; however, older parents have expressed dismay at the shift in attitudes toward filial responsibility that their adult children display.

Studying Ethnic Variations

For all Hispanic groups, researchers are studying the types of ethnic communities and institutions that tend to develop in given localities and their impact on the lives of elders. Mexican Americans, for example, participate heavily in senior citizen clubs. Actually, the senior citizen culture is strong in the various representations of Hispanic community (Torres-Gil, 1988). Though minority elders tend to underutilize government and health services, high ethnic population density seems to correlate with higher rates of utilization. The status of the elders in the various Hispanic groups is better in large, fully developed ethnic communities than in small or scattered ones. Here are some statistics about high ethnic population density:

- Eighteen percent of all Hispanics live in Los Angeles

- Twelve percent of all Hispanics live in New York

- New York's Puerto Rican population is double that of San Juan, Puerto Rico

- Seventy-seven percent of immigrants from the Dominican Republic live in urbanized New York

- Laredo, Texas, is 94 percent Hispanic, and the proportion of Hispanics is nearly that high in several other Texas border towns

- Cubans are clustered in Miami and other cities of southeastern Florida

- Panamanians are the most geographically diverse

- Other groups cluster in enclaves of large cities, according to national origin (Winsberg, 1994)

Another area of research is the unique cultural traditions that are maintained in each Hispanic group. Cuban elders, for example, tend to be much more politically active than Mexican Americans. A professor from Miami describes some unique aspects of Cuban culture as they affect elders (Hernandez, 1992): Cuban culture is a blend of whites from the Iberian Peninsula and blacks from Africa. The Afro-Cuban culture emphasizes respect for elders, stemming from their folk healing beliefs and practices. Familism (adherence to strong family values) is strong in Cuban culture and evokes guilt when members do not fulfill expected roles. For example, adult children are likely to feel great guilt if they do not care for aged parents. Cu-

ban women tend to marry older men who care for them financially; however, a culture of *marianismo* is often present, which is characterized by a belief in female superiority and the expectation that women are capable of enduring all suffering (Hooyman & Kiyak, 2002). Eventually the younger wife cares for the aged husband in an atmosphere of respect, dictating expectations of how others should treat us and be treated. Complete dependence on family members, such as adult children or spouses, is welcomed and encouraged by the culture and not interpreted as pathology.

Neglected areas of research are social stratification within ethnic groups, rate of return migration, and degree of cultural adaptation. Hispanic elders who lived most of their lives in their native countries and do not immigrate until late adulthood no doubt experience more culture shock and isolation, but this phenomenon needs to be explored.

Asian Americans

The term Asian American refers in the broadest sense to persons of Chinese, Korean, Japanese, Filipino, East Indian, Thai, Vietnamese, Burmese, Indonesian, Laotian, Malayan, and Cambodian descent who live in the United States. Each group represents a culture with its own history and religion, its own language and values. Asian Americans, like Hispanics, are not a homogeneous group. Most **Asian American elders** are concentrated in California, Hawaii, New York, Illinois, Washington, and Massachusetts. Elders represent around 6 percent of the non-Hispanic Asian and Pacific Islander population; they make up approximately 16 percent of the population of elders living in poverty (Administration on Aging, 1999).

A single description cannot encompass the Asian communities in the United States. Differences of culture, language, and religion make each group unique (see Table 13.2). Asians are alike, however, in the sense that they all have encountered language barriers and racism.

American laws have discriminated against Asians for some time. The Chinese Exclusion Act of 1882, passed during a period of high unemployment by fearful whites, made all Chinese immigration illegal. It was amended twice to allow immigration under certain circumstances and then in 1924 became totally exclusionary again. The act was not repealed until 1943, when China became a U.S. ally in World War II. The legislative history is not an honorable one and has important social implications:

> Laws discriminating against Asians are numerous, ranging from . . . the Japanese Alien Land Law of 1913, the Executive Order of 1942 for the internment of 110,000 persons of Japanese ancestry, denial of citizenship to first-generation Asians in 1922, the anti-miscegenation statue of 1935, and more recently Public Law 95-507 excluding Asians as a protected minority under the definition of "socially and economically disadvantaged" (US Commission on Civil Rights, 1979). Such legislation, combined with a history of prejudice and discrimination, has contributed to feelings of mistrust, injustice, powerlessness, and fear of government among many Pacific Asian elders, and thus a reluctance to utilize services. (Hooyman & Kiyak, 1996, p. 455)

The current generation of Asian Americans, conditioned to traditional American social and cultural folkways and mores, may be just as likely to regard their elders as an unwelcome burden, just as many middle-class white Americans seem to do. According to traditional culture in China, Japan, and Korea, the eldest son assumes responsibility for his elderly parents. **Filial piety** is a custom demanding that family members respect and care for elders. Japanese American families have preserved to some extent the norm of *enryo,* a pattern of deference and modesty, as well as *amaeru,* the valuing of dependency, which encourages special dependent relationships (Johnson, 1996). These patterns are carried into respectful attitudes toward elders; however, they contrast markedly

Asian American elders represent a large number of different ethnicities. Meeting elder needs with appropriate cultural sensitivity is the challenge for elder services.

with dominant American values. As children and grandchildren become more enculturated, intergenerational tensions are bound to result. This becomes a moral "generation gap" between young Asian Americans and their elders. Older family members hold on to traditions, especially those concerning moral propriety, while the young move away from them.

Because health and welfare agencies have few bilingual staff members, and because they therefore have difficulty publicizing their available services to the Asian community, outreach programs to Asian American seniors have been limited in their success. These deficits, in addition to their socially conditioned reluctance to seek aid from their adopted land, result in neglect of Asian American elders.

Japanese Americans

Most of the Japanese who first came to the United States were single men, oftentimes younger sons who did not inherit any family wealth. The bulk of the Japanese immigration, which took place between 1870 and 1924, was made up of men who wanted to have traditional families. Many waited until they could afford a wife and then paid for one to come from Japan. This pattern reinforced traditional values of high status for men and elders. The survivors of that earliest immigration period, called *issei,* are now mostly women because the men, who were much older, have died.

The first generation worked primarily on farms or as unskilled laborers or service workers. However, within 25 years of entering the United States, they showed great economic mobility. Though their internment during World War II was economically as well as morally devastating, Japanese Americans as a group rebounded remarkably. First-generation Japanese, the *issei,* learned to live socially segregated from American culture. The children of the *issei,* the *nissei,* generally born between 1910 and 1940, are more likely to be integrated into the American mainstream. Most *nissei* are now over 65 and doing well economically and socially.

Japanese American elders, on the whole, have adequate savings or family support in their retirement years. Through the normative values of *amaeru,* filial piety, and other Confucian moral principles, Japanese Americans have largely replicated the traditional pattern of family care for elders: 46 percent live with an adult child in addition to or in lieu of a spouse. In traditional Japanese society, upon retirement the retiree joined the ranks of elders and assumed religious duties in the community. This particular tradition is lacking in the United States (Markides & Mindel, 1987).

Chinese Americans

Because past restrictive immigration laws denied entry to wives or children, a disproportionate share of Chinese American and Filipino American elders are men. Male immigrants have outnumbered females by at least three to one in census counts. These Asian men were valuable as cheap labor in U.S. mines, canneries, farms, and railroads, but their wives and children were neither needed nor wanted. Though we cannot fully assess the damage this caused to the family life of the elderly Chinese American, such damage has no doubt been extensive, traumatic, and demoralizing.

The immigration law of 1924, which halted Asian immigration, forbade males of Chinese descent from bringing their foreign-born wives to the United States. As a result, many Chinese men in the United States could not marry. Although the men who originally came in the early 1900s are a rapidly vanishing group, a few are still around, typically living in poverty and without close family ties.

Chinese Americans retain a tradition of respect for elders based on Confucian ethics. Traditionally, the Chinese family was embedded in a larger system of extended family and clans than was the Japanese family. Older family members held wealth and power, not only in their immediate family but all the way up the family hierarchy to the encompassing clan. Though this traditional structure has never been reproduced in the United States, respect for elders persists. The Chinese American pattern is for adult children to bring a widowed parent into their household.

Increasing numbers of Chinese elders are second generation. This generally means that they are more educated and acculturated and have a more comfortable financial situation. There is a vast difference between the lifestyles of those who are foreign born and who have never learned English and those who were born in the United States. The second generation is retiring with pensions and savings, reaping the harvest of their hard work in this country. Despite discrimination, Chinese Americans have achieved a high rate of occupational mobility; many have gone from restaurant and laundry businesses to educating children who have entered professional and technical occupations.

Southeast Asian Americans

The settlement of Vietnamese, Cambodians, and Laotians in the United States has included a small percentage of elders who enter a world alien in all facets of life, from language, dress, and eating habits to religious beliefs. Family ties are strong for most of these people. Traditionally, extended families are standard. Southeast Asians have a special respect for their elders, especially for fathers and grandfathers.

Though immigration policy places Southeast Asians throughout the entire United States, once on their own many gradually migrate to areas where the weather is similar to that in their native countries. California has by far the largest number of Southeast Asians. Studies of Southeast Asian refugees show that, like other Asian groups, they adjust fairly well to U.S. culture. Older first-generation immigrants who have suffered, living near or below the poverty line, take pride in children or grandchildren who have achieved financial and other successes.

In Los Angeles, a study that interviewed 19 older Hmong refugees and their families clearly demonstrated the pain and culture shock of displacement (Hays, 1987). In Laos, they lived in extended families with households containing as many as 35 members. Order and authority were maintained through respect for age. The oldest male of each clan sat on a governing council that handled all problems. Both male and female elders enjoyed high status within the village.

The Hmong believed that they would be resettled in the United States in a large group, possibly on a reservation. Being scattered in cities was a major blow. They were shocked to learn about American housing standards; they were unable to understand, for example, why a family of 10 could not live in a two-bedroom apartment. One elder Hmong recalled, "When I found out that some of my children would not live with me, my life stopped." The older Hmong had had no formal education in Laos, and many could not face the rigors of learning English in an American classroom.

The role of elders in the Hmong family has changed. In Laos, the elders acted as counselors for adult children experiencing marital difficulties. In the United States, by contrast, they are more out of touch with young couples' marital problems, and they rarely act as advisers or mediators. The older women try to help with child care, but the men don't have much to do. Many would like a farm and animals to tend. Elderly Hmong have experienced loss of function, mobility, religious customs, and status. Some are very depressed. Studies of Southeast Asian refugees find that, because of the language barrier and lack of communication with the larger society, displacement is more difficult for the elderly than for the young.

Native Americans

Measured by numbers alone, older American Indians constitute a small percentage of American society. Only 13 percent of American Indians will live to be 65 years and older (compared with 19.5 percent of the U.S. population); however, the proportion of Native Americans in the oldest-old category will at least double in the first two decades of the twenty-first century (NIH, 2000). By any social or economic indicator of living conditions, Native American elders are possibly *the most* deprived of all ethnic groups in the United States. The Indian Health Service (IHS) has worked diligently in the past 30 years to eliminate infectious diseases and meet Native American acute-care needs earlier in life; this is reflected by a life expectancy increase of 20 years from 1940 and 1980 (NIH, 2000).

Many of the problems of Native American elders are due to poverty rather than to age. American Indians on reservations and in rural areas experience extremely high unemployment rates. Few jobs exist on the reservations, and those who leave in search of work pay the high price of losing touch with their family, lifestyle, and culture. Many houses on reservations are substandard, and, despite substantial improvements in health, disparities still exist, especially in sanitation and nutrition. Accurate sociocultural accounts of Native Americans are difficult: they are a diverse population, and many urban American Indians do not live on reservations. Their living conditions and needs are therefore less visible.

The value of elders in any culture depends to a great extent on the degree to which the older generation is able to pass on important cultural information to a younger generation.

© Joel Gordon

Cultural Uniformity and Diversity

Native Americans are a diverse group: there are nearly 535 federally recognized tribes, an estimated 100 unrecognized tribes, and approxi-

mately 300 federally recognized reservations (NIH, 2000). Nearly 300 languages are spoken, and cultural traditions vary widely. Native Americans do share some values, however, that distinguish them from the larger society. Their lifestyle and spirituality dictate a deep reverence for the land, animals, and nature; and generally, they believe in attaining harmony between human beings and nature.

Family structure, values, and norms among Native American tribes are diverse. Generally speaking, Native Americans have close family ties and favor tribal autonomy. Though many family structures are patriarchal, a wide variety of descent systems exists. The largest tribe, the Navajo, follows a matrilineal structure. Native Americans generally share the characteristics of nonlinear thinking, the use of indirect communication and styles, and a historical suspicion of authority (Hooyman & Kiyak, 2002). The position of elders varies from tribe to tribe, as does emphasis on peace versus war and many other values. And, although some tribes are rivals, there exists today an extensive pan-Indian network that promotes intertribal networking, visiting, and cooperation. Marriage between members of different tribes is also more common than it once was (Kitano, 1991).

Population Data

For many years, despite rapid growth in the population of the country as a whole, the American Indian population declined. At the time of the first European settlement in what is now the United States, the number of Indians is estimated to have been between 1 and 10 million. By 1800, the native population had declined to approximately 600,000; by 1850, it had shrunk to 250,000. This mortifying decrease, the result of malnutrition, disease, and an all-out military assault on Native Americans, was a unique occurrence in our national history. However, the population eventually stabilized and is now increasing (Kitano, 1991). Because of early childbearing, it is common for Native Americans to

Physical aging and cultural values interact to create the experience of being old, which varies in different cultures. This Inuit elder, a respected hunter, is a valued and central part of his family and community.

© Lionel Delevingne/Stock, Boston

longer than Native American men. Women comprise almost 60 percent of the American Indian elders (NIH, 2000).

Native Americans who leave the reservations are usually scattered throughout urban areas, rather than forming ethnic enclaves. Over 48,000 Native Americans, for example, live throughout the Los Angeles area. San Francisco, Tulsa, Denver, New York City, Seattle, Minneapolis, Chicago, and Phoenix all have sizable Native American populations; Minneapolis has a Native American enclave. Although a multitude of tribes are scattered throughout the United States, 44 percent of all Native Americans reside in California, Oklahoma, Arizona, and New Mexico (Kitano, 1991). Findings for one tribe cannot be generalized to include all others; values and behavior vary greatly. Specific patterns of aging need to be examined in each tribe.

become grandparents in their mid- to late 30s. By comparison, grandparenthood usually comes to whites in their mid-50s (John, 1991).

Many older Native Americans live on reservations, staying behind while the young seek work in the city. Young or old, those who go to the city often expect to return to rural reservations to retire. Although the American population as a whole is more urban than rural, the reverse is largely true for the Native American population. Native Americans are the most rural of any ethnic group in the country. Fifty-three percent live in nonmetropolitan areas, 22 percent live in central cities, and the rest live in suburban areas outside central cities (Schick & Schick, 1994).

Life expectancy among Native Americans is substantially lower than that for whites. The Native American population is largely young, with a median age of 27 years, compared to 34 years for the general population. Their current life expectancy is 65 years—about 8 years less than for the white population. As in the white population, Native American women live

Education, Employment, and Income

The educational attainment of Native Americans today is behind that of whites. A sizable percentage of unemployed Navajo adults, for example, cannot speak English; nor can they read or write it. Among Native American youths, the school dropout rate is twice the national average. Because education has been a traditional means of social advancement in the United States, these data suggest that future generations of Native American elders may continue to suffer from functional illiteracy. A high percentage of Native American elders have graduated neither from elementary nor from high school.

Unemployment creates a problem in the Native American community. An extremely high percentage of the Native American workforce is unemployed, and most of those who work hold menial jobs with low pay and few, if any, fringe benefits. Because they have often paid only small amounts into Social Security, retirement for Native Americans is a great hardship. White Americans often associate major difficulties of growing old with retirement from the work-force. Native Americans usually have no work from which to retire. For most over 65, old age merely continues a state of poverty and jobless-ness that has lasted a lifetime.

Health Characteristics

Native American elders are more likely to suffer from chronic illnesses and disabilities than any other ethnic aged group, and they have the low-est life expectancy. However, though the mor-tality rates for younger Navajos are relatively high, mortality rates among elder Navajos are lower than those for non-Indians of the same age. This paradox represents an instance of the mortality "crossover" (Kunitz & Levy, 1989). Native Americans are more likely than the gen-eral population to die from diabetes, alcohol-ism, influenza, pneumonia, suicide, and homi-cide (Hobbs & Damon, 1996). Lack of income leads to poor nutrition and health care, and is associated with lower education levels, which compound other variables. The Native Ameri-can accident rate, for example, is high. Native Americans are more likely than the general pop-ulation to be killed in motor-vehicle accidents; and death from other types of accidents is also more likely. Native Americans suffer dispropor-tionately from alcoholism and alcohol-related diseases. American Indians are generally dis-posed genetically to have a low alcohol toler-ance; however, the abuse rate of alcohol in the Native American population is probably related to the stressors of minority status and poverty. Health problems are compounded by the alien nature of the dominant health-care system to the traditional culture of Native Americans.

Older Native Americans remain an enor-mously needy group. Today, Native Americans suffer both from dependency on the federal government and from the impact of conflicting federal policies. They are sometimes denied as-sistance from various government agencies un-der the excuse that the Bureau of Indian Affairs (BIA) is responsible for providing the denied

© David Strickler / The Image Works

In the next century minority women will represent a far larger proportion of elders than in the past. This shift to greater diversity in later life will impact social policy.

service. According to the *United States Govern-ment Manual 1989/90,* the principal objectives of the BIA are to "actively encourage and train Indian and Alaska Native people to manage their own affairs under the trust relationship to the Federal Government; to facilitate, with maximum involvement of Indian and Alaska Native people, full development of their human and natural resource potential; to mobilize all public and private aids to the advancement of In-dian and Alaska Native people for use by them; and to utilize the skill and capabilities of Indian and Alaska Native people in the direction and management of programs for their benefit." The BIA has 12 area offices in the United States, so that the distance between the service provider, the work site, and the reservation (place of resi-dence) compounds the difficulties of eligibility and availability of assistance.

Improving the Status of Ethnic Elders

A large number of minority elders spend the last years of their lives with inadequate income and housing, poor medical care, and few necessary services. Aging accentuates the factors that have contributed to a lifetime of social, economic, and psychological struggle. Rather than achieving comfort and respect with age, minority persons may get pushed further aside.

Upgrading the status of ethnic elders in the short term requires, first, recognition of the various factors that prevent them from utilizing services and, second, outreach programs designed to overcome those factors. The object should be to expand culturally appropriate health care and education services, to develop more self-help programs, to increase the **bilingual** abilities and cultural competence of social service professionals, and to recruit staff members from the ethnic groups they serve. In doing so, cultural isolation and the perceived stigma of utilizing services (especially in mental health) will be reduced.

With these goals in mind, the Administration of Aging (AOA) has funded four national organizations to improve the well-being of minority elders:

1. National Caucus and Center on Black Aged (NCCBA) in Washington, D.C.
2. National Indian Council on Aging (NICOA) in Albuquerque, New Mexico
3. Asociación Nacional Pro Personas Mayores (National Association for Hispanic Elderly) in Los Angeles, California
4. National Pacific/Asian Resource Center on Aging (NP/ARCA) in Seattle, Washington

These centers educate the general public and advocate for their groups.

Ultimately, though, spending a bit of extra money and adding a few services will not solve the real problem. The disadvantages tend to derive from economic marginality that has lasted a lifetime. One's work history is a central factor in how one fares in later life. A work history that allows for a good pension or maximum Social Security benefits is a big step toward economic security in old age. Also, those who have made good salaries have had a chance to save money for their retirement years—a safety net not possible for low-wage earners. Until members of minority groups are from birth accorded full participation in the goods and services our society offers, they will continue to suffer throughout their lives. The critical perspective in sociology calls for addressing these basic inequalities and taking major steps toward making all citizens equal.

Chapter Summary

Women, including older ones, in the United States, are in a minority status. They do not participate equally in the political and economic structures. Older women are victims of the double standard of aging—a standard that judges them more harshly as they age. A large percentage of elders in poverty are female.

Ethnic elders suffer from inequality in the United States. Older blacks are poorer than older whites and have a lower life expectancy, poorer health, worse housing, and fewer material comforts. Although some older African Americans are well-to-do, others are impoverished. Family ties, religion, and a resolve to persevere are their special strengths. Hispanic elders are not a homogeneous group. About half of all Hispanic elders are Mexican Americans; others come from Cuba, Puerto Rico, and various Central and South American countries. Hispanic elders have suffered major linguistic and cultural barriers to assimilation, and their socioeconomic status has remained low. Asian-American elders also come from many countries. They, too, have encountered racial hatred, language barriers, and discrimination. Native American elders are a small group. But by any social or economic indicator, they are possibly the most deprived group in the United States. More efforts need to be directed at correcting inequities for ethnic minorities and women.

Key Terms

African American
    elders
age terrorism
amaeru
Asian American elders
bilingual
double standard
    of aging
enryo

ethnic groups
ethnicity
familism
filial piety
Hispanic elders
late midlife
    astonishment
minority
minority elder

Questions for Discussion

1. What special problems do older women experience? Older African Americans? Hispanics? Asian Americans? Native Americans? White Americans? In what ways are older women's issues unique to their ethnic or cultural background, and in what ways are their issues ones shared by all older women?

2. What are the primary gender-gap issues that arise between generations in each of the five cultural or racial groups above? Describe some *particular* cultural values that are held by the older generation but not shared as

deeply by the next generation for different cultural groups.

Fieldwork Suggestions

Interview an older person from a racial minority. Note carefully the person's lifestyle and outlook on life. What past and present discrimination has he or she experienced?

Internet Activities

1. Locate the AARP home page and search for information on retired women's issues. Now search for information on minority issues. What levels of analysis do you find? Are the issues of retired women and minorities well addressed, or are they addressed as being "other" to the dominant (white male) population of retired persons?

2. Go to the U.S. Bureau of the Census home page and search out the number of children living with grandparents in the country. Can you locate this information by race and ethnicity? Does your home state have parallel information? Where else might you search for data on ethnicity and family household structure?

3. Seek out Internet information on minority elder status, other than U.S. Census data. Maintain a log of your Internet "travels." How easy or hard was it for you to locate the information? Who is the intended audience of the information you have?

Death and Dying

15

A Death Doctor's Strange Obsessions

James Risen

He was a bright young doctor at a time when the United States was just beginning its post–World War II ascent, and Jack Kevorkian, University of Michigan Medical School Class of 1952, could have—should have—had it all.

But he had this nagging, inexplicable fascination with the dying and the dead, a personal obsession, really, one that was all the more peculiar because it first appeared during an optimistic era of limitless possibilities and unquestioning faith in the resiliency of American life.

Perhaps it was reinforced during his brief time as a U.S. Army doctor in Korea; certainly it was there during his residency at the University of Michigan Medical Center in the mid-1950s. . . .

"I don't like to watch someone die," he insists. "It is a traumatic, wrenching experience. . . ."

Over the years, Kevorkian's obsession would cost him dearly. On the fringes of medicine, he would become permanently unemployed in his mid-50s—rejected even for a job as a paramedic.

His last patients were acquaintances who would stop him in the street to ask his advice on minor ailments. He would complain that American medical journals refused to publish his ideas. By the onset of the 1990s, Kevorkian had retreated into a private world. . . .

And so when Janet Adkins came to him eager to end her life, eager to stop the suffering of Alzheimer's disease before she became mentally incompetent, Kevorkian was ready.

He already had traveled the slippery ethical slope that leads from medicine to euthanasia. In his own mind, he was no longer a practicing pathologist.

Instead, he printed up new business cards. On them, he called himself an "obitiatrist," with its root in the word "obituary"; a doctor of death. "The world's first," he says.

On June 4, 1990, Adkins, a 54-year-old mother of three from Portland, Oregon, climbed into the back of Kevorkian's rusting old Volkswagen van in a rural Michigan park not far from Pontiac and allowed Kevorkian to connect her to his homemade "suicide machine."

She then pushed a button three times to ensure the machine's death-inducing drugs would course through her veins. According to Kevorkian, "Thank you, thank you," were her last words.

Author's Note: This was Kevorkian's first physician-assisted suicide widely publicized by the media. In March 1998, the Kevorkian-assisted suicide of a 66-year old man with lung cancer marked the 100th suicide assist of Jack Kevorkian (age 69), his lawyer Geoffrey Fieger stated publicly. Kevorkian, who lost his license to practice medicine in Michigan in 1991, has been acquitted in three trials in Michigan, the last one in 1997. In that trial, Fieger provided a video of Kevorkian's latest subjects begging to be allowed to die, and stated that "Government has no business telling you what to do." The controversy surrounding

Kevorkian continues because he helps people die who are not necessarily in extreme pain nor in the final months of terminal illness, the two major criteria in Holland for physician-assisted suicides.

Source: James Risen, "Death Doctor's Strange Obsession," *San Francisco Chronicle* (26 June 1990): A8. Copyright © 1990 Los Angeles Times. Reprinted with permission.

Adapted from: New York Times, 1998 Associated Press. "Kevorkian Deaths Total 100," *New York Times,* March 15, 1998 v 147, p14(N), p 18(L).

Death is one of the few certainties of life. This statement is neither pessimistic nor morbid. Despite our wildest fantasies about immortality, no one has yet escaped death permanently. Despite its universality, however, death is not easily discussed in American society. People tend to be sensitive and shy about discussing the topic openly.

Facing death, dealing with the fact of death in a rational way, and exerting control over the manner of one's dying are all difficult situations in a society that denies death. Just because one is old does not mean that one does not fear death or that one welcomes dying. In this chapter, we will examine the ability of the older individual to experience a "good" death to the extent our society permits it.

> *Life itself is a sexually transmitted, terminal condition.*

A Death-Denying Society?

Our words, attitudes, and practices suggest that ours is a **death-denying society.** Have you ever used the word "died" and had the uncomfortable feeling that those with whom you were talking considered the word too direct and in bad taste? "Passed away" might be the preferred phrase, or "passed on"—but not "dead." There are dozens of euphemisms for the process of dying. Funerals, presenting an embalmed and painted body, try to project an illusion of life. There is even a sort of prescribed script that mourners follow: "She looks just like she did yesterday when I was talking to her," or "He looks so natural." Those selling cemetery plots advise us not to buy a grave but to invest in a "pre-need memorial estate." The funeral industry in the United States is enormous, now offering services, in addition to burial, from funeral planning to bereavement counseling.

Watching death on television or killing after violent killing in the movies is not facing death. The violent deaths portrayed in cartoons and action films do not evoke the human emotions—the deep sorrow, anger, and guilt—that the actual death of a loved one would. "Sensitive" television dramas that depict the death of a family member tend to be just as unrealistic.

At the end of the nineteenth century, dying and death were household events that encompassed not only elders, but the young and middle-aged as well. At the end of the twentieth century, death is characterized by life-extending medical procedures, hospital and insurance bureaucracies, and secularism. As chronic diseases and increased technology keep people in a prolonged state of dying, bureaucracy makes the setting impersonal, and a secular society robs a person of the religious significance of dying. These three trends promote the impersonalization of the process through which the dying individual must go. Small wonder that death is perceived as such a fearful, lonely experience.

Death avoidance is not unique to modern times, however. Dealing with the unknowable, whatever its outcome, is anxiety producing for humans, whose driving desire is toward understanding. The French philosopher Montaigne (1533–1592) argued in the sixteenth century that to become free of death's grip we must immerse ourselves in all the aspects and nuances of death:

> We come and we go and we trot and we dance, . . . and never a word about death. All well and good. Yet when death does come—to them, their wives, their children, their friends—catching them unawares and unprepared, then what storms of passion overwhelm them, what cries, what fury, what despair! . . . To begin depriving death of its greatest advantage over us, let us adopt a way clean contrary to that common one; let us deprive death of its strangeness, let us frequent it, let us get used to it; let us have nothing more often in mind than death. . . . We do not know where death awaits us: so let us wait for it everywhere. To practice death is to practice freedom. [One] who has learned how to die has unlearned how to be a slave. (Montaigne, quoted in Marrone, 1997, p. 328)

Denial of death is possible on a grand scale now not because we choose to deny it more than our ancestors did, but because we have greater institutional resources for helping us to avoid its reality.

About 85 percent of American deaths occur in hospital rooms and convalescent hospitals (Marrone, 1997). The final moments of life are seldom observed, even by family. Health professionals and paraprofessionals are the predominant care providers for the dying, but health professionals are seldom trained in the process of death. They are trained to extend life, and death is a failure of the promise of that training. Death is often as hard a reality to health professionals as it is to everyone else.

Despite social customs that decrease the interaction of the living with death and dying, interest in the topic has escalated in the last decade or so. College courses on death and dying, seminars instructing health professionals and clergy in understanding the dying person, and many books on the subject have become available.

Fear of Death

Fear of death is a normal human condition—we struggle for life, and for the lives of others, and we desperately desire to avoid unknowns. But are people more fearful, or less fearful, at different ages?

Old people are commonly stereotyped as waiting fearlessly for death. And, though any given individual may be an exception to the rule, elders as a group do seem less fearful than younger persons. The thanatologist Richard Kalish (1987) attributed this difference to three things: (1) many elders feel they have completed the most important tasks of life, (2) they are more likely to be in pain or to be suffering from chronic diseases and thus view death as an escape from that pain, and (3) they have lost many friends and relatives. Those losses have made death more a reality.

Some people who work with elders, however, believe that old people may fear death *more* because they are closer to it. There is less time available to complete important life tasks, to make amends, to say goodbye. Other observers say that fear is the greatest in late middle age, when midlife brings a heightened awareness of aging and death. Once that transitory phase passes, however, fears usually decline. Most observers and philosophers agree that fear of death is innate in all individuals, regardless of age, and that it provides direction for life's activities. Understanding that we will die may be a precondition for a fuller and deeper understanding of life.

There are two ways of not thinking about death: The way of our technological civilization, which denies death and refuses to talk about it; and the way of traditional civilization, which is not a denial but a recognition of the impossibility of thinking about it directly or for very long because death is too close and too much a part of daily life.

ARIES, 1981

Given painful experiences, and the power of storytelling and imagination, people have many reasons to fear death itself or to have **fears about dying.** People fear a long, painful death; illness, such as cancer; cognitive impairment; the unknown; judgment in the afterlife; and the fate of one's body. They fear dying alone or, conversely, being watched; fear dying in a hospital or nursing home; and fear the loss of bodily control. Some of the fears are of death itself; others are fears about the process of dying, such as the imagined pain, helplessness, and dependence. Fear of the *condition* of death—of being dead—as well as fear of the *process* of dying are important to understand if we are to help people who are dying and to help ourselves in our own deaths.

Some fears seem normal, that is, justified and within reason. Others seem to be exaggerated. The term **fear of death** is usually used when such apprehension has a specific, identifiable source. In comparison, **death anxiety** describes feelings of apprehension and discomfort that lack an identifiable source. **Death competency,** on the other hand, is our capability and skill in dealing with death. But how fearful, anxious, or competent are people? Does an individual's fear of death or overriding anxiety about death affect his or her process of grieving, or shape his or her own death? If we knew more about which aspects of death were most problematic for a given person, could that person be better assisted through a "good" death, or with grief and mourning over the death of someone beloved?

Several measures of death fear have been developed in an attempt to understand more about the fears and anxieties surrounding death for groups of people and to provide a better understanding about a particular person. The questions generally cover a range of fears, such as fear of dependency, fear of pain, fear of indignity, fear of isolation or loneliness, fears related to an afterlife, fear of leaving people we love, and fear of the fate of the body (Lemming & Dickinson, 1994; Neiman, 1994). Findings from more general research provide a road map for understanding individual issues with death and dying.

Traditional religious beliefs that include "heaven" and survival of the body after death have been found to be related to a decrease in fears of death, as are beliefs in the paranormal, such as sightings of angels or other personal guides (Alvardo et al., 1995; Lange & Houran, 1997). People with lower death depression scores seem to have greater strength of conviction and greater belief in an afterlife, and they are less likely to say that *the* most important aspect of religion is that it offers the possibility of life after death (Alvarado et al., 1995). Research consistently finds that the strength of belief—whatever that belief might be—is more closely related to lower death anxiety scores than knowledge of dogma, attitudes toward mortality, or frequency of church attendance (Lonetto & Templer, 1986; Conn et al., 1996; Thorson & Powell, 1996). This reinforces the suggestion that fear of death is an internal, psychological relationship with the state of dying, based on an individual's beliefs and values. We die as we live; we are the same person as we "go into that dark night" as we were before the specter of death was upon us.

This might give us pause to consider just how we choose to live—our coping skills, our choices, our personality patterns are what we will have to help us cope in our own deaths.

Though the experience of death will be different for every person, in general, our fears about the suffering of death may be at least somewhat unfounded. Most people die relatively painless deaths. In most cases, an individual's health does not deteriorate until he or she is very close to death. Most people are in good or excellent health a year before they die, and many are in good health the week of their death. It is the haunting stories of lingering, painful, lonely death that many people carry in their heads when they think of death that feeds our innate fears. In reality, the more we know and understand about death, the less fearful it will seem.

Elders' fears and concerns about dying must be dealt with as openly as possible, difficult as that might be. Because of their own anxieties about death, adult children often will not allow parents or grandparents to fully express their views on the subject. Older people often attempt a discussion about their own death and/or about what the family will do after (or just before) the elder dies, only to be told in many different ways, "Oh, you don't have to think about this yet! You have a lot of time for that." Yet this "death talk" can be realistic, practical, and therapeutic. Family members would be wise to listen.

Living Fully until Death

The marginal status of elders in our society affects their ability to live fully until death. Richard Kalish discovered that although the death of an elder is less disturbing than the death of a younger person in our American culture, this attitude is not universal. He told this story:

> I once asked a group of about two dozen Cambodian students in their mid-twenties whether, given the necessity for choice, they would save the life of their mother, their wife or their daughter. All responded immediately

that they would save their mother, and their tone implied that only an immoral or ignorant person would even ask such a question. (Kalish, 1985, p. 116)

Although we all hope to live fully from the moment of birth until death, for some elders, living fully until death may not be possible. Some spend their final years confined to nursing homes or other caretaking institutions. Oddly, researchers have generally found a more positive attitude toward death among institutionalized elderly than among those living in their own homes. Upon closer examination, this positive attitude may not represent an acceptance of dying as much as it represents a desire not to continue living. Elders living in nursing homes are generally more frail and less physically competent than elders living at home. Death for some elders, rather than being a point of acceptance, is one simply of resignation in a life that is no longer meaningful.

During her pioneer work in hospitals with death and the dying, Elisabeth Kübler-Ross invited dying patients to share their wants, anxieties, and fears with professionals involved in their care. Though talking about death was off-limits for doctors, it was definitely not so for the dying patients:

> With few exceptions, the patients were surprised, amazed, and grateful. Some were plain curious and others expressed their disbelief that a . . . doctor would sit with a dying old woman and really care to know what it is like. In the majority of cases the initial outcome was [like] opening floodgates. . . . The patients responded with great relief to sharing some of their last concerns, expressing their feelings without fear of repercussions. (Kübler-Ross, 1969, pp. 157–158)

Kübler-Ross's work provided the foundation for modern thanatology—she moved dying out of the medical closet, in which it had lived throughout the twentieth century.

The following section summarizes Kübler-Ross's theory of the process of dying. Although

Telling the story of one's life is a way of confirming values, recognizing the growth and development that has occurred over time, and connecting with other people.

Stage 2: Anger

Following the initial shock, a new reaction sets in: anger, or resentment of those whose lives will continue. "Why me? I have [young children] . . . [finally found love in life] . . . [responsibilities to family] . . . [not yet done something important] . . ." or a myriad of other realities that give our lives meaning. This anger often becomes displaced to the doctors, who are no good; the nurses, who do everything wrong; the family, which is not sympathetic; and the world, which is a mess. I'm not dead yet—so pay attention to me! Do not abandon me with my fears. The anger serves to give vent to feelings of helplessness, despair, and frustration; it can be a very important process in helping the dying person move vague anxieties to a psychological point at which he or she can deal more openly with the experience of dying. Understanding that anger has a function for the dying person can help the people around him or her to cope with those expressions of dissatisfaction or rage.

Stage 3: Bargaining

Bargaining is an attempt to postpone the inevitable. If life can only be extended until they can do the one thing they have always wanted to do, or until they can make amends for something they have regretted, or until they can see someone again, they promise to accept death. Some pledge their life to God or to service in the church in exchange for additional time. Others might promise to give their bodies to science, if only life could be extended. Bargaining is a compromise stage that follows the realization that death cannot be denied or escaped and functions to help the individual cope with the reality of the approaching death.

Stage 4: Depression

When terminally ill patients can no longer deny an illness because of its advancing symptoms, a profound sense of loss is experienced. The loss may be of physical parts of the body re-

articulated as stages, Kübler-Ross found that a person might be in any stage or in several stages simultaneously, and the "stages" are not necessarily sequential. People might move back and forth or in and out of the categorizations or skip some altogether. The Kübler-Ross stage model provided the most fundamental groundwork for developing a greater understanding of the process of dying. It also provides a good framework to understand the process of grief and **bereavement,** which might, indeed, be what the dying person experiences.

Stage 1: Denial and shock

Of the more than 300 dying patients interviewed by Kübler-Ross, most reported first reacting to the awareness of a terminal illness with statements such as, "No, not me, it can't be true." The reactions of denial and shock are necessary to give us time to come to terms with the reality of the impending death.

moved by surgery, of money that is being spent on treatment, of functions that no longer can be performed, or of relationships with family and friends. A deep sorrow generally accompanies the recognition that death is undeniable. The depression might be **reactive** (the reaction to loss) or **preparatory** (preparation for one's impending loss of life; such preparation facilitates a state of acceptance), but it comes with the profound recognition that there is nothing that can be done about the approaching death.

Stage 5: Acceptance

Most people ultimately move into a weak, quiet state of submission to that which fate has to offer. Kübler-Ross referred to this as acceptance, but it is apparently a time devoid of emotion—it is a twilight for the dying person, who is often sleepy or half-conscious, but no longer depressed or angry. "The struggle for survival is over," and the dying person seems to be taking "a final rest before the long journey," said one of Kübler-Ross's patients (Kübler-Ross, 1969). The individual's vital capacity has ebbed and interaction seems unimportant. At this time, the dying person often wants to be with only one particular, special person. Despite the disinclination to engage at this time, Kübler-Ross emphasized the profound importance for the dying person to be touched and spoken to, as a loving reminder of the context of their life.

Facing death is a difficult task upon which age, status, and experience have little bearing, if any. Young children, old people, and those in between seem to experience a similar process. We die as we have lived, the saying goes. Whether we are angry, or energetic fighters, or philosophers—those will be the characteristics we bring with us to the process of our death. People do have choice in the way they die, however. Lynne Lofland (1979) proposed that four dimensions of choice shape the role of a dying person: (1) how much "life space" to devote to the dying role—the degree of activity to give over to dying; (2) whether to surround oneself with others who are dying; (3) whether to share information about the facts and feelings of one's death with others; and (4) the sort of personal philosophy one wishes to express in the dying role.

Making decisions about the way in which one will die might be the final act of self-determination the dying person can make. Understanding the process makes the possibility of addressing it and making choices about it far more possible.

The Life Review

The study of geropsychology attempts to provide insight into the factors most likely to affect the life satisfaction of older people. According to Erikson (1982) and Butler (1981), **reminiscence** provides a source for life satisfaction for the elderly, allowing for the integration of past experiences (who I was then) with the present (who I am now), to make reasonable projections about the future (who I will be, what will happen to me).

During reminiscence, a person progressively remembers more of past experiences and reexamines and reintegrates unresolved conflicts with the present. This process can bring new significance and meaning to life, reduce anxiety, and prepare one for death. It may well occur in all individuals in the final days of their lives. Though a life review can occur at a younger age, the drive to put one's life in order seems strongest in old age—and it seems to be a necessary process in order for a person to make sense of his or her life as lived.

At some point in late life, the individual develops a particularly vivid imagination and memory for the past and can recall with sudden and remarkable clarity events of early life, seemingly moving thoughts from their subconscious to their conscious mind. This process allows people to grapple with their vulnerability and mortality as they reassess the meaning of life. The life review that results from this process may be told to other people, or it may be preserved as private reflection. Finding the process of expression therapeutic, some older people will tell their life history to anyone who will listen; others share their thoughts with no one. Those who cannot resolve the issues their life review uncovers may become anxious or depressed, or may even enter a state of terror or panic. Those who cannot face or accept the resolution of their life conflicts may become deeply depressed or even commit suicide. Others gain a sense of satisfaction, a sense of tranquility, a capacity to enjoy to the utmost the remainder of their life. Counselors are advised to be attentive and ready to question and to listen about life and about dying with patients. By creating the opportunity for a dying elder to talk about his or her life in terms of the integration of past, present, and future, the listener helps the dying person to deal more effectively with stress (Puentes, 1998).

Butler's ideas have generated much research, and though the terms life review and reminiscence have often been used interchangeably in the accompanying literature, some researchers have separated the concepts by considering the life review to be one of many forms of reminiscence. Reminiscence may provide materials for life review or it may be just storytelling for fun or social activity. By comparison, **life review** is that form of reminiscence in which the reviewer actively evaluates the past and attempts to resolve conflicts. It is not always comfortable; the reviewer is not glossing lightly over a topic, creating a good story for the benefit of the listener. In the life review processes, the listener is merely the excuse for the elder's process of working with past material. Indeed, some older people proceed with the process of life review through their writing—of journals, of stories, of letters. Butler, on introducing the concept, said:

Life review is a naturally occurring, universal mental process characterized by the progressive return to consciousness of past experiences, and particularly, the resurgence of unresolved conflicts; simultaneously, and normally, these revived experiences and conflicts can be surveyed and reintegrated.

Presumably this process is prompted by the realization of approaching dissolution and death, and the inability to maintain one's sense of personal invulnerability. It is further shaped by contemporaneous experiences and its nature and outcome are affected by the lifelong unfolding of character. (Butler, 1963, p. 66)

It is possible that people more commonly engage in life review in their later years, though it is not limited to that period of the life course. Butler contends that thoughts of death initiate the life review, which is, developmentally, more expected as one nears the end of life.

Although it may seem that older people, whether close to death or not, are wasting time by talking of the past and dwelling on details that have little meaning to younger listeners, these elders may be engaging in life review. Bernice Neugarten (1987) coined the term "interiority" to refer to a process common in mid- and later life of becoming more focused on internal messages and stories and less focused on outside, social issues. This disengagement from the social may accurately describe what happens just prior to death: people turn inward, mentally evaluate their lives, and gradually reduce connections with the larger social world. In contrast, seeking to remain actively, externally connected may potentially damage the self-concept of the dying person by discouraging this reflection, reevaluation, and resolution.

Older residents in nursing homes who belong to reminiscing groups seem to have higher rates of life satisfaction than do residents who do not engage in reminiscing (Cook, 1997). In the early 1980s a sense of closeness to death among nursing home residents was examined. Researchers named this "awareness of finitude" and found that this awareness was a better predictor of disengagement than chronological age. The residents who gave a shorter estimate had altered their behavior by constricting their life space and had already become more introverted (Still, 1980).

Awareness of finitude

Care of the Dying in Hospitals

The medical anthropologist Sharon Kaufman identifies a conflict between the **medicalization paradigm** (belief in scientific answers to health), and the paradigm of **individualism and autonomy** (belief in noninterference in personal choice). She suggests it is this conflict that is the source of the "problem" of frailty in old age in American society (Kaufman, 1994) and by extension, the "problem" of dying in a hospital.

In their pioneering study of patient-staff interactions in a number of hospitals, the sociologists Barney Glazer and Anselm Strauss (1966) created a typology of **awareness contexts of dying** for terminally ill patients: (1) closed awareness, (2) suspicion awareness, (3) the ritual drama of mutual pretense, (4) open awareness, and (5) disconnection.

Closed Awareness —Doct. doesn't tell

The patient does not yet know that he or she is going to die. The physician in charge decides to keep the patient from knowing or even suspecting the actual diagnosis, and the rest of the staff do all they can to maintain the patient's lack of knowledge. The physician gains the patient's trust and at the same time avoids revealing the fact of his or her impending death.

Suspicion Awareness

The patient suspects the truth, but no one will confirm his or her suspicions. Because the patient is afraid to ask outright questions, he or she therefore receives no clear answers. Still, the patient, who wants evidence, tries to interpret what the staff says and does. Peeking at medical charts, eavesdropping on medical conversations, and watching listeners' reactions after declaring "I think I'm dying" are typical behaviors.

Ritual Drama of Mutual Pretense

This is the third type of awareness. *Denial* Both patient and staff now know that death is impending, but both choose to act as if it is not. The patient tries to project a healthy, well-groomed appearance, and behaves as if he or she will be leaving the hospital soon; the staff makes comments such as "You're looking well today"; and both follow the script as if acting out a drama. Blatant events that expose the mutual pretense are ignored.

Open Awareness —healthiest

This may or may not extend to the time of death and mode of dying, but both patient and staff openly acknowledge that the patient is dying. Game playing is eliminated.

Disconnection

Doctors and nurses for whom daily encounters with dying patients produce painful and bewildering emotions can be distant and tense with dying people. To face a dying person is a reminder in the health care context that they are a "failure" at keeping that person alive and vigorous, as well as a reminder of their own mortality and the finality of death. Some hospital staff members react to the dying person by withdrawing emotionally at a time when the patient most needs their support.

Fortunately, in no small part because of hospice and chaplaincy services, the health care system is showing an increased sensitivity to issues about death and dying. If health professionals can face their own mortality, they can more easily face mortality in others and are less likely to transmit their fear, shock, or horror to the dying person. Generally, the goal for hospital staff is to maintain an open awareness context, as appropriate to the patient. Sometimes other contexts are called for; closed awareness, for example, may be appropriate if the patient indicates a strong desire not to know any details about his or her condition and clearly denies his or her own illness.

Care of the dying in a hospital involves more than the decision to tell or not to tell a patient of his or her fate. A number of other problems are evident.

Labeling

One problem occurs when doctors and nurses stereotype or label a terminally ill person as "the dying patient." The word "dying" fades all other facets of the individual's personality and colors others' behavior toward him or her. Forgetting that the person is still alive, aware, and unique, staff members may talk as if the patient were insensate or absent. Paradoxically, the full richness of the human being often is not acknowledged, at the very time such validation is central for the dying person to reassess his or her shifting identity.

Encouragement

How much hope to offer the dying patient is another task health care professionals must face. Some degree of hope can be helpful to the terminally ill. A glimpse of hope can maintain a person through tests, surgery, and suffering. Patients show the greatest confidence in doctors who offer hope without lying, who share with them the hope that some unforeseen develop-

ment will change the course of events. Hope does not particularly mean that people who understand they are dying believe they will live. It means they have something to live for a little while longer.

The "Dying Person's Bill of Rights," drawn up by those who nurse cancer patients, includes this statement about hope: "I have the right to be cared for by those who can maintain a sense of hopefulness, however changing this might be."

Professionals' fears

For two decades, the National Cancer Institute has offered a seminar to physicians planning to specialize in the care of cancer patients. The physicians meet to come to grips with their own anxieties about death and to better understand their interactions with dying patients and their families. Doctors and nurses often feel an involuntary anger at the dying patient, who comes to represent their own sense of failure and helplessness. "When you've exhausted everything you can do for a patient medically, it becomes difficult to walk into the room every day and talk to that patient." The seminar seems to relieve stress on the cancer ward's nurses, who used to regularly ask for transfers to other wards. It also teaches the staff to be more comfortable in discussing death and other potentially sensitive topics with the patient.

Courses in death and dying are now available at Harvard, Tufts, and other medical schools. Nine out of ten medical schools in the country have at least one or two lectures for students on the topic, but only six medical schools offer an entire course on death and dying. In only half of the schools with such a course is it required; in the other half it is an elective. Personal involvement of students with dying patients was minimal in almost every course at every medical school. One exception is the Yale School of Medicine, which developed a course enabling medical students to interact with very sick patients. The course tries to help students develop and demonstrate their compassion without being afraid.

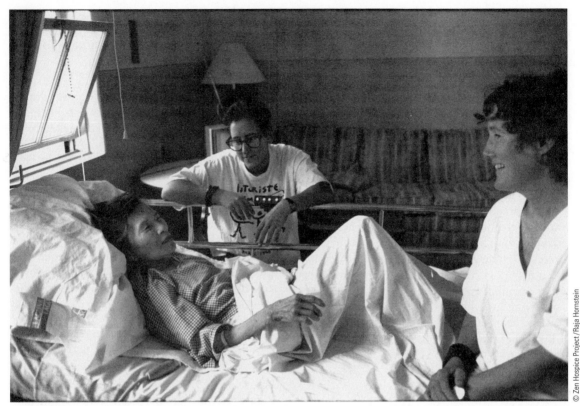

The hospice movement has revolutionized end-of-life care in the United States. Quality of life at end of life is now a priority for most medical institutions.

Elders, as we might expect, have a higher death rate than any other age group. Morbidity and mortality statistics indicate that health declines and the death rate increases at the upper age levels. Care of the dying, then, has special relevance to older persons, especially the very old, who stand to benefit the most from improved care for the dying.

funeral plans, which also involve the matter of choice, have special implications for elders.

Did you know . . .
Searching the medical literature for articles on "death" will yield more articles on cell death than on human death.

HORGAN, 1997

A Matter of Choice

Individuals who face the prospect of imminent death increasingly seek to expand their rights in determining the manner of their dying. Deciding to die at home or to not prolong life by artificial means are becoming two areas of choice for terminally ill patients. In addition, suicide and

The Hospice Movement

Hospice was virtually unheard of in this country until the mid-1970s. It received a tremendous boost in 1982, when Medicare payments were authorized to cover care for terminally ill patients. In 1989 a federal law raised disbursement rates for hospice services by 20 percent, and

20% hospice.

another surge of interest occurred (Worsnop, 1996). In 1996 the Hospice Association of America reported that over 2,100 Medicare-certified hospice programs were in operation across the country, compared with 158 in 1985.

The hospice model, which stresses effective pain relief for terminal cancer patients, is designed to care for the dying person—the whole person, not the disease. The term "hospice" can be any organization that provides support services to dying patients and their loved ones in the place where that care is given, whether it is in the home, in a hospital, or in a nursing home (Worsnop, 1997).

Palliative care—pain control—is the core of the practice, in which an individual's death is neither hastened nor prolonged. It provides, in the words of Christine Cassel (1996), "aggressive comfort care." Tremendous advances in the management of pain have occurred in the final decade of the twentieth century: drugs can be delivered through skin patches, through topical creams, and by intravenous pumps. Some new drugs and drug delivery systems have helped to minimize the side effects of many painkillers, such as grogginess, nausea, and reduced mental clarity (Horgan, 1997).

Social attitudes that have limited prescriptions of analgesics—opiates such as morphine, particularly—have shifted somewhat in recent years. The Pain and Policy Studies Group at the University Wisconsin has conducted some outstanding research on attitudes of the public and of physicians about painkillers and found changing perceptions regarding the use of "addicting" drugs for pain control (Horgan, 1997). It is striking to note that medical research in the field of pain control has been directed not by humanitarian philosophy, but by the market potential brought about by longevity and by governmental funding through Medicare for palliative care.

The first hospice program in the United States, Hospice of Connecticut, in New Haven, offers a model of care for the dying. The New Haven hospice began as a home care program.

Outreach workers visited and counseled patients, and they also provided home nursing to the dying. Family members could receive individual or group counseling throughout the dying process to get support from others experiencing the same shock and grief. The program later developed a residential hospice in which families and friends could be with the dying person, away from the home.

Hospice works with an interdisciplinary team of workers, including nurses, health aides, counselors, physical therapists, nutritionists, chaplains, volunteer visitors, doctors, and long-term care administrators. Volunteers provide care so family members can get out of the house or feel comfortable leaving the bedside. Volunteers also might do light housekeeping, laundry, meal preparations, and errands for the family or the ill person.

Some hospitals run hospice programs, and programs are becoming available at nursing homes as well. These programs offer an integrated approach to death in which medical and nursing staffs, chaplains and visiting clergy, and social service staff members work together to meet the physical, spiritual, and psychological needs of the dying.

Awareness of hospitals as potentially grim and depersonalized places to die has encouraged a trend toward dying at home. Some health-care organizations enable patients to go home to die by providing doctors and nurses who will counsel the family, monitor the patient's drug intake, and provide emotional support.

A dying person often takes a renewed interest in life when he or she finds people who are sensitive to both medical needs and emotions. The hospice or the hospice wing of a hospital often does not appear to be institutional. In the visitors' area, the radio may play upbeat music while rambunctious children play in the hallways. Visitors are welcome over a wide range of hours—indeed, the model encourages open interactions designed around the needs of real people, rather than requiring that those people fit their needs into an institutional format.

Hospice care in the 1990s has focused a great deal of attention on AIDS patients. Nursing homes that, until recently, have cared mostly for elders now provide facilities for young adult AIDS patients. Hospice care, though stretching to meet the needs of all clients, is, nevertheless, overburdened in areas where the numbers of AIDS patients are high. Additionally, they have becoming far more bureaucratized and regulated, especially where Medicaid and Medicare reimbursements apply (Magno, 1990). The AIDS epidemic, with no cure in sight, has underscored the need for the hospice orientation, an approach that emphasizes care when there is no cure. Hospice care promotes the philosophy that comfort and quality of life are in and of themselves worthwhile and essential goals to the end of one's life.

Although most people, when asked, express a desire to die at home, only a small percentage actually do. Not everyone should die at home. For a patient who has an unhappy or unstable family or who needs complicated nursing care, a hospital or nursing home may be a better option. Parents and grandparents sometimes choose to die in hospitals in order to avoid traumatizing young children. However, some psychiatrists believe that the very fact of a death occurring at home can ward off psychological damage to the family. The child who is involved throughout the dying process does not have to face the sudden, unexplained disappearance of a parent or grandparent. In contrast, children who are not involved may believe, for example, that they are somehow responsible for the death. Keeping a dying family member at home can both make it easier for relatives to accept the death and prevent the patient from being alone in the dying process.

Reframing the Craft of Dying

Lynne Lofland (1979) refers to the hospice movement and a number of other groups that work toward improving attitudes and conditions surrounding death as the **happy death movement.** This movement opposes the conventional view that the dying person be stoic, strong, and silent. It began, she says, in academia and filtered out to ordinary citizens who are embracing the concept (in Hoefler, 1994). Lofland notes that although the new movement has helped some people to freely express their fears, others still refuse to express their concerns.

The new movement has advocated the view that dying can be a learning, growing, and positive experience. Lofland observes that this emphasis, in itself, may pressure dying people to assume a certain way of thinking. Those who will not or cannot share their thoughts and feelings, or who do not develop positive attitudes, may feel like failures. Additionally, it is not culturally appropriate among all people to discuss their intimate feelings, and surely little can be so intimate as one's own process of dying. Lofland believes that alternative ideologies are critical to providing dying people the greatest degree of choice in their mental preparation for death.

In a similar vein, some who work in the field of death and dying have criticized the phrase "death with dignity" as placing too much emphasis on being proper or accepting (Nuland, 1994). "Dignity" has a Latin root, *dignitas,* meaning "worthiness" (Meyer, 1995). The potential is there for "death with dignity" to communicate to the dying individual the burden of expectations of a particular behavior, rather than its intended meaning—to create an environment in which the dying person is helped to be aware of his or her worthiness.

Did you know . . .
In 1937 a nationwide Gallup Poll reported that 46 percent of Americans interviewed favored "mercy deaths under government supervision for hopeless individuals."
Worsnop, 1996

The Right to Die

We have grappled with the **right-to-die issue** for many decades. The first bill to legalize doctor-assisted suicide was introduced in 1906 in the state of Ohio, which proposed that a doctor could ask a terminally ill person in the presence of three witnesses whether he or she wished to die. If the answer was yes, and three other physicians agreed that the patient's condition was hopeless, they could assist in his suicide. Opponents feared a lack of safeguards, and the measure was defeated.

The issue slowly grew in public acceptance, fermenting until the liberation of the Nazi death camps in 1945 at the end of World War II. The full horror of medically assisted death—systematic termination of life—suddenly became so abhorrent a concept that **assisted suicide** ceased to be a public topic (Worsner, 1996).

In the 1970s, the parents of Karen Quinlan, a 21-year-old woman in a permanent vegetative state, initiated a court battle in the state of New Jersey for the right to disconnect the life-support machines to which Karen was attached. Though a trial judge initially ruled against them, in 1976, after taking the case to the New Jersey Supreme Court, the Quinlans were allowed to have the machines removed. Karen lived in a comatose state another nine years.

A second case that galvanized the public's awareness was that of *Cruzan v. Missouri Department of Health*. Following an auto accident that left her in a vegetative state, Nancy Cruzan had been kept alive for seven years by a feeding tube. In a suit filed in 1988, her parents, acting on her behalf, requested that her food and fluids be stopped. A lengthy and extraordinarily expensive process ensued for the Cruzans. In a summary of the case in the *Congressional Quarterly*, Richard Worsnop reported:

> *The Missouri Department of Health appealed the decision to the State Supreme Court, which reversed it. As a result, the Cruzans appealed to the U.S. Supreme Court, which held on June 25, 1990, that a person whose wishes were clearly known had a constitutional right to refuse life-sustaining medical treatment. At the same time, however, it ruled that states could require that comatose patients be kept alive unless there was "clear and convincing evidence" that they would not want to live under such conditions. Such evidence, said the court, was lacking in the* Cruzan *case.*
>
> *Instead of giving up, the Cruzans returned to Jasper County Circuit Court. Three of Nancy's former co-workers now testified that she had told them years earlier she would not want to live out her days in a coma. . . . [The court ruled that] this disclosure amounted to clear and convincing evidence. . . . The Cruzans had the right to order the removal of their daughter's feeding tube. (Worsnop, 1996, p. 780).*

Nancy died 12 days following removal of the feeding tube. Her death came two months after a U.S. law requiring hospitals and other health care facilities receiving Medicare or Medicaid payments to inform patients of their right to execute living wills or other advance directives (Worsnop, 1996).

Families are still fighting similar court battles today. Doctors traditionally have felt they must prolong life as long as possible without questioning the circumstances, an idea that constitutes an intrinsic part of the Hippocratic oath. However, values and laws traditionally lag behind technological advancements; and the value system doctors have followed for centuries is now in a state of flux. The right to die is but one of many issues confronting **medical ethics** in the new century.

In the following sections, we will discuss that issue and several others. The issues are complex: At what point should the decision not to prolong life be made? Who should make the decision? Does an individual have the right to choose death when life could be extended in some fashion? Some of the right-to-die issues can be stated as specific questions:

1. What is the difference between killing and allowing a person to die?
2. What is the difference between stopping treatment and not beginning it?
3. Are there reasonable and unreasonable treatments?

The answers to these questions, which cannot be easily answered, vary on both moral and legal grounds.

In an odd way, the right-to-die movement has improved the quality of care of the dying in America. After Measure 16 passed [in Oregon] in 1994, the health profession started sponsoring seminars and lectures on pain control and set up task forces on end-of-life care. Now people reckon Oregon is the finest place to die in America. Doctors and nurses here will do their very best for you so that you don't ask for assisted dying.

DEREK HUMPHRY, HEMLOCK
SOCIETY FOUNDER, 1997

Theoretically, there are a number of ways that medical personnel could hasten the end for patients who wish to die. The terminally ill patient could be killed by injection. The decision could be made not to begin an intravenous drip or a respirator, or to stop one that was being used. A decision could be made to avoid antibiotic use with a patient with pneumonia. A fatally high dose of a narcotic or barbiturate could be administered. The legal consequences of these alternatives vary, and doctors vary, as well, in their attitudes toward assisted death. Some use code words on charts for "hopeless case" patients. Such a patient may be labeled "Code 90 DNR" (do not resuscitate), for example, or "CMO" (comfort measures only). Both indicate that extraordinary lifesaving measures

should not be applied (DeSpelder & Strickland, 1991).

Advance directives

Margaret Jones's 88-year-old mother was in the terminal stage of brain cancer. When Margaret arrived to visit, she found her mother unconscious on the bathroom floor. Margaret telephoned 911; when the paramedics arrived, they resuscitated the elder Mrs. Jones, as required by law. The painful intubation procedure and a portable ventilator kept Mrs. Jones alive for the remainder of the month, when she finally died. She had no advance directives. In trying to be sensitive to Mrs. Jones's sense of hope, Margaret probably did her mother a great disservice.

Though nearly 90 percent of all Americans will have a "managed death" in a hospital or skilled nursing facility that can lengthen life for up to several years through medical and nursing interventions, only about 15 percent of patients have advance directives (Haynor, 1998). Figure 15.1 is an example of a **living will,** one form of advance directive.

Two terms are important to a discussion of the right to die: (1) **passive euthanasia,** or the process of allowing persons to die without using "extraordinary means" to save their lives; and (2) **active euthanasia,** or performing a deliberate act to end a person's life, such as administering a fatal injection. There are acts between active and passive euthanasia that are difficult to categorize. Not treating a person for pneumonia is one example. Is the intentional lack of action in itself "active?"

The Patient Self-Determination Act (PSDA)

The **Patient Self-Determination Act (PSDA)** of 1991 requires all health care facilities receiving Medicare and Medicaid funding to recognize the living will and durable power of attorney for health care (health care proxy) as advance directives. It further requires "all hospitals,

FIGURE 15.1

Example of living will

The following document is only a guide. It should not replace necessary consultation with a qualified legal professional regarding your state's regulations regarding a living will's length of effectiveness, requirements for witnesses, or other factors.

LIVING WILL OF [**fill in your name**]

To my physician, attorney, family, friends, and any medical facility or health care professional whose care I may come under or happen to be under and all others who may be responsible for decision making with respect to my health or well-being:

On this [**fill in ordinal number, e.g., first, second**] day of [**fill in month**], [**fill in year**], I, [**fill in first name, middle name, and last name**], born [**fill in birth date**], being of sound mind, willfully and voluntarily direct that my dying and death shall not be artificially prolonged under the circumstances set forth in this declaration:

If, at any time:

1. I should be in a coma or persistent vegetative state and, in the opinion of two physicians who have personally examined me, one of whom shall be my attending physician, have no known hope of regaining awareness and higher mental functions no matter what is done; or

2. I should have an incurable injury, disease, or illness certified to be a terminal condition by two physicians who have personally examined me, one of whom shall be my attending physician, and the physicians have determined that my death will occur as a result of such incurable injury, disease or illness, whether or not life-sustaining procedures are utilized, and where the application of such procedures would serve only to prolong artificially a hopeless illness or the dying process, I direct that life-sustaining or -prolonging treatments or procedures (including the artificial administration of food and water, whether intravenously, by gastric tube, or by any other similar means) shall not be used and I do not desire any such treatment to be provided and/or continued.

3. I would like to live out my last days at home rather than in a hospital, long-term care facility, nursing home, or other health care facility if it does not jeopardize the chance of my recovery to a meaningful life and does not put undue hardship on my family or significant other.

4. I direct that I be permitted to die naturally, with only the administration of medication and/or the performance of any medical procedure deemed necessary to provide me with comfort and/or to alleviate pain. In the absence of my ability to give directions regarding the use of such life-sustaining procedures, it is my intention that this document and my wishes with respect to dying shall be honored by my family and physicians as a definitive expression of my legal right to refuse medical or surgical treatment and to accept the consequences from such refusal.

As a consequence of the foregoing instructions, I hereby direct my Personal Representative, my Trustee, the beneficiaries under my Will, and my heirs that none of them may or shall maintain or cause to be maintained any legal or administrative action that has as its foundation or as one of its claims or causes of action the failure of a physician, nurse, hospital, clinic, or any other natural or legal person or entity whatsoever to prolong my life while, because of an incurable injury, disease, or illness certified to be a terminal condition, under the procedures described above.

This statement is made after careful consideration and is in accordance with my strong convictions and beliefs. I want the wishes and directions here expressed carried out to the full extent permitted by law. Those concerned with my health and well-being are asked to take whatever action is needed (including legal) to realize my preferences, wishes, and instructions. Insofar as they are not legally enforceable, let those to whom this is addressed regard themselves morally bound by these provisions.

(continued)

FIGURE 15.1

Example of living will—continued

I am an adult of sound mind and otherwise legally competent to make this Declaration, and I understand its full import.

Signed by: [**print your full name and address**]

Signature of the above:
Date: [**fill in date**]

Under penalty of perjury, we state that this Declaration was signed by [name of individual signing] in the presence of the undersigned, who, at the Declarant's request, in the Declarant's presence, and in the presence of each other, have hereunto signed our names as witnesses this [**fill in ordinal number, e.g., first, second**] day in the month of [**fill in month**], in the year of [**fill in year**].

Each of us individually states that: The Declarant is personally known to me, and I believe the Declarant to be of sound mind. I did not sign the Declarant's signature to this Living Will Declaration.

Based upon information and belief, I am not related to the Declarant by blood or marriage, a creditor of he Declarant, entitled to any portion of the estate of the Declarant under any existing testamentary instrument of the Declarant, financially or other wise responsible for the Declarant's medical care, or an employee of any such person or institution.

Name: [**fill in name**]   Name: [**fill in name**]
Address: [**fill in address**]   Address: [**fill in address**]
Date: [**fill in day, month, year**]   Date: [**fill in day, month, year**]

Copies of this Living Will have been distributed to:

Name: [**fill in name**]   Name: [**fill in name**]
Address: [**fill in address**]   Address: [**fill in address**]

The original Living Will is located in [**fill in**] at [**fill in address**].

nursing homes, health maintenance organizations, hospices, and health care companies that participate in Medicare or Medicaid to provide patients with written information on their rights concerning advance directives under state and federal law" (Duffield & Podzamsky, 1996). The PSDA created no new rights for patients, but it reaffirmed the common-law right of self-determination as guaranteed in the Fourteenth Amendment (Haynor, 1998).

The decision to commit suicide with the assistance of another may be just as personal and profound as the decision to refuse unwanted medical treatment, but it has never enjoyed similar legal protection. Indeed, the two acts are widely and reasonably regarded as quite distinct. . . . First, when a patient refuses life-sustaining medical treatment, he dies from an underlying fatal disease or pathology; but if a patient ingests lethal medication prescribed by a physician, he is killed by that medication.

SUPREME COURT CHIEF JUSTICE
WILLIAM H. REHNQUIST, 1997

Suicide and assisted suicide

Adults of all ages support the right to die by refusing treatment, as reflected in living will legislation in all 50 states. When it comes to actively hastening death, or physician-assisted suicide, people are less certain. Between 40 and 50 percent of physicians believe that physician-assisted suicide may be an ethically permissible practice, and around 66 percent of the general public favors its legalization (Koenig et al., 1996). Polls, however, have included only a small proportion of older adults (a proportionally representative sample).

In November 1997 Oregon voters overwhelmingly—by 60 percent—reaffirmed their support for the nation's only law allowing physician-assisted suicide. The legislation was originally passed in 1994 and was brought to a second vote in 1997 by political referendum. The law includes a 15-day waiting period after a terminally ill person has requested physician assistance with suicide. At least two doctors must agree that the patient's condition is terminal, and the patient must request the drugs in writing and administer the drugs to him- or herself.

When older patients are asked about their attitudes toward physician-assisted suicide and the types of assistance that should be provided, interesting differences in attitude emerge. In two separate studies, elderly patients were found to be less likely than their relatives to support physician-assisted suicide. Those patients who oppose the practice represent a particularly vulnerable portion of society: women, African Americans, the poor, and people with lower educational achievement (Duffield & Podzamsky, 1996; Koenig et al., 1996). This implies that special protection might be necessary for some groups of individuals who by tradition have less of a voice in the system.

Whether anyone has the right to take his or her own life is a complicated issue with moral implications. Older persons may first contemplate, then commit, suicide because they feel life no longer holds meaning, or because they are in pain that feels unbearable. Some deaths of elders lie between accident and suicide. Older people who are disappointed and frustrated with life may refuse to eat, keep to themselves, and refuse care, with fatal consequences. Such deaths may not be officially regarded as suicides.

Suicides such as these pose the question of whether people have a right to choose death by suicide. Several groups, such as the Hemlock Society, advocate control over one's dying, which includes committing suicide, if necessary, to escape profound pain or great bodily deterioration. AIDS advocates, often argue for the right to commit suicide if that is the choice of the suffering person. But no one has received as much publicity in terms of assisted suicide as Dr. Jack Kevorkian—"Doctor Death."

By 1998, Dr. Kevorkian had helped 100 people commit suicide. All of his suicide patients have been in the terminal stage of disease, generally accompanied by excruciating pain. He has referred to assisted suicide as "patholysis" (Greek for freedom from suffering) and has dedicated his life and career to bringing to public awareness the need, from his perspective, for the legalization of assisted suicide. He was eventually arrested and was charged initially with violating the state statute prohibiting assisted suicide. That charge was dropped, however, and in 1999 he was sent to prison, was convicted of second-degree murder for delivering a controlled substance without a license (PBS, 2004).

Patients of Dr. Kevorkian who requested assistance with their suicide were interviewed by telephone at length by him and his associates, usually for several weeks before actually meeting with him. His agreement to provide assistance was based on his assessment of the mental competence and the physical condition of the patient, among other factors. If Kevorkian agreed to provide assistance, the patient met with Kevorkian and his attorney for personal interviews and to review the case. Documents assuring the patient's competence and desire to commit suicide were signed. Those people willing to do so also made a videotaped personal statement, often in interview format with Kevorkian and/or his attorney.

Examples of people whose deaths were assisted by Kevorkian are a 72-year-old woman, a double amputee in severe pain from rheumatoid arthritis and advanced osteoporosis, and a person with multiple sclerosis who was unable to sit or lie down because of excruciating pain. People who completed their suicide with Kevorkian's assistance left a note directing family and/or police to the location of their body; generally the note included a personal statement articulating the person's choice in the matter. A 78-year-old Canadian immigrant from India with severe Parkinson's disease left a note including the statement, "I am grateful to the merciful hands of Dr. Kevorkian . . . to bring about a happy deliverance—Maha Samadhi—a final embrace with the divine" (U.S. News Bulletins, 1997).

Kevorkian and his associates, including his attorney and his assistants, attempted to challenge the legal system into making a definitive ruling on the legal status of physician-assisted suicide. His objectives were to make it an accepted medical practice. "It's time to clear the air," said Kevorkian in a news interview. "I admit I assisted in the [deaths of 100 people]. If there was a crime committed, charge me. If there isn't, don't bother me" (U.S. News Bulletins, 1998).

In 1996 a Michigan jury acquitted Jack Kevorkian of charges that he assisted in two suicides. In the same time period, California and New York struck down state prohibitions against physician-assisted suicide. In 1998 Kevorkian was convicted of second-degree murder charges, based on his delivery of a controlled substance without a license. In 2004 his attorney requested the state parole board to recommend he be released from prison for health reasons. He was 76 and had served five and a half years of a 10-to-25-year prison sentence, during which time his health deteriorated. He is eligible for parole in 2007 (ABC News, 2004).

Assisted Suicide

Law in the United States did not uphold assisted suicide—whether the assistant is a physician, friend, or family member—until November 1997, when Oregon became the first state in the country to pass a law allowing doctors to hasten death for the terminally ill. The law provides that a doctor may prescribe but not administer a lethal dose of medication to a patient who has less than six months to live. Two doctors must agree that the patient is mentally competent and that the decision is voluntary. The Oregon State Health Division reviewed the first year of the law's implementation and concluded that the law was working well and had not been abused.

This option is illegal in all but a handful of other states; over 30 states have statutes specifically prohibiting assisted suicide (PBS, 2004). In other states, the assistant might be prosecuted under a general charge of manslaughter; in still others, the law is unclear and not vigorously pursued. The issue has created intense public debate and split the health care community.

A review by John Horgan summarized:

> The American Medical Association (AMA), the American Nursing Association, the National Hospice Organization and dozens of other groups have filed briefs with the Supreme Court opposing physician-assisted suicide. Supporters of legalization include the American Medical Student Association, the Coalition of Hospice Professionals, and Marcia Angell, editor of the New England Journal of Medicine.
>
> Nonetheless, the dispute masks a deep consensus among health care experts that much can and should be done to improve the care of the dying. (Horgan, 1997, p. 100)

At the federal level the only legislation addressing the issue (by 2001) was the Assisted

Suicide Funding Restriction Act, which prohibited federal money from being used in support of physician-assisted suicide. In 2002 legislation was introduced at the federal level—but not enacted—to revoke the license to prescribe controlled drugs of any doctor who participated in assisted suicide. Capitol Hill watchers expect new legislation to emerge.

The arguments both in support of and against assisted suicide touch upon powerful issues of ethics and American values. On the one hand is fear that laws allowing physician-assisted suicide will start us down a slippery slope toward involuntary euthanasia. Ethicists worry that the power to decide who should live and who should die will get into the hands of the wrong person. The ability to make a decision as powerful as this might move to the next step of making the determination for a "medically defective" person, or someone who is "too old" or "too poor" to warrant expensive medical care.

On the other hand is the belief that self-determination by competent individuals is an inviolable right and essential to the maintenance of human dignity. Validation for this perspective comes in part from teaching hospitals, which report that 40 percent of terminally ill patients experience severe pain "most of the time" (Horgan, 1997). The perspective also emerges from a greater sensitivity to cultural diversity. The Japanese, for example, have a less restrictive attitude toward suicide than do European Americans. It is seen as a "sad but not morally ambiguous response to human relational struggles" (Matzo, 1997).

Those in the center of the argument believe the stage is set for an assisted suicide if doctor and patient have thoroughly explored all options and if the patient is not depressed. If the patient is terminally ill and near death and cannot face either the pain of the disease or the agonizing efforts of more useless treatments, then physician-assisted suicide is acceptable, according to this position.

> *Even in the very shadow of death, one's living experience can give rise to accomplishment. Dying is just a time of living. It's a particularly difficult time of living that has a propensity for problems and suffering. . . . People are dignified even in their dying, even in their physical dependency, if they're treated in a dignified manner.*
>
> IRA BYOCK, 1996

Another approach to end-of-life comfort and control is to sidestep the issues of ethics and morality and address the need for pain control. The capability exists to control pain far better than is often done. Pain control simply is not made available in all cases (Matzo, 1997). The seriously ill may become trapped in a cycle of intensifying distress in which chronic pain becomes more severe over time, leading to psychological distress, making the pain more difficult to endure. Even with advances in pain medications and their delivery, pain is not adequately addressed by health care services (Beresford, 1997). Too little, too late creates too much suffering.

Informed Consent to Treatment

Norms have radically changed in acceptable medical practice in the past 30 years. Issues of autonomy, self-determination, and quality of life now make a huge difference in how medicine is delivered. Somewhere around 85 percent of deaths in the United States occur in institutions, and 70 percent of those involve elective withholding of life-sustaining treatment (Matzo, 1997). The role of the patient as an autonomous individual responsible for making medical and life decisions has preempted the role of patient passivity.

As recently as the 1970s, doctors felt comfortable making all informed decisions for their patients, certain that their judgment, though imperfect, was the best judgment available. Nurses acquiesced without question in the doctor's judgments—they were considered technicians whose job it was to do the physician's bidding. This is no longer the case. Patients have the right—and are given the responsibility—to accept or reject any treatment or prescription that their physician may offer them, and they have the right to be informed of their choices. Those suffering a serious or life-threatening illness for which several treatment plans are possible or optional now are in the difficult position of needing to select what they believe to be the best plan, under the informed guidance of their physician. This requires an enormous level of information and confidence on the part of the patient. Clearly, this is not always the case. For example, surgery, radiation, chemotherapy, and special diets are all available as treatment options for cancer. Patients have an obligation to inform themselves of both the options and risks involved with each option and then base their consent to treatment on three principles:

1. They are competent to give general consent

2. They give consent freely (they are not coerced by, e.g., economic situation or relatives)

3. They have a full understanding of the meaning of the options (DeSpelder & Strickland, 1991)

Informed consent means that patients share in their health care decision making by becoming informed and by basing their choice, acceptance, or rejection of treatment on the information available to them.

More Ethics in Aging

Other ethical issues have been arisen now that medical technology has the capacity to prolong life almost indefinitely, and disease control keeps more people alive into advanced age. Here are some of those issues:

1. What is the appropriate level of direction family members and the health care system should provide when dealing with a person who is losing competency? For example, is the person with early Alzheimer's allowed self-determination in deciding whether to drive a car? With more advanced Alzheimer's, how is a "wanderer" restrained and who makes the decision? (Moody, 1992)

2. With regard to the ethics of nursing home placement and ethical dilemmas in the nursing home, how much self-determination and autonomy is allowed the older person to make decisions and act for himself or herself?

3. Should we ration health care on the grounds of age? Using formulas of cost and age, who decides when the cost gets too high and when the very old are not "worth" being saved?

4. What kind of research can legally and morally be conducted on older subjects? Effects of various drugs and therapeutic procedures are constantly under study. Yet ethical guidelines for research with aged patients is not discussed nearly as much as with younger patients (Wicclair, 1993)

5. What obligations do adult children have for the financial, physical, and emotional support of frail elderly parents?

Funerals

Dying in institutions is depersonalized for the dying individual and dissociates society from the process of dying. The person dies, usually alone. The body is sent to a funeral parlor, where it is prepared for burial by strangers, who never knew the living person. Preparation in-

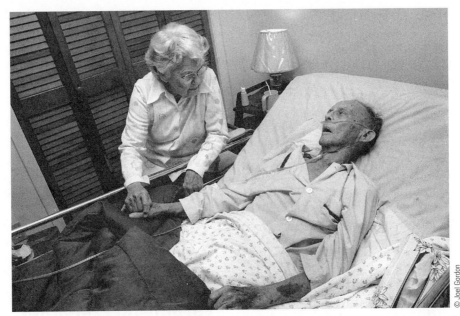

Perhaps the most precious gift to be given is to be with someone else on the journey into death. To help someone with dying, one's own death must have been squarely addressed.

cludes washing the body; it often includes injecting preservatives; dressing it for burial in whatever garment the family or caretaker chooses; applying flesh-colored makeup to whatever skin is exposed after dressing; arranging the hair; and arranging the facial expression to give the impression of peaceful slumber. It is often *after* this point that family members spend time with the body, to say goodbye to the person who has died.

The majority of Americans who die are buried, but cremations are more frequently chosen now than in the past. Between 1990 and 1996, cremations increased from 17 percent to 21 percent, and the number of people who plan a cremation for themselves increased from 37 to 42 percent (Cassel, 1996). Both burial and cremation, however, allow for a funeral or memorial service at which the grieving friends and family can commemorate the life of the person they loved. These rituals serve as a way for families or groups to share their identity and reestablish their collective presence in the absence of the person who has died.

Old and young alike can be victims of coercion when arranging funerals for themselves or for their loved ones. Some of the criticisms leveled at the modern funeral industry are commercialization, unnecessary extravagance, and deception. An individual is vulnerable after the death of a spouse or relative and, wanting to do the very best for the deceased person, easily persuaded to spare no expense for a funeral.

Some funeral directors play on the emotions of the bereaved. They may, for example, persuade a grief-stricken relative to buy an expensive casket to show how much he or she loved the deceased. The cost of the casket can be one financial trap; embalming can be another. Funeral directors are hesitant to mention that no law requires embalming or that no casket is required for cremation.

The cost of cemetery plots also can be high. Charges for limousines, burial clothes, use of the viewing room, and a headstone are not necessarily mere marketing ploys. In this culture, mortuaries are a necessary business, operating for profit. Consumers should not be pressured into spending thousands of dollars on a funeral that will create financial hardship; however, once again, vast cultural differences exist.

Some organizations help to provide simple, dignified funerals for their members. Cremation, which costs about one-eighth as much as a conventional funeral, is becoming more common and is appealing especially to those who believe that cemeteries are a needless waste of land. Individuals should be aware that they do have choices in these matters and that the range of choices is from the very simple to the elaborate. Making choices in the grips of grief, however, can make people vulnerable to exploitation by unethical funerary operatives.

Because of complaints about the funeral industry, the Federal Trade Commission (FTC) ruled in 1984 that funeral directors must provide itemized lists of goods and services and their prices. This may keep prices from varying depending on a client's vulnerability, and it shows clearly that a price range exists. The FTC also ruled that misrepresentation of state laws concerning embalming and cremation is against the law. In addition, funeral parlors must itemize on a funeral bill every charge—the cost of flowers, death notices in newspapers, the provision of hearses and limousines, guest registers, and other related services (Aiken, 1994).

Consumer groups still need to educate the public about the laws governing the funeral industry and to inform individuals about their rights and choices. An individual needs to know about the itemized price list, for example, to ensure that he or she asks for and receives one. The average cost of a funeral is now more than $7,000. But no one has to spend that much. For example, inexpensive caskets are available, but family members of the deceased may not know this. Sometimes family members feel guilty if they purchase a casket made of, say, particleboard rather than wood, not realizing that a particleboard casket can be just as beautiful as a wooden one. It's helpful to family members if these matters can be discussed before death occurs.

Some people buy their plots and tombstones long before they are near death. A person who is in good health and has a clear mind is in the best position to discuss funeral decisions with his or her family. If a person can give specific instructions about the kind of funeral and burial he or she wants, the surviving spouse and children or other relatives are less likely to be led into agonizing and/or expensive choices they will regret.

Facing and Preparing for Death

Realizing that death is the ultimate destiny for each of us, we need to understand, regardless of our age, the importance of preparing for it. Facing death, or at least easing personal anxiety about it, can improve the quality of an individual's life. Whether you have thought about or have already answered any of the following questions tells something about your degree of preparation for dying:

1. Do you have a will?

2. Do you have life insurance?

3. Did you prepare advance directives?

4. Are you willing to have an autopsy done on your body?

5. Are you willing to donate the organs of your body for use after you die?

6. Do you know how you want your body disposed of (buried, cremated, donated to a medical school)?

7. What kind of last rites do you desire (funeral, memorial services, a party)?

When we reduce our own fears of death and dying, we can offer others, including the terminally ill, better care and help them cope. If our thoughts of death elicit thoughts of satisfaction with a life well lived, we have reached what psychologist Erik Erikson means by integrity, his final stage of psychosocial development. In the later years of life, those with a sense of integrity reflect on their past with satisfaction; those filled with despair dwell on missed opportunities and missed directions. With luck and understanding, the path each person takes will prepare them for death, which Kübler-Ross calls "the final stage of growth."

Bereavement

The loss of a loved one is generally the most tragic event an individual experiences in a lifetime. It is an experience that occurs some time or another in nearly everyone's life. In old age, these events occur with increasing frequency, as friends and family members die. Social scientists believe that their goal, after empathizing with another person's suffering, is to step aside from the maze of emotion and sensation and to make sense of it—what is the function of suffering to the human condition? Folk wisdom holds that "pain is inevitable; suffering is not." Is that so? If we can understand more about bereavement, we can understand more about supporting those who are bereaved.

Bereavement theory and research are expanding into unknown areas, such as why some bereaved people themselves die soon after their loved one. Though there are vast individual differences, bereaved persons tend to recover within a two-year period, yet a smaller, high-risk group of people simply cannot.

Complicated mourning is a cognitive disorganization and emotional chaos that can lead some people into profound depressions that do not move toward resolution (Rando, 1995). Types of complicated mourning reactions in-clude chronic grief reactions, masked grief reactions, exaggerated grief reactions, and chronic depression (Aiken, 1994; Marrone, 1997).

Chronic grief reactions involve reactions to death that are of long duration and do not lead to resolution. The survivor feels sorrow for years after the loss.

Masked grief reactions are the complete absence of grief reactions, accompanied by substitute psychosomatic complaints (headaches, insomnia, pain). The broken-heart syndrome, referring to findings that a widow or widower is more likely to die within the first two years following the death of his or her spouse, may be connected to this type of grief reaction (Stroebe & Stroebe, 1987).

Exaggerated grief reactions are repressed reactions to former grief-causing situations that erupt in response to a current loss. Old losses that were covered up erupt as phobias, psychosomatic symptoms, psychiatric disorders, and so forth (Marrone, 1997).

Clinical depression is similar to the profound sadness and depression experienced in mourning; however, its effects are more powerful, and it lasts longer. Clinical depression is considered to be a mood disorder that includes sadness, helplessness, guilt, and a pervasive sense of suffering. The inability to concentrate and general apathy accompany clinical depression.

Complicated grief reactions occur based on personality characteristics of the bereaved individual, the degree of support available to him or her in the grief process, and the relationship of the deceased person with the bereaved individual. Feelings of ambivalence toward the deceased person can bring about a complicated grief reaction, as can the circumstances of the death.

Mourning is a profoundly individual matter. Bereavement is a state of loss—to bereave, in fact, means "to take away from, to rob, to dispossess" (Kalish, 1985). The ways in which we respond to that loss will be as different as are our personalities and our life experiences.

Chapter Summary

Death is one of the few certainties of life, yet denial of death is common. We have euphemisms for the word death, we protect children from hearing about it, and the "deaths" we see enacted on TV are unreal. Instead, death is disassociated with everyday events because it typically occurs in a hospital setting. Elders, just like any other age group, may have fears about dying. The phases that a terminally ill person goes through include (1) denial and isolation, (2) anger, (3) bargaining, (4) depression, and (5) acceptance. Efforts must be made so terminally ill patients are given care, concern, and support. Elders are being given more choices in dying, but suicide is still not socially accepted. Yet changes are slowly taking place to broaden choices for the dying.

Physician-assisted suicide has become a topic of wide debate and has been legalized in Oregon. The hospice movement has supported people in their choice to die at home and to refuse life-extending measures that bring pain and discomfort. Medical ethics is challenging the assumption that lives should be extended at any cost. Patients are being informed of their rights, especially the right to refuse treatment. The right-to-die movement has gained momentum. Social scientists are now seriously exploring the issue of near-death experiences. It is important for elders to face death and prepare for it.

Key Terms

active euthanasia
assisted suicide
awareness contexts
   of dying
bereavement
chronic grief reactions
clinical depression
complicated mourning
death anxiety
death competency

death-denying society
exaggerated grief
   reactions
fear of death
fears about dying
happy death movement
hospice
individualism and
   autonomy
informed consent

life review
living will
masked grief reactions
medical ethics
medicalization paradigm
palliative care
passive euthanasia

Patient Self-
   Determination
   Act (PSDA)
preparatory
reactive
reminiscence
right-to-die issue

Questions for Discussion

1. Why do death and dying evoke fear? Why might a person fear death?
2. What is the function of the life review?
3. What are the arguments for and against euthanasia?
4. Imagine being told that you have six months to live. What would be your reaction? Explain in depth. What would you think? Where would you go? What would you do?

Fieldwork Suggestions

1. Go to a cemetery, walk around, and examine your own feelings about death and dying.
2. Talk with three people about their attitudes toward physician-assisted suicide. What do they think about Dr. Kevorkian? Did you find anyone who is not familiar with his name?
3. Ask five people about their fear of death. How do people go about talking about their fears (or lack of fears)—that is, what *themes* do you hear?

Internet Activities ✦

1. Locate the website for Batesville Casket Company (http://www.batesville.com). What products and services are offered through this corporation? To whom is the marketing addressed? What is your assessment of this

website? Can you think of ways in which it might be improved or otherwise changed?

2. Find information on cremation and other online resources for burial and body disposal. What did you locate? How difficult was it to find this information? Who do you think uses this site, and for what purpose?

3. Find information on estate and funeral planning; on living wills, legal assistance, and directories concerning other advance directives. How difficult was it to locate this information? To whom is it directed? If you were in the terminal stages of a disease, would the information you have found be useful for you in developing a living will or other advance directive?

16 Politics, Policies, and Programs

Mandela's Journey Perhaps Unsurpassed in History of Human Spirit

Rener Tyson

On trial for sabotage at Pretoria's Palace of Justice, Nelson Mandela knew he faced the gallows. But he would have his say even if it cost him his life.

That was April 20, 1961. Mandela was 45 years old. The charge against him, which carried the death sentence, was sabotage with intent to overthrow the white government. It was a charge he readily admitted.

Thirty years later, Mandela used the exact words he spoke to the judge during that 1961 trial as he campaigned for the presidency of South Africa.

"During my lifetime I have dedicated myself to this struggle of the African people," Mandela told the Pretoria court. "I have fought against white domination, and I have fought against black domination.

"I have cherished the ideal of a democratic and free society in which all persons live together in harmony and with equal opportunities. It is an ideal which I hope to live for and to achieve. But if it needs be, it is an ideal for which I am prepared to die."

Mandela lived to achieve that ideal. At the age of 75, he became South Africa's first black president—the victor in the country's first all-races election that sounded the death knell of apartheid.

Born into African aristocracy (July 18, 1918), Mandela was groomed to rule from childhood.

When Mandela was 12, his father died. The youngster was placed under the care and instruction of his guardian uncle, Chief Jonquintaba, at the nearby village of Maekezweni.

"In my youth in the Tranaei, I listened to the elders of my tribe telling stories of the old days," Mandela told the Pretoria court back in 1961.

Eager to learn and always a good student, Mandela enrolled at the University of Fort Mars in South Africa's eastern Cape Province, where he met a reserved but highly intelligent student named Oliver Tambo. Their friendship was to prove a powerful force in the struggle for freedom. Later they opened South Africa's first black law firm in Johannesburg.

But after two years at Fort Mars, both Mandela and Tambo were expelled for protesting poor food and living conditions.

In Soweta, a sprawling black township on the southwestern edge of Johannesburg, Mandela took refuge in the modest home of real estate agent Walter Sisulu. It was a move that shaped his life forever.

Sisulu encouraged Mandela to attend law school in Johannesburg. Mandela, Sisulu, along with Tambo and other young turks, took over direction of the moribund ANC (African National Congress—the major native African political organization) through its youth league. At that time the Afrikaner-dominated National Party had just come to power and began imposing apartheid.

Tall, handsome, an amateur boxer, Mandela, now a lawyer, quickly emerged as the liberation movement's main man.

He led the passive resistance Defiance Campaign of 1952, which aimed at getting white officials to hear black grievances about discrimination. White officials banned him from public activities. A court convicted him under the Suppression of Communism Act, but gave him a suspended sentence. He was tried and acquitted for treason.

In 1960, the government of Prime Minister Henrik Varwoard, apartheid's architect, declared the ANC unlawful and banned it. The ANC went underground. . . .

Mandela was captured near the Natal town of Howick. Last year, Mandela made a visit to Howick and remarked how after his arrest, "I went on a long holiday."

On July 12, 1961, Mandela, Sisulu and six other leaders were sentenced to life in prison. Mandela's powerful and emotional speech in court probably saved his life and the lives of his compatriots.

In prison, Mandela excited the passions of human rights activists around the world. Even though he was behind bars, he gained stature year by year as a symbol of the fight against apartheid.

On February 11, 1990, President F. W. de Klerk, who was to share the Nobel Peace Prize in 1993 with the former political prisoner, released Mandela from prison to make the walk to freedom and into the presidency, completing a journey perhaps unsurpassed in the history of the human spirit.

To judge strength by size alone, the older population of the United States is stronger than ever before. Numbers command political power at the voting booth and in lobbying efforts; however, because of fiscally conservative federal policies in the 1980s, harsh economic turns in the 1990s, and the extraordinary need in 2001 to reevaluate the balance between social programs and national security, the United States has a general political environment that ignores special needs of elders as well as other requests of local, state, and federal budgets. Though elders have made significant strides over the last 50 years in gaining the wherewithal to maintain healthy and meaningful lives, their progress, like that of our society in general, depends primarily on the condition of the U.S. economic system.

In the twenty-first century the nation will see a demographic evolution of revolutionary proportion, as the huge baby-boomer cohort approaches retirement. Whereas proactive social policy is necessary if we are to adequately meet the changing needs of our citizens, it takes specific, targeted, cause-based organizational dedication to make that social policy happen.

The threat of cutbacks in government programs looms in most of the nations of Europe and will grow larger in the next 20 years as the global boomers of the World War II era reach age 65. The Netherlands provides a clear example of threatened cutbacks; their social welfare policies provide substantial benefits to elders that they have come to take for granted. A conservative political environment has now challenged these policies. In the early 1990s, in a country of 11 million, some 15,000 Dutch citizens over the age of 65 marched into a soccer stadium to rally, shouting to opposing political parties, "Keep your hands off our pensions" (Drozdiak, 1994). For the next 10 years the General Old People's Union, along with another senior citizens' party, won six seats in the Dutch parliament. The political awakening of elders is gathering momentum as their numbers increase. The cost of social welfare in Holland, however, has gone off the charts. The Dutch now spend over $100 billion a year on health and social security costs, or about 10 times what they pay for their military defense. The older population fears a decrease in their standard of living as cost-cutting measures become inevitable, and they support political candidates who do not advocate the reduction of their entitlements.

We begin this chapter by briefly reviewing periods during which elder political activism in the United States flourished. Today's political climate can then be examined in the light of these earlier decades of struggle and progress.

Early Rumblings

Political movements are the combined result of social, economic, and historical events. Circumstances develop that make political action imperative. Those who are affected respond by joining forces and asserting their need to improve their situation. This happened in the early 1900s, when a large proportion of older people were living in poverty. Although retirement had increasingly become mandatory, pensions were not yet generally available, which often left the elderly with neither work nor money. In 1921 a limited pension system was established for federal employees, but the vast majority of elders still had no pensions at all. In 1928, 65 percent of those over 65 were receiving assistance of some sort from children. The depression had wiped out the pensions and savings of millions, leaving elders in the most desperate poverty of any age group. Kevin Starr described the situation in *Endangered Dreams*:

> With 12 million people out of work by 1933, voluntary assistance to parents plummeted along with the rest of the economy. To whom could the elderly now turn? Not to government. American culture had no discernible tradition of old-age pensions from government. Only 6 American states had any form of old-age assistance program. By 1934 a mere 180,000 elderly, out of a

> total population of 15 million–plus senior citizens, were receiving any form of legally mandated assistance. Yet fully 50 percent of the elderly in America were in need of some form of outside aid if they were to make it through the slump. (Starr, 1996, p. 134)

Their plight created the social environment for the nation's first elderly uprising, which took political form as the **Townsend plan.** Named after the retired physician Francis E. Townsend, who headed the program, the Townsend plan was organized through local clubs. By 1935 a half million Americans had joined Townsend Clubs, and by the end of 1936 about 2.2 million people belonged (Starr, 1996). The Townsend plan proposed placing $200 of government funds per month in the hands of persons age 60 and older, with the requirements that the recipients be retired and spend the money within 30 days. The plan was to end the economic problems of elders, solve unemployment, and introduce new spending to stimulate the economy. It would not increase the deficit, because it was funded by a multiple sales tax.

The plan was resoundingly criticized: the political Left argued that the transactions tax was regressive; the political Right feared the tax would cut profits and the spending would undermine the incentive to work (Amenta et al., 1992). Scholars and policy experts felt the tax implied higher levies on finished goods and thought it would not work to register farmers for the tax. Ultimately, following internal conflict among Townsend plan leaders over charges of graft, plus vigorous opposition from the Roosevelt administration, less than 4 percent of the national electorate approved the Townsend plan (Starr, 1996). The plan was not a utopian scheme, however. It provided for the aged to have a large national pension, whose size would be determined by an earmarked tax (Amenta et al., 1992). It provided the model for old-age assistance to come.

The Social Security Act, part of the New Deal legislation, adopted one of Townsend's main interests—a pension for elders. However, the Social Security Act was a more conservative measure. Rather than "giving" pensions to the retired, it paid pensions out of sums collected from workers; and the amount of each pension was determined by each individual's employment record. Those who did not work were not eligible for benefits. In the decades that followed, amendments to the Social Security Act added coverage for more kinds of workers and their dependents.

Few Californians could be found in the inner circle of President Roosevelt or at the helm of New Deal agencies. While eager for a myth of individualism and self-improvement, Californians seemed incapable, the majority of them, of moving to an expression of such ambitions beyond the instant solution of an old-age pension plan. The affluence and altered attitudes of the 1950s and 1960s would reverse this orientation and make of California, briefly, the very model of the social democratic experiment.

STARR, 1966

Other political movements, many of which originated in California, attempted to help the elderly during this era. Even before the Townsend plan, there had been EPIC (End Poverty in California). The EPIC movement was based on campaign promises Upton Sinclair made when he ran for governor of California in 1934. His platform of sweeping social reform was energized by utopianism, which had popular support in California at the same time. The movement's slogan was decidedly socialist in orientation: "Production for Use, Not Profit."

Also from California, the **Ham and Eggs movement** proposed that the government issue a large amount of special scrip, the value of which would expire at the end of a year; therefore, the elderly pensioners who received it would spend it promptly and stimulate the economy. In the late 1940s George McLain, a leader of the Ham and

Eggs movement, lobbied the California legislature and advocated his reforms through a daily radio program. He believed that all elderly were entitled to pension increases, low-cost government housing, medical aid, and elimination of a financial means test. Before any of his proposals were widely adopted, the McLain movement, which drew a membership of about 7 percent of those aged 65 and over in California, ended in 1965 with McLain's death.

A significant characteristic of the various movements in the 1930s and 1940s, including McLain's, was that they extracted great sums of money from older people themselves. Indeed, although the movements set a precedent for political organization, they also demonstrated how vulnerable elders could be to corrupt leaders who preyed on their trust:

> *Certainly old-age power was helped to grow because of them; however, the secretiveness, greed, and paranoia with which the advocates held power stymied grassroots growth. (Kleyman, 1974, p. 70)*

Although the civil rights movement began in the 1950s, this decade is often described as a time of political inactivity and apathy, an era of general economic prosperity chiefly characterized by inattention to needy groups. The early 1960s brought more fervor to the civil rights movement, and in 1964 President Lyndon B. Johnson declared the War on Poverty. The high incidence of poverty among some groups—racial minorities, the rural, and elders—began to attract public attention. With the advent of the antiwar movement and the hippie lifestyle, the 1960s also saw increasing political activism among students and other adults. Gay liberation and the women's movement evolved in the 1970s as civil libertarian ideals gathered support. The women's movement in particular dealt with the issue of aging by attacking job discrimination against middle-aged and older women. The National Organization for Women (NOW) established an energetic task force of older women to identify issues and organize political action.

The 1970s also ushered in the advocacy of rights for the disabled. These humanistic movements created an environment in which one movement could combine forces with another. In this sense, all of the social movements of the 1960s and 1970s contributed to the social movement of **senior power**. A number of pro-senior interest groups and programs materialized in the 1960s; their chief accomplishments were the passage of the Older Americans Act (1965) and Medicare (1966).

The early 1970s brought forth a more visible and vital seniors' movement. For the first time since the Great Depression, older people, with cries of "gray power" and slogans such as "Don't Agonize—Organize," showed evidence of considerable political activism. Demonstrations, sit-ins, and sleep-ins by oldsters wearing "Senior Power" buttons made the headlines. The new militancy of old-age groups such as the Gray Panthers presented a surprising and exciting image for those who had once been stereotyped as powerless, dependent, slow, and unenthusiastic. The name Gray Panthers captured the new consciousness of the elderly. It suggested strength, power, and radical—if not revolutionary—political and social behavior.

The political activism of elders often targets issues that are at national and international levels. This woman is an AIDS activist, providing leaflets to shoppers in New York City.

Political Activity Today

Voting

When enough older people turn out to vote on a given issue and vote as a bloc, they wield considerable power. Approximately 90 percent of Americans over age 50 are registered to vote, compared with an overall national figure of less than 75 percent. In all recent elections; older people are more likely to vote than younger ones (Hooyman & Kiyak, 2002). Citizens in their 80s are more likely to vote than those in their early 20s—in fact, older voter turnout (those 65 and over) is generally double the voter turnout of young adults under 25 years of age. Thus, the voting power of older people is greater than

their actual numbers in the population would indicate, even though disability and lack of transportation keep some elders from the polls. Only one subgroup of older voters shows low turnout—homemakers, virtually all of whom are women.

Despite generally large voter turnout among elders, there is no old-age voting bloc—not even on old-age issues. In national politics, people of similar social classes are more likely to vote alike than are people of similar age groups. The wealthy older person, for example, might not support welfare measures for older people living in poverty; neither would the wealthy younger voter. Political organization and mobilization would be necessary to encourage elders to use their potential power by voting as a bloc.

Older people are neither more nor less conservative than younger people, unlike the common stereotype that people grow more conservative with age. Older people's politics are balanced fairly equally between the Republican and Democratic parties. The 75-plus age group has been more likely to vote in the last five presidential elections than those voters under 35. When older voter turnout is low, factors such as gender, ethnic minority, and education are more important than age: Only just over 50 percent of African American elders voted in the 1996 presidential election, and less than 50 percent of the older Hispanic voters regularly vote (Hooyman & Kiyak, 2002).

Office Holding

Another measure of political power is the ability to be elected or appointed to public office. Only two U.S. presidents have entered office after the age of 65: William Henry Harrison (age 68) and Ronald Reagan (age 69). Many more have turned 65 while in office. Because life expectancy has increased greatly since George Washington's time, one might guess that presidents have entered office at increasingly older ages; however, this has not happened. Though the first American presidents were 57 or older, the nation has seen some very young presidents. The youngest was Theodore Roosevelt (age 42), followed by John F. Kennedy, who was 43 years old at his inauguration in 1961. Bill Clinton was age 47 at his inauguration in 1993.

Children, believe me: Things were not better in the old days. . . . I remember black people riding in the back of the bus. I remember summer being a season of fear because summer was when polio stalked the neighborhood, crippling and killing. I remember cars being cranked by hand and seeing men with arms broken from cranking carelessly. I remember headlines about gangsters spraying crowded streets with Tommy guns, remember hoboes at kitchen doors begging for sandwiches. . . . Just like right now, back then was chock full of meanness.

BAKER, 1996

Members of Congress, because they are elected officials, are not subject to mandatory retirement laws. Some members have served into their 80s and, occasionally, into their 90s. Since 1974, the average age has risen to over 50; in 1996, many congressional members were over age 65. The seniority system in Congress allows older members who have served many years to wield the most power, often as heads of important committees.

Cabinet members and ambassadors tend to be older, perhaps because they are appointed by the president rather than elected. These positions, which imply years of experience, are often filled by men and women who, in any other area of work, might have been forced by age alone to retire. Supreme Court justices also tend to be older. There is no mandatory retirement for them, and they generally serve as long as their health allows. In 1991 the controversial appointment of Clarence Thomas, age 43, made him the youngest justice to serve on the Court. All other appointments, including subsequent appointments, were made when the appointee was 50 or older—60 years of age in the instance of the sole female justice, Ruth Bader Ginsberg.

Despite the representation of elders in elected and appointed positions, we do not seem to be headed toward a gerontocracy—rule by the old. Both young and old are involved in the political arena. Although it has long been acceptable for members of Congress to be middle-aged or older, a youthful political image has been favorable since the time of Teddy Roosevelt. In addition, even among old politicians, age does not appear to be a major variable affecting their position on political issues. A presidential candidate or member of Congress does not support old-age measures simply because he or she is near age 65. The support that Congresspersons give to issues reflects not only their political ideology but, ideally, the wishes of their constituents as well. Supreme Court justices make decisions based on philosophy and ideology; impartiality dictates that age not be an influencing variable. Older politicians and other elders involved in the political process provide good role models and typically work hard at their jobs.

Political Associations

Interest groups representing older Americans have increased in number and political effectiveness over the past several decades.

One type of specialized interest group is the **trade association.** Trade associations represent specific concerns and lobby to achieve their purposes and goals. Some examples are the American Association of Homes for the Aging, the American Nursing Home Association, the National Council of Health Care Services, and the National Association of State Units on the Aging. There are also **professional associations,** such as the Gerontological Society, the Association for Gerontology in Higher Education, and the American Society of Aging, composed primarily of academicians in the field of aging. States and regions also have professional associations, such as the California Coalition for Gerontology and Geriatrics. Other **interest groups,** such as the National Association of Retired Federal Employees (NARFE) and the National Retired Teachers Association (NRTA), are composed of retired persons.

A few organizations representing older persons have enjoyed special growth, success, and media attention. Here we consider six of them: the American Association of Retired Persons, the National Committee to Preserve Social Security and Medicare, the National Council of Senior Citizens, the National Council on the Aging, the National Caucus and Center on the Black Aged, and the Gray Panthers.

American Association of Retired Persons

Currently the premier lobbyist for elder causes in the United States is the **American Association of Retired Persons (AARP).** Its 32 million members are all over 50, and two-thirds of them are over 65 (Morris, 1996). Although the goals of some groups have always been to exert political influence, the primary goals of AARP have only recently become political.

The group's founder, Ethel Percy Andrus, was an educator—the first woman in California to become a high school principal. She founded the National Retired Teachers Association (NRTA) in 1947 when she was forced to retire from her position after reaching the age of 65. She was 76 in 1958 when she created AARP as a parallel organization to bring benefits of the NRTA to elders who had not been teachers. The organization's co-founder was Leonard Davis, a young insurance agent who developed the group health insurance plan for NRTA members. It has been suggested that Davis financed the creation of AARP to expand his own mail-order health insurance market. Until forced out in the early 1980s, Davis was in control of AARP, which was "operating as a sales network to hawk very high-priced insurance and a host of other . . . products to old people" (Morris, 1996, p. 10). He left the organization a very wealthy man.

In 2005 the AARP's operating budget reportedly was $900 million—about three times that of the National Rifle Association (Kaiser, 2006). Known for defending the interests of elders in a broad range of political initiatives, the AARP is not a nonprofit and therefore can maintain lobbying functions at the state and national governmental level. Services available through the organization include reduced rates for members at automobile rental companies, at motel and hotel chains, and at various tourist attractions. In addition, it provides health insurance, special prescription rates, an auto club, education, income tax counseling, and training services.

Membership makes the AARP one of the largest voluntary organizations represented in Washington and one of the nation's largest lobbying groups. The group, which tries to remain nonpartisan, has directed its political efforts at improving pensions, opposing mandatory retirement, and improving Social Security benefits, widely shared goals that unite the association's members. Their congressional lobbyists support causes for poor elders, and their magazine, *Modern Maturity,* stresses an image of well-to-do, healthy aging.

Nineteen-sixties style, hit-the-streets protesting is the model of choice for some advocacy groups. The Gray Panthers has a tradition of speaking out with noise on local and national-level issues needing the immediate attention of voters.

ship for more focus on social reform from the organization and less emphasis on their marketing of insurance and other financial services to members:

> *According to* BusinessWeek *(3/14/2005) at least $300 million of that $900 million income comes from the sale of insurance and other financial services to members. . . . How can we expect AARP to vigorously represent us in issues like prescription drug coverage with such a glaring conflict of interest? Even the $10 million of our membership dollars it spends to convince us to use generic drugs will no doubt have a positive impact on their insurance bottom line. (Kaiser, 2006)*

On the other hand, in 2003 AARP's positions influenced the U.S. Congress's support for the Medicare Prescription Drug, Improvement, and Modernization Act providing baseline legislation for development of Medicare Part D, and it mobilized resistance to changes in Social Security in 2005 (Wikipedia, 2006). The organization grows and changes as cohorts of older people change.

National Committee to Preserve Social Security and Medicare

Founded by James Roosevelt (the son of President Franklin Roosevelt) in 1983, the **National Committee to Preserve Social Security and Medicare** is concerned about the solvency of the Social Security Trust Funds. Now boasting 5 million members, it is a nonprofit organization funded entirely by membership fees and donations. Its 59-member staff works to protect and improve Social Security and Medicare benefits. Many of the staff are full-time lobbyists.

National Council of Senior Citizens

The **National Council of Senior Citizens** (**NCSC**) originated in 1961 as a pressure group to support the enactment of Medicare legislation. Its leadership has always come from labor

In recent years, as the more socially active boomers approach retirement, the AARP has found itself under fire for not being more effective in helping develop a special-interest voting bloc. Emphasis is growing by AARP member-unions, mainly the AFL-CIO and other industrial unions. From a small, highly specialized group, the NCSC has grown to include a general membership of over one million. It is now an organization of autonomous senior citizens' clubs, associations, councils, and other groups. Their aims are to support Medicare, increases in Social Security, reductions in health costs, and increased social programs for seniors.

The organization's stated goals are broad and straightforward: "We work with, persuade, push, convince, testify, petition, and urge Congress, the Administration, and government agencies to get things done on behalf of the aged." The council, located in Washington, D.C., lobbies for Social Security revision, a national health insurance program, higher health and safety standards in nursing homes, and adequate housing and jobs for elders. The membership base is composed primarily of labor union retirees, but membership is open to anyone age 55 or older.

National Council on the Aging

Founded in 1950, the **National Council on the Aging,** a confederation of social welfare agencies and professionals in the field of aging, has been at the forefront of advocacy, policy, and program development on all issues affecting the quality of life for older Americans. The organization, headquartered in Washington, D.C., has regional offices in New York and California. The council publishes books, articles, and journals on aging; sponsors seminars and conferences; and funds eight special-interest groups:

National Association of Older Worker Employment Services (NAOWES)

National Center on Rural Aging (NCRA)

National Institute on Adult Day Care (NIAD)

National Institute on Community-Based Long-Term Care (NICLC)

National Institute of Senior Centers (NISC)

National Institute of Senior Housing (NISH)

National Voluntary Organizations for Independent Living for the Aging (NVOILA)

The Health Promotion Institute (HPI)

National Caucus and Center on Black Aged

Formed in 1980 when two groups—the National Caucus on Black Aged and the National Center on Black Aged—merged, the **National Caucus and Center on Black Aged (NCCBA)** attempts to improve the quality and length of life for senior African Americans. The NCCBA, which believes that problems can be resolved through effective and concentrated political action on behalf of and by older African Americans, was initially formed as an ad hoc group of African American and white professionals who shared a concern for older African Americans. NCCBA activities have been largely national, focusing on such areas as income, health, and housing. An annual conference is held every May. The National Center on Black Aged in Washington, D.C., established by the NCCBA through federal funding, is the location for various activities: training, research, legislative development, and assistance to black elders.

The five groups discussed so far are neither revolutionary nor radical. Rather than advocating a redistribution of wealth, they work to improve the status of the elders by ensuring that more federal money is channeled to them. For example, they have successfully lobbied the Department of Health and Human Services, the Department of Education, the Office of Economic Opportunity, the Administration on Aging, and other government agencies to increase resources for the older population.

Gray Panthers

One pro-age political group that identifies itself as a radical nonviolent group is the **Gray Panthers,** a loosely organized group that includes young people as well as old ("age and youth in action") to fight ageism in U.S. society. It received a great deal of media attention when it was formed in the 1970s.

The best age is the age you are.

MAGGIE KUHN, GRAY PANTHERS FOUNDER

Maggie Kuhn (1905–1995), a dynamic woman who was unwillingly retired at age 65, founded the movement in her search for new ways to constructively use her energies. She and the group's other members describe themselves as a consciousness-raising activist group. Drawn together by deeply felt concerns for human liberation and social change, the Gray Panthers operate out of an office in a West Philadelphia church. From that office, a small staff and a group of volunteers maintain a center for the entire organization—thousands of concerned persons in several hundred chapters in cities and towns across the nation. Their goals are to bring dignity to old age, to eliminate poverty and mandatory retirement, to reform pension systems, and to develop a new public consciousness of the aging person's potential.

Describing themselves as a movement rather than an organization, the Gray Panthers have no formal membership requirements and collect no membership dues. They have opposed the national budget deficit, the nuclear arms race, and cuts in Social Security. Currently, the group advocates a national health insurance program. These views are similar to those who espouse the critical perspective in sociology.

The Gray Panthers espouse their views in a newsletter called *Network*. Writes one member:

We stand firm in our commitment to oppose all forms of discrimination and to challenge harmful prejudiced attitudes and values. Now, we reaffirm our pledge to help create a world that is fair to all people regardless of their gender, race, ethnicity, national-ity, sexual orientation, religion, income, physical or mental abilities, or age. (Kerr-Layton, 1993)

Gray Panthers also defend the rights of gays, lesbians, and AIDS victims and their friends. They are opposed to violence and abuse of any kind and draw special attention to the presence of hate crimes in our society. They also sponsor jointly with other organizations an international People's Summit for Peace and work for world peace in any way they can. In 2006 the Panthers drafted statements on immigration, the need to strengthen Social Security for the future, a call for better disaster preparedness (following Hurricane Katrina's devastation of New Orleans), and a call on Congress to investigate allegations of international human rights violations by the United States, among others. In short, the organization is a politically liberal one, functioning to focus the interests and skills of aging, socially active citizens.

Legislative influence

Researchers offer divergent views on the political impact of the "gray lobby." In some areas they are organized and strong. The AARP, along with the other organizations, has been effective in staving off large cuts in Medicare. Reductions in Social Security benefits proposed by the Clinton administration and again by the Bush administration have been thwarted or abandoned as politically dangerous because of the "gray lobby" groups. On the other hand, the state of the economy (the national debt, the trade imbalance, worldwide recession, the realignment of economic priorities following 9/11), and the growing number of elders, along with the shrinking workforce, are not factors the "gray lobby" can control.

Assessing the impact of the senior movement is difficult because it is so complex—representing, as it does, the vast diversity of that collection of Americans who happen to be 65 years old or older.

The Older Americans Act and Other Programs

The **Older Americans Act (OAA)** attempts to alter state and local priorities to ensure that older people's needs are represented in social services allocations. It was created to form a national network for comprehensive planning and delivery of aging services. Funding for the Older Americans Act comes up for Congressional renewal every four years; therefore, the U.S. political and economic climate is a major determinant of the OAA's level of funding.

The OAA was adopted by Congress in 1965, during a period very favorable to programs for the aging. (Medicare was enacted during the same general time period.) Whereas the 1960s and 1970s saw budget increases and expanded programs under the OAA, the 1980s and 1990s brought decreases in funding. Since participation rates in many OAA services have been highest among middle-income older persons, cuts in funding alongside proposals for cost sharing have been introduced in Congress. The major portion of OAA funds is devoted to congregate or group meals, senior centers, and transportation programs.

The Older Americans Act contains six major sections, or titles, which outline the intentions and objectives of the act. Title II establishes the Administration on Aging (AOA) in Washington, D.C., the organization that administers the programs and services that the act mandates. Title III provides for the distribution of money to establish state and community agencies—Area Agencies on Aging, or AAAs. These agencies disseminate information about available social services and are responsible for planning and coordinating such services for the elderly in local settings. A local community that has a council or center on aging is probably receiving federal funds through Title III. Title IV, which had its funding slashed in the 1980s and not increased in the 1990s, provides funds for training people to work in the field of aging as well as for

research and education on aging. Other titles provide funds for multipurpose senior centers to serve as community focal points for the development and delivery of social services.

The specific titles of the act are intended to achieve the following objectives for older citizens, as spelled out in Title I: (1) adequate income, (2) good physical and mental health, (3) suitable housing at reasonable cost, (4) full restorative services for those who require institutional care, (5) equal employment opportunities, (6) retirement with dignity, (7) a meaningful existence, (8) efficient, coordinated community services, (9) benefits of knowledge from research, and (10) freedom, independence, and individual initiative in the planning and management of one's life.

The act's major programs are developed to address these goals at local levels, with guidance from state units and the AOA. Funding comes partially from the federal government and partially from state and local governments and charity organizations. Some of the programs funded and administered through this system are discussed below.

Meals and Nutrition

The success of pilot projects in the 1960s resulted in federal funding for home-delivered meals and, in 1972, funding for congregate (group) dining projects. Under the OAA, funds are available to all states to deliver meals to the homebound elderly or to serve meals in congregate sites. Meals on Wheels, for example, delivers meals to the homebound at a minimal charge. Congregate dining is aimed at getting the elderly out of their homes and into a friendly environment where they can socialize with other people as well as enjoy a hot meal.

Meals and activities take place in churches, schools, restaurants, or senior centers. Besides serving hot meals, some agencies provide transportation to and from the dining site, information and referral services, nutrition education, health and welfare counseling, shopping assistance, and recreational activities. The act that established the congregate dining program specifies that participants not be asked their income; they may make a contribution if they wish, but there is no set charge.

Friendly Visiting and Telephone Reassurance

The OAA provides limited funding for volunteer community services such as friendly visitor and telephone reassurance programs. Because of decreasing funds, however, local staffs have had to become increasingly adept at fund-raising to keep programs afloat.

The Friendly Visitor Program has improved the quality of life for many people. Visitors are volunteers of all ages who have an interest in developing a friendly relationship with older persons. They are matched with elderly persons in their community on the basis of such things as common interests or location. In some cases, the Friendly Visitor has proved to be a lifeline. The program has a small paid staff that organizes and instructs volunteers.

Telephone reassurance programs have staff, either paid or volunteer, to check on older persons daily by phone at a given time. For the homebound, this call may be an uplifting and meaningful part of the day. If the phone is not answered, a staff member immediately goes in person to check on the elder's welfare.

Employment

The Title V employment program is small but is one of the most politically popular programs. The major program, the Senior Community Service Employment Program (SCSEP), which provides community service work opportunities for unemployed low-income persons age 55 and over, employs 62,500 older applicants in part-time minimum-wage community service jobs throughout the United States.

A related program is Green Thumb. Men and women age 55 and older who live in rural areas may work up to 20 hours per week at minimum wage in public projects that include landscaping, horticulture, and highway maintenance.

Adult Day Centers

The Older Americans Act partially funds multipurpose day programs to provide services on an outpatient basis to the many older people who need services on a daily or weekly basis but do not need 24-hour institutional care. Older people may come to such centers for health care, meals, social activities, physical exercise, or rehabilitation. Practitioners from the centers may, on occasion, deliver home services. These centers allow people to enjoy the advantages of both institutional care and home living.

Other Services

Local agencies on aging may offer legal services to low-income elders for civil matters such as landlord disputes; other agencies may offer home health services as well. Still others may offer housing services such as counseling on housing options, home equity conversion information, and assistance in locating affordable housing. Information and referral is a hallmark of agencies on aging.

Considering the budget constraints within which the AOA must work, fulfilling all its goals is largely impossible. In 1999, for example, Social Security and Medicare payments to older persons totaled between $500 and $600 billion, vastly more than the $22 billion AOA appropriation. Nevertheless, the AOA provides an excellent outreach structure for elders across the United States. Vast numbers have enjoyed and appreciated the services the act offers. Those who think they might be eligible for any of these programs are advised to call their local agency on aging. Though the limited funds cannot reach far enough to include those above the poverty line as well as those below it, many elders living in modest if not meager circumstances do meet eligibility requirements.

In a controversial effort to expand the efficacy of a decreasing AOA budget, in 2001 the Bush administration established a Center for Faith-Based and Community Initiatives and issued an executive order for similar units to be established in federal agencies (Administration on Aging; 2006). The controversy is based on the fundamental American philosophy demanding separation of church and state. In 2002, however, the Republican-controlled Congress appropriated a $30 million Compassion Capital Fund (CCF)—the first federal dollars specifically targeting faith-based grassroots organizations. Because of their grassroots nature, local organizations are presumed to better understand local and regional needs of their entire populations than can the federal government.

Two Programs Not Funded by the OAA

Elderhostel

Certainly not all successful programs for older persons have been funded by the Older Americans Act. Some have sprung up locally and are funded by local tax dollars. Others are funded by private donations or charity organizations or sponsored by churches or various federal or state government agencies separate from the Administration on Aging. **Elderhostel** is a program made available through a combination of state colleges and universities and private payment.

Offering special one-week or summer residential academic programs for citizens age 55 and over, the very successful Elderhostel program is designed to meet some of the educational interests of older people. From its Boston headquarters, the program, inspired by the youth hostels and folk schools of Europe, directs a network of several thousand high schools, universities, national parks, environmental education centers, and other educational institutions throughout the United States, Canada, and more than 100 overseas locations. Hostelers can go to school (a different school every week, if desired) as many

weeks as they wish and take up to three courses per week. Noncredit courses with no exams, no grades, and no required homework are offered in multitudinous subjects; no-cost extracurricular activities are also provided. Scholarships are available, and students are charged a reasonable flat fee for class, room, and board. Elderhostel offers personal assistance with overseas travel arrangements. The program has been enormously popular among older "students of life."

Foster Grandparent Program

Funded through participating states and ACTION (the principal federal agency that administers volunteer service programs), the **Foster Grandparent Program (FGP)** allows low-income citizens age 60 or older to use their time and talents to provide much-needed love, care, and attention to disadvantaged youngsters. Begun in 1965, FGP was the first federally sponsored program to offer challenging activity to retirees. The FGP provides opportunities for close relationships to two different groups: low-income elders who want to feel needed and who want to participate in and contribute to children's lives, and institutionalized children and/or children with special or exceptional needs.

Foster grandparents exist in every state. Participating elders receive 40 hours of orientation in the specific area of their choice. In most cases, they work four hours a day, five days a week, assisting youngsters in physical or speech therapy or with their homework. Their main task is to provide for the emotional, mental, and physical well-being of children by affording them intimate and continuing relations through uncomplicated activities such as going for a walk or reading stories, or within family intervention structures. Foster grandparents receive a nontaxable stipend of an amount per hour that is approximately minimum wage, transportation if needed, a meal each day that they work, accident and liability insurance coverage, and an annual physical exam. Sometimes nonstipended volunteers may enroll in the program under certain conditions. Many seniors work in this program for years both because they need the extra income and, more important, because their "grandchildren" love them.

Activism and Advocacy

Activism connotes more than simply voting or joining an organization. The term political activist brings to mind an individual who is politically committed to a cause and who uses a variety of means to push for social change.

Elders and those interested in their causes participate in community activities by serving on boards of trustees, advisory councils, and committees in all kinds of social service agencies. Interested persons may get involved in police-community relations, join voluntary organizations, and enter local politics as either campaign workers or candidates. They may lobby to maintain or increase funding for federal programs, including those of the Older Americans Act. Legal activity is another area for activism. Class-action lawsuits can be brought against organizations and institutions that discriminate against or do not properly serve elders. Voter registration drives are important. They ensure that older persons can support those who support Social Security, Medicaid, home-delivered meals, public housing, employment programs, improved transportation, health benefits, and dozens of other programs for the elderly. Grievance procedures can be initiated to aid complaints against Social Security or welfare departments. Collective activity is a good tactic for the activist who

Respect for cultural differences enriches society and validates the knowledge, experience, and culture of our diverse elder population.

joins with others in membership drives, marches, and demonstrations. That activism can be high profile, such as a Gray Panthers–sponsored march, or it can be on a far smaller scale. In either case, it involves taking responsibility for putting one's values into action, and the result can be profoundly validating.

The expansion of the Internet has dramatically shifted the ability of all people, whatever their interest or age group, to communicate with like-minded persons and advocacy organizations. The Alliance for Retired Americans, for example, advertises itself as "an advocacy organization, NOT an insurance company." One particularly well-organized website called Suddenly Senior (http://www.suddenlysenior.com) has on its home page a button for "222 Best Senior Links" that includes government agencies, retail price comparison sites, and alphabetized and monitored sources for just about any need or interest. Such sites serve to inform, to connect, and, potentially, to organize a forum for political bases. How effective this will be in influencing social policy remains yet to be seen.

Resistance activity can be an effective form of social activity. It includes boycotts, rent strikes, wheelchair sit-ins, and voting against bond issues. Designated individuals may act as watchdogs on agencies that serve the elderly. In any type of organized activity, the media can provide an important tool in airing the interests and concerns of elders.

Advocacy is a term widely used in the field of aging, perhaps because of numerous individuals and organizations doing just that. Advocacy involves using one's resources and power for the benefit of a special-interest group, such as the elderly. Stereotypes of the 1950s and 1960s portrayed elders as dependent and passive, in need of someone to advocate for them. The 1970s and 1980s changed that idea. The Gray Panthers were in the forefront of creating a stronger, more forceful image for elders. It is becoming quite clear that older persons are capable of advocating for themselves; nonetheless, they do appreciate all the help they can get. In the first decades of the new century, advocacy

will ideally combine the efforts of individuals, regardless of age, who desire to promote a more satisfying later life for all U.S. citizens.

The Equity Issue

Generational equity is a controversial issue that was first popularized by the media in the mid-1980s. Critics of elder programs, who fear that the older generation is advancing at the expense of the younger one, have described older people as selfishly demanding programs targeting their age group only, at the expense of children and children's programs. An example of the argument in action is the criticism of a politician who supports Meals-on-Wheels programs for elders but votes to cut federal nutrition programs for school lunches. The reason? "The elderly vote, and children don't," goes the usual reply. Perhaps so, perhaps not. The issue of social programs for special-needs groups is far too complex to be dealt with simplistically. From a national policy perspective, decisions on programmatic support must be made in the context of the total net of services available as well as the need for those services. Sloganism brought to the public by a media searching for the 20-second sound bite does not provide reasoning adequate to make decisions that will affect millions of American citizens, whatever their ages.

Those who advocate generational equity believe that younger generations will suffer because of the older population's unprecedented size and affluence. Around the country, suburbs have a growing number of older residents. Older residents have no direct stake in the public school systems, and the constituency for supporting schools and other youth services is shrinking proportionally as the nation ages.

The idea, however, that increased affluence for elders leads to decreased moneys for children is unsound. The improved financial status of elders is due largely to better Social Security coverage, and, indeed, benefit increases should keep pace with inflation. Although they dramatically reduce poverty rates among seniors, such essentially small increases in benefits are not the reason for poverty among children and other younger generations. Nor is the increased cost of medical care for elders. If, as some suggest, Medicare premiums tripled in cost for the well-to-do and expensive surgeries were rationed for the very old, women and children would still be poor in this country. The growing number of older people is hardly the major reason for spiraling health care costs. It is just one contributing factor in a complex economic system. The basic reason for the poverty of children is their parents' unemployment or underemployment and the increasing number of female-headed families with low incomes. To protect children, our economic house must be in order.

Economic prosperity and public support for education are strongly associated. American industry must have workers capable of making informed decisions, learning new tasks, and following complex instructions. A system of public education in the United States has provided competent workers in the past and must be strong enough to do so for the future. Blaming either Medicare and Social Security on the one hand, or poor parents on the other, does not address issues necessary for national-level, workable, effective policy for caring for America's citizens.

In 1950 Social Security was amended to establish a program of aid to permanently and totally disabled persons and to broaden aid to dependent children to include a relative with whom the child lives. Social Security actually provides benefits to many different age groups, and every worker can rest easier knowing that, despite recent doubts about the program's continued solvency, he or she will likely be covered in retirement. A working father or mother who has paid into Social Security can know that, should he or she die before the children are grown, they will be provided for to some extent by Social Security. Social Security is a retirement *and disability* program—in reality, an intergenerational safety net to reduce poverty.

Public policy based on the competition to "get" limited resources will ultimately be unworkable because it will not meet the needs of

The physical health and social well-being of elders is strong and getting stronger in the new century.

those who require assistance, and it flies in the face of the deeply held value of interdependence across generations. Rather than competing for human services dollars—dividing the piece of pie into yet smaller sections—politicians and citizens need to be reformulating the way in which the pie is sliced.

In 2002 the Social Security payroll tax was 15.3 percent of wages up to $84,900, with half of this percentage coming from the employees' checks and the other half paid by employers (U.S. Social Security Administration, 2002). This is a bigger tax burden on most households than personal income tax. Additionally, Medicare plus the means-tested Medicaid benefits for the aged costs as much as the Social Security pensions. Together these programs cost about 10 percent of the gross domestic product. This is around 25 percent more than the entire revenue from personal income tax (Feldstein, 1997).

What must a nation do to address dramatic shifts in the age of its population? With advances in medical science and improvements in lifestyles, it is possible that people will live even longer than current projections predict. The "contract between generations" is the relationship of expectations between older and younger age groups in a context of changing resources and values. The relationship goes beyond parents and children to that of generations in a nation: who owes what to whom and how, and when is it transferred. The exchanges, or **intergenerational transfers,** are based on the question, "To what extent do we hold older generations accountable for the effect of current policies on future generations?" At the beginning of the twenty-first century, we might take a lesson from ancient Native American philosophy: the consequences of all actions must be considered through the seventh generation. In what ways do my actions (my political perspective) affect those generations surrounding me, as well as future generations?

Epilogue: A New Generation of Older Adults

What does the future hold for older individuals? In some respects, the future looks bright. Elders are living longer and healthier lives, and they are becoming more visible not only in numbers, but also in political activism. They have required, and to some degree have received, a bigger slice of that pie than did their parents, who were not as long-lived. As a result of dollars put into health, education, nutrition, and socialization for elders, the quality of life for the average older person has dramatically improved over that of several decades past.

On the other hand, the future is uncertain. The line between paying for programs for the well-being of elders and seeing thousands of elders live in poverty, as many elders once did, is a fine one. The nation is faced with a stark, "no-fault" reality: people are not growing old because they are mean-hearted or self-centered. Longevity has increased so suddenly in terms of human history that those who are currently living into very old age are at the cutting edge. They have few role models, and they did not "plan" to live to be 80, 90, and older. The questions are of the nation itself: Where do national values lie with respect to the country's responsibility to provide for its elders now and in the future? What services should be provided; who should be targeted to receive those services; and what cost, if any, should participants pay for those services?

The 1997 reauthorization of the Older Americans Act provided an opportunity (and requirement) for advocates and policymakers to debate the role and future of OAA—essentially, to develop a plan for the future of services to elders (Wacker et al., 1998). Two options are to target services and to introduce cost sharing.

Targeting services to low-income individuals by developing financial eligibility standards is energetically endorsed by many policymakers, particularly those whose bottom-line criterion is the budget (Wacker et al., 1998). Using income eligibility standards, however, might undermine the social-insurance principle that has provided broad public support for Social Security and Medicare. Including the middle class along with the lower class provides a very broad base of programmatic support that otherwise might not be there.

Implementing a format of *cost sharing,* another option being discussed, is supported by many elder advocates. This plan would provide for an income-based sliding scale of shared cost responsibility similar to the theoretical income tax. Low-income individuals would have services paid for, and higher-income individuals would shoulder a proportion of the cost, depending on income. In this way, continued popular support for programs could be maintained. The image of a large administrative overhead looms for many people in this proposal, however. The choices are not easy, the task is enormous, and the outcomes are monumental for the shaping of the lives of elders in the twenty-first century.

The most exciting part of the future, however, is that the turn of the century brings with it a new generation of elders. Foremost, their parents' generation will have given them the experience of extended longevity. They will know much more about living to be 90, and more of them will *expect* to do so, than did their parents. They will have made plans, even if those plans are psychological and not practical. The gift of the previous generation is an understanding that the possible is likely to be the probable. The new generation of elders will have a better understanding of the relationship between lifestyle and health, and they will have lived in greater affluence than did their parents and have had greater opportunity to make lifestyle choices. They will bring with them the ability to redefine the timing of life-course transactions. They just might choose to work (or introduce the possibility) until they are 55, then work for five years, take two years off, and repeat the cycle until they become completely unable to do so. They will bring with them different attitudes toward marriage, responsibility to the community, and responsibility for personal growth.

The future is a very exciting place. The present responsibility is to understand the ways in which an aging nation and globe will shape that future, economics will shape that future, and both will combine to shape the cultural environment of the nation.

Chapter Summary

Judging by numbers, the political power of elders is stronger than ever before. However, numbers do not tell the whole story. The political environment for elders is dependent on the economy as well as national priorities established by the current presidential administration.

In earlier times, there have been examples of social movements by and for elders. The Townsend plan and Ham and Eggs movement in the 1930s are two examples. The activism of the 1970s symbolized by the Gray Panthers is a third example.

Today there are a number of indicators that older people have reasonable political clout. They vote in larger numbers than do younger persons. We have recently seen two presidents (Reagan and the first Bush) over 65, and the seniority system in Congress ensures power to elder members. A number of political associations are strong—the leading one being the American Association of Retired Persons. The Older Americans Act of 1965 authorizes taxpayer spending on elders. However, funding has *not* proportionally increased in the twenty-first century. The major funding goes to congregate meals, senior centers, and transportation programs. Only if there is effective advocacy and activism can these programs remain in place.

The question of generational equity will continue to raise its head as the percentage and number of elders continues to increase while funding for social programs decreases. It is unfortunate when the old are posited against the young. People of all ages should unite to improve the quality of life for everyone.

Key Terms

advocacy
American Association of Retired Persons (AARP)
Elderhostel
Foster Grandparent Program (FGP)
generational equity
Gray Panthers
Ham and Eggs movement
interest groups

intergenerational transfers
National Caucus and Center on Black Aged (NCCBA)
National Committee to Preserve Social Security and Medicare
National Council of Senior Citizens (NCSC)
National Council on the Aging

Older Americans
  Act (OAA)
professional
  associations

resistance activity
senior power
Townsend plan
trade association

Questions for Discussion

1. What do you predict will be the future social movements for seniors? Why? How politically active do you expect these seniors to be?

2. Do you think ageism will be reversed in the future? Why or why not?

3. Do you expect to be politically active as an elder? If so, why? If not, why not?

4. What organization(s) will you join? What measures do you support? Do you see yourself as being an activist when you are 60, 70, 80, 90? Explain.

Fieldwork Suggestions

1. Interview the head of the AARP in your area. How politically active is this person? Do you think that the AARP will represent your best interests when you are eligible to join? If you are eligible to join, are you a member? Why or why not? How well informed are the people you know about the AARP?

2. Locate the nearest chapter of the Gray Panthers. Write for information on their activities.

What activities are they focused upon? Who is attracted as a member to this group?

3. Interview an old person who considers himself or herself to be an activist or radical, or to have been one at an earlier point in life. What were the issues that brought the person into activism? What issues has he or she addressed since?

Internet Activities 🌐

1. Multidisciplinary resource centers for gerontology are funded by the Administration on Aging. They include the Institute of Gerontology, University of Michigan; gerontology studies at Wayne State University; Andrus Gerontology at University of Southern California; and the Center for Aging and Human Development at Duke University. Updates on the status of the centers are posted on the Community Resources for Older Adults Web page. Locate this page and develop a summary of the current status of resource centers supported by AOA funding.

2. Locate the AARP home page and create a list of resources available from that website.

3. Using the resource list at the back of the text, locate an appropriate agency or interest group and write an analysis of (1) the description and content of the site, and (2) your evaluation of its intent and purpose.

INTERNET INFORMATION RESOURCES

Administration on Aging
http://www.aoa.dhhs.gov/
Extensive links to other national organizations
and programs.

Administration on Aging
Eldercare Search
http://www.eldercare.gov/Eldercare/Public/Home.asp
The Eldercare Locator connects older Americans and their
caregivers with sources of information on senior services.

Administration on Aging
Elder Rights
http://www.aoa.gov/eldfam/Elder_Rights/Elder
_Rights.asp
Elder rights and resources.

Administration on Aging
Family Caregiver Options
http://www.aoa.gov/eldfam/For_Caregivers/
For_Caregivers.asp
Good place for information about respite and caregiver
support services. Updated frequently.

Aging Network Services
http://www.agingnets.com/
A guide for children who are coping with their aging
parents.

Alliance of Information and Referral Systems (AIRS)
http://www.airs.org/
More than 1,000 information and service providers.

Alzheimer's Association
http://www.alz.org/
Provides details on Alzheimer's research and support for
patients and their families.

Alzheimer's Association
Treatment Options for Alzheimer's Disease
http://www.alz.org/AboutAD/Treatments.asp
Latest research on Alzheimer's Disease.

Alzheimer's Association
What Is Alzheimer's Disease?
http://www.alz.org/AboutAD/WhatIsAD.asp
Information on Alzheimer's Disease, with fact sheets
and resource lists.

American Association of Retired Persons (AARP)
http://www.aarp.org/internetresources/
Guide to Internet Resources; includes alphabetical list
of sites.

BenefitsLink
http://benefitslink.com/index.html
Links to benefit-plan information.

Canada Pension Plan (CPP)
http://www.sdc.gc.ca/en/isp/cpp/cpptoc.shtml
Compare Canada's retirement pension program with the
U.S. Social Security program.

Caregiver's Handbook
http://www.sdc.gc.ca/en/isp/cpp/cpptoc.shtml
Complete caregiver's handbook; also guide to choosing
a residential facility.

East Bay (California) Elder Abuse Prevention
http://www.elderabuseprevention-eastbay.org/
Definition of elder abuse, how to recognize it, who must
report it, and where to report it.

ElderWeb
http://www.elderweb.com/home/
Information for caregivers and older adults.

Family Caregiver Alliance
http://www.caregiver.org/caregiver/jsp/home.jsp
Assistance to caregivers of persons with Alzheimer's,
Parkinson's, and other brain disorders.

FedStats
http://www.fedstats.gov/
Charts and graphs of population projections.

FindLaw
Living Wills
http://estate.findlaw.com/estate-planning/living-wills.html
Information on living wills, legal assistance, and
directories and associations on advance directives.

Florida Health Stat
http://www.floridahealthstat.com/fit_nh.shtml
Tips on finding a nursing home; good resource even for
non-Floridians.

Gay and Lesbian Retirement Communities
http://www.ourtownvillages.com/ or
http://www.gaylesbianretiring.org/
Information regarding retirement communities
for gay adults.

The Gerontologist
http://www.cpr.maxwell.syr.edu/gerontologist/ira/
Internet resources on aging. Includes a guide to other
resources.

GriefNet
http://www.griefnet.org/
Resources related to death, dying, bereavement, and major
emotional and physical losses.

Hospice Foundation of America
http://www.hospicefoundation.org/
A resource for locating a hospice organization, with
related links.

Institute of Gerontology
http://www.iog.wayne.edu/
Wayne State University resource for researchers, educators,
and practitioners.

Mental Health Net Directory
http://www.mentalhealth.net/
For locating a mental health professional in your
community.

Mental Help Net
http://mentalhelp.net/
Help for individuals on a variety of mental health topics.

Mid-America Congress on Aging
http://www.lgrossman.com/macareso.htm
Internet resources for the aging; many links to associations
and support services.

National Association for Home Care and Hospice
http://www.nahc.org/
Information about state organizations; consumer and
legislative information.

National Center on Elder Abuse
http://www.elderabusecenter.org/
Information and statistics about elder abuse; links and
publications listing.

National Coalition for the Homeless (NCH)
http://www.nationalhomeless.org/
A national advocacy network of homeless persons,
activists, and service providers.

National Coalition for Homeless Veterans
http://www.nchv.org/
Resources to governmental, legislative, advocacy, and
political issues. With guides and brochures for veterans.

National Institute on Aging
http://www.nia.nih.gov/
Information on aging research, clinical trials, grants,
and scientific resources.

National Senior Citizens Law Center
http://www.nsclc.org/
Information on Social Security, Supplemental Security
Income, Medicare, Medicaid, age discrimination and
mandatory retirement, and the Older Americans Act.

Resources for Aging
http://www.ageinfo.com/
Seeks to empower the growing number of informal
caregivers to be more effective and efficient in managing
the care process.

Resources for Caregivers
http://www.stls.org/caregiver/DevelopmentalDisabilities/
CGLinks_1.htm
Central listing on personal and professional caregiving.

SAMHSA's Mental Health Information Resources
http://www.mentalhealth.samhsa.gov/
Substance Abuse and Mental Health Services
Administration provides mental illness facts, services,
and tips.

SeniorLaw Home Page
http://www.seniorlaw.com/
Specialists in elder law.

Seniorlink
http://www.seniorlink.com/content/view/12/59/
Elder care resource, with referral and consultation services
for older adults, families, and care providers.

Senior Sites
http://www.seniorsites.com/
Information on long-term care and housing for older
adults.

Seniors-Site.com
http://www.seniors-site.com/
Concerns about aging; financial information.

Social Security Online
http://www.ssa.gov/
Comprehensive site. Visitors can request earnings record, review statistical information about benefits and beneficiaries, and review information on history and legislation on Social Security.

Stress Management and Emotional Wellness Links
http://www.imt.net/~randolfi/StressLinks.html
Links to emotional wellness sites.

U.S. Census Bureau
http://www.census.gov/
U.S. Census Bureau links, with data tools, population estimates, and a list of publications.

U.S. Department of Housing and Urban Development
http://www.hud.gov/
Information about housing policy and programs.

U.S. Department of Labor
http://www.dol.gov/
Labor resources and links to pension information.

Abbott, D. W.; deZwaan, M.; Mussell, M. P.; Raymond, N. C.; Seim, H. C.; Crow, S. J.; Crosby, R. D.; & Mitchell, J. E. (1998). Onset of binge eating and dieting in overweight women: Implications for etiology, associated features and treatment. *Journal of Psychosomatic Research, 44* (3–4), 367–374.

Abel, E. K., & Sankar, A. (1995). The uses and evaluation of qualitative research: It's not what you do when you don't have data or don't know statistics. *Research on Aging, 17* (1), 3–7.

Abel, S. A. (1998). Social Security retirement benefits: The last insult of a sexist society. *Family and Conciliation Courts Review, 36* (1), 54–64.

Achenbaum, W. A. (1996). Historical perspectives on aging. In R. H. Binstock and L. K. George (Eds.), *Handbook of aging and the social sciences* (4th ed). San Diego: Academic Press.

Achenbaum, W. A., & Bengtson, V. L. (1994). Reengaging the disengagement theory of aging. *Gerontologist, 34* (6), 756–763.

Achenbaum, W. A., & Binstock, R. H. (1993). Making sense of dementia, *Gerontologist, 33* (5), 695.

Adami, S.; Passerl, M.; & Ortolani, S. (1995). Effects of oral alendronate and intranasal salmon calcitonin in bone mass and biochemical markers of bone turnover in postmenopausal women with osteoporosis. *Bone, 17,* 383–390.

Adams, R. G. (1983). Friendship and aging. *Generations, 10,* 40–43.

Adams, R. G., & Blieszner, R. (1994). An integrative conceptual framework for friendship research. *Journal of Social and Personal Relationships, 11,* 163–184.

Adams, R. G., & Blieszner, R. (1995). Aging well with family and friends. *American Behavioral Scientist, 38* (2), 209–224.

Adams, T. (1996). Informal family caregiving to older people with dementia: Research priorities for community psychiatric nursing. *Journal of Advanced Nursing, 24,* 703–710.

Aday, R. H.; Sims, C. R.; & Evans, E. (1991). Youth's attitudes toward the elderly: The impact of intergenerational partners. *Journal of Applied Gerontology, 19* (3), 372–384.

Aday, R. H.; Sims, C. R.; McDuffie, W.; & Evans, E. (1996). Changing children's attitudes toward the elderly: The longitudinal effects of an intergenerational partners program. *Journal of Research in Childhood Education, 10* (2), 143–151.

Adelman, R. (1987, April). A community-oriented geriatric rehabilitation unit in a nursing home. *Gerontologist, 27,* 143–146.

Ade-Ridder, L., & Kaplan, L. (1993). Marriage, spousal caregiving, and a husband's move to a nursing home. *Journal of Gerontological Nursing, 19* (10), 13–23.

Adkins, G.; Martin, P.; & Poon, L. W. (1996). Personality traits and states as predictors of subjective well being in centenarians, octogenarians, and sexagenerians. *Psychology and Aging, 11* (3), 408–416.

Administration on Aging. (1997). *Profile of older Americans: 1997.* Program Resources Department, American Association of Retired Persons and the Administration on Aging, U.S. Department of Health and Human Services.

Administration on Aging. (1999). *Older Americans update 2000: Key indicators of well-being.* www.agingstats.gov, accessed June 20, 2006.

Administration on Aging. (1999). *Profile of older Americans: 1999.* Program Resources Department, American Association of Retired Persons and the Administration on Aging, U.S. Department of Health and Human Services.

Administration on Aging. (2001). *Profile of older Americans: 2001.* Program Resources Department, American Association of Retired Persons and the Administration on Aging, U.S. Department of Health and Human Services.

Administration on Aging. (2002). *Profile of older Americans: 2002.* Program Resources Department, American Association of Retired Persons and the Administration on Aging, U.S. Department of Health and Human Services.

Administration on Aging. (2006). *Profile of older Americans: 2006.* Program Resources Department, American Association of Retired Persons and the Administration on Aging, U.S. Department of Health and Human Services.

Aiken, L. (1994). *Dying, death, and bereavement* (3rd ed.). Boston: Allyn & Bacon.

Akiyama, H.; Antonucci, T.C.; & Campbell, R. (1997). Exchange and reciprocity among two generations of Japanese and American women. In J. Sokolovsky (Ed.), *The cultural context of aging* (3rd ed.). Westport, CT: Bergin & Garvey.

Akiyama, H.; Elliott, K.; & Antonucci, T. C. (1996). Same-sex and cross-sex relationships. *Journal of Gerontology: Psychological Sciences, 51B* (6), P374–382.

Aldwin, C. M., & Sutton, K. J. (1996). The development of coping resources in adulthood. *Journal of Personality, 64* (4), 837–871.

Alexy, B., & Belcher, J. (1997). Rural elderly present need for nursing continuity. *Nursing Economics, 15* (3), 146–150.

Allain, T. J.; Matenga, J. A.; Gomo, Z.; Adamchak, D. J.; & Wilson, A. O. (1996). Determinants of happiness and life satisfaction in elderly Zimbabweans. *Central African Journal of Medicine, 42* (11), 308–311.

Allan, M. A. (1998). Elder abuse: A challenge for home care nurses. *Home Healthcare Nurse, 16* (2), 103–110.

Almberg, B. E., & Grafstrom, W. (2000). Caregivers of relatives with dementia: Experiences encompassing social support and bereavement, *Aging and Mental Health, 4* (1), 82–89.

Amenta, E.; Carruthers, B. G.; & Zylan, Y. (1992). A hero for the aged? The Townsend movement, the political mediation model, and US old-age policy, 1934–1950. *American Journal of Sociology, 98* (2), 308–339.

American Association of Retired Persons. (1990). *Using the experience of a lifetime.* Booklet #D13353. Washington, DC: American Association of Retired Persons.

American Association of Retired Persons. (1995). *Women's issues.* http://www.aarp/webplace, accessed March 30, 1997.

American Association of Retired Persons. (1997). *Profile of older Americans: 1997.* Administration on Aging, U.S. Department of Health and Human Services, Washington, DC.

American Cancer Society. (1996). *Cancer facts and figures.* Atlanta, GA: American Cancer Society.

American Psychiatric Association. (1994). *Diagnostic and statistical manual for mental disorders* (4th ed.). Washington, DC: American Psychiatric Association.

American Psychiatric Association. (1997). Practice guidelines for the treatment of patients with schizophrenia. *American Journal of Psychiatry, 15* (suppl.), 1–63.

American Psychological Association. (1997). *The graying of America: An aging revolution in need of a national research agenda.* John C. Cavanaugh & Denise C. Park, co-chairs, Division 20, Vitality for Life Committee, Washington, DC.

American Psychological Association. (2001). *Older adults' health and age-related changes: Reality vs. myth.* www.apa.org/pi/aging/publications.html, accessed March 18, 2006.

Amir, Y. (1969). Contact hypothesis in ethnic relations. *Psychological Bulletin, 71,* 319–342.

Anderson, D. C. (1997, July 13). Aging behind bars. *New York Times,* 28–32.

Anstey, K.; Lord, S. R.; & Williams, P. (1997). Strength in the lower limbs, visual contrast sensitivity, and simple reaction time predict cognition in older women. *Psychology and Aging, 12* (1), 137–144.

Antonucci, T. C., & Akiyama, H. (1987). Social networks in adult life: A preliminary examination of the convoy model. *Journal of Gerontology: Social Sciences, S42,* 512–527.

Antonucci, T. C., & Akiyama, H. (1995). Convoys of social relations: Family and friendships within a life span context. In R. Blieszner & V. H. Bedford (Eds.), *Handbook of aging and the family.* Westport, CT: Greenwood.

Antonucci, T. C.; Fuhrer, R.; & Dartigues, J.-F. (1997). Social relations and depressive symptomatology in a sample of community-dwelling French older adults. *Psychology and Aging 12* (1), 189–195.

Apple, D. D. (1956). The social structure of grandparenthood. *American Anthropologist, 58,* 656–663.

Aquino, J. A.; Russell, D. W.; Cutrona, C. E.; & Altmaier, E. M. (1996). Employment status, social support, and life satisfaction among the elderly. *Journal of Counseling Psychology, 43* (6), 480–489.

Archbold, P. (1983). Impact of parent caring on women. *Family Relations, 32,* 39–45.

Ardelt, M. (1997). Wisdom and life satisfaction in old age. *Journal of Gerontology: Psychological Sciences, 52B,* P15–P27.

Aries. E. J., & Johnson, F. L. (1983). Close friendship in adulthood: Conversational content between same-sex friends. Sex Roles: A Journal of Research, 9, 1183–1196.

Arnold, S. E., & Trojanowski, J. Q. (1996). Cognitive impairment in elderly schizophrenia: A dementia (still) lacking distinctive histopathology. *Schizophrenia Bulletin, 22* (1), 5–9.

Associated Press. (1987, September 20). Elderly unpersons. *Santa Rosa Press Democrat,* 1, A11.

Atchley, R. (1976). *The sociology of retirement.* Cambridge, MA: Schenkman.

Austad, S. N. (1997). *Why we age: What science is discovering about the body's journey through life.* New York: Wiley.

Baba, S. (1993). The super-aged society. *World Health, 46* (3), 9–11.

Bahr, Sr. R. T. (1994). An overview of gerontological nursing. In M. O. Hogstel (Ed.), *Nursing care of the older adult* (3rd ed., pp. 2–25). Albany, NY: Delmar.

Bailik, R. (1992). Family care of the elderly in Mexico. In J. Kosberg (Ed.), *Family care of the elderly.* Newbury Park, CA: Sage.

Baltes, P. (1991). The many faces of human aging: Toward a psychological culture of old age. *Psychological Medicine, 21,* 827–854.

Baltes, P. (1993). The aging mind: Potential and limits. *Gerontologist, 33* (5), 580–594.

Baltes, P. B., & Horgas, A. L. (1996). Long-term care institutions and the maintenance of competence. In S. L. Willis, K. W. Schaie, & M. Hayward (Eds.), *Social mechanisms for maintaining competence in old age.* New York: Springer.

Baltes, P. B., & Lindenberger, U. (1997). Emergence of a powerful connection between sensory and cognitive functions across the adult life span: A new window to the study of cognitive aging? *Psychology and Aging, 12*, 12–21.

Bank, S. P. (1995). Before the last leaves fall: Sibling connections among the elderly. *Journal of Geriatric Psychology, 28* (2), 183–195.

Barazan, M. (1994). Fear of crime and its consequences among urban elderly individuals. *International Journal of Aging and Human Development, 38* (2), 99–116.

Barbato, C. A., & Freezel, J. D. (1987). The language of aging in different age groups. *Gerontologist, 27*, 527–531.

Bargh, J. A.; Chen, M.; & Burrows, L. (1996). Automaticity of social behaviors: Direct effects of trait construct and stereotype activation on action. *Journal of Personality and Social Psychology, 71*, 230–244.

Barinaga, M. (1991). How long is the human life span? *Science, 254*, 936–941.

Barker, W. H., & Mullooly, J. P. (1997). Stroke in a defined elderly population, 1967–1985: A less lethal and disabling but no less common disease. *Stroke, 28* (2), 284–290.

Barrow, G. M. (1994). College student attitudes toward older people. Unpublished report. Santa Rosa Community College, CA.

Bartels, S. J.; Muester, K. T.; & Miles, K. M. (1997). Functional impairments in elderly patients with schizophrenia and major affective illness in the community: Social skills, living skills, and behavior problems. *Behavior Therapy, 28*, 43–63.

Barusch, A. S. (1997). Self-concepts of low-income older women: Not old or poor, but fortunate and blessed. *International Journal of Aging and Human Development, 44* (4), 269–282.

Bash, A. (1995, February 17). Field wields clout within "Means." *USA Today*, 24.

Bauer, J. J., & McAdams, D. D. (2004). Growth goals, maturity, and well-being. *Developmental Psychology, 40* (1), 114–127.

Bazargan, M. (1994). The effects of health, environmental, and socio-psychological variables on fear of crime and its consequences among urban black elderly individuals. *International Journal of Aging and Human Development, 38* (2), 99–115.

Beard, B. B. (1991). *Centenarians: The new generation.* Westport, CT: Greenwood Press.

Beauvoir, S. de. (1973). *The coming of age.* New York: Warner Communications.

Bechara, A.; Damasio, H.; Tranel, D.; & Anderson, S. W. (1998). Dissociation of working memory from decision making within the human prefrontal cortex. *Journal of Neuroscience, 18* (1), 428–437.

Beck, J. G., & Stanley, M. A. (1997). Anxiety disorders in the elderly: The emerging role of behavior therapy. *Behavior Therapy, 28*, 83–100.

Beck, M. (1990, July 16). Trading places. *Newsweek*, 48–54.

Beckman, L. J. (1981). Effects of social interaction and children's relative inputs on older women's psycho-

logical well-being. *Journal of Personality and Social Psychology, 4*, 1075–1086.

Beckman, M. (2004). Low-cal connections. *Science of Aging Knowledge & Environment, 2004* (25), n. 60.

Bellandi, D. (1997, August 25). Seniors on patrol. *Modern Healthcare*, 44–45.

Belliveau, F., & Richter, L. (1970). *Understanding human sexual inadequacy.* New York: Bantam Books.

Bengtson, V. L., & Achenbaum, W. A. (1993). *The changing contract across generations.* New York: Aldine de Gruyter.

Bengtson, V. L.; Burgess, E. O.; & Barrott, T. M. (1997). Theory, explanation, and a third generation of theoretical development in social gerontology. *Journal of Gerontology: Social Sciences, 52B* (2), S72–S88.

Bengtson, V. L., & Dowd, J. J. (1981). Sociological functionalism, exchange theory and life-cycle analysis: A call for more explicit theoretical bridges. *International Journal of Aging and Human Development, 12* (2), 55–73.

Bennett, K. M. (2005). Psychological wellbeing in later life: The longitudinal effects of marriage, widowhood and marital status change. *International Journal of Geriatric Psychiatry, 20* (3), 280–284.

Beresford, L. (1997). The good death. *Hospitals and Health Networks, 71* (12), 60–62.

Berry, J. M., and Jobe, J. B. (2002). At the intersection of personality and adult development, *Journal of Research in Personality, 36* (4), 283.

Berzlanovich, M.; Leil, W.; Waldhoer, T.; Sim, E.; Fasching, P.; & Fazeny-Dorner, B. (2005). Do centenarians die healthy? An autopsy study. *Journals of Gerontology, Series A: Biological Sciences and Medical Sciences, 60*, 862–865.

Binstock, R. (1983). The aged as scapegoats. *Gerontologist, 23*, 136–143.

Blazer, D. (1990). *Emotional problems in later life.* New York: Springer.

Blieszner, R., & Bedford, V. H. (1995). The family context of aging: Trends and challenges. In R. Blieszner & V. H. Bedford (Eds.), *Handbook of aging and the family.* Westport, CT: Greenwood.

Bliwise, N. (1987). The epidemiology of mental illness in late life. In E. Lurie and J. Swan (Eds.), *Serving the mentally ill elderly* (pp. 179–202). Lexington, MA: D.C. Health.

Block, J. H., & Block, J. (1980). The role of ego-control and ego-resiliency in the organization of behavior. In W. A. Collins (Ed.), *Minnesota symposia on child psychology* (pp. 39–101). Hillsdale, NJ: Lawrence Erlbaum Associates.

Blouin, A. S., & Brent, N. J. (1996). Downsizing and potential discrimination based on age. *Journal of Nursing Administrators, 26* (11), 3–5.

Botkin, D. R.; Weeks, M. O.; & Morris, J. E. (2000). Changing marriage role expectations, 1961–1996. *Sex Roles, 42* (9), 933–942.

Boudreau, J. W., Boswell, W. R., & Judge, T. A. (2001). Effects of personality on executive career success in the United States and Europe. *Journal of Vocational Behavior, 58,* 53–81.

Bould, S.; Sanborn, B.; & Reif, L. (1989). *Eighty-five plus: The oldest old.* Belmont, CA: Wadsworth.

Bowen, J.; Teri, L.; Kukull, W.; McCormick, W.; McCurry, S. M.; & Larson, E. B. (1997). Progression to dementia in patients with isolated memory loss. *Lancet, 349,* 763–765.

Bowling, A. (1997). The effects of illness on quality of life: Findings from a survey of households in Great Britain. *Journal of Epidemiology and Community Health, 50,* 149–155.

Bowling, A.; Grundy, E.; & Farquhar, M. (1995). Changes in network composition among the very old living in inner London. *Journal of Cross-Cultural Gerontology, 10,* 331–347.

Boxer, A. M. (1997). Gay, lesbian, and bisexual aging into the twenty-first century: An overview and introduction. *Journal of Gay, Lesbian, and Bisexual Identity, 2* (3/4), 187–193.

Boynton, S. (1993, March 22). Aging boomers! The graying of a generation. *Santa Rosa Press Democrat,* B1.

Brackley, M. H. (1994). The plight of American family caregivers: Implications for nursing. *Perspectives in Psychiatric Care, 30* (4), 14–20.

Brandtstadter, J. (1999). Sources of resilience in the aging self: Toward integrating perspectives. In T. M. Hess & F. Blanchard-Fields (Eds.), *Social cognition and aging* (pp. 123–141). San Diego: Academic Press.

Braus, P. (1994, June). Groceries over grandchildren. *American Demography,* 33.

Brecher, E. (1984). *Love, sex and aging: A Consumers' Union report.* Boston: Little, Brown.

Brecht, S. B. (1996). Trends in the retirement housing industry. *Urban Land, 55* (11), 32–39.

Bretschneider, J., & McCoy, N. (1988). Sexual interest and behavior in healthy 80 to 102 year olds. *Archives of Sexual Behavior, 17* (2), 102–129.

Brignolo, D. (1998, March 10). Investment fiasco ends in sentencing. *San Jose Mercury News,* 1B.

Brody, E. (1984). Caregivers, daughters and their local siblings: Perceptions, strains, and interactions. *Gerontologist, 29* (4), 529–538.

Brody, E. (1985). *Women in the middle: Their parent care years.* New York: Springer.

Brown, A. (1990). *Social processes of aging and old age.* Englewood Cliffs, NJ: Prentice-Hall.

Brown, A. S., & Nix, L. A. (1996). Age-related changes in tip-of-the-tongue experience. *American Journal of Psychology, 109* (1), 79–91.

Brown, P. L. (2000, August 24). Raising more than consciousness now. *New York Times,* www.nytimes.com/library/home/082400thea-group.html, accessed May 12, 2006.

Brown, R. (1993). Do health maintenance organizations work for Medicare? *Health Care Financing Review, 15* (1), 7–24.

Bryant, H., & Fernald, L. (1997). Nursing knowledge and use of restraint alternatives: Acute and chronic care. *Geriatric Nursing, 18* (2), 57–60.

Buckwalter, J. A. (1997). Decreased mobility in the elderly: The exercise antidote. *Physician and Sportsmedicine, 25* (9), 127–133.

Buckwalter, J. A.; Woo, S. L.; & Goldberg, V. M. (1993). Current concepts review: Soft-tissue aging and musculoskeletal function. *Journal of Bone and Joint Surgery, 75* (10), 1533–1548.

Buckwalter, K.; Smith, M.; & Martin, M. (1993). Attitude problem. *Nursing Times, 89* (5), 54–57.

Buhrich, N., & Teesson, M. (1996). Impact of a psychiatric outreach service for homeless persons with schizophrenia. *Psychiatric Services, 47* (6), 644–646.

Bureau of Justice Statistics. (1992). *Criminal victimization in the United States, 1991.* Washington, DC: US Government Printing Office.

Bureau of Justice Statistics. (2000). *Criminal victimization in the United States, 1999: The National Crime Victimization Survey.* NCJ-174446.

Burger, J. M.; Horita, M.; Kinoshita, L.; Roberts, K.; & Vera, C. (1997). Effects of time on the norm of reciprocity. *Basic and Applied Social Psychology, 19* (1), 91–100.

Burgess, E. W. (1960). *Aging in Western societies.* Chicago: University of Chicago Press.

Burke, J. L. (1981). Young children's attitudes and perceptions of older adults. *International Journal of Aging and Human Development, 14,* 205–221.

Burkhauser, R. V. (1996). Editorial: Touching the third rail; Time to return the retirement age for early social security benefits to 65. *Gerontologist, 36* (6), 726–727.

Burkhauser, R. V.; Couch, K. A.; & Phillips, J. W. (1996). Who takes early Social Security benefits? The economic and health characteristics of early beneficiaries. *Gerontologist, 36* (6), 789–799.

Burl, M. R. (1993). *Hunger among the elderly: Local and national comparisons.* Washington, DC: Urban Institute.

Burnette, D. (1999). Grandparents rearing grandchildren: A school-based small group intervention. *Research on Social Work Practice, 8* (1), 10–27.

Busan, T. (1991). *Use your perfect memory.* New York: Plume Division, Penguin Books.

Butler, R. (1969). Ageism: Another form of bigotry. *Gerontologist, 9,* 243–246.

Butler, R. (1975). *Why survive?* New York: Harper & Row.

Butler, R. N. (1963). The life review: An interpretation of reminiscence in the aged. *Psychiatry, 26,* 65–76.

Butler, R. N. (1981). Ageism: A forward. *Journal of Social Issues, 36,* 8–11.

Butler, R. N. (1994). *Love and Sex after 60.* New York: Ballantine.

Butler, S. S., & DePoy, E. (1996). Rural elderly women's attitudes toward professional and governmental assistance. *AFFILIA, 11* (1), 76–94.

Byock, I. (1996). *Dying Well*. New York: Riverhead.

Cahill, S.; South, K.; & Spade, J. (2001). *Outing age: Public policy issues affecting gay, lesbian, bisexual and transgender elders*. New York: Policy Institute of the National Gay and Lesbian Task Force.

Calabrese, R. L., & Barton, A. M. (1995). Mexican-American male students and Anglo female teachers: Victims of the policies of assimilation. *High School Journal, 78* (3), 115–123.

Camp, C., & Camp, G. (1996). *The corrections yearbook*. South Salem, NY: Criminal Justice Institute.

Carr, M. (1997). Not at your age! *Accountancy: International Edition, 41,* 4.

Carstensen, L.; Mason, S. E.; & Caldwell, E. C. (1982). Children's attitudes toward the elderly: An intergenerational technique for change. *Educational Gerontology, 8,* 291–301.

Carstensen, L. L.; Gross, J. J.; & Fung, H. H. (1997). The social context of emotional experience. In K. W. Schaie & M. P. Lawton (Eds.), *Annual review of gerontology and geriatrics, vol. 17* (pp. 325–352). New York: Springer.

Cassel, C. K. (1996). Overview on attitudes of physicians toward caring for the dying patient. In American Board of Internal Medicine (Ed.), *Caring for the dying: Identification and promotion of physician competency.* Washington, DC: AMA.

Cavanaugh, J., & Blanchard-Fields, F. (2006). *Adult development and aging* (5th ed.). Belmont, CA: Wadsworth/Thomson Learning.

Centers for Disease Control and Prevention. (1996). *Suicide among older persons: United States, 1980–1992.* U.S. Department of Health and Human Services *MMWR, 45* (1), 3–6.

Ceridian, Control Data Systems settle age bias lawsuits (1997, March 6). *Wall Street Journal*, P13.

Chappell, N. (1991). Living arrangements and sources of caregiving. *Journals of Gerontology, 46* (1), S1–S8.

Chatard, J.-C.; Boutet, C.; Tourny, C.; Garcia, S.; Berthouze, S.; & Guezennec, C.-Y. (1998). Social comparison, self-stereotyping, and gender differences in self-construals. *European Journal of Applied Physiology, 77* (1–2), 157–163.

Cherlin, A. J., & Furstenberg, F. F., Jr. (1994). Stepfamilies in the United States: A reconsideration. *Annual Review of Sociology, 20,* 359–381.

Chestnut, C. H.; McClung, M. R.; & Ensrud, K. E. (1995). Alendronate treatment of the postmenopausal osteoporotic woman: Effect of multiple dosages on bone mass and bone remodeling. *American Journal of Medicine, 99,* 144–152.

Chew, S. C. (1962). *The pilgrimage of life*. New Haven, CT: Yale University Press.

Chodzko-Zajko, W. (1997). Translating theory in practice: A formidable challenge for the future. *Journal of Aging and Physical Activity, 5,* 283–284.

Choi, N. G. (1994a). Changes in labor force activities and income of the elderly before and after retirement: A longitudinal analysis. *Journal of Sociology and Social Welfare, 21* (2), 5–26.

Choi, N. G. (1994b). Pattern and determinants of social service utilization: Comparison of the childless elderly and elderly parents living with or apart from their children. *Gerontologist, 34* (3), 353–362.

Choi, N. G. (1996). Changes in the living arrangements, work patterns, and economic status of middle-aged single women, 1971–1991. *Affilia, 11* (2), 164–178.

Choi, N. G., & Wodarski, J. S. (1996). The relationship between social support and health status of elderly people: Does social support slow down physical and functional deterioration? *Social Work Research, 20* (1), 52–63.

Christy, M. (1993, April 15). At 71 she's still a Cosmo girl. *Santa Rosa Press Democrat*, D1.

Cicirelli, V. G. (1981). Kin relationships of childless and one-child elderly in relation to social services. *Journal of Gerontological Social Work, 4* (1), 19–33.

Cicirelli, V. G. (1997). Relationship of psychosocial and background variables to older adults' end-of-life decisions. *Psychology and Aging, 12* (1), 137–151.

Clark, D. E.; Knapp, T. A.; & White, N. E. (1996, Summer). Personal and location-specific characteristics and elderly interstate migration. *Growth and Change, 27,* 327–351.

Cloninger, S. C. (1996). *Theories of personality: Understanding persons* (2nd ed.). Newark, NJ: Prentice Hall.

Cohen, C. I. (1999). Aging and homelessness. *Gerontologist, 39,* 5–14.

Cohen, E., & Kruschwitz, A. (1990). Old age in America represented in nineteenth- and twentieth-century popular sheet music. *Gerontologist, 30* (3), 345–354.

Cohen, G., & Taylor, S. (1997). Reminiscence and ageing. *Ageing and Society, 18,* 601–610.

Cohen, G. D. (1988). Psychopathology and mental health in the mature and elderly adult. In J. E. Birren and K. W. Schaie (Eds.), *Handbook of the Psychology of Aging*, (3rd ed.), San Diego: Academic Press.

Cohen, H. J. (1997). Cancer and the functional status of the elderly. *Cancer, 80* (10), 1883–1886.

Cohen, J.; Fihn, S.; & Boyko, E. E. A. (1994). Attitudes toward assisted suicide and euthanasia among physicians in Washington State. *New England Journal of Medicine, 331* (2), 89–94.

Cohn, L. D., & Adler, N. E. (1992). Female and male perceptions of ideal body shapes. *Psychology of Women Quarterly, 16,* 69–79.

Colburn, D. (1987, April 14). Facing the certainty of death. *Washington Post*, 16.

Cole, T. (1992). *The journey of life: A cultural history of aging in America*. New York: Cambridge University Press.

Collins, C., & Frantz, D. (1994, June). Let us prey: Cults and the elderly. *Modern Maturity,* 22–26.

Colsher, P. L.; Wallace, R. B.; Loeffelholz, P. L.; & Sales, M. (1992, June). Health status of older male prisoners. *American Journal of Public Health, 82* (6), 881–884.

Comfort, A. (1976, November–December). Age prejudice in America. *Social Policy, 7* (3), 3–8.

Commonwealth Fund. (1993, November). *The untapped resource: Americans over 55 at work.* New York: Commonwealth Fund.

Congressional Budget Office. (1993). *Displaced workers: Trends in the 1980s and implications for the future.* Washington, DC: Congress of the United States.

Connidis, I. (1994). Sibling support in old age. *Journal of Gerontology, 49,* 5309–5317.

Connidis, I., & Campbell, L. D. (1995). Closeness, confiding, and contact among siblings in middle and late adulthood. *Journal of Family Issues, 16* (6), 722–745.

Connidis, I. A., & Rosenthal, C. J. (1996). The impact of family composition on providing help to older parents, *Research on Aging, 18* (4), 402.

Cook, E. A. (1997). The effects of reminiscence on psychological measures of ego integrity in elderly nursing home residents. *Archives of Psychiatric Nursing, 5* (5), 292–298.

Cooley, C. H. (1902). *Human nature and the social order.* New York: Charles Scribner's Sons.

Cooper, M. H. (1998). Caring for the elderly. *Congressional Quarterly, 8* (7), 147–166.

Corbin, D. E.; Metal-Corbin, J.; & Barg, C. (1989). Teaching about aging in the elementary school: A one-year follow-up. *Educational Gerontology, 15,* 103–110.

Corder, E. H.; Saundres, A. M.; & Strittmatter, W. J. (1993). Gene dose of apolipoprotein E type 4 allele and the risk of Alzheimer's disease in late onset families. *Science, 261,* 921–923.

Costa, P. T., & McCrae, R. R. (1987). The case for personality stability. In G. Maddox & E. Busse (Eds.), *Aging: The universal human experience.* New York: Springer.

Costa, P. T.; Metter, E. J.; & McCrae, R. R. (1994). Personality stability and its contribution to successful aging. *Journal of Gerontological Psychology, 27* (1), 41–59.

Council on Scientific Affairs. (1996). American Medical Association Council report: Alcoholism in the elderly. *Journal of the American Medical Association, 275* (10), 797–801.

Coupland, N.; Coupland, J.; & Giles, H. (1991). *Language, society and the elderly.* Oxford: Basil Blackwell.

Courneya, K. S. (1995). Understanding readiness for regular physical activity in older individuals: An application of the theory of planned behavior. *Health Psychology, 14* (1), 80–87.

Courtenay, B. C.; Poon, L. W.; Martin, P.; Clayton, G. M.; & Johnson, M. A. (1992). Religiosity and adaptation in the oldest-old. *International Journal of Aging and Human Development, 34* (1), 47–56.

Couzin, J., & Vogel, H. (2004). Renovating the heart. *Science, 304* (5668), 192–194.

Covey, H. C. (1988). Historical terminology used to represent older people. *Gerontologist, 28,* 291–297.

Covey, H. C. (1991). Old age and historical examples of the miser. *Gerontologist, 31* (5), 573–678.

Coward, R. T.; Cutler, S. J.; Lee, G. R.; Danigelis, N. L.; & Netzer, J. (1996). Racial differences in the household composition of elders by age, gender, and area of residence. *International Journal of Aging and Human Development, 42* (3), 205–227.

Cowgill, D. (1974). Aging and modernization: A revision of the theory. In J. F. Gubrium (Ed.,), *Late life communities and environmental policy.* Springfield, IL: Charles C. Thomas.

Cowgill, D. (1986). *Aging around the world.* Belmont, CA: Wadsworth.

Cowley, M. (1980). *The view from eighty.* New York: Viking Press.

Crandall, R. C. (1980). *Gerontology: A behavioral approach.* Reading, MA: Addison-Wesley.

Crane, M. (1994). Elderly homeless people: Elusive subjects and slippery concepts. *Ageing and Society, 14,* 631–640.

Crenshaw, A. (1992, September 27). Living trusts lure some people not to be trusted. *Washington Post,* H3.

Crispell, D. (1993, September 13). Rank of older wives swell in work force. *Wall Street Journal,* B1 (W), B11 (E).

Crockett, W., & Hummert, M. L. (1987). Perceptions of aging and the elderly. In B. A. Maher (Ed.), *Progress in experimental personality research* (vol. 2, pp. 217–241). New York: Academic Press.

Cronk, M. (1998, March 21). Thief poses as Cupertino City worker, steals cash. *San Jose Mercury News,* 2B.

Crystal, S., & Beck, P. (1992, October). A room of one's own: The SRO and the single elderly. *Gerontologist, 32* (5), 684–692.

Cumming, E., & Henry, W. E. (1961). *Growing old: The process of disengagement.* New York: Basic Books.

Cummins, R. A. (1996). The domains of life satisfaction: An attempt to order chaos. *Social Indicators Research, 38,* 303–328.

Cunningham, C. M.; Callahan, C. M.; Plucker, J. A.; Roberson, S. C.; & Rapkin, A. (1998). Identifying Hispanic students of outstanding talent: Psychometric integrity of a peer nomination form. *Exceptional Children, 645* (2), 197–209.

Cutler, N. R.; Sramek, J. J.; & Frankiewicz, E. J. (1997). Efficacy and safety of two dosing regiments of buspirone in the treatment of outpatients with persistent anxiety. *Clinical Therapeutics: The International Peer-Reviewed Journal of Drug Therapy, 19* (3), 498–506.

Cyr, D. (1996). Lost and found: Retired employees. *Personnel Journal, 75* (11), 40–46.

Darbonne, A. R. (1969). Suicide and age: A suicide note analysis. *Journal of Consulting and Clinical Psychology, 33,* 46–50.

D'Augelli, A. R., & Garnets, L. D. (1995). Lesbian, gay, and bisexual communities. In A. R. D'Augelli & C. J. Patterson (Eds.), *Lesbian, gay and bisexual identities over the lifespan: Psychological perspectives.* New York: Oxford University Press.

Daniels, W. (1997). "Derelicts," recurring misfortunate, economic hard times and lifestyle choices: Judicial images of homeless litigants and implications for legal advocates. *Buffalo Law Review, 45* (3), 687–736.

Dannefer, D., & Uhlenberg, P. (1999). Paths of the life course: A typology. In V. L. Bengston & K.W. Schaie (Eds.), *Handbook of theories of aging* (pp. 306–326). New York: Springer.

Davidson, M.; Harvey, P. D.; Powchick, P.; Parrella, M.; White, L.; Knobler, H. Y.; Losonczy, M. F.; Keefe, R. S.; Katz, S.; & Frecska, E. (1995). Severity of symptoms in chronically institutionalized geriatric schizophrenic patients. *American Journal of Psychiatry, 152,* 197–207.

Dawson, K. (1982). *Serving the older community.* Sex Education and Information Council of the United States, SIECUS Report.

Day, N. E. (1993). Performance in salespeople: The impact of age. *Journal of Managerial Issues, 5,* 254–278.

Debats, D. L.; van der Lubbe, P. M.; & Wezeman, F. R. A. (1993). On the psychometric properties of the Life Regard Index (LRI): A measure of meaningful life. An evaluation in three independent samples based on the Dutch version. *Personality and Individual Differences, 14,* 337–345.

Delany, S. L., & Hearth, A. H. (1997). *On my own at 107: Reflections on life without Bessie.* San Francisco: Harper.

Dench, G.; Ogg, J.; & Thompson, K. (1999). The role of grandparents. In R. Jowell (Ed.), *British social attitudes: The 16th report* (pp. 136–156). Ashgate, UK: National Centre for Social Research.

Denis, M. (1996). Implications of offering early retirement benefits in exchange for a release from employment claims. *Employment Relations Today, 23* (3), 65–69.

Denney, N. W., & Palmer, A. A. M. (1987). Adult age differences in traditional and practical problem solving measures. *Psychology and Aging, 4,* 438–442.

DeParle, J. (1994). Build single room occupancy hotels. *Washington Monthly,* 52–53.

D'Epiro, N. W. (1996, November). Treating Alzheimer's disease: Today and tomorrow. *Patient Care,* 62–83.

De Rijk, M. C.; Breteler, M. M. B.; Graveland, G. A.; Ott, A.; Grobbee, D. E.; van der Meche, F. G. A.; & Hofman, A. (1995). Prevalence of Parkinson's disease in the elderly: The Rotterdam study. *Neurology, 45,* 2143–2146.

DeSpelder, L. A., & Strickland, D. L. (1991). *The last dance.* Mountain View, CA: Mayfield Press.

Devitt, T. (1991, September/October). Staying young. *On Wisconsin Magazine,* 21–26.

Devlin, S. J., & Arye, L. (1997). The Social Security debate: A financial crisis or a new retirement paradigm? *Generations, 21* (2), 27–33.

Devons, C. A. J. (1996). Suicide in the elderly: How to identify and treat patients at risk. *Geriatrics, 51* (3), 67–72.

DeVries, H. (1991, December 8). An interview with Cher. *San Francisco Chronicle,* Datebook, 37.

Diamond, T. H.; Thornley, S. W.; Sekel, R.; & Smeraely, P. (1997). Hip fracture in elderly men: Prognostic factors and outcomes. *Medical Journal of Australia, 167* (8), 412–415.

Dion, K. K., & Dion, K. L. (1996) Cultural perspectives on romantic love. *Personal Relationships, 3* (1), 5–7.

Dolliver, R. H. (1994). Classifying the personality theories and personalities of Adler, Freud, and Jung with introversion/extraversion. *Individual Psychology, 50* (2), 192–202.

Dolnick, E. (1991, July 16). The mystery of superwoman. *San Francisco Chronicle,* 3–8.

Dorfman, R. (1994). *Aging into the 21st century: The exploration of aspirations and values.* New York: Brunner/Mazel.

Dowd, J. (1984). Beneficence and the aged. *Journal of Gerontology, 39,* 102–108.

Dowd, J. J. (1975). Aging as exchange: A preface to theory. *Journal of Gerontology, 30,* 584–594.

Downe-Wamboldt, B. L., & Melanson, P. M. (1990). Attitudes of baccalaureate student nurses toward aging and the aged: Results of a longitudinal study. *Educational Gerontology, 16,* 49–57.

Drench, M. E. & Losee, R. H. (1996). Sexuality and sexual capacities of elderly people. *Rehabilitation Nursing, 21* (3), 118–123.

Drew, L. A., & Smith, P. K. (1999). The impact of parental separation/divorce on grandparent-grandchild relationships. *International Journal of Aging and Human Development, 48,* 191–216.

Drozdiak, W. (1994, May 3). Elderly Dutch reach for political power in "granny revolution." *Washington Post,* A16.

Duff, C. (1994, April 6). These big clocks actually are made by grandfathers. *Wall Street Journal,* A1(W), A1(E).

Duffield, P., & Podzamsky, J. E. (1996). The completion of advance directives in primary care. *Journal of Family Practice, 42* (4), 378–383.

Duffy, J. M. (1987). The measurement of service productivity and related contextual factors in long-term care facilities. Unpublished Ph.D. diss., University of Texas, Austin.

Dullea, S. (1986, 10 February). When the aged start to steal. *New York Times,* B12.

Dychtwald, K. (1989). *Age wave.* Los Angeles: Tarcher.

Ekstrom, M. (1994). Elderly people's experiences of housing renewal and forced relocation: Social theories and contextual analysis in explanations of emotional experiences. *Housing Studies, 9* (3), 369–391.

Elder, G., & Liker, J. (1982). Hard times in women's lives: Historical influences across forty years. *American Journal of Sociology,* 241–267.

Elder, G. H. (1979). Historical patterns and personality. In P. B. Baltes & O. G. Brim, Jr. (Eds.), *Life-span development and behavior,* vol. 2. New York: Academic Press.

Elder, G. H., & O'Rand, A. M. (1994). Adult lives in a changing society. In K. Cook, G. Fine, & J. S. House (Eds.), *Sociological perspectives on social psychology* (pp. 102–121). New York: Basic.

Emerson, R. W. (1878). The sovereignty of ethics. Reprinted from the *North American Review, 10,* 12.

Encandela, J. A. (1997). Social construction of pain and aging: Individual artfulness within interpretive structures. *Symbolic Interaction, 20* (3), 251–273.

Ensrud, K. E.; Lipschutz, R. C.; Cauley, J. A.; Seeley, D.; Nevitt, M. C.; Scott, J.; Orwoll, E. S.; Genant, H. K.; & Cummings, S. R. (1997). Body size and hip fracture risk in older women: A prospective study. *American Journal of Medicine, 103* (4), 274–280.

Erikson, E. (1963). *Childhood and society* (2d ed.). New York: Norton.

Erikson, E. (1966). Eight ages of man. *International Journal of Psychiatry, 2,* 281–297.

Erikson, E. (1982). *The life cycle completed.* New York: W. W. Norton.

Estes, C. L. (1983). Austerity and aging in the US: 1980 and beyond. In A. Guillemard (Ed.), *Old age and the welfare state.* Beverly Hills: Sage.

Estes, C. L. (1991). The new political economy of aging: Introduction and critique. In M. Minkler & C. L. Estes (Eds.), *Critical perspectives on aging: The political and moral economy of growing old.* New York: Baywood.

Estes, P. (1992). *Women who run with the wolves.* New York: Ballentine.

Estrada, L. (1994, May 9). At the dawn of assisted living centers. *Washington Post,* WB11.

Euler, B. (1992). A flaw in gerontological assessment: The weak relationship of elderly superficial life satisfaction to deep psychological well being. *International Journal of Aging and Human Development, 34,* 299–310.

Evans, M. (1998, March 27). Caregiving daughters suffer stress. *Santa Rosa Press Democrat,* A13.

Evans, W., & Rosenberg, I. H. (1991). *Biomarkers: The 10 determinants of aging you can control.* New York: Simon & Schuster.

Featherman, D. L.; Smith, J.; & Peterson, J. G. (1990). Successful aging in a 'post-retired' society. In P. B. Baltes & M. M. Baltes (Eds.), *Successful aging: Perspectives from the behavioral sciences* (pp. 50–93). New York: Cambridge University Press.

Feder, J.; Lambrew, J.; & Huckaby, M. (1997). Medicaid and long-term care for the elderly: Implications of restructuring. *Milbank Quarterly, 75* (4), 425–459.

Fehring, R. J.; Miller, J. F.; & Shaw, C. (1997). Spiritual well-being, religiosity, hope, depression, and other mood states in elderly people coping with cancer. *Oncology Nursing Forum, 24* (4), 663–671.

Feinberg, Richard J. (1997). Adaptation to mortality at the stage of integrity vs. despair: A case for synthesis of psychoanalytic and existential perspectives on the nature of maturity in later years. *Journal of Aging and Identity, 2* (1), 37–58.

Feldman, P. (1993). Work life improvements for home care workers: Impact and feasibility. *Gerontologist,* 47–54.

Feldstein, I. (1970). *Sex in later life.* Baltimore, MD: Penguin.

Feldstein, M. (1997). The case for privatization. *Foreign Affairs, 76* (4), 24–38.

Field, D. (1991). Continuity and change in personality in old age: Evidence from five longitudinal studies. Special issue, introduction. *Journal of Gerontology: Psychological Sciences, 46* (6), P271–274.

Field, D. (1993, November). Looking back, what period of your life brought you the most satisfaction? Paper presented to the Annual Gerontological Society meeting, New Orleans, LA, November.

Finch, C. E., & Pike, M. C. (1996). Maximum life span predictions for the Gompertz mortality model. *Journal of Gerontology, Biological Sciences, 51A* (3), B183–B194.

Fired executive sues Apple. (1993, September 27). *Washington Post,* NB17.

Fischer, D. H. (1977). *Growing old in America.* New York: Oxford University Press.

Fisk, J. E., & Warr, P. (1996). Age and working memory: The role of perceptual speed, the central executive, and the phonological loop. *Psychology and Aging, 11* (2), 316–323.

Fiske, M., & Chiriboga, D. (1990). *Change and continuity in adult life.* San Francisco, CA: Jossey-Bass.

Fleeson, W., & Heckhausen, J. (1997). More or less "me" in past, present, and future: Perceived lifetime personality during adulthood. *Psychology and Aging, 12* (1), 125–136.

Foley, K. T., & Mitchell, S. J. (1997). The elderly driver: What physicians need to know. *Cleveland Clinic Journal of Medicine, 64* (8), 423–428.

Foner, A. (1996). Age norms and the structure of consciousness: Some final comments. *Gerontologist, 36* (2), 221–223.

Forrester, J. S., & Shah, P. (1997). Using serum cholesterol as a screening test for preventing coronary heart disease: The five fundamental flaws of the American College of Physicians' guidelines. *American Journal of Cardiology, 79* (6), 790–792.

Fowles, D. G. (1995). *A profile of older Americans, 1995.* Washington, DC: American Association of Retired Persons and U.S. Department of Health and Human Services Administration on Aging.

Francheschi, C.; Motta, L.; Valensin, S.; Rapisarda, R.; Franzone, A.; Berardelli, M.; Motta, M.; Moni, D.; Bonafe, M.; et al. (2000). Do men and women follow different trajectories to reach extreme longevity? Italian multicenter study on centenarians. *Aging, 12* (2), 77–84.

Freeman, V. A. (2000). Aggregate changes in severe cognitive impairment among older Americans: 1993 and 1998. *Journals of Gerontology: Psychological Sciences and Social Sciences, 56B* (2), S100–111.

Friend, R. A. (1987). The relationship between group cohesion and the development of pluralism in sexual attitudes as a function of the small group component of SAR seminars. *Dissertation Abstracts International, 47* (7-A), 2466–2467.

Frolik, L. A. (1996). The special housing needs of older persons: An essay. *Stetson Law Review, 26* (2), 647–666.

Frost, J. C. (1997). Group psychotherapy with the aging gay male: Treatment of choice. *Group, 21* (3), 267–285.

Fry, P. S. (2003). Perceived self-efficacy domains as predictors of fear of the unknown and fear of dying among older adults. *Psychology and Aging, 18* (3), 74–82.

Fuller-Thomson, E.; Minkler, M.; & Driver, D. (1997). A profile of grandparents raising grandchildren in the United States. *Gerontologist, 37* (3), 406–411.

Fullmer, H. T. (1984). Children's descriptions of an attitude toward the elderly. *Educational Gerontology, 10,* 22–107.

Gall, T. L.; Evans, D. R.; & Howard, J. (1997). The retirement adjustment process: Changes in the well-being of male retirees across time. *Journal of Gerontology: Psychological Sciences, 52B* (3), P110–P117.

Gamliel, T. (2001). Social version of gerotranscendence: Case study. *Journal of Aging and Identity, 6* (2), 105–114.

Garber, A. M.; Browner, W. S.; & Hulley, S. B. (1996). Cholesterol screening in asymptomatic adults, revisited. *Annals of Internal Medicine, 1224,* 518–531.

Garfein, A. J., & Herzog, R. A. (1995). Robust aging among the young-old, old-old, and oldest-old. *Journal of Gerontology, 50B* (2), 577–587.

Garrard, J.; Cooper, S. L.; & Goertz, C. (1997). Drug use management in board and care facilities. *Gerontologist, 37* (6), 748–756.

George, L. K. (2005). Socioeconomic status and health across the life course: Progress and prospects. *Journals of Gerontology: Series B, Special Issue: Health Inequalities across the Life Course,* 135–139.

Gerstner, C. R. & Day, D. V. (1997). Meta-analytic review of leader-member exchange theory: Correlates and construct issues. *Journal of Applied Psychology, 82* (6), 827–844.

Geyelin, M. (1994, May 17). Age bias verdict. *Wall Street Journal,* B7(W), B5(E).

Gibson, R. (1993). Reconceptualizing retirement for black Americans. In E. Stoller & R. Gibson (Eds.), *Worlds of difference.* Thousand Oaks, CA: Pine Forge Press.

Gilderbloom & Mullins. (1995).

Ginsburg, K., & Heinemann, A. W. (1989). Alcohol use and activity patterns following spinal cord injury. *Rehabilitation Psychology, 34* (3), 191–205.

Glascock, A. P. (1997). When is killing acceptable: The moral dilemma surrounding assisted suicide in America and other societies. In J. Sokolovsky (Ed.), *The cultural context of aging* (3rd ed.). Westport, CT: Bergin & Garvey.

Glasheen, L. (1994, June). Mobile homes. *Bulletin of the American Association of Retired Persons,* 1–16.

Glass, J. C., Jr., & Jolly, G. R. (1997). Satisfaction in later life among women 60 or older. *Educational Gerontology 23,* 297–314.

Glazer, B., & Strauss, A. (1996). *Awareness of dying.* Chicago: Aldine.

Glen, N. D., & Weaver, C. N. (1983–1984). Enjoyment of work by full-time workers in the US, 1955–1980. *Public Opinion Quarterly, 46,* 459–470.

Gliksman, M. D.; Lazarus, R.; Wilson, A.; & Leeder, S. R. (1995). Social support, marital status and living arrangement correlates of cardiovascular disease risk factors in the elderly. *Social Science and Medicine, 40* (6), 811–814.

Goering, P.; Wasylenki, D.; Lindsay, C.; Lemire, D.; & Rhodes, A. (1997). Process and outcome in a hostel outreach program for homeless clients with severe mental illness. *American Journal of Orthopsychiatry, 67* (4), 607–617.

Golant, S. M. (1994). Housing quality of U.S. elderly households: Does aging in place matter? *Gerontologist, 34* (6), 803–814.

Golant, S. M., & LaGreca, A. J. (1994). Differences in the housing quality of white, black, and Hispanic US elderly households. *Journal of Applied Gerontology, 13* (4), 413–437.

Golberg, L.; Gallagher, T. C.; Anderson, R. M.; & Koegel, P. (1997). Competing priorities as a barrier to medical care among homeless adults in Los Angeles. *American Journal of Public Health, 87,* 217–221.

Gold, D. P.; Andres, D.; Etezadi, J.; Arbuckle; T., Schwartzman; A., & Chikelson, J. (1995). Structural equation model of intellectual change and continuity and predictors of intelligence in older men. *Psychology and Aging, 10* (2), 294–303.

Gold, D. T.; Woodbury, M. A.; George, L. K. (1990, March). Relationship classification using grade of membership analysis: A typology of sibling relationships in later life. *Journal of Gerontology, 45* (2), S43–51.

Goldbourt, U. (1997). Physical activity, long-term CHD, mortality and longevity: A review of studies over the last 30 years. *World Review of Nutrition and Dietetics, 82,* 229–239.

Goldman, K. (1993, September 20). Seniors get little respect on Madison Avenue. *Wall Street Journal,* B8.

Goldman, N.; Korenman, S.; & Weinstein, R. (1995). Marital status and health among the elderly. *Social Science and Medicine, 40* (12), 1717–1730.

Goldman, R. J., & Goldman, J. D. (1981). How children view old people and aging: A developmental study of children in four countries. *Australian Journal of Psychology, 33* (3), 405–418.

Goldstein, K. (1980). *Language and language disturbances.* New York: Grune & Stratton.

Goldstein, M. Z.; Pataki, A.; & Webb, M. T. (1996). Alcoholism among elderly persons. *Psychiatric Services, 47* (9), 941–943.

Goronzy, J. (2004). Prognostic markers of radiographic progression in early rheumatoid arthritis. *Arthritis and Rheumatism, 50* (1), 43–54.

Gotthardt, M. (2005, March–April). Across the divide. *AARP: The Magazine,* 106.

Gould, R. L. (1978). *Transformations: Growth and change in adult life.* New York: Simon & Schuster.

Gouldner, A. (1960). The norm of reciprocity: A preliminary statement. *American Sociological Review, 25,* 161–178.

Graham, J. E.; Rockwood, K.; Beattie, B. L.; Eastwood, R.; Gauthier, S.; Tukko, H.; & McDowell, I. (1997). Prevalence and severity of cognitive impairment with and without dementia in an elderly population. *Lancet, 349,* 1793–1796.

Greco, A. J., & Swayne, L. E. (1999, September–October). Sales response of elderly consumers to point-of-purchase advertising. *Journal of Advertising Research,* 43–53.

Greenberg, J. S.; Seltzer, M. M.; & Greenley, J. R. (1993). Aging parents of adults with disabilities: The gratifications and frustrations of later-life caregiving. *Gerontologist, 33,* 542–550.

Greenhalgh, Trisha. (1997). I told you I was ill. *Accountancy, 119* (1241), 16.

Griffin, R. (1994). From sacred to secular. In L. E. Thomas and S. Eisenhandler (Eds.), *Aging and the religious dimension* (pp. 90–112). Westport, CT: Auburn House.

Gruen, R. J.; Silva, R.; Ehrlich, J.; Schweitzer, J. W.; & Friedhoff, A. J. (1997). Vulnerability to stress: Self-criticism and stress-induced changes in biochemistry. *Journal of Personality, 65* (1), 33–47.

Gubrium, J. F. (1975). *Living and dying at Murray Manor.* New York: St. Martin's Press.

Gubrium, J. F., & Holstein, J. A. (1995). Life course malleability: Biographical work and deprivatization. *Sociological Inquiry, 65* (2), 207–223.

Guilford, J. P. (1966). Intelligence: 1965 model. *American Psychologist, 21,* 20–26.

Guillemard, A.-M., & Rein, M. (1993). Comparative patterns of retirement: Recent trends in developed societies. *Annual Review of Sociology, 19,* 469–503.

Gutmann, D. L. (1977). The cross-cultural perspective: Notes toward a comparative psychology of aging. In J. E. Birren and K. W. Schaie (Eds.), *Handbook of the psychology of aging.* New York: Van Nostrand Reinhold.

Gutmann, D. L. (1987). *Reclaimed powers: Toward a new psychology of men and women in later life.* New York: Basic Books.

Gutmann, D. L. (1992). Toward a dynamic geropsychology. In J. Birren, M. Eagle, & D. Welitzky (Eds.), *Interface of psychoanalysis and psychology* (pp. 284–295). Washington, DC: American Psychological Association.

Guyotte, R. L. (1997). Generation gap: Filipinos, Filipino Americans and Americans, here and there, then and now. *Journal of American Ethnic History, 17* (1), 64–70.

Haas, C., & Selkoe, D. J. (1998). A technical KO of amyloid-β peptide. *Nature, 391* (2), 339–340.

Haber, C. (1983). *Beyond sixty-five: The dilemma of old age in America's past.* New York: Cambridge University Press.

Hagenaars, A., & de Vos, K. (1988). The definition and measurement of poverty. *Journal of Human Resources, 23,* 211–221.

Haight, B. K. (1996). Suicide risk in frail elderly people relocated to nursing homes. *Geriatric Nursing, 16* (5), 104–107.

Harman, D. (1995). Free radical theory of aging: Alzheimer's disease pathogenesis. *Age, 18* (3), 97–119.

Harris, E. (1996, September–October). Just quit! *Utne Reader,* 39–44.

Harris, M. B. (1994). Growing old gracefully: Age concealment and gender. *Journal of Gerontology: Psychological Sciences, 49,* 149–158.

Harris, P. (1993). The misunderstood caregiver? A qualitative study of the male caregiver. *Gerontologist, 32,* 551–556.

Hart, V., & Reed, G. (1990). *Living at home program service coordinators: A training and orientation guide.* San Francisco: San Francisco Living at Home Program Services for Seniors.

Hassell, B. L., & Perrewe, P. (1995). An examination of beliefs about older workers: Do stereotypes still exist? *Journal of Organizational Behavior, 16* (5), 457–468.

Havighurst, R. J. (1972). *Developmental tasks and education* (3rd ed.). New York: McKay.

Hawkins, B. A.; Kim, K.-A.; & Eklund, S. J. (1995). Validity and reliability of a five dimensional life satisfaction index. *Mental Retardation, 33* (5), 294–303.

Hayflick, L. (1985). The cell biology of aging. *Clinical Geriatric Medicine, 1* (1), 15–27.

Haynor, P. (1998). Meeting the challenge of advance directives. *American Journal of Nursing, 98* (3), 26–32.

Hays, C. D. (1987). Two worlds in conflict: The elderly Hmong in the United States. In D. Gelfard and C. Barresi (Eds.), *Ethnic dimensions of aging* (pp. 97–112). New York: Springer.

Hays, J. C.; Gold, D. T.; Pieper, C. F. (1997). Sibling bereavement in late life. *Omega, 36* (1), 25–42.

Hayslip, B.; Shore, J.; Henderson, C.; & Lambert, P. (1998). Custodial grandparenting and the impact of grandchildren with problems on role satisfaction and role meaning. *Journal of Gerontology, 53B* (3), S164–173.

Health Care Financing Administration. (1996). *1996 HCFA statistics.* Publication No. 03394. Washington, DC: Health Care Financing Administration.

Health Care Financing Administration. (1997). *1997 HCFA Statistics,* Washington, DC: Health Care Financing Administration.

Health Care Financing Administration. (2000). *2000 HCFA Statistics,* Washington, DC: Health Care Financing Administration.

Heath, J. M. (1993). Outpatient management of chronic bronchitis in the elderly. *American Family Physician, 48* (5), 841–848.

Heckhausen, J.; Dixon, R. A.; & Baltes, P. B. (1989). Losses in development throughout adulthood as perceived by different adult age groups. *Developmental Psychology, 25,* 109–121.

Heidrich, S. L., & Ryff, C. D. (1993). The role of social comparisons processes in the psychological adaptation of elderly adults. *Journal of Gerontology: Psychological Sciences, P48,* 127–136.

Hein, H. O.; Suadicani, P.; Sorensen, H.; & Gyntelberg, F. (1994). Changes in physical activity level and risk of ischemic heart disease. *Scandinavian Journal of Medicine and Science in Sports, 4,* 52–64.

Helson, R., & Roberts, B. W. (1994). Ego development and personality change in adulthood. *Journal of Personality and Social Psychology, 66,* 911–920.

Henderson, C. E. (2003). Grandparent-grandchild attachment as a predictor of psychological adjustment among youth from divorced families. *Dissertation Abstracts International, Section B: The Sciences and Engineering, 63* (9-B), 4371.

Hendricks, J. (1995). Exchange theory in aging. In G. Maddox (Ed.), *The encyclopedia of aging* (2nd ed.). New York: Springer.

Hensley, Wayne E. (1996). A theory of the valenced other: The intersection of the looking-glass-self and social penetration. *Social Behavior and Personality, 24* (3), 293–308.

Herdt, G.; Beeler, J.; & Rawls, T. (1997). Understanding the identities of older lesbians and gay men: A study in Chicago. *Journal of Gay, Lesbian, and Bisexual Identity, 2* (3–4), 231–245.

Hernandez, G. (1992). The family and its aged members: The Cuban experience. In T. Brink (Ed.), *Hispanic aged mental health.* Binghamton, NY: Haworth.

Hevesi, D. (1994, March 27). Anger wins out over fear of a gang. *New York Times,* 31 (L).

Heynen, J. (1990). *One hundred over 100.* Golden, CO: Fulcrum.

Hickey, N. (1990, 20 October). Its audience is aging—so why is TV still chasing the kids? *TV Guide,* 22–24.

Hillier, S. (2004). Classroom exercise: Journey through adulthood. Unpublished manuscript, Sonoma State University, California.

Hillman, J., & Stricker, G. (1996). Predictors of college students' knowledge of an attitudes toward elderly sexuality: The relevance of grandparental contact. *Educational Gerontology, 22,* 539–555.

Hilt, M. L., & Lipschultz, J. H. (1996). Broadcast news and elderly people: Attitudes of local television managers. *Educational Gerontology, 22,* 669–682.

Himes, C. L. (2001). Elderly Americans. *Population Bulletin,* 3–8.

Hinrichsen, G. (1985). The impact of age-concentrated, publicly-assisted housing on older people's social and emotional well-being. *Journal of Gerontology, 40,* 758–760.

Hobbs, F. B., & Damon, B. L. (1996). *65+ in the United States.* http://www.census.gov/prod/1/pop/p23-190/p23190-k.pdf, accessed May 21, 2006.

Hobbs, F. B., & Stoops, B. (2002). *65-Plus in the United States.* http://www.census.gov/prod/1/pop.pdf, assessed June 2, 2006.

Hoefler, J. (1994). *Deathright: Culture, medicine, politics and the right to die.* Boulder, CO: Westview Press.

Hogan, R., & Nicholson, R. A. (1988). The meaning of personality test scores. *American Psychologist, 43,* 621–626.

Holahan, C. J.; Holahan, C. K.; Moos, R. H.; & Brennan, P. (1995). Social support, coping, and depressive symptoms in a late-middle-aged sample of patients reporting cardiac illness. *Health Psychology, 14* (2), 152–163.

Holden, K. C. & Kuo, H.-H. D. (1996). Complex marital histories and economic well-being: The continuing legacy of divorce and widowhood as the HRS cohort approaches retirement. *Gerontologist, 36* (3), 383–390.

Holding, R. (1991, September 12). "Help! I've fallen" firm sued. *San Francisco Chronicle,* A19.

Holliday, R. (1996a). The current status of the protein error theory of aging. *Experimental Gerontology, 31* (4), 449–452.

Holliday, R. (1996b). The evolution of human longevity. *Perspectives in Biology and Medicine, 40* (1), 100–107.

Holmes, T., & Rahe, R. (1967). The Social Readjustment Rating Scale. *Journal of Psychosomatic Research,* 213–218.

Holstein, M. (1995). Qualitative gerontology: Methodology and meaning. *Research on Aging, 17* (1), 114–116.

Homeless Voices Page [Internet site maintained by the National Coalition for the Homeless]. http://nch.ari.net, accessed 1998.

Hong, L. K., & Duff, R. W. (1997). Relative importance of spouses, children and friends in the life satisfaction of retirement community residents. *Journal of Clinical Geropsychology, 3* (4), 275–282.

Hooker, K.; Frazier, L. D.; & Monahan, D. J. (1994). Personality and coping among caregivers of spouses with dementia. *Gerontologist,* 386–392.

Hooker, K., & Kaus, C. R. (1994). Health-related possible selves in young and middle adulthood. *Psychology and Aging, 9,* 126–133.

Hooyman, N. R., & Kiyak, H. A. (2002). *Social gerontology: A multidisciplinary perspective* (6th ed.). Boston, MA: Allyn & Bacon. (First published 1996.)

Horgan, J. (1997, May). Seeking a better way to die. *Scientific American,* 100–105.

Hosen, R. (1996). The benign comparison scale and its relevance to subjective well-being research. *Psychology: A Journal of Human Behavior, 33* (2), 63–67.

Hostetler, A. J., & Cohler, B. J. (1997). Partnership, singlehood, and the lesbian and gay life course: A research agenda. *Journal of Gay, Lesbian, and Bisexual Identity, 2* (3–4), 199–230.

Hoyert, D. L., & Rosenberg, H. M. (1997). Alzheimer's disease as a cause of death in the United States. *Public health reports, 112,* 497–505.

Huang, B.; Rodriguez, B. L.; Burchfiel, C. M.; Chyou, P.-H; Curb, J. D.; & Sharp, D. S. (1997). Associations of adiposity with prevalent coronary heart disease among elderly men: The Honolulu heart program. *International Journal of Obesity and Research, 21* (5), 340–348.

Hueston, W. J.; Mainous, A. G. III; & Schilling, R. (1996). Patients with personality disorders: Functional status, health care utilization, and satisfaction with care. *Journal of Family Practice, 42* (1), 54–60.

Hummert, M. L. (1995). Judgments about stereotypes of the elderly: Attitudes, age associations, and typicality ratings of young, middle-aged, and elderly adults. *Research on Aging, 17* (2), 168–189.

Hummert, M. L. (1999). A social cognitive perspective on age stereotypes. In T. M. Hess & F. Blanchard-Fields (Eds.), *Social cognition and aging* (pp. 175–196). San Diego: Academic Press.

Hummert, M. L.; Garetka, T. A.; Shaner, J. L.; & Strahm, S. (1994). Stereotypes of the elderly held by young, middle-aged, and elderly adults. *Journal of Gerontology: Psychological Sciences, P49*, P240–49.

Humphry, D. (1985). *Let me die before I wake.* Los Angeles: Hemlock Society and Grove Press.

Humphry, D. (1991). *Final exit.* New York: Dell Trade.

Huyck, M. H. (2001). Romantic relationships in later life. *Generations, 25* (2), 9–17.

Hwang, S. W.; Orav, E. J.; O'Connell, J. J.; Lebow, J. M.; & Brennan, T. A. (1997). Causes of death in homeless adults in Boston. *Annuals of Internal Medicine, 126*, 625–628.

IBM's Japan unit offers early retirement plan. (1993, February 19). *Wall Street Journal*, B12(W), B2(E).

Ikels, C. (1997). Long-term care and the disabled elderly in urban China. In J. Sokolovsky (Ed.), *The cultural context of aging* (3rd ed.). Westport, CT: Bergin & Garvey.

Intrieri, R. C.; Kelly, J. A.; Brown, M. M.; & Castilla, C. (1993). Improving medical students' attitudes toward and skills with the elderly. *Gerontologist, 33*, 373–378.

Italian Multicenter Study on Centenarians. (1997). Epidemiological and socioeconomic aspects of Italian centenarians. *Archives of Gerontology and Geriatrics, 25*, 149–157.

Jacob, M., & Guarnaccia, V. (1997). Motivational and behavioral correlates of life satisfaction in an elderly sample. *Psychological Reports, 80*, 811–818.

Jacobs, J. (1975). *Older persons and retirement communities: Case studies in social gerontology.* Springfield, IL: Charles C. Thomas.

Jacobs, R. (1994). *Be an outrageous older woman: ARASP.* Manchester, CT: Knowledge, Ideas and Trends.

Jail doctor wins age-bias settlement (1998, January 5). *New York Times*, A13.

James, G. (1994). Man is held in swindles of elderly. *New York Times*, 29, B3 (L).

James, J. B.; Lewkowicz, C.; Libhaber, J.; & Lachman, M. (1995). Rethinking the gender identity crossover hypothesis: A test of a new model. *Sex Roles, 32* (314), 185–207.

Jazwinski, S. M. (1996). Longevity, genes, and aging. *Science, 273*, 54–59.

Job applicants face age bias, study finds. (1994, February 23). *New York Times*, A7(N), A15(L).

Job, E. M. (1983). Retrospective life span analysis: A method for studying extreme old age. *Journal of Gerontology, 38*, 367–374.

Johansson, C.; Mellstrom, D.; Rosengren, K.; & Rundgren, A. (1993). A prevalence of vertebral fractures in 85 year olds. Radiological examination. *Acta Orthopedics of Scandinavia, 64*, 25–27.

John, R. (1991). Family support networks among elders in a Native American community: Contact with children and siblings among the Prairie Band Potawatomi. *Journal of Aging Studies, 5* (1), 45–59.

Johnson, C. L. (1996). Cultural diversity in the latelife family. In R. Blieszner & V. H. Bedford (Eds.), *Aging and the family: Theory and research* (pp. 218–223). Westport, CT: Praeger.

Joseph, J. (1997). Fear of crime among black elderly. *Journal of Black Studies, 27* (5), 698–717.

Jung, C. (1955). *Modern man in search of a soul.* San Diego, CA: Harcourt-Brace.

Jung, C. (1965). *Two essays on analytical psychology.* New York: Meridian. (First published 1916.)

Jung, C. G. (1959). *Aion: Researches into the phenomenology of the self* (2nd ed.; Trans. R. F. C. Hull). Princeton, NJ: Princeton University Press. (First published 1918.)

Kahana, E.; Redmond, C.; Hill, G. J.; Kercher, K.; Kahana, B.; Johnson, J. R.; & Young, R. F. (1995). The effects of stress, vulnerability and appraisals on the psychological well-being of the elderly. *Research on Aging, 17* (4), 459–489.

Kaiser, F. (2006). Suddenly senior: When will AARP grow some balls? http://www.suddenlysenior.com/aaarpgrowballs.html; accessed April 2, 2006.

Kalish, R. A. (1985). *Death, grief, and caring relationships* (2nd ed.). Belmont, CA: Brooks/Cole.

Kalish, R. A. (1987). Death and dying. In G. Busse (Ed.), *Elderly as pioneers* (pp. 360–385). Bloomington: Indiana University Press.

Kalymun, M. (1992). Board and care vs. assisted living. *Adult Residential Care Journal, 6* (1), 35–44.

Kanacki, L. S.; Jones, P. S.; & Galbraith, M. E. (1996). Social support and depression in widows and widowers. *Journal of Gerontological Nursing, 22* (2), 39–45.

Kane, D. (1996). A comparison of job satisfaction and general well-being for job sharing and part-time female employees. *Guidance and Counseling, 11* (3), 27–30.

Kane, R. (1992). The literature lives: Generations of applied gerontological research. *Gerontologist, 32* (6), 724–725.

Kant, G. L.; D'Zurilla, T. J.; & Maydeu-Olivares, A. (1997). Social problem solving as a mediator of stress-related depression and anxiety in middle-aged and elderly community residents. *Cognitive Therapy and Research, 21* (1), 73–96.

Karp, D. A. (1988). A decade of reminders: Changing age consciousness between fifty and sixty years old. *Gerontologist, 28* (6), 727–738.

Karpinski, J. (1997). Engaging and treating the self-neglecting elder. *Journal of Geriatric Psychiatry, 42,* 133–151.

Karr, A. (1993, February 4). Imperiled promises: Risk to retirees rises as firms fail to fund pensions they offer. *Wall Street Journal,* A1.

Kastenbaum, R. (1992). Death, suicide, and the older adult. In A. Leenaars (Ed.), *Suicide and the older adult.* New York: Guilford Press.

Kaufman, A. S., & Horn, J. L. (1996). Age changes on tests of fluid and crystallized ability for women and men on the Kaufman adolescent and adult intelligence test (KAIT) at ages 17–94 years. *Archives of Clinical Neuropsychology, 11* (2), 97–121.

Kaufman, S. (1986). *The ageless self: Sources of meaning in later life.* Madison: University of Wisconsin Press.

Kaufman, S. (1993). Reflections on the ageless self. *Generations, 17,* 13–16.

Kausler, D. H. & Kausler, B. C. (1996). *The graying of America.* Chicago, IL: University of Illinois Press.

Kaye, R. A. (1993). Sexuality in the later years. *Ageing and Society, 13,* 415–426.

Kazan, Elia. (1988, June 19). Famed director reflects on Hollywood life. Interview by Alvin P. Sanoff. *San Francisco Chronicle,* 11.

Keating, N., and Jeffrey, B. (1983). Women's work careers. *Gerontologist, 23,* 416–421.

Keeton, K. (1992). *Longevity.* New York: Viking.

Keil, K. L. (1998). An intimate profile of generation X. *American Enterprise, 9* (1), 49–51, 59.

Keith, P. M. (1983). Patterns of assistance among parents and the childless in very old age: Implications for practice. *Journal of Gerontological Social Work, 6* (1), 49–59.

Kelley, P. (1997). Grandparents raising grandchildren in the inner city. *Families in Society, 78* (5), 492.

Kelley, S. J.; Yorker, B. C.; & Whitley, D. (1997). To grandmother's house we go . . . and stay: Children raised in intergenerational families. *Journal of Gerontological Nursing, 23* (1), 12–20.

Kemnitz, J. W.; Weindruck, R.; Roecker, E. B.; Crawford, K.; Kaufman, P. O.; & Ershler, W. B. (1994). Dietary restriction of adult male rhesus monkeys: Design, methodology, and preliminary findings from the first year of study. *Journals of Gerontology, 48* (10), B17–B26.

Kemper, S. (1994). "Elderspeak": Speech accommodation to older adults. *Aging and Cognition, 1,* 17–28.

Kendig, H. L., & Wells, Y. D. (1988, April). Confidants and family structure in old age. *Journal of Gerontology, 43,* 531–540.

Kennedy, G. E. (1996). Grandparenthood literature for family life educators: Updating for curriculum development. *Journal of Family and Consumer Sciences Education, 14* (2), 4.

Kerr-Layton, D. (1993, November). Gray panthers discrimination update. *Network Newsletter,* 1.

King, V., & Elder, G. H. (1997). The legacy of grandparenting: Childhood experiences with grandparents and current involvement with grandchildren. *Journal of Marriage and the Family, 59,* 848–859.

Kinsey, Alfred. (1948). *Sexual behavior in the human male.* Philadelphia, PA: W. B. Saunders.

Kinsey, Alfred. (1953). *Sexual behavior in the human female.* Philadelphia, PA: W. B. Saunders.

Kirkland, R. I. (1994, February 21). Why we will live longer—and what it will mean. *Fortune,* 66–77.

Kitano, H. (1991). *Race relations.* Englewood Cliffs, NJ: Prentice Hall.

Kivnick, H. Q. (1982). *The meaning of grandparenthood.* Ann Arbor: University of Michigan Press.

Kleemeier, R. W. (1962). Intellectual change in the senium. *Proceedings of the Social Statistics Section of the American Statistical Association, 1,* 290–295.

Klemmack, D., & Roff, L. L. (1984). Fear of personal aging and subjective well-being in later life. *Journal of Gerontology, 39,* 756–758.

Kleyman, P. (1974). *Senior power: Growing old rebelliously.* San Francisco: Glide.

Klitgaard, H.; Zhou, M.; & Schiaffino, S. (1990). Aging alters the hyosin heavy chain composition of single fibers from human skeletal muscle. *Acta Physiology Scandinavia, 140* (1), 55–62.

Klohnen, E. C., & Vandewater, E. A. (1996). Negoatiating the middle years: Ego-resilience and successful midlife adjustment in women. *Psychology and Aging, 11* (3), 431–442.

Knight, B. G.; Lutzky, S. M.; & Macofsky-Urban, F. (1993). A meta-analytic review of interventions for caregiver distress: Recommendations for future research. *Gerontologist, 32,* 249–257.

Koenig, H. G.; Wildman-Hanlon, D.; & Schmader, K. (1996). Attitudes of elderly patients and their families toward physician-assisted suicide. *Archives of Internal Medicine, 156* (9), 2240–2248.

Kolata, G. (1992, February 2). Elderly become addicts to drug-induced sleep. *New York Times,* E4.

Krach, P.; DeVaney, S.; DeTurk, C.; Zink, M. H. (1996). Functional status of the oldest-old in a home setting. *Journal of Advanced Nursing, 25,* 456–464.

Krause, N. (1991). Stress and isolation from close ties in later life. *Journal of Gerontology: Social Sciences, 46,* 183–194.

Krause, N. (1995). Negative interaction and satisfaction with social support among older adults. *Journal of Gerontology: Psychological Sciences, 50B,* P59–P73.

Kruger, Arnold. (1994). The midlife transition: Crisis or chimera? *Psychological Reports, 75,* 1299–1305.

Kruk, E. (1994). Grandparent visitation disputes: Multigenerational approaches to family mediation. *Mediation Quarterly, 12* (1), 37–53.

Kübler-Ross, E. (1969). *On death and dying.* New York: Macmillan.

Kunitz, S., & Levy, J. (1989). Aging and health among Navajo Indians. In K. Markides (Ed.), *Aging and health: Perspectives on gender, race, ethnicity and class* (pp. 120–128). Newbury Park, CA: Sage.

Kutty, N. (1998). The scope for poverty alleviation among elderly home-owners in the United States through reverse mortgages. *Urban Studies, 35* (1), 113–129.

Lachs, M. S.; Williams, C.; O'Brien, S.; Hurst, L.; & Horwitz, R. (1997). Risk factors for reported elder abuse and neglect: A nine-year observational cohort study. *Gerontologist, 37* (4), 469–474.

Lamb, H.; Christie, J.; Singleton, A. B.; Leake, A.; Perry, R. H.; Ince, P. G.; McKeith, I. G.; Melton, L. M.; Edwardson, J. A.; & Morris, C. M. (1998). Apolipoprotein E and alpha-1 antichymotrypsin polymorphism genotyping in Alzheimer's disease and in dementia with Lewy bodies. *Neurology, 50,* 388–391.

Lambert, W., & Woo, J. (1994, April 29). CBS settlement. *Wall Street Journal,* B5 (W), B4 (E).

Lamme, S.; Dykstra, P. A.; & van Groenou, M. I. B. (1996). Rebuilding the network: New relationships in widowhood. *Personal Relationships, 3,* 337–349.

Landau, J. C., & Werbel, J. D. (1995). Sales productivity of insurance agents during the first six months of employment: Differences between older and younger hires. *Journal of Personal Selling and Sales Management, 15* (4), 33–43.

Lang, F. R., & Carstensen, L. L. (1994). Close emotional relationships in late life: Further support for proactive aging in the social domain. *Psychology & Aging, 9* (2), 315–324.

Lanza, M. L. (1996). Divorce experienced as an older woman. *Geriatric Nursing, 17,* 166–170.

Larson, R., & Lee, M. (1995). The capacity to be along as a stress buffer. *Journal of Social Psychology, 136* (1), 5–16.

Larson, R. A. (1997). The emergence of solitude as a constructive domain of experience in early adolescence. *Child Development, 68* (1), 80–93.

Laumann, E.; Michaels, M. R.; & Gagnon, J. (1994). *The social organization of sexuality.* Chicago: University of Chicago Press.

Lavie, C. J., & Milani, R. V. (1997). Benefits of cardiac rehabilitation and exercise training in elderly women. *American Journal of Cardiology, 79* (5), 664–666.

Laws, G. (1995). Understanding ageism: Lessons from feminism and postmodernism. *Gerontologist, 35* (1), 112–118.

Lawton, M. P. (1997). Measures of quality of life and subjective well-being. *Generations, 21* (1), 45–47.

Lee, I.-M.; Hseih, C.-C.; & Pfaffenbarger, R., Jr. (1995). Exercise intensity and longevity in men: The Harvard alumni health study. *Journal of the American Medical Association, 273* (15), 1179–1184.

Lee, J.; Hanna, S. D.; Mok, C. F. J.; & Wang, H. (1997). Apparel expenditure patterns of elderly consumers: A life-cycle consumption model. *Family and Consumer Sciences Research Journal, 26* (2), 109–140.

Lehman, H. (1953). *Age and achievement.* Princeton, NJ: Princeton University Press.

Lemming, M. R., & Dickinson, G. E. (1994). *Understanding dying, death, and bereavement* (3rd ed.). Orlando, FL: Harcourt Brace.

Lester, D., & Savlid, A. C. (1997). Social psychological indicators associated with the suicide rate: A comment. *Psychological Reports, 80,* 1065–1066.

Levinson, D. (1978). *The seasons of a man's life.* New York: Knopf.

Levinson, D. (1996). *The seasons of a woman's life.* New York: Knopf.

Levitt, M. J.; Weber, R. A.; & Guacci, N. (1996). Convoys of social support: An intergenerational analysis. *Psychology and Aging, 8,* 323–326.

Levy, B. (2003). Mind matters: Cognitive and physical effects of aging self-stereotypes. *Journals of Gerontology, Series B: Psychological Sciences and Social Sciences, 58B* (4), 203–211.

Levy, B., & Langer, E. (1994). Aging free from negative stereotypes: Successful memory in China and among the American deaf. *Journal of Personality and Social Psychology, 66* (6), 989–997.

Lewinsohn, P. M.; Seeley, J. R.; Roberts, R. E.; & Allen, N. B. (1997). Center for Epidemiologic Studies Depression Scale (CES-D) as a screening instrument for depression among communityresiding older adults. *Psychology and Aging, 12* (2), 277–287.

Liang, J. (1984). Dimensions of the life satisfaction index A: A structural formulation. *Journal of Gerontology, 39,* 613–622.

Liang, J.; Bennett, J.; Akiyama, H.; & Maeda, D. (1992). The structure of PGC morale scale in American and Japanese aged: A further note. *Journal of Cross-Cultural Gerontology, 7,* 45–68.

Liberto, J. G.; Oslin, D. W.; & Ruskin, P. E. (1992). Alcoholism in older persons: A review of the literature. *Hospital Community Psychiatry, 43,* 975–983.

Lichtenstein, P.; Gatz, M.; Pedersen, N. L.; Berg, S.; & McClearn, G. E. (1996). A co-twin control study of response to widowhood. *Journal of Gerontology: Psychological Sciences, 51B* (5), P279–P289.

Lieberman, M. S., & Tobin, S. (1983). *The experience of old age: Stress, coping, and survival.* New York: Basic Books.

Light, J. M.; Grigsby, J. S.; & Bligh, M. C. (1996). Aging and heterogeneity: Genetics, social structure, and personality. *Gerontologist, 36* (2), 165–173.

Linville, P. W. (1982). The complexity-extremity effect and age-based stereotyping. *Journal of Personality and Social Psychology, 42,* 183–211.

Liu, X.; Liang, J.; & Gu, S. (1995). Flows of social support and health status among older persons in China. *Social Science and Medicine, 41* (3), 1175–1184.

Ljungquist, B., & Berg, S. (1998). The effect of genetic factors for longevity: A comparison of identical and fraternal twins. *Journals of Gerontology, Series A: Biological Sciences and Medical Sciences, 53A* (6), 441.

Loevinger, J. (1976). *Ego development: Conceptions and theories.* San Francisco: Jossey-Bass.

Loevinger, J., & Wessler, R. (1970). *Measuring ego development*. San Francisco: Jossey-Bass.

Lofland, L. H. (1979). *The craft of dying: The modern face of death*. Beverly Hills, CA: Sage.

Lopata, H. Z. (1988). Support systems of American urban widowhood. *Journal of Social Issues, 44* (3), 113–128.

Losyk, B. (1997). Generation X: What they think and what they plan to do. *Public Management, 79* (12), 4–9.

Lovenheim, B. (1990). *Marriage odds: When you are smart, single, and over 35*. New York: William Morrow.

Luborsky, M. R. (1993). The romance with personal meaning in gerontology: Cultural aspects of life themes. *Gerontologist, 33* (4), 445–452.

Luborsky, M., & Sankar, A. (1993, August). Extending the critical gerontology perspective: Cultural dimensions. *Gerontologist, 33* (4), 440–454.

Lussier, G.; Deater-Deckard, K.; Dunn, J.; & Davies, L. (2002). Support across two generations: Children's closeness to grandparents following parental divorce and remarriage. *Journal of Family Psychology, 16* (3), 363–376.

Luszcz, M. A.; Bryan, J.; & Kent, P. (1997). Predicting episodic memory performance of very old men and women: Contributions from age, depression, activity, cognitive ability, and speed. *Psychology and Aging, 12* (2), 340–351.

Luszcz, M. A., & Fitzgerald, K. M. (1986). Understanding cohort differences in cross-generational, self, and peer perspectives. *Journal of Gerontology, 41*, 234–40.

Maas, H. S., & Kuypers, J. A. (1977). *From thirty to seventy*. San Francisco: Jossey-Bass.

Madden, M. M. (1997). Strengthening protection of employees at home and abroad: The extraterritorial application of Title VII of the civil rights act of 1964 and the age discrimination in employment act. *Hamline Law Review, 20* (3), 739–768.

Magno, J. (1990). The hospice concept of care: Facing the 1990s. *Death Studies, 14*, 109–119.

Manchester, J. (1997). Aging boomers and retirement: Who is at risk? *Generations, 21* (2), 19–22.

Mangen, D., & Westbrook, G. (1988). Measuring intergenerational norms. In D. Mangen (Ed.), *Measurement of intergenerational relationships*. Newbury Park, CA: Sage.

Manheimer, R. J., & Moskow-McKenzie, D. (1997). Transforming older adult education: An emerging paradigm from a nationwide study. *Educational Gerontology, 21*, 613–632.

Mannheim, K. (1952). The problem of generations. In D. Kecskemeti (Ed.), *Essays on the sociology of knowledge* (2nd ed., pp. 276–322). London: Oxford University Press.

Mannheim, K. (1993). The sociology of intellectuals. *Theory, Culture and Society, 10*, 69–80.

Manson, M., & Gutfeld, G. (1994, May). Losing the final five. *Prevention Magazine, 46* (5), 22–24.

Marcellini, F.; Sensoli, C.; Barbini, N.; & Fioravanti, P. (1997). Preparation for retirement: Problems and suggestions of retirees. *Educational Gerontology, 23*, 337–388.

Markides, K. S., & Mindel, C. H. (1987). *Aging and ethnicity*. Newbury Park, CA: Sage.

Markson, E. W. (2003). *Social gerontology today: An introduction*. Los Angeles, CA: Roxbury.

Markus, H. R., & Herzog, A. R. (1991). The role of the self-concept in aging. In K. W. Schaie & M. P. Lawton (Eds.), *Annual review of gerontology and geriatrics, vol. 11* (pp. 110–143). New York: Springer.

Marrone, R. (1997). *Death, mourning, and caring*. Pacific Grove, CA: Books/Cole.

Martin, J. D. (1971, May). Power, dependence, and the complaints of the elderly: A social exchange perspective. *Aging and Human Development, 2*, 108–112.

Martin, L. R.; Friedman, H. S.; Tucker, J. S.; Schwartz, J. E.; Criqui, M. H.; & Tomlinson-Keasey, C. (1995). An archival prospective study of mental health and longevity. *Health Psychology, 14* (5), 381–387.

Masters, W. M., & Johnson, V. E. (1966). *Human sexual response*. Boston: Little Brown.

Masters, W. M., & Johnson, V. E. (1970). *Human sexual inadequacy*. Boston: Little Brown.

Matley, S. (1994). Age-related suits increase. *Business Insurance, 28* (3), 1–4.

Matthews, S. H. (1979). *The social world of old women: Management of self-identity*. Newbury Park: Sage.

Matzo, M. L. (1997). The search to end suffering: A historical perspective. *Journal of Gerontological Nursing, 23* (3), 11–17.

Mayeux, R.; Saunders, A.; Shea, S.; Mirra, S.; Evans, D.; Roses, A.; Hyman, B.; Crain, B.; Tang, M.-X.; & Phelps, C. (1998). Utility of the apoliproprotein E genotype in the diagnosis of Alzheimer's disease. *New England Journal of Medicine, 338*, 506–511.

McAdams, D. P. (1995). What do we know when we know a person? *Journal of Personality, 63* (3), 365–375.

McAdams, D. P., & Bowman, P. J. (2001). Narrating life's turning points: Redemption and contamination. In D. P. McAdams, R. Josselson, & A. Lieblich (Eds.), *Turns in the road: Narrative studies of lives in transition* (pp. 3–34). Washington, DC: American Psychological Association.

McAdams, D. P., & de St. Aubin, E. (Eds.). (1992). A theory of generativity and its assessment through self-report, behavioral acts, and narrative themes in autobiography. *Journal of Personality and Social Psychology, 62* (6), 1003–1015.

McAdams, D. P.; Diamond, A.; de St. Aubin, E.; & Mansfield, E. (1997). Stories of commitment: The psychosocial construction of generative lives. *Journal of Personality and Social Psychology, 72* (3), 678–694.

McCarty, E. F. (1996). Caring for a parent with Alzheimer's disease: Process of daughter caregiver stress. *Journal of Advanced Nursing, 23*, 792–803.

McCoy, H. V.; Wooldredge, J. D.; Cullen, F. T.; Dubeck, P. J.; & Browning, S. L. (1996). Lifestyles of the old and not so fearful: Life situation and older persons' fear of crime. *Journal of Criminal Justice, 24* (3), 191–205.

McCrae, R. R., & Costa, P. T. (1995). Trait explanations in personality psychology. *European Journal of Personality, 9,* 231–353.

McCulloch, J., & Kivett, V. R. (1995). Characteristics of and survivorship among the very old. *Family Relations, 44,* 87–94.

McGarry, K. (1996). Factors determining participation of the elderly in supplemental security income. *Journal of Human Resources, 31* (2), 331–358.

McGue, M.; Vaupel, J. W.; Holm, N.; & Harvald, B. (1993). Longevity is moderately heritable in a sample of Danish twins born 1870–1880. *Journal of Gerontology: Biological Sciences, 48B,* B237–B244.

McMorris, F. A. (1997, February 20). Age-bias suits may become harder to prove. *Wall Street Journal,* B1.

Mergenbagen, P. (1994, June). Rethinking retirement. *American Demographics,* 28–34.

MetLife Foundation. (2005). *New face of work survey.* San Francisco, CA: Civic Ventures.

Meyer, D. R., & Bartolomei-Hill, S. (1994). The adequacy of supplemental security income benefits for aged individuals and couples. *Gerontologist, 34* (2), 161–172.

Meyer, M. J. (1995). Dignity, death and modern virtue. *American Philosophical Quarterly, 32* (1), 45–55.

Michaels, S. (1996). The prevalence of homosexuality in the United States. In R. P. Cabaj & T. S. Stein (Eds.), *Textbook of homosexuality and mental health.* Washington, DC, and London: American Psychiatric Press.

Miller, B. & Kaufman, J. E. (1996). Beyond gender stereotypes: Spouse caregivers of persons with dementia. *Journal of Aging Studies, 10* (3), 189–204.

Mills, C. W. (1959). *The sociological imagination.* New York: Oxford University Press.

Minda, G. (1997). Aging workers in the postindustrial era. *Stetson Law Review, 26* (2), 561–597.

Miniter, R. (1997). Generation X does business. *American Enterprise, 8* (4), 38.

Minkler, M. (1996). Critical perspectives on ageing: New challenges for gerontology. *Ageing and Society, 16,* 467–487.

Minker, M., & Estes, C. L. (1991). *Critical perspectives on aging: The political and moral economy of growing old.* Amityville, NY: Baywood.

Minkler, M., & Roe, K. (1993). *Grandmothers as caregivers: Raising children of the crack cocaine epidemic.* Newbury Park, CA: Sage.

Mintz, H. (1998, February 19). Trial opens for thrift accused of elder fraud. *San Jose Mercury News,* 1B.

Mittelman, M. S.; Ferris, S. H.; Shulman, E.; Steinberg, G.; Ambinder, A.; Mackell, J. A.; & Cohen, J. (1995). A comprehensive support program: Effect on depression in spouse-caregivers of AD patients. *Gerontologist, 35* (6), 792–802.

Moody, H. (1992). *Ethics in an aging society.* Baltimore: Johns Hopkins University Press.

Moody, H. R. (2000). *Aging: Concepts and controversies.* Thousand Oaks, CA: Pine Forge Press.

Morgan, D. (1989, February). Adjusting to widowhood: Do social networks make it easier? *Gerontologist, 29* (1), 101–107.

Morgan, D. L.; Neal, M. B.; & Carder, P. C. (1997). Both what and when: The effects of positive and negative aspects of relationships on depression during the first 3 years of widowhood. *Journal of Clinical Geropsychology, 3* (1), 73–91.

Mori, N. (1997). Molecular genetic approaches to the genes of longevity, aging and neurodegeneration in mammals. *Mechanisms of Aging and Development, 98* (3), 223–230.

Morley, J. E., & Kaiser, F. E. (1989). Sexual function with advancing age. *Medical Clinics of North America, 73* (6), 1483–1495.

Morris, J. N. (1996). Exercise in the prevention of coronary heart disease: Today's best buy in public health. *Medicine and Science in Sports and Exercise, 26,* 807–814.

Morris, J. N.; Heady, J. A.; & Raffle, P.A.B. (1953). Coronary heart disease and physical activity at work. *Lancet, 265,* 1053–1105.

Morris, P. L.; Robinson, R. G.; & Samuels, J. (1993). Depression, introversion and mortality following stroke. *Australian and New Zealand Journal of Psychiatry, 23,* 443–449.

Morris, R., & Caro, F. G. (1995). The young-old, productive aging, and public policy. *Generations, 19* (3), 32–37.

Morse, R. M., & Flavin, D. K. (1992). The definition of alcoholism. *Journal of the American Medical Association, 268,* 1012–1014.

Morton, J. (1992). *An administrative overview of the older inmate.* Washington, DC: U.S. Department of Justice and National Institute of Corrections.

Mudrack, P. E. (1997). Protestant work-ethic dimensions and work orientations. *Personality and Individual Differences, 23* (2), 217–225.

Mui, A., & Burnette, D. (1994). Long-term care service used by frail elders: Is ethnicity a factor? *Gerontologist, 34* (2), 190–198.

Mullen, F. (1996). Public benefits: Grandparents, grandchildren, and welfare reform. *Generations, 20* (1), 61–64.

Mulroy, T. M. (1996). Divorcing the elderly: Special issues. *American Journal of Family Law, 10,* 65–70.

Murer, M. J. (1997). Assisted living: The regulatory outlook. *Nursing Homes: Long Term Care Management, 46* (7), 24–29.

Mutter, S. A., & Goedert, K. M. (1997). Frequency discrimination vs. frequency estimation: Adult age differences and the effect of divided attention. *Journal of Gerontology: Psychological Sciences, 52B* (6), P319–P328.

Myers, D. (1991). Work after cessation of career job. *Journal of Gerontology 46* (2), S93–S102.

Mykyta, L. J. (1997). The consequences of osteoporosis in the elderly. *Australian Family Physician, 26* (2), 115–121.

National Center for Health Statistics (1994). *Vital statistics of the United States, 2* (A). Washington: U.S. Public Health Service.

National Center for Health Statistics (1996). *Births and deaths: United States, 1995. U.S. Department of Health and Human Services, 45* (3), suppl. 2. Washington, DC.

National Center for Health Statistics. (1999). *National vital statistics*. Washington, DC: Government Printing Office.

National Center for Health Statistics. (2004). *Older Americans, 2004: Key indicators of well-being*. Federal Interagency Forum on Aging Related Statistics. http://www.agingstats.gov, accessed February 2005.

National Institutes of Health. (2000). *Aging: Medical and social markers*. NIH Publication #102. Bethesda, MD: NIH.

National Institutes of Health. National Institute on Aging (1993). *In search of the secrets of aging*. NIH Publication No. 93-2756. Bethesda, MD: NIH.

National Safety Council. (1993). *Accident facts*. Chicago: National Safety Council.

Nelson, L.; Brown, R.; Gold, M.; Ciemnecki, A.; & Docteur, E. (1997). Access to care in Medicare HMOs, 1996. *Health Affairs, 16* (2), 148–156.

Neugarten, B. L. (1964). *Personality in middle and late life*. New York: Atherton.

Neugarten, B. L. (1977). Personality and aging. In J. E. Birren & K. W. Schaie (Eds.), *Handbook of the psychology of aging* (pp. 77–96). New York: Academic Press.

Neugarten, B. L. (1985). Interpretive social sciences and research on aging. In A. Rossi (Ed.), *Gender and the life course*. New York: Aldine.

Neugarten, B. L.; Havighurst, J.; & Tobin, S. (1961). The measurement of life satisfaction. *Gerontology, 16*, 134–143.

Newbold, K. B. (1996). Determinants of elderly interstate migration in the United States, 1985–1990. *Research on Aging, 18* (4), 451–476.

New FHA Program: Pilot promises elderly money from home. (1988, December). *ABA Banking Journal*, 22–23.

Newman, E. (1984). *Elderly criminals*. Cambridge, MA: Oelgeschlager, Gunn, & Hain.

Newman, R. J. (1993, June 14). Older folks are real people, too. *US News and World Report*, 103.

Niederehe, G. (1997). Future directions for clinical research in mental health and aging. *Behavior Therapy, 28*, 101–108.

Nolan, D. C. (1997). Assisted living: Moving its availability down the income scale. *Nursing homes: Long Term Care Management, 46* (7), 29–31.

Nuland, S. (1994). *How we die: Reflections on life's final chapter*. New York: Alfred A. Knopf, 1994.

Nye, W. (1993, March). Amazing grace: Religion and identity among elderly black individuals. *International Journal of Aging and Human Development, 36* (2), 103–105.

Oates, B.; Shufeldt, L.; & Vaught, B. (1996). A psychographic study of the elderly and retail store attributes. *Journal of Consumer Marketing, 13* (6), 14–27.

O'Brian, B. (1993, March 26). American Airlines sues EEOC to block fine in age-bias case. *Wall Street Journal*, A4(W), A5G(E).

O'Bryant, S. (1991, January). Older widows and independent lifestyles. *International Journal of Aging and Human Development, 32* (1), 41–51.

O'Connell, L. J. (1994). The role of religion in health-related decision making. *Generations, 18* (4), 27–30.

O'Connor, G. T.; Buring, J. E.; & Yusuf, S. (1989). An overview of randomized trials of rehabilitation with exercise after myocardial infarction. *Circulation, 80*, 234–244.

Ogg, J., & Bennett, G. (1992). Elder abuse in Britain. *British Medical Journal, 305*, 988–989.

Olshansky, S. J. (1995). Introduction: New developments in mortality. *Gerontologist, 35*, 563–587.

Olson, S. (1998). Senior housing: A quiet revolution. *Architectural Record, 186* (1), 103–106.

Onega, L. L., & Tripp-Reimer, T. (1997). Expanding the scope of continuity theory: Application to gerontological nursing. *Journal of Gerontological Nursing, 23* (6), 29–35.

Opatrny, S. (1991, March 3). Women who stay vital past seventy. *San Francisco Examiner*, A1–A3.

Orchard, T. J., & Strandness, D. B. (1993). Assessment of peripheral vascular disease in diabetes: Report and recommendations of an international workshop sponsored by the American Diabetes Association and the American Heart Association. *Circulation, 88*, 819–828.

Osgood, N. (1991). *Suicide among the elderly in long-term care facilities*. Westport, CT: Greenwood Press.

Paffenbarger, R. S., Jr.; Hyde, R. T.; Wing, A. L.; & Steinmetz, C. H. (1985). A natural history of athleticism and cardiovascular health. *Journal of the American Medical Association, 252*, 491–495.

Paffenbarger, R. S., Jr., & Lee, I.-M. (1996). Physical activity and fitness for health and longevity. *Research Quarterly for Exercise and Sport, 67* (3), 11–28.

Palmore, E. (2001). The ageism survey: First findings. *Gerontologist, 41*, 572–575.

Palmore, E. B. (1990). *Ageism: Negative and positive*. New York: Springer.

Palmore, E. B.; Nowlin, J. B.; & Wang, H. S. (1985, March). Predictors of function among the old-old: A ten-year follow-up. *Journal of Gerontology, 40* (2), 244–250.

Parker, L. D.; Cantrell, C.; & Demi, A. S. (1997). Older adults' attitudes toward suicide: Are there race and gender differences? *Death Studies, 21*, 282–289.

Parker, R. (1995). Reminiscence: A continuity theory framework. *Gerontologist, 35* (4), 515–525.

Pascual-Leone, J. (1990). An essay on wisdom: Toward organismic processes that make it possible. In R. J. Sternberg (Ed.), *Wisdom: Its nature, origins, and development* (pp. 244–278). Cambridge: Cambridge University Press.

Pascucci, M. A., & Loving, G. L. (1997). Ingredients of an old and healthy life: A centenarian perspective. *Journal of Holistic Nursing, 15* (2), 199–213.

Pearlin, L. I., & LeBlanc, A. J. (1997). Bereavement and the loss of mattering among Alzheimer's caregivers. In J. T. Mullan (Chair), Bereavement and the life course: Some views from AIDS and Alzheimer's caregivers, Symposium presented at the Fiftieth Annual Scientific Meeting of the Gerontological Society of America, Cincinnati, OH.

Pearlman, M. (1993). Late mid-life astonishment: Disruptions to identity and self-esteem. In N. David (Ed.), *Faces of women and aging.* Binghamton, NY: Haworth.

Perdue, C. W., & Gurtman, M. B. (1990). Evidence for the automaticity of ageism. *Journal of Experimental Social Psychology, 11,* 177–186.

Perkins, K. (1994, July 12). Older women forced back to work. *Santa Rosa Press Democrat,* A1.

Perlmutter, M. (1990). *Later life potential.* Washington, DC: Gerontological Society of America.

Perls, T. T. (1995, January). The oldest old. *Scientific American,* 70–75.

Peters, S. H. (1994). Book reviews: Social sciences. *Library Journal, 119* (21), 102.

Peterson, B. E., & Klohnen, E. C. (1995). Realization of generativity in two samples of women at midlife. *Psychology and Aging, 10* (1), 20–29.

Peto, R., & Doll, R. (1997). There is no such thing as aging. *British Medical Journal, 315* (7115), 1030–1032.

Phone swindlers dangle prizes to cheat elderly out of millions. (1997, June 29). *New York Times,* D18.

Pickens, J. (1998). Formal and informal care of people with psychiatric disorders: Historical perspectives and current trends. *Journal of Psychosocial Nursing, 36* (1), 37–43.

Pillemer, K., & Moore, D. (1989, June). Abuse of patients in nursing homes: Findings from a survey of staff. *Gerontologist, 29* (3), 314–320.

Plumb, J. D. (1997). Homelessness: Care, prevention, and public policy. *Annals of Internal Medicine, 126* (12), 973–975.

Podkieks, E. (1992). National survey on abuse of the elderly in Canada. *Journal of Elder Abuse and Neglect, 4,* 5–58.

Poon, L. W. (1992). *The Georgia centenarian study.* Amityville, NY: Baywood.

Posner, R. A. (1995). *Aging and old age.* Chicago: University of Chicago Press.

Preston, D. B. (1995). Marital status, gender roles, stress, and health in the elderly. *Health Care for Women International, 16,* 149–165.

Puentes, W. J. (1998). Incorporating simple reminiscence techniques into acute care nursing practice. *Journal of Gerontological Nursing, 24* (2), 14–20.

Quadagno, J. (1996). *The color of welfare: How racism undermined the war on poverty.* New York: Oxford University Press.

Quadagno, J. (1996). Social Security and the myth of the entitlement "crisis." *The Gerontologist, 36* (3), 391–399.

Quadagno, J. (2005). *Aging and the life course.* Boston: McGraw Hill.

Quadagno, J., & Reid, J. (1999). The political economy perspective in aging. In V. L. Bengston & K. W. Schaie (Eds.), *Handbook of theories of aging* (pp. 344–358). New York: Springer.

Quadagno, J. S. (1982). *Aging in early industrial society.* New York: Academic Press.

Quadagno, J. S. (1991, August). Falling into the Medicaid gap: The hidden long-term care dilemma. *Gerontologist, 31* (4), 521–526.

Quinnan, E. J. (1997). Connection and autonomy in the lives of elderly male celibates: Degrees of disengagement. *Journal of Aging Studies, 11* (2), 115–130.

Rahe, R. H. (1995). Stress and coping in psychiatry. In H. I. Kaplan & B. J. Sadock (Eds.), *Comprehensive textbook of psychiatry* (6th ed., pp. 1545–1559). Baltimore: Williams & Wilkins.

Rahe, R. H., & Arthur, R. T. (1978). Subjects' recent life changes and their near-future illness susceptibility. *Advances in Psychosomatic Medicine, 8,* 2–9.

Rando, T. A. (1995). Grieving and mourning: Accommodating to loss. In H. Wass & R. A. Niemeyer (Eds.), *Dying: Facing the facts.* Washington, DC: Taylor & Francis.

Rantz, M. J.; Mohr, D. R.; Popejoy, L.; Zwygart-Stauffacher, M.; Hicks, L. L.; Grando, V.; Conn, V. S.; Porter, R.; Scott, J.; & Maas, M. (1998). Nursing home care quality: A multidimensional theoretical model. *Journal of Nursing Care Quality, 12* (3), 30–46.

Rathbone-McCuan, E. (1996). Self-neglecting in the elderly: Knowing when and how to intervene. *Aging,* 44–49.

Ray, D. (1987). Differences in psychologists' ratings of older and younger clients. *Gerontologist, 27,* 82–86.

Reday-Mulvey, G. (1996, May 16). Why working lives must be extended. *People Magazine,* 24–29.

Redfoot, D., & Gaberlavage, G. (1991). Housing for older Americans: Sustaining the dream. *Generations,* 35–38.

Reich, K., & Morrison, P. (1986, October 1). Deception in insurance mailers. *Los Angeles Times,* 3.

Reiters, D. C.; Mutran, E. J.; & Verrill, L. A. (1995). Activities and self-esteem. *Research on Aging, 17* (3), 260–277.

Reker, G. T. (1997). Personal meaning, optimism, and choice: Existential predictors of depression in community and institutional elderly. *Gerontologist, 37* (6), 709–716.

Rempel, J. (1985). Childless elderly: What are they missing? *Journal of Marriage and the Family, 47,* 343–348.

Riabowal, K.; Harley, C.; & Goldstein, S. (1995). The maintenance of the accuracy of protein synthesis and its relevance to aging. *Experimental Gerontology, 30,* 5–6.

Richardson, C. A., & Hammond, S. M. (1996). A psychometric analysis of a short device for assessing depression in elderly people. *British Journal of Clinical Psychology, 35* (4), 543–551.

Richardson, E. E. (1909). The will to believe as a basis for the defense of religious faith: A critical study. *Psychological Bulletin, 6* (6), 200–202.

Richardson, J. P., & Lazur, A. (1995). Sexuality in the nursing home patient. *American Family Physician, 51* (1), 10–14.

Richman, J. (1995). From despair to integrity: An Eriksonian approach to psychotherapy for the terminally ill. *Psychotherapy, 32* (2), 317–322.

Rickles, R. E., & Finch, C. E. (1995). *Aging: A natural history.* New York: Scientific American Library, W. H. Freeman.

Riley, M. W., & Riley, J. R. (1994). Age integration and the lives of older people. *Gerontologist, 34* (1), 110–115.

Riordan, C. M.; Griffith, R. W.; & Weatherly, E. W. (2003). Age and work-related outcomes: The moderating effects of status characteristics. *Journal of Applied Social Psychology, 33,* 337–357.

Roan, C. L., & Raley, R. K. (1996). Intergenerational coresidence and contact: A longitudinal analysis of adult children's response to their mother's widowhood. *Journal of Marriage and the Family, 58,* 708–717.

Roan, S. (1993). Measuring progress. *American Fitness, 11* (1), 21.

Roan, S. (1993, January 17). The Ponce de Leon study. *San Francisco Chronicle,* Sunday Punch section, 2.

Roberto, K. A. (1997). Qualities of older women's friendships: Stable or volatile? *International Journal of Aging and Human Development, 44* (1), 1–14.

Roberto, K. A., & Scott, J. (1984–1985). Friendship patterns among older women. *International Journal of Aging and Human Development, 19,* 1–9.

Robinson, B. E. (1997). Guideline for initial evaluation of the patient with memory loss. *Geriatrics, 52* (12), 30–39.

Robinson, J. D., & Skill, T. (1995). The invisible generation: Portrayals of the elderly on primetime television. *Communication Reports, 8* (2), 111–119.

Robinson, L., & Mahon, M. M. (1997). Sibling bereavement: A concept analysis. *Death Studies, 21,* 477–499.

Rogers, C. C. (2000). *Changes in the older population and implications for rural areas.* U.S. Department of Agriculture, Economic Research Service. http://www.ers.usda.gov/publications/rdrr90/, accessed August 8, 2006.

Roha, R. R. (1998, January). Medigap: One size doesn't fit all. *Kiplinger's Personal Finance,* 107–111.

Rosen, M.; Simon, E. W.; & McKinsey, L. (1995). Subjective measure of quality of life. *Mental Retardation, 33,* 31–34.

Rosenkoetter, M. M. (1996). Changing life patterns of the resident in long-term care and the community-residing spouse. *Geriatric Nursing, 17* (6), 267–272.

Rosow, I. (1974). *Socialization to old age.* Berkeley: University of California Press.

Ross, D. W. (1996). Biology of aging. *Archives of Pathological Laboratory Medicine, 120* (12), 114–116.

Rossi, A. S., & Rossi, P. H. (1990). *Of human bonding.* New York: Aldine de Gruyter.

Rowe, J. W. (1997). The new gerontology. *Science, 278* (5337), 367–369.

Rowland, V. T., & Shoemake, A. (1995). How experiences in a nursing home affect nursing students' perceptions of the elderly. *Educational Gerontology, 21,* 735–748.

Rubenstein, J. (1987). A cross-cultural comparison of children's drawings of same- and mixed-sex peer interaction. *Journal of Cross-Cultural Psychology, 18,* 234–250.

Rubenstein, R. (1994). Generativity as pragmatic spirituality. In L. E. Thomas and S. Eisenhandler (Eds.), *Aging and the religious dimension.* Westport, CT: Auburn House.

Ryan, E. B.; Hummert, M. L.; & Boich, L. H. (1995). Communication predicaments of aging: Patronizing behavior toward older adults. *Journal of Language and Social Psychology, 14* (1–2), 144–166.

Ryan, M. (1993, July 18). Undercover among the elderly. *Parade Magazine,* 8.

Salili, Farideh. (1995). Age, sex, and cultural differences in the meaning and dimensions of achievement. *Personality and Social Psychology Bulletin, 20* (6), 5–8.

Saluter, A. F. (1992). Marital status and living arrangements: March, 1991. *Current population reports: Population characteristics.* Series P-20, No. 461. Washington, DC.

Samuels, S. C. (1997). Midlife crisis: Helping patients cope with stress, anxiety, and depression. *Geriatrics, 52,* 55–63.

Sandecki, R. (1993, July 5). Ex-AT&T manager wins verdict. *Los Angeles Times,* C18.

Sandell, S. H., & Iams, H. M. (1997). Reducing women's poverty by shifting Social Security benefits from retired couples to widows. *Journal of Policy Analysis and Management, 16* (2), 279–297.

Sanders, G. F.; Montgomery, J. E.; Pittman, J. F., Jr.; & Blackwell, C. (1984). Youth attitudes toward the elderly. *Journal of Applied Gerontology, 3,* 59–70.

Sarbin, T. R. (1986). The narrative as a root metaphor for psychology. In T. R. Sarbin (Ed.), *Narrative psychol-*

ogy: *The storied nature of human conduct* (pp. 3–21). New York: Praeger.

Savage, R. D.; Britton, P.; Bolton, N.; & Hall, E. H. (1973). *Intellectual functioning in the aged*. London: Methuen.

Sawyer, C. H. (1996). Reverse mortgages: An innovative tool for elder law attorneys. *Stetson Law Review, 26* (2), 617–646.

Schaie, K. W. (1996). *Intellectual development in adulthood: The Seattle longitudinal study*. New York: Cambridge University Press.

Schaie, K. W., & Willis, S. L. (1996). *Adult development and aging* (4th ed.). New York: HarperCollins.

Schick, F., & Schick, R. (1994). *Statistical handbook of aged Americans*. Phoenix, AZ: Oryx.

Schideler, K. (1994, August 8). Everybody gets osteoporosis. *Santa Rosa Press Democrat*, D2.

Schmidt, K. (1993, March 8). No purpose in dying: Staying young longer. *U.S. News and World Report*, 66–73.

Schoonmaker, C. (1993). Aging lesbians: Bearing the burden of triple shame. In N. Davis, E. Cole, & C. Rothblum (Eds.), *Faces of women and aging*. New York: Haworth Press.

Schuchter, S. R., & Zisook, R. (1993). The course of normal grief. In M. S. Stroebe, W. Stroebe, & R. O. Hansson (Eds.), *Handbook of bereavement: Theory, research, and intervention*. Cambridge, UK: Cambridge University Press.

Schutter, M. E.; Scherman, A.; & Carroll, R. S. (1997). Grandparents and children of divorce: Their contrasting perceptions and desires for the postdivorce relationship. *Educational Gerontology, 23*, 213–231.

Schwald, S. J., & Sedlacek, W. E. (1990). Have college students' attitudes toward older people changed? *Journal of College Student Development, 31*, 127–123.

Seals, J. D. R.; Hagberg, J. M.; & Hurley, B. F. (1984). Endurance training in older men and women: Cardiovascular responses to exercise. *Journal of Applied Physiology, 57* (4), 1024–1029.

Seelye, K. Q. (1997, March 27). US of future: Grayer and more Hispanic. *New York Times*, 9.

Segell, M. (1993, September). How to live forever. *Esquire*, 125–132.

Sejnowski, T. (1995). Sleep and memory. *Current Biology, 5* (8), 832–834.

Seligman, M. E. P. (1975). *Helplessness: On depression, development and death*. San Francisco: Freeman.

Selzer, M. M. (1989). The three R's of life cycle sibships: Rivalries, reconstructions, and relationships. *American Behavioral Scientist, 33*, 107–115.

Sengstock, M. C.; McFarland, M. R.; & Hwalek, M. (1990). Identification of elder abuse in institutional settings. *Journal of Elder Abuse and Neglect, 18* (2), 31–50.

Seppa, N. (2006). Looking ahead: Tests might predict Alzheimer's risk. *Science News, 169* (7), 102.

Serafini, M. W. (1997). Brave new world. *National Journal, 29* (33), 163–165.

Seshadri, S.; Wolf, P. A.; Beiser, A.; Au, R.; McNulty, K.; White, R.; & D'Agostino, R. B. (1997). Lifetime risk of dementia and Alzheimer's disease. The impact of mortality on risk estimates in the Framingham study. *Neurology, 49*, 1498–1504.

Severance offers chance to teach (1991, November 26). *USA Today*, 4B.

Sharpley, C. F. (1997). Psychometric properties of the self-perceived stress in retirement scale. *Psychological Reports, 81*, 319–322.

Shea, D.G.; Miles, T.; & Hayward, M. (1996). The health-wealth connection: Racial differences. *The Gerontologist, 36* (3), 342–349.

Sheehy, G. (1976). *Passages*. New York: Dutton.

Sheehy, G. (1995). *New passages: Mapping your life across time*. New York: Ballantine Books.

Shephard, R. J.; Rhind, S.; & Shek, P. N. (1995). The impact of exercise on the immune system: NK cells, interleukins 1 and 2, and related responses. In J. O. Holloszy (Ed.), *Exercise and Sports Sciences Reviews, 23*, 214–241.

Shepherd, M. D., & Erwin, G. (1983). An examination of students' attitudes toward the elderly. *American Journal of Pharmaceutical Education, 47*, 35–38.

Sherman, S. R. (1994). Changes in age identity: Self-perceptions in middle and late life. *Journal of Aging Studies, 8* (4), 397–412.

Sherrard, C. (1997). Subjective well-being in later life. *Ageing and Society, 17*, 609–613.

Shmotkin, D., & Hadari, G. (1996). An outlook on subjective well-being in older Israeli adults: A unified formulation. *International Journal of Aging and Human Development, 42* (4), 271–289.

Shock, N. W.; Greulich, R. C.; Andres, R.; Arenburg, D.; Costa, P. T.; Lakatta, F. G.; & Tobin, J. D. (1989). *Normal human aging: The Baltimore longitudinal study of aging*. NIH Publication No. 84-2450. Washington, DC: US Government Printing Office.

Shoemake, A. F., & Rowland, V. T. (1993). Do laboratory experiences change college students' attitudes toward the elderly? *Educational Gerontology, 19*, 295–309.

Siegel, S. R. (1993). Relationships between current performance and likelihood of promotion for old versus young workers. *Human Resources Development Quarterly, 4* (1), 39–50.

Silberman, P. R.; Weiner, A.; & El Ad, N. (1995). Parent-child communication in bereaved Israeli families. *Omega, 31* (4), 293–306.

Silver, M. (1990, January 30). Retire early at Hewlett-Packard. *Santa Rosa Press Democrat*, B1.

Simmons, L. W. (1949). *The role of the aged in primitive society*. New Haven, CT: Yale University Press.

Simmons, L. W. (1960). Aging in preindustrial societies. In C. Tibbitts (Ed.), *Handbook of social gerontology*. Chicago: University of Chicago Press.

Slotterback, Carole S., & Saarnio, David A. (1996). Attitudes toward older adults reported by young adults: Variation based on attitudinal task and attribute categories. *Psychology and Aging, 11* (4), 563–571.

Small, J. P. (1995). Recent scientific advances in the understanding of memory. *Helios, 22* (2), 156–162.

Smith, D. W. (1996). Cancer mortality at very old ages. *American Cancer Society, 77* (7), 1367–1372.

Smith, D. W. (1997). Centenarians: Human longevity outliers. *Gerontologist, 37* (2), 200–207.

Smyer, T.; Gragert, M. D.; & LaMere, S. (1997). Stay safe! Stay healthy! Surviving old age in prison. *Journal of Psychosocial Nursing, 35* (9), 10–17.

Sokolovsky, J. (Ed.). (1997). *The cultural context of aging* (3rd ed.). Westport, CT: Bergin & Garvey.

Soldo, B. J.; Hurd, M. D.; Rodgers, W. L.; & Wallace, R. B. (1997). Asset and health dynamics among the oldest old: An overview of the AHEAD study. *Journals of Gerontology, 52B* (special issue), 1–20.

Sonnichsen, A. C.; Ritter, M. M.; Mohrle, W.; Richter, W. O.; & Schwandt, P. (1993). The waist-to-hip ratio corrected for body mass index is related to serum triglycerides and high-density lipoprotein cholesterol but not to parameters of glucose metabolism in healthy premenopausal women. *Clinical Investigation, 71,* 913–917.

Stafford, R. S., & Cyr, P. L. (1997). The impact of cancer on the physical function of the elderly and their utilization of health care. *Cancer, 80* (10), 1973–1980.

Stallings, M. E.; Dunham, C. C.; Gatz, M.; Baker, L. A.; & Bengtson, V. L. (1997). Relationship among life events and psychological well-being: More evidence for a two-factor theory of well-being. *Journal of Applied Gerontology, 16* (1), 104–119.

Starr, B., & Weiner, M. (1981). *The Starr-Weiner Report on sex and sexuality in the mature years.* Briarcliff Manor, NY: Stein & Day.

Starr, K. (1996). *Endangered dreams: The Great Depression in California.* New York: Oxford University Press.

Stein, M. B.; Chartier, M. J.; Hazen, A. L.; Kozak, M. V.; Tancer, M. E.; Lander, S.; Furer, P.; Chubaty, D.; & Walker, J. R. (1998). A direct-interview family study of generalized social phobia. *American Journal of Psychiatry, 155* (1), 90–97.

Steinberg, D. (1993, March 13). Seniorities: How fairy tales help perpetuate ageist mythology. *San Francisco Examiner,* C7.

Steinweg, K. K. (1997). The changing approach to falls in the elderly. *American Family Physician, 56* (7), 1815–1822.

Stern, M. R. (1987, April). At 93, blessings and memories. *Washington Post,* 23.

Sternberg, R. J. (1990). *Wisdom: Its nature, origins, and development.* Cambridge University Press: New York.

Stevens, N. (1995). Gender and adaptation to widowhood in later life. *Ageing and Society, 15,* 37–58.

Stewart, A. J., & Ostrove, J. M. (1998). Women's personality in middle age: Gender, history, and midcourse corrections. *American Psychologist, 53* (11), 1185–1194.

Still, J. S. (1980). Disengagement reconsidered: Awareness of finitude. *Gerontologist, 20,* 457–462.

Stokes, G. (1992). *On being old: The psychology of later life.* London: Falmer.

Stolberg, S. (1994, July 27). Many elderly too medicated, study finds. *Los Angeles Times,* A1.

Stolk, R. P.; Lamberts, S. W.; Breteler, M.; Grobbee, D.; Hoffman, A.; Ott, A.; & Pols, H. (1997). Insulin and cognitive function in an elderly population. *Diabetes Care, 20* (5), 792–795.

Stoller, E. (1990). Males as helpers: The role of sons, relatives, and friends. *Gerontologist, 30,* 228–236.

Stolley, J. M., & Koenig, H. (1997). Religion/spirituality and health among elderly African Americans and Hispanics. *Journal of Psychosocial Nursing, 35* (11), 32–38.

Stone, P. (1993). Just another con job on the elderly? *National Journal, 25* (36), 2141–2144.

Stone, R., & Keigher, S. (1994). Toward equitable universal caregiver policy: The potential of financial supports for family caregivers. *Aging and Social Policy, 6,* 57–76.

Strawbridge, W. J.; Wallhagen, M. I.; Shema, S. J.; & Kaplan, G. A. (1997). New burdens or more of the same? Comparing grandparent, spouse, and adult-child caregivers. *Gerontologist, 37* (4), 505–510.

Strom, R.; Collinsworth, P.; Strom, S.; & Griswold, D. (1993). Strengths of black grandparents. *International Journal of Aging and Human Development, 36* (4), 255–259.

Strom, R. D.; Buki, L. P.; & Strom, S. K. (1997). Intergenerational perceptions of English speaking and Spanish speaking Mexican American grandparents. *International Journal of Aging and Human Development, 45* (1), 1–21.

Sue, D. W.; Bingham, R. P.; Porché-Burke, L.; & Vasquez, M. (1999). The diversification of psychology: A multicultural revolution. *American Psychologist, 54,* 1061–1069.

Sweepstakes' fine print tells all. (1998, March 22). Ann Landers's column. *San Jose Mercury News,* 4G.

Sykes, J. T. (1990). Living independently with neighbors who care: Strategies to facilitate aging in place. In D. Tilson (Ed.), *Aging in place: Supporting the frail elderly in residential environments* (pp. 47–56). Glenview, IL: Scott, Foresman.

Szinovacz, M. (1996). Couples' employment/retirement patterns and perceptions of marital quality. *Research on Aging, 18* (2), 243–268.

Szinovacz, M. E. (1998). Grandparents today: A demographic profile. *Gerontologist, 38* (1), 37.

Szinovacz, M.; DeViney, S.; & Atkinson, M. (1999). Effects of surrogate parenting on grandparents' well-being. *Journal of Gerontology, 54B* (6), S376–389.

Talamantes, M. A.; Cornell, J.; Espino, D. V.; Lichenstein, M. J.; & Hazuda, H. P. (1996). SES and ethnic differences in perceived caregiver availability among young-old Mexican Americans and non-Hispanic whites. *Gerontologist, 36* (1), 88–99.

Talbot, M. (1990). The negative side of the relationship between older widows and their children. *Gerontologist, 30* (5), 595–603.

Tandemar Research (1988). *Quality of life among seniors.* Toronto, Ontario: Tandemar Research.

Tanenbaum, L. (1997, March–April). Changing the images makes a big difference. *Extra!, 22–23.*

Tauer, L. (1995). Age and farmer productivity. *Review of Agricultural Economics, 17,* 63–69.

Taylor, H.; Bass, R.; & Harris, L. (1992). *Productive aging: A survey of Americans age 55 and over.* New York: Louis Harris.

Taylor, S. E., & Brown, J. D. (1988). Illusion and well-being: A social psychological perspective on mental health. *Psychological Bulletin, 103,* 193–210.

Tennstedt, S., & Yates, E. (1999). Contributors to and mediators of psychological well-being for informal caregivers, *Journals of Gerontology, Series B: Psychological Sciences & Social Science, 54B* (1), 11–12.

Thomas, J. (1992). *Adult and aging.* Boston: Allyn & Bacon.

Thomas, L. E. (1994). Introduction. In L. E. Thomas & S. Eisenhandler (Eds.), *Aging and the religious dimension* (pp. 1–20). Westport, CT: Auburn House.

Thomas, W. I. (1923). *The unadjusted girl.* Boston: Little, Brown.

Thomas, W. I. (1927). The behavior pattern and the situation. *Publications of the American Sociological Society, 22,* 1–14.

Thomas, W. I., & Thomas, D. S. (1928). *The child in America: Behavior problems and programs.* New York: Alfred A. Knopf.

Thone, R. (1993). *Women and aging: Celebrating ourselves.* Binghamton, NY: Haworth.

Tiberti, C.; Sabe, L.; Kuzis, G.; Cuerva, A. G.; Leiguarda, R.; & Starkstein, S. E. (1998). Prevalence and correlates of the catastrophic reaction in Alzheimer's disease. *Neurology, 50,* 546–548.

Tillman, Ralph A. (1997). The president's page: Elderly—advanced in years or past middle age. *Journal of the Medical Association of Georgia, 86* (2), 73–74.

Tinker, A. (1991). Granny flats: The British experience. *Journal of Housing for the Elderly, 7* (2), 421–456.

Tobin, S. (1991). *Personhood in advanced old age.* New York: Springer.

The top ten health frauds (1990, February). *Consumer's Research Magazine, 34–36.*

Tornstam, L. (1994). Gero-transcendence: A theoretical and empirical exploration. In L. E. Thomas & S. Eisenhandler, *Aging and the religious experience* (pp. 203–225). Westport, CT: Greenwood Press.

Tornstam, L. (1997). Gerotranscendence: The contemplative dimension of aging. *Journal of Aging Studies, 11* (2), 143–154.

Torres-Gil, F. (1988). Interest group politics: Empowerment of the *ancianos.* In S. Applewhite (Ed.), *Hispanic elderly in transition.* New York: Greenwood.

Toughill, E.; Jason, D. J.; Beck, T. L.; & Christopher, M. A. (1993). Health, income, and postretirement employment of older adults. *Public Health Nursing, 10* (2), 100–107.

Townsend, A. L., & Franks M. M. (1997). Quality of the relationship between elderly spouses: Influence on spouse caregivers' subjective effectiveness. *Family Relations, 46,* 33–39.

Tracy, K. R. (1996). Diversifying into adult day care: A learning experience. *Nursing homes: Long Term Care Management, 45* (10), 39–41.

Treas, J. (1997). Older Americans in the 1990s and beyond. *Population Bulletin, 50* (2), 2–46.

Troll, L. E., & Skaff, M. M. (1997). Perceived continuity of self in very old age. *Psychology and Aging, 12* (1), 162–169.

Tuckman, J., & Lorge, I. (1953). Attitudes toward old people. *Journal of Gerontology, 32,* 227–232.

Turjanski, N.; Lees, A. J.; & Brooks, D. J. (1997). In vivo studies on striatal dopamine D_1 and D_2 site binding in L-dopa-treated Parkinson's disease patients with and without dyskinesias. *Neurology, 49,* 717–723.

Turner, L. (1996). Time out with half-time: Job sharing in the nineties. *Canadian Journal of Counseling, 30* (2), 104–113.

Uehara, E. S. (1995). Reciprocity reconsidered: Gouldner's "moral norm of reciprocity" and social support. *Journal of Social and Personal Relationships, 12* (4), 483–502.

Uhlenberg, P. I. (1996). Mutual attraction: Demography and life-course analysis. *Gerontologist, 36* (2), 226–229.

U.S. Bureau of the Census. (1990). *Marital status and living arrangement.* Current population reports (Series P20, No. 455). Washington, DC: U.S. Government Printing Office.

U.S. Bureau of the Census. (1991). *Statistical abstract of the United States, 1990.* Washington, DC: Department of Commerce, Bureau of the Census.

U.S. Bureau of the Census. (1993). *Statistical abstract of the United States.* 113th ed. Washington, DC: U.S. Government Printing Office.

U.S. Bureau of the Census. (1994). *Profiles of general demographic characteristics, 1990 census.* Census of Population and Housing. Washington, DC: U.S. Department of Commerce.

U.S. Bureau of the Census. (2000). *A profile of older Americans.* Current Population Reports.

U.S. Bureau of the Census. (2001). *Aging in the United States.* http://www.census.gov, accessed June 2000.

U.S. Bureau of the Census. (2002). *We the people: Aging in the United States*. http://www.census.gov, accessed January 2005.

U.S. Bureau of the Census. (2003). *Statistical Abstract of the United States*. Washington, DC: U.S. Government Printing Office.

U.S. Bureau of Labor Statistics. (1996). *Employment and Earnings*. 46 (11), 21–22.

U.S. Bureau of Labor Statistics. (2000). *Employment and Earnings*. http://stats.bls.gov, accessed October 2001.

U.S. Bureau of Labor Statistics. (2004). *Employment and Earnings*. http://stats.bls.gov/cpsaatab/00-02.htm#empstat, accessed June 2005.

U.S. Department of Health and Human Services. (1997). *An overview of nursing homes and their current residents: Data from the 1995 national nursing home survey*. Public Health Service 97-1250, Report 280.

U.S. Department of Health and Human Services. (1997). *Physical activity and health: A report of the Surgeon General*. National Center for Chronic Disease Prevention. Atlanta: U.S. Government Printing Office.

U.S. Department of Housing and Urban Development. (1999). *Housing our elders*. Washington, DC: Office of Policy Development and Research.

U.S. Government. (2003). *Older Americans 2000: Key indicators of well-being*. Washington, DC: Federal Interagency Forum on Aging-Related Statistics.

U.S. News Bulletins. (1997, September 21). Kevorkian assists in suicide of Canadian from British Columbia. http://www.rights.org/deathnet/ Usnews_9709.html.

U.S. News Bulletins. (1998, March 1). Kevorkian says: "Charge me—or leave me alone!" http://www.rights .org/deathnet/ Usnews_9803.html.

U.S. Social Security Administration. (1997). Office of Policy Publications. www.ssa.gov/policy, accessed February 2006.

U.S. Social Security Administration. (2002). *Status of the Social Security and Medicare programs: A summary of the 2001 Annual Reports*. http://www.ssa.gov/OACT/ TYRSUM/trsummary.html, accessed February 20, 2006.

van Boxtel, M. P. J.; Paas, F. G. W. C.; Houx, P. J.; Adam, J. J.; Teeken, J. C.; & Jolles, J. (1997). Aerobic capacity and cognitive performance in a cross-sectional aging study. *Medicine and Science in Sports and Exercise, 29* (10), 1357–1365.

van den Hoonaard, D. (1997). Identity foreclosure: Women's experiences of widowhood as expressed in autobiographical accounts. *Ageing and Society, 17*, 533–551.

van Ranst, N., & Marcoen, A. (1997). Meaning in life of young and elderly adults: An examination of the factorial validity and invariance of the Life Regard Index. *Personality and Individual Differences, 22* (6), 877–884.

Vasavada, T.; Masand, P. S.; & Nasra, G. (1997). Evaluations of competency of patients with organic mental disorder. *Psychological Reports, 80* (2), 107–113.

Vasil, L., & Wass, H. (1993). Portrayal of the elderly in the media: A literature review and implications for educational gerontologists. *Educational Gerontology, 19*, 71–85.

Verbrugge, L. M.; Gruber-Baldini, A. L.; & Fozard, J. L. (1996). Age differences and age changes in activities: Baltimore Longitudinal Study on Aging. *Journal of Gerontology: Social Sciences, 51B* (1), S30–S41.

Vertinsky, P. (1991). Old age, gender and physical activity: The biomedicalization of aging. *Journal of Sport History, 18* (1), 64–80.

Verwoerdt, A.; Pfeiffer, E.; & Wang, H. S. (1969). Sexual behaviorism in senescence. *Geriatrics, 24*, 137–153.

Vitt, L. (1995). Persistent inequalities: Wage disparity under capitalist competition. *Work and Occupations, 22* (3), 360–362.

Vogt, M. T.; Wolfson, S. K.; & Kuller, L. H. (1992). Lower extremity arterial disease and the aging process: A review. *Journal of Clinical Epidemiology 45*, 529–542.

Wacker, R. R.; Roberty, K. A.; & Piper, L. E. (1998). *Community resources for older adults: Programs and services in an era of change*. Thousand Oaks, CA: Pine Forge Press.

Walford, R. L. (1983). *Maximum life span*. New York: Norton.

Wallace, S., & Williamson, R. (1992). *The senior movement: References and resources*. New York: G. K. Hall.

Wallis, C. (1995, March 6). How to live to be 120. *Time Magazine*, 85.

Walls, C., & Zarit, S. (1991). Informal support from black churches and the well-being of elderly blacks. *Gerontologist, 31* (4), 490–495.

Walter, P. (1997). Effects of vegetarian diets on aging and longevity. *Nutrition Reviews, 55* (1), S61–S65.

Ward, R. (1993). Marital happiness and household equity in later life. *Journal of Marriage and the Family, 55* (2), 427–438.

Ward, R. A. (1984). The marginality and salience of being old. *Gerontologist, 24*, 227–232.

Ware, J. M. (1996). Differences in four-year health outcomes for elderly and poor, chronically ill patients treated in HMO and fee-for-service systems: Results from the medical outcomes study. *Journal of the American Medical Association, 276* (13), 1039–1047.

Watson, K. (1997, Fall). Current trauma in the lives of older adults: Surviving and healing the wounds of a changing self-concept and self-neglect. Unpublished manuscript, Gerontology of Aging. Rohnert Park, CA: Sonoma State University.

Weaver, C. L. (2000). Private accounts: Political vs. market risk. In H. R. Moody (Ed.), *Aging? Concepts and controversies* (pp. 240–242). Thousand Oaks, CA: Pine Forge Press.

Weaver, C. N. (1997). Has the work ethic in the USA declined? Evidence from nationwide surveys. *Psychological Report, 81*, 491–495.

Weber, M. (1958). *The Protestant ethic and spirit of capitalism* (T. Parsons, Trans.). New York: Scribner. (Original work published 1904–1905.)

Welch, J. (1997, June 26). Intel faces fight over "termination quotas." *People Management,* p. 9.

Wellman, N. S.; Weddle, D. O.; Krantz, S.; & Brain, C. T. (1997). Elder insecurities: Poverty, hunger, and malnutrition. *Journal of the American Dietetic Association, 97* (10), 120–122.

Wells, R. M. (1997, March 1). Subsidies for Section 8 program are on the chopping block. *Congressional Quarterly,* 539–541.

Westinghouse Electric, Northrop settle suits on age discrimination. (1997, November 3). *Wall Street Journal,* A2.

Whaley, D. E., & Ebbeck, V. (1997). Older adults' constraints to participation in structured exercise classes. *Journal of Aging and Physical Activity, 5* (3), 190–213.

White, N., & Cunningham, W. R. (1988). Is terminal drop pervasive or specific? *Journals of Gerontology, 42,* P141–P144.

Whitehead, C., & Finucane, P. (1997). Malnutrition in elderly people. *Australian and New Zealand Journal of Medicine, 27* (1), 68–74.

Whitley, B. E., & Kite, M. E. (2006). *The psychology of prejudice and discrimination.* Belmont, CA: Thompson/Wadsworth Higher Education.

Wicclair, M. (1993). *Ethics and the elderly.* New York: Oxford University Press.

Wick, G., & Grubeck-Loebenstein, B. (1997). The aging immune system: Primary and secondary alterations of immune reactivity in the elderly. *Experimental Gerontology, 32* (4–5), 401–413.

Widowed Services Fact Sheet. (1990). Centers for Disease Control and Precaution: Web-based injury statistics query and reporting system. http://www.cdc.gov/ncipc/wisqars, accessed March 27, 2003.

Wikipedia. (2006). American Associations of Retired Persons. http://en.wikipedia.org/wiki/American_Association_of_Retired_Persons, accessed March 31, 2006.

Wilcox, S. (1997). Age and gender in relation to body attitudes: Is there a double standard of aging? *Psychology of Women Quarterly, 21* (4), 549–565.

Willett, W. C. (1994). Diet and health: What should we eat? *Science, 264,* 532–537.

Williams, A.; Coupland, J.; Folwell, A.; & Sparks, L. (1997). Talking about Generation X: Defining them as they define themselves. *Journal of Language and Social Psychology, 16* (3), 251–277.

Williams, A., & Giles, H. (1997). Communication, age and discrimination. In M. Hecht & J. Baldwin (Eds.), *Communicating prejudices: Tolerance and intolerance.* Thousand Oaks, CA: Sage.

Williams, L. J.; Gavin, M. B.; & Williams, M. L. (1996). Measurement and nonmeasurement processes with negative affectivity and employee attitudes. *Journal of Applied Psychology, 81,* 88–101.

Wiscott, R., & Kopera-Frye, K. (2000). Sharing of culture: Adult grandchildren's perceptions of intergenerational relations. *International Journal of Aging and Human Development, 51* (3), 199–215.

Witkin, G. (1994, January 17). Ten myths about sex. *Santa Rosa Press Democrat, Parade Magazine.*

Wolf, D. A.; Freedman, V.; & Soldo, B. J. (1997). The division of family labor: Care for elderly parents. *Journals of Gerontology, 52B* (special issue), 102–109.

Wolfson, C.; Handfield-Jones, R.; Glass, K. C.; McClaran, J.; & Keyserlingk, E. (1993). Adult children's perceptions of their responsibility to provide care for dependent elderly parents. *Gerontologist, 33* (3), 315–323.

Wolters, G., & Prinsen, A. (1997). Full versus divided attention and implicit memory performance. *Memory and Cognition, 25* (6), 764–771.

Woman, 73, battles intruder and foils rape in apartment. (1991, August 14). *New York Times,* A12(N).

Worsnop, R. I. (1997). Caring for the dying. *Congressional Quarterly Researcher, 7* (33), 769–792.

Wright, E. R. (1995). Personal networks and anomie: Exploring the sources and significance of gender composition. *Sociological Focus, 28* (3), 261–282.

Wynder, E. L. (1995). Editorial: Interdisciplinary centers for tobacco-related cancer research—A health policy issue. *American Journal of Public Health, 85* (1), 14.

Yali, A. M., & Revenson, T. A. (2004). How changes in population demographics will impact health psychology: Incorporating a broader notion of cultural competence into the field. *Health Psychology, 23* (2), 27–33.

Yancik, R. (1993). Ovarian cancer. *Cancer, 71,* 517–523.

Yashin, A. I., & Iachine, I. A. (1995). Genetic analysis of durations: Correlated family model applied to survival of Danish twins. *Genetic Epidemiology, 12,* 529–538.

Zandi, T.; Mirle, J.; & Jarvis, P. (1990). Children's attitudes toward elderly individuals: A comparison of two ethnic groups. *International Journal of Aging and Human Development, 30* (3), 161–174.

Zeiss, A. M., & Breckenridge, J. S. (1997). Treatment of late life depression: A response to the NIH consensus conference. *Behavior Therapy, 28,* 3–21.

Zeiss, A. M., & Kasl-Godley, J. (2001). Sexuality in older adults' relationships. *Generations, 25* (2), 18–25.

PHOTO CREDITS

NAME INDEX

Note: Italic page numbers indicate material in tables or figures.

SUBJECT INDEX

Note: Italic page numbers indicate material in tables or figures.

men (*continued*)
  remarriage and, 142
  sexuality and, 149–50, 151, 152
  Social Security and, 221–22
  as spousal caregivers, 308
  suicide and, 319–20
  widowhood and, 136, 140–41,
    300
  See also gender
menopause
  middle age and, 71–72
  osteoporosis and, 169
  sexuality and, 72, 147, 150, 154
  views of, 345
mental health and mental illness
  caring for mentally ill, 291
  exercise and, 271
  functional disorders, 283–86
  homelessness and, 233, 234
  longevity and, 179–81
  nursing homes and, 261, 266
  oldest old and, 298
  organic mental disorders, 286–90
  promoting mental health, 292
  stereotypes of aging and, 48
  See also psychology
Mercy Housing, 249
metaphors
  definition of, 54
  theories as, 54–56, *55*
Mexican-Americans. *See* Hispanics
Michigan, 245, 252
middle age
  caregiving for elderly and, 305, 308
  employment and, 204
  fear of death and, 368
  generation gap and, 101
  grandparenthood and, 118
  middle-aged displaced homemakers, 346
  midlife crisis and, 66–70
  as stage of life cycle, 63, 70–73
  wealth span and, 215
midlife crisis, 66–70, 72
midlife transitions, 68–69
Midwest
  demographics of, 21, *21*
  migration and, 252
  naturally occurring retirement communities and, 254
  rural areas and, 236
migration
  of Hispanics, 354–55, 356
  living environments and, 249,
    251–53, 254
Milwaukee, Wisconsin, 326
Minneapolis Age and Opportunity
  Center, 256

Minnesota, 252
minorities
  adult development and, 65
  categorization of, 343–44
  definition of, 344
  home ownership and, 245
  poverty and, 396
  status of aged and, 363
  See also culture; ethnicity
minority elders, 350, 363
miracle drugs, and fraud, 335
Mississippi, 236
mnemonics, 282
mobile-home parks, 256, 258
mobile homes, 217, 255–56
modernization theory, 9–10
modified nuclear family, 303
mortality
  attitudes toward, 369
  elder caregiving to adult children
    and, 310
  infant mortality, 16, 20, 352
  race and, 163
motivation, 36
mourning, 389
movies, stereotypes of aging, 46–47
multi-infarct dementia (MID), 290
myocardial infarction, 164
myths
  of depression, 284
  exercise and, 177
  of financial status, 216
  of individualism, 396
  of multigenerational household,
    302
  of nonfunctional nuclear family,
    303
  of older worker, 199–200
  of senility, 283
  of untreatable mental illness, 292
  See also stereotypes

narrative metaphor, 55, *55*
National Affordable Housing Act of
  1990, 249, 259
National Association for the Advancement of Colored People
  (NAACP), 352
National Association of Older
  Worker Employment Services
  (NAOWES), 401
National Association of Retired Federal
  eral Employees (NARFE), 399
National Association of State Units
  on the Aging, 399
National Black Women's Political
  Caucus, 352
National Cancer Institute, 375

National Caucus and Center on Black
  Aged (NCCBA), 363, 401
National Center for Health Statistics,
  319
National Center for Studies of Suicide
  Prevention, 322
National Center on Elder Abuse, 318
National Center on Rural Aging
  (NCRA), 401
National Committee for the Prevention of Elder Abuse, 330
National Committee to Preserve Social Security and Medicare, 400
National Council of Health Care
  Services, 399
National Council of Senior Citizens
  (NCSC), 400–401
National Council on the Aging, 401
National Hospice Organization, 384
National Indian Council on Aging
  (NICOA), 363
National Institute of Senior Centers
  (NISC), 401
National Institute of Senior Housing
  (NISH), 401
National Institute on Adult Day Care
  (NIAD), 401
National Institute on Aging, 53, 180
National Institute on Community-
  Based Long-Term Care (NICLC),
  401
National Opinion Research Center
  (NORC), 324
National Organization for Women
  (NOW), 196, 396
National Pacific/Asian Resource Center on Aging (NP/ARCA), 363
National Retired Teachers Association (NRTA), 399
National Rifle Association, 399
National Voluntary Organizations for
  Independent Living for the Aging
  (NVOILA), 401
Native Americans
  cultural uniformity and diversity of,
    360
  as percent of population, 343, *343,*
    345, 359
  population data on, 360–61
naturally occurring retirement community (NORC), 254
Nazi death camps, 379
near-poor, 236–37
Neighborhood Watch, 325–26, 353
Netherlands, 193, 232, 394–95
network analysis, 123–24
neurotic personality, 79
Nevada, 245, 252